American Casebook Series
Hornbook Series and Basic Legal Texts
Black Letter Series and Nutshell Series

of

WEST PUBLISHING COMPANY
P.O. Box 64526
St. Paul, Minnesota 55164–0526

Accounting

FARIS' ACCOUNTING AND LAW IN A NUT-SHELL, 377 pages, 1984. Softcover. (Text)

FIFLIS' ACCOUNTING ISSUES FOR LAWYERS, TEACHING MATERIALS, Fourth Edition, 706 pages, 1991. Teacher's Manual available. (Casebook)

SIEGEL AND SIEGEL'S ACCOUNTING AND FINANCIAL DISCLOSURE: A GUIDE TO BASIC CONCEPTS, 259 pages, 1983. Softcover. (Text)

Administrative Law

AMAN AND MAYTON'S HORNBOOK ON ADMINISTRATIVE LAW, Approximately 750 pages, 1993. (Text)

BONFIELD AND ASIMOW'S STATE AND FEDERAL ADMINISTRATIVE LAW, 826 pages, 1989. Teacher's Manual available. (Casebook)

GELLHORN AND LEVIN'S ADMINISTRATIVE LAW AND PROCESS IN A NUTSHELL, Third Edition, 479 pages, 1990. Softcover. (Text)

MASHAW, MERRILL, AND SHANE'S CASES AND MATERIALS ON ADMINISTRATIVE LAW—THE AMERICAN PUBLIC LAW SYSTEM, Third Edition, 1187 pages, 1992. (Casebook)

ROBINSON, GELLHORN AND BRUFF'S THE ADMINISTRATIVE PROCESS, Third Edition, 978 pages, 1986. (Casebook)

Admiralty

HEALY AND SHARPE'S CASES AND MATERIALS ON ADMIRALTY, Second Edition, 876 pages, 1986. (Casebook)

MARAIST'S ADMIRALTY IN A NUTSHELL, Sec-

ond Edition, 379 pages, 1988. Softcover. (Text)

SCHOENBAUM'S HORNBOOK ON ADMIRALTY AND MARITIME LAW, Student Edition, 692 pages, 1987 with 1992 pocket part. (Text)

Agency—Partnership

DEMOTT'S FIDUCIARY OBLIGATION, AGENCY AND PARTNERSHIP: DUTIES IN ONGOING BUSINESS RELATIONSHIPS, 740 pages, 1991. Teacher's Manual available. (Casebook)

FESSLER'S ALTERNATIVES TO INCORPORATION FOR PERSONS IN QUEST OF PROFIT, Third Edition, 339 pages, 1991. Softcover. (Casebook)

HENN'S CASES AND MATERIALS ON AGENCY, PARTNERSHIP AND OTHER UNINCORPORATED BUSINESS ENTERPRISES, Second Edition, 733 pages, 1985. Teacher's Manual available. (Casebook)

REUSCHLEIN AND GREGORY'S HORNBOOK ON THE LAW OF AGENCY AND PARTNERSHIP, Second Edition, 683 pages, 1990. (Text)

SELECTED CORPORATION AND PARTNERSHIP STATUTES, RULES AND FORMS. Softcover. Revised 1991 Edition, 953 pages.

STEFFEN AND KERR'S CASES ON AGENCY-PARTNERSHIP, Fourth Edition, 859 pages, 1980. (Casebook)

STEFFEN'S AGENCY-PARTNERSHIP IN A NUTSHELL, 364 pages, 1977. Softcover. (Text)

Agricultural Law

MEYER, PEDERSEN, THORSON AND DAVIDSON'S AGRICULTURAL LAW: CASES AND MATERIALS, 931 pages, 1985. Teacher's Manual avail-

Agricultural Law—Cont'd

able. (Casebook)

Alternative Dispute Resolution

KANOWITZ' CASES AND MATERIALS ON ALTERNATIVE DISPUTE RESOLUTION, 1024 pages, 1986. Teacher's Manual available. (Casebook) 1990 Supplement.

NOLAN–HALEY'S ALTERNATIVE DISPUTE RESOLUTION IN A NUTSHELL, 298 pages, 1992. Softcover. (Text)

RISKIN AND WESTBROOK'S DISPUTE RESOLUTION AND LAWYERS, 468 pages, 1987. Teacher's Manual available. (Casebook)

RISKIN AND WESTBROOK'S DISPUTE RESOLUTION AND LAWYERS, Abridged Edition, 223 pages, 1987. Softcover. Teacher's Manual available. (Casebook)

RISKIN'S DISPUTE RESOLUTION FOR LAWYERS VIDEO TAPES, 1992. (Available for purchase by schools and libraries.)

American Indian Law

CANBY'S AMERICAN INDIAN LAW IN A NUTSHELL, Second Edition, 336 pages, 1988. Softcover. (Text)

GETCHES AND WILKINSON'S CASES AND MATERIALS ON FEDERAL INDIAN LAW, Second Edition, 880 pages, 1986. (Casebook)

Antitrust—see also Regulated Industries, Trade Regulation

BARNES AND STOUT'S ECONOMIC FOUNDATIONS OF REGULATION AND ANTITRUST LAW, 102 pages, 1992. Softcover. Teacher's Manual available. (Casebook)

FOX AND SULLIVAN'S CASES AND MATERIALS ON ANTITRUST, 935 pages, 1989. Teacher's Manual available. (Casebook) 1993 Supplement.

GELLHORN'S ANTITRUST LAW AND ECONOMICS IN A NUTSHELL, Third Edition, 472 pages, 1986. Softcover. (Text)

HOVENKAMP'S BLACK LETTER ON ANTITRUST, Second Edition approximately 325 pages, April 1993 Pub. Softcover. (Review)

HOVENKAMP'S HORNBOOK ON ECONOMICS AND FEDERAL ANTITRUST LAW, Student Edition, 414 pages, 1985. (Text)

POSNER AND EASTERBROOK'S CASES AND ECONOMIC NOTES ON ANTITRUST, Second Edi-

tion, 1077 pages, 1981. (Casebook) 1984–85 Supplement.

SULLIVAN'S HORNBOOK OF THE LAW OF ANTITRUST, 886 pages, 1977. (Text)

Appellate Advocacy—see Trial and Appellate Advocacy

Architecture and Engineering Law

SWEET'S LEGAL ASPECTS OF ARCHITECTURE, ENGINEERING AND THE CONSTRUCTION PROCESS, Fourth Edition, 889 pages, 1989. Teacher's Manual available. (Casebook)

Art Law

DUBOFF'S ART LAW IN A NUTSHELL, Second Edition, approximately 325 pages, 1993. Softcover. (Text)

Banking Law

BANKING LAW: SELECTED STATUTES AND REGULATIONS. Softcover. 263 pages, 1991.

LOVETT'S BANKING AND FINANCIAL INSTITUTIONS LAW IN A NUTSHELL, Third Edition, 470 pages, 1992. Softcover. (Text)

SYMONS AND WHITE'S BANKING LAW: TEACHING MATERIALS, Third Edition, 818 pages, 1991. Teacher's Manual available. (Casebook)

Statutory Supplement. *See Banking Law: Selected Statutes*

Bankruptcy—see Creditors' Rights

Business Planning—see also Corporate Finance

PAINTER'S PROBLEMS AND MATERIALS IN BUSINESS PLANNING, Second Edition, 1008 pages, 1984. (Casebook) 1990 Supplement.

Statutory Supplement. *See Selected Corporation and Partnership*

Civil Procedure—see also Federal Jurisdiction and Procedure

AMERICAN BAR ASSOCIATION SECTION OF LITIGATION—READINGS ON ADVERSARIAL JUSTICE: THE AMERICAN APPROACH TO ADJUDICATION, 217 pages, 1988. Softcover. (Coursebook)

CLERMONT'S BLACK LETTER ON CIVIL PROCEDURE, Third Edition, approximately 350 pages, May, 1993 Pub. Softcover. (Review)

COUND, FRIEDENTHAL, MILLER AND SEXTON'S

Civil Procedure—Cont'd

CASES AND MATERIALS ON CIVIL PROCEDURE, Fifth Edition, 1284 pages, 1989. Teacher's Manual available. (Casebook)

COUND, FRIEDENTHAL, MILLER AND SEXTON'S CIVIL PROCEDURE SUPPLEMENT. 476 pages, 1991. Softcover. (Casebook Supplement)

FEDERAL RULES OF CIVIL PROCEDURE—EDUCATIONAL EDITION. Softcover. 761 pages, 1992.

FRIEDENTHAL, KANE AND MILLER'S HORNBOOK ON CIVIL PROCEDURE, Second Edition, approximately 1000 pages, May 1993 Pub. (Text)

KANE AND LEVINE'S CIVIL PROCEDURE IN CALIFORNIA: STATE AND FEDERAL 1992 Edition, 551 pages. Softcover. (Casebook Supplement)

KANE'S CIVIL PROCEDURE IN A NUTSHELL, Third Edition, 303 pages, 1991. Softcover. (Text)

KOFFLER AND REPPY'S HORNBOOK ON COMMON LAW PLEADING, 663 pages, 1969. (Text)

LEVINE, SLOMANSON AND WINGATE'S CALIFORNIA CIVIL PROCEDURE, CASES AND MATERIALS, 546 pages, 1991. Teacher's Manual available. (Casebook)

MARCUS, REDISH AND SHERMAN'S CIVIL PROCEDURE: A MODERN APPROACH, 1027 pages, 1989. Teacher's Manual available. (Casebook) 1991 Supplement.

MARCUS AND SHERMAN'S COMPLEX LITIGATION–CASES AND MATERIALS ON ADVANCED CIVIL PROCEDURE, Second Edition, 1035 pages, 1992. Teacher's Manual available. (Casebook)

PARK AND MCFARLAND'S COMPUTER-AIDED EXERCISES ON CIVIL PROCEDURE, Third Edition, 210 pages, 1991. Softcover. (Coursebook)

SIEGEL'S HORNBOOK ON NEW YORK PRACTICE, Second Edition, Student Edition, 1068 pages, 1991. Softcover. (Text) 1992 Supplemental Pamphlet.

SLOMANSON AND WINGATE'S CALIFORNIA CIVIL PROCEDURE IN A NUTSHELL, 230 pages, 1992. Softcover. (Text)

Commercial Law

BAILEY AND HAGEDORN'S SECURED TRANSACTIONS IN A NUTSHELL, Third Edition, 390 pages, 1988. Softcover. (Text)

EPSTEIN, MARTIN, HENNING AND NICKLES' BASIC UNIFORM COMMERCIAL CODE TEACHING MATERIALS, Third Edition, 704 pages, 1988. Teacher's Manual available. (Casebook)

HENSON'S HORNBOOK ON SECURED TRANSACTIONS UNDER THE U.C.C., Second Edition, 504 pages, 1979, with 1979 pocket part. (Text)

MEYER AND SPEIDEL'S BLACK LETTER ON SALES AND LEASES OF GOODS, Approximately 300 pages, 1993. Softcover. (Review)

NICKLES' BLACK LETTER ON COMMERCIAL PAPER, 450 pages, 1988. Softcover. (Review)

NICKLES, MATHESON AND DOLAN'S MATERIALS FOR UNDERSTANDING CREDIT AND PAYMENT SYSTEMS, 923 pages, 1987. Teacher's Manual available. (Casebook)

NORDSTROM, MURRAY AND CLOVIS' PROBLEMS AND MATERIALS ON SALES, 515 pages, 1982. (Casebook)

NORDSTROM, MURRAY AND CLOVIS' PROBLEMS AND MATERIALS ON SECURED TRANSACTIONS, 594 pages, 1987. (Casebook)

RUBIN AND COOTER'S THE PAYMENT SYSTEM: CASES, MATERIALS AND ISSUES, 885 pages, 1989. Teacher's Manual Available. (Casebook)

SELECTED COMMERCIAL STATUTES. Softcover. 1897 pages, 1992.

SPEIDEL, SUMMERS AND WHITE'S COMMERCIAL LAW: TEACHING MATERIALS, Fourth Edition, 1448 pages, 1987. Teacher's Manual available. (Casebook)

SPEIDEL, SUMMERS AND WHITE'S COMMERCIAL PAPER: TEACHING MATERIALS, Fourth Edition, 578 pages, 1987. Reprint from Speidel et al., Commercial Law, Fourth Edition. Teacher's Manual available. (Casebook)

SPEIDEL, SUMMERS AND WHITE'S SALES: TEACHING MATERIALS, Fourth Edition, 804 pages, 1987. Reprint from Speidel et al., Commercial Law, Fourth Edition. Teacher's Manual available. (Casebook)

SPEIDEL, SUMMERS AND WHITE'S SECURED

Commercial Law—Cont'd

TRANSACTIONS: TEACHING MATERIALS, Fourth Edition, 485 pages, 1987. Reprint from Speidel et al., Commercial Law, Fourth Edition. Teacher's Manual available. (Casebook)

STOCKTON AND MILLER'S SALES AND LEASES OF GOODS IN A NUTSHELL, Third Edition, 441 pages, 1992. Softcover. (Text)

STONE'S UNIFORM COMMERCIAL CODE IN A NUTSHELL, Third Edition, 580 pages, 1989. Softcover. (Text)

WEBER AND SPEIDEL'S COMMERCIAL PAPER IN A NUTSHELL, Third Edition, 404 pages, 1982. Softcover. (Text)

WHITE AND SUMMERS' HORNBOOK ON THE UNIFORM COMMERCIAL CODE, Third Edition, Student Edition, 1386 pages, 1988. (Text)

Community Property

MENNELL AND BOYKOFF'S COMMUNITY PROPERTY IN A NUTSHELL, Second Edition, 432 pages, 1988. Softcover. (Text)

VERRALL AND BIRD'S CASES AND MATERIALS ON CALIFORNIA COMMUNITY PROPERTY, Fifth Edition, 604 pages, 1988. (Casebook)

Comparative Law

BARTON, GIBBS, LI AND MERRYMAN'S LAW IN RADICALLY DIFFERENT CULTURES, 960 pages, 1983. (Casebook)

FOLSOM, MINAN AND OTTO'S LAW AND POLITICS IN THE PEOPLE'S REPUBLIC OF CHINA IN A NUTSHELL, 451 pages, 1992. Softcover. (Text)

GLENDON, GORDON AND OSAKWE'S COMPARATIVE LEGAL TRADITIONS: TEXT, MATERIALS AND CASES ON THE CIVIL LAW, COMMON LAW AND SOCIALIST LAW TRADITIONS, 1091 pages, 1985. (Casebook)

GLENDON, GORDON AND OSAKWE'S COMPARATIVE LEGAL TRADITIONS IN A NUTSHELL. 402 pages, 1982. Softcover. (Text)

Computers and Law

MAGGS, SOMA AND SPROWL'S COMPUTER LAW—CASES, COMMENTS, AND QUESTIONS, 731 pages, 1992. Teacher's Manual available. (Casebook)

MAGGS AND SPROWL'S COMPUTER APPLICATIONS IN THE LAW, 316 pages, 1987. (Coursebook)

MASON'S USING COMPUTERS IN THE LAW: AN INTRODUCTION AND PRACTICAL GUIDE, Second Edition, 288 pages, 1988. Softcover. (Coursebook)

Conflict of Laws

CRAMTON, CURRIE AND KAY'S CASES–COMMENTS–QUESTIONS ON CONFLICT OF LAWS, Fourth Edition, 876 pages, 1987. (Casebook)

HAY'S BLACK LETTER ON CONFLICT OF LAWS, 330 pages, 1989. Softcover. (Review)

SCOLES AND HAY'S HORNBOOK ON CONFLICT OF LAWS, Student Edition, 1160 pages, 1992. (Text)

SIEGEL'S CONFLICTS IN A NUTSHELL, 470 pages, 1982. Softcover. (Text)

Constitutional Law—Civil Rights—see also First Amendment and Foreign Relations and National Security Law

ABERNATHY'S CIVIL RIGHTS AND CONSTITUTIONAL LITIGATION, CASES AND MATERIALS, Second Edition, 753 pages, 1992. (Casebook)

BARNES AND STOUT'S THE ECONOMICS OF CONSTITUTIONAL LAW AND PUBLIC CHOICE, 127 pages, 1992. Softcover. Teacher's Manual available. (Casebook)

BARRON AND DIENES' BLACK LETTER ON CONSTITUTIONAL LAW, Third Edition, 440 pages, 1991. Softcover. (Review)

BARRON AND DIENES' CONSTITUTIONAL LAW IN A NUTSHELL, Second Edition, 483 pages, 1991. Softcover. (Text)

ENGDAHL'S CONSTITUTIONAL FEDERALISM IN A NUTSHELL, Second Edition, 411 pages, 1987. Softcover. (Text)

FARBER AND SHERRY'S HISTORY OF THE AMERICAN CONSTITUTION, 458 pages, 1990. Softcover. Teacher's Manual available. (Text)

FISHER AND DEVINS' POLITICAL DYNAMICS OF CONSTITUTIONAL LAW, 333 pages, 1992. Softcover. (Casebook Supplement)

GARVEY AND ALEINIKOFF'S MODERN CONSTITUTIONAL THEORY: A READER, Second Edition, 559 pages, 1991. Softcover. (Reader)

LOCKHART, KAMISAR, CHOPER AND SHIFFRIN'S CONSTITUTIONAL LAW: CASES–COMMENTS–QUESTIONS, Seventh Edition, 1643 pages,

Constitutional Law—Civil Rights—Cont'd
1991. (Casebook) 1992 Supplement.

LOCKHART, KAMISAR, CHOPER AND SHIFFRIN'S THE AMERICAN CONSTITUTION: CASES AND MATERIALS, Seventh Edition, 1255 pages, 1991. Abridged version of Lockhart, et al., Constitutional Law: Cases–Comments–Questions, Seventh Edition. (Casebook) 1992 Supplement.

LOCKHART, KAMISAR, CHOPER AND SHIFFRIN'S CONSTITUTIONAL RIGHTS AND LIBERTIES: CASES AND MATERIALS, Seventh Edition, 1333 pages, 1991. Reprint from Lockhart, et al., Constitutional Law: Cases–Comments–Questions, Seventh Edition. (Casebook) 1992 Supplement.

MARKS AND COOPER'S STATE CONSTITUTIONAL LAW IN A NUTSHELL, 329 pages, 1988. Softcover. (Text)

NOWAK AND ROTUNDA'S HORNBOOK ON CONSTITUTIONAL LAW, Fourth Edition, 1357 pages, 1991. (Text)

ROTUNDA'S MODERN CONSTITUTIONAL LAW: CASES AND NOTES, Fourth Edition, approximately 1100 pages, April, 1993 Pub. (Casebook)

VIEIRA'S CONSTITUTIONAL CIVIL RIGHTS IN A NUTSHELL, Second Edition, 322 pages, 1990. Softcover. (Text)

WILLIAMS' CONSTITUTIONAL ANALYSIS IN A NUTSHELL, 388 pages, 1979. Softcover. (Text)

Consumer Law—see also Commercial Law
EPSTEIN AND NICKLES' CONSUMER LAW IN A NUTSHELL, Second Edition, 418 pages, 1981. Softcover. (Text)

SELECTED COMMERCIAL STATUTES. Softcover. 1897 pages, 1992.

SPANOGLE, ROHNER, PRIDGEN AND RASOR'S CASES AND MATERIALS ON CONSUMER LAW, Second Edition, 916 pages, 1991. Teacher's Manual available. (Casebook)

Contracts
BARNES AND STOUT'S THE ECONOMICS OF CONTRACT LAW, 127 pages, 1992. Softcover. Teacher's Manual available. (Casebook)

CALAMARI AND PERILLO'S BLACK LETTER ON CONTRACTS, Second Edition, 462 pages, 1990. Softcover. (Review)

CALAMARI AND PERILLO'S HORNBOOK ON CONTRACTS, Third Edition, 1049 pages, 1987. (Text)

CALAMARI, PERILLO AND BENDER'S CASES AND PROBLEMS ON CONTRACTS, Second Edition, 905 pages, 1989. Teacher's Manual Available. (Casebook)

CORBIN'S TEXT ON CONTRACTS, One Volume Student Edition, 1224 pages, 1952. (Text)

FESSLER AND LOISEAUX'S CASES AND MATERIALS ON CONTRACTS—MORALITY, ECONOMICS AND THE MARKET PLACE, 837 pages, 1982. Teacher's Manual available. (Casebook)

FRIEDMAN'S CONTRACT REMEDIES IN A NUTSHELL, 323 pages, 1981. Softcover. (Text)

FULLER AND EISENBERG'S CASES ON BASIC CONTRACT LAW, Fifth Edition, 1037 pages, 1990. (Casebook)

HAMILTON, RAU AND WEINTRAUB'S CASES AND MATERIALS ON CONTRACTS, Second Edition, 916 pages, 1992. Teacher's Manual available. (Casebook)

KEYES' GOVERNMENT CONTRACTS IN A NUTSHELL, Second Edition, 557 pages, 1990. Softcover. (Text)

SCHABER AND ROHWER'S CONTRACTS IN A NUTSHELL, Third Edition, 457 pages, 1990. Softcover. (Text)

SUMMERS AND HILLMAN'S CONTRACT AND RELATED OBLIGATION: THEORY, DOCTRINE AND PRACTICE, Second Edition, 1037 pages, 1992. Teacher's Manual available. (Casebook)

Copyright—see Patent and Copyright Law

Corporate Finance—see also Business Planning
HAMILTON'S CASES AND MATERIALS ON CORPORATION FINANCE, Second Edition, 1221 pages, 1989. (Casebook)

OESTERLE'S THE LAW OF MERGERS, ACQUISITIONS AND REORGANIZATIONS, 1096 pages, 1991. (Casebook) 1992 Supplement.

Corporations
HAMILTON'S BLACK LETTER ON CORPORATIONS, Third Edition, 732 pages, 1992. Softcover. (Review)

HAMILTON'S CASES AND MATERIALS ON CORPORATIONS—INCLUDING PARTNERSHIPS AND

Corporations—Cont'd

LIMITED PARTNERSHIPS, Fourth Edition, 1248 pages, 1990. Teacher's Manual available. (Casebook) 1990 Statutory Supplement.

HAMILTON'S THE LAW OF CORPORATIONS IN A NUTSHELL, Third Edition, 518 pages, 1991. Softcover. (Text)

HENN'S TEACHING MATERIALS ON THE LAW OF CORPORATIONS, Second Edition, 1204 pages, 1986. Teacher's Manual available. (Casebook)

> Statutory Supplement. *See Selected Corporation and Partnership*

HENN AND ALEXANDER'S HORNBOOK ON LAWS OF CORPORATIONS, Third Edition, Student Edition, 1371 pages, 1983, with 1986 pocket part. (Text)

SELECTED CORPORATION AND PARTNERSHIP STATUTES, RULES AND FORMS. Revised 1991 Edition, 953 pages. Softcover.

SOLOMON, SCHWARTZ AND BAUMAN'S MATERIALS AND PROBLEMS ON CORPORATIONS: LAW AND POLICY, Second Edition, 1391 pages, 1988. Teacher's Manual available. (Casebook) 1992 Supplement.

> Statutory Supplement. *See Selected Corporation and Partnership*

Corrections

KRANTZ' THE LAW OF CORRECTIONS AND PRISONERS' RIGHTS IN A NUTSHELL, Third Edition, 407 pages, 1988. Softcover. (Text)

KRANTZ AND BRANHAM'S CASES AND MATERIALS ON THE LAW OF SENTENCING, CORRECTIONS AND PRISONERS' RIGHTS, Fourth Edition, 619 pages, 1991. Teacher's Manual available. (Casebook)

Creditors' Rights

BANKRUPTCY CODE, RULES AND OFFICIAL FORMS, LAW SCHOOL EDITION. 910 pages, 1992. Softcover.

EPSTEIN'S DEBTOR-CREDITOR LAW IN A NUTSHELL, Fourth Edition, 401 pages, 1991. Softcover. (Text)

EPSTEIN, LANDERS AND NICKLES' CASES AND MATERIALS ON DEBTORS AND CREDITORS, Third Edition, 1059 pages, 1987. Teacher's Manual available. (Casebook)

EPSTEIN, NICKLES AND WHITE'S HORNBOOK

ON BANKRUPTCY, Approximately 1000 pages, January, 1992 Pub. (Text)

LOPUCKI'S PLAYER'S MANUAL FOR THE DEBTOR-CREDITOR GAME, 123 pages, 1985. Softcover. (Coursebook)

NICKLES AND EPSTEIN'S BLACK LETTER ON CREDITORS' RIGHTS AND BANKRUPTCY, 576 pages, 1989. (Review)

RIESENFELD'S CASES AND MATERIALS ON CREDITORS' REMEDIES AND DEBTORS' PROTECTION, Fourth Edition, 914 pages, 1987. (Casebook) 1990 Supplement.

WHITE AND NIMMER'S CASES AND MATERIALS ON BANKRUPTCY, Second Edition, 764 pages, 1992. Teacher's Manual available. (Casebook)

Criminal Law and Criminal Procedure—see also Corrections, Juvenile Justice

ABRAMS' FEDERAL CRIMINAL LAW AND ITS ENFORCEMENT, 866 pages, 1986. (Casebook) 1988 Supplement.

BUCY'S WHITE COLLAR CRIME, CASES AND MATERIALS, 688 pages, 1992. Teacher's Manual available. (Casebook)

DIX AND SHARLOT'S CASES AND MATERIALS ON CRIMINAL LAW, Third Edition, 846 pages, 1987. (Casebook)

GRANO'S PROBLEMS IN CRIMINAL PROCEDURE, Second Edition, 176 pages, 1981. Teacher's Manual available. Softcover. (Coursebook)

HEYMANN AND KENETY'S THE MURDER TRIAL OF WILBUR JACKSON: A HOMICIDE IN THE FAMILY, Second Edition, 347 pages, 1985. (Coursebook)

ISRAEL, KAMISAR AND LaFAVE'S CRIMINAL PROCEDURE AND THE CONSTITUTION: LEADING SUPREME COURT CASES AND INTRODUCTORY TEXT. 802 pages, 1992 Edition. Softcover. (Casebook)

ISRAEL AND LaFAVE'S CRIMINAL PROCEDURE—CONSTITUTIONAL LIMITATIONS IN A NUTSHELL, Fourth Edition, 461 pages, 1988. Softcover. (Text)

JOHNSON'S CASES, MATERIALS AND TEXT ON CRIMINAL LAW, Fourth Edition, 759 pages, 1990. Teacher's Manual available. (Casebook)

JOHNSON'S CASES AND MATERIALS ON CRIMI-

Criminal Law and Criminal Procedure—Cont'd

NAL PROCEDURE, 859 pages, 1988. (Casebook) 1992 Supplement.

KAMISAR, LAFAVE AND ISRAEL'S MODERN CRIMINAL PROCEDURE: CASES, COMMENTS AND QUESTIONS, Seventh Edition, 1593 pages, 1990. (Casebook) 1992 Supplement.

KAMISAR, LAFAVE AND ISRAEL'S BASIC CRIMINAL PROCEDURE: CASES, COMMENTS AND QUESTIONS, Seventh Edition, 792 pages, 1990. Softcover reprint from Kamisar, et al., Modern Criminal Procedure: Cases, Comments and Questions, Seventh Edition. (Casebook) 1992 Supplement.

LAFAVE'S MODERN CRIMINAL LAW: CASES, COMMENTS AND QUESTIONS, Second Edition, 903 pages, 1988. (Casebook)

LAFAVE AND ISRAEL'S HORNBOOK ON CRIMINAL PROCEDURE, Second Edition, 1309 pages, 1992 with 1992 pocket part. (Text)

LAFAVE AND SCOTT'S HORNBOOK ON CRIMINAL LAW, Second Edition, 918 pages, 1986. (Text)

LOEWY'S CRIMINAL LAW IN A NUTSHELL, Second Edition, 321 pages, 1987. Softcover. (Text)

LOW'S BLACK LETTER ON CRIMINAL LAW, Revised First Edition, 443 pages, 1990. Softcover. (Review)

SALTZBURG AND CAPRA'S CASES AND COMMENTARY ON AMERICAN CRIMINAL PROCEDURE, Fourth Edition, 1341 pages, 1992. Teacher's Manual available. (Casebook) 1992 Supplement.

SUBIN, MIRSKY AND WEINSTEIN'S THE CRIMINAL PROCESS: PROSECUTION AND DEFENSE FUNCTIONS, Approximately 450 pages, February, 1993 Pub. Softcover. Teacher's Manual available. (Text)

VORENBERG'S CASES ON CRIMINAL LAW AND PROCEDURE, Second Edition, 1088 pages, 1981. Teacher's Manual available. (Casebook) 1990 Supplement.

Domestic Relations

CLARK'S HORNBOOK ON DOMESTIC RELATIONS, Second Edition, Student Edition, 1050 pages, 1988. (Text)

CLARK AND GLOWINSKY'S CASES AND PROB-

LEMS ON DOMESTIC RELATIONS, Fourth Edition. 1150 pages, 1990. Teacher's Manual available. (Casebook) 1992 Supplement.

KRAUSE'S BLACK LETTER ON FAMILY LAW, 314 pages, 1988. Softcover. (Review)

KRAUSE'S CASES, COMMENTS AND QUESTIONS ON FAMILY LAW, Third Edition, 1433 pages, 1990. (Casebook)

KRAUSE'S FAMILY LAW IN A NUTSHELL, Second Edition, 444 pages, 1986. Softcover. (Text)

KRAUSKOPF'S CASES ON PROPERTY DIVISION AT MARRIAGE DISSOLUTION, 250 pages, 1984. Softcover. (Casebook)

Economics, Law and—see also Antitrust, Regulated Industries

BARNES AND STOUT'S CASES AND MATERIALS ON LAW AND ECONOMICS, 538 pages, 1992. Teacher's Manual available. (Casebook)

GOETZ' CASES AND MATERIALS ON LAW AND ECONOMICS, 547 pages, 1984. (Casebook)

MALLOY'S LAW AND ECONOMICS: A COMPARATIVE APPROACH TO THEORY AND PRACTICE, 166 pages, 1990. Softcover. (Text)

Education Law

ALEXANDER AND ALEXANDER'S PUBLIC SCHOOL LAW, Third Edition, 880 pages, 1992. Teacher's Manual available. (Coursebook)

ALEXANDER AND ALEXANDER'S THE LAW OF SCHOOLS, STUDENTS AND TEACHERS IN A NUTSHELL, 409 pages, 1984. Softcover. (Text)

YUDOF, KIRP AND LEVIN'S EDUCATIONAL POLICY AND THE LAW, Third Edition, 860 pages, 1992. (Casebook)

Employment Discrimination—see also Gender Discrimination

ESTREICHER AND HARPER'S CASES AND MATERIALS ON THE LAW GOVERNING THE EMPLOYMENT RELATIONSHIP, Second Edition, 966 pages, 1992. (Casebook) Statutory Supplement.

JONES, MURPHY AND BELTON'S CASES AND MATERIALS ON DISCRIMINATION IN EMPLOYMENT, (The Labor Law Group). Fifth Edition, 1116 pages, 1987. (Casebook) 1990 Supplement.

PLAYER'S FEDERAL LAW OF EMPLOYMENT DIS-

Employment Discrimination—Cont'd

CRIMINATION IN A NUTSHELL, Third Edition, 338 pages, 1992. Softcover. (Text)

PLAYER'S HORNBOOK ON EMPLOYMENT DISCRIMINATION LAW, Student Edition, 708 pages, 1988. (Text)

PLAYER, SHOBEN AND LIEBERWITZ' CASES AND MATERIALS ON EMPLOYMENT DISCRIMINATION LAW, 827 pages, 1990. Teacher's Manual available. (Casebook) 1992 Supplement.

Energy and Natural Resources Law—see also Oil and Gas

LAITOS' CASES AND MATERIALS ON NATURAL RESOURCES LAW, 938 pages, 1985. Teacher's Manual available. (Casebook)

LAITOS AND TOMAIN'S ENERGY AND NATURAL RESOURCES LAW IN A NUTSHELL, 554 pages, 1992. Softcover. (Text)

SELECTED ENVIRONMENTAL LAW STATUTES— EDUCATIONAL EDITION. Softcover. 1296 pages, 1992.

Environmental Law—see also Energy and Natural Resources Law; Sea, Law of

BONINE AND MCGARITY'S THE LAW OF ENVIRONMENTAL PROTECTION: CASES—LEGISLATION—POLICIES, Second Edition, 1042 pages, 1992. (Casebook)

FINDLEY AND FARBER'S CASES AND MATERIALS ON ENVIRONMENTAL LAW, Third Edition, 763 pages, 1991. Teacher's Manual available. (Casebook)

FINDLEY AND FARBER'S ENVIRONMENTAL LAW IN A NUTSHELL, Third Edition, 355 pages, 1992. Softcover. (Text)

PLATER, ABRAMS AND GOLDFARB'S ENVIRONMENTAL LAW AND POLICY: NATURE, LAW AND SOCIETY, 1039 pages, 1992. Teacher's Manual available. (Casebook)

RODGERS' HORNBOOK ON ENVIRONMENTAL LAW, 956 pages, 1977, with 1984 pocket part. (Text)

SELECTED ENVIRONMENTAL LAW STATUTES— EDUCATIONAL EDITION. Softcover. 1296 pages, 1992.

Equity—see Remedies

Estate Planning—see also Trusts and Estates; Taxation—Estate and Gift

LYNN'S INTRODUCTION TO ESTATE PLANNING IN A NUTSHELL, Fourth Edition, 352 pages, 1992. Softcover. (Text)

Evidence

BERGMAN'S TRANSCRIPT EXERCISES FOR LEARNING EVIDENCE, 273 pages, 1992. Teacher's Manual available. (Coursebook)

BROUN AND BLAKEY'S BLACK LETTER ON EVIDENCE, 269 pages, 1984. Softcover. (Review)

BROUN, MEISENHOLDER, STRONG AND MOSTELLER'S PROBLEMS IN EVIDENCE, Third Edition, 238 pages, 1988. Teacher's Manual available. Softcover. (Coursebook)

CLEARY, STRONG, BROUN AND MOSTELLER'S CASES AND MATERIALS ON EVIDENCE, Fourth Edition, 1060 pages, 1988. (Casebook)

FEDERAL RULES OF EVIDENCE FOR UNITED STATES COURTS AND MAGISTRATES. Softcover. 549 pages, 1992.

FRIEDMAN'S THE ELEMENTS OF EVIDENCE, 315 pages, 1991. Teacher's Manual available. (Coursebook)

GRAHAM'S FEDERAL RULES OF EVIDENCE IN A NUTSHELL, Third Edition, 486 pages, 1992. Softcover. (Text)

LEMPERT AND SALTZBURG'S A MODERN APPROACH TO EVIDENCE: TEXT, PROBLEMS, TRANSCRIPTS AND CASES, Second Edition, 1232 pages, 1983. Teacher's Manual available. (Casebook)

LILLY'S AN INTRODUCTION TO THE LAW OF EVIDENCE, Second Edition, 585 pages, 1987. (Text)

MCCORMICK, SUTTON AND WELLBORN'S CASES AND MATERIALS ON EVIDENCE, Seventh Edition, 932 pages, 1992. Teacher's Manual available. (Casebook)

MCCORMICK'S HORNBOOK ON EVIDENCE, Fourth Edition, Student Edition, 672 pages, 1992. (Text)

ROTHSTEIN'S EVIDENCE IN A NUTSHELL: STATE AND FEDERAL RULES, Second Edition, 514 pages, 1981. Softcover. (Text)

Federal Jurisdiction and Procedure

CURRIE'S CASES AND MATERIALS ON FEDERAL COURTS, Fourth Edition, 783 pages, 1990. (Casebook)

CURRIE'S FEDERAL JURISDICTION IN A NUTSHELL, Third Edition, 242 pages, 1990.

Federal Jurisdiction and Procedure—Cont'd
Softcover. (Text)

FEDERAL RULES OF CIVIL PROCEDURE—EDUCATIONAL EDITION. Softcover. 761 pages, 1992.

REDISH'S BLACK LETTER ON FEDERAL JURISDICTION, Second Edition, 234 pages, 1991. Softcover. (Review)

REDISH'S CASES, COMMENTS AND QUESTIONS ON FEDERAL COURTS, Second Edition, 1122 pages, 1989. (Casebook) 1992 Supplement.

VETRI AND MERRILL'S FEDERAL COURTS PROBLEMS AND MATERIALS, Second Edition, 232 pages, 1984. Softcover. (Coursebook)

WRIGHT'S HORNBOOK ON FEDERAL COURTS, Fourth Edition, Student Edition, 870 pages, 1983. (Text)

First Amendment

GARVEY AND SCHAUER'S THE FIRST AMENDMENT: A READER, 527 pages, 1992. Softcover. (Reader)

SHIFFRIN AND CHOPER'S FIRST AMENDMENT, CASES—COMMENTS—QUESTIONS, 759 pages, 1991. Softcover. (Casebook) 1992 Supplement.

Foreign Relations and National Security Law

FRANCK AND GLENNON'S FOREIGN RELATIONS AND NATIONAL SECURITY LAW, 941 pages, 1987. (Casebook)

Future Interests—see Trusts and Estates

Gender Discrimination—see also Employment Discrimination

KAY'S TEXT, CASES AND MATERIALS ON SEX-BASED DISCRIMINATION, Third Edition, 1001 pages, 1988. (Casebook) 1992 Supplement.

THOMAS' SEX DISCRIMINATION IN A NUTSHELL, Second Edition, 395 pages, 1991. Softcover. (Text)

Health Law—see Medicine, Law and

Human Rights—see International Law

Immigration Law

ALEINIKOFF AND MARTIN'S IMMIGRATION: PROCESS AND POLICY, Second Edition, 1056 pages, 1991. (Casebook)
  Statutory Supplement. *See Immigra-*

tion and Nationality Laws

IMMIGRATION AND NATIONALITY LAWS OF THE UNITED STATES: SELECTED STATUTES, REGULATIONS AND FORMS. Softcover. 519 pages, 1992.

WEISSBRODT'S IMMIGRATION LAW AND PROCEDURE IN A NUTSHELL, Third Edition, 497 pages, 1992. Softcover. (Text)

Indian Law—see American Indian Law

Insurance Law

DEVINE AND TERRY'S PROBLEMS IN INSURANCE LAW, 240 pages, 1989. Softcover. Teacher's Manual available. (Coursebook)

DOBBYN'S INSURANCE LAW IN A NUTSHELL, Second Edition, 316 pages, 1989. Softcover. (Text)

KEETON'S COMPUTER-AIDED AND WORKBOOK EXERCISES ON INSURANCE LAW, 255 pages, 1990. Softcover. (Coursebook)

KEETON AND WIDISS' INSURANCE LAW, Student Edition, 1359 pages, 1988. (Text)

WIDISS AND KEETON'S COURSE SUPPLEMENT TO KEETON AND WIDISS' INSURANCE LAW, 502 pages, 1988. Softcover. Teacher's Manual available. (Casebook)

WIDISS' INSURANCE: MATERIALS ON FUNDAMENTAL PRINCIPLES, LEGAL DOCTRINES AND REGULATORY ACTS, 1186 pages, 1989. Teacher's Manual available. (Casebook)

YORK AND WHELAN'S CASES, MATERIALS AND PROBLEMS ON GENERAL PRACTICE INSURANCE LAW, Second Edition, 787 pages, 1988. Teacher's Manual available. (Casebook)

International Law—see also Sea, Law of

BERMANN, DAVEY, FOX AND GOEBEL'S CASES AND MATERIALS ON EUROPEAN COMMUNITY LAW, Approximately 1200 pages, 1993. (Casebook) Statutory Supplement. *See European Economic Community: Selected Documents*

BUERGENTHAL'S INTERNATIONAL HUMAN RIGHTS IN A NUTSHELL, 283 pages, 1988. Softcover. (Text)

BUERGENTHAL AND MAIER'S PUBLIC INTERNATIONAL LAW IN A NUTSHELL, Second Edition, 275 pages, 1990. Softcover. (Text)

EUROPEAN ECONOMIC COMMUNITY: SELECTED DOCUMENTS. Approximately 550 pages,

International Law—Cont'd
1993. Softcover

FOLSOM'S EUROPEAN COMMUNITY LAW IN A NUTSHELL, 423 pages, 1992. Softcover. (Text)

FOLSOM, GORDON AND SPANOGLE'S INTERNATIONAL BUSINESS TRANSACTIONS—A PROBLEM-ORIENTED COURSEBOOK, Second Edition, 1237 pages, 1991. Teacher's Manual available. (Casebook) 1991 Documents Supplement.

FOLSOM, GORDON AND SPANOGLE'S INTERNATIONAL BUSINESS TRANSACTIONS IN A NUTSHELL, Fourth Edition, 548 pages, 1992. Softcover. (Text)

HENKIN, PUGH, SCHACHTER AND SMIT'S CASES AND MATERIALS ON INTERNATIONAL LAW, Second Edition, 1517 pages, 1987. (Casebook) Documents Supplement.

INTERNATIONAL LITIGATION AND ARBITRATION: SELECTED TREATIES, STATUTES AND RULES. Approximately 275 pages, 1993. Softcover

INTERNATIONAL ORGANIZATIONS IN THEIR LEGAL SETTING: SELECTED DOCUMENTS. Approximately 500 pages, March, 1993 Pub. Softcover

JACKSON AND DAVEY'S CASES, MATERIALS AND TEXT ON LEGAL PROBLEMS OF INTERNATIONAL ECONOMIC RELATIONS, Second Edition, 1269 pages, 1986. (Casebook) 1989 Documents Supplement.

KIRGIS' INTERNATIONAL ORGANIZATIONS IN THEIR LEGAL SETTING, Second Edition, approximately 1150 pages, March, 1993 Pub. Teacher's Manual available. (Casebook) Statutory Supplement.

LOWENFELD'S INTERNATIONAL LITIGATION AND ARBITRATION, Approximately 875 pages, 1993. (Casebook) Statutory Supplement. *See International Litigation: Selected Documents*

WESTON, FALK AND D'AMATO'S INTERNATIONAL LAW AND WORLD ORDER—A PROBLEM-ORIENTED COURSEBOOK, Second Edition, 1335 pages, 1990. Teacher's Manual available. (Casebook) Documents Supplement.

Interviewing and Counseling

BINDER AND PRICE'S LEGAL INTERVIEWING

AND COUNSELING, 232 pages, 1977. Softcover. Teacher's Manual available. (Coursebook)

BINDER, BERGMAN AND PRICE'S LAWYERS AS COUNSELORS: A CLIENT–CENTERED APPROACH, 427 pages, 1991. Softcover. (Coursebook)

SHAFFER AND ELKINS' LEGAL INTERVIEWING AND COUNSELING IN A NUTSHELL, Second Edition, 487 pages, 1987. Softcover. (Text)

Introduction to Law—see Legal Method and Legal System

Introduction to Law Study

HEGLAND'S INTRODUCTION TO THE STUDY AND PRACTICE OF LAW IN A NUTSHELL, 418 pages, 1983. Softcover. (Text)

KINYON'S INTRODUCTION TO LAW STUDY AND LAW EXAMINATIONS IN A NUTSHELL, 389 pages, 1971. Softcover. (Text)

Judicial Process—see Legal Method and Legal System

Jurisprudence

CHRISTIE'S JURISPRUDENCE—TEXT AND READINGS ON THE PHILOSOPHY OF LAW, 1056 pages, 1973. (Casebook)

SINHA'S JURISPRUDENCE (LEGAL PHILOSOPHY) IN A NUTSHELL. Approximately 350 pages, 1993. Softcover. (Text)

Juvenile Justice

FOX'S JUVENILE COURTS IN A NUTSHELL, Third Edition, 291 pages, 1984. Softcover. (Text)

Labor and Employment Law—see also Employment Discrimination, Workers' Compensation

FINKIN, GOLDMAN AND SUMMERS' LEGAL PROTECTION OF INDIVIDUAL EMPLOYEES, (The Labor Law Group). 1164 pages, 1989. (Casebook)

GORMAN'S BASIC TEXT ON LABOR LAW—UNIONIZATION AND COLLECTIVE BARGAINING, 914 pages, 1976. (Text)

LESLIE'S LABOR LAW IN A NUTSHELL, Third Edition, 388 pages, 1992. Softcover. (Text)

NOLAN'S LABOR ARBITRATION LAW AND PRAC-

Labor and Employment Law—Cont'd

TICE IN A NUTSHELL, 358 pages, 1979. Softcover. (Text)

OBERER, HANSLOWE, ANDERSEN AND HEINSZ' CASES AND MATERIALS ON LABOR LAW—COLLECTIVE BARGAINING IN A FREE SOCIETY, Third Edition, 1163 pages, 1986. Teacher's Manual available. (Casebook) Statutory Supplement. 1991 Case Supplement.

RABIN, SILVERSTEIN AND SCHATZKI'S LABOR AND EMPLOYMENT LAW: PROBLEMS, CASES AND MATERIALS IN THE LAW OF WORK, (The Labor Law Group). 1014 pages, 1988. Teacher's Manual available. (Casebook) 1988 Statutory Supplement.

WOLLETT, GRODIN AND WEISBERGER'S COLLECTIVE BARGAINING IN PUBLIC EMPLOYMENT, (The Labor Law Group). Fourth Edition, approximately 600 pages, April, 1993 Pub. (Casebook)

Land Finance—Property Security—see Real Estate Transactions

Land Use

CALLIES AND FREILICH'S CASES AND MATERIALS ON LAND USE, 1233 pages, 1986. (Casebook) 1991 Supplement.

HAGMAN AND JUERGENSMEYER'S HORNBOOK ON URBAN PLANNING AND LAND DEVELOPMENT CONTROL LAW, Second Edition, Student Edition, 680 pages, 1986. (Text)

WRIGHT AND GITELMAN'S CASES AND MATERIALS ON LAND USE, Fourth Edition, 1255 pages, 1991. Teacher's Manual available. (Casebook)

WRIGHT AND WRIGHT'S LAND USE IN A NUTSHELL, Second Edition, 356 pages, 1985. Softcover. (Text)

Legal History—see also Legal Method and Legal System

PRESSER AND ZAINALDIN'S CASES AND MATERIALS ON LAW AND JURISPRUDENCE IN AMERICAN HISTORY, Second Edition, 1092 pages, 1989. Teacher's Manual available. (Casebook)

Legal Method and Legal System—see also Legal Research, Legal Writing

ALDISERT'S READINGS, MATERIALS AND CASES IN THE JUDICIAL PROCESS, 948 pages, 1976. (Casebook)

BERCH, BERCH AND SPRITZER'S INTRODUCTION TO LEGAL METHOD AND PROCESS, Second Edition, 585 pages, 1992. Teacher's Manual available. (Casebook)

BODENHEIMER, OAKLEY AND LOVE'S READINGS AND CASES ON AN INTRODUCTION TO THE ANGLO-AMERICAN LEGAL SYSTEM, Second Edition, 166 pages, 1988. Softcover. (Casebook)

DAVIES AND LAWRY'S INSTITUTIONS AND METHODS OF THE LAW—INTRODUCTORY TEACHING MATERIALS, 547 pages, 1982. Teacher's Manual available. (Casebook)

DVORKIN, HIMMELSTEIN AND LESNICK'S BECOMING A LAWYER: A HUMANISTIC PERSPECTIVE ON LEGAL EDUCATION AND PROFESSIONALISM, 211 pages, 1981. Softcover. (Text)

KEETON'S JUDGING, 842 pages, 1990. Softcover. (Coursebook)

KELSO AND KELSO'S STUDYING LAW: AN INTRODUCTION, 587 pages, 1984. (Coursebook)

KEMPIN'S HISTORICAL INTRODUCTION TO ANGLO-AMERICAN LAW IN A NUTSHELL, Third Edition, 323 pages, 1990. Softcover. (Text)

MEADOR'S AMERICAN COURTS, 113 pages, 1991. Softcover. (Text)

REYNOLDS' JUDICIAL PROCESS IN A NUTSHELL, Second Edition, 308 pages, 1991. Softcover. (Text)

Legal Research

COHEN AND OLSON'S LEGAL RESEARCH IN A NUTSHELL, Fifth Edition, 370 pages, 1992. Softcover. (Text)

COHEN, BERRING AND OLSON'S HOW TO FIND THE LAW, Ninth Edition, 716 pages, 1989. (Text)

COHEN, BERRING AND OLSON'S FINDING THE LAW, 570 pages, 1989. Softcover reprint from Cohen, Berring and Olson's How to Find the Law, Ninth Edition. (Coursebook)

    Legal Research Exercises, 4th Ed., for use with Cohen, Berring and Olson, 253 pages, 1992. Teacher's Manual available.

ROMBAUER'S LEGAL PROBLEM SOLVING—ANALYSIS, RESEARCH AND WRITING, Fifth Edition, 524 pages, 1991. Softcover. Teacher's Manual with problems availa-

Legal Research—Cont'd

ble. (Coursebook)

STATSKY'S LEGAL RESEARCH AND WRITING: SOME STARTING POINTS, Fourth Edition, approximately 270 pages, 1993. Softcover. Teacher's Manual available. (Coursebook) Student Workbook.

TEPLY'S LEGAL RESEARCH AND CITATION, Fourth Edition, 436 pages, 1992. Softcover. (Coursebook)

Student Library Exercises, Fourth Edition, 276 pages, 1992. Answer Key available.

Legal Writing and Drafting

CHILD'S DRAFTING LEGAL DOCUMENTS: PRINCIPLES AND PRACTICES, Second Edition, 425 pages, 1992. Softcover. Teacher's Manual available. (Coursebook)

DICKERSON'S MATERIALS ON LEGAL DRAFTING, 425 pages, 1981. Teacher's Manual available. (Coursebook)

FELSENFELD AND SIEGEL'S WRITING CONTRACTS IN PLAIN ENGLISH, 290 pages, 1981. Softcover. (Text)

GOPEN'S WRITING FROM A LEGAL PERSPECTIVE, 225 pages, 1981. (Text)

MARTINEAU'S DRAFTING LEGISLATION AND RULES IN PLAIN ENGLISH, 155 pages, 1991. Softcover. Teacher's Manual available. (Text)

MELLINKOFF'S DICTIONARY OF AMERICAN LEGAL USAGE, 703 pages, 1992. Softcover. (Text)

MELLINKOFF'S LEGAL WRITING—SENSE AND NONSENSE, 242 pages, 1982. Softcover. Teacher's Manual available. (Text)

PRATT'S LEGAL WRITING: A SYSTEMATIC APPROACH, Second Edition, approximately 550 pages, April, 1993 Pub. Teacher's Manual available. (Coursebook)

RAY AND COX'S BEYOND THE BASICS: A TEXT FOR ADVANCED LEGAL WRITING, 427 pages, 1991. Softcover. Teacher's Manual available. (Text)

RAY AND RAMSFIELD'S LEGAL WRITING: GETTING IT RIGHT AND GETTING IT WRITTEN, 250 pages, 1987. Softcover. (Text)

SQUIRES AND ROMBAUER'S LEGAL WRITING IN A NUTSHELL, 294 pages, 1982. Softcover.

(Text)

STATSKY AND WERNET'S CASE ANALYSIS AND FUNDAMENTALS OF LEGAL WRITING, Third Edition, 424 pages, 1989. Teacher's Manual available. (Text)

TEPLY'S LEGAL WRITING, ANALYSIS AND ORAL ARGUMENT, 576 pages, 1990. Softcover. Teacher's Manual available. (Coursebook)

WEIHOFEN'S LEGAL WRITING STYLE, Second Edition, 332 pages, 1980. (Text)

Legislation—see also Legal Writing and Drafting

DAVIES' LEGISLATIVE LAW AND PROCESS IN A NUTSHELL, Second Edition, 346 pages, 1986. Softcover. (Text)

ESKRIDGE AND FRICKEY'S CASES AND MATERIALS ON LEGISLATION: STATUTES AND THE CREATION OF PUBLIC POLICY, 937 pages, 1988. Teacher's Manual available. (Casebook) 1992 Supplement.

NUTTING AND DICKERSON'S CASES AND MATERIALS ON LEGISLATION, Fifth Edition, 744 pages, 1978. (Casebook)

STATSKY'S LEGISLATIVE ANALYSIS AND DRAFTING, Second Edition, 217 pages, 1984. Teacher's Manual available. (Text)

Local Government

FRUG'S CASES AND MATERIALS ON LOCAL GOVERNMENT LAW, 1005 pages, 1988. (Casebook) 1991 Supplement.

MCCARTHY'S LOCAL GOVERNMENT LAW IN A NUTSHELL, Third Edition, 435 pages, 1990. Softcover. (Text)

REYNOLDS' HORNBOOK ON LOCAL GOVERNMENT LAW, 860 pages, 1982 with 1990 pocket part. (Text)

VALENTE AND MCCARTHY'S CASES AND MATERIALS ON LOCAL GOVERNMENT LAW, Fourth Edition, 1158 pages, 1992. Teacher's Manual available. (Casebook)

Mass Communication Law

GILLMOR, BARRON, SIMON AND TERRY'S CASES AND COMMENT ON MASS COMMUNICATION LAW, Fifth Edition, 947 pages, 1990. (Casebook)

GINSBURG, BOTEIN AND DIRECTOR'S REGULATION OF THE ELECTRONIC MASS MEDIA: LAW

Mass Communication Law—Cont'd

AND POLICY FOR RADIO, TELEVISION, CABLE AND THE NEW VIDEO TECHNOLOGIES, Second Edition, 657 pages, 1991. (Casebook) Statutory Supplement.

ZUCKMAN, GAYNES, CARTER AND DEE'S MASS COMMUNICATIONS LAW IN A NUTSHELL, Third Edition, 538 pages, 1988. Softcover. (Text)

Medicine, Law and

FISCINA, BOUMIL, SHARPE AND HEAD'S MEDICAL LIABILITY, 487 pages, 1991. Teacher's Manual available. (Casebook)

FURROW, JOHNSON, JOST AND SCHWARTZ' HEALTH LAW: CASES, MATERIALS AND PROBLEMS, Second Edition, 1236 pages, 1991. Teacher's Manual available. (Casebook)

FURROW, JOHNSON, JOST AND SCHWARTZ' BIOETHICS: HEALTH CARE LAW AND ETHICS, Reprint from Furrow et al., Health Law, Second Edition. Softcover. Teacher's Manual available. (Casebook)

FURROW, JOHNSON, JOST AND SCHWARTZ' THE LAW OF HEALTH CARE ORGANIZATION AND FINANCE, Reprint from Furrow et al., Health Law, Second Edition. Softcover. Teacher's Manual available.

FURROW, JOHNSON, JOST AND SCHWARTZ' LIABILITY AND QUALITY ISSUES IN HEALTH CARE, Reprint from Furrow et al., Health Law, Second Edition. Softcover. Teacher's Manual available. (Casebook)

HALL AND ELLMAN'S HEALTH CARE LAW AND ETHICS IN A NUTSHELL, 401 pages, 1990. Softcover (Text)

JARVIS, CLOSEN, HERMANN AND LEONARD'S AIDS LAW IN A NUTSHELL, 349 pages, 1991. Softcover. (Text)

KING'S THE LAW OF MEDICAL MALPRACTICE IN A NUTSHELL, Second Edition, 342 pages, 1986. Softcover. (Text)

SHAPIRO AND SPECE'S CASES, MATERIALS AND PROBLEMS ON BIOETHICS AND LAW, 892 pages, 1981. (Casebook) 1991 Supplement.

Military Law

SHANOR AND TERRELL'S MILITARY LAW IN A NUTSHELL, 378 pages, 1980. Softcover. (Text)

Mining Law—see Energy and Natural Resources Law

Mortgages—see Real Estate Transactions

Natural Resources Law—see Energy and Natural Resources Law, Environmental Law

Negotiation

GIFFORD'S LEGAL NEGOTIATION: THEORY AND APPLICATIONS, 225 pages, 1989. Softcover. (Text)

TEPLY'S LEGAL NEGOTIATION IN A NUTSHELL, 282 pages, 1992. Softcover. (Text)

WILLIAMS' LEGAL NEGOTIATION AND SETTLEMENT, 207 pages, 1983. Softcover. Teacher's Manual available. (Coursebook)

Office Practice—see also Computers and Law, Interviewing and Counseling, Negotiation

HEGLAND'S TRIAL AND PRACTICE SKILLS IN A NUTSHELL, 346 pages, 1978. Softcover (Text)

MUNNEKE'S LAW PRACTICE MANAGEMENT: MATERIALS AND CASES, 634 pages, 1991. Teacher's Manual available. (Casebook)

Oil and Gas—see also Energy and Natural Resources Law

HEMINGWAY'S HORNBOOK ON THE LAW OF OIL AND GAS, Third Edition, Student Edition, 711 pages, 1992. (Text)

KUNTZ, LOWE, ANDERSON AND SMITH'S CASES AND MATERIALS ON OIL AND GAS LAW, Second Edition, approximately 1000 pages, 1993. Teacher's Manual available. (Casebook) Forms Manual. Revised.

LOWE'S OIL AND GAS LAW IN A NUTSHELL, Second Edition, 465 pages, 1988. Softcover. (Text)

Partnership—see Agency—Partnership

Patent and Copyright Law

CHOATE, FRANCIS AND COLLINS' CASES AND MATERIALS ON PATENT LAW, INCLUDING TRADE SECRETS, COPYRIGHTS, TRADEMARKS, Third Edition, 1009 pages, 1987. (Casebook)

HALPERN, SHIPLEY AND ABRAMS' CASES AND MATERIALS ON COPYRIGHT, 663 pages, 1992. (Casebook)

Patent and Copyright Law—Cont'd

MILLER AND DAVIS' INTELLECTUAL PROPERTY—PATENTS, TRADEMARKS AND COPYRIGHT IN A NUTSHELL, Second Edition, 437 pages, 1990. Softcover. (Text)

NIMMER, MARCUS, MYERS AND NIMMER'S CASES AND MATERIALS ON COPYRIGHT AND OTHER ASPECTS OF ENTERTAINMENT LITIGATION—INCLUDING UNFAIR COMPETITION, DEFAMATION, PRIVACY, ILLUSTRATED, Fourth Edition, 1177 pages, 1991. (Casebook) Statutory Supplement. See *Selected Intellectual Property Statutes*

SELECTED INTELLECTUAL PROPERTY AND UNFAIR COMPETITION STATUTES, REGULATIONS AND TREATIES. Softcover.

Products Liability

FISCHER AND POWERS' CASES AND MATERIALS ON PRODUCTS LIABILITY, 685 pages, 1988. Teacher's Manual available. (Casebook)

PHILLIPS' PRODUCTS LIABILITY IN A NUTSHELL, Third Edition, 307 pages, 1988. Softcover. (Text)

Professional Responsibility

ARONSON, DEVINE AND FISCH'S PROBLEMS, CASES AND MATERIALS IN PROFESSIONAL RESPONSIBILITY, 745 pages, 1985. Teacher's Manual available. (Casebook)

ARONSON AND WECKSTEIN'S PROFESSIONAL RESPONSIBILITY IN A NUTSHELL, Second Edition, 514 pages, 1991. Softcover. (Text)

LESNICK'S BEING A LAWYER: INDIVIDUAL CHOICE AND RESPONSIBILITY IN THE PRACTICE OF LAW, 422 pages, 1992. Softcover. Teacher's Manual available. (Coursebook)

MELLINKOFF'S THE CONSCIENCE OF A LAWYER, 304 pages, 1973. (Text)

PIRSIG AND KIRWIN'S CASES AND MATERIALS ON PROFESSIONAL RESPONSIBILITY, Fourth Edition, 603 pages, 1984. Teacher's Manual available. (Casebook)

ROTUNDA'S BLACK LETTER ON PROFESSIONAL RESPONSIBILITY, Third Edition, 492 pages, 1992. Softcover. (Review)

SCHWARTZ, WYDICK AND PERSCHBACHER'S PROBLEMS IN LEGAL ETHICS, Third Edition, approximately 400 pages, 1993. (Coursebook)

SELECTED STATUTES, RULES AND STANDARDS ON THE LEGAL PROFESSION. Softcover. 940 pages, 1992.

SMITH AND MALLEN'S PREVENTING LEGAL MALPRACTICE, 264 pages, 1989. Reprint from Mallen and Smith's Legal Malpractice, Third Edition. (Text)

SUTTON AND DZIENKOWSKI'S CASES AND MATERIALS ON PROFESSIONAL RESPONSIBILITY FOR LAWYERS, 839 pages, 1989. Teacher's Manual available. (Casebook)

WOLFRAM'S HORNBOOK ON MODERN LEGAL ETHICS, Student Edition, 1120 pages, 1986. (Text)

WYDICK AND PERSCHBACHER'S CALIFORNIA LEGAL ETHICS, 439 pages, 1992. Softcover. (Coursebook)

Property—see also Real Estate Transactions, Land Use, Trusts and Estates

BARNES AND STOUT'S THE ECONOMICS OF PROPERTY RIGHTS AND NUISANCE LAW, 87 pages, 1992. Softcover. Teacher's Manual available. (Casebook)

BERNHARDT'S BLACK LETTER ON PROPERTY, Second Edition, 388 pages, 1991. Softcover. (Review)

BERNHARDT'S REAL PROPERTY IN A NUTSHELL, Second Edition, 448 pages, 1981. Softcover. (Text)

BOYER, HOVENKAMP AND KURTZ' THE LAW OF PROPERTY, AN INTRODUCTORY SURVEY, Fourth Edition, 696 pages, 1991. (Text)

BROWDER, CUNNINGHAM, NELSON, STOEBUCK AND WHITMAN'S CASES ON BASIC PROPERTY LAW, Fifth Edition, 1386 pages, 1989. Teacher's Manual available. (Casebook)

BRUCE, ELY AND BOSTICK'S CASES AND MATERIALS ON MODERN PROPERTY LAW, Second Edition, 953 pages, 1989. Teacher's Manual available. (Casebook)

BURKE'S PERSONAL PROPERTY IN A NUTSHELL, Second Edition, approximately 400 pages, May, 1993 Pub. Softcover. (Text)

CUNNINGHAM, STOEBUCK AND WHITMAN'S HORNBOOK ON THE LAW OF PROPERTY, Second Edition, approximately 900 pages, May, 1993 Pub. (Text)

DONAHUE, KAUPER AND MARTIN'S CASES AND MATERIALS ON PROPERTY, AN INTRODUCTION TO THE CONCEPT AND THE INSTITUTION, Third

Property—Cont'd

Edition, approximately 1000 pages, 1993. Teacher's Manual available. (Casebook)

HILL'S LANDLORD AND TENANT LAW IN A NUTSHELL, Second Edition, 311 pages, 1986. Softcover. (Text)

JOHNSON, JOST, SALSICH AND SHAFFER'S PROPERTY LAW, CASES, MATERIALS AND PROBLEMS, 908 pages, 1992. Teacher's Manual available. (Casebook)

KURTZ AND HOVENKAMP'S CASES AND MATERIALS ON AMERICAN PROPERTY LAW, Second Edition, approximately 1350 pages, March, 1993 Pub. Teacher's Manual available. (Casebook)

MOYNIHAN'S INTRODUCTION TO REAL PROPERTY, Second Edition, 239 pages, 1988. (Text)

Psychiatry, Law and

REISNER AND SLOBOGIN'S LAW AND THE MENTAL HEALTH SYSTEM, CIVIL AND CRIMINAL ASPECTS, Second Edition, 1117 pages, 1990. Teacher's Manual available. (Casebook) 1992 Supplement.

Real Estate Transactions

BRUCE'S REAL ESTATE FINANCE IN A NUTSHELL, Third Edition, 287 pages, 1991. Softcover. (Text)

MAXWELL, RIESENFELD, HETLAND AND WARREN'S CASES ON CALIFORNIA SECURITY TRANSACTIONS IN LAND, Fourth Edition, 778 pages, 1992. Teacher's Manual available. (Casebook)

NELSON AND WHITMAN'S BLACK LETTER ON LAND TRANSACTIONS AND FINANCE, Second Edition, 466 pages, 1988. Softcover. (Review)

NELSON AND WHITMAN'S CASES AND MATERIALS ON REAL ESTATE TRANSFER, FINANCE AND DEVELOPMENT, Fourth Edition, 1346 pages, 1992. (Casebook)

NELSON AND WHITMAN'S HORNBOOK ON REAL ESTATE FINANCE LAW, Second Edition, 941 pages, 1985 with 1989 pocket part. (Text)

Regulated Industries—see also Mass Communication Law, Banking Law

GELLHORN AND PIERCE'S REGULATED INDUSTRIES IN A NUTSHELL, Second Edition, 389 pages, 1987. Softcover. (Text)

MORGAN, HARRISON AND VERKUIL'S CASES AND MATERIALS ON ECONOMIC REGULATION OF BUSINESS, Second Edition, 666 pages, 1985. (Casebook)

Remedies

DOBBS' HORNBOOK ON REMEDIES, Second Edition, approximately 1000 pages, April, 1993 Pub. (Text)

DOBBS' PROBLEMS IN REMEDIES. 137 pages, 1974. Teacher's Manual available. Softcover. (Coursebook)

DOBBYN'S INJUNCTIONS IN A NUTSHELL, 264 pages, 1974. Softcover. (Text)

FRIEDMAN'S CONTRACT REMEDIES IN A NUTSHELL, 323 pages, 1981. Softcover. (Text)

LEAVELL, LOVE AND NELSON'S CASES AND MATERIALS ON EQUITABLE REMEDIES, RESTITUTION AND DAMAGES, Fourth Edition, 1111 pages, 1986. Teacher's Manual available. (Casebook)

O'CONNELL'S REMEDIES IN A NUTSHELL, Second Edition, 320 pages, 1985. Softcover. (Text)

SCHOENBROD, MACBETH, LEVINE AND JUNG'S CASES AND MATERIALS ON REMEDIES: PUBLIC AND PRIVATE, 848 pages, 1990. Teacher's Manual available. (Casebook) 1992 Supplement.

YORK, BAUMAN AND RENDLEMAN'S CASES AND MATERIALS ON REMEDIES, Fifth Edition, 1270 pages, 1992. Teacher's Manual available. (Casebook)

Sea, Law of

SOHN AND GUSTAFSON'S THE LAW OF THE SEA IN A NUTSHELL, 264 pages, 1984. Softcover. (Text)

Securities Regulation

HAZEN'S HORNBOOK ON THE LAW OF SECURITIES REGULATION, Second Edition, Student Edition, 1082 pages, 1990. (Text)

RATNER'S SECURITIES REGULATION IN A NUTSHELL, Fourth Edition, 320 pages, 1992. Softcover. (Text)

RATNER AND HAZEN'S SECURITIES REGULATION: CASES AND MATERIALS, Fourth Edition, 1062 pages, 1991. Teacher's Manual available. (Casebook) Problems and Sample Documents Supplement.

Statutory Supplement. *See Securities*

Securities Regulation—Cont'd

Regulation, Selected Statutes

SECURITIES REGULATION, SELECTED STATUTES, RULES, AND FORMS. Softcover. Approximately 1375 pages, 1993.

Sports Law

CHAMPION'S SPORTS LAW IN A NUTSHELL,. Approximately 300 pages, January, 1993 Pub. Softcover. (Text)

SCHUBERT, SMITH AND TRENTADUE'S SPORTS LAW, 395 pages, 1986. (Text)

Tax Practice and Procedure

GARBIS, RUBIN AND MORGAN'S CASES AND MATERIALS ON TAX PROCEDURE AND TAX FRAUD, Third Edition, 921 pages, 1992. Teacher's Manual available. (Casebook)

MORGAN'S TAX PROCEDURE AND TAX FRAUD IN A NUTSHELL, 400 pages, 1990. Softcover. (Text)

Taxation—Corporate

KAHN AND GANN'S CORPORATE TAXATION, Third Edition, 980 pages, 1989. Teacher's Manual available. (Casebook) 1991 Supplement.

SCHWARZ AND LATHROPE'S BLACK LETTER ON CORPORATE AND PARTNERSHIP TAXATION, 537 pages, 1991. Softcover. (Review)

WEIDENBRUCH AND BURKE'S FEDERAL INCOME TAXATION OF CORPORATIONS AND STOCKHOLDERS IN A NUTSHELL, Third Edition, 309 pages, 1989. Softcover. (Text)

Taxation—Estate & Gift—see also Estate Planning, Trusts and Estates

MCNULTY'S FEDERAL ESTATE AND GIFT TAXATION IN A NUTSHELL, Fourth Edition, 496 pages, 1989. Softcover. (Text)

PEAT AND WILLBANKS' FEDERAL ESTATE AND GIFT TAXATION: AN ANALYSIS AND CRITIQUE, 265 pages, 1991. Softcover. (Text)

PENNELL'S CASES AND MATERIALS ON INCOME TAXATION OF TRUSTS, ESTATES, GRANTORS AND BENEFICIARIES, 460 pages, 1987. Teacher's Manual available. (Casebook)

Taxation—Individual

DODGE'S THE LOGIC OF TAX, 343 pages, 1989. Softcover. (Text)

GUNN AND WARD'S CASES, TEXT AND PROB-LEMS ON FEDERAL INCOME TAXATION, Third Edition, 817 pages, 1992. Teacher's Manual available. (Casebook)

HUDSON AND LIND'S BLACK LETTER ON FEDERAL INCOME TAXATION, Fourth Edition, 410 pages, 1992. Softcover. (Review)

MCNULTY'S FEDERAL INCOME TAXATION OF INDIVIDUALS IN A NUTSHELL, Fourth Edition, 503 pages, 1988. Softcover. (Text)

POSIN'S FEDERAL INCOME TAXATION, Second Edition, approximately 650 pages, May, 1993 Pub. Softcover. (Text)

ROSE AND CHOMMIE'S HORNBOOK ON FEDERAL INCOME TAXATION, Third Edition, 923 pages, 1988, with 1991 pocket part. (Text)

SELECTED FEDERAL TAXATION STATUTES AND REGULATIONS. Softcover. 1686 pages, 1993.

Taxation—International

DOERNBERG'S INTERNATIONAL TAXATION IN A NUTSHELL, 325 pages, 1989. Softcover. (Text)

KAPLAN'S FEDERAL TAXATION OF INTERNATIONAL TRANSACTIONS: PRINCIPLES, PLANNING AND POLICY, 635 pages, 1988. (Casebook)

Taxation—Partnership

BERGER AND WIEDENBECK'S CASES AND MATERIALS ON PARTNERSHIP TAXATION, 788 pages, 1989. Teacher's Manual available. (Casebook) 1991 Supplement.

BISHOP AND BROOKS' FEDERAL PARTNERSHIP TAXATION: A GUIDE TO THE LEADING CASES, STATUTES, AND REGULATIONS, 545 pages, 1990. Softcover. (Text)

BURKE'S FEDERAL INCOME TAXATION OF PARTNERSHIPS IN A NUTSHELL, 356 pages, 1992. Softcover. (Text)

SCHWARZ AND LATHROPE'S BLACK LETTER ON CORPORATE AND PARTNERSHIP TAXATION, 537 pages, 1991. Softcover. (Review)

Taxation—State & Local

GELFAND AND SALSICH'S STATE AND LOCAL TAXATION AND FINANCE IN A NUTSHELL, 309 pages, 1986. Softcover. (Text)

HELLERSTEIN AND HELLERSTEIN'S CASES AND MATERIALS ON STATE AND LOCAL TAXATION, Fifth Edition, 1071 pages, 1988. (Case-

Taxation—State & Local—Cont'd book)

Torts—see also Products Liability

BARNES AND STOUT'S THE ECONOMIC ANALYSIS OF TORT LAW, 161 pages, 1992. Softcover. Teacher's Manual available. (Casebook)

CHRISTIE AND MEEKS' CASES AND MATERIALS ON THE LAW OF TORTS, Second Edition, 1264 pages, 1990. (Casebook)

DOBBS' TORTS AND COMPENSATION—PERSONAL ACCOUNTABILITY AND SOCIAL RESPONSIBILITY FOR INJURY, 955 pages, 1985. Teacher's Manual available. (Casebook) 1990 Supplement.

KEETON, KEETON, SARGENTICH AND STEINER'S CASES AND MATERIALS ON TORT AND ACCIDENT LAW, Second Edition, 1318 pages, 1989. (Casebook)

KIONKA'S BLACK LETTER ON TORTS, 339 pages, 1988. Softcover. (Review)

KIONKA'S TORTS IN A NUTSHELL, Second Edition, 449 pages, 1992. Softcover. (Text)

PROSSER AND KEETON'S HORNBOOK ON TORTS, Fifth Edition, Student Edition, 1286 pages, 1984 with 1988 pocket part. (Text)

ROBERTSON, POWERS AND ANDERSON'S CASES AND MATERIALS ON TORTS, 932 pages, 1989. Teacher's Manual available. (Casebook)

Trade Regulation—see also Antitrust, Regulated Industries

MCMANIS' UNFAIR TRADE PRACTICES IN A NUTSHELL, Third Edition, approximately 450 pages, 1993. Softcover. (Text)

SCHECHTER'S BLACK LETTER ON UNFAIR TRADE PRACTICES, 272 pages, 1986. Softcover. (Review)

WESTON, MAGGS AND SCHECHTER'S UNFAIR TRADE PRACTICES AND CONSUMER PROTECTION, CASES AND COMMENTS, Fifth Edition, 957 pages, 1992. Teacher's Manual available. (Casebook)

Trial and Appellate Advocacy—see also Civil Procedure

APPELLATE ADVOCACY, HANDBOOK OF, Second Edition, 182 pages, 1986. Softcover. (Text)

BERGMAN'S TRIAL ADVOCACY IN A NUTSHELL,

Second Edition, 354 pages, 1989. Softcover. (Text)

BINDER AND BERGMAN'S FACT INVESTIGATION: FROM HYPOTHESIS TO PROOF, 354 pages, 1984. Teacher's Manual available. (Coursebook)

CARLSON'S ADJUDICATION OF CRIMINAL JUSTICE: PROBLEMS AND REFERENCES, 130 pages, 1986. Softcover. (Casebook)

CARLSON AND IMWINKELRIED'S DYNAMICS OF TRIAL PRACTICE: PROBLEMS AND MATERIALS, 414 pages, 1989. Teacher's Manual available. (Coursebook) 1990 Supplement.

CLARY'S PRIMER ON THE ANALYSIS AND PRESENTATION OF LEGAL ARGUMENT, 106 pages, 1992. Softcover. (Text)

DESSEM'S PRETRIAL LITIGATION IN A NUTSHELL, 382 pages, 1992. Softcover. (Text)

DESSEM'S PRETRIAL LITIGATION: LAW, POLICY AND PRACTICE, 608 pages, 1991. Softcover. Teacher's Manual available. (Coursebook)

DEVINE'S NON-JURY CASE FILES FOR TRIAL ADVOCACY, 258 pages, 1991. (Coursebook)

GOLDBERG'S THE FIRST TRIAL (WHERE DO I SIT? WHAT DO I SAY?) IN A NUTSHELL, 396 pages, 1982. Softcover. (Text)

HAYDOCK, HERR, AND STEMPEL'S FUNDAMENTALS OF PRE-TRIAL LITIGATION, Second Edition, 786 pages, 1992. Softcover. Teacher's Manual available. (Coursebook)

HAYDOCK AND SONSTENG'S TRIAL: THEORIES, TACTICS, TECHNIQUES, 711 pages, 1991. Softcover. (Text)

HEGLAND'S TRIAL AND PRACTICE SKILLS IN A NUTSHELL, 346 pages, 1978. Softcover. (Text)

HORNSTEIN'S APPELLATE ADVOCACY IN A NUTSHELL, 325 pages, 1984. Softcover. (Text)

JEANS' HANDBOOK ON TRIAL ADVOCACY, Student Edition, 473 pages, 1975. Softcover. (Text)

LISNEK AND KAUFMAN'S DEPOSITIONS: PROCEDURE, STRATEGY AND TECHNIQUE, Law School and CLE Edition. 250 pages, 1990. Softcover. (Text)

MARTINEAU'S CASES AND MATERIALS ON APPELLATE PRACTICE AND PROCEDURE, 565 pages, 1987. (Casebook)

Trial and Appellate Advocacy—Cont'd

SONSTENG, HAYDOCK AND BOYD'S THE TRI-ALBOOK: A TOTAL SYSTEM FOR PREPARATION AND PRESENTATION OF A CASE, 404 pages, 1984. Softcover. (Coursebook)

WHARTON, HAYDOCK AND SONSTENG'S CALIFORNIA CIVIL TRIALBOOK, Law School and CLE Edition. 148 pages, 1990. Softcover. (Text)

Trusts and Estates

ATKINSON'S HORNBOOK ON WILLS, Second Edition, 975 pages, 1953. (Text)

AVERILL'S UNIFORM PROBATE CODE IN A NUTSHELL, Second Edition, 454 pages, 1987. Softcover. (Text)

BOGERT'S HORNBOOK ON TRUSTS, Sixth Edition, Student Edition, 794 pages, 1987. (Text)

CLARK, LUSKY AND MURPHY'S CASES AND MATERIALS ON GRATUITOUS TRANSFERS, Third Edition, 970 pages, 1985. (Casebook)

DODGE'S WILLS, TRUSTS AND ESTATE PLANNING–LAW AND TAXATION, CASES AND MATERIALS, 665 pages, 1988. (Casebook)

McGOVERN, KURTZ AND REIN'S HORNBOOK ON WILLS, TRUSTS AND ESTATES–INCLUDING TAXATION AND FUTURE INTERESTS, 996 pages, 1988. (Text)

MENNELL'S WILLS AND TRUSTS IN A NUTSHELL, 392 pages, 1979. Softcover. (Text)

SIMES' HORNBOOK ON FUTURE INTERESTS,

Second Edition, 355 pages, 1966. (Text)

TURANO AND RADIGAN'S HORNBOOK ON NEW YORK ESTATE ADMINISTRATION, 676 pages, 1986 with 1991 pocket part. (Text)

UNIFORM PROBATE CODE, OFFICIAL TEXT WITH COMMENTS. 863 pages, 1991. Softcover.

WAGGONER'S FUTURE INTERESTS IN A NUTSHELL, 361 pages, 1981. Softcover. (Text)

Water Law—see also Energy and Natural Resources Law, Environmental Law

GETCHES' WATER LAW IN A NUTSHELL, Second Edition, 459 pages, 1990. Softcover. (Text)

SAX, ABRAMS AND THOMPSON'S LEGAL CONTROL OF WATER RESOURCES: CASES AND MATERIALS, Second Edition, 987 pages, 1991. Teacher's Manual available. (Casebook)

TRELEASE AND GOULD'S CASES AND MATERIALS ON WATER LAW, Fourth Edition, 816 pages, 1986. (Casebook)

Wills—see Trusts and Estates

Workers' Compensation

HOOD, HARDY AND LEWIS' WORKERS' COMPENSATION AND EMPLOYEE PROTECTION LAWS IN A NUTSHELL, Second Edition, 361 pages, 1990. Softcover. (Text)

LITTLE, EATON AND SMITH'S CASES AND MATERIALS ON WORKERS' COMPENSATION, 537 pages, 1992. Teacher's Manual available. (Casebook)

HEALTH LAW
CASES, MATERIALS AND PROBLEMS
Second Edition

By

Barry R. Furrow
Professor of Law
Widener University

Sandra H. Johnson
Professor of Law, Professor of Law in
Health Care Administration and
Associate Professor of Law
in Internal Medicine
St. Louis University

Timothy S. Jost
Professor of Law and of Hospital and
Health Services Administration
Ohio State University

Robert L. Schwartz
Professor of Law
University of New Mexico

AMERICAN CASEBOOK SERIES®

WEST PUBLISHING CO.
ST. PAUL, MINN., 1991

American Casebook Series, the key symbol appearing on the front
cover and the WP symbol are registered trademarks of West Publishing
Co. Registered in U.S. Patent and Trademark Office.

Library of Congress Cataloging-in-Publication Data

Health law : cases, materials, and problems / by Barry R. Furrow . . .
    [et al.]. — 2nd ed.
      p.   cm. — (American casebook series)
    Includes index.
    ISBN 0–314–83133–9
    1. Medical laws and legislation—United States—Cases.
  2. Hospitals—Law and legislation—United States—Cases.
  I. Furrow, Barry R. II. Series.
  KF3821.A7H43 1991
  344.73'041—dc20
  [347.30441]

                                                    91–369
                                                     CIP

ISBN 0–314–83133–9

    (F., J., J. & S.) Health Law, 2d Ed. ACB
    2nd Reprint—1993

To Donna Jo, Elena, Michael, Nicholas, Eva, and Robert

B.R.F.

To Bob, Emily, and Kathleen

S.H.J.

To Ruth, Jacob, Micah, and David

T.S.J.

To Jane, Mirra, Elana, and Bryn

R.L.S.

This book is also dedicated to the memory of our friend and colleague, Professor Nancy Rhoden, who contributed so much to the health law community, and to us individually.

*

Preface

In the four years since the first edition of this book was published health law has certainly not stood still. Indeed, it has moved on at a flat-out sprint. Access to health care has become increasingly prominent on the agenda of the state and federal governments as the specter of over thirty million without health insurance, most of them working women and men, becomes an increasing embarrassment. Health care cost control has become ever more urgent as the cost of health care continues to consume an ever greater share of our national productivity. Strategies to contain costs have, however, become ever more complex and diffuse, as the search for an overall regulatory solution has, for the time, been abandoned and private industry and government struggle separately to control the costs of their own health care programs. Major Supreme Court pronouncements in *Webster* and *Cruzan*, as well as further developments in the state courts and legislatures, have raised new issues and challenged the established law in the area of bioethics. Though the malpractice crisis of the early 1980s seems to have abated somewhat at the end of the decade, new ideas for malpractice reform continue to emerge, as do new data illuminating malpractice reforms of the mid-1970s and early 1980s. A whole new sector of law governing the business relationships among health care institutions and professionals has clearly emerged and warrants academic study. It is time for a second edition.

This second edition maintains and enhances the features that made the first edition of this book so popular among health law teachers and students. Our goal continues to be to produce a teachable book. We retain, often in updated form, many of the problems from the first edition and have added new problems, allowing students to struggle with applying the law in situations similar to those they might encounter in practice. We continue to supply an ample store of legal material—cases, statutes, and regulations—supplemented, but not supplanted, by readings in health policy. We have attempted to retain as many materials as possible from the first edition to ease preparation for teaching the second edition, replacing or supplementing only where new developments necessitate updating. We also continue to present all sides of policy issues, not to evangelize for any political, economic, or social agenda of our own.

We have updated and improved the first edition, often in response to helpful comments from those who used the first edition. We have added new sections on private insurance and on physician/hospital contracts and physician recruitment. We have reorganized chapter one of the book to allow an early introduction of all of the elements in the

v

health care industry, reflecting our belief that an understanding of the operations of the health care industry is at least as important to our students as is an understanding of legal doctrine. Chapter five has been expanded and reorganized to focus on business relationships within the health care industry. The access and cost control chapters of the book have been extensively revised, reflecting changing strategies for dealing with these important subjects. The order of these chapters has also been switched to permit a more logical order of presentation. Materials on AIDS, presented separately in the first teachers manual and supplement, have been integrated into the book, illustrating how the AIDS epidemic has pervasively influenced the health care industry. Chapter nine has been completely rewritten to reflect new medical and legal developments in the areas of human reproduction and birth. Finally, chapters on malpractice and on patients rights (bioethics) have been updated to include important new developments in these areas.

We thank many of you who have offered helpful comments for this revision. In particular, we thank Charles Baron, Arnold Celnicker, Dr. Stewart Duban, Margaret Farrell, Michael Gerhart, Dr. Joan Melver Gibson, Thomas Greaney, Jay Healey, Arthur LaFrance, Pam Lambert, Antoinette Sedillo Lopez, Thomas Mayo, Vicki Michel, Ben Rich, Arnold Rosoff, Karen Rothenberg, George Smith, Sheila Taub, Michael Vitiello, and William Winslade for the benefit of their wisdom and experience. We welcome continued dialogue with you, the users of this book, as we struggle together with this important, exciting, and ever-changing field.

We thank those who assisted our research: Karen Biaggi, Tina Boradiansky, John Brady, Laura Holleman, Eric Jackson, Jonathan Lord, Aleda Oetinger, Angela Puco, Philip Rothermich, Kenneth Schmitt, Denise Simmons, and Lynn Wieland.

Finally, we thank our Deans for their support: Dean Anthony Santoro; Dean Francis X. Beytagh; Dean Rudolph C. Hasl; and Deans Theodore Parnall and Leo Romero.

Introduction

Subject Matter, Themes and Organization

This book is about law as it affects the professionals and institutions that deliver health care in the United States. The health care industry is one of the largest industries in the United States. It consumes 12% of the gross national product and 13% of federal expenditures. Moreover, its significance to us cannot be measured in mere economic terms. Health law exists because health care is not a thing so much as it is a relationship between individuals. As the doctor and the patient, the patient and his family, health care providers and health care institutions meet, there are both joint decisions and conflicts. Health care by definition is concerned with our health, and thus affects each of us personally and immediately. Health law struggles with issues of personhood that arise at the start of life in reproduction and birth; at the end of life at death surrounded by medical technology; and continuously in the professional-patient relationship. Health law attempts to insure that health care is of acceptable quality and to reduce or eliminate medical error. Health law articulates our society's often ambivalent commitment to universal and equitable access to health care: a primary human right to a primary human need.

Health law is both broader and narrower than law and medicine as it has been traditionally taught in American law schools. Law and medicine has in the past generally focused on two issues—professional malpractice and forensic medicine. In recent years law and medicine courses have expanded to cover new issues that arise at the interface of law and medicine. This book grows out of a belief that no longer can one course cover all the issues that now arise from the interaction of law and medicine, and that any attempt to do so will inevitably be unfocused. We therefore leave to other courses forensic medicine, proof of medical facts, and some of the more advanced issues of professional malpractice or bioethics. We do cover many subjects not previously covered in depth in law and medicine texts: health care financing and cost control, organization and management of health care institutions, and access of the poor to health care, to name a few. We shift the focus from law and medicine to law as it affects the health care industry, and examine this law as an integrated whole.

Who are the people and institutions that deliver health care in the United States? The first professional that comes to mind is the physician. This is not surprising, for although doctoring is only one of the more than 200 occupations in the health care industry and physicians make up only about 9% of the health care workforce, they control most important health care decisions. But many other professionals also provide health care, including dentists, optometrists, podiatrists, chiropractors, nurses and allied medical professionals.

The hospital has traditionally been the key institution for the delivery of health care in the United States. The nursing home, the pharmacy, and the mental hospital have, however, long existed alongside the hospital. In recent years other health care institutions have proliferated, providing specialized services formerly found only in the hospital: emergicenters, hospices, surgicenters, birthing centers, and other specialized clinics. The health care industry is dependent on other institutions and programs that finance care—Medicare, Medicaid, Blue Cross and Blue Shield, commercial insurance companies, health maintenance organizations and preferred provider organizations. Other institutions regulate health care, including state and federal agencies and private entities like the Joint Commission on Accreditation of Healthcare Organizations or physician specialty certification boards.

The sources of the law that regulate health care are varied. In the first year of law school students become accustomed to searching for law in cases decided by courts. Many court cases involve medical care, particularly medical malpractice. Much of the law that affects health is found not in cases, however, but in statutes, regulations, manuals, contracts, by-laws and protocols. A lawyer counseling a medical professional or institution often must interpret dense and complex statutes or regulations, without guidance from prior court decisions. The statute or regulation may be too recent to have generated litigation, or may raise problems that are not readily subject to judicial review. It is, therefore, essential that lawyers who practice health law have a thorough grounding in health policy; that they understand the problems that bring forth statutes or regulations and previous governmental approaches to those problems; and that they realize how an issue relates to other concerns of the government agency that enforces the statute or regulation, or the professionals or institutions affected. Lawyers representing, advising, regulating, or suing health care professionals and institutions must also understand the organization of the health care industry, its origins and directions. For these reasons, many of the chapters of this book bear little resemblance to the traditional casebook, presenting few cases, but rather lengthy textual notes examining the policies behind regulatory or financing programs and the history of the implementation of those policies.

Health law addresses four major concerns. The first of these is the quality of health care. Much relevant law assumes that the free market upon which we largely rely to assure the quality of most products cannot assure the quality of health care. Consumers cannot be certain of receiving health care of adequate quality, for the products of health care are too complex and information about them too costly to obtain. States have licensed health care providers and institutions as a way of addressing this market failure. The malpractice system also addresses quality problems by retroactively compensating those who receive care of inadequate quality and attempting to deter those who would otherwise commit medical errors. Hospitals and other health care institutions assure the quality of the care they provide through risk management and quality assurance programs. Finally, the JCAHO and other private organizations police the quality of health care, with varying legal consequences.

A second concern of health law is cost. As the proportion of our gross national product and of the federal and state budgets claimed by the health care industry climbs steadily upward, the issue of cost has become increasingly urgent. The diagnosis is again market failure, the prescription legal intervention (sometimes intervention to regulate, sometimes to restore competitive conditions). Public policy directed at controlling health care expenditures has found articulation in programs that have attempted to control the supply of health care resources, limit utilization of health care, or constrain rates charged by health care providers. The use of the antitrust laws or of regulatory strategies to force the health care industry to become more competitive also reflects cost concerns.

A third concern of health law is equitable access. Although our society has rejected the notion that all ought to have equal wealth, it has to some degree accepted the argument that health care is different, that everyone should receive some level of health care. This has resulted in legal intervention to force health care providers to provide "free" care, that is, care financed by other patients, and in government programs to pay for health care directly. As costs have risen, society's commitment to access to health care has been reexamined. New technologies such as organ transplants, which are subject to limitations other than cost, have further tested the meaning and commitment to equal access.

A final concern of health law is respect for the person of the patient. Medicine has traditionally taken the paternalistic approach exemplified by the use of the word "patient"—one who suffers passively—to identify the object of health care. The law has taken on the role of protecting the autonomy of the patient. This concern is reflected in the doctrine of informed consent, protection of confidentiality of medical information, and the patient's right to choose an abortion or to terminate life support systems under certain circumstances.

Chapters 1, 2, and 4 of this book focus primarily on how the law regulates the quality of health care, through licensure, institutional quality control programs and the tort system. Chapter 5 deals with a variety of issues that arise in health care institutions. Chapter 6 examines access issues. Chapters 7 and 8 are concerned with control of health care costs through regulation, competition and the antitrust laws. Chapters 3, 9, 10, 11 and 12 discuss respect for personhood in the context of the professional-patient relationship, medical intervention in the processes of reproduction and death, health care decisionmaking, and medical research.

This book does not follow traditional casebook form, in that we have adapted the material to the legally relevant resources for particular issues. Although the medical malpractice chapter makes extensive use of cases, for example, the chapters on cost control and access rely on text, statutory and regulatory material. This book also departs from traditional casebook form in its use of problems. The problems are intended to be used to integrate and to focus classroom discussion of wide-ranging materials. In some sections they test the students' mastery of statutory or regulatory materials presented in the text. Most of these problems are relatively complex. Some raise issues that are currently unresolved and for which there are no answers. The more sophisticated problems may be used either to begin discussion or after there has been an analysis in the classroom of the cases and materials in the text. We believe the problem approach is particularly useful in health law because the lawyer practicing in the area is so often called upon to be a problem solver.

Editorial Style:

Elipses in the text of quoted material indicate an omission of material within the quoted paragraph. Centered elipses indicate the omission of a paragraph or more. Brackets indicate the omission of citations.

All authors acknowledge the editorial assistance of Joyce Coleman.

BARRY R. FURROW
SANDRA H. JOHNSON
TIMOTHY S. JOST
ROBERT L. SCHWARTZ

Acknowledgments

The authors gratefully acknowledge permission to quote from the following materials:

Abraham, Medical Liability Reform: A Conceptual Framework, 260 Journal of the American Medical Association 68–72 (1988). Copyright © 1988, American Medical Association.

Annas, Impact of Gene Maps on Law and Society, Trial 42 (July 1990). Reprinted with permission of the author.

C.R. Austin, Human Embryos: The Debate On Assisted Reproduction (1989). Copyright 1989, Oxford University Press. Reprinted with permission of the Oxford University Press.

Battin, The Least Worst Death, 13 Hastings Center Report (2) 13 (April 1983). Copyright 1983, the Hastings Center. Reprinted with permission of the Hastings Center.

Beardsley, Profile: Gene Doctor, Scientific American 33 (August 1990). Copyright 1990, Scientific American, Inc. Reprinted with permission of Scientific American, Inc.

Bernat, Culver, and Gert, Defining Death in Theory and Practice, 12 Hastings Center Report (1) 5 (February 1982). Copyright 1982, the Hastings Center. Reprinted with permission of the Hastings Center.

Brahams, Medicine and the Law: Court of Appeal Endorses Medical Decision to Allow Baby to Die, Lancet 969 (April 29, 1989). Copyright 1989, The Lancet Ltd. Reprinted with permission of The Lancet Ltd.

Callahan, Morality in Contemporary Culture: The President's Commission and Beyond, 6 Cardozo L.Rev. 347. Copyright 1984, Cardozo Law Review. Reprinted with permission of the Cardozo Law Review.

Callahan, Special Supplement, 19 Hastings Center Report (Jan./Feb.) 4 (1989). Copyright 1989, the Hastings Center. Reprinted with permission of the Hastings Center.

Capron, Alternative Birth Technologies: Legal Challenges, 20 U.C. Davis L.Rev. 679 (1987). Copyright 1987 by the Regents of the University of California. Reprinted with permission.

Capron and Kass, A Statutory Definition of the Standards for Determining Human Death: An Appraisal and a Proposal, 121 U.Pa.L.Rev. 87 (1972). Copyright 1972, the University of Pennsylvania Law Review. Reprinted with permission of the University of Pennsylvania Law Review.

Danzon, P., Medical Malpractice: Theory, Evidence, and Public Policy, 1st Ed., (Cambridge, Mass., Harvard University Press, 1985) 3–4, 39, 91, 225–227. Reprinted by permission of Harvard University Press.

Donabedian, Avedis, The Definition of Quality and Approaches to Its Assessment, 1st Ed., (Ann Arbor, MI Health Administration Press, 1980), 4–6, 7, 13, 14, 27, 79–84, 102, 119. Reprinted from Avedis Donabedian, The Definition of Quality and Approaches to Its Assessment, vol. 1 of Explorations in Quality Assessment and Monitoring. Health Administration Press, Ann Arbor, Michigan. Copyright © 1980. Reprinted with permission.

Englehardt, Fashioning an Ethic for Life and Death in a Post-Modern Society, Spec. Supp., 19 Hastings Center Report (Jan./Feb.) 7 (1989). Copyright 1989, the Hastings Center. Reprinted with permission of the Hastings Center.

Evans, Tension, Compression and Shear: Directions, Stresses, and Outcomes of Health Care Cost Control, 15 Journal of Health Politics, Policy and Law 101 (1990). Copyright © 1990, Duke University Press. Reprinted by permission of the publisher.

Fletcher, Drawing Moral Lines in Fetal Therapy, 29 Clin. Obstetrics & Gynecology 595 (1986). Copyright 1986. Reprinted with permission of J.B. Lippincott Company.

Fletcher, Humanhood, in Humanhood, Essays in Biomedical Ethics. Copyright 1979, the Hastings Center. Reprinted with permission of the Hastings Center.

Gibson and Kushner, Ethics Committees: How are they Doing?, 16 Hastings Center Report (3) 9 (June 1986). Copyright 1986, the Hastings Center. Reprinted with permission of the Hastings Center.

Gibson and Schwartz, Physicians and Lawyers, Art and Conflict, 6 Am. J.L. Med. 173. Copyright 1981, the American Society of Law and Medicine. Reprinted with permission of American Society of Law and Medicine.

Ginsburg, Physician Payment Policy in the 101st Congress, 8 Health Affairs 5 (Spring 1988). Copyright © 1988 by Project HOPE, (Millwood, VA). Reprinted by permission of Health Affairs.

Johnson, Phillips, Orentlicher and Hatlie, The American Medical Association/Specialty Society Tort Reform Proposal: A Fault-Based Administrative System, 1 Courts, Health Science and the Law 84–86 (1990). Reprinted with permission of Courts, Health Science and the Law.

Kass, Death as an Event, A Commentary on Robert Morison, 173 Science 698. Copyright 1971 by the AAAS. Reprinted with permission of the AAAS.

Katz, Jay, The Silent World of Doctor and Patient, The Free Press, a Division of Macmillan, Inc., 1, 79, 82–83, 102, 228–229. Copyright © 1984 by Jay Katz. Excerpted with permission of The Free Press, a Division of Macmillan, Inc. from THE SILENT WORLD OF DOCTOR AND PATIENT by Jay Katz.

I. Kennedy and A. Grubb, Medical Law (1989). Copyright 1989. Reprinted with permission of Butterworth Legal Publishers.

Korbin, Comment—Confidentiality of Genetic Information, 30 UCLA L.Rev. 1283. Copyright 1983, the Regents of the University of California. All rights reserved. Reprinted with permission of the Regents of the University of California.

Laing, The Politics of the Family and Other Essays. Copyright 1971, Random House, Inc. Reprinted with permission of Random House.

Lidz, Neisel, Zerubavel, Carter, Sestak, and Roth, Informed Consent: A Study of Decision-making in Psychiatry, 318, 326, 333–334 (New York, The Guilford Press, 1984). Copyright © 1984 by The Guilford Press. Reprinted with permission of The Guilford Press.

Morison, Death: Process or Event, 173 Science 694. Copyright 1971 by the AAAS. Reprinted with permission of the AAAS.

National Conference of Commissioners of Uniform State Laws, Uniform Probate Code. Copyright, National Conference of Commissioners on Uniform State Law. This Act has been reprinted through the permission of the National Conference of Commissioners on Uniform State Laws, and copies of the Act may be ordered from them at a nominal cost at 676 North St. Clair Street, Suite 1700, Chicago, Illinois 60611, (312) 915–0195.

National Conference of Commissioners of Uniform State Laws, Uniform Rights of the Terminally Ill Act. Copyright 1989, National Conference of Commissioners on Uniform State Law. This Act has been reprinted through the permission of the National Conference of Commissioners on Uniform State Laws, and copies of the Act may be ordered from them at a nominal cost at 676 North St. Clair Street, Suite 1700, Chicago, Illinois 60611, (312) 915–0195.

National Conference of Commissioners of Uniform State Laws, Uniform Determination of Death Act. Copyright 1980, National Conference of Commissioners on Uniform State Law. This Act has been reprinted through the permission of the National Conference of Commissioners on Uniform State Laws, and copies of the Act may be ordered from them at a nominal cost at 676 North St. Clair Street, Suite 1700, Chicago, Illinois 60611, (312) 915–0195.

National Conference of Commissioners of Uniform State Laws, Uniform Parentage Act. Copyright 1973, National Conference of Commissioners on Uniform State Law. This Act has been reprinted through the permission of the National Conference of Commissioners on Uniform State Laws, and copies of the Act may be ordered from them at a nominal cost at 676 North St. Clair Street, Suite 1700, Chicago, Illinois 60611, (312) 915–0195.

National Conference of Commissioners of Uniform State Laws, Uniform Anatomical Gift Act. Copyright 1987, National Conference of Commissioners on Uniform State Law. This Act has been reprinted through the permission of the National Conference of Commissioners on Uniform State Laws, and copies of the Act may be ordered from them at a nominal cost at 676 North St. Clair Street, Suite 1700, Chicago, Illinois 60611, (312) 915–0195.

Oetinger, Drawing of the Reproductive Process. Copyright © 1991 by Aleda Oetinger. Reprinted with permission of Aleda Oetinger.

Rapp, Chromosomes of Communication: The Discourse of Genetic Counseling, 2 Med. Anthropology Q. 143 (1988). Copyright 1988, American Anthropological Association. Reproduced by permission of the American Anthropological Association. Not for sale or further reproduction.

Report of the Commission of inquiry into "Human Fertilisation and Embryology" (Cmnd 9314) (1984). Copyright 1984, Her Majesty's Stationery Office. Reprinted with permission of the Controller of Her Majesty's Stationery Office.

Rigter, Euthanasia in the Netherlands: Distinguishing Fact from Fiction, Spec. Supp., 19 Hastings Center Report (Jan./Feb.) 7 (1989). Copyright 1989, the Hastings Center. Reprinted with permission of the Hastings Center.

Robin E., Matters of Life and Death: Risks vs. Benefits of Medical Care, 57, 65, 73, & 147 (New York, W.H. Freeman and Company Publishers, 1984). Copyright © 1984 by Eugene D. Robin. Reprinted with permission by W.H. Freeman and Company.

Ross, Case Consultation: The Committee or the Clinical Consultant, 2 Hospital Ethics Committee Forum 289 (1990). Copyright 1990. Reprinted by permission of the Hospital Ethics Committee Forum.

Roth, Meisel & Lidz, Tests of Competency to Consent to Treatment, 134 Am. J. of Psychiatry 279. Copyright 1977, American Psychiatric Association. Reprinted with permission of the American Psychiatric Association and the authors.

Rowinski, Genetic Testing in the Work Place, 4 J. of Contemp. Health L. and Policy 375 (1988). Copyright 1988. Reprinted with permission of the Journal of Contemporary Health Law and Policy.

Schifrin, Weissman, and Wiley, Electronic Fetal Monitoring and Obstetrical Malpractice, 13 Law, Medicine & Health Care 100, 104 (1985). Copyright © 1985, the American Society of Law and Medicine. Reprinted with permission of the American Society of Law and Medicine, Boston, Massachusetts.

Showalter, Determining Death: The Legal and Theological Aspects of Brain-Related Criteria, 27 Catholic Lawyer 112 (1982). Copyright 1982, Catholic Lawyer. Reprinted with permission of the Catholic Lawyer.

Sinsheimer, Whither the Genome Project?, 20 Hastings Center Report (July/Aug.) 5 (1990). Copyright 1990, the Hastings Center. Reprinted with permission of the Hastings Center.

Somerville, Therapeutic Privilege: Variations on the Theme of Informed Consent, 12 Law, Medicine & Health Care 4 (1984). Copyright © 1984, the American Society of Law and Medicine. Reprinted with permission of the American Society of Law and Medicine, Boston, Massachusetts.

Thomas, Dylan, "Do Not Go Gentle Into That Good Night", Dylan Thomas: Poems of Dylan Thomas. Copyright 1952 by Dylan Thomas. Reprinted by permission of New Directions Publishing Company.

Ulrich, Reproductive Rights and Genetic Disease, in J. Humber and R. Almeder, eds., Biomedical Ethics and the Law. Copyright 1976, Plenum Press. Reprinted with permission of Plenum Press and the author.

Veatch, Correspondence—What it Means to be Dead, 12 Hastings Center Report (5) 45 (October 1982). Copyright 1982, the Hastings Center. Reprinted with permission of the Hastings Center.

Wennberg, John E., "Dealing with Medical Practice Variations: A Proposal for Action", Vol. 3 Health Affairs, 7, 9, (Millwood, VA, Project Hope 1984). Copyright © 1984 by Project HOPE, (Millwood, VA). Reprinted by permission of Health Affairs.

*

Summary of Contents

Table of Contents

1

1

1

1

1

*

Table of Problems

Table of Cases

The principal cases are in bold type. Cases cited or discussed in the text are roman type. References are to pages. Cases cited in principal cases and within other quoted materials are not included.

HEALTH LAW
CASES, MATERIALS AND PROBLEMS

*

Chapter 1

REGULATING THE QUALITY OF HEALTH CARE

This chapter will consider first the definition and evaluation of quality; then examine the problem of medical error; next consider methods of quality assessment; and then consider two methods through which the quality of health care is currently controlled: (1) licensing and (2) institutional quality assessment and risk management. Quality concerns are addressed again in chapters 2 and 4, which examine the malpractice system and its reform; and throughout this book.

I. QUALITY AND ERROR

Lawyers become involved with quality of health care issues through a variety of routes. They file, or defend against, malpractice suits when a patient is injured because of a doctor's deviation from a standard of medical practice. They handle medical staff privilege cases that frequently turn on the quality of the staff doctor's performance. They represent the government in administering programs that aim to cut the cost of health care and improve its quality and providers that must adjust to these programs. Quality is a central concern in health care politics and law.

A. DEFINING SICKNESS

Before examining the meaning of quality in health care, consider the meaning of health and of sickness. We all have an operational definition of health and sickness. I know when I am depressed, have a broken leg, a headache or a hangover. In these circumstances I consider myself to be in ill health because I am not functioning as well as I usually do, even though I may lack a scientific medical explanation of my malaise. But am I in poor health because my arteries are gradually becoming clogged, a process that probably began when I was a teenager? Am I sick or in poor health if I am obese, or addicted to alcohol or drugs, or if I am very old and enfeebled?

We need some definition of health in order to assess the quality of care needed to promote or restore it. A malpractice suit or medical quality audit depends on an ability to distinguish a bad from a good

1

medical care outcome. An understanding of the nature of sickness and health is required to determine what health care society should provide the poor and how much society ought to spend on health care. Should Medicaid (a federal/state health care program for the poor) or a commercial insurer, for example, cover in vitro fertilization or abortions? Does the possibility of organ transplantation mean that replacement hearts should become the normal treatment for a condition that formerly inevitably ended in death? Should organ transplantation be available to all, without regard to the ability to pay? If the state of being old becomes a state of sickness (and particularly if that sickness must be "cured" at public expense), what will be the cost? Is this cost justified? Finally, the definition of health raises questions of autonomy, responsibility and personhood. Should health be defined by the doctor as scientist or the patient as person, or both? Is the drunkard or serial killer diseased or sinning or both or neither?

The Constitution of the World Health Organization defines health as "[A] State of complete physical, mental and social well-being and not merely the absence of disease or infirmity." When did you last feel that way? Can health ever be achieved under this definition, or is everyone always in a state of ill health? How much can physicians and hospitals contribute to health under this definition? A further provision of the WHO Constitution provides that "Governments have a responsibility for the health of their peoples which can be fulfilled only by the provision of adequate health and social measures." What are the political ramifications of these principles?

Health can be viewed in a more limited sense as the performance by each part of the body of its "natural" function. Definitions in terms of biological functioning tend to be more descriptive and less value-laden. As Englehardt writes, "The notion required for an analysis of health is not that of a good man or a good shark, but that of a good specimen of a human being or shark." Englehardt, "The Concepts of Health and Disease," in Concepts of Health and Disease 552 (A. Caplan, H. Engelhardt, and J. McCartney, eds. 1981) (hereafter Concepts). Boorse compares health to the mechanical condition of a car, which can be described as good because it conforms to the designers' specifications, even though the design is flawed. Disease is then a biological malfunction, a deviation from the biological norm of natural function. Boorse, "On the Distinction Between Disease and Illness," in Concepts, supra at 553.

Illness can be defined as a subset of disease. Boorse writes:
> An illness must be, first, a reasonably *serious* disease with incapacitating effects that make it undesirable. A shaving cut or mild athlete's foot cannot be called an illness, nor could one call in sick on the basis of a single dental cavity, though all these conditions are diseases. Secondly, to call a disease an illness is to view its owner as deserving special treatment and diminished moral accountability * * *. Where we do not make the appropriate normative judgments or activate the social institutions, no amount of disease will lead us to use the term

"ill." Even if the laboratory fruit flies fly in listless circles and expire at our feet, we do not say they succumbed to an illness, and for roughly the same reasons as we decline to give them a proper funeral.

There are, then, two senses of "health". In one sense it is a theoretical notion, the opposite of "disease." In another sense it is a practical or mixed ethical notion, the opposite of "illness."

Illness is thus a socially constructed deviance. Something more than a mere biological abnormality is needed. To be ill is to have deviant characteristics for which the sick role is appropriate. The sick role, as Parsons has described it, exempts one from normal social responsibilities and removes individual responsibility. See T. Parsons, The Social System (1951). Our choice of words reflects this: an alcoholic is sick; a drunkard is not.

A sick person can be assisted by treatment defined by the medical model. He becomes a patient, an object of medical attention by a doctor. The doctor has the right and the ability to label someone ill, to determine whether the lump on a patient's skin is a blister, a wart or a cancer. The doctor can thus decide whether a patient is culpable or not, disabled or malingering. Illness also enjoins the physician to action to restore the patient to health.

Illness thus has many ramifications. First, it affects the individual. It relieves responsibility. The sick person need not report for work at 8:00; the posttraumatic stress syndrome or premenstrual syndrome victim may be declared not guilty for an assault. It means loss of control. The mild pain may have disproportionate effects on the individual who sees it as the harbinger of cancer or a brain tumor. The physician can restore control by providing a rational explanation for the experience of impairment. Illness costs the patient money, in lost time and in medical expenses. And someone receives that money for trying to treat that patient's illness.

But our understanding of illness also affects society. Defining a condition as an illness, to be aggressively treated, rather than as a natural condition of life to be accepted and tolerated, has significant economic effects. Medical care is also a good, the object of economic choice. Yet it is a good that many perceive to be different from other goods, possessing greater, sometimes immeasurable value. Thus, it is argued, persons are willing to pay far more for medical care than they would for other goods, or, more typically, to procure insurance that will deliver them from ever having to face the choice of paying for health care and abandoning all else. And society may also feel a special obligation to pay for the medical expenses of those who need treatment and lack resources to pay for it.

TRAYNOR v. TURNAGE

Supreme Court of the United States, 1988.
485 U.S. 535, 108 S.Ct. 1372, 99 L.Ed.2d 618.

Justice White delivered the opinion of the Court.

These cases arise from the Veterans' Administration's refusal to grant two recovered alcoholics extensions of time in which to use their veterans' educational benefits. We must decide whether the Veterans' Administration's decision is subject to judicial review and, if so, whether that decision violates § 504 of the Rehabilitation Act of 1973, 87 Stat. 394, 29 U.S.C. § 794, which requires that federal programs not discriminate against handicapped individuals solely because of their handicap.[1]

I

Veterans who have been honorably discharged from the United States Armed Forces are entitled to receive educational assistance benefits under the Veterans' Readjustment Benefit Act of 1966 ("G.I. Bill") to facilitate their readjustment to civilian life. See 38 U.S.C. § 1661. These benefits generally must be used within 10 years following discharge or release from active duty. § 1662(a)(1). Veterans may obtain an extension of the 10–year delimiting period, however, if they were prevented from using their benefits earlier by "a physical or mental disability which was not the result of [their] own willful misconduct." *Ibid.*

Petitioners are honorably discharged veterans who did not exhaust their educational benefits during the decade following their military service. They sought to continue to receive benefits after the expiration of the 10–year delimiting period on the ground that they had been disabled by alcoholism during much of that period. The Veterans' Administration determined that petitioners' alcoholism constituted "willful misconduct" under 38 CFR § 3.301(c)(2) (1987),[2] and accordingly denied the requested extensions.

* * *

III

Congress historically has imposed time limitations on the use of "G.I. Bill" educational benefits. * * * The delimiting period under the current "G.I. Bill" was raised from 8 years to 10 years in 1974. [ ] In 1977, Congress created an exception to this 10–year delimiting period for veterans who delayed their education because of "a physical or

---

1. Section 504, 29 U.S.C. § 794, provides, in pertinent part, that "[n]o otherwise qualified handicapped individual … shall, solely by reason of his handicap, be excluded from the participation in, be denied the benefits of, or be subjected to discrimination under any program or activity receiving Federal financial assistance or under any program or activity conducted by any Executive agency."

2. The applicable regulation, 38 CFR § 3.301(c)(2) (1987), provides:

"*Alcoholism:* The simple drinking of alcoholic beverage is not of itself willful misconduct. The deliberate drinking of a

known poisonous substance or under conditions which would raise a presumption to that effect will be considered willful misconduct. If, in the drinking of a beverage to enjoy its intoxicating effects, intoxication results proximately [*sic*] and immediately in disability or death, the disability or death will be considered the result of the person's willful misconduct. Organic diseases and disabilities which are a secondary result of the chronic use of alcohol as a beverage, whether out of compulsion or otherwise, will not be considered of willful misconduct origin."

mental disability which was not the result of [their] own willful misconduct." Pub.L. 95–202, Tit. II, § 203(a)(1), 91 Stat. 1429, 38 U.S.C. § 1662(a)(1).

Congress did not use the term "willful misconduct" inadvertently in § 1662(a)(1). The same term had long been used in other veterans' benefits statutes. * * * The Veterans' Administration had long construed the term "willful misconduct" for purposes of these statutes as encompassing primary alcoholism (i.e., alcoholism that is not "secondary to and a manifestation of an acquired psychiatric disorder"). [ ]

* * * The legislative history confirms that Congress intended that the Veterans' Administration apply the same test of "willful misconduct" in granting extensions of time under § 1662(a)(1) as the agency already was applying in granting disability compensation under § 310 and § 521. * * * These criteria therefore are among the "standards" that * * * Congress intended to be utilized in determining eligibility for extended educational benefits.

It is thus clear that the 1977 legislation precluded an extension of time to a veteran who had not pursued his education because of primary alcoholism. If Congress had intended instead that primary alcoholism not be deemed "willful misconduct" for purposes of § 1662(a)(1), as it had been deemed for purposes of other veterans' benefits statutes, Congress most certainly would have said so.

It was the same Congress that one year later extended § 504's prohibition against discrimination on the basis of handicap to "any program or activity conducted by any Executive agency." [ ] Yet, in enacting the 1978 Rehabilitation Act amendments, Congress did not affirmatively evince any intent to repeal or amend the "willful misconduct" provision of § 1662(a)(1). Nor did Congress anywhere in the language or legislative history of the 1978 amendments expressly disavow its 1977 determination that primary alcoholism is not the sort of disability that warrants an exemption from the time constraints of § 1662(a)(1).

Accordingly, petitioners can prevail under their Rehabilitation Act claim only if the 1978 legislation can be deemed to have implicitly repealed the "willful misconduct" provision of the 1977 legislation or forbade the Veterans' Administration to classify primary alcoholism as willful misconduct. They must thereby overcome the " 'cardinal rule * * * that repeals by implication are not favored.' " [ ]

As we have noted, the 1978 legislation did not expressly contradict the more "narrow, precise, and specific" 1977 legislation. Moreover, the 1978 legislation is not rendered meaningless, even with respect to those who claim to have been handicapped as a result of alcoholism, if the "willful misconduct" provision of § 1662(a)(1) is allowed to retain the import originally intended by Congress.

First, the "willful misconduct" provision does not undermine the central purpose of § 504, which is to assure that handicapped individuals receive "evenhanded treatment" in relation to nonhandicapped individuals. [ ] This litigation does not involve a program or activity that is alleged to treat handicapped persons less favorably than non-handicapped persons. [ ] Rather, petitioners challenge a statutory provision that treats disabled veterans more favorably than able-bodied veterans: The former may obtain extensions of time in which to use their educational benefits so long as they did not become disabled as a result of their own "willful misconduct"; the latter are absolutely precluded from obtaining such extensions regardless of how compelling their reasons for having delayed their schooling might be. In other words, § 1662(a)(1) merely provides a special benefit to disabled veterans who bear no responsibility for their disabilities that is not provided to other disabled veterans or to any able-bodied veterans.

* * *

Furthermore, § 1662(a)(1) does not deny extensions of the delimiting period to all alcoholics but only to those whose drinking was not attributable to an underlying psychiatric disorder. It is estimated by some authorities that mental illness is responsible for 20% to 30% of all alcoholism cases. Brief for American Medical Association as *Amicus Curiae* 7. Each veteran who claims to have been disabled by alcoholism is entitled under § 1662(a)(1) to an individualized assessment of whether his condition was the result of a mental illness.

Petitioners, however, perceive an inconsistency between § 504 and the conclusive presumption that alcoholism not motivated by mental illness is necessarily "willful." They contend that § 504 mandates an individualized determination of "willfulness" with respect to each veteran who claims to have been disabled by alcoholism. It would arguably be inconsistent with § 504 for Congress to distinguish between categories of disabled veterans according to generalized determinations that lack any substantial basis. If primary alcoholism is not always "willful," as that term has been defined by Congress and the Veterans' Administration, some veterans denied benefits may well be excluded solely on the basis of their disability. We are unable to conclude that Congress failed to act in accordance with § 504 in this instance, however, given what the District of Columbia Circuit accurately characterized as "a substantial body of medical literature that even contests the proposition that alcoholism is a disease, much less that it is a disease for which the victim bears no responsibility." [ ] Indeed, even among many who consider alcoholism a "disease" to which its victims are genetically predisposed, the consumption of alcohol is not regarded as wholly involuntary. See Fingarette, The Perils of *Powell:* In Search of a Factual Foundation for the "Disease Concept of Alcoholism," 83 Harv.L.Rev. 793, 802–808 (1970). As we see it, § 504 does not demand inquiry into whether factors other than mental illness rendered an individual veteran's drinking so entirely beyond his control as to negate any degree of "willfulness" where Congress and the Veterans' Administration have reasonably determined for purposes of the veterans' benefits statutes that no such factors exist.

In sum, we hold that a construction of § 1662(a)(1) that reflects the original congressional intent that primary alcoholics not be excused from the 10–year delimiting period for utilizing "G.I. Bill" benefits is not inconsistent with the prohibition on discrimination against the handicapped contained in § 504 of the Rehabilitation Act. * * *

IV

This litigation does not require the Court to decide whether alcoholism is a disease whose course its victims cannot control. It is not our role to resolve this medical issue on which the authorities remain sharply divided. Our task is to decide whether Congress intended, in enacting § 504 of the Rehabilitation Act, to reject the position taken on the issue by the Veterans' Administration and by Congress itself only one year earlier. In our view, it is by no means clear that § 504 and the characterization of primary alcoholism as a willfully incurred disability are in irreconcilable conflict. If petitioners and their proponents continue to believe that this position is erroneous, their arguments are better presented to Congress than to the courts.

* * *

JUSTICE BLACKMUN, with whom JUSTICE BRENNAN and JUSTICE MARSHALL join, concurring in part and dissenting in part.

I join Parts I and II of the Court's opinion, for I agree that, under § 504 of the Rehabilitation Act of 1973, 87 Stat. 394, as amended, 29 U.S.C. § 794, the "final and conclusive" language of 38 U.S.C. § 211(a) does not bar judicial review of petitioners' claims. Similarly, I acknowledge the legality (a) of the 10–year delimiting period imposed by 38 U.S.C. § 1662(a) upon veterans' educational assistance, and (b) of that statute's alleviation of the delimiting period in cases of disability except where that disability is the result of a veteran's "own willful misconduct."

My dispute with the Court centers in its upholding of the regulation, 38 CFR § 3.301(c)(2) (1987), whereby the Veterans' Administration (VA) presumes, *irrebuttably,* that primary alcoholism always is the result of the veteran's "own willful misconduct." This is the very kind of broad social generalization that § 504 of the Rehabilitation Act is intended to eliminate. The petitioners in these cases ask only that their situations be given individualized evaluation. Because I think this is what the Rehabilitation Act clearly requires, I dissent from the Court's conclusion to the contrary.[1]

I

Petitioner Eugene Traynor began drinking when he was eight or nine years old. He drank with increasing frequency throughout his teenage years, and was suffering alcohol-related seizures by the time he was on active military duty in Vietnam. During the four years follow-

---

1. It perhaps is worth noting that, despite much comment in the popular press, these cases are not concerned with wheth-er alcoholism, simplistically, is or is not a "disease."

ing his honorable discharge in 1969, Mr. Traynor was hospitalized repeatedly for alcoholism and related illnesses.

By the end of 1974, however, petitioner Traynor had conquered his drinking problem. He attended college part-time beginning in 1977, and continued working toward his degree until the 10–year period for using his veteran's educational benefits expired for him in 1979. Mr. Traynor applied for the extension of time available under 38 U.S.C. § 1662(a)(1) to one whose disability had prevented him from completing a program of education within the 10–year period. Because he was unable to establish that his alcoholism was due to an underlying psychiatric disorder, his condition was labeled "primary alcoholism." Pursuant to the regulation cited above, Mr. Traynor was presumed to have brought his alcoholism upon himself through "willful misconduct." The requested extension therefore was denied.

[The discussion of petitioner McKelvey's history of drinking is omitted.]

II

The VA's reliance on its irrebuttable presumption that all primary alcoholism is attributable to willful misconduct cannot be squared with the mandate against discrimination contained in § 504 of the Rehabilitation Act. Just last year, in *School Bd. of Nassau County v. Arline,* ___ U.S. ___, 107 S.Ct. 1123, 94 L.Ed.2d 307 (1987), this Court explained in no uncertain terms that § 504 bars the generic treatment of any group of individuals with handicaps based on archaic or simplistic stereotypes about attributes associated with their disabling conditions. Instead, § 504 requires an individualized assessment of each person's qualifications, based on "reasoned and medically sound judgments." *Id.,* at 285. In sanctioning the VA's irrebuttable presumption that any veteran suffering from primary alcoholism brought the ailment upon himself through willful misconduct, the Court ignores the lesson of *Arline,* and the clear dictate of the Rehabilitation Act.

In these cases, the Court is called upon, not to make its own medical judgments about the causes of alcoholism, but to interpret § 504. * * *

It is beyond dispute that petitioners, as alcoholics, were handicapped individuals covered by the Act. [ ] Nor is it disputed that § 504 of the Act prohibits federal agencies, such as the VA, from denying benefits to petitioners solely because they are alcoholics. [ ]

* * *

The VA seems to suggest that generalizations about attributes associated with individuals suffering from a particular disability can be relied upon to assess those individuals' qualifications, as long as the generalizations are shown to be reasonable. But reliance on generalizations, even "reasonable" ones, is clearly prohibited under *Arline.* In that case, the Court ruled that § 504 prevented the Nassau County School Board from generalizing about the contagiousness of tuberculosis. ___ U.S., at ___-___, 107 S.Ct., at 1127–30. Acknowledging that in some cases contagiousness would justify altering or perhaps terminating a tuberculosis sufferer's employment in order to avoid infecting others, *id.*, at 1131, n. 16, the Court nevertheless found impermissible a generalization built on that less-than-perfect correlation between disability and qualification. The Court explained:

> "The fact that *some* persons who have contagious diseases may pose a serious health threat to others under certain circumstances does not justify excluding from the coverage of the Act *all* persons with actual or perceived contagious diseases. Such exclusion would mean that those accused of being contagious would never have the opportunity to have their condition evaluated in light of medical evidence and a determination made as to whether they were 'otherwise qualified.' Rather, they would be vulnerable to discrimination on the basis of mythology—precisely the type of injury Congress sought to prevent." 480 U.S., at ___-___, 107 S.Ct., at 1130 (emphasis in original).

The myth to which the Court was referring was not that some tuberculosis sufferers were contagious, but that they *all* were. The parallel myth in the present cases, of course, is that *all* primary alcoholics became disabled as a result of their own willful misconduct. Just as § 504 entitles each person suffering from tuberculosis to an individualized determination, based on sound medical evidence, as to whether that person is contagious and therefore not "otherwise qualified" for a job, 29 U.S.C. § 794, the statute entitles each alcoholic veteran to an individualized determination, based on the medical evidence in his own case, of the causes of his disability. If this individualized assessment leads the adjudicator to conclude that the particular veteran's alcoholism was brought on by willful misconduct, that veteran will have been adjudicated to be not "otherwise qualified" to collect the education benefits. But only after this individualized inquiry has been conducted, can the VA deprive him of benefits available to all whose disabilities were not caused by willful misconduct.

B

The VA's attempt to justify its reliance upon the irrebuttable presumption that primary alcoholism is caused by willful misconduct is further undermined by the meagerness of the medical support it summons. Nothing in the record suggests that the VA based its continuing reliance on the presumption, after § 504 was amended, on any factual findings of the kind found to be required in *Arline*. And its *post hoc* rationalization of that reliance in this litigation consists of a hodgepodge of medical conclusions, some of only marginal relevance. For example, the VA relies upon the comments of a number of "medical writers" who note that "volition plays a significant role" in the *treatment* of alcoholism. [ ] While cure and cause are likely to be somewhat related, the fact that alcoholism is "highly treatable, but * * * will require great responsibility from the patient," [ ] provides little assistance in assessing whether the original onset of the disability can always be ascribed to willful misconduct.

In contrast, ample evidence supports petitioner's contrary contention that the degree of willfulness associated with the onset of alcoholism varies from case to case. Recent medical research indicates that the causes of primary alcoholism are varied and complex, only some of which conceivably could be attributed to a veteran's will. Indeed, even the VA acknowledges that "alcoholism is not a unitary condition [but rather] has multiple forms and ranges of severity." [ ] A sensitivity to this case-to-case variation is precisely what § 504 requires of employers and federal agencies in their assessments of the qualifications for employment or benefits of an individual with handicaps. As the medical community's understanding of the causes of alcoholism continues to develop, § 504 requires the VA to take these new developments into account in making "sound medical judgments" about the source of a particular veteran's alcoholism. Presumably, evidence concerning the circumstances surrounding a veteran's development of alcohol dependence—including his age, home environment, and psychological health—always will be relevant to this assessment.

C

Finally, in asserting that its automatic association of primary alcoholism with willful misconduct is supported by medical evidence, the VA adopts, perhaps for purposes of this litigation alone, a definition of willful misconduct which is inconsistent with the definition articulated in the VA's own regulations and practices. According to the VA, primary alcoholism is appropriately attributed to willful misconduct because medical evidence suggests that "many alcoholics are *not completely helpless*," in controlling their disability. [ ] But a "not completely helpless" test is not the standard the VA has established for determining whether other disabilities are incurred willfully.

The VA defines willful misconduct as "an act involving conscious wrongdoing or known prohibited action," 38 CFR § 3.1(n) (1987), and "the intentional doing of something either with the knowledge that it is likely to result in serious injury or with a wanton and reckless disregard of its probable consequences." VA Manual M21-1, change 239, subch. I, § 14.04a (Aug. 21, 1979).[9] This definition of willful misconduct is a far cry from a "not completely helpless" standard. While some primary alcoholics may well owe their disability to willful misconduct, as delineated by the regulation, the VA has failed to demonstrate that *all* primary alcoholics had any awareness that their initial drinking was likely to result in serious injury. Nor, in many cases, would it be

---

9. Outside the alcoholism context, the Board of Veterans Appeals has found willful misconduct when, for example, a veteran "placed [a] gun to his head and pulled the trigger," No. 86–22–350 (March 23, 1987); or intentionally put his arm through window glass, No. 85–31–331 (Feb. 14, 1986); or attempted to ride his motorcycle on one wheel, No. 84–33–060 (May 13, 1985); or engaged in an altercation, No. 81–10–510 (June 12, 1981); or drove about 100 miles per hour in a 25–mile–per–hour zone on a wet road at dusk, No. 80–31–502 (June 5, 1981).

appropriate to describe one's gradual development of alcohol dependency as evidence of "wanton and reckless disregard of [drinking's] probable consequences." Indeed, I wonder how one meaningfully can ascribe such intent and appreciation of long-range consequences to a 9– or 13–year–old boy who follows the lead of his adult role models in taking his first drinks.[10]

* * *

Individuals suffering from a wide range of disabilities, including heart and lung disease and diabetes, usually bear some responsibility for their conditions. And the conduct that can lead to this array of disabilities, particularly dietary and smoking habits, is certainly no less voluntary than the consumption of alcohol. Nevertheless, the VA has expressed an unwillingness to extend the definition of willful misconduct to all voluntary conduct having some relation to the development of a disability. In justifying the exclusion of secondary organic effects of alcoholism, such as cirrhosis of the liver, from the reach of the willful-misconduct presumption, the VA has explained:

> "[H]istorically, the question of willful misconduct has never been raised in other related situations where personal habits or neglect are possible factors in the incurrence of disability. For example, the harmful effects of tobacco smoking on circulation and respiration were known long before tobacco was incriminated as a causative factor in the high incidence of cancer, emphysema and heart disease. Yet smoking has not been considered misconduct. It is unreasonable and illogical to apply one set of rules with respect to alcohol and a different one in a situation closely analogous." *Ibid.*

In deferring to the VA's "reasonable" determination that all primary alcoholism is attributable to willful misconduct, the Court obscures the meaning of "willful misconduct" in a similar fashion. The Court discusses the propriety of denying benefits to those who "bear some responsibility for their disabilities," and suggests that the attribution of all primary alcoholism to willful misconduct is justified because "the consumption of alcohol is not regarded as wholly involuntary." *Ante,* at 549, 550. The degree of personal responsibility for their disability attributed to alcoholics by the VA in its brief and echoed by the Court in its opinion is clearly not of the magnitude contemplated by the VA's general definition of willful misconduct.

* * *

Notes and Questions

1. What else hinges on the characterization of alcoholism as a "disease"? What difference does it make? Drinking can cause problems for an individual, and those around him. What are the characteristics of alcohol

10. That puzzle, of course, would have to be worked out by the VA when considering petitioners' claims on remand.

consumption that justify the label "disease"? See Milhorn, The Diagnosis of Alcoholism, AFP 175 (June 1988) ("... alcoholism can be defined as the continuation of drinking when it would be in the patient's best interest to stop.")

2. The debate rages around the appropriate role and responsibility of the individual in handling his problems. Herbert Fingarette, whose 1970 law review article is cited by the court, argues that alcoholism is not a disease. Fingarette, the author of Heavy Drinking: The Myth of Alcoholism as a Disease (1988), contends that "... heavy drinking has many causes which vary from drinker to drinker, from one drinking pattern to another." Drinking patterns can vary dramatically in different settings, and alcoholics can limit their drinking in response to a variety of stimuli. Neither biological nor genetic factors cause heavy drinking, although they are linked to it in a small minority of people, according to Fingarette.

Fingarette's concern is that "when behavior is labeled a disease, it becomes excusable because it is regarded as involuntary.... Thus special benefits are provided to alcoholics in employment, health, and civil rights law, provided they can prove that their drinking is persistent and very heavy. The effect is to reward people who continue to drink heavily." See Fingarette, We Should Reject the Disease Concept of Alcoholism, 6 The Harvard Medical School Mental Health Letter 4 (Feb.1990).

George Vaillant, author of The Natural History of Alcoholism (1983), responds:

(1) drinking, like hypertension or other diseases, lies on a continuum without sharp lines of demarcation. Use of the "disease" label, however, helps to "... underscore that a person has lost the capacity to control consistently how much and how often he or she drinks"; continued drinking can cause substantial harm to self and others;

(2) alcoholism is affected by situational and psychological factors, so that drinking is often reactive; but so is a disease like hypertension, which also has a psychological component.

(3) labelling someone an alcoholic, rather than diminishing their responsibility and free will, will help that drinker to take responsibility for self cure. A diagnosis of alcoholism, and a patient's acceptance of it, helps the patient get medical treatment, and also provides him access to emergency rooms, detoxification clinics, and medical insurance.

Vaillant's main point is that "[c]alling alcoholism a disease rather than a behavior disorder is a useful device both to persuade the alcoholic to acknowledge the problem and to provide a ticket for admission to the health care system." See Vaillant, We Should Retain the Disease Concept of Alcoholism, 6 The Harvard Medical School Mental Health Letter 4, 5 (1990).

4. What other emerging clinical "syndromes" or diseases can you think of that raise troubling problems for the medical model of disease? How about anorexia? Obesity? "Battered wife" syndrome? What forces have led to the proliferation of these new syndromes or diseases?

5. A new disease category, "HIV disease", has been proposed to replace and expand the present disease of AIDS. It would include those infected with the HIV virus as well as those who subsequently develop the disabling symptoms of ARC or AIDS. This would arguably help those infected to think about early treatment and would extend medical benefits to cover early treatment. A class action suit has been filed against the Department of Health and Human Services on behalf of five plaintiffs who are HIV-infected, whose applications for Social Security disability benefits have been delayed or denied. See Staver, Suit Seeks Expansion of AIDS Disability Criteria, American Medical News 6 (October 19, 1990). Are there any negative repercussions in expanding the definition of disease? Garrison, Redefining the Scope of AIDS: New Term Broadens View of Who's Ill, San Francisco Examiner at 1, col. 6 (July 24, 1988).

Problem: *The Couple's Illness*

You represent Thomas and Jill Henderson, a couple embroiled in a dispute with their health insurance plan over coverage of infertility treatments. The Hendersons have been having trouble getting pregnant. Thomas has a low sperm count and motility, while Jill has irregular ovulation. They have undergone infertility treatment successfully in the past and have one child. They again sought further treatment, in order to have a second child. A simple insemination procedure failed. The health and disability group benefit plan of Thomas's employer, Clarion, paid their health benefits for this procedure.

They were then advised to try a more complex and expensive procedure, called Protocol I, which involved treating Thomas' sperm to improve its motility. Drug therapy was prescribed for Jill to induce ovulation. Semen was then taken from Thomas, and put through an albumin gradient to improve its mobility. The semen was then reduced to a small pellet size and injected directly into the uterine cavity at the time of ovulation.

The Hendersons underwent Protocol I and submitted a bill to Clarion, which refused to pay it. Clarion cited a provision in its plan, Article VI, section 6.7, which provided:

> If a covered individual incurs outpatient expenses relating to injury or illness, those expenses charged, including but not limited to, office calls and for diagnostic services such as laboratory, x-ray, electro-cardiography, therapy or injections, are covered expenses under the provisions of [the plan].

Under section 2.24 of the plan, "illness" was defined as "any sickness occurring to a covered individual which does not arise out of or in the course of employment for wage or profit." Clarion denied the Henderson's claim on the grounds that the medical services were not performed because of any illness of Jill, as required under section 6.7. No provisions in the plan specifically excluded fertilization treatments like Protocol I.

What arguments can you make on behalf of the Hendersons that their situation is an "illness"? What arguments can you make for the insurance company that it is not?

See Witcraft v. Sundstrand Health and Disability Group Benefit Plan, 420 N.W.2d 785 (Iowa 1988).

B. DEFINING THE NATURE OF QUALITY IN HEALTH CARE

AVEDIS DONABEDIAN, THE DEFINITION OF QUALITY AND APPROACHES TO ITS ASSESSMENT

(Vol. 1) (1980) 4–6.

The search for a definition of quality can usefully begin with what is perhaps the simplest complete module of care: the management by a physician, or any other primary practitioner, of a clearly definable episode of illness in a given patient. It is possible to divide this management into two domains: the technical and the interpersonal. Technical care is the application of the science and technology of medicine, and of the other health sciences, to the management of a personal health problem. Its accompaniment is the management of the social and psychological interaction between client and practitioner. The first of these has been called the science of medicine and the second its art * * *.

There may also be a third element in care which could be called its "amenities". * * * In a way, the amenities are properties of the more intimate aspects of the settings in which care is provided. But the amenities sometimes seem to be properties of the care itself * * *.

* * * At the very least, the quality of technical care consists in the application of medical science and technology in a manner that maximizes its benefits to health without correspondingly increasing its risks. The degree of quality is, therefore, the extent to which the care provided is expected to achieve the more favorable balance of risks and benefits.

What constitutes goodness in the interpersonal process is more difficult to summarize. The management of the interpersonal relationship must meet socially defined values and norms that govern the interaction of individuals in general and in particular situations. These norms are reinforced in part by the ethical dicta of health professions, and by the expectations and aspirations of individual patients. It follows that the degree of quality in the management of the interpersonal relationship is measured by the extent of conformity to these values, norms, expectations, and aspirations. * * * All these postulates lead us to a unifying concept of the quality of care as that kind of care which is expected to maximize an inclusive measure of patient welfare, after one has taken account of the balance of expected gains and losses that attend the process of care in all its parts.

Notes and Questions

1. Donabedian is a leader in the theory of health care assessment. Does his definition capture most of what you find important in thinking about quality health care?

The Joint Commission on Accreditation of Healthcare Organizations offers this definition of quality:

> The degree to which patient-care services increase the probability of desired patient outcomes and reduce the probability of undesired outcomes, given the current state of knowledge.

Joint Commission on Accreditation of Healthcare Organizations, 1990 Accreditation Manual for Hospitals (1989)

The Institute of Medicine, in assessing the Medicare program, has developed its own definition:

> ... quality of care is the degree to which health services for individuals and populations increase the likelihood of desired health outcomes and are consistent with current professional knowledge.

Institute of Medicine, Medicare: A Strategy for Quality Assurance, Vol. I, 20 (K. Lohr, Ed.1990)

Do these definitions differ from Donabedian's? If so, what is the difference? Does the difference matter?

2. Unnecessary care that causes harm, by Donabedian's criteria, is poor in quality, since such care that causes harm unnecessarily is not counterbalanced by any expectation of benefit. How about care that is unnecessary yet harmless, like over-the-counter medicines that contain no therapeutic ingredients? Or medical interventions that have no proven value? Donabedian argues that such care should be judged as poor in quality.

> First, such care is not expected to yield benefits. Second, it can be argued that it causes reductions in individual and social welfare through improper use of resources. By spending time and money on medical care the patient has less to use for other things he values. Similarly, by providing excessive care to some, society has less to offer to others who may need it more. Finally, the use of redundant care, even when it is harmless, indicates carelessness, poor judgment, or ignorance on the part of the practitioner who is responsible for care. (Id. at 6–7).

A proposed new methodology for determining whether Medicare should cover new medical technologies hopes to use cost-effectiveness as a test for coverage of new treatments.

> Cost-effectiveness means having improved health outcomes for Medicare patients that justify additional expenditures... We believe that the regular application of these principles by HCFA, as well as by those proposing new technologies for coverage, would vastly improve our knowledge base and be a deterrent to coverage or procedures that may be costly, but have little or no impact on improving health outcomes. Proposed on January 30, 1989, 54 Fed.Reg. 4,302, not yet a final rule, at p. 17, 18.

Should cost-effectiveness be the sole criterion for evaluating medical care? Is it an appropriate criterion?

Higher quality care may cost more, raising the question of cost-effectiveness. But higher quality care may also be obtained for less money, as by cutting out ineffective services. Medicare reforms designed to contain the system's escalating costs, such as Diagnosis–Related Groups (DRGs), have been based on the assumption that the costs of caring for the elderly can be cut without affecting quality, that the corpus of health care delivery has substantial fat that can be trimmed. Empirical evidence to date supports this hypothesis. See Chapter 6, infra. See also Volume 264, No. 15 (1990) of the Journal of the American Medical Association (J.A.M.A.); the whole issue is devoted to a study of the prospective payment system and its effects on the quality of medical care.

4. What is the role of the patient and her values in the delivery of medical care? Donabedian's definition of quality combines the doctor's technical management with the patient's expectations and values, as well as cost considerations. An "absolutist" medical view, on the other hand, might define quality as a doctor's management of a patient's problems in a way that the doctor expects will best balance health benefits and risks. Donabedian characterizes this position as follows: "[i]t is the responsibility of the practitioner to recommend and carry out such care. All other factors, including monetary costs, as well as the patient's expectations and valuations, are thereby regarded as either obstacles or facilitators to the implementation of the standard of quality." (Donabedian, supra at 13). Consider this position when you read the materials on informed consent in Chapter 3, and the discussion of utilization review in Chapter 6.

A second view, also reflected in the judicial discussions of informed consent, is described by Donabedian as an "individualized" definition of quality:

> A long and honorable tradition of the health professions holds that the primary function of medical care is to advance the patient's welfare. If this is so, it is inevitable that the patient must share with the practitioner the responsibility for defining the objectives of care, and for placing a valuation on the benefits and risks that are expected as the results of alternative strategies of management. In fact, it can be argued that the practitioner merely provides expert information, while the task of valuation falls on the patient or on those who can, legitimately, act on his behalf. Donabedian, supra at 13–14.

How do cost considerations fit into this individualized definition of quality? If the patient has no insurance and probably cannot pay for an expensive surgical procedure, or if the patient decides to forego a treatment after making his or her own cost tradeoffs, how should the doctor respond? Must the doctor be satisfied with giving the patient less medical care than would be possible, and than would in fact help the patient?

> [I]n real life, we do not have the option of excluding monetary costs from the individualized definition of quality. Their inclusion means that the practitioner does for each patient what the patient has decided his circumstances allow. In so doing, the practitioner has discharged his responsibility to the patient, provided that he has helped the patient to discover and use every available means of paying for care. Donabedian, supra at 27.

Patients' insurance status significantly affects the procedures they receive to treat various medical problems. A study of in-hospital cardiac procedures found that patients with private health insurance, compared to patients with either Medicaid or no insurance, were 80% more likely to receive angiography, 40% more likely to receive bypass grafting, and 28% more likely to receive angioplasty. See Wenneker, et al., The Association of Payer with Utilization of Cardiac Procedures in Massachusetts, 264 J.A.M.A. 1255 (1990).

Even in a society with comprehensive social benefits, such as a national health insurance program, costs must be considered by the practitioner, who is still constrained by the resources available for health care. The doctor as citizen must choose whether to help the patient as much as possible, with the taxpayers absorbing the costs; or to stop short of giving the individual the maximum help. See discussion in Chapters 6 and 7, infra.

5. The common law of battery has been applied in cases where a doctor performed a procedure on a patient against the patient's will or without his or her consent. What if the doctor's decision was correct, in the technical sense of achieving a good outcome for the patient? Consider Donabedian:

> Taken by and large, outcomes tend to be inherently valid, in the sense that there is usually no need to argue whether they are, in themselves, good or bad. For example, there is general agreement that life is preferable to death, functional integrity preferable to disability, and comfort preferable to pain. By contrast, the validity of the elements of process is fundamentally derivative, because it depends on the contribution of process to desired outcomes. But there are important exceptions. * * * [T]here are some attributes of the interpersonal process that are valid in themselves, because they represent approved or desirable behaviors in specified social situations. Attributes such as these may be valued and preserved even though they make it more difficult to achieve certain outcomes. Donabedian, supra at 102.

Should the legal system allow an individual to rank a value higher than his or her health, or than life itself? See the discussions in Chapter 3 and Chapter 11.

6. A third definition of quality adds a social dimension, looking at the distribution of benefits within a population. As a society, we may value different segments of our population differently, based on our political choice, indifference, or social values. For example, various Federal cutbacks in maternity and child care benefits in the early 1980s disproportionately affected minorities and lower class families, reflecting political choices that seriously reduced the quality of health care received by a significant percentage of the U.S. population. Organ transplantation practices may have unduly disadvantaged African–Americans and other minorities in terms of access to organs. Access will be used as a major measure of the quality of the American health care system. See Chapter 5.

See generally Avedis Donabedian, A Primer of Quality Assurance and Monitoring in Medical Care, 20 Toledo L.Rev. 401 (1989); A. Donabedian, The Definition of Quality and Approaches to Its Assessment (1980); A. Donabedian, The Criteria and Standards of Quality (1982); A. Donabedian, The Methods and Findings of Quality Assessment and Monitoring: An

Illustrated Analysis (1985). See also Havighurst and Blumstein, Coping with Quality/Cost Trade–Offs in Medical Care: The Role of PSRO's, 70 Nw.U.L.Rev. 6 (1975); Furrow, Medical Malpractice and Cost Containment: Tightening the Screws, 36 Case W.Res.L.Rev. 985 (1986); Veatch, DRGs and the Ethical Reallocation of Resources, 16 Hastings Center Report 32 (1986).

C. ASSESSING QUALITY

Thus far we have attempted to give some content to a definition of "quality" in health care. The next step is to examine how to evaluate quality. We need to take the definition of quality, and particularize it to describe acceptable medical procedures, and institutional structures and processes.

The elements of such an evaluation have again been provided by Donabedian, whose trichotomy is generally accepted as a starting point for thinking about the evaluation of health care.

AVEDIS DONABEDIAN, THE DEFINITION OF QUALITY AND APPROACHES TO ITS ASSESSMENT

Vol. 1 (1980) 79–84.

[T]he primary object of study is a set of activities that go on within and between practitioners and patients. This set of activities I have called the "process" of care. A judgment concerning the quality of that process may be made either by direct observation or by review of recorded information * * *. But, while "process" is the primary *object* of assessment, the *basis* for the judgment of quality is what is known about the relationship between the characteristics of the medical care process and their consequences to the health and welfare of individuals and of society, in accordance with the value placed upon health and welfare by the individual and by society.

With regard to technical management, the relationship between the characteristics of the process of care and its consequences is determined, in the abstract, by the state of medical science and technology at any given time. More specifically, this relationship is revealed in the work of the leading exponents of that science and technology; through their published research, their teachings, and their own practice these leaders define, explicitly or implicitly, the technical norms of good care.

Another set of norms governs the management of the interpersonal process. These norms arise from the values and the ethical principles and rules that govern the relationships among people, in general, and between health professionals and clients, in particular. * * *

It follows, therefore, that the quality of the "process" of care is defined, in the first place, as normative behavior. * * *

* * *

I have argued, so far, that the most direct route to an assessment of the quality of care is an examination of that care. But there are * * * two other, less direct approaches to assessment: one of these is the assessment of "structure", and the other the assessment of "outcome."

By "structure" I mean the relatively stable characteristics of the providers of care, of the tools and resources they have at their disposal, and of the physical and organizational settings in which they work. The concept of structure includes the human, physical, and financial resources that are needed to provide medical care. The term embraces the number, distribution, and qualifications of professional personnel, and so, too, the number, size, equipment, and geographic disposition of hospitals and other facilities. [Donabedian goes on to include within structure the organization of financing and delivery, how doctors practice and how they are paid, staff organization, and how medical work is reviewed in institutions] * * * The basic characteristics of structure are that it is relatively stable, that it functions to produce care or is a feature of the "environment" of care, and that it influences the kind of care that is provided.

* * * Structure, therefore, is relevant to quality in that it increases or decreases the probability of good performances. * * * But as a means for assessing the quality of care, structure is a rather blunt instrument; it can only indicate general tendencies.

* * *

I believe that good structure, that is, a sufficiency of resources and proper system design, is probably the most important means of protecting and promoting the quality of care. * * * As a source of accurate current information about quality, the assessment of structure is of a good deal less importance than the assessment of process or outcome.

* * *

The study of "outcomes" is the other of the indirect approaches that I have said could be used to assess the quality of care. [Outcome is] * * * a change in a patient's current and future health status that can be attributed to antecedent health care. * * * I shall include improvements of social and psychological function in addition to the more usual emphasis on the physical and physiological aspects of performance. By still another extension I shall add patient attitudes (including satisfaction), health-related knowledge acquired by the patient, and health-related behavioral change.

* * *

* * * [T]here are three major approaches to quality assessment: "structure," "process," and "outcome." This three-fold approach is possible because there is a fundamental functional relationship among the three elements, which can be shown schematically as follows:

Structure → Process → Outcome

This means that structural characteristics of the settings in which care takes place have a propensity to influence the process of care so that its quality is diminished or enhanced. Similarly, changes in the process of care, including variations in its quality, will influence the effect of care on health status, broadly defined.

Notes and Questions

1. Quality assurance strategies depend on evaluation tools that apply the definition of quality to a health care professional or institution. Structure evaluation is the easiest to do. Personnel, equipment, and buildings can be counted or described; internal regulations and staff organization measured against specific criteria; and budgets critiqued. Structure evaluation is the least useful, however, since the connection between structural components and quality of care is not necessarily direct.

Hospitals are accredited by the Joint Commission on Accreditation of Healthcare Organizations (JCAHO) (formerly the Joint Commission on Accreditation of Hospitals, or JCAH). JCAHO review has traditionally looked at "bricks and mortar" structural considerations. Part of the structure required by JCAHO, however, is the existence of internal institutional committees to review process as well as morbidity and other aspects of patient outcome. See Chapter 5.

2. Process evaluation of health care has several advantages over structural evaluations. It allows doctors to specify criteria and standards of good care or to establish a range of acceptable practice before all the research evidence is in; it assures documentation in the medical record for preventive and informative purposes; and it permits attribution of responsibility for discrete clinical decisions.

The process perspective has three major drawbacks, however. First, "[t]he major drawback * * * is the weakness of the scientific basis for much of accepted practice. The use of prevalent norms as a basis for judging quality may, therefore, encourage dogmatism and help perpetuate error." Donabedian, supra at 119. Second, the emphasis on the need for technical interventions may lead to high cost care. Third, the interpersonal process is slighted, since process evaluation focuses on the technical proficiency of the doctor.

How should process review take place within a medical practice? Within a hospital? Should surgeons or internists assess each other's work? What if an errant colleague is spotted? Consider these questions as you read Gonzales v. Nork, infra.

A new approach to improving the processes of health care delivery is modelled after Japanese management practices. This "ethic of continuous improvement" has been proposed as a model for promoting high quality, cost effective health care. It adopts managerial principles to improve quality:

(1) active visible support from clinical and managerial leadership for the continuous improvement of quality;

(2) focus on processes as the objects of improvement;

(3) elimination of unnecessary variation; and

(4) revised strategies for personnel management.

This ethic of continuous improvement assumes that processes are complex and frequently characterized by unnecessary rework and waste, whose reduction might both improve quality and reduce cost. It combines outcome measures with process technology and emphasis on personnel management, treating staff as resources central to quality improvement. Its application in health care was suggested by Berwick, Continuous Improvement as an Ideal in Health Care, 320 N.Eng.J.Med. 53 (1989). See Laffel and Blumenthal, The Case for Using Industrial Quality Management Science in Health Care Organizations, 262 J.A.M.A. 2869, 2872 (1989). The methodology was developed for use by industrial organizations by W. Demin, in Quality, Productivity, and Competitive Position (1982) and J. Juran, Managerial Breakthrough (1964).

3. Outcome evaluation has substantial advantages over both process and structure measures. It provides a flexible approach that focuses on what works and on integrated care that includes consideration of the patient's own contribution. The goal of all health care is, after all, the best possible outcome for the patient.

Outcome measures also have their problems, however: the duration, timing, or extent of outcomes of optimal care are often hard to specify; it is often hard to credit a good outcome to a specific medical intervention; and the outcome is often known too late to affect practice. Attempts to better relate the process of care to good outcomes have borne fruit in recent studies. See Kahn, et al., Measuring Quality of Care With Explicit Process Criteria Before and After Implementation of the DRG–Based Prospective Payment System, 264 N.Eng.J.Med. 1969 (1990). For a summary of many of these current outcome-based research projects, see 7 Health Affairs 145–150 (1988); Fifer, The Evolution of Quality Assurance Systems in Health Care—A Personal Retrospective, 4 The Medical Staff Counselor 11 (1990).

Are outcome measures useful for comparing hospitals? Consider the Department of Health and Human Services' recent release of mortality figures for various medical procedures at hospitals around the country. Hospitals had widely differing mortality and morbidity rates and success rates for different procedures. This seems to be a pure outcome indicator, a kind of Consumer Reports rating of hospitals to be used comparatively for purposes of consumer information. Is release of such statistics desirable? Does it benefit the health care consumer? Does the consumer care?

It appears that even before such explicit data became available, the relative quality of hospitals played a part in the choices made by admitting physicians and their patients. It is likely that the admitting physicians were aware of hospital differences, and chose selectively for their patients. The proliferation of specific comparative data might accelerate these tendencies to stratify hospitals by their mortality and morbidity records. Luft et al., Does Quality Influence Choice of Hospital? 263 J.A.M.A. 2899 (1990). See generally Hartz et al., Hospital Characteristics and Mortality Rates, 321 N.Eng.J.Med. 1720 (1989); Berwick and Wald, Hospital Leaders' Opinions of the HCFA Mortality Data, 263 J.A.M.A. 247 (1990).

The Health Care Financing Administration (HCFA) is developing regulations to strengthen the link between substandard care, poor outcomes and payment denials by Professional Review Organizations (PROs) (see Chapter 6, infra). See Proposed Rule, Denial of Payment for Substandard Quality Care and Review of Beneficiary Complaints, 54 FR 1956–01 (Jan. 18, 1989).

We believe that Medicare payment should be denied for substandard quality care that results in either of the following:

• It results in an actual, significant, adverse effect on the beneficiary, that is, patient management that results in—

• Unnecessarily prolonged treatment of the patient;

• Complications in medical conditions;

• Readmission to the hospital;

• Physiological or anatomical impairment;

• Disability; or

• Death.

• It presents an imminent danger to the health, safety, or well-being of the beneficiary, or places the beneficiary unnecessarily in a high-risk situation, so as to constitute a gross and flagrant violation of the obligations . . .

As of 1986 the JCAHO announced a plan to provide outcome review for the nation's accredited hospitals. Under this plan, the JCAHO will gather clinical information in order to predict outcomes and provide an ongoing survey of the clinical activities in the 5000 hospitals which it accredits (out of a total of approximately six thousand hospitals in the country). The goal is to develop clinical indicators, using outcomes data produced by hospitals, to spot potential quality control problems. See Outcomes in Action: the JCAHO's Clinical Indicators, Hospital 34 (Oct. 5, 1990). See Chapter 5.

A concept of outcomes management has been articulated for the health care industry, as a reaction to the increasing volume of outcomes data that is currently being produced. It has been defined by Ellwood as based on a "permanent national medical data base that uses a common set of definitions for measuring quality of life to enable patients, payers, and providers to make informed health choices . . ." Ellwood, Shattuck Lecture—Outcomes Management: A Technology of Patient Experience, 318 N.Eng.J. Med. 1549, 1555 (1988). Ellwood writes that outcomes management:

. . . consists of a common patient-understood language of health outcomes; a national data base containing information and analysis on clinical, financial, and health outcomes that estimates as best we can the relation between medical interventions and health outcomes, as well as the relation between health outcomes and money; and an opportunity for each decision-maker to have access to the analyses that are relevant to the choices they must make. Id. at 1551.

Outcomes management systems are being developed to track the effects of medical care on patients over time, measuring patient clinical condition, functional status, and satisfaction with care. One study has used generic (non-disease specific) health measures for the purpose of monitoring progress and for use as outcomes in studies of patients with chronic conditions. The factors include: physical functioning; role functioning; social functioning; mental health; health perceptions; and bodily pain. Stewart, et al., Functional Status and Well-being of Patients With Chronic Conditions, 262 J.A.M.A. 907, 912 (1989). See also Tarlov, et al., The Medical Outcomes Study: An Application of Methods for Monitoring the Results of Medical Care, 262 J.A.M.A. 925 (1989) (new paradigm for monitoring results of health care, using a new database.) Such management combines health assessment of patients, by collecting the available databases into a national system and developing algorithms of practice.

Such approaches are currently primitive, given deficiencies in studies and information gathering. Beller, Outcome Measurement and Effectiveness Research: Players and Principles, 6 HealthSpan 12 (1989) One of the risks of such systems is that deceptively objective measures can be easily misapplied. In assessing hospital based care, particularly mortality, the severity of the patient's illness at admission needs to be considerably refined before many such outcome comparisons can be trusted. Green, et al., The Importance of Severity of Illness in Assessing Hospital Mortality, 263 J.A.M.A. 241 (1990).

Patient satisfaction, as measured through a survey, is a central part of the outcome assessment. See Koska, Outcomes Management Stresses Patient Input, Hospitals 32 (Nov. 5, 1989).

4. A new study by the Office of Technology Assessment proposes a variety of indicators of good or bad quality health care. Some of these quality-of-care indicators include:

    a.   hospital mortality rates;

    b.   adverse events that affect patients, such as nosocomial infections in hospitals;

    c.   formal disciplinary actions taken by state medical boards against physicians;

    d.   malpractice awards;

    e.   process evaluation of physicians' performance in treating a particular condition, such as hypertension screening and management;

    f.   physician specialization;

    g.   patient self-assessment of their own care;

    h.   scope of hospital services, evaluated by external guidelines like those of the JCAHO.

See Sisk, et al., Assessing Information for Consumers on the Quality of Medical Care, 27 Inquiry 263 (1990)

Which of these indicators are structure measures? Which are process or outcome based? These indicators could be used in a variety of ways, but one common proposal is to give health care consumers information about comparative performance of providers using several of these measures. This market approach would then allow the consumers to select higher quality providers. Are individual patients likely to be good consumers? How can individuals be helped to process the kind of quantitative comparative information that can be produced? Might the other consumers of health care, such as insurers and employers, be better able to use such information than individual patients? How?

See McClure, Buying Right: How to Do It, 2 Bus. & Health 41 (1985); Office of Technology Assessment, The Quality of Medical Care: Information for Consumers (1988); General Accounting Office, Medicare: Improved Patient Outcome Analyses Could Enhance Quality Assessment (1988). For a discussion of the legal and regulatory issues, see Mehlman, Assuring the Quality of Medical Care: The Impact of Outcome Measurement and Practice Standards, 18 Law, Medicine & Health Care 368 (1990); Furrow, The Changing Role of the Law in Promoting Quality in Health Care: From Sanctioning Outlaws to Managing Outcomes, 26 Houston L.Rev. 147 (1989); Jost, The Necessary and Proper Role of Regulation to Assure the Quality of Health Care, 25 Houston L.Rev. 525 (1988).

D. THE PROBLEM OF MEDICAL ERROR

How prevalent is medical error? How often does such error injure patients? How should a regulatory regime handle medical error that does not result in injury? If we discover that a substantial number of patients are injured by medical error, what should the legal system do about it? Even if we conclude that errors are infrequent, how do we "raise the average" of medical practice?

Medical error is a major source of iatrogenesis—disease or illness induced by medical treatment or diagnosis. Such iatrogenesis has also been characterized as medical misadventure, and we will use the two terms interchangeably. As you read through the chapter, critically evaluate the perspectives presented with an eye toward developing your own position on the problem of medical error and how to handle it through the legal system.

1. Medical Iatrogenesis: Sources and Solutions

Injury caused by doctors and health care institutions, or iatrogenesis, is the inverse of quality medicine. It is thus helpful to refine our understanding of injury, medical error, and medical fault, as part of our inquiry into the meaning of quality in health care. The literature on iatrogenesis is surprisingly sparse, considering the importance of the subject.

GONZALES v. NORK

N. 228566 (Superior Court, Sacramento County, Cal., Nov. 19, 1973).*

[The plaintiff Albert Gonzales suffered from lower back pain and went to Dr. Nork for relief. Dr. Nork recommended, and performed, a laminectomy on Gonzales. His surgery was negligently performed, by

---

* A longer excerpt from Judge Goldberg's opinion can be found as Appen- dix, S. Law and S. Polan, Pain and Profit: The Politics of Malpractice 215 (1978).

Nork's own admission. Gonzales suffered after surgery from arachnoiditis, a painful and disabling condition that is permanent, inoperable, and progressive. It is the result of poor technique and not an inherent risk of the procedure. At trial, Dr. Nork admitted that he was a "secret drug user", using both Preludin and Equanol. He had failed the examinations of the American Board of Orthopedic Surgeons.]

GOLDBERG, J.

Dr. Nork's formal and testimonial admissions that he treated the plaintiff improperly and his testimonial admissions that he treated other patients improperly are corroborated by the appalling list of patients on whom he performed surgery that was either unnecessary, or bungled, or both. Evidence was adduced as to 38 patients and, since several underwent multiple surgeries, something in excess of 50 operations. * * *

* * *

Dr. Nork made a practice of operating not only on the basis of inadequate preoperative findings, but also on the basis of false findings. Drs. Jones and Bernstein testified from a recapitulation of 26 laminectomies Dr. Nork performed between 1966 and 1970. They found that Dr. Nork's preoperative findings were statistically inconceivable in a sample of this size. * * *

Another practice followed by Dr. Nork was to operate on patients without giving them a period of conservative treatment within the hospital. * * *

Another deficiency of Dr. Nork was his faulty myelographic technique. * * *

One of Dr. Nork's least endearing habits was that of inducing patients to undergo surgery. Some he actually terrorized; others he merely gulled. * * *

* * *

Dr. Nork's treatment of the plaintiff was in accordance with the pattern of professional misconduct. * * * He performed a perfunctory examination of Gonzales, made no substantial effort to treat the patient conservatively, discouraged consultation, hurried him into unnecessary surgery, which he bungled, and achieved a bad result, which he concealed. Gonzales' case differs from the others in that one of the consequences of the unnecessary and bad surgery was to upset his ability to cope with life to such a degree that it impaired his amenability to treatment for cancer. In a nutshell: Dr. Nork not only harmed Gonzales' back, but he also ruined his personality. * * *

The plaintiff first saw Dr. Nork on November 1, 1967, in his office. Dr. Nork now admits he should have been aware even then of his own incompetence from the sorry history related above. His own witness, Dr. Hanzel, agrees. Nevertheless, he undertook to treat Mr. Gonzales, examined him, and hospitalized him forthwith with the diagnosis

"Acute slipped spondylolisthesis (traumatic) L5—S1 & acute disc herniation L4—5." Dr. Nork placed the plaintiff in traction and reported that he was intermittently better and worse. * * *

After Gonzales had been in traction about a week, he no longer had his original severe pain and thought the traction was helping. But Dr. Nork denied it was helping and said a myelogram and surgery were needed * * *

* * *

[After a myelogram, which the radiologist read as normal, conservative treatment would have been appropriate, as Dr. Bernstein testified.]

The point here is not that Dr. Nork's surgery was unnecessary, because he has admitted not only that it was unnecessary but incompetently performed. The point is the fact that the surgery was unnecessary was obvious. Indeed, Dr. Bernstein concluded that Gonzales did not even have the herniated disc Dr. Nork purported to find. * * *

The surgery was performed on November 17 by Dr. Nork with Dr. Stanford assisting. * * * The patient was under anesthetic for 4 hours and 25 minutes, and received 5 units, 2500cc of blood. Dr. Nork conceded that this amount of blood was "grossly excessive." It was needed because he had to withdraw the bone graft for the fusion, repack the site, and start over. He believes that he performed the surgery negligently.

* * *

[Dr. Nork had staff privileges at Mercy Hospital, which had failed to detect his pattern of fraudulent and iatrogenic surgeries. Mercy was JCAHO (then JCAH) accredited, and complied with requirements for record keeping and peer review of the quality of patients' treatment.] Judge Goldberg described the hospital's diligence:

* * * the methods of review required by JCAH in 1967, and before, were random, casual, subjective and uncritical. They would have disclosed Dr. Nork's frauds only by accident. * * *

* * *

* * * the performance of a laminectomy is such that no one in the operating room can tell whether the surgeon is mishandling the dura or nerve roots * * * Thus there was, in the operating room, no easy way to detect Dr. Nork's clumsiness. His ineptitude has to be inferred from the histories of his patients.

Mercy Hospital did not become aware of the fact that it had a problem with Dr. Nork until May of 1970, when Dr. Dresel, its administrator, heard a rumor that Dr. Nork's malpractice insurance had been cancelled. * * * It inquired and found the rumor was true * * *

* * *

Whatever the reason for the cancellation, Mercy acted promptly and put Dr. Nork under a monitoring program, under which he was forbidden to operate without another designated surgeon present. And Dr. Nork did no further back surgery at either Mercy General or Mercy San Juan after June 1970.

* * *

[Judge Goldberg noted that the hospital satisfied JCAH standards, but refused to immunize Mercy from liability on the basis of such compliance.]

* * * It is no more a matter of medical science to require a hospital to tally up a doctor's lapses than it is to require a nurse to count sponges.

[He further noted that the review of physician work was subjective, random, infrequent, and "casual, uncritical and sandwiched in between the doctors' other work". The reviews did not compare physician progress records and nurses notes. And "[n]o protocol, profile or record was made of doctors' deficiencies so that there was no common fund of knowledge available to the hospital."]

[Judge Goldberg summarized his bases for holding the hospital liable for the acts of Dr. Nork.]

The hospital has a duty to protect its patients from malpractice by members of its medical staff when it knows or should have known that malpractice was likely to be committed upon them. Mercy Hospital had no actual knowledge of Dr. Nork's propensity to commit malpractice, but it was negligent in not knowing. It was negligent in not knowing, because it did not have a system for acquiring knowledge; it did not use the knowledge available to it properly; it failed to investigate the Freer case, which would have given it knowledge; and it cannot excuse itself on the ground that its medical staff did not inform it.

* * *

[Judge Goldberg ordered Dr. Nork and Mercy Hospital to pay Gonzales $1,710,447.17 in compensatory damages and $2,000,000 in punitive damages, dividing these sums between them.]

Notes and Questions

1. What are the sources of iatrogenesis in Gonzales v. Nork? What kinds of medical errors did Nork made? Mercy Hospital? Does the word "error" capture the range of problems that led to patient injury in this case?

2. Consider a spectrum of sources of patient injury.

a. *Willful or reckless acts.* Both lawyers and doctors generally view intentional deviation from professional norms of good practice, without good cause, as culpable error. Dr. Nork, performing multiple operations that he knew were beyond his abilities, committed acts in this category. The large punitive damage award in the *Nork* case demonstrates the court's willingness to add a quasi-criminal sanction to the normal range of tort damages when the errors are as egregious as those of Dr. Nork. He was a "bad apple" among physicians. Many quality control mechanisms now in place, such as licensing and medical board disciplinary actions, seem to be aimed at these "bad apples." See Section II, infra.

b. *Negligent acts.* A negligence standard measures a physician's actions against accepted norms of practice. A doctor may fall short, injuring a patient for a number of reasons:

1. Inattentiveness on a particular occasion, even though the doctor is otherwise skillful and well trained;

2. A systematic failure of training resulting from failure to keep up with the field of practice or to be properly educated generally. In Darling v. Charleston Community Memorial Hospital, 33 Ill.2d 326, 211 N.E.2d 253 (1965), the defendant doctor had not read the latest texts on setting bone fractures;

3. A personal incapacity of the doctor to deal with this particular disease or patient, because of his or her own impairment, or inability to carry out the procedure with technical proficiency.

We feel no unfairness in generally holding doctors accountable for wilful misconduct, or for negligence based on inattentiveness, failures of education, or personal incapacity. They have failed to live up to the level of competence that their professional membership indicates they should have achieved.

3. Two categories of patient injury are usually viewed as based on nonculpable conduct, since it is argued that the doctor could not have done any better.

a. *Error due to patient variation.* The argument has been made that doctors cannot be held responsible for some errors because their knowledge of particular patients is necessarily limited. Each patient is unique, more than just the sum total of physical and chemical mechanisms. Each patient is a product of his or her own history. Perfect knowledge is thus impossible. If a bad result occurs, therefore, the fault lies not with any scientific ignorance but, rather, with an unavoidable "ignorance of the contingencies of the environmental context." Gorovitz and MacIntyre, Toward a Theory of Medical Fallibility, 1 J.Med.Phil. 51 (1976). Given the uncertain results of therapeutic intervention on a given patient, regardless of the state of general knowledge about interventions of that type, every therapeutic intervention is an experiment that risks hurting the patient.

b. *Injuries of ignorance.* Much of medical treatment is still primitive: the etiologies and optimal treatments for many illnesses are not known; many treatment techniques, such as cancer chemotherapy, create substantial side-effects. Iatrogenic effects often result from the infant nature of the medical specialty. Use of the word "error" is arguably inappropriate, since the concept of error implies that an alternative error-free way of treatment exists.

The argument of medical ignorance is justified to a large extent. Can we in fairness ask a doctor to do more than medical science and his or her specialty have said is possible? But what if a whole profession has lagged behind, failing to discover the benefits of a desirable new practice or the risks of a generally accepted older practice. A specialty may have failed to try to transcend the limits of its existing treatments. We might like more research, more efforts to bring specialty consensus on diagnosis and treatment, more systematic efforts at analysis of cost-effective medicine. Iatrogenesis due to ignorance and patient variation is, therefore, reducible with further research. Medicine is not static.

Consider the case of Beshada v. Johns–Manville Products Corp., 90 N.J. 191, 447 A.2d 539 (1982), involving plaintiff workers who had developed asbestosis, allegedly from exposure to asbestos in the workplace. The New Jersey Supreme Court pushed strict product liability doctrine to its limits, imposing liability for a failure to warn of dangers which were undiscoverable at the time of manufacture.

> Defendants have treated the level of technological knowledge at a given time as an independent variable not affected by defendant's conduct. But this view ignores the important role of industry in product safety research. The "state-of-the-art" at a given time is partly determined by how much industry invests in safety research. By imposing on manufacturers the costs of failure to discover hazards, we create an incentive for them to invest more actively in safety research.

Are you comfortable with applying this argument to medicine? What is the responsibility of the individual physician to invest in medical research?

4. Is a concept of error also important to us as lawyers? Do lawyers have a similar set of problems with the iatrogenic effects of legal practice? Think of the harm that lawyers can do, and how it compares to the harm that doctors can do. Are the two professions comparable? Or is the doctor burdened with a heavier responsibility, and correspondingly heavier costs of error?

In Healing the Wounds: A Physician Looks at His Work (1986), Dr. David Hilfiker explores the stresses experienced by a doctor. He chronicles the stresses in the practice of medicine—the drains on a physician's time and energy, fears of making a wrong decision, lack of time to integrate experiences, and difficulties in keeping up with rapidly changing medical specialties. A busy physician—buffeted by the pressures of uncertainties in decisionmaking, the need to keep up, and the demands of a schedule—makes mistakes. As Hilfiker writes,

> it is not only in the emergency room, the operating room, the intensive care unit, or the delivery room that a doctor can blunder into tragedy. Errors are always possible, even in the midst of the humdrum routine of daily care. * * * A doctor has to confront the possibility of a mistake with every patient visit. Id. at 82.

The well trained physician may simply be inattentive on a particular occasion; he may have failed to keep up with new developments; he may have problems dealing with a particular patient for personal reasons. Some of these causes of error can be addressed by particular correctives—an eased schedule, an expanded collegial support setting, the transfer of a patient to another doctor. How should the law respond to these exigencies in medical malpractice litigation? In disciplinary actions?

5. As you become familiar with the health care enterprise, and the role of physicians and other professionals within that enterprise, think about the range of regulatory tools that might be valuable in improving the quality of health care. Consider the deficiencies in Mercy Hospital's system for monitoring physician errors and iatrogenesis. Although Dr. Nork was the active agent in causing patient harm, the hospital provided the indispensable workplace for his activities. Dr. Nork was an "impaired" physician. Can a health care institution also be "impaired", i.e., suffering from a systemic problem that impairs its functioning?

6. The law has historically focused on physician "error". Until recently, malpractice cases were brought against the treating physician and not his institution because of a variety of legal rules that shielded the hospital. State licensing boards brought disciplinary actions against the individual errant doctor. Staff privilege cases involved the individual doctor's qualifications. The narrow focus on individual error facilitated a clear definition of "bad medicine". Bad medicine was what bad doctors did, "bad apples", doctors like the infamous Dr. Nork and others whose incompetence was obvious and offensive.

Consider the traditional malpractice suit for a moment. Suppose that a doctor followed generally accepted, "customary," community practice in the use of a drug to control heart problems (See Chapter 2 infra), yet his patient died. In most jurisdictions, the doctor would not be liable, since he or she conformed to an accepted community practice. Now suppose that we introduce an outcome measure into our assessment. Can you design a liability rule that would take an outcome approach? Would it be desirable to apply this rule to most of medical practice?

This focus on individual responsibility and error has been the starting point for quality assessment, even though it misses many causes of poor quality health care. Such a concept of error provides a necessary starting point, but bad outcomes at the individual physician level typically occur too infrequently to identify poor or good physicians. The larger problem of quality in medical care must also address systemic failures, poor administrative design for review of health care, inadequacies in training of physicians, and the nature of practice incentives.

See Brook and Kosecoff, Commentary: Competition and Quality, 7 Health Affairs 150, 157 (1988).

E. ROBIN, MATTERS OF LIFE & DEATH: RISKS VS BENEFITS OF MEDICAL CARE
57, 58 (1984).

Iatrogenic (Greek, *iatros* = doctor, *genic* = arising from or developing from) literally means disease or illness caused by doctors. This definition, however, is too broad. Almost everything a doctor does has potential risks as well as potential benefits. Should we consider every mishap related to treatment as an iatrogenic episode? No. There are many circumstances in which the doctor deliberately places the patient at risk because the potential benefits outweigh the risks.

* * *

Part of the doctor's job is to risk harming patients in order to help them. When he does this consciously and deliberately, with knowledge of the risks but in the belief that the benefits outweigh the risks, even if the patient is harmed, he has not created a mishap.

In an iatrogenic episode a patient is harmed as a result of an error in diagnosis or treatment, or as a result of a mishap during medical care. The harm is independent of the natural progression of the patient's illness and treatment and represents part of the risk that the patient *must* assume as an inevitable component of management.

Notes and Questions

1. Customary medical practice, faithfully followed, can sometimes cause injury to patients. The history of medicine is replete with examples, such as blood-letting during the 1600s and 1700s. If a medical practice, such as the routine performance of tonsillectomies in children during the 1950s, proves to have little therapeutic value and to have significantly harmed many patients, is this an iatrogenic effect?

2. How should the legal system treat such "iatroepidemics," as Dr. Robin refers to them?

Iatroepidemic is a term I have coined to denote an epidemic, or plague, caused by doctors. * * * Iatroepidemics develop because of systematic errors incorporated into medical practice. The application of these errors to masses of patients results in harm or death to large numbers. Unlike iatrogenic episodes, which are random and accidental, iatroepidemics are systematic and their causes are predictable—and therefore potentially preventable.

* * *

[Iatroepidemics] share several characteristics: A practice was introduced into medicine on the basis of a fundamentally unsound idea or poorly interpreted experience. The practice took hold without adequate studies to establish its efficacy and then developed a life of its own. It was supported by a group of experts whose opinions encouraged its continued use. Their own reputations or positions partially depended on the practice and, when challenged, they leaped to its defense. As a result, changes were slow to come. Because the idea was fundamentally unsound, many patients were harmed. This process, repeated time and again, fosters iatroepidemics. Robin, supra at 65, 73.

A detailed account of psychosurgery, one of Robin's case studies of iatroepidemics, is provided by Elliot Valenstein, Great and Desperate Cures: The Rise and Decline of Psychosurgery and Other Radical Treatments for Mental Illness (1986).

2. *The Extent of Medical Misadventures*

Medical errors that cause iatrogenic harms to patients also impose costs on society, including the cost of correcting the bad result (when it can be corrected) and the loss to society of that patient's productivity. How extensive are such medical mishaps?

PATIENTS, DOCTORS, AND LAWYERS: MEDICAL INJURY, MALPRACTICE LITIGATION, AND PATIENT COMPENSATION IN NEW YORK

The Report of the Harvard Medical Practice Study to the State of New York (1990).

[The Harvard Medical Practice Study in New York looked at the incidence of injuries resulting from medical interventions, "adverse events," beginning with a sample of more than 31,000 New York hospital records drawn from the study year 1984. The review was conducted by medical record administrators and nurses in the screening phase, and by board certified physicians for the physician-review phase.]

* * *

We analyzed 30,121 (96%) of the 31,429 records selected for the study sample. After preliminary screening, physicians reviewed 7,743 records, from which a total of 1,133 adverse events were identified that occurred as a result of medical management in the hospital or required hospitalization for treatment. Of this group, 280 were judged to result from negligent care. Weighting these figures according to the sample plan, we estimated the incidence of adverse events for hospitalizations in New York in 1984 to be 3.7%, or a total of 98,609. Of these, 27.6%, 27,179 cases, or 1.0% of all hospital discharges, were due to negligence.

Physician confidence in the judgments of causation of adverse events spanned a broad range, but only 1.3% of all discharges were in the close-call range (defined as a confidence in causation of just under or just over 50–50). An even smaller fraction, 0.7% of discharges were close-call negligent adverse events, but they constituted a larger proportion of total negligent adverse events.

The majority of adverse events (57%) resulted in minimal and transient disability, but 14% of patients died at least in part as a result of their adverse event, and in another 9% the resultant disability lasted longer than 6 months. Based on these figures, we estimated that about 2,500 cases of permanent total disability resulted from medical injury in New York hospitals in 1984. Further, we found evidence that medical injury contributed at least in part to the deaths of more than 13,000 patients in that year. Many of the deaths occurred in patients who had greatly shortened life expectancies from their underlying diseases, however. Negligent adverse events resulted, overall, in greater disability than did non-negligent events and were associated with 51% of all deaths from medical injury.

RISK FACTORS

The risk of sustaining an adverse event increased with age. When rates were standardized for DRG level, persons over 65 years had twice the chance of sustaining an adverse event of those in the 16–44 years group. Newborns had half the adverse event rate of the 16–44 years group. The percent of adverse events resulting from negligence was increased in elderly patients. We found no gender differences in adverse event or negligence rates. Although the rates were higher in the self-pay group than in the insured categories, the differences were not significant. Blacks had higher rates of adverse events and adverse events resulting from negligence, but these differences overall were not significant. However, higher rates of adverse events and negligent events were found in hospitals that served a higher proportion of minority patients. At hospitals that cared for a mix of white and minority patients, blacks and whites had nearly identical rates.

Adverse event rates varied 10–fold between individual hospitals, when standardized for age and DRG level. Although standardized adverse event and negligence rates for small hospitals (fewer than 8,000 discharges/year) were less than for larger hospitals, these differences were not significant. Hospital ownership (private, non-profit, or government) also was not associated with significantly different rates of adverse events. The fraction of adverse events due to negligence in government hospitals was 50% higher than in non-profit institutions, however, and three times that in proprietary hospitals. These differences were significant. The standardized rate of adverse events in upstate, non–MSA hospitals was one-third that of upstate metropolitan hospitals and less than one-fourth that in New York City. These differences were highly significant. The percent of adverse events due to negligence was not significantly different across regions. Non-teaching hospitals had half the adverse event rates of university or affiliated teaching hospitals, but university teaching hospitals had rates of negligence that were less than half those of the non-teaching or affiliated hospitals.

THE NATURE OF ADVERSE EVENTS

Nearly half (47%) of all adverse events occurred in patients undergoing surgery, but the percent caused by negligence was lower than for non-surgical adverse events (17% vs 37%). Adverse events resulting from errors in diagnosis and in non-invasive treatment were judged to be due to negligence in over three-fourths of patients. Falls were considered due to negligence in 45% of instances.

The high rate of adverse events in patients over 65 years occurred in three categories: non-technical postoperative complications, complications of non-invasive therapy, and falls. A larger proportion of adverse events in younger patients was due to surgical failures. The operating room was the site of management for the highest fraction of adverse events, but relatively few of these were negligent. On the other hand, most (70%) adverse events in the emergency room resulted from negligence.

The most common type of error resulting in an adverse event was that involved in performing a procedure, but diagnostic errors and prevention errors were more likely to be judged negligent, and to result in serious disability.

The more severe the degree of negligence the greater the likelihood of resultant serious disability (moderate impairment with recovery taking more than six months, permanent disability, or death).

2. Litigation data

We estimated that the incidence of malpractice claims filed by patients for the study year was between 2,967 and 3,888. Using these figures, together with the projected statewide number of injuries from medical negligence during the same period, we estimated that eight times as many patients suffered an injury from negligence as filed a malpractice claim in New York State. About 16 times as many patients suffered an injury from negligence as received compensation from the tort liability system.

These aggregate estimates understate the true size of the gap between the frequency of malpractice claims and the incidence of adverse events caused by negligence. When we identified the malpractice claims actually filed by patients in our sample and reviewed the judgments of our physician reviewers, we found that many cases in litigation were brought by patients in whose records we found no evidence of negligence or even of adverse events. Because the legal system has not yet resolved many of these cases, we do not have the information that would permit an assessment of the success of the tort litigation system in screening out claims with no negligence.

* * *

Notes and Questions

1. The Harvard Study was designed to produce empirical data to better inform the debate about reform of the tort system, including no-fault reforms. Do the findings of the study, as to level of patient injury attributable to medical error, surprise you?

A study based upon insurance company closed malpractice claims files for anesthesia-related patient injuries concluded that payment was made in more than 80% of the claims filed by patients judged to have received substandard anesthetic care. The claims were reviewed by expert anesthesiologists and divided into inappropriate and appropriate care. The authors found that a patient was much more likely to be paid if the care received was substandard. These favorable odds for payment cut across all severities of injury. The authors also concluded that when a patient files suit for anesthesia-related injury, and the care was judged to be appropriate by peers, payment was made to the patient in 42% of the cases. The authors concluded that "... the tort-based system of patient compensation for injury clearly favors payment to the injured patient, but inequities exist for both patient and physician." See Cheney et al., Standard of Care and Anesthesia Liability, 261 J.A.M.A. 1599 (1989).

Do these conclusions support the existing tort system's value as a quality control system in detecting and deterring error? Or do they support the need for reform?

See Chapter 4 infra for further discussion of these issues. The study and its methodology is critiqued in Mehlman, saying "No" to No–Fault: What the Harvard Malpractice Study Means for Medical Malpractice Reform, (N.Y. State Bar Association 1991).

For an exploration of the role of the tort system in insuring against inadvertent negligence or accidents not caused by a professional failure, see Grady, Why Are People Negligent? Technology, Nondurable Precautions, and the Medical Malpractice Explosion, 82 Nw.Univ.L.Rev. 293 (1988).

2. As you read Chapter 2, try to sort out the various tort doctrines and rules of admissibility to see whether they protect or ferret out medical error. Do liability doctrines adequately attack medical errors? Do the defenses available to doctors adequately protect non-errant doctors?

3. Other studies have also concluded that the hospital setting exposes patients to significant risks of iatrogenic illness. One study found that more than 36% of the patients admitted to a hospital developed iatrogenic illnesses, either a major or minor complication. Nine percent had major complications, and 2% of all patients died for reasons related to the iatrogenic illness. Exposure to drugs was an important factor in patient complications. Steel et al., Iatrogenic Illness on a General Medical Service at a University Hospital, 304 N.Eng.J.Med. 638, 641 (1981).

4. Surgery is also risky. One study concluded that patients experiencing care on a surgical ward experienced about a 1% incidence or mishap rate. Diagnostic errors, and delay in performing a procedure, were major contributors to the mishaps. More than half the medical errors surveyed were errors of commission, including unnecessary or contraindicated surgery, defective execution of an indicated operation, and performance of an improper surgical procedure. The authors of the study concluded that " * * * in 31 instances, or 90 per cent of the errors of therapeutic commission, the mistakes were those of unnecessary, contraindicated, or technically defective surgical activity." Couch et al., The High Cost of Low–Frequency Events, 304 N.Eng.J.Med. 634, 635 (1981).

5. These medical mishaps are expensive. The hospital based study found that costs attributable to error were 1.3% of the hospital's patient-service billings for the year. The research confirmed an earlier study, which had concluded that medical misadventure contributed significantly to the costs of health care. Zook and Moore, High Cost Users of Medical Care, 302 N.Eng.J.Med. 996 (1980).

Other studies have confirmed that many medical interventions are costly, not just in terms of dollars spent on technology and personnel, but also in terms of the iatrogenic injuries inflicted. Almost every intervention risks causing adverse side effects that can entail extra treatment, added hospitalization, or even death. The medical profession has long known that the best treatment may harm. See Barr, Hazards of Modern Diagnosis and Therapy—The Price We Pay, 159 J.A.M.A. 1452 (1955); Moser, Diseases of Medical Progress, 255 N.Eng.J.Med. 606 (1956). As many as 15% of the hospitalized patient population may react adversely to the drugs given them. Karch and Lasagna, Adverse Drug Reactions: A Critical Review, 234 J.A.M.A. 1236 (1975). The existence of a whole specialty of legal practice—drug liability—reflects the prevalence of drug-induced side-effects. Doctors have recognized that a deceptively simple and commonplace procedure, such as drawing blood for testing, may produce unnecessary iatrogenic effects. Smoller, Kruskall, Phlebotomy for Diagnostic Laboratory Tests in Adults: Pattern of Use and Effect on Transfusion Requirements, 314 N.Eng.J.Med. 1233 (1986). Standard procedures such as intraortic balloon pumping and tracheostomy may also lead to complications, a significant percentage of them life threatening. Burnum, Medical Vampires, 314 N.Eng.J.Med. 2250 (1986).

3. *Origins of Clinical Standards of Practice*

The standard of care applied in a tort suit or a hospital peer review process does not normally derive from an external authority such as a government standard. In the medical profession, as in other professions, standards develop in a complicated way involving the interaction of leaders of the profession, professional journals and meetings, and networks of colleagues. Neither the Food and Drug Administration, the National Institutes of Health, the Department of Health and Human Services, nor state licensing boards have had much to do with shaping medical practice. Most clinical policies derive from a flow of reports in the literature, at meetings, and in peer discussions. Over a period of time, hundreds of separate comments come together to form a clinical policy. If this becomes generally accepted, we can call it "standard practice." See generally Eddy, Clinical Policies and the Quality of Clinical Practice, 307 N.Eng.J.Med. 343 (1982).

This decentralized process of policy setting has some advantages, as Eddy notes: the individual doctor benefits from collective wisdom; unwarranted bursts of enthusiasm are dampened; the policies are tested by the best minds (through statistical and other tools); and flexibility, allowing adaptation to local skills and values, is promoted. Such a policy making process also has drawbacks: oversimplification may ignore side-effects, costs and risks; overbroad conclusions may be drawn from a few observations; examples may be chosen that tend to support the expected result; incentives may favor overuse rather than underuse; an advocacy system may arise in which proponents push and counterarguments may be ignored; the policy consensus may be based upon little more than repetition by the largest or loudest voices; and the inertia inherent in the status quo may dominate.

The diffusion of new medical technologies of diagnosis and treatment poses special problems for the individual physician. Most doctors will note new ideas as they show up in the literature. But they may not be appropriately skeptical. In spite of insufficient evidence of efficacy, doctors in various specialties have been quick to adopt new technologies such as respirator therapy, gastric freezing of ulcers, and other now-discredited techniques. Other tools, such as the CT scan and magnetic resonance imaging, have proliferated rapidly before the evidence on their efficacy was in. The adoption of what has been termed "slam-bang" technologies often precedes careful evaluation.

Even if a cautious and conscientious doctor is skeptical, the data and opinions available are often inadequate to allow evaluation of research findings. The studies may have defects; they may fail, for example, to explain how to translate limited clinical research into practice or may inadequately evaluate controversy over earlier studies. Or the doctor may not be aware of the unique nature of clinical trials.

See Young, Communications Linking Clinical Research and Clinical Practice, Biomedical Innovation 177 (1981); 1 Intern.J.Tech.Ass. in Health Care (No. 3, 1985) (issue devoted to assessment of magnetic resonance-imaging and spectroscopy); Saverbruch et al., Fragmentation of Gallstones by Extracorporeal Shock Waves, 314 N.Eng.J.Med. 818 (1986); Mulley, Shock–Wave Lithotripsy: Assessing a Slam–Bang Technology, 314 N.Eng.J.Med. 845 (1986).

The phenomenon of medical practice variation highlights the role of uncertainty in the setting of medical standards. Wennberg, whose studies in this area are often cited, looked at states and at regions within states for variation in surgical and other practices:

> [I]n Maine by the time women reach seventy years of age in one hospital market the likelihood they have undergone a hysterectomy is 20 percent while in another market it is 70 percent. In Iowa, the chances that male residents who reach age eighty-five have undergone prostatectomy range from a low of 15 percent to a high of more than 60 percent in different hospital markets. In Vermont the probability that resident children will undergo a tonsillectomy has ranged from a low of 8 percent in one hospital market to a high of nearly 70 percent in another.

Wennberg, Dealing with Medical Practice Variations: A Proposal for Action, 3 Health Affairs 6, 9 (1984).

Physician variation in treatment approaches is greatest with aging-related conditions, where the outcomes of conservative treatment are unknown. By contrast, the procedures least subject to variation are those "for which there is a professional consensus on the preferred place or style of treatment." Wennberg, supra. A study of a range of medical and surgical services used by Medicare beneficiaries during 1981 confirm Wennberg's findings. The study documented large variations "linked directly to the degree of medical consensus concerning the indications for use." Chassin et al., Variations in the Use of Medical and Surgical Services by the Medicare Population, 314 N.Eng.J.Med. 285, 288 (1986).

The appropriateness of much medical treatment has been questioned. Wide variation has been noted in the use of laboratory tests, prescription drugs, X-rays, return appointments, and telephone consultations among similarly trained doctors in a wide variety of practice settings. Research on appropriateness indicates that from one quarter to one third of medical services may be of no value to patients. Brook and Lohr, Will We Need to Ration Effective Medical Care?, Issues in Science and Technology 68 (Fall 1986). The extent of inappropriate hospital use is also significant. One recent study concluded that 21% of pediatric hospital use is medically inappropriate. Kemper, Medically Inappropriate Hospital Use in a Pediatric Population, 318 N.Eng.J. Med. 1033 (1988). Other studies have found that between 20% and 40% of hospital ancillary services are unnecessary. Hughes, The Ancillary Services Review Program in Massachusetts: Experience of the 1982 Pilot Project, N.Eng.J.Med. 1727 (1984). Carotid enterectomies, procedures that remove clots in arteries leading to the brain, were judged as appropriate in only 35% of the cases surveyed. Chassin, et al., How Coronary Angiography Is Used, J.A.M.A. 2543 (1988).

In another study, the researchers looked at implantation of permanent cardiac pacemakers in a large population. They found that 44% of the implants were definitely indicated, 36% possibly indicated, and 20% were not indicated. Seventy-three percent of the hospitals had an incidence of 10% or more unwarranted implantations, regardless of type of hospital. Goldman, et al., Costs and Effectiveness of Routine Therapy with Long–Term Beta–Adrenergic Antagonists After Acute Myocardial Infarction, 318 N.Eng.J.Med. 152 (1988). One study found a seventeen-fold variation in lab use among internists dealing with clinical patients. Schroeder et al., Use of Laboratory Tests and Pharmaceutical Variation Among Physicians and Effect of Cost Audit on Subsequent Use, 225 J.A.M.A. 969 (1973).

The attitudes of individual doctors influence the range of variation where consensus is lacking; Wennberg has termed this the "practice style factor." This style can exert its influence in the absence of scientific information on outcomes; in other cases it may be unrelated to controversies.

> Physicians in some hospital markets practice medicine in ways that have extremely adverse implications for the cost of care, motivated perhaps by reasons of their own or their patients' convenience, or because of individualist interpretations of the requirements for defensive medicine. Whatever the reason, it certainly is not because of adherence to medical standards based on clinical outcome criteria or even on statistical norms based on average performance.

Wennberg, supra at 7. See also Wennberg, The Paradox of Appropriate Care, 258 J.A.M.A. 2568 (1987). See generally, J. Eisenberg, Doctors' Decisions and the Cost of Medical Care (1986).

E. IMPROVING THE DELIVERY OF HEALTH CARE SERVICES

Doctors make mistakes, and some of these errors injure patients. The frequency of medical misadventures in the nation's hospitals and clinical settings is substantial. Much health care is of unproven value, but consumes consumer and governmental resources. The American health care system is therefore not of optimal quality, and could stand improvement. We have a definition of quality, we have criteria and standards for its evaluation. How do we translate the criteria into a strategy to modify behavior and performance to improve the quality of care delivered?

Several approaches to quality improvement can be pursued. We can rely on the traditional forces of professional ethics and socialization. We can expand the role of the marketplace, using dissemination of quality information to consumers and buyers of health, on the theory that prudent buyers will reject lower quality providers. We can improve the current modes of self-regulation of the medical profession and the industry, which include accreditation, medical staff privileges, and medical licensing actions. The process by which a patient sues for malpractice can be improved. And the government, as a primary source of financing for much health care in the United States, can intervene, setting standards and demanding better processes and outcomes. We will examine each of these methods of quality improvement in later sections and chapters.

The combined problems of variation in medical practice and lack of evidence of efficacy of many treatment approaches has launched a movement toward practice parameters. Specialty societies and now the Medicare program have moved to study practices, to articulate consensus on acceptable practice, and to disseminate information on the consensus. The development of practice parameters or protocols has intensified in recent years, as the medical profession attempts to sift through the available research knowledge and reduce variation in medical practice. A new agency within the Public Health Service, the Agency for Health Care Policy and Research, was created to further such research efforts. 42 U.S.C.A., Title ix, section 901. Promotion of quality work is done within this new Agency by the Office of the Forum for Quality and Effectiveness in Health Care. 42 U.S.C.A. 201, § 911.

Measuring appropriateness and developing parameters has its problems: it is easier to study overuse than underuse because of difficulties in defining relevant populations; the scientific evidence is always incomplete, requiring reliance on expert judgment; and parameters are slow and expensive to develop in many areas of medical practice. Brook, Practicing Guidelines and Practicing Medicine: Are They Compatible? 262 J.A.M.A. 3027 (1989).

Given the patterns of variation in medical practice, and the unscientific way in which various medical treatments diffuse into common use, is it likely that newly developed practice parameters will be adopted by physicians in practice? One study evaluated the effect of distributing practice guidelines generated under the auspices of a national specialty association—the 1986 Canadian guidelines advocating a lower rate of cesarean sections. The dissemination of guidelines had little effect on actual physician practice. Physician awareness of them was high, and the attitudes of obstetricians were positive toward the recommendations. One third of the obstetricians and hospitals reported changing their practices because of the guidelines.

> * * * [T]his high level of awareness, the apparently positive attitudes, and the reported changes in practice coexisted with a demonstrated poor knowledge of the actual recommendations and very little actual change in practices. These results agree with the findings in other evaluations in this area.

See Lomas et al, Do Practice Guidelines Guide Practice? The Effect of a Consensus Statement on the Practice of Physicians, 32 N.Eng.J.Med. 1306 (1989). The authors speculated that many forces besides research evidence affect physician decisions, including financial incentives favoring one approach over another, patient pressure, and fears of malpractice. "In the absence of any accompanying strategies to overcome these other influences, the dissemination of research evidence in the form of practice guidelines issues by a national body is unlikely to have much effect on inappropriate practices that are sustained by powerful non-scientific forces." Id. at 1310.

Earlier studies on continuing medical education have generally failed to confirm any link between practitioner knowledge and quality, concluding that educational approaches had little proven effect on either physician performance or on overall quality of care. In one study, the authors surveyed almost 250 studies of CME interventions and found only one that supported improvement in outcomes linked to CME. Haynes et al., A Critical Appraisal of the Efficacy of Continuing Medical Education, 251 J.A.M.A. 61 (1984). A second study of the effect of learning packages on quality of care found little effect, with a control group who did not receive the packages showing equal improvement. Sibley, et al., A Randomized Trial of Continuing Medical Education, 306 N.Eng.J.Med. 511 (1982). In a third study, CME materials on hypertension were mailed to primary care physicians, and no effect on these physicians' performance in lowering blood pressure was demonstrated in the learner group. Evans, Does a Mailed Continuing Education Program Improve Physician Performance, 255 J.A.M.A. 501 (1986).

Part II will examine licensing of health care professionals. Part III will look at government quality control of health care institutions, with particular attention on nursing homes. Part IV will look at hospitals and quality control. As you become familiar with the various approaches to quality assessment and control, ask yourself what mix of strategies is likely to be most effective, least intrusive on the physician-patient relationship, and least expensive.

II. LICENSING OF HEALTH CARE PROFESSIONALS

Medical licensing statutes are justified as protective of the health, safety and general welfare of the community and thus are supported by the police power of the states. Through the licensing statutes, physicians control entry into the medical profession, disciplinary actions against their colleagues and the delivery of health care services by persons other than physicians. Allocation of these functions to the medical profession itself furthers the public interest, it is argued, because the lay public is incapable of adequately evaluating the quality of medical services. Only the professionals themselves have sufficient control over the specialized knowledge required for such an evaluation.

The medical profession in the United States did not always have such power. In fact, during the nineteenth century, the medical profession was divided within itself by competing theories of health care and was too weak to exert control over medical education or practice. Its ascendence to power is attributable to a combination of social and political forces over time. P. Starr, The Social Transformation of American Medicine (1982). See also, Rose, Professional Regulation: The Current Controversy, 7 Law and Human Behavior 103 (1983), which is part of a symposium on professional regulation; and Gellhorn, The Abuse of Occupational Licensing, 44 U.Chi.L.Rev. 6 (1976).

Currently, all professional self-regulation is under strong attack. Professional entry requirements are criticized as homogenizing services through mandating uniformity of professional education and qualifying exams at the expense of innovation and diversity. The entry requirements set by occupational licensing are also criticized as discriminating against the poor and minorities. The legal authority accorded professionals both to define and to implement the prohibition of unauthorized practice gives professionals the ability to control their market. As Paul Starr comments, "Power abhors competition about as intensely as nature abhors a vacuum. Professional organization is one form resistance to the market may take." (Id. at 23.) Critics maintain that professional entry requirements do not improve the quality of the services available and so do not justify their negative effects. See, e.g., Dorsey, Occupational Licensing and Minorities, 7 Law and Human Behavior 171 (1983); Hogan, The Effectiveness of Licensing: History, Evidence, and Recommendations, 7 Law and Human Behavior 117 (1983); Rayack, Professional Power and American Medicine: The Economics of the American Medical Association 147 (1967); W. Gellhorn, Individual Freedom and Governmental Restraints 144 (1956).

In addition to controlling entry, licensing systems governing professionals generally defer to the profession in the discipline of its own members. Critics of this deference argue that the professions are ineffective in monitoring the competence of their colleagues. The popular perception of fraternal leniency undermines public support for professional control of discipline and encourages the development of other quality-control mechanisms, such as malpractice litigation and other forms of government regulation. Law and Polan, Pain and Profit: The Politics of Malpractice (1978); Derbyshire, Medical Licensure and Discipline in the United States (1969).

Licensing continues to be viewed as an important public concession to the professions. The following sections examine two issues raised by medical licensure. The first section examines professional discipline through licensure and the second, the practice of medicine by unlicensed practitioners and by non-physician, licensed health care providers.

A. LICENSING AND DISCIPLINE OF PHYSICIANS

IN THE MATTER OF DONALD R. WILLIAMS, M.D.
Court of Appeals of Ohio (1990).
1990 WL 63027.

BRYANT, JUDGE.

Defendant-appellant, State Medical Board of Ohio, appeals from a judgment of the Franklin County Common Pleas Court reversing appellant's order suspending plaintiff-appellee's medical license for a three-year probationary period. . . .

By letter dated March 12, 1987, appellant notified appellee that his prescribing practices allegedly violated several provisions of R.C. 4731.-22(B): (1) that he had failed to use reasonable care discrimination in administering drugs, or had failed to employ acceptable scientific methods in the selection of drugs or other modalities for treatment of disease, (2) that he was selling, prescribing or giving away or administering drugs other than for legal or legitimate therapeutic purposes, and (3) that his prescribing practices were a departure from, or a failure to conform to, the minimal standards of care of similar practitioners under the same or similar circumstances, whether or not any patient sustained actual injury. Included in the letter were a list of patients, the dates on which appellee had prescribed a controlled substance, primarily Biphetamine, to each patient, and the amount of the controlled substance prescribed on each date. Biphetamine is a Schedule II FDA-approved prescription drug used for the suppression of appetite in connection with the treatment of obesity.

A hearing on the foregoing charges was held before a hearing officer of the State Medical Board of Ohio. Appellant presented appellee's testimony as on cross-examination, as well as a number of exhibits, including the patient records for fifty-one patients which formed the basis for the information contained in appellant's March 12, 1987 letter to appellee. Appellant also presented excerpts from the 1979 Physicians' Desk Reference regarding Biphetamine, an excerpt from the 1979 Physicians' Desk Reference regarding Obetrol, and an excerpt from Facts and Comparisons regarding amphetamines.

Appellee presented not only his own testimony, but that of Eljorn Don Nelson, a doctor of pharmacology, John P. Morgan, M.D., and Sister Mary George Boklege, president of the Clermont Mercy Hospital in Batavia, Ohio, as well as various articles and treatises pertaining to the prescription of drugs for purposes of weight control.

Based on the evidence presented to her, the hearing officer prepared a written report, including findings of fact and conclusions of law. The hearing officer's findings of fact are essentially as follows:

1. Appellee wrote or otherwise authorized prescriptions for the patients at issue.

2. With noted exceptions, appellee prescribed either Biphetamine or Obetrol for those patients for purposes of weight control. Generally, he continued such treatment over extended periods of time, often for well over a year, but each patient was required to return for weight and usually blood pressure checks in order to obtain additional prescriptions. In the case of four separate patients, amphetamines were prescribed for weight control over periods from seven to nine years.

3. Appellee was aware that the Physicians' Desk Reference recommended that Biphetamine or Obetrol be used for control of obesity only as a short-term adjunct to a regimen of weight reduction.

4. Upon beginning a weight control program with his patients, appellee gave the patient diet information in addition to a drug prescription. He discussed exercise and sometimes behavior modification with the patients. His therapeutic regimen was based on the oral history given by the patient. As a result, he often prescribed Schedule II amphetamines at the outset of treatment because the patient related the ineffectiveness of other past medications.

5. Appellee first became aware of appellant's November 1986 rule concerning the prescription of controlled substances for weight control sometime around the last week of December 1986. See Ohio Adm.Code 4731–11–03. Since that time, appellee has discontinued prescribing Schedule II controlled substances for purposes of weight control in accordance with the rule.

Based thereon, the hearing examiner concluded that appellee's patient records "fail to reflect that he selected treatment modalities based upon individual evaluation" of the patients at issue. In particular, the hearing officer noted that appellee "utilized long-term treatment with amphetamines in cases of mild, as well as severe, obesity"; and that such "treatment was generally continued, apparently without regard to the amount of weight the patient lost or gained." Although noting several of appellee's contentions, and giving passing reference to the testimony of Dr. Morgan, the hearing officer concluded that:

"Dr. Williams' prescribing practices not only disregarded the recognized risks of long-term amphetamine use, but also bore no perceivable relationship to the severity of the obesity or to the significance of results achieved from such therapy. Such practice, even when no harm to patients is shown, simply falls below minimal standards of care for medical practitioners. Furthermore, such prescribing for purposes of maintaining weight or preventing possible weight increases, especially for those patients who had not been diagnosed as obese has no legitimate therapeutic purpose. * * * "

Based thereon, the hearing officer determined that appellee had in fact violated the provisions of R.C. 4731.22(B) as alleged in appellant's March 12, 1987 letter. She further recommended that appellee's license to practice medicine be revoked, but that the revocation be stayed subject to a probationary term of three years with certain terms and conditions, including a requirement that appellee keep a log of all controlled substances prescribed, dispensed, or administered during the probationary period.

The board as a whole considered the hearing examiner's report and recommendation, and adopted the report, including the findings of fact and conclusions of law. However, contrary to the recommendation of the hearing officer, the board revoked appellee's license for a period of three years, and stayed the revocation pending a suspension for a minimum of one year, to be followed by a probationary term of not less than five years on certain terms and conditions, including a permanent suspension of appellee's ability to prescribe, administer, dispense, order, or possess controlled substances.

Appellee appealed to the common pleas court, which, on review of the transcript of the proceedings before the medical board, found the board's order not to be supported by reliable, substantial, and probative evidence and not in accordance with law. Appellant appeals therefrom, contending that the common pleas court erred in its determination.

* * *

[T]he issue before the medical board was whether appellee's prescribing of Schedule II controlled substances for purposes of weight control fell below the reasonable standard of care and had no legitimate therapeutic purpose. The issue presented to the common pleas court was whether the medical board's determination was supported by substantial, reliable, and probative evidence and was in accordance with law. By contrast, the issue presented to us is whether the common pleas court abused its discretion in finding that the medical board's order was not supported by substantial, reliable, and probative evidence and was not in accordance with law.

While appellant presented no witnesses regarding the appropriate standard of care in this case, appellee presented the testimony of two expert witnesses, both of whom testified to a "majority" view and a "minority" view regarding the prescription of amphetamines for purposes of weight control. According to their testimony, the majority view holds that amphetamines, and Schedule II controlled substances in general, should not be prescribed for more than short periods of four to six weeks in efforts to control weight. On the other hand, the minority view believes that the prescription of amphetamines for weight control may properly extend over long periods of time. While neither of appellee's experts themselves subscribed to the minority view, both acknowledged it as a viable theory for weight control. As a result, in response to an inquiry as to whether the record contained any evidence that appellee had sold, prescribed, or given away or administered drugs for other than legitimate therapeutic purposes, Dr. Nelson responded: "The opinion is that I don't see any indication of that in the records that I was given to review." When both experts were asked if appellee departed from minimal standards of care of similar practitioners under the same or similar circumstances, Dr. Nelson responded: "My opinion is that the standard of care that's expressed in the records is consistent with the standards for prescribing these medications for the time period that's indicated." Similarly, Dr. Morgan stated: "Williams did not depart from medical standards of care."

Given the foregoing, appellee suggests that the referee properly concluded that appellant had simply failed to provide enough evidence on which to find appellee in violation of R.C. 4731.22(B). Appellant, however, relying on *Arlen v. State* (1980), 61 Ohio St.2d 168, contends that it was not required to present testimony that appellee's conduct fell below the standard of care. Specifically, appellant relies on the language of *Arlen* which states:

"[E]xpert testimony as to a standard of practice is not mandatory in a license revocation hearing and the board may rely on its own expertise to determine whether a physician failed to conform to minimum standards of care." Id. at 172.

* * *

The court [in *Arlen*] concluded:

" * * * The very purpose for having such a specialized technical board would be negated by mandating that expert testimony be presented. Expert opinion testimony can be presented in a medical board proceeding, but the board is not required to reach the same conclusion as the expert witness. The weight to be given to such expert opinion testimony depends upon the board's estimate as to the propriety and reasonableness, but such testimony is not binding upon such an experienced and professional board." Id. at 174.

Appellant urges that we apply *Arlen* in this case, and relieve the medical board of any obligation to present expert testimony regarding the standard of care appropriate to the facts herein. We note, though, that, just as the record indicates the existence of "majority" and "minority" views on the subject of prescribing amphetamines, majority and minority views exist on the issue of the need for expert testimony supporting a specialized board's decision. On the latter subject, Ohio takes the minority view, in that a majority of the jurisdictions in which the highest court has considered the issue requires that expert testimony supporting a board's decision appear in the record. [ ]

The primary rationale for the majority approach to the issue of expert testimony is the need to preserve a record for judicial review. The Supreme Judicial Court of Massachusetts in [*Arthurs v. Board*, 418 N.E.2d 1236 (1981)], stated the rationale as follows:

" * * * The board, however, argues that since most of the members of the board are experts, the board can use its expertise without the evidentiary basis of that expertise appearing in the record. 'This startling theory, if recognized, would not only render absolute a finding opposed to uncontradicted testimony but would render the right of appeal completely inefficacious as well. A board of experts, sitting in a quasi-judicial capacity, cannot be silent witnesses as well as judges.' * * * " [   ]

The approach of the majority jurisdictions would also tend to lessen the problems of lack of notice and lack of an opportunity to cross-examine. In essence, appellant's contentions would require a physician to determine, without the benefit of cross-examination or explicit testimony, what the board's expert opinion, individually or collectively, might be, and then to present evidence to refute that opinion. Indeed, in some instances, the physician would be relegated to presenting some expert testimony in the offhand chance that the testimony may be able to persuade the board that its own opinion, whatever that may be, is invalid.

We do not intend to suggest that the Supreme Court incorrectly decided *Arlen* or that we are not bound by the *Arlen* decision. Nevertheless, *Arlen* is not entirely dispositive of the present case, since *Arlen* merely held that expert testimony is unnecessary. The *Arlen* court did not find that judicial review, notice, or meaningful cross-examination were unnecessary.

* * *

In addition, reliance upon *Arlen* in the present case would be an extension of *Arlen* beyond its original factual context. More particularly, in this case, appellee presented two experts who testified that a valid and viable minority view exists which holds that long-term prescription of amphetamines for purposes of weight control is a legitimate therapeutic course of treatment and conforms with a reasonable standard of care. While appellee unquestionably failed to comply with the majority view, the record reveals nothing to suggest that appellee deviated from the minority view or that that view falls below reasonable standards of care. Whether or not the board subscribes to the minority view does not eliminate, on the evidence in the record, the minority view and appellee's compliance therewith.

In contrast, the physician in *Arlen* presented no expert testimony that his practice conformed to an accepted medical view. Moreover, a specific provision in R.C. 3709.06(A) prohibited Dr. Arlen's conduct. *Arlen* thus seems closer to a case in which no expertise is needed to determine the matter because the case involves the commission of acts which are blatantly illegal or improper.

We therefore conclude that, although the board does not have to base its decisions on testimony, the board's decisions ordinarily require the support of reliable, probative, and substantial evidence in the record. In addition, in cases in which the board relies upon specialized medical knowledge, the board must provide the physician with notice of and an opportunity to refute the evidence upon which the board relies.

The facts of the present case illustrate the difficulty of reviewing a decision of the board when the basis of the decision does not appear in the record. Subsequent to the time in which appellee committed the alleged violations for which he was sanctioned, appellant promulgated Ohio Adm.Code 4731–11–03, entitled "Schedule II controlled stimulants." The rule reflects the position that appellee's witnesses characterized as the majority view. The rule also states that a violation constitutes grounds for discipline under R.C. 4731.22(B)(2), (B)(3), and (B)(6), which were the statutory provisions that formed the basis for the charges against appellee. Given the lack of evidence on the standard of care used by the board, one could well conclude on this record that the board simply ignored appellee's evidence on the minority view and retroactively applied Ohio Adm.Code 4731–11–04. Admittedly, the board can, in its discretion, choose to resolve a dispute through adjudication as well as rule-making. [ ] However, the board arguably could not apply the rule retroactively without considering whether appellee's conduct conformed to the standard that existed at the time. [ ] In short, we conclude that the common pleas court did not abuse its discretion in finding the order of the board not supported by substantial, reliable, and probative evidence.

In addition, we find aspects of the board's order which are not in accordance with the law. First, the hearing officer's report is deficient. While the hearing officer reported some of the evidence, she completely failed to mention other pertinent testimony, such as that of the expert witness, Dr. Morgan. Similarly, she failed to report certain aspects of appellee's testimony regarding his prescribing Biphetamine. [ ]

Finally, although the case law indicates that our authority to review penalties imposed by an agency is relatively limited in cases in which reliable, probative, and substantial evidence supports the agency's findings, [ ] we find it necessary to briefly comment on the penalty imposed upon appellee. Specifically, the hearing officer recommended a three-year probationary period during which time appellee would be allowed to continue to prescribe controlled substances under the supervision of the board. In rejecting the hearing officer's recommendation, the board revoked appellee's license for three years, stayed that revocation pending a one-year suspension and a three-year probationary period. However, appellee was to be deprived permanently of his ability to prescribe all controlled substances. For a general practitioner, deprivation of the right to prescribe all controlled substances in effect virtually deprives him or her of the ability to practice medicine. While that may be an appropriate punishment in certain instances, the facts of this case do not support such a severe sanction, as the evidence indicates that appellee at all times complied with the reasonable standard of care as held by the minority view; and that when he learned of the board's order prohibiting the prescription of amphetamines for purposes of weight control, he ceased the prohibited activity immediately. In such circumstances, a total revocation of appellee's ability to prescribe controlled substances in any aspect of this practice is unduly harsh and unnecessarily deprives appellee of the ability to practice medicine.

Accordingly, we overrule appellant's single assignment of error. The judgment of the common pleas court is affirmed.

Judgment affirmed.

[The Medical Board has appealed to the Ohio Supreme Court.]

In re GUESS

Supreme Court of North Carolina, 1990.
327 N.C. 46, 393 S.E.2d 833.

MITCHELL, JUSTICE.

* * *

The facts of this case are essentially uncontested. The record evidence tends to show that Dr. George Albert Guess is a licensed physician practicing family medicine in Asheville. In his practice, Guess regularly administers homeopathic medical treatments to his patients. Homeopathy has been defined as:

> A system of therapy developed by Samuel Hahnermann on the theory that large doses of a certain drug given to a healthy person will produce certain conditions which, when occurring spontaneously as symptoms of a disease, are relieved by the same drug in small doses. This [is] * * * a sort of "fighting fire with fire" therapy.

Stedman's Medical Dictionary 654 (24th ed. 1982); *see* Schmidt's Attorneys' Dictionary of Medicine H–110 (1962). Homeopathy thus differs from what is referred to as the conventional or allopathic system of medical treatment. Allopathy "employ[s] remedies which affect the body in a way *opposite* from the effect of the disease treated." Schmidt's Attorneys' Dictionary of Medicine A–147 (emphasis added); *see* Stedman's Medical Dictionary 44.

* * * On 25 June 1985, the Board charged Dr. Guess with unprofessional conduct, pursuant to N.C.G.S. § 90–14(a)(6), specifically based upon his practice of homeopathy. In a subsequent Bill of Particulars, the Board alleged that in his practice of medicine, Guess utilized "so-called 'homeopathic medicines' prepared from substances including, but not limited to, moss, the night shade plant and various other animal, vegetable and mineral substances." * * *

Following notice, a hearing was held by the Board on the charge against Dr. Guess. The hearing evidence chiefly consisted of testimony by a number of physicians. Several physicians licensed to practice in North Carolina testified that homeopathy was not an acceptable and prevailing system of medical practice in North Carolina. In fact, there was evidence indicating that Guess is the only homeopath openly practicing in the State. Guess presented evidence that homeopathy is a recognized system of practice in at least three other states and many foreign countries. There was no evidence that Guess' homeopathic treatment had ever harmed a patient, and there was anecdotal evidence that Guess' homeopathic remedies had provided relief to several patients who were apparently unable to obtain relief through allopathic medicine.

Following its hearing, the Board revoked Dr. Guess' license to practice medicine in North Carolina, based upon findings and conclusions that Guess' practice of homeopathy "departs from and does not conform to the standards of acceptable and prevailing medical practice in this State," thus constituting unprofessional conduct as defined and prohibited by N.C.G.S. § 90–14(a)(6). The Board, however, stayed the revocation of Guess' license for so long as he refrained from practicing homeopathy.

Guess appealed the Board's decision. * * * After review, the Superior Court entered an order on 20 May 1987 which reversed and vacated the Board's decision. The Superior Court found and concluded that Guess' substantial rights had been violated because the Board's findings, conclusions and decision were "not supported by competent, material and substantial evidence and [were] arbitrary and capricious."

* * * [T]he Court of Appeals rejected the Superior Court's reasoning to the effect that the Board's findings, conclusions and decision were not supported by competent evidence. *In re Guess,* 95 N.C.App. 435, 437, 382 S.E.2d 459, 461 (1989). The Court of Appeals, nonetheless, affirmed the Superior Court's order reversing the Board's decision,

> because the Board neither charged nor found that Dr. Guess' departures from approved and prevailing medical practice either endangered or harmed his patients or the public, and in our opinion the revocation of a physician's license to practice his profession in this state must be based upon conduct that is detrimental to the public; it cannot be based upon conduct that is merely different from that of other practitioners.

Id. at 437, 382 S.E.2d at 461. We granted the Board's Petition for Discretionary Review, and now reverse the Court of Appeals.

I.

The statute central to the resolution of this case provides in relevant part:

§ 90–14. Revocation, suspension, annulment or denial of license.

(a) The Board shall have the power to deny, annul, suspend, or revoke a license * * * issued by the Board to any person who has been found by the Board to have committed any of the following acts or conduct, or for any of the following reasons:

* * *

(6) Unprofessional conduct, including, but not limited to, *any departure* from, or the failure to conform to, the *standards of acceptable and prevailing medical practice,* or the ethics of the medical profession, *irrespective of whether or not a patient is injured thereby.* * * *

N.C.G.S. § 90–14 (1985) (emphasis added). The Court of Appeals concluded that in exercising the police power, the legislature may properly act only to protect the public from harm. [ ] Therefore, the Court of Appeals reasoned that, in order to be a valid exercise of the police power, the statute must be construed as giving the Board authority to prohibit or punish the action of a physician only when it can be shown that *the particular action in question* poses a danger of harm to the patient or the public. Specifically, the Court of Appeals held that:

> Before a physician's license to practice his profession in this state can be lawfully revoked under G.S. 90–14(a)(6) for practices contrary to acceptable and prevailing medical practice that *it must also appear that the deviation complained of posed some threat of harm to either the physician's patients or the public.* [ ]

The Board argues, and we agree, that the Court of Appeals erred in construing the statute to add a requirement that each particular practice prohibited by the statute must pose an actual threat of harm. Our analysis begins with a basic constitutional principle: the General Assembly, in exercising the state's police power, may legislate to protect the public health, safety and general welfare. [ ]

Turning to the subject of this case, regulation of the medical profession is plainly related to the legitimate public purpose of protecting the public health and safety. [ ] State regulation of the medical profession has long been recognized as a legitimate exercise of the police power. As the Supreme Court of the United States has pointed out:

> The power of the State to provide for the general welfare of its people authorizes it to prescribe all such regulations as in its judgment will secure *or tend to secure* them against the consequences of ignorance and incapacity as well as of deception and fraud. * * *

> Few professions require more careful preparation by one who seeks to enter it than that of medicine. It has to deal with all those subtle and mysterious influences upon which health and life depend. * * * The physician must be able to detect readily the presence of disease, and prescribe appropriate remedies for its removal. Everyone may have occasion to consult him, but comparatively few can judge of the qualifications of learning and skill which he possesses. Reliance must be placed upon the assurance given by his license, issued by an authority competent to judge in that respect, that he possesses the requisite qualifications. * * * The same reasons which control in imposing conditions, upon compliance with which the physician is allowed to practice in the

first instance, may call for further conditions as new modes of treating disease are discovered, or a more thorough acquaintance is obtained of the remedial properties of vegetable and mineral substances, or a more accurate knowledge is acquired of the human system and of the agencies by which it is affected.

Dent v. West Virginia, 129 U.S. 114, 122–23, 9 S.Ct. 231, 233, 32 L.Ed. 623, 626 (1889) (emphasis added). [   ]

* * * We conclude that the legislature, in enacting N.C.G.S. § 90–14(a)(6), reasonably believed that a general risk of endangering the public is *inherent* in *any* practices which fail to conform to the standards of "acceptable and prevailing" medical practice in North Carolina. We further conclude that the legislative intent was to prohibit any practice departing from acceptable and prevailing medical standards without regard to whether the particular practice itself could be shown to endanger the public. Our conclusion is buttressed by the plain language of N.C.G.S. § 90–14(a)(6), which allows the Board to act against *any* departure from acceptable medical practice "irrespective of whether or not a patient is injured thereby." By authorizing the Board to prevent or punish *any* medical practice departing from acceptable and prevailing standards, irrespective of whether a patient is injured thereby, the statute works as a regulation which "tend[s] to secure" the public generally "against the consequences of ignorance and incapacity as well as of deception and fraud," even though it may not immediately have that direct effect in a particular case.

* * *

II.

* * *

Dr. Guess also contends that the Board's decision was arbitrary and capricious and, therefore, must be reversed under N.C.G.S. § 90–14.10. He argues that the Board's arbitrariness is revealed in its "selective" application of the statute against him. He seems to contend that if the Board is to take valid action against him, it must also investigate and sanction every physician who is the "first" to utilize any "new" or "rediscovered" medical procedure. We disagree. The Board properly adhered to its statutory notice and hearing requirements, and its decision was amply supported by uncontroverted competent, material and substantial evidence. We detect no evidence of arbitrariness or capriciousness.

Dr. Guess strenuously argues that many countries and at least three states recognize the legitimacy of homeopathy. While some physicians may value the homeopathic system of practice, it seems that others consider homeopathy an outmoded and ineffective system of practice. This conflict, however interesting, simply is irrelevant here in light of the uncontroverted evidence and the Board's findings and conclusion that homeopathy is not currently an "acceptable and prevailing" system of medical practice in North Carolina.

While questions as to the efficacy of homeopathy and whether its practice should be allowed in North Carolina may be open to valid debate among members of the medical profession, the courts are not the proper forum for that debate. The legislature may one day choose to recognize the homeopathic system of treatment, or homeopathy may evolve by proper experimentation and research to the point of being recognized by the medical profession as an acceptable and prevailing form of medical practice in our state; such choices, however, are not for the courts to make.

We stress that we do not intend for our opinion in this case to retard the ongoing research and development of the healing arts in any way. The Board argues, and we agree within our admittedly limited scope of medical knowledge, that preventing the practice of homeopathy will not restrict the development and acceptance of new and beneficial medical practices. Instead, the development and acceptance of such new practices simply must be achieved by "acceptable and prevailing" methods of medical research, experimentation, testing, and approval by the appropriate regulatory or professional bodies.

* * *

Reversed and Remanded.

FRYE, JUSTICE, dissenting.

* * *

I believe that the majority has construed subsection (6) of N.C.G.S. § 90–14(a) in a manner inconsistent with its purpose and legislative intent. * * *

* * *

* * * All of the evidence tended to show that Dr. Guess is a highly qualified practicing physician who uses homeopathic medicines as a last resort when allopathic medicines are not successful. He takes 150 credits of continuing medical education approved by the American Medical Association every three years and from fifty to eighty hours of homeopathic continuing medical education each year. The homeopathic medications prescribed by him are listed in the Homeopathic Pharmacopoeia of the United States and are regulated by the United States Federal Food, Drug and Cosmetic Act. The homeopathic approach is often preferred, in Dr. Guess' words, "primarily because of its well documented safety." This is not a case of a quack beguiling the public with snake oil and drums, but a dedicated physician seeking to find new ways to relieve human suffering. The legislature could hardly have intended this practice to be considered "unprofessional conduct" so as to revoke a physician's license in the absence of some evidence of harm or potential harm to the patients or to the public. Nothing in the record before the Board or this Court justifies so broad a sweep in order to secure the public "against the consequences of ignorance and incapacity as well as of deception and fraud." [ ]

* * *

* * * I do not believe that the General Assembly would require a physician to undergo a possibly lengthy wait for legislative action while it is attending to other matters before allowing him to make non-dangerous, beneficial treatments available to members of the public who knowingly consent. Where there is no showing of danger, I do not believe specific legislative approval is a prerequisite to a physician engaging in a practice which is by all indications helpful when used wisely.

* * *

Notes and Questions

1. What implications do the arguments presented in the first section of this chapter, concerning the meaning and measurement of quality in medical care, have for the issues raised in these two cases?

The State Medical Board of Ohio promulgated a rule, cited in *Williams,* requiring that physicians meet the "majority" standard regarding the prescription of controlled substances for weight control. Should licensure boards establish standards of care or practice guidelines, or should they simply acknowledge and reflect the full range of actual medical practices? Would your answer depend on whether the board was acting in a rulemaking or in an adjudicatory role?

2. Could the Ohio State Medical Board satisfy the court's requirement of expert testimony by designating one of its physician members to present the case and be available for cross-examination? Would this address the court's concerns? Was the problem in *Williams* that there was no expert testimony submitted by the board? Does *Williams* stand for the proposition that a physician conforming to a "minority view" is safe from discipline? Can you distinguish *Williams* and *Guess?*

3. The Inspector General of the Department of Health and Human Services reported that there have been "strikingly" few disciplinary actions for malpractice and incompetence. He also reported that approximately 75 percent of all disciplinary actions were based on drug and alcohol abuse by the physician or for inappropriate prescription for drugs. Report of the Inspector General, Department of Health and Human Services, June 5, 1986.

The Inspector General reported that early 1986 figures showed that "things are just beginning to come together for the boards." Brinkley, "State Medical Boards Disciplined Record Number of Doctors in '85", N.Y. Times, Nov. 8, 1986 at 6, col. 1. The Inspector General expressed the opinion that "years of criticism had finally begun to bring results" and that "the raising of public interest in medical incompetence has had a positive impact and prompted the states to better support their boards." Id. at 13, col. 3.

The Inspector General issued a second, follow-up report in 1990. In this later report, the Inspector General identified the following continuing impediments to effectiveness: limitations on the boards' authority; limitations on the authority of other agencies to share information; standards of proof calling for clear and convincing evidence; lack of clear-cut standards concerning competent medical care; and infrequent information sharing among state boards concerning investigative approaches. Case backlogs and understaffing continue to be serious problems. The OIG reported that, upon close examination, reported increases in disciplinary actions were quite "modest." The OIG report states that reports to the Federation of State Medical Boards tend to over-report the number of disciplinary actions. In reviewing the types of behavior triggering discipline, the report states that the majority involve actions in a doctor's office and the fewest involve actions in nursing homes. There continues to be a wide range among the states, with one state taking 2.6 actions per 1,000 licensees and another taking 32.2 actions. As before, the majority of disciplinary actions involved improper use of drugs or alcohol (57%) and far fewer involved incompetence (11.5%). A significant number of disciplinary actions involve "private" remedies, such as a private letter of concern, reprimand or warning.

The Federation of State Medical Boards reported in 1990 that "for the first time in five years," state medical licensure agencies had failed to increase disciplinary actions despite great increases in the number of complaints. The Patient's Advocate, Washington Post, Page Z17 (9–4–90); Winn, Breaden and Shelton, Official 1988 Federation Summary of Reported Disciplinary Actions, 77 Federation Bulletin 227 (August 1990).

How would you measure whether the number of disciplinary actions per 1000 doctors in your state was "enough?" See also, Dolan and Urban, The Determinants of the Effectiveness of Medical Disciplinary Boards, 1960–1977, 7 Law and Human Behavior 203 (1983).

4. State licensure boards charged with enforcement are frequently understaffed. See, Derbyshire, How Effective is Medical Self–Regulation?, 7 Law and Human Behavior 193, 199 (1983); Inspector General's Report, supra note 3. The boards also may have a difficult time in securing the legal services needed to prosecute disciplinary actions because the licensure boards are only one of many agencies who may have a claim on the services of the office of the state attorney general. How might their access to legal services affect their decisions, if at all?

If the boards must set priorities due to limited funding, what should those priorities be? Should the boards make responding to complaints a priority? Should they focus on the more easily proven cases? Should they make cases of "incompetency" a priority?

5. The collegial nature of the professions discourages voluntary reporting of colleagues to disciplinary boards. The President of the Federation of State Medical Boards comments that when he first served on a licensure board many years ago, it was a "good old boys' club" in which the board would occasionally discipline "the drunk doctor or the one who was having an affair." But, he states that this has changed in part because of state statutes requiring mandatory reporting of information relating to unprofessional conduct. Jacott, Modern Medical Discipline, 14 State Health Legislation Report 1, 3 (1986). See, e.g., N.Y.—McKinney's Pub. Health Law § 230(11)(a), Ill.Rev.Stat. ch. 111, par. 4400–23 (1988).

For a discussion of these statutes, see Fama, Reporting Incompetent Physicians: A Comparison of Requirements in Three States, 11 Law,

Medicine & Health Care 111 (1983); Cullinane, New Rules for an Old Problem—The Problem Physician, 72 Ill.B.J. 426 (1983), commenting on the Illinois mandatory reporting system; and Mandatory Reporting of Impaired Physicians, 12 State Health Legislation Report 22 (1984) for a survey of statutes mandating reporting.

6. Medical licensure is controlled by each state. This has in the past allowed doctors disciplined in one state to practice in another, at least until the disciplinary action happened to be discovered. Although the Federation of State Medical Boards and the AMA maintained data on disciplined physicians, the data was not comprehensive as states were not required to report. In order to address this problem, Congress enacted the Health Care Quality Improvement Act in 1986 (42 U.S.C.A. §§ 11101–11152 (1990)). The statute provides immunity for peer review actions that meet the statutory requirements (as discussed in Chapter 8) and establishes a national data bank for information on physicians. The National Practitioner Data Bank, in operation as of October 1, 1990, will serve as a central source of information related to physician disciplinary actions which are related to professional competence or conduct and medical malpractice payments and settlements. State boards and health care entities, including hospitals, that participate in peer review are required to report disciplinary actions. Hospitals have a statutory duty to request information from the data bank whenever a physician applies for admission to the medical staff or clinical privileges, and at least every two years for all medical-staff or privileged physicians. Failure to request such information creates a presumption that the hospital has knowledge of the information in the data bank and may also result in the loss of the statutory immunity. The data bank will not be accessible to the general public, and attorneys for plaintiffs in suits against a hospital may access the information under very limited circumstances. 54 Fed.Reg. 42,722; to be codified 45 C.F.R. § 60. If you were legal counsel to a hospital, how would you advise it to handle the application of a physician against whom a malpractice settlement or judgment has been reported? What is the rationale for prohibiting public access to the information?

7. The impaired physician presents a serious problem for quality-control regulation. Estimates of the incidence of physician impairment due to alcoholism or drugs vary. The A.M.A. has estimated that seven to eight percent of practicing physicians are alcoholics. The drug addiction rate for physicians is thirty to a hundred times higher than the rate for the general public. A survey indicated that over half of the doctors age 40 and under had used drugs "recreationally" at some time and that 38% of those under 40 reported a continuing use of marijuana, cocaine or other drugs. Twenty-five percent of the 500 physicians surveyed reported that they had treated themselves with mind-affecting drugs in the year prior to the survey and 42% had done so at some time in their lives. McAuliffe, et al., Psychoactive Drug Use among Practicing Physicians and Medical Students, 315 N.Eng.J.Med. 805 (1986). As of 1981, forty-seven states had passed legislation authorizing state medical boards to establish special committees to intervene with impaired physicians. This legislation typically establishes a system that co-exists with the disciplinary system and that focuses on the rehabilitation, rather than punishment, of the impaired physician.

Although the statute may require colleagues or institutions to report a physician's impairment, they generally shield the impaired physician from disciplinary action so long as the physician agrees to limit his practice and participate in a rehabilitation program. Thus, these programs are coercive, but not punitive. Other programs are strictly voluntary and do not threaten the physician with referral for disciplinary action. In either type of program, the physician is guaranteed confidentiality at least during the course of rehabilitation unless there is a threat to the welfare of patients.

Two issues raised by impaired physician statutes are the point at which intervention should occur and the appropriate role of the public in the process. "Can coercive intervention be justified where the likelihood of harm is slight, either because the impairment is mild or because the doctor is insulated from possible victims of harm? Is it important to differentiate among a severely alcoholic surgeon, an elderly general practitioner with a small practice who now and then experiences memory lapses, and an addicted medical researcher who conducts clinical trials on human subjects?" Morrow, Doctors Helping Doctors, 14 Hastings Center Report, 32, 38 (Dec. 1984). In reference to the participation of the public in these nondisciplinary committees, Morrow notes:

> In medicalizing the problem of addicted, alcoholic, and psychiatrically disturbed doctors, impaired physician programs embrace the principle of "doctor helping doctor," that is, mutual assistance among nonimpaired, recovered, and currently impaired doctors. By implication, committees relying on reports from the public or otherwise involving the public have failed to act as their brother's keeper and, in the words of one doctor I interviewed, risk "shooting the credibility of the program" and transforming mutual assistance into a "watchdog committee or a witchhunt."

Is the public's interest in the problem of the impaired physician better served by rehabilitation or discipline? Should there be public participation in the "doctor helping doctor" programs?

See, Walzer, Impaired Physicians: An Overview and Update of the Legal Issues, 11 J.Leg.Med. 131 (1990); Comment, The Impaired Physician: An Old Problem Creates the Need for New Legislation, 26 St. Louis U.L.J. 727 (1982); Comment, The Chemically–Dependent Physician: Liability for Colleagues and Hospitals in California, 21 San Diego L.Rev. 431 (1984); Petty, The Impaired Physician: A Failed Healer, Legal Aspects of Medical Practice 5 (July 1984), (describing the range of state legislative responses to the impaired physician).

Problem: Among Friends

One of your best friends, Peter Anderson, is a doctor in Illinois. You have known Peter since college. You remained friends while you went to law school, and he went to medical school. You see him socially at parties and at ball games. Peter has always been a gregarious individual. He has always been able to drink more than most and still "hold his liquor." Recently you've become concerned because he seems to be drinking a little more, although not ordinarily to the extent that you would consider him too drunk to drive. Also, Peter has told you that he has begun to use cocaine periodically and finds it very invigorating. Will you report Peter to the disciplinary committee of the state medical board? Will you report him to one of the substance abuse assistance programs set up to help impaired doctors? Would your decision or concerns be different if, in addition to being Peter's friend, you were a colleague at the hospital? In either case, would you report Peter if he were not a practicing physician, but rather did research not involving human subjects?

B. THE REGULATION OF NON–PHYSICIAN HEALTH CARE PROVIDERS

1. *Unlicensed Health Care Providers*

The state medical practice acts define the practice of medicine quite broadly and indeterminately and prohibit any but licensed physicians and other licensed health care professionals, within the bounds of their own licensure, from practicing medicine. This prohibition is enforced by criminal sanctions against the unlicensed practitioner and license revocation against any physician who aids and abets the unlicensed practitioner.

The state administrative board charged with supervising the licensure of physicians generally has the primary responsibility for enforcing the prohibition against the unauthorized practice of medicine. Cases in which a board has found an unlicensed practitioner guilty of the unauthorized practice of medicine give a glimpse of the definitional problems associated with this prohibition and the impact that its broad definition has on the delivery of health care services.

For example, cases against unlicensed practitioners have involved services such as nutrition counseling, ear piercing and other activities provided both by physicians and by lay practitioners. The statutory definition of the practice of medicine leads to such reaching. For example, in Medical Licensing Board of Indiana v. Stetina, 477 N.E.2d 322 (Ind.App.1985), the court affirmed an injunction against a woman who practiced "iridology." The court relied on the state's statutory definition of the practice of medicine:

> "(1) Holding oneself out to the public as being engaged in the diagnosis, treatment, correction or prevention of any disease, ailment, defect, injury, infirmity, deformity, pain or other condition of human beings, or the suggestion, recommendation or prescription or administration of any form of treatment, without limitation, or the performing of any kind of surgical operation upon a human being, including tattooing, or the penetration of the skin or body orifice by any means, for the intended palliation, relief, cure or prevention of any physical, mental or functional ailment or defect of any person;

> "(2) The maintenance of an office or place of business for the reception, examination or treatment of persons suffering from disease, ailment, defect, injury, infirmity, deformity, pain or other conditions of body or mind; ..."

The court found that Stetina had examined an investigator's eyes for "clues or hints" and had used an iridology chart developed by a chiropractor that related spots in the eyes to certain physical conditions. Stetina had explained to her "client" that she was prohibited from making a diagnosis. Stetina recommended a colonic irrigation and a particular diet and supplements. The court held that Stetina had made a diagnosis and so was engaged in the unlicensed practice of medicine.

Notes and Questions

Would the prohibition against the unauthorized practice of medicine, as defined in the Indiana statute, extend to services offered by a health club, which may include "physical condition assessment" and advice on a particular nutritional regimen designed to remedy specific weaknesses? Would it extend to the recommendation of over-the-counter medications for particular aches, pains or illnesses by a volunteer making friendly visits to homebound elderly?

What is the underlying rationale of the medical practice acts' prohibition of "diagnosis" and "prescription" if the practitioner discloses to the patient that she is not a doctor? Are there any alternative regulatory methods that might be used to serve the purposes of the prohibition of unauthorized practice? For example, rather than prohibiting practice by defendant, a statute could require particular disclosures, or even warnings, to consumers. What would be the comparative advantages and disadvantages of disclosure as against prohibition? Consider this question in relation to the following case.

THE PEOPLE OF THE STATE OF ILLINOIS V. MARGARET JIHAN

Supreme Court of Illinois, 1989.
127 Ill.2d 379, 130 Ill.Dec. 422, 537 N.E.2d 751.

The question presented by this appeal is whether provisions of the now repealed Illinois Medical Practice Act (the Act) [   ] which prohibited the unlicensed practice of midwifery, were unconstitutionally vague under the due process clauses of the United States and Illinois Constitutions.

In 1986, appellee, Margaret Jihan, was convicted of practicing midwifery without a license in violation of the Act (the Act was not repealed until December 31, 1987) for the role she played in assisting Hanizah Hashim in the delivery of her baby. The only witness who testified at the trial was a Carbondale police officer to whom appellee had given a statement describing what had occurred at the birthing. The officer testified that, according to appellee, Hashim had originally planned on delivering her baby at a birthing center. However, when it became apparent that the center would not open in time for the birth, her doctor recommended that she contact appellee to assist her in delivering the baby at home. Hashim and her husband met appellee for the first time six to eight weeks before the birth. The purpose of the meeting "was for education and awareness of child birthing at home."

On May 16, 1985, Hashim telephoned appellee and told her that "her bag of waters had broke." Appellee then advised her of various methods of inducing labor including breast stimulation, long walks and hot showers. Appellee saw Hashim that day and again on May 17, when she spent most of the day and night at Hashim's apartment. During these visits, appellee observed the progress of Hashim's labor and monitored the child's heartbeat. Hashim's active labor began on the morning of May 18.

At about 7 o'clock on the evening of May 18, Hashim passed a bloody discharge in which meconium was present. Meconium is a fecal material which a fetus can ingest into its lungs, causing blocked airways. Meconium must be removed immediately after childbirth to allow the baby to breathe normally. The presence of the meconium indicated to appellee that a special delivery of the baby would be necessary, one that would require extensive suctioning of the baby to remove the meconium and possibly even resuscitation to revive the baby's breathing. Appellee suggested at this point that Hashim go to the hospital, but Hashim wanted to stay at home. Consequently, appellee continued to monitor Hashim, conducted an internal exam with a sterile glove, determined that Hashim was dilated eight centimeters, and checked the baby's heartbeat every 15 minutes with a stethoscope.

At about 10 o'clock that evening, Hashim began to deliver her baby. The baby's head was delivered first, and appellee saw meconium present and so wiped the baby's face and began suctioning the baby's nose with a rubber ball syringe. After the remainder of the baby was delivered, appellee continued suctioning and removing the meconium, began to massage the baby, placed the baby on top of the mother, and clamped and cut the umbilical cord. The baby had failed to breathe after birth. Appellee then instructed an assistant who was also present at the delivery to begin massaging Hashim's abdomen. Appellee also told the assistant to call an ambulance while appellee took the baby into the bathroom of the apartment and turned on the hot water to create steam. When the baby became unresponsive, appellee began administering cardiovascular pulmonary resuscitation, but could not get oxygen into the baby's lungs. Appellee then wrapped the baby in sterile blankets and took it out of the bathroom. Appellee then began massaging Hashim's abdomen because the assistant had failed to do so. When the ambulance arrived, appellee took the baby out to the ambulance crew and gave them a brief history of the birth. Appellee then returned to Hashim and continued massaging her abdomen. Seeing that the placenta had attached itself, thus requiring an emergency procedure, appellee called for another ambulance. While waiting for the ambulance to arrive, appellee assisted Hashim with her breathing and gave her a glass of cold tea with honey. The baby was taken by ambulance to a hospital, where it was pronounced dead on arrival.

In her statement to the police officer, appellee described herself as a "labor-coach and patient advocate." She explained that she charges two to five dollars per hour for her attendance at births. She also gave the officer a "Release" that she had Hashim and her husband sign. The release said, in part:

"We initiated the relationship with (appellee) and asked her to be present at the birth of our child as a midwife. We are fully aware that she is not a doctor or a nurse, and has no medical or nursing training, and agree that she is not representing that she can or will perform any tasks which require such training. We understand that her experiences are limited to having given birth three times herself and having attended a few other births as a lay midwife or as an assistant to a doctor.

We further realize that (appellee) does not have a license as a midwife, and that Illinois does not license midwives. We understand that (appellee) does not hold herself out to the public as a midwife, but is only agreeing to attend our birth because she feels she could be of help to us."

Appellee was charged by indictment with involuntary manslaughter and practicing midwifery without a license. [ ] The circuit court dismissed the manslaughter charge but convicted appellee of practicing midwifery without a license. Appellee was sentenced to one year of probation and, as a condition of probation, was ordered to serve six months of "electronic home confinement" from 10 p.m. until noon six days per week.

* * *

The Medical Practice Act prohibited any person from the "practice * * * (of) midwifery" without a State license to do so. A person who "practice(d) midwifery" without a license was guilty of a Class 4 felony [ ]. The terms "practice" and "midwifery" were not defined in the Act.

Appellee claims that the undefined term "midwifery" was vague and so contends that we should affirm the appellate court's decision that the statute was unconstitutional. The State, on the other hand, argues that appellee does not have standing to raise a vagueness challenge because appellee's conduct was clearly prohibited by the Act. The State further argues that even if appellee does have standing, the term "midwife" has a common and ordinary meaning that is easily understood by the average person and so the appellate court's finding that the statute was vague was incorrect.

* * *

The State first claims that appellee clearly practiced midwifery because appellee, as evidenced by the "Release" she had Hashim sign, with its language that appellee would be present at the birth as a "midwife," understood herself to be a midwife. However, the issue here is not, Did appellee think that her conduct constituted midwifery? Rather the question is, Did the Act clearly specify that appellee's conduct was prohibited? To answer this question, we must first ascertain what conduct occurred and then decide if that conduct was clearly prohibited by the language of the Act.

* * *

We find that there is ambiguity in the term "midwifery" and that this ambiguity is demonstrated by the State's argument itself. The indictment in this case read that appellee "committed the offense of practice of midwifery without a license in that she delivered the child of Hanizah Hashim, without being licensed to do so in the State of Illinois. Similarly, the State in its reply brief and during oral argument stated that the act of midwifery is the act of delivering a child. Although the meaning of the term "delivery" may be as vague as that of "midwifery," we find that it connotes the playing of a major role in physically removing or extracting a baby from its mother's womb. The term "assisting at childbirth," however, encompasses a far broader range of activity than the mere physical delivery of the baby, and could include everything from educating the mother weeks before the delivery to caring for the mother and child immediately after birth. It is therefore unclear whether the term "midwifery" has the broad meaning of assisting at childbirth, as the State contends at times, or if it has the more narrow meaning of actually delivering the child at birth.

Clearly, appellee assisted at the birth of Hashim's child. However, there has been no showing that appellee delivered Hashim's child.

* * *

The testimony [at trial] only establishes that appellee monitored, examined and assisted Hashim with her birth and cared for the baby during and after the delivery. It is not clear from the evidence whether appellee actually delivered the child in the sense of physically removing or extracting it from its mother's womb. Because the language of the Act could be read as merely prohibiting persons not licensed as midwives from delivering babies, rather than the State's more broad reading that it prohibits such persons from assisting at birth, and because there is no evidence that appellee delivered Hashim's baby, we conclude that the Act did not clearly prohibit the conduct engaged in by appellee in this case. Accordingly, we find that the Act was unconstitutionally vague as applied to appellee in that it did not provide sufficient notice that appellee's conduct in this case was prohibited.

We note in closing that the Act in question here has been repealed by the General Assembly and replaced by the Medical Practice Act of 1987. [ ] The new act makes no reference to the practice of midwifery or to midwives, and so our holding here has no effect upon the current statutory scheme which governs the practice of medicine in Illinois.

Notes and Questions

1. Was the release signed by Hanizah Hashim relevant to the issue of the statutory prohibition? Why or why not? Should the legislature, or the board, or the court take into account the reasons women may choose lay midwives whether these be religious (for example, perhaps Jihan was the only female childbirth assistant available to Hashim whose religion prohibited male assistance) or economic or other reasons? Would Jihan's acts constitute the unauthorized practice of medicine?

2. In Leigh v. Board of Registration in Nursing, 395 Mass. 670, 481 N.E.2d 1347, 1353 (1985), the Massachusetts Supreme Court distinguishes "ordinary assistance in the normal cases of childbirth" from a situation in which a lay midwife used "obstetrical instruments" and "printed prescriptions or formulas." The court in *Leigh* found that assistance at normal childbirth is not the practice of medicine but left standing the holding in a previous case (Commonwealth v. Porn, 82 N.E. 31 (1907)) that the use of obstetrical instruments and prescriptions by a midwife is the unauthorized practice of medicine.

3. The prohibition of lay midwifery in many states has generated claims that the prohibition constitutes an unconstitutional interference with a pregnant woman's right to privacy as embodied in the right to choose the manner of and the attendant for childbirth. Several courts have rejected this claim. See, e.g., *Bowland; Leigh;* Board of Registration for Healing Arts v. Southworth, 704 S.W.2d 219 (Mo.1986). See also, Caldwell, Bowland v. Municipal Court Revisited: A Defense Perspective on Unlicensed Midwife Practice in California, 15 Pac.L.J. 19 (1983) (reassessing *Bowland* in light of the expansion of the right of privacy in California); Note, A Matter of the Quality of Birth: Mothers and Midwives Shackled by the Medical Establishment and Pennsylvania Law, 23 Duquesne L.Rev. 171 (1984) (suggesting challenges based on family privacy including deference to the parents in choosing health care for children); Evenson, Midwives: Survival of An Ancient Profession, 7 Women's Rts.L.Rep. 313 (1982). For an excellent review of midwifery and analysis of current statutes and case law concerning lay midwifery see Note, Choice in Childbirth: Parents, Lay Midwives, and Statutory Regulation, 30 St. Louis U.L.J. 985 (1986).

2. Other Health Care Professionals: Nurses and Physician Assistants

a. Nurses

The medical practice acts exempt non-physician, licensed health care professionals acting within the scope of their own licensure from sanctions against the unauthorized practice of medicine. These professions include nursing, which is licensed under state nursing practice acts. Nursing practice acts parallel the medical practice acts in establishing entry requirements, discipline and definitions of the practice of nursing. The jurisdictional claims of each profession may overlap because the "practice of medicine" and the "practice of nursing" can involve the same functions. The recent rapid growth in the participation of non-physician health care providers in health care delivery and the expansion of the role of nursing have caused clashes between physicians and nurses on the regulatory level, as in the following case.

SERMCHIEF v. GONZALES

Supreme Court of Missouri, 1983.
660 S.W.2d 683.

WELLIVER, JUDGE.

This is a petition for a declaratory judgment and injunction brought by two nurses and five physicians[1] employed by the East Missouri Action Agency (Agency) wherein the plaintiff-appellants ask the Court to declare that the practices of the Agency nurses are authorized under the nursing law of this state, § 335.016.8, RSMo 1978 and that such practices do not constitute the unauthorized practice of medicine under Chapter 334 relating to the Missouri State Board of Registration For the Healing Arts (Board). * * * The holding below was against appellants who make direct appeal to this Court alleging that the validity of the statutes is involved. Mo. Const. art. V, § 3. * * *

I

The facts are simple and for the most part undisputed. The Agency is a federally tax exempt Missouri not-for-profit corporation that maintains offices in Cape Girardeau (main office), Flat River, Ironton, and Fredericktown. The Agency provides medical services to the general public in fields of family planning, obstetrics and gynecology. The services are provided to an area that includes the counties of Bollinger, Cape Girardeau, Perry, St. Francis, Ste. Genevieve, Madison, Iron and Washington. Some thirty-five hundred persons utilized these services during the year prior to trial. The Agency is funded from federal grants, Medicaid reimbursements and patient fees. The programs are directed toward the lower income segment of the population. Similar programs exist both statewide and nationwide.

Appellant nurses Solari and Burgess are duly licensed professional nurses in Missouri pursuant to the provisions of Chapter 335 and are employed by the Agency. Both nurses have had post-graduate special training in the field of obstetrics and gynecology. Appellant physicians are also employees of the Agency and duly licensed to practice medicine (the healing arts) pursuant to Chapter 334. Respondents are the members and the executive secretary of the Missouri State Board of Registration for the Healing Arts (Board) and as such are charged with the enforcement, implementation, and administration of Chapter 334.

The services routinely provided by the nurses and complained of by the Board included, among others, the taking of history; breast and pelvic examinations; laboratory testing of Papanicolaou (PAP) smears,

1. The physicians are joined for the reason that they are charged with aiding and abetting the unauthorized practice of medicine by the nurses.

gonorrhea cultures, and blood serology; the providing of and giving of information about oral contraceptives, condoms, and intrauterine devices (IUD); the dispensing of certain designated medications; and counseling services and community education. If the nurses determined the possibility of a condition designated in the standing orders or protocols that would contraindicate the use of contraceptives until further examination and evaluation, they would refer the patients to one of the Agency physicians. No act by either nurse is alleged to have caused injury or damage to any person. All acts by the nurses were done pursuant to written standing orders and protocols signed by appellant physicians. The standing orders and protocols were directed to specifically named nurses and were not identical for all nurses.

The Board threatened to order the appellant nurses and physicians to show cause why the nurses should not be found guilty of the unauthorized practice of medicine and the physicians guilty of aiding and abetting such unauthorized practice. Appellants sought Court relief in this proceeding.

* * * [T]he trial court described in its memorandum opinion as the ultimate issues for determination:

A. Does the conduct of plaintiff nurses Solari and Burgess constitute "Professional Nursing" as that term is defined in § 335.016.8, RSMo?

B. If the Court finds and concludes that any act or acts of plaintiff nurses Solari and Burgess does not or do not constitute(s) "professional nursing" and, constitutes the unauthorized practice of medicine under § 334.010, RSMo the Court must then determine if § 334.010, RSMo is unconstitutionally vague and uncertain on its face and, thus, is in violation of the specificity requirements of the Fifth and Fourteenth Amendments to the United States Constitution and of Article 1, § 10 of the Missouri Constitution.

* * *

In our opinion the trial court correctly defined the issues of the case, both of which we deem to be matters of law to be determined by the Court.

* * *

III

The statutes involved are:

It shall be unlawful for any person not now a registered physician within the meaning of the law to practice medicine or surgery in any of its departments, or to profess to cure and attempt to treat the sick and others afflicted with bodily or mental infirmities, or engage in the practice of midwifery in this state, except as herein provided.

Section 334.010.

This Chapter does not apply to dentists licensed and lawfully practicing their profession within the provisions of chapter 332, RSMo; *to nurses licensed and lawfully practicing their profession within the provisions of chapter 335, RSMo;* to optometrists licensed and lawfully practicing their profession within the provisions of chapter 336, RSMo; to pharmacists licensed and lawfully practicing their profession within the provisions of chapter 338, RSMo; to podiatrists licensed and lawfully practicing their profession within the provisions of chapter 330, RSMo; or to chiropractors licensed and lawfully practicing their profession within the provisions of chapter 331, RSMo.

Section 334.155, RSMo Supp.1982 (emphasis added).

Definitions.—As used in sections 335.011 to 335.096, unless the context clearly requires otherwise, the following words and terms shall have the meanings indicated:

* * *

(8) "Professional nursing" is the performance for compensation of any act which requires substantial specialized education, judgment and skill based on knowledge and application of principles derived from the biological, physical, social and nursing sciences, including, but not limited to:

(a) Responsibility for the teaching of health care and the prevention of illness to the patient and his family; or

(b) Assessment, nursing diagnosis, nursing care, and counsel of persons who are ill, injured or experiencing alterations in normal health processes; or

(c) The administration of medications and treatments as prescribed by a person licensed in this state to prescribe such medications and treatments; or

(d) The coordination and assistance in the delivery of a plan of health care with all members of the health team; or

(e) The teaching and supervision of other persons in the performance of any of the foregoing;

Section 335.016.8(a)–(e).

At the time of enactment of the Nursing Practice Act of 1975, the following statutes were repealed:

2. A person practices professional nursing who for compensation or personal profit performs, *under the supervision and direction of a practitioner authorized to sign birth and death certificates,* any professional services requiring the application of principles of the biological, physical or social sciences and nursing skills in the care of the sick, in the prevention of disease or in the conservation of health.

Section 335.010.2, RSMo 1969 (emphasis added).

Nothing contained in this chapter shall be construed as conferring any authority on any person to practice medicine or osteopathy or to undertake the treatment or cure of disease.

Section 335.190, RSMo 1969.

The parties on both sides request that in construing these statutes we define and draw that thin and elusive line that separates the practice of medicine and the practice of professional nursing in modern day delivery of health services. A response to this invitation, in our opinion, would result in an avalanche of both medical and nursing malpractice suits alleging infringement of that line and would hinder rather than help with the delivery of health services to the general public. Our consideration will be limited to the narrow question of whether the acts of these nurses were permissible under § 335.016.8 or were prohibited by Chapter 334.

* * *

The legislature substantially revised the law affecting the nursing profession with enactment of the Nursing Practice Act of 1975.[5] Perhaps the most significant feature of the Act was the redefinition of the term "professional nursing," which appears in § 335.016.8. Even a facile reading of that section reveals a manifest legislative desire to expand the scope of authorized nursing practices. Every witness at trial testified that the new definition of professional nursing is a broader definition than that in the former statute. A comparison with the prior definition vividly demonstrates this fact. Most apparent is the elimination of the requirement that a physician directly supervise nursing functions. Equally significant is the legislature's formulation of an open-ended definition of professional nursing. The earlier statute limited nursing practice to "services * * * in the care of the sick, in the prevention of disease or in the conservation of health." § 335.010.2, RSMo 1969. The 1975 Act not only describes a much broader spectrum of nursing functions, it qualifies this description with the phrase "including, but not limited to." We believe this phrase evidences an intent to avoid statutory constraints on the evolution of new functions

5. The impetus for the legislation was the ongoing expansion of nursing responsibilities. Several national commissions investigated the causes of and the implications of this phenomenon during the early 1970's. One committee concluded: "Professional nursing * * * is in a period of rapid and progressive change in response to the growth of biomedical knowledge, changes in patterns of demand for health services, and the evolution of professional relationships among nurses, physicians and other health professions." Secretary's Committee to Study Extended Roles for Nurses, Dep't. of Health, Education and Welfare, Pub. No. (HSM) 73–2037, "Extending the Scope of Nursing Practice: A Report of the Secretary's Committee to Study Extended Roles for Nurses" 8 (1971). *See also* National Comm'n for the Study of Nursing and Nursing Education, An Abstract for Action (1970); National Comm'n for the Study of Nursing and Nursing Education, From Abstract Into Action (1973). The broadening of nursing roles necessitated altering existing nursing practice laws to reflect the changes in a nurse's professional duties. At the time the Missouri legislature acted, thirty states had amended their laws regulating the nursing profession. *See* Comment, "Interpreting Missouri's Nursing Practice Act," 26 St. Louis U.L.J. 931, 931 n. 1 (1982). Forty states currently have broadened nursing practice statutes similar to § 335.016.8. *See infra* note 6.

for nurses deliverying [sic] health services.   Under § 335.016.8, a nurse
may be permitted to assume responsibilities heretofore not considered
to be within the field of professional nursing so long as those responsibilities are consistent with her or his "specialized education, judgment
and skill based on knowledge and application of principles derived from
the biological, physical, social and nursing sciences."   § 335.016.8.

The acts of the nurses herein clearly fall within this legislative
standard.   All acts were performed pursuant to standing orders and
protocols approved by physicians.   Physician prepared standing orders
and protocols for nurses and other paramedical personnel were so well
established and accepted at the time of the adoption of the statute that
the legislature could not have been unaware of the use of such practices.   We see nothing in the statute purporting to limit or restrict their
continued use.

Respondents made no challenge of the nurses' level of training nor
the degree of their skill.   They challenge only the legal right of the
nurses to undertake these acts.   We believe the acts of the nurses are
precisely the types of acts the legislature contemplated when it granted
nurses the right to make assessments and nursing diagnoses.   There
can be no question that a nurse undertakes only a nursing diagnosis, as
opposed to a medical diagnosis, when she or he finds or fails to find
symptoms described by physicians in standing orders and protocols for
the purpose of administering courses of treatment prescribed by the
physician in such orders and protocols.

The Court believes that it is significant that while at least forty
states [6] have modernized and expanded their nursing practice laws
during the past fifteen years neither counsel nor the Court have
discovered any case challenging nurses' authority to act as the nurses
herein acted.

The broadening of the field of practice of the nursing profession
authorized by the legislature and here recognized by the Court carries
with it the profession's responsibility for continuing high educational
standards and the individual nurse's responsibility to conduct herself or
himself in a professional manner.   The hallmark of the professional is
knowing the limits of one's professional knowledge.   The nurse, either
upon reaching the limit of her or his knowledge or upon reaching the
limits prescribed for the nurse by the physician's standing orders and
protocols, should refer the patient to the physician.   There is no
evidence that the assessments and diagnoses made by the nurses in this
case exceeded such limits.

* * *

Having found that the nurses' acts were authorized by § 335.016.8,
it follows that such acts do not constitute the unlawful practice of
medicine for the reason that § 334.155 makes the provisions of Chapter

6.   [The court cites the nursing practice   acts of these states.]

334 inapplicable "to nurses licensed and lawfully practicing their profession within the provisions of Chapter 335 RSMo."

This cause is reversed and remanded with instructions to enter judgment consistent with this opinion.

Notes and Questions

1. The nursing practice act in *Sermchief* contains an open-ended definition of the practice of nursing. The court believed the open-ended definition indicated a legislative "intent to avoid statutory constraint on the evolution of new functions for nurses delivering health services." The trend toward non-specific legislation generally has led to an increased reliance on rulemaking by the administrative agencies and a change in the role of the judiciary from limiting agency activity substantively to monitoring the process by which rules are developed. Stewart, The Reformation of American Administrative Law, 88 Harv.L.Rev. 1667 (1975); Bazelon, The Judiciary: What Role in Health Improvement? 211 Science 792 (1981). What implications might the allocation of authority between the administrative agency and the judiciary have for the regulation of non-physician providers? What is the regulatory impact of using a phrase such as "diagnosis" to define the practice of medicine or nursing?

2. Some states authorize and regulate specific categories of nurses such as nurse-midwives and nurse-anesthetists. See, e.g., West's Ann.Cal. Bus. & Prof.Code § 2746 (regulating nurse midwifery), § 2825 (regulating nurse anesthetists) and § 2834 (regulating nurse practitioners). Each section describes the particular nursing practice regulated and specifies entry requirements for the nurse specialty.

Could this type of statute have an impact on the scope of nursing practice? Assume that your state has a general nursing practice act such as that of Missouri. Could the board of nursing in your state prohibit nurses from acting as nurse-anesthetists? As nurse-midwives? See, Leigh v. Board of Registration in Nursing, 395 Mass. 670, 481 N.E.2d 1347 (1985).

3. Interprofessional "territorial" disputes have occurred not only between doctors and nurses, but among other health care providers as well: for example, radiologists and chiropractors in Brodie v. State Board of Medical Examiners, 177 N.J.Super. 523, 427 A.2d 104 (App.Div.1981), and nurses and physician assistants in Washington State Nurses Ass'n v. Board of Medical Examiners, 93 Wash.2d 117, 605 P.2d 1269 (1980).

4. The American Medical Association has been involved in shaping the regulation of nursing. For example, the Joint Practice Commission of the American Medical Association and the American Nurses Association unanimously recommended non-specific legislation, such as found in the statute in *Sermchief*. This Joint Practice Commission noted that "[i]n view of their growing interdependence, it becomes increasingly evident that successful or effective delivery of health care cannot be achieved through unilateral determination of functions by either medicine or nursing." Quoted in V. Hall, Statutory Regulation of the Scope of Nursing Practice: A Critical Survey (1975). A joint professional or interprofessional board is one that includes among its members representatives of each profession

regulated by the statutes licensing or certifying health care practitioners. The experience of a successful joint professional effort is described in Booth, Legal Accommodation of the Nurse Practitioner Concept—The Process in North Carolina, 1 Nurse Prac. 13 (Nov.–Dec. 1976). What is gained or lost in mandating interprofessional cooperation in the definition of the legitimate scope of practice of licensed professionals?

5. The statutory interpretation problems involved in *Sermchief* are discussed in Johnson, Regulatory Theory and Prospective Risk Assessment in the Limitation of Scope of Practice, 4 J.Leg.Med. 447 (1983); Greenlaw, *Sermchief v. Gonzales* and the Debate over Advanced Nursing Practice Legislation, 12 Law, Medicine & Health Care 30 (1984); Wolff, Court Upholds Expanded Practice Role for Nurses, 12 Law, Medicine & Health Care 26 (1984); and Note, Interpreting Missouri's Nursing Practice Act, 26 St. Louis U.L.J. 931 (1982). See also B. Bullough, Law and the Expanding Nursing Role 60 (1980).

b. Physician Assistants

Physician assistants (PAs) perform functions delegated to them by a physician. In contrast to nurses, the PA is considered a *dependent* practitioner because the PA may practice only under the supervision of a physician. Physician assistants may function in the absence of specific statutory authority because the medical practice acts do not prohibit a licensed physician from employing or utilizing an assistant to perform delegated tasks. The permissible scope of delegation in the absence of specific statutory authorization depends on the prevailing custom and usage of the medical profession, the degree of supervision and control exercised by the doctor, and the expertise of the supervising doctor who, because of the nature of delegation, must delegate only functions that are within the doctor's competence. The drive for professionalization by physician assistants, among other factors, has led most states to provide for certification or registration of physician assistants with established entry criteria and a specified permissible scope of delegation. Such statutes provide that physician assistants may not exercise independent judgment or diagnose the patient's condition. See e.g., West's Ann.Ind.Code 25–22.5–1–2. Under these statutes, physician assistants must act only under the direction or supervision of a licensed physician. Some statutes specifically limit the number of physician assistants each licensed physician may supervise (generally, limited to one) and may require the PA to wear a name tag identifying him or her as a PA. See e.g., Ill.Rev.Stat. Ch. 111, par. 4602–4612.

What are the relative advantages and disadvantages of specific authorizing legislation over the common law authority to delegate? Why wasn't the D.C. Commission on Licensure, described in the following case, more specific in its description of the scope of licensure of physician assistants?

JACOBS v. UNITED STATES

Court of Appeal, District of Columbia, 1981.
436 A.2d 1286.

NEBEKER, ASSOCIATE JUDGE:

* * *

Appellant was convicted [in a jury trial] of aiding and abetting a licensed paramedical assistant employed by him. An implied exception to the proscriptions [against the unauthorized practice of medicine] is contained in D.C.Code 1978 Supp., § 2–123(d)(10), which provides:

[P]rofessional misconduct * * * means * * * [k]nowingly practicing medicine with an unlicensed physician except in an accredited preceptorship or residency training program; or aiding or abetting such unlicensed persons in the practice of medicine. *This provision shall not apply to accepted use of qualified paramedical personnel.* (Emphasis added.)

* * *

I

At trial, the government produced evidence revealing that appellant was a physician licensed to practice medicine by the District of Columbia. Appellant employed Fernando Morales as a paramedic, or physician's assistant, at appellant's National Health Care Plan Clinic in the District of Columbia. Morales was not licensed to practice medicine. On November 8, 1977, an investigator from the District of Columbia Department of Economic Development inspected the clinic and met with Morales. Appellant was not present during the inspection. Morales showed the investigator a pad of prescription blanks which had been signed by appellant. Seven days later, a covert investigator from the Metropolitan Police Department visited the clinic. He complained of pain in his right shoulder and was examined and treated by Morales. Morales gave the investigator a number of pain pills which, upon analysis, were discovered to be a controlled substance. Morales also filled out and gave the investigator a prescription for a different controlled substance. The prescription form had been pre-signed by appellant, but it was Morales who wrote in the drug name and gave the slip to the patient.

Morales testified under a grant of immunity from the government. He testified that appellant came to the clinic once a week or once every two weeks, and that approximately 200 people came to the clinic for treatment between July and November 1977. Appellant performed the initial examinations of ten to twenty of the patients. Fifty to sixty of the patients were never seen by appellant. Appellant authorized Morales to give prescriptions when appellant was not present in the clinic, and a pad of 50 pre-signed prescriptions was given to Morales for that purpose. Morales wrote approximately 75 to 80 prescriptions during that time. Twenty-five percent of these were written after consulting with appellant in person or over the phone.

II

* * * Morales is unlicensed as a physician and was engaged in the diagnosis and treatment of "illnesses." He is, however, licensed as a paramedical assistant. The issue becomes, then, whether the appellant's use of Morales at the clinic was an "accepted use" within the meaning of the statute permitting paramedical assistance of physicians.

Appellant asserts that the statutory exception provides inadequate notice of the degree of supervision that is necessary to qualify his conduct as an "accepted use." In a case such as this, the alleged vagueness of the statute must be measured in terms of the actual conduct of the appellant in the case at hand.[ ] If this particular appellant could reasonably have comprehended that his conduct was prohibited by the statute, the statute provides sufficient notice and is not unconstitutional.

* * *

Whether a particular profession or a particular individual in that regulated profession is on notice as to the nature of prohibited conduct depends on whether the statutory prohibition has a comprehensible meaning in the context of regulations, custom, usage, and training in that field.[ ] Appellant, a licensed physician, should have been aware of what conduct constitutes "accepted use" of a paramedic, and should have known that in this instance, his conduct departed dramatically from that use.

III

* * *

Since we are dealing with a criminal charge, we ought not to rely only on assumptions regarding the professional awareness of appellant and other physicians. Supporting our holding is the stark reality of the conduct which appellant did permit, aid, and abet. The evidence shows that as a licensed physician, he willfully and knowingly: (1) utilized an employee who was not licensed to practice medicine in the District of Columbia to run a medical clinic, nearly autonomous in its operations; (2) permitted that employee to examine and to treat patients without his consultation and with minimal supervision; (3) permitted that employee, as part of such treatment, to fill out and distribute drug prescriptions which he had pre-signed; (4) did not require that the employee seek his approval before prescribing drugs; and (5) did not review the prescriptions for several days in some cases.

We are further supported in this view by the evidence presented at trial by appellant's own experts. Karl Katterjohn, the director of the Physicians' Assistants Program at George Washington University and a board-certified physician's assistant, testified as to certain accepted uses of paramedics. He testified that it was not an accepted use for a physician to give a paramedical assistant a pre-signed prescription pad. In addition, Mr. Katterjohn testified that accepted use requires that the physician be located in the same building as the physician's assistant.

Accepted use, according to his testimony, also requires that the physician approve each prescription before it is issued, particularly those for controlled substances. Should the physician not actually see the patient, the "24–hour rule" mandates that the physician review the charts within that time.

Noel H. McFarlane, the Assistant Director of the Physicians' Assistant Department at Howard University and a board-certified physician's assistant, also testified as an expert for appellant. McFarlane described the use of pre-signed prescription pads as a common practice, and asserted there is no common standard governing the length of time that properly may pass before review of work by the physician. He testified, however, that where a physician's assistant writes a prescription, accepted practice requires its review within 48 to 72 hours.

From the testimony of appellant's own experts, it appears that he ought to have been aware of the impropriety of his conduct. * * * Testimony revealed that, on occasion, appellant did not review the charts of some patients treated by Morales for as long as two weeks after their visits.

Standards propounded in this jurisdiction by the D.C. Commission on Licensure—of which appellant is presumptively aware as a licensed physician—further narrow the definition of accepted use contained in D.C.Code 1978 Supp., § 2–123(d)(10). In a 1972 policy statement, the Licensure Commission approved the use of physicians' assistants, but set forth these standards: (1) that they not make judgment decisions; and (2) that they only assist and not replace the physician. * * *

Appellant's action grossly violated this policy statement. He set up the clinic, manned it with physician assistants, and then paid the operation scant personal attention. Appellant was present only weekly or every two weeks, and then only for a few hours. Often he was out of town, and the clinic continued operation. He never saw the majority of patients, nor was he consulted in advance of or contemporaneously with their treatment.

Other specific professional standards of conduct put appellant on notice that his manner of operation did not constitute an accepted use of a paramedic. Regulations of the Food and Drug Administration provide that "All prescriptions for controlled substances shall be dated as of, and signed on, the day when issued." 21 C.F.R. § 1306.05 (1977). Appellant's distribution of pre-signed prescription pads to the physician's assistant with no meaningful restrictions on their use, other than infrequent oral review, constitutes the most serious and obvious violation of "accepted use."

* * *

Under all of the circumstances—to which we must look in determining whether appellant was on notice of the illegality of his conduct—we hold that appellant was able to have reasonably comprehended that his conduct was not an "accepted use" of a paramedic and, therefore, a violation of the licensing statute.

Furthermore, that appellant aided and abetted conduct falling within the proscriptions [of the statutes] was supported by sufficient evidence to permit the jury reasonably to conclude his guilt beyond a reasonable doubt.

Problem: Physicians, Physician Assistants and Nurses

Drs. Allison Jones and Emily Johnson have a practice in Jerrold, Allstate, which is located in south St. Louis County. Both Drs. Jones and Johnson are board-certified internists with a rather broad family practice. They would like to expand their practice to Jackson County, a primarily rural area about sixty miles south of Jerrold. They are especially interested in Tesson, a town of approximately 6,000 that is centrally located among the four or five small towns in the area. They are interested in Tesson because it has a small community hospital and is located close to the interstate highway. They also believe the town is underserved by physicians. The town has one internist. It has no obstetricians, although there is an obstetrician in a small town about eighteen miles distant from Tesson. There is also no pediatrician in Tesson, although there is one twenty miles away.

Drs. Jones and Johnson would like to open an office in Tesson and employ a physician assistant, a nurse-midwife and a pediatric nurse practitioner to staff the office full time. Either Dr. Jones or Dr. Johnson would have office hours at that office once a week. They are interested in the nurse-midwife and nurse practitioner because they hope to serve the needs of Tesson by establishing active obstetrical and pediatric practices.

They have a physician assistant in their office in Jerrold and have been impressed with her handling of the "routine" patients that come to the office with minor injuries such as cuts and sprains and illnesses such as chicken pox and strep throat. In most cases, the assistant examines the patient, decides on a course of treatment and prescribes medication using pre-signed prescription slips. In more difficult cases, the physician assistant asks for advice from one of the physicians.

For their Tesson office, they would like to find a physician assistant with extensive experience in trauma so that the assistant could care for the high incidence of farming and hunting injuries expected in that area. This PA, then, would complement the doctors' own skills as the doctors have had little experience with trauma victims.

Drs. Jones and Johnson have come to you for advice concerning their plans. They have many questions, but their first concerns the Board of Healing Arts, which supervises the licensing and discipline of physicians in Allstate, and whether their plans are consistent with the laws regulating practice in Allstate.

Please specify how they might comply with the law while maintaining a "low cost" practice. If for some reason the Board decides to take action against them, what is the likelihood of the physicians' success in challenging the Board's action?

III. GOVERNMENT QUALITY–CONTROL REGULATION OF HEALTH CARE INSTITUTIONS

The previous section examined licensure and discipline of individual health care professionals as a mechanism for assuring the quality of health care services. Even though only licensed health care professionals such as doctors and nurses can practice the "healing arts," a quality-control system that stopped with the individual professional would be incomplete. Although hospitals, nursing homes and other health care facilities cannot "practice medicine," the quality of the institution itself has a very significant impact on the quality of care received by the patients. The range of institutional quality issues is very broad and extends from building and equipment design, maintenance and sanitation, through the fiscal and managerial soundness of the operation, through the selection, training and monitoring of the individuals directly involved in health care delivery within the institution, and so on.

A major challenge for any quality-control regulatory policy is the vast and changing structure of health care facilities. To illustrate the range of "health care" institutions, consider the Illinois Public Health and Safety Code, which includes specific regulatory requirements for the following institutional health care providers, as defined by the statute:

Hospitals ("any institution * * * devoted primarily to the maintenance and operation of facilities for the diagnosis and treatment or care of * * * persons admitted for overnight stay or longer in order to obtain medical * * * care of illness, disease, injury, infirmity, or deformity.")

Nursing homes ("a private home, institution * * * or any other place * * * which provides * * * personal care, sheltered care or nursing * * * not includ[ing] a hospital.")

Home health agencies ("a public agency or private organization that provides skilled nursing services [in a patient's home] and at least one other home health service.")

Life care facilities ("a place * * * [that provides] a resident with nursing services, medical services or personal care services * * * pursuant to a life care contract.")

Hospices ("a coordinated program of home and inpatient care providing * * * palliative and supportive medical, health and other services to terminally ill patients and their families.")

Ambulatory surgical treatment centers ("any institution * * * devoted primarily to the performance of surgical procedures * * * not provid[ing] beds or other accommodations for overnight stay of patients * * * [P]atients shall be discharged in an ambulatory condition. * * * [Not including a hospital.]")

Clinical laboratories (providers of laboratory services other than licensed hospitals.)

Ambulance operations ("all ambulance service providers and specialized emergency medical services vehicle providers.")

Other familiar institutional health care providers include the various "care units" for chemical dependencies or psychiatric care; free-standing emergicenters, which provide some basic level of emergency care; and rehabilitation facilities, for persons who can return to some level of functioning after an acute episode. In addition, hospitals are frequently involved in offering "intra-institutional" specialty services such as birthing centers, wellness centers, and occupational health testing and rehabilitation programs.

While nearly all institutional health care providers in the United States are regulated by state and federal government agencies, the character and scope of that regulation is dependent on the nature and history of the particular type of institution. Some differences in the regulatory posture among health care institutions are attributable to historical accident. But many differences relate to the type of health care provided, the strength of private accreditation, the effectiveness of private malpractice litigation and the character of the people served by the facility, among other factors. This section reviews government quality-control regulation of health care institutions, with a particular emphasis on long-term care.

The long-term care industry merits independent treatment because it is a critically important and growing portion of our nation's health care sector. Nursing homes are subject to a high degree of public quality-control regulation by both federal and state governments, especially as contrasted to hospitals, home health agencies and other organizations. The enforcement of nursing home standards over the past two decades, particularly by the states, has created an informative case study of enforcement of quality-control regulation in health care. The impact of a dual federal-state regulatory system is best studied in relation to long-term care. Finally, the contrast between long-term care providers and acute-care hospitals illustrate the importance of understanding the distinctions among health care institutions.

CHARACTERISTICS OF LONG–TERM CARE INSTITUTIONS

Unlike hospital patients, long-term care patients are chronically rather than acutely ill. The average length of stay for nursing home patients is much longer than the average length of stay for patients in acute care hospitals. A study conducted by the Institute of Medicine in 1976, found that 63% of new residents either died or were discharged within three months of admission; but 70% of all residents in a facility at any one time had been there at least eighteen months.

Long-term care patients are not limited to the elderly. Approximately 13% are younger patients, the majority of whom are mentally impaired. Thirteen percent of nursing home residents have no visitors in the course of a year. The 1980 report of the National Center for Health Statistics reported that 86% of nursing home residents were dependent in bathing; 69%, in dressing; 66%, in transferring; 45%, in continence; and 33%, in eating. Each of these categories demonstrated sizable increases in the rates of dependency among nursing home residents over the previous 1973–74 survey. About 1.4 million persons live in nursing homes. Seven out of eight nursing home residents are over 65. While only one in sixty persons between the ages of 65 and 74 in the United States lives in a nursing home, one out of five over the age of 85 lives in such a facility.

The characteristics of this population have limited their ability to themselves bring suit to remedy harms suffered as a result of breaches of established standards of care. Physical injuries such as broken bones and bruises in very frail elderly persons may be caused either by ordinary touching or by poor care or abuse. Causation is, therefore, difficult to prove. The mental impairment of many nursing home patients makes them poor witnesses. Their limited life-span and their disabilities minimize legally recognizable damages for injury or death. They do not suffer lost wages and the costs of medical care for injuries are covered largely by public programs. Their access to private attorneys has been limited because small damage awards discourage contingent fee arrangements and because of the isolation of institutionalization.

While hospitals developed in the United States as charitable institutions under the direction of physicians, nursing homes developed originally as "mom-and-pop" enterprises, in which individuals boarded elderly persons in private homes. Most long-term care institutions do not focus on sophisticated medical or skilled nursing care. Advances in medical treatment and technology, which led to greater physician control within the hospital, historically did not dominate nursing home care. The admitting staff privileges system of the hospital has not developed to any comparable extent in nursing homes.

While professional nurses dominate direct patient care in hospitals, the role of the registered nurse in the majority of long-term care institutions is that of supervisor with most of the direct patient care rendered by nonprofessional nurses' aides. Nursing homes typically have to deal with a turnover rate of 70 to 100 percent each year in these persons who provide direct patient care.

The nursing home industry has been the subject of several widely-publicized scandals concerning poor patient care. Although the number of facilities actually involved in these charges could be small, the public and legislative perception of the industry has been affected by this history.

The strong demand for nursing home spaces (occupancy rates in metropolitan areas are well over 90%, and in some areas approach nearly 100%) leaves a potential nursing home resident or the resident's family with little or no choice among facilities once the essential factors of source of payment (if Medicare, Medicaid or other public assistance) and level of care required are considered. Proximity to family and friends is a significant concern in light of the typically long stay. Choice is further limited by the short length of time available for placement and the stress accompanying such a severe change. Such constraints on consumer choice limit the power of the market over quality. This market failure in the nursing home context is exacerbated because the resident, who is the actual consumer of services, is often not the one making the choice. Further, the ability of residents to leave one facility for another if a bad choice is made is limited by the physical and mental frailty of many residents and the lack of effective family control.

What impact, if any, might the distinctions between hospitals and long-term care facilities have on the nature of government regulation of nursing homes as contrasted with regulation of hospitals?

A rapidly growing type of facility that can be characterized as offering "long-term care" is the life-care or continuous-care facility. Life-care communities generally guarantee residents "on-campus" apartment style housing and some degree of food service while the resident is relatively independent. Should the resident require skilled nursing care, it is generally provided in an on-campus facility. Residents purchase this lifetime guarantee while they are capable of independent living at the facility by paying a lump-sum entrance fee and monthly maintenance fees. The entrance fee may be a specific amount generally ranging between $35,000 and $60,000 or may be stipulated as "all assets" of the resident. The monthly maintenance fee is often set at an amount related to that expected to be available to the resident from government sources, such as Social Security. Life-care communities are very attractive to the elderly, who often fear personal bankruptcy should they need nursing home care in the future; however, the great majority of elderly persons never require long-term institutionalization.

Several states have passed statutes that specifically regulate life-care communities. These regulations are very different from the states' regulation of nursing homes. Which traits are relevant in distinguishing between life-care communities and nursing homes? How would you expect the regulation of life-care communities to differ from that of nursing homes? What would justify these differences? See, e.g., Ill.S.H.A. ch. 111 § 4160–1 et seq. See also Note, The Ties That Bind: Life Care Contracts and Nursing Homes, 8 Am.J.Law & Med. 153 (1982).

Long-term health care increasingly includes health care provided in the home. Both Medicare and Medicaid provide some reimburse-

ment for home health care, as do some private insurance policies. At
least 38 states license some home health care agencies, and agencies
receiving federal reimbursement must meet federal certification standards. Home health care includes both palliative care and technologically sophisticated and complex care. Patients often contract with
agencies for the provision of health care in their homes. Home health
agencies in turn contract with other agencies or with individuals to
provide care. Almost all patients receive care both from agency personnel and from family members or volunteers. Many patients receive
care from more than one agency. In addition, providers of durable
medical equipment for the home often provide some services. Reported
negligence cases against home health agencies are very rare. See
Johnson, Quality–Control Regulation of Home Health Care, 26 Houston
L.Rev. 901 (1989). As you read the following materials on enforcement
of regulations in nursing homes, consider whether different problems
would be faced in the implementation of public standards in reference
to home health care.

A. GOVERNMENT REGULATION THROUGH LICENSURE

1. Statute, Regulation and Litigation

The source of the states' power to regulate health care institutions
is the police power, which is retained by the states in our federal
system. Under the police power, the state's regulation of health care
institutions must further the health, safety and general welfare. In
reviewing legislation challenged as lying beyond the scope of the state's
police power, courts will uphold the legislation if its contribution to
health, safety and general welfare is at least fairly debatable. Challenges to state nursing home regulations arguing that the regulations
are beyond the scope of the police power have seldom succeeded. See,
for example, Eagleton v. Patrick, 370 S.W.2d 254 (Mo.1963).

Licensing is the primary mechanism chosen by state legislatures to
regulate nursing homes. Compliance with standards is required as a
condition of holding the required operating license. Instead of developing specific standards of performance, the legislature typically delegates that task to an administrative agency. In delegating this task to
an administrative agency, the legislature is confined by the nondelega-
tion doctrine. This doctrine requires the legislature to establish boundaries and guidelines for the agency's discretion in rulemaking so as not
to delegate a legislative function to the agency. The state courts have,
however, generally been willing to accept very broad, non-determina-
tive standards as sufficient. See, for example, Levine v. Whalen, 50
A.D.2d 503, 378 N.Y.S.2d 800 (1976) modified, 39 N.Y.2d 510, 384
N.Y.S.2d 721, 349 N.E.2d 820 (1976). For a case in which the court
declared a provision of a nursing home statute an unconstitutional
delegation, see High Ridge Management Corporation v. State, 354 So.2d
377 (Fla.1977).

The administrative agency both promulgates and enforces regulations under the statute. Both of these activities are governed by rules and procedures established in the nursing home statute itself and in the state's administrative procedures act. In enforcing the promulgated standards, the agency must follow procedures established by these two statutes. See, for example, Somers Manor Nursing Home, Inc. v. Whalen, 52 A.D.2d 998, 383 N.Y.S.2d 445 (1976). Agency procedures also are subject to scrutiny under constitutional due process.

Judicial review of agency enforcement actions is limited. A facility ordinarily must exhaust available administrative remedies. Exhaustion is not required if these remedies are inadequate or if the plaintiff will suffer irreparable harm if required to pursue these procedures. These exceptions generally are narrowly construed. Evidence not presented to the state agency at the administrative hearing ordinarily cannot be presented later in court unless the evidence is newly discovered and could not have been ascertained earlier with reasonable diligence. This rule has been applied both to facilities and to enforcement agencies. See, for example Zieverink v. Ackerman, 1 Ohio App.3d 10, 437 N.E.2d 319 (1981) and Valley View Convalescent Home v. Department of Social and Health Services, 24 Wash.App. 192, 599 P.2d 1313 (1979). The court must uphold the agency's action if it is supported by substantial evidence in this record. See, for example, Boswell, Inc. v. Harkins, 230 Kan. 610, 640 P.2d 1202 (1982) and Geriatrics, Inc. v. Colorado State Department of Health, 650 P.2d 1288 (Colo.App.1982), both of which upheld the agency's action, and Schultz v. Public Health Council, 46 A.D.2d 580, 364 N.Y.S.2d 566 (1975), overturning the agency's action.

THOMPSON v. DIVISION OF HEALTH OF MISSOURI

Court of Appeals of Missouri, 1980.
604 S.W.2d 802.

MANFORD, JUDGE.

This is an appeal from an administrative order suspending a nursing home license. The circuit court entered judgment affirming the suspension order. The judgment is reversed with directions.

* * *

Review of this matter is of the record of the administrative agency and not of the circuit court. [ ] Neither the circuit court nor this court can substitute its judgment for that of the administrative agency. Review is limited to the determination of whether or not the agency, in the instant case the Division of Health, had the authority to act in the manner in which it did, and secondly, whether or not the finding and order of the agency was supported by competent and substantial evidence.

* * *

In addressing appellant's final point, a review of the pertinent facts must first be made to determine whether or not the administrative order was supported by competent and substantial evidence.   * * *

Appellant was a lessee of the property which houses her nursing home operation. Appellant is an "operator" within the nursing home law. [ ] The issue of appellant as "lessee" was presented for two purposes: first, the fact that appellant purchased the property just a short time prior to these proceedings was elicited to show that many of the violations could not be corrected by appellant as lessee; and second, that after appellant purchased the property, she in fact corrected many of the specific violations.

Appellant was notified, by letter, of 28 deficiencies related to patient care and dietary services. This was the result of an inspection of June 1, 1978. The notice letter advised appellant of a license revocation hearing for July 28, 1978. The July date was later changed to August 8, 1978. The letter afforded appellant notice of charged deficiencies in dietary service, patient care, fire safety and sanitation, all of which existed since August 23, 1965. At the August 8, 1978 hearing, two witnesses for respondent agency, both inspectors, testified that a 45–day delay would not be detrimental to the patients of the facility and that the 45–day delay would be ample time to correct the deficiencies.

The matter was continued to October 5, 1978, when a full hearing was held. At this hearing, it was stipulated that the dietary deficiencies had been corrected and were no longer a part of the hearing. The hearing was limited to deficiencies allegedly found during the June 1, 1978 inspection. All sanitation deficiencies had been corrected, except for one crusted urinal. The inspector for the agency testified that the vast majority of the deficiencies had been corrected, except in the areas of medical care, treatment and record keeping.

Subsequent to the August 8, 1978 date (on this date the matter was continued for 45 days), inspections were held on September 26 and 29, 1978. The main criticisms offered by the agency were (a) medical charting, (b) lack of employee health records (on four out of 20 employees) and (c) deficiency in staffing schedules. The agency's witness, who was also the inspecting party, testified that her major concern was the charting of medical distribution in pencil rather than pen, not administering medicines ordered by physicians and the giving of medicines which had not been ordered.

Appellant offered testimony by employees and a resident of the facility as to the general good quality of the care and service at the facility. Appellant advised the court of the improvements she had provided, introduced various receipts showing payment for the improvements and testified that she provided clothing and medications for patients unable to purchase such items. Appellant stated that she had been reprimanded for entering medical information in pencil, but could not go back and trace over the penciled entry with pen, so those records would have to stand. Appellant further testified she kept medical records locked but made them available for inspections. She said she had employee staffing schedules, but at the time of the inspection, the schedules were at her home because she was working on them. She testified that she had corrected the medical deficiencies and offered to show the inspector the records related to this matter, but the inspector declined by saying, "You will have your day in court" or words to that effect. Appellant stated she was personally seeing to these matters and that all the deficiencies would be corrected.

On November 28, 1978, almost seven weeks following the hearing, the hearing examiner entered his order, finding the allegations, relating to the quality of patient care as set forth under the notice of June 23, 1978, to be substantially true. The examiner found appellant's facility not to be in substantial compliance and suspended appellant's license. The suspension order, however, contained two provisos. First, the effective date of the suspension was to be January 22, 1979, some three months in the future from the October hearing date. Second, the order provided that if a letter from respondent agency verified the facility was in compliance, the suspension would be vacated.

The record fails to reveal that any inspection was held subsequent to the November 28, 1978 order. The record also fails to reveal that any further inspection was ordered. In fact, nothing happened in regard to further inspections or the order, and this was conceded by respondent on oral argument.

When this case was argued before this court, a question was asked as to why no inspection occurred subsequent to the November 28, 1978 order and prior to its projected effective date of January 22, 1979. No answer was provided. On oral argument, it was developed that appellant was issued a valid license for the year 1979–80. The expiration date for the license was April 26, and appellant received her license effective April 26, 1979 to April 26, 1980.

Appellant then applied for a license from April 26, 1980 to April 26, 1981 and pursuant to that, was informed that a reinspection would have to be completed prior to the issuance of the 1980–81 license. This court is without information as to whether that reinspection has ever occurred.

From the above facts, a serious question arises, that being whether or not the alleged deficiencies for the year 1978 can, in fact, be inspected, and whether or not any such inspection would have any real meaning. The reason this is so is because of the lengthy lapse of time, the intervening reissuance of a valid license and a supposed inspection relative to the 1980–81 license.

It could be argued that the issue has become moot because of the intervention of time and the reissuance of a valid license, but regarding the inspections, there is no time limit upon them as they relate to deficiencies. Thus, in other words, the reissuance of an annual license does not prevent inquiry into past violations. [   ]

After review of the record and all documents herein, this court cannot conclude there was substantial and competent evidence to find that appellant's nursing home facility was not in compliance on January 22, 1979, the effective date of the examiner's order.

It is apparent from the record of this case that substantial compliance with listed deficiencies had occurred. There is no evidence to determine if total compliance had been reached by the January 22, 1979 order. Neither the inspectors nor the examiner considered the deficiencies of a grave nature. If the deficiencies had been so detrimental to the patient's welfare, why does the record reveal by testimony of the inspectors that a 45–day delay would not be detrimental to the patients? Further, if the deficiencies were of such a grave nature, why would a suspension order have been given an effective date some three months in the future?

The order of suspension was predicated upon the lack of quality of patient care. The effective date was January 22, 1979. There was no order or directive for a reinspection following the date the order was issued and its effective date thereof. It cannot follow there was, under the attending facts and circumstances of this case, competent and substantial evidence to support the order of the examiner. The only manner by which such order could have validity, by its effective date, was to have been supported by competent and substantial evidence. That evidence necessitated a reinspection between November 28, 1978 and January 22, 1979. No such evidence exists in this case and this court cannot determine whether in fact appellant was or was not in compliance on January 22, 1979.

Notes and Questions

1. Should the enforcement agency take into account the fact that Mrs. Thompson had just purchased the property a short time prior to the problems in 1978? If so, how? Why did the agency give the suspension order an effective date three months after its issuance? How was the agency deficient in handling this facility?

2. Sources on litigation of nursing home standards include Johnson, Terry and Wolff, Nursing Homes and the Law: State Regulation and Private Litigation (Harrison Co.1985); Butler, A Long–Term Care Strategy for Legal Services, 14 Clearinghouse Review 612 (1980); and Goldberg and Harkins, Recent Developments in Long Term Care Litigation in Long Term Care and the Law (S.H. Johnson, ed. Nat'l Health Law Pub. 1983).

2. Implementation

A major reform of state nursing home licensing statutes occurred in the 1970s. A primary focus of this reform was to create for the state agencies the enforcement tools, called intermediate sanctions, needed to implement nursing home standards. Prior to these changes, the only penalty the states generally had for violation of standards was revocation or denial of the operating license. Closing a substandard facility is not always a successful enforcement strategy, however, because it disrupts the lives and may injure the health of the residents and may aggravate a shortage of nursing home beds. License revocation also threatens serious economic harm to the facility's owners and so is accompanied by necessary procedures that are time-consuming, often delaying enforcement for several years and making heavy demands on the inspection and legal services resources of the enforcement agencies. Although delicensure is appropriate for seriously deficient facilities, it is not useful for the enforcement of many important nursing home standards. In light of these limitations, it is not surprising that license revocation is used only rarely.

The goal of intermediate sanctions is to relate the severity of sanctions to the severity of violations more precisely and to create sanctions that could be imposed quickly and efficiently. Two of the more common intermediate sanctions are civil fines and receiverships. Although the state statutes vary, there is enough similarity to allow generalization in discussing these sanctions.

Among the most effective of the intermediate sanctions is the civil fine. With an appropriate range, the amount of the fine can be adjusted to reflect the severity of the particular violation and the history of the facility. Civil fines can increase the cost and decrease the benefit of violations. The most serious threat to the effectiveness of civil fines is persistent, systemic delay, which may occur if the civil penalty system is not well-designed. Civil fines can be effective with facilities that have repeated violations if the statute allows amplified penalties and the agency develops a method for aggressively monitoring repeated violations.

In a receivership, the provider retains ownership of the facility, but a court-appointed receiver controls and manages the facility. The receivership is a powerful tool for the protection of the health and safety of nursing home residents. The receivership can be used to maintain a facility in operation while the residents are safely transferred. It can also be used to upgrade a seriously substandard facility for continued operation under previous or new owners. In implementing receiverships, the most important statutory provisions are those that specify the grounds for the appointment of a receiver, that provide the funds necessary for the receiverships and that set a termination date for the receivership. Absent statutory provision for nursing home receiverships, some courts have appointed a receiver under their equitable powers.

Other intermediate sanctions include suspension of admissions (which requires a substandard facility to cease either all admissions or all public-pay admissions), public monitor (which allows the state agency to appoint a person to be present in the facility constantly to monitor a troubled facility's performance) and criminal sanctions for violation of certain standards such as reimbursement fraud and abuse of patients.

Notes and Questions

1. If the enforcement agency is authorized to levy fines from $100 to $10,000, what criteria should it use to set the amount of a fine against a facility for particular violations? Assume that your state either does not have a nursing home receivership statute or has a statute that allows the court to specify the powers of the receiver. What powers should a receiver have? How would you balance the enforcement agency's interests and goals with those of the facility's owner? Would any of these sanctions have been effective with the facility in *Thompson?* (The Missouri Supreme Court in Villines v. Division of Aging and Missouri Department of Social Services, 722 S.W.2d 939 (Mo.1987), overturned the agency's revocation of a nursing home's state license. The agency had based the revocation on a single incident that was not in itself life-threatening. The court held that the enactment of intermediate sanctions in the state's Omnibus Nursing Home Reform Act required the agency to select a sanction that was not more severe than necessary to remedy the violation involved.)

2. Sources on intermediate sanctions include ABA Commission on Legal Problems of the Elderly, Model Recommendations: Intermediate Sanctions for Enforcement of Quality Care in Nursing Homes (ABA, 1981); Johnson, State Regulation of Long–Term Care: A Decade of Experience with Intermediate Sanctions, 13 Law, Medicine & Health Care 173 (1985); and Symposium on Nursing Home Law, 24 St. Louis U.L.J. 617–852 (1981).

Problem: Restful Manor

Restful Manor is a skilled nursing facility licensed by the state and operating in its largest city. It has 117 residents, all of whom are elderly. Only twenty percent of the residents are ambulatory. Until eighteen months ago, the home had a good record of compliance with state nursing home standards. The facility has begun to have problems with compliance, although it still consistently has corrected violations or has submitted an acceptable plan of correction. The facility has also experienced some financial difficulties recently.

The most recent inspection of the facility took place four months ago. At that time, the facility was out of compliance with several standards relating to the quality of the food, the cleanliness of the kitchen and maintenance of patients' medical records. The facility also had some staffing problems. Other problems included the lack of a qualified dietitian and a high, though not unacceptable, rate of errors in the administration of medications by the nurses. As a result of this inspection report, the facility was required to submit a written plan of correction in which it agreed to remedy the violations. The next on-site inspection was scheduled to take place within six to eight weeks.

Prior to that inspection, however, an investigative news team from a local television station visited the facility with a hidden camera. The news team posed as potential out-of-town buyers of the facility. The visit revealed several patients who were soiled and unattended and several others who were restrained in wheelchairs. A recorded conversation with the Director of Nursing, an R.N., indicated that there was one nurses' aide for every ten patients, which the R.N. thought was probably "not enough to do a good job for some of these patients." When asked about these incidents, the owner attributed these "temporary" problems to financial constraints and to his inability to hire a good administrator who was willing to work within a reasonable budget.

The news team showed portions of the videotape on the nightly news. Three days later it followed up with a report that one of the ambulatory, mentally-impaired patients at the facility had wandered out of the building. A passerby had found the patient walking aimlessly along the main thoroughfare near the facility and called the police.

The state agency felt pressured to respond. It conducted an unannounced inspection two days after the latest news report. The surveyor conducting this inspection cited the facility for violations of several regulations including the following:

1. Each resident should receive adequate skin care that supports his or her health and well-being and avoids decubitus ulcers. (The surveyor found two patients with two or more bedsores measuring at least eight centimeters and one patient who had been admitted to the hospital for serious bedsores.) This is a Class I standard, see statute infra.

2. Each resident shall be kept clean and well-groomed. (The surveyor reported that "several residents had on dirty clothes" and "several smelled of urine.") This is a Class III standard.

3. The facility shall provide a nursing staff that is appropriately trained and adequate in number to care for the residents of the facility. (The surveyor wrote in his report that the facility provided one nurses' aide for every ten patients and that this was "inadequate in light of the dependency of the residents.") This is a Class I standard.

4. The facility shall employ a certified dietitian. (The surveyor noted that "the facility currently does not employ a certified dietitian but reports that it has been trying to hire one for the last three months.") This is a Class II standard.

5. The nurses of the facility shall administer ordered medications safely and adequately. An error rate in excess of 5% in the administration of medication is unacceptable and shall constitute a violation of this standard. (The surveyor reported an error rate of 6%.) This is a Class I standard.

Even though the facility is currently in violation of several standards, families of Restful Manor's patients have rallied to the facility's support. They believe the care is good despite the problems cited. The Department disagrees.

The statute provides the following remedies for violation of nursing home standards:

198.036 Revocation of License—grounds—notice required

(1) The department may revoke a license in any case in which it finds that the operator:

(a) Failed or refused to comply with Class I or II standards as established by the department; or failed or refused to comply with Class III standards as established by the department, where the aggregate effect of such noncompliance presents an imminent danger to the health, safety or welfare of any resident or a substantial probability that death or serious physical harm would result, or

(b) Demonstrated financial incapacity to operate and conduct the facility.

(2) Upon revocation of a license, the director of the department shall so notify the operator in writing setting forth the reason and grounds for the revocation.

198.028   Noncompliance, how determined, procedure to correct, notice reinspection

(1) Whenever a duly authorized representative of the department finds a violation of a Class I or Class II standard, a written report shall be prepared of any deficiency, and a copy of such report and a written correction order shall be sent to the operator or administrator.

(2) The operator or administrator shall have ten working days following receipt of the report and correction order to request any conference and to submit a plan of correction for the department's approval which contains specific dates for achieving compliance.

(3) A reinspection shall be conducted within fifty-five days after the original inspection to determine if deficiencies are being corrected as required in the approved correction plan or any subsequent authorized modification. If the facility is not in substantial compliance with the standards established, and the operator is not correcting the noncompliance in accordance with the time schedules in his approved plan of correction, the department shall issue a notice of noncompliance.

198.067   Noncompliance with law—injunction, when—civil penalties

Any facility which received a notice of noncompliance is liable to the state for civil penalties of up to one hundred dollars for each day that noncompliance continues after the notice of noncompliance is received. The attorney general shall upon the request of the department, bring an action in a circuit court of competent jurisdiction to recover the civil penalty. The court shall have the authority to determine the amount of civil penalty to be assessed.

198.099   Petition for appointment of receiver—when

(1) The attorney general, either on his own initiative or upon the request of the department or of any other state governmental agency having an interest in the matter, a resident or residents or the guardian of a resident of a facility or the owner or operator of a facility may petition for appointment of a receiver for a facility when any of the following conditions exist:

(a) The operator is operating without a license;

(b) The department has revoked the license of an operator or refused to grant an application for a license to the operator;

(c) The department has initiated revocation procedures and has determined that the lives, health, safety, or welfare of the residents cannot be adequately assured pending a full hearing on license revocation;

(d) The facility is closing or intends to close and adequate arrangements for relocation of residents have not been made at least thirty days prior to closure;

(e) An emergency exists in the facility; or

(f) The operator is insolvent.

(2) The receiver shall have the powers granted by the court.

The Department of Health expects litigation as a result of any enforcement action it takes in this case. It has come to the office of the state's Attorney General for advice. The Director of the Department wants to be aggressive in this case in part because the poor condition of the facility has become public knowledge. She believes that the agency's effectiveness has been challenged and that the facility is seriously deficient and heading for more problems.

Several students should serve as the assistant A.G. who has been assigned to this case. Please advise the Department on the course of action they should follow in this instance.

Other students should serve in the role of attorneys representing the facility. Please identify any defenses available to the facility, your strategy and the course the dispute is likely to take.

Having worked through these provisions, what recommendations for change would you make to this state's legislature, both as to enforcement mechanisms and as to the standards?

B. GOVERNMENT REGULATION THROUGH FINANCING

While the states have authority to regulate health care facilities under their police power, the federal government's authority arises from its role as purchaser of health care. The states have relied on licensure as their major form of quality-control regulation of health care institutions. The federal government, as purchaser, regulates through provider "certification." In order to receive payments under Medicare or Medicaid, an institutional provider must be certified and must sign a provider agreement. The federal government has used its purchasing power to require facilities to meet standards that go beyond the federal payment system. For example, Medicare now requires that providers receiving Medicare payments meet standards concerning the screening, treatment and discharge of any patient, including patients who are not Medicare beneficiaries, presenting at the facility's emergency room. (See discussion in Chapter 6.)

Given the immense sums the federal government spends on medical care ($196 billion in 1990), it would appear to have considerable power to assure that beneficiaries receive care of adequate quality. At least until recently, however, it has appeared hesitant to exercise this power, preferring to defer to the states. The federal enforcement process in relation to nursing homes, including the relation between state and federal enforcement agencies, and the federal government's traditional approach to it, are described in the following case.

IN RE THE ESTATE OF MICHAEL PATRICK SMITH v. HECKLER

United States Court of Appeals, Tenth Circuit, 1984.
747 F.2d 583.

McKAY, CIRCUIT JUDGE:

Plaintiffs, seeking relief under 42 U.S.C. § 1983 (1982), brought this class action on behalf of Medicaid recipients residing in nursing homes in Colorado. They alleged that the Secretary of Health and Human Services (Secretary) has a statutory duty under Title XIX of the Social Security Act, 42 U.S.C. § 1396–1396n (1982), commonly known as the Medicaid Act, to develop and implement a system of nursing home review and enforcement designed to ensure that Medicaid recipients residing in Medicaid-certified nursing homes actually receive the optimal medical and psychosocial care that they are entitled to under the Act. The plaintiffs contended that the enforcement system developed by the Secretary is "facility-oriented," not "patient-oriented" and thereby fails to meet the statutory mandate. The district court found that although a patient care or "patient-oriented" management system is feasible, the Secretary does not have a duty to introduce and require the use of such a system. *In re Estate of Smith v. O'Halloran*, 557 F.Supp. 289, 295 (D.Colo.1983).

The primary issue on appeal is whether the trial court erred in finding that the Secretary does not have a statutory duty to develop and implement a system of nursing home review and enforcement which focuses on and ensures high quality patient care. * * *

BACKGROUND

The factual background of this complex lawsuit is fully discussed in the district court's opinion. *In re Estate of Smith v. O'Halloran*, 557 F.Supp. 289 (D.Colo.1983). Briefly, plaintiffs instituted the lawsuit in an effort to improve the deplorable conditions at many nursing homes. They presented evidence of the lack of adequate medical care and of the widespread knowledge that care is inadequate. Indeed, the district court concluded that care and life in some nursing homes is so bad that the homes "could be characterized as orphanages for the aged." *Id.* at 293.

* * *

THE MEDICAID ACT

An understanding of the Medicaid Act (the Act) is essential to understand plaintiffs' contentions. The purpose of the Act is to enable the federal government to assist states in providing medical assistance to "aged, blind or disabled individuals, whose income and resources are insufficient to meet the costs of necessary medical services, and * * * rehabilitation and other services to help such * * * individuals to attain or retain capabilities for independence or self care." 42 U.S.C. § 1396 (1982). To receive funding, a state must submit to the Secretary and have approved by the Secretary, a plan for medical assistance which meets the requirements of 42 U.S.C. § 1396a(a).

* * * A state seeking plan approval must establish or designate a single state agency to administer or supervise administration of the state plan, 42 U.S.C. § 1396a(a)(5), and must provide reports and information as the Secretary may require. *Id.* § 1396a(a)(6). Further, the state agency is responsible for establishing and maintaining health standards for institutions where the recipients of the medical assistance under the plan receive care or services. *Id.* § 1396a(a)(9)(A). The plan must include descriptions of the standards and methods the state will use to assure that medical or remedial care services provided to the recipients "are of high quality." *Id.* § 1396a(a)(22)(D).

The state plan must also provide "for a regular program of medical review * * * of each patient's need for skilled nursing facility care * * *, a written plan of care, and, where applicable, a plan of rehabilitation prior to admission to a skilled nursing facility. * * * " *Id.* § 1396a(a)(26)(A). Further, the plan must provide for periodic inspections by medical review teams of:

> (i) the care being provided in such nursing facilities * * * to persons receiving assistance under the State plan; (ii) with respect to each of the patients receiving such care, the adequacy of the services available in particular nursing facilities * * * to meet the current health needs and promote the maximum physical well-being of patients receiving care in such facilities * * *; (iii) the necessity and desirability of continued placement of such patients in such nursing facilities * * *; and (iv) the feasibility of meeting their health care needs through alternative institutional or non-institutional services. *Id.* § 1396a(a)(26)(B).

The state plan must provide that any skilled nursing facility receiving payment comply with 42 U.S.C. § 1395x(j), which defines "skilled nursing facility" and sets out standards for approval under a state plan. *Id.* § 1396a(a)(28). The key requirement for purposes of this lawsuit is that a skilled nursing facility must meet "such other conditions relating to the health and safety of individuals who are furnished services in such institution or relating to the physical facilities thereof as the Secretary may find necessary. * * * " *Id.* § 1395x(j)(15).

The state plan must provide for the appropriate state agency to establish a plan, consistent with regulations prescribed by the Secretary, for professional health personnel to review the appropriateness and quality of care and services furnished to Medicaid recipients. *Id.* § 1396a(a)(33)(A). The appropriate state agency must determine on an ongoing basis whether participating institutions meet the requirements for continued participation in the Medicaid program. *Id.* § 1396a(a)(33)(B). While the state has the initial responsibility for determining whether institutions are meeting the conditions of participation, section 1396a(a)(33)(B) gives the Secretary the authority to "look behind" the state's determination of facility compliance, and make an independent and binding determination of whether institutions meet the requirements for participation in the state Medicaid plan. Thus, the state is responsible for conducting the review of facilities to determine whether they comply with the state plan. In conducting the review, however, the states must use federal standards, forms, methods, and procedures. 42 C.F.R. § 431.610(f)(1) (1983). * * *

Implementing Regulations

Congress gave the Secretary a general mandate to promulgate rules and regulations necessary to the efficient administration of the functions with which the Secretary is charged by the Act. 42 U.S.C. § 1302 (1982). Pursuant to this mandate the Secretary has promulgated standards for the care to be provided by skilled nursing facilities and intermediate care facilities. See 42 C.F.R. § 442.200–.516 (1983). * * *

The Secretary has established a procedure for determining whether state plans comply with the standards set out in the regulations. This enforcement mechanism is known as the "survey/certification" inspection system. Under this system, the states conduct reviews of nursing homes pursuant to 42 U.S.C. § 1396a(a)(33). The Secretary then determines, on the basis of the survey results, whether the nursing home surveyed is eligible for certification and, thus, eligible for Medicaid funds. The states must use federal standards, forms, methods, and procedures in conducting the survey. 42 C.F.R. § 431.610(f)(1). At issue in this case is the form SSA–1569, [   ], which the Secretary requires the states to use to show that the nursing homes participating in Medicaid under an approved state plan meet the conditions of participation contained in the Act and the regulations. Plaintiffs contend that the form is "facility-oriented," in that it focuses on the theoretical capability of the facility to provide high quality care, rather than "patient-oriented," which would focus on the care actually provided. The district court found, with abundant support in the record, that the "facility-oriented" characterization is appropriate and that the Secretary has repeatedly admitted that the form is "facility-oriented." [   ]

The Plaintiffs' Claims

Plaintiffs contend that the statutory requirements regarding the content of state plans create a correlative entitlement for Medicaid recipients to quality care. They argue that the Secretary has an enforcement obligation to insure compliance with the approved state plan. More specifically, plaintiffs argue that the Secretary has a statutory duty to develop an enforcement system whereby to receive Medicaid funds states would be forced to use a patient care management system. Such a system would ensure, through the review process of section 1396a(a)(33), that Medicaid recipients residing in nursing homes certified for Medicaid participation are "actually, continuously receiving their Medicaid entitlements to optimal medical and psychosocial care in a safe, sanitary, rehabilitatively supportive, accessible, personalized environment and in a context of full civil liberties as a condition of such facilities' receipt of federal and state financial reimbursement from the Medicaid Program." *In re Estate of Smith*, 557 F.Supp. at 292.

The plaintiffs do not challenge the substantive medical standards, or "conditions of participation," which have been adopted by the Secretary and which states must satisfy to have their plans approved. See 42 C.F.R. § 405.1101–.1137. Rather, plaintiffs challenge the enforcement mechanism the Secretary has established. The plaintiffs contend that the federal forms, form SSA–1569 in particular, which states are required to use, evaluate only the physical facilities and theoretical capability to render quality care. The surveys assess the care provided almost totally on the basis of the records, documentation, and written policies of the facility being reviewed. [ ] Further, out of the 541 questions contained in the Secretary's form SSA–1569 which must be answered by state survey and certification inspection teams, only 30 are "even marginally related to patient care or might require any patient observation. * * * " [ ] Plaintiffs contend that the enforcement mechanism's focus on the facility, rather than on the care actually provided in the facility, results only in "paper compliance" with the substantive standards of the Act. Thus, plaintiffs contend, the Secretary has violated her statutory duty to assure that federal Medicaid monies are paid only to facilities which meet the substantive standards of the Act—facilities which actually provide high quality medical, rehabilitative, and psychosocial care to resident Medicaid recipients.

THE DISTRICT COURT'S HOLDING

After hearing the evidence, the district court found the type of patient care management system advocated by plaintiffs clearly feasible and characterized the current enforcement system as "facility-oriented." [ ] However, the court concluded that the failure to implement and require the use of a "patient-oriented" system is not a violation of the Secretary's statutory duty. [ ] The essence of the district court's holding was that the State of Colorado, not the federal government, is responsible for developing and enforcing standards which would assure high quality care in nursing homes and, thus, the State of Colorado, not the federal government, should have been the defendant in this case. [ ]

* * *

THE SECRETARY'S DUTY

After carefully reviewing the statutory scheme of the Medicaid Act, the legislative history, and the district court's opinion, we conclude that the district court improperly defined the Secretary's duty under the statute. The federal government has more than a passive role in handing out money to the states. The district court erred in finding that the burden of enforcing the substantive provisions of the Medicaid Act is on the states. The Secretary of Health and Human Services has a duty to establish a system to adequately inform herself as to whether the facilities receiving federal money are satisfying the requirements of the Act, including providing high quality patient care. This duty to be adequately informed is not only a duty to be informed at the time a facility is originally certified, but is a duty of continued supervision.

Nothing in the Medicaid Act indicates that Congress intended the physical facilities to be the end product. Rather, the purpose of the Act is to provide medical assistance and rehabilitative services. 42 U.S.C. § 1396. The Act repeatedly focuses on the care to be provided, with facilities being only part of that care. For example, the Act provides that health standards are to be developed and maintained, *id.* § 1396a(a)(9)(A), and that states must inform the Secretary what methods they will use to assure high quality care. *Id.* § 1396a(a)(22). In addition to the "adequacy of the services available," the periodic inspections must address "the care being provided" in nursing facilities. *Id.* § 1396a(a)(26)(B). State plans must provide review of the "appropriateness and quality of care and services furnished," *id.* § 1396a(a)(33)(A), and do so on an ongoing basis. *Id.* § 1396a(a)(33)(B).

While the district court correctly noted that it is the state which develops specific standards and actually conducts the inspection, there is nothing in the Act to indicate that the state function relieves the Secretary of all responsibility to ensure that the purposes of the Act are being accomplished. The Secretary, not the states, determines which facilities are eligible for federal funds. [ ] While participation in the program is voluntary, states who choose to participate must comply with federal statutory requirements. [ ] The inspections may be conducted by the states, but the Secretary approves or disapproves the state's plan for review. Further, the inspections must be made with federal forms, procedures, and methods.

It would be anomalous to hold that the Secretary has a duty to determine whether a state plan meets the standards of the Act while holding that the Secretary can certify facilities without informing herself as to whether the facilities actually perform the functions required by the state plan. The Secretary has a duty to ensure more than paper compliance. The federal responsibility is particularly evident in the "look behind" provision. 42 U.S.C. § 1396a(a)(33)(B) (1982). We do not read the Secretary's "look behind" authority as being "nothing more than permitted authority * * *," 557 F.Supp. 296, as the district court found. Rather, we find that the purpose of that section is to assure that compliance is not merely facial, but substantive.

* * *

By enacting section 1302 Congress gave the Secretary authority to promulgate regulations to achieve the functions with which she is charged. The "look-behind" provision and its legislative history clearly show that Congress intended the Secretary to be responsible for assuring that federal Medicaid money is given only to those institutions that actually comply with Medicaid requirements. The Act's requirements include providing high quality medical care and rehabilitative services. In fact, the quality of the care provided to the aged is the focus of the Act. Being charged with this function, we must conclude that a failure to promulgate regulations that allow the Secretary to remain informed, on a continuing basis, as to whether facilities receiving federal money are meeting the requirements of the Act, is an abdication of the Secretary's duty. While the Medicaid Act is admittedly very complex and the Secretary has "exceptionally broad authority to prescribe standards for applying certain sections of the Act," *Schweiker v. Gray Panthers*, 453 U.S. 34, 43 (1981), the Secretary's authority cannot be interpreted so as to hold that that authority is merely permissive authority. The Secretary must insure that states comply with the congressional mandate to provide high quality medical care and rehabilitative services.

The district court made a factual finding that the Secretary's current method of informing herself as to whether the facilities in question are satisfying the statutory requirements is "facility-oriented," rather than "patient-oriented." 557 F.Supp. at 295. This characterization is fully supported by the record. Having determined that the purpose and the focus of the Act is to provide high quality medical care, we conclude that by promulgating a facility-oriented enforcement system the Secretary has failed to follow that focus and such failure is arbitrary and capricious. [   ]

Reversed and Remanded.

Notes and Questions

1. What explains the opposition of the federal government to a patient-oriented nursing home evaluation program? *Smith* was filed in 1975 and opposed by a succession of administrations. Is this explained by the inherent difficulties of designing such a system? Or is the primary problem that of enforcing a patient-oriented quality evaluation system through the Medicaid and Medicare decertification system? Or may the explanation simply be that the preferences of nursing home owners for a system they can easily manipulate have prevailed in the political marketplace over the interests of the citizenry, i.e. the regulator has been captured? Why require the active participation of the federal government if the state is already inspecting facilities and enforcing standards?

2. In 1986, the Secretary issued final regulations to implement a new survey system as ordered by the court in *Smith*. The Secretary commented in the introduction to the regulations: "The current survey system, which has been in effect since 1974, was designed to address the many shortcomings in nursing home care that became evident in the late 1960s and 1970s. The process focused on structural requirements * * * more than on resident outcomes, because at the time this was the area of the most serious deficiencies. Now that the current survey system has largely succeeded in improving the structural problems, it has become clear that further improvements can be made in the quality of nursing home care by focusing more heavily on resident outcomes." The survey adopted in the final rules, which had been tested in several demonstration projects, included interviews with residents and the examination of the condition and care of a representative sampling of residents. The Secretary refused to include the survey instrument itself in the regulations, however: "[T]he new forms and instructions are not set forth in these regulations, and any future changes will be implemented through general instructions, without further changes in these regulations. This allows flexibility to revise and improve the survey process as experience is gained." 51 Fed.Reg. 21,550 (6/13/86). What else does this allow the agency to do?

The federal district court rejected the final rules and held the Secretary in contempt of court. The judge stated:

The Secretary contends that the principles for determining compliance set forth [in the regulations] adequately describe and will mandate the use of the fundamental features of the methodology that will make it "patient oriented." The Secretary also asserts that "quality health care" cannot be legislatively defined, and that the surveyors exercising their professional judgment will give meaning to that phrase. This court disagrees with both these contentions. The principles in the rule state that the survey process is the means and federal forms will be used. What is the process and what are the forms? They can be changed at any time for any reason and the Secretary is not bound because the rule does not articulate any methodology. * * * Moreover, the Secretary's benign approach in relying on professional judgment rings hollow when there is no federal requirement of professionals on the survey team. Smith v. Bowen, 675 F.Supp. 586 (D.Colo.1987).

What is the judge's concern here? If the Secretary promulgated quality standards, would the judge have any basis for review? Does the use of a survey instrument that has not been promulgated as a regulation (and has not been the subject of general publication and formal comment and may be changed without the type of notice required for change of regulations) present a problem for patient advocates? For providers? Does the Secretary's recognition of the role of "professional judgment" during the survey process benefit providers? Disadvantage providers?

3. In 1987, as part of the Omnibus Budget Reconciliation Act (OBRA), Congress enacted comprehensive nursing home reform legislation. This legislation adopted many of the recommendations of the Institute of Medicine of the National Academy of Sciences, which were developed during its Congressionally commissioned study of nursing homes. See, Improving the

Quality of Care in Nursing Homes (National Academy of Sciences Press 1986). In OBRA of 1987, Congress, following the lead of state licensing systems, mandated the adoption of intermediate sanctions by both the state and federal governments. The sanctions required by OBRA are denial of payment, civil monetary penalties, temporary management, monitors and authority to close facilities and transfer residents in emergencies. 42 U.S.C.A. §§ 1395i–3(h) and 1396r(h). The statute also required that a new state and federal survey process be in place by October 1, 1990. This survey was to be process- and outcome-focused. The requirements in OBRA enjoyed the support of both resident advocates and provider groups; however, in the three years since the statute, the Department of Health and Human Services has failed to issue final regulations for several major questions, and the broad support for the reform has diminished. Providers argue that they cannot comply with the law if there are no final regulations on substantial requirements and if additional funding is not forthcoming. Advocacy groups argue that "a major change in public policy has been thwarted by the mismanagement of officials who simply had other priorities." The federal agency has stated that it is ready to enforce the new requirements and has trained 2500 surveyors to implement the act. The agency responsible for developing regulations failed to do so because they were deluged with work. Pear, As Deadline Nears, U.S. Lags on Rules for Nursing Care, N.Y. Times p. 1 col. 1 (9/17/90).

Problem: Residents' Rights

In OBRA, Congress enacted residents' rights provisions. Violation of these provisions subjects the facility to enforcement action. One of the requirements that has attracted the most attention is the limitation on the use of physical restraints, such as straps used to tie residents to beds or chairs or vests that wrap around the resident and then are tied to the bed or chair, and drugs used to control behavior.

Assume that you are the attorney for Pine Acres Nursing Home, located in an older section of the city. The administrator has approached you regarding a problem with certain patients. One patient, Francis Scott, aged 82, has been a resident of the facility for six months. Scott's mental and physical condition has been deteriorating slowly for several years. His family placed him in the nursing home because they wanted him to be safe. He had often left his apartment and become lost on the way back. Scott is angry about the placement, tends to be rude and insists on walking through the hallways and around the grounds of the facility. He has always been an early riser and likes to take his shower at the crack of dawn. He refuses to be assisted by a nurses' aide. In addition, his friends from the neighborhood like to visit. They like to play pinochle when they come, and they usually bring a six-pack.

Another patient, Emma Kaitz, has fallen from her bed twice. The staff is very concerned that she will be hurt. They have begun using "soft restraints" (cloth straps on her hands) to tie her to the bedrails, but she becomes agitated and cries. She says she feels like a dog when they tie her up. She is receiving a sedative to help her relax, but it also tends to make her appear confused.

The administrator wants to know what he should do. The physician who is medical director of the facility will write an order for "restraints as needed" for any resident upon the request of the administrator. How should he deal with Francis' friends? Francis seems to be more trouble than he is worth. He is a Medicaid patient. Can the administrator discharge him? What would you advise this administrator? The OBRA provisions follow.

(b) REQUIREMENTS RELATING TO PROVISION OF SERVICES—

    (1) QUALITY OF LIFE.—

      (A) IN GENERAL.—A nursing facility must care for the residents in such a manner and in such an environment as will promote maintenance or enhancement of the quality of life of each resident.

* * *

(c) REQUIREMENTS RELATING TO RESIDENTS' RIGHTS—

    (1) GENERAL RIGHTS.—

      (A) SPECIFIED RIGHTS.—A nursing facility must protect and promote the rights of each resident, including each of the following rights:

        (i) FREE CHOICE.—The right to choose a personal attending physician, to be fully informed in advance about care and treatment, to be fully informed in advance of any changes in care or treatment that may affect the resident's well-being, and (except with respect to a resident adjudged incompetent) to participate in planning care and treatment or changes in care and treatment.

        (ii) FREE FROM RESTRAINTS.—The right to be free from physical or mental abuse, corporal punishment, involuntary seclusion, and any physical or chemical restraints imposed for purposes of discipline or convenience and not required to treat the resident's medical symptoms. Restraints may only be imposed—

          (I) to ensure the physical safety of the resident or other residents, and

          (II) only upon the written order of a physician that specifies the duration and circumstances under which the restraints are to be used (except in emergency circumstances specified by the Secretary) until such an order could reasonably be obtained.

        (iii) PRIVACY.—The right to privacy with regard to accommodations, medical treatment, written and telephonic communications, visits, and meetings of family and of resident groups.

* * *

(v) ACCOMMODATION OF NEEDS.—The right—

(I) to reside and receive services with reasonable accommodations of individual needs and preferences, except where the health or safety of the individual or other residents would be endangered, and

(II) to receive notice before the room or roommate of the resident in the facility is changed.

(vi) GRIEVANCES.—The right to voice grievances with respect to treatment or care that is (or fails to be) furnished, without discrimination or reprisal for voicing the grievances and the right to prompt efforts by the facility to resolve grievances the resident may have, including those with respect to the behavior of other residents.

* * *

(ix) PARTICIPATION IN OTHER ACTIVITIES.—The right of the resident to participate in social, religious, and community activities that do not interfere with the rights of other residents in the facility.

* * *

Clause (iii) shall not be construed as requiring the provision of a private room.

* * *

(C) RIGHTS OF INCOMPETENT RESIDENTS.—In the case of a resident adjudged incompetent under the laws of a State, the rights of the resident under this title shall devolve upon, and, to the extent judged necessary by a court of competent jurisdiction, be exercised by, the person appointed under State law to act on the resident's behalf.

(D) USE OF PSYCHOPHARMACOLOGIC DRUGS.—Psychopharmacologic drugs may be administered only on the orders of a physician and only as part of a plan (included in the written plan of care ...) designed to eliminate or modify the symptoms for which the drugs are prescribed and only if, at least annually an independent, external consultant reviews the appropriateness of the drug plan of each resident receiving such drugs.

(2) TRANSFER AND DISCHARGE RIGHTS.—

(A) IN GENERAL.—A nursing facility must permit each resident to remain in the facility and must not transfer or discharge the resident from the facility unless—

(i) the transfer or discharge is necessary to meet the resident's welfare and the resident's welfare cannot be met in the facility;

(ii) the transfer or discharge is appropriate because the resident's health has improved sufficiently so the resident no longer needs the services provided by the facility;

(iii) the safety of individuals in the facility is endangered;

(iv) the health of individuals in the facility would otherwise be endangered;

(v) the resident has failed, after reasonable and appropriate notice, to pay * * * an allowable charge imposed by the facility for an item or service requested by the resident and for which a charge may be imposed * * *

(vi) the facility ceases to operate.

In each of the cases described in clauses (i) through (v), the basis for the transfer or discharge must be documented in the resident's clinical record. In the cases described in clauses (i) and (ii), the documentation must be made by the resident's physician, and in the case described in clause (iv) the documentation must be made by a physician. * * *

(B) PRE–TRANSFER AND PRE–DISCHARGE NOTICE.—

(i) IN GENERAL.—Before effecting a transfer or discharge of a resident, a nursing facility must—

(I) notify the resident (and, if known, a family member of the resident or legal representative) of the transfer or discharge and the reasons therefor,

(II) record the reasons in the resident's clinical record * * * and

(III) include in the notice the items described in clause (iii). [concerning appeal of transfer]

(ii) TIMING OF NOTICE.—The notice under clause (i)(I) must be made at least 30 days in advance of the resident's transfer or discharge except—

(I) in a case described in clause (iii) or (iv) of subparagraph (A);

(II) in a case described in clause (ii) of subparagraph (A), where the resident's health improves sufficiently to allow a more immediate transfer or discharge;

(III) in a case described in clause (i) of subparagraph (A), where a more immediate transfer or discharge is necessitated by the resident's urgent medical needs; or

* * *

(IV) in a case where a resident has not resided in the facility for 30 days.

In the case of such exceptions, notice must be given as many days before the date of the transfer or discharge as is practicable.

* * *

(3) ACCESS AND VISITATION RIGHTS.— A nursing facility must—

(A) permit immediate access to any resident by any representative of the Secretary, by any representative of the State, by an ombudsman * * *, or by the resident's individual physician;

(B) permit immediate access to a resident, subject to the resident's right to deny or withdraw consent at any time, by immediate family or other relatives of the resident;

(C) permit immediate access to a resident, subject to reasonable restrictions and the resident's right to deny or withdraw consent at any time, by others who are visiting with the consent of the resident;

(D) permit reasonable access to a resident by any entity or individual that provides health, social, legal, or other services to the resident, subject to the resident's right to deny or withdraw consent at any time; and

(E) permit representatives of the state ombudsman (* * *), with the permission of the resident (or the resident's legal representative) and consistent with State law, to examine a resident's clinical records.

* * *

(e)(3) STATE APPEALS PROCESS FOR TRANSFERS.—The State, for transfers from nursing facilities effected on or after October 1, 1989, must provide for a fair mechanism, * * * for hearing appeals on transfers of residents of such facilities. * * *

* * *

Consider the civil liability issues raised by this problem after you have studied the materials in Chapter 2. See also, Johnson, The Fear of Liability and the Use of Restraints in Nursing Homes, 18 Law, Medicine & Health Care 263 (1990). The Ohio Court of Appeals considered the effect of public regulations concerning restraints in litigation for negligence against a facility in Fine v. Woodside Manor Nursing and Convalescent Home, 1984 WL 6860. The court allocated both duty and burden of proof according to its reading of the regulations. See also, Kujawski v. Arbor View Health Care Center, 139 Wis.2d 455, 407 N.W.2d 249 (1987).

What do you think your client expects of you in this problem? What role should you play?

How should an inspector who interviews Scott interpret his reports of dissatisfaction? Would Kaitz' complaints be treated in the same way or differently? Why?

What sanctions are appropriate for residents rights violations? Should different sanctions be used than those used for enforcing other standards? Do residents rights relate to the quality of care? What competing values do you see in standard setting for nursing homes?

Note: *Private Accreditation of Health Care Facilities*

The previous sections examined the regulation of quality of care in nursing homes, revealing a high level of government involvement in developing and enforcing standards. In contrast to the regulation of nursing homes, the public regulation of quality of care in hospitals defers to a great extent to accreditation by the Joint Commission on Accreditation of Healthcare Organizations (JCAHO, formerly the Joint Commission on

Accreditation of Hospitals), which is the leading health care facility accreditation organization.

The JCAHO is a not-for-profit private association, and accreditation is, in theory, strictly voluntary. For law schools, the equivalent accrediting body is the American Bar Association. In most states, graduation from an ABA-accredited law school is required for admission to the bar. The accreditation program offered by the ABA is still considered "voluntary" on the part of law schools, just as JCAHO accreditation is considered voluntary for any health care organization. In other words, law schools lacking ABA accreditation may still operate, but their graduates will not be allowed to take the bar exam.

The JCAHO, and the many other private, voluntary accreditation organizations in the health care system, represent a classic form of self-regulation. The professionals and institutions participating in such programs both establish the standards of quality and survey the participating facilities. The governing and policy-making members of the JCAHO include the American Medical Association, the American Hospital Association, the American College of Surgeons, and the American College of Physicians. The JCAHO is the successor to the American College of Surgeons Hospital Standardization Program, which was established in 1919. (For a further discussion of the history of the JCAHO and an analysis of each of the issues identified below see, Jost, The Joint Commission on Accreditation of Hospitals: Private Regulation of Health Care and the Public Interest, 24 B.C.L. Rev. 835 (1983).)

Under the Medicare statute, JCAHO accreditated hospitals are deemed to meet most requirements for Medicare certification. (42 U.S.C.A. §§ 1395x(e), 1395bb). Many states, 38 as of 1983, have to a greater or lesser degree incorporated JCAHO accreditation into their hospital licensure standards. JCAHO accreditation is a prerequisite for payment by some health insurance plans and is required in practice for a hospital to be approved for a residency program. Over 80% of acute care hospitals in the United States, including virtually all hospitals with more than 25 beds, are JCAHO accredited. In recognition of the broad acceptance of JCAHO standards within the hospital industry, violation of the standards has been used as proof of the standard of care in corporate negligence cases against hospitals. See discussion in Chapter 2. While the JCAHO offers accreditation programs for a variety of health care providers, including nursing homes and home health care, for example, none of these other programs have a participation level comparable to their hospital accreditation program.

While the high degree of participation on the part of hospitals would indicate that the program is successful on some level, critics have described the JCAHO inspection process as inadequate and have attacked the control exercised by provider groups. A recent article in the Wall Street Journal claimed: "Although the joint commission is the first to learn of a hospital's sloppiness, it is usually the last to act decisively. While bureaucratic fumbling may occasionally play a role, the commission appears subject to a fundamental conflict." Bogdanich, Prized by Hospitals, Accreditation Hides Perils Patients Face, Wall St. Journal, p. 1 col. 1 (Oct. 12, 1988). The same article reports that in random checks of 58 accredited hospitals, government officials found approximately one in three seriously deficient. In responding to such criticisms, the JCAHO identifies its goal as assisting hospitals in improving their performance: "We keep as many institutions as possible within the pale of our influence, so we can keep lifting them up. You get more things fixed with a cooperative arrangement." Id. Individual hospitals complain that government inspectors, in contrast to the JCAHO surveyors, exaggerate minor or temporary problems. Id.

It should be said that, until the early 1980s, the focus of nursing home regulation was also one of consultation rather than enforcement. In 1981, the Reagan administration proposed accepting JCAHO accreditation of nursing homes in lieu of federal certification for participation in federal payment programs. This proposal was vigorously opposed by consumer advocates and was withdrawn. Should nursing homes be treated differently than hospitals on this issue? Is such treatment justified on policy grounds or is it simply explained by timing? (JCAHO accreditation was accepted as adequate for hospital certification for Medicare in 1965.) Do the differences between hospitals and nursing homes described earlier explain this distinction?

Similarly, JCAHO accreditation standards have suffered from many of the limitations previously described in relation to quality standards established by the government. The JCAHO standards have emphasized structural indicators that demonstrated the *capacity* to provide quality care, rather than clinical indicators used to examine the quality of care actually provided. JCAHO standards have established professional control of the organization, for example, through a hospital's medical staff, as itself an indicator of quality. Responding to criticism of their standards, JCAHO has adopted an "Agenda for Change," which would develop clinical indicators for use in accreditation.

The most controversial quality-control issue concerning private accreditation is the fusing of private accreditation with public regulation. This occurs when private accreditation is used as a substitute for public regulation, as it is under the Medicare hospital certification program described previously. Does such reliance on JCAHO accreditation improperly delegate government authority? See, Cospito v. Heckler, 742 F.2d 72 (3d Cir.1984). Should JCAHO accreditation or compliance with JCAHO standards demonstrate that medical conditions in a prison comply with the Eighth and Fourteenth Amendments or that a mental hospital provides constitutionally adequate treatment? Should violation of JCAHO accreditation standards establish the existence of unconstitutional conditions? See, for example, Woe by Woe v. Cuomo, 559 F.Supp. 1158 (E.D.N.Y.1983); 729 F.2d 96, 106–107 (2d Cir.1984); 638 F.Supp. 1506 (E.D.N.Y.1986) (describing JCAHO standards and procedures); 801 F.2d 627 (2d Cir.1986) (reversing permanent injunction but affirming preliminary injunction). What are the advantages and disadvantages of relying on a private, provider-controlled organization for quality-control regulation? See generally, Jost, The Necessary and Proper Role of Regulation to Assure the Quality of Health Care, 25 Houston L.Rev. 525 (1988); Lawrence, Private Exercise of Governmental Power, 61 Ind.L.J. 647 (1986).

Other legal issues also arise in private accreditation activities. Because private accrediting organizations are dominated by the professionals or institutions that are to be accredited, there have been claims that these organization's standards or enforcement policies are used to restrain competition within the particular accredited group or by entities outside the dominant group. The antitrust implications of these claims are discussed in Chapter 8.

A final issue concerns the legal standards applied to an accrediting body's behavior when challenged by an institution denied accreditation. For constitutional challenges, such as violation of due process, under what circumstances would a private accrediting agency's activities satisfy the requirements for state action? With the important benefits at stake in a private accreditation decision, do institutions denied accreditation have any rights to fairness in the procedures of the accreditation body? For each of these issues, see St. Agnes Hospital v. Riddick, 748 F.Supp. 319 (D.Md. 1990), in which a Catholic hospital challenged the denial of accreditation for its residency program in obstetrics and gynecology by the Accreditation Council for Graduate Medical Education (ACGME). ACGME discontinued accreditation because it found the program to provide inadequate experience in retropubic surgery, tubal surgery, family planning, and in the subspecialties of oncology and endocrinology. St. Agnes refused to perform or to provide clinical training in elective abortions, sterilizations and artificial contraception as a matter of its religious institutional philosophy. The state of Maryland required graduation from a residency program accredited by ACGME, or its equivalent, as a condition of licensure for medical doctors.

IV. QUALITY CONTROL IN THE INSTITUTIONAL SETTING

A. RISK MANAGEMENT AND QUALITY ASSURANCE

While professional licensing and credentialing may assure that those entering practice possess minimal qualifications, they are much less effective at removing from practice those who cease to be qualified, and even less effective at assuring that patients receive health care of optimal quality. Other methods of quality control, however, have proven more effective in regulating the quality of health care. Among the most important of these are the quality assurance systems that exist within hospitals and other health care institutions.

Most hospitals employ two distinct but closely related systems to oversee the quality of care: risk management and quality assurance. The goals of an effective risk management program are to eliminate the causes of loss experienced by the hospital and its patients, employees, and visitors; lessen the operational and financial effects of unavoidable losses; and cover inevitable losses at the lowest cost. As such, risk management is concerned not only with the quality of patient care delivered by a hospital but also with the safety and security of the hospital's employees, visitors, and property. The risk manager also administers claims against the hospital if injuries occur and oversees the hospital's insurance programs, determining which risks the hospital ought to insure against and which it ought to retain through self-insurance or high deductibles. Finally, the risk manager must be concerned with public and patient relations, as dissatisfied patients are more likely to sue for medical errors.

The most important tool of the risk manager is the incident report. Hospitals require incident reports on occurrences not consistent with routine patient care or hospital operation that have resulted or could have resulted in hospital liability or patient dissatisfaction. Examples include sudden deaths, falls, drug errors or reactions, injuries due to faulty equipment, threats of legal action, and unexplained requests from attorneys for medical records. The filing of incident reports (usually prepared by nurses) is the responsibility of department heads or supervisors. Incident reports are directed to the hospital risk manager, who investigates them as necessary. The risk manager also informs appropriate administrative and medical staff about the incident. By compiling data from incident reports, the risk manager can identify problem areas within the hospital and thus help prevent errors and injuries. Incident reports also assist in claims management, permitting the hospital to avoid costly lawsuits by quickly coming to terms with injured patients where liability seems clear and facilitating early coordination with an attorney to plan a defense where litigation seems unavoidable. Some malpractice insurance contracts include reservation of rights clauses, which permit the insurer to refuse to pay claims based on unreported incidents, underscoring the importance of incident reports.

On risk management and incident reporting and investigation, see B. Brown, Risk Management for Hospitals: A Practical Approach (1979); J. Orlikoff, W. Fifer, G.H. Greeley, Malpractice Prevention and Liability Control for Hospitals (1981); Blake, Incident Investigation, A Complete Guide, 15 Nursing Mgmt. 36 (Nov.1984); Sielicki, Current Philosophy of Risk Management, 9 Topics in Health Care Financing 1 (Spring 1983).

Hospital quality assurance programs are directly concerned with assessing and improving patient care. Quality assurance focuses more narrowly on patient care than does risk management. It is broader than risk management, however, in that it considers a wide range of quality concerns, not just discrete mishaps.

Incident reports play a major role in quality assurance, as they permit the hospital to identify serious quality deficiencies. The most significant tools of hospital quality assurance, however, are the hospital committees that oversee the quality of various hospital functions. These committees carry out functions mandated by JCAHO accreditation standards, and are in some states required by state law or regulation. See West's Ann.Cal.Admin.Code tit. 22, § 70703(e); N.Y.— McKinney's Pub.Health Law § 2805–j. Common hospital committees include a tissue committee, which oversees the quality and necessity of surgery; an infections committee, which evaluates patients' infections and oversees the disposal of infectious material and the use of antibiotics; a pharmacy and therapeutics committee, which monitors the use and handling of drugs; a medical records committee, which assures the quality and completeness of medical records; a utilization review committee, which assures that patients are not admitted inappropriately or hospitalized too long; and medical audit committees, which review the quality of care provided in the hospital as a whole or in certain departments. Some hospitals also have an overall quality control committee, which coordinates quality assurance efforts throughout the hospital. Two other very important committees are the executive and credentials committees. The former serves as the cabinet of the medical staff, and in this capacity oversees all efforts of the medical staff to ensure quality. The credentials committee passes on applications for medical staff appointments and reappointments, and establishes and reviews physician clinical privileges; i.e., it determines which doctors can practice in the hospital and what procedures they may perform. As such, it has a vital role in assuring the quality of care provided by the hospital.

Some committees, such as the credentials or executive committee, are medical staff committees; i.e., they are composed of and answerable to physicians who practice in the hospital. Others, such as the quality assurance or infections control committees, are likely to be hospital committees, answerable to the hospital administration and including other professionals besides physicians. In many hospitals, committees play an active role in assuring the quality of care; in others, they exist primarily to meet accreditation requirements and do little.

See, discussing quality control in hospitals, N. Graham, Quality Assurance in Hospitals (1982); JCAHO, 1991 Accreditation Manual for Hospitals, 215–222 (1990).

Risk management is outcome oriented—it operates primarily by reacting to bad outcomes. Quality assurance is more process oriented. Some quality assurance activities involve concurrent review of the care process, such as the proctoring of doctors with probationary staff privileges. Quality assurance may also include retrospective review of care, another form of process review. Risk management is a managerial function, while quality assurance is predominantly a clinical function. See, comparing risk management and quality assurance, Orlikoff & Lanham, Why Risk Management and Quality Assurance Should be Integrated, 55 Hospitals 54 (June 1, 1981).

B. LEGAL ISSUES CONCERNING QUALITY ASSURANCE AND RISK MANAGEMENT

A hospital's risk management and quality assurance functions can figure in a variety of legal problems. The most important of these— whether a hospital is liable in tort for injuries caused by its failure to oversee adequately the quality of care provided by its employees or medical staff—will be discussed at length in chapter 2. A second—when and how a hospital may exclude a high risk, poor quality physician—will be considered in Chapter 5. Several other questions will be considered here. Are hospital committee proceedings or incident reports immune from discovery? Is information from them admissible as evidence? Can the members of a hospital's committee be sued for defamation by a physician whose activities are criticized in the committee?

Plaintiffs in malpractice actions frequently seek discovery of the proceedings of hospital quality assurance committees. They may request production of a committee's minutes or reports, propound interrogatories about the committee process or outcome, or ask to depose committee members concerning committee deliberations. If the plaintiff is suing a health care professional whose work was reviewed by the committee, the discovery may seek to confirm the negligence of the professional or to uncover additional evidence substantiating the plaintiff's claim. If the suit is against the hospital on a theory of corporate liability (i.e., claiming that the hospital itself was negligent in appointing or failing to supervise a professional), evidence of committee proceedings may prove vital to establishing the hospital's liability.

These discovery requests are usually met with a claim that information generated within or by hospital committees is not discoverable. The following case involves such a claim.

COBURN v. SEDA

Supreme Court of Washington, En Banc, 1984.
101 Wash.2d 270, 677 P.2d 173.

UTTER, JUSTICE.

Petitioner Kadlec Hospital challenges a trial court order to answer an interrogatory and produce records of a hospital committee, asserting that the requested information is immune from discovery under RCW 4.24.250 and the common law. We hold RCW 4.24.250 applies to this medical malpractice action and affords an immunity from discovery to the written records, proceedings, and reports of hospital committees which review the quality of patient care.

Respondents, Angeline Coburn and her children, brought this medical malpractice action against Dr. Peter Seda and Kadlec Hospital following the death of Denny Coburn. Mr. Coburn died during a heart catheterization procedure performed by Dr. Seda at Kadlec Hospital.

As part of discovery, respondents propounded an interrogatory and request for production seeking information about a hospital review committee. The interrogatory, request for production, and the responses of appellant were as follows:

28. Does the hospital have a review committee that reviews the quality of patient care? If so, state:

(a) The name of the committee.

(b) The names and addresses of the members of the committee.

(c) Did the committee review the incident which is the subject of this lawsuit?

(d) If so, where and when and who was present?

(e) Was a written report prepared by the committee concerning the incident?

ANSWER: Defendant objects to this inquiry for the reason that any in-hospital reviews of quality of patient care are privileged and confidential and are protected by common law privilege [ ] as well as by statutory privilege [ ].

Request for Production No. 9. Produce the written report identified in your answer to the foregoing interrogatory and the minutes of the committee meeting.

N/A

Following petitioner's refusal to divulge the requested information, respondents brought a motion to compel Kadlec Hospital to answer the interrogatory and produce the written report. The trial judge granted this motion, ruling that no statutory or common law privilege applied. The trial judge found RCW 4.24.250 applied only to actions brought by one health care provider against another, not to medical malpractice actions. The plain language of the statute compels us to rule otherwise.

I.

RCW 4.24.250 provides:

Any health care provider as defined in RCW 7.70.020(1) and (2) as now existing or hereafter amended who, in good faith, files charges or presents evidence against another member of their profession based on the claimed incompetency or gross misconduct of such person before a regularly constituted review committee or board of a professional society or hospital whose duty it is to evaluate the competency and qualifications of members of the profession, including limiting the extent of practice of such person in a hospital or similar institution, or before a regularly constituted committee or board of a hospital whose duty it is to review and evaluate the quality of patient care, shall be immune from civil action for damages arising out of such activities. The proceedings, reports, and written records of such committees or boards, or of a member, employee, staff person, or investigator of such a committee or board, shall not be subject to subpoena or discovery proceedings in any civil action, except actions arising out of the recommendations of such committees or boards involving the restriction or revocation of the clinical or staff privileges of a health care provider as defined above.

The statute, on its face, prohibits discovery of certain records in "*any* civil action" with a single exception: actions arising out of committee recommendations which involve restriction or revocation of staff privileges. * * *

Thus, all civil actions not falling within the specific exception are subject to the statutory provision shielding certain information from discovery. The discovery prohibition therefore applies to medical malpractice actions.

II.

What is the nature of the statutory protection granted the proceedings, reports and written records of quality review committees? A matter may be nondiscoverable either because it is subject to an immunity from discovery or a privilege. Courts often use the terms "privilege" and "immunity" interchangeably, hence the definitional distinction between the two is somewhat muddy. [ ] Despite this lack of clarity, it appears that immunity is a subset of privilege. An immunity may make a matter nondiscoverable but does not control its potential admissibility at trial. In contrast, privilege is a rule of evidence expressly incorporated into the rules of discovery. * * *

Policies favoring both discovery immunities and evidentiary privileges underlie RCW 4.24.250. The discovery protection granted hospital quality review committee records, like work product immunity, prevents the opposing party from taking advantage of a hospital's careful self-assessment. The opposing party must utilize his or her own experts to evaluate the facts underlying the incident which is the subject of suit and also use them to determine whether the hospital's care comported with proper quality standards.

The discovery prohibition, like an evidentiary privilege, also seeks to protect certain communications and encourage the quality review process. Statutes bearing similarities to RCW 4.24.250 prohibit discovery of records on the theory that external access to committee investigations stifles candor and inhibits constructive criticism thought necessary to effective quality review. Courts determining that hospital quality review records should be subject to a common law privilege have advanced this same rationale. As the court stated in *Bredice v. Doctors Hosp., Inc.*, 50 F.R.D. 249, 250 (D.D.C.1970), *aff'd*, 479 F.2d 920 (D.C.Cir.1973):

> Confidentiality is essential to effective functioning of these staff meetings; and these meetings are essential to the continued improvement in the care and treatment of patients. Candid and conscientious evaluation of clinical practices is a *sine qua non* of adequate hospital care * * *. Constructive professional criticism cannot occur in an atmosphere of apprehension that one doctor's suggestion will be used as a denunciation of a colleague's conduct in a malpractice suit.

* * *

RCW 4.24.250 does grant an immunity from discovery to the reports, records, and proceedings of hospital quality review boards. * * *

What is the scope of the statute's grant of immunity from discovery? The protection afforded by the statute was nonexistent at common law [ ]. Further, the prohibition of discovery is in sharp contrast to the general policy favoring broad discovery [ ]. As a statute in derogation of both the common law and the general policy favoring discovery, RCW 4.24.250 is to be strictly construed and limited to its purposes. [ ].

The statute may not be used as a shield to obstruct proper discovery of information generated outside review committee meetings. The statute does not grant an immunity to information otherwise available from original sources. * * *

What is the statute's impact on this action? RCW 4.24.250 will have an effect on the scope of discovery only if the committee in question is "a regularly constituted committee or board of [the] hospital whose duty it is to review and evaluate the quality of patient care." * * * On the sparse record before us, we are unable to conclude whether the committee falls within the statute's requirements. We remand so that the trial court may determine whether Kadlec Hospital's committee satisfies the statutory definition.

In making this determination, the trial court may wish to consider, in addition to other relevant evidence, the guidelines and standards of the Joint Commission on Accreditation of Hospitals and the bylaws and internal regulations of Kadlec Hospital. These materials may aid the trial court in ascertaining the organization and function of the committee as well as whether it is "regularly constituted" [ ]. A further factor which the trial judge should take into account is whether the committee's function is one of current patient care or retrospective review. [ ].

Assuming without deciding that the Kadlec Hospital committee meets the statutory definition, the Request for Production seeks the report of the hospital review committee and falls squarely within the statutory language protecting "written reports" from discovery. As such it would be nondiscoverable.

While Interrogatory 28 does not explicitly request disclosure of "proceedings, reports, and written records", it does seek information which would be included within committee records. The statute's application to the interrogatory must therefore be determined by deciding whether disclosure would interfere with the statutory purposes. Disclosure of the existence and name of the quality review committee would have no detrimental effect on open discussion during committee investigations. Similarly, discovery of the location and time of the review would also be unlikely to inhibit criticism. This data is not the type of substantive information about specific cases and individuals generated in the course of committee meetings the statute seeks to protect. Disclosure of the remainder of the information requested in the interrogatory, however, could well prevent a review committee from operating in a fully effective manner. Individuals may be hesitant to participate in peer or quality review proceedings if anonymity is not assured.

* * *

The trial court's ruling is reversed and remanded * * *.

Notes and Questions

1. Most states have statutes affording hospital quality assurance proceedings some degree of protection from discovery. See Roach, Discoverability and Admissibility of Medical Staff Committee Records: A State by State Analysis, Topics in Medical Records Management 17 (Sept. 1981); Note, Discovery of Peer Review Records, 53 U.M.K.C.L.Rev. 663, 664, note 7 (1985). The policies supporting these statutes are discussed in the principal case. Critics of discovery immunity, on the other hand, argue that immunity deprives plaintiffs, particularly those claiming hospital corporate negligence, of necessary evidence. Moreover, they argue, JCAHO and licensing requirements, plus the threat of tort liability, provide ample incentives for hospital quality assurance efforts so that immunity is unnecessary. See, arguing the immunity question, Flanagan, Rejecting a General Privilege for Self–Critical Analysis, 51 Geo.Wash.L.Rev. 551 (1983); Southwick & Slee, Quality Assurance in Health Care: Confidentiality of Information and Immunity for Participants, 5 J.Leg.Med. 343 (1984); Note, The Privilege of Self–Critical Analysis, 96 Harv.L.Rev. 1083 (1983); Comment, Anatomy of the Conflict Between Hospital Medical Staff Peer Review Confidentiality and Medical Malpractice Plaintiff Recovery, 24 Santa Clara L.Rev. 661 (1984).

2. Statutes protecting committee proceedings from discovery are often subject to exceptions, either explicitly or through judicial interpretation. One common exception affords discovery to physicians challenging the results of committee action against them. Thus a physician whose staff privileges were revoked may discover information from the credentialing committee, Schultz v. Superior Court, 66 Cal.App.3d 440, 446, 136 Cal.Rptr. 67 (1977). This seems to be required by notions of fair process. On the other hand, do statutes that grant physicians access to information that is denied to malpractice plaintiffs violate equal protection? See Jenkins v. Wu, 102 Ill.2d 468, 82 Ill.Dec. 382, 468 N.E.2d 1162, 1166–8 (1984). If a court in a public proceeding grants a physician access to the transcript of a committee hearing under such an exception, must it subsequently grant a patient access to further information regarding the same proceeding? See Henry Mayo Newhall Memorial Hospital v. Superior Court, 81 Cal.App.3d 626, 146 Cal.Rptr. 542 (1978).

Statutes barring discovery of committee information in "civil proceedings" have been interpreted to permit discovery in administrative proceedings brought by a state licensing body, Unnamed Physician v. Commission on Medical Discipline of Maryland, 285 Md. 1, 400 A.2d 396 (1979); but see Attorney General v. Bruce, 124 Mich.App. 796, 335 N.W.2d 697 (1983) (forbidding discovery in administrative proceedings). Some state statutes have been interpreted to protect only opinions presented in committee proceedings and not factual matter considered by the committee, Tucson Medical Center, Inc. v. Misevch, 113 Ariz. 34, 545 P.2d 958 (1976). Does severance of fact from opinion require *in camera* review of all committee records? See Walker v. Alton Memorial Hospital Association, 91 Ill.App.3d 310, 46 Ill.Dec. 797, 414 N.E.2d 850 (1980).

3. In the absence of a statute providing immunity from discovery, a few courts have refused discovery of peer review committee proceedings under the court's inherent power to control discovery. See Bredice v. Doctors Hospital, Inc., 50 F.R.D. 249, 250 (D.D.C.1970), affirmed, 479 F.2d 920 (D.C.Cir.1973); Dade County Med. Ass'n v. Hlis, 372 So.2d 117 (Fla.App. 1979). More courts have rejected common law immunity, holding that the plaintiff's need for evidence outweighs the defendant's claim to protection. See State ex rel. Chandra v. Sprinkle, 678 S.W.2d 804 (Mo.1984); Wesley Medical Center v. Clark, 234 Kan. 13, 669 P.2d 209 (1983).

4. A number of statutes immunizing committee proceedings from discovery do not explicitly render information from those committees privileged from admission into evidence if the plaintiff can obtain it otherwise. But would such information be otherwise admissible? Would it be hearsay? If so, would it be subject to the business records exception? See Fed.R.Evid. 803(6). Might committee records indicating that a hospital was concerned about the performance of a physician be admissible as an admission in a subsequent corporate negligence action against the hospital? See Fed.R.Evid. 801(d)(2)(D). Might a plaintiff's expert be permitted to testify on the basis of information gleaned from committee records, even though those records were themselves hearsay? See Fed.R.Evid. 703. In a suit brought by one particular patient, would committee records documenting errors made by a physician in the treatment of other patients be relevant? Might opinions concerning a physician's negligence found in committee records or reports invade the province of the jury? See, addressing these questions, Dunn & Holbrook, Legal Issues Concerning Peer Review Documents, Topics In Health Record Mgmt., 9, 13–14 (Sept.1981); Holbrook & Dunn, Medical Malpractice Litigation: The Discoverability and Use of Hospitals' Quality Assurance Records, 16 Washburn L.J. 54, 68–70 (1976); Hall, Hospital Committee Proceedings and Reports: Their Legal Status, 1 Am.J.L. & Med. 245, 277–81 (1975).

5. When a plaintiff seeks discovery of incident reports rather than committee proceedings, policy considerations are somewhat different. Hospitals have greater incentives to investigate untoward events than they have to carry on continuing quality review, and are less dependent on voluntary participation. The incident report would usually be more directly relevant to a single claim for malpractice than would general committee investigations. Possibly for these reasons, immunity statutes that protect committee proceedings less often protect incident reports, and courts have been less willing to immunize incident reports from discovery. On the other hand, since incident reports are more directly related to litigation of specific mishaps, two privileges can be asserted to protect them that would seldom apply to committee proceedings: the work product immunity and attorney client privilege.

These issues are discussed in St. Louis Little Rock Hospital, Inc. v. Gaertner, 682 S.W.2d 146, 150–51 (Mo.App.1984):

> To constitute work product, materials must be prepared in anticipation of litigation. Rule 56.01(b)(3). Accordingly, we must look to the nature and purpose of the incident report in this case. Relator has attached as exhibits to its brief the *Compton Hills Medical Center Safety Manual*. The section thereof labelled "Incident/Accident Reporting System," provides for the preparation in triplicate of reports of all incidents. One copy is sent to the hospital administration, one to the head of the involved department, and one to the hospital's insurance company. It is significant to note that this third copy is sent to the insuror not immediately after the incident, but "on a monthly basis." The insurance company "feeds these reports into a computer and sends back to the hospital a computer printout." After review by the Incident Report Coordinator and the Safety Committee, the report forms the basis for corrective and preventive action. It is a further significance that the incident report form, although containing the name of the insurance company, is headed as follows:

> PATIENT INCIDENT REPORT
> NOT A NOTICE OF LOSS

> For Loss Prevention Purposes Only.

> The use served by these incident reports is obviously that of future loss prevention, an important and praiseworthy objective. But they are not documents prepared in anticipation of litigation so as to invoke application of the work product exception to discovery.

> We turn next to the question of applicability of the attorney-client privilege.

> * * *

> At the outset, we note that the fact that the incident report was communicated to relator's insuror rather than directly to relator's attorney does not preclude assertion by relator of the privilege. A communication falls within the attorney-client privilege even though the attorney was not yet actually representing the client, provided that the communication was made between the client as an insured to his liability insuror during the course of an existing insured-insuror relationship. [ ]. Nevertheless, relator's incident report does not fall within the scope of the attorney-client privilege. In order to be privileged, a communication between a client and his attorney, or between an insured and his insuror, must be within the context of the attorney-client relationship. [ ]. In other words, the purpose of the communication must be to secure legal advice from the client's attorney. [ ]. The purpose of the incident report was not to enable relator or its insuror to obtain legal advice, but rather to help relator reduce the number of accidents at its facility. The incident report form called for the nurse to fill in answers coded so that a computer would be able to read the responses. There is no indication that the coded responses were decipherable by relator's attorneys or that an incident report ever found its way into an attorney's hands. Moreover, the fact that the

form indicates it was for loss prevention purposes only militates not only against finding that the incident report was prepared in anticipation of litigation, but also against finding that the report was prepared for the purpose of seeking professional legal advice.   * * * That the incident report may have been subsequently used by relator's attorney or insuror is irrelevant.   A document which is not privileged does not become privileged by the mere act of sending it to an attorney.

Gaertner is consistent with other authorities considering the work product and attorney-client privilege issues.   See also Kay Laboratories, Inc. v. District Court, 653 P.2d 721 (Colo.1982); Bernardi v. Community Hospital Ass'n, 166 Colo. 280, 443 P.2d 708 (1968); Wiener v. Memorial Hospital for Cancer, etc., 114 Misc.2d 1013, 453 N.Y.S.2d 142 (1982); Shibilski v. St. Joseph's Hospital, Inc., 83 Wis.2d 459, 266 N.W.2d 264 (1978); but see Sierra Vista Hospital v. Superior Ct., 248 Cal.App.2d 359, 56 Cal.Rptr. 387 (1967).   See also Dwyer, Hospital Incident Reports: Protected from Discovery?   63 Hospital Progress 38 (Oct.1982); Roach, Legal Review: Hospital Incident Reports, Topics in Health Records Management 85 (Dec. 1981).

If a physician criticizes another physician before a hospital quality review committee, or if a committee issues a report critical of a physician, may the criticized physician recover for defamation?   If professionals or institutions could be held liable for defamation in such cases, this could obviously have a considerable chilling effect on the frank discussion necessary for effective peer review.   On the other hand, a critical committee report, particularly one that results in termination or suspension of medical staff privileges, can have a considerable impact on the reputation of a physician.

MATVIUW v. JOHNSON

Court of Appeals of Illinois, 1979.
70 Ill.App.3d 481, 26 Ill.Dec. 794, 388 N.E.2d 795.

MCNAMARA, JUSTICE:

Plaintiff, Dr. William D. Matviuw, appeals from an order of the circuit court of Cook County dismissing his complaint for compensatory and punitive damages arising from certain allegedly defamatory remarks made by defendant, Dr. Jeffrey B. Johnson.   The trial court found that defendant's remarks were absolutely privileged and were therefore non-actionable as a matter of law.

In November 1976, both plaintiff and defendant were members of the Department of Obstetrics and Gynecology of the Alexian Brothers Medical Center, a hospital located in Elk Grove Village, Illinois.

Plaintiff's complaint charged that on November 23, 1976, a special meeting of Alexian's executive committee was convened in reference to two letters written by plaintiff.   Plaintiff addressed the committee and departed.   The complaint further alleged that subsequently defendant addressed the committee and made several statements regarding plaintiff's professional capabilities.   Defendant expressed an unwillingness to continue to work with plaintiff because of plaintiff's dishonest and unethical practices. Defendant also stated that the majority of plaintiff's colleagues had a very low opinion of the latter's abilities. Defendant advised that he had warned several people regarding plaintiff's shoddy practices on occasion and that one such practice had prompted plaintiff's dismissal from another hospital. As an example of plaintiff's alleged incompetence, defendant cited an instance where plaintiff's method of delivery resulted in serious injury to an infant. Defendant also stated that pediatricians' reports of "battered babies" prompted a departmental audit.

In his complaint, plaintiff further alleged that defendant made the statements with knowledge of their falsity or with reckless disregard of their truth or falsity. Plaintiff charged that defendant neither consulted hospital records nor made any investigation to determine the accuracy of his accusations and that defendant was prompted to make the statements out of a desire to injure plaintiff's medical practice and to benefit his own. Plaintiff alleged that as a result of defendant's defamatory remarks he was not reappointed to the Alexian staff, had lost several patients and had been unable to obtain new patients.

Defendant moved to dismiss the complaint pursuant to sections 45 and 48 of the Civil Practice Act. * * * On April 14, 1978, the trial court dismissed plaintiff's complaint on the ground that the remarks made by defendant to the committee were absolutely privileged.

Plaintiff contends that the trial court erred in holding that the Medical Studies Act creates an absolute privilege to defame. Plaintiff argues that the Act offers only a qualified privilege to statements made before the executive committee of a hospital. He maintains that such a privilege did not warrant dismissal of his complaint.

Appellees argue that the language of the Medical Studies Act, as well as its legislative purpose, supports a construction which accords an absolute privilege to statements made before Alexian's executive committee. They cite the public policy which is promoted by allowing staff members to speak freely on matters regarding the evaluation of their colleagues' performance and improvement of patient care. Appellees suggest that the purpose and effectiveness of hospital committees will be seriously undermined if those testifying cannot be certain that their testimony will not subject them to civil liability. Moreover, appellees maintain that an absolute privilege is necessary to avoid the situation in which a witness would be required to guess beforehand whether the statements will be protected.

The issue of whether sections 1, 2, and 3 of the Medical Studies Act confer an absolute privilege upon statements made before an executive committee of a hospital is one of first impression in this state. We first note that since an absolute privilege completely forecloses a remedy in a civil action, the class of absolute privileges has traditionally been very limited. (*Cook v. East Shore Newspapers* (1945), 327 Ill.App. 559, 64 N.E.2d 751.) We must therefore look to the language and purpose of the Act to determine the legislative intent with reference to privilege.

Section 1 of the Act provides that all "information, interviews, reports, statements, memoranda or other data" of medical executive committees shall be strictly confidential and used only for the purposes enumerated therein. Section 1 also contains an exception permitting a physician to gain access to or use data upon which a decision regarding his staff privileges was based.

Plaintiff's complaint alleged that as a direct result of the statements made by defendant before the executive committee, plaintiff was not reappointed to Alexian's medical staff. Thus, plaintiff falls within the exception set forth in section 1 and was therefore properly permitted access to and use of the substance of defendant's statements before the committee.

Appellees contend that the phrase "use of" should be narrowly construed to permit use of the data by a physician to rebut charges made against him and to appeal from a committee decision through the hospital's internal appeal procedure and, ultimately, judicial review. Under this interpretation, no civil action would be within the permitted use of such information.

We perceive no such limitation in the language used in the statute. The phrase "use of data" is not qualified or limited in any manner. On the basis of statutory language, we find no bar to plaintiff's action for defamation. Furthermore, we cannot accept appellees' contention that the construction of section 1 urged by plaintiff will defeat the Act's purpose and the legislature's intent. We agree that, through the Medical Studies Act, the legislature intended to bolster the effectiveness of in-hospital peer group review committees. To this end, the Act provided for a general policy of confidentiality for information obtained by such committees to insure that those providing the information could speak freely. Nevertheless, an individual's interest in his personal and professional reputation must be recognized and protected. * * *

In-hospital peer group review committees have need of candid commentary in order to function effectively. It does not follow, however, that those testifying before such committees must be accorded an absolute privilege to defame. Defamatory statements, motivated by ill-will or malice, have no place in a forum convened to determine the qualifications of an individual to continue in the practice of his profession. If anything, such statements serve to detour the committee from its proper channel of investigation. There is no useful purpose to be served by allowing one physician to defame another before a medical executive committee and prohibiting the defamed party from seeking a remedy. Section 1 of the Act does not expressly provide for an absolute privilege and our examination of the legislative history does not mandate a finding that an absolute privilege is what the legislature intended. We hold, therefore, that, on the basis of section 1, a qualified privilege is accorded to those testifying before the executive committee of a hospital.

* * *

A qualified privilege is by no means inadequate to protect those who offer a candid evaluation of a colleague's performance in response to a medical executive committee's inquiry. As long as the person testifying does so in good faith and with a reasonable belief as to the truth of his statements, the testimony is protected by the privilege, even though it may later be discovered that the statements were, in fact, false. We believe a qualified privilege adequately protects those physicians who, motivated by a sense of duty, respond to a medical executive committee's inquiry regarding another staff member's level of performance. Those motivated to falsely accuse out of ill-will or malice would not and should not be protected.

We also reject appellees' contention that Alexian's executive committee is a quasi-judicial office and, therefore, defendant's statements were absolutely privileged. Cases cited by the *amicus curiae* involve proceedings conducted by public governmental bodies. [ ] Such proceedings are readily distinguishable from hearings conducted by the executive committee of a hospital.

* * *

Since the trial court concluded that plaintiff's complaint was barred by the defense of absolute privilege the case must be reversed and remanded. In light of our holding that sections 1, 2, and 3 of the Medical Studies Act create a qualified privilege, we believe plaintiff's complaint contains sufficient allegations of bad faith and malice to withstand the motion to dismiss the complaint.

* * *

Notes and Questions

1. The great majority of states have adopted statutes extending a defamation privilege to participants in hospital peer review proceedings. Most of the courts that have considered the defamation issue have held the peer review privilege to be qualified rather than absolute. Only participants who act in good faith and without malice are therefore protected. See Spencer v. Community Hospital of Evanston, 87 Ill.App.3d 214, 42 Ill.Dec. 272, 408 N.E.2d 981 (1980); Mayfield v. Gleichert, 437 S.W.2d 638 (Tex.Civ.App.1969); Raymond v. Cregar, 38 N.J. 472, 185 A.2d 856 (1962); Campbell v. St. Mary's Hospital, 312 Minn. 379, 252 N.W.2d 581 (1977). A few courts have extended to participants in the peer review process an absolute privilege from defamation liability, Goodley v. Sullivant, 32 Cal. App.3d 619, 108 Cal.Rptr. 451 (1973); Franklin v. Blank, 86 N.M. 585, 525 P.2d 945 (App.1974). How does an absolute privilege benefit peer review participants more than a qualified privilege if they have in fact acted in good faith and without malice? What other defenses might a peer review participant raise in a defamation action? Should a hospital make medical staff privileges contingent on a physician's prospectively releasing the hospital and its medical staff from liability arising from the peer review or credentialing process? See, discussing these and related issues, Southwick & Slee, Quality Assurance in Health Care: Confidentiality of Information and Immunity for Participants, 5 J. Legal Med. 343, 381–393 (1984); Note, The Legal Liability of Medical Peer Review Participants for Revocation of Hospital Staff Privileges, 28 Drake L.Rev. 692 (1978–79).

2. The Health Care Quality Improvement Act of 1986 [Public Law 99–660, Title IV] provides:

Sec. 411. (a)

* * *

(2) *Protection for those providing information to professional review bodies.*—Notwithstanding any other provision of law, no person (whether as a witness or otherwise) providing information to a professional review body regarding the competence or professional conduct of a physician shall be held, by reason of having provided such information, to be liable in damages under any law of the United States or of any State (or political subdivision thereof) unless such information is false and the person providing it knew that such information was false.

* * *

The Act provides immunity against state law claims commenced after October 14, 1989. As amended by the Omnibus Budget Reconciliation Act of 1989, the Act does not preempt state laws providing additional "incentives, immunities or protection" for professional review. The principal impact of the Act is on medical staff privileges proceedings, discussed in Chapter 5, and as a defense to antitrust liability, discussed in Chapter 8.

Problem: Quality Assurance and Risk Management

Your firm represents a large (1500–bed) hospital and has handled all its tort litigation for about 15 years. The hospital is currently the defendant in two cases your firm is handling. Until three months ago, Dr. Carter was a member of the medical staff at the hospital and had general surgical privileges. Eight months ago he performed a relatively routine repair of a herniated disk. The patient, Anne Jefferson, experienced severe pain after the surgery, and a subsequent X-ray disclosed that Dr. Carter had operated on the wrong disk. A second surgery, performed by Dr. Mendoza, was necessary to correct the damage done by Dr. Carter. An incident report was filed regarding the operation, which was referred to the administrator, the hospital's insurer, the head of the surgery department, and, two months later, to your firm. After reviewing the report, the chief of surgery instigated an investigation of Dr. Carter's surgical practice at the hospital. This investigation revealed that Dr. Carter had performed an unusually large number of back surgeries at the hospital, a number of which seemed not to be indicated given the symptoms complained of, the radiologic and laboratory evidence prior to the surgery, and the results obtained. The medical audit committee referred its findings to the credentials committee, which began proceedings to reassess Dr. Carter's staff privileges at the hospital.

At these proceedings, Dr. Mendoza testified concerning Dr. Carter's qualifications. He claimed that he had frequently smelled alcohol on Dr. Carter's breath at the hospital, and had observed an open bottle of scotch behind Dr. Carter's desk one recent morning. He alleged that Dr. Carter's alcohol problem had caused him severe financial difficulties in the past three years and that Dr. Carter had carried out several unnecessary surgeries to make up for his financial losses. Dr. Mendoza asserted that he had complained frequently to the chief of the surgery department about the threat Dr. Carter posed to patients, and that it was high time some action be taken. After reviewing the report of the medical audit committee and hearing the testimony of several other witnesses, the committee asked Dr. Carter, who had been present throughout the proceedings, to leave. After deliberating for about an hour, the committee informed Dr. Carter that his privileges were being revoked.

Both Ms. Jefferson and Dr. Carter have sued the hospital. Ms. Jefferson has sued under a corporate negligence theory, claiming that the hospital was negligent for keeping Dr. Carter on its medical staff and for failing to supervise his practice. Dr. Carter has sued, claiming that his medical staff privileges were improperly terminated. He has also sued Dr. Mendoza, alleging that his remarks before the credentials committee were defamatory. Your firm is defending this suit under an agreement between the hospital and the medical staff to defend the staff for any actions arising out of hospital peer review proceedings.

Ms. Jefferson has propounded a request for production of all documents relating to Dr. Carter's conduct at the hospital, including any incident reports about her surgery or any surgery performed by Dr. Carter on any other patients, as well as the minutes, transcripts, and reports of any hospital committee that has reviewed Dr. Carter's practice. Ms. Jefferson has also noticed Dr. Mendoza to appear for a deposition, and has propounded interrogatories to the hospital inquiring when and how it became aware of deficiencies in Dr. Carter's practice.

Dr. Carter has sent you a request for production of all documents relating to the credentials review process, including minutes and transcripts of the meeting at which his staff privileges were revoked. He has also noticed for deposition Dr. Gunderson, the head of the credentials committee, intending to ask him about the committee's deliberations in executive session.

You have moved for a protective order to quash all interrogatories regarding committee proceedings and all requests for production of documents. You have also moved for a protective order to keep the depositions of Dr. Mendoza and Dr. Gunderson from going forward. Finally, you have moved to dismiss Dr. Carter's suit against Dr. Mendoza, asserting that Dr. Mendoza's comments before the committee were absolutely privileged, and claiming the benefit of a hospital medical staff bylaw which states that by accepting medical staff privileges at the hospital, all physicians waive any actions they may have against participants in hospital committee proceedings. The following statutes govern these matters in your jurisdiction:

WEST'S ANN.CAL.EVID.CODE § 1157, WEST'S
ANN.CAL.CIV.CODE §§ 43.7, 43.8, 47.2

§ 1157. Proceedings and records of medical, medical-dental, podiatric, registered dietitian, psychological or veterinary staff review committees; local medical, dental, dental hygienist, podiatric, dietetic, veterinary, chiropractic society, or state or local psychological review committees

(a) Neither the proceedings nor the records of organized committees of medical * * * staffs in hospitals having the responsibility of evaluation and improvement of the quality of care * * * shall be subject to discovery.

(b) Except as hereinafter provided, no person in attendance at a meeting of any of those committees shall be required to testify as to what transpired at that meeting.

(c) The prohibition relating to discovery or testimony does not apply to the statements made by any person in attendance at a meeting of any of those committees who is a party to an action or proceeding the subject matter of which was reviewed at that meeting, or to any person requesting hospital staff privileges, or in any action against an insurance carrier alleging bad faith by the carrier in refusing to accept a settlement offer within the policy limits.

§ 43.7 Immunity from liability; members of professional society or staff; peer review or insurance underwriting committees; hospital governing boards

There shall be no monetary liability on the part of, and no cause of action for damages shall arise against, * * * any duly appointed member of a committee * * * of a professional staff of a licensed hospital (provided the professional staff operates pursuant to written bylaws that have been approved by the governing board of the hospital), for any act or proceeding undertaken or performed within the scope of the functions of the committee * * * or any member of any peer review committee whose purpose is to review the quality of medical * * * services rendered by physicians and surgeons, * * * which committee is composed chiefly of physicians and surgeons, * * * for any act or proceeding undertaken or performed in reviewing the quality of medical * * * services rendered by physicians and surgeons, * * * or any member of the governing board of a hospital in reviewing the quality of medical services rendered by members of the staff if the committee or board member acts without malice, has made a reasonable effort to obtain the facts of the matter as to which he or she acts, and acts in reasonable belief that the action taken by him or her is warranted by the facts known to him or her after the reasonable effort to obtain facts. * * *

§ 43.8 Immunity from liability, communication on evaluation of practitioner of healing or veterinary arts or law; duration of section

In addition to the privilege afforded by Section 47, there shall be no monetary liability on the part of, and no cause of action for damages shall arise against, any person on account of the communication of information in the possession of such person to any hospital, hospital medical staff, * * * professional society, medical, dental, podiatric school, * * * professional licensing board or division, committee or panel of such licensing board, peer review committee, quality assurance committees * * * when such communication is intended to aid in the evaluation of the qualifications, fitness, character, or insurability of a practitioner of the healing * * * arts and * * * does not represent as true any matter not reasonably believed to be true. The immunities afforded by this section and by Section 43.7 shall not affect the availability of any absolute privilege which may be afforded by Section 47.

§ 47. Privileged publication or broadcast

A privileged publication or broadcast is one made—

2. In any (1) legislative or (2) judicial proceeding, or (3) in any other official proceeding authorized by law.

What arguments do you present in support of your motions? Assume further that Dr. Mendoza has informed you that he believes Ms. Jefferson's complaint is justified, and would like to testify in her behalf. Can you prevent his testimony? Assume that the federal legislation discussed in Note 2 above is now in force. How do you now advise your clients?

C. PEER REVIEW ORGANIZATIONS

The quality of medical care provided in hospitals and nursing homes was a primary focus of the Professional Standards Review Organization (PSRO) Program from 1974 through 1982, and is an important concern of the current Peer Review of Utilization and Quality of Health Care Services (PRO) program. These programs attempt to identify services that are provided inappropriately or unnecessarily to Medicare or Medicaid beneficiaries and to discourage providers from providing inappropriate care through the use of education, peer pressure, and, in extreme cases, exclusion from federal reimbursement or fines. The quality review functions of the PSROs were carried out, by and large, through medical care evaluations which audited particular problem areas of medical care delivery in health care institutions. PROs attempt not only to keep hospitals from overutilizing potentially hazardous treatments, but also to avoid underutilization that might be encouraged by Diagnosis–Related Group per case reimbursement. Since the primary focus of the federal peer review programs has been to police cost containment, the PSRO and PRO programs are discussed in Chapter 7.

Chapter 2

PROFESSIONAL LIABILITY

In the previous chapter we considered various measures of the quality of medical care and the problems of medical error. This chapter will examine the framework for a malpractice suit against health care professionals and institutions and the doctrinal and evidentiary dimensions of such litigation. As you read the chapter, think about the cases and materials on three levels. First, how is the plaintiff's case proved and how does the defendant counter it? Second, how does tort doctrine respond to different categories of medical error? And third, is malpractice litigation an appropriate way to assure the quality of medical care?

I. THE HEALTH CARE PROFESSIONAL AS MALPRACTICE DEFENDANT

A. THE STANDARD OF CARE

HALL v. HILBUN

Supreme Court of Mississippi, 1985.
466 So.2d 856.

ROBERTSON, JUSTICE, for the Court:

I.

This matter is before the Court on Petition for Rehearing presenting primarily the question whether we should, as a necessary incident to a just adjudication of the case at bar, refine and elaborate upon our law regarding (a) the standard of care applicable to physicians in medical malpractice cases and (b) the matter of how expert witnesses may be qualified in such litigation.

* * *

When this matter was before the Court on direct appeal, we determined that the judgment below in favor of the surgeon, Dr. Glyn R. Hilbun, rendered following the granting of a motion for a directed verdict, had been correctly entered. * * *

For the reasons set forth below, we now regard that our original decision was incorrect. * * *

II.

Terry O. Hall was admitted to the Singing River Hospital in Jackson County, Mississippi, in the early morning hours of May 18, 1978, complaining of abdominal discomfort. Because he was of the opinion his patient had a surgical problem, Dr. R.D. Ward, her physician, requested Dr. Glyn R. Hilbun, a general surgeon, to enter the case for consultation. Examination suggested that the discomfort and illness were probably caused by an obstruction of the small bowel. Dr. Hilbun recommended an exploratory laporatomy [sic]. Consent being given, Dr. Hilbun performed the surgery about noon on May 20, 1978, with apparent success.

Following surgery Mrs. Hall was moved to a recovery room at 1:35 p.m., where Dr. Hilbun remained in attendance with her until about 2:50 p.m. At that time Mrs. Hall was alert and communicating with him. All vital signs were stable. Mrs. Hall was then moved to a private room where she expired some 14 hours later.

On May 19, 1980, Glenn Hall commenced this wrongful death action by the filing of his complaint * * *.

* * *

At trial Glenn Hall, plaintiff below and appellant here, described the fact of the surgery. He then testified that he remained with his wife in her hospital room from the time of her arrival from the recovery room at approximately 3:00 p.m. on May 20, 1978, until she ultimately expired at approximately 5:00 a.m. on the morning of May 21. Hall stated that his wife complained of pain at about 9:00 p.m. and was given morphine for relief, after which she fell asleep. Thereafter, Hall observed that his wife had difficulty in breathing which he reported to the nurses. He inquired if something was wrong and was told his wife was all right and that such breathing was not unusual following surgery. The labored breathing then subsided for an hour or more. Later, Mrs. Hall awakened and again complained of pain in her abdomen and requested a sedative, which was administered following which she fell asleep. Mrs. Hall experienced further difficulty in breathing, and her husband reported this, too. Again, a nurse told Hall that such was normal, that patients sometimes make a lot of noise after surgery.

After the nurse left the following occurred, according to Hall.

> [A]t this time I followed her [the nurse] into the hall and walked in the hall a minute. Then I walked back into the room, and walked back out in the hall. Then I walked into the room again and I walked over to my wife and put my hand on her arm because she had stopped making that noise. Then I bent over and flipped the light on and got closer to her where I could see her, and it looked like she was having a real hard problem breathing and she was turning pale or a bluish color. And I went to screaming.

Dr. Hilbun was called and came to the hospital immediately only to find his patient had expired. The cause of the death of Terry O. Hall was subsequently determined to be adult respiratory distress syndrome (cardio-respiratory failure).

Dr. Hilbun was called as an adverse witness and gave testimony largely in accord with that above. * * *.

Dr. Hilbun stated the surgery was performed on a Saturday. Following the patient's removal to her room, he "went home and was on call that weekend for anything that might come up." Dr. Hilbun made no follow-up contacts with his patient, nor did he make any inquiry that evening regarding Mrs. Hall's post-operative progress. Moreover, he was *not* contacted by the nursing staff or others concerning Mrs. Hall's condition during the afternoon or evening of May 20 following surgery, or the early morning hours of May 21, although the exhibits introduced at trial disclose fluctuations in the vital signs late in the evening of May 20 and more so, in the early morning hours of May 21. Dr. Hilbun's next contact with his patient came when he was called by Glenn Hall about 4:55 or 5:00 that morning. By then it was too late.

* * *

The autopsy performed upon Mrs. Hall's body revealed the cause of death and, additionally, disclosed that a laporatomy [sic] sponge had been left in the patient's abdominal cavity. The evidence, however, without contradiction establishes that the sponge did not contribute to Mrs. Hall's death. Although the sponge may ultimately have caused illness, this possibility was foreclosed by the patient's untimely death.

Plaintiff's theory of the case centered around the post-operative care provided by Dr. Hilbun. Two areas of fault suggested were Dr. Hilbun's failure to make inquiry regarding his patient's post-operative course prior to his retiring on the night of May 20 and his alleged failure to give appropriate post-operative instructions to the hospital nursing staff.

When questioned at trial, Dr. Hilbun first stated that he had practiced for 16 years in the Singing River Hospital and was familiar with the routine of making surgical notes, i.e., a history of the surgery. He explained that the post-operative orders were noted on the record out of courtesy by Dr. Judy Fabian, the anesthesiologist on the case. He stated such orders were customarily approved by his signature or he would add or subtract from the record to reflect the exact situation.

[Dr. Hilbun testified as to the post-operative orders noted in the medical records as of May 20, 1978. Mrs. Hall had a nasogastric tube, an i.v., a catheter; she was receiving medications for pain, nausea, and infections.] His testimony continued:

Q. Now after this surgery, while Mrs. Hall was in the recovery room did I understand you to say earlier that you checked on her there?

A. When I got through operating on Mrs. Hall, with this major surgical procedure in an emergency situation—and I always do—I went to the recovery room with Mrs. Hall, stayed in the recovery room with Mrs. Hall, listened to her chest, took her vital signs, stayed there with her and discharged her to the floor. The only time I left the recovery room was to go into the waiting room and tell Mr. Hall. Mrs. Hall waked up, I talked to her, she said she was cold. She was completely alert.

* * *

Q. Now, you went to the recovery room to see her because you were still her physician following her post-surgery?

A. I was one of her physicians. I operated on her, and I go to the recovery room with everybody.

Q. Okay. You were the surgeon and you were concerned about the surgical procedures and how she was doing post-operatively, or either you are not concerned with your patients, how they do post-operatively?

A. As I said, I go to the recovery room with every one of my patients.

Q. Then you are still the doctor?

A. I was one of her physicians.

Q. Okay. And you customarily follow your patients following the surgery to see how they are doing as a result of the surgery, because you are the surgeon. Is that correct?

A. Yes.

* * *

Q. How long do you follow a patient like Terry Hall?

A. Until she leaves the hospital.

Q. Okay. So ever how long she is in the hospital, you are going to continue to see her?

A. As long as my services are needed.

Insofar as the record reflects, Dr. Hilbun gave the nursing staff no instructions regarding the post-operative monitoring and care of Mrs. Hall beyond those [summarized above]. Dr. Hilbun had no contact with Mrs. Hall after 3:00 p.m. on May 20. Fourteen hours later she was dead.

The plaintiff called Dr. S.O. Hoerr, a retired surgeon of Cleveland, Ohio, as an expert witness. The record reflects that Dr. Hoerr is a *cum laude* graduate of the Harvard Medical School, enjoys the respect of his peers, and has had many years of surgical practice. Through him the plaintiff sought to establish that there is a national standard of surgical practice and surgical care of patients in the United States to which all surgeons, including Dr. Hilbun, are obligated to adhere. Dr. Hoerr conceded that he did not know for a fact the standard of professional skill, including surgical skills and post-operative care, practiced by general surgeons in Pascagoula, Mississippi, but that he did know what the standard should have been.

* * * [T]he trial court ruled that Dr. Hoerr was not qualified to give an opinion as to whether Dr. Hilbun's post-operative regimen departed from the obligatory standard of care. * * *.

* * *

Parts of Dr. Hoerr's testimony excluded under the trial judge's ruling follow:

A. My opinion is that she [Mrs. Hall] did not receive the type of care that she should have received from the general surgical specialist and that he [Dr. Hilbun] was negligent in not following this patient; contacting, checking on the condition of his patient sometime in the evening of May 20th. *It is important in the post-operative care of patients to remember that very serious complications can follow abdominal operations, in particular in the first few hours after a surgical procedure.* And this can be inward bleeding; it can be an explosive development in an infection; or *it can be the development of a serious pulmonary complication, as it was in this patient. As a result of her condition, it is my opinion that he lost the opportunity to diagnose a condition, which in all probability could have been diagnosed at the time by an experienced general surgeon, one with expertise in thoracic surgery. And then appropriate treatment could have been undertaken to abort the complications and save her life.*

There are different ways that a surgeon can keep track of his patient—"follow her" as the expression goes—besides a bedside visit, which is the best way and which need not be very long at all, in which the vital signs are checked over. The surgeon gets a general impression of what's going on. He can delegate this responsibility to a competent physician, who need not be a surgeon but could be a knowledgeable family practitioner. He could call in and ask to speak to the registered nurse in charge of the patient and determine through her what the vital signs are, and if she is an experienced Registered Nurse what her evaluation of the patient is. *From my review of the record, none of these things took place, and there is no effort as far as I can see that Dr. Hilbun made any effort to find out what was going on with this patient during that period of time.* I might say or add an additional belief that I felt that the nursing responsibility which should have been exercised was not exercised, particularly at the 4:00 a.m. level when the pulse rate was recorded at 140 per minute without any effort as far as I can see to have any physician see the patient or to get in touch with the operating surgeon and so on.

There is an additional thing that Dr. Hilbun could have done if he felt that the nursing services might be spotty—sometimes good, sometimes bad. This is commonly done in Columbus, Ohio, in Ashtabula, Pascagoula, etcetera. *He could put limits on the degree in which the vital signs can vary, expressing the order that he should be called if they exceeded that.* Examples would be: Call me if the pulse rate goes over 110; call me if the temperature exceeds 101; call me if the blood pressure drops below 100. There is a simple way of spelling out for the nursing services what the limits of discretion belong to them and the point at which the doctor should be called.

* * *

Dr. Hilbun did not place any orders on the chart for the nurses to call him in the event of a change in the vital signs of Mrs. Hall. He normally made afternoon rounds between 4:00 and 5:00 p.m. but didn't recall whether he went by to see her before going home. Dr. Hilbun was on call at the hospital that weekend for anything which might come up. Subsequent to the operation and previous to Mrs. Hall's death, he was called about one other person on the same ward, one door down, twice during the night. He made no inquiry concerning Mrs. Hall, nor did he see or communicate with her.

Dr. Donald Dohn, of expertise unquestioned by plaintiff and with years of practical experience, gave testimony for the defendant. He had practiced on the staff at the Cleveland Clinic Foundation in Cleveland, Ohio, beginning in 1958. Fortuitously, he had moved to Pascagoula, Mississippi, about one month before the trial. Dr. Dohn stated he had practiced in the Singing River Hospital for a short time and there was a great difference in the standard of care in medical procedures in Cleveland, Ohio, and those in Pascagoula, Mississippi. Although he had practiced three weeks in Pascagoula, he was still in the process of acquainting himself with the local conditions. He explained the differences as follows:

Well, there are personnel differences. There are equipment differences. There are diagnostic differences. There are differences in staff responsibility and so on. For example, at the Cleveland Clinic on our service we had ten residents that we were training. They worked with us as our right hands. Here we have no staff. So it is up to us to do the things that our residents would have done there. There we had a team of five or six nurses and other personnel in the operating room to help us. Here we have nurses in the operating room, but there is no assigned team. You get the luck of the draw that day. I am finding out these things myself. Up there it is a big center; a thousand beds, and it is a regional center. We have tremendous advantages with technical systems, various types of x-ray equipment that is [sic] sophisticated. Also in terms of the intensive care unit, we had a Neurosurgical Intensive Care with people who were specially trained as a team to work there. From my standpoint personally, I seldom had to do much paperwork there as compared to what I have to do now. I have to dictate everything and take all my notes. So, as you can see, there is a difference.

Finally, he again stated the standard of care in Ohio and the standard of care in the Singing River Hospital are very different, although it is obvious to the careful reader of Dr. Dohn's testimony that in so doing he had reference to the differences in equipment, personnel and resources and not differences in the standards of skill, medical knowledge and general medical competence a physician could be expected to bring to bear upon the treatment of a patient.

At the conclusion of the plaintiff's case, defendant moved for a directed verdict on the obvious grounds that, the testimony of Drs. Hoerr and Sachs having been excluded, the Plaintiff had failed to present a legally sufficient quantum of evidence to establish a prima facie case. The Circuit Court granted the motion. * * *

III.

A. GENERAL CONSIDERATIONS

Medical malpractice is legal fault by a physician or surgeon. It arises from the failure of a physician to provide the quality of care required by law. When a physician undertakes to treat a patient, he takes on an obligation enforceable at law to use minimally sound medical judgment and render minimally competent care in the course of the services he provides. A physician does not guarantee recovery. If a patient sustains injury because of the physician's failure to perform the duty he has assumed under our law, the physician may be liable in damages. A competent physician is not liable *per se* for a mere error of judgment, mistaken diagnosis or the occurrence of an undesirable result.

The twin principles undergirding our stewardship of the law regulating professional liability of physicians have always been reason and fairness. For years in medical malpractice litigation we regarded as reasonable and fair what came to be known as the "locality rule" (but which has always consisted of at least two separate rules, one a rule of substantive law, the other a rule of evidence).

* * *

Both "prongs" of the locality rule have fallen under attack in recent years. It is urged that the circumstances which have given rise to the rules have passed out of existence. The practice of medicine in general and medical malpractice litigation in particular are said to have achieved a level of sophistication that require a modernization of our law. There is merit in the attack. Suffice it to say that the rules we have heretofore employed do not seem nearly so consonant with reason and fairness as they once did.

* * *

C. THE PHYSICIAN'S DUTY OF CARE: A PRIMARY RULE OF SUBSTANTIVE LAW

1. The Backdrop

* * *

2. *The Inevitable Ascendency of National Standards*

* * *

We would have to put our heads in the sand to ignore the "nationalization" of medical education and training. Medical school admission standards are similar across the country. Curricula are substantially the same. Internship and residency programs for those entering medical specialities have substantially common components. Nationally uniform standards are enforced in the case of certification of specialists. Differences and changes in these areas occur temporally, not geographically.

Physicians are far more mobile than they once were. They frequently attend medical school in one state, do a residency in another, establish a practice in a third and after a period of time relocate to a fourth. All the while, they have ready access to professional and scientific journals and seminars for continuing medical education from across the country. Common sense and experience inform us that the laws of medicine do not vary from state to state in anything like the manner our public law does.

Medicine is a science, though its practice be an art (as distinguished from a business). Regarding the basic matter of the learning, skill and competence a physician may bring to bear in the treatment of a given patient, state lines are largely irrelevant. That a patient's temperature is 105 degrees means the same in New York as in Mississippi. Bones break and heal in Washington the same as in Florida, in Minnesota the same as in Texas. * * *

It is absurd to think that a physician examining a patient in his or her office would, by reference to the genuine health care needs of the patient, say: Because I practice in Mississippi (or the Deep South), I will make this diagnosis and prescribe this medication and course of treatment, but if I were in Iowa, I would do otherwise. We are confident (as the medical community of this state is no doubt confident) that Mississippi's physicians are capable of rendering and do in fact render a quality of care on a par with that in other parts of the country.

3. *The Competence–Based National Standard of Care: Herein Of the Limited Role Of Local Custom*

All of the above informs our understanding and articulation of the competence-based duty of care. Each physician may with reason and fairness be expected to possess or have reasonable access to such medical knowledge as is commonly possessed or reasonably available to minimally competent physicians in the same specialty or general field of practice throughout the United States, to have a realistic understanding of the limitations on his or her knowledge or competence, and, in general, to exercise minimally adequate medical judgment. Beyond that, each physician has a duty to have a practical working knowledge of the facilities, equipment, resources (including personnel in health related fields and their general level of knowledge and competence), and options (including what specialized services or facilities may be available in larger communities, e.g., Memphis, Birmingham, Jackson, New Orleans, etc.) reasonably available to him or her as well as the practical limitations on same.

In the care and treatment of each patient, each physician has a non-delegable duty to render professional services consistent with that objectively ascertained minimally acceptable level of competence he may be expected to apply given the qualifications and level of expertise he holds himself out as possessing and given the circumstances of the particular case.   The professional services contemplated within this duty concern the entire caring process, including but not limited to examination, history, testing, diagnosis, course of treatment, medication, surgery, follow-up, after-care and the like.

* * *

Mention should be made in this context of the role of good medical judgment which, because medicine is not an exact science, must be brought to bear in diagnostic and treatment decisions daily.   Some physicians are more reluctant to recommend radical surgery than are other equally competent physicians.   There exist legitimate differences of opinion regarding medications to be employed in particular contexts. "Waiting periods" and their duration are the subject of bona fide medical controversy.   What diagnostic tests should be performed is a matter of particularly heated debate in this era of ever-escalating health care costs.   We must be vigilant that liability never be imposed upon a physician for the mere exercise of a bona fide medical judgment which turns out, with the benefit of 20–20 hindsight (a) to have been mistaken, and (b) to be contrary to what a qualified medical expert witness in the exercise of his good medical judgment would have done. We repeat: a physician may incur civil liability only when the quality of care he renders (including his judgment calls) falls below minimally acceptable levels.

Different medical judgments are made by physicians whose offices are across the street from one another.   Comparable differences in medical judgment or opinion exist among physicians geographically separated by much greater distances, and in this sense local custom does and must continue to play a role within our law, albeit a limited one.

We recognize that customs vary within given medical communities and from one medical community to another.   Conformity with established medical custom practiced by minimally competent physicians in a given area, while evidence of performance of the duty of care, may never be conclusive of such compliance.   [   ] The content of the duty of care must be objectively determined by reference to the availability of medical and practical knowledge which would be brought to bear in the treatment of like or similar patients under like or similar circumstances by minimally competent physicians in the same field, given the facilities, resources and options available. The content of the duty of care may be informed by local medical custom but never subsumed by it.

* * *

4. The Resources–Based Caveat to the National Standard of Care

The duty of care, as it thus emerges from considerations of reason and fairness, when applied to the facts of the world of medical science and practice, takes two forms: (a) a duty to render a quality of care consonant with the level of medical and practical knowledge the physician may reasonably be expected to possess and the medical judgment he may be expected to exercise, and (b) a duty based upon the adept use of such medical facilities, services, equipment and options as are reasonably available. With respect to this second form of the duty, we regard that there remains a core of validity to the premises of the old locality rule.

* * *

A physician practicing in Noxubee County, for example, may hardly be faulted for failure to perform a CAT scan when the necessary facilities and equipment are not reasonably available. In contradistinction, objectively reasonable expectations regarding the physician's knowledge, skill, capacity for sound medical judgment and general competence are, consistent with his field of practice and the facts and circumstances in which the patient may be found, *the same everywhere.*

* * *

As a result of its resources-based component, the physician's nondelegable duty of care is this: given the circumstances of each patient, each physician has a duty to use his or her knowledge and therewith treat through maximum reasonable medical recovery, each patient, with such reasonable diligence, skill, competence, and prudence as are practiced by minimally competent physicians in the same specialty or general field of practice throughout the United States, who have available to them the same general facilities, services, equipment and options.

* * *

As we deal with general principles, gray areas necessarily exist. One involves the case where needed specialized facilities and equipment are not available locally but are reasonably accessible in major medical centers—New Orleans, Jackson, Memphis. Here as elsewhere the local physician is held to minimally acceptable standards. In determining whether the physician's actions comport with his duty of care, consideration must always be given to the time factor—is the physician confronted with what reasonably appears to be a medical emergency, or does it appear likely that the patient may be transferred to an appropriate medical center without substantial risk to the health or life of the patient? Consideration must also be given to the economic factors—are the proposed transferee facilities sufficiently superior to justify the trouble and expense of transfer? Further discussion of these factors should await proper cases.

D. Who May Qualify As Expert Medical Witness In Malpractice Case: A rule of evidence

As a general rule, if scientific, technical or other specialized knowledge will assist the trier of fact to understand the evidence or to determine a fact in issue, a witness qualified as an expert by knowledge, skill, experience, training or education (or a combination thereof), coupled with independence and lack of bias, may testify thereto in the form of an opinion or otherwise. Medical malpractice cases generally require expert witnesses to assist the trier of fact to understand the evidence. [ ]

Generally, where the expert lives or where he or she practices his or her profession has no relevance *per se* with respect to whether a person may be qualified and accepted by the court as an expert witness. There is no reason on principle why these factors should have *per se* relevance in medical malpractice cases.

* * *

In view of the refinements in the physician's duty of care * * * we hold that a qualified medical expert witness may without more express an opinion regarding the meaning and import of the duty of care * * *, given the peculiar circumstances of the case. Based on the information reasonably available to the physician, i.e., symptoms, history, test results, results of the doctor's own physical examination, x-rays, vital signs, etc., a qualified medical expert may express an opinion regarding the conclusions (possible diagnoses or areas for further examination and testing) minimally knowledgeable and competent physicians in the same specialty or general field of practice would draw, or actions (not tied to the availability of specialized facilities or equipment not generally available) they would take.

Before the witness may go further, he must be familiarized with the facilities, resources, services and options available. This may be done in any number of ways. The witness may prior to trial have visited the facilities, etc. He may have sat in the courtroom and listened as other witnesses described the facilities. He may have known and over the years interacted with physicians in the area. There are no doubt many other ways in which this could be done, but, significantly, we should allow the witness to be made familiar with the facilities (and customs) of the medical community in question via a properly predicated and phrased hypothetical question.

Once he has become informed of the facilities, etc. available to the defendant physician, the qualified medical expert witness may express an opinion what the care duty of the defendant physician was and whether the acts or omissions of the defendant physician were in compliance with, or fell substantially short of compliance with, that duty.

At this point it is appropriate to note the earnestness with which counsel for Dr. Hilbun, no doubt purporting to speak on behalf of the medical community generally, begs for protection from the circuit-riding charlatan, the man from out of town with a briefcase. The instrument with which they would have us afford this protection is too blunt.   * * *

* * *

V.   DISPOSITION OF THE CASE AT BAR

* * *

Without further ado, and applying to the facts of this case the legal principles stated above, we hold as follows: to the extent that the testimony of Drs. Hoerr and Sachs was excluded because these two physicians lived and had their practices in Cleveland, Ohio, the trial court erred. To the extent that the testimony of each of these physicians was excluded in its entirety because they were supposedly not familiar with the standard of care in Pascagoula, Mississippi, in general or in the Singing River Hospital in particular, the trial court erred.

Without the testimony of Drs. Hoerr and Sachs, Plaintiff Hall has no case. With that testimony, Plaintiff Hall has a fighting chance to survive a motion for a directed verdict. We say this because the trial judge, when he considered and granted defendant's motion for a directed verdict, was proceeding without reference to the testimony of Drs. Hoerr and Sachs which had been excluded. The core holding of today's decision is that the trial judge erred when he directed a verdict for defendant without taking into account the testimony of plaintiff's two out of state experts. That error was prejudicial because the testimony of Drs. Hoerr and Sachs does suggest a basis on which reasonable minds might determine that Dr. Hilbun breached the duty of care he owed to Terry O. Hall. The judgment below is reversed, and this case is remanded for a new trial.

* * *

Notes and Questions

1. How did the court in *Hall v. Hilbun* view the customary practice of the defendant's medical specialty? Why did it adopt this position? How much of a burden might it be for a defendant to rebut the plaintiff's evidence on customary practice?

2. The standards by which the delivery of professional medical services is judged are not normally established by either judge or jury. The medical profession itself sets the standards of practice and the courts enforce these standards in tort suits. Defendants trying to prove a standard of care normally present expert testimony describing the actual pattern of medical practice, without any reference to the effectiveness of that practice. Many jurisdictions give professional medical standards con-

clusive weight, so that the trier of fact is not allowed to reject the practice as improper. See, e.g., Holt v. Godsil, 447 So.2d 191 (Ala.1984); Senesac v. Associates in Obstetrics and Gynecology, 141 Vt. 310, 449 A.2d 900 (1982). See generally Morris, Custom and Negligence, 42 Colum.L.Rev. 1147 (1942).

Should conformity to customary practice be a conclusive shield for a health care professional? What justifies judicial deference? In tort litigation not involving professionals, courts are willing to reject customary practice if they find the practice dangerous or out of date. See King, In Search of a Standard of Care for the Medical Profession—the "Accepted Practice" Formula, 28 Vand.L.Rev. 1213, 1236 (1975). Critics such as King worry that standard practice may at times be little more than a routine into which physicians have drifted by default, whereas what is needed is aspiration to standards set by professional leaders.

3. Could a plaintiff use the studies cited in Chapter 1 to support a position that the efficacy of a standard practice is not proven? How would a court react to such studies?

Note: The Locality Rule

Hall provides an excellent discussion of the locality rule, which determines what kind of medical expert can testify for the plaintiff in a malpractice case. Courts have been moving from the locality rule to a similar locality or a national standard, in part due to worries about a "conspiracy of silence" that unfairly limits the pool of available experts. Doctors do not like to testify against one another, as the court noted in Mulder v. Parke Davis & Co., 288 Minn. 332, 181 N.W.2d 882 (1970):

> All too frequently, and perhaps understandably, practicing physicians are reluctant to testify against one another. Unfortunately, the medical profession has been slow to fashion machinery for making impartial and objective assessments of the performance of their fellow practitioners. Consequently, in actions of this kind claimants are required to rely on licensed physicians who are not in the mainstream of the practice.

For a first hand account of this conspiracy by an M.D.–J.D., see Robinson, Why the Conspiracy of Silence Won't Die, Medical Economics 180 (Feb. 20, 1984). See also Pearson, The Role of Custom in Medical Malpractice Cases, 51 Ind.L.J. 528 (1976).

The locality rule has been viewed as a subsidy for rural areas, one of the bundle of incentives to attract doctors to areas that they won't otherwise find attractive. Rural communities face substantial difficulties in getting doctors: salaries are lower, availability of peers is limited, health insurance for doctor and patient may be harder to get. Absent the added protection of the locality rule, it is argued, rural areas will suffer even more from little or no medical care. Karlson and Erwin, Medical Malpractice: Informed Consent to the Locality Rule, 12 Ind.L.Rev. 653, 664–657 (1979).

The response of the court in *Hall* and that of other courts to this "subsidy" justification and to the locality rule generally is that technology and training have made medical practice national in scope. See also

Shilkret v. Annapolis Emergency Hospital Ass'n., 276 Md. 187, 349 A.2d 245 (1975).

Access by physicians to computer databases makes information on advances in medical knowledge instantly available whether the doctor is rural or urban. MEDLINE, the largest, has available over five million references and articles from 4,000 journals. The level of skill required to access such a database has steadily decreased, with more user friendly command structures and access through commercial services such as MED-LARS and MEDIS. A physician with a phone, a modem and a personal computer can pay a monthly subscription fee and then call up information 24 hours a day. While no case has yet required an individual physician to have access to such a service, the argument is a plausible one.

Does computerized research create a nationwide standard of care against which to judge physicians in all areas? Not only will such access continue to diminish the importance of the locality rule or its manifestations, but it may also limit the "respectable minority" rule and other judgment rules by narrowing the range of variation in medical opinion as to what is acceptable. A physician relying on a contraindicated drug, an outdated surgical technique, or an inappropriate description of risk factors in getting a patient's informed consent may be attacked by the plaintiff using the results of a computer search. See Warrick v. Giron, 290 N.W.2d 166 (Minn.1980) (the defendants introduced a computerized search they had conducted, revealing no evidence that the surgical and anesthesiological techniques utilized by the defendants were improper.)

Research findings put in question the rural practice subsidy justification for a locality rule. One study of causes of the frequency and severity of malpractice claims concluded that urbanization was the "single most powerful predictor" of the frequency and severity of claims. P. Danzon, Medical Malpractice 82–83 (1985). Danzon qualified this in a later study, concluding that urbanization predicts frequency of claims filed, but is negatively related to the number of paid claims. This may suggest that more "frivolous" claims are filed in urban areas. See Danzon, The Frequency and Severity of Medical Malpractice Claims: New Evidence, 49 Law & Contemp.Probs. 57, 69 (1986). Other factors, such as complexity of medical facilities and per capita income, did not account for urban litigiousness. For poorly understood reasons, rural practitioners are not likely to get sued, perhaps because of more personal relationships with their patients or the attitudes of rural residents generally toward litigation.

A national standard of practice may not exist for many procedures, and the "highest and best" practice may not be the safest or most effective in the long run. Substantial regional variations exist in the use of many procedures, with no apparent differences in outcome (life expectancy, morbidity, days missed from work). Different practice styles exist in different regions, and even within states, based on local concepts of good practice.

What do these findings suggest? Why might the level of claims filed be higher in urban areas than in rural areas? Does the evidence on variation in medical practice among regions support the locality rule? Might it be better to allow the locality rule in a tort suit as a way of supporting local practices against a monolithic national practice under some circumstances? When might this make sense?

The debate over the locality rule has been largely won by the national standard test, as *Hall* evidences. But many courts, like *Hall,* also allow evidence describing the practice limitations under which the defendant labors. *Hall*'s "resource component" allows the trier of fact to consider the facilities, staff and other equipment available to the practitioner in the institution, following the general rule that courts should take into account the locality, proximity of specialists and special facilities for diagnosis and treatment. Blair v. Eblen, 461 S.W.2d 370 (Ky.1970); Restatement (Second) of Torts, sec. 299A, Comment g. ("Allowance must be made also for the type of community in which the actor carries on his practice. A country doctor cannot be expected to have the equipment, facilities, experience, knowledge or opportunity to obtain it, afforded him by a large city.")

1. Raising the Standard

The customary or accepted practice standard follows the general tort rule that an expert is held to the standard of his profession, not merely the standard of a reasonable and prudent person. Evolving medical practices often create tensions for the physician, particularly where the older practice may be dangerous in light of new evidence. The following case raises issues not only of the standard of care in the face of changing practices, but also of medical research and its costs.

BURTON v. BROOKLYN DOCTORS HOSPITAL

Supreme Court of New York, Appellate Division, 1982.
88 A.D.2d 217, 452 N.Y.S.2d 875.

SULLIVAN, JUSTICE.

Plaintiff, blind since infancy from a disease known as retrolental fibroplasia (RLF), caused by his exposure to a prolonged liberal application of oxygen, has recovered a substantial judgment for medical malpractice against New York Hospital, where he was treated as a premature infant, and two of its physicians, all of whom appeal.

Born five to six weeks premature at Brooklyn Doctors Hospital on July 3, 1953, plaintiff, who weighed only 1362 grams or three pounds at birth, was transferred the next day to New York Hospital, which had been designated by the City of New York as a premature nursery care center. Transfer was automatic in cases where an infant weighed less than 1500 grams. At the time, more than half of all premature babies of plaintiff's size died in infancy; many of the survivors either sustained brain damage or were blinded by RLF, a disease which, first identified in 1942, reached epidemic proportions in this country in the late 1940's and early 1950's. The increase in the incidence of RLF coincided with the widespread advances in the development of life-saving techniques in treating premature infants, all of which revolved around the liberal use of oxygen.

RLF is a progressive disease consisting of five stages. Initially, the blood vessels to the retina constrict. In the second stage the vessels enlarge, causing hemorrhaging into the retina. Further bleeding into the inside of the eye develops in the third stage, and in the fourth a localized tear in the retina ("retinal detachment") occurs. Finally, the retina detaches and a fibroid mass develops over the crystalline lens of the eye. The disease is irreversible in the fourth and fifth stages.

In the summer of 1953 a significant segment of the medical community continued to believe that the liberal administration of oxygen to prematures was important in preventing death or brain damage. Yet, a respected body of medical opinion believed that oxygen contributed to RLF. Thus, the medical profession was confronted with a terrible dilemma—the antidote to two problems, death and brain damage, appeared to be the cause of another, blindness. One court, commenting on the perplexity of the problem, spoke of the anxiety of those physicians who "tried to steer their tiny patients between the Scylla of blindness and the Charybdis of brain damage." [ ]

On July 1, 1953, just two days before plaintiff's birth and after years of uncoordinated and inconclusive independent investigation, a national human research study known as the Cooperative Study of Retrolental Fibroplasia and the Use of Oxygen was undertaken in an attempt to determine the role of oxygen in RLF and the effect of its withdrawal or curtailment. The Cooperative Study, whose conclusions were announced on September 19, 1954 and published in October of 1956, found that prolonged liberal use of oxygen was the critical factor in the development of RLF, and that curtailment of the supply of oxygen to premature infants after 48 hours to clinical need decreased the incidence of RLF without increasing the risk of death or brain damage.

While liberal exposure to oxygen continued to be routine treatment for premature babies at the time of plaintiff's birth, the view that increased oxygen was a necessary life saver had, as already noted, become suspect. New York Hospital, for instance, had, from January 1952 to June 1953, conducted its own study of the effects of oxygen on premature infants and concluded "that prolonged oxygen therapy may be related to the production of RLF * * *." The results of that 18 month study were announced by the hospital on June 16, 1953 at a meeting attended by its pediatricians and ophthalmologists. Because the preliminary results of its investigation were considered to be insufficient, however, the hospital decided to become a participant in the Cooperative Study. This was the situation that existed on July 4, 1953 when plaintiff entered New York Hospital.

[The infant plaintiff was in good condition when he entered the hospital on July 4, 1953, "a vigorous premature infant * * *". He was placed on the "serious" list, however, because of weight loss. Dr. Lawrence Ross, a pediatric resident, had ordered the plaintiff placed in an incubator with oxygen at three to four liters.]

At 11:15 that evening Dr. Ross, aware that oxygen had been implicated as a cause of RLF, ordered that oxygen be "reduced * * * as tolerated." Dr. Ross testified that the order to reduce oxygen was "good medical practice and in accordance with [my] judgment." * * * [The nurses reduced the oxygen from three to two and one-half liters, and plaintiff's condition remained good.]

* * *

On July 6th at 2:10 p.m., Dr. Mary Engle, a member of the hospital staff and an instructor in pediatrics at New York Hospital's affiliate, * * * on instructions from Dr. Levine, the Chairman of the Department of Pediatrics, entered an order in the hospital record, "Oxygen study: In prolonged oxygen at concentration greater than 50%." At the time Dr. Engle was serving as Dr. Levine's assistant for purposes of coordinating the hospital's participation in the Cooperative Study. Dr. Engle conceded that she countermanded Dr. Ross's order without examining plaintiff and without ever speaking to his parents. She testified further that she had no responsibility for the care and treatment of premature infants or the supervision of residents.

The Cooperative Study's methodology was to enter and observe prematures of 1500 grams or less at birth after 48 hours. Its protocol provided that one out of every three such premature infants be placed in an increased oxygen environment, while two out of three be placed in reduced oxygen. This method of distribution was designed to subject the least number of babies to the risk of blindness that statistics would permit. Of the approximately 760 babies who were placed in the Study throughout the United States, only 68 were placed in increased oxygen.

As a result of Dr. Engle's order the concentrations of oxygen went from 2½ to 5 liters in one day, and, over a span of 28 days in increased dosages up to a high of 9 liters, and from an environment of 30% oxygen to a high of 82%. Dr. Engle testified that at the time of plaintiff's birth the medical community was unsure whether premature babies were better or worse off in routine (increased) oxygen, but conceded that the doctors familiar with the earlier New York Hospital study, of which she was a co-author, had concluded that increased oxygen might be unnecessary for premature babies. Nevertheless, she stated, prolonged oxygen was the routine practice. New York Hospital's manual on the "Management of Premature Infants", which set forth the hospital's rules relating to premature care, provided for the liberal administration of oxygen.

* * *

[The plaintiff's eyes were examined two or three times during the 28 day high oxygen state, and by August 19 examinations revealed that " * * * the swelling had totally enveloped the eyes."]

* * *

Except for faint light perception in his left eye plaintiff is totally blind. He suffers daily pain and irritation, which has worsened in recent years and which he eases by rubbing and pressing his eyes. Except for a brief stint in his family's business answering phones, and a part time job as an interviewer with the Blind Guild he has been unable to find employment. Eventually, because his eyes are shrinking, they will have to be enucleated and replaced with plastic ones.

In 1975 plaintiff commenced this action against New York Hospital, Dr. Ross and Dr. Engle, alleging medical malpractice and the failure to obtain informed consent from his parents before placing him in an increased oxygen environment. The jury absolved Dr. Ross from liability for malpractice, but found him liable for failing to obtain informed consent. New York Hospital and Dr. Engle were found liable under both theories.

Plaintiff's proof clearly established that the prolonged liberal administration of oxygen to which he was subjected caused his blindness, and defendants do not challenge this finding. Since 1954 prolonged exposure to oxygen has been uniformly recognized as the leading cause of RLF. Of the several issues raised defendants' principal contention, as it was at trial, is that the treatment which plaintiff received at New York Hospital was in accordance with applicable 1953 community standards. The question presented to the jury was whether defendants followed sound medical practice in 1953 in permitting plaintiff to be exposed to an increased oxygen environment for a prolonged period, even though it was a common practice at the time, when they were aware of the possibility that RLF might result. Ancillary to that question was whether, even if defendants exercised proper medical judgment, they should have informed plaintiff's parents of the risks involved, and obtained their consent.

We believe that the evidence supports a finding that Dr. Engle and the hospital failed in their duty to plaintiff in both respects and, thus, the verdict of liability against them should stand. We further find that Dr. Ross, who did not order the increase in oxygen, and whose own order to reduce oxygen was countermanded, should not have been found liable at all.

Any analysis of defendants' liability must take into account that when plaintiff arrived at New York Hospital he was a healthy baby, without any unusual conditions, except that he was premature and had lost some weight, a not atypical post-birth phenomenon. The treating resident, Dr. Ross, initially placed him in a higher than average oxygen environment, as was common practice at the time, but, recognizing the baby's good health, directed that the oxygen be reduced as tolerated. Yet, Dr. Engle, who was not plaintiff's physician, and who admitted that she had neither examined the baby nor had any responsibility for the care of premature infants, changed the oxygen supply and ordered a drastic increase. No adverse change in the baby's medical condition had been noted at the time. He was progressing well, and indicated no need for additional oxygen. Thus, it seems reasonably clear that Dr. Engle's order to increase the oxygen supply was an administrative judgment, based upon a random allocation of babies into one of two groups for monitoring as part of the Cooperative Study. Neither the hospital nor Dr. Engle offered any medical reason for placing plaintiff in routine (increased) oxygen. Both Dr. Engle and the hospital were aware of the dangers of excess oxygen, and, more importantly, knew or are charged with the knowledge that plaintiff was progressing well in a curtailed oxygen environment.

Although the conventional medical wisdom at the time believed that increased oxygen was essential to the survival of premature babies, the hospital and Dr. Engle cannot avail themselves of the shield of acceptable medical practice when a number of studies, including their own, had already indicated that increased oxygen was both unnecessary and dangerous, particularly for an otherwise healthy baby, and especially when the attending physician, who had primary responsibility for the patient's health, had recommended a decrease. * * *

Furthermore, the jury had before it evidence that symptoms of RLF had begun to appear during the 28 day period of increased oxygen. Yet, the hospital permitted a healthy infant to remain in a precarious position after symptoms of a disease of which it was aware and, indeed, was studying, had been detected. Thus, the jury could find that even if the hospital had been justified in placing plaintiff in increased oxygen, it should have removed him from the high oxygen environment long before it did because of the results of the periodic ophthalmoscopic examinations.

Moreover, that increased oxygen was the only accepted practice at the time of the study is belied to an extent by the hospital's own involvement in the Cooperative Study. Two out of three premature babies were given curtailed oxygen, while only one out of three was placed in increased oxygen. Thus, by testing two out of three babies, the hospital was acting contrary to its own routine. Without in any way challenging the legitimacy of the debate within the medical community as to the effect of the curtailment of oxygen on premature infants, we find it difficult to believe that any reputable institution would permit two out of three of its patients to receive unusual treatment, which might result in death or brain damage, unless it was fairly convinced that the conventional wisdom no longer applied.

Since compelling evidence was introduced that New York Hospital and Dr. Engle, whatever their uncertainty, were aware that plaintiff's life would not have been jeopardized if Dr. Ross's order to reduce oxygen had been followed and of the risk of blindness inherent in the high oxygen environment which they ordered, the jury's finding of malpractice should not be disturbed. The issue was submitted to the jury under a proper charge. "If a physician fails to employ his expertise or best judgment, and that omission causes injury, he should not automatically be freed from liability because in fact he adhered to acceptable practice."

Notes and Questions

1. Dr. Ross had elected the emerging standard of lower oxygen levels, although 1953 standards still called for higher levels. What if the infant had died because of insufficient oxygen? Should Dr. Ross have been held liable for deviating from community practice? Or should tort doctrine leave some leeway for these kinds of professional decisions? How?

In an earlier New York case, Toth v. Community Hospital at Glen Cove, 22 N.Y.2d 255, 292 N.Y.S.2d 440, 239 N.E.2d 368 (1968), the defendant doctor had ordered a reduction in the flow of oxygen to the plaintiff, and the nursing staff had failed to carry out the order.

> * * * evidence that the defendant followed customary practice is not the sole test of professional malpractice. If a physician fails to employ his expertise or best judgment, and that omission causes injury, he should not automatically be freed from liability because in fact he adhered to acceptable practice. There is no policy reason why a physician, who knows or believes there are unnecessary dangers in the community practice, should not be required to take whatever precautionary measures he deems appropriate.

2. What flaws do you see in the study as the hospital implemented it? Can you think of any other way in which such a study might be conducted to avoid the kind of injury suffered by the plaintiff? Or is the threat of a malpractice suit a barrier to scientific research that puts one group of subjects at risk? Should a properly obtained informed consent relieve the researcher or institution of liability? From whom should the hospital have sought informed consent in this case? Given knowledge of the hospital's own study, why would anyone consent? Should this research have been permitted? Would it be today? See Chapter 12 infra, for a discussion of human experimentation.

3. *Practice Guidelines.* American physicians have in recent years put forth substantial efforts toward standard setting, specifying treatments for particular diseases. Clinical practice protocols (also referred to as practice parameters) have been developed by specialty societies such as the American Academy of Pediatrics; by the government, through the National Institutes of Health; and by individual hospitals in the clinical setting. What effect will this development of standards in many areas of medicine have on the proof of a malpractice case? The development of practice standards and guidelines by national medical organizations will accelerate the process of moving all medical practice toward a national one.

Such guidelines provide a particularized source of standards against which to judge the conduct of the defendant physician. A widely accepted clinical standard may be presumptive evidence of due care, but expert testimony will still be required to introduce the standard and establish its sources and its relevancy. See generally Kinney and Wilder, Medical Standard Setting in the Current Malpractice Environment: Problems and Possibilities, 22 U.Cal.Dav.L.Rev. 421 (1989). The source of the study will determine the weight to be given it. See generally Legal Impediments to Physician Efforts to Increase Appropriateness of Care, in Physician Payment Review Commission: Annual Report to Congress 1990.

Might medical societies that develop guidelines expose themselves to liability if poorly crafted guidelines lead to injury, or if they fail to keep the guidelines up-to-date as medical knowledge advances? See Chassin, Standards of Care in Medicine, 25 Inquiry 437 (1988).

Medical practice guidelines or practice protocols might be used as an affirmative defense by a physician in a malpractice suit, to show that he complied with accepted practice. Maine has passed legislation to immunize physicians from suit if they practiced in accordance with such standards. Me.Gen.Laws, Ch. 931 (1990). The law was premised on concerns that physicians practiced too much "defensive medicine" in response to liability fears, ordering tests primarily to protect themselves from subsequent suits. If given some protection in the liability area, they could change their practice patterns without fear of liability. The Maine legislation includes physicians in emergency medicine, anesthesia, and obstetrics and gynecology. Physicians who elect to participate can assert compliance with established practice parameters and risk management protocols as an affirmative defense in any malpractice suit brought against them during the five years of the demonstration project. The practice parameters and risk management protocols will be developed by advisory committees in each of the practice areas.

The Maine statute provides:

> * * * in any claims for professional negligence against a physician or the employer of a physician participating in the project in which a violation of standard of care is alleged, only the physician or the physician's employer may introduce into evidence as an affirmative defense the existence of the practice parameters and risk management protocols developed pursuant to the project.

Outside experts will not be able to challenge the standard, and the physician is not bound by the standard in a case in which he deviated from the protocol. The project will not take effect until 50% in any specialty elect to participate. See Smith, Maine's Liability Demonstration Project—Relating Liability to Practice Parameters, 18 State Health Legislation Report 1 (1990).

2. Proving the Plaintiff's Case

The standard of practice in the defendant doctor's specialty or area of practice is normally established through the testimony of medical experts. The cases above illustrate the burden that the plaintiff bears. In any jurisdiction, plaintiffs, to withstand a motion for a directed verdict, must 1) qualify their medical witnesses as experts; 2) satisfy the court that the expert's testimony will assist the trier of fact; and 3) have the witnesses testify based upon facts that support their expert opinions. The requirement that the expert be of the same specialty as the defendant typically governs the qualifying of the expert for testifying at trial.

A plaintiff must offer proof that the defendant physician breached the legally required standard of care and was thus negligent. Expert testimony is needed to establish both the standard of proper professional skill or care and a failure by the defendant to conform. The expert does not have to testify explicitly that the conduct was "malpractice." "In medical malpractice cases, it is proper for the trier of fact to draw inferences and reach conclusions from facts that are found to be proved." Campbell v. Palmer, 20 Conn.App. 544, 568 A.2d 1064, 1067 (1990) (radiologist testified for plaintiff as to what he and his peers would do).

The abolition of the locality rule has been one way to ease the plaintiff's burden of proof, broadening the plaintiff's choices of available experts. Plaintiff's experts normally must be in the same specialty as the defendant. Under some circumstances, however, courts have allowed physicians in other specialties to testify, so long as the alleged negligence involved matters within the knowledge of every physician. A general surgeon can testify as to the standard of care of a plastic surgeon performing elective surgery, as to general surgical issues as to whether nerves in the forehead should have been protected. Hauser v. Bhatnager, 537 A.2d 599 (Me.1988). In Miller v. Silver, 181 Cal.App.3d 652, 226 Cal.Rptr. 479 (1986), a psychiatrist was allowed to testify as to the standard of post-operative care for a patient receiving breast implants. The court found that the psychiatrist, because of his medical education and internship, had "the ability to research the role prophylactic antibiotics play in implant patients who have experienced life threatening complications from recent surgery." See also Searle v. Bryant, 713 S.W.2d 62 (Tenn.1986) (expert in infectious diseases could testify as to the standard of care for a surgeon, where the patient developed an abdominal infection following surgery.)

An expert need not be board certified in the subject of the suit, so long as he has the appropriate education and experience. Hanson v. Baker, 534 A.2d 665 (Me.1987). The liberal view is that an expert need not possess a medical degree so long as he has the medical knowledge. " * * * [B]efore one may testify as an expert, that person must be shown to know a great deal regarding the subject of his testimony. Thompson v. Carter, 518 So.2d 609 (Miss.1987) (toxicologist allowed to testify as to side effects of a drug prescribed by defendant physician). See also Pratt v. Stein, 298 Pa.Super. 92, 444 A.2d 674 (1982); Cornfeldt v. Tongen, 262 N.W.2d 684 (Minn.1977) (nurse anesthetist competent to testify); Hudgins v. Serrano, 186 N.J.Super. 465, 453 A.2d 218 (1982).

Some jurisdictions adopt a narrower view, requiring that the expert have practiced in the same area as the defendant. See Lundgren v. Eustermann, 370 N.W.2d 877 (Minn.1985) (licensed psychologist could not testify as to standard of a physician); Bell v. Hart, 516 So.2d 562 (Ala.1987) (pharmacist and toxicologist testimony disallowed). For a general discussion, see Carlson, Policing the Basis of Modern Expert Testimony, 39 Vand.L.Rev. 577 (1986).

The standard of care may be based upon the expert's own practice and education. As discussed above, the emergence of practice guidelines or parameters, particularly statements by medical societies as to good practice, will provide a ready-made particularized standard that an expert can use as a benchmark against which to test a defendant's conduct.

Other Methods of Proving Negligence. The plaintiff will usually use his own experts to establish a standard of care, defendant's deviation from it, and causation, as was done in *Hall.* Negligence can also be established by:

1. examination of defendant's expert witnesses. The plaintiff may establish the standard of care through defense witnesses, leaving the issue of breach within the province of the fact finder, not the trial court on summary disposition. Porter v. Henry Ford Hospital, 181 Mich.App. 706, 450 N.W.2d 37 (1989). See also McDermott v. Manhattan Eye, Ear and Throat Hospital, 15 N.Y.2d 20, 255 N.Y.S.2d 65, 203 N.E.2d 469 (1964).

2. pharmaceutical package insert instructions and warnings. Package inserts may be used to establish the standard of care for use of the particular drug. In Thompson v. Cater, 518 S.2d 609 (Miss.1987), the physician used Bactrim, a sulfonamide antibiotic, to treat the plaintiff's kidney infection. She developed Stevens Johnson Syndrome, a severe allergic reaction associated with use of Bactrim. The court allowed the admission of the package insert, holding:

> " * * * the package insert contains prima facie proof of the proper method of use of Bactrim * * * [ ] The package insert can be given weight as authoritative published compilation by a pharmaceutical manufacturer. It is some evidence of the standard of care, but it is not conclusive evidence. The prescribing physician can be permitted to rebut this implication and explain its deviation from the manufacturer's recommended use on dosage. The holding will shift the burden of persuasion to the physician to provide a sound reason for his deviating from the directions for its use, and will require corroborative evidence to determine whether the physician met or violated the appropriate standard." Id. at 613.

Accord, Mueller v. Mueller, 88 S.D. 446, 221 N.W.2d 39 (1974) (holding insert to be not only admissible but also "essential" in showing the physician's lack of care); Garvey v. O'Donoghue, 530 A.2d 1141 (D.C. App.1987) (relevant evidence of the medical standard of care). But see Tarter v. Linn, ___ Pa.Super. ___, 578 A.2d 453 (1990) (sustaining trial court's refusal to allow plaintiff to establish the standard of care by introducing information on adverse drug reactions to the drug Diamox from the Physician's Desk Reference); Ramon v. Farr, 770 P.2d 131 (Utah 1989) (allowing package insert only as "some evidence" but not prima facie evidence of standard of care for Marcaine).

3. judicial standard setting. In U.S. v. Zwick, 413 F.Supp. 113, 115 (N.D.Ohio 1976), the U.S. District court considered an action for injunctive relief brought by the United States against a physician who had prescribed over 3,800,000 doses of anorectic controlled substances

in a three year period. The court issued an injunction, declaring that minimum standards of medical practice for physicians in bariatric practice require that such drugs not be used as a routine part of treatment of obesity. " * * * [I]t is not proper for the physician dispensing and prescribing anorectic controlled drugs to adopt a unitary approach to the treatment of obesity in that no standard approach to treatment exists." The court cited, as support for its articulation of medical standards, a monograph by the National Institutes of Health; a New England Journal of Medicine article; two treatises; Food and Drug Administration regulations; and standards set forth by the American Society of Bariatric Physicians, "Standards of Bariatric Practice".

4. substantive use of a learned treatise. At the common law, a treatise could be used only to impeach the opponent's experts during cross-examination. It could only undercut the expert's testimony, not function substantively to build the plaintiff's case. The concern was hearsay, since the author of the treatise was not available for cross-examination as to statements contained in the treatise. Federal Rule of Evidence (FRE) 803(18) creates an exception to the hearsay rule, so that the learned treatise can be used for substantive purposes, so long as the treatise is accepted as reliable. An expert must be on the stand to explain and assist in the application of the treatise. Tart v. McGann, 697 F.2d 75 (2d Cir.1982). The treatise must be declared reliable by the trial court, after a motion by the moving lawyer to use the treatise substantively under FRE 803(18) or its state equivalent. Maggipinto v. Reichman, 481 F.Supp. 547 (E.D.Pa.1979). See also Comment, Substantive Admissibility of Learned Treatises and the Medical Malpractice Plaintiff, 71 Nw.U.L.Rev. 678 (1977).

5. an admission by the defendant that he or she was negligent. In Grindstaff v. Tygett, 698 S.W.2d 33 (Mo.App.1985), the defendant described a delivery in the hospital records as a "tight midforceps rotation". In his deposition, when asked what this phrase meant, he described the rotation as "[o]ne in which you would have to apply excessive pressure to effect the maneuver." This was held to be sufficient to submit the case to the jury. In Helm v. Shields, No. 85–CA–1326–MR (Ky.App.1986), the physician admitted that he had cut the patient's bile duct because he had misidentified various vessels. See also Senesac v. Associates in Obstetrics and Gynecology, 141 Vt. 310, 449 A.2d 900 (1982).

An implicit admission of culpability can be found through evidence of intimidation by defendant of plaintiff's expert witnesses, which a jury is allowed to consider as defendant's consciousness of the weakness of his case. "This, in conjunction with the other evidence in the case, may lead to the further inference that appellee considers his case to be weak because he, in fact, is guilty of the negligence which appellant asserts he committed. Such inferences are, of course, merely permissible * * *." Meyer v. McDonnell, 40 Md.App. 524, 392 A.2d 1129 (1978).

6. testimony by the plaintiff, in the rare case where he or she is a medical expert qualified to evaluate the doctor's conduct. Lamont v. Brookwood Health Services, Inc., 446 So.2d 1018 (Ala.1983).

7. common knowledge in situations where a layperson could understand the negligence without the assistance of experts. Bauer v. Friedland, 394 N.W.2d 549 (Minn.1986); Hastings v. Baton Rouge General Hospital, 498 So.2d 713 (La.1986); Therrell v. Fonde, 495 So.2d 1046 (Ala.1986).

A physician's obvious or admitted ignorance of an illness or a procedure may create a duty to investigate and consult another physician. In Largess v. Tatem, 130 Vt. 271, 291 A.2d 398 (1972), the defendant, a general practitioner in Vermont, treated the plaintiff, a 77 year old woman, for a fracture of her left hip. He called in a specialist in orthopedic surgery, who implanted a Jewett nail. This fixation device was not designed to permit full early weight bearing. Dr. Tatem was not familiar with the postoperative instructions for such a device and released the patient without instructions. The device broke and a second surgery was required. The court held that expert testimony was not required:

> Under the circumstances of this case, the evidence presented to the trier of fact clearly indicated the failure of the defendant to inquire prior to making a judgment concerning the weight bearing of the plaintiff was a gross violation of the due care owed by a physician to a patient. This violation of that due care being so apparent to be comprehensible to the lay trier of fact, expert medical testimony is not needed to substantiate the violation which is already apparent. Id. at 403.

But see Ward v. Levy, 27 Mass.App.Ct. 1101, 534 N.E.2d 308 (1989)— plaintiff needs expert; not a "common knowledge" situation sufficient to dispense with need for expert.

8. negligence per se, as when the defendant physician clearly violated a clearly articulated practice within his specialty. See Deutsch v. Shein, 597 S.W.2d 141 (Ky.1980), where the defendant was negligent per se in ordering radiology and other tests on the pregnant plaintiff, injuring the fetus.

9. use of res ipsa loquitur, as discussed infra, pp. 147–151.

Problem: Evidentiary Hurdles

You have been approached by Clinton Scott, whose wife Diane died of toxemia at the end of pregnancy. The facts are as follows. Clinton tells you that Diane had experienced symptoms of blurred vision, headaches, chest pains and swelling in the second half of pregnancy, with worsening symptoms in early February. Diane had described these symptoms to her obstetrician, Dr. Fowles, during her January examination, and then early in February when they got markedly worse. In mid-February Diane was admitted to the hospital after Dr. Fowles had diagnosed pre-eclampsia (toxemia). Drugs were administered to control Diane's condition, but she went into convulsions a few hours later. Later that day the staff failed to detect fetal heart tones and a C-section was promptly performed. A stillborn baby girl was delivered. Six days later, Diane's brain had ceased to function. She was taken off life-support with Clinton's approval, and died.

In your preliminary discovery, you have had trouble finding a local obstetrician to testify against Dr. Fowles, who is the president of the local medical society and is quite well-respected among his peers. Your jurisdiction follows the *Hall* rule, so you could hire an expert from elsewhere in the state or region, but you would prefer to use someone who can claim familiarity with local practices and who would cost you less in discovery costs as well.

Consider the following evidence issues. Will you be successful in getting this evidence admitted? In getting the case to the jury? In winning a jury trial?

1. You took the deposition of Dr. Fowles, who was forthright and candid during the examination. The following questions and answers are particularly interesting.

Q. Is the standard of care when managing a pregnant patient that where you have a condition of persistent headaches, blurred vision, fatigue, significant epigastraic pain, and developing edema of the feet, that the physician managing the woman should suspect pre-eclampsia as a cause?

A. Yes, those symptoms should put a doctor on notice of the potential of toxemia. When you suspect this, you should promptly treat the patient, since immediate treatment increases the likelihood of a cure without the development of any adverse complications.

Q. Would earlier diagnosis and treatment of Diane have prevented her brain death and the loss of the infant?

A. That is impossible to say.

2. You have interviewed a nurse-practitioner in obstetrics in the area, who examined the medical records and talked with Clinton. She is willing to testify that based upon her experience as an obstetric nurse for over 10 years, Dr. Fowles was negligent in failing to immediately treat Diane when her symptoms were first related to him. She has also done a literature search of recent studies of toxemia. These studies urge early treatment at the slightest suspicion of the onset of the problem.

3. Williams on Obstetrics states the following:

Since eclampsia is preceded in most cases by premonitory signs and symptoms, its prophylaxis is in many ways more important than its cure and is identical with the treatment of pre-eclampsia. Indeed, a major aim in treating of pre-eclampsia is to prevent convulsions. The necessity of regular and frequent blood pressure measurements thus becomes clear, as well as the importance of detection of rapid gain of weight and of proteinuria, and the immediate institution of appropriate dietary and medical treatment as soon as the earliest signs and symptoms appear. By the employment of these precautionary mea-

sures and by prompt termination of pregnancy in those cases that do not improve or that become progressively worse under treatment, frequency of eclampsia will be greatly diminished and many lives will be saved. Prophylaxis, while valuable, is not invariably successful.
* * *

The relevant rules of evidence in your jurisdiction are identical to the Federal Rules of Evidence below.

Federal Rule of Evidence 701

If the witness is not testifying as an expert, his testimony in the form of opinions or inferences is limited to those opinions or inferences which are (a) rationally based on the perception of the witness and (b) helpful to a clear understanding of his testimony or the determination of a fact in issue.

Federal Rule of Evidence 702

If scientific, technical, or other specialized knowledge will assist the trier of fact to understand the evidence or to determine a fact in issue, a witness qualified as an expert by knowledge, skill, experience, training, or education, may testify thereto in the form of an opinion or otherwise.

Federal Rule of Evidence 703

The facts or data in the particular case upon which an expert bases an opinion or inference may be those perceived by or made known to him at or before the hearing. If of a type reasonably relied upon by experts in the particular field in forming opinions or inferences upon the subject, the facts or data need not be admissible in evidence.

Federal Rule of Evidence 704

Testimony in the form of an opinion or inference otherwise admissible is not objectionable because it embraces an ultimate issue to be decided by the trier of fact.

Federal Rule of Evidence 705

The expert may testify in terms of opinion or inference and give his reasons therefore without prior disclosure of the underlying facts or data, unless the court requires otherwise. The expert may in any event be required to disclose the underlying facts or data on cross-examination.

Federal Rule of Evidence 803(18)

To the extent called to the attention of an expert witness upon cross-examination or relied upon by him in direct examination, statements contained in published treatises, periodicals, or pamphlets on a subject of history, medicine, or science or art, established as a reliable authority by the testimony or admission of the witness or by other expert testimony or by judicial notice. If admitted, the statements may be read into evidence but may not be received as exhibits.

3. Altering the Burden of Proof

In the typical malpractice case, the plaintiff must introduce expert testimony as to the standard of care or face a nonsuit. The courts have developed several doctrines that ease the plaintiff's burden of proof, shifting either the burden of production of evidence or the burden of persuasion onto the defendant.

a. *Res Ipsa Loquitur*

The best known of these evidentiary devices is the doctrine of *res ipsa loquitur* (Latin for "The thing speaks for itself"), which eliminates the plaintiff's need to present expert testimony as to negligence of the defendant. *Ybarra* is the classic statement of the justifications for the doctrine in a medical malpractice case.

YBARRA v. SPANGARD

Supreme Court of California, 1944.
25 Cal.2d 486, 154 P.2d 687.

GIBSON, CHIEF JUSTICE.

This is an action for damages for personal injuries alleged to have been inflicted on plaintiff by defendants during the course of a surgical operation. The trial court entered judgments of nonsuit as to all defendants and plaintiff appealed.

On October 28, 1939, plaintiff consulted defendant Dr. Tilley, who diagnosed his ailment as appendicitis, and made arrangements for an appendectomy to be performed by defendant Dr. Spangard at a hospital owned and managed by defendant Dr. Swift. Plaintiff entered the hospital, was given a hypodermic injection, slept, and later was awakened by Drs. Tilley and Spangard and wheeled into the operating room by a nurse whom he believed to be defendant Gisler, an employee of Dr. Swift. Defendant Dr. Reser, the anesthetist, also an employee of Dr. Swift, adjusted plaintiff for the operation, pulling his body to the head of the operating table and, according to plaintiff's testimony, laying him back against two hard objects at the top of his shoulders, about an inch below his neck. Dr. Reser then administered the anesthetic and plaintiff lost consciousness. When he awoke early the following morning he was in his hospital room attended by defendant Thompson, the special nurse, and another nurse who was not made a defendant.

Plaintiff testified that prior to the operation he had never had any pain in, or injury to, his right arm or shoulder, but that when he awakened he felt a sharp pain about half way between the neck and the point of the right shoulder. He complained to the nurse, and then to Dr. Tilley, who gave him diathermy treatments while he remained in the hospital. The pain did not cease but spread down to the lower part of his arm, and after his release from the hospital the condition grew worse. He was unable to rotate or lift his arm, and developed paralysis and atrophy of the muscles around the shoulder. He received further treatments from Dr. Tilley until March, 1940, and then returned to work, wearing his arm in a splint on the advice of Dr. Spangard.

Plaintiff also consulted Dr. Wilfred Sterling Clark, who had X-ray pictures taken which showed an area of diminished sensation below the shoulder and atrophy and wasting away of the muscles around the shoulder. In the opinion of Dr. Clark, plaintiff's condition was due to trauma or injury by pressure or strain applied between his right shoulder and neck.

Plaintiff was also examined by Dr. Fernando Garduno, who expressed the opinion that plaintiff's injury was a paralysis of traumatic origin, not arising from pathological causes, and not systemic, and that the injury resulted in atrophy, loss of use and restriction of motion of the right arm and shoulder.

Plaintiff's theory is that the foregoing evidence presents a proper case for the application of the doctrine of res ipsa loquitur, and that the inference of negligence arising therefrom makes the granting of a nonsuit improper. Defendants take the position that, assuming that plaintiff's condition was in fact the result of an injury, there is no showing that the act of any particular defendant, nor any particular instrumentality, was the cause thereof. They attack plaintiff's action as an attempt to fix liability "en masse" on various defendants, some of whom were not responsible for the acts of others; and they further point to the failure to show which defendants had control of the instrumentalities that may have been involved. * * * We are satisfied, however, that these objections are not well taken in the circumstances of this case.

The doctrine of res ipsa loquitur has three conditions: "(1) the accident must be of a kind which ordinarily does not occur in the absence of someone's negligence; (2) it must be caused by an agency or instrumentality within the exclusive control of the defendant; (3) it must not have been due to any voluntary action or contribution on the part of the plaintiff." [ ] It is applied in a wide variety of situations, including cases of medical or dental treatment and hospital care. [ ]

* * *

The present case is of a type which comes within the reason and spirit of the doctrine more fully perhaps than any other. * * * [I]t is difficult to see how the doctrine can, with any justification, be so restricted in its statement as to become inapplicable to a patient who submits himself to the care and custody of doctors and nurses, is rendered unconscious, and receives some injury from instrumentalities used in his treatment. Without the aid of the doctrine a patient who received permanent injuries of a serious character, obviously the result of some one's negligence, would be entirely unable to recover unless the doctors and nurses in attendance voluntarily chose to disclose the identity of the negligent person and the facts establishing liability. [ ] If this were the state of the law of negligence, the courts, to avoid gross injustice, would be forced to invoke the principles of absolute liability, irrespective of negligence, in actions by persons suffering injuries during the course of treatment under anesthesia. But we think this juncture has not yet been reached, and that the doctrine of res ipsa loquitur is properly applicable to the case before us.

The condition that the injury must not have been due to the plaintiff's voluntary action is of course fully satisfied under the evidence produced herein; and the same is true of the condition that the accident must be one which ordinarily does not occur unless some one was negligent. We have here no problem of negligence in treatment, but of distinct injury to a healthy part of the body not the subject of treatment, nor within the area covered by the operation. The decisions in this state make it clear that such circumstances raise the inference of negligence and call upon the defendant to explain the unusual result.
[   ]

* * *

We have no doubt that in a modern hospital a patient is quite likely to come under the care of a number of persons in different types of contractual and other relationships with each other. For example, in the present case it appears that Drs. Smith, Spangard and Tilley were physicians or surgeons commonly placed in the legal category of independent contractors; and Dr. Reser, the anesthetist, and defendant Thompson, the special nurse, were employees of Dr. Swift and not of the other doctors. But we do not believe that either the number or relationship of the defendants alone determines whether the doctrine of res ipsa loquitur applies.   * * *

* * *

It may appear at the trial that, consistent with the principles outlined above, one or more defendants will be found liable and others absolved, but this should not preclude the application of the rule of res ipsa loquitur. The control at one time or another, of one or more of the various agencies or instrumentalities which might have harmed the plaintiff was in the hands of every defendant or of his employees or temporary servants. This, we think, places upon them the burden of initial explanation. Plaintiff was rendered unconscious for the purpose of undergoing surgical treatment by the defendants; it is manifestly unreasonable for them to insist that he identify any one of them as the person who did the alleged negligent act.

The other aspect of the case which defendants so strongly emphasize is that plaintiff has not identified the instrumentality any more than he has the particular guilty defendant. Here, again, there is a misconception which, if carried to the extreme for which defendants contend, would unreasonably limit the application of the res ipsa loquitur rule. It should be enough that the plaintiff can show an injury resulting from an external force applied while he lay unconscious in the hospital; this is as clear a case of identification of the instrumentality as the plaintiff may ever be able to make.

An examination of the recent cases, particularly in this state, discloses that the test of actual exclusive control of an instrumentality has not been strictly followed, but exceptions have been recognized where the purpose of the doctrine of res ipsa loquitur would otherwise be defeated. * * *

In the face of these examples of liberalization of the tests for res ipsa loquitur, there can be no justification for the rejection of the doctrine in the instant case. As pointed out above, if we accept the contention of defendants herein, there will rarely be any compensation for patients injured while unconscious. A hospital today conducts a highly integrated system of activities, with many persons contributing their efforts. There may be, e.g., preparation for surgery by nurses and interns who are employees of the hospital, administering of an anesthetic by a doctor who may be an employee of the hospital, an employee of the operating surgeon, or an independent contractor; performance of an operation by a surgeon and assistants who may be his employees, employees of the hospital, or independent contractors; and post surgical care by the surgeon, a hospital physician, and nurses. The number of those in whose care the patient is placed is not a good reason for denying him all reasonable opportunity to recover for negligent harm. It is rather a good reason for re-examination of the statement of legal theories which supposedly compel such a shocking result.

We do not at this time undertake to state the extent to which the reasoning of this case may be applied to other situations in which the doctrine of res ipsa loquitur is invoked. We merely hold that where a plaintiff receives unusual injuries while unconscious and in the course of medical treatment, all those defendants who had any control over his body or the instrumentalities which might have caused the injuries may properly be called upon to meet the inference of negligence by giving an explanation of their conduct.

The judgment is reversed.

Notes and Questions

1. What justifications did the court cite in favor of applying res ipsa loquitur? Does RIL operate here purely as a recognition of the probability of negligence, or as something more?

See also Nixdorf v. Hicken, 612 P.2d 348 (Utah 1980) (doctor repaired a cystocele in patient, losing curved cutting needle used for suturing; needle remained in patient); Beaudoin v. Watertown Memorial Hospital, 32 Wis.2d 132, 145 N.W.2d 166 (1966) (after having a bleeding polyp removed from her vaginal canal patient developed blisters on her buttocks).

In most states, res ipsa loquitur operates as an inference of negligence. That is, the jury may infer that the defendant was in some way negligent, but it is not compelled to conclude negligence. It can reject the inference as well as accepting it. A few states treat res ipsa as a presumption, so that a plaintiff who proves a res ipsa case should win unless the defendant comes forward with some evidence to rebut the presumed negligence. See generally D. Dobbs, Torts and Compensation: Personal Accountability and

Social Responsibility for Injury 173–174 (1985); W. Prosser & P. Keeton, Torts secs. 39–40 (5th ed. 1984).

The doctrine has become increasingly unpopular, with many jurisdictions reluctant to apply the doctrine in medical malpractice cases out of concern that doctors might be held liable for rare bad outcomes, whether or not they were related to any negligence by the defendant. As Justice Gibson, author of *Ybarra,* wrote in Siverson v. Weber, 57 Cal.2d 834, 22 Cal.Rptr. 337, 372 P.2d 97 (1962), " * * * this would place too great a burden upon the medical profession and might result in an undesirable limitation on the use of operations or new procedures involving an inherent risk of injury even when due care is used."

See also Priest v. Lindig, 583 P.2d 173 (Alaska 1978); Van Zee v. Sioux Valley Hospital, 315 N.W.2d 489 (S.D.1982); Zeno v. Lincoln General Hospital, 404 So.2d 1337 (La.App.1981); Baker v. Chastain, 389 So.2d 932 (Ala.1980). See Seidelson, Res Ipsa Loquitur: The Big Umbrella, 25 Duq.L. Rev. 387 (1987).

Many states have eliminated the availability of res ipsa loquitur by statute as part of malpractice reform packages. See Chapter 4.

2. *Ybarra* relaxed the requirement of exclusive control of the instrumentality, by shifting to the defendants the burden of explanation. For a recent case rejecting *Ybarra,* see Hoven v. Rice Memorial Hospital, 396 N.W.2d 569 (Minn.1986).

3. *Conditional Res Ipsa Loquitur.* A few states have developed a version of RIL termed "conditional RIL", in which expert testimony as to the probable causes of the injury can establish an inference of negligence. In Spidle v. Steward, 79 Ill.2d 1, 37 Ill.Dec. 326, 402 N.E.2d 216 (1980), the patient underwent a supracervical hysterectomy necessitated by problems with pelvic inflammatory disease. After the operation, she developed a vaginal fecal fistula and a drainage sinus at the lower part of the surgical incision, indicating a "communication between the vagina, colon, and abdominal wall." The plaintiff's expert had testified that the formation of a fecal vaginal fistula was "a rare and unusual complication of hysterectomies." Id. at 8, 402 N.E.2d at 219.

What is the court doing here, in applying conditional RIL? The expert says little more than that the plaintiff's condition is a rare and adverse outcome. Is he really saying that only a medical error leads to this outcome? How is this case different from other cases in which the court demands expert testimony as to the standard of care and deviation from it?

See also Quintal v. Laurel Grove Hospital, 62 Cal.2d 154, 41 Cal.Rptr. 577, 397 P.2d 161 (1964); Mayor v. Dowsett, 240 Or. 196, 215–219; 400 P.2d 234, 243–44 (1965) (court allows RIL where, " * * * in addition to the rarity of the injury and the fact that there is no problem of negligence in treatment, but of distinct injury to a healthy part of the body not the subject of treatment or surgery, we have expert testimony that such an injury is not to be expected where due care is observed in the administration of the anesthetic.")

b. Shifting the Burden of Persuasion

Courts have in special situations used a variety of burden-shifting devices to ease the plaintiff's burden of proof. Res ipsa loquitur, as applied in *Ybarra, supra,* obviated the plaintiff's need to prove a special error by the defendants. In rare cases, courts have shifted the burden of persuasion onto the defendants, requiring that they present evidence to exonerate themselves, or face liability. The rule in such cases approximates strict liability in its impact on the defendants.

ANDERSON v. SOMBERG

Supreme Court of New Jersey, 1975.
67 N.J. 291, 338 A.2d 1.

[The facts of the case can be summarized as follows. The plaintiff was undergoing a laminectomy performed by Dr. Somberg. During surgery, the tip of a pituitary rongeur broke off in the plaintiff's spinal canal. The surgeon tried to retrieve the metal fragment but was unable to do so. He then terminated the operation. The imbedded fragment caused medical complications and further surgical interventions were required. The rongeur had been used five times a year, or in about twenty previous surgical procedures. The rongeur had been purchased from the distributor, Reinhold, about four years before; the distributor obtained it from the manufacturer, Lawton.

The plaintiff sued Dr. Somberg for medical malpractice, alleging that the doctor's negligent action caused the rongeur to break; St. James Hospital for negligently furnishing a defective surgical instrument; the medical supply distributor on a warranty theory and the manufacturer of the rongeur, on a strict liability in tort claim, alleging that the rongeur was a defective product.

Dr. Somberg testified that he had not examined the rongeur prior to the day of surgery, that he then inspected it visually, and that he had not twisted it while performing the laminectomy. Dr. Graubard, a general surgeon testifying for the plaintiff, stated that the rongeur was a delicate instrument that might break if twisted. He testified that "a rongeur used properly and not defective would not break."

The manufacturer called a metallurgist who testified that the broken rongeur exhibited neither structural defects nor faulty workmanship. His microscopic examination revealed a secondary crack near the main crack but he could not explain where the crack came from. The expert opined that the instrument had been strained, probably because of "an improper 'twisting' of the tool. The strain, however, could have been cumulative, over the course of several operations, and the instrument could conceivably have been cracked when handed to Dr. Somberg and broken in its normal use."

The plaintiff was left with multiple defendants, a range of hypothetical causes for the rongeur's failure, and an inability to prove either the cause of the defect or the source of it.]

In short, when all the evidence had been presented, no theory for the cause of the rongeur's breaking was within reasonable contemplation save for the possible negligence of Dr. Somberg in using the instrument, or the possibility that the surgeon had been given a defective instrument, which defect would be attributable to a dereliction of duty by the manufacturer, the distributor, the hospital or all of them.

* * *

In the ordinary case, the law will not assist an innocent plaintiff at the expense of an innocent defendant. However, in the type of case we consider here, where an unconscious or helpless patient suffers an admitted mishap not reasonably foreseeable and unrelated to the scope of the surgery (such as cases where foreign objects are left in the body of the patient), those who had custody of the patient, and who owed him a duty of care as to medical treatment, or not to furnish a defective instrument for use in such treatment can be called to account for their default. They must prove their nonculpability, or else risk liability for the injuries suffered.

* * *

The rule of evidence we set forth does not represent the doctrine of *res ipsa loquitur* as it has been traditionally understood. * * * Imposition of the burden of proof upon multiple defendants, even though only one could have caused the injury, is no novelty to the law, as where all defendants have been clearly negligent. [ ] As against multiple defendants where there is no evidence as to where culpability lies, the rule is not generally available, according to Prosser, because it might impose an equal hardship on an innocent defendant as on an innocent plaintiff. Prosser notes exceptional special cases, as where defendant owes a special responsibility to plaintiff, and in those instances the burden of proof can in fact be shifted to defendants. [ ] The facts of this case disclose just such a special responsibility, and require a shifting of the burden of proof to defendants.

We hold that in a situation like this, the burden of proof in fact does shift to defendants. All those in custody of that patient or who owed him a duty, as here, the manufacturer and the distributor, should be called forward and should be made to prove their freedom from liability. The rule would have no application except in those instances where the injury lay outside the ambit of the surgical procedure in question; for example, an injury to an organ, when that organ was itself the object of medical attention, would not by itself make out a prima facie case for malpractice or shift the burden of proof to defendants. [ ]

Further, we note that at the close of all the evidence, no reasonable suggestion had been offered that the occurrence could have arisen because of plaintiff's contributory negligence, or some act of nature; that is, there was no explanation for the occurrence in the case save for negligence or defect on the part of someone connected with the manufacture, handling, or use of the instrument. (Any such proof would be acceptable to negative plaintiff's prima facie case.) Since all parties had been joined who could reasonably have been connected with that negligence or defect, it was clear that one of those parties was liable, and at least one could not succeed in his proofs.

In cases of this type, no defendant will be entitled to prevail on a motion for judgment until all the proofs have been presented to the court and jury. The judge may grant any motion bearing in mind that the plaintiff must recover a verdict against at least one defendant. Inferences and doubts at this stage are resolved in favor of the plaintiff. If only one defendant remains by reason of the court's action, then, in fact, the judge is directing a verdict of liability against that defendant.

Notes and Questions

1. Why is the court willing to shift the burden of proof to the defendants in *Anderson*? Are the court's arguments convincing? What evidence might defendants produce to meet their burden of proof? As counsel for one of the defendants, would you move to join all of the doctors who had previously used the rongeur? After all, if they could not prove that they did *not* weaken it negligently, shouldn't they be liable for a portion of the damages? How does the use of a medical device complicate the problem of multiple defendants?

See section E. 2., infra., for a discussion of multiple defendants and judicial handling of causation complexities.

2. A "missing witness" instruction has been upheld in a few jurisdictions, allowing the jury to presume negligence and causation from the mere absence of a crucial piece of evidence. In Welsh v. United States, 844 F.2d 1239 (6th Cir.1988), the court shifted the burden of persuasion to the defendants, holding that "acts by the hospital surgeons in this case create a rebuttable presumption of negligence and proximate causation against the defendant—the negligent destruction of a skull bone flap after the second [of two] operations, and the consequent failure at that time to undertake a pathological examination of this evidence * * * ". Id at 1239–40. See also C. McCormick, McCormick on Evidence, § 273, at 810 at n. 20 (3rd Ed. 1984). Rejecting "missing evidence" as substantive proof that shifts the burden, see Battocchi v. Washington Hospital Center, 581 A.2d 759 (D.C. App.1990) (limiting the effect of a showing of missing evidence to an instruction allowing the jury to draw an adverse inference against the defendants, upon a showing of gross indifference to or reckless disregard for the relevance of the evidence to a possible claim).

c. Strict Liability

HOVEN v. KELBLE

Supreme Court of Wisconsin, 1977.
79 Wis.2d 444, 256 N.W.2d 379.

[The court considered an appeal from the granting of the defendant anesthesiologist's demurrer to the count in the plaintiff's complaint for

strict liability for medical services provided by the defendant anesthesiologist. The plaintiff Robert Hoven, while undergoing a lung biopsy,
suffered a cardiac arrest and injury to his nervous system and brain
tissue. The court sustained the defendant's demurrer to the plaintiff's
strict liability cause of action. The plaintiff had pleaded that Kelble
was a seller of medical services, i.e., anesthesiology, that the services
rendered were defective, and that plaintiff suffered injury as a result of
the defect. This was essentially the test of the Restatement of the Law,
Torts, 2d, sec. 402A, which Wisconsin had adopted for product defect
cases. The court wrestled with the merits of the strict liability cause of
action before rejecting it.]

Application of this standard of liability to the rendition of medical
services of course would require that some definition of a "defective"
medical service be formulated. Plaintiff's briefs suggest that a suitable
and acceptable governing principle is the "reasonable expectations of
the consumer," as described by Greenfield in Consumer Protection in
Service Transactions—Implied Warranties and Strict Liability in Tort,
1974 Utah L.Rev. 661.

* * *

[T]he essence of plaintiffs' position appears to be that if a plaintiff
could show that a hypothetical virtually perfectly informed doctor,
working in a perfectly equipped hospital, could have avoided the untoward result, the plaintiff could recover, notwithstanding that the
defendants exercised reasonable care in all respects. If attainment of
the goal, or avoidance of the maloccurrence is possible, then failure to
attain the goal or to avoid the maloccurrence renders the service
defective.

This court has stated in respect to products that the doctrine of
strict liability does not make the seller an insurer. [ ] Plaintiffs in
the case at bar recognize this and deny that the theory they advocate
would have any such effect. Under plaintiffs' theory if there is no
known cure the plaintiffs would not recover. However, it is apparent
that adoption of the plaintiffs' theory of liability * * * would set the
standard of performance for the entire medical profession at the zenith
of that profession's achievement, a level at which by definition virtually
no one could perform all the time. That which might possibly have
been done would be required, or liability would result, and inevitably,
the matter would be judged with the acuity of vision which hindsight
provides.

* * *

To date this court has not applied * * * strict liability beyond the
context of damages resulting from the sale of a defective and unreasonably dangerous product. * * * Several cases have allowed recovery on
the basis of strict liability or implied warranty where "defective services" have been rendered, but these services have been of a relatively
routine or simple nature. Where "professional" services are in issue
the cases uniformly require that negligence be shown. We have found

no decision of any court applying strict liability to the rendition of professional medical services.

* * *

The usual reasons given for applying strict liability in tort to transactions in goods are the following:

1. It is the seller who in the first instance creates the risk by placing the defective product on the market, and it is the seller, as opposed to the consumer, who has the superior knowledge and opportunity to control the risk.

2. The consumer relies on the skill, care and reputation of the seller and on the apparent safety of the product. The seller generally stimulates this reliance through advertising and other promotion of the goods.

3. The seller is in a better position than the consumer to bear the loss caused by defects and to distribute the costs of the risks created by the sale of the defective product over all his customers. The seller may pass the cost on to consumers as a group in the form of increased prices and may protect himself by purchasing insurance or by a form of self-insurance.

4. The burden of proof on a purchaser of goods may be unreasonably difficult if the consumer must trace a particular item through the distribution and production systems to the source of the defect and prove that the defect resulted from negligence.

5. Strict liability promotes the public interest in the protection of human life, health and safety. Strict liability is an effective deterrent; it deters the creation of unnecessary risks, or to put it positively, strict liability is an incentive to safety.

The plaintiffs argue that the mere fact that a transaction involves a "service" rather than a sale of goods does not render these considerations inapplicable or preclude application of strict liability, and we might well agree. Moreover, it may be admitted that many of the justifications for strict liability have force regarding professional medical services.

The provider of medical services appears to stand in substantially the same position with respect to the patient as the seller of goods does with the consumer. The typical purchaser of medical services cannot evaluate the quality of care offered because medical services are complex and infrequently bought. The medical care market gives the purchaser little assistance in enabling the purchaser to evaluate what he or she is buying. It is generally the physician—not the patient— who determines the kind of services to be rendered and how often. It is the physician not the patient who prescribes other goods and services, *e.g.,* drugs, therapy, and hospitalization, that should supplement the physician's services. The physician is in a better position than the patient to determine and improve the quality of the services, and the patient's reliance on the doctor's skill, care and reputation is perhaps greater than the reliance of the consumer of goods. The difficulties faced by plaintiffs in carrying the burden of proving negligence on the part of a doctor are well known. [ ] The hospital and doctor are in a better position than the patient to bear and distribute the risk of loss.

However, other considerations call for caution in moving in the direction the plaintiffs advocate. There are differences between the rendition of medical services and transactions in goods (or perhaps other types of services as well). Medical and many other professional services tend often to be experimental in nature, dependent on factors beyond the control of the professional, and devoid of certainty or assurance of results. Medical services are an absolute necessity to society, and they must be readily available to the people. It is said that strict liability will inevitably increase the cost for medical services, which might make them beyond the means of many consumers, and that imposition of strict liability might hamper progress in developing new medicines and medical techniques.

There have been many studies on the delivery of health care in this country and of the problems of the malpractice concept of tort liability. Although there may be general dissatisfaction with our present tort medical injury compensation system, moving from the malpractice concept—even with its many problems—to a strict liability system at the present time appears to be a dubious move. Strict liability has been far from a panacea in products cases, and there has been reluctance to advocate the extension of the principle to medical services.
* * *

* * *

Order affirmed.

Notes and Questions

1. Are you convinced by the court's arguments in *Hoven*? Consider the arguments in *Ybarra*. Can you reconcile the different outcomes?

2. The courts have generally resisted applying strict liability (or implied warranty) to a health care professional or institution. The reasons are well stated in *Hoven*. The court distinguishes between medicine and other "commercial" enterprises. Does this argument seem convincing in light of the growth of modern corporate health care? For a proposal to apply strict liability to a particular medical specialty, based on an outcomes analysis, see Furrow, Defective Mental Treatment: A Proposal for the Application of Strict Liability to Psychiatric Services, 58 B.U.L.Rev. 391 (1978).

For a collection of cases, see Annotation, Liability of Hospital or Medical Practitioner Under Doctrine of Strict Liability in Tort, or Breach of Warranty, for Harm Caused by Drug, Medical Instrument, or Similar Device Used in Treating Patient, 54 ALR 3d 258.

B. JUDICIAL RISK—BENEFIT BALANCING

HELLING v. CAREY

Supreme Court of Washington, 1974.
83 Wash.2d 514, 519 P.2d 981.

HUNTER, ASSOC. JUSTICE.

The plaintiff suffers from primary open angle glaucoma. Primary open angle glaucoma is essentially a condition of the eye in which there is an interference in the ease with which the nourishing fluids can flow out of the eye. Such a condition results in pressure gradually rising above the normal level to such an extent that damage is produced to the optic nerve and its fibers with resultant loss in vision. The first loss usually occurs in the periphery of the field of vision. The disease usually has few symptoms and, in the absence of a pressure test, is often undetected until the damage has become extensive and irreversible.

The defendants (respondents), Dr. Thomas F. Carey and Dr. Robert C. Laughlin, are partners who practice the medical specialty of ophthalmology. Ophthalmology involves the diagnosis and treatment of defects and diseases of the eye.

The plaintiff first consulted the defendants for myopia, nearsightedness, in 1959. At that time she was fitted with contact lenses. She next consulted the defendants in September, 1963, concerning irritation caused by the contact lenses. Additional consultations occurred in October, 1963; February, 1967; September, 1967; October, 1967; May, 1968; July, 1968; August, 1968; September, 1968; and October, 1968. Until the October 1968 consultation, the defendants considered the plaintiff's visual problems to be related solely to complications associated with her contact lenses. On that occasion, the defendant, Dr. Carey, tested the plaintiff's eye pressure and field of vision for the first time. This test indicated that the plaintiff had glaucoma. The plaintiff, who was then 32 years of age, had essentially lost her peripheral vision and her central vision was reduced to approximately 5 degrees vertical by 10 degrees horizontal.

Thereafter, in August of 1969, after consulting other physicians, the plaintiff filed a complaint against the defendants alleging, among other things, that she sustained severe and permanent damage to her eyes as a proximate result of the defendants' negligence. During trial, the testimony of the medical experts for both the plaintiff and the defendants established that the standards of the profession for that specialty in the same or similar circumstances do not require routine pressure tests for glaucoma upon patients under 40 years of age. The reason the pressure test for glaucoma is not given as a regular practice to patients under the age of 40 is that the disease rarely occurs in this age group. Testimony indicated, however, that the standards of the profession do require pressure tests if the patient's complaints and symptoms reveal to the physician that glaucoma should be suspected.

The trial court entered judgment for the defendants following a defense verdict. The plaintiff thereupon appealed to the Court of Appeals, which affirmed the judgment of the trial court. [ ] The plaintiff then petitioned this Court for review, which we granted.

* * * [T]he plaintiff contends * * * that she was unable to argue her theory of the case to the jury that the standard of care for the specialty of ophthalmology was inadequate to protect the plaintiff from the incidence of glaucoma, and that the defendants, by reason of their special ability, knowledge and information, were negligent in failing to give the pressure test to the plaintiff at an earlier point in time which, if given, would have detected her condition and enabled the defendants to have averted the resulting substantial loss in her vision.

We find this to be a unique case. The testimony of the medical experts is undisputed concerning the standards of the profession for the specialty of ophthalmology. It is not a question in this case of the defendants having any greater special ability, knowledge and information than other opthalmologists which would require the defendants to comply with a higher duty of care than that "degree of care and skill which is expected of the average practitioner in the class to which he belongs, acting in the same or similar circumstances." [ ] The issue is whether the defendants' compliance with the standard of the profession of ophthalmology, which does not require the giving of a routine pressure test to persons under 40 years of age, should insulate them from liability under the facts in this case where the plaintiff has lost a substantial amount of her vision due to the failure of the defendants to timely give the pressure test to the plaintiff.

The defendants argue that the standard of the profession, which does not require the giving of a routine pressure test to persons under the age of 40, is adequate to insulate the defendants from liability for negligence because the risk of glaucoma is so rare in this age group. * * *

The incidence of glaucoma in one out of 25,000 persons under the age of 40 may appear quite minimal. However, that one person, the plaintiff in this instance, is entitled to the same protection, as afforded persons over 40, essential for timely detection of the evidence of glaucoma where it can be arrested to avoid the grave and devastating result of this disease. The test is a simple pressure test, relatively inexpensive. There is no judgment factor involved, and there is no doubt that by giving the test the evidence of glaucoma can be detected. The giving of the test is harmless if the physical condition of the eye permits. The testimony indicates that although the condition of the plaintiff's eyes might have at times prevented the defendants from administering the pressure test, there is an absence of evidence in the record that the test could not have been timely given.

Justice Holmes stated [ ] in Texas & Pac. Ry. v. Behymer, [ ]:

What usually is done may be evidence of what ought to be done, but what ought to be done is fixed by a standard of reasonable prudence, whether it usually is complied with or not.

In The T.J. Hooper, 60 F.2d 737 * * *, Justice Hand stated:

[I]n most cases reasonable prudence is in fact common prudence; but strictly it is never its measure; a whole calling may have unduly lagged in the adoption of new and available devices. It never may set its own tests, however persuasive be its usages. *Courts must in the end say what is required; there are precautions so imperative that even their universal disregard will not excuse their omission.*

(Italics ours.)

Under the facts of this case reasonable prudence required the timely giving of the pressure test to this plaintiff. The precaution of giving this test to detect the incidence of glaucoma to patients under 40 years of age is so imperative that irrespective of its disregard by the standards of the ophthalmology profession, it is the duty of the courts to say what is required to protect patients under 40 from the damaging results of glaucoma.

We therefore hold, as a matter of law, that the reasonable standard that should have been followed under the undisputed facts of this case was the timely giving of this simple, harmless pressure test to this plaintiff and that, in failing to do so, the defendants were negligent, which proximately resulted in the blindness sustained by the plaintiff for which the defendants are liable.

* * *

Notes and Questions

1. Is the court correct in imposing its own risk-benefit result on the specialty of ophthalmology? Certainly its view of the tradeoff between blindness and a low-cost test seems to lead inevitably to the *Helling* conclusion. A survey of Washington ophthalmologists subsequent to the *Helling* decision found that they did test for glaucoma with some regularity before *Helling*, with 20.3% reporting that they tested "quite often", and 30.1% testing "virtually always". Wiley, "The Impact of Judicial Decisions on Professional Conduct: An Empirical Study", 55 S.Cal.L.Rev. 345, 383 (1981). Yet the expert testimony in the case was that testing was not the practice for patients under forty.

The court assumed that the test was harmless as well as low in cost: "the giving of the test is harmless if the physical condition of the eye permits." This view ignores both the costs of false-positives and the merits of treatment when a true positive result was found. It has been estimated that more than 15 patients per one million population go blind from glaucoma annually. Screening for glaucoma using tonometry (the pressure test in *Helling*) is recommended on the theory that early treatment will stop the progression of glaucoma into blindness.

The value of tonometry is questionable, however. First, the false positive rate for tonometry is very high. Patients who test abnormally high who actually have glaucoma is less than 1 percent. 99 percent of those who test positive therefore have to undergo further testing and are subjected to considerable worry for a disease they do not have. Second, patients who are correctly diagnosed as having glaucoma or at least elevated intraocular pressure may not gain much from this knowledge. Conventional drug treatments do not produce significant improvements, nor does evidence support the theory that early treatment will halt the progression of glaucoma. See generally E. Robin, Matters of Life & Death: Risks v. Benefits of Medical Care 147 (1984); Fortess and Kapp, Medical Uncertainty, Diagnostic Testing, and Legal Liability, 13 Law, Medicine & Health Care 213 (1985) (because of high false-positive rate, followup testing would cost a great deal, and patients who tested positive falsely would also suffer unnecessary anxiety about incipient glaucoma.)

2. Do these opinions change your view of the rightness of the court's position in *Helling*? Why didn't the defendant ophthalmologists make these arguments to justify the conservative non-testing approach? Why did the defense fail to prove that a significant minority, or even a majority of Washington ophthalmologists, used the pressure test routinely? Should we be reluctant to encourage courts to move beyond the customary practice, given the complexity inherent in medical practice? Or should courts be aggressive in judging the community standard, so long as the parties present full evidence as to the pros and cons of the procedure at issue?

It can be argued that courts should more often articulate clear standards for practice. Such standards are more likely to be heeded by health care professionals in their practice, where the rule is a relatively simple one. Givelber, Bowers, and Blitch, Tarasoff, Myth and Reality: An Empirical Study of Private Law In Action, 1984 Wisc.L.Rev. 443, 485–486. Givelber et al. concluded, after surveying 2875 psychotherapists nationwide, that therapists now warn third parties when a patient utters a threat. They feel bound by *Tarasoff,* even though the case is binding only on California therapists. Therapists feel capable of assessing dangerousness and were comfortable with warning victims.

The authors argued that

" * * * [I]f an appellate court desires to change behavior, it should use judicially established standards of behavior, not jury determined standards. The judicially determined rule of *Tarasoff I,* protect through warning, appears to have affected therapist attitudes, knowledge and behavior to a far greater degree than *Tarasoff II.* Id. at 487.

3. *Helling v. Carey* is one of a small number of cases rejecting the customary practice. See also Lundahl v. Rockford Memorial Hospital Association, 93 Ill.App.2d 461, 465, 235 N.E.2d 671, 674 (1968) ("what is usual or customary procedure might itself be negligence"); Favalora v. Aetna Casualty & Surety Company, 144 So.2d 544 (La.App.1962); Toth v. Community Hospital at Glen Cove, 22 N.Y.2d 255, 263, 292 N.Y.S.2d 440, 447–48, 239 N.E.2d 368, 373 (1968) ("evidence that the defendant followed customary practice is not the sole test of professional malpractice"). These cases have involved a readily understandable therapy or diagnostic proce-

dure, and the courts have allowed the trier of fact to weigh without expert testimony the relative risks of using the procedure or omitting it. Most jurisdictions have been reluctant to follow *Helling* in replacing the established medical standard of care with a case-by-case judicial balancing.

Note: The Effects of Tort Suits on Provider Behavior

Are tort suits likely to change potentially dangerous patterns of medical practice? Malpractice litigation in theory operates as a quality control mechanism. From the economist's perspective, tort doctrine should be designed to achieve an optimal prevention policy, reducing the sum total of the costs of medical accidents and the costs of preventing them. In theory, the tort system deters accident producing behavior. How? The existence of a liability rule and the resulting threat of a lawsuit and judgment encourages health care providers to reduce error and patient injury in circumstances where patients themselves lack the information (and ability) to monitor the quality of care they receive. Potential defendants will take precautions to avoid error and will buy insurance to cover any errors that injure patients. By finding fault and assessing damages against a defendant, a court sends a signal to health care providers that if they wish to avoid similar damages in the future they may need to change their behavior.

How does the existence of malpractice insurance alter this analysis? If the insurer does not employ experience rating to distinguish the litigation-prone providers from their colleagues, it is in effect causing an inaccurate signal to be sent. The existence of such insurance may therefore dilute or eliminate the financial incentives for physicians or other providers to change their behavior. Malpractice insurers, particularly the physician-owned companies in many states, engage in aggressive review of claims. These companies insure about 40% of physicians in active patient care. They routinely use physicians to review applications for insurance and to review the competence of those sued. Physicians with claims due to negligence, as assessed by the peer reviews, may be terminated, may be surcharged, or have restrictions on practice imposed.

> * * * [T]he data suggest that the PIAA companies are effective agents in detecting negligence-prone behavior and also play an important role in deterring substandard behavior. Surcharges and restrictions on practice put physicians on notice that the company is dissatisfied with their performance. * * * [T]he threat of termination of coverage and the problems that will then ensue are likely to provide a powerful stimulus to improved performance.

Schwartz and Mendelson, The Role of Physician–Owned Insurance Companies in the Detection and Deterrence of Negligence, 262 J.A.M.A. 1342 (1989). If a physician loses his malpractice insurance, he may quit, switch jobs, or go without insurance. He may also go to a surplus-lines insurance company that charges much higher premiums for coverage. Claims exposure thus can lead to a direct financial impact on the physician forced to carry such expensive insurance. See Schwartz and Mendelson, Physicians Who Have Lost Their Malpractice Insurance, 262 J.A.M.A. 1335 (1989).

Does this model realistically describe the likely effect of being named a defendant? How might a provider modify her behavior to avoid or reduce negligent behavior? She may spend more time on exams or patient histories, invest in further training, increase support staff or stop doing procedures that she does not do well. The few available studies have found that physicians who have been malpractice defendants often alter their practice as a reaction, even if they win the litigation. They also suffer chronic stress until the trial is over. See, for example, Charles, Wilbert, and Kennedy, Physicians' Self–Reports of Reactions to Malpractice Litigation, 141 Am.J.Psychiatry 563, 565 (1984) ("A malpractice suit was considered a serious and often a devastating event in the personal and professional lives of the respondent physicians").

Malpractice litigation does affect medical practice, making anxious providers either overestimate the risks of a suit or at least adjust their practice to a new assessment of the risk of suit, regardless of the incentive effects of judgments and premium increases. Physicians perceive a threat from the system, judging their risk of being sued as much higher than it actually is. The Harvard New York Study, surveying New York physicians, found that physicians who had been sued were more likely to explain risks to patients, to restrict their scope of practice, and to order more tests and procedures. Patients, Doctors, and Lawyers: Medical Injury, Malpractice Litigation, and Patient Compensation in New York 9–29 (1990). Physicians surveyed in the New York study felt that the malpractice threat was important in maintaining standards of care. Id. at 9–24. The Report notes that " * * * the perception of incentives largely shapes the behavior that ultimately affects patient care." Id. at 3–19. Perceived risk is thus important to physician conduct. See Bell, Legislative Intrusions in the Common Law of Medical Malpractice: Thoughts About the Deterrent Effect of Tort Liability, 35 Syracuse L.Rev. 939, 973–90 (1984). Hospitals have instituted risk management offices and quality assurance programs; informed consent forms have become ubiquitous; medical record-keeping with an eye toward proof at trial has become the rule. One economist has estimated (based upon admittedly limited data) that "* * * the current non-trivial incidence of injury due to negligence would be at least 10 percent higher, were it not for the incentives for injury prevention created by the one in ten incidents of malpractice that result in a claim." Danzon, An Economic Analysis of the Medical Malpractice System, 1 Behavioral Sciences & the Law 39 (1983). See also P. Danzon, Medical Malpractice 10 (1984); G. Calabresi, The Costs of Accidents (1970); Schwartz and Komesar, Doctors, Damages and Deterrence: An Economic View of Medical Malpractice, 298 New Eng.J.Med. 1282 (1978); The Economics of Medical Malpractice (S. Rottenberg, ed. 1978). For a skeptical view of the signalling effect of tort litigation generally, see Sugarman, Doing Away with Tort Law, 73 Cal.L.Rev. 555 (1985); critiquing Sugarman's view, see Latin, Problem–Solving Behavior and Theories of Tort Liability, 73 Cal.L.Rev. 677, 740 (1985).

What other forces and incentives affect the quality of health care delivery by physicians, other professionals, and institutions? If you were a physician or a nurse who conscientiously wanted to reduce medical errors in your own practice, what steps would you consider? A technological innovation for example may reduce both the level of medical injury for a procedure and the risks of being sued. Consider the pulse oximeter, which monitors a patient's blood oxygen to indicate when his oxygen level drops due to breathing problems or overuse of anesthesia. This can give physicians three or four minutes to correct a problem before brain damage results. In 1984, no hospital operating room had such a device, but by 1990 all operating rooms did. Patients under anesthesia now suffer fewer injuries as a result.

C. OTHER THEORIES

1. Negligent Infliction of Mental Distress

Most medical malpractice suits are negligence suits for physical injury and lost wages suffered by the patient, or in a wrongful death action, for damages that include harm to the deceased's relatives. Recent cases however have allowed plaintiffs to sue a health care provider for the negligent infliction of emotional distress under particularly egregious circumstances.

OSWALD v. LeGRAND

Supreme Court of Iowa, 1990.
453 N.W.2d 634.

NEUMAN, JUSTICE.

This appeal challenges a grant of summary judgment for medical professionals in a case involving the spontaneous abortion of a 19–22 week-old fetus. The trial court barred the plaintiffs from introducing expert testimony due to their failure to timely designate an expert in accordance with Iowa Code section 668.11(2) (1987). Accordingly, the district court determined that plaintiffs could not generate a material issue of fact concerning the defendants' negligence. Because we conclude that expert testimony is crucial to some but not all of plaintiffs' claims, we affirm in part, reverse in part, and remand for further proceedings.

I.   * * *

To establish a prima facie case of medical malpractice, a plaintiff must produce evidence that (1) establishes the applicable standard of care, (2) demonstrates a violation of this standard, and (3) develops a causal relationship between the violation and the injury sustained. [ ] Ordinarily, evidence of the applicable standard of care—and its breach—must be furnished by an expert. [ ] This court has recognized two exceptions to this rule:

> One is where the physician's lack of care is so obvious as to be within the comprehension of a lay[person] and requires only common knowledge and experience to understand. The other exception is really an example of the first situation. It arises when the physician injures a part of the body not being treated.

[   ] It is the "common knowledge" exception upon which plaintiffs base their argument for reversal in the present case.

II.   * * * [W]e accept the following facts as established for purposes of this appeal.

Plaintiffs Susan and Larry Oswald have been married for ten years and are the parents of two healthy sons. During Susan's third pregnancy, she began experiencing bleeding and painful cramping just prior to her five-month checkup. At that time, she was under the care of a family practice physician, defendant Barry Smith. He ordered an ultrasound test and Susan was then examined in his office by one of his colleagues, defendant Larry LeGrand, an obstetrician. Neither the test nor the examination revealed an explanation for the bleeding and Susan was instructed to go home and stay off her feet. Later that day, however, Susan began to bleed heavily. She was taken by ambulance to defendant Mercy Health Center. The bleeding eventually stopped, Dr. Smith's further examination failed to yield a cause of the problem, and Susan was discharged the following day with directions to take it easy.

The following day, Susan's cramping and bleeding worsened. Susan thought she was in labor and feared a miscarriage. She was unable to reach Dr. Smith by telephone and so Larry drove her to the emergency room at Mercy. There Dr. Christopher Clark, another physician in association with Smith and LeGrand, examined her. He advised her there was nothing to be done and she should go home. Larry was angered by this response and insisted Susan be admitted to the hospital. Dr. Clark honored this request and Susan was transferred to the labor and delivery ward.

In considerable pain and anxious about her pregnancy, Susan's first contact on the ward was with a nurse who said, "What are you doing here? The doctor told you to stay home and rest." Susan felt like "a real pest." A short while later, while attached to a fetal monitor, Susan was told by another nurse that if she miscarried it would not be a baby, it would be a "big blob of blood." Susan was scared.

The next morning, an argument apparently ensued over which physician was responsible for Susan's care. Standing outside Susan's room, Dr. Clark yelled, "I don't want to take that patient. She's not my patient and I am sick and tired of Dr. Smith dumping his case load on me." At the urging of Larry and a nurse, Dr. Clark apologized to Susan for this outburst. He assured her that he would care for her until he left for vacation at noon that day when he was scheduled to go "off call" and Dr. LeGrand would take over.

Around 9:00 a.m. Susan began experiencing a great deal of pain that she believed to be labor contractions. Dr. Clark prescribed Tylenol and scheduled her for an ultrasound and amniocentesis at 11:00 a.m. By that time, Susan was screaming in pain and yelling that she was in labor. Dr. Clark arrived in the x-ray department halfway through the ultrasound procedure and determined from viewing the sonogram that there was insufficient fluid in the amniotic sac to perform an amniocentesis. He told the Oswalds that the situation was unusual but did not reveal to them his suspicion that there was an infection in the uterus. He examined Susan abdominally but did not do a pelvic exam. By all accounts, Susan was hysterical and insisting she was about to deliver. Dr. Clark wanted her transferred upstairs for further monitoring. He told Larry to calm her down. Then he left on vacation, approximately one-half hour before the end of his scheduled duty.

Within minutes, Susan began delivering her baby in the hallway outside the x-ray lab. When Larry lifted the sheet covering Susan and "saw [his] daughter hanging from her belly" he kicked open a glass door to get the attention of hospital personnel. Susan was quickly wheeled to the delivery room where two nurses delivered her one-pound baby girl at 11:34 a.m.

After visually observing neither a heartbeat nor any respiratory activity, one of the nurses announced that the baby was stillborn. The nurse wrapped the infant in a towel and placed her on an instrument tray. Ten minutes later, Dr. LeGrand arrived and delivered the placenta. At Susan's request, he checked the fetus for gender. He made no further examination of the infant, assuming it to be a nonviable fetus. After assuring himself that Susan was fine, and offering his condolences to the disappointed parents, he returned to his office.

Meanwhile, Larry called relatives to advise them of the stillbirth. Upon his return to Susan's room, he touched the infant's finger. Much to his surprise, his grasp was returned. Larry told a nurse in attendance that the baby was alive but the nurse retorted that it was only a "reflex motion." The nurses subsequently determined that the baby *was* alive. After having left her on an instrument tray for nearly half an hour, the nurses rushed the infant to the neonatal intensive care unit. The infant, registered on her birth certificate as Natalie Sue, received comfort support measures until she died about twelve hours later. Further facts will be detailed as they become pertinent to the issues on appeal.

III. In January 1987, the Oswalds sued the hospital and doctors Clark, Smith and LeGrand on theories of negligence, negligent loss of chance of survival, breach of implied contract and breach of implied warranty. As to Dr. LeGrand and the hospital, Oswalds additionally alleged gross negligence. Factually, these causes of action were premised on violation of the standard of prenatal care owed to Susan Oswald and alleged negligence in the examination and treatment of Natalie Sue including failure to recognize signs of an imminent premature birth, failure to properly prepare for such delivery, and delaying timely and vital treatment to the infant upon her birth. The Oswalds claimed damages for Natalie Sue's lost chance to live, their loss of society and companionship flowing from Natalie Sue's death, severe emotional distress and anxiety resulting from the defendants' negligence in the care of both Susan and Natalie Sue, and severe emotional distress and mental anguish caused by witnessing the negligent treatment of their newborn infant.

* * *

IV.   * * *

A. *Evidence not within common knowledge.*   To begin, there is no evidence in this record that more prompt or heroic efforts to sustain Natalie Sue's life would have been successful.   * * *

Similarly, the record contains no evidence that the doctors' or hospital's treatment of Susan in any way prompted Susan's premature delivery or could have, in any way, prevented it.   * * *

B. *Evidence within the "common knowledge" exception.*   Beyond these fundamental treatment issues, however, lie plaintiffs' claims that the care provided by defendants Clark, LeGrand, and Mercy Hospital fell below the standard of medical professionalism understood by laypersons and expected by them.   Into this category fall Nurse Slater's unwelcoming remarks upon Susan's arrival at the birthing area; Nurse Gardner's deprecating description of a fetus as a "big blob of blood"; Dr. Clark's tirade outside Susan's door; Dr. Clark's insensitivity to Susan's insistence that she was in the final stage of labor, leaving her in a hysterical state minutes before her delivery in a hospital corridor while he went "off call"; Nurse Flynn's determination that the fetus was stillborn, only to discover it gasping for breath half-an-hour later; and Dr. LeGrand's admitted failure to make an independent determination of the viability of the fetus, conceding it was his obligation to do so. Larry and Susan contend that they have suffered severe emotional distress as a result of these alleged breaches of professional conduct.

We note preliminarily that because the Oswalds can sustain no claim of physical injury, they would ordinarily be denied recovery in a negligence action for emotional distress. [ ] An exception exists, however, where the nature of the relationship between the parties is such that there arises a duty to exercise ordinary care to avoid causing emotional harm. [ ] Such claims have been recognized in the negligent performance of contractual services that carry with them deeply emotional responses in the event of breach as, for example, in the transmission and delivery of telegrams announcing the death of a close relative, [ ] and services incident to a funeral and burial. [ ] Under the comparable circumstances demonstrated by this record, we think liability for emotional injury should attach to the delivery of medical services. As we observed by way of analogy in *Meyer,* the birth of a child involves a matter of life and death evoking such "mental concern and solicitude" that the breach of a contract incident thereto "will inevitably result in mental anguish, pain and suffering." *Meyer,* 241 N.W.2d at 920 (quoting *Stewart v. Rudner,* 349 Mich. 459, 84 N.W.2d 816). * * * [ ]

Insofar as the sufficiency of damages are concerned, the Oswalds' claim appears undisputed.[2] The question is whether these six incidents, if proven at trial, would demonstrate a breach of professional medical conduct so obvious as to be within the common knowledge of laypersons without the aid of expert testimony; or, in the alternative, whether plaintiffs could prove the standard of care and its breach through defendants' own testimony. In other words, is the evidence presented by plaintiffs' resistance to the motion sufficient to overcome summary judgment on defendants' claim that no material dispute exists with respect to the issues of negligence and causation? We are persuaded that it is.

The first three incidents described above raise commonly understood issues of professional courtesy in communication regarding a patient's care and treatment. No expert testimony is needed to elaborate on whether the statements by the nurses and Dr. Clark were rude and uncaring; a lay fact finder could easily evaluate the statements in light of the surrounding circumstances to determine whether the language used or message conveyed breached the standard of care expected of medical professionals, and determine the harm, if any, resulting to the plaintiffs. In reaching this conclusion we hasten to emphasize that our decision in this case is closely limited to its facts. We in no way suggest that a professional person must ordinarily answer in tort for rudeness, even in a professional relationship. In order for liability to attach there must appear a combination of the two factors existing here: extremely rude behavior or crass insensitivity coupled with an unusual vulnerability on the part of the person receiving professional services.

We are similarly convinced that a lay jury is also capable of evaluating the professional propriety of Dr. Clark's early departure from the hospital, knowing that he had left Susan Oswald unattended in a hospital corridor screaming hysterically that she was about to give birth.   * * *

* * *

C.   *Evidence demonstrable through defendants' admissions.*   * * *

* * *

2. Because the trial court determined plaintiffs' proof was insufficient on the elements of negligence and causation, it did not reach the question of damages. The record reveals that both Susan and Larry have undergone psychological counseling in an effort to overcome the stress, anxiety, and depression associated with Susan's fear of becoming pregnant again and Larry's anger and guilt over the extraordinary helplessness he felt as a witness to his wife's painful and humiliating experience at Mercy Hospital. To the extent that the trial court considered, and dismissed, any claim of intentional infliction of emotional distress due to a perceived lack of "outrageousness" in defendants' conduct, we note that plaintiffs' emotional distress claim has not been pleaded as an independent tort but rather as an element of damages flowing from the underlying breach of professional conduct. Under such circumstances, the dismissal was not warranted because proof of outrageous conduct need not be shown.

Defendants argue that because Natalie Sue's death was inevitable, the emotional distress suffered by the Oswalds is understandable but not compensable. What defendants overlook is the colorable claim of severe emotional distress proximately caused by the equivocation of these health care professionals on the very question of her life or death. Under this record, we think the plaintiffs have produced evidence minimally sufficient to overcome summary judgment on this claim of malpractice.

* * *

In conclusion, we affirm in part, reverse in part, and remand this case for further proceedings not inconsistent with this opinion.

Affirmed in part, reversed in part, and remanded.

Notes and Questions

1. *Oswald* focuses on the vulnerability of the plaintiffs, coupled with the "crass insensitivity" of the medical staff. Consider, as a companion case, Wargelin v. Sisters of Mercy Health Corporation, 149 Mich.App. 75, 385 N.W.2d 732 (1986). In *Wargelin*, a series of obstetric disasters befell the plaintiffs. The obstetrician made only two visits during labor, even though a Caesarean section was indicated due to the plaintiff's lopsided uterus; the fetal monitor indicated distress, but the staff failed to react; an intern subsequently delivered the plaintiff's child, not breathing and blue in color, and placed it on her stomach as if it were a healthy child; the obstetrician then grabbed the child and began to pound on its chest and administer electrical shocks to revive it; a call for a pediatrician to help went unanswered; and after fifteen minutes the rescue attempt was abandoned.

The Michigan court applied the bystander rule, which allows that a member of the family witnessing an injury to a third person may recover if they are present or suffer shock "fairly contemporaneous" with the accident. The court held that the series of events related above, including negligent acts, were sufficient. " * * * [T]he cumulative effect of all the events surrounding the stillbirth of the child, if proven to be negligent at trial, are sufficient to cause a parent to suffer emotional and mental distress."

Do *Oswald* and *Wargelin*, read together, expand the applicability of the tort of negligent infliction of mental distress? They indicate judicial sensitivity to hospital failures to provide sensitive, well-trained health care, and willingness to extend the bystander doctrine to allow recovery in these highly charged situations.

2. Negligent infliction of mental distress cases typically involve "bystanders" who witness injury to a loved one. Dillon v. Legg, 68 Cal.2d 728, 69 Cal.Rptr. 72, 441 P.2d 912 (1968) was the first case to articulate a general test of foreseeability of harm, a primary guideline being whether the distress resulted from the "sensory and contemporaneous observance of the accident." Parents would thus need to "observe" the accident or trauma in jurisdictions following the *Dillon* approach.

The California Supreme Court limited the *Dillon* "foreseeability" approach in Thing v. La Chusa, 48 Cal.3d 644, 257 Cal.Rptr. 865, 771 P.2d 814 (1989). The court noted that " * * * [t]he emotional distress for which monetary damages may be recovered * * * ought not to be that form of acute emotional distress or the transient emotional reaction to the occasional gruesome or horrible incident to which every person may potentially be exposed in an industrial and sometimes violent society." The court then said that a plaintiff could recover only if he:

(1) is closely related to the injury victim; (2) is present at the scene of the injury producing event at the time it occurs and is then aware that it is causing injury to the victim; and (3) as a result suffers serious emotional distress—a reaction beyond that which would be anticipated in a disinterested witness and which is not an abnormal response to the circumstances.

In Johnson v. Ruark Obstetrics and Gynecology Associates, P.A., 327 N.C. 283, 395 S.E.2d 85 (1990), the expectant parents of a stillborn fetus sued the physicians for the negligent infliction of mental distress. The parents alleged they had observed events surrounding the death of the fetus. The North Carolina Supreme Court, in ruling on the defendant's motion to dismiss, allowed a cause of action for the negligent infliction of emotional distress based on a test of reasonably foreseeable consequences.

In Frame v. Kothari, 212 N.J.Super. 498, 515 A.2d 810 (1985), the defendant physician's misdiagnosis of a cerebellar hemorrhage and acute hydrocephalus due to blunt trauma to the skull was held to be an event perceived by the parents. First, the parents' discussion with the defendant about their son's deteriorating condition was an "observation;" and second, their distress was foreseeable after the doctor was informed of the condition and failed to properly treat it. See also Ochoa v. Superior Court of Santa Clara County, 39 Cal.3d 159, 216 Cal.Rptr. 661, 703 P.2d 1 (1985), where a mother suffered distress after visiting her son who was receiving "woefully inadequate" medical care in a juvenile detention home.

Consider the following situations:

• Parents are standing outside the operating room waiting for their baby to undergo surgery. He is negligently burned during the surgery, and they discover the burn when he is brought out. Smelko v. Brinton, 241 Kan. 763, 740 P.2d 591 (1987) (merely seeing the bad result is not sufficient for recovery).

• A physician negligently diagnoses a pregnant woman's condition as requiring an abortion, when the abortion is not necessary. The woman aborts the fetus, and then discovers the abortion was not needed. Martinez v. Long Island Jewish Hillside Medical Center, 70 N.Y.2d 697, 518 N.Y.S.2d 955, 512 N.E.2d 538 (1987) (recovery allowed); Lynch v. Bay Ridge Obstetrical and Gynecological Associates, P.C., 72 N.Y.2d 632, 536 N.Y.S.2d 11, 532 N.E.2d 1239 (1988) (recovery allowed).

• A physician negligently performs amniocentesis on a pregnant woman, with the result that her child is stillborn. Tebbutt v. Virostek, 65 N.Y.2d 931, 493 N.Y.S.2d 1010, 483 N.E.2d 1142 (1985) (no recovery, since the observation of another's death must be "contemporaneous").

3. If a contractual relationship forms the basis for liability for emotional distress, some jurisdictions have held that the injured party need not have observed the disaster, as foreseeability is not required. In Newton v. Kaiser Hospital, 184 Cal.App.3d 386, 228 Cal.Rptr. 890 (1986) the plaintiffs' baby was born partially paralyzed as the result of the doctor's failure to perform a caesarian section. The father was not present and the mother was unconscious, but both were allowed to sue for their emotional distress. The court held that "[t]he mother had a contract with Kaiser by which it undertook, for consideration, to provide care and treatment for the delivery of a healthy fetus. Kaiser's contract was the source of its duty and a determination of foreseeability is unnecessary to establish a duty of care". (Id. at 894).

In Rowe v. Bennett, 514 A.2d 802 (Me.1986), a lesbian psychotherapist continued to treat her lesbian patient even though she had developed an emotional relationship with the patient's lover. The Maine Supreme Court held that the nature of the therapist-patient relationship could provide the basis for a claim of emotional distress. The court wrote:

> Given the fact that a therapist undertakes the treatment of a patient's mental problems and that the patient is encouraged to divulge his innermost thoughts, the patient is extremely vulnerable to mental harm if the therapist fails to adhere to the standards of care recognized by the profession. Any psychological harm that may result from such negligence is neither speculative nor easily feigned. Unlike evidence of mental distress occurring in other situations, objective proof of the existence vel non of a psychological injury in these circumstances should not be difficult to obtain. (Id. at 819–20).

Are the courts in *Newton* and *Rowe* expanding notions of fiduciary obligations arising out of professional relationships to justify emotional distress damages? The vulnerable plaintiff is the theme that ties together many of these cases.

4. In Strachan v. John F. Kennedy Memorial Hospital, 109 N.J. 523, 538 A.2d 346 (1988), a brain-dead twenty-year old patient was kept on life support for three days after the parents had requested it be discontinued. The parents saw him on life-support during that time, and, because of this, claimed the negligent infliction of mental distress, with the hospital's negligence its failure to have proper procedures in place for removing life support or releasing dead person to family. The New Jersey Supreme Court did not decide whether the parents had an emotional distress claim for damages suffered directly, absent physical injury; they based their damage award instead on the general duty of a hospital to act reasonably in honoring the parents' requests to have their son's dead body turned over to them. See also Burgess v. Perdue, 239 Kan. 473, 721 P.2d 239 (1986) (plaintiff's son died during emergency treatment; mother agreed to limited autopsy, but coroner did a complete autopsy and removed son's brain to a storage jar. The treating physician found the brain three weeks after the son's funeral, called the mother, told her he had Stephen's brain in a jar, and asked what she wanted done with it. Held: not extreme and outrageous under the Restatement (Second) test of section 46(1) (1963)).

2. Fraud and Concealment Actions

In a few jurisdictions, courts have allowed a separate intentional tort theory to be pleaded along with a negligence claim, where the physician has deliberately altered records to create misleading entries, or has knowingly made a false material representation to a plaintiff. These claims have three purposes: (1) to show fraudulent concealment by the physician of obvious negligence, so that the statute of limitations will be tolled; (2) to void the patient's informed consent to a procedure, so that a battery theory may be used; (3) as a separate theory of recovery. See generally D. Louisell and H. Williams, Medical Malpractice, para. 8.11, p. 8–144 (1984). Fraudulent concealment will toll the statute of limitations.

The party seeking to take advantage of a defendant's fraudulent concealment has the burden of proving that the defendant affirmatively concealed the facts upon which the cause of action is based. As one court noted, however, " * * * the close relationship of trust and confidence between patient and physician gives rise to duties of disclosure which may obviate the need for a patient to prove an affirmative act of concealment." Koppes v. Pearson, 384 N.W.2d 381 (Iowa 1986).

In Simcuski v. Saeli, 44 N.Y.2d 442, 406 N.Y.S.2d 259, 265, 377 N.E.2d 713 (1978), a physician negligently injured a nerve in plaintiff's neck during surgical excision of a node from her neck. He then falsely told her that her postoperative pains were transient and would disappear if she would continue a regimen of physiotherapy which he prescribed. She learned four years later that her injury was caused by surgery, and that it was now too late to try to correct the nerve damage. The court required the plaintiff to show by clear and convincing evidence that (1) the physician knew of the fact of his malpractice and the injury suffered by his patient as a consequence; (2) "the physician thereafter made material, factual misrepresentation to the patient with respect to the subject matter of the malpractice and the therapy appropriate to its cure, on which the patient justifiably relied", knowing it to be false; (3) that the condition caused by the malpractice could have been corrected or alleviated absent the fraud. The court stated as to this that "if there is not an available, efficacious remedy or cure which the plaintiff is diverted from undertaking in consequence of the intentional, fraudulent misrepresentation—as in many instances of medical malpractice there may not be—there will normally be only minimal damages, if any."

An action for deceit requires proof that a false representation of a material fact was made and was relied upon by the patient in ignorance, and that damage resulted. The representation must be made fraudulently, since an intention to deceive by the physician is needed. See Harris v. Penninger, 613 S.W.2d 211 (Mo.App.1981). In Hart v. Browne, 103 Cal.App.3d 947, 163 Cal.Rptr. 356 (1980), a physician was sued for fraud when he advised the lawyer for a surgeon's patient that the surgeon's conduct was not negligent, although the records he had examined in fact showed abundant negligence. See also Henry v. Deen, 310 N.C. 75, 310 S.E.2d 326 (1984) (civil conspiracy and a punitive damages claim allowed); Krueger v. St. Joseph's Hospital, 305 N.W.2d 18 (N.D.1981) (a claim in fraud allowed based upon the physician's false representations.)

Some commentators have advocated development of this rather sparse line of caselaw into a new theory of a duty to disclose. This would require negligent health care providers to confess their negligence to the patients injured by it. Vogel and Delgado, To Tell The Truth: Physicians' Duty to Disclose Medical Mistakes, 28 U.C.L.A.L. Rev. 52 (1980); LeBlang and King, Tort Liability for Nondisclosure: the Physician's Legal Obligations to Disclose Patient Illness and Injury, 89 Dick.L.Rev. 1 (1984). How likely are health care professionals to make such disclosures in the face of the indefinite risks of being sued?

D. DEFENSES TO A MALPRACTICE SUIT

1. *The Respectable Minority Exception*

HENDERSON v. HEYER–SCHULTE CORP.

Court of Civil Appeals of Texas, 1980.
600 S.W.2d 844.

PEDEN, JUSTICE.

Carol Henderson appeals from a take-nothing judgment in a medical malpractice suit. * * *

Defendant-appellee Dr. Philip Rothenberg is a specialist in plastic surgery who has practiced in Houston since 1973. In September of 1974, Dr. Rothenberg performed a mammary augmentation operation on Mrs. Henderson, inserting artificial breast implants manufactured by Heyer–Schulte Corporation. The implants consisted of silicone envelopes filled with a soft silicone gel. After inserting each implant, Dr. Rothenberg intentionally slit the envelope to allow the gel to escape into the retro-mammary pockets.

Several days after the surgery, Mrs. Henderson began experiencing swelling, soreness, and inflammation of her breasts. She returned to Dr. Rothenberg, who examined her and diagnosed a hematoma (collection of blood) behind her left breast. She was hospitalized immediately, and Dr. Rothenberg removed the implant from her left breast, drained the hematoma, inserted a new Heyer–Schulte implant, and again ruptured the envelope.

While Mrs. Henderson continued seeing Dr. Rothenberg for post-operative care until early December, she continued to experience pain and inflammation. She later developed numerous small lumps or nodules under the skin of her chest and abdomen; these were later diagnosed as siliconomas, caused by accumulations of migrating silicone gel. The testimony is in dispute as to whether the siliconomas arose after other doctors had operated on her. Although she has undergone over twenty surgical operations to remove the siliconomas, they continue to appear. In addition, Mrs. Henderson has suffered several deformities in the shape and placement of her breasts. She has consulted many other physicians and has undergone subsequent augmentation procedures, some of which were sought to further increase the size of her breasts.

Mrs. Henderson sued both Dr. Rothenberg and Heyer–Schulte Corporation, alleging that Dr. Rothenberg was negligent in his care and treatment of her and that Heyer–Schulte was guilty of both negligence and breach of warranty in manufacturing a defective product. The defendants sued each other for indemnity or contribution. Prior to the trial, Heyer–Schulte settled with Mrs. Henderson, but it remained in the suit because of the doctor's cross-action. The case was tried before a jury and a take-nothing judgment was rendered.

The evidence established that the surgical technique or procedure followed by Dr. Rothenberg in this case was taught to him at Baylor College of Medicine and was utilized by various qualified and respected plastic surgeons in the Houston area at one time. It is also uncontroverted that the use of such technique is no longer recognized or accepted. The heart of the controversy in this case was submitted to the jury in the first two special issues: was the defendant negligent in using that technique in September of 1974, and if so, was that negligence a proximate cause of damage to the plaintiff?

* * *

Mrs. Henderson first complains about an instruction given by the trial judge, saying it was not a correct statement of the law, was inconsistent with the proper standard of care required of physicians in choosing surgical procedures, was in conflict with the decision of the Texas Supreme Court in *Hood v. Phillips,* 554 S.W.2d 160 (1977), and constituted a comment on the weight of the evidence to such an extent as to amount to a directed verdict. The instruction reads:

> If you find from the credible evidence that other plastic surgeons recognized more than one method for performing augmentation mammoplasties at the time in question you are instructed that Dr. Rothenberg was at liberty to select any of such methods. A doctor is not negligent merely because he made a choice of a recognized alternative method for the procedures he followed in the treatment of a patient, if he exercised the required skill and care in administering and following the method of his choice. This would be true even though other medical witnesses may not agree with the choice he made.

* * *

Mrs. Henderson made a timely objection to the instruction and later requested an amendment to the charge instructing the jury to disregard it.

We agree that the instruction should not have been given. The Supreme Court of Texas in *Hood v. Phillips,* supra, established the proper test for the standard of care in a medical malpractice case where the plaintiff attacks the surgical procedure selected and employed by the doctor. After discussing several tests which had been followed in this and in other jurisdictions, the Court concluded:

> We are of the opinion that the statement of the law most serviceable to this jurisdiction is as follows: A physician who undertakes a mode or form of treatment which a reasonable and prudent member of the medical profession would undertake under the same or similar circumstances shall not be subject to liability for harm caused thereby to the patient. The question which conveys to the jury the standard which should be applicable is as follows: Did the physician undertake a mode or form of treatment which a reasonable and prudent member of the medical profession would not undertake under the same or similar circumstances? [ ]

The court expressly rejected standards which would release doctors from liability when a "respectable minority" or a "considerable number" of physicians adhere to the procedures in question. As Mrs. Henderson points out, the instruction given in this case does not even go that far in establishing a minimal threshold. It simply directs the jury to consider whether "other plastic surgeons" recognized the method used by Dr. Rothenberg. There is no requirement that the "other" surgeons be reasonable or prudent or that they be prepared to employ that method under circumstances similar to those Dr. Rothenberg faced, the two factors most stressed in *Hood.*

* * *

[The court concluded that the instruction was harmless error, and that the plaintiff's evidence was insufficient to show that the "rupture method" was no longer in use by reasonable plastic surgeons.]

The judgment is affirmed.

Notes and Questions

1. The court adopts the test of Hood v. Phillips, 554 S.W.2d 160 (Tex.1977), replacing the "respectable minority" test with a "reasonable and prudent" physician test. Is this an improvement? What are the Texas courts worried about? What about the experimenter who wants to try something new? Does the Texas test provide her with any protection, or is it a test based in reality on customary majority practice?

2. States that instruct on "two schools of thought" often impose restrictions on the defense.

a. Size of the respectable minority. Pennsylvania limits the doctrine to cases involving schools of thought followed by a "considerable number of physicians." Duckworth v. Bennett, 320 Pa. 47, 181 A. 558 (1935), cited with approval by the court in D'Angelis v. Zakuto, 383 Pa.Super. 65, 556 A.2d 431, 433 (1989).

b.   Failures to properly diagnose. Where the critical issue is what the diagnosis is, as for example whether the patient had a localized or a generalized infection, then the "two schools of thought" or "alternative means of treatment" instruction may not be appropriate where there is only one agreed approach to each type of infection. See Hutchinson v. Broadlawns Medical Center, 459 N.W.2d 273 (Iowa 1990). In D'Angelis v. Zakuto, 383 Pa.Super. 65, 556 A.2d 431, 433 (1989), the Superior Court held that the instruction is intended for situations where medical experts may disagree among themselves. It is however not appropriately given where "the symptoms of a disease or the effects of an injury are so well known that a reasonably competent and skillful physician or surgeon ought to be able to diagnose the disease or injury * * *" (quoting Morganstein v. House, 377 Pa.Super. 512, 547 A.2d 1180 (1988).

c.   Weight given to plaintiff experts as to good practice. In Ourada v. Cochran, 234 Neb. 63, 449 N.W.2d 211 (1989), the court rejected a jury instruction that seemed to give the jury too much leeway to reject the plaintiff's experts' testimony. The rejected instruction read:

> A physician who is a specialist is not bound to use any particular method of procedure; and if, among physicians of ordinary skill and learning in that specialty, more than one method of procedure is recognized as proper, it is not negligence for a physician to adopt any of such methods. The fact that some other method of procedure exist, or the fact that some other physician in that specialty testified in this case that he might or would have used or advised another or a different method, does not, standing alone, establish that the specialist used an improper procedure; nor would it be an act of negligence or impropriety for the specialist not to have adopted another method.

But see DiFilippo v. Preston, 53 Del. 539, 173 A.2d 333 (1961): choice by defendant surgeon of one of two acceptable techniques is not negligence.

3.   Consider Chumbler v. McClure, 505 F.2d 489 (6th Cir.1974). The plaintiff was injured in an electrical explosion. Dr. McClure diagnosed his illness as cerebral vascular insufficiency and prescribed a female hormone, estrogen, produced and marketed commercially as Premarin. Premarin's known side effects included enlargement of the breasts and loss of libido. The trial court directed a verdict for the defendant on the grounds that the plaintiff failed to show any deviation from accepted medical practice. The testimony in the case was that Dr. McClure was the only neurosurgeon, out of nine in Nashville, using such therapy for cerebral vascular disease. One expert admitted that there was no specific established treatment for the disease. The court, in affirming the directed verdict, wrote:

> The record in this case is devoid of evidence of such deviation. The most favorable interpretation that may be placed on the testimony adduced at trial below is that there is a division of opinion in the medical profession regarding the use of Premarin in the treatment of cerebral vascular insufficiency, and that Dr. McClure was alone among neurosurgeons in Nashville in using such therapy. The test for malpractice and for community standards is not to be determined solely by a plebiscite. Where two or more schools of thought exist among competent members of the medical profession concerning proper medi-

cal treatment for a given ailment, each of which is supported by responsible medical authority, it is not malpractice to be among the minority in a given city who follow one of the accepted schools.

In *Chumbler,* the minority of which the defendant was a part seems to have consisted only of himself, which hardly seems "respectable". By what measure should the courts measure a respectable minority practice? Is this doctrine just a judicial acknowledgement of the medical profession's uncertainty over how to treat diseases such as cerebral vascular insufficiency?

4. The "respectable minority" rule allows for variation in clinical judgment: " * * * a physician does not incur liability merely by electing to pursue one of several recognized courses of treatment." Downer v. Veilleux, 322 A.2d 82, 87 (Me.1974). If a defendant established that distinctive practices are supported by a minority within the professional group, the judge may direct a verdict for the defendant rather than leaving the issue to the jury. Hamilton v. Hardy, 37 Colo.App. 375, 549 P.2d 1099 (1976). In the typical case, the minority approach is followed by at least a few doctors, and is often the "best available" for a certain problem. Leech v. Bralliar, 275 F.Supp. 897 (D.Ariz.1967) (prolotherapy for whiplash; 65 doctors in the country used this treatment, with a claimed 85% success rate; the defendant was held liable because he varied the treatment and therefore became a minority of one within the respectable minority.)

5. The "respectable minority" standard is sometimes applied in medical license revocation hearings under state Medical Practice Acts. In Clark v. Department of Professional Regulation, Board of Medical Examiners, 463 So.2d 328 (Fla.App.1985), the Florida Board of Medical Examiners had revoked the license of Dr. Clark and the revocation was upheld on appeal. Florida law empowered the Board of Medical Examiners to revoke, suspend or otherwise discipline a licensed medical doctor for: "Gross or repeated malpractice or the failure to practice medicine with that level of care, skill, and treatment which is recognized by a reasonably prudent similar physician as being acceptable under similar conditions and circumstances." Dr. Clark diagnosed a patient as having cancer, and treated her with chemotherapy in conjunction with metabolic therapy, using Laetrile. Chemotherapy and metabolic therapy are incompatible and should not be used together. The hearing examiner concluded that subsection t had been violated by Clark, " * * * by failing to properly stage and treat Ms. Burroughs' disease", and by administering metabolic therapy, "a form of cancer treatment not generally accepted by the medical profession or by a respectable minority of the medical profession * * *."

463 So.2d at 330–331.

6. The "honest error in judgment" doctrine is a corollary of the "respectable minority" rule. The respectable minority rule allows for a choice between alternative approaches to diagnosis or treatment; the honest error in judgment doctrine allows for a range of uncertainty in choosing between alternative treatments. A typical jury instruction reads:

> a [physician] is not a guarantor of a cure or a good result from his treatment and he is not responsible for an honest error in judgment in choosing between accepted methods of treatment.

This was a standard Minnesota instruction, which was rejected in Ouellette v. Subak, 391 N.W.2d 810 (Minn.1986). In Ouellette, the court held that this instruction is misleading and subjective. The court proposed an instruction that focussed the jury's attention on both the diagnostic workup and its adequacy, and on the accepted nature of the treatment choice:

> A doctor is not negligent simply because his or her efforts prove unsuccessful. The fact a doctor may have chosen a method of treatment that later proves to be unsuccessful is not negligence if the treatment chosen was an accepted treatment on the basis of the information available to the doctor at the time a choice had to be made; a doctor must, however, use reasonable care to obtain the information needed to exercise his or her professional judgment, and an unsuccessful method of treatment chosen because of a failure to use such reasonable care would be negligence.

Is the court's reshaping of the doctrine in its proposed instructions an improvement over the previous "honest error in judgment" instruction? What are the court's concerns? Does their instruction address those concerns?

In Haase v. Garfinkel, 418 S.W.2d 108 (Mo.1967), the doctor, a heart specialist, failed to treat his patient with anticoagulants. At the time, the profession was divided upon the use of these drugs because of powerful side-effects. The court wrote: "Even if defendant had been mistaken about their use in Mr. Haase's case he was entitled to a wide range in the exercise of his judgment and discretion and could not be found guilty of negligence 'unless it be shown that the course pursued was clearly against the course recognized as correct by the profession generally. As long as there is room for an honest difference of opinion among competent physicians, a physician who uses his own best judgment cannot be convicted of negligence, even though it may afterward develop that he was mistaken.'[   ]"

Problem: To Monitor or Not?

You are general counsel for the Columbia Hospital for Women. The head obstetric resident has just walked into your office to get your advice regarding hospital policy. Jane Rudd, pregnant with her second child, has just been admitted to the Obstetrics Ward at term and in labor. The charts reveal that her first delivery of a healthy 7½ pound baby boy had been uncomplicated. Upon admission, she asked not to be given intravenous fluids and stated that she does not want continuous fetal monitoring (EFM). Rather, she wished to be free to walk around with her husband during labor. The nurses told her that hospital policy requires electronic monitoring of all women in labor. The patient responded that she did not need EFM during her first labor, which went well, and expects the same experience again. She has appealed to the resident, who has discussed the request with the staff.

The staff split over the issue. One doctor argued that the policy is a wise measure intended to protect infants. Further, EFM shields staff from accusations that the best care was not provided, if a bad outcome occurs. Another doctor opposed routine EFM, arguing that unmonitored fetuses run an extremely small risk of fetal distress or intrapartum death. In

1965, without monitoring the intrapartum death rate was only 1.5 per 1,000 among all labors involving infants who weighed 5½ pounds or more. The mother's risk status is altered, however, since the likelihood of a Caesarean section is increased. This doctor pointed out that a careful British study of low-risk patients revealed that the rate of C-sections doubled, from 4.4 to 9%, when EFM was used. An American study found that the number of Caesareans performed on women hospitalized for delivery between 1980 and 1987 jumped 48%, much of this increase traceable to fetal monitoring.

If Ms. Rudd is allowed to labor with reasonable staff surveillance by auscultation, i.e. use of the stethoscope by staff on a regular basis, and if the obstetric unit can resuscitate her infant if the unexpected occurs, then, this doctor argued, the risks for both mother and child are very low.

You have done some further reading, and have uncovered the following legal discussions. Consider the comments of Schifrin, Weissman, and Wiley:

> [T]he standard of care today requires EFM for all high-risk patients. It is recommended that EFM be used in low-risk patients as well, despite the fact that authoritative guidelines find auscultation acceptable in such patients. While no guidelines to define minimal standards of interpretation of fetal heartrate patterns exist, given the current climate, the decision to forego EFM requires documentation of the reasons and a discussion with the patient.

> Electronic Fetal Monitoring and Obstetrical Malpractice, 13 Law, Medicine & Health Care 100, 104 (1985).

One study compared universal continuous monitoring with selective monitoring, grouping patients into high- or low-risk categories. The authors concluded that universal monitoring changed obstetric practices, increasing the C-section rate at the hospital studied, "but did not significantly improve perinatal outcome * * * We conclude that not all pregnancies * * * need continuous electronic fetal monitoring during labor." Leveno et al., A Prospective Comparison of Selective and Universal Electronic Fetal Monitoring in 34,995 Pregnancies, 315 N.Eng.J.Med. 615, 618 (1986). The authors estimated, however, that more than two thirds of U.S. pregnancies are continuously monitored. Fetal monitoring has a high false positive rate and low specificity.

A second study analyzed the neurologic development of premature infants. The authors compared the early development of children born prematurely whose heart rates were monitored electronically during delivery, compared to children born prematurely whose heart rates were monitored by auscultation. The authors found that not only had the infants' neurologic development not improved with monitoring, compared with auscultation, but there was a 2.9–fold increase in the odds of having cerebral palsy with the monitored infants. Shy et al., Effects of Electronic Fetal–Heart–Rate Monitoring, As Compared with Periodic Auscultation, on the Neurologic Development of Premature Infants, 322 N.Eng.J.Med. 588 (1990). The authors noted, however, that the trials for the study had dedicated nurses assigned to the auscultation group, "a circumstance that is not always possible in a busy clinical setting."

In another study, the authors found that "[w]hen fetal accidents, such as prolapsed cord or abruptio placentae, have occurred on our service, *they were diagnosed not by continuous FHR monitoring but by the standard technique of intrapartum surveillance and good nursing care.*" Goodlin & Haesslein, When Is It Fetal Distress? 128 Am.J.Obst. & Gyn. 442 (1977). For an argument against fetal monitoring as customary practice, see Gilfix, Electronic Fetal Monitoring: Physician Liability and Informed Consent, 10 Am.J.Law & Med. 31 (1984).

The American College of Obstetricians and Gynecologists advise that patients at high risk have either continuous electronic fetal monitoring or intermittent auscultation every 15 minutes in the first stage of labor and every 5 minutes in the second stage. Low risk patients are advised to have auscultation every 30 minutes in the first stage and every 15 minutes in the second.

What policies will minimize the hospital's liability exposure while also respecting the patient's wishes whenever it is safe to do so? How do the tort doctrines we have discussed interact?

2. *Clinical Innovation*

BROOK v. ST. JOHN'S HICKEY MEMORIAL HOSPITAL

Supreme Court of Indiana, 1978.
269 Ind. 270, 380 N.E.2d 72.

HUNTER, JUSTICE.

This case is before us on the petition to transfer of Warren E. Fischer, M.D. The Court of Appeals [ ] reversed a jury verdict in Dr. Fischer's favor. The Court of Appeals held that the trial court committed reversible error in failing to give certain of the plaintiffs' tendered instructions and ordered a new trial as to Dr. Fischer on that basis. We have granted transfer on the petition of Dr. Fischer. We find that the Court of Appeals committed error in reversing the judgment of the trial court as to Dr. Fischer and hereby affirm the trial court.

This case began as an action by Tracy Lynn Brook and her father (Arthur) against St. John's Hickey Memorial Hospital, Guy E. Ross, M.D., Lawrence Allen, M.D., and Dr. Fischer. The record discloses that Tracy was diagnosed by a specialist as having a possible urological disorder and that X-rays taken with a contrast medium would be necessary to confirm the diagnosis. The Court of Appeals summarized Dr. Fischer's role in Tracy's treatment as follows:

"Dr. Fischer, a radiologist, injected the contrast medium into the calves of both of Tracy's legs, because he was unable to find a vein which he could use. The package insert, which contained the manufacturer's directions for injecting the contrast medium, recommended that the contrast medium be injected into the gluteal muscles (buttocks). * * *

"A short while [four months later] after being discharged from the hospital Tracy began to have trouble with her right leg. Her leg was stiff and her heel began to lift off the ground. Tracy's problem was later diagnosed as a shortening of the achilles tendon, which *may* have been precipitated by some kind of trauma to her ankle or calf muscle. After two operations and other expensive treatment, including the wearing of a leg brace, Tracy's problem was substantially corrected."   368 N.E.2d 264, 266, 267 [emphasis added].

* * *

* * * [T]he Brooks contended that the trial court erred in refusing to give to the jury plaintiffs' tendered instruction No. 4 which reads as follows:

"You are instructed that a Radiologist is not limited to the most generally used of several modes of procedure and the use of another mode known and proved by the profession is proper, but every new method of procedure should pass through an experimental stage in its development and a Radiologist is not authorized in trying untested experiments on patients."

The Brooks alleged that Dr. Fischer was negligent in choosing an injection site which had not been specifically recommended by the medical community and that this choice of an unusual injection site was a medical experiment. The trial court refused to give this instruction on the basis that since no substantial evidence of a medical experiment had been introduced, it would be erroneous to give an instruction covering medical experiments. We agree.

The Court of Appeals found that since there was no evidence presented which showed that any other doctors had used the calf muscles as an injection site, Dr. Fischer's use of them may have been a medical experiment. We disagree. The record clearly shows that Dr. Fischer had several compelling, professional reasons for choosing the calf muscles as an injection site for the contrast medium in this case.

First, the record shows that Dr. Fischer had read medical journals which cautioned against the injection of the contrast medium into the buttocks (gluteal area) and thighs of infants and small children. * * *.

Tracy Brook was only twenty-three months old when the injection was given. Dr. Fischer testified that other articles had also warned against the use of the thighs in young children. Because Dr. Fischer was trying to avoid any damage to the sciatic nerve, he chose the next largest muscle mass "away from the trunk" as the site for the injection.

Second, Dr. Fischer had used this injection site successfully on children on prior occasions. He also testified that he had never read or heard anything that proscribed the selection of the calf muscles as an injection site.

Too often courts have confused judgmental decisions and experimentation. Therapeutic innovation has long been recognized as permissible to avoid serious consequences. The everyday practice of medicine involves constant judgmental decisions by physicians as they move from one patient to another in the conscious institution of procedures, special tests, trials and observations recognized generally by their profession as effective in treating the patient or providing a diagnosis of a diseased condition. Each patient presents a slightly different problem to the doctor. A physician is presumed to have the knowledge and skill necessary to use some innovation to fit the peculiar circumstances of each case.

Thus, the choice of the calf muscles as the site for the injection of a contrast medium in a two-year old child, based upon prior successful uses of this same injection site, is not a medical experiment where the use of more common sites had been warned against and where it was reasonably and prudently calculated by the physician [radiologist] to accomplish the intended purpose of diagnosis of the patient's condition.

* * *

The judgment of the trial court is in all respects affirmed.

Notes and Questions

1. If you disagree with the Supreme Court of Indiana, what do you think Dr. Fischer should have done? Should he have refused to treat Tracy? Should he have explained that his treatment was experimental? How would that have helped Tracy? See Chapter 12 for a discussion of legal limitations on human research.

2. Should the law allow a defense such as clinical innovation? Are clinicians likely to be trained scientists, keeping careful records and publishing their results for peer review? Medical researchers have criticized such clinical "experiments," calling instead for randomized scientifically valid trials. See Guyatt et al., Determining Optimal Therapy—Randomized Trials in Individual Patients, 314 N.Eng.J.Med. 889 (1986).

3. Experiments are acceptable to the courts when conventional treatments are largely ineffective or where the patient is terminally ill and has little to lose by experimentation with potentially useful treatments. Organ transplantation often involves therapeutic innovation. The classic case is Karp v. Cooley, 493 F.2d 408 (5th Cir.1974), where Dr. Denton Cooley was sued for the wrongful death of Haskell Karp. Dr. Cooley had implanted the first totally mechanical heart in Mr. Karp, who died some 32 hours after the transplant surgery. The court directed a verdict for Dr. Cooley on the issue of experimentation. It held:

> A Texas court bound in traditional malpractice actions to expert medical testimony to determine how a reasonably careful and prudent physician would have acted under the same or similar circumstances * * * would not likely vary that evidentiary requirement for an experimentation charge. This conclusion is also suggested by the few reported cases where experimentation has been recognized as a separate basis of liability. The record contains no evidence that Mr. Karp's treatment was other than therapeutic and we agree that in this context an action for experimentation must be measured by traditional malpractice evidentiary standards. Whether there was informed consent is necessarily linked to the charge of experimentation, and Mr.

Karp's consent was expressly to all three stages of the operation actually performed—each an alternative in the event of a preceding failure.

The court excluded testimony by Dr. DeBakey that the heart pump he himself had tested was not ready for use in humans and that he would not have recommended its use.   Dr. DeBakey refused however to give his opinion on the pump used by Dr. Cooley, except that it was similar to his pump.

4.   New surgical procedures and treatments, other than drugs and medical devices, fall into a regulatory gap.   Drugs and medical devices are carefully regulated by the Food and Drug Administration through licensing.   See the Federal Food, Drug, and Cosmetic Act, 21 U.S.C.A. § 301 et seq.   Human experimentation generally, if the institution is funded by the federal government in whole or part, is governed by regulations of the Department of Health and Human Services.   The regulations require the institution sponsoring the research to establish Institutional Review Boards (IRBs).   These evaluate the research proposals before any experimentation begins, in order to determine whether human subjects might be "at risk" and if so, how to protect them.   See 45 C.F.R. § 46.101(a) (1985) and Chapter 12 infra.

It is generally not difficult to determine whether a new drug or device is being used experimentally.   It is often very difficult to determine whether a particular surgical procedure is experimental.   Surgeons tend to view themselves as artists rather than scientists, custom-tailoring a treatment for a patient's ailment.

5.   Most clinical innovation falls somewhere between standard practice and experimental research.   Much of this innovation is unregulated by the government.   What kinds of controls, direct or indirect, apply to innovation in medicine?   The absence of controls over experimentation has worried some commentators, who have argued that the patient's informed consent is not a sufficient protection against untested procedures.   Such experimentation has been termed "nonvalidated practice," since the most salient attribute of a novel practice is the lack of suitable validation of its safety and efficacy.   The National Commission for the Protection of Human Subjects of Biomedical and Behavioral Research, discussing innovation, wrote:

> Radically new procedures * * * should * * * be made the object of formal research at an early stage in order to determine whether they are safe and effective.   Thus, it is the responsibility of medical practice committees, for example, to insist that a major innovation be incorporated into a formal research project.

For a good discussion of the problem, see Cowan and Bertsch, Innovative Therapy: The Responsibility of Hospitals, 5 J.Leg.Med. 219 (1984).

3. Good Samaritan Acts

Forty-nine states and the District of Columbia have adopted Good Samaritan legislation to protect health care professionals who render emergency aid from civil liability for damages for any injury they cause or enhance. The statutes take a variety of forms. West's Ann.Cal.Bus. & Prof.Code § 2395, for example, states, in relevant part:

> No licensee, who in good faith renders emergency care at the scene of an emergency, shall be liable for any civil damages as a result of any acts or omissions by such person in rendering the emergency care.

> "The scene of an emergency" as used in this section shall include, but not be limited to, the emergency rooms of hospitals in the event of a medical disaster. * * *

The following case applies the California statute in a hospital setting.

McKENNA v. CEDARS OF LEBANON HOSPITAL

Court of Appeal of California, 1979.
93 Cal.App.3d 282, 155 Cal.Rptr. 631.

Mrs. Evangeline McKenna underwent a therapeutic abortion and tubal ligation at Cedars of Lebanon Hospital on January 17, 1974. That afternoon, she had a seizure and was treated by a resident of the hospital. She stopped breathing and went into a coma from which she never recovered. She died over a week later. Her husband and children sued Dr. Margolin, her physician; Dr. Gilman, the anesthesiologist; Dr. Warner, the resident who responded to an alert from his beeper; and Cedars of Lebanon Hospital. The jury verdict was 10–2 in favor of the hospital and Dr. Warner and against plaintiffs. Plaintiffs appeal from the judgment. The primary issue here is whether there can be an emergency, as that term is used in the "Good Samaritan" statute within a hospital, so as to invoke that statute's application as a defense to the malpractice action against the doctor and hospital.

FACTS:

Mrs. McKenna entered Cedars of Lebanon Hospital January 16, 1974. Dr. Margolin, her gynecologist, performed a therapeutic abortion and a tubal sterilization on Mrs. McKenna on the morning of January 17, 1974. She was taken to the recovery room at 9:25 a.m. and stated that she had some difficulty breathing. The recovery room records show that later that morning she stated she felt much better and was returned to her room at about 10:45 a.m. She had lunch at 12:30, and the regular diet was "taken well."

At about 2 p.m., Mrs. McKenna started having seizures. The patient sharing the room with Mrs. McKenna called for assistance. The nurse's notes reveal "Unable to get pulse. Dr. Weirner [sic] called stat * * *." The nurse who originally arrived testified that the patient was "moving her arms and her legs in an uncoordinated, rigid manner which appeared to be some type of seizure activity at that time." Dr. Warner was on the floor above when his beeper sounded. He picked up the phone, spoke to the page operator, and "dashed" to Mrs. McKenna's room. About one minute elapsed from the time he heard his beeper to the time a nurse guided him into Mrs. McKenna's room.

Dr. Warner testified that he observed the patient having a grand-mal type seizure. He observed the patient, asked for Valium from a nurse, and slowly gave the patient approximately five milligrams of Valium into the I.V. tubing in order to stop the convulsions. The patient's convulsions stopped; she had a cardiac arrest and complete cessation of breathing. An anesthesiologist inserted an endotracheal tube; Dr. Warner was giving external cardiac massage, and he called for a Code Blue cardiac pulmonary resuscitation team. The patient was eventually transferred to the intensive care unit where she remained in a coma until her death on January 28, 1974. Appellants claim malpractice by Dr. Warner. As is usual in this type of case, appellants produced a doctor who testified that Dr. Warner's response to the patient's seizure fell below the standard of care and the respondents produced evidence that Dr. Warner's conduct was proper.

* * *

The jury in the case at bench was instructed: "No licensed physician, who in good faith renders emergency care at the scene of the emergency, shall be liable for any civil damages as a result of any of his acts or omissions in rendering the emergency care." * * * Appellants contend that the policy behind the Good Samaritan Statute does not apply to hospital emergencies and that the instruction should not have been given.   * * *

Business and Professions Code section 2144 applies to "emergency care at the scene of the emergency * * *." There is no limitation as to the situs of the "scene of the emergency." A 1976 amendment to the statute defined "the scene of the emergency" and included, but did not limit, that phrase to "the emergency rooms of hospitals in the event of a medical disaster." Nothing in the statute itself precludes application of the Good Samaritan Statute to emergency situations in hospitals.

* * *

Dr. Warner in the case at bench was on duty as chief resident the afternoon of the emergency; appellants have failed to demonstrate that he had any legal duty to respond to an emergency call. He was, in essence, a medical volunteer, called to the scene of an emergency from the floor above where he was conducting a routine pelvic examination. Mrs. McKenna was another doctor's patient; there is no showing Dr. Warner had a legal duty to render emergency treatment arising from his contract of employment with Cedars. In such a situation, the legislative intent of encouraging emergency medical care by doctors who have no legal duty to treat a patient is carried out by applying Business and Professions Code section 2144 to Dr. Warner.

* * *

* * * [T]he "need to encourage physicians to render emergency medical care when they otherwise might not" prevails over the policy of vindicating the rights of a malpractice victim.

In the instant case, Dr. Warner proved he was not "on call" for emergencies, was not a member of the hospital team whose job it was to respond to emergencies and did not have a previous physician-patient relationship with Mrs. McKenna. In short, at the time he responded to Mrs. McKenna's emergency, Dr. Warner was truly a volunteer. Since there was evidence showing that Dr. Warner rendered emergency care to Mrs. McKenna in good faith at the place where her emergency occurred, the Good Samaritan statute applied on its face.

Notes and Questions

1. What kinds of situations do the Good Samaritan statutes cover? Suppose a physician walking down the street on Sunday morning to buy her New York Times sees a man fall to the pavement, gasping for breath and turning blue. The physician does not have her black bag, never met the victim before, and is aware of a gathering crowd. If she attempts to help the man and is negligent in administering aid, should she be sued for malpractice? Certainly physicians have worried about such situations. Is the setting of *McKenna* distinguishable from the street rescue situation? In McCain v. Batson, 233 Mont. 288, 760 P.2d 725 (1988), a physician on vacation sutured a hiker's wound at his condominium, using limited medical supplies on hand. The court held that this was an "emergency" within the meaning of statute.

2. The majority of state statutes exclude medical services rendered in the hospital from the coverage of the statutes, either by excluding emergency services provided in the ordinary course of work or services that doctors render to those with whom they have a doctor-patient relationship or to whom they owe a pre-existing duty. Guerrero v. Copper Queen Hospital, 112 Ariz. 104, 537 P.2d 1329 (1975) (statute not applicable to services in hospital); Colby v. Schwartz, 78 Cal.App.3d 885, 144 Cal.Rptr. 624 (1978) (normal course of practice not protected); Gragg v. Neurological Associates, 152 Ga.App. 586, 263 S.E.2d 496 (1979) (crisis during operating procedure is not emergency within meaning of statute).

Hospital-based emergency assistance by a physician is often protected, however, where the physician is not on duty at the time of the call for help. See Gordin v. William Beaumont Hospital, 180 Mich.App. 488, 447 N.W.2d 793 (1989), where the plaintiff's decedent was admitted to the emergency room after a car accident. The ER physician called for the on-call surgeon to assist, but the surgeon was unavailable. He then called Dr. Howard, who was not officially on call. The court held that the Good Samaritan Statute applied. The plaintiff argued that the statute should only be applied in the "biblical" Good Samaritan situation, to a doctor who renders care outside his training, not to a trained surgeon summoned to the hospital to render care for which he was trained and compensated. As in *McKenna*, however, the Michigan statute had been amended to include hospital settings and off-duty physicians. In Kearns v. Superior Court, 204 Cal.App.3d 1325, 252 Cal.Rptr. 4 (2 Dist.1988), a physician happened to be in the hospital treating his own patients when another surgeon asked his help during the course of an operation. The assisting physician was held to be rendering assistance in an "emergency" for purposes of California's Good Samaritan law.

3. Some statutes protect health care professionals, while others protect all Good Samaritans, without regard to their profession. Some states grant statutory immunity from suit to emergency medical personnel unless gross negligence is shown. Mallory v. City of Detroit, 181 Mich.App. 121, 449 N.W.2d 115 (1989). Is there any reason, except for the political power of doctors, to limit the application of such statutes to doctors or health care professionals? See generally Anno., Construction of 'Good Samaritan' Statutes Excusing from Civil Liability One Rendering Care in Emergency, 39 A.L.R.3d 222.

4. The malpractice crisis of 1974 undoubtedly played a role in the push by state legislatures to enact such laws. They are an interesting example of a protective response to a low risk of suit. There is no reason to believe that physicians have any idea as to whether the state in which they practice has a Good Samaritan law, or what its terms might be. Nor can evidence be found to establish that such laws have encouraged emergency treatment. In a study over twenty years ago, the American Medical Association found that the existence of Good Samaritan legislation made no difference to the willingness of physicians to stop and assist. 51.5% said they would stop to furnish emergency aid if the statutes were in effect, and 48.8% if no statute was in effect. Law Dept. of the AMA 1963 Professional Liability Survey, 189 J.A.M.A. 859 (1964). See Hessel, Good Samaritan Laws: Bad Legislation, 2 J.Leg.Med. 40 (1974). For a proposal for a uniform statute, see Comment, Good Samaritan Statutes: Time for Uniformity, 27 Wayne L.Rev. 217 (1980).

5. If the purpose of Good Samaritan statutes is to encourage emergency aid, should they instead impose a civil or criminal penalty on those who fail to offer such assistance? That is the case in many European countries, and—on the books—in Vermont, which imposes a $100 fine for failure to render aid under some circumstances. See 12 Vt.Stat.Ann. § 519. Should we require even more in the way of a duty to rescue?

For an interesting discussion of the duty to rescue, see Levmore, Waiting for Rescue: An Essay on the Evolution and Incentive Structure of the Law of Affirmative Obligations, 72 Va.L.Rev. 879 (1986).

4. Contributory Fault of the Patient

Patients through their own mistakes or lifestyle often enhance, or even cause, their injuries. People don't take their doctor's advice; they fall off their diets, stop exercising, start smoking, or act in a variety of ways counterproductive to their health. Very few tort cases have raised the issue directly, by raising a patient's lifestyle choice as a defense to a malpractice claim. Consider the following case.

OSTROWSKI v. AZZARA

Supreme Court of New Jersey, 1988.
111 N.J. 429, 545 A.2d 148.

O'HERN, J.

This case primarily concerns the legal significance of a medical malpractice claimant's pre-treatment health habits. Although the parties agreed that such habits should not be regarded as evidencing comparative fault for the medical injury at issue, we find that the instructions to the jury failed to draw the line clearly between the normal mitigation of damages expected of any claimant and the concepts of comparative fault that can preclude recovery in a fault-based system of tort reparation. Accordingly, we reverse the judgment below that disallowed any recovery to the diabetic plaintiff who had bypass surgery to correct a loss of circulation in a leg. The need for this bypass was found by the jury to have been proximately caused by the physician's neglect in performing an improper surgical procedure on the already weakened plaintiff.

I

As noted, the parties do not dispute that a physician must exercise the degree of care commensurate with the needs of the patient as she presents herself. This is but another way of saying that a defendant takes the plaintiff as she finds her. The question here, however, is much more subtle and complex. The complication arose from the plaintiff's seemingly routine need for care of an irritated toe. The plaintiff had long suffered from diabetes attributable, in unfortunate part perhaps, to her smoking and to her failure to adhere closely to her diet. Diabetic patients often have circulatory problems. For purposes of this appeal, we shall accept the general version of the events that led up to the operation as they are set forth in defendant-physician's brief.

On May 17, 1983, plaintiff, a heavy smoker and an insulin-dependent diabetic for twenty years, first consulted with defendant, Lynn Azzara, a doctor of podiatric medicine, a specialist in the care of feet. Plaintiff had been referred to Dr. Azzara by her internist whom she had last seen in November 1982. Dr. Azzara's notes indicated that plaintiff presented a sore left big toe, which had troubled her for approximately one month, and calluses. She told Dr. Azzara that she often suffered leg cramps that caused a tightening of the leg muscles or burning in her feet and legs after walking and while lying in bed. She had had hypertension (abnormally high blood pressure) for three years and was taking a diuretic for this condition.

Physical examination revealed redness in the plaintiff's big toe and elongated and incurvated toenails. Incurvated toenails are not ingrown; rather, they press against the skin. Diminished pulses on her foot indicated decreased blood supply to that area, as well as decreased circulation and impaired vascular status. Dr. Azzara made a diagnosis of onychomycosis (a fungous disease of the nails) and formulated a plan of treatment to debride (trim) the incurvated nail. Since plaintiff had informed her of a high blood sugar level, Dr. Azzara ordered a fasting blood sugar test and a urinalysis; she also noted that a vascular examination should be considered for the following week if plaintiff showed no improvement.

Plaintiff next saw Dr. Azzara three days later, on May 20, 1983. The results of the fasting blood sugar test indicated plaintiff's blood sugar was high, with a reading of 306. The urinalysis results also indicated plaintiff's blood sugar was above normal. At this second visit, Dr. Azzara concluded that plaintiff had peripheral vascular disease, poor circulation, and diabetes with a very high sugar elevation. She discussed these conclusions with plaintiff and explained the importance of better sugar maintenance. She also explained that a complication of peripheral vascular disease and diabetes is an increased risk of losing a limb if the diabetes is not controlled. The lack of blood flow can lead to decaying tissue. The parties disagree on whether Dr. Azzara told plaintiff she had to return to her internist to treat her blood sugar and circulation problems, or whether, as plaintiff indicates, Dr. Azzara merely suggested to plaintiff that she see her internist.

In any event, plaintiff came back to Dr. Azzara on May 31, 1983, and, according to the doctor, reported that she had seen her internist and that the internist had increased her insulin and told her to return to Dr. Azzara for further treatment because of her continuing complaints of discomfort about her toe. However, plaintiff had not seen the internist. Dr. Azzara contends that she believed plaintiff's representations. A finger-stick glucose test administered to measure plaintiff's non-fasting blood sugar yielded a reading of 175. A physical examination of the toe revealed redness and drainage from the distal medial (outside front) border of the nail, and the toenail was painful to the touch. Dr. Azzara's proposed course of treatment was to avulse, or remove, all or a portion of the toenail to facilitate drainage.

Dr. Azzara says that prior to performing the removal procedure she reviewed with Mrs. Ostrowski both the risks and complications of the procedure, including nonhealing and loss of limb, as well as the risks involved with not treating the toe. Plaintiff executed a consent form authorizing Dr. Azzara to perform a total removal of her left big toenail. The nail was cut out. (Defendant testified that she cut out only a portion of the nail, although her records showed a total removal.)

Two days later, plaintiff saw her internist. He saw her four additional times in order to check the progress of the toe. As of June 30, 1983, the internist felt the toe was much improved. While plaintiff was seeing the internist, she continued to see Dr. Azzara, or her associate, Dr. Bergman. During this period the toe was healing slowly, as Dr. Azzara said one would expect with a diabetic patient.

During the time plaintiff was being treated by her internist and by Dr. Azzara, she continued to smoke despite advice to the contrary. Her internist testified at the trial that smoking accelerates and aggravates peripheral vascular disease and that a diabetic patient with vascular disease can by smoking accelerate the severity of the vascular disease by as much as fifty percent. By mid-July, plaintiff's toe had become more painful and discolored.

At this point, all accord ceases. Plaintiff claims that it was the podiatrist's failure to consult with the patient's internist and defendant's failure to establish by vascular tests that the blood flow was sufficient to heal the wound, and to take less radical care, that left her with a non-healing, pre-gangrenous wound, that is, with decaying tissue. As a result, plaintiff had to undergo immediate bypass surgery to prevent the loss of the extremity. If left untreated, the pre-gangrenous toe condition resulting from the defendant's nail removal procedure would have spread, causing loss of the leg. The plaintiff's first bypass surgery did not arrest the condition, and she underwent two additional bypass surgeries which, in the opinion of her treating vascular surgeon, directly and proximately resulted from the unnecessary toenail removal procedure on May 31, 1983. In the third operation a vein from her right leg was transplanted to her left leg to increase the flow of blood to the toe.

At trial, defense counsel was permitted to show that during the pre-treatment period before May 17, 1983, the plaintiff had smoked cigarettes and had failed to maintain her weight, diet, and blood sugar at acceptable levels. The trial court allowed this evidence of the plaintiff's pre-treatment health habits to go to the jury on the issue of proximate cause. Defense counsel elicited admissions from plaintiff's internist and vascular surgeon that some doctors believe there is a relationship between poor self-care habits and increased vascular disease, perhaps by as much as fifty percent. But no medical expert for either side testified that the plaintiff's post-treatment health habits could have caused her need for bypass surgery six weeks after defendant's toenail removal. Nevertheless, plaintiff argues that defense counsel was permitted to interrogate the plaintiff extensively on her post-avulsion and post-bypass health habits, and that the court allowed such evidence of plaintiff's health habits during the six weeks after the operation to be considered as acts of comparative negligence that could bar recovery rather than reduce her damages. The jury found that the doctor had acted negligently in cutting out the plaintiff's toenail without adequate consideration of her condition, but found plaintiff's fault (fifty-one percent) to exceed that of the physician (forty-nine percent). She was therefore disallowed any recovery. On appeal the Appellate Division affirmed in an unreported decision. We granted certification to review plaintiff's claims. [ ] We are told that since the trial, the plaintiff's left leg has been amputated above the knee. This was foreseen, but not to a reasonable degree of medical probability at the time of trial.

II

Several strands of doctrine are interwoven in the resolution of this matter. The concepts of avoidable consequences, the particularly susceptible victim, aggravation of preexisting condition, comparative negligence, and proximate cause each play a part. It may be useful to unravel those strands of doctrine for separate consideration before considering them in the composite.

Comparative negligence is a legislative amelioration of the perceived harshness of the common-law doctrine of contributory negligence. [   ] In a fault-based system of tort reparation, the doctrine of contributory negligence served to bar any recovery to a plaintiff whose fault contributed to the accident. Whatever its conceptual underpinnings, its effect was to serve as a "gatekeeper." Epstein, "The Social Consequences of Common Law Rules," 95 *Harv.L.Rev.* 1717, 1736–37 (1982). Any fault kept a claimant from recovering under the system. Fault in that context meant a breach of a legal duty that was comparable to the duty of the other actors to exercise such care in the circumstances as was necessary to avoid the risk of injury incurred. Its prototype was the carriage driver who crossed the train tracks as the train was approaching the crossing. [   ] Harsh, but clear.

Comparative negligence was intended to ameliorate the harshness of contributory negligence but should not blur its clarity. It was designed only to leave the door open to those plaintiffs whose fault was not greater than the defendant's, not to create an independent gatekeeping function. Comparative negligence, then, will qualify the doctrine of contributory negligence when that doctrine would otherwise be applicable as a limitation on recovery. * * *

* * * The doctrine [of avoidable consequences] proceeds on the theory that a plaintiff who has suffered an injury as the proximate result of a tort cannot recover for any portion of the harm that by the exercise of ordinary care he could have avoided. [   ] * * * Avoidable consequences, then, normally comes into action when the injured party's carelessness occurs *after* the defendant's legal wrong has been committed. Contributory negligence, however, comes into action when the injured party's carelessness occurs *before* defendant's wrong has been committed or concurrently with it. [   ]

A counterweight to the doctrine of avoidable consequences is the doctrine of the particularly susceptible victim. This doctrine is familiarly expressed in the maxim that "defendant 'must take plaintiff as he finds him.'" [   ] * * * It is ameliorated by the doctrine of aggravation of a preexisting condition. While it is not entirely possible to separate the doctrines of avoidable consequence and preexisting condition, perhaps the simplest way to distinguish them is to understand that the injured person's conduct is irrelevant to the consideration of the doctrine of aggravation of a preexisting condition. Negligence law generally calls for an apportionment of damages when a plaintiff's antecedent negligence is "found not to contribute in any way to the original accident or injury, but to be a substantial contributing factor in increasing the harm which ensues." *Restatement (Second) of Torts,* § 465 at 510–11, comment c. Courts recognize that a defendant whose acts aggravate a plaintiff's preexisting condition is liable only for the amount of harm actually caused by the negligence. [   ] * * *

Finally, underpinning all of this is that most fundamental of risk allocators in the tort reparation system, the doctrine of proximate cause. * * *

We have sometimes melded proximate cause with foreseeability of unreasonable risk. * * *

We have been candid in New Jersey to see this doctrine, not so much as an expression of the mechanics of causation, but as an expression of line-drawing by courts and juries, an instrument of "overall fairness and sound public policy." [   ] * * * In this term of Court, we have been required to resolve varying aspects of the problem of proximate causation and the avoidance of damages in the context of the special duty of the health care provider to protect patients against their own self-destructive acts, [   ] or in the context of requiring the occupant of an automobile to wear a seat belt as a method of avoiding damages. [   ]

III

Each of these principles, then, has some application to this case.[3] Plaintiff obviously had a preexisting condition. It is alleged that she failed to minimize the damages that she might otherwise have sustained due to mistreatment. Such mistreatment may or may not have been the proximate cause of her ultimate condition.

But we must be careful in reassembling these strands of tort doctrine that none does double duty or obscures underlying threads. In particular, we must avoid the indiscriminate application of the doctrine of comparative negligence (with its fifty percent qualifier for recovery) when the doctrines of avoidable consequences or preexisting condition apply.

The doctrine of contributory negligence bars any recovery to the claimant whose negligent action or inaction *before* the defendant's wrongdoing has been completed has contributed to cause actual invasion of plaintiff's person or property. By contrast,

> "[t]he doctrine of avoidable consequences comes into play at a later stage. Where the defendant has already committed an actionable wrong, whether tort or breach of contract, then this doctrine [avoidable consequences] limits the plaintiff's recovery by disallowing only those items of damages which could reasonably have been

---

3. Each principle, however, has limitations based on other policy considerations. For example, the doctrine of avoidable consequences, although of logical application to some instances of professional malpractice, is neutralized by countervailing policy. Thus, a physician who performed a faulty tubal litigation cannot suggest that the eventual consequences of an unwanted pregnancy could have been avoided by termination of the fetus. [   ] Thus, too, a physician who asserts the defense of aggravation of preexisting condition must bear a special burden of proof on that issue. [   ] We offer these observations not for the correctness of their conclusion, but merely to show the mutations that every principle undergoes in its common-law evolution.

averted * * * [.]"   "[C]ontributory negligence is to be asserted as a complete defense, whereas the doctrine of avoidable consequences is not considered a defense at all, but merely a rule of damages by which certain particular items of loss may be excluded from consideration * * *."   * * *

Hence, it would be the bitterest irony if the rule of comparative negligence, designed to ameliorate the harshness of contributory negligence, should serve to shut out any recovery to one who would otherwise have recovered under the law of contributory negligence. Put the other way, absent a comparative negligence act, it would have never been thought that "avoidable consequences" or "mitigation of damages" attributable to post-accident conduct of any claimant would have included a shutout of apportionable damages proximately caused by another's negligence.   * * *

* * *

In this context of post-injury conduct by a claimant, given the understandable complexity of concurrent causation, expressing mitigation of damages as a percentage of fault which reduces plaintiff's damages may aid juries in their just apportionment of damages, provided that the jury understands that neither mitigation of damages nor avoidable consequences will bar the plaintiff from recovery if the defendant's conduct was a substantial factor without which the ultimate condition would not have arisen.

* * * In the field of professional health care, given the difficulty of apportionment, sound public policy requires that the professional bear the burden of demonstrating the proper segregation of damages in the aggravation context. [   ] The same policy should apply to mitigation of damages. [   ]   Hence, overall fairness requires that juries evaluating apportionment of damages attributable in substantial part to a faulty medical procedure be given understandable guidance about the use of evidence of post-treatment patient fault that will assist them in making a just apportionment of damages and the burden of persuasion on the issues. This is consistent with our general view that a defendant bear the burden of proving the causal link between a plaintiff's unreasonable conduct and the extent of damages. [   ]   Once that is established, it should be the "defendant who also has the burden of carving out that portion of the damages which is to be attributed to the plaintiff." [   ]

IV

As noted, in this case the parties agree on certain fundamentals. The pre-treatment health habits of a patient are not to be considered as evidence of fault that would have otherwise been pled in bar to a claim of injury due to the professional misconduct of a health professional. This conclusion bespeaks the doctrine of the particularly susceptible victim or recognition that whatever the wisdom or folly of our lifestyles, society, through its laws, has not yet imposed a normative life-style on its members; and, finally, it may reflect in part an aspect of that policy judgment that health care professionals have a special responsibility with respect to diseased patients. [   ]

This does not mean, however, that the patient's poor health is irrelevant to the analysis of a claim for reparation. While the doctor may well take the patient as she found her, she cannot reverse the frames to make it appear that she was presented with a robust vascular condition; likewise, the physician cannot be expected to provide a guarantee against a cardiovascular incident. All that the law expects is that she not mistreat such a patient so as to become a proximate contributing cause to the ultimate vascular injury.

However, once the patient comes under the physician's care, the law can justly expect the patient to cooperate with the health care provider in their mutual interests. Thus, it is not unfair to expect a patient to help avoid the consequences of the condition for which the physician is treating her. * * *

Hence, we approve in this context of post-treatment conduct submission to the jury of the question whether the just mitigation or apportionment of damages may be expressed in terms of the patient's fault. If used, the numerical allocation of fault should be explained to the jury as a method of achieving the just apportionment of the damages based on their relative evaluation of each actor's contribution to the end result—that the allocation is but an aspect of the doctrine of avoidable consequences or of mitigation of damages. In this context, plaintiff should not recover more than she could have reasonably avoided, but the patient's fault will not be a bar to recovery except to the extent that her fault caused the damages.

An important caveat to that statement would be the qualification that implicitly flows from the fact that health care professionals bear the burden of proving that their mistreatment did not aggravate a preexisting condition: that the health care professional bear the burden of proving the damages that were avoidable.

Finally, before submitting the issue to the jury, a court should carefully scrutinize the evidence to see if there is a sound basis in the proofs for the assertion that the post-treatment conduct of the patient was indeed a significant cause of the increased damages. Given the short onset between the contraindicated surgery and the vascular incident here, plaintiff asserts that defendant did not present proof, to a reasonable degree of medical probability, that the plaintiff's post-treatment conduct was a proximate cause of the resultant condition. Plaintiff asserts that the only evidence given to support the defense's theory of proximate cause between plaintiff's post-treatment health habits and her damages was her internist's testimony regarding generalized studies showing that smoking increases vascular disease by fifty percent, and her vascular surgeon's testimony that some physicians believe there is a relationship among diabetes, smoking, and vascular impairment. Such testimony did not address with any degree of medical probability a relationship between her smoking or not between May 17,

1983, and the plaintiff's need for bypass surgery in July 1983. Defendant points to plaintiff's failure to consult with her internist as a cause of her injury, but the instruction to the jury gave no guidance on whether this was to be considered as conduct that concurrently or subsequently caused her injuries. [   ]

V

We acknowledge that it is difficult to parse through these principles and policies in the course of an extended appeal. We can well imagine that in the ebb and flow of trial the lines are not easily drawn. There are regrettably no easy answers to these questions.

* * *

[The court noted the factual complexities of the case, and concluded that "the instructions to the jury in this case did not adequately separate or define the concepts that were relevant to the disposition of the plaintiff's case." The case was remanded for a new trial.]

Notes and Questions

1. Do you advocate applying contributory negligence, or comparative negligence (depending upon the jurisdiction), to situations such as that of *Ostrowski*? Such cases raise fundamental questions about the limits of medicine and the role of patients in their own illnesses. Can a smoker easily stop? Is it fair to bar his recovery when his smoking is not a simple, easily abandoned, choice? See Sawka v. Prokopowycz, 104 Mich.App. 829, 306 N.W.2d 354 (1981), where the plaintiff sued the defendant for his failure to diagnose lung cancer. The court rejected the claim that the plaintiff's continued smoking and failure to return for further examination as instructed were contributory negligence.

Would you treat an overzealous jogger who had cardiac arrest while running in the same way as a chain smoking or obese sedentary patient? How much of your decision is based on your desire to punish the smoker or glutton for immoral or irresponsible behavior which may be virtually impossible to control?

2. A finding of contributory negligence was upheld in Ray v. Wagner, 286 Minn. 354, 176 N.W.2d 101, 104 (1970), where the physician performed a pap smear on the plaintiff, got back a positive test result, and was unable to reach the plaintiff by telephone for five months. The court noted:

> Ordinarily, a patient can rely on a doctor's informing her if the results of a test are positive. Here, however, plaintiff gave the doctor somewhat misleading information as to her status, she had no phone at the address where she lived, and she did not live at the address where she had a phone.

See also Harlow v. Chin, 405 Mass. 697, 545 N.E.2d 602 (1989) (plaintiff failed to return for further treatment when pain got worse; plaintiff held to be 13% comparatively negligent.)

The theory is typically invoked when a patient failed to follow a physician's instructions after a procedure was performed, or while in the hospital. Thus in Butler v. Berkeley, 25 N.C.App. 325, 213 S.E.2d 571 (1975), the plaintiff removed the nasogastric tube that had been inserted to prevent wounds from being contaminated by food after plastic surgery. This action might have caused the infection that the patient then developed, and the court granted summary judgment for the surgeon on grounds of contributory negligence. In Musachia v. Rosman, 190 So.2d 47 (Fla.App. 1966), the decedent left the hospital over the objections of, and contrary to the advice of, the defendants. He drank liquor and ignored instructions to eat only baby food. He then died from fecal peritonitis due to small perforations in the bowel, and his recovery was barred on the basis of contributory negligence. See also Faile v. Bycura, 297 S.C. 58, 374 S.E.2d 687 (1988) (patient refused to wear a medically prescribed postoperative orthotic device after foot surgery); Grippe v. Momtazee, 705 S.W.2d 551 (Mo.App.1986).

3. Contributory negligence is rarely applied against a patient. In Weil v. Seltzer, 873 F.2d 1453 (D.C.Cir.1989), the defendant argued that the patient was contributorily negligence in failing to discover that the medication given him over a twenty year period was steroids rather than antihistamines as told by the defendant; the court strongly rejected this argument, holding that while a patient must cooperate with her physician, "[i]t is a quantum leap * * * to permit a duty to be placed on a patient * * * " [quoting Stager v. Schneider, 494 A.2d 1307, 1312 (D.C.1985)]. The court also rejected the assumption of the risk defense, since there was no evidence that the plaintiff knew of the danger of prolonged steroid use and voluntarily accepted the risks. (1459)

In Windisch v. Weiman, 555 N.Y.S.2d 731 (App.Div., N.Y.1990), the court held that the failure of a physician to properly followup a patient, resulting in a missed diagnosis of lung cancer, may provide the basis for imposing liability even when the patient is partially responsible for the delay in diagnosis. See also Jensen v. Archbishop Bergan Mercy Hospital, 236 Neb. 1, 459 N.W.2d 178 (1990) (the court held that a patient's failure to lose weight may have been causally related to his pulmonary embolism, but it was not contributory negligence with respect to a subsequent malpractice claim against the hospital for treatment of the embolism.)

4. Some 35 states have adopted comparative fault, simplifying the issue by eliminating the harsh all-or-nothing effect of contributory negligence. Courts in comparative fault jurisdictions are likely to become more willing to allow evidence of plaintiffs' contributions to their injuries. See generally V. Schwartz, Comparative Negligence (2nd ed. 1986); W. Prosser and P. Keeton, *Torts* sec. 67 (5th ed. 1984).

5. Assumption of the risk. The doctrine of assumption of the risk is a viable defense even in many comparative fault jurisdiction. In Schneider v. Revici, 817 F.2d 987, 995 (2d Cir.1987), the Second Circuit considered whether a patient undergoing unconventional treatment for breast cancer after signing a consent form had waived all her rights to sue or assumed the risk of injury from the treatment. The court held that the consent form was not clear and unequivocal as a covenant not to sue, but that the doctrine of assumption of risk was available:

* * * we see no reason why a patient should not be allowed to make an informed decision to go outside currently approved medical methods in search of an unconventional treatment. While a patient should be encouraged to exercise care for his own safety, we believe that an informed decision to avoid surgery and conventional chemotherapy is within the patient's right to "determine what shall be done with his own body," [   ].

The court held that the jury could consider assumption of the risk as a total bar to recovery, based on the language of the signed consent form and the patient's general awareness of the risks of treatment.

Assumption of the risk is rarely argued except in cases of obvious defects of which the patient should have been aware, such as hazards in the hospital room. See, e.g., Charrin v. Methodist Hospital, 432 S.W.2d 572 (Tex.Civ.App.1968) (plaintiff tripped over television cord in hospital room; she knew it was there, having previously pointed it out to the staff.) The problem of assumption of the risk, in the sense of a conscious explicit assumption of medical risks, blends into the issues of informed consent and waivers of liability, discussed in Chapter 3, infra.

E. CAUSATION PROBLEMS: DELAYED, UNCERTAIN, OR SHARED RESPONSIBILITY

1. *The Discovery Rule*

MASTRO V. BRODIE

Supreme Court of Colorado, 1984.
682 P.2d 1162.

NEIGHBORS, JUSTICE.

* * *

On February 5, 1977, Mastro surgically removed a small nodule from the back of Brodie's shoulder. He obtained Brodie's consent to the surgery after explaining that she would have a scar, "but it wouldn't be a bad one." Several months later, however, the scar from the surgery became "large, unsightly and uncomfortable." Brodie returned to Mastro in July 1977, but received no further treatment and no explanation of what had happened. He told her only that "there was nothing else he could do about [the scar]." Since that time, Brodie has had no contact with Mastro. She received treatment, including a series of injections into the scar, from two other physicians during the next two years. She also discussed the scar with at least two attorneys for whom she worked during this time period. Her scar, however, has remained approximately the same in size and appearance as when she first became aware of it. In August 1979, a physician at the University of Colorado Medical Center informed Brodie that she had developed a "keloid"[3] on her shoulder. Further, he told her that a surgical proce-

---

3. *Dorland's Illustrated Medical Dictionary* 695 (26th ed. 1981) defines "keloid" as "a sharply elevated, irregularly-shaped, progressively enlarging scar due to the for-

dure on the shoulder of young, dark-skinned individuals frequently results in the formation of a keloid, which, while unpredictable, does occur in a percentage of such patients. He indicated to Brodie's attorney that "the risk of keloid should have been anticipated" and that Mastro should have warned Brodie of such a risk before operating on her shoulder.[4]

Three months later, in November 1979, Brodie filed a complaint against Mastro * * * alleging medical malpractice. She claimed that, when she consulted him about the nodule on her shoulder, Mastro knew or should have know of the inherent risk of keloid development in a person with her physical characteristics, and that he knew or should have known that disclosure of this risk "would be of great significance to a person in [Brodie's] position in deciding to submit to surgery." Since Mastro was "under a duty to inform [Brodie] of any substantial or special risks inherent in the procedure," his failure to mention keloid scarring before the surgery prevented her from making "an intelligent choice as to alternative treatments consonant with the underlying premise of informed consent." As a result, Brodie suffered "a serious, permanent disfiguring injury" in the form of "a large, unsightly growth" that was "plainly visible on her shoulder." While admitting that she was aware of the scar by July 1977, Brodie concluded by alleging that she was not aware and could not reasonably have been aware of "[Mastro's] negligence in failing to inform her" of the high risk of keloid formation until she consulted the physician at the medical center in August 1979, at the direction of her attorney.

After depositions of the parties were taken, Mastro filed a motion for summary judgment, claiming that the two-year statute of limitations for medical malpractice actions based on lack of informed consent barred Brodie's claim. [ ] Under this provision, the two-year period begins to run when the injured person discovers or in the exercise of reasonable diligence should have discovered "the injury." Mastro claimed that there was no genuine issue of material fact since Brodie "has admitted that she knew of the injury (unsightly scar) more than two years prior to initiation of her Complaint."

Brodie filed a memorandum opposing the summary judgment motion. * * *

The district court granted the motion for summary judgment. It concluded that the two-year statute of limitations began to run no later than July 1977, when Brodie returned to Mastro's office "to complain about the enlarged scar," and expired in July 1979, four months before she filed her complaint. * * *

* * *

mation of excessive amounts of collagen [fibrous tissue] * * * during connective tissue repair."

4. Brodie is a dark-skinned woman. She described her racial background in her deposition as "half black and half Mexican." Brodie's father had been a patient of Mastro's before her surgery.

We conclude that the pivotal question in this case is whether Brodie filed suit within two years after she "discovered, or in the exercise of reasonable diligence and concern should have discovered, the *injury*." Section 13–80–105(1) (emphasis added). Therefore, we must interpret the word "injury" as it appears in the statute of limitations governing medical malpractice cases.

* * *

C.

There are at least three possible interpretations of the word "injury": (1) the alleged negligent act or omission; (2) the physical damage or manifestation resulting from the act or omission; or (3) the legal injury, i.e., all the essential elements of a claim for medical malpractice.

At least two courts have adopted the first definition. [ ] We reject this interpretation of the word. The legislature clearly intended that the word "injury" have a different meaning than "act or omission" because the three words are each used in the malpractice statute. [ ] A claimant must file suit within two years after discovering the "injury" and, in no event, more than three years after the date of the "act or omission." Moreover, such a construction defeats the purpose of the discovery rule which has been specifically adopted by the legislature.

Likewise, we reject the interpretation that the "injury" occurs for purposes of the statute of limitations on the date that the injury manifests itself in a physically objective and ascertainable manner. The physical damage test fails to account adequately for all relevant factors. In some cases, such as the discovery of a sponge left in the patient during surgery * * * the discovery of the physical injury may occur simultaneously with the discovery of the only possible cause, i.e., the doctor's negligence. However, where the injury is consistent with post-operative recovery and treatment is continued by the treating doctor who reassures the patient that there is no permanent damage, the patient who reasonably trusts the doctor and relies upon the physician's advice would be unfairly barred from bringing suit. In addition, the physical injury standard requires a claimant to immediately file suit against a physician, even though the plaintiff has no knowledge of any wrongful conduct on the part of the doctor. Courts should not adopt a construction of a statute which may encourage the filing of frivolous claims. * * *

* * *

We hold that the statute of limitations begins to run when the claimant has knowledge of facts which would put a reasonable person on notice of the nature and extent of an injury and that the injury was caused by the wrongful conduct of another. The overwhelming majority of state appellate courts which have addressed the issue here have adopted the "legal injury" construction of the word "injury" used in statutes of limitation governing medical malpractice actions. The focus is on the plaintiff's knowledge of facts, rather than on discovery of applicable legal theories. * * *

The judgment of the court of appeals is affirmed.

Notes and Questions

1. Has the discovery rule simplified or complicated malpractice litigation? The older cases generally held that a cause of action accrued when the right to bring an action arose, i.e. when the medical error had occurred. Consider Shearin v. Lloyd, 246 N.C. 363, 98 S.E.2d 508 (1957). The defendant surgeon removed the plaintiff's appendix in July of 1951. Plaintiff subsequently complained of pain near the incision during his checkups. In November, 1952 the defendant admitted that something must be wrong. X-rays showed a sponge in the abdomen. This was removed later in November, but then a series of "knots" occurred. In the fall of 1953 defendant told plaintiff he needed another operation. Plaintiff severed his relationship with the defendant, and sued in November of 1955. The statute of limitations was three years and plaintiff was nonsuited. The court held that "plaintiff's cause of action accrued on July 20, 1951, when defendant closed the incision without first removing the lappack. * * * Defendant's failure thereafter to detect or discover his own negligence in this respect did not affect the basis of his liability therefore." See also Goldsmith v. Howmedica, Inc., 67 N.Y.2d 120, 500 N.Y.S.2d 640, 491 N.E.2d 1097 (1986) (plaintiff received a total hip replacement in 1973; in 1981 the hip broke and plaintiff sued in 1983. Held: action accrued in 1973 and was barred by the statute of limitations.)

This older rule has the advantage of a bright line approach to the statute of limitation. The newer discovery rule was created to be fair to patients who suffered latent injuries. What does such a rule cost? Can the malpractice insurance crisis be traced in some small way to the uncertainties bred by such a rule? The discovery rule makes it actuarially difficult for a malpractice insurer to predict losses, by creating a long period of time after a medical intervention during which a claim can be "discovered." As a result, insurers must raise premiums to compensate for the uncertainty of future unknown claims not barred by a rigid statute of limitations rule. Or they might change the design of policies to a claims-made basis to eliminate this uncertainty about future claims. See Chapter 4 infra.

2. The modern discovery rule creates difficult problems. Does the statute begin to run when the initial harm surfaces, or when the injury matures or worsens? See Burns v. Hartford Hosp., 192 Conn. 451, 472 A.2d 1257 (1984) (patient had infection due to contaminated IV tube. Court held that " * * * the harm need not have reached its fullest manifestation before the statute begins to run.")

3. In suits against the federal government, the statute of limitations begins to run when the plaintiff learns of an injury's existence and cause, rather than when he learns the injury was negligently inflicted. Once the injury and its causes are known, the plaintiff can "protect himself by seeking advice in the medical and legal community." United States v.

Kubrick, 444 U.S. 111, 100 S.Ct. 352, 62 L.Ed.2d 259 (1979) (suit against government under Tort Claims Act).

2. Multiple Defendants

a. Joint Tortfeasor Doctrine

In the typical malpractice case in which the parties acted together to commit the wrong, or the parties' acts, if independent, unite to cause a single injury, multiple defendants are considered joint rather than separate tortfeasors. In determining whether to assess liability jointly, the courts have considered factors such as whether each defendant has a similar duty; whether the same evidence will support an action against each; the indivisible nature of the plaintiff's injury; and identity of the facts as to time, place or result. For a contemporary application of these tests, see Riff v. Morgan Pharmacy, 353 Pa.Super. 21, 508 A.2d 1247 (1986). For a clear explanation of joint and several liability, see Dobbs, supra at 620–623; W. Prosser & P. Keeton, Torts § 50 (5th Ed.1984).

What if a doctor fails to diagnose a patient's problem, and subsequently another doctor is negligent in treating it? The first negligent treating doctor might be liable to the injured plaintiff for all foreseeable injuries resulting from the later negligent medical treatment of a second doctor. See 1 D. Louisell & H. Williams, Medical Malpractice, para. 16.06 (1986). Two or more physicians who fail to make a proper diagnosis on successive occasions are co-tortfeasors under contribution statutes. Foote v. United States, 648 F.Supp. 735 (N.D.Ill.1986). See, e.g., Gilson v. Mitchell, 131 Ga.App. 321, 205 S.E.2d 421 (1974):

> " * * * if the separate and independent acts of negligence of several persons combine naturally and directly to produce a single indivisible injury, and a rational basis does not exist for an apportionment of damages, the actors are joint tortfeasors."

Where an existing injury is aggravated by malpractice, the innocent plaintiffs are not required to establish that share of expenses, pain, suffering, disability or impairment attributable solely to malpractice. The burden of proof shifts to the culpable defendant, who is responsible for all damages unless he can demonstrate that the damages for which he is responsible are capable of some reasonable apportionment. W. Prosser & P. Keeton, Torts § 50 (5th Ed.1984).

b. Multiple Defendants and Burden Shifting

Where only one of several defendants could have caused the plaintiff's injuries, but the plaintiff cannot adduce evidence as to which defendant is responsible, the courts have developed special rules to protect the obviously deserving plaintiff. Cases like Ybarra v. Spangard, and Anderson v. Somberg, supra, reflect judicial attempts to use doctrines like *res ipsa loquitur* to cover multiple defendant/uncertain proof situations. An equitable doctrine of burden shifting is derived from the exception in the Restatement (Second) Torts, § 433B(3) (1965):

> Where the conduct of two or more actors is tortious, and it is proved that harm has been caused to the plaintiff by only one of them, but there is uncertainty as to which one has caused it, the burden is upon each actor to prove that he has not caused the harm.

The reason for this burden shift is " * * * the injustice of permitting proved wrongdoers, who among them have inflicted an injury upon the entirely innocent plaintiff, to escape liability merely because the nature of their conduct and the resulting harm has made it impossible to prove which of them has caused the harm." Id., comment f.

The DES cases, involving the marketing of drugs and multiple defendants, have taken burden shifting well beyond the common law precedents, with the courts developing a variety of special tests. In Hymowitz v. Eli Lilly and Co., 73 N.Y.2d 487, 541 N.Y.S. 941, 539 N.E.2d 1069 (1989), cert. denied, ___ U.S. ___, 110 S.Ct. 350, 107 L.Ed.2d 338 (1989), New York's highest court chronicled the efforts by other courts to come to grips with the difficulties inherent in identifying the manufacturer of the particular DES that injured the plaintiff. The court noted the rationale behind burden-shifting generally, to force defendants to come forward or else be held jointly and severally liable.

The Iowa Supreme Court, in Mulcahy v. Eli Lilly & Co, 386 N.W.2d 67 (1986), described this "market share" theory as follows:

> The "market share" theory, fashioned in Sindell [v. Abbott Laboratories, 26 Cal.3d 588, 163 Cal.Rptr. 132, 607 P.2d 924 (1980),] apportions liability among defendants based on their respective shares of the "relevant" market. The plaintiff must first join "the manufacturers of a substantial share of the DES which her mother might have taken," and also meet her burden as to all other elements. [ ] The burden of proof then shifts to the defendants to demonstrate they could not have manufactured the DES that caused the plaintiff's injuries. [ ] If a defendant fails to meet this burden, the court fashions a "market share" theory to apportion damages according to the likelihood that any of defendants supplied the product by holding each defendant liable "for the proportion of the judgment represented by its share of that market." [ ] The intended result under this approach is that "each manufacturer's liability for an injury would be approximately equivalent to the damage caused by the DES it manufactured." [ ]

The law review article that gave rise to the market share theory in Sindell v. Abbott is Comment, DES and a Proposed Theory of Enterprise Liability, 46 Fordham L.Rev. 963 (1978). The best articles on the subject, with full citations to other literature, are Rosenberg, The Causal Connection in Mass Exposure Cases: A "Public Law" Vision of the Tort System, 97 Harv.L.Rev. 851 (1984), and Wright, Causation in

Tort Law, 73 Cal.L.Rev. 1735 (1985). For a useful analysis of the
trauma experienced by DES daughters, see R. Apfel and S. Fisher, To
Do No Harm: DES and the Dilemmas of Modern Medicine (1984).

The market share theories, while developed in the DES cases, have
also been allowed in other drug cases. In Shackil v. Lederle Laboratories, 530 A.2d 1287, 1302 (N.J.Super.A.D.1987), New Jersey applied a
modified market share approach to manufacturers of the pertussis
antigen component of a diphtheria, pertussis and tetanus toxoid vaccine
(DPT). The court noted that its approach followed the guiding principles established in Anderson v. Somberg, supra.

F. DAMAGE INNOVATIONS

1. Loss or Reduction of a Plaintiff's Chances of Survival

HERSKOVITS v. GROUP HEALTH COOPERATIVE
OF PUGET SOUND

Supreme Court of Washington, 1983.
99 Wash.2d 609, 664 P.2d 474.

DORE, JUSTICE.

This appeal raises the issue of whether an estate can maintain an
action for professional negligence as a result of failure to timely
diagnose lung cancer, where the estate can show probable reduction in
statistical chance for survival but cannot show and/or prove that with
timely diagnosis and treatment, decedent probably would have lived to
normal life expectancy.

Both counsel advised that for the purpose of this appeal we are to
assume that the respondent Group Health Cooperative of Puget Sound
and Dr. William Spencer negligently failed to diagnose Herskovits'
cancer on his first visit to the hospital and *proximately* caused a 14
percent reduction in his chances of survival. It is undisputed that
Herskovits had less than a 50 percent chance of survival at all times
herein.

The main issue we will address in this opinion is whether a patient,
with less than a 50 percent chance of survival, has a cause of action
against the hospital and its employees if they are negligent in diagnosing a lung cancer which reduces his chances of survival by 14 percent.

* * *

I

The complaint alleged that Herskovits came to Group Health
Hospital in 1974 with complaints of pain and coughing. In early 1974,
chest x-rays revealed infiltrate in the left lung. Rales and coughing
were present. In mid–1974, there were chest pains and coughing,
which became persistent and chronic by fall of 1974. A December 5,
1974 entry in the medical records confirms the cough problem. Plaintiff contends that Herskovits was treated thereafter only with cough

medicine. No further effort or inquiry was made by Group Health concerning his symptoms, other than an occasional chest x-ray. In the early spring of 1975, Mr. and Mrs. Herskovits went south in the hope that the warm weather would help. Upon his return to the Seattle area with no improvement in his health, Herskovits visited Dr. Jonathan Ostrow on a private basis for another medical opinion. Within 3 weeks, Dr. Ostrow's evaluation and direction to Group Health led to the diagnosis of cancer. In July of 1975, Herskovits' lung was removed, but no radiation or chemotherapy treatments were instituted. Herskovits died 20 months later, on March 22, 1977, at the age of 60.

At hearing on the motion for summary judgment, plaintiff was unable to produce expert testimony that the delay in diagnosis "probably" or "more likely than not" caused her husband's death. The affidavit and deposition of plaintiff's expert witness, Dr. Jonathan Ostrow, construed in the most favorable light possible to plaintiff, indicated that had the diagnosis of lung cancer been made in December 1974, the patient's possibility of 5–year survival was 39 percent. At the time of initial diagnosis of cancer 6 months later, the possibility of a 5–year survival was reduced to 25 percent. Dr. Ostrow testified he felt a diagnosis perhaps could have been made as early as December 1974, or January 1975, about 6 months before the surgery to remove Mr. Herskovits' lung in June 1975.

Dr. Ostrow testified that if the tumor was a "stage 1" tumor in December 1974, Herskovits' chance of a 5–year survival would have been 39 percent. In June 1975, his chances of survival were 25 percent assuming the tumor had progressed to "stage 2". Thus, the delay in diagnosis may have reduced the chance of a 5–year survival by 14 percent.

Dr. William Spencer, the physician from Group Health Hospital who cared for the deceased Herskovits, testified that in his opinion, based upon a reasonable medical probability, earlier diagnosis of the lung cancer that afflicted Herskovits would not have prevented his death, nor would it have lengthened his life. He testified that nothing the doctors at Group Health could have done would have prevented Herskovits' death, as death within several years is a virtual certainty with this type of lung cancer regardless of how early the diagnosis is made.

Plaintiff contends that medical testimony of a reduction of chance of survival from 39 percent to 25 percent is sufficient evidence to allow the proximate cause issue to go to the jury. Defendant Group Health argues conversely that Washington law does not permit such testimony on the issue of medical causation and requires that medical testimony must be at least sufficiently definite to establish that the act complained of "probably" or "more likely than not" caused the subsequent disability. It is Group Health's contention that plaintiff must prove that Herskovits "probably" would have survived had the defendant not been allegedly negligent; that is, the plaintiff must prove there was at least a 51 percent chance of survival.

II

* * *

This court heretofore has not faced the issue of whether, under § 323(a), [of the Restatement (Second) of Torts (1965)] proof that the defendant's conduct increased the risk of death by decreasing the chances of survival is sufficient to take the issue of proximate cause to the jury. Some courts in other jurisdictions have allowed the proximate cause issue to go to the jury on this type of proof. [ ] These courts emphasized the fact that defendants' conduct deprived the decedents of a "significant" chance to survive or recover, rather than requiring proof that with absolute certainty the defendants' conduct caused the physical injury. The underlying reason is that it is not for the wrongdoer, who put the possibility of recovery beyond realization, to say afterward that the result was inevitable. [ ]

Other jurisdictions have rejected this approach, generally holding that unless the plaintiff is able to show that it was *more likely than not* that the harm was caused by the defendant's negligence, proof of a decreased chance of survival is not enough to take the proximate cause question to the jury. [ ] These courts have concluded that the defendant should not be liable where the decedent more than likely would have died anyway.

The ultimate question raised here is whether the relationship between the increased risk of harm and Herskovits' death is sufficient to hold Group Health responsible. Is a 36 percent (from 39 percent to 25 percent) reduction in the decedent's chance for survival sufficient evidence of causation to allow the jury to consider the possibility that the physician's failure to timely diagnose the illness was the proximate cause of his death? We answer in the affirmative. To decide otherwise would be a blanket release from liability for doctors and hospitals any time there was less than a 50 percent chance of survival, regardless of how flagrant the negligence.

III

We are persuaded by the reasoning of the Pennsylvania Supreme Court in *Hamil v. Bashline,* [481 Pa. 256, 392 A.2d 1280 (1978)] * * *. The plaintiff's decedent was suffering from severe chest pains. His wife transported him to the hospital where he was negligently treated in the emergency unit. The wife, because of the lack of help, took her husband to a private physician's office, where he died. In an action brought under the wrongful death and survivorship statutes, the main medical witness testified that if the hospital had employed proper treatment, the decedent would have had a substantial chance of surviving the attack. The medical expert expressed his opinion in terms of a 75 percent chance of survival. It was also the doctor's opinion that the substantial loss of a chance of recovery was the result of the defendant hospital's failure to provide prompt treatment. The defendant's expert witness testified that the patient would have died regardless of any treatment provided by the defendant hospital.

The *Hamil* court reiterated the oft-repeated principle of tort law that the mere occurrence of an injury does not prove negligence, but the defendant's conduct must be a proximate cause of the plaintiff's injury. The court also referred to the traditional "but for" test, with the qualification that multiple causes may culminate in injury. The court held that once a plaintiff has introduced evidence that a defendant's negligent act or omission increased the risk of harm to a person in plaintiff's position, and that the harm was in fact sustained, "it becomes a question for the jury as to whether or not that increased risk was a substantial factor in producing the harm". [ ].

The *Hamil* court distinguished the facts of that case from the general tort case in which a plaintiff alleges that a defendant's act or omission set in motion a force which resulted in harm. In the typical tort case, the "but for" test, requiring proof that damages or death probably would not have occurred "but for" the negligent conduct of the defendant, is appropriate. In *Hamil* and the instant case, however, the defendant's act or omission failed in a *duty* to protect against harm from *another source*. Thus, as the *Hamil* court noted, the fact finder is put in the position of having to consider not only what *did* occur, but also what *might have* occurred.

* * *

The *Hamil* court held that once a plaintiff has demonstrated that the defendant's acts or omissions have increased the risk of harm to another, such evidence furnishes a basis for the jury to make a determination as to whether such increased risk was in turn a substantial factor in bringing about the resultant harm.

* * *

Under the *Hamil* decision, once a plaintiff has demonstrated that defendant's acts or omissions in a situation to which § 323(a) applies have increased the risk of harm to another, such evidence furnishes a basis for the fact finder to go further and find that such increased risk was in turn a substantial factor in bringing about the resultant harm. The necessary proximate cause will be established if the jury finds such cause. It is not necessary for a plaintiff to introduce evidence to establish that the negligence resulted in the injury or death, but simply that the negligence increased the *risk* of injury or death. The step from the increased risk to causation is one for the jury to make.

* * *

Where percentage probabilities and decreased probabilities are submitted into evidence, there is simply no danger of speculation on the part of the jury. More speculation is involved in requiring the medical expert to testify as to what would have happened had the defendant not been negligent.

CONCLUSION

* * * We reject Group Health's argument that plaintiffs *must show* that Herskovits "probably" would have had a 51 percent chance of survival if the hospital had not been negligent. We hold that medical testimony of a reduction of chance of survival from 39 percent to 25 percent is sufficient evidence to allow the proximate cause issue to go to the jury.

Causing reduction of the opportunity to recover (loss of chance) by one's negligence, however, does not necessitate a total recovery against the negligent party for all damages caused by the victim's death. Damages should be awarded to the injured party or his family based only on damages caused directly by premature death, such as lost earnings and additional medical expenses, etc.

We reverse the trial court and reinstate the cause of action.

PEARSON, J., concurring.

* * *

* * * I am persuaded * * * by the thoughtful discussion of a recent commentator. King, *Causation, Valuation, and Chance in Personal Injury Torts Involving Preexisting Conditions and Future Consequences,* 90 Yale L.J. 1353 (1981).

* * *

Under the all or nothing approach, typified by *Cooper v. Sisters of Charity of Cincinnati, Inc.,* 27 Ohio St.2d 242, 272 N.E.2d 97 (1971), a plaintiff who establishes that but for the defendant's negligence the decedent had a 51 percent chance of survival may maintain an action for that death. The defendant will be liable for all damages arising from the death, even though there was a 49 percent chance it would have occurred despite his negligence. On the other hand, a plaintiff who establishes that but for the defendant's negligence the decedent had a 49 percent chance of survival recovers nothing.

This all or nothing approach to recovery is criticized by King on several grounds, 90 Yale L.J. at 1376–78. First, the all or nothing approach is arbitrary. Second, it

> subverts the deterrence objectives of tort law by denying recovery for the effects of conduct that causes statistically demonstrable losses * * *. A failure to allocate the cost of these losses to their tortious sources * * * strikes at the integrity of the torts system of loss allocation.

90 Yale L.J. at 1377. Third, the all or nothing approach creates pressure to manipulate and distort other rules affecting causation and damages in an attempt to mitigate perceived injustices. [ ] Fourth, the all or nothing approach gives certain defendants the benefit of an uncertainty which, were it not for their tortious conduct, would not exist. * * * Finally, King argues that the loss of a less than even chance is a loss worthy of redress.

These reasons persuade me that the best resolution of the issue before us is to recognize the loss of a less than even chance as an actionable injury. Therefore, I would hold that plaintiff has established a prima facie issue of proximate cause by producing testimony that defendant probably caused a substantial reduction in Mr. Herskovits' chance of survival. * * *

Finally, it is necessary to consider the amount of damages recoverable in the event that a loss of a chance of recovery is established. Once again, King's discussion provides a useful illustration of the principles which should be applied.

> To illustrate, consider a patient who suffers a heart attack and dies as a result. Assume that the defendant-physician negligently misdiagnosed the patient's condition, but that the patient would have had only a 40% chance of survival even with a timely diagnosis and proper care. Regardless of whether it could be said that the defendant caused the decedent's death, he caused the loss of a chance, and that chance-interest should be completely redressed in its own right. Under the proposed rule, the plaintiff's compensation for the loss of the victim's chance of surviving the heart attack would be 40% of the compensable value of the victim's life had he survived (including what his earning capacity would otherwise have been in the years following death). The value placed on the patient's life would reflect such factors as his age, health, and earning potential, including the fact that he had suffered the heart attack and the assumption that he had survived it. The 40% computation would be applied to that base figure.

(Footnote omitted.) 90 Yale L.J. at 1382.

I would remand to the trial court for proceedings consistent with this opinion.

WILLIAM H. WILLIAMS, C.J., and UTTER and STAFFORD, JJ., concur.

BRACHTENBACH, JUSTICE (dissenting).

I dissent because I find plaintiff did not meet her burden of proving proximate cause. While the statistical evidence introduced by the expert was relevant and admissible, it was not alone sufficient to maintain a cause of action.

Neither the majority nor Justice Dolliver's dissent focus on the key issue. Both opinions focus on the significance of the 14 percent differentiation in the patient's chance to survive for 5 years and question whether this statistical data is sufficient to sustain a malpractice action. The issue is not so limited. The question should be framed as whether all the evidence amounts to sufficient proof, rising above speculation, that the doctor's conduct was a proximate cause of the patient's death. While the relevancy and the significance of the statistical evidence is a subissue bearing on the sufficiency of the proof, such evidence alone neither proves nor disproves plaintiff's case.

II

Furthermore, the instant case does not present evidence of proximate cause that rises above speculation and conjecture. The majority asserts that evidence of a statistical reduction of the chance to survive for 5 years is sufficient to create a jury question on whether the doctor's conduct was a proximate cause of the death. I disagree that this statistical data can be interpreted in such a manner.

Use of statistical data in judicial proceedings is a hotly debated issue. [ ] Many fear that members of the jury will place too much emphasis on statistical evidence and the statistics will be misused and manipulated by expert witnesses and attorneys. [ ]

Such fears do not support a blanket exclusion of statistical data, however. Our court system is premised on confidence in the jury to understand complex concepts and confidence in the right of cross examination as protection against the misuse of evidence. Attorneys ought to be able to explain the true significance of statistical data to keep it in its proper perspective.

Statistical data should be admissible as evidence if they are relevant, that is, if they have

> any tendency to make the existence of any fact that is of consequence to * * * the action more probable or less probable than it would be without the evidence.

ER 401. The statistics here met that test; they have some tendency to show that those diagnosed at stage one of the disease may have a greater chance to survive 5 years than those diagnosed at stage two.

The problem is, however, that while this statistical fact is relevant, it is not sufficient to prove causation. There is an enormous difference between the "any tendency to prove" standard of ER 401 and the "more likely than not" standard for proximate cause.

* * *

Thus, I would not resolve the instant case simply by focusing on the 14 percent differentiation in the chance to survive 5 years for the different stages of cancer. Instead, I would accept this as an admissible fact, but not as proof of proximate cause. To meet the proximate cause burden, the record would need to reveal other facts about the patient that tended to show that he would have been a member of the 14 percent group whose chance of 5 years' survival could be increased by early diagnosis.

Such evidence is not in the record. Instead, the record reveals that Mr. Herskovits' cancer was located such that corrective surgery "would be more formidable". This would tend to show that his chance of survival may have been less than the statistical average. Moreover, the statistics relied on did not take into consideration the location of the tumor, therefore their relevance to Mr. Herskovits' case must be questioned. Clerk's Papers, at 41.

In addition, as the tumor was relatively small in size when removed (2 to 3 centimeters), the likelihood that it would have been detected in 1974, even if the proper test were performed, was less than average. This uncertainty further reduces the probability that the doctor's failure to perform the tests was a proximate cause of a reduced chance of survival.

Other statistics admitted into evidence also tend to show the inconclusiveness of the statistics relied on by the majority. One study showed the *two*-year survival rate for this type of cancer to be 46.6 percent for stage one and 39.8 percent for stage two. Mr. Herskovits lived for 20 months after surgery, which was 26 months after defendant allegedly should have discovered the cancer. Therefore, regardless of the stage of the cancer at the time Mr. Herskovits was examined by defendant, it cannot be concluded that he survived significantly less than the average survival time. Hence, it is pure speculation to suppose that the doctor's negligence "caused" Mr. Herskovits to die sooner than he would have otherwise. Such speculation does not rise to the level of a jury question on the issue of proximate cause. Therefore, the trial court correctly dismissed the case. [   ]

The apparent harshness of this conclusion cannot be overlooked. The combination of the loss of a loved one to cancer and a doctor's negligence in diagnosis seems to compel a finding of liability. Nonetheless, justice must be dealt with an even hand. To hold a defendant liable without proof that his actions *caused* plaintiff harm would open up untold abuses of the litigation system.

Cases alleging misdiagnosis of cancer are increasing in number, perhaps because of the increased awareness of the importance of early detection. These cases, however, illustrate no more than an inconsistency among courts in their treatment of the problems of proof. *See* Annot., *Malpractice in Connection with Diagnosis of Cancer*, 79 A.L. R.3d 915 (1977). Perhaps as medical science becomes more knowledgeable about this disease and more sophisticated in its detection and treatment of it, the balance may tip in favor of imposing liability on doctors who negligently fail to promptly diagnose the disease. But, until a formula is found that will protect doctors against liability imposed through speculation as well as afford truly aggrieved plaintiffs their just compensation, I cannot favor the wholesale abandonment of the principle of proximate cause. For these reasons, I dissent.

Notes and Questions

1. How would damages be figured under the majority's approach? Under the Pearson/King theory? What is the relationship between causation and damages in these cases? The majority and Pearson opinions would effectively permit recovery but reduce damages as the causation link weakens. Is this a reasonable approach?

2. What problems do you foresee with the application of the "loss of a chance" doctrine to medical practice? Note that the evidence as to risk

must be put in probabilistic form for the jury to consider. What about Judge Brachtenbach's concerns about the weight to be given statistical evidence? Would his concerns always prevent the use of statistics in litigation? Or can you offer some solutions to his problems?

3. One judicial attempt at calculating the loss of a chance is found in McKellips v. St. Francis Hospital, Inc., 741 P.2d 467 (Okl.1987):

> To illustrate the method in a case where the jury determines from the statistical findings combined with the specific facts relevant to the patient, the patient originally had a 40% chance of cure and the physician's negligence reduced the chance of cure to 25%, (40%–25%) 15% represents the patient's loss of survival. If the total amount of damages proved by the evidence is $500,000, the damages caused by defendant is 15% × $500,000 or $75,000 * * *".

This has come to be called the percentage apportionment of damages method. See also Mays v. United States, 608 F.Supp. 1476 (D.Colo.1985).

4. A more detailed application of the percentage apportionment approach is found in Boody v. United States, 706 F.Supp. 1458 (D.Kan.1989). The U.S. District Court for Kansas, interpreting Kansas law, adopted the *Herskovits* approach and worked through the calculations. The plaintiff's decedent was found to have lost a 51% chance of surviving five years due to failure of the defendant, Dr. Tuason, to note atelectasis in her right lung during his review of a lateral chest x-ray. Cancer was the most common cause of the atelectasis, or collapsed area of lung. By the time the cancer was detected, it was Stage III, and had metastasized to the brain, leaving a very small five year survival chance. Plaintiff asked for $1,364,729.25 in damages, arguing that decedent lost a 51% chance of survival, and that plaintiff should be compensated for the entire value of decedent's life.

> The court considered three approaches to resolving the damages issue.

> First, the court or jury, without explicit guidance, could arrive at a compensation figure. While simple in formulation and fully allowing a decision maker to render justice, this rule is flawed. The decision maker needs some circumscription to properly evaluate the compensation necessary for the loss of a fractional right. The damages inquiry, when possible, should be more precise. As explained below, the loss of chance theory lends itself to precision. The first option is rejected.

> A second method would provide full compensation for the loss of life regardless of the decedent's less than even chance of survival. [ ] This approach is too onerous for defendants. They should not have to compensate a plaintiff for the percentage of the harm they did not cause or that would have occurred naturally. [ ] The second method should not apply here.

> The most logical approach is to compensate plaintiffs for what they lost: the approximate percentage chance of living or surviving for a fixed period of time. For example, if a person would have had a thirty percent chance to survive a heart attack with proper treatment but died because of negligent treatment, the plaintiff recovers thirty percent of the value placed on the decedent's life. Thus if the jury

believed decedent's life was worth two million dollars, plaintiff would recover $600,000. [ ]

* * *

The court determines the percentage allocation is the most reasonable method and the one the Kansas Supreme Court would adopt. This method is preferable because it apportions damages in direct relation to the harm caused; it neither over compensates plaintiffs or unfairly burdens defendants with unattributable fault. Second, the percentage method gives juries and judges concrete guidelines on how to measure damages, alleviating the "pulling out of the hat" problem identified with the first method. If the decision maker believes plaintiff's expert(s) on causation, the percentage of chance lost, then it makes the usual finding on the value of a life ($X) and multiplies $X by the percentage of chance lost to arrive at the compensation for the lost chance to survive.

An application of the damage formula to the instant facts is straightforward. The court first calculates the total value of the decedent's life. * * *

Plaintiff requests one million dollars under the survival statute for decedent's pain and suffering from 1984 until her death in December 1987. * * * Therefore, in the absence of any contrary evidence and the fraction to be applied, the court somewhat reluctantly finds the one million dollar valuation to be within reason and the evidence.

* * *

The total amount of recovery for decedent's loss of life is $24,377 of medical expenses + $5,353.25 of funeral expenses + $100,000 nonpecuniary loss + $1,000,000 pain and suffering award = $1,129,729.25.

The second step is to determine the percentage of her total life that decedent lost because of Dr. Tuason's negligence. This step is a more complex task than in the usual case. Her lost chance was not in terms of life expectancy but in a percentage of surviving five years. The court reasons that to adhere to the percentage method described above requires the following calculations. Decedent was forty-eight when the negligent act occurred. Her life expectancy at that age was an additional 32.9 years. [ ] Decedent had a significant (51%) chance of living five years. While she may have lived longer than five years, she had a 49% chance of living less than five years. The court determines that five years is the most reasonable amount of time that the negligence deprived her of living. Five years represented 15.2% of her remaining life (5 divided by 32.9). The 15.2% of her remaining life is the loss recoverable under *Roberson*.

The final step is to multiply the two figures: the total value of life by the percentage of life lost. Plaintiff recovers $171,718.83 or 15.2% of $1,129,729.25.

It is by the Court therefore Ordered that judgment in the amount of $171,718.83 plus costs is entered in favor of plaintiff.

5. Some jurisdictions have applied § 323(a) as compensating for the lost chance for treatment itself (McKellips). Others have interpreted § 323(a) as lessening the plaintiff's burden of proof on causation (*Herskovits, Hamil*). Once the plaintiff shows that the defendant's negligence increased the risk that the plaintiff's injury would occur, § 323(a) allows the trier of fact to determine whether the negligence was a substantial factor in causing the injury.

The court in Ehlinger v. Sipes, 155 Wis.2d 1, 454 N.W.2d 754, 759 (Wis.1990), rejected the majority view, refusing to shift the burden of proof onto the defendant.

> We conclude that in a case of this nature, where the causal relationship between the defendant's alleged negligence and the plaintiff's harm can only be inferred by surmising as to what the plaintiff's condition would have been had the defendant exercised ordinary care, to satisfy his or her burden of production on causation, the plaintiff need only show that the omitted treatment was intended to prevent the very type of harm which resulted, that the plaintiff would have submitted to the treatment, and that it is more probable than not the treatment *could* have lessened or avoided the plaintiff's injury had it been rendered. It is then for the trier of fact to determine whether the defendant's negligence was a substantial factor in causing the plaintiff's harm. Id. at 761.

The court rejected the idea that an expert must testify as to what more probably than not would have happened had the defendant rendered appropriate care. This would constitute speculation by a physician as to the success of a particular treatment, "a fact which inherently is incapable of proof to a reasonable certainty". Id. The trier of fact may consider evidence of the likelihood of success of proper treatment; if the defendant's negligence is found to have a substantial factor in causing the harm, the trier of fact may also consider evidence of the likelihood of success of proper treatment in determining the amount of damages to be awarded. Id. at 763.

Compare Alfonso v. Lund, 783 F.2d 958 (10th Cir.1986) (New Mexico unlikely to adopt "lost chance" approach to harm; proximate cause must be shown by a probability, not possibility); DeBurkarte v. Louvar, 393 N.W.2d 131, 135 (Iowa 1986) (jury could have found that the defendant's failure to diagnose and treat breast cancer probably caused a substantial reduction in the plaintiff's chances to survive it); Cullum v. Siefer, 1 Cal.App.3d 20, 81 Cal.Rptr. 381 (1969) (evidence that prompt biopsy might have lengthened life or increased patient's comfort level held sufficient for new trial); Monahan v. Weichert, 82 A.D.2d 102, 442 N.Y.S.2d 295 (1981) (even if defendant's acts merely speeded up an inevitable result, recovery should be allowed to the extent that negligence brought the condition on prematurely). Pillsbury–Flood v. Portsmouth Hospital, 128 N.H. 299, 512 A.2d 1126 (1986) (doctrine rejected; "causation is a matter of probability, not possibility"); Gooding v. University Hosp. Bldg., Inc., 445 So.2d 1015 (Fla.1984) ("Health care providers could find themselves defending cases simply because a patient fails to improve or where serious disease processes are not arrested because another course of action could possibly bring a better result.")

6. Can a person recover for the loss of a chance, if a physician negligently fails to diagnose AIDS, or improperly performs the tests for the HIV virus? See Herman, AIDS: Malpractice and Transmission Liability, 58 Colo.L.Rev. 63 (1986/87).

7. Law review articles discussing the "loss of a chance" problem include: King, Causation, Valuation and Chance in Personal Injury Torts Involving Preexisting Conditions and Future Consequences, 90 Yale L.J. 1353 (1981); Note, Increased Risk of Harm: A New Standard for Sufficiency of Evidence of Causation in Medical Malpractice Cases, 65 Boston Univ.L.Rev. 275 (1985); Comment, Proving Causation in "Loss of a Chance" Cases: A Proportional Approach, 34 Cath.U.L.Rev. 747 (1985).

Extended analysis and criticism of the "loss of a chance" doctrine can be found in Health Care Law and Ethics (R.M.F. Southby and H.L. Hirsh, Eds.1989).

Problem: The Patient's Choice?

Jane Rogers was an attractive pale skinned blonde woman in her early thirties. She had worked every summer during high school and college as a lifeguard at the beach. While she was in graduate school, one of her sisters was diagnosed as having melanoma, a deadly cancer that is often fatal if not detected and treated early. Melanoma is more prevalent in people who have fair complexions, and prolonged exposure to the sun over time, particularly severe sun burns, are a risk factor for the cancer.

Ms. Roger's sister died. The family physician, Dr. James, told the family members that they should all get a thorough physical to check for signs of skin tumors that might be precancerous. Ms. Rogers went to the University Student Clinic, and requested a physical examination. She explained why she was worried. Dr. Gillespie, an older physician who had retired from active practice and now helped out part-time at the Clinic, examined her. He observed a nodule on her upper back, but incorrectly diagnosed it as a birthmark. He told her not to worry. She continued her lifeguarding and water safety instruction activities during the summer, to pay for her graduate education.

At a party one Friday night, Ms. Rogers met a young physician who was a resident at the University hospital. She was wearing a shoulderless dress, and the resident, Dr. Wunch, noted a mole on her shoulder. He recognized it as a melanoma. He pointed it out to her, and told her that she really ought to get it checked. He gave her his card, with his phone number, and said he would be glad to set her up with an appointment with a good cancer specialist at the hospital. Ms. Rogers called, made an appointment, and filled out the forms required by the University Hospital, but then missed her appointment. She never went back.

A year later, during a routine physical as part of an employment application, the examining physician found several large growths on Ms. Roger's back. She was diagnosed as having melanoma, which had spread into her blood and had metastasized into her lymph nodes. She was dead within a year.

What problems do you see with the suit by her estate against the available defendants?

2. *Fear of the Future*

PETRIELLO v. KALMAN

Supreme Court of Connecticut, 1990.
215 Conn. 377, 576 A.2d 474.

[The court considered two issues on appeal. First, plaintiff alleged that the defendant hospital had a duty to ensure that the plaintiff had given her informed consent to surgery before she was medicated. The court held no such duty existed. Second, the defendant physician contended that the plaintiff could not be rewarded damages for increased risk of future injury.]

SHEA, ASSOC. J.

* * *

The jury could reasonably have found the following facts from the evidence. On April 13, 1984, the plaintiff, who was sixteen weeks pregnant, was seen by the defendant Kalman regarding her complaints of low back pain and vaginal bleeding. Kalman, a specialist in obstetrics,[1] had been treating the plaintiff throughout her pregnancy. As a result of his examination, Kalman diagnosed a possible missed abortion or threatened abortion and, therefore, admitted the plaintiff to the Griffin Hospital later that evening. On the basis of his belief that the plaintiff's child had died, an ultrasound examination was performed the next morning. This test revealed that the child had in fact died in utero. Kalman was advised of the ultrasound results and he then telephoned the plaintiff, who remained at the hospital, informing her that the results of the test indicated fetal death and that he intended to perform, later that afternoon, a surgical procedure known as a dilatation and curettage to remove the fetus from the plaintiff's womb.

* * *

That afternoon, during the procedure to remove the fetus, Kalman, utilizing a suction device, perforated the plaintiff's uterus and drew portions of her small intestine through the perforation, through her uterus and into her vagina. The plaintiff's expert, Phillip Sullivan, an obstetrician, testified that Kalman had used excessive force in the operation of the suction device and that the perforation had resulted from a deviation from the prevailing standard of care. Kalman, in an attempt to repair the damage to the uterine wall, made a transverse incision on the plaintiff's abdomen and requested the assistance of Jose Flores, a general surgeon. Because he could not adequately explore the

1. The defendant was not employed by the hospital, but, rather, was an independent physician possessing privileges at the hospital.

plaintiff's abdomen, Flores made another incision perpendicular to the one made by the defendant. Flores repaired the injury to the plaintiff's intestine by means of a bowel resection, removing approximately one foot of the intestine and connecting the two ends of the remaining intestine.

Flores, testifying for the plaintiff, stated that, as a result of the bowel resection, adhesions had more probably than not formed in the plaintiff's abdomen. He also testified that the plaintiff faces an increased risk of future bowel obstruction as a result of these adhesions, but that he thought the risk was remote. Flores stated that, in his experience, adhesions were a prominent cause of small bowel obstruction and that he had advised the plaintiff, after the surgery, that adhesions would form in her abdomen and that they could result in a future bowel obstruction. The plaintiff testified that she was also advised of this increased risk of future bowel obstruction by Flores' partner, who was also a physician. The plaintiff's expert, Sullivan, also testified that the plaintiff was subject to an increased risk of future bowel obstruction and that, based on literature he had consulted, she had an 8 to 16 percent chance of developing such an obstruction.

The plaintiff brought her revised complaint in two counts, alleging that Kalman was negligent in that he: (1) performed the dilatation and curettage without first attempting other nonsurgical methods; (2) perforated the plaintiff's uterus during the surgical procedure; (3) suctioned out portions of the plaintiff's small intestine during the surgical procedure; and (4) made an improper incision in the plaintiff's abdomen during his attempt to repair the plaintiff's small intestine.   * * *

I

* * *

II

In his appeal, the defendant claims that the trial court erred by: (1) allowing expert testimony concerning the plaintiff's increased risk of a bowel obstruction; (2) charging the jury that the plaintiff could be compensated for her fear that such an obstruction will occur; and (3) charging the jury that the plaintiff could be compensated for the increased risk that she will suffer a future bowel obstruction. We conclude that the expert testimony was admissible and that the court correctly instructed the jury.

A

The defendant claims that the plaintiff should not have been permitted to present any testimony regarding her increased susceptibility to a future bowel obstruction resulting from the defendant's actions. * * * During a hearing conducted as a result of the defendant's motion in limine, the plaintiff argued that the evidence concerning her increased risk of bowel obstruction was admissible for three reasons: (1) as evidence of her fear of future disability; (2) as evidence that her fear was rational; and (3) as evidence of a presently compensable injury. We conclude that the evidence was admissible for all three purposes.

The defendant has chosen to ignore the fact that the plaintiff, in her revised complaint, alleged that as a result of the defendant's actions she "experienced extreme emotional distress." At trial, she sought to prove that her emotional distress was caused, at least in part, by her fear of suffering an obstruction of her bowel at some later date and that she should be compensated for that fear. We have previously held that evidence concerning an increased risk of injury, although insufficient to justify an award of damages based upon the occurrence of that injury in the future, may, nevertheless, be presented to the jury as evidence of emotional distress. * * * [T]he jury was entitled, in this case, to hear testimony that the plaintiff had been informed of the increased risk of future bowel obstruction, as well as testimony regarding any anxiety this information produced in the plaintiff's mind.

The expert testimony, regarding the plaintiff's increased risk of suffering a future bowel obstruction, was also admissible on the issue of whether the plaintiff's anxiety was rationally based. Although "[s]ome courts have permitted recovery where there is not even a possibility that the feared disability will develop * * * [m]ore often there is a requirement that the plaintiff's anxiety have some reasonable basis." D. Faulkner & K. Woods, "Fear of Future Disability—An Element of Damages in a Personal Injury Action," 7 W.New Eng.L.Rev. 865, 877–78 (1985). [ ] Thus, the evidence objected to by the defendant was admissible to show that the plaintiff's anxiety regarding the possibility of a future bowel obstruction was both subjectively held and objectively reasonable.

Finally, given that we resolve the question of the compensability of an increased risk of future injury in favor of the plaintiff, the expert testimony, regarding the extent of that risk in this case, was also admissible for the purpose of showing how likely it was that the plaintiff would experience a bowel obstruction at some later date.

B

The defendant also claims that, even if the expert testimony was admissible, the court erred in allowing the jury to award the plaintiff compensation for her fear of a future bowel obstruction, since the evidence established that there was only a possibility that the plaintiff would develop a bowel obstruction and this possibility was too speculative to support the inclusion in the verdict of damages for such a fear. The defendant argues that "the Plaintiff's [chance] of incurring a bowel obstruction is 'so remote' that it is not a proper element of damages." We conclude that the evidence presented was sufficient to establish a reasonable basis for the plaintiff's fear that she will suffer from a future bowel obstruction and, therefore, was also sufficient to support compensation for that fear. Although one of the plaintiff's expert witnesses, Flores, testified that there was a "very remote" chance that such a blockage would occur, the testimony of another expert, Sullivan, presented to the jury the results of research conducted by him which indicated that, according to two studies he consulted, there was between an 8 and 16 percent chance that the plaintiff would suffer a future bowel obstruction as a result of the bowel resection necessitated by the defendant's actions. Thus, even if Flore's [sic] testimony was insufficient to establish a reasonable ground for the plaintiff's anxiety, we conclude that the jury could have found a sufficient basis in the opinion rendered by Sullivan. [ ] We conclude, therefore, that the court correctly instructed the jury that it might award the plaintiff damages for her fear of the increased risk that she will someday suffer from a bowel obstruction.

C

The defendant's principal claim on appeal is that the court erred by instructing the jury that the plaintiff could be awarded compensation for the increased risk that the defendant's negligence would cause her to experience a bowel obstruction at some future date. The defendant excepted to this instruction at trial upon the ground that the "intestinal blockage [was] purely speculation" and had not been shown to be "reasonably probable." He raises essentially the same claim on appeal.

The defendant contends that the evidence in this case established no reasonable probability that the plaintiff would suffer a bowel obstruction at some future date, and, therefore, the trial court incorrectly instructed the jury that the plaintiff should be compensated for whatever risk there was of some future injury. The jury heard expert testimony that the risk of the plaintiff suffering a future bowel obstruction was somewhere between 8 and 16 percent. There is no question that such a degree of probability of the occurrence of future injury would not support an award of damages to the same extent as if that injury had in fact occurred. In *Healy v. White,* supra, at 444, 378 A.2d 540, we reasoned that in order to be awarded full compensation for an injury that has not yet manifested itself, a plaintiff must show that there exists a reasonable probability that the injury will in fact occur.
* * *

In *Healy,* we affirmed our adherence to the prevailing all or nothing standard for compensating those who have either suffered present harm and seek compensation as if the harm will be permanent, or have suffered present harm and seek compensation for possible future consequences of that harm. * * * By denying any compensation unless a plaintiff proves that a future consequence is more likely to occur than not, courts have created a system in which a significant number of persons receive compensation for future consequences that never occur and, conversely, a significant number of persons receive no compensation at all for consequences that later ensue from risks not rising to the level of probability. This system is inconsistent with the goal of compensating tort victims fairly for all the consequences of the injuries they have sustained, while avoiding, so far as possible, windfall awards for consequences that never happen.

In seeking to enforce their right to individualized compensation, plaintiffs in negligence cases are confronted by the requirements that they must claim all applicable damages in a single cause of action; [   ] and must bring their actions no "more than three years from the date of the act or omission complained of." General Statutes § 52–584. Under these circumstances, no recovery may be had for future consequences of an injury when the evidence at trial does not satisfy the more probable than not criterion approved in *Healy*, despite a substantial risk of such consequences. Conversely, a defendant cannot seek reimbursement from a plaintiff who may have recovered for a future consequence, which appeared likely at the time of trial, on the ground that subsequent events have made that consequence remote or impossible. Our legal system provides no opportunity for a second look at a damage award so that it may be revised with the benefit of hindsight.
* * *

If the plaintiff in this case had claimed that she was entitled to compensation to the extent that a future bowel obstruction was a certainty, she would have been foreclosed from such compensation solely on the basis of her experts' testimony that the likelihood of the occurrence of a bowel obstruction was either very remote or only 8 to 16 percent probable. Her claim, however, was for compensation for the increased risk that she would suffer such an obstruction sometime in the future. If this increased risk was more likely than not the result of the bowel resection necessitated by the defendant's actions, we conclude that there is no legitimate reason why she should not receive present compensation based upon the likelihood of the risk becoming a reality. When viewed in this manner, the plaintiff was attempting merely to establish the extent of her present injuries. She should not be burdened with proving that the occurrence of a future event is more likely than not, when it is a present risk, rather than a future event for which she claims damages. In our judgment, it was fairer to instruct the jury to compensate the plaintiff for the increased risk of a bowel obstruction based upon the likelihood of its occurrence rather than to ignore that risk entirely. The medical evidence in this case concerning the probability of such a future consequence provided a sufficient basis for estimating that likelihood and compensating the plaintiff for it.

This view is consistent with the Second Restatement of the Law of Torts, which states, in § 912, that "[o]ne to whom another has tortiously caused harm is entitled to compensatory damages for the harm if, but only if, he establishes by proof the extent of the harm and the amount of money representing adequate compensation with as much certainty as the nature of the tort and the circumstances permit." Damages for the future consequences of an injury can never be forecast with certainty. With respect to awards for permanent injuries, actuarial tables of average life expectancy are commonly used to assist the trier in measuring the loss a plaintiff is likely to sustain from the future effects of an injury. Such statistical evidence does, of course, satisfy the more likely than not standard as to the duration of a permanent injury. Similar evidence, based upon medical statistics of the average incidence of a particular future consequence from an injury, such as that produced by the plaintiff in this case, may be said to establish with the same degree of certitude the likelihood of the occurrence of the future harm to which a tort victim is exposed as a result of a present injury. Such evidence provides an adequate basis for measuring damages for the risk to which the victim has been exposed because of a wrongful act.

The probability percentage for the occurrence of a particular harm, the risk of which has been created by the tortfeasor, can be applied to the damages that would be justified if that harm should be realized. We regard this system of compensation as preferable to our present practice of denying any recovery for substantial risks of future harm not satisfying the more likely than not standard. We also believe that such a system is fairer to a defendant, who should be required to pay damages for a future loss based upon the statistical probability that such a loss will be sustained rather than upon the assumption that the loss is a certainty because it is more likely than not. We hold, therefore, that in a tort action, a plaintiff who has established a breach of duty that was a substantial factor in causing a present injury which has resulted in an increased risk of future harm is entitled to compensation to the extent that the future harm is likely to occur. [ ]

Applying this holding to the facts of this case, we conclude that the trial court correctly instructed the jury that the plaintiff could be awarded compensation for the increased likelihood that she will suffer a bowel obstruction some time in the future. The court's instruction was fully in accord with our holding today. * * *

The judgment of the trial court is affirmed.

* * *

Notes and Questions

1. *Petriello* allows a plaintiff to recover for the risk of future harm, and for the fear that such a risk will materialize. Is this double recovery? *Herskovits* and other "loss of a chance" cases involve missed diagnoses, usually in oncology situations. *Petriello* involves a botched procedure, leaving the plaintiff at an enhanced risk of future injury. What kind of evidence may the plaintiff produce as to the fear of future harm? How do *Petriello* and *Herskovits* differ?

2. Recovery for fear of future harm, based on increased risk, is relatively rare in American case law. See Ferrara v. Galluchio, 5 N.Y.2d 16, 176 N.Y.S.2d 996, 152 N.E.2d 249 (1958); Howard v. Mt. Sinai Hospital, Inc., 63 Wis.2d 515, 217 N.W.2d 383 (1974).

Problem: The Fatal Cavity

You have been approached by the family of a young woman, Kim Brennan, to explore the possibilities of a tort suit. Kim, a twenty-one year old college student, has recently undergone dental work, having several wisdom teeth extracted by Dr. James.

Kim has heard rumors that Dr. James is gay. She is concerned that he might have AIDS, or be HIV-positive. She has been tested for the HIV virus and her last test was negative. She has been reading up on AIDS, however, and learned that some individuals can carry the HIV virus and not seroconvert for long periods of time, so that they will not test positive. She is terrified of entering into romantic relationships now, and feels constantly anxious. She has never had any sexual relationships, nor has she ever used drugs.

What do you need to know to prepare a complaint against Dr. James? Assuming that Dr. James in fact is HIV-positive, can Kim recover for her fear of becoming HIV-positive? What evidence will you need to produce?

II. THE INSTITUTION AS DEFENDANT: FROM CHARITY TO TARGET

INTRODUCTION

The modern hospital—with its operating theaters, stainless steel equipment, and its large staffs of nurses, doctors, and support personnel—has come to symbolize the delivery of medical care. It was not always so. For centuries, in Europe and in America, hospitals tended the sick and the insane but made no attempt to treat or cure. They were supported by the philanthropy of the wealthy and by religious groups. In the 1870's it could be said that only a small minority of doctors practiced in hospitals, and even they devoted only a small portion of their practice to such work. A person seeking medical care before 1900 did not consider hospitalization, since doctors made house calls and even operated in the home. By the late 1800's, however, developments in medical knowledge moved the hospital toward a central position in health care. The development of antiseptic and aseptic techniques reduced the previously substantial risk of infection within hospitals; the growing scientific content of medicine made hospitals a more attractive place for medical practice.

Therapeutic and diagnostic improvements became identified with hospital doctors. These doctors, the product of the modernization of medicine, discovered that the hospital was well suited to their practice needs. Control over the hospital began to shift from the trustees to the doctors during the early 1900's. For an analysis of the role and history of the hospital in the United States, see Chapter 5, infra. For an excellent extended discussion of the history of the hospital, see P. Starr, The Social Transformation of American Medicine (1982), particularly Chapter 4.

As the hospital evolved, physicians became increasingly dependent upon hospital affiliation. By 1975, no doctor would consider practicing without the resources that a hospital offered, and 25 percent of the 330,000 active physicians practiced fulltime in a hospital.

Traditionally, the relationship of doctor to hospital was that of independent contractor, rather than employee. The hospital was therefore not regularly targeted as a defendant in a malpractice suit. Only if the doctor whose negligence injured a patient was an employee could the hospital be reached through the doctrine of vicarious liability. The hospital was independently liable only if it were negligent in its administrative or housekeeping functions, for example causing a patient to slip and fall on a wet floor. Otherwise, the hospital was often immune from liability.

A. FROM IMMUNITY TO VICARIOUS LIABILITY

Until recently hospitals have been considered as charitable institutions, as such exempted from the general rule that a corporation is responsible for the acts of its employees. The doctrine of charitable immunity protected hospitals from liability in any form through the 1940's. In the 1950's, however, courts began to observe the increasing importance of the hospital in providing health care and supervising their staffs.

BING v. THUNIG

Supreme Court of New York, 1957.
2 N.Y.2d 656, 163 N.Y.S.2d 3, 143 N.E.2d 3.

The doctrine declaring charitable institutions immune from liability was first declared in this country in 1876. McDonald v. Massachusetts Gen. Hosp., 120 Mass. 432. Deciding that a charity patient, negligently operated upon by a student doctor, could not hold the hospital responsible, the court reasoned that the public and private donations that supported the charitable hospital constituted a trust fund which could not be diverted. * * * The second reason which the court advanced was that the principle of *respondeat superior* was not to be applied to doctors and nurses. It was the court's thought that, even though employed by the hospital, they were to be regarded as independent contractors rather than employees because of the skill they exercised and the lack of control exerted over their work—and yet, we pause again to interpolate, the special skill of other employees (such as airplane pilots, locomotive engineers, chemists, to mention but a few) has never been the basis for denying the application of *respondeat superior* and, even more to the point, that very principle has been invoked to render a public hospital accountable for the negligence of its doctors, nurses and other skilled personnel. [ ]

Nor may the exemption be justified by the fear, the major impetus originally behind the doctrine, that the imposition of liability will do irreparable harm to the charitable hospital. At the time the rule originated, in the middle of the nineteenth century, not only was there the possibility that a substantial award in a single negligence action might destroy the hospital, but concern was felt that a ruling permitting recovery against the funds of charitable institutions might discourage generosity and "constrain * * * [them], as a measure of self-protection, to limit their activities." Schloendorff v. New York Hosp., supra, 211 N.Y. 125, 135, 105 N.E. 92, 95, 52 L.R.A.,N.S., 505. Whatever problems today beset the charitable hospital, and they are not to be minimized, the dangers just noted have become less acute. Quite apart from the availability of insurance to protect against possible claims and lawsuits, we are not informed that undue hardships or calamities have overtaken them in those jurisdictions where immunity is withheld and liability imposed. * * * In any event, today's hospital is quite different from its predecessor of long ago; it receives wide community support, employs a large number of people and necessarily operates its plant in businesslike fashion.

The conception that the hospital does not undertake to treat the patient, does not undertake to act through its doctors and nurses, but undertakes instead simply to procure them to act upon their own responsibility, no longer reflects the fact. Present-day hospitals, as their manner of operation plainly demonstrates, do far more than furnish facilities for treatment. They regularly employ on a salary basis a large staff of physicians, nurses and interns, as well as administrative and manual workers, and they charge patients for medical care and treatment, collecting for such services, if necessary, by legal action. Certainly, the person who avails himself of "hospital facilities" expects that the hospital will attempt to cure him, not that its nurses or other employees will act on their own responsibility.

Hospitals should, in short, shoulder the responsibilities borne by everyone else. There is no reason to continue their exemption from the universal rule of *respondeat superior*. The test should be, for these institutions, whether charitable or profit-making, as it is for every other employer, was the person who committed the negligent injury-producing act one of its employees and, if he was, was he acting within the scope of his employment.

The rule of nonliability is out of tune with the life about us, at variance with modern day needs and with concepts of justice and fair dealing. * * *

In sum, then, the doctrine according the hospital an immunity for the negligence of its employees is such a rule, and we abandon it. The hospital's liability must be governed by the same principles of law as apply to all other employers.

The judgment of the Appellate Division should be reversed and a new trial granted, with costs to abide the event.

* * *

Note: Elimination of Immunity

Most hospitals prior to 1940 were protected from suit either by charitable or governmental immunity. The reasons were related to hospital difficulties in obtaining liability insurance and the fiscal fragility of many hospitals in a time before government reimbursement of health care was extensive.

The trend over the past few decades has been to impose full tort liability on all hospitals, whatever their form or origins. The charitable immunity doctrine disappeared with remarkable speed from American law. Prior to 1942, some form of immunity was recognized by most American jurisdictions. The case of President and Directors of Georgetown College v. Hughes, 130 F.2d 810 (D.C.Cir.1942) was a watershed case eliminating immunity. Since that case, over 30 jurisdictions have abrogated charitable immunity, while the remainder retain immunity to the extent of statutory ceilings on recoverable damages, or only up to available coverage, or as to charity care. See Etheridge v. Medical Center Hospitals, 237 Va. 87, 376 S.E.2d 525 (1989); Cutts v. Fulton–DeKalb Hosp. Auth., 192 Ga.App. 517, 385 S.E.2d 436 (1989).

Governmental immunity has proved more resistant to elimination by the courts. State courts have split on governmental immunity, with some eliminating it, others leaving it to the legislatures, and others retaining immunity in various forms. The Federal Tort Claims Act (FTCA), 28 U.S.C.A. §§ 1346(b) and 2671–2680, defines the extent to which the Federal government can be sued. Section 2680 provides for an exception to the Federal government's waiver of immunity for claims based upon "the exercise or performance or the failure to exercise or perform a discretionary function or duty on the part of a federal agency or an employee of the Government, whether or not the discretion involved be abused." Several states have adopted acts similar to the FTCA, and "discretionary" has been narrowly construed by both the federal courts and state courts to cover primarily policy making of a broad sort. See Hyde v. University of Mich. Board of Regents, 426 Mich. 223, 393 N.W.2d 847 (1986), granting immunity to state hospitals. Municipal and county immunity has likewise seen erosion by the courts. For a detailed state-by-state analysis of the intricacies of governmental immunity, see Louisell and Waltz, 2 Medical Malpractice sect. 17.18 (1984).

Judicial and legislative actions have left most hospitals responsible for the torts of their employees, including doctors. Principles of vicarious liability became applicable to health care institutions once charitable and governmental immunities were abrogated. A master-servant relationship, a partnership, or a joint venture could lead to liability. The hospital came to be viewed as an enterprise liable for the acts of its employees, and the physician became liable for the acts of her employees, a partner, or another physician working jointly with her.

1. The Captain of the Ship Doctrine

The Captain of the Ship doctrine provides that a physician who exercises control and authority over nurses and other health care professionals should be held liable for their negligence. It is a harsher version of the "borrowed servant" doctrine, which provides that a surgeon borrows nurses or support personnel during surgery. In the typical case, the surgeon is held responsible for an error in a sponge count done by the nursing staff after surgery, even though the surgeon does not participate in such sponge counts. See Ravi v. Williams, 536 So.2d 1374 (Ala.1988) (surgeon liable to patient for failure to remove sponge, even though he had delegated that task to nurse). If the surgeon is held liable, of course, the hospital will not be, since the nurses are considered to have been "borrowed" by the physician, so that temporarily the hospital is not vicariously liable for their errors. See Restatement (Second) of Agency § 227. See also Krane v. St. Anthony Hosp. Systems, 738 P.2d 75 (Colo.App.1987); Rudeck v. Wright, 218 Mont. 41, 709 P.2d 621 (1985).

The Captain of the Ship doctrine is a special application of this agency rule of borrowed servant in the medical context, on the theory that the surgeon is in complete control of the operating room. It is a strict liability theory, often predicated on the surgeon's "right to control", rather than actual control. As the court noted in Truhitte v. French Hospital, 128 Cal.App.3d 332, 348, 180 Cal.Rptr. 152, 160 (1982). " * * * the 'captain of the ship' doctrine arose from the need to assure plaintiffs a source of recovery for malpractice at a time when many hospitals enjoyed charitable immunity."

Accord, Northeast Alabama Regional Medical Center v. Robinson, 548 So.2d 439 (Ala.1989). In a later California decision, Schultz v. Mutch, 165 Cal.App.3d 66, 211 Cal.Rptr. 445, 450 (1985), another California court of appeal rejected the *Truhitte* position, based on the patient's reliance on the physician's competence and expertise. Both courts referred to *Ybarra v. Spangard,* supra, which addressed the helplessness of hospital patients and the impersonal nature of hospital care.

Should the Captain of the Ship doctrine have continuing vitality? Or is it better to focus liability on the hospital for its staff's errors? See Price, The Sinking of the "Captain of the Ship": Reexamining the Vicarious Liability of an Operating Surgeon for the Negligence of Assisting Hospital Personnel, 10 J.Leg.Med. 323 (1989). See also Franklin v. Gupta, 81 Md.App. 345, 567 A.2d 524 (1990) (rejecting doctrine.)

2. Stretching Vicarious Liability Doctrine

Hospitals continued through the sixties to be protected from most litigation for patient injuries by a treating physician, even though charitable immunity was abrogated, since most doctors were independent contractors. The courts then began to articulate doctrines to give the plaintiff a possible defendant, where the hospital had immunity or where vicarious liability would not work. Thus the "borrowed servant" rule and the "Captain of the Ship" doctrine placed the doctor in the position of responsibility in some specialized situations.

In the last four decades the courts have begun to grapple with the independent doctor's connection to the institution, using a number of doctrines to circumvent vicarious liability limitations. For an overview, see A. Southwick, The Law of Hospital and Health Care Administration, Chapter XIV (2d ed. 1988); Note, Theories for Imposing Liability Upon Hospitals for Medical Malpractice: Ostensible Agency and Corporate Liability, 11 Wm. Mitchell L.Rev. 561 (1985).

a. The Control Test

The first judicial approach was simply to test whether the doctor was an employee or subject to the control of the hospital, applying a number of standard criteria for evaluating the existence of a master-servant relationship. If the contract gave the hospital substantial control over the doctor's choice of patients or if the hospital furnished equipment, then an employee relationship might be found. The case-law reflects divergent applications of the "control" test, because of the breadth of the factors involved. See Mduba v. Benedictine Hospital, 52 A.D.2d 450, 384 N.Y.S.2d 527 (3d Dept.1976) (doctor failed to give blood to patient, resulting in his death; hospital in the contract between doctor and hospital had guaranteed doctor's salary and controlled his activities. Court held doctor to be an employee); Kober v. Stewart, 148 Mont. 117, 417 P.2d 476 (1966) (contract establishes the method by which hospital hired a doctor as supervisor).

b. The "Ostensible Agency" Test

Some courts concluded that in some settings, such as the emergency room or the radiology labs, the hospital holds itself out as offering services to the patient through a doctor, even though the doctor who renders the service is not an employee. The following case illustrates a modern application of this test to a contemporary contractual relationship between a hospital and a physician.

JACKSON v. POWER

Supreme Court of Alaska, 1987.
743 P.2d 1376.

BURKE, JUSTICE.

This case presents an issue of first impression in this state, concerning health care delivery in hospital emergency rooms. The question that we must resolve is whether a hospital may be held vicariously liable for negligent health care rendered by an emergency room physician who is not an employee of the hospital, but is, instead, an independent contractor. We hold that the hospital in this case had a non-delegable duty to provide non-negligent physician care in its emergency room and, therefore, may be liable.

I

On the evening of May 22, 1981, sixteen year old Brett Jackson was seriously injured when he fell from a cliff. Jackson was airlifted to

Fairbanks Memorial Hospital (FMH). Shortly after midnight, he was received in the hospital's emergency room.

Jackson was examined by respondent John Power, M.D., one of two emergency room physicians on duty at the time. Dr. Power's examination revealed multiple lacerations and abrasions of the patient's face and scalp, multiple contusions and lacerations of the lumbar area, several broken vertebrae and gastric distension, suggesting possible internal injuries. Dr. Power ordered several tests, but did not order certain procedures that could have been used to ascertain whether there had been damage to the patient's kidneys. Jackson had, in fact, suffered damage to the renal arteries and veins which supply blood to and remove blood from the kidneys. This damage, undetected for approximately 9 to 10 hours after Jackson's arrival at FMH, ultimately caused Jackson to lose both of his kidneys.

II

Jackson and his mother, Linda Estrada, (hereinafter referred to collectively as Jackson) filed suit. In their complaint they alleged negligence in the diagnosis, care and treatment Jackson received at FMH. Jackson moved for partial summary judgment seeking to hold FMH vicariously liable as a matter of law for the care rendered by Dr. Power. In support of his motion, Jackson advanced three separate theories: (1) enterprise liability; (2) apparent authority; and (3) non-delegable duty. [The court's discussion of non-delegable duty is found at pp. 266–270 infra.]

* * *

III

Initially, it is important to clarify the exact issue that we have been asked to resolve. Jackson has conceded, for purposes of this appeal, that Dr. Power was not an employee of FMH, but an independent contractor employed by respondent Emergency Room, Inc. (ERI), and that ERI and FMH are separate legal entities. Traditional rules of *respondeat superior* are, therefore, inapposite. Jackson also makes no claim that FMH was itself negligent in its selection, retention, or supervision of Dr. Power. Consequently, we have no occasion to consider the doctrine of corporate negligence.[2] Jackson asks us to resolve only whether a hospital should be vicariously liable, as a matter of public policy, for the negligence or malpractice of an independent contractor/physician, committed while treating a patient in the hospital's emergency room, under theories of (1) enterprise liability; (2) apparent authority; or (3) non-delegable duty.

IV

As previously noted, this case presents this court with an issue of first impression.

2. The doctrine of corporate negligence holds that a hospital owes an independent duty to its patients to use reasonable care to insure that physicians granted hospital privileges are competent, and to supervise the medical treatment provided by members of its medical staff. [ ]

The generally accepted rule is that, where an employment relationship exists between the physician and the hospital, the hospital will be liable, under the traditional rule of *respondeat superior,* for any negligence or malpractice which results in injury to a hospital patient. [ ] Conversely, no liability attaches to the hospital when the physician is an independent contractor. [ ]

Jackson concedes that Dr. Power was an independent contractor; however, he asserts that Alaska's law of *respondeat superior* mandates a result different than that which would be reached under the general rule. Jackson argues that our decision in *Fruit v. Schreiner,* 502 P.2d 133 (Alaska 1972), establishes that the law of "vicarious legal responsibility" in Alaska is "enterprise liability." Thus, he contends, if the enterprise impacts society and the negligent act occurred during an activity performed for the benefit or in the interest of the enterprise, the enterprise is liable.

[The court rejects Jackson's argument that vicarious liability is equivalent to enterprise liability.]

V

Jackson next argues that the trial court erred in holding that genuine issues of material fact prevented it from granting summary judgment on his theory of apparent authority.

Although we have recognized the doctrine of apparent authority in other contexts, [ ] this is the first time we have been asked to apply this doctrine to a hospital-independent contractor/physician relationship.

Cases from other jurisdictions show a strong trend toward liability against hospitals that permit or encourage patients to believe that independent contractor/physicians are, in fact, authorized agents of the hospitals. These courts have held hospitals vicariously liable under a doctrine labeled either "ostensible" or "apparent" agency or "agency by estoppel." [ ] Although courts and commentators often use these terms interchangeably, they are not theoretically identical.

The "ostensible" or "apparent" agency theory is based on Section 429 of the Restatement (Second) of Torts (1965), which provides:

One who employs an independent contractor to perform services for another which are accepted in the reasonable belief that the services are being rendered by the employer or by his servants, is subject to liability for physical harm caused by the negligence of the contractor in supplying such services, to the same extent as though the employer were supplying them himself or by his servants.

Two factors are relevant to a finding of ostensible agency: (1) whether the patient looks to the institution, rather than the individual physician, for care; and (2) whether the hospital "holds out" the physician as its employee. [ ]

"Agency by estoppel," in contrast, is predicated on the arguably stricter standard of the Restatement (Second) of Agency § 267 (1958). Section 267 provides:

> One who represents that another is his servant or agent and thereby causes a third person justifiably to rely upon the care or skill of such apparent agent is subject to liability to the third person for harm caused by the lack of care or skill of the one appearing to be a servant or other agent as if he were such.

Under this theory, there must be actual reliance upon the representations of the principal by the person injured. [ ]

Jackson, in essence, asks us to adopt a rule of ostensible agency. FMH, on the other hand, requests that we * * * refuse to apply this doctrine in the hospital-physician context or, alternatively, that we adopt a rule which is essentially estoppel by agency. Although we find nothing antithetical about applying the doctrine of apparent authority to a hospital-independent contractor/physician relationship, we perceive no reason to adopt a special rule in this area. We believe that traditional rules of apparent authority provide sufficient guidelines.

* * *

Drawing all reasonable inferences in the light most favorable to FMH, the record shows the following: at the time of Jackson's accident, FMH was the only civilian hospital north of Anchorage providing emergency room services in Alaska. Two road signs in Fairbanks note the location of the hospital. However, neither of these signs specifically refer to the existence of emergency room services. The signs were not constructed or situated by FMH. In fact, FMH does no advertising at all.

From the time of its establishment in 1972, FMH has never staffed its emergency room with its own physician employees, but has always relied upon local physicians to provide that service. Prior to the formation of ERI in 1977, FMH's emergency room was serviced by three local clinics, each providing one physician on a nightly basis. After 1977, ERI provided one physician on a nightly basis who worked a 14–hour graveyard shift (6:00 p.m. to 8:00 a.m.).[8] While on duty in the emergency room, the ERI physician was "in charge" and no FMH personnel were responsible for either scheduling or monitoring the emergency room physicians. No contractual arrangement existed between FMH and ERI for the provision of emergency room physicians.

In apparent non-life threatening situations the first person an incoming patient sees at the emergency room is the admissions clerk. Immediately adjacent to the clerk's desk is a sign which indicated that physicians from ERI were working in the emergency room. Although the exact state of Jackson's awareness is not entirely clear, there is

---

8. The clinics continued to provide an additional physician for the graveyard shift on a rotation basis.

evidence suggesting that he was admitted in a conscious state.[9] Neither Jackson nor his mother selected FMH as the place of treatment nor Dr. Power as Jackson's physician.

From the above, a jury could conclude that FMH held itself out as providing emergency care services to the public. A jury could also find that Jackson reasonably believed that Dr. Power was employed by the hospital to deliver emergency room service. It is also possible, however, that a jury could find to the contrary.[10]

Unless the evidence allows but one inference, the question of apparent authority is one of fact for the jury. [ ] In the case at bar, the record is not susceptible to a single inference. Thus, the trial court properly denied summary judgment on this issue.

HARDY v. BRANTLEY

Supreme Court of Mississippi, 1985.
471 So.2d 358.

[The plaintiff decedent was admitted to the emergency room diagnosed as having heat exhaustion, and released. He died soon thereafter from a perforated duodenal ulcer and peritonitis. The estate sued both the emergency room doctor and the hospital. The defendant doctor was a member of the Hinds Emergency Group (HEG) which had a detailed contract with the hospital. The contract provided in part that the group was an independent contractor.]

We see no reason why cases of this sort should be outside the mainstream of the general tort law. We note that Restatement (Second) of Torts § 429 (1966) provides:

> One [Hinds General] who employs an independent contractor [Dr. Brantley and his group] to perform services for another [Brad Ewing] which are accepted in the reasonable belief that the services are being rendered by the employer or by his servants, is subject to liability for physical harm caused by the negligence of the contractor in supplying such services, to the same extent as though the employer were supplying them himself or by his servants.

* * * No longer are hospitals merely physical facilities where physicians practice their professions. Hospitals hold themselves out to

---

9. Jackson testified at his deposition that he recalled being placed in the helicopter but had no recollection of being removed from it, being taken to FMH, or of meeting the doctor who treated him. On the other hand, the medical records indicate that Jackson appeared to be neurologically stable, completely oriented and gave no indication that he was unconscious or in distress. Moreover, at his deposition, Dr. Power testified that "Jackson was talking" and "completely oriented."

10. In this regard, we agree with the weight of authority that application of apparent authority in the hospital/emergency cy room physician situation does not require an express representation to the patient that the treating physician is an employee of the hospital. Nor is direct testimony as to reliance required absent evidence that the patient knew or should have known that the treating physician was not a hospital employee when the treatment was rendered. *See* cases cited *supra* p. 1380.

the public as offering and rendering quality health care services. We notice a marked increase in advertisement and other forms of solicitations of patients as hospitals compete for the health-care dollar.

It goes without saying that hospitals such as Hinds General are corporate entities capable of acting only through human beings whose services the hospital engages. In arrangements such as that existing between Hinds General and HEG, the hospital places a great portion of its eggs in the baskets of the emergency room physicians. If they do their job well, the hospital succeeds in its chosen mission, profiting financially and otherwise from the quality of emergency care so delivered. On such facts, anomaly would attend the hospital's escape from liability where the quality of care so delivered was below minimally acceptable standards. All of this is surely so whether the high or low quality of emergency care is delivered by physician, nurse, paramedic or any other person engaged by the hospital.

Reason dictates the validity of the above premises without regard to the details of any undisclosed agreement between the hospital and the person acting in its behalf. We say this in the context of the fact that patients often seek emergency care and treatment from the hospital, not from any particular physician. The patient entering the hospital emergency room seldom knows the name of the physician who will treat him. Although there may be important factual variations from case to case, a patient's non-selection of his physician is often the rule in the case of anesthesiologists, radiologists and particularly emergency room physicians. We are presented such a situation here. Larry Ewing testified he and Brad sought emergency care of Hinds General, that they had never heard of Dr. Brantley, but were content to accept his care as in their view he had been furnished by the hospital. Under such circumstances, it seems only reasonable that the hospital should be estopped to deny responsibility for the neglect of its emergency room physicians. [   ]

Having in mind the considerations and premises set forth in the above authorities, we have concluded that the better rule to be followed in this state henceforth is this: Where a hospital holds itself out to the public as providing a given service, in this instance, emergency services, and where the hospital enters into a contractual arrangement with one or more physicians to direct and provide the service, and where the patient engages the services of the hospital without regard to the identity of a particular physician and where as a matter of fact the patient is relying upon the hospital to deliver the desired health care and treatment, the doctrine of respondeat superior applies and the hospital is vicariously liable for damages proximately resulting from the neglect, if any, of such physicians. By way of contrast and distinction, where a patient engages the services of a particular physician who then admits the patient to a hospital where the physician is on staff, the hospital is not vicariously liable for the neglect or defaults of the physician.

c.   The Inherent Function Test

A third approach, the inherent function doctrine, is discussed in the following case.

BEECK v. TUCSON GENERAL HOSPITAL

Supreme Court of Arizona, 1972.
18 Ariz.App. 165, 500 P.2d 1153.

[The plaintiff contracted pneumonia as the result of the insertion of a needle into her spine during a lumbar myelogram, due to the collision by the x-ray machine screen with the needle. She brought a malpractice suit against Tucson General and the radiologists who administered the test. The trial court granted the hospital's motion for summary judgment on the ground that Dr. Rente was an independent contractor. Plaintiff appealed.]

Having undertaken one of mankind's most critically important and delicate fields of endeavor, concomitantly therewith the hospital must assume the grave responsibility of pursuing this calling with appropriate care. The care and service dispensed through this high trust, however technical, complex and esoteric its character may be, must meet standards of responsibility commensurate with the undertaking to preserve and protect the health, and indeed, the very lives of those placed in the hospital's keeping. [   ]

* * *

The radiology department of Tucson General was operated virtually on a monopoly basis. Dr. Rente and his colleagues were the only ones authorized to perform x-ray work for the department. Any choice by Mrs. Beeck was eliminated. The hospital had chosen for her. It had placed the "hospital radiologists" in the position of exclusive radiologists for the hospital. Further, the hospital furnished everything. The equipment belonged to the hospital and the radiologist paid no rent for use of the equipment or for space at the hospital. Working hours, vacation time, billing and employment of technicians were all controlled by the hospital. The radiology services were obviously furnished under the auspices of Tucson General. Clearly the hospital could regulate operation of its x-ray department to the extent of requiring that the descent-arresting stop be in place before undertaking the type of procedure in question here. Checklists are commonly used in operating complicated equipment. Furthermore, it is well known that hospitals undertake control of the highly technical service with which they deal through overseeing boards and supervisors and peer group mechanisms of various types. [   ]

* * * Further, the hospital had the right to control the standards of performance of this chosen radiologist. The radiologist was employed by the hospital for an extended period of time (five years) to

perform a service which was an inherent function of the hospital, a function without which the hospital could not properly achieve its purpose. All facilities and instrumentalities were provided by the hospital together with all administrative services for the radiology department.

* * * [W]e hold that an employee-employer relationship existed between Dr. Rente and the hospital and the doctrine of respondeat superior applies.

* * *

For the reasons given, the judgment is reversed and the case remanded for further proceedings consistent with this opinion.

Notes and Questions

1. Do the above cases reflect the changing balance of power between health care institutions and physicians? The control test is closest to vicarious liability principles, looking to the terms of the contract and the actual relationship between the hospital and the physician. The ostensible agency or apparent authority test, articulated in Jackson v. Power, then looks to the patient and his or her expectations as to treatment. See e.g. Porter v. Sisters of St. Mary, 756 F.2d 669, where the court held that the plaintiff failed to prove, under s. 267 of the Restatement (Second) Agency, that he relied upon representations that the physician was an agent of the hospital. When the plaintiff entered the emergency room with a collapsed lung, an employee of the hospital said that he had called Dr. Schneider, "and he's our best person for the job." The court held that statement was insufficient to satisfy the requirements to prove apparent authority; plaintiff had then deliberated for several days before selecting Dr. Schneider to perform further surgery which gave rise to his injuries.

The inherent function test takes the inquiry one step further, looking at those functions of a hospital which are essential to its operation. Radiology labs and emergency rooms are two such functions. See, e.g., Adamski v. Tacoma General Hospital, 20 Wash.App. 98, 579 P.2d 970 (1978). This notion of "inherent function" overlaps substantially with the "nondelegable duty" rule in agency law, as expressed in corporate negligence cases, as discussed in Jackson v. Power, section II.b.3, infra.

2. Several jurisdictions have allowed cases to proceed past summary judgment motions, or to go to the jury, on theories of ostensible agency or apparent authority. The courts use agency principles to hold a hospital liable for negligent acts of independent contractors such as radiologists or emergency room physicians. Thus hospitals have been held liable for the acts of radiologists, residents, emergency room physicians, and surgeons, even though these persons were not hospital employees.

The number of courts that have adopted exceptions to vicarious liability is increasing. See Shepard v. Sisters of Providence, 89 Or.App. 579, 750 P.2d 500 (1988) (resident clothed in ostensible authority when he assisted private surgeon in an operation with a private patient, in the hospital); Pamperin v. Trinity Memorial Hospital, 144 Wis.2d 188, 423 N.W.2d 848 (1988) (radiologists); Thompson v. The Nason Hospital, 370 Pa.Super. 115,

535 A.2d 1177 (1988) (surgeons); Richmond County Hospital Authority v. Brown, 257 Ga. 507, 361 S.E.2d 164 (1987) (emergency room physicians); Martell v. St. Charles Hospital, 137 Misc.2d 980, 523 N.Y.S.2d 342 (1987) (emergency room physicians); Strach v. St. John Hospital Corp. 160 Mich. App. 251, 408 N.W.2d 441 (1987) (physicians referred to surgery unit as part of hospital's team and surgery team doctors exercised direct authority over hospital employees.); Barrett v. Samaritan Health Services, Inc., 153 Ariz. 138, 735 P.2d 460 (1987) (emergency room physicians).

Problem: Creating a Shield

You represent Bowsman Hospital, a small rural hospital in Iowa. The hospital has until now relied on Dr. Francke for radiology services. It provides him with space, equipment and personnel for the radiology department, sends and collects bills on his behalf, and provides him with an office. It also pays him $300 a day in exchange for which Dr. Francke agrees to be at the hospital one day a week. Bowsman is one of several small hospitals in this part of Iowa that use Dr. Francke's services. Bowsman advertises in the local papers of several nearby communities. Its advertisements stress its ability to handle trauma injuries, common in farming areas. The ads say in part:

"Bowsman treats patient problems with big league medical talent. Our physicians and nurses have been trained for the special demands of farming accidents and injuries."

What advice can you give as to methods of shielding Bowsman from liability for the negligent acts of Dr. Francke? Must it insist that Dr. Francke operate his own outside laboratory? Or furnish his own equipment? Pay his own bills? Should the hospital hire its own radiologist?

Develop guidelines to protect the hospital from liability for medical errors of the radiologist. Consider in doing so the two following cases.

Estates of Milliron v. Francke, 243 Mont. 200, 793 P.2d 824 (1990). The plaintiff was referred to the hospital and the radiologist who practiced there by his family physician, for evaluation of prostatis and uropathy. The radiologist used an intravenous pyelogram, to which the plaintiff had a reaction. The patient suffered brain damage. The hospital provided space, equipment and personnel for the radiology department, sent and collected bills on his behalf, and provided him with an office. The court granted summary judgment for the defendant on the ostensible agency claim. The court noted that this was a small hospital in a rural area, and the radiologist rotated between this and several other small hospitals. This was an ordinary practice in smaller communities in Montana.

> Providing these traveling physicians with offices at the hospital simply helps ensure that these smaller and more remote communities will be provided with adequate medical care and is not a sufficient factual basis to establish an agency relationship. Id. at 827.

Gregg v. National Medical Health Care Services, Inc., 145 Ariz. 51, 699 P.2d 925 (1985). Gregg went to the hospital's emergency room at 3 a.m. after having three episodes of crushing substernal chest pain accompanied by nausea and vomiting. The court noted that the hospital's right to control the physician was critical to its liability for the physician's acts, and held that the facts raised a jury question. The physician was paid $300 per week to commute from his office to the hospital clinic to act as a consultant. He was required to be at the hospital at least once a week.

B. INSTITUTIONAL LIABILITY

1. *Negligence*

WASHINGTON v. WASHINGTON HOSPITAL CENTER
District of Columbia Court of Appeals, 1990.
579 A.2d 177.

[The Court considered two issues: whether the testimony of the plaintiff's expert was sufficient to create a issue for the jury; and whether the hospital's failure to request a finding of liability of the settling defendants or to file a cross claim for contribution against any of the defendants defeated the hospital's claim for a pro rata reduction in the jury verdict. The discussion of the first issue follows.]

FARRELL, ASSOCIATE JUDGE:

This appeal and cross-appeal arise from a jury verdict in a medical malpractice action against the Washington Hospital Center (WHC or the hospital) in favor of LaVerne Alice Thompson, a woman who suffered permanent catastrophic brain injury from oxygen deprivation in the course of general anesthesia for elective surgery * * *

* * *

I. THE FACTS

On the morning of November 7, 1987, LaVerne Alice Thompson, a healthy 36–year-old woman, underwent elective surgery at the Washington Hospital Center for an abortion and tubal ligation, procedures requiring general anesthesia. At about 10:45 a.m., nurse-anesthetist Elizabeth Adland, under the supervision of Dr. Sheryl Walker, the physician anesthesiologist, inserted an endotracheal tube into Ms. Thompson's throat for the purpose of conveying oxygen to, and removing carbon dioxide from, the anesthetized patient. The tube, properly inserted, goes into the patient's trachea just above the lungs. Plaintiffs alleged that instead Nurse Adland inserted the tube into Thompson's esophagus, above the stomach. After inserting the tube, Nurse Adland "ventilated" or pumped air into the patient while Dr. Walker, by observing physical reactions—including watching the rise and fall of the patient's chest and listening for breath sounds equally on the patient's right and left sides—sought to determine if the tube had been properly inserted.

At about 10:50 a.m., while the surgery was underway, surgeon Nathan Bobrow noticed that Thompson's blood was abnormally dark, which indicated that her tissues were not receiving sufficient oxygen, and reported the condition to Nurse Adland, who checked Thompson's vital signs and found them stable. As Dr. Bobrow began the tubal ligation part of the operation, Thompson's heart rate dropped. She suffered a cardiac arrest and was resuscitated, but eventually the lack of oxygen caused catastrophic brain injuries. Plaintiffs' expert testified that Ms. Thompson remains in a persistent vegetative state and is totally incapacitated; her cardiac, respiratory and digestive functions are normal and she is not "brain dead," but, according to the expert, she is "essentially awake but unaware" of her surroundings. Her condition is unlikely to improve, though she is expected to live from ten to twenty years.

* * *

The plaintiffs alleged that Adland and Walker had placed the tube in Thompson's esophagus rather than her trachea, and that they and Dr. Bobrow had failed to detect the improper intubation in time to prevent the oxygen deprivation that caused Thompson's catastrophic brain injury. WHC, they alleged, was negligent in failing to provide the anesthesiologists with a device known variously as a capnograph or end-tidal carbon dioxide monitor which allows early detection of insufficient oxygen in time to prevent brain injury.

* * *

II. WASHINGTON HOSPITAL CENTER'S CLAIMS ON CROSS-APPEAL

A. *Standard of Care*

On its cross-appeal, WHC first asserts that the plaintiffs failed to carry their burden of establishing the standard of care and that the trial court therefore erred in refusing to grant its motion for judgment notwithstanding the verdict.

* * *

In a negligence action predicated on medical malpractice, the plaintiff must carry a tripartite burden, and establish: (1) the applicable standard of care; (2) a deviation from that standard by the defendant; and (3) a causal relationship between that deviation and the plaintiff's injury. [ ] Because these issues are "distinctly related to some science, profession, or occupation," [ ] expert testimony is usually required to establish each of the elements, [ ] except where the proof is so obvious as to lie within the ken of the average lay juror, [ ].

Generally, the "standard of care" is "the course of action that a reasonably prudent [professional] with the defendant's specialty would have taken under the same or similar circumstances." [ ] With respect to institutions such as hospitals, this court has rejected the "locality" rule, which refers to the standard of conduct expected of other similarly situated members of the profession in the same locality or community, [ ] in favor of a national standard. [ ] Thus, the question for decision is whether the evidence as a whole, and reasonable inferences therefrom, would allow a reasonable juror to find that a reasonably prudent tertiary care hospital,[3] at the time of Ms. Thomp-

---

3. Plaintiffs' expert defined a tertiary care hospital as "a hospital which has the facilities to conduct clinical care management of patients in nearly all aspects of medicine and surgery."

son's injury in November 1987, and according to national standards, would have supplied a carbon dioxide monitor to a patient undergoing general anesthesia for elective surgery.

WHC argues that the plaintiffs' expert, Dr. Stephen Steen, failed to demonstrate an adequate factual basis for his opinion that WHC should have made available a carbon dioxide monitor. The purpose of expert opinion testimony is to avoid jury findings based on mere speculation or conjecture. [ ] The sufficiency of the foundation for those opinions should be measured with this purpose in mind. * * *

* * *

* * * [WHC] asserts that * * * Steen gave no testimony on the number of hospitals having end-tidal carbon dioxide monitors in place in 1987, and that he never referred to any written standards or authorities as the basis of his opinion. We conclude that Steen's opinion * * * was sufficient to create an issue for the jury.

Dr. Steen testified that by 1985, the carbon dioxide monitors were available in his hospital (Los Angeles County—University of Southern California Medical Center (USC)), and "in many other hospitals." In response to a question whether, by 1986, "standards of care" required carbon dioxide monitors in operating rooms, he replied, "I would think that by that time, they would be [required]." As plaintiffs concede, this opinion was based in part on his own personal experience at USC, which cannot itself provide an adequate foundation for an expert opinion on a national standard of care. But Steen also drew support from "what I've read where [the monitors were] available in other hospitals." He referred to two such publications: The American Association of Anesthesiology (AAA) Standards for Basic Intra–Operative Monitoring, approved by the AAA House of Delegates on October 21, 1986, which "encouraged" the use of monitors, and an article entitled *Standards for Patient Monitoring During Anesthesia at Harvard Medical School,* published in August 1986 in the Journal of American Medical Association, which stated that as of July 1985 the monitors were in use at Harvard, and that "monitoring end-tidal carbon dioxide is an emerging standard and is strongly preferred."

WHC makes much of Steen's concession on cross-examination that the AAA Standards were recommendations, strongly encouraged but not mandatory, and that the Harvard publication spoke of an "emerging" standard. In its brief WHC asserts, without citation, that "[p]alpable indicia of widespread *mandated* practices are necessary to establish a standard of care" (emphasis added), and that at most the evidence spoke of "recommended" or "encouraged" practices, and "emerging" or "developing" standards as of 1986–87. A standard of due care, however, necessarily embodies what a *reasonably prudent* hospital would do, [   ] and hence care and foresight exceeding the minimum required by law or mandatory professional regulation may be necessary to meet that standard. It certainly cannot be said that the 1986 recommendations of a professional association (which had no power to issue or enforce mandatory requirements), or an article speaking of an "emerging" standard in 1986, have no bearing on an expert opinion as to what the standard of patient monitoring equipment was fully one year later when Ms. Thompson's surgery took place.

Nevertheless, we need not decide whether Dr. Steen's testimony was sufficiently grounded in fact or adequate data to establish the standard of care. The record contains other evidence from which, in combination with Dr. Steen's testimony, a reasonable juror could fairly conclude that monitors were required of prudent hospitals similar to WHC in late 1987. The evidence showed that at least four other teaching hospitals in the United States used the monitors by that time. In addition to Dr. Steen's testimony that USC supplied them and the article reflecting that Harvard University had them, plaintiffs introduced into evidence an article entitled *Anesthesia at Penn,* from a 1986 alumni newsletter of the Department of Anesthesia at the University of Pennsylvania, indicating that the monitors were then in use at that institution's hospital, and that they allowed "instant recognition of esophageal intubation and other airway problems. * * *" Moreover, WHC's expert anesthesiologist, Dr. John Tinker of the University of Iowa, testified that his hospital had installed carbon dioxide monitors in every operating room by early 1986, and that "by 1987, it is certainly true that many hospitals were in the process of converting" to carbon dioxide monitors.[5]

Perhaps most probative was the testimony of WHC's own Chairman of the Department of Anesthesiology, Dr. Dermot A. Murray, and documentary evidence associated with his procurement request for carbon dioxide monitors. In December 1986 or January 1987, Dr. Murray submitted a requisition form to the hospital for end-tidal carbon dioxide units to monitor the administration of anesthesia in each of the hospital's operating rooms, stating that if the monitors were not provided, the hospital would "fail to meet the national standard of

---

5. In its reply brief, WHC argues that the fact that four teaching hospitals used CO_2 monitors during the relevant time period is almost irrelevant. Institutions with significantly enhanced financial resources and/or government grants which accelerate their testing and implementation of new and improved technologies would naturally have available to them items which, inherently, were not yet required for the general populace of hospitals.

In fact, Dr. Steen, in voir dire examination on his qualification as an expert on the standard required of hospitals in WHC's position in regard to equipment, testified that his review of WHC's President's Report for 1986–87 led him to conclude that WHC was a teaching hospital. Counsel for the hospital could have identified and probed fully before the jury any differences between WHC and the hospitals relied on to establish the standard of care. To the extent the record was not so developed, the jury could credit Steen's testimony that WHC was required to adhere to the standard applicable to teaching hospitals.

care." The monitors were to be "fully operational" in July of 1987.[6] Attempting to meet this evidence, WHC points out that at trial

> Dr. Murray was *never asked to opine,* with a reasonable degree of medical certainty, that the applicable standard of care at the relevant time *required* the presence of CO_2 monitors. Indeed, his testimony was directly to the contrary. Moreover, the procurement process which he had initiated envisioned obtaining the equipment * * * over time, not even beginning until fiscal year 1988, a period ending June 30, 1988. [Emphasis by WHC.]

Dr. Murray opined that in November 1987 there was *no* standard of care relating to monitoring equipment. The jury heard this testimony and Dr. Murray's explanation of the procurement process, but apparently did not credit it, perhaps because the requisition form itself indicated that the equipment ordered was to be operational in July 1987, four months before Ms. Thompson's surgery, and not at some unspecified time in fiscal year 1988 as Dr. Murray testified at trial.

On the evidence recited above, a reasonable juror could find that the standard of care required WHC to supply monitors as of November 1987. The trial judge therefore did not err in denying the motion for judgment notwithstanding the verdict.

* * *

Notes and Questions

1. Does the plaintiff present sufficient evidence that the carbon dioxide monitor is now standard equipment for tertiary care hospitals? Is the Washington Hospital Center stuck in a zone of transition between older precautions and emerging technologies that improve patient care? Why did they not purchase such monitors earlier?

A companion device to the carbon dioxide monitor is the blood-monitoring pulse oximeter, which has become a mandatory device in hospital operating rooms. By 1990 all hospitals used oximeters in their operating rooms; in 1984, no hospital had them. The device beeps when a patient's blood oxygen drops due to breathing problems or overuse of anesthesia. That warning can give a vital three or four minutes warning to physicians, allowing them to correct the problem before the patient suffers brain damage. These devices have so improved patient safety that malpractice insurers have lowered premiums for anesthesiologists. See Appleby, Pulse Oximeters Pump Up Bottom Lines and Patient Safety, Deflate Malpractice Risk, HealthWeek 17–18 (October 9, 1990).

2. A health care institution, whether hospital, nursing home, or clinic, is liable for negligence in maintaining its facilities, providing and maintaining medical equipment, hiring, supervising and retaining nurses and other staff, and failing to have in place procedures to protect patients. Basic negligence principles govern hospital liability for injuries caused by

---

6. As supporting documentation for the requisition, Dr. Murray attached a copy of the Journal of the American Medical Association article on standards at Harvard University. The requisitions, with attachments, were exhibits admitted in evidence.

other sources than negligent acts of the medical staff. As *Washington* holds, hospitals are generally held to a national standard of care for hospitals in their treatment category.

The professional duty of a hospital " * * * is primarily to provide a safe environment within which diagnosis, treatment, and recovery can be carried out. Thus if an unsafe condition of the hospital's premises causes injury to a patient, as a result of the hospital's negligence, there is a breach of the hospital's duty *qua* hospital." Murillo v. Good Samaritan Hospital, 99 Cal.App.3d 50, 56–57, 160 Cal.Rptr. 33 (1979) (failure to properly set the bedrails on a patient's bed). The test is " * * * whether the negligent act occurred in the rendering of services for which the health care provider is licensed." Id. at 57.

a. Hospitals must have minimum facility and support systems to treat the range of problems and side effects that accompany procedures they offer. In Hernandez v. Smith, 552 F.2d 142 (5th Cir.1977), for example, an obstetrical clinic that lacked surgical facilities for caesarean sections was found liable for " * * * the failure to provide proper and safe instrumentalities for the treatment of ailments it undertakes to treat * * *." See also Valdez v. Lyman–Roberts Hosp., Inc., 638 S.W.2d 111 (Tex.App.1982).

b. Staffing must be adequate. Short staffing has been rejected as a defense where the available staff could have been juggled to achieve closer supervision of a problem patient. Horton v. Niagara Falls Memorial Medical Center, 51 A.D.2d 152, 380 N.Y.S.2d 116 (1976).

c. Equipment must be adequate for the services offered, although it need not be the state of the art. See Emory University v. Porter, 103 Ga.App. 752, 120 S.E.2d 668, 670 (1961); Lauro v. Travelers Ins. Co., 261 So.2d 261 (La.App.1972). If a device such as an expensive CT scanner has come into common use, however, a smaller less affluent hospital can argue that it should be judged by the standards of similar hospitals with similar resources. This variable standard, reflecting resource differences between hospitals, would then protect a hospital in a situation where its budget does not allow purchase of some expensive devices. If an institution lacks a piece of equipment that has come to be recognized as essential, particularly for diagnosis, it may have a duty to transfer the patient to an institution that has the equipment. In Blake v. D.C. General Hospital (discussed in Mehlman, Rationing Expensive Lifesaving Medical Treatments, 1985 Wisc. L.Rev. 239) the trial court allowed a case to go to the jury where the plaintiff's estate claimed that she died because of the hospital's lack of a CT scanner to diagnose her condition. The court found a duty to transfer in such circumstances.

d. A hospital and its contracting physicians may be liable for damages caused by inadequate or defective systems they develop and implement, particularly where emergency care is involved. In the case of Marks v. Mandel, 477 So.2d 1036 (Fla.App.1985), the plaintiff brought a wrongful death action against the hospital, alleging negligence based on the failure of the on-call system to produce a thoracic surgeon and failure of the hospital staff to send the patient to a hospital with a trauma center. The Florida Supreme Court held that the trial court erred in excluding from evidence the hospital's emergency room policy and procedure manual.

This manual set out in detail how the on-call system should operate and itemized procedures for responding to calls made from ambulances. The court held that evidence was sufficient to go to the jury on the issue of liability of the hospital and the emergency room supervisor for the failure of the on-call system to produce a thoracic surgeon in a timely fashion. See also Habuda v. Trustees of Rex Hospital, 3 N.C.App. 11, 164 S.E.2d 17 (1968), where the hospital was liable for inadequate rules for handling, storing, and administering medications; Herrington v. Miller, 883 F.2d 411 (5th Cir.1989) (failure to provide for adequate 24–hour anesthesia service). See also Ball Memorial Hosp. v. Freeman, 245 Ind. 71, 196 N.E.2d 274 (1964).

2. Negligence Per Se

The usual American practice in a tort case not involving health care is to treat violation of a statute as negligence per se, giving rise to a rebuttable presumption of negligence. If the defendant fails to rebut the presumption, the trier of fact must find against him on the negligence issue. The classic statement of the rule is found in Martin v. Herzog, 228 N.Y. 164, 126 N.E. 814 (1920). Negligence per se is usually applied in cases where a statute is used to show a standard of care. In malpractice cases, however, standards are typically used to create only a permissive inference of negligence, allowing the plaintiff to get the jury which can then accept or reject the inference of fault.

Hospitals are regulated by their states. The majority are also subject generally to the standards of the Joint Commission on Accreditation of Healthcare Organizations (JCAHO). The standard of care that the courts have applied reflects a baseline mandated by JCAHO standards, including peer review through internal committee structures. This baseline has largely doomed the locality rule for hospitals. See Shilkret v. Annapolis Emergency Hospital Association, 276 Md. 187, 349 A.2d 245 (1975). As to the JCAHO generally, see Jost, The Joint Commission on Accreditation of Hospitals: Private Regulation of Health Care and the Public Interest, 24 B.C.L.Rev. 835 (1983). See also Dickinson v. Mailliard, 175 N.W.2d 588 (Iowa 1970); Greenberg v. Michael Reese Hospital, 83 Ill.2d 282, 47 Ill.Dec. 385, 415 N.E.2d 390 (1980).

The court in the Darling case, infra, allowed evidence of JCAHO standards, which the trier of fact could accept or reject. The JCAHO Guidelines therefore operated to create a permissive inference of negligence.

Courts have proved resistant to the application of negligence per se to health care institutions, even to create an inference of negligence, unless the standard is specific and supported by expert testimony. In Van Iperen v. Van Bramer, 392 N.W.2d 480 (Iowa 1986), the court considered the effect of JCAHO standards on a hospital. The plaintiff had argued that the hospital should have provided drug monitoring services, based on JCAHO accreditation standards requiring that a hospital provide drug monitoring services through its pharmacy, including a medication record or drug profile and a review of the patient's drug regimen for potential problems.

In nursing home litigation, some courts have likewise resisted the use of external standards to establish negligence. Thus in Makas v. Hillhaven, Inc., 589 F.Supp. 736 (M.D.N.C.1984), the court rejected the plaintiff's attempt to use the Nursing Home Patients' Bill of Rights to establish negligence, holding that the Bill of Rights was "so general and nebulous that a trier of fact could not determine whether the standard had been violated." Id. at 742. Such a standard could only be used very generally in a negligence case to show a patient's expectations of nursing home care. Accord, Stogsdill v. Manor Convalescent Home, Inc., 35 Ill.App.3d 634, 343 N.E.2d 589 (1976). In general, the more specific the standards, whether of the JCAHO or other agent of the state, the more likely that a court will be willing to use them to invoke the negligence per se doctrine.

3. Strict Liability

KARIBJANIAN v. THOMAS JEFFERSON UNIVERSITY HOSPITAL

United States District Court, Eastern District of Pennsylvania, 1989.
717 F.Supp. 1081.

OPINION

JOSEPH S. LORD, III, SENIOR DISTRICT JUDGE.

Plaintiff claims that her husband died as a result of exposure in 1956 to the substance Thorotrast, a form of thorium dioxide, with which he was injected during a diagnostic medical procedure called a cerebral arteriography.[1] She alleges Thorotrast is an inherently unsafe product and that defendants knew or should have known that it is so. Defendant Thomas Jefferson University Hospital ("Hospital") moves to dismiss several paragraphs of the complaint, pursuant to Fed.R.Civ.P. 12(b)(6). * * *[ ]

* * *

Finally, the Hospital asks me to dismiss paragraphs 80 and 81 of the complaint, which allege

80. [The Hospital] sold, supplied and/or distributed a defective and dangerous product, Thorotrast, which was administered to plaintiff's decedent substantially unchanged from the form that it was received in.

---

1. According to *Stedman's Medical Dictionary*, 5th Ed. (1982), a cerebral arteriography, also called a cerebral angiography, is "visualization of an artery or arteries by x-rays after injection of a radiopaque contrast medium." "[I]njection may be made by percutaneous puncture or after exposure. * * *" It appears from the complaint that Thorotrast was used as the contrast medium.

81. [The Hospital] is strictly liable to plaintiff's decedent for the injuries and resulting death sustained under §§ 402A and/or 519 and 520 of the *Restatement (Second) of Torts* as adopted in the Commonwealth of Pennsylvania.

Section 402A provides, in part, that

(1) One who sells any product in a defective condition unreasonably dangerous to the user or consumer * * * is subject to liability * * * if (a) the seller is engaged in the business of selling such a product. * * *

The Hospital cites two Superior Court decisions which hold that a hospital cannot be liable under § 402A when a defective surgical tool injures a patient during an operation. *Podrat v. Codman–Shurtleff,* ___ Pa.Super. ___, 558 A.2d 895 (1989) (forceps); *Grubb v. Albert Einstein Medical Center,* 255 Pa.Super. 381, 387 A.2d 480 (1978) (bone plug cutter).[4] The *Podrat* court reasoned that a hospital is primarily in the business of supplying services, and "supplies" surgical tools only incidentally; and that the medical service (a back operation) could not have been performed without the use of the instrument. ___ Pa.Super. at ___, 558 A.2d at 898. The Hospital contends that likewise it was not in the "business of selling" Thorotrast; rather that it was in the business of providing services.

Plaintiff seeks to limit the holding in *Podrat* to products which are approved but turn out to be defective; she argues that Thorotrast, because it is alleged to be inherently unsafe, is distinguishable. I do not find this proposed distinction persuasive.

It might be supposed that surgical tools like the forceps in *Podrat* and the bone plug cutter in *Grubb* are different from contrast media because those surgical tools may be reused on a number of patients, while a dose of Thorotrast is completely consumed by a single patient. However, in *Francioni v. Gibsonia,* 472 Pa. 362, 372 A.2d 736, 739 (1977), the court held that lessors of durable products are liable to the same degree as sellers of such products.

A decision of a state's intermediate appellate court "is a datum for ascertaining state law which is not to be disregarded by a federal court unless it is convinced by other persuasive data that the highest court of the state would decide otherwise." [ ] There are, I think, significant data which suggest Pennsylvania's Supreme Court would in some circumstances hold a hospital liable under § 402A as a seller of a product like Thorotrast, if it is the product itself rather than the procedure by which it was administered which is alleged to have been defective.

Comment (f) to § 402A explains what the *Restatement's* authors meant by the "business of selling."

4. In *Grubb,* the per curiam opinion states that a hospital can be liable under § 402A; however, four of the seven judges dissented from this statement, and the hospital was held liable only under a negligence theory.

> It is not necessary that the seller be engaged solely in the business of selling such products. Thus the rule applies to the owner of a motion picture theatre who sells popcorn or ice cream, either for consumption on the premises or in packages to be taken home.

> The rule does not, however, apply to the occasional seller of food or other such products who is not engaged in that activity as a part of his business. Thus it does not apply to the housewife who, on one occasion, sells to her neighbor a jar of jam. * * *

So long as a hospital *regularly* supplies contrast media to its patients, albeit as an incidental part of its service operations, it seems to fall within § 402A as explained by comment (f). The comment draws no distinction between suppliers of goods who also supply services, and those suppliers who simply supply goods.

Pennsylvania's Supreme Court recently cited comment (f) to § 402A with approval in *Musser v. Vilsmeier Auction Co.,* ___ Pa. ___, 562 A.2d 279 (1989). The *Musser* court held that an auctioneer who never owns, operates or controls the products he auctions is not a "seller" of the products for § 402A purposes, unless he or she has a "direct continuous course of dealing with a manufacturer or sales organization for their specific products." ___ Pa. at ___, 562 A.2d at 283. Besides citing comment (f), the *Musser* court reviewed the purposes behind § 402A as they were expressed in *Francioni,* 472 Pa. at 368–69, 372 A.2d at 739:

> (1) In some instances the lessor, like the seller, may be the only member of the marketing chain available to the injured plaintiff for redress; (2) As in the case of the seller, imposition of strict liability upon the lessor serves as an incentive to safety; (3) The lessor will be in a better position than the consumer to prevent the circulation of defective products; and (4) The lessor can distribute the cost of compensating for injuries resulting from defects by charging for it in his business, i.e. by adjustment of the rental terms.

The *Musser* court reasoned that the auctioneer should not be liable because the injured party could always sue the owner of the item auctioned, rather than the auctioneer; and because the auctioneer would be in no better position than the consumer to influence the safety of the design or manufacture of the product. The auctioneer had not been shown to have a continuing relationship with the manufacturer; rather he was "an ad hoc salesman of the goods of another for a specific purpose and a specific time." *Id.* at ___ ___, 562 A.2d at 283. While the auctioneer might have been in a position to distribute the costs of compensation, that factor alone did not justify imposing liability under § 402A, the court said.

It is not beyond doubt that plaintiff can prove no facts which would establish that the Hospital was a seller of Thorotrast for purposes of § 402A. Unlike the product auctioned in *Musser,* the Thorotrast allegedly came from the Hospital's own inventory, ¶ 33, which I take to mean the Hospital owned it until it supplied it to plaintiff's decedent, via his physician, and that the Hospital regularly supplied Thorotrast to other patients. Plaintiff must be given the opportunity to present evidence concerning the other factors identified in *Musser* and *Francioni.*

I am also influenced by the thoughtful discussion of Judge Pollak in *Villari v. Terminix,* 677 F.Supp. 330, 333–334 (E.D.Pa.1987), in which he held that a professional pesticide application firm could be liable under § 402A even though it provided services as well as the pesticides themselves.[5] Judge Pollak noted that the defendant was the sole "retail" supplier of the pesticide, and that it told its customers that the product was safe. On the other hand, at least one court, in California, has held that hospitals cannot be liable under § 402A for defective drugs, under reasoning similar to that in *Podrat. Carmichael v. Reitz,* 17 Cal.App.3d 958, 95 Cal.Rptr. 381 (1971). *See also Flynn v. Langfitt,* 710 F.Supp. 150, 152 (E.D.Pa.1989) (hospital not liable under § 402A for defective tissue graft).

I will deny the Hospital's motion to dismiss ¶¶ 80 and 81 of the complaint. Plaintiff will, however, have to establish the factual bases I outlined above before she can recover against the Hospital under § 402A. Neither party has briefed the question of whether the Hospital can be liable under § 519 and § 520 of the *Restatement (Second) of Torts,* dealing with abnormally dangerous activities. I will leave that imaginative theory of liability for another day.

Notes and Questions

1. The hospital in *Karibjanian* considers Pennsylvania Superior Court cases rejecting the application of Restatement (Second) Torts, section 402A, to hospitals for defective surgical tools. It then rejects these decisions as predictive of what the Pennsylvania Supreme Court might do.

In Podrat v. Codman–Shurtleff, Inc., 384 Pa.Super. 404, 558 A.2d 895 (1989) (involving forceps that broke, leaving piece in patient's disc space), the court stressed the hospital's actual function of providing a service to a patient. The instrument's use is simply incidental to the provision of this service.

> In sum, we conclude that the trial court did not err in finding that the hospital could not be liable under a theory of strict liability because the hospital was not in the business of selling this instrument, its use was only incidental to the hospital's primary function of providing medical services and the medical services could not have been rendered without the use of this product. Id. at 898.

---

5. To offer another analogy, a restaurant patron who enjoys an exquisite souffle values the services of the chef more than the eggs with which it is made, since the eggs could be had for less than a dollar at any store. Nonetheless, if fate has it that the eggs are bad, the restaurant would be liable under § 402A as a supplier of eggs, even though the eggs were but an incidental part of what the patron paid for. And this is not to mention the services of the maitre d' who seats her, and the waiter who serves her.

In Grubb v. Albert Einstein Medical Center, 255 Pa.Super. 381, 387 A.2d 480 (1978) (defective plug cutter), the per curiam opinion stated that a hospital could be liable under § 402A; however, since four of the seven judges dissented, the hospital was liable only under a negligence theory.

What is the "persuasive data" that leads the court to reject these lower court decisions? The court does not seem impressed by the argument that providers of medical services should be treated specially. It cites as analogous activities auctioneering and pesticide application. What are the tests that the *Musser* and *Villari* cases seem to require? What facts must the plaintiff now establish before she can recover against the hospital?

How about the analogy in footnote 5? Is the provision of expensive restaurant food and service an apt comparison to hospital-based care involving drugs and devices? A chef cannot, after all, make a souffle without eggs; neither can a surgeon operate on a patient with medical devices, nor a radiologist do testing without contrast media. A plurality of the Pennsylvania Superior Court in *Grubb*, supra, in dicta, stated that " * * * if a hospital supplies equipment to an operating physician the hospital must appraise themselves of the risks involved and adopt every effort to insure the safety of the equipment chosen."

2. The court also suggests, in a tantalizing last paragraph, that the hospital might be liable under sections 519 and 520 of the Restatement (Second) of Torts, Abnormally Dangerous Activities, which the plaintiffs had pleaded. Is the court kidding? Or is there a possible argument to be made against hospital-based health care? See the discussion in Chapter 1 on iatrogenic injury.

3. The devices that a hospital furnishes its staff and patients, as part of the provision of medical service, must be properly maintained. Strict liability arguments imported from product defects litigation have made some inroads in lawsuits against hospitals. Both implied warranty doctrine and Section 402A of the Restatement, Second, have on rare occasions been applied to devices used in hospitals. The growth of technological medicine has made physicians increasingly dependent upon diagnostic machinery, computer-assisted tests, and drugs and devices. Many of the *res ipsa loquitur* cases, for example, involve medical devices that failed during surgery. These devices are bought by a hospital's purchasing department, subject to the controls imposed by the hospital's administration. The standard use of devices such as fetal monitors and CT scanners implicate the hospital as middleman in a stream of commerce of the sort courts discuss in products liability cases.

In Skelton v. Druid City Hosp. Board, 459 So.2d 818 (Ala.1984), a suture needle broke off in the patient during ventral hernia repair. These needles were reused several times by the hospital, and there was no way to be sure exactly how many times. Section 2–315 of the Uniform Commercial Code, implied warranty of fitness for a particular purpose, was applied to this "hybrid" service-product transaction between hospital and patient. The court held:

> The gist of an action under this section is reliance. Patients are rarely in a position to judge the quality of the medical supplies and other goods sold to them and used in their care; often, those supplies

are of an inherently dangerous nature. The complete dependence of patients on the staff of a hospital to choose fit products justifies the imposition of an implied warranty under s. 7–2–315, whether the hospital is a "merchant" or not.

But see, rejecting strict liability for devices, Hector v. Cedars–Sinai Medical Center, 180 Cal.App.3d 493, 225 Cal.Rptr. 595 (2 Dist.1986) (pacemaker); Perlmutter v. Beth David Hospital, 308 N.Y. 100, 123 N.E.2d 792 (1954).

Hospitals often reuse medical devices, such as pulmonary catheters, hemodialyzers, biopsy needles, electrosurgical devices, and endotracheal tubes. Kobren, Lowe–Clements, and Hedrick, Medical Device Reuse: The FDA Perspective, 2 HealthSpan 6 (1985). The pressure to contain costs is one of the primary reasons for this practice. When a reused device proves defective and a patient is injured as a result, liability may fall on the manufacturer, the retailer, the hospital, and health care professionals. Strict liability and breach of warranty theories, as well as negligence, are likely to be attractive doctrines to apply, by analogy to the products liability area generally. Kahan and Gibbs, Reuse of Disposable Medical Devices: Regulatory and Liability Issues, 2 HealthSpan 12 (1985).

4. Drugs are normally prescribed by the treating physician, and are purchased by the patient from third party pharmacies. In the hospital setting, however, the patient is usually administered a variety of drugs as part of treatment and these drugs come from hospital supplies. Should a duty to warn a patient of possible side-effects of the drug fall on the hospital as well as the treating physician? The court in *Karibjanian* allowed the plaintiff's cause of action claiming a hospital duty to supervise physicians, which included ensuring that informed consent was obtained. This has not been a popular position. See, e.g., Kirk v. Michael Reese Hospital and Medical Center, 117 Ill.2d 507, 111 Ill.Dec. 944, 513 N.E.2d 387 (1987), cert. denied, 485 U.S. 905, 108 S.Ct. 1077, 99 L.Ed.2d 236 (1988), where the Illinois Supreme Court held that a hospital which had dispensed and administered psychotropic drugs to the plaintiff as an in-patient had no duty to warn him of the drug's side effects upon discharge a few hours later.

5. Hospital administrative and mechanical services have been held to be subject potentially to strict liability, *Johnson v. Sears,* 355 F.Supp. 1065, 1067 (E.D.Wis.1973), as have hospital operations that are not "integrally related to its primary function of providing medical services", *Silverhart v. Mount Zion Hospital,* 20 Cal.App.3d 1022, 98 Cal.Rptr. 187 (1971) (gift shop as example of such a nonessential function).

Problem: The Monitor Failed

Jane Rudd has approached you as to the merits of a suit for injuries sustained by her infant during childbirth. Ms. Rudd went into labor at full term and was admitted to the Columbia Hospital. She was examined, placed in a labor room, and attached to a fetal monitor. She objected to the use of the monitor, but the Chief Resident, after a lengthy debate with the staff, strongly urged her to use it. She finally acquiesced. The monitor is manufactured by Rohm Instruments and leased to the hospital by Medex

Equipment Ltd. Medex maintains the monitors it leases to hospitals on a monthly basis, or as needed.

The nurse responsible for Ms. Rudd checked the monitor printout several times an hour. The machine has a warning buzzer that sounds if abnormal fetal heart rates are detected. It did not sound at any time. Neither the doctor nor the nurses checked the fetal heart rate with a stethoscope after the first two hours. At 6 a.m. on Sunday morning, the doctor on duty delivered Ms. Rudd's baby. Its umbilical cord was wrapped tightly around its neck and it showed signs of fetal distress at delivery. The child has extensive brain damage due to oxygen deprivation.

Because of comments made by the delivery room nurse, Ms. Rudd believes that the monitor may have malfunctioned and failed to either detect or print out variations in fetal heartrate near the end of labor.

What tort doctrines can you invoke in drafting a complaint? What defendants might you pursue? What further information do you need?

C. THE EMERGENCE OF CORPORATE NEGLIGENCE

The courts' stretching of vicarious liability doctrine to sweep in doctors as conduits to hospital liability led inevitably to the direct imposition of corporate negligence liability on the hospital. The courts effectively made the medical personnel who used the hospital part of this "enterprise", whether they were staff employees or independent contractors.

1. The Duty to Protect Patients From Medical Staff Negligence

The next step was to hold the hospital directly liable for the failure of administrators and staff to properly monitor and supervise the delivery of health care within the hospital. The leading case is *Darling v. Charleston Community Memorial Hospital.*

DARLING v. CHARLESTON COMMUNITY MEMORIAL HOSPITAL

Supreme Court of Illinois, 1965.
33 Ill.2d 326, 211 N.E.2d 253, certiorari denied 383 U.S. 946, 86 S.Ct.
1204, 16 L.Ed.2d 209 (1966).

This action was brought on behalf of Dorrence Darling II, a minor (hereafter plaintiff), by his father and next friend, to recover damages for allegedly negligent medical and hospital treatment which necessitated the amputation of his right leg below the knee. The action was commenced against the Charleston Community Memorial Hospital and Dr. John R. Alexander, but prior to trial the action was dismissed as to Dr. Alexander, pursuant to a covenant not to sue. The jury returned a verdict against the hospital in the sum of $150,000. This amount was reduced by $40,000, the amount of the settlement with the doctor. The judgment in favor of the plaintiff in the sum of $110,000 was affirmed on appeal by the Appellate Court for the Fourth District, which granted a certificate of importance. 50 Ill.App.2d 253, 200 N.E.2d 149.

On November 5, 1960, the plaintiff, who was 18 years old, broke his leg while playing in a college football game. He was taken to the emergency room at the defendant hospital where Dr. Alexander, who was on emergency call that day, treated him. Dr. Alexander, with the assistance of hospital personnel, applied traction and placed the leg in a plaster cast. A heat cradle was applied to dry the cast. Not long after the application of the cast plaintiff was in great pain and his toes, which protruded from the cast, became swollen and dark in color. They eventually became cold and insensitive. On the evening of November 6, Dr. Alexander "notched" the cast around the toes, and on the afternoon of the next day he cut the cast approximately three inches up from the foot. On November 8 he split the sides of the cast with a Stryker saw; in the course of cutting the cast the plaintiff's leg was cut on both sides. Blood and other seepage were observed by the nurses and others, and there was a stench in the room, which one witness said was the worst he had smelled since World War II. The plaintiff remained in Charleston Hospital until November 19, when he was transferred to Barnes Hospital in St. Louis and placed under the care of Dr. Fred Reynolds, head of orthopedic surgery at Washington University School of Medicine and Barnes Hospital. Dr. Reynolds found that the fractured leg contained a considerable amount of dead tissue which in his opinion resulted from interference with the circulation of blood in the limb caused by swelling or hemorrhaging of the leg against the construction of the cast. Dr. Reynolds performed several operations in a futile attempt to save the leg but ultimately it had to be amputated eight inches below the knee.

The evidence before the jury is set forth at length in the opinion of the Appellate Court and need not be stated in detail here. The plaintiff contends that it established that the defendant was negligent in permitting Dr. Alexander to do orthopedic work of the kind required in this case, and not requiring him to review his operative procedures to bring them up to date; in failing, through its medical staff, to exercise adequate supervision over the case, especially since Dr. Alexander had been placed on emergency duty by the hospital, and in not requiring consultation, particularly after complications had developed. Plaintiff contends also that in a case which developed as this one did, it was the duty of the nurses to watch the protruding toes constantly for changes of color, temperature and movement, and to check circulation every ten to twenty minutes, whereas the proof showed that these things were done only a few times a day. Plaintiff argues that it was the duty of the hospital staff to see that these procedures were followed, and that either the nurses were derelict in failing to report developments in the case to the hospital administrator, he was derelict in bringing them to the attention of the medical staff, or the staff was negligent in failing to take action. Defendant is a licensed and accredited hospital, and the plaintiff contends that the licensing regulations, accreditation standards, and its own bylaws define the hospital's duty, and that an infraction of them imposes liability for the resulting injury.

* * *

The basic dispute, as posed by the parties, centers upon the duty that rested upon the defendant hospital. That dispute involves the effect to be given to evidence concerning the community standard of care and diligence, and also the effect to be given to hospital regulations adopted by the State Department of Public Health under the Hospital Licensing Act (Ill.Rev.Stat.1963, chap. 111½, pars. 142–157.), to the Standards for Hospital Accreditation of the American Hospital Association, and to the bylaws of the defendant.

As has been seen, the defendant argues in this court that its duty is to be determined by the care customarily offered by hospitals generally in its community. Strictly speaking, the question is not one of duty, for " * * * in negligence cases, the duty is always the same, to conform to the legal standard of reasonable conduct in the light of the apparent risk. What the defendant must do, or must not do, is a question of the standard of conduct required to satisfy the duty." (Prosser on Torts, 3rd ed. at 331.) * * * Custom is relevant in determining the standard of care because it illustrates what is feasible, it suggests a body of knowledge of which the defendant should be aware, and it warns of the possibility of far-reaching consequences if a higher standard is required. [ ] But custom should never be conclusive.

In the present case the regulations, standards, and bylaws which the plaintiff introduced into evidence, performed much the same function as did evidence of custom. This evidence aided the jury in deciding what was feasible and what the defendant knew or should have known. It did not conclusively determine the standard of care and the jury was not instructed that it did.

"The conception that the hospital does not undertake to treat the patient, does not undertake to act through its doctors and nurses, but undertakes instead simply to procure them to act upon their own responsibility, no longer reflects the fact. Present-day hospitals, as their manner of operation plainly demonstrates, do far more than furnish facilities for treatment. They regularly employ on a salary basis a large staff of physicians, nurses and interns, as well as administrative and manual workers, and they charge patients for medical care and treatment, collecting for such services, if necessary, by legal action. Certainly, the person who avails himself of 'hospital facilities' expects that the hospital will attempt to cure him, not that its nurses or other employees will act on their own responsibility." (Fuld, J., in Bing v. Thunig (1957), 2 N.Y.2d 656, 163 N.Y.S.2d 3, 11, 143 N.E.2d 3, 8.) The Standards for Hospital Accreditation, the state licensing regulations and the defendant's bylaws demonstrate that the medical profession and other responsible authorities regard it as both desirable and feasible that a hospital assume certain responsibilities for the care of the patient.

* * * Therefore we need not analyze all of the issues submitted to the jury. Two of them were that the defendant had negligently: "5. Failed to have a sufficient number of trained nurses for bedside care of all patients at all times capable of recognizing the progressive gangrenous condition of the plaintiff's right leg, and of bringing the same to the attention of the hospital administration and to the medical staff so that adequate consultation could have been secured and such conditions rectified; * * * 7. Failed to require consultation with or examination by members of the hospital surgical staff skilled in such treatment; or to review the treatment rendered to the plaintiff and to require consultants to be called in as needed."

We believe that the jury verdict is supportable on either of these grounds. On the basis of the evidence before it the jury could reasonably have concluded that the nurses did not test for circulation in the leg as frequently as necessary, that skilled nurses would have promptly recognized the conditions that signalled a dangerous impairment of circulation in the plaintiff's leg, and would have known that the condition would become irreversible in a matter of hours. At that point it became the nurses' duty to inform the attending physician, and if he failed to act, to advise the hospital authorities so that appropriate action might be taken. As to consultation, there is no dispute that the hospital failed to review Dr. Alexander's work or require a consultation; the only issue is whether its failure to do so was negligence. On the evidence before it the jury could reasonably have found that it was.

[The remainder of the opinion, discussing expert testimony and damages, is omitted.]

Notes and Questions

1. Consider the issues submitted to the jury. It is alleged that both the nurses and the administrators were negligent in not taking steps to curtail Dr. Alexander's handling of the case. How can a nurse "blow the whistle" on a doctor without risking damage to her own career? See the section on labor law in health care institutions, Chapter 5, infra. How can a nurse exercise medical judgment in violation of Medical Practice statutes? See Chapter 1, supra.

In Jensen v. Archbishop Bergan Mercy Hospital, 236 Neb. 1, 459 N.W.2d 178, 183 (1990), the plaintiffs alleged that the nursing staff should have altered the attending physician's orders if they had reason to believe they were wrong. The court disagreed, holding that "* * * hospital staff members lack authority to alter or depart from an attending physician's order for a hospital patient and lack authority to determine what is a proper course of medical treatment for a hospitalized patient. The foregoing is recognition of the realities and practicalities inherent in the physician-hospital nurse relationship."

2. Darling disclosed the prevailing attitude of hospital administrators toward affiliated doctors, reflecting the earlier concept of the doctor as independent contractor. The hospital administrator was subjected to a prolonged cross-examination by the plaintiff's attorney exploring his obli-

gations to evaluate doctor training and conduct. The administrator testified:

> "As the Board's representative, I did nothing to see that Dr. Alexander
> reviewed his operating techniques for the handling of broken bones.
> So far as I know, Dr. Alexander may not have reviewed his operating
> techniques since he was first licensed to practice in 1928. No examina-
> tions were ever given. I never asked questions of the doctor about this
> matter. The governing board, neither through me nor through any
> other designated administrative representative, ever checked up on the
> ability of Dr. Alexander as compared by medical text books. I had
> access at the hospital to some good orthopedic books. * * * Other than
> buying these books, I never made any effort to see that Dr. Alexander,
> or any other physician admitted to practice more than thirty years ago,
> read them." Darling v. Charleston Community Memorial Hosp., 50
> Ill.App.2d 253, 295, 200 N.E.2d 149, 171 (1964).

How can a hospital administrator devise procedures to trigger an
alarm when a physician is incompetent? See Gonzales v. Nork, Chapter 1,
infra. Must the administrator himself be an M.D.? Can you think of
methods that would have avoided the Darling tragedy?

In Albain v. Flower Hospital, 50 Ohio St.3d 251, 553 N.E.2d 1038, 1046
(1990), the Ohio Supreme Court recognized a hospital's independent duty to
exercise due care in granting staff privileges and retaining competent
physicians, but qualified the duty:

> A physician's negligence does not automatically mean that the hospital
> is liable, and does not raise a presumption that the hospital was
> negligent in granting the physician staff privileges. [ ] Nor is a
> hospital required to constantly supervise and second-guess the activi-
> ties of its physicians, beyond the duty to remove a known incompetent.
> Most hospital administrators are laypersons with no medical training
> at all. [ ] In any event, only licensed physicians, not hospitals, are
> permitted to practice medicine or surgery in this state. [ ]
>
> * * *
>
> * * * [ ] In short, the hospital is not an insurer of the skills of
> physicians to whom it has granted staff privileges.

In Thompson v. Nason Hospital, 370 Pa.Super. 115, 535 A.2d 1177,
1182 (1988), the court noted that

> for a hospital to be charged with negligence for failing to supervise the
> quality of care or competence of its staff, it is necessary to show that
> the hospital had actual or constructive knowledge of the procedures
> utilized. [ ] Moreover, the negligence of the hospital must have been
> a substantial factor in bringing about the harm to the plaintiff. [ ]

3. See, for a description of the Darling case by the plaintiff's lawyer,
Appelman, Hospital Liability for Acts of Nonsalaried Staff Physicians,
Personal Injury Annual 161 (1964); see also (describing the case), Spero,
Hospital Liability, 15 Trial 22 (Sept. 1979). For an older case imposing
direct liability for the failure of a hospital to control the use of its facilities,
see Hendrickson v. Hodkin, 276 N.Y. 252, 11 N.E.2d 899 (1937) (hospital
liable for allowing a quack to treat a patient on its premises).

WILLIAMS v. ST. CLAIRE MEDICAL CENTER

Court of Appeals of Kentucky, 1983.
657 S.W.2d 590.

MILLER, JUDGE.

This is a medical negligence case in which the plaintiff appeals from a summary judgment entered by the Rowan Circuit Court in favor of the defendant hospital, St. Claire Medical Center. The entry of summary judgment under CR 56.03, which is only proper in absence of a genuine issue of a material fact, [   ] sets up two ultimate questions for our consideration: (1) Does a hospital owe a duty to private patients of staff physicians to enforce its published rules and regulations pertaining to patient care, the breach of which may result in independent liability of the hospital, and (2) may vicarious liability be imposed upon a hospital for the negligence of independent staff personnel in the care and treatment of patients, under the doctrine of apparent authority or ostensible agency. Upon careful evaluation of available precedent and with realistic understanding of present day society we answer both questions in the affirmative.

FACTS AND PROCEDURAL HISTORY

Appellant, Delbert Junior Williams, suffered permanent brain damage on October 30, 1980, while being administered anesthetics prior to undergoing an arthroscopy at St. Claire Medical Center (hospital), the appellee herein. Appellant was having problems with his left knee and was admitted to the hospital on October 29, 1980, as a private patient of Dr. Thomas Fossett, an orthopedic surgeon with staff privileges. At that time appellee had no anesthesiologist on staff and thus all anesthetics were administered by nurse anesthetists. Dr. Fossett was chairman of the Department of Surgery at the hospital and also acting chairman of the Department of Anesthesiology, although he had no medical training in general anesthesia.

The nurse anesthetists who worked at St. Claire Medical Center were not employees of the hospital, but rather were employed by Cave Run Clinic, a professional service corporation in the area comprised of medical doctors. Ed Johnson, the nurse who anesthetized appellant, was not a certified registered nurse anesthetist at the time of the incident causing appellant's injury. He had only graduated from nurse anesthetist school one month prior to treating appellant and had not yet taken the examinations necessary to obtain certification. He was employed by Cave Run Clinic on July 26, 1980, and was simultaneously granted temporary staff privileges at the hospital. His staff privileges were, however, limited to those instances when he was under the direct supervision of Jerri Reis, certified registered nurse anesthetist, (CRNA), pending completion of nurse anesthetist training and eligibility for board certification.

The hospital's published anesthesiology policies in force in October, 1980, pertinent to this appeal provided as follows:

* * *

III. The Certified Registered Nurse Anesthetists are under the supervision of the Chairman of the Anesthesia Service.

IV. When giving anesthesia, the CRNA will have been in communication with the anesthesiologist and surgeon or obstetrician except in emergent procedures when the anesthesiologist is not available for consultation.

V. Anesthetics will be administered only by a CRNA or qualified physician.

* * *

Appellant was first introduced to nurse Johnson in his hospital room the day before the scheduled surgery on October 29, 1980, at which time Johnson solicited information from appellant for the purpose of determining an anesthetic plan. Although a spinal anesthetic would normally be administered for an arthroscopy, Johnson determined that a general anesthesia should be used in deference to the fact that appellant had previously had a myelogram. Johnson testified that he did not recall having any conferences with Dr. Fossett between the time he interviewed appellant on the 29th and when he anesthetized him the next day.

Although Johnson was to perform his nursing services only under the direct supervision of Jerri Reis, CRNA, neither Ms. Reis, nor any other certified registered nurse anesthetist, nor Dr. Fossett, was in the operating room on the morning of October 30, 1980, when Johnson anesthetized appellant. Thus the type of anesthetic and the amount given were entirely left to the discretion of Johnson who administered same to appellant with no direct supervision.

About twenty minutes after Johnson began administering the anesthetic he noticed that appellant was getting "dusky" from the neck up. He immediately asked Dr. Fossett to step into the operating room. Another doctor was called and the two doctors administered closed chest massage to resuscitate appellant. Appellant was then transferred to the University of Kentucky Medical Center where he remained in a coma for 10 to 12 days.

* * *

INDEPENDENT LIABILITY OF HOSPITAL

* * *

There is abundant evidence in the record which creates a jury issue of whether or not the hospital breached its duty to appellant, and if so, whether or not the breach thereof was a substantial factor in bringing about appellant's injuries. The various depositions show that the appellee had established written procedures for the administration of anesthetics, that it had limited Johnson's ability to administer anesthetics to those times when he was under the direct supervision of a CRNA or M.D. Neither a CRNA or M.D. was in the operating room when Johnson anesthetized appellant, that Fossett, acting chairman of the anesthesiology department of the hospital, was aware both of the fact that restrictions had been imposed on Johnson and that the morning of October 30, 1980, Johnson was unsupervised. There is ample basis for believing appellant suffered permanent brain damage immediately following the anesthesia procedure. The record further contains the deposition of appellant's expert witness, Dr. I.V. Malhotra, who testified that the hospital was negligent, in his opinion, for not having a trained anesthesiologist on staff, for allowing the attending surgeon to be in charge of anesthesia and for not insuring that a physician was present in the operating room when Johnson anesthetized appellant. Thus in order for the summary judgment to be affirmed, it must be determined, as a matter of law, that the hospital owed no duty to appellant to enforce its anesthesiology policies, or to establish procedures to insure that those with limited staff privileges did not exceed the authority to treat patients as restricted by the hospital.

* * *

The legal duty in the case at bar, which appellant claims the hospital owed him and which he claims is breached, is not the duty to supervise or review the medical treatment given him, but the duty to enforce its policies which, if followed, would have precluded his receiving any anesthetic treatment in the first place solely from an unqualified, uncertified, inexperienced nurse with temporary, limited staff privileges.

* * *

* * * [W]hile the patient must accept all the rules and regulations of the hospital, he should be able to expect that the hospital will follow its rules established for his care. Whether a patient enters a hospital through the emergency room or is admitted as a private patient by a staff physician, the patient is entering the hospital for only one reason recognized by this court's predecessor many years ago in *University of Louisville v. Hammock,* 127 Ky. 564, 106 S.W. 219, 220 (1907), wherein the court said:

> Indeed, the sick leave their homes and enter hospitals because of the superior treatment there promised them.

There is no rational reason or public policy why a hospital's duty to properly administer its policies should be any less to one patient than another depending upon how the patient initially arrived at the hospital.

* * *

We believe the record reflects facts which, when taken in light of prevailing case law, create a genuine issue of the hospital's breach of duty to appellant by failing to enforce its own rules and regulations regarding the administering of anesthesia. Therefore, summary judgment on this issue was erroneous.

* * *

[The Court then considered vicarious liability principles, including apparent authority and ostensible agency]

In applying the above legal principles to the situation here presented, it logically follows that the appellant justifiably believed Johnson to be a hospital employee. By taking no action to give appellant notice otherwise, the hospital "held-out" Johnson as an employee, thus creating an apparent agency. Therefore the hospital should be held liable for the negligence, if any, of nurse Johnson.

* * *

We believe it to be axiomatic that the general public, unless otherwise directed, in seeking medical services from public hospitals, acts in total reliance upon the hospital staff as though they are agents and servants of the hospital in a traditional sense. We believe this view is one prevailing in contemporary judicial thought. [ ] Therefore, we believe the trial court was also in error in entering a summary judgment on the issue of apparent authority or ostensible agency. Although it may well be that a hospital owes no duty to admit a patient in absence of a clear emergency or an order from an attending physician, [ ] we are not here required to approve or disapprove the wisdom of such a rule. However, it appears to us that when a hospital has received a patient, under whatever circumstance, and has undertaken treatment, that patient is owed a duty by the hospital through its employees and staff, including independent staff personnel, to exercise appropriate care to provide for the patient's well-being and to promote his cure. A breach of this duty may expose the hospital to liability in tort. Any lesser rule would be insensible to the true role of a hospital as an institution in present day society.

For the foregoing reasons the judgment of the lower court is reversed and this cause is remanded for proceedings consistent with this opinion.

* * *

Notes and Questions

1. What is the holding of *Williams* with regard to the negligence count? That a hospital is strictly liable when any breach of its administrative rules causes patient injury? What effect does the court give to the hospital's violation of its own bylaws? Is this administrative negligence per se, analogous to a statutory violation which leads to negligence per se?

Is it clear that the nurse, Ed Johnson, made an error in administering the anesthesia? Might this bad result have merely been one of the low risk bad outcomes of any anesthesia procedure, no matter who performed it? The court says that the record supports the finding that his act was a "substantial" factor in the plaintiff's injury. Or is the court applying a rule of circumstantial proof?

2. The court finds that the agency doctrine of apparent authority applies. But does the penultimate paragraph of the opinion suggest that the court is extending agency principles further?

Note: *The Duty to Properly Select and Retain Medical Staff*

A typical hospital has several categories of practicing physicians. The largest category is comprised of private physicians with staff privileges. These privileges include the right of the physicians to admit and discharge their private patients to the hospital and the right to use the hospital's facilities. Hospitals will also have physicians in training present, including interns, residents, and externs. Hospitals will often also have full-time salaried physicians, including teaching hospital faculty, and physicians under contract with the hospital to provide services for an agreed upon price. Classen, Hospital Liability for Independent Contractors: Where Do We Go From Here?, 40 Ark.L.Rev. 469, 478 (1987).

The organized medical staff of a hospital, private physicians with privileges, comprises the largest group of hospital-based physicians. The medical staff governs the hospital's provision of medical services. The typical medical staff operates under its own bylaws, elects its own officers, and appoints its own committees. It is not simply another administrative component of the hospital, under the authority of the governing board of the hospital. While the hospital board must approve the staff's bylaws and can approve or disapprove particular staff actions, it cannot usually discipline individual physicians directly or appoint administrative officers to exercise direct authority. A hospital's medical staff is therefore a powerful body within the larger organization. See generally Havighurst, Doctors and Hospitals: An Antitrust Perspective on Traditional Relationships, 1984 Duke L.J. 1071, 1084–92. The requirement of staff self-governance under JCAHO standards maintains and reinforces this physician authority within hospitals.

The process by which the medical staff is selected is of crucial importance. See Chapter Five, infra, for discussion of the other legal issues arising out of staff privileges. A hospital has an obligation to its patients to investigate the qualifications of medical staff applicants. The Wisconsin Supreme Court elaborated on this obligation in Johnson v. Misericordia Community Hospital, 99 Wis.2d 708, 301 N.W.2d 156, 174–75 (1981).

> In summary, we hold that a hospital owes a duty to its patients to exercise reasonable care in the selection of its medical staff and in granting specialized privileges. The final appointing authority resides in the hospital's governing body, although it must rely on the medical staff and in particular the credentials committee (or committee of the whole) to investigate and evaluate an applicant's qualifications for the requested privileges. However, this delegation of the responsiblity to investigate and evaluate the professional competence of applicants for clinical privileges does not relieve the governing body of its duty to appoint only qualified physicians and surgeons to its medical staff and periodically monitor and review their competency. The credentials committee (or committee of the whole) must investigate the qualifications of applicants. The facts of this case demonstrate that a hospital

should, at a minimum, require completion of the application and verify the accuracy of the applicant's statements, especially in regard to his medical education, training and experience. Additionally, it should: (1) solicit information from the applicant's peers, including those not referenced in his application, who are knowledgeable about his education, training, experience, health, competence and ethical character; (2) determine if the applicant is currently licensed to practice in this state and if his licensure or registration has been or is currently being challenged; and (3) inquire whether the applicant has been involved in any adverse malpractice action and whether he has experienced a loss of medical organization membership or medical privileges or membership at any other hospital. The investigating committee must also evaluate the information gained through its inquiries and make a reasonable judgment as to the approval or denial of each application for staff privileges. The hospital will be charged with gaining and evaluating the knowledge that would have been acquired had it exercised ordinary care in investigating its medical staff applicants and the hospital's failure to exercise that degree of care, skill and judgment that is exercised by the average hospital in approving an applicant's request for privileges is negligence. This is not to say that hospitals are *insurers* of the competence of their medical staff, for a hospital will not be negligent if it exercises the noted standard of care in selecting its staff.

See also Bell v. Sharp Cabrillo Hospital, 211 Cal.App.3d 1339, 260 Cal.Rptr. 37 (4th Dist.1989):

Although once established the medical staff may well be self-governing, it is the hospital which is responsible for organizing and implementing procedures to select and reappoint staff. Thus, we conclude the competent selection and review of medical staff is precisely the type of professional service a hospital is licensed and expected to provide, for it is in the business of providing medical care to patients and protecting them from an unreasonable risk of harm while receiving medical treatment. * * * [T]he competent performance of this responsibility is "inextricably interwoven" with delivering competent quality medical care to hospital patients.

In *Bell*, the Chief of Surgery had failed to investigate the adverse information concerning the surgeon's loss of privileges at two hospitals he had listed on the reappointment application. He had failed to investigate a discrepancy between the surgeon's admission on the reappointment form and a report from the medical board, and he had never asked for an explanation of the adverse information.

See also Elam v. College Park Hospital, 132 Cal.App.3d 332, 183 Cal.Rptr. 156 (1982); Purcell v. Zimbelman, 18 Ariz.App. 75, 500 P.2d 335 (1972); Oehler v. Humana Inc., 775 P.2d 1271 (Nev.1989).

2. The hospital must also have proper procedures developed to detect impostors. Insinga v. LaBella, Humana, et al., 543 So.2d 209 (Fla.1989) (non physician fraudulently obtained an appointment to the medical staff, after having assumed the name of a deceased Italian physician; the court

applied corporate negligence, noting that at least seventeen jurisdictions had adopted the doctrine.)

3.   A hospital should also properly restrict the clinical privileges of staff physicians who are incompetent to handle certain procedures, or detect concealment by a staff doctor of medical errors. See Cronic v. Doud, 168 Ill.App.3d 665, 119 Ill.Dec. 708, 523 N.E.2d 176 (1988); Corleto v. Shore Memorial Hospital, 138 N.J.Super. 302, 350 A.2d 534 (1975).

4.   The medical staff has also been held liable in a few cases independently for its failure to supervise and regulate the activity of its members. *Corleto,* supra.

5.   Under the Health Care Quality Improvement Act of 1986 (HCQIA), hospitals must check a central registry, a national database maintained by the Unisys Corporation under contract with the Department of Health and Human Services, before a new staff appointment is made. This database contains information on individual physicians who have been disciplined, had malpractice claims filed against them, or had privileges revoked or limited. If the hospital fails to check the registry, it is held constructively to have knowledge of any information it might have gotten from the inquiry. See discussion of staff privileges in Chapter 5, infra.

Problem: Proctoring Peers

You have been asked by Hilldale Adventist Hospital to advise them on the implications of their use of proctors for assessing candidates for medical staff privileges, in light of a recent lawsuit brought by a patient injured during surgery, joining both the proctor and the hospital. They have used Dr. Hook, a surgeon certified by the American Board of Orthopedic Surgery, as a proctor in two different operations on the plaintiff Frances Bacon, at two different hospitals during the process of evaluation of Dr. Frank DiBianco for staff privileges. Dr. Hook had been asked to observe ten surgeries by Dr. DiBianco and then file a report. He observed an operation on the plaintiff during one of these observations. Two months later, he was again asked to proctor Dr. DiBianco at another hospital, and he again observed a second procedure on the plaintiff by Dr. DiBianco at this hospital. Prior to each procedure, Dr. Hook had reviewed the x-rays, discussed the operative plan, but otherwise took no part in the care and treatment of the plaintiff. He did not participate in the operations, did not scrub in, and always observed from outside the "sterile field". He got no payment for his proctoring efforts, and he had never met the plaintiff nor had any other contact with her.

Can Hilldale be liable for their use of Dr. Hook as a proctor? Can Dr. Hook be directly liable for failing to stop negligent work by Dr. DiBianco?

2. The Duty to Protect Non-patients

Darling for the first time imposed a duty on the hospital administrators to supervise and evaluate care delivered by physicians within the hospital. The court drew on JCAHO standards, the hospital's own bylaws, and other documents in outlining the extent of the responsibility. Later cases refined and limited the concept of corporate negligence.

PEDROZA v. BRYANT

Supreme Court of Washington, 1984.
101 Wn.2d 226, 677 P.2d 166.

The issue before us is whether a hospital may be held liable under a theory of corporate negligence for its action in granting privileges to a nonemployee doctor who allegedly commits malpractice while in private practice off the hospital premises.

In December of 1978, Maria Pedroza was in her 35th week of pregnancy and under the care of Dr. Ben Bryant. During the week of December 3 through 9, Maria became ill and exhibited the classical symptoms of preeclampsia (a toxemia of pregnancy), namely, hypertension, headaches, and edema of the lower extremities. Mrs. Pedroza visited Dr. Bryant's office on December 6 and 7, and telephoned him on December 8. Dr. Bryant prescribed no medicine other than bed rest and aspirin. He did not refer Mrs. Pedroza to another health care provider.

On December 9, 1978, Maria Pedroza was admitted, comatose, to defendant Skagit Valley Hospital. She was admitted to surgery, with a diagnosis of irreversible cerebral death due to intracerebral hemorrhage resulting from eclampsia. Dr. Bryant was neither the admitting nor the treating physician for this hospitalization. Indeed, the hospital had, on April 13, 1977, limited Dr. Bryant's obstetrical and newborn privileges to Class II for the years 1977 and 1978. Dr. Bryant was thus required to consult with a Class I physician on all "seriously ill patients," including pregnancies with "major medical complications" and "[l]ate or severe toxemia of pregnancy." Thus, Dr. Bryant would not have been allowed to treat Maria Pedroza for eclampsia in the hospital.

In surgery, Mrs. Pedroza's child was successfully delivered by emergency cesarean section. After family consent was obtained, respiratory support for Mrs. Pedroza was discontinued on December 15, 1978, whereupon she died.

It should be noted at the outset that plaintiff is not claiming that defendant hospital is vicariously liable for the negligence of Dr. Bryant under the theory of respondeat superior. Dr. Bryant is an independent contractor, not an employee of defendant hospital. Plaintiff is instead relying solely on the doctrine of corporate negligence, which differs from respondeat superior in that it imposes on the hospital a nondelegable duty owed directly to the patient, regardless of the details of the doctor-hospital relationship. Plaintiff contends that defendant hospital owed a duty to Maria Pedroza of carefully selecting and reviewing the competency of its staff physicians. ("Staff physicians" are those doctors who have been given "staff privileges" at the hospital. A physician must be a member of the hospital's medical staff in order to regularly admit patients to the hospital.) Plaintiff alleges that defendant hospital breached this duty by allowing Dr. Bryant to possess staff privileges at the hospital, and that this breach was the proximate cause of Mrs. Pedroza's death.

II.

The first question we must address, then, is whether the doctrine of corporate negligence applies to hospitals in Washington. * * *

[The court adopted the doctrine of corporate negligence in Washington, citing several justifications:

(1) "the public's perception of the modern hospital as a multifaceted health care facility responsible for the quality of medical care and treatment rendered, and the public's subsequent reliance on the hospital";

(2) the hospital's "superior position to monitor and control physician performance", given its opportunities to observe professional practices on a daily basis, to adopt procedures to detect problems, and the use of its medical staff to monitor quality;

(3) incentives on hospitals, created by imposing corporate negligence, "to insure the competency of their medical staffs", thereby reducing their malpractice insurance costs.

The court then adopted the theory of corporate negligence, noting that "[n]early every jurisdiction that has addressed the issue in the last 15 years has adopted corporate negligence."]

III.

Having adopted the doctrine of corporate negligence, we turn now to the task of defining the standard of care to which hospitals will be held. [The court noted that hospitals are members of national organizations such as the Joint Commission on Accreditation of Healthcare Organizations, subject to accreditation requirements.]

* * *

Also relevant to a hospital's standard of care are the hospital's own bylaws. [ ] Hospitals are required by statute and regulation to adopt bylaws with respect to medical staff activities. [ ] It is "recommended" that the organization and functions of the medical staff under the bylaws be in accord with the JCAH standards. [ ] Bylaws are therefore based on national standards, and their use in defining a standard of care for hospitals is appropriate. * * *

IV.

Our decision to adopt the doctrine of corporate negligence as enunciated by other jurisdictions does not necessarily entitle plaintiff in the case at bar to a reversal of the summary judgment against him. The alleged acts of malpractice committed by Dr. Bryant occurred entirely outside the hospital. Mrs. Pedroza was not a patient of the hospital at the time. For plaintiff to prevail, we must decide that the duty of care owed by hospitals under the corporate negligence doctrine extends not only to hospital patients, but also to patients treated by hospital staff members in those staff members' private office practices, where the hospital is not involved. No other jurisdiction appears to have done this; all the cases involve acts of malpractice committed at the hospital.

Defendant argues that extending a hospital's duty of care to patients outside the hospital would require a hospital to supervise and, if necessary, limit the private medical practices of its staff members outside the hospital. Such intervention could adversely affect the delicate physician-patient relationship. Substantial administrative problems would probably result as well.

This argument appears to be based upon a misconception of the doctrine of corporate negligence. The doctrine does not impose vicarious liability on a hospital for the acts of a medical staff member. The pertinent inquiry is whether the hospital exercised reasonable care in the granting, renewal, and delineation of staff privileges. This inquiry focuses on the procedures for the granting and renewal of staff privileges set forth in the hospital bylaws. In no case adopting corporate negligence premised upon a hospital's independent duty to select and maintain a competent medical staff has there been a suggestion that a hospital, in order to fulfill its duty of reasonable care, must supervise a physician's office practice. Acts of malpractice committed by a staff physician outside the hospital are relevant only if the hospital has actual or constructive notice of them, and where failure to take some action as a result of such notice is negligence. *Fridena v. Evans,* 127 Ariz. 516, 622 P.2d 463 (1980).

Plaintiff argues that defendant hospital's independent duty of care should extend to Maria Pedroza because she was a foreseeable plaintiff. Foreseeability determines the extent and scope of duty. [ ] Plaintiff alleges that Maria Pedroza used Dr. Bryant's services only because Dr. Bryant possessed admitting and obstetrical privileges at defendant hospital (each of Maria Pedroza's seven children had been born at Skagit Valley Hospital), and that it was, therefore, foreseeable that the hospital's alleged negligence in the granting or renewal of Dr. Bryant's staff privileges might result in harm to his obstetrical patients. Plaintiff argues that it should make no difference whether the harm occurred in or out of the hospital, as long as the harm was foreseeable. The doctrine of corporate negligence focuses on the negligence of the hospital in failing to rescind Dr. Bryant's privileges.

The fact remains, however, that every jurisdiction that has adopted corporate negligence has based the hospital's liability on the duty owed by the hospital *to its patients.* * * * The hospital holds itself out to the community as a competent provider of medical care. The hospital does *not* hold itself out as an inspector or insurer of the private office practices of its staff members. The delineation of staff privileges by the hospital can only affect the procedures used by staff members while they are inside hospital walls. The public cannot reasonably expect anything more.

This court has in the past recognized a hospital's independent duty of care only in those situations where the plaintiff was a patient of the hospital. [ ] RCW 70.41, which controls the licensing and regulation of hospitals, supports the limitation of a hospital's duty of care to those who are patients in the hospital. RCW 70.41.010 provides in pertinent part: "The primary purpose of this chapter is to promote safe and adequate care of individuals in hospitals * * *."

Extending the hospital's duty of care to those who are not its patients would be undesirable in that it would likely grant those people a windfall, as any increased hospital costs resulting from such an extension of liability would be spread among hospital patients, rather than those who would benefit from the extended liability.

Accordingly, we hold that a hospital's duty of care under the doctrine of corporate negligence extends only to those who are patients within the hospital. Defendant Skagit Valley Hospital owed no duty to Maria Pedroza under the doctrine because she was not a hospital patient when the harm occurred. The fact that she had been a patient at defendant hospital in years past does not make her a patient for purposes of this case. Each of those prior hospital-patient relationships ended upon her discharge from the hospital; they did not continue indefinitely.

Since there are no allegations of negligence after Mrs. Pedroza was admitted to the hospital, we affirm the trial court's order of summary judgment.

Notes and Questions

1. Washington later applied its new corporate negligence doctrine in Schoening v. Grays Harbor Community Hospital, 40 Wash.App. 331, 698 P.2d 593 (1985). The plaintiff was treated in the emergency room for an infection. The plaintiff's expert, in his affidavit, wrote that the hospital should have been aware of "obvious negligence." The court held that where the care by the attending physician is questionable and the patient's condition is deteriorating, the hospital staff should have continuously monitored and observed the patient and sought additional evaluations. The court held that a fact question was raised by the expert's affidavit as to the hospital's duty to intervene.

See, rejecting the doctrine of corporate negligence, Albain v. Flower Hospital, 50 Ohio St.3d 251, 553 N.E.2d 1038 (1990).

2. Can you make a stronger argument that a hospital should be responsible, under some circumstances, for the negligent acts of physicians in their private practice, so long as they have staff privileges? What if the hospital is on notice of a long history of malpractice claims against one of its staff, resulting from negligence in that physician's private practice? If

the physician has performed adequately while treating patients within the hospital, should the hospital have any further responsibility?

Consider the case of Copithorne v. Framingham Union Hospital, 401 Mass. 860, 520 N.E.2d 139 (1988). The plaintiff, Copithorne, was a technologist at Framingham Union Hospital who was drugged and sexually assaulted by a physician with staff privileges at the hospital. The Massachusetts Supreme Judicial Court imposed liability on the hospital. The court summarized the facts as follows:

> At the time of the incident, Helfant was a practicing neurosurgeon and a visiting staff member of the hospital. He was not a hospital employee, but had been affiliated with the hospital for about seventeen years, having been reappointed to the visiting staff each year since his initial appointment. Copithorne was a hospital employee. In the course of her employment, she injured her back, and, aware of Helfant's reputation within the hospital as a good neurosurgeon and a specialist in back injuries, she sought his professional assistance. In the course of treating her, Helfant made a house call to Copithorne's apartment, where he committed the drugging and rape for which he was convicted and which caused the injuries for which Copithorne seeks compensation. [Helfant had been convicted in 1985 of rape and drugging a person for unlawful sexual intercourse.]

The court assumed, as did the trial court, that the hospital was negligent in retaining Dr. Helfant on staff.

> We think that a jury reasonably could find that the hospital owed a duty of care to Copithorne, as an employee who, in deciding to enter a doctor-patient relationship with Helfant, reasonably relied on Helfant's good standing and reputation within the hospital community, and that the hospital violated this duty by failing to take sufficient action in response to previous allegations of Helfant's wrongdoing.

The hospital had received actual notice, prior to the assault on the plaintiff, of at least two prior incidents of sexual assault in which Helfant had caressed and otherwise improperly fondled female patients in the hospital. One of these patients filed a complaint with the Board of Registration in Medicine, copying the complaint to the hospital. The hospital then took action.

> * * * Dr. Byrne [Chief of Surgery] met with Helfant, who denied any wrongdoing. Dr. Byrne then instructed Helfant to have a chaperon present in the future when visiting female patients in the hospital. Based on Helfant's "excellent record" at the hospital, Dr. Bryne "felt that no further action was necessary as it was his opinion that the had no need to worry about Dr. Helfant harming a patient. In effect, Dr. Helfant was given an oral warning." Dr. Bryne also told the nurses on the floor to "keep an eye on Dr. Helfant."

Walckner, the hospital administrator,

> "inquired of hospital personnel, through department heads at management meetings, if there was any awareness of sexual harassment at the hospital in general involving either employees or patients." Following receipt of a copy of Kathleen's letter to the Board of Registration in

Medicine, Walckner wrote to the board, but received no response, and took no further action.

The court found that the facts would support a jury finding that

> the risk of injury to Copithorne was within the range of foreseeable consequences of the hospital's negligence in continuing Helfant's staff privileges. Where the hospital had received actual notice of allegations that Helfant had sexually assaulted patients, both on the hospital premises and off the premises in his office and in a patient's home, and yet took only the limited measures indicated, it was not unforeseeable that Helfant would continue to act in a consistent, if not worse, manner.

The court also rejected the trial judge's ruling that the withdrawal of Helfant's staff privileges would not have prevented his assault on the plaintiff.

> Copithorne asserted that, by reason of her employment, she was aware of Helfant's good reputation within the hospital, and that she relied on this reputation in entering in a doctor-patient relationship with him; that as an employee, any change in Helfant's status would have become known to her; and that, if she had had any reason to know that the hospital has suspended Helfant's staff privileges or imposed any disciplinary sanctions on him, she would not have entered into a doctor-patient relationship with him. A different question would be presented if a member of the general public claimed that the hospital was liable for similar harm simply because Helfant was a staff member and should not have been.

The court reversed the summary judgment in favor of the defendant, and remanded the case for further proceedings.

> Judge Lynch, dissenting, noted that corporate negligence typically is imposed because of a duty of care owed by a hospital to its patients on its premises.

> > Sound policy may suggest that a hospital have some responsibility for acts occurring on its premises in order to ensure that a hospital exercises care in supervising the activities that occur within its boundaries. Since it can have no control over the activities that occur off hospital premises, imposing liability would only increase the already skyrocketing cost of inpatient hospital care [ ], because of conduct over which the hospital has no control. * * *

* * *

> > * * * the hospital responded to the complaints by prohibiting Helfant from unchaperoned contact with its female patients. If the hospital had failed to act, it may have been foreseeable that Helfant would commit sexual assaults on hospital premises, but the hospital's response would appear to have eliminated that possibility. Helfant's hospital staff privileges had no relation to Helfant's ability to assault his private patients sexually in their homes or at his office. That opportunity existed in the absence of his visiting staff privileges.

How broad is the holding in *Copithorne?* Does this case contradict *Pedroza,* or is it distinguishable? Analyze the relationship of the hospital to the plaintiff and the defendant. Is the employer-employee relationship between the hospital and the nurse crucial to the holding? Or does this simply reinforce the reliance by the plaintiff on the defendant's implied representation that its staff is trustworthy? As hospitals devote more attention to staff privileges, driven by their need to avoid liability and achieve the best possible staffs, and as physicians come to restrict their privileges to fewer hospitals, or just one, does the reliance interest of the public increase?

Are your encouraged by the action of the medical disciplinary board of the state, which did nothing? See Doctors Rarely Lose Licenses: Maryland Panel Allowed Rapist to Keep Practicing, Washington Post, Part I, p. 1, January 10, 1988.

Problem: Referrals

You represent Chadds Hospital, a small nonprofit hospital that is trying to increase its patient count. One of the strategies it is contemplating is a physician referral service. The hospital plans to advertise, in local newspapers and on the radio, that individuals should call Chadds Hospital for the name of a doctor for specific problems. The referral service operator will then offer to make the appointment for the caller with the particular doctor, to be seen in his office practice. The draft of the advertising copy that the hospital marketing staff has prepared states: "You can trust the high quality of these doctors because they are members of the medical staff of Chadds Hospital, and our doctors are the best."

What is your advice to the hospital in light of the above cases? Do you foresee any legal risks in this marketing strategy?

3. Non-delegable Duties: The Hospital as Public Utility

JACKSON v. POWER

Supreme Court of Alaska, 1987.
743 P.2d 1376.

[The facts of the case, and the portion of the opinion that addresses the issue of ostensible agency, is reproduced on pp. 226–230, supra.]

VI

Jackson's final point is that the trial court erred in refusing to rule, as a matter of law, that FMH, as a general acute care hospital, has a non-delegable duty to provide non-negligent physician care in its emergency room. In essence, Jackson's position is that when a hospital undertakes to operate an emergency room as an integral part of its health care enterprise, public policy dictates that it not be allowed to insulate itself from liability by shunting that responsibility onto another.

FMH, on the other hand, argues that a hospital does not have a non-delegable duty to guarantee safe treatment in its emergency room.

Physicians, not hospitals, FMH asserts, have a duty to practice medicine non-negligently. Thus, according to FMH, a hospital cannot be held to have delegated away a duty it never had.

The trial court ruled that "[t]here cannot be a non-delegable duty if there is no contractual relationship." Since it was unclear from the evidence whether or not there was any contractual relationship between ERI and FMH, the court denied Jackson's motion for summary judgment. Initially, we note the trial court's erroneous characterization of the issue. By holding that there can be no "non-delegable duty if there is no contractual relationship," the court confused the question of the existence of a duty with the issue of whether a duty is non-delegable. The flaw in this reasoning is self-evident. As FMH points out, a party cannot be held to have delegated away a duty it never had. Thus, the threshold question is whether FMH had a duty to provide emergency room care. Only if it did, is it necessary to determine what that duty entailed.

FMH is licensed as a "general acute care hospital."[11] As such, it is required to comply with state regulations designed to promote "safe and adequate treatment of individuals in hospitals in the interest of public health, safety and welfare." AS 18.20.060. These regulations provided, at the time of Jackson's accident, that an acute care hospital *shall* "insure that a physician is available to respond to an emergency at all times." Former 7 AAC 12.110(c)(2).[12] Thus, at a minimum, the law imposed a duty on FMH to provide emergency care physicians on a 24–hour basis.

FMH, however, voluntarily assumed a much broader duty. At the time of Jackson's accident, FMH was accredited by the Joint Committee on the Accreditation of Hospitals (JCAH.) In order to receive and maintain accreditation, FMH had to comply with the JCAH's standards promulgated in the *Accreditations Manual For Hospitals, Emergency Services*. Standard I mandates that all accredited hospitals implement a well defined plan for emergency care based on community need and the capability of the hospital. The JCAH standards also mandate, among other things, that: (1) FMH's emergency room be directed by a physician member of the active medical staff (Standard II); (2) FMH's emergency room be integrated with other units and departments of the hospital (Standard III); (3) that emergency care be guided by written policies and procedures; and (4) that the quality of care be continually reviewed, evaluated and assured through establishment of quality control mechanisms (Standard V).

Additionally, FMH's own bylaws provided for the establishment and maintenance of an emergency room. Article X, section 1(d)(1)(b) of FMH's Medical Bylaws provides for an emergency room as one of the

---

11. A general acute care hospital is a "facility which provides hospitalization for inpatient medical care of acute illness or injury and obstetric care." 7 AAC 12.100.

12. In 1983, this regulation was amended to provide that "[a] general acute care hospital *must* provide * * * [among other services not relevant here] emergency care services." 7 AAC 12.105 (emphasis added).

services of the hospital. Article XI, section 3(e) provides for the creation of an emergency room committee which is required among other things to:

(a) formulate rules and regulations for the continuous coverage of the emergency room; and

(b) supervise the clinical work in that department.

Based upon the above, it cannot seriously be questioned that FMH had a duty to provide emergency room services and that part of that duty was to provide physician care in its emergency room. Having so determined, we must next ascertain whether FMH's duty to provide physician care in the emergency room is non-delegable. That is, we must determine whether, having assumed the duty to staff an emergency room, FMH should be allowed to avoid responsibility for the care rendered therein by claiming that the physicians it provides are not its employees. We conclude that it cannot.

A non-delegable duty is an established exception to the rule that an employer is not liable for the negligence of an independent contractor. W. Keeton, D. Dobbs, R. Keeton, D. Owen, *Prosser and Keeton on The Law of Torts*, § 71 at 511–12 (5th ed. 1984). * * *

It is difficult to suggest any criterion by which the non-delegable character of such duties may be determined, other than *the conclusion of the courts that the responsibility is so important to the community that the employer should not be permitted to transfer it to another.*

Id. at 512 (emphasis added). *Accord, Alaska Airlines v. Sweat*, 568 P.2d 916, 925–26 (Alaska 1977).

Our principal decision on non-delegable duty is *Sweat*, 568 P.2d 916. In that case, Sweat sued Alaska Airlines for injuries sustained in an air crash while traveling aboard a Chitina Air Service plane. *Id.* at 922. Chitina had been engaged under a contract with Alaska Airlines to service a portion of Alaska Airlines' regularly scheduled routes. *Id.* at 921, 922. Alaska Airlines contended that Chitina was an independent contractor and therefore it was not liable for Chitina's negligence. *Id.* at 923. The trial court found Alaska Airlines vicariously liable based on Restatement (Second) of Torts § 428. *Id.* On appeal, we affirmed the trial court's decision on the alternative ground that Alaska Airlines owed a common law nondelegable duty of safety to its passengers. *Id.* at 925. We reasoned:

We believe that the responsibility of a common carrier for the safety of its passengers is so important that the carrier should not be permitted to transfer it to another. A scheduled common carrier such as Alaska is given a monopoly or semi-monopoly primarily for the purpose of furnishing safe and reliable scheduled air transportation. It should not be permitted to barter away its responsibility to the traveling public by means of contracts with other carriers. If this were permissible, an air carrier could avoid liability by engaging in independent contracts for furnishing food, maintenance of its planes and conceivably even for supplying crews. Regardless of whether such contracts may be permitted by regulatory authorities, the traveling public is entitled to look for protection to the certificated carrier responsible for the scheduled route.

Id. at 926.

We have little trouble concluding that patients, such as Jackson, receiving treatment at a hospital emergency room are as deserving of protection as the airline passengers in *Sweat.* Likewise, the importance to the community of a hospital's duty to provide emergency room physicians reveals the importance of the common-carriers' duty for the safety of its passengers. We also find a close parallel between the regulatory scheme of airlines and hospitals. Undoubtedly, the operation of a hospital is one of the most regulated activities in this state. Besides the license, and certificate of need, requirements mentioned above, a hospital must comply with state regulations promulgated to control its activities, AS 18.20.070, 7 AAC 12.610; adopt a state approved risk management program "to minimize the risk of injury to patients," AS 18.20.075; and undergo "annual inspections and investigations" of its facilities, AS 18.20.080. Failure to comply with these statutory requirements can lead to suspension or revocation of the hospital's license. AS 18.20.050.

The hospital regulatory scheme and the purpose underlying it (to "provide for the development, establishment, and enforcement of standards for the care and treatment of hospital patients that promote safe and adequate treatment" AS 18.20.010), along with the statutory definition of a hospital, (an institution devoted primarily to providing diagnosis, treatment or care to individuals, AS 18.20.130(3)), manifests the legislature's recognition that it is the hospital as an institution which bears ultimate responsibility for complying with the mandates of the law. It is the hospital that is required to ensure compliance with the regulations and thus, relevant to the instant case, it is the hospital that bears final accountability for the provision of physicians for emergency room care. We, therefore, hold that a general acute care hospital's duty to provide physicians for emergency room care is non-delegable. Thus, a hospital such as FMH may not shield itself from liability by claiming that it is not responsible for the results of negligently performed health care when the law imposes a duty on the hospital to provide that health care.

We are persuaded that the circumstances under which emergency room care is provided in a modern hospital mandates the rule we adopt today. Not only is this rule consonant with the public perception of the hospital as a multifaceted health care facility responsible for the quality of medical care and treatment rendered, it also treats tort liability in the medical arena in a manner that is consistent with the commercialization of American medicine. Finally, we simply cannot fathom why liability should depend upon the technical employment status of the emergency room physician who treats the patient. It is the hospital's duty to provide the physician, which it may do through any means at its disposal. The means employed, however, will not change the fact that the hospital will be responsible for the care rendered by physicians it has a duty to provide.

This holding is necessarily limited. We do not change the standard of care with which a physician must comply, nor do we extend the duty which we find non-delegable beyond its natural scope. Our holding does not extend to situations where the patient is treated by his or her own doctor in an emergency room provided for the convenience of the doctor. Such situations are beyond the scope of the duty assumed by an acute care hospital. Rather our holding is limited to those situations where a patient comes to the hospital, as an institution, seeking emergency room services and is treated by a physician provided by the hospital. In such situations, the hospital shall be vicariously liable for damages proximately caused by a physician's negligence or malpractice.

In the instant case, Jackson came to FMH as an institution seeking emergency room services. Dr. Power was a physician FMH had a non-delegable duty to provide. FMH is, therefore, vicariously liable as a matter of law for any negligence or malpractice that Dr. Power may have committed. Accordingly, the trial court's ruling on this issue must be reversed. Jackson is entitled to partial summary judgment on the issue of FMH's vicarious liability.

VII

For the reasons outlined above, the trial court's denial of summary judgment on Jackson's theories of enterprise liability and apparent authority are AFFIRMED. However because we hold that FMH has a non-delegable duty to provide non-negligent physician care in its emergency room, the trial court's denial of summary judgment on the theory of non-delegable duty, is REVERSED and REMANDED with instructions to enter partial summary judgment on the issue of FMH vicarious liability in favor of Jackson.

* * *

Notes and Questions

1. Has the Alaska Supreme Court done anything new or expansionary in *Jackson?* Is there any clear stopping point to expansion of hospital liability, given the *Jackson* court's reliance on the heavily regulated nature of institutionally provided health care and the need for centralized control over physicians? Is the court merely applying the vicarious liability principles we have developed in this chapter? The court limits its holding to emergency rooms, and yet its discussion of the pervasively regulated nature of health care institutions seems open to expansion.

2. Is a hospital like a public utility? The health care industry is pervasively regulated, particularly by the federal government. See Chapters 6 and 7, infra. Health care generally is viewed as an inappropriate

industry for free market principles. Health care is considered a necessity. See Chapter 1, supra. The special tax exemptions given hospitals depend on their supplanting governmental functions for indigent care. See Chapter 6, infra. Given the extent of government regulation and the special status of health care, doesn't the *Jackson* court properly elevate hospitals to the status of public utilities? See Corley, Hospitals as a Public Utility: or "Work with Us Now or Work for Us Later," 2 J.Health Pol.Poly. & L. 304 (1978); Priest, Possible Adaptation of Public Utility Concepts in the Health Care Field, 35 L. & Contemp.Prob. 839 (1970).

3. The application of the non-delegable duty doctrine to hospitals was rejected in Estates of Milliron v. Francke, 243 Mont. 200, 793 P.2d 824 (1990) (distinguishing *Jackson* since it involved radiology, not emergency room practice) and Albain v. Flower Hospital, 50 Ohio St.3d 251, 553 N.E.2d 1038 (1990) (noting that the normal application of nondelegable duty doctrine is premised on peculiar risks and special precautions attendant to the work itself. "The practice of medicine in a hospital by an independent physician with staff privileges does not involve the type of risks and precautions required * * *.")

4. Malpractice litigation based on theories of corporate negligence and ostensible agency reflects judicial perceptions of the value of institutional mechanisms for controlling the provision of health care. Such judicial decisions may lead to changes in the behavior of institutional providers. Consider, for example, the impact of the decision by the Alaska Supreme Court in *Jackson*. The decision caused plaintiffs attorneys in Alaska to include hospitals in every suit they brought against individual physicians. Some hospitals in Alaska reportedly responded to this by deciding to hire their own emergency room physicians so the hospital would not have to worry about being joined in suits brought against independent contractor physicians. See *HealthWeek,* June 6, 1988, P. 1, 33.

5. Some states by statute have adopted corporate negligence for institutional providers. Florida, for example, has by statute incorporated "institutional liability" or "corporate negligence" in its regulation of hospitals. Hospitals and other providers will be liable for injuries caused by inadequacies in the internal programs that are mandated by the statute. West's Fla.Stat.Ann. § 768.60.

Problem: The Birthing Center

You have been approached by Rosa Hernandez to handle a tort suit for damages for the death of her infant during delivery at the Hastings Birthing Center. Discovery reveals the following facts.

The death of the infant is attributable to the negligence of Dr. Jones, the physician who attended Ms. Hernandez at the Center during delivery. The death was caused in part by the infant's aspiration of meconium into the lungs. Although the Center is equipped to suction meconium and other material from a newborn's throat, it is not equipped to perform an intubation and attach the infant to a ventilator. To intubate the infant, it would have to be transferred to the hospital. Even if the infant had been transferred, it would probably have suffered brain damage due to oxygen deprivation before the procedure could have been undertaken.

Dr. Jones has a spotless record, but over the two weeks preceding the incident he had appeared at the hospital smelling of alcohol and evidencing other signs of intoxication. He was apparently having marital problems at the time. Nurses at the hospital had reported this behavior to their supervisor and had watched the physician's work very carefully, calling his attention to things he missed. The nurse supervisor had reported the situation to the head of OB/GYN, who said he would "look into it". Ms. Hernandez noticed the smell of liquor on Dr. Jones' breath during her labor, and was upset by his apparent intoxication. Dr. Jones has also dropped his malpractice insurance coverage, a fact of which the hospital is aware.

Further discovery has revealed that the nurse-midwife had observed that Dr. Jones' acts were questionable, but she had not intervened because she knew of his excellent reputation. She knew that doctors were resentful of the independence of nurse-midwives at the Center, and she believed she could "compensate" for his mistakes during the delivery. By the time she realized the extent of Dr. Jones' intoxication and took over the delivery, it was too late.

In exploring the relationship between the Columbia Hospital and the Hastings Birthing Center, you find that they have a complicated connection. The hospital found that it had needed to increase its patient census. To do this and to better serve the community, it has joined in the establishment of the Hastings Birthing Center. The hospital also receives a percentage of the profits of the Center.

The Center is located in a former convent one block from the hospital. The hospital owns the building and rents it to the Center. This particular birthing center, according to its promotional literature, offers "both a home-like setting for the delivery of your child and the security of the availability of back-up physicians and hospital care." The Center is separately incorporated and has its own Board of Directors. It is totally self-governing and is solely responsible for staff, provision of equipment, and policy.

The phone listing in the Yellow Pages describes the Hospital as a "cooperating hospital that will provide hospital care for mother and child if needed." Columbia has a contract with the Center requiring the Center to "establish a screening program that will exclude high-risk patients and that doctors attending patients at the Center have privileges at Columbia Hospital." The hospital allows the employees of the Center to participate in the hospital's group health and pension plans. Nurses from the hospital moonlight at the Center. When they do so, they receive a separate paycheck from the Center.

Although the Center's by-laws provide for a committee to review the qualifications of physicians who attend at the Center, it has instead relied on the hospital's review of qualifications, since the hospital has a better opportunity to review credentials and performance. It is not clear that the hospital is aware of this; while it does notify the Center of the suspension, denial or revocation of privileges, it does not provide the Center with information used in investigations.

If you decide to litigate, should you sue both the Center and the hospital as well as Dr. Jones? Describe your theories, based on the information you have discovered to date, and consider what other facts you would like to know.

D. HEALTH MAINTENANCE ORGANIZATIONS

Managed care organizations are increasingly the defendants in liability suits, facing the same theories that hospitals face. "Managed care" is a phrase often used to describe organizational groupings that attempt to control the utilization of health care services through a variety of techniques, including prepayment by subscribers for services on a contract basis, use of physicians as "gatekeepers" for hospital and specialty services, and others. See generally Chapter 7, infra, for further definitions and discussions.

Health Maintenance Organizations (HMOs) and Independent Practice Associations (IPAs) have emerged as a force in health care delivery primarily because they promise lower cost care at a time when employers and the government are worried about the escalating costs of that care. HMOs and IPAs in theory face the same vicarious and corporate liability questions as hospitals, since they provide services through physicians, whether the physicians are salaried employees or independent contractors. These issues have emerged in recent litigation.

BOYD v. ALBERT EINSTEIN MEDICAL CENTER
Superior Court of Pennsylvania, 1988.
377 Pa.Super. 609, 547 A.2d 1229.

OLSZEWSKI, JUDGE:

This is an appeal from the trial court's order granting summary judgment in favor of defendant/appellee, Health Maintenance Organization of Pennsylvania (hereinafter HMO). Appellant asserts that the trial court erred in granting the motion for summary judgment when there existed a question of material fact as to whether participating physicians are the ostensible agents of HMO. For the reasons stated below, we reverse the grant of summary judgment.

The facts, as averred by the parties in their pleadings and elicited through deposition testimony, reveal that at the time of her death, decedent and her husband were participants in the HMO. HMO is a medical insurance provider that offers an alternative to the traditional Blue Cross/Blue Shield insurance plan.[1] Decedent's husband became eligible for participation in a group plan provided by HMO through his

---

1. "A Health Maintenance Organization is an organized system of health care which provides or arranges for a comprehensive array of basic and supplemental health care services. These services are provided on a prepaid basis to voluntarily enrolled members living within a prescribed geographic area. Responsibility for the delivery, quality and payment of health care falls to the managing organization—the HMO." Physicians Office Coordinator Training Manual citing *HMOs An Alternative to Today's Health Care System.* A Towers, Perrin, Forster, and Crosby Background Study, December 1975.

employer. Upon electing to participate in this plan, decedent and her husband were provided with a directory and benefits brochure which listed the participating physicians. Restricted to selecting a physician from this list, decedent chose Doctor David Rosenthal and Doctor Perry Dornstein as her primary care physicians.

In June of 1982, decedent contacted Doctor David Rosenthal regarding a lump in her breast. Doctor Rosenthal ordered a mammogram to be performed which revealed a suspicious area in the breast. Doctor Rosenthal recommended that decedent undergo a biopsy and referred decedent to Doctor Erwin Cohen for that purpose. Doctor Cohen, a surgeon, is also a participating HMO physician. The referral to a specialist in this case was made in accordance with the terms and conditions of HMO's subscription agreement.[2]

On July 6, 1982, Doctor Cohen performed a biopsy of decedent's breast tissue at Albert Einstein Medical Center. During the procedure, Doctor Cohen perforated decedent's chest wall with the biopsy needle, causing decedent to sustain a left hemothorax. Decedent was hospitalized for treatment of the hemothorax at Albert Einstein Hospital for two days.

In the weeks following this incident decedent complained to her primary care physicians, Doctor David Rosenthal and Doctor Perry Dornstein, of pain in her chest wall, belching, hiccoughs, and fatigue. On August 19, 1982, decedent awoke with pain in the middle of her chest. Decedent's husband contacted her primary care physicians, Doctors Rosenthal and Dornstein, and was advised to take decedent to Albert Einstein hospital where she would be examined by Doctor Rosenthal. Upon arrival at Albert Einstein emergency room, decedent related symptoms of chest wall pain, vomiting, stomach and back discomfort to Doctor Rosenthal. Doctor Rosenthal commenced an examination of decedent, diagnosed Tietz's [sic] syndrome,[3] and arranged for tests to be performed at his office where decedent underwent x-rays, EKG, and cardiac ioenzyme tests.[4] Decedent was then sent home and told to rest.[5]

---

2. Doctor Rosenthal admitted in his deposition that HMO limited specifically the doctors to whom decedent could have been referred. Deposition, p. 70.

3. Tietze's Syndrome is an inflammatory condition affecting the costochondral cartilage. It occurs more commonly in females, generally in the 30 to 50 age range. Deposition of Doctor Rosenthal, p. 48.

4. HMO avers that decedent was returned to the doctor's office for testing because it was more comfortable and convenient for her. Appellant, however, asserts that the tests were performed in the doctor's office, rather than the hospital, in accordance with the requirements of HMO

whose primary interest was in keeping the medical fees within the corporation.

5. Appellant contends that Doctor Rosenthal acted negligently in ordering the tests to be performed in his office when decedent exhibited symptoms of cardiac distress. The safer practice, avers appellant, would have been to perform the tests at the hospital where the results would have been more quickly available. Appellant further contends that, despite Doctor Rosenthal's diagnosis of Tietze's Syndrome, the nature of the tests he ordered indicates that he was concerned about the possibility of a heart attack.

During the course of that afternoon, decedent continued to experience chest pain, vomiting and belching. Decedent related the persistence and worsening of these symptoms by telephone to Doctors Rosenthal and Dornstein, who prescribed, without further examination, Talwin, a pain medication. At 5:30 that afternoon decedent was discovered dead in her bathroom by her husband, having expired as a result of a myocardial infarction.

Appellant's complaint and new matter aver that HMO advertised that its physicians and medical care providers were competent, and that they had been evaluated for periods of up to six months prior to being selected to participate in the HMO program as a medical provider. The complaint further avers that decedent and appellant relied on these representations in choosing their primary care physicians. The complaint then avers that HMO was negligent in failing to "qualify or oversee its physicians and hospital who acted as its agents, servants, or employees in providing medical care to the decedent nor did HMO of Pa. require its physicians, surgeons and hospitals to provide adequate evidence of skill, training and competence in medicine and it thereby failed to furnish the decedent with competent, qualified medical care as warranted." Paragraph 39, plaintiff's amended complaint. Finally, appellant's new matter avers that HMO furnished to its subscribers documents which identify HMO as the care provider and state that HMO guarantees the quality of care. Plaintiff's new matter, paragraph 18.

Appellant's theory of recovery before the trial court was primarily one of vicarious liability under the ostensible agency theory. [ ] In granting defendant HMO's motion for summary judgment, the trial court found that plaintiff/appellant had failed to establish either of the two factors on which the theory of ostensible agency, as applied to hospitals in *Capan,* is based. On appeal, appellant contends that the evidence indicates that there exists a question of fact regarding whether HMO may be held liable under this theory.

* * *

* * * In adopting the theory of ostensible agency, [based on the Restatement (Second) of Torts, § 429 (1968)] we noted that several jurisdictions had applied the concept to cases involving hospital liability for the negligence of independent contractor physicians. [ ] We also noted two factors which contributed to the conclusion by other courts that, although a physician holds independent contractor status with respect to the hospital, he may nevertheless be an agent of the hospital with respect to the patient. First, there is a likelihood that patients will look to the institution rather than the individual physician for care due to the changing role of the hospital in today's society. Second, "where the hospital 'holds out' the physician as its employee[,]" a justifiable finding is that there is an ostensible agency relationship between the hospital and the physician. [ ] We recognized that a holding out occurs "when the hospital acts or omits to act in some way

which leads the patient to a *reasonable* belief he is being treated by the hospital or one of its employees." *Capan, [supra,]* at 370, 430 A.2d at 649. (Citation omitted) (Emphasis in original).

[ ]

We must, therefore, consider appellant's claim in light of Section 429 and decide whether there is an issue of material fact as to participating physicians being the ostensible agents of HMO. In order to make these determinations, we will discuss, initially, the arrangement between HMO and participating doctors and their relationship with HMO members.

The record reflects that, through his employer, appellant became eligible for and ultimately chose to participate in a group plan provided by the Health Maintenance Organization of Pennsylvania (hereinafter HMO).[6] As part of its services, HMO provided its members with a brochure explaining, in general outline form only, the main features of the program of benefits. Appellant's brief, appendix E. The brochure also provided a directory of participating primary physicians and declared that the complete terms and conditions of the plan were set forth in the group master contract. *Id.*

The group master contract provides that HMO "operates a comprehensive prepaid program of health care which provides health care services and benefits to Members in order to protect and promote their health, and preserve and enhance patient dignity." Group master contract, Form HMOPA/GM-6 (5/83) of record [hereinafter group master contract].[7] HMO was incorporated in 1975 under the laws of Pennsylvania and converted from a nonprofit to a for-profit corporation in 1981. Training manual of record at 1. HMO is based on the individual practice association model (hereinafter IPA), which means that HMO is comprised of participating primary physicians who are engaged in part in private practice in the HMO service area. *Id.* Under the plan, IPA contracts with HMO to provide medical services to HMO members. *Id.* at 1–2. IPA selects its primary and specialist physicians and enters into an agreement with them obligating the physician to perform health services for the subscribers of HMO. Primary physician agreement of record at 1.

---

6. In a document entitled "Why offer HMO–PA?", Appellee's brief at 55b, HMO reasoned to employers that HMO "is a total care program which not only insures its subscribers, but provides medical care, guarantees the quality of the care and controls the costs of health care services." The document also claimed that "HMO–PA is more than just another health insurance plan. HMO–PA is an entire health care system. HMO–PA provides the physicians, hospitals and other health professionals needed to maintain good health. HMO–PA assures complete security, when illness or injury arises." Appellee's brief at 58b. Finally, the document provided that HMO–PA "[a]ssumes responsibility for quality and accessibility." Appellee's brief at 61b.

7. The introduction to the group master contract also provides that "HMOPA operates on a direct service rather than indemnity basis. The interpretation of the Contract shall be guided by the direct service nature of HMOPA's prepaid program." Group master contract at 1.

"A physician applying for membership in the IPA of the HMO–PA should expect a four to six months review process prior to admission to the organization." Document entitled Membership Process of the IPA of record at 1. When an interested physician calls the IPA, the Provider relations representative reviews the physician's credentials and the reasons for his interest in HMO. The physician then subsequently receives an application packet that requests the applicant's *curriculum vitae,* four letters of recommendation, copies of the state license, and evidence of malpractice insurance. Soon thereafter, the IPA coordinator visits the applicant's practice in order to: (1) observe how the office is run, how the office personnel treat patients, and the ability of the office to absorb a number of new patients; (2) inspect the actual physical plant to ensure that appropriate procedures, space, and necessary medical equipment are available; (3) explain the payment system, the incentive program, and the rights and responsibilities of an IPA physician; and (4) set up a medical director's interview. *Id.* at 1–2.

After interviewing the applicant,[8] the medical director makes a recommendation that is forwarded to the membership committee, which thoroughly discusses and determines whether the applicant has met all the criteria for membership. The criteria include: Twenty-four-hour-a-day coverage provided with another IPA member for office and hospital patients, with any exclusions being approved by the executive committee; prior routine hospitalization of patients on his own service at a participating HMO hospital; specific routinely performed procedures including minor surgery and office gynecology; scheduling of appointments at a rate of no more than five patients per hour per doctor; and office records that are legible, reproducible, and pertinent. *Id.* at 3–4.

The membership committee makes a recommendation to the executive committee, which makes the final decision regarding the applicant. Those accepted into the IPA are called by an IPA coordinator, who schedules an office orientation.

The primary physician's role is defined as the "gatekeeper into the health care delivery system." Document entitled Role of the Primary Physician of record at 1. "An HMO member must consult with his primary physician before going to a specialist and/or the hospital." *Id;* Group master contract at II B. If the primary physician deems it necessary, he arranges a consultation with an HMO participating specialist, which constitutes a second opinion. Role of the Primary Physician at 1. "Basically, with the primary physicians 'screening' the members' illnesses, excessive hospitalization and improper use of specialists can be reduced." *Id.*

Member-patients use a physician directory and choose a conveniently located office of a participating primary physician. HMO

---

8. During the interview, the medical director reviews applicant's understanding of the HMO and IPA, the physician's referral pattern, how he would handle various medical problems, and his medical charts.

members will only receive reimbursement from non-participating providers when the condition requiring treatment was of an immediate nature. Determinations of immediacy are made by the HMO quality assurance committee. In any event, persons desiring emergency non-provider benefits must notify HMO or their primary physician of the emergency within forty-eight hours and must give written proof of the occurrence within ninety days after service is rendered. Group master contract at 13. Reimbursement for emergency care by a non-participating provider is limited to expenses incurred prior to the time the member's condition, "in the opinion of HMOPA, reasonably permitted him or her to travel or be transported to the nearest HMOPA Participating Provider, or to receive follow-up care from a Participating Provider, upon referral by the Member's Participating Primary Physician." *Id.* at 14.

Primary physicians are paid through a mechanism termed "capitation." Capitation is an actuarially determined amount prepaid by HMO to the primary physician for each patient who has chosen his office. Revised attachment AA to primary physician agreement. The dollar amount is based upon a pre-determined rate per age group. The primary physicians are paid 80% of the capitation amount and the remaining 20% is pooled by IPA and goes back into a pooled risk-sharing fund as a reserve against specialty referral costs and hospital stays. Each primary care office has its own specialist fund and hospital fund established by allocating a pre-determined amount each month for each member who has chosen that primary care office. The surplus from the specialist fund is returned to the primary care office. The hospital fund, however, is governed by a hospital risk/incentive-sharing scheme which anticipates a number of inpatient days per members per year. If the actual hospital utilization is less than anticipated, the HMO and IPA each receive 50% of the savings. IPA must place the savings in the Special IPA risk-sharing account and must use the funds to offset losses resulting from unanticipated physician costs. Attachment B to primary physician agreement. If utilization is greater than anticipated, IPA is responsible for 50% of the loss up to the amount of uncommitted funds in the Special IPA risk sharing account. *Id.*

Appellant asserts that he has raised a question of material fact as to whether the treating physicians were the ostensible agents of HMO. As delineated *supra,* Pennsylvania courts have determined that the two factors relevant to a finding of ostensible agency are: (1) whether the patient looks to the institution, rather than the individual physician for care, and (2) whether the HMO "holds out" the physician as its employee. * * *

* * *

HMO asserts that because the theory of ostensible agency has been applied in Pennsylvania only to the relationship between hospitals and independent contractor physicians, the theory is not appropriate in the instant situation. We emphasize, however, that when this Court introduced the concept of ostensible agency to this Commonwealth in *Capan,* *supra,* we based that decision in large part upon "the changing role of the hospital in society [which] creates a likelihood that patients will look to the institution" for care. *Id.* 287 Pa.Super. at 368, 430 A.2d at 649. Because the role of health care providers has changed in recent years, the *Capan* rationale for applying the theory of ostensible agency to hospitals is certainly applicable in the instant situation.

Therefore, while *Capan* is distinguishable on its facts, it is instructive in our resolution of the instant matter. Moreover, we are guided not so much by facts of *Capan* and its progeny as their delineation of the theory of ostensible agency as contained in Restatement (Second) of Torts and their justification for implementing the theory.

We find that the facts indicate an issue of material fact as to whether the participating physicians were the ostensible agents of HMO. HMO covenanted that it would "[provide] health care services and benefits to Members in order to protect and promote their health. * * *" Group master contract at 1. "HMOPA operates on a direct service rather than an indemnity basis." *Id.* Appellant paid his doctor's fee to HMO, not to the physician of his choice. Then, appellant selected his primary care physicians from the list provided by HMO. Regardless of who recommended appellant's decedent to choose her primary care physician, the fact remains that HMO provides a limited list from which a member must choose a primary physician. Moreover, those primary physicians are screened by HMO and must comply with a list of regulations in order to honor their contract with HMO. *See* discussion and footnote 8, *supra.*

Further, as mandated by HMO, appellant's decedent could not see a specialist without the primary physician's referral. As HMO declares, the primary physician is the "gatekeeper into the health care delivery system." Document entitled Role of the Primary Physician of record at 1. "An HMO member must consult with his primary physician before going to a specialist and/or the hospital." *Id.* Moreover, appellant's decedent had no choice as to which specialist to see. In our opinion, because appellant's decedent was required to follow the mandates of HMO and did not directly seek the attention of the specialist, there is an inference that appellant looked to the institution for care and not solely to the physicians; conversely, that appellant's decedent submitted herself to the care of the participating physicians in response to an invitation from HMO. *See* comment (a), Restatement (Second) Agency § 267.

Summary judgment should be granted only where there is not the slightest doubt as to the absence of a triable issue of fact. [ ] Based on the foregoing, we find that there is an issue of material fact as to whether the participating physicians were the ostensible agents of HMO. We conclude, therefore, that the trial court erred when it granted HMO's motion for summary judgment on the ground that the participating physicians were not the ostensible agents of HMO.

The order granting summary judgment is reversed and the case remanded for proceedings consistent with this opinion. Jurisdiction is relinquished.

Notes and Questions

1. Does a subscriber to an IPA-style managed care organization look to it for care rather than solely to the individual physicians? In an IPA, there is no central office, staffed by salaried physicians; the subscriber instead goes to the individual offices of the primary care physicians or the specialists. What is the predicate for the court's willingness to extend ostensible agency doctrine to this arrangement?

2. HMOs generally carry "vicarious liability" coverage, to cover the managed care plan for acts committed by contracting providers. Such coverage can cost over $100,000 per year. A verdict for $10 million against FHP International Corporation, a California owner of six HMOs, was rendered by a Los Angeles jury in July of 1990. HMO exposure to malpractice suits, whether they are staff plan or IPA model HMOs, is undoubtedly on the increase. See FHP Loses Negligence Suit, Hikes Malpractice Fund, HealthWeek 6 (August 13, 1990).

3. Another potential shield against HMO liability is the "corporate practice of medicine" doctrine, which some states still follow. In Sloan v. The Metropolitan Health Council of Indianapolis, Inc., 516 N.E.2d 1104 (Ind.App. 1 Dist.1987), the Sloans sued Metro, a Health Maintenance Organization, alleging a negligent failure to diagnose. Metro claimed that its physicians were independent in their practice of medicine, and that Metro did not control their judgment in diagnosis or treatment decisions. It therefore invoked the "corporate practice of medicine" doctrine, which made it unlawful for a corporation to practice medicine. The defendant argued that physician may not accept directions in diagnosing and treating ailments from a corporation, and is therefore an independent contractor.

The court rejected this defense, finding it to be a "non sequitur to conclude that because a hospital cannot practice medicine or psychiatry, it cannot be liable for the actions of its employed agents and servants who may be so licensed." An HMO likewise should not be insulated from liability. The court noted that Metro's staff physicians were under the control of its medical director, a physician, and "[t]he circumstances establish an employment relationship where the employee performed acts within the scope of his employment". Id. at 1109.

4. The effect of legislative restrictions on the corporate practice of medicine turns upon the language of a particular state's statutes. It may also depend on the structure of the HMO. In Williams v. Good Health Plus, Inc., 743 S.W.2d 373 (Tex.App.—San Antonio 1987), the court considered whether HealthAmerica, a health maintenance organization, provided medical treatment to Mrs. Williams or held itself out as a provider of medical treatment. Mrs. Williams had been treated in her right thumb nail, which became infected and had to be surgically removed. The court examined the various Texas statutes that defined the practice of medicine, including the Texas Health Maintenance Organization Act. The HMO Act specifically stated that the HMO has powers including "the furnishing of or

arranging for medical care services only through physicians or groups of physicians who have independent contracts with the health maintenance organizations.   * * * "

HealthAmerican therefore argued that it could not be liable as a matter of law, first because "it was incapable of practicing medicine in the state of Texas", and second because its physicians were independent contractors."   (376) The HMO was not a staff plan, as in *Sloan*, but rather an Independent Practice Association, as in *Boyd*, with groups of physicians contracting with the HMO. The court held:

> In the instant case, HealthAmerica established as a matter of law that it could not practice medicine, so as to be subjected to liability for the alleged failure to diagnose and properly treat the thumbnail staph infection and drug-induced lupus erythematosus condition or for failure to order the usual and customary lab work for a person taking the medications prescribed for Mrs. Williams. Any act or omission alleged to constitute negligence against HealthAmerica necessarily involves the practice of medicine, which HealthAmerica is barred from doing by statute. * * * HealthAmerica exercises no right of direction or control over either the physicians involved in the treatment of Mrs. Williams, or over Southwest Medical Group. * * * Id. at 378.

Could Mrs. Williams have amended her pleadings to make out a cause of action on some theory against HealthAmerica? Or did the "corporate practice of medicine" rule simply bar her from any chance of success? The court noted that Mrs. Williams failed to allege any basis for a "holding out" theory, suggesting that they might have viewed the case differently with such evidence.

5. Some states have explicitly immunized health services corporations, including HMOs, against tort liability. Missouri's statute, RSMo 1978, Section 354.125, is illustrative:

> A health services corporation shall not be liable for injuries resulting from neglect, misfeasance, malfeasance or malpractice on the part of any person, organization, agency or corporation rendering health services to the health services corporation's members and beneficiaries.

Health maintenance organizations have been held to be Health Services Corporations under this section, which applies to Blue Cross type not-for-profit corporations that either provided health care services or made reimbursement for services provided by others. See Harrell v. Total Health Care, Inc., 781 S.W.2d 58, 61 (Mo.1989), where the Supreme Court of Missouri upheld the constitutionality of this section. The court observed:

> The purpose of the statutes authorizing this kind of corporation is to sanction one method of combatting the cost of health care. Just as the ancient Chinese are reputed to have paid their doctors while they remained well, a person may elect to pay fixed dues in advance so that medical services may be available without additional cost when they are needed.

>   * * *

> * * * The legislature well might have considered that one in the position of this plaintiff has an adequate remedy against the persons

actually guilty of malpractice, who are licensed physicians, and does not heed an additional source of recompense from a not-for-profit corporation. * * *

* * *

* * * People are concerned both about the cost and the unpredictability of medical expenses. A plan such as Total offered would allow a person to fix the cost of physicians' services. The legislature might easily perceive that the costs of a plan would be substantially increased if the Health Services Organization were to be subject to claims originating in malpractice, that the cost of these claims would necessarily be shared by other plan members, and that malpractice liability might threaten the solvency of the plan. * * *

Is this rebirth of immunity motivated by the same legislative concerns that supported charitable immunity doctrine in its heyday, that is, protecting the solvency of a particular type of health care enterprise? Are the justifications convincing?

Chapter 3

THE RELATIONSHIP OF PROVIDER AND PATIENT

INTRODUCTION

Health care today is most often delivered within institutions, whether hospitals, ambulatory care clinics, or HMO offices, but it is still the individual physician who sees the patient, diagnoses the problem, and prescribes the treatment. Professional liability, discussed in Chapter 2, supra, focuses upon a breach of duty of care owed by the physician to a particular patient. The threshold question is whether the doctor had a relationship with the patient sufficient to create a duty of care.

A physician-patient relationship is a prerequisite to a professional malpractice suit against a doctor. When for example a doctor employed by an insurance company examines an individual for the purpose of qualifying him for insurance coverage, most courts considering the issue have held that a doctor owes no duty to the individual to treat or to disclose problems discovered during the examination. See Ervin v. American Guardian Life Assur., 376 Pa.Super. 132, 545 A.2d 354 (1988) (no duty owed by doctor employed by an insurance company to the plaintiff, where doctor examined the plaintiff for purposes of insurance and failed to discover or disclose his cardiac abnormalities to him; plaintiff died a month after the examination from his heart condition); accord, Keene v. Wiggins, 69 Cal.App.3d 308, 138 Cal.Rptr. 3 (1977). Workplace examinations of employees may however give rise to a physician-patient relationship. In Green v. Walker, 910 F.2d 291 (5th Cir.1990), the U.S. Court of Appeals for the Fifth Circuit, interpreting Louisiana law in a diversity action, held that the physician-patient relationship should be expanded to include employees examined by a company physician for employment purposes. The court held that "[t]his relationship imposes upon the examining physician a duty to conduct the requested tests and diagnose the results thereof, exercising the level of care consistent with the doctor's professional training and expertise, and to take reasonable steps to make information available timely to the examinee of any findings that pose an imminent danger to the examinee's physical or mental well-being."

283

I. THE CONTRACT BETWEEN PATIENT AND PHYSICIAN

A. EXPRESS AND IMPLIED CONTRACT

The physician-patient relationship can be considered initially as a contractual one. Physicians in private practice may contract for their services as they see fit, and retain substantial control over the extent of their contact with patients. Physicians may limit their specialty, their scope of practice, their geographic area, and the hours and conditions under which they will see patients. They have no obligation to offer services that a patient may require that are outside the physician's competence and training; or services outside the scope of the original physician-patient agreement, where the physician has limited the contract to a type of procedure, to an office visit, or to consultation only. They may transfer responsibility by referring patients to other specialists. They may refuse to enter into a contract with a patient, or to treat patients, even under emergency conditions. Hiser v. Randolph, 126 Ariz. 608, 617 P.2d 774, 776 (1980).

Physicians may also expressly contract with a patient for a specific result. Stewart v. Rudner, 349 Mich. 459, 84 N.W.2d 816, 822–23 (1957) (couple contracted with physician to have wife's child delivered by Caesarian section, as she had had two stillbirths and was worried about normal vaginal delivery; the court held that "a doctor and his patient * * * have the same general liberty to contract with respect to their relationship as other parties entering into consensual relationship with one another, and a breach thereof will give rise to a cause of action."). Courts will sometimes allow parol evidence to fill in the terms of these contracts, where the patient has signed other consent forms. Murray v. Univ. of Penn. Hospital, 340 Pa.Super. 401, 490 A.2d 839 (1985) (court allowed parol evidence to show the existence of an oral agreement to guarantee the prevention of future pregnancies by a tubal ligation).

Once the physician-patient relationship has been created, however, physicians are subject to an obligation of "continuing attention." Ricks v. Budge, 91 Utah 307, 64 P.2d 208 (1937). Termination of the physician-patient relationship, once created, is subject in some jurisdictions to a "continuous treatment" rule to determine when the statute of limitations is tolled. Treatment obligations cease if the physician can do nothing more for the patient, or ceases to attend the patient. See Jewson v. Mayo Clinic, 691 F.2d 405 (8th Cir.1982). Accord, Wells v. Billars, 391 N.W.2d 668 (S.D.1986).

An express written contract is rarely drafted for specific physician-patient interactions. An implied contract is usually the basis of the relationship between a physician and a patient. A physician who talks with a patient by telephone may be held to have an implied contractual obligation to that patient. Bienz v. Central Suffolk Hospital, 557 N.Y.S.2d 139 (2d Dept., 1990); O'Neill v. Montefiore Hospital, 11 A.D.2d

132, 202 N.Y.S.2d 436 (1960). Likewise, a physician, such as a pathologist, who renders services to a patient but has not contracted with him, is nonetheless bound by certain implied contractual obligations.

When a patient goes to a doctor's office with a particular problem, he is offering to enter into a contract with the physician. When the physician examines the patient, she accepts the offer and an implied contract is created. The physician is free to reject the offer and send the patient away, relieving herself of any duty to that patient. See, e.g., Childs v. Weis, 440 S.W.2d 104 (Tex.Civ.App.1969). Some courts state as a starting principle that " * * * [a]s a practical matter, health professionals cannot be required to obtain express consent before each touch or test they perform on a patient. Consent may be express or implied; implied consent may be inferred from the patient's action or seeking treatment or some other act manifesting a willingness to submit to a particular course of treatment * * * ." Jones v. Malloy, 226 Neb. 559, 412 N.W.2d 837, 841 (1987). See Tisdale v. Pruitt, infra, for judicial difficulties with contextual consent.

Physicians who practice in institutions must provide health care within the limits of the health plan coverage or their employment contracts with the institution. In this case, the contact between the physician and the patient is preceded by an express contract spelling out the details of the relationship. Physicians who are members of a health maintenance organization have a duty to treat plan members, as part of their contractual obligation to the HMO. In these situations, the express contract is between the physician and the HMO, and the subscriber and the HMO, with an implied contract between the subscriber and the treating physician. See generally Rodgers, Boyd & Wilson, The HMO Contract and Quality of Care, 78 Iowa Med. 466 (1988); Comment, Contractual Theories of Recovery in the HMO Provider–Subscriber Relationship: Prospective Litigation for Breach of Contract, 36 Buffalo L.Rev. 119 (1987). Members of a hospital staff may also be expressly bound to treat patients, particularly in the emergency room when they are on call. Hiser, supra. They have waived their rights to refuse to treat particular patients, as a result of their contract obligations to the hospital. Certain contractual obligations therefore flow from the employment setting, binding physicians to treat individual subscribers. And the traditional scope of the contractual relationship may also include obligations, such as completing a variety of benefit forms for a patient. If these forms are not properly and timely completed, and a patient suffers an economic detriment, courts have held that a suit for breach of contract will lie. Chew v. Meyer, M.D., P.A., 72 Md.App. 132, 527 A.2d 828 (1987).

The apparent voluntariness of the physician-patient relationship, and its reciprocity, i.e., a fee for a service, or consideration, makes the relationship look like a traditional contract. In other ways, however, the analogy to a contract is weak. First, the terms of the contract are largely fixed in advance of any bargaining, by standard or customary practices that the physician must follow at the risk of liability for malpractice. The exact nature of the work to be done by the physician is usually left vaguely defined at best. The relationship seems closer to quasi-contract, where we impute to both the physician and the patient standard intentions and reasonable expectations. See Goodin, Protecting the Vulnerable 63, 64–65 (1985).

Second, professional ethics impose fiduciary obligations on physicians in a variety of ways, as the cases in Section II reveal. Courts often look outside the parameters of contract law analysis in judging the obligations of a physician to treat a patient. The courts stress that the physician's obligation to his patient, while having its origins in contract, is governed also by fiduciary obligations and other public considerations "inseparable from the nature and exercise of his calling * * * ." Norton v. Hamilton, 92 Ga.App. 727, 89 S.E.2d 809, 812 (1955) (doctor withdrew from case at time when wife was in premature labor; while husband searched for a substitute, wife delivered child). See Chatman v. Millis, 257 Ark. 451, 453 517 S.W.2d 504, 505 (1975) (malpractice action requires a doctor-patient relationship, a duty owed from doctor to patients, although "[w]e do not flatly state that a cause for malpractice must be predicated upon a contractual agreement between a doctor * * * and patient * * * .").

Third, professionals are constrained in their ability to withdraw from their contracts by judicial caselaw defining patient abandonment. A doctor who withdraws from the physician-patient relationship before a cure is achieved or the patient is transferred to the care of another may be liable for abandonment. To escape liability, the physician must give the patient time to find alternative care. See Norton v. Hamilton, 92 Ga.App. 727, 89 S.E.2d 809 (1955). Implied abandonment is a negligence-based theory judged by the overall conduct of the physician. See Meiselman v. Crown Heights Hosp., 285 N.Y. 389, 34 N.E.2d 367 (1941); Ascher v. Gutierrez, 533 F.2d 1235 (D.C.Cir.1976). See Comment, The Action of Abandonment in Medical Malpractice Litigation, 36 Tul.L.Rev. 834 (1962).

B. SPECIFIC PROMISES AND WARRANTIES OF CURE

A contract claim may have several advantages for the plaintiff. The statute of limitations is typically longer than for a tort action. The plaintiff need not establish the medical standard of care and thus may not need to present expert testimony. A contract claim may be viable even when the doctor has made the proper risk disclosure, satisfying the requirements of the tort doctrine of informed consent. Finally, a contract claim offers a remedy to the plaintiff who underwent the procedure because of the enticements of the physician.

The contract between physician and patient can be breached in a variety of ways. The physician may promise to use a certain procedure and then use an alternative procedure. See Stewart v. Rudner, 349 Mich. 459, 84 N.W.2d 816 (1957) (breached promise by physician to perform Caesarean section); Moser v. Stallings, 387 N.W.2d 599 (Iowa 1986) (plastic surgeon did not perform chin implant as part of cosmetic surgery on plaintiff, after telling patient that implant would be a part of the procedure; court in dicta suggested that patient might have had a contract claim). Contra, see Labarre v. Duke University, 99 N.C.App. 563, 393 S.E.2d 321 (1990), where the pregnant plaintiff had been assured that if, during delivery she needed an epidural anesthetic, the Director of Obstetric Anesthesia or another fully-trained faculty anesthesiologist would administer it. Instead, a resident administered the anesthesia, causing the plaintiff to suffer injury. The court held that the promise was not supported by consideration and was therefore unenforceable.

A breach may also be found where the doctor promises a particular result which fails to occur. The classic case is Guilmet v. Campbell, 385 Mich. 57, 188 N.W.2d 601 (1971), where the physician treated the patient for a bleeding ulcer. The doctor had allegedly told the patient prior to the operation:

> Once you have an operation it takes care of all your troubles. You can eat as you want to, you can drink as you want to, you can go as you please. Dr. Arena and I are specialists, there is nothing to it at all—it's a very simple operation. You'll be out of work three to four weeks at most. There is no danger at all in this operation. After the operation you can throw away your pill box. 385 Mich. 57, 68, 188 N.W.2d 601, 606 (1971).

The patient suffered serious aftereffects, and the jury found for the plaintiff on a breach of contract theory.

The remedial options for a breach by a physician of a warranty of good results are discussed in Sullivan v. O'Connor, 363 Mass. 579, 296 N.E.2d 183 (1973), where the surgeon promised the plaintiff, a professional entertainer, that he would improve the appearance of her nose. He failed, and her nose ended up bulbous and asymmetrical. Justice Kaplan noted the problems with the application of a contract theory to the medical enterprise:

> It is not hard to see why the courts should be unenthusiastic or skeptical about the contract theory. Considering the uncertainties of medical science and the variations in the physical and psychological conditions of individual patients, doctors can seldom in good faith promise specific results. Therefore it is unlikely that physicians of even average integrity will in fact make such promises. Statements of opinion by the physician with some optimistic coloring are a different thing, and may indeed have therapeutic value. But patients may transform such statements into firm promises in their own minds, especially when they have been disappointed in the event, and testify in that sense to sympathetic juries. If actions for breach of promise can be readily maintained, doctors, so it is said, will be frightened into practicing "defensive medicine." On the other hand, if these actions were outlawed, leaving only the

possibility of suits for malpractice, there is fear that the public might be exposed to the enticements of charlatans, and confidence in the profession might ultimately be shaken. [ ] The law has taken the middle of the road position of allowing actions based on alleged contract, but insisting on clear proof. Instructions to the jury may well stress this requirement and point to tests of truth, such as the complexity or difficulty of an operation as bearing on the probability that a given result was promised.

The measure of damages in a breach of contract suit might be "expectancy" damages, that amount sufficient to place the plaintiff in the position he would be in if the contract had been performed, or "restitution" damages, an amount equivalent to the benefit conferred by the plaintiff upon the defendant. In *Sullivan,* the Massachusetts Supreme Judicial Court considered an intermediate position, a "reliance" basis, a more lenient standard for breach of an agreement "to effect a cure, attain a stated result, or employ a given medical method: * * * the substance is that the plaintiff is to recover any expenditures made by him and for other detriment * * * following proximately and foreseeably upon the defendant's failure to carry out his promise." The Court allowed pain and suffering as an item of damages, as a foreseeable consequence of a surgical operation which fails.

See also Stewart v. Rudner, supra, where the court noted that ordinarily damages are not recoverable for mental anguish or disappointment. "Yet not all contracts are purely commercial in their nature. Some involve rights we cherish, dignities we respect, emotions recognized by all as both sacred and personal. In such cases the award of damages for mental distress and suffering is a commonplace, even in actions ex contractu."

Courts will sometimes allow contract claims, but then define the "contract" restrictively. Courts typically distinguish "therapeutic assurances" from express warranties to effect a cure. See Rogala v. Silva, 16 Ill.App.3d 63, 305 N.E.2d 571 (1973). In Ferlito v. Cecola, 419 So.2d 102 (La.App.1982), the court held that a dentist's statement that crown work would make the plaintiff's teeth "pretty" did not constitute a guarantee. Other courts have imposed evidentiary burdens, requiring proof by clear and convincing evidence. See Burns v. Wannamaker, 281 S.C. 352, 315 S.E.2d 179 (1984). Even if the burden of proof is not elevated from the preponderance test to clear and convincing evidence, the jury will be instructed that they must find that the physician "clearly and unmistakably [gave] a positive assurance [that he or she would] produce or * * * avoid a particular result * * * ." Scarzella v. Saxon, 436 A.2d 358 (D.C.App.1981). In some states, the Statute of Frauds specifically requires that for agreements guaranteeing therapeutic results to be enforceable, they must be in writing and signed. See, e.g., West's Ann.Ind.Code 16–915–1–4. See also Powers v. Peoples Community Hospital Authority, 183 Mich.App. 550, 455 N.W.2d 371 (1990).

What effect might such a requirement have?

For further reading, see Note, Express Contracts to Cure: The Nature of Contractual Malpractice, 50 Ind.L.J. 361 (1975); Comment, Physicians and Surgeons—Sullivan v. O'Connor: A Liberal View of the Contractual Liability of Physicians and Surgeons, 54 N.C.L.Rev. 885 (1976).

C. EXCULPATORY CLAUSES

TUNKL v. REGENTS OF UNIV. OF CALIFORNIA

Supreme Court of California, 1963.
60 Cal.2d 92, 82 Cal.Rptr. 33, 383 P.2d 441.

TOBRINER, JUSTICE.

This case concerns the validity of a release from liability for future negligence imposed as a condition for admission to a charitable research hospital. For the reasons we hereinafter specify, we have concluded that an agreement between a hospital and an entering patient affects the public interest and that, in consequence, the exculpatory provision included within it must be invalid under Civil Code section 1668.

Hugo Tunkl brought this action to recover damages for personal injuries alleged to have resulted from the negligence of two physicians in the employ of the University of California Los Angeles Medical Center, a hospital operated and maintained by the Regents of the University of California as a nonprofit charitable institution. Mr. Tunkl died after suit was brought, and his surviving wife, as executrix, was substituted as plaintiff.

The University of California at Los Angeles Medical Center admitted Tunkl as a patient on June 11, 1956. The Regents maintain the hospital for the primary purpose of aiding and developing a program of research and education in the field of medicine; patients are selected and admitted if the study and treatment of their condition would tend to achieve these purposes. Upon his entry to the hospital, Tunkl signed a document setting forth certain "Conditions of Admission." The crucial condition number six reads as follows: "RELEASE: The hospital is a nonprofit, charitable institution. In consideration of the hospital and allied services to be rendered and the rates charged therefor, the patient or his legal representative agrees to and hereby releases The Regents of the University of California, and the hospital from any and all liability for the negligent or wrongful acts or omissions of its employees, if the hospital has used due care in selecting its employees."

Plaintiff stipulated that the hospital had selected its employees with due care. The trial court ordered that the issue of the validity of the exculpatory clause be first submitted to the jury and that, if the jury found that the provision did not bind plaintiff, a second jury try the issue of alleged malpractice. When, on the preliminary issue, the jury returned a verdict sustaining the validity of the executed release, the court entered judgment in favor of the Regents.[1] Plaintiff appeals from the judgment.

We shall first set out the basis for our prime ruling that the exculpatory provision of the hospital's contract fell under the proscription of Civil Code section 1668; we then dispose of two answering arguments of defendant.

We begin with the dictate of the relevant Civil Code section 1668. The section states: "All contracts which have for their object, directly or indirectly, to exempt anyone from responsibility for his own fraud, or willful injury to the person or property of another, or violation of law, whether willful or negligent, are against the policy of the law."

* * *

In one respect, as we have said, the decisions are uniform. The cases have consistently held that the exculpatory provision may stand only if it does not involve "the public interest."

* * *

If, then, the exculpatory clause which affects the public interest cannot stand, we must ascertain those factors or characteristics which constitute the public interest. * * *

* * * It concerns a business of a type generally thought suitable for public regulation. The party seeking exculpation is engaged in performing a service of great importance to the public, which is often a matter of practical necessity for some members of the public. The party holds himself out as willing to perform this service for any member of the public who seeks it, or at least for any member coming within certain established standards. As a result of the essential nature of the service, in the economic setting of the transaction, the party invoking exculpation possesses a decisive advantage of bargaining strength against any member of the public who seeks his services. In exercising a superior bargaining power the party confronts the public with a standardized adhesion contract of exculpation, and makes no provision whereby a purchaser may pay additional reasonable fees and obtain protection against negligence. Finally, as a result of the transaction, the person or property of the purchaser is placed under the control of the seller, subject to the risk of carelessness by the seller or his agents.

* * *

1. Plaintiff at the time of signing the release was in great pain, under sedation, and probably unable to read. At trial plaintiff contended that the release was invalid, asserting that a release does not bind the releasor if at the time of its execution he suffered from so weak a mental condition that he was unable to compre- hend the effect of his act. [ ] The jury, however, found against plaintiff on this issue. Since the verdict of the jury established that plaintiff either knew or should have known the significance of the release, this appeal raises the sole question of whether the release can stand as a matter of law.

In the light of the decisions, we think that the hospital-patient contract clearly falls within the category of agreements affecting the public interest. To meet that test, the agreement need only fulfill some of the characteristics above outlined; here, the relationship fulfills all of them. Thus the contract of exculpation involves an institution suitable for, and a subject of, public regulation. [ ] That the services of the hospital to those members of the public who are in special need of the particular skill of its staff and facilities constitute a practical and crucial necessity is hardly open to question.

The hospital, likewise, holds itself out as willing to perform its services for those members of the public who qualify for its research and training facilities. While it is true that the hospital is selective as to the patients it will accept, such selectivity does not negate its public aspect or the public interest in it. The hospital is selective only in the sense that it accepts from the public at large certain types of cases which qualify for the research and training in which it specializes. But the hospital does hold itself out to the public as an institution which performs such services for those members of the public who can qualify for them.

In insisting that the patient accept the provision of waiver in the contract, the hospital certainly exercises a decisive advantage in bargaining. The would-be patient is in no position to reject the proffered agreement, to bargain with the hospital, or in lieu of agreement to find another hospital. The admission room of a hospital contains no bargaining table where, as in a private business transaction, the parties can debate the terms of their contract. As a result, we cannot but conclude that the instant agreement manifested the characteristics of the so-called adhesion contract. Finally, when the patient signed the contract, he completely placed himself in the control of the hospital; he subjected himself to the risk of its carelessness.

* * *

We turn to a consideration of the * * * arguments urged by defendant to save the exemptive clause. Defendant contends that while the public interest may possibly invalidate the exculpatory provision as to the paying patient, it certainly cannot do so as to the charitable one. * * *

* * *

In substance defendant here asks us to modify our decision in *Malloy*, which removed the charitable immunity; defendant urges that otherwise the funds of the research hospital may be deflected from the real objective of the extension of medical knowledge to the payment of claims for alleged negligence. Since a research hospital necessarily entails surgery and treatment in which fixed standards of care may not yet be evolved, defendant says the hospital should in this situation be excused from such care. But the answer lies in the fact that possible plaintiffs must *prove negligence;* the standards of care will themselves reflect the research nature of the treatment; the hospital will not become an insurer or guarantor of the patient's recovery. To exempt the hospital completely from any standard of due care is to grant it immunity by the side-door method of a contractual clause exacted of the patient. We cannot reconcile that technique with the teaching of *Malloy*.

* * *

The judgment is reversed.

Notes and Questions

1. Why shouldn't a patient be able to waive the right to sue in exchange for lower cost or free treatment? Is there something special about medical care in general, or Tunkl's situation in particular, that makes such a choice by a patient suspect? Do the court's arguments convince you as to the reasons for invalidating such attempts by health care institutions to limit their liability? Short of a complete waiver of a right to sue, how else might hospitals or doctors protect themselves? Can a patient be asked to waive the right to sue for punitive damages? Could the parties agree on liquidated damages? Could the parties agree that an action would be brought in the local state court? Could treatment be conditioned on the patient submitting any malpractice claim to an administrative body, or to arbitration? See Chapter 4, infra.

For a thoughtful analysis of *Tunkl*, and a proposal to allocate medical risks by contract, see Robinson, Rethinking the Allocation of Medical Malpractice Risks Between Patients and Providers, 49 Law & Contemp. Probs. 173 (1986).

2. Courts are generally hostile to attempts by health care providers to limit their liability by contract. The typical case involves a poor plaintiff asked to trade off his common law right to sue in exchange for low cost or free treatment. See Emory University v. Porubiansky, 248 Ga. 391, 282 S.E.2d 903 (1981) (dental clinic could not ask patients to waive right to sue for negligence; the court noted however that the clinic could enter into binding contracts with patients, asking patients for example to waive the right to insist on complete treatment.)

In Abramowitz v. New York University Dental Center, College of Dentistry, 110 A.D.2d 343, 494 N.Y.S.2d 721 (2 Dept.1985), a patient sued the dental clinic based on the negligence of a post-graduate dental student. The clinic pleaded the affirmative defense of a waiver and release. The waiver was held to be insufficient to exculpate. First, the waiver was buried in the middle of a longer "Registration Form" in an untitled, almost illegible section, and was given to the plaintiff for signature, without explanation, while he was being examined, reclining, with a dental examination light in his eyes. Second, even if the plaintiff had read the paragraph carefully, it was poorly drafted. "The word 'negligence' was never mentioned, and construing the language strictly against its drafter, it simply cannot be said to unmistakenly express an intention on the part of the plaintiff to absolve the defendant of liability for its own negligence." (494 N.Y.S.2d at 724). While complete waivers are suspect, *Abramowitz* suggests implicitly that a waiver might be effective if carefully executed and properly presented to the patient.

The problem of waivers arises in informed consent and arbitration settings. Consider the following cases.

Reaves v. Mandell, 209 N.J.Super. 465, 507 A.2d 807 (1986): plaintiff claimed to have received no information by defendant doctor as to the risks of a total abdominal hysterectomy and left salpingo-oophorectomy. The doctor testified that he could not remember the details of any conversation with the plaintiff, but that he had performed over 1000 hysterectomies, of which 50 involved a fibroid uterus of the type the plaintiff had. He always told his patients details about the procedure, alternatives, and side-effects. It was a "fixed procedure". Held: " * * * the physician's behavior was so consistent over the years, considering the uniformity of response and the adequacy of the prior instances, when confronted with a similarly presenting patient, to rise to the level of habit." [See also Federal Rule of Evidence 406].

Guertin v. Marrella, 149 Mich.App. 420, 385 N.W.2d 805 (1986): plaintiff sued defendant for malpractice, and the defendant moved to compel arbitration on the basis of a signed arbitration agreement. Plaintiff claimed that no one explained the agreement to him and that he did not receive the required informational booklet. The clerk of the hospital testified as to her usual procedures at admission, including an explanation of the agreement and provision of the booklet. Held: the burden of establishing that the agreement was executed in compliance with the Michigan statute should lie with the defendant. "Presumptions regarding the construction of contract documents, such as the presumption that a person had read what he or she has signed, should not prevail over the presumption against the waiver of a constitutional right * * * Once the defendant has established that the arbitration agreement complied with the statutory requirements, the burden would be on the plaintiff to establish the grounds to avoid the arbitration agreement." 385 N.W.2d at 806. Contra, Feinberg v. Straith Clinic, 151 Mich.App. 204, 390 N.W.2d 697 (1986) (burden on plaintiff to show that agreement was invalid; waiver is based upon "voluntariness" standard, and there is some room for constructive notice, and here the plaintiff was "careless about the admission procedure because his wife and her friend had undergone successful cosmetic surgery through the same clinic".)

The cases suggest the importance of institutional routine in proving that a patient received information affecting his rights.

3. Some physicians such as obstetricians and emergency physicians have curtailed their services in response to liability insurance concerns. Indigent patients create a special problem, since these patients create a liability risk, yet physicians cannot recover their liability insurance costs because there is no compensation for their services. State legislatures, often as part of malpractice reform packages, have responded to this "access" problem by providing immunity from tort liability for certain categories of physician services. See 16 State Health Legislation Report (May 1988). In particular, physicians or other health professionals who

provide free health care services have been granted tort immunity if they provided uncompensated care, unless the care was grossly negligent. Ariz. Rev.Stat. § 12–571; West's Fla.Stat. Ann. § 768.13; Official Ga.Code Ann. § 51–1–29.1; Ill.Rev.Stat. ch. 111, § 4405; Me.Rev.Stat.Ann. tit. 24, § 2904; S.C.Code Ann. § 33–55–210; Va.Code § 54–276.12.

How do these protective immunity statutes square with judicial hostility to waivers or limitations on liability, as manifested in *Tunkl?*

D. PARTIAL LIMITATIONS ON THE RIGHT TO SUE

SHORTER v. DRURY

Supreme Court of Washington, 1985.
103 Wn.2d 645, 695 P.2d 116.

DOLLIVER, JUSTICE.

This is an appeal from a wrongful death medical malpractice action arising out of the bleeding death of a hospital patient who, for religious reasons, refused a blood transfusion. Plaintiff, the deceased's husband and personal representative, appeals the trial court's judgment on the verdict in which the jury reduced plaintiff's wrongful death damages by 75 percent based on an assumption of risk by the Shorters that Mrs. Shorter would die from bleeding. The defendant doctor appeals the judgment alleging that a plaintiff-signed hospital release form completely barred the wrongful death action. Alternatively, defendant asks that we affirm the trial court's judgment on the verdict. Defendant does not appeal the special verdict in which the jury found the defendant negligent.

The deceased, Doreen Shorter, was a Jehovah's Witness, as is her surviving husband, Elmer Shorter. Jehovah's Witnesses are prohibited by their religious doctrine from receiving blood transfusions.

Doreen Shorter became pregnant late in the summer of 1979. In October of 1979, she consulted with the defendant, Dr. Robert E. Drury, a family practitioner. Dr. Drury diagnosed Mrs. Shorter as having had a "missed abortion". A missed abortion occurs when the fetus dies and the uterus fails to discharge it.

When a fetus dies, it is medically prudent to evacuate the uterus in order to guard against infection. To cleanse the uterus, Dr. Shorter recommended a "dilation and curettage" (D and C). There are three alternative ways to perform this operation. The first is with a curette, a metal instrument which has a sharp-edged hoop on the end of it. The second, commonly used in an abortion, involves the use of a suction device. The third alternative is by use of vaginal suppositories containing prostaglandin, a chemical that causes artificial labor contractions. Dr. Drury chose to use curettes.

Although the D and C is a routine medical procedure there is a risk of bleeding. Each of the three principal methods for performing the D and C presented, to a varying degree, the risk of bleeding. The record below reflects that the curette method which Dr. Drury selected posed the highest degree of puncture-caused bleeding risk due to the sharpness of the instrument. The record also reflects, however, that no matter how the D and C is performed, there is always the possibility of blood loss.

Dr. Drury described the D and C procedure to Mr. and Mrs. Shorter. He advised her there was a possibility of bleeding and perforation of the uterus. Dr. Drury did not discuss any alternate methods in which the D and C may be performed. Examination of Mr. Shorter at trial revealed he was aware that the D and C posed the possibility, albeit remote, of internal bleeding.

The day before she was scheduled to receive the D and C from Dr. Drury, Mrs. Shorter sought a second opinion from Dr. Alan Ott. Mrs. Shorter advised Dr. Ott of Dr. Drury's intention to perform the D and C. She told Dr. Ott she was a Jehovah's Witness. Although he confirmed the D and C was the appropriate treatment, Dr. Ott did not discuss with Mrs. Shorter the particular method which should be used to perform it. He did, however, advise Mrs. Shorter that "she could certainly bleed during the procedure" and at trial confirmed she was aware of that possibility. Dr. Ott testified Mrs. Shorter responded to his warning by saying "she had faith in the Lord and that things would work out. * * *"

At approximately 6 a.m. on November 30, Mrs. Shorter was accompanied by her husband to Everett General Hospital. At the hospital the Shorters signed the following form (underlining after heading indicates blanks in form which were completed in handwriting):

GENERAL HOSPITAL OF EVERETT
REFUSAL TO PERMIT BLOOD TRANSFUSION

Date November 30, 1979 Hour 6:15 a.m.

I request that no blood or blood derivatives be administered to

Doreen V. Shorter

during this hospitalization. I hereby release the hospital, its personnel, and the attending physician from any responsibility whatever for unfavorable reactions or any untoward results due to my refusal to permit the use of blood or its derivatives and I fully understand the possible consequences of such refusal on my part.

> [/s/ Doreen Shorter]
> Patient
> [/s/ Elmer Shorter]
> Patient's Husband or Wife

The operation did not go smoothly. Approximately 1 hour after surgery, Mrs. Shorter began to bleed internally and go into shock. Emergency exploratory surgery conducted by other surgeons revealed Dr. Drury had severely lacerated Mrs. Shorter's uterus when he was probing with the curette.

Mrs. Shorter began to bleed profusely. She continued to refuse to authorize a transfusion despite repeated warnings by the doctors she would likely die due to blood loss. Mrs. Shorter was coherent at the time she refused to accept blood. While the surgeons repaired Mrs. Shorter's perforated uterus and abdomen, Dr. Drury and several other doctors pleaded with Mr. Shorter to permit them to transfuse blood into Mrs. Shorter. He likewise refused. Mrs. Shorter bled to death. Doctors for both parties agreed a transfusion in substantial probability would have saved Doreen Shorter's life.

Mr. Shorter thereafter brought this wrongful death action alleging Dr. Drury's negligence proximately caused Mrs. Shorter's death; the complaint did not allege a survival cause of action. The release was admitted into evidence over plaintiff's objection. Plaintiff took exception to jury instructions numbered 13 and 13A which dealt with assumption of the risk.

The jury found Dr. Drury negligent and that his negligence was "a proximate cause of the death of Doreen Shorter". Damages were found to be $412,000. The jury determined, however, that Mr. and/or Mrs. Shorter "knowingly and voluntarily" assumed the risk of bleeding to death and attributed 75 percent of the fault for her death to her and her husband's refusal to authorize or accept a blood transfusion. Plaintiff was awarded judgment of $103,000. Both parties moved for judgment notwithstanding the verdict. The trial court denied both motions. Plaintiff appealed and defendant cross-appealed to the Court of Appeals, which certified the case pursuant to RCW 2.06.030(d).

The three issues before us concern the admissibility of the "Refusal to Permit Blood Transfusion" (refusal); whether assumption of the risk is a valid defense and if so, whether there is sufficient evidence for the jury to have found the risk was assumed by the Shorters; and whether the submission of the issue of assumption of the risk to the jury violated the free exercise clause of the First Amendment. The finding of negligence by Dr. Drury is not appealed by defendant.

I

Plaintiff argues the purpose of the refusal was only to release the defendant doctor from liability for not transfusing blood into Mrs. Shorter had she required blood during the course of a nonnegligently performed operation. He further asserts the refusal as it applies to the present case violates public policy since it would release Dr. Drury from the consequences of his negligence.

Defendant concedes a survival action filed on behalf of Mrs. Shorter for her negligently inflicted injuries would not be barred by the refusal since enforcement would violate public policy. Defendant argues, however, the refusal does not release the doctor for his negligence but only for the consequences arising out of Mrs. Shorter's voluntary refusal to accept blood, which in this case was death.

While the rule announced by this court is that contracts against liability for negligence are valid except in those cases where the public interest is involved [ ], the refusal does not address the negligence of Dr. Drury. This being so it cannot be considered as a release from liability for negligence. * * *

Plaintiff categorizes the refusal as an all or nothing instrument. He claims that if it is a release of liability for negligence it is void as against public policy and if it is a release of liability where a transfusion is required because of nonnegligent treatment then it is irrelevant. We have already stated the document cannot be considered as a release from liability for negligence. The document is more, however, than a simple declaration that the signer would refuse blood only if there was no negligence by Dr. Drury. * * *

We find the refusal to be valid. There was sufficient evidence for the jury to find it was not signed unwittingly but rather voluntarily. * * *

We also hold the release was not against public policy. We emphasize again the release did not exculpate Dr. Drury from his negligence in performing the surgery. Rather, it was an agreement that Mrs. Shorter should receive no blood or blood derivatives. The cases cited by defendant, Tunkl v. Regents of Univ. of Cal., Colton v. New York Hosp., 98 Misc.2d 957, 414 N.Y.S.2d 866 (1979); Olson v. Molzen, 558 S.W.2d 429 (Tenn.1977), all refer to exculpatory clauses which release a physician or hospital from all liability for negligence. The Shorters specifically accepted the risk which might flow from a refusal to accept blood. Given the particular problems faced when a patient on religious grounds refuses to permit necessary or advisable blood transfusions, we believe the use of a release such as signed here is appropriate. [ ] Requiring physicians or hospitals to obtain a court order would be cumbersome and impractical. Furthermore, it might subject the hospital or physician to an action under 42 U.S.C. § 1983. [ ] The alternative of physicians or hospitals refusing to care for Jehovah's Witnesses is repugnant in a society which attempts to make medical care available to all its members.

We believe the procedure used here, the voluntary execution of a document protecting the physician and hospital and the patient is an appropriate alternative and not contrary to the public interest.

If the refusal is held valid, defendant asserts it acts as a complete bar to plaintiff's wrongful death claim. We disagree. While Mrs. Shorter accepted the consequences resulting from a refusal to receive a blood transfusion, she did not accept the consequences of Dr. Drury's negligence which was, as the jury found, a proximate cause of Mrs. Shorter's death. Defendant was not released from his negligence. We next consider the impact of the doctrine of assumption of the risk on this negligence.

II

Plaintiff argues the trial court erred in admitting jury instructions 13 and 13A on the ground that assumption of the risk is no longer a recognized defense in Washington, except in products liability. Plaintiff alternatively argues that even if assumption of the risk remains a viable defense, there was no evidence in the present case from which the jury may have found that Mrs. Shorter, in signing the release form, knowingly and voluntarily assumed the risk that Dr. Drury would negligently perform the D and C, proximately causing her death.

Defendant argues the assumption of the risk doctrine remains viable after enactment of the former comparative negligence statute (RCW 4.22) in cases in which the plaintiff expressly, as opposed to impliedly, assumes the risk of the defendant's negligence. He further asserts Mrs. Shorter, when she signed the blood transfusion release, expressly assumed the risk of bleeding to death even though her chances of bleeding to death may have been increased by his negligence.

* * *

Courts and commentators have struggled with the issue as to whether and to what extent the defense of "reasonable" assumption of risk survives the enactment of comparative negligence statutes. [   ] To determine whether the giving of the assumption of risk jury instruction was error, the type of risk the Shorters are alleged to have assumed must be identified.

Prosser classifies the forms of assumption of risk as follows: express, implied primary, implied reasonable, and implied unreasonable. * * * We confine our analysis to the validity of express assumption of risk and the extent to which it applies in the circumstances of this case.

Express assumption of the risk is a defense when:

[T]he plaintiff, in advance, has given his *express* consent to relieve the defendant of an obligation of conduct toward him, and to take his chances of injury from a known risk arising from what the defendant is to do or leave undone.

W. Keeton, *supra* § 68, at 480. Jurisdictions with comparative negligence statutes have generally held that the defense of express assumption of the risk survives the enactment of these statutes. [   ]

* * *

The next question is whether the Shorters could be found by the jury to have expressly assumed the risk that Dr. Drury's performance of the D and C could be negligent, thereby increasing Mrs. Shorter's chances of bleeding to death. * * *

The general rule is that for persons to assume a risk, they must be aware of more than just the generalized risk of their activities; there must be proof they knew of and appreciated the specific hazard which caused the injury. [   ] From this rule, plaintiff argues that while he and his wife were aware of the generalized risk of bleeding to death, they did not understand Mrs. Shorter's chances of bleeding to death would be greatly increased by Dr. Drury's negligence. The Shorters, however, did not merely assume a "generalized risk". They assumed the specific risk that Mrs. Shorter might die from bleeding if she refused to permit a blood transfusion.

The Shorters signed the refusal which stated that they waived professional liability for "unfavorable reactions" or "untoward results" due to Mrs. Shorter's refusal to permit the use of blood. Mrs. Shorter consulted with Drs. Drury and Ott, both of whom advised her that the D and C, even if nonnegligently performed, could result in fatal bleeding. Furthermore, the Shorters were repeatedly advised Mrs. Shorter was bleeding and that without a transfusion her death was imminent.

Plaintiff calls our attention to the common law principle that a person cannot assume the risk of another's negligence. * * * While we do not question the rule, we disagree with plaintiff's assertion that it applies in this case.

* * * Defendant argues, and we agree, that the Shorters could be found by the jury to have assumed the risk of death from an operation which had to be performed without blood transfusions and where blood could not be administered under any circumstances including where the doctor made what would otherwise have been correctable surgical mistake. The risk of death from a failure to receive a transfusion to which the Shorters exposed themselves was created by, and must be allocated to, the Shorters themselves.

* * *

III

Finally, plaintiff asserts the submission of the issue of assumption of the risk to the jury violated the free exercise clause of the First Amendment. Plaintiff concedes he has found no cases involving the effect of a patient's refusal of blood in a malpractice action. Nevertheless, plaintiff claims error in the refusal of the trial court to give his proposed instruction 24 which would have told the jury compensation could not be denied because of a refusal of blood for religious reasons. While the Supreme Court has stated the free exercise clause of the First Amendment forbids the "state condition[ing] receipt of an important benefit upon conduct proscribed by a religious faith", *Thomas v. Review Bd.*, 450 U.S. 707, 717, 101 S.Ct. 1425, 1432, 67 L.Ed.2d 624 (1981), a prerequisite for First Amendment cases is that there be some state action or interference. *Sherbert v. Verner*, 374 U.S. 398, 83 S.Ct. 1790, 10 L.Ed.2d 965 (1963); *Thomas v. Review Bd., supra.* There is none here. This is a dispute between private individuals; plaintiff is denied no rights under the First Amendment.

* * *

Affirmed.

Notes and Questions

1. Jehovah's Witnesses rarely sue physicians who respect their decisions not to receive blood. A decision to vitiate the partial release in *Shorter* might have discouraged surgeons from agreeing to treat Jehovah's Witnesses consistent with their religious beliefs.

The refusal by Jehovah's Witnesses to accept blood transfusions has its origins in their interpretation of the Bible. Their religious doctrine mandates that they "abstain from blood":

> A human is not to sustain his life with the blood of another creature. (Genesis 9:3, 4) When an animal's life is taken, the blood representing that life is to be 'poured out,' given back to the Life–Giver. (Leviticus 17:13, 14) And as decreed by the apostolic council, Christians are to 'abstain from blood,' which applies to human blood as well as to animal blood." (Acts 15:28, 29.)

Jehovah's Witnesses and the Question of Blood 17 (1977).

Jehovah's Witnesses make no distinction between taking blood in by mouth and into the blood vessels, and treat the issue of blood as involving "the most fundamental principles on which they as Christians base their lives. Their relationship with their Creator and God is at stake." Id. at 19. The Jehovah's Witnesses have prepared brochures for health care professionals that explain these beliefs, stating that they will sign consent forms that relieve doctors of any responsibility for possible adverse consequences of blood refusal.

2. How does the court support its allowance of the partial release? What does the court fear might happen to patients with particular religious beliefs? Can you think of any other methods by which a hospital or doctor might protect against the risk of lawsuits by patients who refuse certain kinds of medical interventions? Is the contract an adhesion contract, as were the contracts in *Tunkl* or *Porubianksy?*

3. *Shorter* offers a defense of a partial waiver, under a special set of circumstances. The issue is important for two reasons. First, providers would like to limit their liability exposure in order to keep malpractice premiums under control. Second, economists and other reformers of the tort system advocate the use of contracts that allocate risk by agreement.

Chapter 4 will explore in more detail the contract approach along with other reform proposals. Several states have already adopted contract approaches, such as elective arbitration contracts that allow the provider and the patient to change the forum for resolving the dispute. See Morris v. Metriyaked, at Chapter 4, infra. Similarly, living wills and durable powers of attorney allow a patient to control the extent of treatment, while protecting the treating doctor from liability for complying with the patient's refusal of treatment.

4. The contract approach to allocating the risks of health care has been advocated by many commentators. See Ginsburg et al., Contractual Revisions to Medical Malpractice Liability, 49 Law & Contemp.Probs. 253 (1986); Havighurst, Reforming Malpractice Law Through Consumer

Choice, 3 Health Affairs 63 (1984); P. Danzon, Medical Malpractice: Theory, Evidence and Public Policy (1985) (Chapter 12); Epstein, Medical Malpractice: The Case For Contract, 1976 A.B.F.Res.J. 87; Epstein, Medical Malpractice, Imperfect Information, and the Contractual Foundation for Medical Services, 49 Law & Contemp.Probs. 201 (1986); Epstein, Market and Regulatory Approaches to Medical Malpractice: The Virginia Obstetrical No–Fault Statute, 74 Va.L.Rev. 1451 (1988); Henderson, Agreements Changing the Forum for Resolving Malpractice Claims, 49 Law & Contemp. Probs. 244 (1986).

Reliance on provider-patient contracts have also been criticized. See Mehlman, Fiduciary Contracting: Limitations on Bargaining Between Patients and Health Care Providers, 51 Univ.Pitt.L.Rev. 365 (1990); Atiyah, Medical Malpractice and the Contract/Tort Boundary, 49 Law & Contemp. Probs. 287, 302 (1986) ("So American reformers turn, as a last resort, to the law of contract, however unsatisfactory this may be as an instrument of legal change compared with legislation or appropriate changes in common law doctrine."); Law, A Consumer Perspective on Medical Malpractice, 49 Law & Contemp.Probs. 305 (1989).

Problem: Arbitrating Disaster

Rhoda Cumin went to the Gladstone Clinic in Las Vegas, Nevada to get a prescription for an oral contraceptive. Her medical history put her at a higher risk of a stroke from use of birth control pills. She did not know this, but her medical records and history would have alerted an obstetrician to the risk. She obtained a prescription for the pills, and began taking them. Six months later she suffered a cerebral incident that left her partially paralyzed.

Ms. Cumin has asked you to handle her suit against the clinic. Your investigation determines that the clinic was negligent in prescribing the contraceptive in light of Ms. Cumin's history. You file a negligence action. The clinic then moves to stay the lawsuit pending arbitration, and for a court order to compel arbitration. Its affidavit states that the clinic requires all patients to sign an arbitration agreement before receiving treatment. This agreement provides that all disputes must be submitted to binding arbitration and that the parties expressly waive their right to a trial. The clinic's standard procedure is to have the receptionist hand the patient the agreement along with two information sheets, informing her that any questions will be answered. The patient must sign the agreement before receiving treatment; the physician signs later. If the patient refuses to sign, the clinic refuses treatment. The agreement, signed by Rhoda Cumin, is attached to the affidavit.

Ms. Cumin tells you that she does not remember either signing the agreement or having it explained to her, and you file an affidavit to that effect. Prepare a memorandum of law in support of your motion in opposition to arbitration.

II. CONFIDENTIALITY AND DISCLOSURE IN THE PHYSICIAN–PATIENT RELATIONSHIP

A. BREACHES OF CONFIDENCE

One of the most important obligations owed by a professional to a patient is the protection of confidences revealed by the patient to the professional. There is also an emerging trend to impose on professionals a duty to disclose to the patient information which the professional has regarding the patient. These obligations are discussed in this section.

HUMPHERS v. FIRST INTERSTATE BANK OF OREGON

Supreme Court of Oregon, In Banc, 1985.
298 Or. 706, 696 P.2d 527.

LINDE, JUSTICE.

We are called upon to decide whether plaintiff has stated a claim for damages in alleging that her former physician revealed her identity to a daughter whom she had given up for adoption.

In 1959, according to the complaint, plaintiff, then known as Ramona Elwess or by her maiden name, Ramona Jean Peek, gave birth to a daughter in St. Charles Medical Center in Bend, Oregon. She was unmarried at the time, and her physician, Dr. Harry E. Mackey, registered her in the hospital as "Mrs. Jean Smith." The next day, Ramona consented to the child's adoption by Leslie and Shirley Swarens of Bend, who named her Leslie Dawn. The hospital's medical records concerning the birth were sealed and marked to show that they were not public. Ramona subsequently remarried and raised a family. Only Ramona's mother and husband and Dr. Mackey knew about the daughter she had given up for adoption.

Twenty-one years later the daughter, now known as Dawn Kastning, wished to establish contact with her biological mother. Unable to gain access to the confidential court file of her adoption (though apparently able to locate the attending physician), Dawn sought out Dr. Mackey, and he agreed to assist in her quest. Dr. Mackey gave Dawn a letter which stated that he had registered Ramona Jean Peek at the hospital, that although he could not locate his medical records, he remembered administering diethylstilbestrol to her, and that the possible consequences of this medication made it important for Dawn to find her biological mother. The latter statements were untrue and made only to help Dawn to breach the confidentiality of the records concerning her birth and adoption. In 1982, hospital personnel, relying on Dr. Mackey's letter, allowed Dawn to make copies of plaintiff's medical records, which enabled her to locate plaintiff, now Ramona Humphers.

Ramona Humphers was not pleased. The unexpected development upset her and caused her emotional distress, worry, sleeplessness, humiliation, embarrassment, and inability to function normally. She sought damages from the estate of Dr. Mackey, who had died, by this action against defendant as the personal representative. After alleging the facts recounted above, her complaint pleads for relief on five different theories: First, that Dr. Mackey incurred liability for "outrageous conduct"; [1] second, that his disclosure of a professional secret fell short of the care, skill and diligence employed by other physicians in the community and commanded by statute; third, that his disclosure wrongfully breached a confidential or privileged relationship; fourth, that his disclosure of confidential information was an "invasion of privacy" in the form of an "unauthorized intrusion upon plaintiff's seclusion, solitude, and private affairs;" and fifth, that his disclosures to Dawn Kastning breached a contractual obligation of secrecy. The circuit court granted defendant's motion to dismiss the complaint on the grounds that the facts fell short of each theory of relief and ordered entry of judgment for defendant. On appeal, the Court of Appeals affirmed the dismissal of the first, second, and fifth counts but reversed on the third, breach of a confidential relationship, and the fourth, invasion of privacy. [ ] We allowed review. We hold that if plaintiff has a claim, it arose from a breach by Dr. Mackey of a professional duty to keep plaintiff's secret rather than from a violation of plaintiff's privacy.

A physician's liability for disclosing confidential information about a patient is not a new problem. In common law jurisdictions it has been more discussed than litigated throughout much of this century.[2] There are precedents for damage actions for unauthorized disclosure of facts conveyed in confidence, although we know of none involving the disclosure of an adoption. Because such claims are made against a variety of defendants besides physicians or other professional counselors, for instance against banks [ ], and because plaintiffs understandably plead alternative theories of recovery, the decisions do not always rest on a single theory.

Sometimes, defendant may have promised confidentiality expressly or by factual implication, in this case perhaps implied by registering a patient in the hospital under an assumed name. Plaintiffs were allowed to proceed on implied contract claims in *Horne v. Patton,* 291 Ala. 701, 287 So.2d 824 (1973), in *Hammonds v. Aetna Casualty & Surety Company,* 243 F.Supp. 793 (N.D.Ohio 1965), and in *Doe v. Roe,* 93 Misc.2d 201, 400 N.Y.S.2d 668 (Sup.Ct.1977) (psychiatrist). * * * A contract claim may be adequate where the breach of confidence causes

---

1. This court has attempted, so far unsuccessfully, to discourage the idea that there is a general tort of "outrageous conduct," partly because the phrase misleadingly suggests potential recovery of damages whenever someone's conduct could be said to deserve this epithet. [ ] Plaintiff in this case actually alleged the factual elements of intentional or reckless inflic-

tion of severe emotional distress as well as "outrageous" conduct.

2. *See, e.g.,* Hanning and Brady, *Extrajudicial Truthful Disclosure of Medical Confidences: A Physician's Civil Liability,* 44 Den.L.J. 463 (1967) (citing the earlier literature); Boyle, *Medical Confidence—Civil Liability for Breach,* 24 N.Ire.Leg.Q. 19 (1973).

financial loss, and it may gain a longer period of limitations; but contract law may deny damages for psychic or emotional injury not within the contemplation of the contracting parties, [ ] though perhaps this is no barrier when emotional security is the very object of the promised confidentiality. A contract claim is unavailable if the defendant physician was engaged by someone other than the plaintiff [ ] and it would be an awkward fiction at best if age, mental condition, or other circumstances prevent the patient from contracting; yet such a claim might be available to someone less interested than the patient, for instance her husband, [ ].

Malpractice claims, based on negligence or statute, in contrast, may offer a plaintiff professional standards of conduct independent of the defendant's assent. * * * Finally, actions for intentional infliction of severe emotional distress, *see supra* note 1, fail when the defendant had no such intention or * * * when a defendant was not reckless or did not behave in a manner that a factfinder could find to transcend "the farthest reaches of socially tolerable behavior." [ ] Among these diverse precedents, we need only consider the counts of breach of confidential relationship and invasion of privacy on which the Court of Appeals allowed plaintiff to proceed. Plaintiff did not pursue her other theories * * * and we express no view whether the dismissal of those counts was correct.

PRIVACY

Although claims of a breach of privacy and of wrongful disclosure of confidential information may seem very similar in a case like the present, which involves the disclosure of an intimate personal secret, the two claims depend on different premises and cover different ground. Their common denominator is that both assert a right to control information, but they differ in important respects. Not every secret concerns personal or private information; commercial secrets are not personal, and governmental secrets are neither personal nor private. Secrecy involves intentional concealment. * * *

For our immediate purpose, the most important distinction is that only one who holds information in confidence can be charged with a breach of confidence. If an act qualifies as a tortious invasion of privacy, it theoretically could be committed by anyone. In the present case, Dr. Mackey's professional role is relevant to a claim that he breached a duty of confidentiality, but he could be charged with an invasion of plaintiff's privacy only if anyone else who told Dawn Kastning the facts of her birth without a special privilege to do so would be liable in tort for invading the privacy of her mother.

Whether "privacy" is a usable legal category has been much debated in other English-speaking jurisdictions as well as in this country, especially since its use in tort law, to claim the protection of government against intrusions by others, became entangled with its use in constitutional law, to claim protection against rather different intrusions by government. No concept in modern law has unleashed a comparable flood of commentary, its defenders arguing that "privacy" encompasses related interests of personality and autonomy, while its critics say that these interests are properly identified, evaluated, and protected below that exalted philosophical level. Indeed, at that level, a daughter's interest in her personal identity here confronts a mother's interest in guarding her own present identity by concealing their joint past. But recognition of an interest or value deserving protection states only half a case. Tort liability depends on the defendant's wrong as well as on the plaintiff's interest, or "right," unless some rule imposes strict liability. One's preferred seclusion or anonymity may be lost in many ways; the question remains who is legally bound to protect those interests at the risk of liability.

* * *

In this country, Dean William L. Prosser and his successors, noting that early debate was more "preoccupied with the question whether the right of privacy existed" than "what it would amount to if it did," concluded that invasion of privacy "is not one tort but a complex of four" * * * Prosser and Keeton, Torts 851, § 117 (5th ed. 1984). They identify the four kinds of claims grouped under the "privacy" tort as, first, appropriation of the plaintiff's name or likeness; second, unreasonable and offensive intrusion upon the seclusion of another; third, public disclosure of private facts; and fourth, publicity which places the plaintiff in a false light in the public eye. *Id.* at 851–66. The same classification is made in the Restatement (Second) Torts §§ 652A to 652E. * * *

This court has not adopted all forms of the tort wholesale. * * *

* * *

* * * The Court of Appeals concluded that the complaint alleges a case of tortious intrusion upon plaintiff's seclusion, not by physical means such as uninvited entry, wiretapping, photography, or the like, but in the sense of an offensive prying into personal matters that plaintiff reasonably has sought to keep private. *See* Prosser and Keeton, *supra* at 854–55, § 117.[11] We do not believe that the theory fits this case.

Doubtless plaintiff's interest qualifies as a "privacy" interest. That does not require the judgment of a court or a jury; it is established by the statutes that close adoption records to inspection without a court order. ORS 7.211, 432.420. * * * But as already stated, to identify an interest deserving protection does not suffice to collect damages from anyone who causes injury to that interest. Dr. Mackey helped Dawn

---

11. Hospital patients have recovered on a variety of theories for what courts recognized as an injury to privacy when the patient, without knowing consent, was exposed to nonmedical personnel, beginning with *DeMay v. Roberts*, 46 Mich. 160, 9 N.W. 146 (1881) (finding the nonmedical stranger's touch to be a battery). *See* Le-

Blang, *Invasion of Privacy: Medical Practice and the Tort of Intrusion*, 18 Washburn L.J. 205, 219–39 (1979). This court recognized that intrusive surveillance could be a tort, though not made out on the facts, in *McLain v. Boise Cascade Corp.*, 271 Or. 549, 533 P.2d 343 (1975).

Kastning find her biological mother, but we are not prepared to assume that Ms. Kastning became liable for invasion of privacy in seeking her out. Nor, we think, would anyone who knew the facts without an obligation of secrecy commit a tort simply by telling them to Ms. Kastning.

Dr. Mackey himself did not approach plaintiff or pry into any personal facts that he did not know; indeed, if he had written or spoken to his former patient to tell her that her daughter was eager to find her, it would be hard to describe such a communication alone as an invasion of privacy. The point of the claim against Dr. Mackey is not that he pried into a confidence but that he failed to keep one. If Dr. Mackey incurred liability for that, it must result from an obligation of confidentiality beyond any general duty of people at large not to invade one another's privacy. We therefore turn to plaintiff's claim that Dr. Mackey was liable for a breach of confidence, the third count of the complaint.

BREACH OF CONFIDENCE

It takes less judicial innovation to recognize this claim than the Court of Appeals thought. A number of decisions have held that unauthorized and unprivileged disclosure of confidential information obtained in a confidential relationship can give rise to tort damages. *See, e.g., Horne v. Patton, supra; McDonald v. Clinger*, 84 A.D.2d 482, 446 N.Y.S.2d 801 (1982); * * *.

One commentator, upon analyzing the cases allowing or denying recovery on a variety of theories, concluded that the tort consists in a breach of confidence in a "nonpersonal" confidential relationship, using the word "nonpersonal" to exclude liability for failing to keep secrets among members of a family or close friends. Note, *Breach of Confidence: An Emerging Tort*, 82 Colum.L.Rev. 1426 (1982). The problem with this formulation of civil liability lies in identifying the confidential relationships that carry a duty of keeping secrets. The writer suggests that the duty arises in all nonpersonal relationships "customarily understood" to carry such an obligation. *Id.* at 1460–61. In any such relationship, a person who discloses personal information conveyed in confidence would have the burden of showing that the disclosure was justified or privileged.

We do not think the law casts so wide a net. It requires more than custom to impose legal restraints on "the right to speak, write, or print freely on any subject whatever." Or. Const., Art. I, § 8. Tort liability, of course, may be a remedy for "injury to person, property, or reputation," Or. Const., Art. I, § 10, even by speech. [ ] But a legal duty not to speak, unless voluntarily assumed in entering the relationship, will not be imposed by courts or jurors in the name of custom or reasonable expectations. Tort liability is the consequence of a nonconsensual duty of silence, not its source.

In the case of the medical profession, courts in fact have found sources of a nonconsensual duty of confidentiality. Some have thought such a duty toward the patient implicit in the patient's statutory privilege to exclude the doctor's testimony in litigation, enacted in this state in OEC 504–1(2). *See, e.g., Berry v. Moench,* 8 Utah 2d 191, 331 P.2d 814 (1958); *Hammonds v. Aetna Cas. & Sur. Co., supra;* [ ]. More directly in point are legal duties imposed as a condition of engaging in the professional practice of medicine or other occupations.[15]

As early as 1920, the Supreme Court of Nebraska, where a medical licensing statute defined professional misconduct to include "betrayal of a professional secret to the detriment of the patient," wrote in *Simonsen v. Swenson, supra,* 104 Neb. at 227, 177 N.W. 831:

> "By this statute, it appears to us, a positive duty is imposed upon the physician, both for the benefit and advantage of the patient as well as in the interest of general public policy. The relation of physician and patient is necessarily a highly confidential one. It is often necessary for the patient to give information about himself which would be most embarrassing or harmful to him if given general circulation. This information the physician is bound, not only upon his own professional honor and the ethics of his high profession, to keep secret, but by reason of the affirmative mandate of the statute itself. A wrongful breach of such confidence, and a betrayal of such trust, would give rise to a civil action for the damages naturally flowing from such wrong."

Professional regulations were similarly cited in *Hammonds v. Aetna Cas. & Sur. Co., supra,* in *Doe v. Roe, supra,* and in *Clark v. Geraci,* 29 Misc.2d 791, 208 N.Y.S.2d 564 (Sup.Ct.1960). [ ]

This strikes us as the right approach to a claim of liability outside obligations undertaken expressly or implied in fact in entering a contractual relationship. [ ] The contours of the asserted duty of confidentiality are determined by a legal source external to the tort claim itself.

* * *

Because the duty of confidentiality is determined by standards outside the tort claim for its breach, so are the defenses of privilege or justification. Physicians, like members of many ordinary confidential professions and occupations, also may be legally obliged to report medical information to others for the protection of the patient, of other individuals, or of the public. *See, e.g.,* ORS 418.750 (physician's duty to report child abuse); ORS 433.003, 434.020 (duty to report certain diseases). * * * Even without such a legal obligation, there may be a privilege to disclose information for the safety of individuals or important to the public in matters of public interest. [ ] Some cases have found a physician privileged in disclosing information to a patient's spouse, *Curry v. Corn,* 52 Misc.2d 1035, 277 N.Y.S.2d 470 (Sup.Ct.1966) or perhaps an intended spouse, *Berry v. Moench, supra.* In any event,

---

15. *See, e.g., In re Lasswell,* 296 Or. 121, 124–26, 673 P.2d 855 (1983) (sustaining professional constraints on disclosure if disclosure is incompatible with professional function and sanction is limited to the professional role or relationship). * * *

defenses to a duty of confidentiality are determined in the same manner as the existence and scope of the duty itself. They necessarily will differ from one occupation to another and from time to time. A physician or other member of a regulated occupation is not to be held to a noncontractual duty of secrecy in a tort action when disclosure would not be a breach or would be privileged in direct enforcement of the underlying duty.

A physician's duty to keep medical and related information about a patient in confidence is beyond question. It is imposed by statute. ORS 677.190(5) provides for disqualifying or otherwise disciplining a physician for "wilfully or negligently divulging a professional secret."
* * *

It is less obvious whether Dr. Mackey violated ORS 677.190(5) when he told Dawn Kastning what he knew of her birth. She was not, after all, a stranger to that proceeding. * * * If Ms. Kastning needed information about her natural mother for medical reasons, as Dr. Mackey pretended, the State Board of Medical Examiners likely would find the disclosure privileged against a charge under ORS 677.190(5); but the statement is alleged to have been a pretext designed to give her access to the hospital records. If only ORS 677.190(5) were involved, we do not know how the Board would judge a physician who assists at the birth of a child and decades later reveals to that person his or her parentage. But as already noted, other statutes specifically mandate the secrecy of adoption records. * * * Given these clear legal constraints, there is no privilege to disregard the professional duty imposed by ORS 677.190(5) solely in order to satisfy the curiosity of the person who was given up for adoption.

For these reasons, we agree with the Court of Appeals that plaintiff may proceed under her claim of breach of confidentiality in a confidential relationship. The decision of the Court of Appeals is reversed with respect to plaintiff's claim of invasion of privacy and affirmed with respect to her claim of breach of confidence in a confidential relationship, and the case is remanded to the circuit court for further proceedings on that claim.

Notes and Questions

1. Every time a person consults a medical professional, is admitted to a health care institution, or receives a medical test, a medical record is created or an entry is made in an existing record. Billions of such records exist in the United States, most of which will be retained from 10 to 25 years. Many of these records contain very personal information—revelations to psychotherapists or documentation of treatment for alcoholism or venereal disease, for example—the disclosure of which could prove devastating to the patient. Yet most records are available to many users for a variety of legitimate and more questionable purposes. One commentator estimated that an average of 75 persons have access to any patient record, American College of Hospital Administrators, Medical Confidentiality, Can it be Protected? 2–3, 1983. The conflict between the need for confidentiali-

ty and various claims to access have traditionally been resolved by professional ethics and institutional management practices, but is increasingly being litigated in legal forums.

2. Who uses medical information? Professional and non-professional medical staff must have access to records of patients in medical institutions for treatment purposes. Consent to such access is commonly presumed. Third party payors are the most common requestors of medical records outside the treatment setting. Access to records also is sought routinely for a variety of medical evaluation and support purposes. For example, in-house quality assurance committees, JCAHO accreditation inspection teams, and state institutional licensure reviewers all must review medical records to assess the quality of hospital care. Medical researchers frequently use information from medical records. If researchers are affiliated with the institution holding the records, access is routinely granted; if they are external to the institution, a request to review records may be reviewed more carefully, but will often be granted. See, discussing protection of confidentiality in the research setting, Adams, Medical Research and Personal Privacy, 30 Vill.L.Rev. 1077 (1985). State public health laws require medical professionals and institutions to report a variety of medical conditions and incidents: venereal disease, contagious diseases, wounds inflicted by violence, poisonings, industrial accidents, abortions, and child abuse.

Access to medical records is also sought for secondary, nonmedical, purposes. Law enforcement agencies, for example, often seek access to medical information. A moderate-size Chicago hospital reported that the FBI requested information about patients as often as twice a month. Attorneys seek medical records to establish disability, personal injury, or medical malpractice claims for their clients. Though they most commonly will ask for records of their own clients, they may also want to review records of other patients to establish a pattern of knowing medical abuse by a physician or the culpability of a hospital for failing to supervise a negligent practitioner. Life, health, disability and liability insurers often seek medical information, as do employers and credit investigators. Disclosure of information from medical records may occur without a formal request. Though secondary users of medical information commonly receive information pursuant to patient record releases, they have been known to seek and compile information surreptitiously. See Privacy Protection Study Commission, Personal Privacy in an Information Society, 285, 286 (1977) [hereafter Personal Privacy]. Another study found that 51% of doctors and 70% of medical students discuss confidential information at parties. Obviously these secondary disclosures of medical information are of great import to patients, as disclosure can result in loss of employment or denial of insurance or credit, or, at least, severe embarrassment.

The volume of requests for medical information is impressive. The director of the medical record department of a 600–bed university hospital testified to the Privacy Protection Study Commission that his hospital received 2,700 information requests a month: 34% from third-party payors; 37% from other physicians; 8% in the form of subpoenas; and 21% from other hospitals, attorneys, and miscellaneous sources. An attorney for the Mayo clinic testified to the same Commission that the clinic receives

300,000 requests a year, 88% related to reimbursement, Personal Privacy, supra, at 280. On handling the disclosure of medical information, see J. Bruce, Privacy and Confidentiality in Health Care (1984); W. Roach, S. Chernoff, C. Esley, Medical Records and the Law 59–116 (1985) [hereafter Roach, Chernoff & Esley]. On disclosure of records of non-litigants in litigation, see Hirsh, The Great Wall About Nonparty Patient Medical Records is Crumbling, 31 Med.Trial Tech.Q. 434 (1985).

3. What legal devices protect the confidentiality of medical information? The physician-patient privilege comes first to mind, but in fact it plays a very limited role. First, and most important, it is only a testimonial privilege, not a general obligation of maintaining confidentiality: though it may permit a doctor to refuse to disclose medical information in court, it does not require the doctor to keep information from employers or insurers. Second, it is a statutory privilege or one created through judicial rulemaking and does not exist in all jurisdictions. According to the Privacy Protection Study Commission 43 states have some form of testimonial privilege, yet some of these are only applicable to psychiatrists. Third, as a privilege created by state statute, it does not apply in non-diversity federal court proceedings, Personal Privacy, supra, at 284. Fourth, the privilege is in most states subject to many exceptions. In California, it is subject to twelve exceptions, including cases where the patient is a litigant, criminal proceedings, will contests, and physician licensure proceedings. State privilege statutes often cover physicians only, who today deliver only about 5% of health care. Finally, the privilege applies only to confidential disclosures made to a physician in the course of treatment and is easily waived. See, criticizing the usefulness of the privilege for protecting confidentiality, Boyer, Computerized Medical Records and the Right to Privacy: The Emerging Federal Response, 25 Buffalo L.Rev. 37, 75–79 (1975); Gellman, Prescribing Privacy: The Uncertain Role of the Physician in the Protection of Patient Privacy, 62 N.C.L.Rev. 255, 272–274 (1984); Turkington, Legal Protection for the Confidentiality of Health Care Information in Pennsylvania: Patient and Client Access, Testimonial Privilege, Damage Recovery for Unauthorized Extra-Legal Disclosure, 32 Vill.L.Rev. 262, 302–377 (1987).

4. Several federal and state statutes protect the confidentiality of medical information. Most notable among these are amendments to the Drug Abuse and Treatment Acts and Comprehensive Alcohol Abuse and Alcoholism Prevention, Treatment, and Rehabilitation Act, 42 U.S.C.A. §§ 290dd–3, 390ee–3 (West 1982 & Supp.1986), and implementing regulations, 42 C.F.R. Part 2 (1985), which impose rigorous requirements on the disclosure of information from alcohol and drug abuse treatment programs. Some state statutes provide civil penalties for disclosure of confidential information. See Ill.Rev.Stat. ch. 91½, § 815; West's Fla.Stat.Ann. § 395.018.

5. State courts have imposed liability on doctors for violating a duty of confidentiality expressed or implied in state licensure or privilege statutes. See Berry v. Moench, 8 Utah 2d 191, 331 P.2d 814 (1958); Felis v. Greenberg, 51 Misc.2d 441, 273 N.Y.S.2d 288 (1966). Several common law theories have also been advanced to impose liability on professionals who disclose medical information. Two of these, invasion of privacy and breach

of confidential relationship, are discussed in the principal case. Other theories that have been argued, some of which are mentioned in the principal case, include breach of contract, Hammonds v. Aetna Casualty and Surety Co., 237 F.Supp. 96 (N.D.Ohio 1965) and 243 F.Supp. 793 (N.D.Ohio 1965); Doe v. Roe, 93 Misc.2d 201, 400 N.Y.S.2d 668 (1977); medical malpractice, Clark v. Geraci, 29 Misc.2d 791, 208 N.Y.S.2d 564 (1960) (rejecting argument); and defamation, Gilson v. Knickerbocker Hospital, 280 App.Div. 690, 116 N.Y.S.2d 745 (1952) (rejecting argument). Where an accurate disclosure of information is made in good faith for a legitimate purpose, courts are generally reluctant to impose liability. See, discussing liability theories, Roach, Chernoff, and Esley, supra, at 141–157; Cooper, The Physician's Dilemma: Protection of the Patient's Right to Privacy, 22 St. Louis U.L.J. 397, 412–419 (1978); Turkington, supra; Anno., Physician's Tort Liability for Unauthorized Disclosure of Confidential Information About Patient, 48 A.L.R. 4th 668.

6. Does a patient have a right to review his or her own records? Since access to medical information is commonly granted pursuant to patient consent, it would seem that the answer to this question would obviously be yes. Surprisingly, however, a provider may still deny a patient access to medical records in a number of jurisdictions. Medical records are the property of the institution or practitioner that creates them, McGarry v. J.A. Mercier Co., 272 Mich. 501, 262 N.W. 296 (1935), though some courts have recognized a property right of the patient in the information the records contain, Pyramid Life Insurance Co. v. Masonic Hospital Association, 191 F.Supp. 51 (W.D.Okl.1961). Many (though certainly not all) doctors argue that patients should not have access to their records, or should have access only under tight controls. They contend that patients cannot understand the information found in the records, may become anxious and upset by what they find, and may rely on medical information to engage in harmful self-treatment. They argue that patient access to medical information may violate confidences of third parties and discourage physician frankness in recording, and will impose administrative costs on institutions. Patient advocates argue that greater access will improve patient understanding of and compliance with treatment, physician-patient relations, and continuity of care. They also contend that patients cannot give informed authorization for disclosure of records to others if they do not know the contents of their own records, and thus access is important. Most of the evidence available supports the arguments for greater access—there is little evidence that patients are harmed by disclosure, some that they are helped, Privacy Protection Commission, supra, at 297; Roth, Wolford, & Meisel, Patient Access to Records: Tonic or Toxin? 137 Am.J.Psychiatry 592 (1980).

Several states have enacted statutes permitting patients access to their medical records, though these are often subject to exceptions. Some statutes, for example, only provide access subsequent to discharge, West's Colo.Rev.Stat.Ann. §§ 25–1–801 & 802; Conn.Gen.Stat.Ann. § 4–104; 22 Me.Rev.Stat.Ann. § 1711; others permit the institution to provide only a summary of the records; West's Ann.Cal.Health & Safety Code § 25256; Or.Rev.Stat. 192.525; Minn.Stat.Ann. § 144.335; and others require the patient to show good cause for access, Tenn.Code Ann. § 53–1322(A);

Miss.Code 1981, § 41–9–65. Absent statutory authority, a number of courts have permitted patients access to records under a property theory, Wallace v. University Hospital of Cleveland, 164 N.E.2d 917 (Ohio C.P.1959), modified, 170 N.E.2d 261 (1960), appeal dismissed, 171 Ohio St. 486, 172 N.E.2d 459 (1961); or fiduciary theory, Hutchins v. Texas Rehabilitation Commission, 544 S.W.2d 802 (Tex.Civ.App.1976); Emmett v. Eastern Dispensary and Casualty Hospital, 396 F.2d 931 (D.C.Cir.1967). Some courts, however, have denied patients access to their records, Gotkin v. Miller, 379 F.Supp. 859 (E.D.N.Y.1974). On access generally, see Adams, Medical Research and Personal Privacy, 30 Vill.L.Rev. 1077 (1985); Winslade, Confidentiality of Medical Records, 3 J.Legal Med. 497 (1982); Tucker, Patient Access to Medical Records, Legal Aspects of Medical Practice 45 (Oct. 1978); Note, Toward a Uniform Right to Medical Records: A Proposal for a Model Patient Access and Information Practices Statute, 30 UCLA L.Rev. 1349 (1983).

7. Medical records often play a pivotal role in medical malpractice cases. By the time a malpractice action comes to trial memories may have dimmed as to what actually occurred at the time negligence is alleged to have taken place, leaving the medical record as the most telling evidence. Medical records, if properly authenticated, will usually be admitted under the business records exception to the hearsay rule. Because either documentation of inadequate care or inadequate documentation of care may result in liability, physicians are sometimes tempted to destroy records or to alter them to reflect the care they wish in retrospect they had rendered. There is nothing wrong with correcting records, so long as corrections are made in such a way as to leave the previous entry clearly readable and the new entry clearly identified as a corrected entry. Conscious concealment, fabrication, or falsification of records may result in an inference of awareness of guilt, Pisel v. Stamford Hospital, 180 Conn. 314, 340, 430 A.2d 1, 15 (1980); Thor v. Boska, 38 Cal.App.3d 558, 113 Cal.Rptr. 296 (1974); or punitive damages. It may also toll the statute of limitations. Finally, premature disposition of records could result in negligence liability, Fox v. Cohen, 84 Ill.App.3d 744, 40 Ill.Dec. 477, 406 N.E.2d 178 (1980).

8. The duty to maintain confidentiality occasionally comes in conflict with a duty to disclose information. Such a duty to disclose may be based on a statute, such as a child abuse or venereal disease reporting act, or on the common law duty of psychotherapists to warn identifiable persons threatened by their patients. See section B, infra. Consider the following problem.

Problem: Confidentiality or Disclosure?

David Anderson was charged with three counts of criminal sexual conduct for allegedly having sexual contact with his ten-year-old stepdaughter and eleven-year-old niece. After he was released on bond, he voluntarily entered therapy at the crisis intervention unit of Bethesda Lutheran Medical Center for acute alcoholism and depression. While in treatment he related his sexual experiences with young girls during one-on-one counselling sessions with a registered nurse and a medical student, during the taking of his social history by a registered nurse and during confidential group therapy sessions. The state seeks to discover these inculpatory disclosures for use in prosecution. The defendant claims that disclosure of the information would violate the federal alcohol treatment statutes and regulations, 42 U.S.C.A. § 4582 (West 1983) and 42 C.F.R. §§ 2.1–.67 (1985) which provide for confidentiality of alcohol treatment records, and the state physician-patient and registered nurse-patient privilege statutes. The state claims that the state child abuse reporting statute, Minn.Stat.Ann. § 626.556, enacted pursuant to federal child abuse legislation, 42 U.S.C.A. § 5101–07 (West 1983 & Supp.1986) and 45 C.F.R. §§ 1340.3–3 & 3.4 (1985) requires disclosure of the information. § 626.556 reads as follows:

> [n]o evidence regarding the child's injuries shall be excluded in any proceeding arising out of the alleged neglect or physical or sexual abuse. Minn.Stat.Ann. § 626.556, subd. 8.

How should this conflict be resolved? Should the disclosures made in group therapy be more open to disclosure than those made in confidence to a medical professional? See State v. Andring, 342 N.W.2d 128 (Minn.1984).

B. EXTENDING THE CONTRACT: THE DUTY TO PROTECT THIRD PARTIES

The obligations of health professionals normally extend only to the patients with whom they have a legal relationship, either under an implied or an express contract. They are not under an obligation to enter into a relationship with a patient, and cannot be compelled to treat someone outside the boundaries of this contractual relationship. The Good Samaritan laws, discussed supra in Chapter 2, reflect legislative reinforcement of the absence of a duty to rescue at the common law. But what if doctors have information about a patient which if disclosed might prevent harm to others? Requirements of confidentiality of the physician-patient relationship militate against disclosure generally, and disclosure may expose the physician to potential liability, as the *Humphers* case indicates.

Physicians and other health professionals have in many jurisdictions an affirmative obligation to protect third parties against hazards created by their patients.

SHEPHARD v. REDFORD COMMUNITY HOSPITAL

Court of Appeals of Michigan, 1986.
151 Mich.App. 242, 390 N.W.2d 239.

Plaintiff commenced an action as personal representative of the estate of her son Eric. She alleged that her son's death was proximately caused by the negligence of employees of the defendant hospital. Defendant moved for summary judgment pursuant to GCR 1963, 117.-2(1), on the basis that no physician-patient relationship existed between any employee of the hospital and Eric, therefore, defendant owed Eric no duty of care. The circuit court agreed that defendant owed no legal duty to plaintiff's decedent and, accordingly, dismissed plaintiff's complaint on January 7, 1985. Plaintiff appeals as of right. We reverse.

On April 4, 1981, plaintiff went to the defendant hospital for treatment of her complaints of high fever, leg pain, congestion, headaches and weakness. She was examined by an emergency room doctor and diagnosed as suffering from an upper respiratory problem. The doctor prescribed an antibiotic and instructed plaintiff to return if her fever did not subside.

Plaintiff returned home and entrusted care of five-year-old Eric to her parents because she felt physically unable to care for him. However, she retained custody of her three-year-old daughter Christina. Over the next two days, plaintiff's fever subsided, but her condition otherwise worsened: she became nauseated, her neck was stiff and her headaches became more severe. She did not, however, return to the hospital for further evaluation.

On April 6, 1981, plaintiff's mother noticed that Eric was quiet, feverish, and nauseated. She called a hospital and was instructed to give him aspirin. The next morning, Eric's fever was down but he had a rash on his chest and face. His grandmother again called a hospital and was told that the rash was a typical response to a high fever. However, Eric became increasingly unresponsive, so his grandmother called a taxi and rushed him to Mt. Carmel Hospital. Eric died one-half hour later. The cause of death was determined to be spinal meningitis.

After Eric's cause of death was determined, plaintiff also was admitted to Mt. Carmel and was determined also to be suffering from the highly infectious condition. She was immediately isolated and her other family members were notified.

On September 14, 1981, plaintiff filed her complaint as personal representative of Eric's estate and also individually, along with her husband, Eric's father. She alleged that defendant, by and through its agents and employees, undertook to diagnose and treat her condition but was negligent and failed to exercise that degree of care and skill ordinarily exercised by similar hospital facilities by:

"a. failing to obtain from plaintiff an adequate history;

"b. failing to perform on plaintiff an adequate examination;

"c. failing to conduct diagnostic testing reasonably required given plaintiff's symptoms;

"d. failing to immediately hospitalize or otherwise commence proper treatment for plaintiff's highly infectious condition;

"e. failing to notify plaintiff and her family of her condition and inform plaintiff and her family of the immediate, critical necessity of examination and testing of plaintiff and her family, given plaintiff's infectious condition."

* * *

The question in this case is whether defendant owed any duty to Eric. More specifically, we are asked to decide whether the absence of a physician-patient relationship between defendant and Eric precludes finding a duty. We hold that it does not.

Duty is an issue of law and for the court to decide. [ ] A duty arises from the relationship of the parties and the decision as to its existence involves a determination of whether the defendant has any obligation to avoid negligent conduct for the benefit of the plaintiff (or her decedent, as here). [ ] Generally, a party has no duty to protect another who is endangered by a third person absent a special relationship with either the dangerous person or the potential victim. [ ]

In the instant case, defendant had a physician-patient relationship with plaintiff. This was a special relationship with the one who allegedly infected Eric, leading to his death. Accordingly, a duty of reasonable care may arise.

Because defendant had a special relationship with plaintiff, we conclude that defendant owed a duty of reasonable care to Eric. As plaintiff's son and a member of her household, Eric was a foreseeable potential victim of defendant's conduct. [ ]

Defendant argues, however, that the law as discussed above, while applicable to negligence actions, should not apply to medical malpractice actions. Defendant contends that the instant case is in reality a medical malpractice case. Like the *Duvall* Court with the claim before it for review, we are not persuaded to characterize plaintiff's complaint as an action for medical malpractice. Even if the complaint did sound in malpractice, we would not exalt form over substance so as to deny plaintiff her day in court. [ ]

Defendant further appeals to considerations of public policy in arguing that we should find no duty. Defendant raises legitimate concerns about confidentiality in the physician-patient relationship and the present medical malpractice crisis. These concerns have been brought to the attention of this Court previously in such cases as *Welke, Duvall,* and *Davis v. Lhim,* 124 Mich.App. 291, 335 N.W.2d 481 (1983), *remanded* 422 Mich. 875 (1985). We are satisfied that these concerns are not sufficient to nullify the duty imposed on defendant on the facts of this case.

Reversed and remanded.

Notes and Questions

1. *Shephard* is one of a long line of cases involving risks of contagious diseases. Physicians have been held liable for failing to warn the daughter of a patient with scarlet fever, a wife about the danger of infection from a patient's wounds, a neighbor about the patient's smallpox. Family members are foreseeable third parties, as are neighbors. See Skillings v. Allen, 143 Minn. 323, 173 N.W. 663 (1919); Edwards v. Lamb, 69 N.H. 599, 45 A. 480 (1899); Freese v. Lemmon, 210 N.W.2d 576 (Iowa 1973); Jones v.

Stanko, 118 Ohio St. 147, 160 N.E. 456 (1928). See generally Physicians and Surgeons, 61 Am.Jur.2d 170 (1964); McDonald, Ethical Problems for Physicians Raised by AIDS and HIV Infection: Conflicting Legal Obligations of Confidentiality and Disclosure, 22 Univ.Cal.Davis L.Rev. 557 (1989).

2. Medication Side–effects. The court in *Shephard* relies on two earlier cases, one involving psychiatric dangerousness and one drug side-effects. In Welke v. Kuzilla, 144 Mich.App. 245, 375 N.W.2d 403 (1985), the court required all physicians to use reasonable care to protect foreseeable third parties against risks created by their patients. In *Welke,* the wife of the plaintiff was killed in a car collision with Kuzilla, a patient of Dr. Capper. Dr. Capper had prescribed medication for Kuzilla on the evening prior to the accident and was therefore joined as a codefendant. The court held:

> * * * the threshold question of whether a duty is owed to plaintiff by defendant is a question of law for the court's resolution. Whether such a duty exists depends "in part on foreseeability—whether it is foreseeable that the actor's conduct may create a risk of harm to the victim * * *" [ ] Further, in the narrow circumstances of this case, the concept of foreseeability entails the finding of some "special relationship" with either the dangerous person or the potential victim.[ ] This "special relationship" exists where the physician determines or, pursuant to the standard of care, should determine that his patient poses a serious threat of danger to a third person.

Welke is part of another line of caselaw requiring physicians to warn third parties about, or take steps to protect them from, patients who are taking medication. These steps might include warning the patient about the effects of medication, or even refusing to prescribe the medication if the patient might still drive. In Myers v. Quesenberry, 144 Cal.App.3d 888, 193 Cal.Rptr. 733 (1983), the physician failed to warn his patient, a diabetic, of the dangers of driving. In Gooden v. Tips, 651 S.W.2d 364 (Tex.Ct.App. 1983), the physician failed to warn the patient of the dangers of driving while taking tranquilizers. In Watkins v. United States, 589 F.2d 214 (5th Cir.1979) the plaintiff was injured in a collision with a patient of the defendant. The defendant had prescribed a 50 day supply of Valium without checking the patient's psychiatric history and the patient proceeded to drink alcohol and take the pills. He then tried to kill himself by deliberately driving his car into the plaintiff's car. Held: defendant was negligent as to anyone who would be endangered by the patient's predictably irresponsible behavior. In Freese v. Lemmon, 210 N.W.2d 576 (Iowa 1973), liability was found where the doctor failed to warn the patient about the risk of a sudden seizure, and the patient then drove into the plaintiff during a fainting spell. In Kaiser v. Suburban Transportation System, 65 Wash.2d 461, 398 P.2d 14 (1965) amended, 65 Wash.2d 461, 401 P.2d 350 (1965), the doctor prescribed a drug for a patient, a bus driver, but neglected to tell him that it might make him sleepy. The doctor was held liable to the bus passengers and other third persons who were harmed when the driver fell asleep at the wheel. But see Forlaw v. Fitzer, 456 So.2d 432 (Fla.1984) (doctor prescribed Quaaludes to a known addict, who then drove into a child riding a bicycle and killed her. The court ruled that there was no negligence per se, because there had been no violation of the Florida controlled substances statute).

3. Psychiatric Dangerousness. The *Shephard* court also relied on Davis v. Lhim, 124 Mich.App. 291, 335 N.W.2d 481 (1983), in which the Michigan Supreme Court held that a psychiatrist owes a professional duty of care to those who could be foreseeably injured by his patient. This obligation first appeared in the psychiatric context in Tarasoff v. Regents of the Univ. of Cal., 17 Cal.3d 425, 131 Cal.Rptr. 14, 551 P.2d 334 (1976). In *Tarasoff,* a psychotherapist at the University of California was treating a patient, Poddar, who had uttered explicit threats toward his former girl-friend during the therapy sessions. No one, including the defendant, attempted to warn the young woman, and Poddar ultimately killed her. The parents sued, alleging negligence in the therapist's failure to warn. The California Supreme Court held that a therapist treating a mentally ill patient owes a duty of reasonable care to warn threatened persons against foreseeable danger created by the patient's condition. The relationship between the physician or therapist and the patient is sufficient to create a duty to protect others. See also McIntosh v. Milano, 168 N.J.Super. 466, 403 A.2d 500 (1979); Hedlund v. Superior Court of Orange County, 34 Cal.3d 695, 194 Cal.Rptr. 805, 669 P.2d 41 (1983); Lipari v. Sears, Roebuck & Co., 497 F.Supp. 185 (D.Neb.1980).

Problem: The Stubborn Patient

You represent Dr. Will Toma, a physician specializing in gerontology. He regularly examines and treats elderly patients, and has come to you for advice. One of his patients, Harry Glint, 86 years old, has a mild neurolog-ical disorder that causes blurred or double vision at times. Harry com-plains that his double vision is worst when he drives at night, when, he says, "The middle line becomes double and I have trouble staying on my side of the road." The problem is not treatable and it will worsen over time (although changes in prescriptions of eyeglasses may reduce the problem at times). Dr. Toma has admonished Mr. Glint never to drive at night, and to stop driving during the day as soon as possible. Mr. Glint is adamant about the importance of his driving, which he says keeps him young and active.

Dr. Toma is worried about his potential liability if Mr. Glint has a car accident which injures others. What are his liability risks, and what steps can he take to minimize them?

Problem: Confidentiality and Disclosure of AIDS–Related Information

One of your established clients, Joel Feinberg, an internist, has consult-ed you concerning a problem that has arisen in his practice. Two weeks ago one of his patients, Dr. Alan Miller, a resident at Mercy hospital where Dr. Feinberg is on staff, came in for a physical. Dr. Feinberg met Dr. Miller last year when Dr. Miller did an internal medicine rotation under Dr. Feinberg's supervision, and they have seen each other socially from time to time since. After his blood had been drawn for routine blood work, Dr. Miller requested that an HIV test be done on the blood. The test results came back positive for HIV antibodies. Dr. Feinberg immediately called Dr. Miller to tell him of the results. Dr. Miller, however, told Dr. Feinberg not to worry, the test was undoubtedly a false positive, and assured him that he would follow up with further testing later when he could find the time.

Dr. Feinberg has been deeply troubled by the test and by Dr. Miller's response to it. First, Dr. Feinberg knows that Dr. Miller is scheduled for orthopedic surgery to correct an old knee injury next month. He wonders whether he should inform the surgeon who will be doing the surgery, a colleague, of the test results. He also wonders whether nurses, surgical assistants, laboratory personnel and others who may be exposed to body fluids from the surgery should be informed. Second, he knows that Dr. Miller has applied for permanent staff privileges at Mercy hospital. Should the hospital medical staff or administration be informed of the test results? Does Dr. Feinberg have any obligation under state law to inform the public health department of the results? Should he inform the state medical licensure board? Finally, he knows that Dr. Miller is planning to marry another intern, Dr. Anne Bowen, early next year. When he asked Dr. Miller whether he would inform Anne of the test results, however, Dr. Miller said he would rather not bother her with results that were probably wrong in any event. Dr. Feinberg wants to know whether he should tell Dr. Bowen himself, ask the Department of Health to contact her through its contact-tracing program, or say nothing? Dr. Feinberg is well aware of his general obligation to keep patient confidences, but wonders whether any exceptions apply in this situation or whether, in fact, he has any obligations to disclose.

Notes and Questions

1. Special characteristics of AIDS and of the AIDS epidemic present new and unique challenges to health care workers trying to understand their general duty to keep confidences and their specific obligations, under some circumstances, to disclose medical information. First, widespread continuing fear of AIDS and ignorance about how it is spread, combined with a history of prejudice and discrimination against gay men among whom AIDS has been most common, have made concerns of privacy and confidentiality even more urgently important. If information about a person's AIDS infection or HIV positivity reaches employers, insurers, schools, family, or acquaintances it may have disastrous consequences. It is widely believed, therefore, that maintenance of the strictest confidentiality is essential if voluntary AIDS testing programs are to succeed—that any risk of disclosure will discourage persons who may possibly be HIV infected or who have AIDS or ARC from seeking testing and counselling.

Second, the fact that the HIV virus cannot be spread through casual contact, unlike many other contagious diseases, limits the need for disclosure of information about infection. The fact that the rate of infection through heterosexual genital intercourse is very low (about .001 per exposure) may argue against a duty to warn heterosexual partners, since it is unlikely that casual heterosexual partners will be infected, or may argue in favor of a warning, since it is possible that longer term partners may have not yet been infected. The possibility of transmission to unborn children may also argue for warning potentially infected persons who may potentially bear children.

Third, the fact that AIDS is presently incurable makes prevention all the more essential. Does this argue for maintaining strict confidentiality, so that persons who may be infected will come forward to be tested and thereafter modify their behavior voluntarily to avoid infecting others? Or does it argue for limited disclosure to protect persons who may be exposed to possible infection? Does the emergence of new treatment modalities like AZT, which may slow the infection process, argue for greater confidentiality or broader disclosure?

What is the relevance to questions of confidentiality and disclosure of the fact that HIV testing results in a significant number of false positives in low-risk populations? Of what significance is the fact that HIV positivity may not show up in testing until months, perhaps years, after a person becomes HIV infected?

2. Should medical records or laboratory specimens of patients in health care institutions who are HIV positive be specially marked to permit special precautions to protect against infection? Might doing so unduly risk further disclosure of confidential information, while offering little additional protection to health care workers who should be observing universal precautions against infection in any event? Might such special identification lull health care workers into unwarranted complacency in dealing with patients and specimens not so identified, despite the fact that patients may be infected but untested or that tests may have resulted in false negatives? Should infected medical personnel be reported to licensure agencies? What action, if any, should licensure agencies take based upon this information?

3. Health care workers should certainly counsel HIV-infected patients to take special precautions to avoid infecting others and to tell their sexual or needle-sharing partners to seek testing, counseling, and treatment. If patients indicate, however, that they will not do so, does the health care worker have an obligation to warn others? Should the health care worker rather notify the state health department of the patient's infected status and of persons who may have been infected by the patient, to permit contact tracing? Even if the health care worker has no duty to warn, is the worker permitted to do so, or does the health care worker face liability for violating confidentiality requirements if she or he proceeds to warn potentially infected persons?

Consider the AMA position on this question:

Where there is no statute that mandates or prohibits reporting of seropositive individuals to public health authorities and it is clear that the seropositive individual is endangering an identified third party, the physician should (1) attempt to persuade the infected individual to cease endangering the third party; (2) if persuasion fails, notify authorities; and (3) if authorities take no action, notify and counsel the endangered third party.

HIV Blood Test Counseling: A.M.A. Physician Guidelines (1988)

4. The states have adopted a variety of legislative and administrative approaches to confidentiality and disclosure of information regarding HIV-positivity, ARC, and AIDS status. All states now require physicians to report AIDS cases to the state health department. A number also require reporting of cases of asymptomatic HIV infection. Several states have adopted statutes mandating strict confidentiality of AIDS-related information. See Cal.Health & Safety Code, § 199.21; West's Fla.Stat.Ann. § 14A § 381.609(2)(f); Mass.Gen.L. Ch. 111 § 70F. Other states have adopted laws permitting disclosure of HIV test results to certain persons or under certain circumstances. See Vernon's Ann.Tex.Rev.Civ.Stat. art. 4419b–1, § 9.03, (disclosure to spouse permitted); Ga.Code Ann. § 38–723(g) (disclosure to spouse, sexual partner or child permitted under some circumstances); McKinney's–N.Y.Pub.Health Law § 2782(4)(a) & (b) (physician may disclose information to persons in significant risk of infection if already infected person will not do so after counselling and physician warns that person of the physician's intention to disclose.) The identity of the infected person cannot be disclosed. The physician is protected from liability whether he discloses or chooses not to disclose the information.) For an excellent recent review of state statutes, see Price, Between Scylla and Charybdis: Charting A Course to Reconcile The Duty of Confidentiality and the Duty to Warn in the AIDS Context, 94 Dick.L.Rev. 435 (1990).

A number of states permit public health authorities to engage in contact tracing or partner notification with respect to persons with AIDS or who are HIV infected. Five different approaches to contact tracing have been identified: 1) solicitation of the names of all sexual and needle-sharing contacts of AIDS- and HIV-infected persons with subsequent notification of all identified contacts (with offers for testing and counselling); 2) limited contact tracing focusing on high risk or especially vulnerable groups who are likely to be unaware of the risk of infection (heterosexual contacts of individuals with AIDS); 3) voluntary contact tracing: infected persons are asked to notify potentially infected persons voluntarily and assistance is offered to those who want help in notifying others; 4) notification in special circumstances, as to rescue or emergency personnel potentially infected in the line of duty; 5) notification of specific persons in specific situations, such as those exposed to infected blood. See Rothenberg, et al. The AIDS Project: Creating a Public Health Policy—Rights and Obligations of Health Care Workers, 48 Md.L.Rev. 94, 181–183 (1989). Colorado has been particularly active in contact tracing, and claims that its program has resulted in the identification and treatment of a number of individuals who would not otherwise have been aware of their HIV positive status. See Partner Notification for Preventing Immunodeficiency Virus (HIV) Infection—Colorado, Idaho, South Carolina, Virginia, 260 J.A.M.A. 613 (1988). Does the fact that contact tracing usually depends on voluntary disclosure of sexual and needle-sharing partners by the infected person render it ineffective in situations where the infected person refuses to notify others voluntarily?

5. One particular situation in which the disclosure of the identify of HIV-infected persons has been frequently sought is where a person who has become HIV infected through tainted blood seeks disclosure of the identity of the donor who donated the infected blood, either to assist in establishing negligence on the part of the blood service or to permit a suit against the

donor. These cases have tended to deny discovery, relying on various privacy, physician patient privilege, or discovery protection theories and on the importance of protecting the identity of blood donors to encourage voluntary blood donations. See Krygier v. Airweld, Inc., 137 Misc.2d 306, 520 N.Y.S.2d 475 (Sup.Ct.1987); Rasmussen v. South Florida Blood Service, Inc., 500 So.2d 533 (Fla.1987); contra, see Gulf Coast Regional Blood Center v. Houston, 745 S.W.2d 556 (Tex.App.1988); Tarrant County Hosp. Dist. v. Hughes, 734 S.W.2d 675 (Tex.Ct.App.1987), cert. denied 484 U.S. 1065, 108 S.Ct. 1027, 98 L.Ed.2d 991 (1988). See Bellow & Lapp, Protecting the Confidentiality of Blood Donors' Identities in AIDS Litigation, 37 Drake L.Rev. 343 (1988).

6. See, among the many sources on confidentiality and disclosure of AIDS-related information, Association of State and Territorial Health Officials, Guide to Public Health Practice: AIDS Confidentiality and Anti–Discrimination Principles (1988); Douard, AIDS, Stigma, and Privacy, 5 AIDS & Pub.Pol.J. 37 (1990); Edgar & Sandomire, Medical Privacy Issues in the Age of AIDS: Legislative Options, 16 Am.J.L. & Med. 155 (1990); Fox, From TB to AIDS: Value Conflicts in Reporting Disease, 16 Hastings Center Rep. 11 (Supp.Dec.1986); Gostin, Hospitals, Health Care Professionals, and AIDS: The "Right to Know" the Health Status of Professionals and Patients, 48 Md.L.Rev. 12 (1989); Hermann & Gagliano, AIDS, Therapeutic Confidentiality, and Warning Third Parties, 48 Md.L.Rev. 55 (1989); McDonald, Ethical Problems for Physicians Raised by AIDS and HIV Infection: Conflicting Legal Obligations of Confidentiality and Disclosure, 22 U.C.D.L.Rev. 557 (1989); North and Rothenberg, The Duty to Warn "Dilemma"—A Framework for Resolution, 4 AIDS & Pub.Policy J. 133 (1989); Price, supra; Rothenberg, supra; Turkington, Confidentiality Policy for HIV–Related Information: An Analytical Framework for Sorting Out Hard and Easy Cases, 34 Vill.L.Rev. 872 (1989); Note, AIDS: A Crisis in Confidentiality, 62 So.Calif.L.Rev. 1702 (1989).

III. INFORMED CONSENT: THE PHYSICIAN'S OBLIGATION

A. ORIGINS OF THE INFORMED CONSENT DOCTRINE

Informed consent has developed out of strong judicial deference toward individual autonomy, reflecting a belief that an individual has a right to be free from nonconsensual interference with his or her person, and a basic moral principle that it is wrong to force another to act against his or her will. This principle was articulated in the medical context by Justice Cardozo in Schloendorf v. Society of New York Hospital, 211 N.Y. 125, 105 N.E. 92 (1914): "Every human being of adult years and sound mind has a right to determine what shall be done with his own body * * * ". Informed consent doctrine has guided medical decisionmaking by setting boundaries for the doctor-patient relationship and is one of the forces altering the attitudes of a new generation of doctors toward their patients. It has provided the starting point for federal regulations on human experimentation, and is now reflected in consent forms that health care institutions require all patients to sign upon admission and before various procedures are performed.

Professor Alexander Capron has argued that the doctrine can serve six salutory functions. It can:

1) protect individual autonomy;

2) protect the patient's status as a human being;

3) avoid fraud or duress;

4) encourage doctors to carefully consider their decisions;

5) foster rational decision-making by the patient; and

6) involve the public generally in medicine.

Capron, "Informed Consent in Catastrophic Disease Research and Treatment," 123 U.Penn.L.Rev. 340, 365–76 (1974).

This chapter will return later to an examination of how informed consent doctrine has in fact affected medical practice and the relationship of physician and patient. First, however, it will examine how the doctrine developed and how it now functions as a litigation tool in American jurisdictions.

Informed consent has been an unnatural graft onto medical practice. As Jay Katz wrote in The Silent World of Doctor and Patient 1 (1984), " * * * disclosure and consent, except in the most rudimentary fashion, are obligations alien to medical thinking and practice." The function of disclosure historically has been to get patients to agree to what the doctors wanted. In ancient Greece, patients' participation in decision-making was considered undesirable, since the doctor's primary task was to inspire confidence. Medieval medical writing likewise viewed conversations between doctors and patients as an opportunity for the former to offer comfort and hope, but emphasized the need for the doctor to be manipulative and even deceitful. Authority needed to be coupled with obedience to create a patient's faith in the cure. By the Enlightenment, the view had emerged that patients had a capacity to listen to the doctor, but that deception was still needed to facilitate patient management. By the nineteenth century, the profession was split over such issues as disclosure of a dire prognosis, although the majority of doctors still argued against disclosure. The beginnings of the twentieth century showed no progress in the evolution of the doctor-patient relationship toward collaboration.

The judicial development of informed consent into a distinct doctrine can be roughly divided into three periods, according to Katz. During the first period, up to the mid-twentieth century, courts built upon the law of battery and required little more than disclosure by doctors of their proposed treatment. The second period saw an emerging judicial feeling that doctors should disclose the alternatives to a proposed treatment and their risks, as well as of risks of the proposed treatment itself. The third period, from 1972 to the present, has seen legislative retrenchment and judicial inertia.

As you read the cases in this section, ask how far the courts have gone toward permitting patients to control treatment decisions that affect them. Consider also what a plaintiff must show to make out an informed consent case in various jurisdictions. Finally, ask if any other processes are likely to serve the purposes of informed consent more efficiently, and with less adverse effect on the doctor-patient relationship.

PERNA v. PIROZZI

Supreme Court of New Jersey, 1983.
92 N.J. 446, 457 A.2d 431.

[The appeal raised three issues: (1) the validity of the practice of pre-submission of malpractice claims to a panel of a judge, lawyer and physician; (2) whether the plaintiff may cross-examine a defendant doctor about prior inconsistent statements at a panel hearing or show the bias of a panel-doctor; (3) the nature of the cause of action of a patient who consents to surgery by one surgeon but is operated on by another surgeon.]

IV

We now address the nature of the claim resulting from the performance of the operation by a physician other than the one named in the consent form, so-called "ghost surgery." If the claim is characterized as a failure to obtain informed consent, the operation may constitute an act of medical malpractice; if, however, it is viewed as a failure to obtain any consent, it is better classified as a battery.

Informed consent is a negligence concept predicated on the duty of a physician to disclose to a patient information that will enable him to "evaluate knowledgeably the options available and the risks attendant upon each" before subjecting that patient to a course of treatment. [ ] Under the doctrine, the patient who consents to an operation is given the opportunity to show that the surgeon withheld information concerning "the inherent and potential hazards of the proposed treatment, the alternatives to that treatment, if any, and the results likely if the patient remains untreated." [ ] If the patient succeeds in proving that the surgeon did not comply with the applicable standard for disclosure, the consent is vitiated. [ ]

In an action predicated upon a battery, a patient need not prove initially that the physician has deviated from a professional standard of care. Under a battery theory, proof of an unauthorized invasion of the plaintiff's person, even if harmless, entitles him to nominal damages. [ ] The plaintiff may further recover for all injuries proximately caused by the mere performance of the operation, whether the result of negligence or not. [ ] If an operation is properly performed, albeit by a surgeon operating without the consent of the patient, and the patient suffers no injuries except those which foreseeably follow from the operation, then a jury could find that the substitution of surgeons did not cause any compensable injury. Even there, however, a jury could award damages for mental anguish resulting from the belated knowledge that the operation was performed by a doctor to whom the patient had not given consent. Furthermore, because battery connotes an intentional invasion of another's rights, punitive damages may be assessed in an appropriate case. [ ]

The plaintiffs here do not challenge the adequacy of the disclosure of information relating to risks inherent in the operation performed. Nor do they contend that Mr. Perna would have decided not to undergo the operation if additional facts had been provided to him. In short, they concede Perna consented to an operation by Dr. Pirozzi. However, plaintiffs contend that two other surgeons operated on him without his consent. If that contention is correct, the operating surgeons violated the patient's right to control his own body. [ ]

Any non-consensual touching is a battery. [ ] Even more private than the decision who may touch one's body is the decision who may cut it open and invade it with hands and instruments. Absent an emergency, patients have the right to determine not only whether surgery is to be performed on them, but who shall perform it. A surgeon who operates without the patient's consent engages in the unauthorized touching of another and, thus, commits a battery. [ ] A nonconsensual operation remains a battery even if performed skillfully and to the benefit of the patient. The medical profession itself recognizes that it is unethical to mislead a patient as to the identity of the doctor who performs the operation. American College of Surgeons, Statements on Principles, § I.A. (June 1981). Participation in such a deception is a recognized cause for discipline by the medical profession. See American College of Surgeons, Bylaws, art. VII, § 1(c) (as amended June 1976). By statute, the State Board of Medical Examiners is empowered to prevent the professional certification or future professional practice of a person who "[h]as engaged in the use or employment of dishonesty, fraud, deception, misrepresentation, false promise or false pretense * * * " N.J.S.A. 45:1–21. Consequently, a statutory, as well as a moral, imperative compels doctors to be honest with their patients.

A different theory applies to the claim against Dr. Pirozzi. As to him, the action follows from the alleged breach of his agreement to operate and the fiduciary duty he owed his patient. With respect to that allegation, the Judicial Council of the American Medical Association has decried the substitution of one surgeon for another without the consent of the patient, describing that practice as a "deceit." A patient has the right to choose the surgeon who will operate on him and to refuse to accept a substitute. Correlative to that right is the duty of the doctor to provide his or her personal services in accordance with the agreement with the patient. Judicial Council of the American Medical Ass'n, Op. 8.12 (1982).

Few decisions bespeak greater trust and confidence than the decision of a patient to proceed with surgery. Implicit in that decision is a willingness of the patient to put his or her life in the hands of a known and trusted medical doctor. Sometimes circumstances will arise in which, because of an emergency, the limited capacity of the patient, or some other valid reason, the doctor cannot obtain the express consent of the patient to a surrogate surgeon. Other times, doctors who practice in a medical group may explain to a patient that any one of them may perform a medical procedure. In that situation, the patient may accept any or all the members of the group as his surgeon. In still other instances, the patient may consent to an operation performed by a resident under the supervision of the attending physician. The point is that a patient has the right to know who will operate and the consent form should reflect the patient's decision. Where a competent patient consents to surgery by a specific surgeon of his choice, the patient has every right to expect that surgeon, not another, to operate.

The failure of a surgeon to perform a medical procedure after soliciting a patient's consent, like the failure to operate on the appropriate part of a patient's body, is a deviation from standard medical care. It is malpractice whether the right surgeon operates on the wrong part or the wrong surgeon operates on the right part of the patient. In each instance, the surgeon has breached his duty to care for the patient. Where damages are the proximate result of a deviation from standard medical care, a patient has a cause of action for malpractice. Although an alternative cause of action could be framed as a breach of the contract between the surgeon and the patient, generally the more appropriate characterization of the cause will be for breach of the duty of care owed by the doctor to the patient. The absence of damages may render any action deficient, but the doctor who, without the consent of the patient, permits another surgeon to operate violates not only a fundamental tenet of the medical profession, but also a legal obligation.

The judgment below is reversed and the matter remanded for trial consistent with our opinion. On remand, the court shall conduct a new pretrial conference at which all parties should have the opportunity to amend their pleadings to conform to this opinion.

Notes and Questions

1. What is at stake in the battery-based consent cases? Patient autonomy in medical decisionmaking is the underlying principle in all consent cases, whether based in battery or negligence. The doctrine of battery protects a patient's physical integrity from harmful contacts and her personal dignity from unwanted bodily contact. The doctrine requires only that the patient show that she was not informed of the very nature of the medical touching, typically a surgical procedure. Physical injury is not necessary. When a surgeon, in the course of surgery, removes or operates upon an organ other than the one he and the patient discussed, a battery action lies. The most obvious medical battery cases, e.g., where a surgeon amputates the wrong leg, can be readily brought as a negligence case. Is

there any reason to treat any informed consent issue as a battery, rather than negligence? In what kind of case would a battery theory permit recovery, but a negligence case would not?

2.   The procedural and other advantages of a battery-based action tip the scales substantially in the favor of the patient. First, the focus is on the patient's right to be free from a touching different from that to which she consented. The physician has few defenses to a battery. Second, the plaintiff need not prove through expert testimony what the standard of care was; the proof is only that the particular physician failed to explain to the patient the nature and character of the particular procedure. Third, to prove causation, the plaintiff need only show that an unconsented-to touching occurred. Under a negligence theory the plaintiff must show that he would have declined a procedure if he had known all the details and risks. See generally Kohoutek v. Hafner, 383 N.W.2d 295 (Minn.1986). In Chouinard v. Marjani, 21 Conn.App. 572, 575 A.2d 238 (1990), the plaintiff sued the defendant surgeon, claiming that the surgeon had performed bilateral breast surgery although the plaintiff had consented only to surgery on her left breast. She admitted that if the surgeon had asked, she would have consented to the surgery on her right breast. The court applied battery doctrine, holding that plaintiff did not need to present either expert testimony nor testify that she would not have consented if the surgeon had asked.

3.   Use of a battery theory therefore reduces the need for medical testimony, restricting the scope of physicians' beliefs about what patients should know and might want as therapy. A judicial sense that medical judgment should be allowed more leeway has led to a movement from battery to negligent nondisclosure over the years. "A physician sued in a battery case has relatively little 'elbow room' in which to establish a defense. A physician sued for medical negligence in failing to disclose hazards has many possibilities on which to base a defense under the circumstances that existed." Plante, An Analysis of 'Informed Consent', 36 Fordham L.Rev. 639 (1968). Malpractice reform in the states has often included abrogation of the battery basis of informed consent. See Rubino v. DeFretias, 638 F.Supp. 182 (D.Ariz.1986) (holding statute unconstitutional on grounds that the Arizona constitution establishes a fundamental right to bring an action against a physician based on common law theory of battery.)

4.   What might motivate a physician in a hospital, a group practice or an HMO to tell his patient that he will treat or operate on a patient when he knows that one of his colleagues will do the procedure? Must a surgeon disclose that a surgical resident is likely to take part in the surgery, and may even be allowed to take over? Must a patient be told that a nurse-anesthetist, rather than the physician-anesthesiologist, is likely to administer the anesthesia? See Labarre v. Duke University, 99 N.C.App. 563, 393 S.E.2d 321 (1990) (No).

5.   Battery theory normally applies when the surgery is completely unauthorized. Negligence covers situations where surgery was authorized but the consent was uninformed. F. Rosovsky, Consent to Treatment, A Practical Guide, § 1.2 at 6 (1984); 2 D. Louisell & H. Williams, Medical

Malpractice, § 22.04 at 22–16 (1987). Fraud and deceit in obtaining a patient's consent has always sounded in battery. The burden of proving fraudulent inducement is a heavy one. See Tonelli v. Khanna, 238 N.J.Super. 121, 569 A.2d 282 (1990) (plaintiff alleged that defendant surgeon rushed her into surgery for his own financial gain; no intentional tort found.) In *Perna,* the issue of physician deceit is explicitly discussed by the court as justification for the result.

6. One advantage of the battery-based action in informed consent is the possibility of getting punitive damages, even where actual damages are small. Punitive damages have been criticized as unfair and out of control in tort litigation generally. In malpractice cases, courts are not willing to allow such damages except under extreme circumstances. Deceit and breach of fiduciary obligations by a physician are examples of causes of action that may justify such damages. In Bommareddy v. Superior Court, 222 Cal.App.3d 1017, 272 Cal.Rptr. 246 (1990), Dr. Bommareddy performed a cataract extraction with an intraocular lens implant on the plaintiff's right eye without her knowledge or consent. She had consented only to tear duct surgery on her left eye. Her first cause of action was for a battery. The court upheld the plaintiff's claim for punitive damages as part of her battery count, noting that "professional negligence" as defined in the California Code did not include battery, and therefore a claim for punitive damages was not limited by the Code.

For an excellent discussion of punitive damages generally, see Dobbs, Ending Punishment in "Punitive Damages": Deterrence–Measured Remedies, 40 Ala.L.Rev. 831 (1989). For an argument in favor of punitive damages for failure to obtain informed consent, particularly in research settings, see McClellan, Informed Consent to Medical Therapy and Experimentation, 3 J.Leg.Med. 81 (1982).

7. Pennsylvania continues to treat a physician's failure to get a patient's informed consent to surgery as a battery, rendering the defendant liable for all injuries the plaintiff suffers from the invasion. A plaintiff need not show that a reasonable person in his place, having been properly advised by his doctor, would not have consented to surgery. "We refuse to eviscerate the doctrine of informed consent by predicating materiality and, thus, the mandate for disclosure of risks and alternatives, upon a factfinder's determination that a plaintiff-patient would have declined treatment had the disclosures been made." Gouse v. Cassel, 385 Pa.Super. 521, 561 A.2d 797, 800 (1989); Moure v. Raeuchele, 387 Pa.Super. 127, 563 A.2d 1217 (1989). Pennsylvania appears to be the only state that grounds informed consent on a battery theory.

B. THE LEGAL FRAMEWORK: NEGLIGENCE AS A BASIS FOR RECOVERY

CANTERBURY v. SPENCE

United States Court of Appeals, District of Columbia Circuit, 1972.
464 F.2d 772.

SPOTTSWOOD W. ROBINSON, III, CIRCUIT JUDGE:

This appeal is from a judgment entered in the District Court on verdicts directed for the two appellees at the conclusion of plaintiff-appellant Canterbury's case in chief. His action sought damages for personal injuries allegedly sustained as a result of an operation negligently performed by appellee Spence, a negligent failure by Dr. Spence to disclose a risk of serious disability inherent in the operation, and negligent post-operative care by appellee Washington Hospital Center. On close examination of the record, we find evidence which required submission of these issues to the jury. We accordingly reverse the judgment as to each appellee and remand the case to the District Court for a new trial.

I

The record we review tells a depressing tale. A youth troubled only by back pain submitted to an operation without being informed of a risk of paralysis incidental thereto. A day after the operation he fell from his hospital bed after having been left without assistance while voiding. A few hours after the fall, the lower half of his body was paralyzed, and he had to be operated on again. Despite extensive medical care, he has never been what he was before. Instead of the back pain, even years later, he hobbled about on crutches, a victim of paralysis of the bowels and urinary incontinence. In a very real sense this lawsuit is an understandable search for reasons.

At the time of the events which gave rise to this litigation, appellant was nineteen years of age, a clerk-typist employed by the Federal Bureau of Investigation. In December, 1958, he began to experience severe pain between his shoulder blades. He consulted two general practitioners, but the medications they prescribed failed to eliminate the pain. Thereafter, appellant secured an appointment with Dr. Spence, who is a neurosurgeon.

Dr. Spence examined appellant in his office at some length but found nothing amiss. On Dr. Spence's advice appellant was x-rayed, but the films did not identify any abnormality. Dr. Spence then recommended that appellant undergo a myelogram—a procedure in which dye is injected into the spinal column and traced to find evidence of disease or other disorder—at the Washington Hospital Center.

Appellant entered the hospital on February 4, 1959. The myelogram revealed a "filling defect" in the region of the fourth thoracic vertebra. Since a myelogram often does no more than pinpoint the location of an aberration, surgery may be necessary to discover the cause. Dr. Spence told appellant that he would have to undergo a laminectomy—the excision of the posterior arch of the vertebra—to correct what he suspected was a ruptured disc. Appellant did not raise any objection to the proposed operation nor did he probe into its exact nature.

Appellant explained to Dr. Spence that his mother was a widow of slender financial means living in Cyclone, West Virginia, and that she could be reached through a neighbor's telephone. Appellant called his mother the day after the myelogram was performed and, failing to contact her, left Dr. Spence's telephone number with the neighbor.

When Mrs. Canterbury returned the call, Dr. Spence told her that the surgery was occasioned by a suspected ruptured disc. Mrs. Canterbury then asked if the recommended operation was serious and Dr. Spence replied "not any more than any other operation." He added that he knew Mrs. Canterbury was not well off and that her presence in Washington would not be necessary. The testimony is contradictory as to whether during the course of the conversation Mrs. Canterbury expressed her consent to the operation. Appellant himself apparently did not converse again with Dr. Spence prior to the operation.

Dr. Spence performed the laminectomy on February 11 at the Washington Hospital Center. Mrs. Canterbury traveled to Washington, arriving on that date but after the operation was over, and signed a consent form at the hospital. The laminectomy revealed several anomalies: a spinal cord that was swollen and unable to pulsate, an accumulation of large tortuous and dilated veins, and a complete absence of epidural fat which normally surrounds the spine. A thin hypodermic needle was inserted into the spinal cord to aspirate any cysts which might have been present, but no fluid emerged. In suturing the wound, Dr. Spence attempted to relieve the pressure on the spinal cord by enlarging the dura—the outer protective wall of the spinal cord—at the area of swelling.

For approximately the first day after the operation appellant recuperated normally, but then suffered a fall and an almost immediate setback. Since there is some conflict as to precisely when or why appellant fell, we reconstruct the events from the evidence most favorable to him. Dr. Spence left orders that appellant was to remain in bed during the process of voiding. These orders were changed to direct that voiding be done out of bed, and the jury could find that the change was made by hospital personnel. Just prior to the fall, appellant summoned a nurse and was given a receptacle for use in voiding, but was then left unattended. Appellant testified that during the course of the endeavor he slipped off the side of the bed, and that there was no one to assist him, or side rail to prevent the fall.

Several hours later, appellant began to complain that he could not move his legs and that he was having trouble breathing; paralysis seems to have been virtually total from the waist down. Dr. Spence was notified on the night of February 12, and he rushed to the hospital. Mrs. Canterbury signed another consent form and appellant was again taken into the operating room. The surgical wound was reopened and Dr. Spence created a gusset to allow the spinal cord greater room in which to pulsate.

Appellant's control over his muscles improved somewhat after the second operation but he was unable to void properly. As a result of this condition, he came under the care of a urologist while still in the hospital. In April, following a cystoscopic examination, appellant was operated on for removal of bladder stones, and in May was released from the hospital. He reentered the hospital the following August for a

10–day period, apparently because of his urologic problems. For several years after his discharge he was under the care of several specialists, and at all times was under the care of a urologist. At the time of the trial in April, 1968, appellant required crutches to walk, still suffered from urinal incontinence and paralysis of the bowels, and wore a penile clamp.

In November, 1959 on Dr. Spence's recommendation, appellant was transferred by the F.B.I. to Miami where he could get more swimming and exercise. Appellant worked three years for the F.B.I. in Miami, Los Angeles and Houston, resigning finally in June, 1962. From then until the time of the trial, he held a number of jobs, but had constant trouble finding work because he needed to remain seated and close to a bathroom. The damages appellant claims include extensive pain and suffering, medical expenses, and loss of earnings.

II

* * *

At the close of appellant's case in chief, each defendant moved for a directed verdict and the trial judge granted both motions. The basis of the ruling, he explained, was that appellant had failed to produce any medical evidence indicating negligence on Dr. Spence's part in diagnosing appellant's malady or in performing the laminectomy; that there was no proof that Dr. Spence's treatment was responsible for appellant's disabilities; and that notwithstanding some evidence to show negligent post-operative care, an absence of medical testimony to show causality precluded submission of the case against the hospital to the jury. The judge did not allude specifically to the alleged breach of duty by Dr. Spence to divulge the possible consequences of the laminectomy.

We reverse. The testimony of appellant and his mother that Dr. Spence did not reveal the risk of paralysis from the laminectomy made out a prima facie case of violation of the physician's duty to disclose which Dr. Spence's explanation did not negate as a matter of law.
* * *

III

* * *

* * * True consent to what happens to one's self is the informed exercise of a choice, and that entails an opportunity to evaluate knowledgeably the options available and the risks attendant upon each. The average patient has little or no understanding of the medical arts, and ordinarily has only his physician to whom he can look for enlightenment with which to reach an intelligent decision. From these almost axiomatic considerations springs the need, and in turn the requirement, of a reasonable divulgence by physician to patient to make such a decision possible.[15]

15. The doctrine that a consent effective as authority to form therapy can arise only from the patient's understanding of alternatives to and risks of the therapy is

A physician is under a duty to treat his patient skillfully but proficiency in diagnosis and therapy is not the full measure of his responsibility. The cases demonstrate that the physician is under an obligation to communicate specific information to the patient when the exigencies of reasonable care call for it. Due care may require a physician perceiving symptoms of bodily abnormality to alert the patient to the condition. It may call upon the physician confronting an ailment which does not respond to his ministrations to inform the patient thereof. It may command the physician to instruct the patient as to any limitations to be presently observed for his own welfare, and as to any precautionary therapy he should seek in the future. It may oblige the physician to advise the patient of the need for or desirability of any alternative treatment promising greater benefit than that being pursued. Just as plainly, due care normally demands that the physician warn the patient of any risks to his well-being which contemplated therapy may involve.

The context in which the duty of risk-disclosure arises is invariably the occasion for decision as to whether a particular treatment procedure is to be undertaken. To the physician, whose training enables a self-satisfying evaluation, the answer may seem clear, but it is the prerogative of the patient, not the physician, to determine for himself the direction in which his interests seem to lie. To enable the patient to chart his course understandably, some familiarity with the therapeutic alternatives and their hazards becomes essential.

A reasonable revelation in these respects is not only a necessity but, as we see it, is as much a matter of the physician's duty. It is a duty to warn of the dangers lurking in the proposed treatment, and that is surely a facet of due care. It is, too, a duty to impart

commonly denominated "informed consent." See, *e.g.*, Waltz & Scheuneman, Informed Consent to Therapy, 64 Nw.U.L. Rev. 628, 629 (1970). The same appellation is frequently assigned to the doctrine requiring physicians, as a matter of duty to patients, to communicate information as to such alternatives and risks. See, *e.g.*, Comment, Informed Consent in Medical Malpractice, 55 Calif.L.Rev. 1396 (1967). While we recognize the general utility of shorthand phrases in literary expositions, we caution that uncritical use of the "informed consent" label can be misleading. See, *e.g.*, Plante, An Analysis of "Informed Consent," 36 Ford.L.Rev. 639, 671–72 (1968).

In duty-to-disclose cases, the focus of attention is more properly upon the nature and content of the physician's divulgence than the patient's understanding or consent. Adequate disclosure and informed consent are, of course, two sides of the same coin—the former a *sine qua non* of the latter. But the vital inquiry on duty to disclose relates to the physician's performance of an obligation, while one of the difficulties with analysis in terms of "informed consent" is its tendency to imply that what is decisive is the degree of the patient's comprehension. As we later emphasize, the physician discharges the duty when he makes a reasonable effort to convey sufficient information although the patient, without fault of the physician, may not fully grasp it. See text *infra* at notes 82–89. Even though the factfinder may have occasion to draw an inference on the state of the patient's enlightenment, the factfinding process on performance of the duty ultimately reaches back to what the physician actually said or failed to say. And while the factual conclusion on adequacy of the revelation will vary as between patients—as, for example, between a lay patient and a physician-patient—the fluctuations are attributable to the kind of divulgence which may be reasonable under the circumstances.

information which the patient has every right to expect. The patient's reliance upon the physician is a trust of the kind which traditionally has exacted obligations beyond those associated with arms-length transactions. His dependence upon the physician for information affecting his well-being, in terms of contemplated treatment, is well-nigh abject. As earlier noted, long before the instant litigation arose, courts had recognized that the physician had the responsibility of satisfying the vital informational needs of the patient. More recently, we ourselves have found "in the fiducial qualities of [the physician-patient] relationship the physician's duty to reveal to the patient that which in his best interests it is important that he should know." We now find, as a part of the physician's overall obligation to the patient, a similar duty of reasonable disclosure of the choices with respect to proposed therapy and the dangers inherently and potentially involved.

This disclosure requirement, on analysis, reflects much more of a change in doctrinal emphasis than a substantive addition to malpractice law. It is well established that the physician must seek and secure his patient's consent before commencing an operation or other course of treatment. It is also clear that the consent, to be efficacious, must be free from imposition upon the patient. It is the settled rule that therapy not authorized by the patient may amount to a tort—a common law battery—by the physician. And it is evident that it is normally impossible to obtain a consent worthy of the name unless the physician first elucidates the options and the perils for the patient's edification. Thus the physician has long borne a duty, on pain of liability for unauthorized treatment, to make adequate disclosure to the patient.[36] The evolution of the obligation to communicate for the patient's benefit as well as the physician's protection has hardly involved an extraordinary restructuring of the law.

IV

Duty to disclose has gained recognition in a large number of American jurisdictions, but more largely on a different rationale. The majority of courts dealing with the problem have made the duty depend on whether it was the custom of physicians practicing in the community to make the particular disclosure to the patient. If so, the physician may be held liable for an unreasonable and injurious failure to divulge, but there can be no recovery unless the omission forsakes a practice prevalent in the profession. We agree that the physician's noncompliance with a professional custom to reveal, like any other departure

---

36. We discard the thought that the patient should ask for information before the physician is required to disclose. Caveat emptor is not the norm for the consumer of medical services. Duty to disclose is more than a call to speak merely on the patient's request, or merely to answer the patient's questions; it is a duty to volunteer, if necessary, the information the patient needs for intelligent decision. The patient may be ignorant, confused, over-

awed by the physician or frightened by the hospital, or even ashamed to inquire. [ ] Perhaps relatively few patients could in any event identify the relevant questions in the absence of prior explanation by the physician. Physicians and hospitals have patients of widely divergent socio-economic backgrounds, and a rule which presumes a degree of sophistication which many members of society lack is likely to breed gross inequities. [ ]

from prevailing medical practice, may give rise to liability to the patient. We do not agree that the patient's cause of action is dependent upon the existence and nonperformance of a relevant professional tradition.

There are, in our view, formidable obstacles to acceptance of the notion that the physician's obligation to disclose is either germinated or limited by medical practice. To begin with, the reality of any discernible custom reflecting a professional concensus [sic] on communication of option and risk information to patients is open to serious doubt. We sense the danger that what in fact is no custom at all may be taken as an affirmative custom to maintain silence, and that physician-witnesses to the so-called custom may state merely their personal opinions as to what they or others would do under given conditions. We cannot gloss over the inconsistency between reliance on a general practice respecting divulgence and, on the other hand, realization that the myriad of variables among patients makes each case so different that its omission can rationally be justified only by the effect of its individual circumstances. Nor can we ignore the fact that to bind the disclosure obligation to medical usage is to arrogate the decision on revelation to the physician alone. Respect for the patient's right of self-determination on particular therapy demands a standard set by law for physicians rather than one which physicians may or may not impose upon themselves.

* * * The caliber of the performance exacted by the reasonable-care standard varies between the professional and non-professional worlds, and so also the role of professional custom. * * *

We have admonished, however, that "[t]he special medical standards are but adaptions of the general standard to a group who are required to act as reasonable men possessing their medical talents presumably would." There is, by the same token, no basis for operation of the special medical standard where the physician's activity does not bring his medical knowledge and skills peculiarly into play. And where the challenge to the physician's conduct is not to be gauged by the special standard, it follows that medical custom cannot furnish the test of its propriety, whatever its relevance under the proper test may be. The decision to unveil the patient's condition and the chances as to remediation, as we shall see, is ofttimes a non-medical judgment and, if so, is a decision outside the ambit of the special standard. Where that is the situation, professional custom hardly furnishes the legal criterion for measuring the physician's responsibility to reasonably inform his patient of the options and the hazards as to treatment.

The majority rule, moreover, is at war with our prior holdings that a showing of medical practice, however probative, does not fix the standard governing recovery for medical malpractice. Prevailing medical practice, we have maintained, has evidentiary value in determinations as to what the specific criteria measuring challenged professional conduct are and whether they have been met, but does not itself define the standard. That has been our position in treatment cases, where the physician's performance is ordinarily to be adjudicated by the special medical standard of due care. We see no logic in a different rule for nondisclosure cases, where the governing standard is much more largely divorced from professional considerations. And surely in nondisclosure cases the factfinder is not invariably functioning in an area of such technical complexity that it must be bound to medical custom as an inexorable application of the community standard of reasonable care.

Thus we distinguished, for purposes of duty to disclose, the special- and general-standard aspects of the physician-patient relationship. When medical judgment enters the picture and for that reason the special standard controls, prevailing medical practice must be given its just due. In all other instances, however, the general standard exacting ordinary care applies, and that standard is set by law. In sum, the physician's duty to disclose is governed by the same legal principles applicable to others in comparable situations, with modifications only to the extent that medical judgment enters the picture. We hold that the standard measuring performance of that duty by physicians, as by others, is conduct which is reasonable under the circumstances.

V

Once the circumstances give rise to a duty on the physician's part to inform his patient, the next inquiry is the scope of the disclosure the physician is legally obliged to make. The courts have frequently confronted this problem but no uniform standard defining the adequacy of the divulgence emerges from the decisions. Some have said "full" disclosure, a norm we are unwilling to adopt literally. It seems obviously prohibitive and unrealistic to expect physicians to discuss with their patients every risk of proposed treatment—no matter how small or remote—and generally unnecessary from the patient's viewpoint as well. Indeed, the cases speaking in terms of "full" disclosure appear to envision something less than total disclosure, leaving unanswered the question of just how much.

The larger number of courts, as might be expected, have applied tests framed with reference to prevailing fashion within the medical profession. Some have measured the disclosure by "good medical practice," others by what a reasonable practitioner would have bared under the circumstances, and still others by what medical custom in the community would demand. We have explored this rather considerable body of law but are unprepared to follow it. The duty to disclose, we have reasoned, arises from phenomena apart from medical custom and practice. The latter, we think, should no more establish the scope of the duty than its existence. Any definition of scope in terms purely of a professional standard is at odds with the patient's prerogative to decide on projected therapy himself. That prerogative, we have said, is at the very foundation of the duty to disclose, and both the patient's right to know and the physician's correlative obligation to tell him are diluted to the extent that its compass is dictated by the medical profession.

In our view, the patient's right of self-decision shapes the boundaries of the duty to reveal. That right can be effectively exercised only if the patient possesses enough information to enable an intelligent choice. The scope of the physician's communications to the patient, then, must be measured by the patient's need, and that need is the information material to the decision. Thus the test for determining whether a particular peril must be divulged is its materiality to the patient's decision: all risks potentially affecting the decision must be unmasked. And to safeguard the patient's interest in achieving his own determination on treatment, the law must itself set the standard for adequate disclosure.

Optimally for the patient, exposure of a risk would be mandatory whenever the patient would deem it significant to his decision, either singly or in combination with other risks. Such a requirement, however, would summon the physician to second-guess the patient, whose ideas on materiality could hardly be known to the physician. That would make an undue demand upon medical practitioners, whose conduct, like that of others, is to be measured in terms of reasonableness. Consonantly with orthodox negligence doctrine, the physician's liability for nondisclosure is to be determined on the basis of foresight, not hindsight; no less than any other aspect of negligence, the issue on nondisclosure must be approached from the viewpoint of the reasonableness of the physician's divulgence in terms of what he knows or should know to be the patient's informational needs. If, but only if, the fact-finder can say that the physician's communication was unreasonably inadequate is an imposition of liability legally or morally justified.

Of necessity, the content of the disclosure rests in the first instance with the physician. Ordinarily it is only he who is in position to identify particular dangers; always he must make a judgment, in terms of materiality, as to whether and to what extent revelation to the patient is called for. He cannot know with complete exactitude what the patient would consider important to his decision, but on the basis of his medical training and experience he can sense how the average, reasonable patient expectably would react. Indeed, with knowledge of, or ability to learn, his patient's background and current condition, he is in a position superior to that of most others—attorneys, for example—who are called upon to make judgments on pain of liability in damages for unreasonable miscalculation.

From these considerations we derive the breadth of the disclosure of risks legally to be required. The scope of the standard is not subjective as to either the physician or the patient; it remains objective with due regard for the patient's informational needs and with suitable leeway for the physician's situation. In broad outline, we agree that "[a] risk is thus material when a reasonable person, in what the physician knows or should know to be the patient's position, would be likely to attach significance to the risk or cluster of risks in deciding whether or not to forego the proposed therapy."

The topics importantly demanding a communication of information are the inherent and potential hazards of the proposed treatment, the alternatives to that treatment, if any, and the results likely if the patient remains untreated. The factors contributing significance to the dangerousness of a medical technique are, of course, the incidence of injury and the degree of the harm threatened. A very small chance of death or serious disablement may well be significant; a potential disability which dramatically outweighs the potential benefit of the therapy or the detriments of the existing malady may summon discussion with the patient.

There is no bright line separating the significant from the insignificant; the answer in any case must abide a rule of reason. Some dangers—infection, for example—are inherent in any operation; there is no obligation to communicate those of which persons of average sophistication are aware. Even more clearly, the physician bears no responsibility for discussion of hazards the patient has already discovered, or those having no apparent materiality to patients' decision on therapy. The disclosure doctrine, like others marking lines between permissible and impermissible behavior in medical practice, is in essence a requirement of conduct prudent under the circumstances. Whenever nondisclosure of particular risk information is open to debate by reasonable-minded men, the issue is for the finder of the facts.

Notes and Questions

1. Although states are almost equally divided, a slight majority has adopted the professional disclosure standard, measuring the duty to disclose by the standard of the reasonable medical practitioner similarly situated. Expert testimony is required to establish the content of a reasonable disclosure. Keel v. St. Elizabeth Medical Center, 1990 W.L. 115094 (Ky.App.1990); Jones v. Malloy, 226 Neb. 559, 412 N.W.2d 837 (1987); Ritz v. Florida Patient's Compensation Fund, 436 So.2d 987 (Fla. App.1983); Magana v. Elie, 108 Ill.App.3d 1028, 64 Ill.Dec. 511, 439 N.E.2d 1319 (1982); Cowman v. Hornaday, 329 N.W.2d 422 (Iowa 1983); Eichelberger v. Barnes Hosp., 655 S.W.2d 699 (Mo.App.1983); Beattie v. Thomas, 99 Nev. 579, 668 P.2d 268 (1983); Ogden v. Bhatti, 92 A.D.2d 658, 460 N.Y.S.2d 166 (1983). For a full list of citations, see LeBlang, Informed Consent–Duty and Causation: A Survey of Current Developments, 18 Forum 280 (1983). This professional standard is justified by three arguments. First, it protects good medical practice—the primary duty of physicians is to advance their patients' best interests, and they should not have to concern themselves with the risk that an uninformed lay jury will later decide they acted improperly. Woolley v. Henderson, 418 A.2d 1123 (Me.1980). Second, a patient-oriented standard would force doctors to spend unnecessary time discussing every possible risk with their patients, thereby interfering with the flexibility that they need to decide on the best form of treatment. Louisell and Williams, 2 Medical Malpractice: Physicians and Related

Professions, § 22:06. Third, only physicians can accurately evaluate the psychological and other impact that risk would have on particular patients.

These jurisdictions ordinarily require the plaintiff to offer medical testimony to establish 1) whether a reasonable medical practitioner in the same or similar community would make this disclosure, and 2) that the defendant did not comply with this community standard. Fuller v. Starnes, 268 Ark. 476, 597 S.W.2d 88 (1980). Expert testimony is essential, since determination of what information needs to be disclosed is viewed as a medical question.

2. The *Canterbury* rule, using the "reasonable patient" as the measure of the scope of disclosure, has won over several states in the last few years. See Pauscher v. Iowa Methodist Medical Center, 408 N.W.2d 355 (Iowa 1987); Wheeldon v. Madison, 374 N.W.2d 367 (S.D.1985) and cases cited. The South Dakota Supreme Court in *Wheeldon,* in following *Canterbury,* expressed the concern that medical practice might conflict with patient needs. "We agree that the right to know—to be informed—is a fundamental right personal to the patient and should not be subject to restrictions by medical practices that may be at odds with the patient's information needs * * *. Materiality, therefore, is the cornerstone upon which the physician's duty to disclose is based." See also Festa v. Greenberg, 354 Pa.Super. 346, 511 A.2d 1371 (1986).

Judge Robinson suggests that the *Canterbury* standard is nothing more than the uniform application of the negligence principle to medical practice. However, the negligence principle normally evaluates the conduct of a reasonable actor—not the expectations of a reasonable victim. The values served by the doctrine—patient autonomy and dignity—are unrelated to the values served by the doctrine of negligence. Informed consent really serves the values we otherwise identify with the doctrine of battery. It is ironic that a doctrine developed to foster and recognize individual choice should be measured by an objective standard.

3. The effect of a patient-oriented disclosure standard is to ease the plaintiff's burden of proof, since the trier of fact could find that a doctor acted unreasonably in failing to disclose, in spite of unrebutted expert medical testimony to the contrary. The question of whether a physician disclosed risks which a reasonable person would find material is for the trier of fact, and technical expertise is not required. Pedersen v. Vahidy, 209 Conn. 510, 552 A.2d 419 (1989); Cooper v. Roberts, 220 Pa.Super. 260, 286 A.2d 647 (1971). In Savold v. Johnson, 443 N.W.2d 656 (S.D.1989), the South Dakota Supreme Court held that expert testimony as to informed consent information was not needed, where a factual dispute exists as to whether any information of the material risks was given at all. Expert testimony is still needed, however, to clarify the treatments and their probabilities of risks. Thus in Cross v. Trapp, __ W.Va. __, 294 S.E.2d 446, 455 (1982), the court held that experts were needed to establish " * * * (1) the risks involved concerning a particular method of treatment, (2) alternative methods of treatment, (3) the risks relating to such alternative methods of treatment and (4) the results likely to occur if the patient remains untreated." Accord, Festa v. Greenberg, 354 Pa.Super. 346, 511 A.2d 1371 (1986); Sard v. Hardy, 281 Md. 432, 379 A.2d 1014 (1977). See

Haligan, The Standard of Disclosure by Physicians to Patients: Competing Models of Informed Consent, 41 La.L.Rev. 9 (1980); Katz, Informed Consent—A Fairy Tale? Law's Vision, 39 U.Pitt.L.Rev. 137 (1977).

4. *Information to be disclosed.* The doctor must consider disclosure of a variety of factors:

a. diagnosis. This includes the medical steps preceding diagnosis, including tests and their alternatives. The right of informed refusal, as established in Truman v. Thomas, 27 Cal.3d 285, 165 Cal.Rptr. 308, 611 P.2d 902 (1980), requires disclosure of the risks of foregoing a diagnostic procedure.

b. the nature and purpose of the proposed treatment.

c. the risks of the treatment. Risks that are remote can be omitted. The threshold of disclosure, as the *Canterbury* court suggests, varies with the product of the probability and the severity of the risk. Thus a five percent risk of lengthened recuperation might be ignored, while a one percent risk of paralysis, as in *Canterbury,* or an even smaller risk of death, should be disclosed. Cobbs v. Grant, 8 Cal.3d 229, 104 Cal.Rptr. 505, 502 P.2d 1 (1972). In Hartke v. McKelway, 707 F.2d 1544, 1549 (D.C.Cir.1983) the doctor performed a laparoscopic cauterization to prevent pregnancy of the plaintiff, who later became pregnant and had a healthy child. "In this case, the undisclosed risk was a .1% to .3% chance of subsequent pregnancy. For most people this risk would be considered very small, but this patient was in a particularly unusual position. In view of the very serious expected consequences of pregnancy for her—possibly including death—as well as the ready availability of ways to reduce the risk * * * a jury could conclude that a reasonable person in what Dr. McKelway knew to be plaintiff's position would be likely to attach significance to the risk here."

d. the probability of success. One case has proposed that the doctor should disclose both the general statistical success rate for a given procedure, and his particular experience with that procedure. Hales v. Pittman, 118 Ariz. 305, 576 P.2d 493 (1978) (discussing the battery count of the plaintiff's complaint).

e. treatment alternatives. Doctors should disclose those alternatives that are generally acknowledged within the medical community as feasible, Holt v. Nelson, 11 Wash.App. 230, 523 P.2d 211 (1974), their risks and consequences, and their probability of success. Even if the alternative is more hazardous, some courts have held that it should be disclosed. Logan v. Greenwich Hospital Association, 191 Conn. 282, 465 A.2d 294 (1983). In Wenger v. Oregon Urology Clinic, P.C., 102 Or.App. 665, 796 P.2d 376 (1990), the court held that defendants failed to properly inform plaintiff of several treatment alternatives to treat Peyonie's disease, a male genital condition which can impair sexual function. The procedure used by the defendant caused an infection, ultimately leading to the amputation of the plaintiff's penis.

Courts may further limit disclosure by concluding that some alternatives are not legitimate treatment options. See Lienhard v. State,

431 N.W.2d 861 (Minn.1988) (managing pregnancy at home rather than in hospital not a choice between alternative methods of treatment; disclosure therefore not required).

5. The British courts had not articulated a judicial position on informed consent until 1985, when the House of Lords ruled in Sidaway v. Bethlem Royal Hospital Governors, 1 All ER 643 (House of Lords, 1985). Amy Sidaway, the plaintiff, had persistent pain in the shoulders and neck. Her surgeon, Dr. Falconer, advised an operation on her spinal column, failing to inform her of the 1% chance of spinal cord damage that could cause great pain and paralysis. The majority ruled that the test in England for a physician's duty to disclose the risks of treatment is the same as that applicable to diagnosis and treatment: accepted medical practice, as established by the physician's peers. Lord Diplock observed:

> No doubt, if the patient in fact manifested this attitude by means of questioning, the doctor would tell him whatever it was the patient wanted to know; but we are concerned here with volunteering unsought information about risks of the proposed treatment failing to achieve the result sought or making the patient's physical or mental condition worse rather than better. The only effect that mention of risks can have on the patient's mind, if it has any at all, can be in the direction of deterring the patient from undergoing the treatment which in the expert opinion of the doctor it is in the patient's interest to undergo. To decide what risks the existence of which a patient should be voluntarily warned and the terms in which such warning, if any, should be given, having regard to the effect that the warning may have, is as much an exercise of professional skill and judgment as any other part of the doctor's comprehensive duty of care to the individual patient, and expert medical evidence on this matter should be treated in just the same way. Id. at 659.

Is this deference to the medical profession simply a judicial recognition of the importance of upholding the power of the English medical profession? In a country where limited resources are committed to the National Health Service, does this approach to informed consent serve to keep patients uninformed and therefore undemanding? If so, won't it help to conserve medical resources, since patients will not be familiar with alternative expensive treatment options? See Schwartz and Grubb, Why Britain Can't Afford Informed Consent, 16 Hastings Center Report 22 (1986); Miller, Informed Consent for the Man on the Clapham Omnibus: An English Cure for the "American Disease"?, 9 W.New Eng.L.Rev. 169 (1987).

TRUMAN v. THOMAS

Supreme Court of California, 1980.
27 Cal.3d 285, 165 Cal.Rptr. 308, 611 P.2d 902.

BIRD, C.J.

This court must decide whether a physician's failure to inform a patient of the material risks of not consenting to a recommended pap smear, so that the patient might make an informed choice, may have breached the physician's duty of due care to his patient, who died from cancer of the cervix.

I

Respondent, Dr. Claude R. Thomas, is a family physician engaged in a general medical practice. He was first contacted in April 1963 by appellants' mother, Rena Truman, in connection with her second pregnancy. He continued to act as the primary physician for Mrs. Truman and her two children until March 1969. During this six-year period, Mrs. Truman not only sought his medical advice, but often discussed personal matters with him.

In April 1969, Mrs. Truman consulted Dr. Casey, a urologist, about a urinary tract infection which had been treated previously by Dr. Thomas. While examining Mrs. Truman, Dr. Casey discovered that she was experiencing heavy vaginal discharges and that her cervix was extremely rough. Mrs. Truman was given a prescription for the infection and advised to see a gynecologist as soon as possible. When Mrs. Truman did not make an appointment with a gynecologist, Dr. Casey made an appointment for her with a Dr. Ritter.

In October 1969, Dr. Ritter discovered that Mrs. Truman's cervix had been largely replaced by a cancerous tumor. Too far advanced to be removed by surgery, the tumor was unsuccessfully treated by other methods. Mrs. Truman died in July 1970 at the age of 30.

Appellants are Rena Truman's two children. They brought this wrongful death action against Dr. Thomas for his failure to perform a pap smear test on their mother. At the trial, expert testimony was presented which indicated that if Mrs. Truman had undergone a pap smear at any time between 1964 and 1969, the cervical tumor probably would have been discovered in time to save her life. There was disputed expert testimony that the standard of medical practice required a physician to explain to women patients that it is important to have a pap smear each year to "pick up early lesions that are treatable rather than having to deal with [more developed] tumor[s] that very often aren't treatable. * * * "[1]

Although Dr. Thomas saw Mrs. Truman frequently between 1964 and 1969, he never performed a pap smear test on her. Dr. Thomas testified that he did not "specifically" inform Mrs. Truman of the risk involved in any failure to undergo the pap smear test. Rather, "I said, 'You should have a pap smear.' We don't say by now it can be Stage Two [in the development of cervical cancer] or go through all of the different lectures about cancer. I think it is a widely known and generally accepted manner of treatment and I think the patient has a high degree of responsibility. We are not enforcers, we are advisors."

1. Dr. Thomas conceded at the trial that it is the accepted standard of practice for physicians in his community to recommend that women of child-bearing age undergo a pap smear each year. His records indicate that during the period in which he acted as Mrs. Truman's family physician he performed between 10 and 20 pap smears per month.

However, Dr. Thomas' medical records contain no reference to any discussion or recommendation that Mrs. Truman undergo a pap smear test.

For the most part, Dr. Thomas was unable to describe specific conversations with Mrs. Truman. For example, he testified that during certain periods he "saw Rena very frequently, approximately once a week or so, and I am sure my opening remark was, 'Rena, you need a pap smear,' .. I am sure we discussed it with her so often that she couldn't [have] fail[ed] to realize that we wanted her to have a complete examination, breast examination, ovaries and pap smear." Dr. Thomas also testified that on at least two occasions when he performed pelvic examinations of Mrs. Truman she refused him permission to perform the test, stating she could not afford the cost. Dr. Thomas offered to defer payment, but Mrs. Truman wanted to pay cash.

Appellants argue that the failure to give a pap smear test to Mrs. Truman proximately caused her death. Two instructions requested by appellants described alternative theories under which Dr. Thomas could be held liable for this failure. First, they asked that the jury be instructed that it "is the duty of a physician to disclose to his patient all relevant information to enable the patient to make an informed decision regarding the submission to or refusal to take a diagnostic test. [¶] Failure of the physician to disclose to his patient all relevant information including the risks to the patient if the test is refused renders the physician liable for any injury legally resulting from the patient's refusal to take the test if a reasonably prudent person in the patient's position would not have refused the test if she had been adequately informed of all the significant perils." Second, they requested that the jury be informed that "as a matter of law ... a physician who fails to perform a Pap smear test on a female patient over the age of 23 and to whom the patient has entrusted her general physical care is liable for injury or death proximately caused by the failure to perform the test." Both instructions were refused.

The jury rendered a special verdict, finding Dr. Thomas free of any negligence that proximately caused Mrs. Truman's death. This appeal followed.

II

The central issue for this court is whether Dr. Thomas breached his duty of care to Mrs. Truman when he failed to inform her of the potentially fatal consequences of allowing cervical cancer to develop undetected by a pap smear.

* * *

* * * The scope of a physician's duty to disclose is measured by the amount of knowledge a patient needs in order to make an informed choice. All information material to the patient's decision should be given. [ ]

Material information is that which the physician knows or should know would be regarded as significant by a reasonable person in the patient's position when deciding to accept or reject the recommended medical procedure. [   ] To be material, a fact must also be one which is not commonly appreciated. [   ] If the physician knows or should know of a patient's unique concerns or lack of familiarity with medical procedures, this may expand the scope of required disclosure. [   ]

Applying these principles, the court in *Cobbs* stated that a patient must be apprised not only of the "risks inherent in the procedure [prescribed, but also] the risks of a decision not to undergo the treatment, and the probability of a successful outcome of the treatment." [   ] This rule applies whether the procedure involves treatment or a diagnostic test. On the one hand, a physician recommending a risk-free procedure may safely forego discussion beyond that necessary to conform to competent medical practice and to obtain the patient's consent. [   ] If a patient indicates that he or she is going to *decline* the risk-free test or treatment, then the doctor has the additional duty of advising of all material risks of which a reasonable person would want to be informed before deciding not to undergo the procedure. On the other hand, if the recommended test or treatment is itself risky, then the physician should always explain the potential consequences of declining to follow the recommended course of action.

Nevertheless, Dr. Thomas contends that *Cobbs* does not apply to him because the duty to disclose applies only where the patient *consents* to the recommended procedure. He argues that since a physician's advice may be presumed to be founded on an expert appraisal of the patient's medical needs, no reasonable patient would fail to undertake further inquiry before rejecting such advice. Therefore, patients who reject their physician's advice should shoulder the burden of inquiry as to the possible consequences of their decision.

This argument is inconsistent with *Cobbs*. The duty to disclose was imposed in *Cobbs* so that patients might meaningfully exercise their right to make decisions about their own bodies. [   ] The importance of this right should not be diminished by the manner in which it is exercised. Further, the need for disclosure is not lessened because patients reject a recommended procedure. Such a decision does not alter "what has been termed the 'fiducial qualities' of the physician-patient relationship," since patients who reject a procedure are as unskilled in the medical sciences as those who consent. [   ] To now hold that patients who reject their physician's advice have the burden of inquiring as to the potential consequences of their decisions would be to contradict *Cobbs*. It must be remembered that Dr. Thomas was not engaged in an arms-length transaction with Mrs. Truman. Clearly, under *Cobbs,* he was obligated to provide her with all the information material to her decision.

Dr. Thomas next contends that, as a matter of law, he had no duty to disclose to Mrs. Truman the risk of failing to undergo a pap smear test because "the danger [is] remote and commonly appreciated to be remote." (*Cobbs, supra,* 8 Cal.3d at p. 245, 104 Cal.Rptr. at p. 516, 502 P.2d at p. 12.) The merit of this contention depends on whether a jury could reasonably find that knowledge of this risk was material to Mrs. Truman's decision.

The record indicates that the pap smear test is an accurate detector of cervical cancer. Although the probability that Mrs. Truman had cervical cancer was low, Dr. Thomas knew that the potential harm of failing to detect the disease at an early stage was death. This situation is not analogous to one which involves, for example, "relatively minor risks inherent in [such] common procedures" as the taking of blood samples. [ ] These procedures are not central to the decision to administer or reject the procedure. In contrast, the risk which Mrs. Truman faced from cervical cancer was not only significant, it was the principal reason why Dr. Thomas recommended that she undergo a pap smear.

Little evidence was introduced on whether this risk was commonly known. Dr. Thomas testified that the risk would be known to a reasonable person. Whether such evidence is sufficient to establish that there was no general duty to disclose this risk to patients is a question of fact for the jury. Moreover, even assuming such disclosure was not generally required, the circumstances in this case may establish that Dr. Thomas did have a duty to inform Mrs. Truman of the risks she was running by not undergoing a pap smear.

Dr. Thomas testified he never specifically informed her of the purpose of a pap smear test. There was no evidence introduced that Mrs. Truman was aware of the serious danger entailed in not undergoing the test. However, there was testimony that Mrs. Truman said she would not undergo the test on certain occasions because of its cost or because "she just didn't feel like it." Under these circumstances, a jury could reasonably conclude that Dr. Thomas had a duty to inform Mrs. Truman of the danger of refusing the test because it was not reasonable for Dr. Thomas to assume that Mrs. Truman appreciated the potentially fatal consequences of her conduct. Accordingly, this court cannot decide as a matter of law that Dr. Thomas owed absolutely no duty to Mrs. Truman to make this important disclosure that affected her life.

* * *

Refusal to give the requested instruction meant that the jury was unable to consider whether Dr. Thomas breached a duty by not disclosing the danger of failing to undergo a pap smear. Since this theory finds support in the record, it was error for the court to refuse to give the requested instruction. [ ] If the jury had been given this instruction and had found in favor of the appellants, such a finding would have had support in the record before us. Reversal is therefore required. [ ]

* * *

The judgment is reversed.

* * *

Notes and Questions

1. Is there such a thing as a "risk-free test or treatment," as the *Truman* court characterizes the choice? Think back to Helling v. Carey and the notes following the case. Why did Mrs. Truman persist in refusing the Pap smear? Was it just the cost, an aversion to the procedure, generalized anxiety over the thought of cancer, or her sense that it wasn't necessary? What if Mrs. Truman had third-party health insurance that covered the full costs of a pap smear? Do you think that Dr. Thomas would have tried harder to convince her of the necessity of the test?

2. Dr. Thomas argued that a patient who rejects her physician's advice has the burden of inquiring as to the consequences of this decision. Isn't this a reasonable position for a physician to take? The court says the 'fiducial qualities' of the physician-patient relationship mandate disclosure, given patient ignorance. How far does this fiduciary obligation extend?

Justice Clark, dissenting, worried about an "intolerable burden" of explanation about every procedure and the risks if it is foregone. He feared that the burden would extend beyond pap smears to "all diagnostic procedures allegedly designed to detect illness which could lead to death or serious complication if not timely treated." Id. at 910.

3. The dissent in *Truman* also talks about "how far a doctor should go in selling his services without alienating the patient from all medical care." Id. at 910. Must the doctor do a "hard sell" in order to avoid the application of the *Truman* rule, manipulating information in order to get the patient to do what he thinks is best therapeutically?

4. Are physicians exposed to conflicting incentives with regard to testing patients? Consider emerging genetic diagnostic technologies. The adoption of such diagnostics by physicians will be driven by both clinical and economic motivations. Genetic testing will proliferate if third party payers reimburse such testing. Providers paid on a fee-for-service basis will adopt them if they are profitable. Malpractice fears will also cause physicians to use new tests if there is any chance of detecting a predisposition to disease. And of course some providers will want the information even if it is of marginal value. Blumenthal and Zeckhauser, Genetic Diagnosis: Implications for Medical Practice, 5 Intl.J.Tech.Assess. in Health Care 579, 585 (1989). See Hillman et al., Frequency and Costs of Diagnostic Imaging in Office Practice—A Comparison of Self–Referring and Radiologist–Referring Physicians, 323 N.Eng.J.Med. 1604 (1990) (finding that physicians who self-referred patients for diagnostic imaging performed imaging from 2½ to 11 times as often as the physician who referred patients to outside radiologists).

5. What is best for the patient therapeutically? Consider new techniques of genetic diagnosis, performed on adults to see if they might be carriers of the gene for Huntington's disease, cystic fibrosis, manic-depressive illness and other neurological disorders. The purpose of these tests is to assess whether the patient will develop a particular condition. However,

the presence of particular genetic structures and the development of clinically relevant disease is not straightforward for diseases such as heart disease, hypertension, mental illness, or cancer. An abnormal gene may not result in clinical disease. In Huntington's chorea, for example, the time of onset varies from early childhood to the seventies. Thus, a patient needs to know a great deal about the likelihood of a disease developing, before it is useful to face the anxiety produced by a positive test result indicating the presence of a genetic marker for a disease.

The very existence of techniques for prenatal diagnosis also produces stress in potential parents. Negative results give relief, alleviating anxiety that the very existence of the tests created. The tests' availability "sharpens what might otherwise be low-level, diffuse concerns that surface only, as one woman put it, 'on bad days,' and turns them into real and dreaded possibilities." Kolker, Advances in Prenatal Diagnosis: Social–Psychological and Policy Issues, 5 Intl.J.Tech.Assess. in Health Care 601, 608 (1989). For further discussion of genetic counseling and screening, see Chapter 9.

Problem: Information Overload

You have been asked by one of your clients, the Gladstone Womens Clinic, to draft some guidelines to help staff physicians handle disclosures to patients who are reluctant to discuss risks of tests or procedures or who are uninsured and therefore careful about medical costs. What are the safe outer limits of physician silence about diagnostic options and their risks? Consider the kinds of tests that might be available to women who come to the clinic:

1. Pap Smears and mammograms to detect cancer;

2. Amniocentesis, chorionic villus sampling (CVS) and ultrasound imaging for evaluating fetal development and health;

3. HIV tests to look for the possibility of the AIDS virus in a woman who may want to get pregnant;

4. Genetic diagnostic technologies used to assess whether a patient will develop a given condition.

C. CAUSATION COMPLEXITIES

CANTERBURY v. SPENCE

United States Court of Appeals, District of Columbia Circuit, 1972.
464 F.2d 772.

VII

No more than breach of any other legal duty does nonfulfillment of the physician's obligation to disclose alone establish liability to the patient. An unrevealed risk that should have been made known must materialize, for otherwise the omission, however unpardonable, is legally without consequence. Occurrence of the risk must be harmful to the patient, for negligence unrelated to injury is nonactionable. And, as in malpractice actions generally, there must be a causal relationship between the physician's failure to adequately divulge and damage to the patient.

A causal connection exists when, but only when, disclosure of significant risks incidental to treatment would have resulted in a decision against it. The patient obviously has no complaint if he would have submitted to the therapy notwithstanding awareness that the risk was one of its perils. On the other hand, the very purpose of the disclosure rule is to protect the patient against consequences which, if known, he would have avoided by foregoing the treatment. The more difficult question is whether the factual issue on causality calls for an objective or a subjective determination.

It has been assumed that the issue is to be resolved according to whether the factfinder believes the patient's testimony that he would not have agreed to the treatment if he had known of the danger which later ripened into injury. We think a technique which ties the factual conclusion on causation simply to the assessment of the patient's credibility is unsatisfactory. To be sure, the objective of risk-disclosure is preservation of the patient's interest in intelligent self-choice on proposed treatment, a matter the patient is free to decide for any reason that appeals to him. When, prior to commencement of therapy, the patient is sufficiently informed on risks and he exercises his choice, it may truly be said that he did exactly what he wanted to do. But when causality is explored at a post-injury trial with a professedly uninformed patient, the question whether he actually would have turned the treatment down if he had known the risks is purely hypothetical: "Viewed from the point at which he had to decide, would the patient have decided differently had he known something he did not know?" And the answer which the patient supplies hardly represents more than a guess, perhaps tinged by the circumstance that the uncommunicated hazard has in fact materialized.

In our view, this method of dealing with the issue on causation comes in second-best. It places the physician in jeopardy of the patient's hindsight and bitterness. It places the factfinder in the position of deciding whether a speculative answer to a hypothetical question is to be credited. It calls for a subjective determination solely on testimony of a patient-witness shadowed by the occurrence of the undisclosed risk.

Better it is, we believe, to resolve the causality issue on an objective basis: in terms of what a prudent person in the patient's position would have decided if suitably informed of all perils bearing significance. If adequate disclosure could reasonably be expected to have caused that person to decline the treatment because of the revelation of the kind of risk or danger that resulted in harm, causation is shown, but otherwise not. The patient's testimony is relevant on that score of course but it would not threaten to dominate the findings. And since that testimony would probably be appraised congruently with the factfinder's belief in its reasonableness, the case for a wholly objective standard for passing on causation is strengthened. Such a standard would in any event ease the fact-finding process and better assure the truth as its product.

* * *

Notes and Questions

1. Causation can only be established if there is a link between the failure of a doctor to disclose and the patient's injury. Two tests of causation have emerged: the objective reasonable patient test and the subjective particular patient test. The former asks what a reasonable patient would have done. The latter asks what the particular patient would have done. *Canterbury* adopted the objective test, after a good deal of vacillation. The court was concerned with patient hindsight testimony that he or she would have foregone the treatment, testimony which the court feared would be " * * * hardly * * * more than a guess, perhaps tinged by the circumstance that the uncommunicated hazard has in fact materialized." The fear is of self-serving testimony.

The risk must be "material" to a reasonable patient in the shoes of the plaintiff. Under this standard, a patient's testimony is not needed to get the issue of causation to the jury. The testimony may be admissible and relevant on causation, but not dispositive. The jury can decide without it "what a reasonable person in that position would have done." Hartke v. McKelway, 707 F.2d 1544 (D.C.Cir.1983). See also Sard v. Hardy, 281 Md. 432, 450, 379 A.2d 1014, 1025 (1977).

2. Is it easy for a jury to put themselves in the shoes of a particular plaintiff? To some extent, that is what the jury is always asked to do in tort cases, particularly as to pain and suffering awards. In that sense, therefore, the courts' rejection of the particular patient test seems unreasonable. Is, however, the jury's empathetic attempt to understand the plaintiff's pain in a personal injury case the same as the jury's collective attempt to second guess the plaintiff's decision whether or not to undergo the diagnosis or treatment proposed by the doctor? Consider the following argument:

> "Interferences with self-determination occur in all situations in which a person's dignitary interests have been violated. They are not limited to those in which physical harm has occurred. Lack of informed consent is itself a violation. It is the harm. The additional presence of physical harm only adds injury to insult * * * As citizens, patients are wronged when physicians begin treatment without fulfilling their disclosure obligation. What patients might or might not have agreed to, if properly informed, is beside the point."

J. Katz, The Silent World of Doctor and Patient 79 (1984). Adoption of an objective standard on causation takes away most of what the *Canterbury* court granted as to risk disclosure. It asks the jury to put themselves in the place of a reasonable person, rather than the particular person. Is a jury likely to find causation in these cases, unless (1) the doctor was clearly negligent, so no reasonable person would have agreed to the treatment; (2) the doctor offered an experimental procedure which a person might refuse in spite of the doctor's urgings; (3) the jury ignores its instructions and applies a subjective standard?

3. One commentator has argued that the subjective state of mind of the plaintiff—who says she would have rejected the chosen treatment if given full information—can be proved objectively, supporting the plaintiff's claim that she would have chosen this particular decision. The courts could consider, for example, testimony about what people generally do when confronted with similar choices, or what they say they would do, when surveyed. See Shultz, From Informed Consent to Patient Choice: A New Protected Interest, 95 Yale L.J. 219, 288–89 (1985). Specific evidence of special circumstances affecting the plaintiff would be admissible to support her claim. See Steele v. St. Paul Fire & Marine Ins. Co., 371 So.2d 843 (La.App.1979), certiorari denied, 374 So.2d 658 (La.1979). Does it make sense to add to the complexity of a malpractice trial by allowing additional expert testimony on opinion surveys or psychological studies? Doesn't the jury do exactly this when evaluating the causation question, by asking themselves what it would have felt like to have been the plaintiff in this situation? If so, why not trust the plaintiff to say this, leaving the assessment of credibility to the jury?

4. The majority of American jurisdictions have adopted the objective test of causality. See Fain v. Smith, 479 So.2d 1150 (Ala.1985) and cases cited. See generally F. Rozovsky, Consent to Treatment 62–63 (§ 1.13.4, "Causation in Negligent Consent") (1984); A. Rosoff, Informed Consent: A Guide for Health Care Providers 151–153 (1981).

D. DAMAGE ISSUES

1. The "Benefits" Doctrine

GRACIA v. MEISELMAN

Superior Court of New Jersey, 1987.
220 N.J.Super. 317, 531 A.2d 1373.

SACHAR, J.S.C.

The complaint in the instant case is couched in terms of malpractice. Those allegations in the complaint that refer to defendant doctor (oral surgeon) as having deviated from accepted medical standards in the performance of the operation were abandoned prior to the commencement of the trial. Plaintiff has proceeded to trial on the remaining allegations of deviation from accepted medical standards in negligently failing to obtain an informed consent to the operation. Defendant signed a standard hospital consent form at St. Elizabeth's Hospital which recites that plaintiff was informed of all risks of the proposed surgery, and consents to the operation. It is plaintiff's contention that defendant doctor did not, in fact, advise him of the risk of medial nerve damage inherent in the operation. Plaintiff has testified that if he had known that there was any risk in the proposed operation, he would have withheld his consent. Defendant, on the other hand, testified that he disclosed the risk of medial nerve damage to plaintiff. While defendant has no specific recollection of the conversation with plaintiff, he testified that it was and is his usual custom to notify all patients who undergo this type of operation of the risk of possible medial nerve involvement.

Plaintiff, 46 years old, had a ninth-grade education in Cuba prior to immigrating to the United States. He had had all of his teeth removed sometime in the past and complained of extreme difficulty in eating or speaking because there was no way for his dentures to adhere to the jawbone that was flat. His protruding lower jaw resulted in his upper and lower teeth not properly coming together, causing an abnormal bite. This condition was congenital. He also had suffered from a pre-existing psychiatric problem which had resulted in marital difficulties prior to seeing defendant. As a result of visits to dentists to rectify what was an intolerable condition with respect to his chewing food and being able to speak, he was told that the only operation that would remedy the condition would be a surgical correction of mandibular prognathism and atrophy of the mandibular alveolar bone. On this basis, he came to see defendant oral surgeon who, after performing requisite x-rays and examination, concurred that this was what should be done and agreed to perform the operation.

The risk, which is the subject of this lawsuit, involves the medial nerve which lies in a channel of the jaw within which the contemplated surgery would be performed. Damage to the nerve need not result either from a touching or cutting of the nerve, but can be caused merely from the proximity of the nerve to the area of the operation. The damage can be caused by hematoma or scarring in the general area of the nerve.

It is undisputed by both parties' experts that the operation was properly performed and improved the conditions for which the operation was undertaken. However, there was resultant permanent sensory loss of the medial nerve extending from the midline of his chin off to the left, and protruding slightly above the left lateral portion of his lower lip. The area measures approximately three centimeters in length and one and a half to two centimeters in width. Plaintiff alleges that he has had post-operative marital problems because he does not want to be kissed by his wife because of the numbness, and that he is angry in general because he is left with the numbness above described.

Informed consent is a negligence concept in which in a medical-legal context, a physician has breached his duty to disclose a risk which a reasonable practitioner would have disclosed to a patient. If there is a finding of proximate cause, i.e., that the operation would not have taken place if the risk had been disclosed, then if the risk materializes and the patient suffers resultant harm, the physician is liable.[1] The damage that defendant is liable for is the subject of this opinion.

1. *Canterbury v. Spence,* 464 *F.*2d 772, 790 (D.C.Cir.1972), *cert. den.,* 409 *U.S.* 1064, 93 *S.Ct.* 560, 34 *L.Ed.*2d 518 (1972) (cited with approval in *Dewes v. Indian Health Service, etc.,* 504 *F.Supp.* 203 (D.S.D.1980)).

* * *

In the case at bar, it is conceded that there was no option of treatment available to the patient to alleviate his dental complaints other than the operation. The benefit that was sought by the patient to alleviate his dental condition could not be achieved without the collateral risk of damage to the medial nerve. The benefits sought and the collateral risk in this case are inseparable by the inherent nature of the operation.

The informed consent doctrine is the creation of equity, growing out of the doctor/patient relationship. The patient, ignorant of medicine, places his trust in the doctor to provide beneficial medical treatment. The patient does not know the relative merits of the options available or risks of treatment. The doctor is under a duty not only to obtain the patient's consent, but to inform the patient of any risks that a reasonable medical practitioner would disclose under the same or similar circumstances.

* * *

The maximum exposure that the doctor is liable for in an informed consent case is the risk that materializes. * * *

* * *

In the case at bar, the cost of the operation (which was properly performed) would have been incurred whether there was or was not resultant nerve damage to the plaintiff. Plaintiff's offer of the medical bill into evidence is accordingly denied. Similarly, the pain and suffering that plaintiff would have incurred from the operation, with or without the resultant nerve damage, is not to be compensated for as damages in this case.

* * *

[The court uses the damage rule from "wrongful birth" and "wrongful life" cases, discussed in Chapter 9.]

In an informed consent case the violation of duty consists of the physician's neglect to inform the patient of an inherent risk in the proposed operation. As a result of the violation of duty to disclose, the operation takes place. The condition to be compared in an informed consent case is (where the risk is the only complication of surgery) the condition that the patient would have been in without having the operation and the condition that the patient is in after having had the operation. In a noninformed consent case, where the physician is negligent in the performance of an operation, the comparison is between the condition that the patient would have been in if the negligence had not taken place, and the condition that the patient has as a result of the physician's negligence. This is because it is the physician's negligence that has caused the injury. But for the physician's negligence, the operation could have been performed without any harm to the patient. In an informed consent case, where there are no alternatives of treatment, the operation could not have been performed without the inherent risk. Therefore, the comparison is between plaintiff's condition without having the operation and plaintiff's condition after having the operation.

* * *

The Court was, in effect, applying the doctrine that where a wrong creates a benefit that would not have existed but for the wrong, the damages flowing from the wrong are offset to the extent of the benefit received. The benefits doctrine is appropriate in an informed consent case, since a collateral risk is an inherent part of the operation and the benefit could not have been achieved without the attendant risk. * * *

This doctrine has also been applied in New Jersey in reducing the damages assessed where the doctor has deviated from the standard of care in the treatment of a patient.

* * *

The benefits doctrine has been applied in New Jersey to wrongful life and wrongful birth cases and accords with general principles of compensatory damages in tort actions. The benefits doctrine is uniformly endorsed in the literature as the appropriate measure of damages for informed consent cases. Since informed consent is an equitable doctrine, the appropriate rule of damages can be molded by the court to fit the circumstances. * * *

The benefits doctrine, wherein complications of surgery are offset by benefits received from surgery, is in accord with the public policy of New Jersey. * * * The State is committed to preserving the health and lives of its citizens. [ ] The medical community strives to maintain the health of society. *See* American Medical Ass'n, *Principles of Medical Ethics* (1982).

It is therefore the opinion of the court that if an operation is properly performed, of overall benefit to the patient, and there are no alternative options for treatment, there should be no compensable damages awarded against the physician. The court's charge will instruct the jury to subtract from the damages proximately caused by the nerve damage the benefits received from the operation.

Notes and Questions

1. Why did the court adopt the benefit rule in this case? Under the normal application of the proximate cause rule in informed consent cases, if a reasonable patient would have gone ahead with the procedure if fully informed of risks, then the plaintiff may not recover. The court merely achieves this result using the damages rule. Why?

2. The court states that the benefit rule applies when there are "no alternative options for treatment". Isn't one option always non-treatment? Is this just an example of a bad case making bad law? The plaintiff's damages seem trivial in light of the benefits he got from the operation, and the damages also seem to be preexisting in the area of the plaintiff's marital difficulties.

2. *Punitive Damages*

TISDALE v. PRUITT, Jr., M.D.

Court of Appeals of South Carolina, 1990.
394 S.E.2d 857.

LITTLEJOHN, J.

In this medical malpractice action, Plaintiff, Laurel S. Tisdale, Respondent (the patient) sued Defendant A. Bert Pruitt Jr., Appellant (Dr. Pruitt) seeking damages alleged to have grown out of an unauthorized dilation and curettage (D & C). The Complaint alleges assault and battery, negligence, recklessness and willfulness and charges that the D & C was performed by the doctor without the informed consent of the patient. The Answer of Dr. Pruitt amounts to a general denial, asserting a medical emergency as justification and alleging the two-year statute of limitations as a bar to the assault and battery claim.

Among the allegations of the Complaint are found the following:

The Defendant's conduct toward the Plaintiff was negligent, reckless, willful, and in conscious disregard of the Plaintiff's rights in the following particulars:

b) In failing to read the Plaintiff's chart in order to determine that the sole purpose of her visit to him was for him to render a second opinion to Dr. Murphy concerning her intended hospital stay.

* * *

d) In failing to obtain her consent prior to performing any procedures upon her other than obtaining a biopsy in order to render a second opinion to Dr. Murphy; * * *.

The trial judge granted a directed verdict by reason of the statute of limitations as to the assault and battery cause of action, and submitted the other causes of action to the jury which returned a verdict for $5,000 actual damages plus $25,000 punitive damages. The doctor appeals. We affirm.

FACTS

The patient had been seeing her own family physician, Dr. Murphy, for approximately ten years. She was having problems with a pregnancy and consulted him. He recommended a D & C and arranged for her to be admitted to St. Francis Hospital for a final diagnosis and for treatment under general anesthesia.

Before hospitalization insurance coverage would be afforded, her carrier required a second opinion, and she was referred by the insurance company to Dr. Pruitt. She went to his office and filled out an information sheet and told his receptionist that she was there for a second opinion. The receptionist initiated a patient's chart and indicated on it in two places that the patient was there for the purpose of a second opinion. Dr. Pruitt admitted that he did not read the chart and placed her on the examination table with feet in stirrups and proceeded not only to examine her so as to supply a second opinion but to perform the D & C. It was not completely satisfactory, and a supplemental D & C was required thereafter; it was performed by Dr. Murphy at the hospital under general anesthesia.

It is the testimony of the patient that she preferred not to have an abortion and if the same was to be performed, she wanted it to be performed by her own doctor rather than by the second opinion doctor whom she had never seen before.

She testified as follows:

Q. And Mrs. Tisdale, if Dr. Pruitt had fully informed you, and asked you for permission, or asked you for your consent to perform a D & C in his office that day, would you have given that consent?

A. No sir. No sir.

Q. Tell the jury why not?

A. I had known Dr. Pruitt for about fifteen minutes. I have known my doctor for over ten years, and I would never consent to have something that painful done in an office, whereas you could go to the hospital and be under general anesthesia, and be confident that everything is all right.

Dr. Pruitt does not with specificity testify as to exactly what he told the patient but says " * * * I explained everything to her * * * " He further testified relative to the patient's consent as follows:

Q. * * * [W]hat were the signals? What made you think that she agreed?

A. I don't know how you would even say. What are vibes? You know, you can sometimes sense hostility, sometimes you can sense grief. Sometimes you can sense disapproval or approval. I could well have missed—I obviously misread Mrs. Tisdale's vibes or signals, or things, but when someone is really upset, that's not hard to do.

ISSUES

While Dr. Pruitt filed thirteen exceptions as appear in the record, the gravamen of his appeal is found in his brief as follows:

* * * Accordingly, the main issue for the Court's decision is whether the evidence presented at trial was sufficient to sustain a verdict based on the doctrine of informed consent. In deciding this issue, the Court is asked to consider the essential elements of *informed consent,* whether the Plaintiff proved causation, and whether the damages awarded were proper. Additionally, the Court is also asked to decide whether consent to a medical procedure may be implied from the patient's conduct and silence, and whether the jury should have been so instructed.

ANALYSIS

* * * Under the doctrine of informed consent, it is generally held that a physician who performs a diagnostic, therapeutic, or surgical procedure has a duty to disclose to a patient of sound mind, in the absence of an emergency that warrants immediate medical treatment, (1) the diagnosis, (2) the general nature of the contemplated procedure, (3) the material risks involved in the procedure, (4) the probability of success associated with the procedure, (5) the prognosis if the procedure is not carried out, and (6) the existence of any alternatives to the procedure.

In a letter (written by Dr. Pruitt to Dr. Murphy after the D & C had been performed) we think that Dr. Pruitt effectively pleads guilty to negligence, recklessness and willfulness. From that letter we quote:

> Again, let me say that I am most distressed that I did not realize Mrs. Tisdale was referred to the office by the Prudential Insurance Co. for a second opinion. Although my receptionist had put this on the chart, I did not notice it, and as I did not realize that D & C's required second opinions, the thought literally never occurred to me. I have been asked on numerous occasions to give second opinions on hysterectomies and other procedures but never for D & C's, especially for missed abortions.
>
>   * * *
>
> I do hope that you will pardon my "goof". I only wish Mrs. Tisdale at the time I was doing the procedure, had mentioned to me more clearly why she was sent to the office. If she did, it fell on deaf ears.

An analysis of Dr. Pruitt's testimony leaves much to be desired in the way of informing a patient of facts upon which an intelligent, informed consent can be made. * * * [W]e hold that the trial judge must be affirmed because of a lack of consent on the part of the patient. The circumstance under which Dr. Pruitt would have us find that the patient consented are relevant in determining whether or not the patient should have ordered Dr. Pruitt to stop what he was doing. She was in the office of a strange doctor recommended by the insurance company. She was greatly disturbed and was crying, experiencing pain. She was on the examining table with her feet in the stirrups. The procedure lasted about five minutes.

Dr. Pruitt's own testimony relative to her acquiescence is relevant. He relies mostly on her silence. He testified as follows:

> * * * I just falsely assumed, or incorrectly assumed that this was what she was there for.
>
>   * * *
>
> * * * Dewey, just for the record—and this may sound offensive, but I obviously, looking back, misread Mrs. Tisdale's feelings,

but when I talked with her during the history taking, she very, very much wanted this pregnancy.

* * * She was just absolutely docile I guess, and I just assumed that she was acquiescing, but I thought I had her consent and her inform—very informed consent * * *

The argument of counsel that the evidence does not make at least a jury issue on whether damages were sustained and proximately caused by Dr. Pruitt's wrongful conduct is without merit. There is testimony that she suffered pain from the procedure without anesthesia; she was deprived of her right to choose the doctor to perform her D & C; in addition, she sustained emotional injury. Both actual and punitive damages are supported by the evidence. We hold that the evidence is not susceptible of the inference that the patient gave an informed consent, expressed or implied. Accordingly, the trial judge properly declined to charge the law of implied consent.

Affirmed.

Notes and Questions

1. The Tisdale court refused to imply consent by the plaintiff, given the context and her passivity. Given the doctor's admissions, the court went further and allowed punitive damages, even though the battery count had been dismissed. Might this kind of award increase a doctor's enthusiasm for conversation with his more quiet patients?

2. Punitive damages are typically awarded as part of the damage claims for an intentional tort such as battery. The focus is on the reprehensible nature of defendant's conduct, which may be reckless or motivated by malice or fraud. Even gross negligence in a malpractice suit usually will not suffice. The circumstances surrounding a tortious act may however warrant an inference of a wilful or wanton attitude, or reckless disregard of the patient's wishes. In *Tisdale*, the physician's cavalier assumptions about the patient's consent, his lack of a conversation with her, and her obvious vulnerability, together constituted reckless behavior, justifying punitive damages.

3. In Strauss v. Biggs, 525 A.2d 992 (Del.Sup.1987), defendant surgeon began to operate on the plaintiff after having worked for sixteen hours straight prior to the surgery; he proposed a procedure that would give only partial relief, when he knew that another procedure would give complete relief, but he was incapable of performing it. He then failed to perform his proposed procedure, but neglected to tell the plaintiff, and continued with surgery after the plaintiff had screamed in pain on the first incision. He finally billed the insurer for procedures both unnecessary and not done. The court found these facts "compelling" for purposes of allowing the jury to find punitive damages. The case seems to add "greed" to "fraud" or "malice" as sufficient to establish physician conduct reprehensible enough for punitive damages.

E. EXCEPTIONS TO THE DUTY TO DISCLOSE

CANTERBURY v. SPENCE

United States Court of Appeals, District of Columbia Circuit, 1972.
464 F.2d 772.

VI

Two exceptions to the general rule of disclosure have been noted by the courts. Each is in the nature of a physician's privilege not to disclose, and the reasoning underlying them is appealing. Each, indeed, is but a recognition that, as important as is the patient's right to know, it is greatly outweighed by the magnitudinous circumstances giving rise to the privilege. The first comes into play when the patient is unconscious or otherwise incapable of consenting, and harm from a failure to treat is imminent and outweighs any harm threatened by the proposed treatment. When a genuine emergency of that sort arises, it is settled that the impracticality of conferring with the patient dispenses with need for it. Even in situations of that character the physician should, as current law requires, attempt to secure a relative's consent if possible. But if time is too short to accommodate discussion, obviously the physician should proceed with the treatment.

The second exception obtains when risk-disclosure poses such a threat of detriment to the patient as to become unfeasible or contraindicated from a medical point of view. It is recognized that patients occasionally become so ill or emotionally distraught on disclosure as to foreclose a rational decision, or complicate or hinder the treatment, or perhaps even pose psychological damage to the patient. Where that is so, the cases have generally held that the physician is armed with a privilege to keep the information from the patient, and we think it clear that portents of that type may justify the physician in action he deems medically warranted. The critical inquiry is whether the physician responded to a sound medical judgment that communication of the risk information would present a threat to the patient's well-being.

The physician's privilege to withhold information for therapeutic reasons must be carefully circumscribed, however, for otherwise it might devour the disclosure rule itself. The privilege does not accept the paternalistic notion that the physician may remain silent simply because divulgence might prompt the patient to forego therapy the physician feels the patient really needs. That attitude presumes instability or perversity for even the normal patient, and runs counter to the foundation principle that the patient should and ordinarily can make the choice for himself. Nor does the privilege contemplate operation save where the patient's reaction to risk information, as reasonably foreseen by the physician, is menacing. And even in a situation of that kind, disclosure to a close relative with a view to securing consent to the proposed treatment may be the only alternative open to the physician.

VIII

In the context of trial of a suit claiming inadequate disclosure of risk information by a physician, the patient has the burden of going forward with evidence tending to establish prima facie the essential elements of the cause of action, and ultimately the burden of proof—the risk of nonpersuasion—on those elements. These are normal impositions upon moving litigants, and no reason why they should not attach in nondisclosure cases is apparent. The burden of going forward with evidence pertaining to a privilege not to disclose, however, rests properly upon the physician. This is not only because the patient has made out a prima facie case before an issue on privilege is reached, but also because any evidence bearing on the privilege is usually in the hands of the physician alone. Requiring him to open the proof on privilege is consistent with judicial policy laying such a burden on the party who seeks shelter from an exception to a general rule and who is more likely to have possession of the facts.

Notes and Questions

1. The common law has long recognized the right of a doctor in a true emergency to act without patient consent, so long as he acts in conformity with customary practice in such emergencies. Jackovach v. Yocum, 212 Iowa 914, 237 N.W. 444 (1931). Some courts hold that consent is presumed in these situations. What constitutes an emergency situation is often unclear; the courts tend to err on the side of permitting arguable emergency treatment without formal consent.

2. Where the patient has consented to a procedure to remedy his condition, he is presumed to have consented to all steps necessary to correct it, even though the procedure in fact used varies from that authorized specifically. Kennedy v. Parrot, 243 N.C. 355, 90 S.E.2d 754 (1956). Does this make sense? If the alternative procedure is part of the repertoire of treatment for the patient's illness, then shouldn't the doctor have advised the patient of the possibility of this procedure as well as the intended one?

3. The most controversial privilege is the therapeutic privilege. Though this privilege is often discussed in dicta, it has not formed the basis for court rulings. *Canterbury* seems to have defined the privilege narrowly: information may be withheld in some situations, since "patients occasionally become so ill or emotionally distraught on disclosure as to foreclose a rational decision." The court used the word *menacing* to describe the patient reaction, but then it equivocated, suggesting that the privilege would be justified where disclosure would complicate or hinder treatment or pose psychological damage to the patient. Given physician unhappiness with requirements of disclosure generally, the therapeutic privilege exception threatens in theory to swallow the informed consent doctrine whole.

Consider the following argument for a narrow application of the exception:

"To the extent that suffering occurs * * * when a person perceives a threat to his integrity or when an individual has no power to control the situation in which he finds himself, informed consent may help to redress the balance. This will occur if adherence to the requirements of the doctrine * * * affirms the personhood of, and gives some measure of control to, the patient. When informed consent is seen as a mechanism for avoiding suffering, any exception, including therapeutic privilege, would need to be narrowly construed. Further, since the doctrine of therapeutic privilege restricts the disclosure of information solely to avoid harm and the suffering that it would entail, the privilege would not be available unless the suffering avoided by applying the doctrine at least outweighed the suffering that resulted from the failure to obtain informed consent."

Somerville, "Therapeutic Privilege: Variation on the Theme of Informed Consent," 12 Law, Med. & Health Care 4 (1984).

How would this balancing test be implemented, and what factors are relevant to it? See also Patterson, The Therapeutic Justification for Withholding Medical Information: What You Don't Know Can't Hurt You, or Can It?, 64 Neb.L.Rev. 721 (1985). In analyzing risks to be disclosed, some courts talk of the need to avoid scaring a patient away from a "needed" procedure, recognizing the effect of disclosure of risks on the patient's choices. Pedersen v. Vahidy, 209 Conn. 510, 552 A.2d 419 (1989).

4. Waiver. Suppose a patient, trusting his doctor to do the best for him, says, "I don't want to know a thing, Doc, just do what you think is best". Should the doctor be able to use this as a defense? It appears that the patient is exercising self-determination in choosing a veil of ignorance. See, e.g., Henderson v. Milobsky, 595 F.2d 654 (D.C.Cir.1978). Meisel, The 'Exceptions' to the Informed Consent Doctrine: Striking a Balance Between Competing Values in Medical Decisionmaking, 1979 Wis.L.Rev. 413, 453–60. Should a patient's waiver be readily allowed, or should a duty to converse be imposed, even in the face of a waiver by the patient of his right to information? Should a patient be forced to listen to a full risk disclosure? If an informed consent form is the primary device for risk disclosure, the patient can choose not to read it as a way of avoidance. Should the patient be forced to read it? See Strasser, "Mill and the Right to Remain Uninformed", 11 J.Med. & Philosophy 65 (1986); Ost, The "Right" Not to Know, 9 J.Med. & Philosophy 301, 306–7 (1984).

5. *Statutory Limits.* More than half of the states have enacted legislation dealing with informed consent, largely in response to the "malpractice crisis" of 1974, or more recent perceived crises in their states. The statutes take a variety of forms, from specific to general, but they all share the common thread of moving the informed consent standard toward greater deference to medical judgment. Given the current state and national mood of legislative limitations on common law tort remedies, it may be expected that the common law of informed consent will continue to be affected by legislative action.

Problem: Whose Benefit Is It Anyway?

You represent Croziere Hospital, a small nonprofit hospital in Northeast Washington, D.C. The Chief of Surgery, Dr. Leaf, has just come into your office seeking your advice on a patient problem. A patient, Mrs. Jan Lee, was admitted to the hospital yesterday through the emergency room in the final stages of labor. She gave birth just an hour ago to a baby boy, healthy in all respects except that his right foot is a club foot. The staff surgeon can easily correct this anomaly now so that the child would be able to walk normally. Without surgery now, the risks of failure are progressively greater.

Mrs. Lee and her husband are Asian immigrants recently arrived in the United States. Dr. Leaf knows from past experience in the military in Asia that Asians from the Lee's area of Asia believe that birth defects are an expression of divine anger, punishing the parents for past misdeeds. The Lees are therefore likely to consider any attempts to correct their son's defects to be an insult to their gods. Dr. Leaf is afraid that if he talks with the Lees, they will refuse the surgery and leave the hospital immediately. They have not yet seen their son and are not aware of the club foot. Dr. Leaf would like to operate on the boy without their permission immediately, given what he sees as the clear benefits of an operation now.

What do you advise him to do, in light of informed consent doctrine and its privileges and exceptions?

F. DISCLOSING CONFLICTS OF INTEREST: THE PHYSICIAN AS FIDUCIARY

Medical professionals are in a position of dominance with regard to their patients. The relationship is inherently unequal. The physician has superior knowledge produced by long years of training and practice, expertise the patient cannot have; the physician is less concerned about the patient's health than is the patient; the patient is often anxious and ill-equipped to process complex medical information; and the physician can usually get another patient more easily than the patient can obtain another doctor. Patients are thus vulnerable, and this vulnerability imposes on physicians a "trust", a fiduciary obligation justified by the physician's dominant position in the relationship.

MOORE v. REGENTS OF THE UNIVERSITY OF CALIFORNIA
Supreme Court of California, 1990.
51 Cal.3d 120, 271 Cal.Rptr. 146, 793 P.2d 479.

[The plaintiff John Moore underwent treatment for hairy-cell leukemia at the Medical Center of the University of California at Los Angeles (UCLA Medical Center). The defendants were Dr. David Golde, the attending physician; the Regents of the University of California, who own and operate the university; Shirley Quan, a researcher at the University; Genetics Institute; and Sandoz Pharmaceuticals Corporation. The Supreme Court granted review to determine whether Moore had stated a cause of action for breach of the physician's disclosure obligations and for conversion. The Court rejected the conversion cause of action.]

* * *

II. FACTS

* * *

Moore first visited UCLA Medical Center on October 5, 1976, shortly after he learned that he had hairy-cell leukemia. After hospitalizing Moore and "withdr[awing] extensive amounts of blood, bone marrow aspirate, and other bodily substances," Golde confirmed that diagnosis. At this time all defendants, including Golde, were aware that "certain blood products and blood components were of great value in a number of commercial and scientific efforts" and that access to a patient whose blood contained these substances would provide "competitive, commercial, and scientific advantages."

On October 8, 1976, Golde recommended that Moore's spleen be removed. Golde informed Moore "that he had reason to fear for his life, and that the proposed splenectomy operation * * * was necessary to slow down the progress of his disease." Based upon Golde's representations, Moore signed a written consent form authorizing the splenectomy.

Before the operation, Golde and Quan "formed the intent and made arrangements to obtain portions of [Moore's] spleen following its removal" and to take them to a separate research unit. Golde gave written instructions to this effect on October 18 and 19, 1976. These research activities "were not intended to have * * * any relation to [Moore's] medical * * * care." However, neither Golde nor Quan informed Moore of their plans to conduct this research or requested his permission. Surgeons at UCLA Medical Center, whom the complaint does not name as defendants, removed Moore's spleen on October 20, 1976.

Moore returned to the UCLA Medical Center several times between November 1976 and September 1983. He did so at Golde's direction and based upon representations "that such visits were necessary and required for his health and well-being, and based upon the trust inherent in and by virtue of the physician-patient relationship. * * *" On each of these visits Golde withdrew additional samples of "blood, blood serum, skin, bone marrow aspirate, and sperm." On each occasion Moore travelled to the UCLA Medical Center from his home in Seattle because he had been told that the procedures were to be performed only there and only under Golde's direction.

"In fact, [however,] throughout the period of time that [Moore] was under [Golde's] care and treatment, * * * the defendants were actively involved in a number of activities which they concealed from [Moore]. * * *" Specifically, defendants were conducting research on Moore's cells and planned to "benefit financially and competitively * * * [by exploiting the cells] and [their] exclusive access to [the cells] by virtue of [Golde's] on-going physician-patient relationship. * * * "

Sometime before August 1979, Golde established a cell line from Moore's T-lymphocytes. On January 30, 1981, the Regents applied for a patent on the cell line, listing Golde and Quan as inventors. "[B]y virtue of an established policy * * *, [the] Regents, Golde, and Quan would share in any royalties or profits * * * arising out of [the] patent." The patent issued on March 20, 1984, naming Golde and Quan as the inventors of the cell line and the Regents as the assignee of the patent. (U.S. Patent No. 4,438,032 (Mar. 20, 1984).)

The Regent's patent also covers various methods for using the cell line to produce lymphokines. Moore admits in his complaint that "the true clinical potential of each of the lymphokines * * * [is] difficult to predict, [but] * * * competing commercial firms in these relevant fields have published reports in biotechnology industry periodicals predicting a potential market of approximately $3.01 Billion Dollars by the year 1990 for a whole range of [such lymphokines]. * * * "

With the Regents' assistance, Golde negotiated agreements for commercial development of the cell line and products to be derived from it. Under an agreement with Genetics Institute, Golde "became a paid consultant" and "acquired the rights to 75,000 shares of common stock." Genetics Institute also agreed to pay Golde and the Regents "at least $330,000 over three years, including a pro-rata share of [Golde's] salary and fringe benefits, in exchange for * * * exclusive access to the materials and research performed" on the cell line and products derived from it. On June 4, 1982, Sandoz "was added to the agreement," and compensation payable to Golde and the Regents was increased by $110,000. "[T]hroughout this period, * * * Quan spent as much as 70 [percent] of her time working for [the] Regents on research" related to the cell line.

* * *

III. Discussion

A. Breach of Fiduciary Duty and Lack of Informed Consent

Moore repeatedly alleges that Golde failed to disclose the extent of his research and economic interests in Moore's cells before obtaining consent to the medical procedures by which the cells were extracted. These allegations, in our view, state a cause of action against Golde for invading a legally protected interest of his patient. This cause of action can properly be characterized either as the breach of a fiduciary duty to disclose facts material to the patient's consent or, alternatively, as the performance of medical procedures without first having obtained the patient's informed consent.

Our analysis begins with three well-established principles. First, "a person of adult years and in sound mind has the right, in the exercise of control over his own body, to determine whether or not to submit to lawful medical treatment." [ ] Second, "the patient's consent to treatment, to be effective, must be an informed consent." [ ] Third, in soliciting the patient's consent, a physician has a fiduciary duty to disclose all information material to the patient's decision. * * * [ ]

(F., J., J. & S.) Health Law, 2d Ed. ACB—10

These principles lead to the following conclusions: (1) a physician must disclose personal interests unrelated to the patient's health, whether research or economic, that may affect the physician's professional judgment; and (2) a physician's failure to disclose such interests may give rise to a cause of action for performing medical procedures without informed consent or breach of fiduciary duty.

To be sure, questions about the validity of a patient's consent to a procedure typically arise when the patient alleges that the physician failed to disclose medical risks, as in malpractice cases, and not when the patient alleges that the physician had a personal interest, as in this case. The concept of informed consent, however, is broad enough to encompass the latter. "The scope of the physician's communication to the patient * * * must be measured by the patient's need, and that need is whatever information is material to the decision." (*Cobbs v. Grant*, supra, 8 Cal.3d at p. 245, 104 Cal.Rptr. 505, 502 P.2d 1.)

Indeed, the law already recognizes that a reasonable patient would want to know whether a physician has an economic interest that might affect the physician's professional judgment. As the Court of Appeal has said, "[c]ertainly a sick patient deserves to be free of any reasonable suspicion that his doctor's judgment is influenced by a profit motive." (*Magan Medical Clinic v. Cal. State Bd. of Medical Examiners* (1967) 249 Cal.App.2d 124, 132, 57 Cal.Rptr. 256.) The desire to protect patients from possible conflicts of interest has also motivated legislative enactments. Among these is Business and Professions Code section 654.2. Under that section, a physician may not charge a patient on behalf of, or refer a patient to, any organization in which the physician has a "significant beneficial interest, unless [the physician] first discloses in writing to the patient, that there is such an interest and advises the patient that the patient may choose any organization for the purposes of obtaining the services ordered or requested by [the physician]." (Bus. & Prof.Code, § 654.2, subd. (a). See also Bus. & Prof.Code, § 654.1 [referrals to clinical laboratories].) Similarly, under Health and Safety Code section 24173, a physician who plans to conduct a medical experiment on a patient must, among other things, inform the patient of "[t]he name of the sponsor or funding source, if any, * * * and the organization, if any, under whose general aegis the experiment is being conducted." (Health & Saf.Code, § 24173, subd. (c)(9).)

It is important to note that no law prohibits a physician from conducting research in the same area in which he practices. Progress in medicine often depends upon physicians, such as those practicing at the university hospital where Moore received treatment, who conduct research while caring for their patients.

Yet a physician who treats a patient in whom he also has a research interest has potentially conflicting loyalties. This is because medical treatment decisions are made on the basis of proportionality—weighing the *benefits* to the patient against the *risks* to the patient. As another court has said, "the determination as to whether the burdens of treatment are worth enduring for any individual patient depends upon the facts unique in each case," and "the patient's interests and desires are the key ingredients of the decision-making process." (*Barber v. Superior Court* (1983) 147 Cal.App.3d 1006, 1018–1019, 195 Cal. Rptr. 484.) A physician who adds his own research interests to this balance may be tempted to order a scientifically useful procedure or test that offers marginal, or no, benefits to the patient. The possibility that an interest extraneous to the patient's health has affected the physician's judgment is something that a reasonable patient would want to know in deciding whether to consent to a proposed course of treatment. It is material to the patient's decision and, thus, a prerequisite to informed consent. [   ]

Golde argues that the scientific use of cells that have already been removed cannot possibly affect the patient's medical interests. The argument is correct in one instance but not in another. If a physician has no plans to conduct research on a patient's cells at the time he recommends the medical procedure by which they are taken, then the patient's medical interests have not been impaired. In that instance the argument is correct. On the other hand, a physician who does have a preexisting research interest might, consciously or unconsciously, take that into consideration in recommending the procedure. In that instance the argument is incorrect: the physician's extraneous motivation may affect his judgment and is, thus, material to the patient's consent.

We acknowledge that there is a competing consideration. To require disclosure of research and economic interests may corrupt the patient's own judgment by distracting him from the requirements of his health. But California law does not grant physicians unlimited discretion to decide what to disclose. Instead, "it is the prerogative of the patient, not the physician, to determine for himself the direction in which he believes his interests lie." (*Cobbs v. Grant,* supra, 8 Cal.3d at p. 242, 104 Cal.Rptr. 505, 502 P.2d 1.)   * * *

Accordingly, we hold that a physician who is seeking a patient's consent for a medical procedure must, in order to satisfy his fiduciary duty [10] and to obtain the patient's informed consent, disclose personal interests unrelated to the patient's health, whether research or economic, that may affect his medical judgment.

1. Dr. Golde

We turn now to the allegations of Moore's third amended complaint to determine whether he has stated such a cause of action. We

10. In some respects the term "fiduciary" is too broad. In this context the term "fiduciary" signifies only that a physician must disclose all facts material to the patient's decision. A physician is not the patient's financial adviser. As we have already discussed, the reason why a physician must disclose possible conflicts is not because he has a duty to protect his patient's financial interests, but because certain personal interests may affect professional judgment.

first discuss the adequacy of Moore's allegations against Golde, based upon the physician's disclosures prior to the splenectomy.

Moore alleges that, prior to the surgical removal of his spleen, Golde "formed the intent and made arrangements to obtain portions of his spleen following its removal from [Moore] in connection with [his] desire to have regular and continuous access to, and possession of, [Moore's] unique and rare Blood and Bodily Substances." Moore was never informed prior to the splenectomy of Golde's "prior formed intent" to obtain a portion of his spleen. In our view, these allegations adequately show that Golde had an undisclosed research interest in Moore's cells at the time he sought Moore's consent to the splenectomy. Accordingly, Moore has stated a cause of action for breach of fiduciary duty, or lack of informed consent, based upon the disclosures accompanying that medical procedure.

We next discuss the adequacy of Golde's alleged disclosures regarding the postoperative takings of blood and other samples. In this context, Moore alleges that Golde "expressly, affirmatively and impliedly represented * * * that these withdrawals of his Blood and Bodily Substances were necessary and required for his health and well-being." However, Moore also alleges that Golde actively concealed his economic interest in Moore's cells during this time period. "[D]uring each of these visits * * *, and even when [Moore] inquired as to whether there was any possible or potential commercial or financial value or significance of his Blood and Bodily Substances, or whether the defendants had discovered anything * * * which was or might be * * * related to any scientific activity resulting in commercial or financial benefits * * *, the defendants repeatedly and affirmatively represented to [Moore] that there was no commercial or financial value to his Blood and Bodily Substances * * * and in fact actively discouraged such inquiries."

Moore admits in his complaint that defendants disclosed they "were engaged in strictly academic and purely scientific medical research. * * * " However, Golde's representation that he had no financial interest in this research became false, based upon the allegations, at least by May 1979, when he "began to investigate and initiate the procedures * * * for [obtaining] a patent" on the cell line developed from Moore's cells.

In these allegations, Moore plainly asserts that Golde concealed an economic interest in the postoperative procedures. Therefore, applying the principles already discussed, the allegations state a cause of action for breach of fiduciary duty or lack of informed consent.

We thus disagree with the superior court's ruling that Moore had not stated a cause of action because essential allegations were lacking. We discuss each such allegation. First, in the superior court's view, Moore needed but failed to allege that defendants knew his cells had potential commercial value *on October 5, 1976* (the time blood tests were first performed at UCLA Medical Center) and had *at that time* already formed the intent to exploit the cells. We agree with the superior court that the absence of such allegations precludes Moore from stating a cause of action based upon the procedures undertaken on October 5, 1976. But, as already discussed, Moore clearly alleges that Golde had developed a research interest in his cells by October 20, 1976, when the splenectomy was performed. Thus, Moore can state a cause of action based upon Golde's alleged failure to disclose that interest before the splenectomy.

The superior court also held that the lack of essential allegations prevented Moore from stating a cause of action based on the splenectomy. According to the superior court, Moore failed to allege that the operation lacked a therapeutic purpose or that the procedure was totally unrelated to therapeutic purposes. In our view, however, neither allegation is essential. Even if the splenectomy had a therapeutic purpose,[11] it does not follow that Golde had no duty to disclose his additional research and economic interests. As we have already discussed, the existence of a motivation for a medical procedure unrelated to the patient's health is a potential conflict of interest and a fact material to the patient's decision.

Notes and Questions

1. In *Moore*, the court explicitly uses both fiduciary duty and informed consent doctrine in order to impose an obligation on the physicians to disclose their research and economic interests. Does a claim of breach of fiduciary duty add anything to an informed consent claim? If so, what? What worries the California Supreme Court? Is it that the patient's medical interests will somehow be impaired, since the physician's judgment during treatment may be corrupted by the promise of financial gain? Or is the court concerned about the patient's economic interests?

Judge Mosk, dissenting, argues that the nondisclosure cause of action is inadequate on three grounds. First, a damage remedy will not give physician-researchers an incentive to disclose conflicts of interest prior to treatment, since it is hard to establish the causal connection between injury and the failure to inform. The patient must show he would have declined, if given full information. Even if the patient claims that he would have refused, he must prove that "no reasonably prudent" person so situated would have declined. Id at 519. Second, " * * * it gives the patient only the right to refuse consent, i.e., the right to prohibit the commercialization of his tissue; it does not give him the right to grant consent to that commercialization on the condition that he share in its proceeds." Id at 520. Third, the cause of action " * * * fails to reach a major class of potential defendants: all those who are outside the strict physician-patient relationship with the plaintiff." Id at 521. This may include other researchers and corporations exploiting the tissue.

11. The record shows that the splenectomy did have a therapeutic purpose. The Regents' patent application, which the superior court and the Court of Appeal both accepted as part of the record, shows that Moore had a grossly enlarged spleen and that its excision improved his condition.

Judge Broussard, concurring and dissenting, disagrees with Judge Mosk as to the efficacy of the nondisclosure action. He argues that the breach of fiduciary duty encompasses the postoperative conduct of defendants as well as the presurgical failure to disclose, so that the plaintiff can recover by "establishing that he would not have consented to some or all of the extensive postoperative medical procedures if he had been fully aware of defendants' research and economic interests and motivations." Id at 500. He also observes that the fiduciary duty, unlike an informed consent cause of action, requires " * * * only that the doctor's wrongful failure to disclose information proximately caused the plaintiff some type of compensable damage." Id at 500. Punitive as well as compensatory damages will be available.

Commentators have contended that the *Moore* nondisclosure cause of action will fail to reach third parties who benefit from the plaintiff's cell line. One commentator has advocated use of the common law tort of invasion of privacy, in particular the appropriateness of likeness for commercial purposes. Restatement (Second) of Torts § 652A (1977). "The tort of invasion of privacy already protects the publication of private writings and the commercialization of one's physical likeness. It is not much of a stretch to extend this protection to the biological body that sports this likeness. * * * If privacy rights exist in biological substances—be they "likenesses" or cells—it follows that they may not be appropriated for commercial use or otherwise without consent." Havens, The Spleen That Fought Back, 20 The Brief 11, 40 (1990).

2. Does the normal treatment setting pose any comparable conflicts of interest, in which the physician's treatment decision may be affected by his financial interests in treating a particular patient? Suppose a physician examines a boy brought into the emergency room of a small community hospital after an auto accident. The boy has an injured leg and foot. The x-ray suggests a dislocated foot. The doctor can either try to reduce the dislocation in the hospital, or he can refer the boy to an orthopedic specialist in a large city a hundred miles away. If the physician chooses to treat, he gets a fee, while the referral generates no further income for him. What should the physician choose to disclose to the boy's parents? The medical risks in either approach? The economic issue that may color his judgment? See D. Hilifiker, Facing Our Mistakes, 310 N.Eng.J.Med. 118, 119 (1984). Ison v. McFall, 55 Tenn.App. 326, 400 S.W.2d 243 (1964); Larsen v. Yelle, 310 Minn. 521, 246 N.W.2d 841 (1976) (physician in general practice liable for failing to refer patient with fractured wrist to orthopedic specialist). See Principles of Medical Ethics of the American Medical Association § 8 (requiring doctor to seek consultation "whenever it appears that the quality of medical services may be enhanced thereby.")

For the incentives on providers to keep patients even if their facilities are inadequate, see Entin, DRGs, HMOs, and PPOs: Introducing Economic Issues in the Medical Malpractice Case, 20 Forum 674 (1985). Are economic motivations so basic that patients can be presumed to be aware of them generally? These issues are discussed further in Chapter 7.

Physicians may at times want to try a new or innovative approach to a patient's problems. What are their obligations to disclose that they are in effect "experimenting" on the patient?

ESTRADA v. JAQUES

Court of Appeals of North Carolina, 1984.
70 N.C.App. 627, 321 S.E.2d 240.

[The plaintiff Estrada had suffered a gunshot wound to his leg. A mass developed in his leg due to a false aneurysm, a weakened spot in the arterial wall caused by the passage of the bullet. The surgeons were advised by the radiologists treating Estrada that the false aneurysm should be treated by a percutaneous steel coil embolization. This was a new procedure involving the insertion of a small steel coil into the weakened artery upstream from the false aneurysm, cutting off the flow of blood and preventing a rupture. The surgeons discussed the procedure with Estrada and obtained a signed consent from him. The embolization did not go well. The surgeons attempted for 16 hours to restore the flow of blood to Estrada's leg, but failed. Estrada's lower leg then had to be amputated.

Estrada argued that the surgeons were negligent in obtaining his consent, in that they did not inform him of the "highly experimental" nature of the steel coil embolization. He charged that the radiologists were similarly negligent in failing to explain the experimental nature of the procedure, as well as negligent in their explanations to the surgeons and in the actual performance of the operation. A statutory provision governed informed consent, requiring that the patient must understand the "procedures or treatments and of the usual and most frequent risks and hazards" inherent in them.]

* * * Obviously, Estrada could only understand *what the surgeons told him.* A careful reading of his whole deposition leads to the conclusion that they informed Estrada only of the risks inherent in the standard surgical procedure and the chance that the embolization might not work. The various depositions of the hospital personnel reflect at best a vague knowledge of the risks of embolization in this sort of case. This knowledge * * * is traceable exclusively to a single medical article and to the ill-defined experience of one of the radiologists, apparently including only one prior operation, with little to suggest he communicated it to the surgeons. There was some evidence that steel coil embolizations had been used in other parts of the body with low risk, but nothing to show why that knowledge should automatically apply to the peripheral arteries operated on in this case.

This omission is critical in light of the evidence that such arteries presented additional difficult problems of size and accessibility. We conclude that this evidence failed to satisfy the surgeons' burden of proof.

* * *

[The court held that the embolization procedure was experimental, and noted that the statute required patient understanding of procedures *"which are recognized and followed by other health care providers."*]   * * *   While the emphasized language is not entirely clear, it appears to require that informed consent be obtained to *established* procedures or treatments.   Obviously, experimental procedures, by their very untested nature, do not fall within the category of practices described.   Just as obviously, on the other hand, medical innovation must go forward, and there will also be some cases in which no recognized procedure will offer any prospect of success.   We do not believe the legislature intended to preclude any valid consent to experimental procedures.

* * *

Instead, we hold that where the health care provider offers an experimental procedure or treatment to a patient, the health care provider has a duty, in exercising reasonable care under the circumstances, to inform the patient of the experimental nature of the proposed procedure.   With experimental procedures the "most frequent risks and hazards" will remain unknown until the procedure becomes established.   If the health care provider has a duty to inform of *known* risks for *established* procedures, common sense and the purposes of the statute equally require that the health care provider inform the patient of any *uncertainty* regarding the risks associated with *experimental* procedures.   This includes the experimental nature of the procedure and the *known or projected most likely risks.*   The evidence presented in this case illustrates the logic of our holding perfectly: taken in Estrada's favor, it shows that the surgeons presented a full picture of the risks of the surgical procedure and simply advised him that the embolization might not work, without informing him of its experimental nature and their consequent lack of knowledge of the risks of whether it would fail or not.   Not surprisingly, Estrada chose the experimental procedure.   * * *

* * *

Our decision that health care providers must inform their patients that proposed procedures are experimental accords with the majority of courts and commentators which have considered the problem.   * * * The underlying tort principles of rationality that require informing before operating clearly demand more information when the proposed procedure is new and untested.   [ ]   Others have recognized that although in some instances the physician may withhold information regarding the experiment, this should only occur in exceptional cases. [ ]   The psychology of the doctor-patient relation, and the rewards, financial and professional, attendant upon recognition of experimental success, increase the potential for abuse and strengthen the rationale for uniform disclosure.   We have found little authority supporting a contrary rule.   Accordingly, we reaffirm our holding that reasonable standards of informed consent to an experimental procedure require disclosure to the patient that the procedure is experimental.

* * *

Affirmed in part; reversed in part; dismissed in part.

Notes and Questions

1. How does the court in *Estrada* define "experimental" for purposes of disclosure to patients? They mention the fact that the surgeons and radiologists were aware of only one previous operation and one article, and that the surgeons had no personal experience. Does the court have the same attitude toward such clinical experimentation as the court did in *Brook,* in Chapter 2, supra?

2. What should be disclosed to a patient about to undergo an experimental procedure? That this is the first time this team has attempted this procedure? That the literature lacks support at present for it? That the surgeons and radiologists will benefit financially or in career recognition if the procedure succeeds? Must the motivations of the team be clearly disclosed to the patient? Should the physicians' motivations even matter, so long as the patient and the physicians believe that the new procedure offers a better chance for the patient?

3. See generally on fiduciary obligations, Mehlman, Fiduciary Contracting: Limitations on Bargaining Between Patients and Health Care Providers, 51 U.Pitt.L.Rev. 365 (1990); Rodwin, Physicians' Conflicts of Interest: The Limitations of Disclosure, 321 N.E.J.M. 1405 (1989); Boyd, Cost Containment and the Physician's Fiduciary Duty to the Patient, 39 DePaul L.Rev. 131 (1989); E.D. Pellegrino and D.C. Thomasma, A Philosophical Basis of Medical Practice 260 (1981); Feldman and Ward, Psychotherapeutic Injury: Reshaping the Implied Contract as an Alternative to Malpractice, 58 N.C.L.Rev. 63 (1979). Many of the cases use the language of fiduciary obligations in discussing informed consent. See Lambert v. Park, 597 F.2d 236 (10th Cir.1979) (physician's fiduciary duty is to obtain patient's informed consent); Ostojic v. Brueckmann, 405 F.2d 302, 304 (7th Cir.1968) (existence of physician's fiduciary duty requires full disclosure); Margaret S. v. Edwards, 488 F.Supp. 181, 207 (E.D.La.1980).

IV. PROMOTING CONVERSATION

A. PERSPECTIVES ON INFORMED CONSENT

The interests at stake in informed consent discussions are varied. Patients may want to be treated as adult decisionmakers equal to the doctor, or they may be ambivalent, with a strong desire to yield to the doctor's professional judgment. The doctor may be most comfortable with a relationship based primarily on the patient's deference to expert judgments, or may seek genuinely to engage the patient in joint decisions. The medical institution—hospital, clinic, HMO—as a bureaucracy struggling to cope with regulations, may perceive consent forms as just another burdensome record-keeping problem. Finally, when a medical accident occurs, the patient's lawyer may see in informed consent another litigation theory, another chance of recovery even though negligent diagnosis or treatment cannot be shown. In the conflict among and convergence of these interests informed consent doctrine is found. Consider the following perspectives on informed consent.

1. *The Legal Arsenal.* Informed consent is valuable to the plaintiff's lawyer for a simple reason: it may allow her to win a tough case without expert medical testimony that the defendant erred in treating or diagnosing. If an informed consent claim is allowed, the defendant may be liable for all injurious consequences of specific undisclosed risks, without the plaintiff having either to allege or prove substandard practice. See Harnish v. Children's Hospital Medical Center, 387 Mass. 152, 439 N.E.2d 240 (1982).

2. *Medical Paternalism.* Historically, the doctor has always been the dominant decisionmaker in doctor-patient relationships. The doctor is the expert, with unique access to information and expertise. The goal of informed consent is simply to disclose enough to get the patient to comply. There is some evidence that this model is losing adherents as a new generation of doctors enters practice.

3. *Patient Autonomy.* Legal doctrine often shifts the balance of power in existing relationships. In the medical relationship, informed consent in theory moves the patient toward collaboration with the doctor in treatment. Equality in decisionmaking thus reallocates power, reducing the doctor's paternalistic grip on treatment decisions. The model makes a valuable point: the various judicial choices—between battery and negligent nondisclosure, between professional or patient-oriented standards—affect the power of doctor and patient.

Respect for patient autonomy is a normative goal in its own right. Even if informed consent doctrine and litigation have little effect on medical practice, the doctrine is still valuable for the norm it upholds. Its goal is personal autonomy, the protection of individual choice in the widest possible range of situations. The deference that others extend to a patient's decisions, even when they appear irrational, preserves individual autonomy, which has meaning only when respected by others. This model leads into complicated ethical issues, but it remains a baseline for evaluating the way doctors approach patients. For a good discussion, see Callahan, Autonomy: A Moral Good, Not a Moral Obsession, 14 The Hastings Center Report 40 (1984); Feinberg, Autonomy, Sovereignty, and Privacy: Moral Ideals in the Constitution? 58 Notre Dame L.Rev. 445 (1983); Dyer, Informed Consent and the Non-autonomous Person, 4 IRB 1 (1982).

4. *Incentives for Change.* A lawsuit against a doctor or a hospital provides an incentive to change future behavior, for three reasons: first, a lawsuit stigmatizes the defendant, whether she wins or loses, and causes anxiety and lost time; second, an award for the plaintiff costs the defendant money, if only in higher malpractice premiums; and third, the norms in the legal rule will be noticed, if not always appreciated, by the target population. Evidence to prove a strong effect on medical behavior is lacking at present, but some studies do support a

trend toward more open medical disclosure, including disclosure of bad prognoses. See President's Commission for the Study of Ethical Problems in Medicine and Biomedical and Behavioral Research, Making Health Care Decisions 72–76 (1982). A 1961 survey found that 90% of physicians preferred not to tell patients of a cancer diagnosis. Oken, What to Tell Cancer Patients: A Study of Medical Attitudes, 175 J.A.M.A. 1120 (1961). Fifteen years later 97% of doctors said they routinely disclosed cancer diagnoses. Novak et al., Changes in Physicians' Attitudes Towards Telling the Cancer Patient, 241 J.A.M.A. 897 (1979). In general, however, the studies have been faulted as poorly designed and executed. Meisel and Roth, Toward an Informed Discussion of Informed Consent: A Review and Critique of the Empirical Studies, 25 Ariz.L.Rev. 265, 340 (1983). See also Lidz et al., Informed Consent: A Study of Decisionmaking in Psychiatry (1984), for a pessimistic view of the positive effects of the doctrine in the psychiatric setting.

5. *Promotion of Conversation.* The informed consent doctrine that the courts have struggled to articulate has focused on the scope of disclosure: low-percentage risks, treatment alternatives, and so on. These elements of disclosure are important, but more important is the comprehension of the patient. While the fact that a litany of risks was disclosed is easy to establish as an evidentiary matter at trial, it is much harder to evaluate true communication from a judicial perspective. It would appear therefore that informed consent doctrine as applied in tort cases can only take us so far in effectuating the values of physician-patient communication. Much new research and writing has attempted to move beyond the bare outlines of informed consent, toward a framework for improving the physician-patient relationship. Consider the following excerpts and ask what the courts, or the legislatures, could do to improve the communication process.

Jay Katz, in his book The Silent World of Doctor and Patient, 82–83, 102, 228–29, builds an elaborate argument in favor of extensive doctor-patient conversation. He argues that the courts have gone in the wrong direction, both in their solicitude for doctors, and in the focus on risk disclosure as the goal of informed consent.

> [C]ourts' all too single-minded emphasis on risk disclosures made the objective of giving patients a greater voice in medical decision making well-nigh unattainable. For such disclosures do little to expand opportunities for meaningful consent, particularly in surrender-prone medical settings, in which a proposed treatment is zealously advocated despite its risks. Treatment decisions are extremely complex and require a more sustained dialogue, one in which patients are viewed as participants in medical decisions affecting their lives.

> * * *

> The new model of trust is grounded in a number of assumptions.

> First, no single right decision exists for how the life of health and illness should be lived. Medical advances have led to a proliferation of

treatment options and a better understanding of their benefits and risks. Alleviation of suffering can be accomplished in a variety of ways and alternative choices must be explained. Physicians alone cannot decide which treatment is best. The patient must be consulted.

Second, physicians and patients bring their own vulnerabilities to the decision-making process. Both are authors and victims of their own individual conflicting motivations, interests, and expectations. Identity of interests cannot be presumed. It can only be established through conversation.

Third, both parties need to relate to one another as equals and unequals. Their equalities and inequalities complement one another. Physicians know more about disease. Patients know more about their own needs. Neither knows at the outset what each can do for the other.

Fourth, all human conduct is influenced by rational and irrational expectations. These expectations can be explored and clarified, at times more readily than at others. Reason and unreason define human beings' essence. Manifestations of the latter should not readily and prematurely lead to presumptions of incompetence. If they did, physicians as well as patients would have to be labeled incompetent.

The new conception of trust advanced here only expands the idea of trust. It asks for mutual trust that extends from physician to patient as well as from patient to physician. This trust cannot be earned through deeds alone. It requires words as well. It relies not only on physicians' *technical* competence but also on their willingness to share the burden of decision making with patients and on their *verbal* competence to do so.

* * *

The radically different climate of physician-patient decision making that I envision cannot be implemented by judicial, legislative, or administrative orders. At best, such outside interventions can prod doctors; at worst, they only substitute bureaucratic authority for professional authority. Meaningful change can come about only through medical education and the education of patients. *Both* physicians and patients must rethink basic assumptions about their relationship and about mutual decision making. Physicians here must take the initiative and lead the way. * * *

* * * Of the many recommendations that will come forth from such explorations, one will most certainly be that physicians and patients must talk more with one another.

This interactive model takes informed consent in the direction of a well developed relationship between a doctor and his patient, in which both struggle to work through their personal fears and anxieties toward an agreed upon approach to the patient's problem. It is an appealing model, and one that would seem to be worth implementing.

B. PROBLEMS WITH ACHIEVING PATIENT CONSENT

1. Patient Decisionmaking Limitations

The courts have struggled to articulate general principles to guide physicians in obtaining patients' informed consent, while researchers have uncovered a spectrum of practical difficulties in obtaining that consent. First, patients have trouble remembering what they are told. One author proposes that doctors " * * * test the patients' comprehension of that information * * *." Jones, Autonomy and Informed Consent in Medical Decisionmaking: Toward a New Self–Fulfilling Prophecy, 47 Wash. & Lee.L.Rev. 379, 429 (1990). One might even require that the patient pass a comprehension test before a procedure could be performed.

Second, patient decisionmaking about medical choices is often irrational, even when information is correctly and fully presented. Patients may undervalue low probability risks because of the difficulty of thinking probabilistically. For example, teenagers may feel invulnerable to a range of harms. Patients may be anxious about treatments for irrational reasons such as fears of the knife or phobic feelings about diseases such as cancer.

Third, patients may have a bias to the near future, giving disproportionate weight to getting benefits and avoiding pain in the short term. One researcher suggests that a scale for comparing risks is needed to help patients compare the odds of a risk of a medical procedure with other life risks they regularly face in driving or flying. See Howard, Microrisks for Medical Decision Analysis, 5 Intl.J.Tech.Assess. in Health Care 357 (1989) (arguing for use of a unit, the microprobability or micromort, to present risks to patients).

Fourth, patients may refuse treatment because of a belief structure that does not make sense, for reasons that may be socially acceptable (religious belief) or not (depression). See generally Brock and Wartman, Sounding Board: When Competent Patients Make Irrational Choices, 322 N.Eng.J.Med. 1595 (1990). While occasionally such patients may be incompetent and a court order can be obtained to compel treatment, such patients may also be legally competent.

Fifth, patients may react to the way choices are framed and articulated, so-called "framing effects". For example, patients told that a given procedure has an 80% survival rate will react differently from those told it has a 20% mortality rate. Patients choose surgery over radiation therapy for lung cancer when outcomes are expressed in terms of the probability of survival rather than the probability of death. McNeil, Pauker, Sox and Tversky, On the Elicitation of Preferences for Alternative Therapies, 306 N.Eng.J.Med. 1259, 1261 (1982).

Do all of these practical problems with rational decisionmaking mean that risk disclosure is useless, since patients often choose irrationally no matter what information they have? Should the physician simply decide to bias the presentation of information to achieve the result she wants?

2. The Nature of Physician Practice

Jay Katz's model of conversation in the therapeutic context is based upon the physician-patient relation in specialty practices such as oncology. Where the physician engages in relatively few procedures, and sees a patient over several visits, it is plausible to advocate an extended conversation about detailed risks and alternatives. Such conversations can be easily recorded, videotaped or otherwise memorialized in writing, achieving both patient consent and physician protection.

The primary care setting, however, poses a severe challenge to the model of conversation. The primary care physician does more procedures to more patients, spending less time with each patient. He is less likely to be fully up-to-date as to drug and treatment alternatives and side-effects, and never sure when disclosure may safely stop. Listing risks may leave out some that turn out with hindsight to have been critical to the particular patient. Discussing risks without also properly balancing the benefits and alternatives for the patient may not properly inform his decision. A full and comprehensive discussion may not be adequate if in fact the patient does not understand, even though he says he does. The task of informed consent may look like it can never be completed satisfactorily. Professor Brody writes:

> * * * physicians are getting a message that informed consent is very different from any other task they are asked to perform in medicine. If physicians conclude that informed consent is therefore not properly part of medicine at all, but is rather a legalistic and bureaucratic hurdle they must overcome at their own peril, blame cannot be atributed to paternalistic attitudes or lack of respect for patient autonomy.

Brody, Transparency: Informed Consent in Primary Care, Hastings Center Report 5, 7 (Sept/Oct 1989).

Brody suggests a "transparency" standard, in which

> "... the physician discloses the basis on which the proposed treatment, or alternative possible treatments, have been chosen; and (2) the patient is allowed to ask questions suggested by the disclosure of the physician's reasoning, and those questions are answered to the patient's satisfaction."

The goal is to render the physician's thinking transparent to the patient, to avoid provider tendencies to present shopping lists of risks to satisfy what is perceived as the law's requirements. What do you think of Brody's proposal? Does it capture something valuable, or merely throw the burden back on the patient? In light of possible sources of patient irrationality in decisionmaking, doesn't Brody simply allow the physician to cop out?

3. *The Utility of Communication*

Any improved model of informed consent aims to preserve patient autonomy, but also to reduce the risk of a lawsuit directed at the physician. Improved conversations with patients may produce more effective care by eliciting patient cooperation and reducing unnecessary procedures, and it may also reduce the risk of malpractice suits by disgruntled patients. If poor communication between physician and patient is the most common cause of malpractice suits, then any increase in physician-patient conversation, it is argued, will reduce the frequency of such suits. Physicians often do spend little time with their patients, and are poor listeners. See Winslow, Sometimes Talk is the Best Medicine: For Physicians, Communications May Avert Suits, Wall St.J., B1, October 5, 1989.

More talk, via the informed consent model, may not be the prophylactic needed for physicians fearful of suit. The sociological literature on who sues doctors seem to confound facile assumptions about communication as a shield against suits. One study of medical disputes in Wisconsin studied the factors relevant to those who sued. The study described patients most likely to sue:

1. patients who more negatively evaluated their doctor's competence prior to the grievance;

2. patients who felt their doctors failed to show concern for them personally;

3. patients who reported serious injuries; merely being dissatisfied is not enough, without the presence of a substantial injury;

4. while status and property ownership were not important, knowledge and experience with both health professionals and legal professionals were connected to likelihood of suit.

The study also concluded that several "informed consent" variables were not significant to patients' decisions to sue: the physician's attempts to involve the patient as partner, to inform him about care, not rushing the visit, and taking personal care about the problem. While informed consent may serve salutary purposes, it does not seem by itself to counteract other forces that lead patients to sue once they suffer serious injury. See May and Stengel, Who Sues Their Doctors? How Patients Handle Medical Grievances, 24 Law & Soc.Rev. 105 (1990).

C. INSTITUTIONAL EFFORTS: THE CONSENT FORM

Consent forms are universally used in institutions, where most health care is provided. Hospitals use them at several points in a patient's progress through the institution—upon admission, when a generic form is signed; and before surgery or anesthesia, when more detailed forms may be offered. These forms have to operate as a legal surrogate for consent, sometimes memorializing an actual physician-patient discussion, sometimes acting simply as a fiction. The courts have had little to say about consent forms.

A consent form, or other written documentation of the patient's verbal consent, is treated in many states as presumptively valid consent to the treatment at issue, with the burden on the patient to rebut the presumption. See West's Florida Statutes Ann. § 766.103(4); Official Code Georgia Ann. § 88–2906.1(b)(2); Idaho Code § 39–4305; Iowa Code Ann. § 147.137; LSA–R.S. 24, Tit. 40, § 1299.40.A; Maine Revised Statutes Ann. § 2905.2; Nevada Revised Statutes § 41A/110; North Carolina G.S., § 90–21.13(b); Ohio Revised Code § 2317.54; Vernon's Ann. Texas Revised Civil Statutes, Art. 4590i, § 6.06; Utah Code Ann. § 78–14–5(2)(e); West's Washington Revised Code Ann. § 7.70.060.

Does the hospital have a duty to see that a patient's informed consent to surgery by a nonemployee attending physician is properly obtained? In Petriello v. Kalman, 215 Conn. 377, 576 A.2d 474 (1990), the Connecticut Supreme Court held that a hospital had no duty to obtain a patient's consent to surgery, nor to conduct any kind of inquiry into the quality of the plaintiff's consent. The plaintiff had suffered a miscarriage, and the treating physician scheduled the plaintiff for a dilation and curettage to remove the fetus. A hospital nurse medicated the plaintiff before the procedure, without getting the plaintiff's signature on the consent form. This violated a hospital policy requiring completion of such forms.

The court held that the responsibility lay with the attending physician, rejecting the plaintiff's claims that the hospital had a duty to get her signature on the form: "This contention is unsound, however, because it equates the signing of the form with the actuality of informed consent, which it is the sole responsibility of the attending physician to obtain." 576 A. at 478.

But see Magana v. Elie, 108 Ill.App.3d 1028, 64 Ill.Dec. 511, 439 N.E.2d 1319 (1982) (hospital has duty to obtain patient's informed consent).

What might be the effect of imposing a duty on the hospital and its staff to ensure that patient consent is properly obtained by attending physicians? Might the hospital not work harder to make sure that consent is properly obtained? Or is deference to physicians too much a part of the hospital-physician relationship? Would it make any difference to the reality of patient consent? See Jones, Autonomy and Informed Consent in Medical Decisionmaking: Toward a New Self–Fulfilling Prophecy, 47 Wash. & Lee.L.Rev. 379, 429 (1990).

A study by Lidz, Meisel, Zerubavel, Carter, Sestak, and Roth, Informed Consent: A Study of Decisionmaking in Psychiatry 326, (1985) puts the role of consent forms in practical perspective:

Consent forms played an insignificant role in the decisionmaking process.

a.   Consent forms were generally presented to patients only after the decision was made and agreed upon by all parties.

b.   The forms were typically too complex for the average patient.

c.   Particularly during the admission process, patients often did not read consent forms before signing them; even when they did, they rarely seemed to have much understanding of the material contained in them.

d.   Decisions were made in a real sense without regard to consent forms. The information in consent forms never changed a decision that had already been made.

e.   Staff viewed consent forms as bureaucratic obstacles to be surmounted before treatment could commence, and thus as something that did not require attention either from them or from patients.

f.   Consent forms were treated by both patients and staff as a ritual for confirming a decision already made, rather than as a step in the decisionmaking process. In effect, consent forms merely symbolized that the patients had agreed to the particular procedure, thus providing some evidence (though of dubious legal value) of consent. If consent forms were meant to ensure that patients understood and consented voluntarily to the decisions, then these consent forms at least were failures.

Id at 318. The fact remains, however, that such written forms will predominate in institutional settings, given bureaucratic pressures for a complete patient record, a desire to protect against litigation, and a sense that something is better than nothing. How can such forms be improved, so that they will facilitate doctor-patient conversation and risk disclosure?

D.   CONCLUSION

To sum up * * * the caselaw provides a general set of principles, backed by the threat of a tort suit; the physician confronts a range of patient limitations in processing risks; the patient is not deterred by a doctor-patient conversation from suing; and bureaucracies treat informed consent as just another record keeping requirement. Where should we go from here? Lidz et al., after their look at the failure of informed consent doctrine in institutions, offer a call to persist.

Before either dismantling the requirement on the one hand or resigning ourselves to winking at it on the other, we believe that bona fide and reasonable efforts at implementation ought to be attempted. Finally, we believe that, over time, as new generations of health care professionals and patients are socialized in a climate that takes informed consent more seriously, informed consent may well be taken more seriously in practice. None of the remedies that we have suggested either singly or together are likely to be solutions for the problems that now exist in the implementation of the informed consent doctrine, and the path to achieving the goal of involving patients in a decision-making partnership will be, at best, a long, slow, gradual, difficult, and winding one. However, the moral commitments of our society do not permit us to turn back.

Lidz et al, id at pp. 333–334.

Problem: Forcing Conversation

You have recently gone to work for the assistant administrator of the Health Care Financing Administration (HCFA) of the Department of Health and Human Services. HCFA is responsible for the Medicare program, which pays physicians for medical services they provide to elderly patients who are Medicare-eligible.

Your superior, Dr. Tuff, is concerned that too many Medicare patients are being treated without much discussion by physicians of the risks of treatment. He reasons that this is due in part to physician attempts to impose their own treatment preferences on patients, thereby maximizing their reimbursement, wherever possible, while also spending as little time as possible with each patient. He would like to use informed consent doctrine as a way of gaining further control over the costs of health care, while also giving the elderly a better level of control over their treatments.

He asks that you consider the following recommendation, to be incorporated into Medicare requirements:

> No Medicare payments for treatments rendered by either individual or institutional health care providers shall be made absent proof that the claimed medical service was consented to by the patient or a suitable surrogate decision maker in a voluntary, competent, and informed manner.

What problems do you foresee with this proposal? What standards for disclosure do you suggest? What modes of proof that consent was obtained? What weight should be given the proof?

See Kapp, "Enforcing Patient Preferences: Linking Payment for Medical Care to Informed Consent," 261 J.A.M.A. 1935, 1936 (1989). For a critical response to Kapp's proposal, see Faden, Editorial: Enforcing Informed Consent Requirements: Form or Substance? 261 J.A.M.A. 1948 (1989).

Chapter 4

REFORMING THE TORT SYSTEM
FOR MEDICAL INJURIES

Litigation over patient injury caused by health care professionals can be found in early English and American law. The application of a negligence test against physicians can be found as early as 1375, in Stratton v. Cavendish, where the King's Bench considered the botched surgery performed by Dr. Swanlon on the hand of the plaintiff. The court compared the surgeon's error to that of a smithy: "If a smith undertakes to cure my horse, and the horse is harmed by his negligence or failure to cure in a reasonable time, it is just that he should be liable". Carleton, Stratton v. Swanlon: The Fourteenth–Century Ancestor of the Law of Malpractice," The Pharos 20 (Fall 1982). The earliest recorded American case is Cross v. Guthery, 1 Am.Dec. 61 (1794) (husband permitted to sue surgeon for damages resulting from an unskillful operation on his wife, causing her death).

As medical practice became more dependent upon technologies such as surgery, drugs, and diagnostic tools, litigation began to increase as well. After World War II, as malpractice insurance coverage became increasingly expensive, the frequency of claims against physicians and hospitals came to be viewed as a source of medical cost inflation. In the 1960s the Federal government began to take on responsibility for financing health care through the Medicare and Medicaid programs, and quality of care and cost issues raised by malpractice became national concerns. By the 1970s, malpractice had become a visible problem. The magnitude of the recent increase in litigation is illustrated by the fact that 80% of the malpractice suits filed between 1935 and 1975 were filed in the last five years of that forty year period.

I. THE SOURCES OF THE MALPRACTICE CRISIS

Malpractice suits require a plaintiff who suffers a medical injury at the hands of a health care provider. Have more patients suffered medical misadventures over the past two decades? In the first detailed look by the federal government at malpractice litigation, the Commission on Medical Malpractice in 1973 speculated as to the causes for the increase in malpractice litigation:

> In part, [the increase] was due to the simple fact that many more people were able to afford, and received, medical care, automatically increasing the exposure to incidents that could lead to suits.

At the same time, innovations in medical science increased the complexities of the health care system. Some of the new diagnostic and therapeutic procedures brought with them new risks of injury; as the potency of drugs increased, so did the potential hazards of using them. Few would challenge the value of these advances, but they did tend to produce a concomitant number of adverse results, sometimes resulting in severe disability.

Medical Malpractice: Report of the Secretary's Commission on Medical Malpractice (1973) at 3.

What was true in 1973 is equally true today. The hazards of health care are substantial. As the Harvard Medical Practice study discovered in surveying medical iatrogenesis in New York hospitals, as many as four percent of hospitalized patients suffer an adverse medical event which results in disability or death. The Harvard Study projected that approximately one percent of all hospital patients suffer injury due to negligently provided care. Harvard Medical Practice Study, Patients, Doctors, and Lawyers: Medical Injury, Malpractice Litigation, and Patient Compensation in New York, Exec.Summ. 3–4 (1990). See Chapter 1 infra.

The emerging technologies of modern medicine held out the prospects of remarkable new treatments for patients. Have patients caused the malpractice crisis by their very litigiousness, driven by unrealistic expectations as to what physicians can deliver? The 1973 Commission on Medical Malpractice, after describing the forces that led to more patient injury, shifted the blame back to patients:

> Lacking an appreciation of the complexities and hazards of modern medical practice, many patients undervalued the inherent risks and assumed negligent conduct when the final outcome was less than had been expected; thus the number of malpractice claims and suits increased.

Id.

Is this a fair assessment? Malpractice suits from this perspective are attributable to a groundswell of consumer assertiveness and insistence on rights, driven by rising and often unrealistic expectations as to entitlements to security and well-being. See also L. Friedman, Total Justice (1985). The malpractice crisis is thus related to a "litigious society", with "a flawed system" that promotes litigation. See Bok, "A Flawed System", Harvard Magazine 38 (May–June 1983).

Some observers have noted that criticism of this "litigiousness" is overblown:

> Portentous pronouncements [about the litigation explosion] were made by established dignitaries and published in learned journals. Could one imagine public health specialists or poultry breeders conjuring up epidemics and cures with such cavalier disregard for the incompleteness of the data and the untested nature of the theory?

Galanter, "Reading the Landscape of Disputes: What We Know and Don't Know (and Think We Know) About Our Allegedly Contentious and Litigious Society", 31 UCLA L.Rev. 4, 70–72 (1983); Saks, In Search of the 'Lawsuit Crisis', 14 Law, Medicine & Health Care 77 (1986). For a further look at the evidence on changing American litigation patterns, see National Center for State Courts, A Preliminary Examination of Available Civil and Criminal Trend Data in State Trial Courts for 1978, 1981, and 1984 (April 1986); Peterson and Priest, The Civil Jury: Trends in Trials and Verdicts, Cook County, Illinois 1960–79 (1982).

A. THE NATURE OF THE INSURANCE INDUSTRY

Any serious analysis of the malpractice "crisis" must begin with the insurance industry. The increase in the frequency of litigation against health care professionals and institutions coincided in the 1970s with a crisis of malpractice insurance availability. The most visible manifestation of the malpractice crisis in the 1970s and again in the 1980s has been increases in premiums for malpractice insurance purchased by health care professionals and institutions. Several insurance carriers dropped out of the malpractice market during the 1970s, while others raised their malpractice premiums precipitously to compensate for investment losses. The insurance market shrank, rates rose, and physicians and hospitals felt the pinch. In the mid–1970s state legislatures passed a first wave of reform legislation, and new insurance entities, such as physician-owned insurance companies, were created. The malpractice problem, as measured by the rate of increase of insurance premiums, seemed to stabilize. Then in the 1980s a new round of premium increases and large visible jury verdicts reignited the debate.

The insurance "crisis" thus began with a rapid escalation in the costs to physicians and health care providers generally of malpractice insurance. The insurance crisis also included product manufacturers, municipalities, and anyone who carried liability insurance. This chapter will examine the effects of this crisis on the health care system generally, but it must be recognized that the problem transcends health care. See "The Insurance Crisis: Now Everyone is in a Risky Business", Business Week 88 (March 10, 1986).

U.S. GENERAL ACCOUNTING OFFICE, MEDICAL MALPRACTICE: NO AGREEMENT ON THE PROBLEMS OR SOLUTIONS

66–72 (1986).

Most health care providers buy medical malpractice insurance to protect themselves from medical malpractice claims. Under the insurance contract, the insurance company agrees to accept financial responsibility for payment of any claims up to a specific level of coverage during a fixed period in return for a fee. The insurer investigates the claim and defends the health care provider.

Medical malpractice insurance is sold by several types of insurers—commercial insurance companies, health care provider owned companies, and joint underwriting associations.

In addition, some large hospitals elect to self-insure for medical malpractice losses rather than purchasing insurance, and a few physicians practice without insurance.

Commercial insurance companies involved in the medical malpractice market may also market other lines of property and casualty insurance. The largest commercial insurer in the malpractice market is the St. Paul Fire and Marine Insurance company. St. Paul's national market share on the basis of direct premiums written in 1984 was 17.9 percent.

* * *

Joint underwriting associations are nonprofit pooling arrangements created by state legislatures to provide medical malpractice insurance to health care providers in the states in which they are established. Although created by a number of states as interim measures to help health care providers find sources of malpractice insurance during the mid–1970s, joint underwriting associations continue to be an important source of coverage in some states.

* * *

Malpractice insurance is written as either an occurrence or claims-made policy. Under an occurrence policy, the insurance company is liable for any incidents that occurred during the period the policy was in force, regardless of when the claim may be filed. A claims-made policy provides for coverage for malpractice incidents for which claims are made while the policy is in force. Premiums for claims-made policies are generally lower and increase each year during the initial 5 years of the policy because the risk exposure is lower. However, usually after 5 years, the premiums mature or stabilize. About one-half of total premiums now written for medical malpractice insurance are for claims-made policies.

To cover claims filed after a claims-made policy has expired, health care providers can purchase insurance known as "tail" coverage.

Typically, medical malpractice insurance policies have a dollar limit on the amount that the insurance company will pay on each claim (per occurrence) and a dollar limit for all claims (in aggregate) for the policy period, which is usually 1 year. Insurance companies usually have minimum and maximum levels of coverage they will write which may vary depending on the risk or physician's specialty.

Malpractice insurance coverage may be purchased in layers because many insurance companies have maximum limits of coverage they will write for individual risks. If the health care provider desires additional coverage above the company's maximum limits, additional coverage may be purchased from one or more other insurance companies. The first layer of coverage is commonly known as basic coverage; the liability coverage above the basic level is known as excess coverage. Umbrella policies usually cover in a single policy professional, personal, and premises liability up to a specified limit. Generally, umbrella policies provide coverage when the aggregate limits of underlying policies have been exhausted.

The objective in establishing insurance rates is to develop rates that will be appropriate for the period during which they apply. To be appropriate, the rates must generate funds to cover (1) losses occurring during the period, (2) the administrative costs of running the company, and (3) an amount for unknown contingencies, which may become a profit if not used. The profit may be retained as capital surplus or returned to stockholders as dividends.

Ratemaking attempts to predict future claims and expenses are based on past experience. For two reasons, ratemaking is very complicated. First, circumstances change over time, and many of these changes affect the number (frequency) of claims or the dollar amount (severity) of losses—the two primary factors that affect the cost of insurance. Inflation increases the average severity of claims, and changes in legal theories may increase the frequency and severity of claims. Second, the use of historical statistics to predict future losses is based on the law of large numbers—as the number of insured physicians and hospitals increases, actual losses will approach more closely expected losses. The medical malpractice insurance market is small, thus the statistical base for making estimates of future losses is relatively small. As a result, it is difficult to set accurate premium prices.

The "long tail" of malpractice insurance (the long length of time that may elapse after an injury occurs before a claim is filed and settled) is a further complicating factor because the data base used for estimating future losses may not reflect current actual losses. For example, the St. Paul Fire and Marine Insurance Company's experience indicates that " * * * 30 percent of its claims are filed in the year of treatment, 30 percent in the year after treatment, 25 percent in the third year, 7 percent in the fourth year, and 8 percent in years five through 10."

* * *

Malpractice insurance rates for physicians vary by specialty and geographic location and generally increase proportionate to the amount and complexity of surgery performed. Rates may vary from state to state and within a state. For rating purposes, insurance companies usually group physician specialties into distinct classes. Each class represents a different level of risk for the company.

The number of and composition of rating classes may vary from company to company. For example, the St. Paul Company uses 8 rating classes for physicians, whereas the Medical Liability Mutual

Insurance Company of New York uses 14. Rates are typically determined based on the claims experience of the rating class rather than on the experience of the individual physician. Some insurance companies assess a surcharge, in addition to the standard rate, for physicians with an unfavorable malpractice claims experience. Malpractice insurance rates for hospitals are frequently based on the malpractice loss experience (in terms of numbers of claims filed and the amount per paid claim) of the individual hospital. For example, in determining its rates, the St. Paul Company includes a factor to adjust its standard rates for the individual hospital's historical malpractice loss experience.

Statutory requirements generally provide that insurance rates be adequate, not excessive, and not unfairly discriminatory. The degree of regulation of medical malpractice insurance rates varies from state to state. For example, New York has "prior approval" authority in which all rates must be filed with the insurance department before use and must be either approved or disapproved by the superintendent of insurance. Arkansas, Indiana, and North Carolina have "file and use" laws, under which the insurers must file their rates with the state's insurance department before the rates become effective; however, the rates may be used without the department's prior approval. The rates may be disapproved if they violate the state's statutory requirements. In California, insurers are not required to file their rates with the state insurance department but may be required to furnish rates and supporting information if requested.

Insurance companies are required by state law to establish reserves to cover future losses from claims. Reserves are liabilities based on estimates of future amounts needed to satisfy claims. In addition to amounts covering indemnity payments, the reserves may also include amounts to cover the company's administrative and legal expenses in handling the claims.

Determining proper reserves for medical malpractice claims presents difficulties for insurance companies because such claims may require years to be resolved. Accurate reserves are difficult to establish because the companies must estimate losses incurred but not reported, losses reported but not paid, and losses partially paid but which continue for several years.

Insurance companies derive investment income from those assets encumbered for loss and loss expense reserves, from unearned premium reserves, and from the company's capital and surplus.

Insurance companies buy reinsurance from other insurers to cover potential losses that may be too large for the individual company to absorb. Reinsurance allows companies to share their risks with other companies and to stabilize insurance losses, which may fluctuate considerably.

Note: Conditions for an Ideal Insurance Market

The market for malpractice insurance fails to satisfy many of the economist's conditions for an ideal insurance market. The ideal market consists of a pooling by the insurer of a large number of homogeneous but independent random events. The auto accident insurance market is perhaps closest to fulfilling this condition. The large numbers of events involved make outcomes for the insurance pool actuarially predictable. Malpractice lacks these desirable qualities of " * * * large numbers, independence, and risk beyond the control of the insured." P. Danzon, Medical Malpractice: Theory, Evidence, and Public Policy 90 (1985) (hereafter Danzon). The pool of potential policyholders is small, as is the pool of claims, and a few states have most of the claims. The awards vary tremendously, with 50% of the dollars paid out on 3% of the claims. In small insurance programs, a single multimillion dollar claim can have a tremendous effect on total losses and therefore average loss per insured doctor.

Second, losses are not independent, since neither claims against an individual doctor nor against doctors as a group are independent; multiple claims against a doctor relate usually to some characteristic of his practice or his technique, and a lawyer can use knowledge gained in one suit in another. Claims and verdicts against doctors generally reflect social forces—shifts in jury attitudes and legal doctrine. Social and legal attitudes toward medicine recently have been in flux. Given the long tail, or time from medical intervention to the filing of a claim, the impact of these shifts is increased.

Finally, the problems of moral hazard and adverse selection distort the market. Moral hazard characterizes the effect of insurance in reducing an insured's incentives to prevent losses, since he is not financially responsible for losses. Adverse selection occurs when an insurer attracts policy holders of above-average risk, ending up with higher claim costs and lower profits as a result. This may have occurred because a competing insurer has attracted away lower risk policyholders through the use of lower rates and selective underwriting. Danzon at 91.

The malpractice crisis is as much a product of the way the insurance industry does business as of changes in the frequency of medical malpractice litigation or the severity of judgments. The cyclical nature of interest rates, as a measure of return on investments, plays a central role in insurers' pricing decisions. The insurance industry engages in cash-flow underwriting, in which insurers invest the premiums they collect. When interest rates and investment returns are high, insurance companies accept riskier exposures to acquire more investable premium and loss reserves. The insurance industry managed to be profitable from 1976 to 1984. If underwriting and investment results are combined during this period, investment gains more than offset losses.

The Government Accounting Office concluded of the insurance "crisis" of the early 1980s that "[t]he underwriting losses resulted, in part, from the industry's cash flow underwriting pricing strategy in which companies sacrificed underwriting gains in an attempt to attract more business and thereby enhance investment gains." Government Accounting Office, Insurance: Profitability of Medical Malpractice and General Liability Lines (1987). See also Zuckerman, Bovbjerg, and Sloan, Effects of Tort Reforms and Other Factors on Medical Malpractice Insurance Premiums, 27 Inquiry 167, 181 (1990).

This underwriting strategy creates instability in the market, since losses have to be paid. If interest rates and investment yields drop, insurance companies must raise their premiums and drop some lines of insurance, in order to compete. Hunter and Borzilleri, The Liability Insurance Crisis, 22 Trial 42, 43 (1986). For other similar critical perspectives, see Posner, Trends in Medical Malpractice Insurance, 1970–1985, 49 Law and Contemp.Problems 37 (1986) (vice-president of Marsh & McLennan, a large professional liability insurer, on the crisis); Olender, The Great Insurance Fraud of the '80s, 8 The National Law Journal 15 (July 21, 1986); Hunter, Taming the Latest Insurance "Crisis", The New York Times, April 13, 1986, at F3.

What measures are possible to improve the market? Remember that insurance depends on actuarially accurate predictions of both the severity of damage awards and the frequency of litigation within a distinct insurance market. As you consider the various tort reforms, ask yourself which ones are likely to have some effect on these insurability issues.

B. INSURANCE AVAILABILITY AND COST: SOME EVIDENCE

Malpractice insurance costs are not a major cost for either hospitals or doctors generally; about ½ of one percent of the total American health care bill goes to pay for malpractice insurance. Real premiums rose at about 5% annually between 1974 and 1986, with some evidence of a faster rate of increase after 1980. Since malpractice recoveries are largely used to pay plaintiff medical bills, and since health care cost inflation has exceeded the general rate of inflation, damage awards have grown progressively larger, with corresponding premium increases. See Zukerman, Bovbjerg, and Sloan, Effects of Tort Reforms and Other Factors on Medical Malpractice Insurance Premiums, 27 Inquiry 167, 178 (1990).

However, for surgical specialties and obstetrics, particularly in five states—California, Florida, Illinois, Michigan, and New York—the problem has been acute. And for young doctors, medical school professors, and physicians with below-average incomes, increases in malpractice premiums can consume a large percentage of gross income. The insurance affordability problem therefore is concentrated in certain areas of medicine. For physicians and hospitals generally, moreover, the shock effect of sudden rapid increases in premium costs has caused a strong reaction by providers. In 1984 such an upward swing occurred, following a four to six year "soft" market. See Posner, Trends in Medical Malpractice Insurance, 1970–1985, 49 Law & Contemp. Probs. 37 (1986).

A comparison of the Minnesota and Florida experiences is instructive. Florida is one of the small number of states in which physicians have experienced substantial increases in premiums, as have physicians in Minnesota and adjoining Midwestern states. A study of the Florida malpractice environment, using malpractice closed claims from 1975 to 1986, has provided the best evidence to date as to the causes of malpractice premium increases. See Nye, Gifford, Webb, and Dewar, "The Causes of the Medical Malpractice Crisis: An Analysis of Claims Data and Insurance Company Finances," 76 Georgetown L.J. 1495 (1988). The authors studied the relative contribution of four potential causes of higher premiums: (1) increased loss payments; (2) excessive insurance company profits; (3) the insurance industry underwriting cycle; (4) the risk classification system used by insurers for rating and pricing purposes.

The Florida study concluded that the primary cause of malpractice premium increases, measured over a nine year period, was the increase in loss payments to claimants. The frequency of claims payments was not primarily responsible for increased claims costs, since the likelihood that a Florida physician would be sued for malpractice has not changed from 1975 to the present. It is rather the "huge increase in the size of claims payments, particularly the increasing frequency of very large payments", that accounted for the total increase in paid losses.

The causes of the increases in claims payments in Florida are not clear. The increases may reflect the belief of defense lawyers and insurance claims managers that their risk at trial would be greater than in 1975. This might be derived from "more serious iatrogenic injuries, a concern that juries are more likely to award larger verdicts and that judges are less likely to control them, a sense that the plaintiffs' trial bar is more able than before, or a concern that the insurer will be held liable under a bad faith claim if it fails to settle within policy limits." Id. at 1560.

Other studies of liability insurance generally, not limited to medical malpractice coverage, have concluded that dramatic premium increases have been due to growth in the discounted value of expected liability losses. Median inflation-adjusted awards in jurisdictions such as California and Illinois appear to have increased substantially over the past three decades. Premiums failed to keep up with losses through 1984, requiring insurers in 1985 and 1986 to impose large premium increases to catch up. See Harrington and Litan, Causes of the Liability Insurance Crisis, 239 Science 737 (1988).

Minnesota's data on insurance claims contrasts with that of Florida. Minnesota's Department of Commerce reviewed all malpractice claims filed with two insurers in Minnesota, North Dakota and South Dakota against physicians from January 1, 1982 to December 31, 1987, comprising the entire insurance market.

The Report concluded:

* The frequency of claims per year did not materially change over the past six years.

* The severity of the claims payment did not materially change over the six year period.

* Fewer than *one-half of one percent* of all malpractice claimants were awarded damages by a jury. This figure remained constant over the period of the study;

* Claims determined by the insurer to be frivolous did not increase over the past six years;

* The likelihood of receiving compensation as a result of filing a malpractice claim was approximately 25 percent. This rate did not materially change over the period of the study;

* No punitive damages were found to be awarded against a physician;

* The average cost of investigation and defending a claim has changed little over the six years. Indeed, the amount appears to be decreasing; and

* Despite unchanging claim frequency and declining loss payments and loss expense, on average, physicians paid approximately triple the amount of premiums for malpractice insurance in 1987 than in 1982.

The Commissioner concluded that the insurance companies overestimated exposure of pending claims by two to three times the amount eventually paid. He noted three reasons for the ability of the insurers to raise premiums in a non-competitive manner. First, physicians are sold policies that do not insure against claims made after the expiration of the policy year. If they try to switch insurers, they must purchase a second policy to cover future claims occurring during the policy year. This "tail endorsement" is expensive. Second, data as to frequency or severity of claims is not available to competitors, making it difficult for them to price a policy. Third, the market is small, failing to attract significant numbers of competing vendors. "Insurers must insure large numbers of policyholders to spread risk * * *."

Other variables that affect insurance premiums have been considered by researchers. Zukerman et al, in their study of insurance closed claims, found that:

* premiums are higher when a population's exposure to iatrogenic injuries increases. A 10% increase in surgery rates increases premiums by 3.8%;

* as the number of practicing physicians increases, premiums fall. This may be due to quality competition or increased monitoring within the profession; or a higher volume of services that improve quality;

* higher real income per capita increases premiums, indicating that plaintiffs with higher incomes are better compensated for lost earnings;

* urbanization is unrelated to premiums (contrary to Danzon's findings), and population mobility lowers premiums, perhaps because it is too difficult to follow through on a claim;

* the percentage of the population over 65 is strongly correlated to premiums, for no clear reason;

* more lawyers do not mean higher premiums;

* premium regulation based on prior approval by the state insurance regulator is associated with lower premiums.

See Zukerman, Bovbjerg, and Sloan, Effects of Tort Reforms and Other Factors on Medical Malpractice Insurance Premiums, 27 Inquiry 167, 180 (1990).

What conclusions do you draw from the somewhat contradictory findings described above? Can you explain some of the discrepancies? What do you recommend based on these findings?

Malpractice insurance rates have recently begun dropping again, declining from 5% to 35% around the country as of 1990. See Pear, Insurers Reducing Malpractice Fees for Doctors in U.S., The New York Times A1, p. 26 (September 23, 1990). Why are the rates dropping? Is the latest crisis over?

II. RESPONSES TO THE CRISIS

The response to the perceived "crisis" in malpractice litigation and insurance availability over the past twenty years has been twofold. First, the availability of insurance has been enhanced by a variety of changes in the structure of the insurance industry. Second, physicians have lobbied with substantial success at the state level for legislation to impede the ability of plaintiffs to bring tort suits and to restrict the size of awards. The effects of these legislative reforms will be considered in Section 2, but criteria for evaluation of reform must first be considered.

A. BENCHMARKS FOR EVALUATING REFORMS

The crisis atmosphere in the 1970s and 1980s has led to a variety of legislative acts their proponents hoped would ease the pain of the crisis. Such malpractice reform proposals can be evaluated by three overall standards. First, do the reforms improve the operation of the tort system for compensating victims of medical injuries? Second, will the reforms create incentives for the reduction of medical error and resulting injury to patients? Third, are changes likely to encourage insurers to make malpractice insurance more available and affordable?

The debate over reform of the tort system is reminiscent of the earlier debate over automobile no-fault insurance in the sixties. The goals against which to evaluate reform efforts are similar. An influential report by the Institute of Medicine of the National Academy of Sciences in 1978 proposed six criteria for judging the effect of various reforms on the tort system.

The criteria, which reflect key characteristics of compensation systems and assure that the various proposals are compared according to certain common elements, are:

* *Access to compensation.* This criterion assesses the relative ease or difficulty of entry to a given compensation system as well as the probability of receiving compensation. The voluntary or compulsory nature of a compensation system and incentives for bringing claims are also analyzed.

* *Scope and depth of compensation.* This criterion includes discussion of predictability of receiving compensation, adequacy of the compensation received, and methods used to limit compensation.

* *Procedures for resolving claims.* This criterion is used to review procedures by which a claim is initiated, validated, and ultimately resolved. The procedural aspects of a compensation system are important because of their implications for overall fairness and efficiency.

* *Costs and Financing.* This criterion was included with the intent of comparing costs of each approach. * * * [T]he committee feels this is an essential element in the development of a compensation scheme, given current interest in cost containment. Financing describes allocation of costs attributable to medically related injuries among providers, patients, and society as a whole.

* *Incentives for injury avoidance.* This criterion looks at the capacity of a compensation scheme for reducing the incidence of medical injury. Injury reduction measures may be direct, indirect, or a combination of both.

* *Relationship to other methods of compensation and quality assurance mechanisms.* This criterion assesses whether specific proposals are freestanding or complementary to existing approaches to compensation. The committee considered the impact of compensation systems on other activities in the health sector, such as quality assurance programs and existing reimbursement mechanisms, as part of this criterion.

Institute of Medicine, Beyond Malpractice: Compensation for Medical Injuries 29–30 (1978). For a federal study which builds upon the Institute of Medicine report, see U.S. General Accounting Office (GAO), Medical Malpractice: No Agreement on the Problems or Solutions (1986). (hereafter GAO Malpractice Report)

Can you think of other goals by which we should test tort reform? Should we rank the goals which the Institute of Medicine proposes in a particular order of priority? If so, what should come first and how do you decide? As you read through these materials, ask yourself if the various reforms are likely to promote or impede particular goals, and at what cost.

B. IMPROVING INSURANCE AVAILABILITY FOR PHYSICIANS

Two major changes, beginning in the mid–70s, have increased the availability of medical malpractice insurance. First, new sources of insurance have been created. Second, the type of policy offered has been changed.

A variety of new sources of insurance have been created, either by the states or by providers. Joint underwriting associations, reinsurance exchanges, hospital self-insurance programs, state funds, and provider owned insurance companies have sprung into being. By the end of 1977, 15 physician-owned insurance companies, most linked to medical societies, covered about 76,000 physicians. By 1984, the number had risen to 30 physician-owned companies writing 50% of malpractice coverage. Hospitals have begun to self-insure. Some states have adopted state programs, such as patient compensation funds, to limit doctor liability to individual patients. The largest insurer, St. Paul Fire and Marine Insurance Company, still has a 15% share of the premium market for physicians, in spite of the new competition.

Medical malpractice insurers changed in the late seventies to writing policies on a claims-made rather than an occurrence basis. Before 1975, most policies had been occurrence policies, covering claims made at any time as long as the insured doctor was covered during the time the medical accident giving rise to the claim occurred. The increase in the frequency and severity of claims in the mid–70s revealed the long tail problem of this kind of insurance. Insurers struggled to reliably predict their future losses and set premium prices, and often failed. Most insurers therefore have shifted to a claims-made policy, allowing them to use more recent claims experience to set premium prices and reserve requirements. The claims-made policy covers claims made during the year of the policy coverage, avoiding the predictability problem of the occurrence policy. Such policies arguably have allowed companies to continue to carry malpractice insurance lines, serving the goal of availability by keeping premium costs lower than they would otherwise have been.

Claims-made policies can however create problems for insured physicians, particularly if they are not careful to keep coverage intact when they change policies or employers. See Langley v. Mutual Fire, Marine, and Inland Insurance Company, 512 So.2d 752 (S.C.Ala.1987) (Dr. Langley, who had been insured under a claims-made policy with the defendant, sued the defendant and its agent for fraud, negligence, and breach of contract, after coverage was denied under the policies for his alleged negligent delivery of a child; the court points out that the very purpose of such policies is to eliminate the actuarial uncertainty inherent in the long tail of occurrence policies. The quid pro quo for the insured physician is a lower premium.) See generally Hutton, Physicians' Suits Against Medical Malpractice Insurers: An Analysis of Current Issues in Professional Liability Insurance Litigation, 11 J.Leg. Med. 225 (1990); Annotation, Event as Occurring Within Period of Coverage of "Occurrence" and "Discovery" or "Claims Made" Liability Policies, 37 A.L.R.4th 382 (1985 & Supp.1989)

C. ALTERING THE LITIGATION PROCESS

Starting in the 1970s, states enacted tort reform legislation. The preamble to the California Medical Injury Compensation Reform Act is typical of the legislative perceptions of the malpractice crisis:

> The Legislature finds and declares that there is a major health care crisis in the State of California attributable to skyrocketing malpractice premium costs and resulting in a potential breakdown of the health delivery system, severe hardships for the medically indigent, a denial of access for the economically marginal, and depletion of physicians such as to substantially worsen the quality of health care available to citizens of this state.

Tort reform measures were intended by their proponents to reduce either the frequency of malpractice litigation or the size of the settlement or judgment. These measures can be subdivided into four groups:

—those affecting the filing of malpractice claims;

—those limiting the award recoverable by the plaintiff;

—those altering the plaintiff's burden of proof through changes in evidence rules and legal doctrine;

—those changing the role of the courts, usually in the direction of substitution of an alternative forum.

This section will outline the nature of these reforms, consider briefly some of the judicial responses to challenges brought against these reforms, and review several comprehensive reform proposals.

1. Common Tort Reforms

a. Reducing the Filing of Claims

If the frequency of litigation is lowered, it is reasonable to assume that insurance companies will have to pay out less money, which in turn should lower premiums. Several reforms are intended to either bar certain claims that could previously have been brought, or create disincentives for the bringing of suits.

(1) Shortened statutes of limitations. Over forty states have now modified their statutes of limitations, in response to the criticism that long statutes of repose complicate insurance prediction of claims and result in uncertainty in portfolio management. Historically, the time period for a medical injury was tolled, or began to run, when the injury was discovered. This created the "long tail" problem. States have reduced the time period, typically by requiring that claims be brought within a short time, for example within two years of the injury or one year of the time that the injury should have been discovered with due diligence. The "discovery rule" and its problems are discussed in Chapter 2.

(2) Controlling legal fees. More than twenty states have regulated attorney fees in a variety of ways, including establishing rigid contin-

gency fee structures or requiring judicial review of the "reasonableness" of the fees. The intended effect of these statutes was to make lawyers more selective in screening out nonmeritorious claims, thus eliminating excessive litigation. Danzon found that contingent fees tend to result in equalizing plaintiff attorney compensation to that of the defense bar (whose income is not controlled), and that controls reduce not only lawyers' income, but also plaintiff compensation. Danzon, supra at 198.

(3) Payment of costs for frivolous claims. Under such a statute or court rule, a malpractice claimant found to have acted frivolously in suing must reimburse the provider for reasonable legal fees, witness fees, and court costs. See American Medical Association Special Task Force on Professional Liability and Insurance, Professional Liability in the '80's, Report II, American Medical Association, (updated as of July 1985) at p. 23.

b. Limiting the Plaintiff's Award

If the previous reforms aim to cut down on the number of cases in court, the next category of reforms is designed to reduce the overall size of the award.

(1) Elimination of the ad damnum clause. This clause, as part of the initial pleading, states the total monetary claim requested by the plaintiff, an amount presumably inflated beyond the level of actual damages suffered. It is feared that such claims expose the defendant to harmful pretrial publicity, damage his reputation, and induce juries to make larger awards than the evidence supports. Thirty-two states have legislated to eliminate the ad damnum clause.

(2) Periodic Payments. Provisions, now in effect in 18 states, allow or require a court to convert awards for future losses from a single lump sum payment into periodic payments over the period of the patient's disability or life. Such a mode of payment is intended to eliminate a windfall payment to heirs if the injured party dies.

(3) Collateral source rule modifications. The collateral source rule has operated to prevent the trier of fact from learning about other sources of compensation (such as medical insurance) which the plaintiff might possess. The rule arguably permits double recovery. The modifications have either required the court to inform juries about payments from other sources to the patient, or to offset against the award some or all of the amount of payment from other sources. Seventeen states have modified this rule.

(4) Limits on liability. The most powerful reform in actually reducing the size of malpractice awards has been a dollar limit, or cap, on awards. Caps may take the form of a limit on the amount of recovery of general damages, typically pain and suffering; or a maximum recoverable per case, including all damages.

Indiana has a $500,000 limit per claim, Nebraska $1 million, South Dakota a limit of $500,000 for general damages, California $250,000 on recovery for noneconomic damages, including pain and suffering.

One interesting reform proposal has been to "schedule" pain and suffering awards, rather than capping them, to narrow the range of variability in jury awards. See Bovbjerg, Sloan, and Blumstein, Valuing Life and Limb in Tort: Scheduling "Pain and Suffering," 83 Northw.Univ.L.Rev. 908 (1989).

c. Altering the Plaintiff's Burden of Proof

Several reforms have altered evidentiary rules or legal doctrine to increase the plaintiff's burden of proof.

(1) Res ipsa loquitur. Res ipsa loquitur was judicially expanded during the 1970's by a number of state courts, creating an inference of negligence (or in three states a presumption) even where expert testimony was needed to establish the "obviousness" of the defendant's negligence. See Chapter 2. Doctors objected that they were forced to shoulder a defense burden for some patient harms that were not the result of their negligence. Ten states now have barred the use of the doctrine or limited its operation.

(2) Expert witness rules. As Chapter 2 demonstrates, the plaintiff is normally required to present expert medical testimony as to the standard of care, the defendant's deviation from it, causation, and damages. Some states have now adopted specific requirements that plaintiff experts be qualified in the particular specialty at issue or devote a large percent of their practice to the specialty. The intent of these reforms is to reduce the ability of the plaintiff to use a so-called "hired gun", a forensic doctor who has never practiced, or no longer practices, in the area of the defendant physician.

(3) Standards of care. The standard of care has evolved from a locality rule to a national standard in most states, not only as to specialists, but also as to general practitioners. Some states have redefined the standard by statute to specify the particular locality (local, similar, state) that governs the litigation. The purpose of these changes has been fairness to rural practitioners, and again to limit the use of forensic experts from other states.

d. Changing the Judicial Role

The role of the jury as trier of fact has been perceived by critics of the tort system as introducing bias against defendants and causing delay in compensating plaintiffs. Some argue that development of either screening or alternative dispute resolution devices (ADRs) will speed resolution of cases and screen out frivolous claims more effectively than common law litigation. These reforms are important, because they set up a complicated parallel track for disputes which reduces the judicial role.

(1) Pretrial screening devices. Twenty-five states have implemented screening panels. These panels are intended to rule on the merits of the case before it can proceed to trial and to speed settlement of cases by pricing them in advance of trial. Screening panel laws vary significantly from state to state, but usually require that all cases be heard by the panel before the plaintiff is entitled to trial. A plaintiff is not prevented from filing suit after a panel's negative finding, but the panel's decision is admissible as evidence at trial. The panels range in size from three to seven members, and often include a judge or a lay person, at least one lawyer, and one or more health care providers from the defendant's specialty or type of institution. The panel conducts an informal hearing in which it hears testimony and reviews evidence. The finding of the panel may cover both liability and the size of the award. For a detailed discussion of such panels, see Macchiaroli, Medical Malpractice Screening Panels: Proposed Model Legislation to Cure Judicial Ills, 58 Geo.Wash.L.Rev. 181 (1990).

Proponents have contended that such panels are less formal and less time consuming, and therefore less expensive as a way of resolving claims. Better informed panel members, including health care professionals, may also reach more accurate decisions than a lay jury could. See generally Institute of Medicine, Beyond Malpractice: Compensation for Medical Injuries, National Academy of Sciences, 33 (1978); GAO Report at 133; Carlin, Medical Malpractice Pre-trial Screening Panels: A Review of the Evidence, Intergovernment Health Policy Project 15 (1980).

The concerns as to the panels are that they will delay dispute resolution, will favor the provider, and will be ignored unless their use is mandatory.

(2) Arbitration. While screening panels supplement jury trials, arbitration is intended to replace them. Thirteen states have laws promoting arbitration of malpractice disputes. The expected advantages of arbitration include diminished complexity in fact-finding, lower cost, fairer results, greater access for smaller claims, and a reduced burden on the courts. See GAO Report at 139–40; American Arbitration Association, Arbitration—Alternative to Malpractice Suits, 5 (1975); Ladimer, Solomon, and Mulvihill, Experience in Medical Malpractice Arbitration, 2 J.Legal Med. 443 (1981). No state requires compulsory arbitration. Like screening panels, the arbitration process uses a panel to resolve the dispute after an informal presentation of evidence. The panel typically consists of a doctor, a lawyer and a layperson or retired judge. The arbitration panel, however, uses members trained in dispute resolution and has the authority to make a final ruling as to both provider liability and damages. The process is initiated only when there is an agreement between the patient and the health care provider to arbitrate any claims.

Problem: Coping With Reform

You represent Marcia Schotz, the mother of Christopher Schotz, a child with severe brain damage and retardation. Marcia has just approached you as to the merits of a lawsuit against the Verdain Hospital, several nurses, Dr. Fred Mulch, her obstetrician at the time of the birth of Christopher, and Dr. Ed James, a pediatrician. The facts are as follows:

Marcia's pregnancy with Chris, her first, had been uneventful. She went into labor on December 18, 1984, and arrived at the hospital at around 11:30 p.m. In the labor room she was attached to a fetal monitor with external electrodes and then examined by nurse Joyce Huzinga. An hour later, Dr. Mulch examined her. He was unable to tell if the baby was presenting headfirst or breech. He therefore ordered an x-ray to resolve his uncertainty. Marcia was then detached from the monitor; while waiting for an orderly to take her for x-rays, her membranes burst. Twenty minutes later she was taken to x-ray, and brought back after an hour. She was then left unsupervised until 2:30. Another nurse, Sally Fields, then came in and discovered that the membranes had ruptured. She attempted to hook up the external monitor again, but her efforts were inept. The monitor therefore failed to register any intelligible information. Dr. Mulch came back at 2:45, confirmed that the membranes had ruptured, but made no attempt to get the fetal heart rate either by monitor or fetoscope until 3:15. At 3:15, an internal monitor was properly connected and fetal distress noted on the printouts. Despite the distress, normal delivery procedures were commenced, including an intravenous anesthetic for Marcia, delaying the birth of Christopher by another 20 minutes, during which time he was being asphyxiated in the uterus. After delivery, Dr. Mulch failed to clear the trachea of meconium (fecal matter) which was then ingested into the lungs. Dr. James, a resident pediatrician, summoned to help in the resuscitation, handled an endotracheal tube in such a way as to cause a hole in one of the baby's lungs and a resulting pneumothorax.

Marcia was unconscious during delivery and had been heavily sedated from about 1:00 on. She was not aware of the errors during delivery since Dr. Mulch said nothing to her afterwards and had altered the medical records and deleted incident reports that would have suggested malpractice. It was only now that Marcia has learned of the possibility of malpractice during the delivery.

This is a complicated case requiring extensive discovery, and expert testimony will be required on a number of issues of nursing, obstetric, and pediatric negligence. Your jurisdiction, Columbia, has just enacted the Medical Malpractice Justice Act and you have not yet had experience with its provisions. Work up the file, considering the theories of recovery, defenses, and potential damages for a brain-damaged infant. Then evaluate the effects of the various reform provisions on the resolution of the case, the possible outcomes, and your fee.

THE COLUMBIA MEDICAL MALPRACTICE JUSTICE ACT

Section 1.

No health care liability claim may be commenced unless the action is filed within two years from the occurrence of the breach or tort or from the date the health care treatment that is the subject of the claim is completed;

provided that minors under the age of 12 shall have until their 14th birthday in which to file or have filed on their behalf, the claim.

Section 2.

(1) In an action for damages alleging medical malpractice against a person or party, damages for noneconomic loss which exceeds $500,000 shall not be awarded.

(2) In awarding damages in an action alleging medical malpractice, the trier of the fact shall itemize damages into economic and noneconomic damages.

(3) "Noneconomic loss" means damages or loss due to pain, suffering, inconvenience, physical impairment, physical disfigurement, or other non-economic loss.

(4) Subsection (1) of this section does not apply to the amount of damages awarded on a health care liability claim for the expenses of necessary medical, hospital, and custodial care received before judgment or required in the future for treatment of the injury.

(5) In any action on a health care liability claim that is tried by a jury in any court in this state, the following shall be included in the court's written instructions to the jurors: Do not consider, discuss, nor speculate whether or not liability, if any, on the part of any party is or is not subject to any limit under applicable law.

Section 3.

In any malpractice action in which the plaintiff seeks to recover for the cost of medical care, custodial care or rehabilitation services, loss of earnings or other economic loss, evidence shall be admissible for considera- tion by the court to establish that any such past or future cost or expense was or will, with reasonable certainty, be replaced or indemnified, in whole or in part, from any collateral source such as insurance, social security, workers' compensation or employee benefit programs. If the court finds that any such cost or expense was or will, with reasonable certainty, be replaced or indemnified from any collateral source, it shall reduce the amount of the award by such finding, minus an amount equal to the premiums paid by the plaintiff for such benefits for the two-year period immediately preceding the accrual of such action and minus an amount equal to the projected future cost to the plaintiff of maintaining such benefits.

Section 4.

(1) An action alleging medical malpractice shall be mediated pursuant to subsection (4).

(2) The judge to whom an action alleging medical malpractice is assigned or the chief judge shall refer the action to mediation by written order not less than 91 days after the filing of the answer or answers.

(3) An action referred to mediation pursuant to subsection (1) shall be heard by a mediation panel selected pursuant to subsection (4).

(4) A mediation panel shall be composed of 5 voting members, 3 of whom shall be licensed attorneys, one of whom shall be a licensed or

registered health care provider selected by the defendant or defendants and one of whom shall be a licensed or registered health care provider selected by the plaintiff or plaintiffs. If a defendant is a specialist, the health care provider members of the panel shall specialize in the same or a related, relevant area of health care as the defendant.

(5) Except as otherwise provided in subsection (1), the procedure for selecting mediation panel members and their qualifications shall be as prescribed by the court rules or local court rules.

(6) A judge may be selected as a member of a mediation panel, but may not preside at the trial of any action in which he or she served as a mediator.

(7) In the case of multiple injuries to members of a single family, the plaintiffs may elect to treat the action as involving one claim, with the payment of one fee and rendering of one lump sum award to be accepted or rejected. If such an election is not made, a separate fee shall be paid for each plaintiff, and the mediation panel shall then make separate awards for each claim, which may be individually accepted or rejected.

(8) At least 7 days before the mediation hearing date, each party shall submit to the mediation clerk five copies of the documents pertaining to the issues to be mediated and five copies of a concise brief or summary setting forth that party's factual or legal position on issues presented by the action. In addition, one copy of each shall be served on each attorney of record.

(9) A party has the right, but is not required, to attend a mediation hearing. If scars, disfigurement, or other unusual conditions exist, they may be demonstrated to the mediation panel by a personal appearance; however, testimony shall not be taken or permitted of any party.

(10) The rules of evidence shall not apply before the mediation panel. Factual information having a bearing on damages or liability shall be supported by documentary evidence, if possible.

(11) Oral presentation shall be limited to 15 minutes per side unless multiple parties or unusual circumstances warrant additional time. The mediation panel may request information on applicable insurance policy limits and may inquire about settlement negotiations, unless a party objects. Following deliberation, the mediation panel shall render an evaluation, to which a majority of the panel must agree.

(12) Statements by the attorneys and the briefs or summaries are not admissible in any subsequent court or evidentiary proceeding.

(13) If a party has rejected an evaluation and the action proceeds to trial, that party shall pay the opposing party's actual costs unless the verdict is more favorable to the rejecting party than the mediation evaluation. However, if the opposing party has also rejected the evaluation, that party is entitled to costs only if the verdict is more favorable to that party than the mediation evaluation.

(14) For the purpose of subsection (13), a verdict shall be adjusted by adding to it assessable costs and interest on the amount of the verdict from the filing of the complaint to the date of the mediation evaluation. After this adjustment, the verdict is considered more favorable to a defendant if

it is more than 10% below the evaluation, and is considered more favorable to the plaintiff if it is more than 10% above the evaluation.

(15) For the purpose of this section, actual costs include those costs taxable in any civil action and a reasonable attorney fee as determined by the trial judge for services necessitated by the rejection of the mediation evaluation.

(16) Costs shall not be awarded if the mediation award was not unanimous.

Section 5.

In an action alleging medical malpractice, if the defendant is a specialist, a person shall not give expert testimony on the appropriate standard of care unless the person is or was a physician licensed to practice medicine or osteopathic medicine and surgery or a dentist licensed to practice dentistry in this or another state and meets both of the following criteria:

(1) Specializes, or specialized at the time of the occurrence which is the basis for the action, in the same specialty or a related, relevant area of medicine or osteopathic medicine and surgery or dentistry as the specialist who is the defendant in the medical malpractice action.

(2) Devotes, or devoted at the time of the occurrence which is the basis for the action, a substantial portion of his or her professional time to the active clinical practice of medicine or osteopathic medicine and surgery or the active clinical practice of dentistry, or to the instruction of students in an accredited medical school, osteopathic medical school, or dental school in the same specialty or a related, relevant area of health care as the specialist who is the defendant in the medical malpractice action.

Section 6.

In order to determine what judgment is to be entered on a verdict in an action to recover damages for dental or medical malpractice under this article, the court shall proceed as follows:

(1) The court shall apply to the findings of past and future damages any applicable rules of law, including set-offs, credits, comparative negligence, additurs, and remittiturs, in calculating the respective amounts of past and future damages claimants are entitled to recover and defendants are obligated to pay.

(2) The court shall enter judgment in lump sum for past damages, for future damages not in excess of two hundred fifty thousand dollars, and for any damages, fees or costs payable in lump sum or otherwise under subsection (3). For the purposes of this section, any lump sum payment of a portion of future damages shall be deemed to include the elements of future damages in the same proportion as such elements comprise of the total award for future damages as determined by the trier of fact.

(3) With respect to awards of future damages in excess of two hundred fifty thousand dollars in an action to recover damages for dental or medical malpractice, the court shall enter judgment as follows:

After making any adjustments prescribed by this subsection and subsection (2), the court shall enter a judgment for the amount of the present value of an annuity contract that will provide for the payment of the remaining amounts of future damages in periodic installments.

Section 7.

(1) Notwithstanding any inconsistent judicial rule, a contingent fee in a medical malpractice action shall not exceed the amount of compensation provided for in the following schedule:

30 percent of the first $250,000 of the sum recovered;

25 percent of the next $250,000 of the sum recovered;

20 percent of the next $500,000 of the sum recovered;

15 percent of the next $250,000 of the sum recovered;

10 percent of any amount over $1,250,000 of the sum recovered.

(2) In the event that claimant's or plaintiff's attorney believes in good faith that the fee schedule set forth in subsection (1) of this section, because of extraordinary circumstances, will not give him adequate compensation, application for greater compensation may be made upon affidavit with written notice and an opportunity to be heard to the claimant or plaintiff and other persons holding liens or assignments on the recovery.

2. *Judicial Responses to Legislative Reform*

Reforms have been challenged on a variety of state and federal constitutional bases and under the common law.

a. *Equal Protection*

Tort reform legislation enacted in the states since the 1970s has generally survived constitutional challenge. The major federal challenges have been based on denial of equal protection and violation of substantive due process guarantees under the 14th Amendment. These challenges have been aimed at state statutes imposing special procedural barriers or damage limitations against medical malpractice claimants, thus singling them out as a class. The courts have generally held that states may discriminate in social and economic matters so long as there is a "rational relationship" between the classification and a permissible state objective. Most state reforms have been held to pass the rational basis test, as they arguably serve the valid state purposes of reducing health and insurance costs and assuring adequate health care delivery.

ETHERIDGE v. MEDICAL CENTER HOSPITALS

Supreme Court of Virginia, 1989.
237 Va. 87, 376 S.E.2d 525.

[In Etheridge, the Virginia Supreme Court upheld the state's $750,000 cap on malpractice awards. The plaintiff had presented the ideal equitable case for the unfairness of a cap on damage awards. She was a 35–year–old mother of three children, a normal, healthy woman. On May 6, 1980, however, she underwent surgery at the hospital to restore a deteriorating jaw bone. The surgery consisted of the removal of five-inch-long portions of two ribs by Trower, a general surgeon, and the grafting of the reshaped rib bone to Wilson's jaw by an oral surgeon. The jury found that both Trower and the hospital were negligent and that their negligence proximately caused Wilson's injuries. The plaintiff Wilson's injuries were severe and permanent. She was brain damaged with limited memory and intelligence, paralyzed on her left side, confined to a wheelchair, and unable to care for herself or her children. Trial evidence was that she had expended more than $300,000 for care and treatment up to the trial and will continue to incur expenses for her care for the rest of her life. Her life expectancy is 39.9 years. She was a licensed practical nurse who had earned almost $10,000 in 1979, the last full year she worked.

The jury returned a verdict for $2,750,000 against both defendants. The trial court then applied the recovery limit prescribed by the Virginia cap in Code § 8.01–581.15 and reduced the verdict to $750,000 and entered judgment in that amount. Plaintiff attacked the validity of this provision on the grounds that it violated the Virginia Constitution's due process guarantee, jury trial guarantee, separation of powers doctrine, prohibitions against special legislation, and equal protection guarantee, as well as certain parallel provisions of the Federal Constitution.

The court noted that the General Assembly passed the Virginia Medical Malpractice Act in large part due to concerns about the "premium cost for, and the availability of, medical malpractice insurance." The legislature had concluded that the increase in the cost of malpractice premiums was causing Virginia physicians to retire early or not enter practice in the state. A crisis of accessibility to health care for the citizens of Virginia was imminent.

The Virginia Supreme Court then applied the rational basis test, holding that "* * * the legislature could have reasonably concluded that the challenged classification would promote a legitimate state purpose."]

The court continued:

Wilson seeks to "second guess" the General Assembly by claiming that its factual findings do not constitute a reasonable basis for limiting recoverable damages in a medical malpractice action. Wilson also claims that "[e]ven if there were some factual premise for the legislation," it must fail because there is no relationship between the General Assembly's goal and the means it chose to attain the goal. We do not agree.

* * * Code § 8.01–581.15 was enacted only after a thorough study had been made of the problem. The General Assembly made specific findings and a legislative judgment as to how the problem

could be best addressed. Bearing in mind that the General Assembly is presumed to have acted within its constitutional powers and according its action the presumption of validity to which it is entitled, we cannot say that the means the General Assembly chose to promote a legitimate state purpose are unreasonable or arbitrary. Accordingly, we hold that the classification does not violate the Equal Protection Clause.

Judge Russell, dissenting, had strong objections to the selective focus of the legislation. He noted:

* * * the unintended consequence of the Act was the creation of a class, described as "health care providers," clothed with a special privilege in the courts. Alone among the multitudes of corporations, associations, groups, and individuals who are daily subjected to tort actions in the courts, the members of this privileged elite (and those who insure them) are granted a special immunity from all damages exceeding $750,000 (now $1,000,000). All defendants not falling within the favored class lack that shield and must pay the full amount a jury may decide to award.

The other side of this unhappy equation is that Code § 8.01–581.15 creates a corresponding disfavored class—those who are so unfortunate as to suffer injury as a result of the negligence of a health care provider. Their right to recover damages is limited by the Act while those injured by the torts of accountants, airlines, architects, barbers, bandits, banks, bus drivers, cooks, dog owners, engineers, financial advisors, horse trainers, golfers, hotel keepers, inebriates, jailors, kidnappers, lawyers, etc., retain an unlimited right of redress in the courts. This is precisely the kind of economic favoritism as which the special-laws prohibitions were aimed.

* * *

I have no doubt that the General Assembly has full constitutional authority to limit or restrict all damages, or all unliquidated damages, or all non-economic damages, or all punitive damages, with respect to all plaintiffs and all defendants regardless of their identities. Having determined that a "liability crisis" exists, the legislature may take rational and proper steps to create a remedy, including limitations on "the practice in, and jurisdiction of the courts." But it must do so evenhandedly. The remedy must not depend upon the identity of the defendant.

The familiar figure holding the scales of justice wears a blindfold. She should not be required to peer around it to ascertain whether the defendant is a "health care provider" before deciding what judgment to pronounce. The Virginia Constitution is particularly emphatic in proscribing laws which protect a select group of defendants or which limit the rights of a select group of plaintiffs to obtain redress in the courts of the Commonwealth.

Notes and Questions

1. Most state courts that have considered caps have rejected equal protection challenges. See Davis v. Omitowoju, 883 F.2d 1155 (3d Cir., 1989); Fein v. Permanente Medical Group, 38 Cal.3d 137, 211 Cal.Rptr. 368, 695 P.2d 665 (1985), appeal dismissed 474 U.S. 892, 106 S.Ct. 214, 88 L.Ed.2d 215 (1985).

2. A few jurisdictions have held a reform provision unconstitutional on Equal Protection grounds, applying a more rigorous and intense level of scrutiny. In Austin v. Litvak, 682 P.2d 41 (Colo.1984), the provision was the three-year statute of repose contained in section 13–80–105, C.R.S. 1973 (1983 Cum.Supp.), as it applied to persons whose claims are premised on a negligent misdiagnosis claim. The statute contained two exceptions to the three-year period of repose. One, the claim is not barred if the person who committed the act or omission knowingly conceals that fact. Two, the claim is excepted from the period of repose if the physician left an unauthorized foreign object in the claimant's body. Under either exception, the medical malpractice action must be filed by the injured person within two years after the claimant discovers or should have discovered the act or omission.

The court analyzed the plaintiff's argument that the provisions of section 13–80–105 violated the plaintiff's right to equal protection of the law.

> We are persuaded that the statutory classification prescribed by section 13–80–105 fails to meet the two-pronged test. The statutory exceptions which permit "foreign object" and "knowing concealment" claimants but not "negligently misdiagnosed" plaintiffs to avoid the three-year statute of repose and to invoke the discovery rule are without a reasonable basis in fact, thereby creating an arbitrary classification. * * * We conclude that the two statutory exemptions substantially undermine the apparent legislative purpose in enacting the strict three-year statute of repose prescribed by section 13–80–105. Claims dependent upon knowing concealment to avoid the repose provision are far more likely to be frivolous or involve stale evidence than claims of negligent misdiagnosis for the reasons stated above. Moreover, the two exceptions created by the legislature also manifest a governmental interest in preserving medical malpractice claims where the claimant has sustained an injury but lacks any reasonable opportunity to discover the act or omission which caused the injury. The classification which results in the denial of the discovery rule to patients whose conditions are negligently misdiagnosed does not further this legitimate governmental interest and, therefore, lacks a rational relationship to that goal.

* * *

See Crier v. Whitecloud, 496 So.2d 305 (La.1986), where the Louisiana Supreme Court upheld the state's statute imposing an absolute bar of three years from the date of the alleged act or omission causing injury.

In Boucher v. Sayeed, 459 A.2d 87 (R.I.1983), the court rejected Rhode Island's mediation panel system for medical malpractice cases. The court concluded that no crisis existed, sufficient to justify differential treatment of malpractice claimants.

> * * * we are unable to sustain the 1981 legislation on the ground that it was enacted as a rational response to a public-health crisis.
>
> Absent a crisis to justify the enactment of such legislation, we can ascertain no satisfactory reason for the separate and unequal treatment that it imposes on medical malpractice litigants. * * * In the absence of an identifiable legitimate governmental interest, these class distinctions constitute a patent violation of one of the most fundamental tenets of equal protection, namely, that persons similarly situated shall be treated in a like manner.

See also Hoem v. State, 756 P.2d 780 (Wyo.1988).

Most state courts that have considered equal protection challenges to malpractice legislation have been deferential to reform legislation, upholding statutes by applying the rational basis test. Hoffman v. Powell, 298 S.C. 338, 380 S.E.2d 821 (1989). Others have backed away from earlier statements of intensified review. Compare Leiker v. Gafford, 245 Kan. 325, 778 P.2d 823 (1989), with Farley v. Engelken, 241 Kan. 663, 740 P.2d 1058 (1987); Meech v. Hillhaven West, Inc., 238 Mont. 21, 776 P.2d 488 (1989). See generally Macchiaroli, Medical Malpractice Screening Panels: Proposed Model Legislation to Cure Judicial Ills, 58 Geo.Wash.L.Rev. 181, 206 (1990).

b. Due Process

Federal constitutional guarantees of due process insure that state action will not deprive a citizen of "life, liberty, or property without due process of law." A cause of action is considered to be property protected by the Due Process clause. See Logan v. Zimmerman Brush Co., 455 U.S. 422, 102 S.Ct. 1148, 71 L.Ed.2d 265 (1982) (employee's right to Fair Employment Practice Act's adjudicatory procedures are property protected by the due process clause). See Smith, "Battling a Receding Tort Frontier: Constitutional Attacks on Medical Malpractice Laws", 38 Okla.L.Rev. 195 (1985); Redish, "Legislative Responses to the Medical Malpractice Insurance Crisis: Constitutional Implications", 55 Tex.L. Rev. 759 (1977). Compensation schemes that eliminate or restrict a patient's ability to bring a negligence action can therefore be challenged as a taking of the patient's property—his right to sue—without due process of law.

The North Dakota Supreme Court, in Arneson v. Olson, 270 N.W.2d 125, 137 (N.D.1978), found that the state's Medical Malpractice Act violated substantive due process requirements.

> Although some of the following provisions of the Act, individually, would not violate due process, we hold that the cumulative effect of the limitation of the application of the Act to only one category of health-care professionals, * * *, the arbitrary requirement of consent under conditions of duress and statutory imposition of "consent" in emergencies * * *, the limitation on use of the doctrine of res ipsa loquitur

* * *, and the near-abolition of the collateral-source doctrine * * * is to violate the right of medical patients in this State to due process of law. We find that the statute is, in respect to these matters, arbitrary and unreasonable and discriminatory, and that the methods adopted have no reasonable relation to the attainment of the results desired.

One of the most interesting debates on these constitutional issues is found in Roa v. Lodi Medical Group, where the California Supreme Court upheld a statutory limitation on contingency fees. The dissent discusses the empirical complexities of legislating and then judging the merits of such legislation.

ROA v. LODI MEDICAL GROUP

Supreme Court of California, 1985.
37 Cal.3d 920, 211 Cal.Rptr. 77, 695 P.2d 164.

KAUS, J.

* * * In this case we address a challenge to Business and Professions Code section 6146, which places limits on the amount of fees an attorney may obtain in a medical malpractice action when he represents a party on a contingency fee basis * * *.[1] [W]hile we express no view as to the wisdom of the measure, we conclude that the legislation is constitutional.

I

This action was brought by Frank Roa, Jr., individually, and by Yvonne Jean Roa, individually and as guardian ad litem for their minor son, Frank Joseph Roa, for injuries allegedly suffered as a result of negligent treatment and care during the child's birth. The complaint named the Lodi Medical Group, Inc., Dr. Gordon B. Roget, the Lodi Community Hospital and numerous Does as defendants.

After some discovery, plaintiffs negotiated a settlement with two of the defendants, the Lodi Medical Group, Inc., and Dr. Roget. The agreement provided for payment of $495,000 to the minor and $5,000 to the parents. Pursuant to Probate Code section 3500, plaintiffs sought

---

1. Section 6146 provides in relevant part: "(a) An attorney shall not contract for or collect a contingency fee for representing any person seeking damages in connection with an action for injury or damage against a health care provider based upon such person's alleged professional negligence in excess of the following limits: [¶] (1) Forty percent of the first fifty thousand dollars ($50,000) recovered. [¶] (2) Thirty-three and one-third percent of the next fifty thousand dollars ($50,000) recovered. [¶] (3) Twenty-five percent of the next one hundred thousand dollars ($100,000) recovered. [¶] (4) Ten percent of any amount on which the recovery exceeds two hundred thousand dollars ($200,000). [¶] The limitations shall apply regardless of whether the recovery is by settlement, arbitration, or judgment, or whether the person for whom the recovery is made is a responsible adult, an infant, or a person of unsound mind. [¶] * * * [¶] (c) For purposes of this section: [¶] (1) 'Recovered' means the net sum recovered after deducting any disbursements or costs incurred in connection with prosecution or settlement of the claim. Costs of medical care incurred by the plaintiff and the attorney's office-overhead costs or charges are not deductible disbursements or costs for such purpose. * * *"

Unless otherwise stated, all section references are to the Business and Professions Code.

court approval of the settlement, advising the court that the $500,000 represented the total policy limits of these two defendants' insurance coverage. The court found the settlement reasonable and approved it.

At the same time, pursuant to Probate Code section 3601, plaintiffs requested that the court approve the payment of fees to their attorneys from the net proceeds of the settlement. * * *

The trial court found (1) that plaintiffs and their attorneys had entered into an understanding that the attorney fee would be 25 percent of the net recovery and (2) that the $122,800 fee which that percentage would yield "is a fair and reasonable amount for attorneys' fees in this case and is in no way disproportionate to the quality or quantity of the legal services provided to the plaintiffs in this case." The court also noted that "were it not for the existence of Business and Professions Code [section] 6146, the amount of attorneys' fees requested" by plaintiffs would be awarded. The court, however, rejected the constitutional challenge to section 6146 and concluded that it was compelled to award fees in accordance with the statutory limitations. Accordingly, it approved a fee of $90,800.

* * *

II

Plaintiffs, and amici on their behalf, contend that section 6146 is unconstitutional as (1) a denial of due process, (2) a violation of equal protection, and (3) a violation of the separation of powers doctrine. We address each of the contentions in turn. [Only the claim of denial of due process follows.]

A

Plaintiffs' due process argument rests on the claim that the statute impermissibly infringes on the right of medical malpractice victims to retain counsel in malpractice actions. Although the right to be represented by retained counsel in civil actions is not expressly enumerated in the federal or state Constitution, our cases have long recognized that the constitutional due process guarantee does embrace such a right. [ ] Section 6146, however, does not in any way abrogate the right to retain counsel, but simply limits the compensation that an attorney may obtain when he represents an injured party under a contingency fee arrangement.

Statutory limits on attorney fees are not at all uncommon, either in California or throughout the country generally. In this state, attorney fees have long been legislatively regulated both in workers' compensation proceedings (Lab.Code, § 4906) and in probate matters. (Prob.Code, §§ 910, 901.) Some states have adopted maximum fee schedules which apply to *all* personal-injury contingency fee arrangements [ ], others have enacted limits which, like section 6146, apply only in a specific area, such as medical malpractice. [ ] Congress has passed numerous statutes limiting the fees that an attorney may obtain in representing claimants in a variety of settings. [ ]

The validity of such legislative regulation of attorney fees is well established.

Plaintiffs contend, however, that even if statutory limitations on attorney fees are generally permissible, the limits established by section 6146 are invalid because the authorized fees are so low that in practice the statute will make it impossible for injured persons to retain an attorney to represent them. The adequacy of the fees permitted by the statute is in large measure an empirical matter, and plaintiffs have made no showing to support their factual claim. Furthermore, a comparison of the fees permitted by section 6146 with the fees authorized under the numerous statutory schemes noted above suggests that section 6146's limits are not usually low. Under the circumstances, we certainly cannot hold that the amount of the fees permitted renders the statute unconstitutional on its face.

Plaintiffs alternatively challenge the "sliding scale" nature of the fee schedule, asserting that the decreasing percentage permitted for larger recoveries creates a conflict of interest between attorney and client, reducing the attorney's incentive to pursue a higher award. As a number of commentators have explained, however, potential conflicts of interest are inherent in all contingent fee arrangements. [ ] On the one hand, whenever a contingency fee agreement provides for either a flat percentage rate regardless of the amount of recovery or a declining percentage with an increase in recovery, "it may be to the lawyer's advantage to settle [the case] quickly, spending as little time as possible on the small claim where the increment in value through rigorous bargaining or trial, while significant to the client, is not significant or perhaps compensatory to the lawyer. * * *" (Mac-Kinnon, *supra,* at p. 198.) On the other hand, "[w]here the rate is graduated according to the stage of litigation at which recovery is attained * * * the increase in the rate of fee may lead the lawyer to bring suit or start trial, for example, solely to increase his rate from 25% to 33⅓%, without actually doing that much additional work and without the likelihood of a comparable increment to the client." (*Ibid.*) Furthermore, no matter how the particular percentage fee is calculated, "[t]he difference in the financial position of the lawyer and client may make for a complete disparity in their willingness to take a risk on a large recovery as against no recovery at all. In the same way the use of delay to increase the eventual recovery on a claim may have an entirely different impact on the injured and uncompensated claimant than it does on the lawyer, who is busy with other claims and regards this as one of a series which are ripening on the vine. * * *" (*Id.* at p. 199.) Thus, though the sliding scale arrangement embodied in section 6146 may affect the settings in which the attorney's and client's interests diverge, it does not create the basic conflict of interest problem.

Indeed, section 6146's decreasing sliding-scale approach has been recommended as the preferable form of regulation by a number of studies that have examined the question. * * * For just these reasons, the Legislature could rationally have determined that this aspect of the statutory scheme would promote the fairness of attorney fees. The sliding scale schedule certainly does not unconstitutionally impinge on a malpractice victim's right to counsel.

Finally, plaintiffs suggest that because the fee limits of section 6146 apply only to medical malpractice actions, the statute will operate to drive the most competent attorneys out of medical malpractice litigation into other areas of personal injury practice; they argue that this amounts to an unconstitutional infringement of a malpractice victim's right to counsel. Once again, plaintiffs have failed to make any showing to support the factual premise of their contention. * * *

* * *

BIRD, CHIEF JUSTICE, dissenting.

I strongly dissent.

Unlike other sections of the Medical Injury Compensation Reform Act (MICRA) which have been upheld by this court, section 6146 of the Business and Professions Code (hereafter section 6146) implicates the fairness of the judicial process itself. [ ] In effect, section 6146 prohibits severely injured victims of medical negligence from paying the general market rate for legal services, while permitting defendants to pay whatever is necessary to obtain high quality representation.

Out of practical necessity, virtually all plaintiffs use contingent fee arrangements in medical malpractice cases. [ ] In fact, for clients of limited means "the contingent fee arrangement offers the only realistic hope of establishing a legal claim." * * *

Section 6146 imposes heavy burdens on the ability of severely injured plaintiffs to obtain adequate legal representation. It sets forth a sliding scale of fee limits—the greater the recovery, the lower the allowable percentage. The effect of this approach is to impose drastically low limits on fees in precisely those cases which require a large recovery to make the plaintiff economically whole. * * *

Other provisions of MICRA interact with section 6146 to further discourage attorneys from representing severely injured plaintiffs. The collateral source provision (Civ.Code, § 3333.1, subd. (a)) can substantially reduce the damage award, and thus the contingent fee, without decreasing the attorney's workload. The periodic payment provision (Code Civ.Proc., § 667.7) may have the same effect and, in addition, could delay the attorney's compensation for years. Further, the $250,-000 limit on noneconomic damages (Civ.Code, § 3333.2) sharply reduces the recovery without relieving the attorney of the most difficult aspects of the malpractice action—proving negligence and causation.

Since section 6146 affects only medical malpractice cases, attorneys may avoid these problems by refusing to represent medical malpractice victims. Only those lawyers not sufficiently competent or well-established to attract unrestricted business have any financial incentive to represent a severely injured medical malpractice victim. [ ]

* * *   Defendants can be expected to concentrate their legal resources on the potential high recovery cases. The statute prohibits plaintiffs from responding in kind. Hence, the legal contest becomes a lopsided mismatch with tort victims on the losing end.

This problem is aggravated by the fact that medical malpractice plaintiffs are even more in need of high quality legal representation than other personal injury plaintiffs. * * *

Further, the risk of a zero recovery is high, and the fees collected in successful cases must also compensate the attorney for his or her work on the unsuccessful ones. [   ]

* * *

II.

Next, plaintiffs contend that section 6146 violates plaintiffs' right to due process of law. * * * The limits imposed by section 6146 must be rationally related to the Legislature's purposes in enacting the statute.

The majority conclude that limiting the compensation that plaintiffs' attorney may receive does not violate due process because it "does not in any way abrogate the right to retain counsel." [   ] However, section 6146 *does* significantly interfere with the right of certain victims of medical malpractice to retain counsel. [   ] Further, it exacerbates the conflict of interest between plaintiffs and their attorneys inherent in the contingent fee arrangement.

In support of their holding, the majority cite a number of existing attorney-fee limits which have withstood legal challenge. * * *

* * *

* * * [F]ee restrictions in the workers compensation and probate contexts are not likely to discourage attorneys from working in those fields, since the legal work is relatively simple, the risks are low and compensation is available which is commensurate to the services performed.

Contrast this situation with that of the plaintiff's attorney in a malpractice action with a contingent fee arrangement. The attorney will receive no compensation unless there is a recovery in the case. One study indicates that over 400 attorney hours are spent on the average malpractice case which results in a "zero recovery" after trial. (*Contingent Fees, supra,* at p. 218, fn. 22.) Faced with the combined effect of the fee limitation and other MICRA provisions (e.g., the collateral source provisions (§ 3333.1), the $250,000 ceiling on noneconomic damages (Civ.Code, § 3333.2), and the periodic installment provision (Code Civ.Proc., § 667.7)), many attorneys can be expected to cease to represent malpractice victims with valid claims. As a result, the most severely injured clients may be unable to secure representation, especially if their cases involve complex or difficult factual issues, problems of proof, or expensive expert testimony.

* * *

* * * [R]eference to the New Jersey and New York schemes highlights two of the most pernicious aspects of section 6146.

First, section 6146 singles out and imposes a burden on only one narrow subclass of personal injury victims. Attorneys may still find ample unrestricted work elsewhere. When the risks and cost associated with general personal injury work are not as great as for medical malpractice, and the potential compensation is much greater, common sense tells us that attorneys will abandon the medical malpractice field. By contrast, the New Jersey and New York schemes restrict broad fields of practice, leaving attorneys little room for escape.

Second, unlike the New Jersey and New York schemes, section 6146 has no provision for higher fees in exceptionally difficult cases. Section 6146 would prohibit a plaintiff from exceeding the limits even where the difficulty of his or her case is so great that a lawyer could not be retained at the specified maximums.

Section 6146 violates due process because it is not sufficiently related to the purposes it was enacted to achieve. Instead of protecting plaintiffs' recoveries, it operates to reduce them. Instead of reducing the number of frivolous claims, it restricts the number of meritorious claims by limiting medical malpractice victims' access to adequate representation.

Simple calculations indicate that section 6146 will often operate to discourage litigation in a manner which results in a *reduction* rather than an increase in a plaintiff's recovery. An example serves to illustrate the point. This example assumes a medical malpractice case which would result in a $250,000 verdict after trial.

Studies indicate that plaintiffs who settle before trial receive approximately 75 percent of their potential verdict. [ ] Plaintiffs and amici note that, prior to MICRA, most plaintiff attorneys employed contingent fee agreements in which the attorney received a greater percentage of the recovery if the case proceeded to trial than if it settled before trial—typically 25 percent to 33 percent if the case settled and 40 percent or more if the case went to trial.

* * *

Hence, after MICRA, if the case settles before trial, the attorney's compensation is not significantly less than if the case had gone to trial. However, the plaintiff's recovery is reduced by almost $55,000. The plaintiff in a malpractice case which settles before trial may recover little more than half his or her actual damages—a smaller percentage and less in absolute terms than would have been received prior to the enactment of section 6146.

This illustration demonstrates how section 6146 exacerbates the conflict of interest between plaintiffs and their attorneys in contingent fee arrangements. [ ] After MICRA, although a plaintiff might significantly increase his or her recovery by going to trial, the marginal increase in attorney fees might not cover the expenses involved in producing expert witnesses, marshalling exhibits, and conducting the trial itself. The pressure on a plaintiff's attorney to settle a meritorious case before trial is overwhelming.

* * *

While discouraging frivolous and meritless suits is a legitimate state interest, there is no evidence that the number of frivolous claims in the medical malpractice field is high, or that such claims contribute to the cost of medical malpractice premiums. On the contrary, the difficulty in proving medical malpractice and the high risk of zero recovery make attorneys very selective about the cases they are willing to pursue. [ ] Even insurers have acknowledged that attorneys reject the vast majority of malpractice claims they see. [ ]

The absence of any evidence that prior to the enactment of MICRA there was an inordinate number of frivolous medical malpractice claims filed strongly suggests that section 6146 actually operates to discourage the filing of *meritorious* claims. The attempt to reduce malpractice premiums by reducing the number of meritorious malpractice claims filed is exactly the sort of "arbitrary and oppressive" legislative action which the due process guarantees must operate to prevent. [ ]

* * *

The attorney fee limitations imposed by section 6146 reduce plaintiffs' recoveries, exacerbate the conflict of interest between attorneys and their clients, and restrict the filing of meritorious claims. The statute does not bear a reasonable relationship to the legislative purposes of protecting plaintiffs' recoveries and lowering malpractice premiums. Thus, it violates the due process guarantees of the state and federal Constitutions.

* * *

Notes and Questions

1. What is the intended purpose of the California fee schedule for contingency fees? Is it to discourage the filing of so-called frivolous claims? Reformers hoped to discourage attorneys from pursuing cases with a high potential award but a low probability of recovery, and to increase the share of a large recovery that ends up in the plaintiff's pocket, rather than the lawyers. What effect will the schedule have on a plaintiff lawyer's incentives to select cases? What kind of cases will be avoided?

2. One recent study concluded that attorney fee controls affect severity of claims, but not premiums, a result that is opposite the intended effect.

This suggests that attorneys may be screening out the small cases and concentrating on cases with greater expected payments; that is, the small cases may no longer be worth their effort, because of large fixed costs of investigation and litigation, even though sliding scales allow a higher percentage fee for small recoveries. However, frequency does not show a corresponding decline and no effect on premiums appears. Thus, we would treat conclusions about this reform tentatively.

Zukerman, Bovbjerg, and Sloan, Effects of Tort Reforms and Other Factors on Medical Malpractice Insurance Premiums, 27 Inquiry 167, 180 (1990). Should this finding be relevant to the constitutional issues? If so, how?

c. *State Constitutional Provisions*

State constitutional law may also be invoked to challenge tort reforms. The right to trial by jury can be asserted to challenge administrative mechanisms that aim to either supplant a jury's resolution of the plaintiff's claims, or to replace the jury completely. Elective arbitration, as in Michigan, substitutes for the common law jury, and screening panels condition the right to a trial upon submission of a claim to the panel. Jury right attacks have generally not been successful where the right to a jury trial was not completely abrogated for malpractice claims. In Keyes v. Humana Hospital Alaska, Inc., 750 P.2d 343 (Alaska 1988), the court held that the panel decision was an expert opinion, to be evaluated by the jury in the same manner it would evaluate any expert's opinion. Accord, Beatty v. Akron City Hospital, 67 Ohio St.2d 483, 424 N.E.2d 586, 21 O.O.3d 302 (1981) (jury remains "final arbiter of all the factual issues presented.") See also Johnson v. St. Vincent Hospital, Inc., 273 Ind. 374, 404 N.E.2d 585, 598 (1980) (panel opinions are evidence to "be considered together with all other evidence presented in arriving at a true verdict or decision."). But see Mattos v. Thompson, 491 Pa. 385, 421 A.2d 190 (1980) (statistical evidence as to delays created by arbitration, held to infringe on the right to a jury); Simon v. St. Elizabeth Medical Center, 355 N.E.2d 903 (Ohio Common Pleas 1976).

Caps on damages have also been attacked as violating a plaintiff's right to a jury trial, or as invading the province of the jury as trier of fact. In Boyd v. Bulala, 647 F.Supp. 781 (W.D.Va.1986), the United District Court had ruled that Virginia Code 1950, § 8.01–581.15, which limits awards in medical malpractice cases to $750,000, violated the federal constitutional right to a jury trial, under the Seventh Amendment, and the right to a jury trial provided by Article 1, section 11 of the Virginia Constitution. The court found that the assessment of damages is a fact issue reserved for jury resolution, and a cap that limits that function is a limitation on the jury's role.

The U.S. Court of Appeals for the Fourth Circuit, in Boyd v. Bulala, 877 F.2d 1191 (4th Cir.1989), reversed the District court:

> As the *Etheridge* court pointed out ... it is not the role of the jury to determine the legal consequences of its factual findings ... That is a matter for the legislature, and here, the Virginia legislature has decided that as a matter of law, damages in excess of $750,000 are not relevant. In so doing, it has not violated the seventh amendment. To paraphrase *Etheridge,* once the jury has made its findings of fact with

respect to damages, it has fulfilled its constitutional function; it may not also mandate compensation as a matter of law.

See Comment, Interpretation of Virginia's Medical Malpractice Act: Boyd v. Bulala, 12 Geo.Mason U.L.Rev. 361 (1990).

In Sofie v. Fibreboard Corp., 112 Wash.2d 636, 771 P.2d 711 (1989), the Washington Supreme Court concluded that the state's damage cap impermissibly invaded the province of the jury. The court concluded that the jury's role extends to the remedies phase of litigation, and unless the underlying substantive law was changed, a damage cap impermissibly deprived a jury of its role in setting damages. A damage cap "adjusts" the jury's award, and "pays lip service to the form of the jury but robs the institution of its function." (771 P.2d at 721.) See also Kansas Malpractice Victims Coalition v. Bell, 243 Kan. 333, 757 P.2d 251 (1988). The United States Supreme Court seems to interpret the Seventh Amendment differently. See Tull v. United States, 481 U.S. 412, 426 n. 9, 107 S.Ct. 1831, 1840 n. 9, 95 L.Ed.2d 365 (1987) ("Nothing in the Amendment's language suggests that the right to a jury trial extends to the remedy phase of a civil trial * * * We have been presented with no evidence that the Framers meant to extend the right to a jury to the remedy phase of a civil trial.")

Any administrative substitute for the tort system, such as the AMA proposal discussed infra, that aims to replace the civil system, including the right to a jury trial, must face a more substantial constitutional challenge. State provisions, whether involving compulsory or elective arbitration or mediation, still allow for the jury to ultimately decide the factual questions. See Beatty above. When the jury is removed altogether from the process, as in a Worker's Compensation type system, constitutional problems become more severe. Worker's Compensation systems have uniformly been held constitutional as not impermissibly burdening a plaintiff's right to a jury. The arguments for their constitutionality has been that workers impliedly consented to the statutory scheme when they accepted employment; and the system imposes a quid pro quo, or tradeoffs on both parties (strict employer liability for exclusivity of the worker's remedy). See, e.g. New York Central Railroad Co. v. White, 243 U.S. 188, 37 S.Ct. 247, 61 L.Ed. 667 (1917). Any proposed new administrative system must therefore not favor physicians more than injured patients, and some semblance of implied consent must be found. Some commentators predict that proposals that try to create new administrative schemes replacing the civil system will founder on constitutional issues. See, e.g. Reynolds, Lockwood, Smart, and Schiferi, A Constitutional Analysis of the American Medical Association's Medical Liability Project Proposal, 1 Courts, Health Science and the Law 58 (1990).

One argument that has succeeded in a few states is that challenged reforms violate the state's "Open Courts" requirement, which provide that citizens have access to the courts in all cases. Thus in Lucas v. United States, 757 S.W.2d 687 (Tex.1988) the court held that the Texas cap of $500,000 on liability violated the Texas constitution. See also Neagle v. Nelson, 685 S.W.2d 11, 12 (Tex.1985) (a statute of limitations provision in the Texas 1977 Medical Liability Act violated the Texas constitution. "The open courts provision of our Constitution protects a citizen, such as Neagle, from legislative acts that abridge his right to sue before he has a reasonable opportunity to discover the wrong and bring suit.") In Kenyon v. Hammer, 142 Ariz. 69, 688 P.2d 961, 967 (1984), the Arizona Supreme Court considered a challenge to a statute of repose that fixed the time of accrual of a malpractice action at the time of the negligent act, thus abrogating the discovery rule. Art. 18, § 6 of the Arizona constitution provided that "The right of action to recover damages for injuries shall never be abrogated, and the amount recovered shall not be subject to any statutory limitation." The court held that "Given the specific provisions of the Arizona Constitution— stronger than the open courts provisions in the Constitution of South Dakota, Florida, North Carolina, Kentucky, and Alabama—we believe that any statute which bars a cause of action before it could legitimately be brought abrogates rather than limits the cause of action and offends Article 18, § 6 * * * ".

The constitutional themes that the courts sound in these cases, evaluating reform schemes that restrict plaintiffs' common law rights, are as follows:

—the legislation fails to provide plaintiffs with a substitute remedy to obtain redress for injuries. The court in *Lucas* noted and rejected the defendants' arguments of a general benefit:

Defendants argue that there is a societal *quid pro quo* in that loss of recovery potential to some malpractice victims is offset by "lower insurance premiums and lower medical care costs for all recipients of medical care." This *quid pro quo* does not extend to the seriously injured medical malpractice victim and does not serve to bring the limited recovery provision within the rationale of the cases upholding the constitutionality of the Workmen's Compensation Act.

—caps are arbitrary, given the differences in injuries among victims;

—the burden of reducing the social costs of high premiums is forced onto only one category of injured parties;

—a special group of defendants is being singled out for special favorable attention.

d. Common Law Arguments

Arbitration and elective no-fault systems involve a contract between a provider and the patient, stipulating the method of resolution of the claim for medical injury. Plaintiffs challenging this provision argue that the provider had superior power and information, or that coercion was exercised in implementing the contract. The contracts can therefore be attacked as voidable either by statute or common law doctrine. The following case illustrates both constitutional and common law arguments against arbitration.

MORRIS v. METRIYAKOOL

Supreme Court of Michigan, 1984.
418 Mich. 423, 344 N.W.2d 736.

These cases concern arbitration of medical malpractice claims. The most significant issue presented is whether the malpractice arbitration act of 1975, M.C.L. § 600.5040 *et seq.;* M.S.A. § 27A.5040 *et seq.,* deprives plaintiffs of constitutional rights to an impartial decisionmaker. We hold that it does not.

The malpractice arbitration act provides that a patient "may, if offered, execute an agreement to arbitrate a dispute, controversy, or issue arising out of health care or treatment by a health care provider", M.C.L. § 600.5041(1); M.S.A. § 27A.5041(1), or by a hospital, M.C.L. § 600.5042(1); M.S.A. § 27A.5042(1). A patient executing such an agreement with a health-care provider may revoke it within 60 days after execution, M.C.L. § 600.5041(3); M.S.A. § 27A.5041(3), or, in the case of a hospital, within 60 days after discharge, M.C.L. § 600.5042(3); M.S.A. § 27A.5042(3), options which must be stated in the agreement. All such agreements must provide in 12–point boldface type immediately above the space for the parties' signatures that agreement to arbitrate is not a prerequisite to the receipt of health care. M.C.L. §§ 600.5041(5), 600.5042(4); M.S.A. §§ 27A.5041(5), 27A.5042(4).

For those who have elected arbitration, the act requires a three-member panel composed of an attorney, who shall be chairperson, a physician, preferably from the respondent's medical specialty, and a person who is not a licensee of the health care profession involved, a lawyer, or a representative of a hospital or an insurance company. M.C.L. § 600.5044(2); M.S.A. § 27A.5044(2). Where the claim is against a hospital only, a hospital administrator may be substituted for the physician. If the claim is against a health-care provider other than a physician, a licensee of the health-care profession involved shall be substituted.

Defendants Detroit Memorial Hospital and Dr. Bloom appeal from the holding [of the Court of Appeals] that the presence of the medical member unconstitutionally created a biased panel. * * *

* * *

No showing of actual bias on the part of a particular arbitration panel is claimed, the parties having appealed from motions for accelerated judgment and no arbitration panel having been convened. That does not prevent a party from claiming that the risk of actual bias is too high to be constitutionally tolerable. * * * Included in those situations is that of a decisionmaker who has a direct or substantial pecuniary interest in the outcome of the controversy. [ ]

Such a pecuniary interest is claimed here—the decisionmaker's interest in lower malpractice insurance premiums will influence his decision towards reducing the number and size of malpractice awards. In their affidavits, the underwriters averred that physicians and hospital administrators have a vested interest in the medical malpractice claims made against others; the claims made do affect the rate of insurance premiums and the availability of insurance. Premium rates for all doctors, they averred, are generally determined by the number of all claims, settlements, and judgments against physicians and hospitals in Michigan. The effect of an arbitration award on insurance rates is thus said to be direct and substantial.

This situation is aggravated, contends plaintiff Jackson, by the composition of the advisory committee, which selects the pool of candidates from which all members of the arbitration panel are chosen. * * *

The medical part of the committee, which includes the malpractice insurance carriers and health-care providers, has a direct interest in reducing the number and size of malpractice awards. There is a substantial possibility, plaintiff Jackson insists, that they will select candidates who are similarly inclined.

All that has been shown here with any degree of certainty is that there is a relationship between the number and size of malpractice awards on the one hand, and the cost and availability of malpractice insurance on the other. This may be taken for granted. It may also be assumed that, because physicians and hospital administrators are concerned with the cost and availability of malpractice insurance, they are members of a class which is affected by the decision in a case between other parties.

* * *

* * * We have been shown no grounds sufficient for us to conclude that these decisionmakers will not act with honesty and integrity. We look for a pecuniary interest which creates a probability of unfairness, a risk of actual bias which is too high to be constitutionally tolerable. It has not been shown here.

Plaintiff Jackson also argues that as a class physicians and hospital administrators possess a subliminal bias against patients who claim medical malpractice.

* * * Neither physicians nor hospital administrators have professional interests that are adverse to patients or even malpractice claimants on a consistent, daily basis. Any identity of interest with respondents is not so strong as to create a subliminal bias for one side and against the other.

* * *

Plaintiffs next argue that the arbitration agreement waives constitutional rights to a jury trial and access to a court. Because these fundamental rights are waived, they say, the burden should rest with the defendants to show a valid contract, which they can only do by showing that the waiver was made voluntarily, knowingly, and intelligently. The burden of showing a voluntary waiver is not an easy one, argue plaintiffs, because the arbitration agreement was offered at the time of admission to the hospital in an atmosphere infected with implicit coercion. Additionally, plaintiffs argue that a knowing and intelligent waiver will not be easily shown because the defendants are chargeable with constructive fraud. * * *

* * *

Plaintiff Jackson contends that the arbitration agreement is a contract of adhesion, the terms of which exceeded her reasonable expectations. She claims that by not stating explicitly that court access with the right to jury trial was waived, this fact was in effect concealed and hence the contract is unconscionable.

Contracts of adhesion are characterized by standardized forms prepared by one party which are offered for rejection or acceptance without opportunity for bargaining * * * Regardless of any possible perception among patients that the provision of optimal medical care is conditioned on their signing the arbitration agreement, we believe that the sixty-day rescission period, of which patients must be informed, fully protects those who sign the agreement. The patients' ability to rescind the agreement after leaving the hospital allows them to obtain the desired service without binding them to its terms. As a result, the agreement cannot be considered a contract of adhesion.

* * *

We also reject plaintiff's claim that the arbitration agreement is unconscionable. According to the record before us, the arbitration agreement signed by plaintiff Jackson is six paragraphs long. The first sentence of the first paragraph begins, "I understand that this hospital and I by signing this document agree to arbitrate any claims or disputes". The first two sentences of the second paragraph state:

> "I understand that Michigan Law gives me the choice of trial by judge or jury or of arbitration. I understand that arbitration is a procedure by which a panel that is either mutually agreed upon or appointed decides the dispute rather than a judge or jury."

This was not a long contract covering different terms, only one of which, obscured among many paragraphs, concerned arbitration. Arbitration was the essential and singular nature of the agreement. We do not believe that an ordinary person signing this agreement to arbitrate would reasonably expect a jury trial. * * *

* * *

Finally, both plaintiffs ask that we find constructive fraud and hold that the agreements are unconscionable because of failure of the contracts to disclose the composition of the panel, the attitudes of physicians, the fact that the medical member of the panel may be intrinsically biased against plaintiffs, and the reasonable probability that malpractice rates are affected by awards in medical malpractice cases.

We decline. We do not believe that the agreements are unconscionable for failing to include plaintiffs' recommendations. Nor do we believe that defendants have breached a legal or equitable duty which has had the effect of deceiving plaintiffs, nor have defendants received an unmerited benefit. *Goodrich v. Waller,* 314 Mich. 456, 462, 22 N.W.2d 862 (1946).

* * *

[W]e affirm.

Notes and Questions

1. Is the tradeoff that the patient is asked to make a reasonable one? The expectation is that arbitration will produce quicker payouts for medical injures that occur in hospitals, even though the payments will be smaller than a jury verdict is likely to be.

2. A study of the Michigan experience concluded that:

—time between patient injury and claim closing was shorter for claims filed in court than for claims filed with arbitration (39.1 versus 41.1 months);

—expenses of defense of claims were lower for arbitration than court claims ($3,652 versus $3,914);

—the median indemnity payment for arbitration claims was less than court claims ($10,000 versus $10,875).

Applied Social Research, Inc., Evaluation: State of Michigan Medical Malpractice Arbitration Program—Summary Report 5, 6, 12 (October, 1984).

A California study looking at a group of Los Angeles area hospitals participating in an arbitration experiment found that hospitals employing voluntary arbitration had 63% fewer claims; closed claims 22% faster; and realized net savings on closed claims of 62%—41% for loss payments and 21% for investigation and defense costs, as compared to those hospitals not employing voluntary arbitration. Heintz, Medical Malpractice Arbitration: A Viable Alternative, 34 Arbitration Journal 18 (1979). Another California based study reached different conclusions, finding that the total amounts of indemnity paid per incident in arbitration and in court were not different; and that although the time from injury to closing the claim was shorter for arbitration, arbitrated cases tended to involve fewer defendants and involve less severe injuries. Ladimer, Solomon, and Mulvihill, Experience In Medical Malpractice Arbitration, 2 J.Leg.Med. 448–450 (1981).

3. See generally Saunders, The Quest for Balance: Public Policy and Due Process in Medical Malpractice Arbitration Agreements, 23 Harv.J. Leg. 267, 271–72 (1986); Terry, The Technical and Conceptual Flaws of Medical Malpractice Arbitration, 30 St. Louis U.L.Journal 571 (1986).

e. Encroachment on the Judicial Function

Many of the reform statutes circumvent existing judicial procedures. Screening panels in particular involve a sharing of judicial
power with lay decisionmakers. The panels can be viewed either as
providing merely an expert assessment of the merits of a case, or as
improperly performing quasi-judicial functions vested by the state constitution in the judiciary alone.

KEYES v. HUMANA HOSPITAL ALASKA, INC.

Supreme Court of Alaska, 1988.
750 P.2d 343.

RABINOWITZ, CHIEF JUSTICE.

Petitioner Melanie Keyes challenges the constitutionality of AS
09.55.536, which provides for mandatory pre-trial review of medical
malpractice claims by an expert advisory panel and makes the panel's
written report admissible in evidence at trial. She specifically argues
that the statute deprives her of due process of law, impairs her right to
a jury trial, and violates separation of powers principles by impermissibly delegating judicial power to members of the panel.

We hold that AS 09.55.536 survives constitutional muster and
therefore affirm the superior court's denial of Keyes' motion for a
protective order.

BACKGROUND.

Petitioner Melanie Keyes filed suit in superior court for personal
injuries arising from an automobile accident against the driver of the
vehicle in which she was a passenger and against the hospitals and
physicians involved in treating her injuries. Her complaint alleged,
inter alia, negligent diagnosis and treatment by each of the defendant
physicians. Most of the acts complained of were allegedly committed in
the emergency rooms of the hospital defendants, by physicians who
were employees or agents of the hospitals.

On September 17, 1986, Keyes filed a motion for a protective order
requesting the superior court not to present her case to an expert
advisory panel as required by AS 09.55.536,[1] based on alleged constitu-

---

1. AS 09.55.536 provides in relevant
part:

(a) In an action for damages due to
personal injury or death based upon the
provision of professional services by a
health care provider when the parties
have not agreed to arbitration of the
claim under AS 09.55.535, the court shall
appoint within 20 days after filing of
answer to a summons and complaint a
three-person expert advisory panel unless the court decides that an expert

advisory opinion is not necessary for a
decision in the case. * * *

(b) The expert advisory panel may
compel the attendance of witnesses, interview the parties, physically examine
the injured person if alive, consult with
the specialists or learned works they consider appropriate, and compel the production of and examine all relevant hospital, medical, or other records or materials relating to the health care in issue.

tional defects of the statute. The medical defendants opposed. The superior court denied the motion and thereafter appointed three physicians to serve as the expert advisory panel in Keyes' case. Subsequently Keyes filed the instant petition.

DISCUSSION.

* * *

C. Delegation of Judicial Power.

Keyes argues that AS 09.55.536 contravenes the separation of powers principles inherent in article IV, section 1 of the Alaska Constitution [22] by vesting judicial power in nonjudicial personnel. Keyes contends that the statute confers judicial authority on the members of the review panel in that they can compel the appearance of witnesses and production of documents, interview the parties, examine the plaintiff's physical condition, AS 09.55.536(b), and ultimately make factual findings and draw legal conclusions concerning issues of liability and damages.[23]

We are aware of only one appellate court that has accepted an argument like Keyes' and held a system of screening panels for medical malpractice cases unconstitutional based on its improper delegation of judicial function. In *Wright v. Central Du Page Hosp. Ass'n*, 63 Ill.2d

The panel may meet in camera, but shall maintain a record of any testimony or oral statements of witnesses, and shall keep copies of all written statements it receives.

(c) Not more than 30 days after selection of the panel, it shall make a written report to the parties and to the court. * * *

* * *

(e) The report of the panel with any dissenting or concurring opinion is admissible in evidence to the same extent as though its contents were orally testified to by the person or persons preparing it. The court shall delete any portion that would not be admissible because of lack of foundation for opinion testimony, or otherwise. Either party may submit testimony to support or refute the report. The jury shall be instructed in general terms that the report shall be considered and evaluated in the same manner as any other expert testimony. Any member of the panel may be called by any party and may be cross-examined as to the contents of the report or of that member's dissenting or concurring opinion.

22. Alaska Const. art. IV, § 1 provides in part:

Judicial Power and Jurisdiction. The judicial power of the State is vested in a supreme court, a superior court, and the courts established by the legislature. The jurisdiction of courts shall be prescribed by law. The courts shall constitute a unified judicial system for operation and administration.

Keyes identifies the separation of powers in this section, placed in opposition to the constitutional provisions which establish separate legislative and executive powers. *See* Alaska Const. art. II, § 1; art. III, § 1.

23. AS 09.55.536(c) directs the panel to make a written report answering the following questions and other questions submitted to it by the court:

(1) What was the disorder for which the plaintiff came to medical care?

(2) What would have been the probable outcome without medical care?

(3) Was the treatment selected appropriate for the case?

(4) Did an injury arise from the medical care?

(5) What is the nature and extent of the medical injury?

(6) What specifically caused the medical injury?

(7) Was the medical injury caused by unskillful care?

* * *

313, 347 N.E.2d 736, 739–40 (Ill.1976), the Illinois Supreme Court invalidated statutes empowering a panel composed of a circuit judge, a practicing physician, and a practicing attorney to make a determination as to liability and, upon finding liability, as to damages. Proceedings before the panel were adversarial, with each party entitled to call and cross-examine witnesses and to introduce evidence. *Id.* 347 N.E.2d at 738. As noted above, the parties could agree to be bound by the panel's decision, in which case judgment would be entered thereon; otherwise, each party had to accept or reject any unanimous decision of the panel, with a failure to reject being deemed an acceptance. *Id.* Whenever the parties had neither agreed to be bound nor accepted the decision, the panel judge conducted a pretrial conference and the case proceeded to trial, during which the panel's decision was not admissible. *Id.* at 738–39.

In reaching its conclusion that this system impermissibly granted judicial power to nonjudicial personnel, the Illinois court observed:

> Section 58.6 * * * provides that the circuit judge member of the medical review panel "shall preside over all proceedings of the panel and shall determine all procedural issues, including matters of evidence." But as to other issues, both legal and factual, the power and function of the lawyer and physician member of the panel are the same as that of the judge. Furthermore, the powers of the judge concerning the determination of "matters of evidence" are diluted by the provision that "The law of evidence shall be followed, except as the panel in its discretion may determine otherwise." (Par. 58.6.) Section 58.7 provides that "The panel shall make its determination according to the applicable substantive law," and by its terms, the lawyer and physician member are vested with authority, equal to that of the judge, to determine and apply the "substantive law."

Id. at 739. The court then concluded that these provisions empowered the nonjudicial members of the panel "to make conclusions of law and fact 'according to the applicable substantive law' over the dissent of the circuit judge" and thereby to exercise a judicial function in violation of the Illinois constitutional provision analogous to Alaska Const. art. IV, § 1. *Id.* at 739–40.

A critical difference between the Illinois and Alaska panel review statutes renders the foregoing reasoning inapplicable to this case: the panel's determination served as the sole basis for entry of judgment in Illinois if the parties so agreed, whereas in Alaska it serves only as an expert opinion at trial. On this basis, courts in all jurisdictions save Illinois which have faced delegation of judicial power attacks on their medical panel review statutes have upheld them. Most have relied on the maxim that "the essence of judicial power is the final authority to render and enforce a judgment," and thus found no separation of powers problems because the actions of the panel are at most advisory and its decision has no more weight than an expert opinion. [ ] We agree with this analysis.

Having found no apposite judicial authority, and no independent basis, for Keyes' claim that the panel review procedure of AS 09.55.536 authorizes an invasion of judicial function by the panel, we decline to invalidate the statute on this ground.

* * *

CONCLUSION.

Petitioner Keyes has failed to overcome the presumption that the legislature acted within constitutional bounds in enacting AS 09.55.536. [ ] She has presented no factual support for her allegations that the expert panel review procedure bears no reasonable or substantial relation to the legislature's goal to encourage settlement and reduce litigation of malpractice claims (and thereby to reduce insurance premiums and ensure the availability of medical care services at reasonable rates). Thus, the asserted deprivation of rights of due process, equal protection, and access to the courts must fail. The claimed violations of a right to a jury trial and of separation of powers principles are ill founded in light of the fact that the parties proceed to a full adjudication of their rights following issuance of the panel's opinion, which is not the sole basis for the entry of judgment but is merely one source of expert evidence available for the jury's consideration. We find no constitutional infirmity in AS 09.55.536.

Affirmed.

* * *

Notes and Questions

1. The court distinguishes Wright v. Central Du Page Hospital Association, 63 Ill.2d 313, 347 N.E.2d 736, 739 (1976), where the Illinois Supreme Court held that medical review panels were constitutionally defective in that they vested essentially judicial functions in non-judicial personnel.

After *Wright*, the Illinois legislature amended the statute to circumvent the judicial objections. The Illinois Supreme Court evaluated review panels again, along with several other reforms, in Bernier v. Burris, 113 Ill.2d 219, 100 Ill.Dec. 585, 497 N.E.2d 763 (1986). The amended statute had granted the judicial member the power to preside over the proceedings and to determine all questions of law, including matters of evidence. It required that the written decision contain the judge's conclusions of law and the panel's conclusions of fact. The court again rejected the statute.

2. See generally Macchiaroli, Medical Malpractice Screening Panels: Proposed Model Legislation to Cure Judicial Ills, 58 Geo.Wash.L.Rev. 181 (1990); Carlin, Medical Malpractice Pre-trial Screening Panels: A Review of the Evidence (Oct. 1980); Daughtrey and Smith, "Medical Malpractice Review Panels in Operation in Virginia", 19 U.Rich.L.Rev. 273 (1985). For a heated attack on Arizona's panels, see Spece, "The Case Against (Arizona) Medical Malpractice Panels", 63 Univ.Det.L.Rev. 7 (1985).

Problem: Designing State Law Reforms

You represent the Columbia Medical Association, which would like to draft model legislation for consideration in the state legislature. The Association membership is interested in three proposals. First, they would like to take advantage of the national trend toward the development of medical practice guidelines or practice protocols. They want you to draft a proposal that allows such protocols to be used as an affirmative defense by a physician in a malpractice suit or by an institutional provider when corporate negligence is alleged, to show compliance with accepted practice.

Second, the Association has concluded that pain and suffering is a source of inflation in malpractice awards. It is also aware that the state trial association is likely to successfully resist any attempt at a flat cap on pain and suffering awards. Try to develop a conceptual approach to pain and suffering that provides a schedule for such damage awards for the jury to evaluate. You have three choices. One approach might create a matrix of values that would award fixed damage amounts according to severity of injury and age of the injured party. A second approach would give juries systematic information on awards based on past experience, providing a small set of paradigmatic injury scenarios with associated dollar values. These would be nonbinding, but would guide the jury's award. A third approach would mandate fixed limits on awards of non-economic damages, but instead of a fixed cap, a system of flexible floors and ceilings would be used, varying with injury severity and victim age.

Third, the Association is interested in amending the rules of civil procedure to require lawyers to advise their clients of alternatives to litigation, such as minitrials, mediation, or court-supervised arbitration. It would like to propose legislation that would impose monetary sanctions on lawyers who fail to advise clients of alternatives or who unreasonably reject an offer to engage in alternative dispute resolution, including legal fees, if delay results.

Elaborate on each of the three areas, trying to develop a Model Act. Consider any constitutional problems that might be presented by your proposals.

III. THE EFFECTS OF REFORM: A PRELIMINARY ASSESSMENT

The Robert Wood Johnson Foundation, the federal government, and others have funded several major studies to determine the effects of reform. The results of these studies are solidifying our understanding of the benefits and the limits of reform.

A. CAPS ON AWARDS AND STATUTES OF LIMITATIONS

Caps on damage awards and reductions in the amount of time the plaintiff has to file suit have proved effective in lowering the amount paid to plaintiffs, by almost 40% according to one study of closed insurance company claims. See Sloan, Mergenhagen & Bovbjerg, Effects of Tort Reforms on the Value of Closed Medical Malpractice Claims: A Microanalysis, 14 J.Health Pol., Pol., & Law 663 (1989).

Limits on payments produce savings per claim, which insurers are passing on to physicians through lower premiums. Shortening statutes of limitations also lowers premiums by reducing the number of claims against physicians, although severity of claims is not affected. See Zukerman, Bovbjerg, and Sloan, Effects of Tort Reforms and Other Factors on Medical Malpractice Insurance Premiums, 27 Inquiry 167, 180 (1990).

B. PRETRIAL SCREENING PANELS

The use of screening panels reduced obstetrics/gynecology premiums by about 7% the year after they were introduced and about 20% in the long run. Zukerman et al. write:

> "The results suggest that panels may be more effective in screening nonmeritorious cases or encouraging out-of-court settlements in claims involving OBGs. Since OBGs are among those incurring the highest insurance expenses and are often a driving force behind reform initiatives, legislators may view this somewhat limited finding of effectiveness as adequate reason for establishing panels." Id at 176.

The study by Zukerman et al. followed up on an earlier study by Sloan, which had evaluated the effect of several reforms on the levels and rates of change in insurance premiums paid from 1974 through 1978 by general practitioners, ophthalmologists, and orthopedic surgeons. Sloan, State Responses to the Malpractice Insurance 'Crisis' of the 1970's: An Empirical Assessment, 9 J.Health Pol., Pol., & Law 629 (1985). Sloan had studied caps on liability, limits on provider payments to plaintiffs, patient compensation funds, limits on res ipsa loquitur, shortened statutes of limitations, informed consent modifications, contingency fee restrictions, collateral source modifications, ad damnum elimination, imposition of a locality rule, screening panels, arbitration, joint underwriting associations, and health care mutual insurance companies. The reforms therefore included both tort system modification and insurance modification. He concluded that only screening panels displayed a statistically significant connection to lower malpractice insurance premiums.

A 1988 study of Maryland arbitration panels concluded that the panel system had reduced the number of claims requiring formal adjudication in the courts and decreased the average length of time for resolution. They also were more likely to find in favor of claimants. See Morlock and Malitz, Nonbinding Arbitration of Medical Malpractice Claims: A Decade of Experience with Pretrial Screening Panels in Maryland (1988); Thurston, Medical Malpractice Dispute Resolution in Maryland, 1 Courts, Health Science & The Law 81 (1990).

Several earlier studies had looked at panels or arbitration. A 1980 study of screening panels concluded that the panels were effective in disposing of claims before trial, resulting in a significant percentage of claims being dropped or settled after a panel hearing, from a high of 88% of claims disposed of after a panel decision in New Jersey to a low of 38% disposed of in Virginia. Carlin, Medical Malpractice Pre–Trial Screening Panels: A Review of the Evidence, 29, 31 (1980). The very threat of a panel hearing seemed to promote early disposition of claims in some states. The panels in some states also processed claims more quickly than conventional litigation. However, some states were having problems that impaired panel operation. In particular, panels were rarely used where their use was voluntary. Carlin at 32, 37, 39.

A study by the Florida Medical Association in 1985 found that the results of panels were mixed, with some states using panels effectively and others experiencing case backlogs and administrative problems. The authors concluded that panel effectiveness was unproven, and that other court efforts such as a special malpractice court, or other procedural reforms, might be more effective. Florida Medical Association, Medical Malpractice Policy Guidebook 188 (1985). Studies by several states of the performance of their panels have not been encouraging. New Jersey and New York both recommended that a mandatory screening approach be dropped in favor of some form of voluntary system, such as optional mediation. See Perna v. Pirozzi, 92 N.J. 446, 457–59, 457 A.2d 431, 437 (1983) (presenting findings of a committee appointed by the New Jersey Supreme Court to evaluate New Jersey's panel system); see also Ad Hoc Committee on Medical Malpractice Panels, described in Bower, Malpractice Panels and Questions of Fact, 14 Trial L.Q. 4 (1982). An Arizona study found several problems with the Arizona panels, concluding that (1) settlements increased and claims filed decreased between 1976 and 1978 (the good news); but (the bad news) (2) neither the frequency or level of recovery by claimants was affected; (3) the time to process the malpractice case was lengthened by the panel system; (4) the panel system aggravated problems of difficulty and expense in handling cases, from the lawyers' and panel members' perspectives; (5) the panel hearings took longer than expected. See National Center for State Courts, Medical Liability Review Panels in Arizona: An Evaluation (1980); Spece, The Case Against (Arizona) Medical Malpractice Panels, 63 U.Det.L.Rev. 7 (1985).

C. OTHER REFORM MEASURES

Earlier studies had evaluated the effects of the reforms of the mid–1970's and 80's. One study looked at the effect of post–1975 reforms on the frequency of claims per capita, the amount per claim paid, and the claim cost per capita, using data from closed claims from 1975 to 1978 by all insurers writing malpractice premiums of a million dollars or more in any year since 1970. Danzon, The Frequency and Severity of Medical Malpractice Claims (1982). Its conclusions were:

> —states with caps on awards had awards 19% lower two years after the effective date of the statutes;

—states with contingency fee limits had a somewhat lower amount paid per claim and total claim cost;

—states eliminating the ad damnum had lower total claim costs; there was otherwise no effect on the frequency or amount paid per claim;

—states requiring collateral source offset had 50% lower awards two years after the statute's effective date, but states admitting evidence of collateral sources without required offset displayed no significant effect;

—several reforms displayed no significant effects, including pretrial screening panels, arbitration, res ipsa loquitur or informed consent limitations, and periodic payments.

Another study by Patricia Danzon updated her earlier studies, based upon analysis of claims nationally over the decade 1975 to 1984, for 49 states in some years, based on data from insurance companies that insured approximately 100,000 physicians. Danzon, The Frequency and Severity of Medical Malpractice Claims: New Evidence, 49 Law & Contemp.Probs. 57 (1986). Her conclusions are:

—the severity of claims rose twice as fast as the Consumer Price Index, a fact related to the fact that health care prices rose faster than consumer prices generally;

—claim severity continues to be higher in urbanized states, consistent with earlier studies, and is also higher in states "with a high ratio of surgical specialists relative to medical specialists," id at 76;

—severity is less in states with larger elderly populations, a fact related to the low wage loss of the elderly and the low potential for damages in a tort suit;

—no correlation was found between the number of lawyers per capita and claim severity;

—the newer data was consistent with earlier findings as to the impact of tort reforms. Statutory caps reduced average severity by 23%. Collateral source offsets appeared to reduce awards by a range of 11 to 18%. Arbitration reduced claim severity by 20%, compared to states without such statutory arbitration. Screening panels did not have a consistent effect in reducing claims severity.

What do these widely varying, and often conflicting, results mean for the future of reform of the tort system? The results reflect to some extent the limits of the studies and the relative novelty of the reforms such as panels or arbitration at the time studied. Time will tell whether procedural reforms, requiring an elaborate administrative structure, will mature and prove effective. But any ultimate conclusions as to the merits and nature of reform still depend upon the goals sought for the system. Some of the reforms, such as caps and collateral source offset, appear to have slowed the growth of awards in some states. Some reforms, such as statutes of repose, reduce claims filings over the longer term. The claims-made insurance policy and mutual insurance companies may also be a more efficient way of allocating risk and protecting insurance availability.

The reforms of the tort system were enacted with the expectation that liability insurance premiums could be lowered, or at least stabilized, by a reduction in the frequency of malpractice suits and the severity of awards in such suits. It has proved difficult to assess the impact of the reforms. The GAO Report of 1985 surveyed six interest groups as to the effect of existing reforms. No consensus was found in their results, although a majority of providers felt that caps had a major impact on the severity of judgments, and a majority of consumers felt that screening panels had a major impact on decreasing the time to close claims. GAO Malpractice Reports, supra.

An assessment of reforms of the tort system and the insurance mechanism leaves the same question: is the conventional, fault-based litigation system worth keeping for medical accidents? In the next section, several proposals are presented as potential candidates to replace the current system.

IV. ALTERNATIVE APPROACHES TO COMPENSATION OF PATIENT INJURY

Several reform proposals would substitute an alternative compensation system for the present tort system. The automobile accident debate of the sixties first focused attention on the problems of common law litigation—the costs of fact finding; the delays involved in court proceedings; unevenness in payments, whereby small claims are overpaid and large claims underpaid; the insufficiency of awards getting to plaintiffs after legal fees and administrative costs. To these criticisms, the malpractice crisis has added the psychological costs upon physicians of being sued and the alleged added social and economic costs of defensive medicine. See Bell, Legislative Intrusions into the Common Law of Medical Malpractice: Thoughts About the Deterrent Effect of Tort Liability, 35 Syracuse L.Rev. 939 (1984).

A. THE RATIONALE FOR AN ALTERNATIVE SYSTEM

THE AMERICAN MEDICAL ASSOCIATION/SPECIALTY SOCIETY TORT REFORM PROPOSAL A FAULT–BASED ADMINISTRATIVE SYSTEM [1]

Johnson, Phillips, Orentlicher, and Hatlie.
1 Courts, Health Science & The Law 6–8 (1990).

* * *

RATIONALE FOR AN ALTERNATIVE SYSTEM

FAILURE OF THE TORT SYSTEM TO SERVE THE GOAL OF COMPENSATION

Under the current tort system, many patients with small damage claims are effectively denied any compensation for injuries caused by medical negligence. For these patients, the potential recovery, and therefore the potential contingency fee, may not be large enough to attract the services of an attorney, particularly if the complexity of the case requires a substantial investment of attorney time [ ]. According to one estimate, most lawyers will not accept a malpractice case unless the expected recovery is at least $50,000. [ ] * * *

A substantial number of potential claims are never brought into the civil justice system. * * *

Moreover, the use of juries is an inefficient way to resolve medical liability disputes. Jurors must make a determination of causation in the face of considerable medical uncertainty about why illnesses strike particular individuals at particular times. In addition, jurors must decide whether the patient was treated appropriately even when experts cannot agree on that question. However, juries cannot evaluate independently the expert testimony introduced in malpractice cases to explain whether the physician failed to meet the appropriate standard of care and whether the physician's failure caused the injury [ ].

Even under the best of circumstances, jurors can never be as effective as specialized triers of fact because jurors are exposed to the medical issues only once; consequently, they cannot develop an institutional memory to aid them in deciding a specific dispute. As a result, medical issues must be redeveloped in their entirety at each trial, thereby increasing costs [ ]. Costs are also increased since juries are not required to articulate reasons for their holdings and therefore their decisions cannot be scrutinized by insurers, lawyers, and claimants to establish reliable predictions for future claims [ ]. The use of a different jury for each case also increases the likelihood of inconsistency across different cases. The uncertainty produced by the system undermines the appearance of legitimacy and aggravates the problems of availability and affordability of insurance.

The inefficiencies of the jury system lead to a very time-consuming process. According to conservative estimates, it takes an average of over 2 years from the filing of a malpractice claim until its disposition [ ]. Cases involving substantial awards may remain open for more than 10 years.

Failure of the Tort System to Serve the Goal of Deterrence

Tort liability does not adequately deter negligent behavior in medical malpractice. * * * [M]ost patients injured by malpractice never file a negligence claim. Patients often do not know whether a bad result was caused by medical malpractice, a preexisting condition, or an inherent risk of their treatment [ ]. Because negligent behavior is not closely related to the likelihood of paying an injured victim, the tort system does not communicate effective signals to physicians.

Moreover, whether an injury results in a claim depends on factors other than the health care provider's culpability. The severity of a patient's injury and the personal relationship between the physician and patient are two often-cited factors contributing to a patient's decision whether to file suit [   ]. Some patients refrain from suing because they rely upon and trust their medical care providers and do not want to disrupt a longstanding relationship [   ].

Claims that do enter the system and reach resolution may result in over deterrence. Liability may be imposed in cases where it is unwarranted. When the physician's practices are viewed in hindsight after they have caused a serious injury, it is easy to overestimate the risks and underestimate the benefits of those practices [   ]. Hence, the effect of tort liability on the quality of each physician's practices is uncertain. This uncertainty increases the use of defensive medicine and undermines deterrence [   ].

An additional failure of the tort system highlights the need for alternative deterrent mechanisms: only negligent behavior that results in an identifiable injury can lead to a claim. This aspect of the tort system, known as the "defendants' lottery," treats similar negligent behavior differently by imposing liability only on the defendant whose unfortunate victim is injured and successfully establishes a compensable claim [   ].

UNJUSTIFIABLY HIGH COSTS TO SOCIETY OF THE CURRENT TORT SYSTEM

Society pays a heavy price for the tort system's deficiencies. Over the past 20 years, the number of malpractice claims has soared. Whereas there was only 1 claim per 37 physicians in 1968, by 1975 there was 1 claim for every 8 physicians [   ]. In some states, there is now 1 claim filed for every 3 or 4 physicians [   ]. Moreover, these increases have occurred without a medical basis for their development. There also have been substantial increases in the severity of claims, measured by the size of damage awards, especially for non-economic damages [   ]. Between 1975 and 1985, the average medical malpractice jury award increased from $220,018 to $1,017,716 [   ].

As a consequence of the increases in the frequency and severity of malpractice claims, malpractice insurance premiums have skyrocketed. In the mid–1970s, insurers imposed increases in premiums of up to 500% [   ], and the total costs for medical liability insurance rose from $60 million in 1960 to nearly $5 billion in 1985.

The high costs of the system for resolving malpractice claims are exacerbated by the system's inefficiencies. According to the best evidence available, only 16 to 40 cents of each dollar paid in malpractice insurance premiums is paid as compensation for an injury caused by medical negligence [   ]. In contrast, the administrative Workers' Compensation System delivers 55 to 70% of premium dollars to the injured claimant [   ]. Moreover, the monies received by injured patients are substantially reduced by their litigation expenses, including attorneys' fees and additional sums for expert witnesses.

The civil justice system also imposes high intangible costs. Both patients and physicians are subject to the anguish and lost productivity of the tort system's lengthy proceedings [   ]. Moreover, the system's adversarial approach is fundamentally at odds with the cooperation between physicians and patients that is vital to the provision of quality medical care. Consequently, the civil justice system often compromises the integrity of the physician-patient relationship [   ].

The costs of the current tort system are threatening the availability and affordability of insurance coverage and health care in many geographic areas in the United States and in many medical specialties. Several of the major national insurance carriers, including Hartford, Fireman's Fund, and Travelers, have stopped writing malpractice insurance [   ]. In response to coverage limitations and enormous increases in premiums for certain specialties, many physicians have curtailed their practices. * * * The crisis in litigation also has led to cutbacks in emergency care. The high cost of malpractice insurance for surgeons forced five of the six hospitals in Dade County, Florida's trauma network to close their trauma units [   ], and 15 of 19 hospitals in Broward County, Florida, to close or restrict their emergency rooms [   ].

* * *

Note: Empirical Responses to Common Criticisms of the Tort System

Criticism 1. The Tort System Sends an Inaccurate Deterrence Signal

Critics often argue that physicians are haphazardly exposed to litigation, regardless of their practice or skill. Physicians believe that claim filings and jury awards bear little relationship to physician negligence. Since jury awards cast a long shadow over the settlement process, irrational jury awards dilute or cancel any deterrent effect of successful plaintiff suits. If awards are largely random, then why should providers reform their practices?

Malpractice suits do not appear to be simply random events that unfairly single out physicians, although the evidence is somewhat contradictory. The authors of a recent study of closed claims for anesthesia-related injuries concluded that payment was made in more than 80% of the claims in which patients were judged to have received substandard anesthetic care. But payment was also made in more than 40% of the claims when the anesthesia care was judged to be appropriate.

The authors concluded that the tort system has a high probability of awarding injuries caused by substandard care (true positives), but also compensates claims that physician reviewers would describe as undeserving (false positives). See Cheney, Posner, Caplan, and Ward, Standard of Care and Anesthesia Liability, 261 JAMA 1599 (1989). However, the burden of persuasion in a jury trial is not the same as the burden imposed by a physician reviewer examining insurance closed claims. It is possible that the tort system intentionally tolerates a higher level of false positives than would physician reviewers, in order to insure that the true positives are more often awarded. See also Sloan and Hsieh, Variability in Medical Malpractice Payments: Is the Compensation Fair?, 24 Law & Soc'y Rev.

997 (1990) (In closed claim review, cases where expert panel agreed that defendant was at fault were more likely to result in payment to claimant.).

Obstetrics has been of the hardest hit of the medical specialties, experiencing a high level of claims and high severity of awards. Obstetrics practice is thus a good test of the hypothesis that juries give large awards based primarily on the sympathy they feel for brain-damaged babies and their families. What evidence justifies blaming irrational juries for large obstetric awards?

One study of jury decisions in obstetric/gynecological cases concluded that (1) juries can distinguish clear violations of a standard of care, (2) they will find for the defendant readily in the absence of such a clear violation, and (3) they will find for the plaintiffs in cases where an older technology, such as the use of oxytocin to speed delivery, is abused in the face of clear limitations and contraindications.

> Only a very small proportion of injury-causing medical errors ever leads to a claim against the physician, and fewer result in a jury trial. Of the small portion of obstetrics and gynecology errors that result in a jury trial, physicians win most of the time. When physicians lose, it is likely to be in situations that do not involve specific procedures but that do involve severe injuries and in situations involving older, well-established technologies. Awards, when plaintiffs are successful, may be high, but they are not excessive, given the seriousness of the injuries. The fact that it is older, established technologies rather than never, frontier technologies that are generally involved suggests that targeted attempts at quality assurance may be more appropriate than radical tort reform in reducing obstetrics and gynecology malpractice litigation.

Daniels and Andrews, The Shadow of the Law: Jury Decisions in Obstetrics and Gynecology Cases, in Institute of Medicine, Medical Professional Liability and the Delivery of Obstetrical Care: An Interdisciplinary Review (Vol. II) 161, 191 (1989). For an interesting account by a thoughtful juror, explaining and justifying a $26 million verdict against defendant physicians in a malpractice case, see Cohen, Malpractice: Behind a $26–Million Award to A Boy Injured in Surgery, New York Magazine Oct. 1, 1990.

The evidence therefore suggests that the litigation process, while far from optimal, is neither as arbitrary nor as unfair as critics suggest. Other studies have provided recent useful data on this issue. Sloan, et al., Medical Malpractice Experience of Physicians: Predictable or Haphazard? 262 J.A.M.A. 3291 (1989) looked at claims in Florida (considered a high malpractice state) between 1975 and the first quarter of 1988. The study grouped physicians into a medical specialty group, an obstetrics-anesthesiology group, and a surgical specialty group.

—In all three groups, a large share of the total paid out by malpractice insurers involved a small number of physicians—more than 85% of payments in the medical specialty group was made on behalf of 3% of the physicians, in obstetrics-anesthesiology, more than 85% on behalf of 6%, and surgical 75% on behalf of 7.8%.

—Having a claim was a rare event for physicians in the low-risk medical specialty group, with 85% having no incident resulting in payment between 1975 and 1980 (compared to 66% of obstetrics-anesthesiology and 52% of surgical specialties having no incidents.

—Twice as many high-payment physicians as no-payment physicians had complaints filed against them with the Florida licensing board, although the sanctions were mild, and none had their licenses revoked or suspended.

—The claims experience of physicians for incidents arising from 1975 to 1980 predicted claims experience for a later period, 1981 to 1983.

—Physicians with high payments may have provided more complex procedures.

The authors looked at various indicators of quality, trying to develop links between indicators of poor quality and physician claims experience, but were unable to draw definite conclusions. Foreign medical training, medical school ranking, solo practice did not correlate to claims experience, but board-certified physicians had more adverse claims experience. Second, a market test was applied to determine if physicians with negative claims experience were more likely to change specialties, retire, or leave the state. No such trends could be found. Finally, a regulatory test was applied to see if physicians with adverse claims experience faced more disciplinary actions by the state licensing board. Fewer than 10% of the physicians with multiple suits were disciplined in any manner, and those who were received letters of guidance and probation.

The lack of a link between discipline and claims experience, according to Sloan et al., " * * * is consistent with two opposing hypotheses: perhaps physicians with adverse claims experience are not bad physicians. Bad claims experience may reflect taking on harder cases or a litigious client. Perhaps such physicians are bad, but the licensing system failed to act. Unfortunately, the data did not permit a rigorous examination of these possibilities." Id at 3297. Claims experience is therefore not at present a valid indicator of physician quality.

Tort litigation has a substantial psychological impact on physicians in excess of the diluted financial incentives created. See generally Bell, Legislative Intrusions into the Common Law of Medical Malpractice: Thoughts About the Deterrent Effect of Tort Liability, 35 Syracuse L.Rev. 939 (1984). For a general discussion of the deterrent value of malpractice suits, see Bovbjerg, Medical Malpractice on Trial: Quality of Care is the Important Standard, 49 Law & Contemp.Probs. 321 (1986). See generally Chapter 1 for an assessment of the merits of malpractice litigation as a quality assurance mechanism.

Criticism 2. The Administrative Costs of the Malpractice System are too High

Another common criticism is that the tort system's administrative costs are too high, with too little of the malpractice premium dollar going to the plaintiff in a malpractice suit. The critics correctly observe that the portion of the health insurance premium dollar that goes to a claimant is much higher that the amount returned by the tort system. Sloan et al. comment:

> An insured seeks out a high-return policy for first-party coverage; the insured's own money is returned to him under circumstances specified by contract. The insured's "entitlement" to payment and the aggregate amounts of payment are relatively clear cut. In contrast, liability insurance defends the insured against claims of negligence (mainly) and also pays compensation to third parties not involved in the insurance contract. Major inquiry by claims adjustors and possibly also by courts and lawyers must individually determine whether payment is due, and, if so, how much. Damages are multifaceted, often with uncertain prospects of future loss. A tort law and insurance system may cost "too much" for the benefits achieved, but they are very different benefits from those of health insurance, so simple comparisons do not advance thoughtful policy. Perhaps provider negligence is dealt with more efficiently and more fairly under a third-party system.

Sloan et al., id at 680.

The question for future research continues to be: is the deterrent value of the tort system worth it? Consider the comments of Patricia Danzon.

Patricia Danzon, Medical Malpractice: Theory, Practice, and Public Policy 225–227 (1985):

> * * * [T]he fault-based system is worth retaining if the benefits, in terms of injuries deterred, exceed the costs of litigating over fault and other associated costs, such as defensive medicine. * * * [W]e can make a very rough calculation of the benefits, in terms of injury reduction, that would be required to offset the additional costs of operating the tort system, rather than simply compensating victims through first-party insurance and forgoing all aim at deterrence. To make this calculation, let us assume initially that both tort and first-party programs fully compensate victims, and that 80 cents of every health insurance premium dollar reaches the patient as compensation, compared to only 40 cents of every malpractice insurance premium dollar. Thus the 40 cents spent litigating to assign fault through the malpractice system is an additional cost worth incurring only if it results in at least equivalent deterrence benefits. In other words, if the tort system deters at least one injury of comparable severity for every injury currently compensated, the deterrence benefits outweigh the additional costs of the liability system.
>
> We do not know how many injuries are actually deterred, but we can estimate the percentage reduction in the rate of negligent injury that is required. Using the 1974 estimate that 1 in 10 incidents of negligence leads to a claim and 1 in 25 receives compensation, only a 4 percent reduction in the rate of negligent injury is required to justify the costs of the tort system. If the rate of compensation per negligent injury is currently, say, twice as high as it was in 1974, then an 8 percent reduction in the rate of negligent injury would be required. Similarly, if the tort system entails significant costs other than the litigation costs considered so far—such as defensive medicine, public

costs of operating the courts, time and psychic costs of litigation to patients and providers—then the deterrence benefits would have to be higher. On the other hand, to the extent that the compensation received by victims through tort understates their willingness to pay for injury prevention, the deterrence necessary to justify the system is less.

This rough calculation suggests that if the number of negligent injuries is, generously, 20 percent lower than it otherwise would be because of the incentives for care created by the malpractice system, the system is worth retaining, despite its costs. Danzon at 225–227.

Criticism 3.   Patient Access to Health Care has been Impaired by Rising Malpractice Insurance Costs and by Physicians' Fears of Suits

Rising malpractice exposure, particularly in obstetrics, has allegedly driven physicians from practice, leaving many rural areas in particular without obstetricians. Rising premium costs have cut deeply into obstetric income, causing physicians to alter their practice patterns. It is claimed that access to care has suffered, with the malpractice system the culprit. Some states such as Virginia have enacted special legislation just to "solve" the "obstetrics" problem, primarily created by a threat by insurers to leave the state and thereby leave obstetricians without any coverage for malpractice.

Income trends suggest that real net income for all physicians has in fact held steady from 1975 to 1985, and that obstetrician-gynecologists as a group have maintained their real net income during the decade. Institute of Medicine, Medical Professional Liability and the Delivery of Obstetrical Care: An Interdisciplinary Review (Vol. I) 105 (1989) (hereafter IOM Study I). Although premium costs between 1982 and 1986 grew by 171%, the average net income of obstetrician-gynecologists grew by 21%. This may mean that these specialists are offering more services, and charging more, since professional liability premium expenses are a higher proportion of expenses for obstetricians than for other specialties, and the percentage is rising. Id at 106–107.

Rural areas have been unattractive locations for physicians for a long time. The reasons transcend malpractice costs and availability, relating as much to the amenities of daily life and the need for professional colleagues. However, the insurance premium costs for family physicians and nurse-midwives have been excessive in relation to their income, and disproportionate to their actual likelihood of being sued. Both availability of coverage and high cost has limited the availability of obstetrical care by nurse-midwives. See IOM Study I at 51. A survey of maternity care centers concluded that the access problem for low-income women is created by unconscionable practices by malpractice insurers. Insurers have imposed "astronomical rates" on physicians and midwives, rates that bear no relation to claims profiles. "In short, malpractice insurers, by denying coverage to qualified center physicians, by discriminating against more experienced physicians, and by contributing to an overall reduction in the financial resources clinics have at their disposal, have succeeded in reduc-

ing the quality and availability of care received by center patients."
Hughes, et al., Obstetrical Care for Low–Income Women: The Effects of
Medical Malpractice on Community Health Centers 59, 74 in Institute of
Medicine, Medical Professional Liability and the Delivery of Obstetrical
Care: An Interdisciplinary Review (Vol. I) 74 (1989) (hereafter IOM Study
II).

Fear of malpractice suits has reduced the willingness of physicians to
treat Medicaid patients, although little evidence exists that poor patients
sue more than other patients. The IOM study noted that while " * * * the
causal relationships between professional liability issues, changes in obstetrical practice, and access to care for low-income women cannot be precisely
documented, the mere perception among physicians that low-income wom-
en pose professional liability problems constitutes a barrier to care." (IOM
Study II at 65). Patient access to health care has thus suffered at least in
some specialties, due to insurance availability and physicians' anxieties.

Develop your own position on the rationales for replacement of the tort
system, in light of the AMA critique, the empirical data that sheds light on
some of the criticisms, and the GAO benchmarks for reform.

B. NO–FAULT REFORMS

Reform proposals aim to eliminate or reduce some of these perceived flaws of the current system. Such proposals can be categorized
in light of several central attributes. The following article offers a
framework for thinking about such reforms.

ABRAHAM, MEDICAL LIABILITY REFORM: A CONCEPTUAL FRAMEWORK

260 Journal of the American Medical Association 68–72 (1988).

* * *

Medical liability reform is essentially an exercise in choosing
variables from a series of categories representing the different components of the system. The variables chosen then can be assembled into a
single package that modifies existing law. There are five categories
from which these variables must be selected: (1) the compensable event,
(2) the measure of compensation, (3) the payment mechanism, (4) the
forum used to resolve disputes, and (5) the method of implementing the
new rights and responsibilities. Traditional medical malpractice law is
just one of many possible combinations of variables from each category.
Virtually every proposed and adopted reform of medical liability is
simply a different combination of these variables. Because each of the
five categories contains several variables, the range of reform alternatives is considerable.

THE COMPENSABLE EVENT

The compensable event is the combination of medical treatment
and resulting injury or disease that triggers a patient's right to compensation. The event may be based on malpractice, on the occurrence of a

treatment-related injury even in the absence of malpractice, or on the occurrence of a defined loss regardless of whether it is related to malpractice or treatment. For convenience, I refer to these three different triggers as *fault, cause,* and *loss.*

Fault

A medical injury caused by malpractice is the compensable event embodied in traditional medical liability law. * * * [I]n theory, malpractice is defined as the failure to conform to an accepted medical standard of performance, although in practice there is often doubt that the jury is capable of understanding and applying such standards. * * *

Cause

Instead of basing the right to compensation on the occurrence of a malpractice-related injury or disease, that right could be triggered whenever the patient suffers an iatrogenic injury or disease or some defined subset of these adverse outcomes. * * * By encompassing a range of compensable injuries far broader than those caused only by malpractice, this approach removes any fault inquiry from the compensation decision.

There are two other important implications, however, entailed in the cause-based approach to compensation. First, because iatrogenic injury is a far more inclusive notion than malpractice-related injury, cause-based compensation may radically expand the number of persons entitled to compensation. For example, one study estimated that only 17% of the potentially compensable events that occur in hospitals result in tort compensation. A system that compensated close to 100% of these injuries would either raise the overall cost of providing compensation or require a reduction in the amount of compensation payable to any given patient.

Also, it is by no means clear that a cause-based standard can be easily applied in practice. Determining what "caused" a patient's injury or disease accounts for a considerable portion of the litigation costs of the current system. * * *

Loss

An even more broadly applicable set of compensable events can be defined by reference to specified losses without regard to cause. This is the method adopted by health and disability insurance whether it is publicly or privately financed. * * *

At present, a loss-based system of compensation composed of health and disability insurance operates parallel to malpractice liability. * * * The loss-based system could be relied on more heavily or exclusively, however, if liability for malpractice were limited or abolished. This could be accomplished either by requiring the universal purchase or provision of private health and disability insurance or through expansion of the governmentally provided forms of social insurance for medical expenses. * * *

The Measure of Compensation

The second important feature of any approach to medical liability is the measure of compensation available to those who suffer compensable events. * * *

Full Tort Damages

A successful plaintiff in any tort liability suit, including those for medical malpractice, is entitled to recover compensation for all losses proximately caused by the defendant's actions. These losses normally include medical expenses and lost wages together with a sum that may vary a great deal from case to case to compensate for the conscious pain and suffering associated with these other losses. * * *

Full Out-of-pocket Losses

An alternative measure of compensation would award no sum for pain and suffering but full compensation for actual expenses incurred in connection with the compensable event. * * *

Partial Out-of-pocket Losses

Most non-tort systems of compensation do not award even full out-of-pocket losses. Rather, they tend to contain copayment provisions—floors in the form of deductibles, ceilings on amounts payable, and coinsurance requirements. * * *

"Scheduled" Damages for Specified Losses

The administrative expense of making individualized loss determinations is a cost of any of the measures of compensation discussed so far. In cause- and loss-based systems this expense is likely to be small, because payments normally are limited to objectively determinable expenses. When the losses in question are subjective, however—damages for pain and suffering payable in the tort system, for example—the cost of determining the extent of a plaintiff's loss can be high. Moreover, jury awards for similar losses are likely to vary considerably precisely because of the subjectivity of both the suffering and each jury's valuation of it.

An alternative to complete denial of compensation for such subjective losses—whether in tort suits or under other approaches—would be to award payments in a way that makes no effort to individualize. This is the compromise struck in workers' compensation, in which there is no explicit award for pain and suffering, but scheduled sums above out-of-pocket losses often are awarded. * * *

In a sense, the legislative ceilings on pain and suffering damages adopted in a number of states in the past several years are a crude example of this approach. * * *

Periodic Payment of Losses

Cutting across the preceding variables is the distinction between lump-sum and periodic payment of losses. Medical liability awards generally are paid in a lump sum to compensate for actual past and estimated future losses. * * * Such awards might of course be calculated only at the time of the trial and then be paid periodically as annuities, but they might also be recalculated periodically to avoid overpayment or underpayment. Many cause- and loss-based systems adopt this latter approach, incurring extra administrative costs to achieve greater accuracy and avoid making windfall payments. * * *

Limits on Counsel Fees

The typical medical malpractice plaintiff pays his or her attorney a percentage of any amount recovered. Since recoveries for pain and suffering are generally understood to help finance such payment, placing limits on counsel fees that can be charged plaintiffs is an indirect method of reducing the measure of compensation. * * *

THE PAYMENT MECHANISM

There are three basic approaches to the payment of compensation for injury and disease and a fourth variation that is largely a hybrid. The payment mechanism adopted depends on the party or parties selected to bear "liability" under the system in force—health care providers, patients, the government, or some combination of the three.

Third–Party Insurance

Third-party insurance is an appropriate financing mechanism when a party other than the patient is responsible for paying compensation. Thus, third-party insurance is the payment mechanism used preponderantly to pay medical malpractice judgments. Third-party insurance could also be used to finance payment under cause-based systems such as medical no-fault. * * *

First–Party and Social Insurance

In contrast, first-party and social insurance are used to finance the payment of compensation under loss-based approaches. Both these forms of insurance, however, could also be used to finance payment under cause-based systems of compensation. Under first-party insurance, patients would purchase coverage before treatment, with premiums roughly calibrated to the probability that the patient (or patients in the same risk class) would suffer a compensable iatrogenic injury. * * *

The Patient Compensation Fund

In some states, ceilings on the amounts for which health care providers are liable in malpractice suits have been adopted, but without restricting the amounts that can be paid to the successful plaintiff. This apparent anomaly is resolved by the creation of a state-operated "Patient Compensation Fund" that is responsible for the portion of any award above the ceiling. Such funds need not be limited to awards above the ceiling, however; they can be employed to finance sums awarded under any of the systems explored so far. Moreover, the method of creating and replenishing the fund might also vary, including assessments against health care providers alone, assessments against patients alone, general revenue, or some combination of these sources. * * *

THE FORUM FOR RESOLUTION OF DISPUTES

The next feature of any approach to liability/compensation issues is the forum that resolves disputes over the rights of patients and providers. This is an important issue, for the identity and qualifications of the decision maker can dramatically influence both the outcome of the dispute and the parties' attitude toward the decision.

Trial by Jury

The chief characteristic of the American jury system that impinges on the medical liability problem is the use of lay jurors. Several consequences follow from this practice. One is potential inconsistency. * * * Moreover, partly because jurors are lay people and partly for reasons of history, trials by jury are highly formal. Rules of evidence apply, information is produced mainly through questions by counsel, and jurors may not question the parties or witnesses. * * * Finally, because of the medical complexity of the issues, because of the need to educate the jury from scratch about both the facts and these medical issues, and because of the formal procedure of the trial itself, the typical medical malpractice case is preceded by years of pretrial information gathering or "discovery". * * *

The great advantage of this approach is its political legitimacy. For the most part, trial by jury in civil cases is constitutionally required at both the state and federal levels. Jury trials are accepted by the public as an important protection for the powerless as well as a means by which decisions about legal rights may be made without relying on an entrenched bureaucracy or on rule by a class of experts. In addition, the right to bring a lawsuit before a lay jury may satisfy the primitive impulse for vindication in a way that should not be overlooked. * * *

Expert Review Panels

One variation on pure trial by jury that would retain the jury is to provide an impartial expert assessment of the technical issues to the parties before the trial and to the jury during the trial. Such an assessment might encourage settlement or guide the jury if a settlement does not occur. The panel may consist exclusively of medical experts (a medical review board) or include legal or lay members as well (a screening panel). Unfortunately, experience in many states over the past decade with different versions of the expert review panel suggests that this device has minimal if any impact on rates of settlement or results at trial.

Bench Trial

This is simply a trial without a jury—that is, a trial before a judge alone. The principal difference between this approach and the use of a jury is that bench trials provide less opportunity for emotionalism and can proceed with somewhat less formality. * * *

Binding Arbitration

Under binding arbitration, an arbitrator or arbitrators chosen by the parties hear a presentation of the claim and the provider's response to it and decide the case. The recent proposal of the American Medical Association Specialty Society Medical Liability Project for fault-based arbitration is a version of this approach. Normally, the arbitrator has some expertise in the subject area of the case, and his or her decision can be appealed to a court only if there is a failure to follow the terms of the arbitration agreement. Because of the arbitrator's expertise, the proceeding can be streamlined and can be shorter than a trial by jury or a bench trial, and it is much less likely to involve emotionalism than trial by jury. * * *

Administrative Panels

Once the requirement of malpractice is eliminated as a feature of the compensable event, there is little need to use any of the above devices to determine whether that event has occurred. Typically, a cause-based system financed by health care providers would use an administrative system of compensation under which a board either in permanent existence or specially convened would determine whether the patient had suffered a compensable event and the amount of the losses suffered. * * *

Insurance Company Determination

In contrast, a cause- or loss-based system based on first-party insurance would not even require administrative panels. Health, life, or disability insurers would simply determine whether the insured compensable event had occurred and award the compensation required by the insurance policy embodying its contract with the claimant.
* * *

THE METHOD OF IMPLEMENTATION

The last determination that must be made in fashioning medical liability reform is how to implement the reformed system. There are two basic approaches: legislation and contract.

Legislation

One legislative alternative would be simply to prescribe a new mandatory system that would replace the current malpractice liability approach. By statute, a new set of variables would be adopted, and patients and health care providers would be required to act accordingly. On the other hand, legislation implementing the new system need not be mandatory; instead, it might be "elective" in one or more ways, specifically authorizing patients and health care providers to fashion their own legal relationship. Such an approach would of course require detailed description of the contract options available and the options (if any) foreclosed.

* * *

CATEGORIES AND CHOICES OF REFORM ALTERNATIVES

Compensable Event	Measure of Compensation	Payment Mechanism	Forum for Resolution of Disputes	Method of Implementation
Fault	Full tort damages	First-party insurance	Jury trial	Legislation
Cause	Full out-of-pocket losses	Third-party insurance	Expert review panels	Mandatory reform
Loss	Partial out-of-pocket losses	Taxation	Bench trial	Elective options
	Scheduled damages	Hybrid funding	Binding arbitration	Private contract
	Lump-sum payment		Administrative boards	
	Periodic payment		Insurance company decision	

Private Contract

The nonlegislative method of implementing reform is for patients and health care providers to fashion their own legal relationship by contract. Under this approach, they might adopt any combination of variables that would constitute their legal rights and responsibilities. The great advantage of this approach, of course, is that it would allow the parties freedom of choice. There are two disadvantages, however, that might be difficult to overcome: (1) It is doubtful that the courts would approve such a contractual approach in the absence of prior legislative authorization, at least in cases in which a patient's legal rights seemed to be limited rather than expanded. (2) The pure contract approach requires the agreement of both parties; in contrast, a legislatively authorized optional system could permit the replacement of malpractice liability at the election of only one of the parties in cases in which this seems desirable. * * *

THE VARIABLES COMBINED: A FULL RANGE OF REFORMS

A full range of reform alternatives can be created by combining the variables chosen from all five of the categories discussed into systems that could replace current medical liability law. The choices available are reflected in the Table. * * *

* * *

In sum, the possibilities for medical liability reform are no longer limited to tinkering with tort law by altering a few technical legal doctrines governing litigation. There is more to potential reform than merely making lawsuits more accurate, predictable, or cost efficient. Retaining the basic model of adversarial litigation is by no means the only available approach. A whole range of alternatives has developed, providing the reformer with a series of choices that must be made on the way to reform. No combination of reforms is without its problems, but no effort to adopt the most appropriate system of liability and compensation should ignore the variety of options that are available to deal with the concerns raised by the critics of reform.

1. The Virginia Reforms

The State of Virginia has led the states in implementing a no-fault system for obstetric mishaps. Effective January 1, 1988, the state enacted the "Birth–Related Neurological Injury Compensation Act", creating a compensation fund for neurologically damaged newborns.

The critical definition for compensation purposes in the Virginia statute is "[b]irth-related neurological injury". This is defined as

"injury to the brain or spinal cord of an infant caused by the deprivation of oxygen or mechanical injury occurring in the course of labor,
delivery or resuscitation in the immediate post-delivery period in a
hospital which renders the infant permanently nonambulatory, apha-
sic, incontinent, and in need of assistance in all phases of daily living.
This definition shall apply to live births only."

A claim under this Act excludes all other tort remedies, with the
exception of a suit "against a physician or a hospital where there is
clear and convincing evidence that such physician or hospital intentionally or willfully caused or intended to cause a birth-related neurological
injury, provided that such suit is filed prior to and in lieu of payment of
an award under this chapter."

Compensation under the statute is for "net economic loss" only,
including medical expenses, rehabilitation expenses, residential and
custodial care and service, special equipment or facilities, and related
travel. Loss of wages from age eighteen (50% of the average weekly
wage in Virginia), and reasonable expenses and attorneys' fees incurred
are also included. Compensation for non-economic loss, "pain and
suffering", is disallowed, as are expenses covered by insurance.

The Industrial Commission of Virginia, the state's worker's compensation commission, handles the claims filed. The Commission will
decide whether the claimed injury falls within the definition of a
birth-related neurological injury, aided by an expert panel of three
impartial physicians. This panel will operate according to guidelines
developed by the deans of the state's medical schools. A hearing must
be held within 120 days of the date of filing. One member of the expert
physician panel must be available to testify at this hearing.

Each claim filed under this program will also be referred automatically to the state Board of Medicine for evaluation to decide whether
the injury resulted from substandard care.

Physicians licensed to practice medicine in Virginia who practice
obstetrics or perform obstetrics either full- or part-time, including
family physicians, may, but are not required to, participate in the
program. Participating physicians must agree in advance with the
state Board of Medicine to submit to a review of their obstetric practice
in the case of a finding of substandard care. They must also certify to
the Commissioner of Health that they will participate in the development of a program to provide maternity care to Medicaid and other
low-income patients.

Participating obstetrician-gynecologists and family physicians will
be required to pay $5,000 into the compensation fund annually, while
all other physicians in the state will be required to pay $250 per year
into the fund. Hospital participation is also voluntary. Participating
hospitals will be required to pay $50 per delivery per year into the
fund, with an absolute cap of $150,000 per hospital per year. Partici-
pating hospitals are also to assist in the development of a state-spon-
sored maternity care program for low-income women.

Both the Virginia $750,000 cap on damages (see *Etheridge*, supra) and the Birth–Related Neurological Injury Compensation Act were responses to the availability of malpractice insurance in the state. In 1986, both St. Paul and Virginia Insurance Reciprocal had declared a moratoria on new obstetric coverage, and PHICO had terminated coverage for all physicians in groups of less than 10. Enactment of the Act in particular led to expansion of malpractice coverage by a new carrier, and the offering of larger policies by another.

It was predicted that the eligibility provisions for brain damage would apply to approximately forty live births in the state each year. In fact, only a handful of claims have qualified each year under the statute, and no claim has been filed. The definition is so narrow that only the most severe injuries are covered, and most of those eligible die as infants. Are the pressures toward participation by physician strong enough? If it is true that very few claims are being filed, what incentives exist for physicians to elect to participate? Can you suggest a redrafting of the eligibility provision to provide for better coverage? The act is now being reconsidered in the Virginia legislature. See Klaidman, Medical Malpractice in Virginia, 1 Courts, Health Science and the Law 75 (1990).

See generally Duff, Compensation for Neurologically Impaired Infants: Medical No–Fault In Virginia, 27 Harv.J.Legis. 391 (1990); Virginia's Birth–Related Neurological Injury Compensation Act: Constitutional and Policy Challenges, 22 U.Rich.L.Rev. 431 (1988). For criticisms of the Virginia system, see Epstein, Market and Regulatory Approaches to Medical Malpractice: The Virginia Obstetrical No–Fault Statute, in Institute of Medicine, Medical Professional Liability and the Delivery of Obstetrical Care: An Interdisciplinary Review (Vol. II), 115 (1989).

2. *Medical Adversity Insurance*

Medical adversity insurance, first proposed by Clark Havighurst and Lawrence Tancredi, is a system whereby a patient experiencing a medical outcome which is on a list of avoidable outcomes would be automatically compensated for certain expenses and losses, and foreclosed from any other recovery for those outcomes. Litigation or arbitration could be pursued for outcomes not covered by the policy.

The lists of adverse outcomes would be developed by panels of doctors, lawyers, and consumers. These outcomes would be clearly described to reduce the potential for claims disputes. The panels would also establish the amounts of compensation for lost wages. Pain and suffering awards could vary based on the temporary or permanent nature of the injury. Panels would periodically review covered outcomes and compensation in order to make adjustments reflecting changes in medical practice and costs.

When the adverse outcome first occurred, the patient or provider would file the claim with the insurer, who would decide whether the injury was covered. If so, it would make prompt payment. Disputes would be resolved through the courts or arbitration.

The plan as proposed would experience rate insurance premiums paid by providers, in order to create incentives for the providers to improve the quality of care, thereby reducing their exposure for the adverse outcomes listed. Provider experience under the plan would also be used to strengthen peer review within hospitals.

The original Havighurst–Tancredi proposal assumed that legislation would be needed to effectuate the plan. More recently, Havighurst has suggested that private contracts rather than legislation should be used. Under the contractual approach, providers would voluntarily contract with insurers to cover certain outcomes, which would then be paid on a no-fault basis. Patients would also contract with the providers to accept those amounts listed in the policy. This would allow more flexibility, with variations possible in both covered events and compensation amounts among providers. Noncovered injuries could be handled through the courts or arbitration.

See Havighurst and Tancredi, "Medical Adversity Insurance—A No–Fault Approach to Medical Malpractice and Quality Assurance", Insurance L.Journal 69 (1974); Havighurst, "Medical Adversity Insurance—Has Its Time Come?", 1975 Duke L.J. 1254; Tancredi, "Designated Compensable Events: A No–Fault Approach to Medical Malpractice", 10 Law, Med. & Health Care 200 (1982); Havighurst, "Reforming Malpractice Law Through Consumer Choice", 3 Health Affairs 63 (1984); Tancredi, Designing a No–Fault Alternative, 49 Law & Contemp. Probs. 277 (1986).

A newer version of the Tancredi concept is called "accelerated-compensation events" (ACEs). The central idea, as with medical adversity insurance, is that lists of medically caused injuries should be drawn up, covering those injuries that should not normally occur and are avoidable if good care is given. These lists are based on professionally selected classes of bad outcomes that medical professionals consider avoidable on a probabilistic basis. See Tancredi and Bovbjerg, Creating a Selective No–Fault System to Replace Malpractice: Methodology of Accelerated–Compensation Events (ACEs), University of Texas Health Science Center Paper (Houston Texas, 1990).

A variation on the Tancredi proposals is provided by Professor O'Connell, who has proposed a variety of elective no-fault options using a list of covered injuries and contract agreements between providers and patients. See O'Connell, No–Fault Insurance for Injuries Arising from Medical Treatment: A Proposal for Elective Coverage, 24 Emory L.J. 35 (1975); O'Connell, Neo–No–Fault Remedies for Medical Injuries: Coordinated Statutory and Contractual Alternatives, 49 Law & Contemp.Probs. 125 (1986); O'Connell, Offers That Can't Be Refused: Foreclosure of Personal Injury Claims by Defendants' Prompt Tender of Claimants' Net Economic Losses, 77 Nw.U.L.Rev. 589 (1982); Institute of Medicine Report at 43.

Notes and Questions

1. What is gained by the Tancredi proposal? It takes certain adverse outcomes out of a fault-based system, and places them in a loss-based system, most likely in the hospital setting. What are the advantages of this approach from the physician's perspective? The hospital's? The patient's?

2. How should the panels set the level below which an adverse event is judged to be avoidable if good care is given? Should national data be used, with this approach implemented on a national basis, perhaps through the Medicare program? Or should this be left state-by-state, or hospital-by-hospital? What approach do you prefer? Why?

3. Proposed Medical Offer and Recovery Act

The proposed Medical Offer and Recovery Act, H.R. Bill 3084, was introduced into the 99th Congress on July 25, 1985. It had been proposed in slightly different form prior to that as the Moore–Gephardt Bill (H.R. 5400). The GAO Malpractice Report summarized the content of the legislation as follows:

The proposal is considered a quasi-no-fault plan because, under the plan, health care providers can selectively decide to foreclose a patient's right to sue the provider for damages from medical malpractice. Under the proposal, health care providers within a designated period of time (180 days from an occurrence) can offer to pay a patient's net economic losses arising from medical injuries and, by tendering the offer, foreclose the patient's right to sue the provider for medical malpractice *except* for cases in which the provider intentionally caused the injury or a wrongful death occurred. Under the proposal, the health care provider and his or her insurer could choose which cases would be in the provider's interest to tender an offer.

Only the patient's economic losses, above amounts paid by other sources such as private health insurance, from the injury would be paid under the proposal. Economic losses include medical expenses, rehabilitation and training expenses, work losses, and replacement services losses. Reasonable attorney's fees to collect benefits would also be allowed. No compensation would be available for any noneconomic losses from the injury, such as pain, suffering, mental anguish, or loss of consortium.

* * * [T]he vast majority of payments would be made to patients as the losses are incurred rather than in lump sum. Patients would submit reasonable proof of net economic losses incurred to the health care provider's insurer, which would be required to make payments within 30 days. Payments would be available as long as the patient's injury continues. However, future payments for the injury would not be available if no payments have been made within the last 5 years. Provisions also allow the health care provider or his insurer to require the injured party to submit to a mental or physical examination if the injured party's mental or physical condition is material and relevant to compensation benefits.

The proposal requires that any lump-sum settlement over $5,000 be reviewed by the court to ensure that it is fair to the injured party.

In cases where the health care provider does not make an offer, the patient can request within 90 days that the claim be resolved by binding arbitration. Recovery from arbitration would be limited to the patient's net economic losses and reasonable attorney fees.

To participate in the program, health care providers would be required to carry sufficient malpractice insurance or post sufficient bond. This provision is designed to protect patients from providers unable to pay compensation.

The proposal includes provisions designed to enhance the quality of medical care. To participate in the program, health care institutional providers are required to report any actions adversely affecting the clinical privileges of a health care professional (other than suspension of privileges for 30 or fewer days or discontinuance of a contract) to the appropriate state health care licensing board. It also provides confidentiality and immunity from suit to those furnishing information regarding the incompetence of a health care professional to a hospital or peer review committee or health care licensing board.

The proposed legislation is designed to serve as model legislation for states to consider in enacting state legislation to encourage prompt payment of patients' economic losses. Unless a state enacts similar legislation by January 1, 1988, the program would apply to beneficiaries of federal health programs, including Medicare, Medicaid, the Federal Employee Health Benefit Program, the Veterans Administration, and the Civilian Health and Medical Program of the Uniformed Services.

Notes and Questions

1. If you represent a hospital, what problems would you see in the Medical Offer and Recovery Act? Why should a provider come forward to inform a patient that he has suffered a compensable injury? What is in it for the provider in an uncertain case? Is the doctor in charge of the case likely to admit error, so that the hospital can present its offer to the patient? How can the hospital encourage staff doctors to come forward? How might legal rules improve the possibilities of disclosure of errors?

2. One of the primary goals in a no-fault system is to reduce the cost of insurance to providers. Measured by this goal, a proposal like the Medical Offer and Recovery Act may fail. The California study in the 1970s estimated that a no-fault system in California could increase malpractice premiums 300% higher than the tort system's insurance costs. California Medical and Hospital Associations, Report on the Medical Insurance Feasibility Study (1977). A critique of the Harvard New York study likewise concluded that the costs of a no-fault system could be greater than the present tort system, when the costs of many more claims and system

administrative costs are combined. See Mehlman, Saying "No" to No-Fault: What the Harvard Malpractice Study Means for Medical Malpractice Reform (New York State Bar Association 1990).

From the insurance industry perspective, these proposals are worrisome, since there seems to be far more malpractice in the world than is ever detected or litigated. A no-fault system may set off an avalanche of litigation. For an account of such fears, see the comments of the Jerry Engelelter, government affairs officer for St. Paul's insurance, in Kleinfield, The Malpractice Crunch at St. Paul, The New York Times, Sunday, February 24, 1985 at p. 4F.

If a compensation system rewards many more claimants, particularly small ones, in an evenhanded and more rapid fashion than does the current tort system, it may well be an improvement. But it is unlikely to be a cheaper system. This suggests that we move directly to a social insurance scheme that moves financing out of the private insurance market and into the taxation structure of the government.

C. The A.M.A. Fault–Based Administrative System

The American Medical Association has proposed an administrative fault-based system for resolving malpractice claims, premised upon physician negligence. The rationale for such system was presented in section A, supra.

A PROPOSED ALTERNATIVE TO THE CIVIL JUSTICE SYSTEM FOR RESOLVING MEDICAL LIABILITY DISPUTES: A FAULT–BASED ADMINISTRATIVE SYSTEM

January 1988.
AMA/Specialty Society Medical Liability Project
Executive Summary.

The American Medical Association ("AMA"), 31 national medical specialty societies and the Council of Medical Specialty Societies have joined together to create the Medical Liability Project to propose a fair and efficient system of resolving medical liability disputes.   * * *

We have endeavored to create a system that is fair and equitable to patients and physicians alike. Medical liability is only a part of the much larger and more important issues concerning the quality of medical care being provided by physicians. Accordingly, in addition to changes in the legal standards for determining medical liability, the proposal includes specific provisions designed to enhance the state medical board's credentialing and disciplinary functions. The administrative scheme proposed in this Report recognizes that physicians, patients and the public have distinct interests which must be respected and evenly balanced in any reasonable attempt to solve the medical liability crisis.

PART I: THE ADMINISTRATIVE ALTERNATIVE TO THE CURRENT MEDICAL LIABILITY SYSTEM AND IMPROVED CREDENTIALING AND DISCIPLINARY PROCESSES

A. Rationale for the Alternative

Our proposal arises out of two basic facts. First, the current judicial system for determining professional liability does not compensate a significant number of patients who have been injured by medical negligence. Individuals who have claims which do not involve a substantial potential recovery have difficulty enlisting the services of private attorneys. Thus, the existing system imposes barriers to the courts which preclude plaintiffs from receiving any compensation for injuries caused by medical negligence.

Second, the current tort system, which relies heavily upon juries, is not optimally suited for resolving medical negligence issues. Under the current system, there have been consistent increases in the size of damage awards, especially for non-economic damages. By their magnitude, these awards are threatening the availability and affordability of insurance coverage and health care in many geographic areas in the United States and in many medical specialties. Moreover, juries have tended to award plaintiffs significantly greater amounts in malpractice cases than in cases which concern identical injuries not involving physicians. In addition, the use of juries can be a time-consuming and inefficient way to resolve medical liability disputes. Currently, less than half of the total dollars spent on malpractice insurance ever reach the injured patient.

* * *

* * * [T]he system of trial by jury has strong historical roots in this country and there are significant constitutional and political limitations on the range of alternatives to the civil justice system that can be implemented even on a limited basis. In particular, there must be meaningful *quid pro quo* provided to patients in order to justify withdrawing their claims from the jury system—as there is in no-fault automobile and workers compensation systems.

The Medical Liability Project does not suggest a general rejection of the tort system, nor does it advocate the abandonment of traditional tort reform. However, the Project has concluded that a persuasive case can be made for employing on an experimental basis an administrative alternative to the tort system for resolving medical liability disputes. The Medical Liability Project therefore proposes that in one or more states broad authority to handle medical liability disputes be granted to an existing medical disciplinary board or to a new agency so that an administrative system of medical liability compensation can be established. This Medical Board would provide several advantages to patients. The most important of these is that the system should permit more injured parties to be compensated than does the current system. At the same time, windfall damage awards would be eliminated, medical liability disputes would be resolved more quickly and efficiently, and certainty and predictability of compensation for medical liability would be increased.

B. The Claims Resolution Function

The administrative system for adjudicating medical liability can be divided into three parts: (1) the pre-hearing and initial hearing state; (2) the final decision of the Board; and (3) judicial review. The proposed system would provide a significant benefit to patients by making available to any patient who has a claim of reasonable merit an experienced attorney from the Medical Board's general counsel's office who will litigate the claim on behalf of the patient free of charge.

Under proposed pre-hearing procedures, claims reviewers from the Medical Board will quickly evaluate claims and dismiss those without merit. For claims with merit, the claims reviewers will submit the matter to an expert in the same field as the health care provider. The expert will review the claim and make a judgment as to whether it has merit. The claims reviewer also will assist the patient in evaluating the claim and any settlement offers.

If the claim is not settled, it will be assigned to one of the Medical Board's hearing examiners. In order to encourage reasonable and timely settlements, blind settlement offers by the parties will be required prior to a hearing. A party would be subject to sanctions if the outcome of the case is not an improvement over a settlement offer that the party has rejected. The hearing examiner also will oversee expedited discovery and ensure that the parties have valid expert evidence available to support their case. At the hearing itself, the examiner will have broad authority to conduct the proceedings, including authority to call an independent expert to provide assistance in deciding the case. The hearing examiner will be required to render a written decision within 90 days of the hearing. In that decision, the hearing examiner will determine whether the health care provider is liable for the claimant's injury and, if so, will determine the size of the damage award.

The hearing examiner's decision will be subject to review by the Medical Board. The Board will have discretion to award fees and costs incurred in an appeal if the appeal presented no substantial question. The Medical Board will hear these cases as an appellate body in panels of three members. The Medical Board will make a full independent determination whether the health care provider's conduct was inadequate and caused the claimant's injury. Appeal from the Medical Board's decision will be to the intermediate appellate court of the state, where the review will be limited to whether the Board acted contrary to statute or the Board's own rules.

This proposed scheme will provide experienced and expert personnel at every level in the decision-making process. Over time, they should be better able than a jury to evaluate medical negligence claims. In addition, the involvement of the board will increase the ability of the decision-making process to be consistent in both liability determinations and the size of damage awards. The proposed administrative system also should be able to resolve disputes more quickly than the current system and thereby save both plaintiffs and defendants the substantial expense incurred in litigating cases for years in court.

In addition to acting as an adjudicator of medical liability claims, the Medical Board also will develop rules and substantive guidelines to complement the statutory standards. The Board will have administrative authority to initiate rulemaking and to solicit public comments. A rule promulgated by the Board will have the force of law and will be subject to judicial review by an appellate court to determine if it is arbitrary, capricious or in excess of the Medical Board's authority.

C. The Performance Monitoring Function

1. In conjunction with its expanded authority to handle medical liability claims, the Board's performance monitoring function will be strengthened. Specifically, all settlements and awards based on medical liability will be reported to the Board's investigative branch. This does not mean that every or even many liability determinations will lead to disciplinary actions. What it means is that every liability determination will give rise to an initial screening of the physician's practices as reported to the Medical Board. The primary purpose of this endeavor, as with all performance monitoring, will be education and rehabilitation. Thus, our proposal is intended to enhance the Board's ability to discover physicians who are impaired, lacking appropriate medical skills or otherwise unable to provide acceptable medical care.

2. In conjunction with the proposals for monitoring physician performance by the Medical Board, our proposal calls for enactment of three categories of changes designed to further strengthen physician credentialing. First, reporting requirements will be increased by requiring hospitals and other health care institutions to conduct periodic physician performance reviews (a modified version of those required by the Joint Commission on the Accreditation of Healthcare Organizations) and to report to the Medical Board any conclusion that a physician's performance has been substandard. Insurers will be required to report cancellations and failures to renew for reasons that are not class based. All physicians will be required to report instances of suspected incompetence, impairment, or drug or alcohol dependence to the hospital credentials committee or other credentialing entity. In order to facilitate physician reporting, the state will provide immunity to physicians who report suspected problems in good faith. All of these reporting requirements are designed to increase substantially the amount of information available on physician performance.

Second, this information must be maintained in a form that is accessible to those who conduct professional review activities under the proposed system. To facilitate this process, the Medical Board will create and maintain a clearinghouse (or utilize the one established pursuant to the Health Care Quality Improvement Act of 1986) for reports from insurers, reports from hospitals and other entities and disciplinary actions taken by other states. Much of the information that will be collected under this proposal overlaps with the required reporting under current federal law. The licensing board will review this information, on a routine basis, every two years. Immediate review is required in the event of certain negative reports. The Board will also have authority to conduct an on-site review of the medical practices of all physicians against whom a medical liability determination (or settlement) has been made where there is reason to believe that the physician's practices pose a threat to patient health. In addition, certain credentialing entities, such as hospitals, will be required to check with the clearinghouse in connection with credentialing and privilege reviews.

Finally, the Project calls for the furtherance of quality assurance/risk prevention goals by requiring all physicians to complete a number of continuing medical education "credit hours" per year. A certain percentage of these hours must be directly relevant to clinical practice. In addition, all physicians will be required to participate in a risk management program. This change is designed to ensure that physicians maintain and enhance their professional skills.

In addition to the settlements and awards that are automatically reported, performance complaints—from hospitals, physicians, the public or employees of the Medical Board—will be sent to a claims reviewer at the Board for investigation. As with claims of medical liability, the claims reviewer will evaluate these complaints and, if appropriate, make a recommendation to the Board's general counsel's office to pursue complaints that appear meritorious. A member of the general counsel's office will then make a decision whether to initiate a disciplinary charge. Once a disciplinary charge is initiated, a member of the general counsel's office will prosecute the charge before a hearing examiner who, after an appropriate due process proceeding, will make a decision as to what, if any, action is appropriate. The examiner's action is subject to review by the Board, which is required to provide notice of any disciplinary action to credentialing entities, insurers and other state Medical Boards.

D. The Structure of the Board

In order to perform the complex and sensitive functions outlined above, the existing Medical Boards will be restructured or a new agency will be created. Membership on the Board will have to become full time, probably for a five year term. Members will be selected by the governor—from a list of nominees selected by a nominating committee—and approved by the legislature. The Project recommends a seven person Board, of which at least two but no more than three members are physicians. It is also crucial that the Medical Board members be widely recognized as experienced and neutral, and that they be committed to attempting a bold new approach to the problems of medical negligence. To ensure the Board's quality, all of its employees, from claims reviewers to hearing examiners, must be selected and retained on the basis of their ability and commitment to resolving claims efficiently and fairly.

Proper implementation of the administrative model also will require that substantial issues of finding be addressed. With respect to the increased funding requirements of the Board itself, because of the substantial benefits to the public and expected lower overall costs, use of general revenue will be necessary and appropriate. In addition, the state could make an initial assessment against insurance companies, which provide medical liability insurance within the state, or physicians and other health care providers.

PART II: THE LEGAL ELEMENTS OF MEDICAL LIABILITY

In order to ensure that the administrative model of medical liability passes constitutional muster, it will be necessary to codify the liability rules to be applied by the Medical Board under the administrative system. It will not be enough simply to incorporate by reference existing common law standards. The statute establishing the Medical Board will have to define specifically the standards under which a claim for medical liability is established, although as noted previously, the Board will be expected to exercise its rulemaking authority to fill in the interstices of the statute. The need for codification of the rules governing medical liability provides an opportunity to revise existing rules in a way that furthers the patient's interests in fair compensation, the physician's interest in predictable awards and the public's interest in standards of liability and damages that can be consistently and efficiently applied. Set forth below is a summary of the most important proposed rules of medical liability.

The rules governing standard of care based on custom and locality would be abolished in favor of a standard that focuses on whether the challenged actions fall within a range of reasonableness, to be determined by reference to the standards of a prudent and competent practitioner in the same or similar circumstances. The hearing examiner would be required to consider a variety of factors in determining the range of reasonableness, including the expertise of and means available to the health care provider, the state of medical knowledge, the availability of facilities and access to transportation and communications facilities. With respect to proof of liability, the statute also would set standards for evidentiary matters such as the qualifications of experts, the use of manufacturer's instructions on drugs and medical devices and the use of medical literature.

A significant modification in the causation standard is also proposed. Traditionally, recovery has been denied unless the physician was at least 50% responsible for the patient's loss. The causation standard would be modified to allow recovery if the physician's negligence was a "contributing factor" in causing the injury. Damages under this standard would be apportioned according to the physician's degree of fault.

The informed consent doctrine would be codified under the current "minority" rule which requires that the adequacy of the disclosure should be measured from the perspective of the reasonable patient. The privilege to withhold information (for therapeutic reasons) and standards for determining individual responsibility for disclosure also would be included in the statutory "informed consent" doctrine.

In the area of damages, non-economic damages (and punitive damages) would be capped at an amount that is tied to a percentage of the average annual wage in the state. Special damages would be awarded under a series of guidelines designed to ensure that those damages represent a realistic "replacement cost." For example, in determining the "lost income" of an unemployed minor, the hearing examiner would be required to award damages based on the average annual income in the state multiplied by the average work life expectancy, absent clear and convincing proof that the loss would be greater or smaller.

The rule of joint and several liability would be abolished so that defendants would be liable for damages only in proportion to their actual liability. In addition, any award of future damages, where the present value of such damages exceeds $250,000, would be made in accordance with a periodic payment schedule. Finally, damages generally would be reduced by collateral source payments.

Notes and Questions

1. Is the AMA proposal likely to speed up and simplify the process of tort litigation? What are its advantages? Consider how injured patients now enter the torts process and find an attorney. Does the AMA proposal improve the process for smaller injuries?

What drawbacks do you see for plaintiffs in the structure proposed? How would you compare the administrative costs of this governmental structure to the costs of the judicial system in handling malpractice cases? As the system is still fault-based, what are its sources of administrative efficiency? How does the AMA proposal measure up to the benchmarks for evaluating reforms, discussed supra.

2. Vermont is considering a medical malpractice compensation board modelled after the AMA proposal. See Senate Bill 205, introduced in 1989. Vermont has on average four malpractice filings per year, which might lead one to wonder as to the administrative savings or other benefits that might be achieved by such a new board.

3. The full text of the AMA proposal can be found in AMA/Specialty Society Medical Liability Project, Tort Reform Codification: Model Medical Liability and Patient Protection Act, 1 Courts, Health Science and the Law 87 (1990) (hereafter Courts). Its relevance to the obstetrics crisis is discussed in Phillips and Esty, A Fault–Based Administrative Alternative for Resolving Medical Malpractice Claims: The AMA–Specialty Society Medical Liability Project's Proposal and Its Relevance to the Crisis in Obstetrics, Institute of Medicine, Medical Professional Liability and the Delivery of Obstetrical Care (Vol. II) 136 (1989). Considerations of the constitutionality

of the AMA proposal are found in Reynolds et al., A Constitutional Analysis of the American Medical Association's Medical Liability Project Proposal, 1 Courts 58 (1990). The proposal is sharply criticized in Peters, Critique of the American Medical Associations Model Liability and Practices Reform Act, 1 Courts 51 (1990) and Bovbjerg, Reforming a Proposed Tort Reform: Improving on the American Medical Association's Proposed Administrative Tribunal for Medical Malpractice, 1 Courts 19 (1990).

4. The only Federal no-fault program now in operation covering a health care related injury is the National Childhood Vaccine Injury Act of 1986. It covers solely those individuals injured or killed by vaccines. It is effective as of October 1, 1988. The program requires a petition to the U.S. Claims Court and an adjudication by that court. The petitioner must elect to accept or reject the judgment of the court. Acceptance bars any tort suit against the manufacturer. The federal government will pay compensation to those who develop specified symptoms or reactions to a vaccine within specified periods of time and suffer a vaccine-related injury that lasts for at least six months. See 42 U.S.C.A. § 300aa–1 et seq., Pub.L. 99–660, tit. III, § 311(a), 100 Stat. 3756 (Nov. 14, 1986).

For an account of the program, and its current operation, by a Special Master who handles petitions filed under the Act, see Hauptly and Mason, The National Childhood Vaccine Injury Act: The Federal No–Fault Compensation Program That Gives a Booster for Tort Reform, 37 Fed.Bar News & J. 452 (1990). See also Prins–Stairs, The National Childhood Vaccine Injury Act of 1986: Can Congressional Intent Survive Judicial Sympathy for the Injured?, 10 J.Leg.Med. 703 (1989); Lenchek, "A Shot in the Arm: The National Childhood Vaccine Injury Act of 1986," 3 The Washington Lawyer 24 (1989).

D. SOCIAL INSURANCE

The last set of proposals draws upon the experience of the United States with the Worker's Compensation System, and that of other countries with pervasive social welfare systems. Such a major reform would achieve the advantages of the other three proposals, plus the advantage of a pure insurance system funded out of general tax revenues.

The common characteristics of such systems, as summarized by the GAO, are:

* Programs are established on the premise that society is better able to bear the cost of adverse outcomes than the injured party.

* Compensation is usually predetermined and limited in amount and duration.

* Benefits are scheduled, that is, a standard formula is applied to the same types of injuries.

* An administering agency processes and validates claims and makes payment of the benefits.

* Determination of fault is usually irrelevant.

* Compensation is essentially automatic for covered losses.

* General tax revenues would fund a "pure" social insurance system.

New Zealand's Accident Compensation Act, effective in 1974, removed all damage claims for accidental injuries from the tort system. All New Zealand residents are covered at all times. The compensation available includes payment for loss of earnings (80% of average weekly earnings at the time of the accident, with a limit of about $340 U.S. dollars per week); reasonable costs of medical treatment; lump sums for permanent disability and pain and suffering and payments to a dependent spouse (with limits on the lump sums), payment to dependents for loss of support, and a variety of other expenses. The Accident Compensation Corporation administers the program. An injured person must file a claim with the Corporation, which then decides whether the claim is covered and if so, how much should be paid. The decision can be appealed to the courts. Forty percent of the claims for medical injury are denied, and awards are generally processed promptly.

Under the New Zealand system, providers help patients to collect compensation. They have an incentive to help their patients qualify for compensation under the no-fault system to avoid direct liability.

See Accident Compensation Corporation, Accident Compensation Coverage—The Administration of the Accident Compensation Act 9 (7th Ed.1983); GAO Malpractice Report at 155; Gellhorn, Medical Malpractice Litigation (U.S.)—Medical Mishap Compensation (N.Z.), 73 Cornell L.Rev. 170 (1988).

Notes and Questions

1. What tradeoffs do the various proposals make, compared to the traditional litigation model? What is lost with a straight social insurance approach?

2. From the perspective of a state legislator who may have to vote to finance such proposals, what problems do you foresee?

3. For a critical perspective on the above reform proposals, see Henderson, The New Zealand Accident Compensation Reform, 48 U.Chi.L. Rev. 781 (1981). Generally, see Law, A Consumer Perspective on Medical Malpractice, 49 Law & Contemp.Probs. 305 (1986).

4. The Swedes and the Finns have also created a self-contained, separate patient compensation scheme. See M. Rosenthal, Dealing with Medical Malpractice: The British and Swedish Experience (1988); Oldertz, The Swedish Patient Insurance System—Eight Years of Experience, 52 Med.–Legal J. 43 (1983); Jost, Quality Assurance in Medical Practice: An International Comparative Study (1990); Braham, No-fault Compensation Finnish Style, Lancet 733 (Sept. 24, 1988)

Problem: Designing a New Approach

You are a lobbyist for the Association of State Public Health Officials, a group which is concerned about the availability and quality of care received by the poor, the rural poor in particular. You are familiar with the new proposals in Congress and in the academic literature. You have been asked by the group to prepare a position paper in which you develop a position for or against the A.M.A. proposal.

Describe the position of poor plaintiffs under the common law litigation system, the goals against which you will measure the proposal, and the strengths and weaknesses of the A.M.A. proposal.

Chapter 5

ORGANIZING HEALTH CARE DELIVERY

INTRODUCTION

Issues of quality, access, cost control and patients' rights inform the legal context for the private business relationships of health care providers and the legal treatment of the structure of health care organizations. This chapter examines some of the legal issues in organizing health care delivery, highlighting those areas in which business relationships in health care are treated differently from those in other service industries.

The chapter begins by considering under what circumstances, if any, health care institutions should have the benefit of exemption from taxation. The case in this first section also provides an introduction to the modern structures of institutional health care delivery. The second section focuses on the legal structure for professional relationships within health care organizations, and ends with an examination of legal issues in the organization of extra-institutional primary care medical practice.

I. HEALTH CARE FACILITIES AS CHARITIES

Eighteenth and nineteenth century hospitals were supported primarily by charitable contributions and provided care to poor sick people who had some chance of recovery. Wealthy persons received medical care in their own homes. In the early twentieth century, the development of aseptic practices, the increasing success of surgery, and the professionalization of nursing eventually made the hospital the preferred location for medical treatment. Medical goals and objectives replaced the earlier religious goals as the primary focus of the hospital. See generally, P. Starr, The Social Transformation of American Medicine (Basic Books 1982) and E. Friedson, The Hospital in Modern Society (Free Press 1963).

The active treatment of acute illness costs far more than the room, board and care provided in hospitals of previous centuries. Increased costs and a broader base of patients desiring hospital-based care have led to substantial government payment programs and higher payments from patients and their insurers. In turn, hospital receipts from government and insurers have displaced philanthropy as the primary source of income. In 1988, over half of U.S. hospitals were not-for-profit and 18% were for-profit, with the remainder owned by governments. In contrast, in 1985, only 19.5% of nursing homes were nonprofit and 75% were proprietary.

In the past decade, not-for-profit hospitals have responded to increased competition and cost containment pressures by engaging in strategies that are similar to those used by for-profit enterprises. In the current stage in the changing nature of health care delivery, not-for-profit hospitals have to be both charitable and businesslike. The balance between business and charity is a critical issue in the tax-exemption for hospitals and other health care facilities.

Tax exemption can refer both to exemption from state and local taxes (such as sales tax, real estate tax and state corporate income tax) and from federal corporate income tax. Requirements for exemption from state taxes vary among the states and depend upon the particular type of taxation involved. Exemption from federal corporate income taxation is governed by § 501(c) of the Internal Revenue Code. Although a great variety of organizations qualify for tax-exempt status under one of the more than twenty major subsections of 501(c), the most desirable of the categories is the 501(c)(3) organization because it alone allows contributions to the exempt organization to be tax deductible for the donor and qualifies the organization for other incidental benefits. In order to qualify for 501(c)(3) status, a hospital must meet an "organizational test," which requires that the hospital's charter limit it to exempt purposes, and an "operational test," which requires that the hospital be operated primarily for exempt purposes. "Charitable," "religious" or "educational" purposes qualify as exempt purposes. Some not-for-profit hospitals qualify for their tax-exempt status as religious organizations. Others must qualify as charities.

Tax exemption is commonly viewed as a public subsidy to the exempt organization, especially when "revenue enhancement" is a government priority. One study estimates the value of exemption from the corporate tax for hospitals at $1.6 billion and the full federal subsidy at over $4 billion. Copeland and Rudney, Federal Tax Subsidies for Not–for–Profit Hospitals, Tax Notes, 3/26/90 p. 1559. This view of tax exemption as subsidy raises two questions. Is the exemption beneficial to the public in general? Is the exemption fair to the exempt organization's competitors?

Each of these questions requires an examination of the distinguishing characteristics of not-for-profit health care. The most prominent general requirement is that the exempt organization be "charitable." The case of *Intermountain Health Care* discusses the standards of charitability in the context of modern tax-exempt hospitals with a particular focus on their duty of providing access to health care as a *quid pro quo* for the public subsidy they receive. The question of competition with for-profit providers most often arises when tax-exempt health care providers behave like for-profit providers in establishing commercial ventures. Under the Internal Revenue Code, federally tax-exempt organizations are restricted in ways that for-profit providers are not. These restrictions serve a variety of policies, but one major concern is to prevent tax-exempt providers from using their public subsidy as a head start in competing in the health care marketplace.

A. CHARITABLE PURPOSES

UTAH COUNTY v. INTERMOUNTAIN HEALTH CARE, INC.

Supreme Court of Utah, 1985.
709 P.2d 265.

DURHAM, JUSTICE:

Utah County seeks review of a decision of the Utah State Tax Commission reversing a ruling of the Utah County Board of Equalization. The Tax Commission exempted Utah Valley Hospital, owned and operated by Intermountain Health Care (IHC), and American Fork Hospital, leased and operated by IHC, from *ad valorem* property taxes. At issue is whether such a tax exemption is constitutionally permissible. We hold that, on the facts in this record, it is not, and we reverse.

IHC is a nonprofit corporation that owns and operates or leases and operates twenty-one hospitals throughout the intermountain area, including Utah Valley Hospital and American Fork Hospital. IHC also owns other subsidiaries, including at least one for-profit entity. It is supervised by a board of trustees who serve without pay. It has no stock, and no dividends or pecuniary profits are paid to its trustees or incorporators. Upon dissolution of the corporation, no part of its assets can inure to the benefit of any private person.

* * *

* * * These [tax] exemptions confer an indirect subsidy and are usually justified as the *quid pro quo* for charitable entities undertaking functions and services that the state would otherwise be required to perform. A concurrent rationale, used by some courts, is the assertion that the exemptions are granted not only because charitable entities relieve government of a burden, but also because their activities enhance beneficial community values or goals. Under this theory, the benefits received by the community are believed to offset the revenue lost by reason of the exemption.

* * *

An entity may be granted a charitable tax exemption for its property under the Utah Constitution only if it meets the definition of a "charity" or if its property is used exclusively for "charitable" purposes. Essential to this definition is the element of gift to the community.

* * * A gift to the community can be identified either by a substantial imbalance in the exchange between the charity and the

recipient of its services or in the lessening of a government burden through the charity's operation.

* * *

Given the complexities of institutional organization, financing, and impact on modern community life, there are a number of factors which must be weighed in determining whether a particular institution is in fact using its property "exclusively for * * * charitable purposes." Utah Const. art. XIII, § 2 (1895, amended 1982). These factors are: (1) whether the stated purpose of the entity is to provide a significant service to others without immediate expectation of material reward; (2) whether the entity is supported, and to what extent, by donations and gifts; (3) whether the recipients of the "charity" are required to pay for the assistance received, in whole or in part; (4) whether the income received from all sources (gifts, donations, and payment from recipients) produces a "profit" to the entity in the sense that the income exceeds operating and long-term maintenance expenses; (5) whether the beneficiaries of the "charity" are restricted or unrestricted and, if restricted, whether the restriction bears a reasonable relationship to the entity's charitable objectives; and (6) whether dividends or some other form of financial benefit, or assets upon dissolution, are available to private interests, and whether the entity is organized and operated so that any commercial activities are subordinate or incidental to charitable ones.
* * *

Because the "care of the sick" has traditionally been an activity regarded as charitable in American law, and because the dissenting opinions rely upon decisions from other jurisdictions that in turn incorporate unexamined assumptions about the fundamental nature of hospital-based medical care, we deem it important to scrutinize the contemporary social and economic context of such care. We are convinced that traditional assumptions bear little relationship to the economics of the medical-industrial complex of the 1980's. Nonprofit hospitals were traditionally treated as tax-exempt charitable institutions because, until late in the 19th century, they were true charities providing custodial care for those who were both sick and poor. The hospitals' income was derived largely or entirely from voluntary charitable donations, not government subsidies, taxes, or patient fees.[7] The function and status of hospitals began to change in the late 19th century; the transformation was substantially completed by the 1920's. "From charities, dependent on voluntary gifts, [hospitals] developed

---

7. Paul Starr, *The Social Transformation of American Medicine* at 150 (1982). "Voluntary" hospitals, like public hospitals (which evolved from almshouses for the dependent poor), performed a "welfare" function rather than a medical or curing function: the poor were housed in large wards, largely cared for themselves, and often were not expected to recover. *See id.* at 145, 149, 160. Early voluntary hospitals had paternalistic, communal social structures in which patients entered at the sufferance of their benefactors, "had the moral status of children," and received more moralistic and religious help than medical treatment. *Id.* at 149, 158. * * *

[Ed. note: The opinion relies on Starr's book extensively. Further citations have been omitted.]

into market institutions financed increasingly out of payments from patients." The transformation was multidimensional: hospitals were redefined from social welfare to medical treatment institutions; their charitable foundation was replaced by a business basis; and their orientation shifted to "professionals and their patients," away from "patrons and the poor."

* * *

Also of considerable significance to our review is the increasing irrelevance of the distinction between nonprofit and for-profit hospitals for purposes of discovering the element of charity in their operations. The literature indicates that two models, described below, appear to describe a large number of nonprofit hospitals as they function today.

(1) The "physicians' cooperative" model describes nonprofit hospitals that operate primarily for the benefit of the participating physicians. Physicians, pursuant to this model, enjoy power and high income through their direct or indirect control over the nonprofit hospitals to which they bring their patients. * * * A minor variation of the above theory is the argument that many nonprofit hospitals operate as "shelters" within which physicians operate profitable businesses, such as laboratories. [ ]

(2) The "polycorporate enterprise" model describes the increasing number of nonprofit hospital chains. Here, power is largely in the hands of administrators, not physicians. Through the creation of holding companies, nonprofit hospitals have grown into large groups of medical enterprises, containing both for-profit and nonprofit corporate entities. Nonprofit corporations can own for-profit corporations without losing their federal nonprofit tax status as long as the profits of the for-profit corporations are used to further the nonprofit purposes of the parent organization.

* * *

* * * Dramatic advances in medical knowledge and technology have resulted in an equally dramatic rise in the cost of medical services. At the same time, elaborate and comprehensive organizations of third-party payers have evolved. Most recently, perhaps as a further evolutionary response to the unceasing rise in the cost of medical services, the provision of such services has become a highly competitive business.

* * *

The stated purpose of IHC regarding the operation of both hospitals clearly meets at least part of the first criterion we have articulated for determining the existence of a charitable use. Its articles of incorporation identify as "corporate purposes," among other things, the provision of "care and treatment of the sick, afflicted, infirm, aged or injured within and/or without the State of Utah." The same section prevents any "part of the net earnings of this Corporation" to inure to the private benefit of any individual. Furthermore, under another section, the assets of the corporation upon dissolution likewise may not be distributed to benefit any private interest.

The second factor we examine is whether the hospitals are supported, and to what extent, by donations and gifts. * * * [W]e have examined the testimony and exhibits in evidence on this question. The latter demonstrate that current operating expenses for both hospitals are covered almost entirely by revenue from patient charges. * * * The evidence was that both hospitals charge rates for their services comparable to rates being charged by other similar entities, and no showing was made that the donations identified resulted in charges to patients below prevailing market rates.

* * *

One of the most significant of the factors to be considered in review of a claimed exemption is the third we identified: whether the recipients of the services of an entity are required to pay for that assistance, in whole or in part. The Tax Commission in this case found as follows:

> The policy of [IHC's hospitals] is to collect hospital charges from patients whenever it is reasonable and possible to do so; however, no person in need of medical attention is denied care solely on the basis of a lack of funds.

The record also shows that neither of the hospitals in this case demonstrated any substantial imbalance between the value of the services it provides and the payments it receives apart from any gifts, donations, or endowments. The record shows that the vast majority of the services provided by these two hospitals are paid for by government programs, private insurance companies, or the individuals receiving care.

* * *

Between 1978 and 1980, the value of the services given away as charity by these two hospitals constituted less than one percent of their gross revenues. Furthermore, the record also shows that such free service as did exist was deliberately not advertised out of fear of a "deluge of people" trying to take advantage of it. Instead, every effort was made to recover payment for services rendered. * * *

The defendants argue that the great expense of modern hospital care and the universal availability of insurance and government health care subsidies make the idea of a hospital solely supported by philanthropy an anachronism. We believe this argument itself exposes the weakness in the defendants' position. It is precisely because such a vast system of third-party payers has developed to meet the expense of modern hospital care that the historical distinction between for-profit and nonprofit hospitals has eroded. * * *

The fourth question we consider is whether the income received from all sources by these IHC hospitals is in excess of their operating and maintenance expenses. Because the vast majority of their services are paid for, the nonprofit hospitals in this case accumulate capital as do their profit-seeking counterparts.

* * *

A large portion of the profits of most for-profit entities is used for capital improvements and new, updated equipment, and the defendant hospitals here similarly expend their revenues in excess of operational expenses. There can be no doubt, in reviewing the references in the record by members of IHC's administrative staff, that the IHC system, as well as the two hospitals in question, has consistently generated sufficient funds in excess of operating costs to contribute to rapid and extensive growth, building, competitive employee and professional salaries and benefits, and a very sophisticated management structure. While it is true that no financial benefits or profits are available to private interests in the form of stockholder distributions or ownership advantages, the user *entity* in this case clearly generates substantial "profits" in the sense of income that exceeds expenses.

* * *

On the question of benefits to private interests, certainly it appears that no individuals who are employed by or administer the defendants receive any distribution of assets or income, and some, such as IHC's board of trustees members, volunteer their services. We have noted, however, that IHC owns a for-profit entity, as well as nonprofit subsidiaries, and there is in addition the consideration that numerous forms of private commercial enterprise, such as pharmacies, laboratories, and contracts for medical services, are conducted as a necessary part of the defendants' hospital operations. The burden being on the taxpayer to demonstrate eligibility for the exemption, the inadequacies in the record on these questions cannot be remedied by speculation in the defendants' favor. * * *

Neither can we find on this record that the burdens of government are substantially lessened as a result of the defendants' provision of services. The record indicates that Utah County budgets approximately $50,000 annually for the payment of hospital care for indigents. Furthermore, the evidence described two instances within a three-month period where, after a Utah County official had declined to authorize payment for a person in the emergency room, Utah Valley Hospital refused to admit the injured person on the basis of that person's inability to pay. The county official was told in these instances to either authorize payment or to "come and get" the person. Such behavior on the hospital's part is inconsistent with its argument that it functions to relieve government of a burden. Likewise, as we have pointed out, there has been no showing that the tax exemption is a significant factor in permitting these defendants to operate, thereby arguably relieving government of the burden of establishing its own medical care providers. In fact, government is already carrying a substantial share of the operating expenses of defendants, in the form of third-party payments pursuant to "entitlement" programs such as Medicare and Medicaid.

* * *

We reverse the Tax Commission's grant of an *ad valorem* property tax exemption to defendants as being unconstitutional.

* * *

STEWART, JUSTICE (dissenting):

* * *

III.   DEFINITION OF CHARITY

* * *

The legal concept of charity does not require, as the majority apparently requires, that a hospital incur a deficit to qualify as a charitable institution. Charitable hospitals need not be self-liquidating.

* * *

It is true that the hospitals in this case receive substantial revenues from third-party payors and patients, but there is not a shred of evidence in this record, much less a finding by the Tax Commission, that one cent of the revenues is used for any purpose other than furthering the charitable purposes of providing hospital services to the sick and infirm. On the contrary, the Tax Commission's findings affirmatively establish that no person has profited from the revenues produced at either Utah Valley or American Fork Hospitals other than patients. Under time-honored legal principles, both hospitals qualify as charitable institutions.

IV.   UTAH VALLEY HOSPITAL'S AND AMERICAN FORK HOSPITAL'S GIFTS TO THE COMMUNITY

* * *

A.   *Direct Patient Subsidies*

* * *

During the years 1978–80, Utah Valley Hospital rendered wholly free services to indigents in the amount of $200,000, and in each of those years the amount increased substantially over the preceding year. During the same period, the hospital subsidized services rendered to Medicare, Medicaid, and worker's compensation patients in the amount of $3,174,024. The corresponding figures for American Fork Hospital were $39,906 in indigent care and $421,306 for subsidization of Medicare, Medicaid, and worker's compensation benefits.

However, the value of the charity extended to indigents is in fact greater than the amounts stated. The cost of the charity extended to patients who are first identified as charity patients *after* admission rather than *at* admission is charged to the "bad debts" account, along with traditional uncollectible accounts or bad debts, instead of being charged to charity.

* * *

In sum, the *direct* cost of patient charity given away by Utah Valley Hospital for the period in question is in excess of $3,374,024, but less than $4,942,779 (which includes bad debts). The *direct* cost of the charity given away by American Fork Hospital is in excess of $461,212, but less than $639,024 (which includes bad debts). * * * Unlike for-profit hospitals, Utah Valley and American Fork have a policy against turning away indigent patients. Therefore, that portion of the hospitals' bad debts which is attributable to indigency is bona fide charity since the charges would have been initially made to the charity account had the patient's indigency been discovered at admission. Those charges are not just ordinary business bad debts experienced by all commercial enterprises, as the majority would have it.

* * *

B. Capital Subsidies and Gifts

The most glaring lapse in the majority opinion, in my view, is its flat-out refusal to recognize that there would be no Utah Valley Hospital—at all—if it had not been given lock, stock, and barrel to IHC by the Church of Jesus Christ of Latter–Day Saints, which initially built the hospital. American Fork Hospital apparently was initially erected by taxpayers' money. At the City's request, IHC took over the operation of the hospital as a lessee of American Fork City to relieve the City of a governmental burden. It follows that all patients at both hospitals, whether indigent, part-paying, or fully paying patients, are direct beneficiaries of large monetary investments in land, buildings, and medical equipment. * * *

In addition to the "gift to the community" of the actual physical facilities, each and every patient benefits from the fact that IHC is a nonprofit corporation whose hospitals make no profit on the value of the assets dedicated to hospital care. The majority's effort to portray IHC hospitals as if they were operated as for-profit entities has no substance in the record whatsoever. A for-profit hospital, unlike a nonprofit hospital, must necessarily price its services to make a profit on its investment if it is to stay in business. The surplus that Utah Valley and American Fork budget for is not by any means the equivalent of profit, as the majority wrongly suggests. * * *

Furthermore, the majority inaccurately asserts that Utah Valley charges rates comparable to other similar entities. The evidence is to the contrary. Utah Valley Hospital, with its 385 beds and expensive, sophisticated acute care equipment, charges rates comparable to the rates charged by Payson Hospital, a small for-profit hospital that renders inexpensive types of services. * * * In addition, there are no "prevailing market rates" for tertiary care hospitals, if by that term the majority means prevailing rates of competitive for-profit hospitals. There is no for-profit tertiary care hospital in the entire state of Utah; all tertiary care hospitals are non-profit institutions. In fact, there is no other tertiary care hospital, whether nonprofit or for-profit, in the immense, sparsely populated area served by the Utah Valley Hospital, which extends from Utah County to the Nevada–Arizona border. Indeed, the facts strongly suggest that a for-profit tertiary care hospital could not survive in the geographical market area served by Utah Valley. * * * The majority wholly dismisses or ignores these facts and focuses on the assertion that "*current operating expenses* for both hospitals are covered almost entirely by revenue from patient charges" (emphasis added) and that "neither of the hospitals in this case demonstrated any substantial imbalance between the value of the services it provides and the payments it receives apart from any gifts, donations, or endowments."

Presumably, only if the hospitals ran deficits, i.e., if the direct expenses of patient care exceeded patient income, would a hospital qualify in the majority's view as a charitable institution. Of course, the deficits would have to be made up by donations, or the hospital would shortly lapse into bankruptcy. As the cases cited above recognize, modern hospitals can hardly be run on the basis that donations must subsidize current expenses.

V.   Tax Exempt Status of Non-Profit Hospitals Under The Majority Opinion

The record also demonstrates that the primary care hospital and the tertiary care hospital involved in this case relieve a significant governmental burden, one of the two alternative tests for determining whether a nonprofit hospital qualifies to be treated as a charitable institution. * * * In the wide-open spaces of the West, where small communities are widely separated, the profit motive has not been sufficient to provide the needed impetus for the building of community hospitals (except in rare instances). Nor has it resulted in the construction of tertiary care hospitals in the more populous parts of the state.

The majority's argument is that no government burden is relieved by providing hospital service to those who can pay for it on a for-profit basis. The argument misses the mark for two reasons. First, the alternatives are not for-profit or nonprofit hospitals. The alternatives are nonprofit hospital care or no hospital care at all, at least within the relevant geographical markets. Second, the charitable status of a hospital does not turn on whether it provides care for patients who can pay. The basic policy is not to tax the sick and infirm irrespective of ability to pay. A county provides many services to rich and poor alike without charging the rich for those services. Parks and playgrounds are but examples. Providing medical services may not be mandatory for counties or cities, but if they do, they most certainly promote the public health, safety, morals, and welfare in a most fundamental way. Surely cities and counties would, as a practical matter, be compelled to provide hospital services if the nonprofit hospitals in this state did not exist.

* * *

VI. DIFFERENCES BETWEEN FOR-PROFIT AND NONPROFIT HOSPITALS

* * *

Two fundamental differences between for-profit and nonprofit corporations are ignored by the majority. First, it is axiomatic that a for-profit hospital must conduct its business to make a profit if it is to remain in business. Second, a for-profit hospital's investment decisions as to what markets or communities to enter and what kinds of equipment to invest in are made from a basically different motive than a nonprofit hospital's. The decisions of a for-profit hospital corporation must be based upon careful calculations as to the rate of return that may be expected on invested capital. If the rate of return is not sufficient, the investment is not made. Whether the surplus is reinvested in part or paid out to investors in dividends in whole or in part, the investor receives personal monetary benefit either in the increased value of his stock or in dividends.

The record indicates that for-profit hospitals in Utah have invested to a limited extent in high-volume, low-cost services such as pediatric, psychiatric, and obstetrical-gynecological services, but not in higher-cost, lower-volume kinds of services. * * *

Nonprofit hospitals must, of course, be concerned with generating sufficient revenue to maintain themselves, but they are not concerned with earning a return on their investment for the benefit of stockholders. Their purposes are altruistic. Any surplus must be used in a manner that aggrandizes no one, such as for the lowering of rates, the acquisition of new equipment, or the improvement of facilities.

* * *

Mr. Jones also testified that IHC's Board of Trustees considers itself a trustee of the health care facilities for the public. "[W]e see ourselves as owned by the community since the corporation owns itself and in effect the church gave the hospitals to the communities, and we're entrusted with the running of the hospitals. We see them as in effect owned by the communities. We have fund raising drives and strive to have the communities feel that [they are] involved."

* * *

Utah Valley Hospital budgets for the projected cost of services plus an additional five to seven percent reserve for contingencies and for replacement of building and equipment and for future expansion. Nothing is budgeted for IHC expansion.

* * *

Notes and Questions

1. Subsequent to the principal case, Intermountain Health Care agreed to expand its charitable services significantly in exchange for retaining its tax exempt status. Intermountain Health Care, according to Health Lawyers News Report, must provide charity care in excess of the

taxes it would otherwise owe and has opened clinics for the homeless, poor persons in rural areas and persons on Indian reservations. The voters rejected in 1986 a constitutional amendment to bar taxes on hospitals. Health Lawyers News Report, May 1988 at 4.

2. Among the states, there are reports of serious scrutiny of exemptions from state taxes, such as property and sales taxes, with a focus on the amount of charity care provided by the facility. The Iowa Supreme Court, for example, denied a nursing home exemption from property taxes because the facility had a strong policy against admitting or retaining residents who were unable to pay. Atrium Village, Inc. v. Board of Review, 417 N.W.2d 70 (Iowa 1987). But see, Callaway Community Hospital Association v. Craighead, 759 S.W.2d 253 (Mo.App.1988).

3. In 1956, the IRS issued a revenue ruling that required a tax-exempt hospital to "be operated to the extent of its financial ability for those not able to pay for the services rendered." In 1958, the Tax Court upheld the denial of exempt status for a hospital that devoted between 2% and 5% of its revenue to care for the indigent (Lorain Avenue Clinic v. Commissioner, 46 T.C. 519). A 1969 Revenue Ruling stated that "the promotion of health * * * is one of the purposes in the general law of charity." Rev.Ruling 69–545. An illustration used in this revenue ruling was a hospital that operated an emergency room that was open to all regardless of ability to pay. In Simon v. Eastern Kentucky Welfare Rights Organization, 426 U.S. 26, 96 S.Ct. 1917, 48 L.Ed.2d 450 (1976), the Supreme Court considered a suit brought by the Welfare Rights Organization challenging the 1969 ruling. The Supreme Court held that the Organization lacked standing to sue the IRS on its claim. In a 1983 Revenue Ruling, a hospital that did not operate an emergency room and usually referred indigent patients to another hospital was described as qualifying for tax-exempt status. The state health planning agency had concluded that the emergency room was not necessary because other hospitals had adequate emergency services. The Revenue Ruling stated that although this hospital could not offer the ER as strong evidence that it was operated for the benefit of the community, "[o]ther significant factors * * * including a board of directors drawn from the community" supported exempt status. Rev.Ruling 83–157.

The IRS manual for examination of tax-exempt organizations instructs agents to "ascertain if admission is denied to patients because of inability to pay [citing Rev.Ruling 69–545]. If so, determine whether the class of persons benefitting directly from the hospital's activities is so small that there is no benefit to the community." Agents are also to "determine the level of activity for the emergency room. Local ambulance services may be instructed to take emergency cases to other hospitals." The IRS and the Department of Health and Human Services recently have agreed to exchange information on patient dumping by tax-exempt hospitals. Proposed federal legislation to require exempt hospitals to accept Medicaid patients in order to qualify to issue tax-exempt bonds is described in Barker, Reexamining the 501(c)(3) Exemption of Hospitals as Charitable Organizations, Tax Notes (7/16/90) 339.

4. A major policy issue in the debate regarding the not-for-profit and for-profit structures in health care delivery is whether the profit motive,

presumed to be diminished seriously in not-for-profit organizations, has a negative impact on the quality or availability of health care.

A Committee Report on for-profit health care produced by the Institute of Medicine of the National Academy of Sciences in 1986 addressed such issues as changes in the ownership, control and configuration of health care services, health care financing and growth, investor ownership and costs, access to care and quality of care. The Committee Report is supplemented in the same volume by fifteen papers presenting research on for-profit/not-for-profit health care and multifacility systems. Institute of Medicine, National Academy of Sciences, For–Profit Enterprise in Health Care (1986). The Committee Report concluded that for-profit "chain" hospitals experienced equal or somewhat higher expenses and charged considerably higher prices than not-for-profit hospitals. In contrast, the Committee Report indicated that the charges of for-profit nursing homes were comparable to those of not-for-profit facilities, but that the expenses of the for-profit facilities were lower. The Report concluded that the expense savings of the for-profit nursing homes arose from savings on patient care expenses. Id. at 74–96.

The Committee Report also examined the impact of for-profit health care on access to care by patients who are unable to pay. The Report concluded:

> The performance of not-for-profit hospitals was more favorable on both measures [admissions of uninsured patients and provision of uncompensated care], although when measured as percentages of total admissions or total revenues, the national differences were not large. Small percentage differences, however, can translate into large numbers of patients, particularly if institutions that provide comparatively small amounts of uncompensated care comprise a relatively large proportion of the market. Id. at 116.

In a supplementary statement to the Committee Report, several Committee members commented on the Report's handling of the access question. They noted that because the committee focused on national data rather than local experience, they were not able "to lay to rest fears expressed by some observers that, particularly in those states, the for-profits are skimming the profitable patients and dumping the unprofitable ones, thus threatening the solvency of hospitals that adhere to a policy of not turning away medically indigent patients." Capron, Freidson, Relman, Schroeder, Sommers, Stevens and Wikler, Supplementary Statement on For–Profit Enterprise in Health Care, Inst. of Med., supra, at 205. For a further discussion of access to health care see Chapter 6.

In addressing the issue of comparative quality of care, the Committee relied primarily on structure and process quality measures rather than outcome measures because of the inadequacy of available outcome data. Data used in the report indicated that 91% of investor-owned chain hospitals; 87% of not-for-profit chain hospitals; 83% of not-for-profit independent hospitals; and 52% of for-profit independent hospitals were JCAHO-accredited in 1983. The percentage of board-certified physicians was 65% for not-for-profit systems hospitals; 61% in investor-owned systems hospitals; and 58% in publicly owned and contract-managed hospitals. Id.

at 128–129. The Committee concluded in regard to nursing homes that "most studies on quality (or surrogate measures) of nursing home care tend to favor the not-for-profit mode of organization" but also noted that most research on nursing homes fails to distinguish investor-owned chains from independent proprietary homes in the for-profit sector. Id. at 136.

The non-profit status of hospitals has come under attack in the academic literature as well. See, e.g., Clark, Does the Nonprofit Form Fit the Hospital Industry? 93 Harv.L.Rev. 1416 (1980), in which Clark argues that nonprofit status does not address the problem of market failure, including the perceived inability of patients to judge quality, that intuitively supports the favorable treatment of non-profits. See also, Etzioni and Doty, Profit in Not-for-Profit Corporations: The Example of Health Care, 91 Political Science Quarterly 433 (1976), in which the authors argue that the nonprofit form does not of itself eliminate "profit-making abuses" in organizations such as nursing homes and day care centers because non-profits are allowed to make "profits" and engage in "profit making" behavior. Hansmann, in The Role of Nonprofit Enterprise, 89 Yale L.J. 835 (1980), examines the theories underlying the nonprofit structure and in The Rationale for Exempting Nonprofit Organizations from Corporate Income Taxation, 91 Yale L.J. 54 (1981), argues in favor of the tax exemption to compensate for constraints on capitalization of nonprofits that operate in transactions characterized by market failure. See also, Institute of Medicine, Nat'l Acad. of Sci., For–Profit Enterprise in Health Care 3–18 (1986); Yoder, Economic Theories of For–Profit and Not–For–Profit Organizations, Id. at 19–25.

Despite arguments that the current business endeavors of not-for-profits makes them indistinguishable from their for-profit counterparts, some authors maintain that not-for-profits share unique characteristics that justify their continued state and federal tax advantages. One often-cited difference is the fiduciary nature of the relationship between the not-for-profit organization and the patient, in which the patient is justified in assuming that the organization's primary goal is to provide health care, and not to exact a profit. Other distinguishing features noted include the mission of providing health care to the entire community; identifying and responding to community health needs; encouragement of voluntarism; continuing medical education and research; and community access to the decision-making processes of the institution. Seay and Vladeck, Mission Matters, in In Sickness and In Health, The Mission of Voluntary Health Care Institutions (J. Seay and B. Vladeck, eds. 1988). Should tax-exempt hospitals be willing to be judged on the basis of their satisfaction of these activities? Could these be included in the requirements for tax-exempt status? How?

Finally, it has been argued that not-for-profit hospitals preserve valuable diversity of mission and method in the hospital industry. Falcone and Warren, The Shadow Price of Pluralism: The Use of Tax Expenditures to Subsidize Hospital Care in the United States, 13 J. Health Policy, Politics and Law 735 (1988).

5. The majority opinion in *Intermountain Health Care* is careful to limit its holding to the "facts of the record" before it. Assume that you

have been asked by the "Sisters of St. Paul," an order of Catholic nuns that has identified health care as part of its mission, to develop the case for exemption from property tax for its hospital in Utah. This hospital is a community hospital in western Utah that offers primary and secondary care but not tertiary care. It operates an emergency room and a variety of services including obstetrics and pediatrics. The nearest hospital is sixty miles away. The hospital provides treatment for all emergency patients but transfers indigent patients to the public hospital once they have been stabilized or if they need treatment unavailable at the hospital. It receives private payments, insurance payments or Medicare and Medicaid for most of the care given. The order does fundraising and, in fact, built the hospital in 1940 with donations from the public and their order. They expanded the hospital in the 1950s with federal funds through the Hill–Burton program. What are their chances for tax exemption under *Intermountain?* What more do you need to know? Can you give the hospital any advice on activities that may increase their chances?

Problem: St. Andrew's Medical Center

St. Andrew's Medical Center is a 750–bed not-for-profit hospital in a metropolitan area. It offers residency programs in Internal Medicine, Obstetrics, Surgery and several other areas. Although St. Andrew's is currently in good financial health, its Board of Directors is concerned about possible cutbacks in federal funds for graduate medical education, further reductions in health care reimbursement and its own inability to raise enough capital for modernization through retained earnings and donations. The Board is hesitant to increase the facility's debt to make capital improvements in its 40–year–old physical plant. It also finds that it gives a significant amount of charity care each year in part because of its self-identified institutional mission and in part because it is one of only three hospitals in the area. The other two hospitals are a for-profit, 250–bed hospital operated by U.S. Healthcare, Inc., which is an investor-owned multi-facility system, and a municipal hospital, which regularly operates at 98% capacity and is often unable to receive transfers from St. Andrew's.

St. Andrew's has been approached by Health Care Enterprises (HCE), a for-profit corporation that owns eighty-five hospitals in thirty states and is interested in acquiring St. Andrew's. HCE has made an initial offer of $200 million for St. Andrew's, which would include the acquisition of all assets of St. Andrew's, including the name itself. The Board is very interested in the offer but is concerned that the provision of charity care continue at St. Andrew's and that HCE conform with the mission of St. Andrew's as a religiously affiliated hospital. For the Board, this latter concern relates, in part, to their interest in having St. Andrew's not offer abortion services.

HCE has suggested to St. Andrew's that St. Andrew's place $150 million (the amount remaining after St. Andrew's pays off outstanding debts) into an endowment for a new St. Andrew's Foundation. The income from this endowment would then be paid to HCE for charity care and the medical education program at St. Andrew's. HCE has also suggested that it is willing to provide "appropriate charity care and adhere to the traditional mission of St. Andrew's." If it fails to do so, HCE has suggested that it would agree to a buy-back by St. Andrew's at a price to be agreed upon.

The community is generally quite upset about the proposal. Many have charged that St. Andrew's is abandoning the community and that HCE is simply seeking to build a reputation by owning a teaching hospital and to "corner the market" by eliminating the only not-for-profit hospital in the metropolitan area.

The Board meeting to decide whether St. Andrew's will be sold to HCE is tomorrow morning. You are a member of the Board. What will you recommend? If the transfer is approved, how would you draft the agreement between St. Andrew's and HCE?

Note: Tax Exempt Status of Alternative Delivery Systems

"Managed care" became a key concept of health care delivery in the cost-conscious 1980s and took on a wide variety of forms and organizations, all intended to manage the use of health care services by consumers. Among the most prominant players in managed care programs are the alternative delivery systems (ADS). The most familiar of these are health maintenance organizations (HMOs), independent practice associations (IPAs), and preferred provider organizations (PPOs), although the organization of ADS is not at all static and new permutations appear constantly.

An HMO delivers both office-based primary care and hospital-based acute care to its subscribers who prepay a predetermined, per capita premium regardless of the amount or cost of medical services actually used. HMOs usually contract with health care facilities for institution-based health care such as inpatient hospital services for their members. For primary care services, HMOs either directly provide the services or contract with individual physicians or physician associations. HMOs generally fit within three models. In the staff model, physicians are direct employees of the HMO. In the group model, physicians are members of a partnership or corporation that contracts with the HMO to provide services to subscribers on a capitation basis. The physicians' partnership or corporation generally pays its member physicians a salary and incentives. Both the staff model and group model typically are located in a center operated by the HMO. The third HMO model is the IPA model. The IPA contracts on behalf of its physician members with the HMO for services provided by the individual doctors in their own offices. Preferred provider organizations are least amenable to a single description, although they generally are groups of providers organized to negotiate fees, including discounts, with payers.

More detailed discussion of the structure of these organizations is included in Chapter 7.

Health maintenance organizations, independent practice associations and preferred provider organizations have all been considered by the IRS for 501(c)(3) status.

Health Maintenance Organizations. A staff model HMO, which provided health services directly to subscribers/members, received 501(c)(3) status in Sound Health Association v. Commissioner, 71 T.C. 158 (1978). In addition to providing services to subscribers/members, the HMO offered emergency medical services at its clinic to all persons regardless of ability to pay. It had even informed ambulance services of the availability of this service. In addition, it had provided free obstetrical care to patients of a family clinic on a referral basis. Finally, it instituted a program of reduced or waived membership fees for indigent persons. This program was to be supported by private charitable contributions raised for that purpose. The IRS had denied its exemption because "preferential treatment will be accorded to * * * member-subscribers" and because the prepayment of medical services was a "form of insurance." The Tax Court reversed, holding that rendering medical care was a charitable purpose and that the HMO could satisfy the qualifications to which hospitals were held, relying on the availability of emergency treatment and the fee waiver program. "If the charitable hospital can, except for emergency cases, restrict its treatment to paying patients, the Association should be able to restrict itself to paying members." The Court was not persuaded by the IRS' claim that the HMO offered a "form of insurance," through spreading the risk of the costs of treatment among subscribers, because this risk-spreading benefit was a public benefit available to a large number of potential subscribers. In 1981, the Service "acquiesced" in *Sound Health Association,* GCM 38735 (5/29/81), but noted that it had not argued that the HMO provided insurance, but that the risk-spreading benefitted only the members of the HMO.

In 1983, the Service denied 501(c)(3) status to an HMO that contracted with an IPA for primary care services, performed utilization review, and paid specialists on a fee-for-service basis. GCM 39057 (11/9/83). The HMO argued that its method of operation eliminated the need for new capital expenditures and duplicative construction. The IRS denied the exemption because the HMO, unlike the HMO in *Sound Health Association,* did not provide emergency services, did not operate a fee waiver program, did not provide for enrollment by Medicaid or Medicare beneficiaries, and would limit membership in the beginning to a defined group of persons. In addition, the board of the HMO consisted of members of the IPA, indicating that it was operated for the private purposes of the physicians. (See also GCM 38894 in which the IRS denied exemption to an IPA: "[the] IPA is similar to a commercial health insurance reimbursement program because it merely serves as an alternate method to the direct billing and collection of fees from patients. * * * Moreover, there is no evidence that [this] IPA will assume the fees of indigent patients that the HMO agreement does not cover. * * * We also think it telling that the organization expects ninety percent of the active physicians of the county to become members. [The] IPA is essentially negotiating on behalf of its physician members with HMOs in determining the permissible fees to be charged and is akin to a collective bargaining representative. * * * Therefore, in our view, [the] IPA exclusively represents physicians who are seeking to maximize their income.")

In 1989, the Service issued a GCM concerning preferred provider organizations. GCM 39799 (10/25/89). Although the applicant organization was an organization of PPOs, the GCM discussed the potential exempt status of PPOs in general. In a statement that will ring true for students, the IRS commented that the "legal structure and tax status of the PPOs [were] not entirely clear. * * * No precise definition exists for what constitutes a preferred provider organization. In general, however, a PPO is a select group of health care providers who agree to charge a negotiated or discounted rate for services to a specific group of patients such as the employees of a particular employer or the policyholders of a particular insurer. Patients are given enhanced benefits or other incentives for utilizing the preferred providers, but otherwise retain freedom of choice. The providers are usually paid on a fee-for-service basis, but are subject to strict utilization review designed to control costs." Citing, American Association of Preferred Provider Organizations, Preferred Provider Organizations (1988). In discussing the exempt status of PPOs, the GCM stated that it would evaluate PPOs under the same standards as it evaluates HMOs, citing GCM 38735. The Service concluded that the PPO, like the non-staff model (IPA model) HMO discussed previously, failed to meet the requirements for 501(c)(3) status.

HMOs have also sought state tax exemptions with little success. See, e.g., New Brunswick v. Rutgers Community Health Plan, 7 N.J.Tax 491 (1985) [denying property tax exemption under a statute providing exemption for property used for "hospital purposes"]; SHARE v. Commissioner, 363 N.W.2d 47 (Minn.1985) and Montgomery County v. Group Health Association, 308 Md. 151, 517 A.2d 1076 (1986) [denying exemption as a "public charity" because the HMO received its support from fees and provided no services without charge].

B. COMPETITION BETWEEN FOR–PROFIT AND NOT–FOR–PROFIT PROVIDERS

Not-for-profit tax-exempt health care organizations compete directly with other non-profit providers and with for-profit providers. Their competitive behavior raises two issues. First, do competitive strategies, such as joint ventures with for-profit providers or physicians, conflict with the charitable purposes of tax-exempt providers? Second, does the subsidy they receive through their tax-exempt status unfairly advantage them in competition against for-profit providers?

This section reviews two limitations on the capacity of federally tax-exempt organizations to diversify their activities through joint ventures. The first relates to whether the joint venture furthers the exempt purpose of the exempt joint venturer. The second limits the ability of an exempt organization to engage in a business that is unrelated to its exempt purpose.

A federally tax-exempt organization must be organized *primarily* for exempt purposes. It is permitted to engage in some non-exempt business activities, but the earnings from non-exempt endeavors are considered "unrelated business taxable income" (UBTI) and are subject to federal corporate taxation. In recent years, the IRS has become more aggressive in requiring that UBTI be reported and in collecting the tax owed. The taxation of UBTI contributes to leveling the playing field when exempt organizations compete with for-profit providers.

The following two private letter rulings, which were issued by the Service in response to requests by a particular organization for review of a proposed activity, indicate how the Service has viewed two common business strategies of tax-exempt providers.

PRIVATE LETTER RULING

8125007.
Undated.

FACTS:

X is a nonprofit general acute care hospital exempt under section 501(c)(3) of the Internal Revenue Code. X has a laboratory department that operates on a twenty-four hour basis. The diagnostic facilities of the laboratory are used by the hospital's inpatients and outpatients, by the patients of hospital staff physicians, and by industrial concerns that submit blood and tissue samples of employees to the hospital for analysis.

Toxicology tests for industrial concerns are of a type very few hospitals perform. * * * The employees do not themselves enter the hospital's facilities as patients. No commercial laboratories in the area perform similar services.

Also performed are tests of tissue specimens of patients of private physicians. * * * The patients do not themselves enter the hospital's facilities. Instead, the samples are collected within the office of the private physician and transmitted to the hospital for analysis.

The [I.R.S.] District concluded that the conduct of diagnostic tests for industrial concerns and for private physicians constituted unrelated business activity giving rise to taxation under section 511 of the Internal Revenue Code.

APPLICABLE LAW:

Section 513 of the Internal Revenue Code provides that the term "unrelated trade or business" means * * * any trade or business the conduct of which is not substantially related to the exercise of the organization of its charitable purpose or function constituting the basis for its exemption under section 501.

Section 1.513–1(d)(2) of the regulations provides that a trade or business is related to the exempt purpose of any organization where the conduct of the business activities has a substantial causal relationship to the exempt purpose. Where the production of goods or performance of services from which the income is derived contributes importantly to the accomplishment of the exempt purposes, the activities will be considered substantially related to those purposes.

RATIONALE:

The primary purpose of the unrelated business tax is the prevention of unfair competition between tax-exempt organizations engaging in business activities unrelated to their exempt purposes, and taxable commercial enterprises with which they compete. [ ] A hospital pharmacy selling pharmaceuticals to the general public is in direct competition with commercial pharmacies. An untaxed hospital pharmacy can undersell its taxable commercial counterparts and adversely affect their business. Revenue Rulings [ ] provide that hospital pharmacies selling to persons other than "patients" of the hospital are conducting an unrelated trade or business.

The patient/nonpatient distinction is also applicable to laboratory testing by tax-exempt hospitals. A tax-exempt hospital performs its exempt function of promoting community health by providing services aiding patient recovery and convenience. Laboratory testing by a hospital of specimens of its own patients is consistent with exemption because such testing serves the convenience of patients at the hospital.

Conversely, a hospital providing laboratory services for persons who are not patients of the hospital is performing an activity that under normal circumstances could be with equal convenience undertaken by commercial laboratories. Consequently, in the usual case, a hospital's performance of laboratory services for non-patients adds nothing to the promotion of community health. * * *

Among the factors to be considered in determining whether special circumstances exist are:

1. Whether the diagnostic testing is highly sophisticated and involves techniques and instruments not offered by commercial laboratories. If commercial laboratories do not offer the service in question, or the hospital possesses testing equipment not available elsewhere in the community, then it may be inconvenient or impossible to refer the specimens to places other than to the hospital. The individual whose specimen is being examined could be inconvenienced by transmittal of the specimen to a distant location. In such a case the hospital serves a community need by providing testing services. Income derived from such services is related to the hospital's exempt function.

2. Whether the diagnostic testing serves to further or contribute to the achievement of other exempt purposes of the hospital, such as medical education. In *St. Lukes Hospital of Kansas City v. United States,* 494 F.Supp. 85 (W.D.Mo.1980), the hospital operated a school to teach the vocation of nursing, and to train medical students and interns. Specimens were used to further the educational purposes of the hospital. The testing was conducted on a small scale, without advertising or solicitation. The activity was found to be related to the exempt purposes of the hospital.

However, even if a hospital's testing activities fall within either of the special circumstances categories listed above, the scale of the activities should also be considered. If the volume of laboratory testing greatly exceeds the community's need for it, or is far in excess of its value for educational or scientific needs, then the evidence is strong that a primarily commercial purpose is being served. In such a case the income from the activity would be income from an unrelated trade or business to the extent the volume of the activity exceeds the amount reasonably necessary for the performance of the exempt function. (See Section 1.513–1(d)(3) of the regulations.)

* * *

If the industrial concerns submitting specimens to X cannot receive the same testing services commercially without loss of time or without other inconvenience, then there is support for the argument that the hospital is performing an activity beneficial to the community. Thus, to the extent that X makes more convenient the testing of specimens of industrial employees, X's industrial toxicology tests can be considered to promote community health, and consequently, to be directly related to its exempt function. There are, in fact, no commercial laboratories performing similar tests in the local area. Because of the lack of availability of alternate laboratories, it is doubtful that the scope of X's toxicology testing is greater than necessary. Moreover, X does not advertise its services, a fact that argues a noncommercial enterprise. [W]e conclude that sufficient special circumstances exist to allow X's industrial toxicology testing to be considered directly related to its exempt function.

We do not have sufficient information to determine whether similar special circumstances exist with respect to X's laboratory testing conducted on specimens of patients of private physicians. Consequently, we are returning the file to the District for further development on that issue.

PRIVATE LETTER RULING
9024085.
3/22/90.

The information submitted indicates that M operates two acute care community hospitals, N and O, in furtherance of its mission to provide high-quality comprehensive health care services to the residents of your geographic area. M has been recognized as exempt under section 501(c)(3) of the Code. * * *

* * *

M plans to install and operate a magnetic resonance imaging (MRI) system at N. The system will be operated as a separate imaging center. The MRI system is a high-tech diagnostic device that penetrates a patient's body and generates an image without the use of x-rays. Its use can be a critical aid to the diagnosis and treatment of tumors and other soft tissue disorders. * * *

M is in the midst of a major realignment and consolidation of its health care facilities. M has committed substantial funds to this several year project in the amount of $y. Because all discretionary funds have been committed, M has decided to finance the acquisition of the MRI equipment rather than pay outright. M has surveyed the physician community and learned that a number of doctors would consider an investment in an MRI system. M believes their participation in the project would also help make the operation of the equipment more successful. In addition, by involving physicians in the financing of the system, M hopes to improve working relationships and increase cooperation between its hospitals and physicians. M believes such cooperation will help improve the quality of care it is able to deliver to its patients.

To secure the financing, a limited partnership will be created. The general partner will be a general partnership consisting of A and B. * * * A and B were selected to handle the partnership business because of their previous experience and expertise in similar transactions. Neither party is a trustee, officer or employee of M.

The Limited Partnership will, by means of a private placement, offer limited partnership interests [Units] to investors. * * * Offers of [Units] will be made primarily to physicians with staff privileges at the two hospitals operated by M. If the Units are not fully sold, M may purchase any unsold Units, though it is under no obligation to do so. In no event will M act as a general partner in the Partnership.

The General Partner will be responsible for the management of the Partnership's business. The Limited Partners will have no voice in the management of the Partnership other than the limited right to remove and replace the General Partner upon the vote of holders of two-thirds of the Units.

You anticipate that the Partnership will purchase the MRI equipment and lease it to M. The Partnership will fund the purchase with the initial cash investment and financing from a third party. M will not finance the Partnership's purchase of the equipment.

The Partnership will lease the equipment to M. You have indicated that the terms of the lease are the result of arm's length negotiations between officers of M, particularly, the Chief Financial Officer, and A. None of the officers of M involved in the negotiations will invest in the Partnership.

You have submitted a draft of the Equipment Lease. The term of the lease will be approximately six years. M will have an option, but not an obligation, to purchase the equipment from the Partnership at the end of the Basic Term for the fair market value of the equipment at the time. M will have the option to renew the lease for one or more one-year renewal terms at a rental rate equal to the fair market rental rate at the time of renewal. M will also have an option to terminate the lease and purchase the equipment for a Termination Price at any time if it determines that the lease in any way jeopardizes its exempt status under section 501(c)(3). In the event of termination under this provision of the lease, M has agreed to a Termination Price defined as the greater of the fair market value of the equipment on the termination date or an amount determined according to a formula designed to make the Partners whole for their investment in the Partnership. The Termination Price does not guarantee any profit to the Partners, but it does guarantee that they will recoup their investment if that is more than the fair market value of the equipment at the time of termination.

During the basic term of the lease, M will be obligated to pay to the Partnership monthly rent denominated as "Basic Rent." In addition to Basic Rent, M will be obligated to pay amounts designated as "Contingent Rent." Contingent Rent payable on an annual basis, will be equal to the lesser of $xx or "Adjusted Net Income" for the year, as defined in the Lease.

Greater use of the MRI System generally will result in a higher Adjusted Income and, therefore, a higher Contingent Rent payment subject to the annual cap. Based on M's projections of usage, revenues and expenses, Contingent Rent will be payable only out of net earnings from its operation of the MRI facility and not out of earnings from its other operations. In any event, you indicate that payments of Contingent Rent will be made only out of cash flow from the operation of the facility and M will not be obligated to pay Contingent Rent out of cash flow from its other operations.

* * *

When considering arrangements between exempt organizations and private enterprises, the initial focus is on whether the arrangement is serving a charitable purpose. Once such a determination is made, the agreement itself must be examined to see whether its terms permit the exempt organization to continue to operate exclusively in furtherance of its exempt purposes and not for the benefit of the private enterprise.

In the instant case, you have indicated that the operation of the MRI facility is in furtherance of M's charitable purposes. * * * [T]he operation of the facility, by improving the hospital's efficiency and the quality of its patient care, is furthering the exempt charitable purposes of the hospital. * * *

* * *

Because M will not be participating in the Partnership, it has no obligation to maximize profits for the Partnership. Under the provisions of the Lease, M will be responsible for the operation of the equipment in a manner designed to further its charitable purposes by providing expanded services to its patients and the community. The Partnership has no role in the operation of the facility. Its only role is as lessor of the equipment. Its decision-making power, exercised solely by its general partner, a non-physician entity, is limited to negotiating the terms of the Lease. Thus, there appears to be no conflict of interest preventing the hospital from operating in an exclusively charitable manner.

The benefits of the Partnership will be limited by the terms of the Lease. The Lease is the result of the arm's length negotiations between officers of M and an unrelated individual representing the General

Partner. The public and charitable interests of M are fully protected under the terms of the Lease. M should be fully compensated each year for the costs of operating the equipment before any Contingent Rent will be paid to the Partnership and thus, M is assured of positive cash flow from the facility before incurring Contingent Rent. M has the right to modify or terminate the Lease if necessary to protect its exempt status. Investors in the Partnership will be limited on their possible return on their investment. The amount of Contingent Rent in any one year will be capped at $xx. All adjusted net income in excess of that amount will benefit M directly. Moreover, an expert in the field has reviewed the proposed arrangement and has concluded that, based on his experience with numerous similar arrangements, the rental arrangement is fair and reasonable.

Based on these facts, we have determined that the benefits to the Partnership and the individual investors are both quantitatively and qualitatively incidental to the public purpose promoted by operation of the MRI facility as part of its overall charitable program. Accordingly, the Lease arrangements proposed will not jeopardize M's status as an organization described in section 501(c)(3) of the Code.

Section 511 of the Code imposes a tax on the unrelated business taxable income of organizations described in section 501(c)(3).

[T]he MRI system is a unique tool which is important in diagnosing and treating disorders common to patients of the two hospitals operated by M and to members of the community. It therefore contributes importantly to the accomplishment of M's exempt purposes as required by section 1.513–1(d)(2) of the regulations. Accordingly, we rule that the operation of the equipment by M in the manner described, will not be an unrelated trade or business within the meaning of section 513(a) of the Code. As in Rev.Rul. 69–269, the income produced from the operation of the facility will not be subject to the tax on unrelated income imposed by section 511 of the Code.

Notes and Questions

1. What standards do you understand the IRS to be applying in deciding whether the MRI joint venture furthers the exempt purpose of the exempt hospital? Do they bear a relationship to the standards for exemption discussed after *Intermountain Health Care?* What function do these standards have?

Proponents of not-for-profit health care institutions argue that these organizations must engage in profitmaking enterprises in order to survive, amid increased competition for health care services, the current emphasis on cost-containment, and diminishing federal resources. Furthermore, profits derived from various business enterprises, health related and otherwise, allow not-for-profit hospitals to expand the range of services they provide. This is particularly important for those services that are frequently operated at a loss; e.g., pediatric intensive care, burn units and emergency room services in economically depressed areas. See, Jones and

DuVal, What Distinguishes the Voluntary Hospital in an Increasingly Commercial Health Care Environment? in In Sickness and In Health, The Mission of Voluntary Health Care Institutions (J. Seay and B. Vladeck, eds. 1988). Does the IRS approach to unrelated business income illustrated in the previous materials relate to this rationale for profitmaking by not-for-profits?

2. How does the IRS decide whether something is unrelated business income? Is there a bright line? What purpose is served by the current IRS approach? Can you offer an alternative approach? Can "M" offer MRI services to patients of hospitals without MRI equipment?

3. The Subcommittee on Oversight of the Ways and Means Committee held hearings in June, 1987, and again in May, 1988. The Subcommittee developed "discussion options" concerning unrelated business ventures of tax-exempt organizations. These included determining whether each income-producing activity was itself tax-exempt and establishing a list of activities (such as sale or rental of medical equipment) that would be categorized as unrelated business and thus subject to tax, rather than relying on a case-by-case approach. Unrelated Business Income Tax: Hearings Before the Subcomm. on Oversight of the House Comm. on Ways and Means, 100th Cong., 1st Sess. (1988); Treimer, Unrelated Business Income: Recent and Proposed Legislative Changes in the Unrelated Business Income Tax, Tax Planning for Non–Profit Health Care Organizations, National Health Lawyers Association (1988). The IRS reported that the amount of tax collected on unrelated business income of tax-exempt organizations nearly quadrupled from 1986 to 1988 due to increased scrutiny of the business ventures of not-for-profit organizations. Health Law Vigil (May 20, 1988).

4. Diversification of services has been a common strategy for hospitals responding to payer cost containment strategies that reduces both utilization of inpatient services and payment levels for those services. In a 1988 survey, the most profitable offerings included freestanding outpatient surgery centers; inpatient rehabilitation programs; women's medicine programs; industrial medical clinics and outpatient psychiatric centers. The profitability of substance abuse treatment centers declined significantly from 1987 to 1988 because of increased supply, revised substance-abuse DRGs and more aggressive utilization review by private payers. Hospitals look to these enterprises for a stream of profits and for increased market share for new and existing services. Sabatino, The Diversification Success Story Continues: A Survey, 63 Hospitals 26 (1989).

5. The physicians who are limited partners in the MRI venture will gain financially if the MRI is used more frequently. These physician limited partners are likely to include doctors who are in a position to refer patients for an MRI. As doctors have increasingly gained an ownership interest in the "tools of the trade," including laboratories, medical equipment suppliers and home health care services, legal and ethical issues in "self-referral" have gained public attention. See, e.g., Physicians and Entrepreneurship in Institute of Medicine, National Academy of Sciences, For–Profit Enterprise in Health Care (1986) at pp. 158–159; Iglehart, The Debate Over Physician Ownership of Health Care Facilities, 321 New

Eng.J.Med. 198 (1989). The federal response to the problems of self-referral in the Medicare and Medicaid programs is discussed in Chapter 7, infra. Some states also regulate self-referral under professional licensure regulation. See, e.g., West's Fla.Stat.Ann. § 458.331(1)(gg), requiring that a physician disclose an ownership interest of 10% or more to the patient referred for services. In Bronstein v. Board of Registration, 403 Mass. 621, 531 N.E.2d 593 (1988), the court examined a lease of office space for an optometrist which included as rent 15% of the gross revenue in excess of $500,000. Bronstein also received an annual $80,000 consulting fee from the lessor. The board of registration had ordered Bronstein to terminate the lease, on the basis that it violated the prohibition against fee-splitting. The trial court overturned the board's conclusion because the lessor exercised no control over the professional practice of the optometrist. For an overview of legal issues concerning health care joint ventures, see Roble and Mason, The Legal Aspects of Health Care Joint Ventures, 24 Duquesne L.Rev. 455 (1986).

6. Some hospital-physician joint ventures represent an attempt by the hospital to "bond" with its medical staff, i.e., to encourage doctors' preference for that hospital for patient admissions. Recall that "M" represented to the IRS that part of their motive in instigating the MRI arrangement was to improve relations with physicians. In a survey on hospital-doctor relationships, financial incentives and technology were influential but quality of care was the top ranked factor in a positive relationship. CEOs also reported that doctor-hospital joint ventures had not generally resulted in a bond between doctor and hospital. Grayson, Survey Spots the Tight Turns in MD–CEO Relations, 62 Hospitals 48 (1988).

II. PROFESSIONAL RELATIONSHIPS IN HEALTH CARE ENTERPRISES

This section presents current legal issues in both the traditional and the more contemporary forms of professional relationships in health care delivery, including hospital privileges, physician contracts, physician recruitment and primary care practice enterprises. In each of these sections, the goal is to highlight those factors which distinguish these health care business relationships from any other.

The last decade has been one of very significant change in the nature of the relationships examined here. One of the major changes has been the erosion of professional hegemony on the part of doctors in health care delivery.

Organized medicine long opposed the "corporate practice of medicine" because the corporate employer or partner inserted a non-physician manager between the physician and the patient. This protection of professional autonomy and control is seen as well in the traditional role of the medical staff in hospital governance. The current dominance of managed care has become the primary arena for the battle over professional control.

Managed care generally refers to health care delivery or payment systems that seek to contain health care costs borne by payers including private insurance providers and employers. The major tools of managed care include utilization review, which involves a third-party review of the frequency and intensity of health care services provided to patients; negotiated discounts for large purchasers of health services, usually using some form of preferred provider organization which negotiates the discounts on behalf of its member providers; and capitation payments. The leading tools of cost containment are discussed in Chapter 7.

Managed care systems have affected nearly the full range of professional relationships discussed in this chapter. The unique legal issues presented by interprofessional relationships in managed care contexts have not been fully developed, but many of the questions have been raised, and will be noted in this section.

A. HOSPITAL PRIVILEGES

A physician or other health care professional may admit or treat patients in a particular hospital only if the practitioner has clinical privileges at that hospital. Thus, hospital privileges are critical to the practice of most physicians and many other health care providers. At the same time, hospitals have become more restrictive in their granting and monitoring of privileges for many reasons, including the hospital's potential liability for failure to adequately monitor the quality of physicians granted privileges at the hospital. The scope of judicial review over decisions of hospitals concerning staff privileges is discussed in the following case.

RAO v. ST. ELIZABETH'S HOSPITAL

Appellate Court of Illinois, 1986.
140 Ill.App.3d 442, 94 Ill.Dec. 686, 488 N.E.2d 685.

JONES, JUSTICE:

The plaintiff, Mallavaropu S. Rao, M.D., brought suit against the defendant, St. Elizabeth's Hospital of the Hospital Sisters of the Third Order of St. Francis, seeking a temporary restraining order, preliminary injunction, and permanent injunction following the defendant's permanent suspension of the plaintiff from its medical staff. The plaintiff sought to enjoin the defendant's suspension of his privileges. The trial court issued a temporary restraining order but after a hearing denied the petition for preliminary injunction. Thereafter the trial court denied the plaintiff's motion to reconsider its order denying the preliminary injunction and still later granted the defendant's motion to dismiss the plaintiff's amended complaint for permanent injunction, for declaratory judgment, and for other relief. The plaintiff has appealed presenting several issues for review.

The facts are largely undisputed. On March 12, 1984, David Rose, M.D., Chairman of the defendant's Department of Medicine and of the Executive Committee of the defendant's Department of Medicine, wrote a letter to the plaintiff stating that the Executive Committee of the Department of Medicine wished to inform him that as of that date he would not be allowed to admit any new patients to the defendant institution or to see any new consultations there and that once any patients he was seeing at the time were discharged all medical privileges would be suspended. Further, all interpretation privileges in the Heart Station would cease according to the same schedule. The letter stated that the Executive Committee had reached this conclusion because of

"the following findings. After careful review of multiple patient records the following has been determined.

1. The number of glucose tolerance tests ordered is excessive and in many cases there is no appropriate indication for a glucose tolerance test.

2. There is serious question of the validity of interpretation of echo cardiograms.

3. The number and appropriateness of the diagnoses of angina pectoris, diabetes mellitus, and hypertension is not substantiated by the patients' records.

4. The number and appropriateness of multiple studies ordered from the Heart Station for each patient appears to be in error."

The letter advised the plaintiff that if he so requested, "pursuant to Article VII, Section 2, Subsection 2 of the Medical Staff Bylaws, you will have the opportunity to have an interview before an Ad Hoc Committee of the Medical Staff of St. Elizabeth's Hospital for review of your suspension." On March 15, 1984, at a special meeting the Executive Committee of the Medical Staff supported unanimously the summary suspension made by Dr. Rose.

On April 4, 1984, the Ad Hoc Committee of the defendant's medical staff conducted a hearing in response to the plaintiff's request for one. * * * The plaintiff was not represented by counsel at the hearing conducted by the Ad Hoc Committee. Dr. Rose was not present at the hearing. In his absence the Ad Hoc Committee entered his letter to the plaintiff of March 12, 1984, into the minutes. Early in the proceedings the plaintiff read a statement from a letter to the chief of defendant's medical staff, Dr. Santiago, in which the plaintiff said, *inter alia,* " 'I regret commissions and omissions inadvertently carried out by me during stressful situations during this [apparently the past few months] while caring for my patients at St. Elizabeth's Hospital. I was rightfully disciplined by my peers of the Medical Staff. This happened in the past and I assure you this will never be repeated.' " He concluded the statement by saying, " 'I only ask that I will be allowed to clear my name by being given another chance. Thank you for anything you might do in my behalf.' " * * *

[Plaintiff had not reviewed all the charts to be discussed at the hearing. He asked for time to do so but eventually agreed to review the charts during the course of the hearing.]

On April 11, 1984, the Ad Hoc Committee submitted its report concerning the plaintiff's suspension to Dr. Santiago. The Ad Hoc Committee confirmed the allegations made in Dr. Rose's letter of March 12, 1984, and reported as a further finding,

> "In addition, it [the committee] discovered a pattern of over and/or inappropriate utilization of laboratory procedures, particularly EKGs and glucose tolerance tests and examples of complaints of illnesses that were not substantially confirmed by subsequent hospital course, and instances of final diagnosis that did not jibe with or were not substantiated by history or laboratory data including serious additions (examples: diverticulitis, spastic colitis, thyrotoxicosis) and omissions (example: cholelithiasis). In the interpretations of glucose tolerance tests, he appeared to ignore existing guidelines."

The Ad Hoc Committee made the following four recommendations:

> "1. Dr. Rao be asked to take a leave of absence for one year;
>
> 2. After that time when he comes back to the Medical Staff, he should not be given privileges to read EKG's, echocardiogram and Holter monitor tests, invasive cardiac or endoscopic procedures;
>
> 3. He should be appropriately proctored for one year; and
>
> 4. If Dr. Rao does not accept the first three recommendations, the alternative recommendation would be suspension."

On May 7, 1984, the Executive Committee held a special meeting to hear the report of the Ad Hoc Committee. At the special meeting the Executive Committee accepted the report of the Ad Hoc Committee but did not accept its recommendations and, instead, voted to suspend the plaintiff permanently from the defendant's medical staff. * * * The Appellate Review Committee met on June 7, 1984, affirmed the Executive Committee's recommendation of permanent suspension, and made a recommendation of permanent suspension of the plaintiff to the defendant's Board of Directors. On June 12, 1984, the defendant's Board of Directors notified the plaintiff of its decision, effective immediately, to suspend him permanently from the defendant's medical staff.

On June 19, 1984, the plaintiff brought suit. * * *

* * *

* * * It is well established in Illinois that a private hospital's refusal to appoint a physician to its medical staff is not subject to judicial review, the rationale behind the rule being the unwillingness of the court to substitute its judgment for that of private hospital authorities. [ ] The only exception to the rule of non-review that has developed in this jurisdiction is that when a physician's existing staff

privileges are revoked or reduced, a private hospital must follow its own bylaws in so doing or be subject to limited judicial review. [ ] Otherwise stated, the general rule is that a court should not act to annul expulsions from hospitals unless unfairness is demonstrated by the fact that the procedures followed violated the constitution or bylaws of the hospital. [ ]

In his brief the plaintiff asserts that "the record in this case clearly demonstrates four major violations of the by-laws and several minor ones as well. Only the major ones will be discussed herein." First, and most importantly in the opinion of the plaintiff, the defendant, a private hospital, failed to follow article VIII, section 3, subsection 2, of its bylaws, which provides:

"The notice of hearing shall state in concise language the acts or omissions with which the practitioner is charged, a list of specific or representative charts being questioned, and/or the other reasons or subject matter that was considered in making the adverse recommendation or decision."

Describing the defendant's alleged omission in this regard as the "most clear and fundamental violation of the by-laws in this case," the plaintiff complains that the defendant failed to give him notice of the hearing of the Ad Hoc Committee in the manner required by this subsection. Specifically, he maintains that the acts or omissions with which he was charged were not stated in concise language and that he did not receive a list of specific or representative charts being questioned. * * * Having reviewed the record, we think that the trial court did not abuse its discretion in finding that the plaintiff acquiesced in the decision of the Ad Hoc Committee to proceed with the hearing as convened. * * * Displeased with the review of his suspension, he will not, after having assured the committee that to proceed was agreeable to him, be heard to say that he was prejudiced by the defendant's failure to provide him in advance of the hearing with the charts being questioned of the defendant's failure otherwise to abide by this provision of its bylaws.

The second violation by defendant of its bylaws alleged by the plaintiff is its failure to follow article VIII, section 5, subsection 8, which provides in pertinent part:

"The Executive Committee, when its action has prompted the hearing, shall appoint one of its members or some other Medical Staff member to represent it at the hearing, to present the facts in support of its adverse recommendation, and to examine witnesses. * * * It shall be the obligation of such representative to present appropriate evidence in support of the adverse recommendation * * *, but the affected practitioner shall thereafter be responsible for supporting his challenge to the adverse recommendation by an appropriate showing that the charges or grounds involved lack any factual basis or that such basis or any action based thereon is either arbitrary, unreasonable or capricious."

The plaintiff contends that

> "[b]ecause no member of the Executive Committee was there to face Dr. Rao and present the facts supporting the adverse recommendation (in other words to act as prosecutor) that function devolved upon the five members of the Ad Hoc Committee itself who were then placed in the position of having to interrogate and prosecute Dr. Rao as opposed to remaining in a neutral and impartial role as hearing and fact finding officers. Thus the committee members were forced to become both 'prosecutors and jury' in considering the charges made against Dr. Rao."

Contrary to the plaintiff's suggestion, the provision does not require the presence of the representative of the Executive Committee at the hearing of the Ad Hoc Committee. Although the representative who is absent from the hearing runs the risk of failing to satisfy his obligation of presenting appropriate evidence in support of the adverse recommendation of the Executive Committee, his or her absence would seem, if anything, to inure to the benefit of the practitioner against whom the representative would be proceeding. We think that, insofar as the plaintiff seeks to equate the procedures outlined in this subsection with the procedures required in a criminal prosecution, his interpretation is unwarranted. Especially is this so in view of the provision of article VIII, section 5, subsection 7, which states that "[t]he hearing need not be conducted strictly according to rules of law relating to the examination of witnesses or presentation of evidence." Inasmuch as subsection 8 does not require the representative of the Executive Committee to be present at the hearing, the absence of the representative from the hearing could not have constituted a violation of this provision of the defendant's bylaws.

The third violation of the bylaws that the plaintiff alleges is related to article VIII, section 5, subsection 9, which provides in pertinent part:

> "The affected practitioner shall have the following rights: to call and examine witnesses, to introduce written evidence, to cross-examine any witness on any matter relevant to the issue of the hearing, to challenge any witness and to rebut any evidence."

According to the plaintiff, the violation consists in the absence of witnesses from the Executive Committee or medical staff whom the plaintiff could cross-examine. However, the subsection provides the right to cross-examine any witness; it does not require the presence of witnesses to be cross-examined. Hence, the absence of witnesses from the Executive Committee or the medical staff could not have constituted a violation of the defendant's bylaws.

The fourth and final violation of the bylaws discussed by the plaintiff is related to article VII, section 2, subsections 1 and 4, concerning summary suspension. Subsection 1 provides:

> "Any one of the following: the Chairman of the Executive Committee, the President of the Medical Staff, the chairman of a

clinical department of the physician, the Chief Executive Officer or the Executive Committee of either the Medical Staff or the Governing Body shall each have the authority, whenever action must be taken immediately in the best interest of patient care in the Hospital, to summarily suspend all or any portion of the clinical privileges of a practitioner, and such summary suspension shall become effective immediately upon imposition."

Subsection 4 provides:

"Immediately upon the imposition of a summary suspension, the Chairman of the Executive Committee or responsible departmental chairman shall have authority to provide for alternative medical coverage for the patients of the suspended practitioner still in the Hospital at the time of such suspension. The wishes of the patients shall be considered in the selection of such alternative practitioner."

The plaintiff maintains that subsection 4 shows that summary suspension is a "drastic measure employed only when a physician's conduct or condition threatens immediate patient harm" and that such was not the case with regard to the conduct of which he was accused. "The inappropriateness of the imposition of summary suspension by the Chairman of the Executive Committee is," the plaintiff urges, "most dramatically highlighted by the fact that in the March 12, 1984, letter, the hospital states that Dr. Rao may continue to see and treat the patients he presently had admitted to the defendant hospital but that he will be no longer allowed to admit new patients. This is clearly inconsistent with the suggestion that 'imminent or immediate patient harm' is threatened by Dr. Rao's conduct." The plaintiff argues that the defendant should have proceeded to investigate his medical practices under another section of the bylaws whereby the affected practitioner is permitted to make an appearance before the Executive Committee prior to the reduction or suspension of clinical privileges. The determination of whether the action of summary suspension must be taken immediately in the best interest of patient care in the hospital would seem to fall within the ambit of judgment best exercised by hospital authorities and for which the court is unwilling to substitute its own judgment. Inasmuch as this determination is properly a medical one to be addressed to the discretion of medical professionals, we consider that aspect of subsection one not to be subject to judicial review. Therefore the determination of whether the Chairman of the Executive Committee needed to suspend the defendant's privileges immediately in the best interest of patient care in the hospital is beyond the scope of judicial review.

* * *

For these reasons the order of the trial court denying the temporary injunction is affirmed, and the order of the trial court granting the defendant's motion to dismiss the plaintiff's amended petition for permanent injunction and declaratory judgment is reversed and the cause remanded to the trial court with the limitations here imposed.

Affirmed in part; reversed in part and remanded with directions.

Notes and Questions

1. Compare the procedural requirements specified in the by-laws at issue in *Rao* with the following two provisions:

> 1) Good Samaritan Hospital is committed to the ideals of fair play and thus guarantees to its medical staff due process protection in any actions reducing or revoking their admitting privileges. The Executive Committee is to develop procedures that meet due process requirements.

> 2) The Board of Trustees of Good Archangel Hospital may limit, suspend or revoke the admitting privileges of any member of the medical staff, upon the recommendation of the Executive Committee of the medical staff. Neither the Executive Committee, nor any other committee, is required to hold a hearing. Rather, they are to notify the physician in writing of their consideration of negative action and are to allow the physician to respond in writing to particular charges.

Which of the three provisions is preferable? Why?

2. The Illinois Supreme Court had the opportunity to re-examine the scope of review of staff privileges decisions in private hospitals in Barrows v. Northwestern Memorial Hospital, 123 Ill.2d 49, 121 Ill.Dec. 244, 525 N.E.2d 50 (1988). The Supreme Court adhered to the rule of nonreviewability of these decisions. The Court of Appeals had held that the courts should review staff privileges decisions and overturn those that are "unreasonable, arbitrary, capricious or discriminatory."

In rejecting the claim of the physician that private staff privileges decisions should be reviewable as a matter of public policy, the Illinois Supreme Court noted that the public policy of Illinois, as expressed in a number of statutes, does not support review and that the "large majority" of states still do not provide judicial review. The Court found the public policy against review in statutes such as the Illinois Medical Practice Act, which gives limited immunity to participants in peer review activities.

As to the existence of a trend toward broader review of privileges decisions by private hospitals, the Court noted that only Arizona, California, Hawaii, New Hampshire, Vermont and New Mexico have adopted some form of the "New Jersey rule" subjecting these decisions to judicial review. The Court found that the rule of reviewability in New Jersey relied on a categorization of private hospitals as "quasi-public" institutions. Of the states identified as following the New Jersey rule, the Court found that New Mexico, Arizona and New Hampshire relied, not on the broader "quasi-public" concept, but rather on the relative lack of hospitals in those states and the near monopoly position of hospitals, especially in rural areas. The Illinois Supreme Court rejected the notion of a trend toward review. Illinois, like many states, however, does require that private hospitals meet standards of "fundamental fairness" in the procedures it uses for staff privileges decisions. Siqueira v. Northwestern Hospital, 132 Ill.App.3d 293, 87 Ill.Dec. 415, 477 N.E.2d 16 (1985).

3.   The Health Care Quality Improvement Act (42 U.S.C.A. § 11111 et seq. (1990)) provides immunity for "professional review actions" from damages under federal or state law (except for laws protecting civil rights). This does not include immunity from claims by non-physician health care professionals. In addition, the statute narrowly defines "professional review action" by establishing limited substantive criteria for such action and by specifying particular procedural standards. The HCQIA was enacted by Congress in response to claims that fear of antitrust liability was chilling the peer review process. The HCQIA and antitrust claims for staff privilege decisions are discussed in Chapter 8. For a comprehensive legislative history of the HCQIA, see Reams, The Health Care Quality Improvement Act of 1986: A Legislative History of Pub.L. 99–660 (1990).

4.   Mark Hall has argued that the "profession's grip on the internal organization of hospitals must be broken in order for cost containment to succeed." Hall, Institutional Control of Physician Behavior: Legal Barriers to Health Care Cost Containment, 137 U.Pa.L.Rev. 431 (1988). Hall reviews the literature on hospital organization, which variously describes the hospital as a "three-legged monster without a head" (referring to the independent lines of authority claimed by the doctors, the administrators and the owners) and as "two separate firms" (referring to the independence of the medical staff as to the "treatment demand function" and to the administration as controlling the "facility supply function"). These critiques of hospital organization refer to the very strong role of the medical staff in the governance of the hospital. The influence of JCAHO accreditation standards has been an important factor supporting this structure, granting to the medical staff the overall responsibility for the quality of the hospital's professional services and viewing the medical staff as independent of the hospital's governing body to the extent that medical staff by-laws are controlled to a significant, though not unilateral, degree by the medical staff itself. Many state hospital licensure statutes have adopted this model of medical staff control. Although the issue has not often been litigated, the medical staff by-laws have been held, by at least one court, to be contractual. In St. John's Hospital Medical Staff v. St. John Regional Medical Center, 245 N.W.2d 472 (S.D.1976), the court prohibited the governing board of a private hospital from amending the medical staff by-laws in the absence of the approval of the medical staff, which was required by the hospital's by-laws. Other historical factors contributing to the power of physicians include the development of antiseptic techniques for surgery and legal barriers to physician employment. For discussions of the development of physician dominance in hospital decisionmaking, see P. Starr, supra; Havighurst, Doctors and Hospitals: An Antitrust Perspective on Traditional Relationships, 1984 Duke L.J. 1071.

Hall comments: "One would expect the resulting lack of integration in function, utility, and authority to undermine the institution. In the past, it has not because the interests of doctors and hospitals traditionally have been directed along parallel, if not congruent paths. Under fee-for-service or cost-based reimbursement, they each benefitted from increased production. Thus, until now, growth of the facility has been the salve for potential hospital/physician conflict. Prospective payment, however, transforms this relationship into a potentially explosive one." Hall offers physician employment and contracting, discussed infra, as desirable alternatives to traditional staff privileges.

6. In *Rao*, the hospital's stated basis for revocation of privileges was the provision of substandard as well as arguably unnecessary care. "Economic credentialing" refers to situations in which hospitals consider the doctor's negative economic effect on the hospital in the privileges decision. What legal issues face a hospital that makes economic performance an explicit criterion for privileges? See Knapp v. Palos Community Hosp., 125 Ill.App.3d 244, 80 Ill.Dec. 442, 465 N.E.2d 554 (1984) (doctor's excessive use of lung scans, medications, pacemakers and other interventions resulted in recommendation for revoking doctor's privileges). See also, Blum, Economic Credentialling: A New Twist in Hospital Appraisal Processes, 12 J.Leg. Med. ___ (1991). Hospitals deny and revoke privileges for other reasons as well.

Among the permissible criteria used by hospitals for the denial of staff privileges are the ability to work with others, the purchase of adequate liability insurance, location of practice or residence in relationship to the hospital and adequate health. For a discussion of the supportability of these and other requirements, see Springer and Casole, Hospitals and the Disruptive Health Care Practitioner: Is the Inability to Work With Others Enough to Warrant Exclusion? 24 Duquesne L.Rev. 377 (1986) and Hein, Hospital Staff Privileges and the Courts: Practice and Prognosis, 34 FIC Quarterly 157 (1984). See also, Everhart v. Jefferson Parish Hosp. Dist. No. 2, 757 F.2d 1567 (5th Cir.1985), in which the court held that the doctor's "ability to work with others" was reasonably related to the purpose of providing adequate medical care and, therefore, a denial of privileges on that basis by a public hospital did not violate the doctor's right to substantive due process. What standards should the courts use to decide whether a particular criterion for privileges is legitimate?

7. Several states have enacted statutes, applying to both public and private hospitals, that limit a hospital's discretion in making clinical privileges decisions. Many of these statutes prohibit discrimination in the granting of staff privileges based on the type of medical degree (e.g., M.D. or D.O.). See, for example, Vernon's Ann.Tex.Rev.Civ.St. art. 4495b; Ohio Rev.Code § 3701.351 (which includes nurse-midwives among those protected from discrimination); and West's Fla.Stat.Ann. § 395.011. These anti-discrimination statutes involve the courts in reviewing the reasonableness of criteria established for the granting of privileges. See, e.g., Dooley v. Barberton Citizens Hospitals, 11 Ohio St.3d 216, 465 N.E.2d 58 (1984), in which the court held that a hospital's two-year residency requirement for staff privileges for podiatrists and a prohibition on surgery by podiatrists was unreasonable in light of the fact that there was no residency program in podiatry in Ohio and only eight to ten percent of podiatrists nationally had completed such a residency. Other state statutes impose specific procedural requirements upon the hospital. See, e.g., N.Y.–McKinney's Public Health Law § 2801, which includes review by the Public Health Council of the denial or diminution of privileges. Should the states limit

the discretion of hospitals in this matter? If so, which type of statute is preferable—the antidiscrimination statute or the procedural statute?

8. Unlike private hospitals, public hospitals must meet due process standards in their privileges proceedings. Cases examining whether a hospital is public or private, for the purposes of judicial review of staff privileges decisions, include Richardson v. St. John's Mercy Hospital, 674 S.W.2d 200 (Mo.App.1984), in which the court held that there was not a sufficiently close nexus between public funds received by the hospital through government reimbursement for care and the Hill–Burton program and the restriction of the physician's privileges, and Kiracofe v. Reid Memorial Hospital, 461 N.E.2d 1134 (Ind.App.1984), in which the court held that the state did not attempt to influence the termination of the physician's privileges and that there was, therefore, no state action despite the fact that the local government appointed four board members, the city held legal title to the land and the hospital's by-laws stated that it was owned by the people.

In Milo v. Cushing Municipal Hospital, 861 F.2d 1194 (10th Cir.1988), the Tenth Circuit considered a case involving a publicly owned hospital leased to and operated by a private hospital management corporation under contract with the city. The contract provided that the management corporation handled medical staff privileges and discipline. Two physicians who were summarily suspended from the hospital brought an action under 42 U.S.C.A. § 1983, which requires state action. The physicians claimed that they had been suspended for reporting the misconduct of another physician on staff.

In addressing the issue of whether the hospital was a public or private entity, the Tenth Circuit relied on Jatoi v. Hurst–Euless–Bedford Hospital Authority, 807 F.2d 1214 (5th Cir.1987). In *Jatoi,* the Fifth Circuit had decided that a public hospital authority that had leased the hospital to a private organization for day-to-day operations, including staff privileges decisions, remained liable for the actions of the hospital due to the degree of financial support and control provided by the authority. The Tenth Circuit followed suit and found that the hospital in *Milo* was a public institution and subject to § 1983.

9. A number of courts have held that Title VII claims alleging racial, sexual, religious or national origin discrimination in staff privileges decisions can prevail without the existence of a formal employer-employee relationship. See e.g., Zaklama v. Mt. Sinai Medical Center, 842 F.2d 291 (11th Cir.1988); Ross v. William Beaumont Hospital, 678 F.Supp. 655 (E.D.Mich.1988); Mousavi v. Beebe Hospital of Sussex County, Inc., 674 F.Supp. 145 (D.Del.1987). But see, Diggs v. Harris Hospital-Methodist, Inc., 847 F.2d 270 (5th Cir.1988).

Problem: Springfield Medical Center

Dr. Michael Carson has had admitting privileges at Springfield Medical Center for the past six years. Springfield Medical Center is incorporated as a not-for-profit corporation. Its by-laws provide that the board members must include the city health commissioner and the mayor or his delegate. The city has a contract with Springfield Medical Center in which SMC agrees to provide care for the indigent patients of the city. Payments to SMC under this contract make up 30% of the hospital's budget. The current health commissioner and mayor have been very active on the board.

Dr. Carson has an abrasive personality and is considered a maverick among physicians in Springfield, a city of 100,000. Although Dr. Carson's relationships at the hospital have never been entirely cordial, there had been no serious problems until recently when Dr. Carson began to expand his practice by employing a nurse practitioner and a physician assistant. Dr. Carson is very vocal about the hostility he perceives on the part of the doctors and nurses at the hospital toward his new employees. He has spoken to the hospital administrator and told the administrator that he would sue the hospital if the administrator, the medical staff or hospital employees interfered with his practice.

The administrator and the president of the medical staff last month received a letter from several doctors on the staff reporting that the nurse practitioner employed by Dr. Carson made house calls for "well-baby" check-ups and that the physician assistant prescribed medications. They also stated that they believed that Dr. Carson's practice had expanded beyond what he could handle and that his supervision of the PA was inadequate. Under a provision identical to that included in *Rao*, the administrator and the president of the medical staff summarily suspended Dr. Carson's staff privileges. Their action was discovered and reported by the local newspaper. Many of Dr. Carson's patients left him, and the nurse practitioner resigned her employment. Although Dr. Carson was offered reinstatement eventually, he has sued the hospital for damages claiming that the summary suspension violated the hospital's by-laws and denied him due process. You are counsel for the hospital. You have been asked to estimate the likelihood that Dr. Carson will be successful in his suit. Explain why you believe Dr. Carson will or will not be successful.

Note: HIV Infection and Health Care Workers

The risk of transmission of the human immunodeficiency virus goes both ways in the health care setting: for health care workers, exposure to HIV, through patients who are seropositive for HIV, is an occupational hazard; for patients, such exposure may come from health care workers who themselves are HIV positive.

Health care workers who are HIV positive may be protected from discrimination under § 504 of the Rehabilitation Act. The U.S. Supreme Court in School Board of Nassau County v. Arline, 480 U.S. 273, 107 S.Ct. 1123, 94 L.Ed.2d 307 (1987) considered the application of § 504 to a teacher who had tuberculosis, and established a framework for analyzing the application of § 504 in the context of transmissible diseases. The Court held that the teacher was within the coverage of § 504 despite claims by the school board that she was dismissed because of her threat to the health of others. In a footnote, the Court refers to the implications its holding might have for persons with AIDS: "[T]he United States [argues] that discrimination solely on the basis of contagiousness is never discrimination on the basis of a handicap. The argument is misplaced in this case, because the handicap here, tuberculosis, gave rise both to a physical impairment *and* to contagiousness." The Court goes on, however, to indicate that the opinion does not intend to resolve the question in regard to persons who are merely seropositive for HIV but who have not experienced any of the symptomatic diseases or impairments of AIDS: "This case does not present, and we therefore do not reach, the questions whether a carrier of a contagious disease such as AIDS could be considered to have a physical impairment, or whether such a person could be considered, solely on the basis of contagiousness, a handicapped person as defined by the Act."

The Act requires handicapped persons to prove that they are "otherwise qualified" for the job. The Supreme Court considered this issue in relation to contagious diseases. It relied on an amicus brief filed by the American Medical Association arguing that the question requires "findings of facts, based on reasonable medical judgments given the state of medical knowledge, about (a) the nature of the risk (how the disease is transmitted), (b) the duration of the risk (how long is the carrier infectious), (c) the severity of the risk (what is the potential harm to third parties) and (d) the probabilities the disease will be transmitted and will cause varying degrees of harm."

The Ninth Circuit, subsequent to *Arline,* held that a teacher with AIDS is protected from dismissal under § 504. Chalk v. United States District Court, 840 F.2d 701 (9th Cir.1988).

After *Arline,* Congress amended the Rehabilitation Act to provide: "For the purpose of section 504 [as it relates to employment], [individual with handicap] does not include an individual who has a currently contagious disease or infection and who, by reason of such disease or infection, would constitute a direct threat to the health or safety of other individuals or who, by reason of the currently contagious disease or infection, is unable to perform the duties of the job." This was generally viewed as "codifying *Arline.*" See AIDS Policy & Law, 3/23/88 (BNA).

Under the *Arline* analysis, policies concerning health care workers with AIDS must consider the actual risk of transmission to patients. Most AIDS policies developed by national organizations focus on distinguishing those health care activities that present such a risk from those that generally do not. For example, the American Medical Association has issued a policy statement that "a physician who knows that he or she is seropositive should not engage in any activity that creates a risk of transmission of the disease to others." AMA Council on Ethical and Judicial Affairs, 259 J.A.M.A. 1360, 1361 (1988). The Centers for Disease Control have been the primary source of authoritative information concerning the risk of transmission. In 1987, CDC issued guidelines concerning the risk of transmission in the health care setting. Centers for Disease Control, Recommendations for Preventing Transmission of HIV in Health–Care Settings, 36 Morbidity & Mortality Weekly Rep. 305 (1987). CDC recently indicated that it would be reviewing its policies concerning screening of health care workers, restrictions in practice and disclosure to patients. AIDS Policy & Law, 8/8/90 (BNA). The CDC recently reported the first case in which it appears that a health care worker transmitted the

AIDS virus to a patient during the course of treatment. This report involved a dentist who was HIV positive and who may have infected a patient on whom he performed two molar extractions. The CDC reported that the dentist wore gloves and a mask and recalled no needlesticks. The patient reported no other risk factors for HIV infection. AIDS Policy & Law, 8/8/90 (BNA).

Cases challenging employment discrimination by health care employers based on HIV status have been percolating through the legal system. In one of the more recent, the counsel for the New York State Division of Human Rights issued a proposed decision that prohibits a hospital from strictly limiting the job duties of a hospital pharmacist who was HIV-positive. The proposed decision cites CDC guidelines in support of its conclusion: the hospital "ignores the clear and unequivocal determination by the CDC that HIV seropositive health care workers performing non-invasive procedures, such as [this pharmacist], need not be restricted from work and do not pose a threat of infection to their patients." The U.S. Office of Civil Rights, pursuant to the pharmacist's claim under § 504, had issued a similar preliminary ruling in the case. AIDS Policy & Law, 8/8/90 (BNA).

In Leckelt v. Board of Commissioners, 714 F.Supp. 1377 (E.D.La.1989), the district court considered the case of a licensed practical nurse who was suspected of having HIV infection and who was dismissed by the hospital-employer when he refused to submit to a test for HIV. The court rejected plaintiff's claim under § 504, finding that he was not handicapped under the Act because the hospital never concluded that he was seropositive. Further, the court found that his dismissal was not based solely on his handicap but on his refusal to take the blood test. The court found that plaintiff was not "otherwise qualified:" "Hospitals are not at liberty to presume, at the risk of the lives of the public, that all employees adhere to their infection control policies at all times. * * * The CDC guidelines call for continuing consultation between the health care institution and the employee's personal physician to determine, on an individualized basis, what job assignments the employee is capable of filling. Although an asymptomatic seropositive individual may present a relatively slight risk to patients, co-workers and himself, and may require relatively little accommodation, a health care institution must know the individual's health status so that it can monitor his condition and determine whether that condition has deteriorated to a point where additional precautions or job modifications are necessary." At 1388. Leckelt was suspected of being HIV positive because his companion of eight years, who was seropositive, had been admitted to defendant hospital. But see, Glover v. Eastern Nebraska Community Office of Retardation, 867 F.2d 461 (8th Cir.1989) in which the court rejected a policy in which the defendant, a provider of residential, vocational and other specialized services for the mentally retarded, required all employees in certain positions to be tested. What advice would you give to hospital clients concerning testing of employees? For a sample of the debate concerning health care workers with AIDS, see Closen, A Call for Mandatory HIV Testing and Restriction of Certain Health Care Professionals, 9 St. Louis U.Pub.L.Rev. 421 (1990) and Isaacman, The Other Side of the Coin: HIV–Infected Health Care Workers, 9 St. Louis U.Pub.L.Rev. 439 (1990).

The Americans with Disabilities Act of 1990 also prohibits employment discrimination based on disability. This act adopts the standards of the Rehabilitation Act as the minimum standards for implementation of the ADA. The employment discrimination protections of the ADA will be enforced by the Equal Employment Opportunity Commission, which now has authority to enforce Title VII and the Age Discrimination in Employment Act, among others.

The risk of HIV transmission from patients to health care workers also raises legal and public policy issues. Risk of transmission, and fear of transmission, has an impact on the availability and quality of health care for persons with AIDS. These issues are discussed in Chapter 6. Studies continue to indicate that the risk of transmission is small and arises most frequently in situations in which there has been an inoculation of contaminated blood through a needlestick. Some health care interventions present higher risks. See, e.g., Peterson, AIDS: The Ethical Dilemma for Surgeons, 17 Law, Medicine & Health Care 139 (1989). The calculus of risk must take into account, of course, the consequences of the infection. Although experience with this disease is relatively recent, it appears that HIV infection will lead to death from AIDS within ten years for approximately 70% of those with the virus.

In 1989, the Occupational Safety and Health Administration issued proposed guidelines for controlling occupational exposure to blood-borne pathogens. The OSHA guidelines rely primarily on risk assessment; post-exposure surveillance; training and education; work practices; engineering controls; labeling; and waste disposal methods. 54 Fed.Reg. 23042.

Health care employers may be liable to health care workers who contract AIDS from patients. Tort claims against health care employers face a number of obstacles. Workers included in the coverage of workers' compensation may be restricted to that system, which limits the losses covered, unless the worker can prove that he fits within an exception to coverage. Beyond the workers' compensation limitation, tort actions would face problems in proving causation (the worker would have to eliminate other possible sources of infection) and in proving negligence (the employer's compliance with CDC and OSHA guidelines would make this difficult). A notorious case of a lawsuit by a doctor against a hospital occupied the front page of the national news in 1990.

Dr. Veronica Prego was an Argentine medical school graduate pursuing her New York state medical license in the "extern" program at the King's County Hospital of New York City. As an extern, she was expected to work uncompensated under the close supervision of intern Dr. Joyce Fogel.

Between November 1982 and January 1983, Dr. Prego alleged that while assisting Dr. Fogel in the collection of blood cultures from an HIV-infected patient, she stuck her finger with an HIV-infected needle left behind by Dr. Fogel among refuse on the patient's bed. In 1984, Dr. Prego took part in a survey regarding the presence of HIV antibodies among health care workers. Although she tested positive for the HIV antibody in this survey, she dismissed this result as she showed no symptoms of AIDS. Furthermore, she attributed some weight loss and fatigue experienced at this time to overwork and marital problems. In 1987, however, she developed symptoms associated with pneumocystis carinii pneumonia (an opportunistic form of pneumonia typically associated as a secondary illness signalling the onset of AIDS). On July 5, 1988, she filed a negligence suit against the City of New York alleging that the hospital failed to provide appropriate disposal receptacles for such needles.

Although this action was settled prior to trial on its merits, two collateral issues of particular importance were raised by the defense as pre-trial motions. The first of these issues concerned the New York Toxic Torts Bill enacted in 1986. This bill retroactively changed the discovery rule setting the date of accrual for a tort action regarding the "latent effects of exposure to any substance." As a result, the date to begin accrual was set as the date the plaintiff knew or should have known of her exposure to a toxic substance in contrast to the date of the exposure itself.

Ruling that HIV qualified under this statute as a substance to which exposure would lead to the latent effects of the AIDS disease, the court held the statute to grant one year and ninety days from the date she knew or should have known of her exposure to the virus to bring her claim. The court declined, however, to find when Dr. Prego should have known of her exposure reserving this issue for the jury. Prego v. City of New York, 147 A.D.2d 165, 541 N.Y.S.2d 995 (1989).

The second issue raised was a workers' compensation defense. The City alleged that Dr. Prego was an employee of the hospital and thus was obligated to bring her claim before the Worker's Compensation Board. This alternative approach would have precluded Dr. Prego from seeking any further recovery from the hospital. Holding that Dr. Prego was not an employee of the hospital, the court noted that Dr. Prego was seeking to fulfill the prerequisites to becoming an employee in the future. In addition, the court ruled that to allow a worker's compensation defense to be raised at this late date would unfairly prejudice Dr. Prego's claim as the Board may find she discovered her exposure more than two years earlier which would then bar her from any recovery at all. New York Law Journal, November 7, 1989.

It was reported in the March 9, 1990, edition of the Los Angeles Times that Dr. Prego settled her claim on March 8, 1990 for an undisclosed sum in an agreement in which neither party admitted fault. She originally claimed $176 million in damages.

An excellent symposium on "Health Care Workers and AIDS" has been published by the Maryland Law Review (48 Md.L.Rev. 1–245 (1989)). It includes an article by Rothenberg, et al., describing an AIDS project in which the situation of AIDS in the health care setting was specifically addressed: Creating a Public Health Policy—Rights and Obligations of Health Care Workers, 48 Md.L.Rev. 95 (1989). Also recommended is Brennan, Ensuring Adequate Health Care for the Sick: The Challenge of the Acquired Immunodeficiency Syndrome as an Occupational Disease, 1988 Duke L.J. 29 (1988).

B. EXCLUSIVE CONTRACTS

The competitive and cost-containment pressures of the 1980s produced a significant change in physician-hospital relationships. No
longer is the traditional privileges system the only structure for this
relationship. Instead, physicians, especially those with hospital-based
practices such as radiology, anesthesiology, and pathology, increasingly
are entering contractual relationships with hospitals. And, in general,
the current generation of new physicians prefer employment-type situations in hospitals, health maintenance organizations or other types of
institutions over the traditional independent solo or small-group practice. These contracts may radically alter the traditional terms of the
physician-hospital relationship.

MATEO–WOODBURN v. FRESNO COMMUNITY HOSPITAL

Court of Appeals, Fifth District, 1990.
221 Cal.App.3d 1169, 270 Cal.Rptr. 894.

Brown, J.

* * *

The medical staff of FCH is governed by its own bylaws, which are
formulated by the physicians and thereafter approved by the board of
trustees, the governing body of FCH. [U]nder the bylaws, medical staff
membership cannot be arbitrarily withheld or terminated without
cause.

* * *

Each plaintiff was a member of the medical staff. * * *

Prior to August 1, 1985, and as early as 1970, the FCH department
of anesthesiology operated as an open staff. The department was
composed of anesthesiologists who were independently competing entrepreneurs with medical staff privileges in anesthesiology. Collectively,
the anesthesiologists were responsible for scheduling themselves for the
coverage of regularly scheduled, urgent and emergency surgeries.
* * *

[E]ach anesthesiologist was rotated, on a daily basis, through a
first-pick, second-pick, etc., sequence whereby each anesthesiologist
chose a particular operating room for that particular date. Usually no
work was available for one or more anesthesiologists at the end of the
rotation schedule. Once an anesthesiologist rotated through first-pick,
he or she went to the end of the line. In scheduling themselves, the
anesthesiologists established a system that permitted each anesthesiologist on a rotating basis to have the "pick" of the cases. This usually
resulted in the "first-pick" physician taking what appeared to be the
most lucrative cases available for that day.

The rotation system encouraged many inherent and chronic vices. For example, even though members of the department varied in their individual abilities, interests, skills, qualifications and experience, often "first-picks" were more consistent with economic advantage than with the individual abilities of the physician exercising his or her "first-pick" option. At times, anesthesiologists refused to provide care for government subsidized patients, allegedly due to economic motivations.

The department chairman had the authority to suggest to fellow physicians that they only take cases for which they were well qualified. However, the chairman was powerless to override the rotation system in order to enforce these recommendations.

Under the open-staff rotation system, anesthesiologists rotated into an "on call" position and handled emergencies arising during off hours. This led to situations where the "on-call" anesthesiologist was not qualified to handle a particular emergency and no formal mechanism was in place to ensure that alternative qualified anesthesiologists would become promptly available when needed.   * * *

* * *

These chronic defects in the system led to delays in scheduling urgent cases because the first call anesthesiologists in charge of such scheduling at times refused to speak to each other. Often, anesthesiologists, without informing the nursing staff, left the hospital or made rounds while one or more of their patients were in post-anesthesia recovery. This situation caused delays as the nurses searched for the missing anesthesiologist.

The trial court found these conditions resulted in breaches of professional efficiency, severely affected the morale of the department and support staff, and impaired the safety and health of the patients. As a result of these conditions, the medical staff (not the board of trustees) initiated action resulting ultimately in the change from an "open" to a "closed" system. We recite the highlights of the processes through which this change took place.

* * *

[Defendant] Helzer, President and Chief Executive Officer of FCH, established an "Anesthesia Task Force" to study the proposed closure. In a subsequent memo to Helzer, dated April 6, 1984, the task force indicated it had considered four alternative methods of dealing with problems in the department of anesthesiology: (1) continuation of the status quo, i.e., independent practitioners with elected department chairman, (2) competitive groups of anesthesiologists with an elected department chairman, (3) an appointed director of anesthesia with independent practitioners and (4) an appointed director with subcontracted anesthesiologists, i.e., a closed staff.

The memo noted that under the third alternative—a director with independent practitioners—the director would have no power to determine who would work in the department of anesthesiology. "Any restriction or disciplinary action recommended by the director would need to go through the usual hospital staff procedure, which can be protracted." It was also noted in the memo that a director with subcontracted practitioners "would have the ability to direct their activities without following usual hospital staff procedures." The committee recommended a director with subcontracted practitioners. [The board held an open meeting to discuss the proposal.]

* * *

[Later], the board rejected [a] counter proposal [offered by Mateo–Woodburn] and authorized the formation of a search committee to recruit a director for the department of anesthesiology. The board also determined that upon appointment of a permanent director, the department would be closed.

Mateo–Woodburn was offered the position of interim director on June 13, 1984, which position she accepted. Mateo–Woodburn was interviewed for the position of director on September 25, 1984. [Dr. William] Hass was interviewed for the position on March 7, 1985.

At a special meeting of the board of trustees held on April 10, 1985, the anesthesia search committee recommended to the board that Hass be hired as director of the department of anesthesiology, and the recommendation was accepted by the board.

At the same April 10 meeting, the board authorized its executive committee to close the department of anesthesiology. On the same day, the executive committee met and ordered the department closed. * * *

* * *

An agreement between FCH and the Hass corporation was entered into on June 7, 1985. On June 18, 1985, Helzer sent a letter to all members of the department of anesthesiology which states in relevant part:

* * *

"The Board of Trustees has now entered into an agreement with William H. Hass, M.D., a professional corporation, to provide anesthesiology services for all hospital patients effective July 1, 1985. The corporation will operate the Department of Anesthesia under the direction of a Medical Director who will schedule and assign all medical personnel. The corporation has appointed Dr. Hass as Medical Director, and the hospital has concurred with the appointment. The agreement grants to the corporation the exclusive right to provide anesthesia services to all hospital patients at all times.

"To provide the services called for by the agreement, it is contemplated that the Hass Corporation will enter into contractual arrangement with individual physician associates who must obtain Medical Staff membership and privileges as required by the staff bylaws. The negotiations with such associates are presently ongoing, and the hospital does not participate in them.

"Effective August 1, 1985, if you have not entered into an approved contractual agreement, with the Hass Corporation, you will not be permitted to engage in direct patient anesthesia care in this hospital. However, at your option, you may retain your staff membership and may render professional evaluation and assessment of a patient's medical condition at the express request of the attending physician."

The contract between the Hass corporation and FCH provided that the corporation was the exclusive provider of clinical anesthesiology services at the hospital; the corporation was required to provide an adequate number of qualified physicians for this purpose; physicians were to meet specific qualifications of licensure, medical staff membership and clinical privileges at FCH, and to have obtained at least board eligibility in anesthesiology; and the hospital had the right to review and approve the form of any contract between the corporation and any physician-associate prior to its execution.

Subject to the terms of the master contract between the Hass corporation and FCH, the corporation had the authority to select physicians with whom it would contract on terms chosen by the corporation subject to the approval of FCH. The contract offered to the anesthesiologists, among many other details, required that a contracting physician be a member of the hospital staff and be board certified or board eligible. The Hass corporation was contractually responsible for all scheduling, billing and collections. Under the contract, the corporation was to pay the contracting physician in accordance with a standard fee arrangement. The contracting physician was required to limit his or her professional practice to FCH except as otherwise approved by the FCH board of trustees.

[The contract also provided:] " * * * Provider shall not be entitled to any of the hearing rights provided in the Medical Staff Bylaws of the Hospital and Provider hereby waives any such hearing rights that Provider may have. However, the termination of this Agreement shall not affect Provider's Medical Staff membership or clinical privileges at the Hospital other than the privilege to provide anesthesiology services at the Hospital."

Seven of the thirteen anesthesiologists on rotation during July 1985 signed the contract. Of the six plaintiffs in this case, five refused to sign the contract offered to them. The sixth plaintiff, Dr. Woodburn, was not offered a contract but testified that he would not have signed it, had one been offered.

* * *

Some of the reasons given for refusal to sign the contract were: (1) the contract required the plaintiffs to give up their vested and fundamental rights to practice at FCH; (2) the 60–day termination clause contained no provisions for due process review; (3) the contract failed to specify amounts to be taken out of pooled income for administrative costs; (4) the contract required plaintiffs to change medical malpractice carriers; (5) the contract required plaintiffs to obtain permission to practice any place other than FCH; (6) the contract imposed an unreasonable control over plaintiffs' financial and professional lives; (7) the contract failed to provide tenure of employment. The Hass corporation refused to negotiate any of the terms of the contract with plaintiffs.

* * *

* * * Numerous cases recognize that the governing body of a hospital, private or public, may make a rational policy decision or adopt a rule of general application to the effect that a department under its jurisdiction shall be operated by the hospital itself through a contractual arrangement with one or more doctors to the exclusion of all other members of the medical staff except those who may be hired by the contracting doctor or doctors. * * *

* * *

[T]he vested rights of a staff doctor in an adjudicatory one-on-one setting, wherein the doctor's professional or ethical qualifications for staff privileges is in question, take on a different quality and character when considered in light of a rational, justified policy decision by a hospital to reorganize the method of delivery of certain medical services, even though the structural change results in the exclusion of certain doctors from the operating rooms. If the justification is sufficient, the doctor's vested rights must give way to public and patient interest in improving the quality of medical services.

It is also noted, where a doctor loses or does not attain staff privileges because of professional inadequacy or misconduct, the professional reputation of that doctor is at stake. In that circumstance, his or her ability to become a member of the staff at other hospitals is severely impaired. On the other hand, a doctor's elimination by reason of a departmental reorganization and his failure to sign a contract does not reflect upon the doctor's professional qualifications and should not affect his opportunities to obtain other employment. The trial court correctly found the decision to close the department of anesthesiology and contract with Hass did not reflect upon the character, competency or qualifications of any particular anesthesiologist.

Plaintiffs list numerous other contentions. Plaintiffs characterize the contract offered to them by Hass as "Draconian" because of the 60–day termination provision and requirement they waive hearing rights contained in the medical staff bylaws, as well as the requirement that permission be obtained prior to practicing at any hospital other than FCH. They also complain of the fact that Lars Bjorkman, assistant director, was offered and accepted a four-year contract with no termination clause, and the fact that cardiac surgery anesthesiologists were allowed to enter into negotiations on a contract with different terms, while Hass refused to negotiate terms with the plaintiffs.

* * *

[I]f the hospital's policy decision to make the change is lawful, and we hold it is, then the terms of the contracts offered to the doctors was part of the administrative decision and will not be interfered with by this court unless those terms bear no rational relationship to the objects to be accomplished, i.e., if they are substantially irrational or they illegally discriminate among the various doctors.

Given the conditions existing under the open rotation method of delivering anesthesia services, including among others the lack of control of scheduling and the absence of proper discipline, we cannot say the terms of the contract were irrational, unreasonable or failed to bear a proper relationship to the object of correcting those conditions. Considered in this light, the terms are not arbitrary, capricious or irrational.

* * *

As to the contract provision which required waiver of hearing rights set forth in the staff bylaws, * * * those rights do not exist under the circumstances of a quasi-legislative reorganization of a department by the board of trustees. This quasi-legislative situation is to be distinguished from a quasi-judicial proceeding against an individual doctor grounded on unethical or unprofessional conduct or incompetency. Accordingly, the waiver did not further detract from or diminish plaintiffs' rights.

* * *

Plaintiffs contend the department of anesthesiology could not be reorganized without amending the bylaws of the medical staff in accordance with the procedure for amendment set forth therein. Closely allied to this argument is the assertion the hospital unlawfully delegated to Hass the medical staff's authority to make staff appointments.

* * * The hospital's action did not change the manner or procedure by which the medical staff passes upon the qualifications, competency or skills of particular doctors in accordance with medical staff bylaws. * * * In fact, plaintiffs remain members of the staff and the contract requires contracting anesthesiologists to be members of the staff. Moreover, it is clear the medical staff does not appoint medical staff members—it makes recommendations to the board of trustees who then makes the final medical staff membership decision. Hass was never given authority to appoint physicians to medical staff and never did so. Hass was merely hired to provide anesthesiology services to the hospital. His decision to contract with various anesthesiologists in order to provide those services was irrelevant to medical staff appointments except that all persons contracting with Hass were required to qualify as members of the medical staff.

We conclude the trial court's determination that the defendants' "actions were proper under the circumstance and that plaintiffs' Medical Staff privileges were not unlawfully terminated, modified or curtailed" is fully supported by the evidence and is legally correct.

Notes and Questions

1. If Fresno Community Hospital had based its decision to contract for anesthesiology on projections that it would save the hospital money, would the result have been the same?

2. Why did Fresno allow the plaintiff doctors to maintain their staff privileges? If the hospital or medical staff by-laws did not allow for reduction or revocation of privileges on this particular basis, should the hospital have been allowed to proceed? Are you persuaded by the court's argument that this type of general policy decision should be treated differently than a decision on an individual's privileges?

3. As discussed earlier in the section on privileges, some states require that the hospital provide procedures for credentialling that are "fundamentally fair." Should a similar requirement be established for physicians providing hospital-based services under contract? Whose interests are served by such a requirement? Do the interests vary in a contract, as opposed to a traditional privileges, situation?

4. In Szczerbaniuk v. Memorial Hospital, 180 Ill.App.3d 706, 129 Ill.Dec. 454, 536 N.E.2d 138 (1989), a radiologist working under an exclusive agreement sued the hospital when his contract and his staff privileges were terminated based on charges that he had sexually harassed hospital employees. The hospital claimed that it was immune from civil damages under an Illinois statute that provided immunity for actions of "a medical utilization review committee, medical review committee, patient care audit committee, medical care evaluation committee, quality review committee, credential committee, peer review committee, or any other committee whose purpose * * * is internal quality control or * * * reduc[ing] morbidity or mortality or * * * improving patient care * * * or for the purpose of professional discipline." While the trial court dismissed plaintiff's claim on this basis, the appellate court reversed. The hospital chief executive officer had investigated the allegations and terminated Dr. Szczerbaniuk's contract and privileges. The executive committee of the hospital's board of directors had informally authorized the CEO to handle the situation as he saw fit and had concurred in the CEO's decision, but had not itself reviewed any of the evidence. The court held that the CEO's action was essentially unilateral and not the action of a committee and further, that the absence of peer review by other health care providers removed the hospital's act from the immunity provided for in the statute. Dr. Szczerbaniuk also claimed breach of contract for the discharge, claiming that the by-laws formed a contract between the hospital and the members of the medical staff. Earlier Illinois cases had stated that the by-laws were contractual in nature. Head v. Lutheran General Hospital, 163 Ill.App.3d 682, 114 Ill.Dec. 766, 516 N.E.2d 921 (1987).

The court held that the contract between Szczerbaniuk and Memorial was unambiguous in displacing the bylaws. The contract provided that if the contract were terminated, medical staff privileges were also terminated. It did not refer to the by-laws and provided that disputes were to be resolved by the executive committee of the board of directors and ultimately by the board itself, which decision would be binding. The contract stated that either party could terminate the agreement, "upon good cause shown," with 180 days' written notice. The court upheld the dismissal of plaintiff's claim for breach of the by-laws. What is left for Dr. Szczerbaniuk in this litigation?

5. The pronounced move toward employment-type relationships between doctors and hospitals, HMOs, or large multi-specialty groups has its proponents and its opponents. Mark Hall, for example, argues that employment/contract relationships are among the most effective cost-containment devices. Hall, Institutional Control of Physician Behavior: Legal Barriers to Health Care Cost Containment, 137 U.Pa.L.Rev. 431 (1988). David Frankford disagrees and argues that greater integration of physicians within employment/contract relationships will not result in cost saving. Instead, Frankford argues, the "trend toward increased employment of physicians within relatively centralized and bureaucratic organizations may be to enhance the power of health care professionals to influence the actions of patients, albeit with a transfer of that influence [and the wealth that results] from the individual professionals to the organizations that employ them. * * * Practice will decreasingly be 'client-dependent' or 'colleague-dependent,' and it will increasingly become 'organization-dependent.'" Frankford, Creating and Dividing the Fruits of Collective Economic Activity: Referrals Among Health Care Providers, 89 Col.L.Rev. 1861, 1931–1932 (1989). What factors support each of these positions? What are the implications of "organization-dependent" practice?

6. For a discussion of the antitrust implications of exclusive contracts, see Chapter 8.

C. PHYSICIAN RECRUITMENT

The bargaining power between doctors and hospitals has not shifted completely toward the hospital. In fact, hospitals continue to depend on physicians for admissions and, despite a prediction of a physician glut, most must recruit physicians who will admit financially desirable patients to the hospital for services favored by current public and private payment systems or identified by the facility as centers of excellence and concentration.

Hospitals and other health care providers, such as health maintenance organizations, may recruit physicians for employment. In many cases, however, hospitals are recruiting physicians who will establish a private practice in a hospital's service area and will admit patients to the hospital. In others, the hospital is attempting to "bond" with physicians who already admit patients to make sure that these physicians continue to do so. Some of the joint ventures discussed in the section on competitive behavior by not-for-profit health care providers are typical of strategies used by hospitals to retain the loyalty of doctors with admitting privileges.

As you might expect, strategies for recruiting physicians are similar to recruiting any other type of individuals and involve the same courting and personal attention you hope for from your future employers or colleagues. But a great deal of physician recruitment relies on financial incentives. See, e.g., Grayson, Physician Recruitment Takes Center Stage, 63 Hospitals 30 (1989); Koska, Physician Recruiting 101: Avoid the Classic Mistakes, 64 Hospitals 46 (1990).

Agreements struck by health care providers and physicians are subject to run-of-the-mill disputes over contractual rights and obligations. For example, in Humana Medical Corporation v. Peyer, 155 Wis.2d 714, 456 N.W.2d 355 (1990), Dr. Peyer sued Humana for failing to respond to his request for references necessary for board certification. Dr. Peyer had established a practice in Florence, Alabama, under the terms of a "Physician Recruitment Agreement" with Humana. Under this agreement, the hospital loaned Peyer the money needed for equipment for his office practice and paid him advances on his projected practice income. Peyer agreed in return to practice in Florence for two years and to pay back the loan and advances over that time. After sixteen months, Peyer asked to be released from the agreement because he opposed the hospital's recruitment of other physicians to the area. The hospital released him from his practice obligation. When Peyer failed to pay back about $9,000 of the amount owed, Humana refused to provide references he requested. Humana later provided the references and filed suit against Peyer. The court held that the agreement governed the duties of the parties, and under the agreement, Humana had no duty to provide the information requested. The court also ordered Dr. Peyer to pay the amount owed.

In Harms Memorial Hospital v. Morton, 112 Idaho 129, 730 P.2d 1049 (1986), the physician recruitment agreement that enticed Dr. Morton to American Falls, Idaho, included a guaranteed income. The hospital guaranteed Dr. Morton a gross monthly income of $12,000, agreeing to provide monthly cash payments to make up any shortfall in Dr. Morton's receipts from his private practice. At the termination of the agreement, or at the end of twelve months, whichever came first, Dr. Morton was to repay the hospital, in eighteen monthly installments, one-half of the amount it had paid him. One month's repayment would be forgiven for each month after termination of the agreement that the doctor remained in practice in American Falls. The hospital terminated the agreement without cause approximately six months after it began, and Dr. Morton moved to Texas three months later, refusing to make any payments. The court ordered Morton to make the payments, holding that the hospital's unilateral termination of the agreement with notice but without cause was allowed under the explicit terms of the agreement. Under the agreement, Morton also had the right to terminate.

Physician recruitment agreements have assumed a vast array of forms. They raise a wide range of legal issues particular to health care. The two most prominent of these issues are the federal prohibition against Medicare fraud and abuse (and similar state prohibitions on fee splitting and self-referrals) and, for 501(c)(3) providers, the prohibition against private inurement. The issues concerning fraud and abuse are discussed in Chapter 7 infra.

The prohibition against private inurement is based on the statutory definition of an exempt organization. In particular, § 501(c)(3) provides that "no part of the net income [of the exempt organization shall inure] to the benefit of any private shareholder or individual." The IRS Manual Handbook sections on the examination procedures for exempt hospitals address this issue:

Examination Procedures for Charitable Organizations (Hospitals)

IRS Manual 4/14/89 Part VII Ch. 300 § 330.3

* * *

* * * Specialists should be alert to any arrangements under which the hospital pays certain personal or business expenses of affiliated doctors and the taxable compensation is not properly reflected as wages on [reports required of the exempt organization.] For example, college and university medical school faculty physicians often have employment contracts with medical schools that limit their compensation to low levels compared to compensation obtainable in private practice. Such physicians often enter into employment contracts as consultant/practitioners with several hospitals or clinics unrelated to the medical schools for which they teach. The written employment contract with such hospitals or clinics may be supplemented by a verbal agreement that provides for the hospital or a third party to pay associated business or personal expenses (e.g., lease of luxury cars, house improvements, country club memberships, etc.) as part of the total annual employment contract amount. * * *

* * *

Review billing rates of the hospital to determine whether billings are increased substantially in departments which use percentage-of-income agreements with department heads. [ ]

* * *

To detect possible inurement of income or serving of private interests, identify the board of trustees or directors, and the key members of administrative and medical staff. Examine any business relationships or dealings with the hospital. Note any pertinent transactions where supplies or services are provided at prices exceeding competitive market or at preferred terms. Be alert for any loan agreements at less than prevailing interest rates. Scrutinize any business arrangements under which hospitals finance the construction of medical buildings owned by staff doctors on favorable financial terms that result in private benefit.

* * *

Determine whether any part of the hospital's property (facilities, space, equipment) or services are used by or rented to doctors or others. Examples of services, facilities, etc., are x-ray and laboratory services or facilities (including lab work for nonpatients), pharmacy departments, laundry services, office space, land and buildings. If so, obtain copies of pertinent leases and contracts to determine whether exempt purposes or private interests are being served or liability for unrelated business tax exists. In determining whether private interests are being served in lease transactions, ascertain whether the lease payment represents fair rental value.

* * *

Review employment arrangements where compensation is based on a percentage of gross or net receipts of a particular department or service. Check for reasonableness of amounts actually paid as this could be a device for distributing profits to those in control.

Review compensation of officers, directors, and physicians to determine if excessive. Specialists should be alert to compensation arrangements, such as open-ended employment contracts or compensation based upon a percentage of a hospital's profits. In addition, specialists should be alert to arrangements employed by hospitals to recruit and/or retain physicians, including such things as: physicians being charged no rent or below market rent for space in hospital-owned office buildings; hospitals providing physicians with practice guarantees; hospitals providing financial assistance to physicians for home purchases and/or the purchase of office equipment; and, outright, cash payments by hospitals to physicians to secure or retain their services. Also arrangements, where a hospital purchases the practice of a physician and subsequently employs the physician (in many instances to operate that same practice) should be scrutinized, giving special attention to the valuation of the practice purchased by the hospital and the compensation paid to the physician-employee. Because of the different and complex compensation arrangements that may be involved in hospital cases, the determination of what constitutes "excess compensation" is a facts and circumstances test.

* * *

In a General Counsel Memorandum, the IRS reviewed recruitment agreements similar to those discussed previously:

G.C.M. 39498
4/24/86.

The Hospital guarantees a newly recruited physician an annual income for a period of two years through a system of subsidies. As proposed, there will be no obligation to repay any subsidies except out of income earned in excess of the guaranteed annual income during the two-year contract period. The income to be guaranteed is established by Hospital officials who are totally independent of the recruited physicians. In setting the amount of income the Hospital officials carefully consider each physician's capabilities and the Hospital's specific needs. Although it is not entirely clear from the administrative file, this apparently means that the Hospital officials consider how much a physician in a particular area of medical specialization, for example, a pediatric surgeon, could earn during a year, and the Hospital's needs for a physician in that area of specialization at a particular level of experience.

In exchange the physician is required to perform several significant services for the Hospital, for example, training and emergency room duties. The guaranteed minimum annual income will be offered when needed to persuade a physician to locate his or her medical practice in the Hospital's service area.

* * *

The Hospital received a ruling letter from the Service * * * which concluded that a guaranteed minimum annual income contract under which the physician is required unconditionally to repay any subsidy paid by the Hospital would not adversely affect the exempt status of the Hospital. The present ruling request relates to the same recruitment device without an unconditional obligation on the part of the recruited physician to repay any subsidies except out of income earned in excess of the guaranteed annual income level during the two-year contract period.

ANALYSIS

* * *

In our opinion, the recruited physicians as employees or as individuals with a close professional working relationship with the Hospital are persons who have a personal and private interest in the activities of the Hospital. Thus, such physicians are subject to the inurement proscription. * * *

* * * In principle we agree that the Hospital must offer incentives or inducements to attract qualified physicians needed in a particular area of specialization to enable the Hospital to provide quality health care. Cf. Rev.Rul. 73.313, 1973 2 CD 174, considered in GCM 35268, I–45–30 (Mar. 14, 1973), (organization formed and supported by residents of isolated, medically underserved, rural community to provide a medical building and facilities at reasonable rent to attract a doctor who would provide medical services to the entire community exempt under section 501(c)(3)); GCM 37789, EE–66–78 (Dec. 18, 1978) (exempt hospital that leases land adjacent to it to its staff members and provides the staff members financing to build a medical center on the land retains exemption). Further, we know that exempt organizations may offer reasonable compensation for services provided to them without violating the requirements for exemption either as respects exclusive operation for exempt purposes or the inurement prohibition. [ ]

It has not been demonstrated, however, nor does it seem possible to demonstrate, that all possible subsidies paid under the Hospital's recruitment program will constitute reasonable compensation. It is logical for the Hospital to consider various factors in determining compensation offers sufficient to attract needed qualified physicians, e.g., the reluctance of a physician to initiate or relocate his or her practice in an unfamiliar area, and the competitive recruitment efforts of other hospitals. However, the method of determining the amount of subsidies to be paid here bears no discernible direct relation to the value of a particular physician to the Hospital. Such subsidies may vary in amount based not on factors directly related to benefits to the Hospital, e.g., increased efficiency or enhanced productivity for the Hospital because of his presence in the hospital's medical service area, but rather on factors that relate principally to the physician's performance in his or her "private" medical practice. Thus, it seems likely that amounts to be paid (and possibly not repaid) as subsidies may fall outside the range of reasonable compensation for the benefit to the Hospital of the doctor's relocation, and result in inurement of the Hospital's net earnings to the recruited physicians. We note the absence of any ceiling on amounts of subsidies to be paid (other than the total annual income guaranteed), or of any requirement that the physician who need not repay a subsidy provide further services or continue to benefit the Hospital after the expiration of the two year contract period. Both of these factors might relate to the reasonableness of the compensation paid recruited physicians under the two year contract.   * * *

[T]he exempt organization states that hospitals often offer recruited physicians [incentives] as follows: expenses of moving a household; expenses of relocating an established medical practice; financial assistance in connection with the purchase of a home * * *; financing office equipment, furniture, and remodeling * * *; assistance in leasing an office (discounted rents, no rent for first year or so with or without interest paid on rental deferred); the provision of various office and administrative services in connection with a physician's private medical practice (use of hospital's secretarial, nursing, billing and record keeping services at or below hospital cost); and a guaranteed minimum annual income contract with an unconditional obligation to repay subsidies granted even after a two year period. These recruitment incentives * * * demonstrate the impossibility of determining in advance that the payment of subsidies under the revised contract will not result in unreasonable compensation or the serving of private interests.

* * *

In considering the private benefit question in GCM 37789, we noted, "[I]f an organization serves a public interest, and also serves a private interest other than incidentally, it is not entitled to exemption under section 501(c)(3)." Further, we reasoned that the term "incidental" has both qualitative and quantitative connotations. We stated our view that to be qualitatively incidental, "a private benefit must be a necessary concomitant of the activity which benefits the public at large; in other words, the benefit to the public cannot be achieved without necessarily benefiting certain private individuals." Without knowing in advance what each physician is offered as additional recruitment incentives, we cannot determine whether the method of determining subsidies to a recruited physician with no obligation to repay subsidies out of income earned after the two year contract period is the only way for the Hospital to achieve its purposes, viz., recruiting an individual physician in a particular area of medical specialization to enable the Hospital to provide quality health care.

Further, the subsidies available under the proposed guaranteed minimum annual income amount are not capped (except by the total income guaranteed). Thus, a subsidy to a recruited physician may be a substantial economic benefit that is not quantitatively incidental to the Hospital's attempt to further the promotion of health through its efforts to recruit the particular physician. * * *

In view of the above we conclude that the provisions of the revised guaranteed minimum annual income contract as part of the Hospital's physician recruitment program may result in the physicians' private interests being served other than incidentally, and inurement of the Hospital's net earnings to individuals having a personal and private interest in the Hospital's activities. Such a conclusion would provide a basis for revocation of the exemption of the Hospital.

Notes and Questions

1. What are the standards used by the IRS in applying the prohibition against private inurement? How would the agreements described in *Peyer* and *Harms* fare under the GCM? If you were counseling the hospital that had requested this opinion, how would you modify the recruitment agreement to avoid the problem? (When you study the Medicare fraud and abuse provisions in Chapter 7 re-examine your solutions for potential conflicts with that statute.)

2. Part of the emphasis on monitoring private inurement emerges from the theory that, in the absence of obligations to shareholders or owners that discipline management of for-profit organizations, not-for-profit organizations tend to distribute earnings to management, or other institutional decisionmakers. Is the IRS correct in including physicians with staff privileges or contracts among those covered by the prohibition on private inurement? Does this GCM approach that issue directly? What impact do you think the prohibition on private inurement would have on the exempt hospital's competitive position?

D. EMPLOYMENT

Doctors, nurses and administrators working in private facilities without an employment contract or under a contract that does not provide for employment security are generally subject to the doctrine of employment at will. While doctors traditionally have had the protection of staff privileges and most continue to have at least the protection of contractual guarantees, this is not uniformly the case. For nurses, the norm has been the absence of job security. Nurses are striving to achieve greater job security. They have begun to find limited success in the courts through actions challenging wrongful discharges. They have made even more significant strides towards greater job security and improved working conditions through organization and collective bargaining under the protection of the National Labor Relations Act.

Until recently, unless nurses had a specific written contract, they served at the will of their employers and could be discharged for good cause, for bad cause, or for no cause. Some courts still take this approach. See Ewing v. Board of Trustees, 486 N.E.2d 1094 (Ind.App. 1985); Williams v. Delta Haven, Inc., 416 So.2d 637 (La.App.1982). This poses an obvious dilemma for the conscientious nurse concerned about patient care within the facility or about her own liability for not protecting patients from substandard treatment. If the nurse criticizes the treatment delivered by a powerful doctor, or complains to the administration about conditions affecting patient care, or reports deficiencies to a state agency, the JCAHO, or the media, can the nurse be discharged without recourse?

McQUARY v. BEL AIR CONVALESCENT HOME, INC.

Court of Appeals of Oregon, 1984.
69 Or.App. 107, 684 P.2d 21.

GILLETTE, PRESIDING JUDGE.

Plaintiff brought this action for wrongful discharge, alleging that she had been fired from her position with defendant because she had threatened to report an instance of staff abuse of one of defendant's patients. A jury found for defendant; plaintiff appeals. The case presents two issues: (1) Does the common law tort of wrongful discharge apply to an employee who is fired for threatening to report alleged nursing care home patient mistreatment to an appropriate state agency; and (2), if it does, must the plaintiff prove that there has been, in fact, "patient abuse"[3] at defendant's nursing care facility in order for her discharge for threatening to report that abuse to be wrongful? We hold that the facts of this case would allow a jury to find that plaintiff was wrongfully discharged and that she needed to prove only that she had a good faith belief that patient abuse had occurred. We therefore reverse and remand.

Defendant is a licensed intermediate care nursing home. Plaintiff was employed as defendant's In–Service Director of Nurses Training and Education. In December, 1979, plaintiff's aunt became a patient at the care center. In the same month, Samuel Lissitz became the home's administrator. Early in the morning of January 26, 1980, a fire broke

---

3. While "patient abuse" has a statutory definition, ORS 441.630(1), the term was used at trial—and is used in this opinion—in its broader, nonstatutory sense.

out in a wastebasket in a corridor near the room plaintiff's aunt occupied. Lissitz concluded that plaintiff's aunt had started the fire by careless smoking and ordered her transferred from the home. Plaintiff was off duty but came to the home when she learned of the transfer. Due to her intercession, her aunt was returned to the home; after a heated conversation with Lissitz, plaintiff agreed to stay at the home that evening until her aunt went to sleep.

The next day, January 27, the facility's fire sprinkler system broke down because of frozen pipes, and the fire department ordered a 24 hour fire watch until it was operable. Plaintiff was again off duty. Plaintiff's aunt called her at her home to complain that Lissitz was yelling at the aunt and calling her a fire bug. Plaintiff came to the care center. After another heated conversation, in the course of which plaintiff threatened to report his actions toward her aunt to the Health Division, Lissitz fired her. His action is the basis for her claim.

The first issue is whether a discharge for such a threat is actionable. An employer may not discharge an employee for fulfilling a societal obligation, [ ] or if the employer acts with a socially undesirable motive. [ ] The evidence in this case would permit a jury to find that Lissitz discharged plaintiff because she had threatened to report his actions to the Health Division and that she believed in good faith that his actions violated her aunt's rights under the Nursing Home Patient's Bill of Rights. [ ] The Health Division is charged with protecting patients' rights under the act, [ ] and a report to it would be a societal obligation of a person who knows of violations. The legislature's desire to protect patients, which reflects a comparable concern on the part of the federal government, [ ] shows that that protection is an important public policy analogous to the performance of jury duty or the avoidance of defamation, policies which the Supreme Court has found to justify wrongful discharge claims. [ ] A discharge for reporting a violation of that policy to the proper authority would thus be a discharge for fulfilling a societal obligation and would be actionable.

Having found that plaintiff has a potential wrongful discharge claim, we turn to the question whether she must prove that Lissitz's actions in fact constituted "patient abuse" in the broad sense of the term, or must only show that she in good faith believed that they did.[5] We are required to choose between competing social values: Either plaintiff must act at her peril in making a complaint, risking her job if the complaint later turns out to be unfounded, or the employer must

---

5. Plaintiff did not actually report this situation to the Health Division until after her termination. She did not have an opportunity to do so before Lissitz fired her, and we do not think that the sequence of events affects her rights. There is no reason that an employee's protection should depend on whether the employer acts before or after the employee is able to file a complaint. In addition, by complaining to Lissitz, plaintiff was bringing the situation to the attention of the proper authority within the nursing home and thus may have already been engaging in protected activity. See ORS 441.057(4) (employee protection under 1981 statute begins with the report of an alleged statutory violation to the administration of the facility) * * *

act at its peril in firing her, risking damages if she turns out to have acted in good faith. On balance, we believe that the social harm from reporting in good faith a complaint that may turn out, after investigation, to be unfounded is potentially far less than the harm of not reporting a well-founded complaint for fear of the consequences. The social benefit from investigating all potentially significant violations of a patient's statutory rights is far greater than the social benefit, if any, from allowing an employer to terminate an employee who in good faith reports to the appropriate authorities situations which prove not to be violations. We therefore hold that an employee is protected from discharge for good faith reporting of what the employee believes to be patient mistreatment to an appropriate authority.

* * *

Reversed and remanded.

Notes and Questions

1. Might the court have held for the nursing home if McQuary had instead contacted the media about her aunt's problems? What would the court do if she had sued the home rather than report it to the health department?

2. Though *McQuary* may signal a modern trend, it runs contrary to the more narrow concept of public policy still observed in many states. In Lampe v. Presbyterian Medical Center, 41 Colo.App. 465, 590 P.2d 513 (1978), a nurse was terminated after complaining that changes in staffing patterns in a hospital jeopardized patient care. The court rejected her claim for wrongful discharge, noting that there was no specific statute that protected the nurse from being fired under these circumstances. It specifically rejected the nurse's argument that her conduct had been in furtherance of the policies of the state nurse practice act, and thus should be protected.

Other emerging exceptions to the employment at will doctrine have also been asserted by hospital employees claiming contractual rights against summary discharge. Duldulao v. St. Mary of Nazareth Hospital Center, 136 Ill.App.3d 763, 91 Ill.Dec. 470, 483 N.E.2d 956 (1985), held that a hospital must comply with the terms of its employee manual in discharging a nurse. Crenshaw v. Bozeman Deaconess Hospital, 693 P.2d 487 (Mont.1984), affirmed a jury verdict against a hospital for $125,000 for compensatory and $25,000 in punitive damages where the hospital breached its judicially imposed obligation of "good faith and fair dealing" by failing to investigate charges against a respiratory therapist before firing her. For a survey of the employment at will doctrine and its exceptions, see Murg & Scharman, Employment at Will: Do the Exceptions Overwhelm the Rule? 23 B.C.L.Rev. 329 (1982). See, arguing in favor of the employment at will doctrine, Power, A Defense of the Employment at Will Rule, 27 St.Louis U.L.J. 881 (1983).

3. In 1974 Congress amended the National Labor Relations Act to extend its coverage to voluntary, non-profit hospitals. Prior to that time the NLRA had only covered proprietary hospitals. By 1980 nearly 30% of

hospitals were organized, and union activity in hospitals seems to be steadily expanding. In extending the protection of the nation's collective bargaining laws to health care employees, Congress was sensitive to the unique nature of the health care industry—to the fact that hospitals minister to acute human needs as well as produce a product. The 1974 amendments, therefore, include several special provisions to minimize disruptive effects of unionization upon health care, including special requirements that health care labor organizations give advance notice of any strike to allow the Federal Mediation and Conciliation Service to Mediate the dispute. (29 U.S.C.A. §§ 158, 183.)

4. The NLRA provides that it is generally an unfair labor practice to terminate the employment of a person for engaging in concerted action to improve the terms and conditions of employment, 29 U.S.C.A. §§ 157, 158(a)(1). Other statutes also prohibit retaliatory discharges for engaging in protected activity. See, e.g. 42 U.S.C.A. § 2000e–3(a). If McQuary had joined with other nurses in complaining to the health department about conditions at Bel Air, would her firing have been an unfair labor practice, permitting the NLRB to order her reinstatement? Consider Misericordia Hospital Medical Center v. NLRB, 623 F.2d 808 (2d Cir.1980) (unfair labor practice to discharge nurse who participated in preparation of report critical of hospital for JCAHO); Community Hospital of Roanoke Valley, Inc. v. NLRB, 538 F.2d 607, 610 (4th Cir.1976) (nurse complaint of hospital staff shortages in television interview protected activity); NLRB v. Mount Desert Island Hospital, 695 F.2d 634 (1st Cir.1982) (unfair labor practice to refuse to rehire employee who was fired for complaining to local newspaper of working conditions and patient care in hospital).

5. Though unionization of health care is often a response to low wages, long hours, and inadequate benefits, health care professionals also attempt to use collective bargaining to achieve other goals more directly related to their professional status. One study, for example, showed that nurses were more concerned with issues like autonomy, professional respect and educational enrichment than they were with more traditional wage and benefit concerns, Ponak, Unionized Professionals and The Scope of Bargaining: A Study of Nurses, 34 Ind. & Lab.Rel.Rev. 396 (1981). Another showed that many nurses favor collective bargaining, and strike if necessary, to improve patient care and their professional status in the decisionmaking structures of the health care facility, Feldbaum, Collective Bargaining in the Health Sector: A Focus on Nurses, 4 J.Health and Hum.Resources Ad. 148 (Fall 1981). Under the National Labor Relations Act, employers must bargain with regard to "wages, hours, and the conditions of employment." 29 U.S.C.A. § 158(d). Under this law, are employers required to bargain with respect to issues like professional autonomy, decisionmaking authority, or the quality of patient care, or are these issues management prerogatives? See Angel, Professionals and Unionization, 66 Minn.L.Rev. 383, 428–9 (1982).

6. The decision of health care professionals to strike raises obvious professional ethical problems. Prior to 1968 the American Nurses' Association (ANA) embraced the position that strikes by nurses were unprofessional, though in the 1960s some nurses engaged in mass resignations in egregious situations, such as one instance where a hospital administrator

refused to meet with nurses to discuss working conditions. In 1968 the
ANA, recognizing the impossibility of engaging in effective collective bargaining without the strike weapon, rescinded its earlier position. Since
then, strikes in the health care industry have become more common,
including one of 570 days from 1980 until 1982. See N. Metzgar, J.
Ferentino, & K. Kruger, When Health Care Employees Strike 53–58 (1984).
Strikes are still much less common in the health care industry than in
other industries, Comment, Labor Relations in the Health Care Industry,
54 Tul.L.Rev. 416, 453 (1980). See, taking different positions on the ethical
issues involved in strikes, Muyskens, Nurses' Collective Responsibility and
the Strike Weapon, 7 J.Med. & Phil.J. 101–12 (Feb. 1982); and Veatch &
Bleich, Interns and Residents on Strike, 5 Hastings Center Rep. 709 (1975).

7. The nature of health care institutions has also caused conflicts
where unions have engaged in solicitation of employees or distribution of
materials within the institution. In two cases in 1978 and 1979 the
Supreme Court upheld NLRB policy permitting solicitation during non-
working hours in non-working areas, including cafeterias and lobbies,
NLRB v. Baptist Hospital Inc., 442 U.S. 773, 99 S.Ct. 2598, 61 L.Ed.2d 251
(1979); Beth Israel Hospital v. NLRB, 437 U.S. 483, 98 S.Ct. 2463, 57
L.Ed.2d 370 (1978). In *Baptist Hospital,* however, the court overruled the
Board's rejection of a hospital rule forbidding solicitation in corridors or
sitting rooms adjacent to patient rooms. Bans on solicitation in patient
rooms, operating rooms and treatment rooms are presumptively valid, so as
to keep union activities from upsetting patients or otherwise interfering
with patient care.

8. Physicians may form unions if they are employees. The National
Labor Relations Board, however, has adopted the position that interns and
residents are students, and not employees, and thus not covered by the
National Labor Relations Act, Cedars–Sinai Medical Center, 223 N.L.R.B.
251 (1976). Moreover, the Board has asserted successfully that, even
though interns and residents are not employees, they are subject to the
jurisdiction of the Board, and thus the grant of state law protection to their
collective bargaining efforts is preempted, N.L.R.B. v. Committee of Interns
and Residents, 566 F.2d 810 (2d Cir.1977). Despite the absence of legal
protection, housestaff have been quite successful in organizing hospitals
and pushing for improved working conditions in some areas. See, House,
Gluckmann, & Bastian, House Staff Organizing, in I. Shepard & A. Doudera, Health Care Labor Law, 1981.

9. Unions have significantly improved wages in many hospitals. One
study showed that nurses earned 8% more in union than in nonunion
hospitals; secretaries and housekeeping staff, 11–12% more, Feldman &
Scheffler, The Union Impact on Hospital Wages and Fringe Benefits, 35
Ind. & Lab.Rel.Rev. 196, 204 (1982). As labor costs constitute 55% of a
hospital's budget, unionization can have a significant impact on efforts to
control costs. The conflict between the drive to control health care costs
and the desire to protect worker's rights explains much of the ambivalence
of Congress about unionization of health care facilities. Arguments that
unionization of interns and residents would lead to escalating health care
costs played an important role in defeating legislation that would have
extended NLRA protection to that group, Note, The Medical House Staff

Labor Dispute: A Judicial Barrier, 25 St. Louis U.L.J. 429, 451 (1981). Even though collective bargaining rights were extended to the nonprofit health care sector in part because of Congressional concerns that wages were low and working conditions poor in the industry, Beth Israel Hospital v. NLRB, 437 U.S. 483, 497–8, 98 S.Ct. 2463, 2471, 57 L.Ed.2d 370 (1978), Congress has also recognized that the cost of improving these conditions will be borne by society, and in large part by the government itself.

10.   One of the most hotly contested issues in the application of NLRA standards to union activity in hospitals is the definition of bargaining units. After years of defining bargaining units on a case-by-case basis, the NLRB issued a rule concerning bargaining units in acute-care hospitals.   The Board's rule recognizes only the following units: physicians, registered nurses, other professional employees, medical technicians, skilled maintenance workers, clerical workers, guards and other nonprofessional employees.   Under the rule, units must have a minimum of six employees for certification. The Seventh Circuit upheld the NLRB rule against challenge by the American Hospital Association. American Hospital Association v. NLRB, 899 F.2d 651 (7th Cir.1990). The court rejected the claim that the NLRB did not have statutory authority to define bargaining units by rule and that the rule itself was arbitrary and capricious. In reviewing the "first significant substantive exertion of rulemaking powers" by the Board, the court identified the interests in contention:

> Labor and management are perennially and systematically at odds over the appropriate number of bargaining units. [   ]

> This is because the smaller and more homogeneous a bargaining unit is, the easier it will be for the members to agree on a mutually advantageous course of collective action, and therefore the more attractive a union will be, unionization being the vehicle for collective action by employees. By the same token, the larger and more heterogeneous the unit is, the harder it will be for the members to agree on a common course of action. The diversity of, often amounting to conflict between, the interests of the members of a large and heterogeneous unit will make collective action difficult, so it will be hard for a union to gain majority support in such a unit or, having gained it, to use it to bargain effectively (for example, by making a credible threat to strike). This is the union's perspective; the employer's perspective is different. The more units there are, the more costly it will be for the employer to negotiate collective bargaining contracts. And work stoppages will be likelier, because there will be more separate decision-making centers each of which can call a strike, and because majority support for a strike call is more likely the more homogeneous a unit is and hence the likelier all members are to benefit if the union wins.

> In making unit determinations the Board is thus required to strike a balance among the competing interests of unions, employees (whose interests are not always identical to those of unions), employers, and the broader public. The statute, though otherwise nondirective, can be read to suggest that the tilt should be in favor of unions, and hence toward relatively many rather than relatively few units. * * * The decision is particularly difficult and delicate in the health care indus

try because the work force of a hospital (or nursing home or rehabilitation center) tends to be at once small and heterogeneous. It may include physicians, registered nurses, psychologists, licensed practical nurses, nurses' aides, lab technicians, orderlies, physical therapists, dieticians, cooks, guards, clerical workers, maintenance workers, and others—but often only a few of each. If the desirability (from the union standpoint) of homogeneous units is stressed, even a hospital of average size might have ten or twenty or even more units, each with a bare handful of workers. The cost of the institution's labor relations and the probability of work stoppages would soar. Wages might soar too (depending, of course, upon competition among hospitals), since proliferation of units fosters unionization and a principal objective of unions is to raise their members' wages. But this is far from certain; workers do not receive wages when they are on strike, and strike-prone workers are worth less to employers.

Work stoppages, heavy bargaining costs, soaring wages, labor unrest— all these are matters of concern in a period of high and rising costs of health care, and indeed, as we shall see, commanded congressional attention even before the tide came in. The sorting out and weighing of these matters are judgmental functions committed to the Board.

The Seventh Circuit has stayed implementation of the rules. The U.S. Supreme Court has granted *certiorari* at the petition of the AHA.

Problem: Nurses and Their Grievances

You are a labor law attorney and have just had a consultation with a group of nurses from Bethesda Methodist Hospital. One of the nurses, Judy Sawatsky, appeared to be the leader of the group. Ms. Sawatsky has worked at Bethesda for five years and has become progressively less happy with conditions in the hospital. The nurses are poorly paid and have little input into work schedules. She is even more upset with the way nurses are treated professionally. She feels that they are not given the respect due their profession, are accorded little discretion in dealing with patients, and are regarded as the handmaidens of the doctors. She feels that patient care suffers because of this.

In the last several months she has become increasingly vocal in her criticism of the treatment she and her patients have received and has discussed these problems frequently with other nurses in her unit. Last week she finally got fed up and wrote a letter to the Chairman of the Hospital Board, complaining generally about the treatment of nurses in the hospital, and also specifically about problems that had recently occurred with two patients in circumstances where physicians had failed to heed warnings raised by nurses concerning the care of the patients. Though the letter was signed only by Ms. Sawatsky, she claimed to speak for all of the nurses in her unit. The letter was referred by the Chairman to the Hospital Administrator, who summarily fired Ms. Sawatsky. When Ms. Sawatsky complained to the Administrator that under the Bethesda's staff manual she was entitled to a hearing before she could be discharged, the Administrator said she had talked to the hospital's lawyer, who had told her that the hospital was not bound by the staff manual.

Ms. Sawatsky is well-liked by other nurses at the hospital, and her discharge came as a shock to them. Several of them got together the following day and began talking seriously about forming a union which might permit them to raise their grievances within the context of collective bargaining. When they began to try to organize the other nurses, however, they were informed by the hospital that it had a firm policy forbidding union solicitation on the premises. This policy, they were told, was necessary to avoid upsetting patients and their families, already under great stress because of their medical problems. Moreover, a number of the nurses they have approached have stated that they are reluctant to join a union because they do not believe they could ever ethically go out on strike. Though these nurses are also concerned about conditions in the hospital, they feel that to strike would violate their professional obligations to care for their patients.

Ms. Sawatsky and the other nurses raise a host of questions. Was Ms. Sawatsky's discharge legally permissible? If not, does she have any remedy? Is the hospital's solicitation policy legal? Can the nurses' grievances be addressed through collective bargaining? Will unionization necessarily lead to a strike? What limitations does the law impose on their ability to strike? Is it ever ethical for a professional to go out on strike if the strike may harm patients (or clients)?

E. PHYSICIAN PRACTICE AGREEMENTS

The traditional form of physician practice enterprise was the fee-for-service solo practice. This form of organization is giving way to physicians working as employees or under contract for hospitals, health maintenance organizations, insurance companies or large physician groups. For those physicians who do not choose employment, solo practice often is not as attractive as practicing in a group of physicians in the same or different specialties. A convergence of economic pressures and technological demands, as well as personal preferences, may be responsible for this shift. Increases in administrative demands by government and insurance payment systems, a more positive attitude toward competition within the profession, and regulatory and economic incentives for the office-based ownership of technology such as laboratories and other equipment have also contributed to this movement. The extent to which voluntary agreements made by physicians in regard to their own practices should be treated specially as a matter of state law is explored in the following cases on "covenants not to compete" and on the prohibition against the "corporate practice of medicine."

1. Restrictive Covenants

Covenants not to compete generally are valid if they are reasonably necessary to protect the employer's business and are reasonable as to geographic area and time. Covenants that have been enforced against physicians as reasonable in scope include a covenant prohibiting practice for three years within a five-mile radius of the previous practice

(Phoenix Orthopaedic Surgeons, Ltd. v. Peairs, 164 Ariz. 54, 790 P.2d 752 (App.1989) and for two years within a thirty mile radius (Gomez v. Chua Medical Corp., 510 N.E.2d 191 (Ind.App.1987). In addition to the generally applicable concerns over scope, restrictive covenants binding physicians may raise public policy issues in the form of concerns over quality and access.

DUFFNER v. ALBERTY

Court of Appeals of Arkansas, 1986.
19 Ark.App. 137, 718 S.W.2d 111

CRACRAFT, CHIEF JUDGE.

David Duffner appeals from an order of the Sebastian County Chancery Court enforcing a covenant not to compete and enjoining him from the practice of medicine within a radius of thirty miles from the offices of Joe Paul Alberty and John Wideman for a period of twelve months from the date of entry of the order. The appellant contends that the covenant is void and unenforceable because it violates the public policy of this state which prohibits unreasonable restraints of trade. We agree.

* * * It is not argued that the geographic restriction was overbroad or that the time limitation was unreasonable. Appellant contends only that there was not a sufficient interference with appellees' business interests to warrant enforcement of the covenant. It is clear that such covenants will not be enforced unless a covenantee had a legitimate interest to be protected by such an agreement and that the law will not enforce a contract merely to prohibit ordinary competition. [ ] The test of reasonableness of contracts in restraint of trade is that the restraint imposed upon one party must not be greater than is reasonably necessary for the protection of the other, and not so great as to injure a public interest.

* * *

Although contracts between individuals ought not to be entered into lightly, all other considerations must give way where matters of public policy are involved. From our review of all the facts and circumstances, we are of the opinion that the contract provision prohibiting appellant from practicing medicine within thirty miles of the City of Fort Smith constitutes an undue interference with the interests of the public right of availability of the orthopedic surgeon it prefers to use and that the covenant's enforcement would result in an unreasonable restraint of trade.

* * *

Although the chancellor found that the appellant had access to appellees' confidential patient files, there was no evidence that he attempted to memorize them or use information from these files to entice any of their former patients to become patients of his new association. Although there was evidence that he obtained the files on twenty-eight persons from the appellees, it was explained that these were not new patients but those who were receiving follow-up medical attention after having undergone surgery by the appellant during his association with the appellees. Other than those twenty-eight persons receiving post-operative care, he testified that he had not seen more than two of appellees' former patients.

We cannot conclude from the evidence that appellant maintained a personal relationship or acquaintance with appellees' patients or that their "stock of patients" was appropriated by the appellant when he left their offices. There was also evidence that appellees' income increased after appellant left the association. We conclude that the enforcement of this covenant would do no more than prohibit ordinary competition.

Notes and Questions

1. In Shankman v. Coastal Psychiatric Associates, 258 Ga. 294, 368 S.E.2d 753 (1988), the Georgia Supreme Court, *per curiam,* upheld the trial court's injunction enforcing a non-competition covenant against a physician, but the dissenting judge argued that covenants not to compete should be "per se" illegal insofar as they apply to physicians: "In my opinion this result is demanded in light of the medical profession's special relationship with the public it serves. * * * The Code of Professional Responsibility for attorneys in Georgia [prohibits lawyers from participating in a partnership or employment agreement that restricts the lawyer's right to practice after termination of the agreement]. I see no reason why doctors should not be held to a similar standard. * * * [M]edical patients should not be forbidden from seeking the best medical treatment from the doctor of their choice simply because of an agreement with a third party. The opinions of the counsel [sic] on Ethical and Judicial Affairs of the American Medical Association, 1986 states [that such agreements are discouraged and do not serve the public interest]. * * * It is unfortunate that patients must be told that they can no longer be treated by their doctor because of an agreement with a third party. Yet, this is what happens when this Court allows doctors to become businessmen instead of healers."

Some states prohibit the enforcement of restrictive covenants against doctors by statute. See, e.g., Colo.Rev.Stat. 8–2–113(3) (1989) and Del.Code tit. 6, § 2707 (1989).

2. Some restrictive covenants include provisions for liquidated damages if the covenant is breached. A liquidated damages clause was upheld in South Bend Clinic v. Paul, 662 F.Supp. 452 (N.D.Ind.1987). South Bend Clinic is a multi-specialty group organized as a partnership. Dr. William Paul joined the group as a salaried associate in 1979. In 1980, he became a partner and signed the partnership agreement, which included a non-competition covenant requiring that a partner resigning from the partnership not practice medicine for one year within a fifty-mile radius of the clinic's main building. The agreement also provided that should the former partner choose to continue practicing during that year in the prohibited area, the partner agreed to pay the partnership 50% of his earnings "for the fiscal year next preceding the year of resignation or withdrawal." Dr.

Paul resigned in 1983 and established his own practice within one mile of the clinic that same day. A week later, the Clinic sent a letter to Paul demanding $109,643, which represented 50% of the $219,286 he had earned at the clinic the previous year. The court, applying Indiana law, held that the liquidated damages clause was reasonable because Paul had generated nearly a half million dollars revenue for the Clinic in the previous year and the Clinic was left with open space and was not likely to be able to recruit another physician in less than a year. In Gomez v. Chua Medical Corporation, 510 N.E.2d 191 (Ind.App.1987), the court upheld a liquidated damages clause as enforceable. Dr. Gomez' had argued that because he did not leave voluntarily but in fact was terminated without cause, the liquidated damages clause should be unenforceable.

Do you think enforcing a restrictive covenant through a liquidated damages clause would be less offensive to the court in *Duffner* or the dissenting judge in *Shankman*? Should patients have any control over the enforcement of these agreements?

2. *Corporate Practice of Medicine*

MORELLI v. EHSAN

Supreme Court of Washington, 1988.
110 Wash.2d 555, 756 P.2d 129.

[Dr. Mike Ehsan and Mr. Tito Morelli formed a partnership to establish and operate the Sunrise Emergency and Family Care Clinic.] The clinic was to provide minor emergency treatment and health care to the general public on an out-patient basis. Morelli told Ehsan that he had consulted his lawyers and had been assured it was legal for a physician and a nonphysician to operate a medical clinic as partners.

Under the [partnership] agreement, Morelli and Ehsan became co-general partners, sharing equally in profits and losses. The agreement provided that, in addition to their share of profits, Morelli and Ehsan could receive a salary for services rendered as employees of the partnership. The agreement also provided that, as general partners, Morelli and Ehsan would have equal rights in the management of the partnership business, and further defined Morelli's areas of responsibility as "Director of Operations" and those of Ehsan as the "Medical Director" of the clinic. The clinic also employed a medical staff, including licensed physicians, who were paid on an hourly basis.

For most of the next 3 years, the clinic operated at a loss, finally showing a small profit in 1984. The partners were obliged to advance additional funds to keep the business going during that time. Morelli's additional contributions to the clinic, totaling $75,000, were later characterized as loans and evidenced by a series of promissory notes, signed by Morelli and Ehsan as co-makers.

During the latter part of 1983, the partners began to have a falling out, and in January 1985, Morelli petitioned the court for a dissolution of the partnership and an accounting. Ehsan moved to dismiss Morelli's complaint, arguing that the partnership agreement was illegal and void.

The trial court granted summary judgment for Ehsan, holding that Morelli's participation in the partnership constituted the unlicensed practice of medicine in violation of former RCW 18.71.020, and as a result, he had no legally cognizable interest in the assets, profits or management of the clinic. The court permanently enjoined Morelli from interfering in any way in the operation of the clinic. Ehsan was ordered to assume all the assets and liabilities of the business, but was held not to be liable for any of the funds contributed by Morelli to the partnership. [   ]

I

In challenging Ehsan's motion for summary judgment, Morelli contends the partnership was legal because his responsibilities and duties were limited strictly to business aspects while Ehsan's authority was limited to the clinic's medical affairs. * * *

At the time of the partnership formation, former RCW 18.71.020 provided:

> Any person who shall practice or attempt to practice or hold himself out as practicing medicine * * * without * * * a valid * * * license * * * shall be guilty of a gross misdemeanor.

The practice of medicine is defined in RCW 18.71.011(1) as anyone who [o]ffers or undertakes to diagnose, cure, advise or prescribe for any human disease, ailment, injury, infirmity, deformity, pain or other condition, physical or mental * * * by means of instrumentality.

Under the Professional Service Corporation Act, RCW 18.100, lawyers, doctors, dentists, optometrists, and other professional specialists are authorized to form a corporate entity within their respective practices. However, the corporation must be organized by "[a]n individual or group of individuals duly licensed * * * to render the same professional services * * *" RCW 18.100.050. Additionally, under RCW 18.100.080, "[n]o professional service corporation * * * shall engage in any business other than the rendering of the professional services for which it was incorporated * * *" The intent of the Legislature to bar other than similarly licensed health care professionals from involvement in professional services is amply delineated.

* * *

[Morelli] was in a general partnership with a physician as an equal partner. While Morelli asserts his only duties were as business manager, the evidence is to the contrary. The partnership agreement clearly establishes Morelli as more than a business manager of the clinic. He was a general partner entitled to equal share of the profits, to equal rights in the management, to hire nurses, and to all the rights and duties of a general partner under the laws of the state of Washington. Furthermore, the record indicates Morelli exercised those rights.

* * *

* * * Both Morelli and Ehsan were violating statutes governing the practice of their respective professions by operating a medical clinic without both being licensed as physicians. The partnership agreement was illegal as a matter of law.

II

* * *

[Despite its own conclusion that the partnership was illegal, the Court of Appeals had remanded to the trial court for an accounting and distribution]. In remanding for an accounting, the Court of Appeals fashioned a "good faith" exception, a new and unprecedented exception to the general rule that the courts will not enforce an illegal agreement where both parties are equally at fault, but will leave the parties where it found them. This exception, apparently effective when both parties believe they were acting within the law, completely undermines the purpose of the rule—deterrence. There is no deterrence from violating a law if parties may claim both were ignorant of the law.   * * *

By denying Morelli an accounting, the trial court followed the law in this jurisdiction and others leaving the parties where it found them. If the court had granted Morelli affirmative relief, as ordered by the Court of Appeals on remand, the parties would be using the court to enforce their illegal partnership agreement. Instead, after finding the agreement illegal, the trial court enjoined Morelli from entering the clinic to prevent his continued participation in the practice of medicine. The court further ordered Ehsan, as the only person authorized to practice medicine, to assume sole liability for all past, present, and contingent liabilities of the clinic. Whether Ehsan continued to practice medicine in the clinic building or go elsewhere, he was still responsible for all liabilities associated with the illegal partnership practice. Ehsan has not appealed from this order. While the order relieved Morelli of any liabilities, it also denied Morelli any recovery from his investment in the illegal partnership.

Finally, Morelli contends that even if an accounting is denied, the court should enforce the promissory notes because they were separate advances to the partnership after its formation. Because the promissory notes were advanced by Morelli, a general partner, in the operation and furtherance of the illegal partnership, allowing Morelli to enforce them would, in effect, sanction the illegal partnership and allow the enforcement of an illegal agreement. [ ]

The trial court correctly denied Morelli any contribution from Ehsan for the promissory note.

To the extent both Morelli and Ehsan violated the law by participating in the illegal partnership, equal fault does exist. The trial court's judgment was correct in finding the partnership agreement illegal and denying an accounting of the partnership.

Notes and Questions

1. The court in *Morelli* comments briefly on the fact that as a general partner, Morelli exercised control over the partnership. In a general partnership, the members function as co-owners of the business, usually sharing equally in the management of the business, profits and rights to partnership property. All partners act as agents of one another and, as such, they are jointly and severally liable for any indebtedness or partnership liability. A limited partnership consists of at least one general and one limited partner. The general partner controls the business operations, while the limited partner is an investor who contributes capital to the business, but does not exercise any significant control over the business. The limited partner has a right to receive a share of the profits, but has no ownership interest in the partnership. Moreover, the limited partner is generally only liable to the extent of his financial contribution to the partnership. See, R. Merrit & M. Helpern, The Partnership Handbook (1986). Should it have made any difference if Morelli had been only a limited partner? What would he have given up had he been a limited instead of general partner?

2. In 1974, a Federal court in Texas upheld the Texas prohibition of "layman corporations" that "practice medicine" by hiring physicians to treat patients. The court found the prohibition to be a rational exercise of the police power: "Without licensed, professional doctors on Boards of Directors, who and what criteria govern the selection of medical and paramedical staff members? To whom does the doctor owe his first duty—the patient or the corporation?" Garcia v. Texas State Board of Medical Examiners, 384 F.Supp. 434 (W.D.Tex.1974), affirmed mem., 421 U.S. 995, 95 S.Ct. 2391, 44 L.Ed.2d 663 (1975). Although *Garcia* involved a health maintenance organization, HMOs are typically exempted from the prohibition against the corporate practice of medicine by state statute. See, HMO Law Manual, *Aspen* Systems Corporation.

3. Early "corporate medical practice" involved corporations contracting with physicians to provide medical care for their employees for a fixed salary or corporations that marketed physicians' services to the public. The AMA considered the corporate practice of medicine the "commercialization" of medicine, and believed that it would increase physician workload, decrease the quality of patient care, and would introduce lay control over the practice of medicine that would interfere with the physician-patient relationship. The AMA promulgated ethical guidelines that restricted or prohibited the corporate practice of medicine. The prohibition against corporate medical practice was enforced by the courts, using statutory prohibitions against the practice of medicine by unlicensed individuals. What does it matter that a doctor is employed by a partnership of doctors or a professional corporation rather than by a lay person or business entity controlled by non-physicians? Should the state eliminate corporate practice prohibitions and pursue quality concerns directly through quality-control regulation or malpractice litigation? What controls respond to the financial incentives presented in fee-for-service practice?

Prohibitions against the corporate practice of medicine are not routinely or consistently enforced: "Obviously, in modern practice the rule against physician employment is honored mainly in the breach. That does not mean that these traditional prohibitions cannot again serve as a basis for hospital liability.... Therefore, it is usually best, whenever possible, to establish true independent contractor arrangements or retain physicians through a separate corporation." Jeddeloh, Physician Contract Audits: A Hospital Management Tool, 21 Journal of Health and Hospital Law 105 (1988).

See also, Rosoff, The Business of Medicine: Problems with the Corporate Practice of Medicine Doctrine, 17 Cumb.L.Rev. 485 (1987).

4. In the early 1970's, physicians pressured states to enact legislation which would make it possible for them to enjoy the same federal tax advantages available to business associations. Virtually all states have established Professional Corporation Acts, which allow state-licensed professionals to incorporate under state law. Frequently states require all shareholders to be licensed to practice the profession, limit the corporate business to that of the specific profession and set requirements for transfer of corporate stock. Generally, corporate shareholders are only liable to the extent of their investment in the corporation and personal liability is limited to a shareholder's own negligent acts. Statutes authorizing professional corporations often extend personal liability for employees who are directly supervised by a shareholder, and in some cases have established joint and several liability for shareholders. See, Note, The Corporate Practice of Medicine Doctrine: An Anachronism in the Modern Health Care Industry, 40 Vand.L.Rev. 445 (1987).

5. Large multi-specialty groups, i.e., a group of physicians of different specialties typically organized as a partnership or professional corporation with some physicians who are employees and others who are partners or shareholders, are proliferating: "This is the most significant development in health care today. It has the potential to eclipse managed care in importance and cripple hospitals' ancillary income. A large practice that generates 5,000 admissions per year for a hospital has considerable bargaining power. * * * Physicians must find a way to deal with the administrative burden of managed care, and forming large group practices [over 50 doctors] also improves their bargaining position with HMOs, allowing them to capture more sole provider contracts." Grayson, Survey Spots the Tight Turns in MD–CEO Relations, 62 Hospitals 48 (1988), quoting a health care consultant.

6. Medical residents surveyed in 1989 strongly preferred group practice or health maintenance organizations as a practice setting. They wanted "a steady paycheck and set practice hours" and were deterred from starting their own medical practice by their large debt loads from medical school and the high cost of self-employed medical practice (estimated by the AMA at $123,700, including $15,000 for liability coverage, annually in 1987). Only 1% of the residents would choose partnership with established physicians, citing fears of "broken promises, personality conflicts, and exaggerated earnings." Koska, Paychecks and Security Will Lure Future M.D.s, 63 Hospitals 56 (1989).

Problem: General Hospital and Doctors' Clinic

A.

General Hospital operates a 501(c)(3) not-for-profit community hospital. Approximately 100 physicians are members of its medical staff. The community at present has no physicians practicing in such specialties as interventional cardiology and rheumatology and inadequate numbers of physicians practicing in other specialties including neurology, nephrology, oncology and hematology. Thus, patients with illnesses requiring treatment by these specialties often must travel to other communities to receive the needed care.

General would like to make a $12 million dollar loan to Doctors' Clinic, a local physician practice group organized as a limited partnership, to finance the renovation and expansion of an office building/clinic owned by the clinic. The new clinic will provide updated facilities and room for expansion, thereby helping Springfield, a small Midwestern community, to attract and retain adequate numbers of physicians and those with needed specialties. Doctors' Clinic engages in most of the physician recruitment for General Hospital's service area, and has determined, on the basis of its recent physician recruitment experiences, that it needs to improve and expand its facilities (which are over 40 years old) in order to attract qualified physicians. Doctors' Clinic believes that the updating and expansion of its facilities is needed for the recruitment and retention of physicians. Therefore, the renovation and expansion of the office building/clinic is expected to encourage physicians who practice the needed specialties to establish or relocate their practices in General Hospital's service area. Clinic physicians representing 19 specialties have reviewed the community's medical needs and have formulated a strategic recruitment and retention plan to match those needs through the mid-1990s. During 1989 Doctors' Clinic began the recruitment efforts necessary to implement this plan. The physician recruitment and retention plan developed by the Clinic will provide for the service of an additional 8 to 12 physicians during a five-year period. The Clinic expects to have recruited approximately one-fourth of these physicians by 1993, at which time the expanded clinic facilities will be needed.

Principal and interest on the loan would be repaid in equal monthly payments over a period of 30 years, and the outstanding principal balance would bear interest at a fixed rate throughout the terms of the loan. The interest rate would be determined at the time the loan agreement is entered into and would not be less than the interest rate then being paid on U.S. Treasury obligations having a similar maturity. The loan would be secured by a first mortgage on the building and payments under the loan agreement would not be conditioned upon the Clinic's success. The loan would be funded from Hospital monies earmarked, or otherwise available, for investment. No current operating funds would be used to fund the loan.

Although Doctors' Clinic would qualify for a loan from other lenders, the interest rate to be charged on the loan from General is expected to be less than the rate that would be charged by a financial institution. General Hospital's approach to the loan is consistent with its overall investment approach. The yield on a 30–year Treasury bond approximates the yield on the hospital's other investments.

It is expected that approximately 40% of General Hospital's annual investment income (excluding investment income of its fundraising foundation) would consist of interest on this loan to the Clinic. Only approximately 2% of the hospital's total revenue would consist of interest paid on the loan.

In addition to the financial terms outlined above, the loan agreement would impose the following conditions and restrictions:

"1. the proceeds of the loan must be used solely to finance the Clinic;

2. Doctors' Clinic physicians must conduct their principal private office practice at the Clinic; and

3. the office space and clinical facilities constructed as part of the Clinic may be leased only to, and used only by, physicians who hold staff membership and clinical privileges at General Hospital, although they may also hold medical staff membership and clinical privileges at other hospitals and may use the facilities for any of their patients."

As counsel for General Hospital, what issues do you see arising in the proposed loan agreement?

B.

Doctors' Clinic is organized as a limited partnership. Most doctors joining the clinic start as employees and after two years may be invited to become limited partners. Healthmed Services, Inc. is the general partner. Dr. Samantha Jones, a board-certified cardiologist, is being recruited by Doctors' Clinic. She has come to you for advice and would like you to review any contract she is offered. What legal issues do you anticipate? Assuming that she retains you to represent her in contract negotiations, what goals will you have? Draft contract language that you would find acceptable as her lawyer on the issues of major concern. Would these be acceptable to the Doctors' Clinic lawyer? Should she also seek a contract with General Hospital?

Chapter 6

ACCESS TO HEALTH CARE

INTRODUCTION

This chapter focuses on the third major theme of this text: access to health care. Although some previously excluded from receiving adequate health care have gained improved access in recent years, there are still significant barriers and inequities. The wealthy, residents of suburban areas, and whites still have better access than do the poor, residents of rural areas or the inner-city, or minorities.

Medicaid, the principal federal effort to assist the poor, currently covers only about 46% of the poor. In the late 1980s, 31.5 million Americans, nearly 15% of the United States population under 65, were wholly without medical insurance. One study of a group of uninsured persons found that 45% of those who had been told by a physician that they should be hospitalized had not sought care and another 10% were rejected by a hospital. Even recipients of Medicaid tend to receive less adequate care and care of questionable quality. One Medicaid HMO clinic, recently audited, had two doctors seeing 400 patients a week, spending slightly over two minutes with each patient. Similarly, minorities receive less care than whites—black children average 3.2 physician visits a year, white children 4.5 a year. 22% of black children have never been to a dentist as compared to 10% of white children. See generally, Health Care for America's Poor: Separate but Unequal, 20 Clearinghouse Rev. 361 (1986).

Is this situation necessarily wrong? Does society in general, or the federal, state or local government in particular have any obligation to change this situation? Consider the following opinions on this subject:

> Physicians who limit their office practice to insured and paying patients declare themselves openly to be merchants rather than professionals. This mercantile approach has several consequences. First, it demeans the individual physician and cheapens the profession. Second, it puts the third-party payer, as a service purchaser, in a position of greater importance than the patient. Third, it fosters the myth that physicians as a group are greedy and self-serving rather than dedicated and altruistic. And most important, it deprives a large segment of our fellow humans of care. Physicians who value their professionalism should treat office patients on the basis of need, not remuneration. Physicians who do not, deserve the contempt and censure of their colleagues.

Peter H. Elias, M.D., letter to editor, 314 New England Journal of Medicine 391 (1986).

What, in the history of the American medical profession, aside from the profession's own rhetoric, should lead a thoughtful person to expect from physicians a conduct significantly distinct from the conduct of other purveyors of goods and service? * * * [I]t has been one of American medicine's more hallowed tenets that piece-rate compensation is the sine qua non of high quality medical care * * *. Ordinary mortals, not blessed by professional courtesy, experience the application of this piece-rate principle whenever they pass the physician's cashier on the way out. * * * As I read [the Hippocratic] oath, I see no reference in it to charity care. It is merely required that physicians do the utmost, without corruption, for patients whose house they do (choose to) enter. * * * My own thoughts on the matter, for what they are worth, are these. Society should not expect private physicians or private hospitals (for-profit or not) to absorb the cost of whatever social pathos washes onto their shores. We as a society have a moral duty to compensate the providers of health care for treating the poor. If providers do give some charity care, our thanks to them.

Letter from Uwe E. Reinhardt to Dr. Arnold S. Relman, Institute of Medicine, Nat'l. Academy of Sciences, For-Profit Enterprise in Health Care 210, at 211, 213 (1986).

* * *

The concept of medical care as the patient's right is immoral because it denies the most fundamental of all rights, that of a man to his own life and the freedom of action to support it. Medical care is neither a right nor a privilege: it is a service that is provided by doctors and others to people who wish to purchase it. It is the provision of this service that a doctor depends upon for his livelihood, and is his means of supporting his own life. If the right to health care belongs to the patient, he starts out owning the services of a doctor without the necessity of either earning them or receiving them as a gift from the only man who has the right to give them: the doctor himself.
* * *

Robert M. Sade, Medical Care as a Right: A Refutation, 285 New England Journal of Medicine 1281, 1289 (Dec. 2, 1971).

A claim that society has an obligation to eliminate inequality of access to health care could take several forms. First, it could be argued that inequality of access to resources is morally wrong: all should have equal rights to all goods and services. Though some political systems are built on this premise, it is not one that currently enjoys wide political support in the United States. Second, health care might be special: access to health care might be necessary even if access to other resources was not. Several arguments can be made for according health care a special status.

First one could argue that health is a fundamental right. Satisfactory health, like education (to which our society does guarantee universal access), is a necessary precondition to realizing every other life opportunity. Therefore, a commitment to equality of opportunity (though not necessarily of result) demands equal access to health care. The fundamental nature of health is also invoked by arguments based on the moral quality of health care. Some claim that because suffering appeals to our humanity and the urge to relieve suffering is basic to humans, availability of health care is morally imperative. Others argue that equal access to health care (like access to sufferage) is basic to a society committed to equal respect of persons.

Others claim that health care is needed by all, and that this need can be objectively defined, thus health care is necessary in a sense that French perfume and high performance automobiles are not. Health is a necessary condition for the human animal to function, and to some extent can be objectively defined. It is universally valued, regardless of personal values or culture. Moreover, the experience of pain is universal and the experience of it is similar to all, thus relief from pain should be equally available to all.

Still other arguments appeal to the indirect effects of ill-health on others, the "externalities" of poor health. These include the loss of productivity it imposes on society and the loss of utility all endure in seeing the suffering of others. A final set of arguments is based on the random and potentially disastrous nature of ill-health. The need for medical care can strike any person at any time with devastating cost and effect on the family, emotionally and financially. Thus, we all gain from the freedom from anxiety afforded when society provides universal access to health care and shares in its cost.

See, developing these arguments, 1 President's Commission for the Study of Ethical Problems in Medicine and Biomedical and Behavioral Research, Securing Access to Health Care, 16–18 (1983) [hereafter Securing Access]; Wikler, Philosophical Perspectives on Access to Health Care, An Introduction, in 2 President's Commission, Securing Access to Health Care, 107 (1983); Daniels, Health Care Needs and Distributive Justice, Gutman, For and Against Equal Access to Health Care in In Search of Equity 1, 43 (Bayer, Caplan and Daniels, eds., 1983).

How do you respond to these arguments? Should health care be treated as just another good that some may be able to afford, others not? Even if you accept the premise that health care is different, and that society has an obligation to grant equal access to health care, does this obligation translate into an enforceable right on the part of any individual? Does a social obligation imply an obligation on government, or might it be met by charity? Even if the government is obligated to provide health care to all, does that obligation logically fall on any particular level of government, federal, state or local? See, 1 Securing Access 25–35.

Recognition of a right to health care does not necessarily require a commitment to providing any particular level of health care. Equity of health care could require equal results, i.e. a commitment to make everyone equally healthy. An 85–year–old cancer patient might have a right to the expenditure of resources necessary to make her as healthy as an 18–year–old athlete. This would not only be impossible, but would require virtually infinite resources devoted both to research and to care. Alternatively, equity could mean that equal health care resources would be expended on each person. However, resource needs vary widely depending on health condition. Devoting the same resources to an 85–year–old cancer patient and an 18–year–old athlete might result in insufficient care for the one, and a waste of resources on the other.

Alternatively, society could commit itself to provide a decent minimum level of care to all, with care beyond this minimum available to those who can afford it through the market. But how do we define this minimum? Perhaps we can agree that it does not include cosmetic breast enlargements or nose reductions, but does it include life support systems to preserve the life of a comatose patient, or annual checkups for a 45-year-old in good health? If, on the other hand, society opted for a definition of equity that guaranteed equal health care to every person, would this necessitate forbidding the purchase of health care in excess of that standard? Without such a prohibition, the wealthy will continue to control the services of the best practitioners and institutions, denying them to others. Would such a prohibition violate the Constitutional rights of the wealthy? Is there any reason to allow the wealthy to buy Lamborghinis and gold coins denied to the poor, but deny them the opportunity to purchase heart transplants or kidney dialysis?

Finally, how do we address access to health care for conditions that are in some sense voluntarily incurred? Does society bear any obligation to provide treatment for the lung cancer of the lifetime heavy smoker who refuses to quit smoking? Must society provide a liver transplant for the alcoholic who has destroyed his own but refuses to stop drinking? Should we give these patients the benefit of the doubt, recognizing that unhealthy behavior is often compulsive, largely beyond the control of the patient, and sometimes the result of genetic propensities? Does the fact that some medical conditions that we now view as beyond the control of the patient (such as most mental illnesses) were once considered to result from moral fault argue against allowing society to deny care to those apparently injured by their own voluntary conduct? Is the issue further clouded by the fact that some medical conditions that some now view as controllable and thus to result from fault of character (such as obesity) were formerly considered healthy and are still considered healthy in other societies? Does society's disagreement over the moral responsibility of some patients, like AIDS sufferers, raise the same problems?

Consider, Engelhardt, Health Care Allocations: Responses to the Unjust, the Unfortunate, and the Undesirable, in Justice and Health Care (E. Shelp, ed. 1981); Fried, Equity and Rights in Medical Care, 6 Hastings Center Report 29 (February 1976); 1 Securing Access, at

35–42. Welch, Health Care Tickets for the Uninsured: First Class, Coach or Standby 321 New.Eng.J.Med. 1261 (1989).

This chapter considers the legal issues presented by each of the various means through which Americans gain access to health care. It first examines private insurance, in particular employment-related group insurance. Next it considers public insurance, focusing on the two major national health insurance programs of the United States, Medicare and Medicaid. It then turns to the problems of the uninsured, and in this context examines the various legal strategies through which professionals and institutions are compelled to provide care for patients regardless of ability to pay. Finally, it studies the problems presented when access to care is impeded not by inability to pay but rather by resource scarcity.

I. ACCESS THROUGH THE MARKET: PRIVATE HEALTH INSURANCE

A. INTRODUCTION TO PRIVATE HEALTH INSURANCE IN THE UNITED STATES AND TO BASIC PRINCIPLES OF HEALTH INSURANCE

In 1986 nearly 180 million Americans had private hospitalization insurance and over 155 million had private major medical expense coverage. Private insurance in 1987 financed approximately 31% of personal health care expenditures, including almost 37% of hospital expenditures. The following excerpts describe the health insurance industry in the United States and basic principles of health insurance:

CONGRESSIONAL RESEARCH SERVICE, HEALTH INSURANCE AND THE UNINSURED: BACKGROUND DATA AND ANALYSIS.

(House Comm. on Education & Labor, Comm. Print, 1988).

CHAPTER 2. A PRIMER ON HEALTH INSURANCE.

I. Description of Health Insurance

A. What is Health Insurance?

Health insurance is provided by a vast and highly complex assortment of insuring entities, including commercial insurance companies, Blue Cross and Blue Shield plans, health maintenance organizations (HMOs), and preferred provider organizations (PPOs). Each insuring entity is in some way distinct, and the nature and practices of the insurance industry are continually evolving. Increasingly, large companies are self-insuring; they assume the risk of health care costs for their employees and use insurance companies only to cover catastrophic expenses and to provide administrative services, if at all. Such variation and constant change make it difficult to characterize the health insurance industry, and generalizations are likely to gloss over important differences in the way individual health insurers operate.

* * *

B. The Historical Development of Health Insurance
in the United States

The first health insurance arrangements were relatively simple, but the industry today is characterized by a variety of complex arrangements. In order to understand why existing arrangements have prevailed over alternatives, the following section describes the historical development of the health insurance industry.

1. Earliest plans

Before the 1930s, few health insurance plans existed; Americans paid over 90 percent of their medical expenses out-of-pocket. The earliest private health insurance plans in the United States were sponsored through employers, unions, or fraternal groups. The railroad, mining, textile, and lumber industries developed the first employee medical care programs. Employers deducted funds from the salaries of workers and contracted with physicians who would treat work-related injuries. In some cases (e.g., the United Mine Workers), workers contributed funds to hire a physician to care for them.

2. Hospital plans

During the Great Depression, increasing numbers of patients were unable to afford medical services. Physicians and hospitals had difficulty remaining solvent because they had too few paying patients. Within this context, hospital-sponsored health insurance arrangements developed to help ensure a more predictable flow of revenue to health care providers. In general, hospital services were made available to those who paid a pre-determined amount directly to the hospital. Initially, these plans involved single hospitals. Later, groups of hospitals banded together to form multiple hospital plans.

* * *

Blue Cross plans.—The non-profit multiple hospital plan served as a model for Blue Cross plans. In 1932, the first Blue Cross plan was established in Sacramento, California. The plan negotiated payment rates with participating hospitals, charged a single community-wide premium rate to subscribers, and guaranteed agreed-upon payments to participating hospitals for the provision of selected services to subscribers.

In the mid–1930s, some State insurance regulators tried to subject multiple hospital plans to their State's insurance regulations, including the reserve requirements. The American Medical Association, along with local hospitals and physicians, promoted State legislative initiatives to exempt Blue Cross plans from certain State insurance regulations. Blue Cross plans were incorporated under separate enabling legislation with their own sets of rules and regulations (e.g., regarding rate-setting and Blue Cross Board composition). In exchange for State tax-exempt status and relief from reserve requirements, States generally charged the plans with the responsibility to serve the entire community and to provide insurance for low- and moderate-income persons. The plans also qualified for Federal tax-exemption as charitable organizations. The combination of negotiated rates with providers and the exemption from taxes gave Blue plans certain financial advantages over other insurers, and by 1945 the plans had expanded to cover 19 million subscribers nationally.

The plans' benefit programs were known as "service benefits" because they provided full coverage for services rather than for a schedule of fixed-dollar payments that might or might not have covered a provider's full charges. Coverage provided by Blue Cross paid for inpatient care in full, and was referred to as "basic coverage."

3. Commercial health insurance

At the same time that Blue Cross plans were developing, commercial insurers began offering health insurance. In 1934, commercial insurers first offered groups "indemnity coverage" against hospital expenses. Unlike service benefit plans, these plans typically paid the amount specified in the policy directly to the enrollee. The enrollee paid the provider and was responsible if the provider's charges exceeded the insurance payment. By the late 1930s, many commercial insurers had expanded their policies to cover surgery and other physician services. This type of coverage was commonly called "comprehensive" and generally covered a variety of services with part of the cost paid by the enrollee. Many commercial insurers also offered "major medical" coverage. This type of plan was established to cover expenses, such as prescription drugs and physician office visits, that were not covered as a basic service through Blue Cross plans.

4. Blue Shield plans

In response to the expansion of commercial health insurance and to the lack of coverage by Blue Cross of physician services, Blue Shield plans were established, often with the assistance of Blue Cross plans. The first Blue Shield physician insurance program, called the California Physician's Service, was developed in 1939. Blue Shield plans reimbursed physicians, initially for the full cost of each service, based on a negotiated payment schedule.

5. Health maintenance organizations

Health maintenance organizations (HMOs) evolved from a variety of arrangements under which physicians contracted to furnish medical care to employers or groups of individuals for a pre-arranged fee. During the 1930s and 1940s, group practice associations were set up to serve specific employers. Among the most successful arrangements of that period were the Group Health Association of Washington, D.C. (GHA), the Kaiser Permanente medical care program of California and the Health Insurance Plan of Greater New York (HIP).

* * *

6. Employer–based health insurance

Before World War II, Blue Cross/Blue Shield arrangements dominated the health insurance industry. However, new economic policies and conditions during the war facilitated the rapid expansion of employer-based health insurance and brought new actors, labor unions and employers, into the health insurance arena.

Health insurance as a benefit.—In the 1940s, wartime price stabilization policies capped wages and thus encouraged employer-worker bargaining over noncash benefits. Employers could not increase wages but often were willing to increase compensation by providing more generous benefit packages in order to attract and retain employees. Health insurance was an attractive benefit for employees because it paid their medical bills. Furthermore, unlike cash compensation, it was a tax-free benefit.

* * *

The growth of employer-based insurance.—Once terms of the benefit package and contributions were agreed upon with the union, the employer generally retained the right to select an insurance carrier. Commercial insurance was especially appealing because it could often offer premiums at rates lower than Blue Cross/Blue Shield plans. Because commercial insurers provided indemnity coverage (reimbursing enrollees for a specified amount or percentage of charges), they offered lower premiums than service-benefit plans which reimbursed providers often for the full value of a service. Premiums were also low for some employers because commercial insurers used experience-rating. That is, instead of computing one premium on the basis of the experience of the entire community, they offered lower premiums to relatively healthy, low-risk groups of employees. In addition, commercial carriers could offer employers an active role in plan administration and benefit design.

* * *

C. The Existing Private Health Insurance Structure

Recent changes in the delivery of health care have been accompanied by changes in health insurance arrangements and a blurring of many of the historical distinctions detailed above. * * *

Competition and cost increases have led to plan design changes, the net effect of which has been to remove many of the differences in plan structure. Deductibles and coinsurance have been added in many cases to the basic coverage of most plans. There is increasing use of mandatory second surgical opinion programs and hospital admission precertification. Most health insurance arrangements cover alternatives to hospital care, such as hospice care, ambulatory surgery, and skilled nursing facility care. Many plans encourage the use of preventive services by covering them in full.

As insurers compete to attract enrollees who will need the least amount of health care, rating practices have been altered. In general, commercial insurers continue to experience-rate, basing the cost per person on the experience of one group of employees. By experience-rating, commercial insurers have been able to attract many low-risk employer groups. Likewise, commercial insurers set commensurate rates for, or decline to cover, high-risk individuals and groups.

In order to attract employers through competitive rates, the Blues have modified their community-rating and underwriting practices. Today, the Blues experience-rate larger groups and are applying this practice to smaller and smaller groups. Some individual Blue Cross/Blue Shield organizations are extending underwriting rules to properly rate (or reject) the worst risks among the smaller employers.

* * *

1. Employer–provided arrangements

* * *

Self–insured plans.—Rising health care costs and the growth in State–mandated benefits and other State insurance regulation have encouraged most large-sized employers, and many medium-sized employers, to turn to one of several forms of self-insurance. The preemption provision in the Employee Retirement Income Security Act (ERISA) which has been interpreted as exempting self-insured employee benefit plans from State mandates has created a strong incentive for companies to self-insure. The incentive increases as State–mandated benefits proliferate. * * *

Self-insured employers have a variety of funding and administrative options. Some employers operate completely self-insured and self-administered health plans. A few employers even run their own health care facilities. Most employers who self-insure, however, retain some of the advantages of the insurance arrangement by using a commercial insurer or the Blues to process claims. Others simply contract with "third-party administrators" to review and process the claims. Employers frequently self-insure for routine health care costs but avoid extreme risks by purchasing "stop-loss" insurance, under which in return for a risk premium an insurer will cover any losses that exceed a certain level, such as 125 percent of expected claims.

* * *

2. Small employer arrangements

Surveys show that small employers are less likely to offer health insurance than large employers. According to the Employee Benefit Research Institute, almost half of all uninsured workers are found in firms with fewer than 25 employees.

A Small Business Administration (SBA) survey in 1987 found that small employers do not offer coverage for a variety of reasons. [ ] Cost is the most prevalent self-reported reason. Over 60 percent of small employers reported that either profits were insufficient to cover the cost of insurance or insurance premiums were too high. * * *

Many small employers cited less generous tax treatment of health insurance premiums for unincorporated firms as an important reason for not offering coverage. While corporations can deduct 100 percent of premium costs for employees as a business expense for purposes of calculating Federal tax liability, self-employed individuals, partnerships and other unincorporated firms are eligible for only a 25 percent deduction.

* * *

From the insurer's point of view, small employers are costly groups, primarily because of the very high turnover and higher administrative costs of small groups. In addition, in small groups the risk is spread over fewer people. Turnover can lead to adverse selection if employees who leave small groups are younger, healthier individuals. In addition, small groups are not large enough to absorb the costs of an employee or family member with extremely high medical expenses. In some cases, small employers have decided to purchase insurance because there is an immediate or predicted need for medical care by the employer, an employee, or family members. * * *

* * *

Only 5 percent of firms with fewer than 100 employees self-insure, compared to rates between 40 and 50 percent for firms over 100. Small firms are less likely to self-insure because of the high risk associated with paying claims out of their own revenues and the administrative burdens associated with self-insurance.

* * *

3. The individual market

Individuals who do not have access to employer-based coverage may obtain health insurance coverage by purchasing it directly from commercial insurers, the Blues, or HMOs. About 14.5 million non-Medicare individuals are enrolled as individuals in "non-group" policies. [ ] Commercial insurers cover the majority of these individuals, Blue Cross/Blue Shield plans insure over 4 million, and HMOs enroll about 1 million.

* * *

Individuals face many of the same restrictions as small employers in their search for health insurance. In order to guard against adverse selection, many insurers underwrite individuals. Some simply do not accept individual enrollees. Other insurers reserve the right to reject individual applicants on the basis of existing health conditions. Commercial insurers and the Blues can offer an individual applicant coverage with an above-average rate or with specific services excluded from coverage. Such coverage is problematic for persons with serious or chronic health problems, who may find it impossible to get insurance because of "pre-existing condition" clauses which exclude treatment for any illness or condition contracted prior to enrollment. * * *

* * *

CONGRESSIONAL RESEARCH SERVICE, INSURING THE UNINSURED: OPTIONS AND ANALYSIS

(House Comm. on Education & Labor, Comm. Print, 1988) [most footnotes deleted.]

II. PRINCIPLES OF HEALTH INSURANCE

A. *The Concept of Risk*

Insurance is a response to risk, to uncertainty about specific outcomes, and to the possibility that those outcomes will be unfavorable. * * * Most people * * * choose to transfer the risk of a financially costly illness to an insurer (or comparable third-party payer). In this way, insurance provides an economic device whereby a person substitutes a certain payment (a premium) for the uncertain financial loss that would occur in the event of an uninsured accident or illness.

The fundamental principle of insurance is, in fact, to minimize the losses of one or a few individuals by spreading the risks (of their medical expenses) among many. In its ideal form, insurance provides a mechanism by which losses can be spread on an equitable basis to all members of the group.

B. *Probability and the Law of Large Numbers*

For insurance to operate, there has to be a way to predict the likelihood or probability that a loss will occur as a result of a specific outcome. Such predictions in insurance are based upon probability theory and the law of large numbers. According to probability theory, "while some events appear to be a matter of chance, they actually occur with regularity over a large number of trials."[5] By examining patterns of behavior over a large number of trials, it is therefore possible for the insurer to infer the likelihood of such behaviors in the future.

* * * Applied to insurance, probability allows the insurer to make predictions on the basis of historical data. In so doing, the insurer "... implicitly says, 'if things continue to happen in the future as they happened in the past, and if our estimate of what has happened in the past is accurate, this is what we may expect.' "[6]

Losses seldom occur exactly as expected, so insurance companies have to make predictions about the extent to which actual experience might deviate from predicted results. For a small group of insured units, there is a high probability that losses will be much greater or smaller than was predicted. For a very large group, the range of probable error diminishes, especially if the insured group is similar in composition to the group upon which the prediction is based. Thus, to predict the probability of a loss, insurers seek to aggregate persons who are at a similar risk for that loss. * * *

5. Vaughan, Emmett J. Fundamentals of Risk and Insurance. 4th Edition. New York. John Wiley and Sons, 1986. p. 22.

6. Ibid., p. 27.

C. *Insurable Risks*

In theory all probabilities of loss can be insured. Insurance could cover any risk for a price. As the probability of loss increases, however, the premium will increase to the point at which it approaches the actual potential pay-out.

To keep premiums competitive, there are in practice some risks that insurers will not accept. In general, insurable risks must meet the following criteria:

- There has to be uncertainty that the loss will occur, and that the loss must be beyond the control of the insured. Insurers will not sell hospital insurance to a person who is on his way to a hospital, nor fire insurance to someone holding a lit match. * * *

- The loss produced by the risk must be measurable. The insurer has to be able to determine that a loss has occurred and that it has a specific dollar value.

- There must be a sufficiently large number of similar insured units to make the losses predictable. * * *

- Generally, the loss must be significant, but there should be a low probability that a very high loss will occur. A person does not need to insure against a trivial loss. However, it would not be prudent for an insurer to accept a risk in which there is a high probability that an expensive loss will occur to a large percentage of the insured units at the same time. Thus, insurers generally do not cover damage that results from acts of war, and insurers often refuse life and health insurance to individual applicants known to be suffering from a costly illness or condition.

* * *

III. RATEMAKING

A. *Introduction*

Ratemaking is the "process of predicting future losses and future expenses and allocating those costs among the various classes of insureds." [14] The outcome of the ratemaking process is a "premium" or price of policy. The premium is made up of expected claims against the insurer and the insurer's "administrative expenses." The term "administrative expenses" is used to mean any expense that the insurance company charges that is not for claims (including reserves for potential claims). * * * In the case of employer group coverage, a third part of the premium is set aside in a reserve held against unexpected claims. This reserve is often refundable to the employer if claims do not exceed expectations.

B. *The Ratemaking Process*

In the textbook descriptions of ratemaking for health insurance, insurers predict losses on the basis of predicted claims costs. This

---

14. Vaughan, 1986, p. 91.

prediction involves an assessment of the likely morbidity (calculated in terms of the number of times the event insured against occurs) and severity (the average magnitude of each loss) of the policyholder or group of policyholders. * * *

* * *

There are different approaches to determining rates. In health insurance, the most frequently used approaches are "experience rating" and "community rating."

Under *experience rating,* the past experience of the group to be insured is used to determine the premium. For employer groups, experience rating would take into account the company's own history of claims and other expenses. * * *

* * *

The advantage of experience rating is that it adjusts the cost of insurance for a specific group in a manner more commensurate with the expected cost of that particular group than is possible through the exclusive use of manual rates. In addition, the increasingly competitive environment among insurers demands that each one "make every effort to retain groups with favorable experience. Unless an insurer can provide coverage to such groups at a reasonable cost, it runs the risk of losing such policyholders to another insurer which more closely reflects the expected costs of their programs in its rates." [18]

Under *community rating,* premium rates are based on the allocation of total costs to all the individuals or groups to be insured, without regard to the past experience of any particular subgroup. The term is related to "class rating," which refers to the practice of computing a rate for a policy that applies to all applicants possessing a given set of characteristics, such as sex, age or locale. Community or class rating has the advantage of allowing an insurer to apply a single rate or set of rates to a large number of people, thus simplifying the process of determining premiums.

* * *

IV. ADVERSE AND FAVORABLE SELECTION

If everyone in the society purchased health insurance, and if everyone opted for an identical health insurance plan, then insurance companies could adhere strictly to the models of prediction and rate-setting described above. However, everyone does not buy insurance, nor do all the purchasers of insurance choose identical benefits. People who expect to need health services are more likely than others to purchase insurance, and are also likely to seek coverage for the specific services they expect to need. * * *

Insurers use the term "adverse selection" to describe this phenomenon. Adverse selection is defined by the health insurance industry as

18. Health Insurance Association of America. A Course in Group Life and Health Insurance. Part A. Washington. 1985 p. 236.

the "tendency of persons with poorer than average health expectations to apply for, or continue, insurance to a greater extent than do persons with average or better health expectations." [27]

* * *

Adjusting premiums for adverse selection results in further adverse selection. As the price of insurance goes up, healthier people are less likely to want to purchase insurance. Each upward rate adjustment will leave a smaller and sicker group of potential purchasers. If there were only a single insurance company, it would serve a steadily shrinking market paying steadily increasing premiums. However, because multiple insurance companies are operating in the market, each company may strive to enroll the lower cost individuals or groups, leaving the higher cost cases for its competitors. In this market, adverse selection consists (from the insurer's point of view) of drawing the least desirable cases from *within the pool of insurance purchasers.* "Favorable" selection occurs if the insurer successfully enrolls lower risk clients than its competitors.

It is thus necessary to distinguish between the more traditional use of "adverse selection," as a term to describe the differences between people who do and do not buy insurance, and the sense in which the term is often used today, to describe the differences among purchasers choosing various insurers or types of coverage. This second type of adverse selection can occur within an insured group, if the individuals in that group are permitted to select from among different insurance options.

Insurers are still concerned about the more traditional type of adverse selection. They use underwriting rules, to exclude or limit the worst risks. Some insurers may also attempt to limit adverse selection by careful selection of where they market and to whom they sell a policy. For example, a company offering a Medicare supplement (Medigap) plan might be more likely to advertise its plan in senior citizen recreation centers, where the patrons tend to be relatively young and healthy, than in nursing homes, where the residents are probably older and have chronic health conditions. Thus, from the perspective of the individual or group applying for insurance, the insurer's attempts to avoid adverse selection may result in lack of availability of coverage, denial of coverage, incomplete coverage or above-average premiums.

* * *

B. STATE AND FEDERAL REGULATION OF PRIVATE INSURANCE

Private health insurance is extensively regulated in the United States. Traditionally, insurance regulation has been the business of

27. Health Insurance Association of America, 1986–1987 Source Book of Health Insurance Data, p. 83, Washington.

the states. The McCarran–Ferguson Act of 1945 confirmed the primacy of the states in the area of insurance regulation and the intention of the federal government not to interfere in this process.

State regulations attempt to assure the solvency of health insurers by prescribing capital and financial reserve requirements. They attempt to protect consumers by requiring disclosure of contract information, standardized printing of terms of coverage, insurance company bonding and auditing. Some states review and approve the rates charged by some insurers to some insureds (e.g. Blue Cross individual policy rates). All states tax the premiums of commercial insurers and more than half also tax Blue Cross and Blue Shield premiums. State laws often require private insurers to provide certain benefits, to pay for the services of certain providers, or to make coverage available to certain persons. State regulations also address coordination of benefits in situations where more than one family member is covered by more than one insurer. Finally, about a third of the states now tax insurance plans to finance risk pools to make insurance available to persons who are otherwise uninsurable.

In recent years, however, the federal government has reasserted its authority over the most common form of health insurance, employee health benefits. The Employee Retirement Income Security Act of 1974 (ERISA) established uniform national standards for employee benefit plans and broadly preempted state regulation of these plans. 29 U.S.C.A. § 1144(a) states that ERISA supercedes state laws to the extent that they "relate to any employee benefit plan" covered by ERISA. This preemption clause is qualified by 29 U.S.C.A. § 1144(b)(2)(A), a "savings clause," which specifies that ERISA does not preempt state laws regulating insurance, banking or securities. This clause is limited, however, by the "deemer clause", 29 U.S.C.A. § 1144(b)(2)(B), which states that self-insured employee benefit plans or trusts will not be considered as engaging in the business of insurance for purposes of any state law "purporting to regulate insurance companies [or] insurance contracts." The interaction of these clauses with state laws that attempt to regulate employee health insurance has caused a great deal of controversy and litigation, discussed below.

Federal involvement in private health insurance was further expanded by the Consolidated Omnibus Budget Reconciliation Act of 1985 (COBRA), which requires extension of group health benefits to certain employees or their dependents beyond the point where benefits would otherwise have terminated. The federal Health Maintenance Organization Act of 1973, discussed in the next chapter, also interjects federal requirements into the administration of health benefit plans.

Finally, the most significant federal impact on private health insurance in the United States comes not through regulation but through the tax laws. Employer contributions for the purchase of employee health insurance are exempt from taxation under the federal income tax laws, resulting in a substantial subsidy ($33.5 billion projected for 1990) for the purchase of employment related health insurance. Individual employees can shelter additional health insurance payments through "salary reduction" or "flexible spending" arrangements, 26 U.S.C.A. § 106, but non-employment related health insurance premiums are only deductible if, when added to other medical expenses, they exceed 7.5% of gross income, 26 U.S.C.A. § 213. The widespread availability of employment-related health insurance in this country is undoubtedly attributable to the liberal subsidies afforded through the tax system.

The combined effect of this rich matrix of federal and state regulation of private insurance is considered in the following materials.

C. ELIGIBILITY FOR PRIVATE INSURANCE

1. *Mandated Coverage: COBRA*

Eighty-five to ninety percent of privately insured persons in the United States are covered through employment-related group insurance policies. Group health insurance costs much less than individual coverage for a variety of reasons: insuring groups avoids the marketing expenses required for individual policies, offers economies of scale in administration, and, most importantly, protects insurance companies from the hazards of adverse selection. A number of states, therefore, have enacted laws attempting to expand eligibility for group coverage to save persons from having to purchase individual coverage. Thirty-eight states, for example, require insurers to cover infants born to insureds, 33 require continued coverage for persons who are mentally or physically handicapped, and 18 require coverage of adopted children. Thirty-three states provide some form of continued coverage for persons who are terminated by employers offering group health insurance. COBRA adopts a federal mandate for such continued coverage:

29 U.S.C.A. § 1161–1167. CONTINUATION COVERAGE UNDER GROUP HEALTH PLANS.

§ 1161. Plans must provide continuation coverage to certain individuals

(a) In general. The plan sponsor of each group health plan shall provide, in accordance with this part, that each qualified beneficiary who would lose coverage under the plan as a result of a qualifying event is entitled, under the plan, to elect, within the election period, continuation coverage under the plan.

(b) Exception for certain plans. Subsection (a) of this section shall not apply to any group health plan * * * if all employers maintaining such plan normally employed fewer than 20 employees on a typical business day during the preceding calendar year.

§ 1162. Continuation coverage

For purposes of section 1161 of this title the term "continuation coverage" means coverage under the plan which meets the following requirements:

(1) Type of benefit coverage. The coverage must consist of coverage which, as of the time the coverage is being provided, is identical to the coverage provided under the plan to similarly situated beneficiaries under the plan with respect to whom a qualifying event has not occurred. If coverage is modified under the plan for any group of similarly situated beneficiaries, such coverage shall also be modified in the same manner for all individuals who are qualified beneficiaries under the plan pursuant to this part in connection with such group.

(2) Period of coverage. The coverage must extend for at least the period beginning on the date of the qualifying event and ending not earlier than the earliest of the following:

(A) Maximum required period.—

(i) General rule for terminations and reduced hours. In the case of a qualifying event described in section 1163(2) of this title, except as provided in clause (ii), the date which is 18 months after the date of the qualifying event.

(ii) Special rule for multiple qualifying events. If a qualifying event (other than a qualifying event described in section 1163(6) of this title) occurs during the 18 months after the date of a qualifying event described in section 1163(2) of this title, the date which is 36 months after the date of the qualifying event described in section 1163(2) of this title.

(iii) Special rule for certain bankruptcy proceedings. In the case of a qualifying event described in section 1163(6) of this title (relating to bankruptcy proceedings), the date of the death of the covered employee or qualified beneficiary (described in section 1167(3)(C)(iii) of this title), or in the case of the surviving spouse or dependent children of the covered employee, 36 months after the date of the death of the covered employee.

(iv) General rule for other qualifying events. In the case of a qualifying event not described in section 1163(2) or 1163(6) of this title, the date which is 36 months after the date of the qualifying event.

(v) Qualifying event involving Medicare entitlement.—In the case of an event described in section 1163(4) of this title (without regard to whether such event is a qualifying event), the period of coverage for qualified beneficiaries other than the covered employee for such event or any subsequent qualifying event shall not terminate before the close of the 36–month period beginning on the date the covered employee becomes entitled to benefits under [Medicare] * * *

In the case of an individual who is determined, * * * [by the Social Security Administration], to have been disabled at the time of a qualifying event described in section 1163(2) of this title, any reference in clause (i) or (ii) to 18 months with respect to such event is deemed a reference to 29 months, * * *.

(B) End of plan. The date on which the employer ceases to provide any group health plan to any employee.

(C) Failure to pay premium. The date on which coverage ceases under the plan by reason of a failure to make timely payment of any premium required under the plan with respect to the qualified beneficiary. * * *

(D) Group health plan coverage or Medicare entitlement. The date on which the qualified beneficiary first becomes, after the date of the election—

(i) covered under any other group health plan (as an employee or otherwise) which does not contain any exclusion or limitation with respect to any preexisting condition of such beneficiary, or

(ii) in the case of a qualified beneficiary other than a qualified beneficiary described in section 1167(3)(C) of this title, entitled to benefits under [Medicare] [   ].

(E) Termination of extended coverage for disability. In the case of a qualified beneficiary who is disabled at the time of a qualifying event described in section 1163(2) of this title, the month that begins more than 30 days after the date of the final determination [by Social Security] * * * that the qualified beneficiary is no longer disabled.

(3) Premium requirements. The plan may require payment of a premium for any period of continuation coverage, except that such premium—(A) shall not exceed 102 percent of the applicable premium for such period, and (B) may, at the election of the payor, be made in monthly installments. * * * In the case of an individual described in the last sentence of paragraph (2)(A), any reference in subparagraph (A) of this paragraph to "102 percent" is deemed a reference to "150 percent" for any month after the 18th month of continuation coverage described in clause (i) or (ii) of paragraph (2)(A).

(4) No requirement of insurability. The coverage may not be conditioned upon, or discriminate on the basis of lack of, evidence of insurability.

(5) Conversion option. In the case of a qualified beneficiary whose period of continuation coverage expires under paragraph (2)(A), the plan must, during the 180–day period ending on such expiration date, provide to the qualified beneficiary the option of enrollment under a conversion health plan otherwise generally available under the plan.

§ 1163. Qualifying event

For purposes of this part, the term "qualifying event" means, with respect to any covered employee, any of the following events which, but for the continuation coverage required under this part, would result in the loss of coverage of a qualified beneficiary:

(1) The death of the covered employee.

(2) The termination (other than by reason of such employee's gross misconduct), or reduction of hours, of the covered employee's employment.

(3) The divorce or legal separation of the covered employee from the employee's spouse.

(4) The covered employee becoming entitled to [Medicare] * * *.

(5) A dependent child ceasing to be a dependent child under the generally applicable requirements of the plan.

(6) A proceeding in a case under Title 11 [bankruptcy], * * *, with respect to the employer from whose employment the covered employee retired at any time.

In the case of an event described in paragraph (6), a loss of coverage includes a substantial elimination of coverage with respect to a qualified beneficiary described in section 1167(3)(C) of this title within one year before or after the date of commencement of the proceeding.

§ 1164.   Applicable premium

For purposes of this part—

(1) In general.   The term "applicable premium" means, with respect to any period of continuation coverage of qualified beneficiaries, the cost to the plan for such period of the coverage for similarly situated beneficiaries with respect to whom a qualifying event has not occurred (without regard to whether such cost is paid by the employer or employee).

(2) Special rule for self-insured plans.   [Self-insured plans may base the premium on a reasonable estimate of the cost of providing coverage to similarly situated beneficiaries, or on the basis of the cost in previous years updated for inflation.]

* * *

§ 1167.   Definitions and special rules for purposes of this part—

* * *

(3) Qualified beneficiary

(A) In general.   The term "qualified beneficiary" means, with respect to a covered employee under a group health plan, any other individual who, on the day before the qualifying event for that employee, is a beneficiary under the plan—(i) as the spouse of the covered employee, or (ii) as the dependent child of the employee.

(B) Special rule for terminations and reduced employment.   In the case of a qualifying event described in section 1163(2) of this title, the term "qualified beneficiary" includes the covered employee.

(C) Special rule for retirees and widows.   In the case of a qualifying event described in section 1163(6) of this title, the term "qualified beneficiary" includes a covered employee who had retired on or before the date of substantial elimination of coverage and any other individual who, on the day before such qualifying event, is a beneficiary under the plan—(i) as the spouse of the covered employee, (ii) as the dependent child of the employee, or (iii) as the surviving spouse of the covered employee.

* * *

Notes and Questions

1. What benefits would COBRA afford in each of the following situations?

a. Mary Robinson is fired from her job because she has been persistently late for work.

b. Six months later she is hired by another employer. The group health policy of that employer, however, excludes coverage for her medical problems related to her high blood pressure because it is a pre-existing condition.

c. John McCarthy retired from his job ten years ago but continues to receive health benefits under his former employer's group insurance plan. His former employer goes bankrupt and terminates its health insurance plan.

d. Lisa Sorensen divorces her husband, David, and is thus terminated from coverage under David's employer's group health plan. She is 55 years old and unemployed, without health coverage on her own.

e. Sue Perkins has just turned 18 and is no longer covered by her mother's group benefits plan. She is in college and has no other insurance.

2. In the cases above in which COBRA applies, would COBRA necessarily provide significant protection? What effect might COBRA have on the employer in cases where it applies? The premium payment for COBRA coverage was set at 102% of the normal group premium to cover additional administrative expenses attributable to COBRA. Why might this premium prove inadequate to cover the actual insurance of COBRA enrollees?. See generally on COBRA, Gottlich & Koblenz, COBRA Continuation Coverage: It's Not Just for Health Lawyers Anymore, 24 Clearinghouse Rev. 538 (1990); Somers, COBRA: An Incremental Approach to National Health Insurance, 5 J. Contemp.Health L. & Pol'y 141 (1989); Perkins & Waxman, The COBRA Continuation Option: Questions and Answers, 21 Clearinghouse Rev. 1315 (1988).

3. Some states provide plan beneficiaries with more generous continuation coverage than does COBRA. Illinois, for example, permits divorced spouses of employees over the age of fifty-five to continue group coverage until they are covered by Medicare. Ill.Ann.Stat. ch. 73 § 979.2. Other statutes permit more limited benefits. Some, for example, allow continuation of coverage at higher premium levels than those permitted by COBRA. Where both COBRA and state statutes apply, which take precedence? See Note: The COBRA Strikes at Group Health Insurance Plans: Divorced Women's Rights to Continue Coverage, 92 Dickinson L.Rev. 253, 276–279 (1987).

4. Who pays for COBRA coverage: employers, insurers, employees, health care insurance consumers?

2. AIDS and Private Health Insurance

AIDS presents a special challenge to the insurance industry and to the conept of insurance. First, the perception of insurers is that the cost of medical care for AIDS could be enormous. In 1988 AIDS-related accident and health claims amounted to $50.3 million for individual policy claims and $248.6 million for group policy claims. This amounted to less than 1% of all health insurance claims nationally, but the amount of claims has been growing very rapidly (the amount for 1988 for group claims was nearly three times the amount for 1986); and some projections see this rapid growth as continuing indefinitely into the future. Some insurance companies fear that AIDS could bankrupt them or make their premiums unaffordable.

The very uncertainty of how high incidence rates and costs of AIDS will go troubles insurers. Insurance underwriting necessarily depends on the ability of insurers to predict the frequency and severity of random events, and when both are uncertain, underwriting is very problematic.

An even greater concern of insurers is the possibility of adverse selection. The incidence of AIDS among persons seeking insurance is not completely random. That is, some people seeking to purchase insurance know, or strongly suspect, that they have been infected by the HIV virus, and thus at high risk for developing AIDS. As discussed earlier in this chapter, insurance underwriting requires the classification of policyholders into categories based on broad risk predictors (such as age, health, or occupational status). Once premiums are set, policyholders for whom risks do not eventuate finance the expenses of those to whom the risk occurs. If a person purchases a policy with the knowledge that the eventuation of a risk is imminent, the other policyholders are unfairly treated. See, Hammond and Shapiro, AIDS and the Limits of Insurability, 64 Milbank Quarterly 143 (1986 Supp. 1).

For these reasons, and perhaps for other reasons, such as homophobia or ignorance, insurers have attempted to avoid insuring persons infected or possibly infected with the AIDS virus. A 1988 Office of Technology Assessment study of AIDS and Health Insurance determined that most insurers that are not legally prohibited from doing so attempt to exclude persons who have AIDS or ARC or are seropositive for HIV, Office of Technology Assessment, AIDS and Health Insurance: An OTA Survey (1988). Additionally, some companies attempt to limit benefits for persons with AIDS.

Should legal limitations be placed on the ability of insurers to exclude persons with AIDS, or people likely to develop AIDS, from coverage? First, serious questions can be raised as to whether the AIDS crisis really threatens the solvency of insurers. The costs of AIDS cases to health insurers, though high, are certainly not as high as the costs of treating other conditions, nor is the incidence of AIDS as high as is the incidence of other high cost conditions. Moreover, insurers have generally only refused coverage to persons with or likely to develop AIDS who are applicants for individual coverage, and not such persons who are members of covered groups. Are these exclusions really likely to make much difference in the insurers financial status, since individual coverage only constitutes 10–15% of health insurance?

Second, serious ethical problems are raised if persons with AIDS are excluded by screening out members of high risk groups, such as gay or bisexual men (or "single males without dependents that are engaged in occupations that do not require physical exertion," a category excluded by one insurer). Exclusion by insurers of members of racial groups because they had a higher risk for certain medical conditions would certainly not be acceptable. Should underwriting on the basis of sexual orientation be any more acceptable? Moreover, exclusion of gays and bisexual men from insurance might make discrimination in other areas, in employment or access to credit for example, more pervasive as well.

Excluding applicants on the basis of positive HIV antibody tests (or rather, on the basis of a battery of positive HIV antibody tests) is perhaps more acceptable. A person with HIV antibodies present is certainly at risk for developing AIDS (though the extent of the risk and how soon it will eventuate are still not clear). Nevertheless, the permissibility of HIV testing is also not beyond dispute. First, if the testing is not accompanied by counselling, it can do considerable emotional harm to the person tested if false, or even true, positive results are obtained. Second, if confidentiality of test results is breached, serious damage could occur to applicants. Insurers can, and often do, share information, much of it through the Medical Information Bureau, an industry-funded organization. In some states insurers are required to report positive AIDS tests to the state. Routine reliance on questions about tests already taken might discourage voluntary testing. Moreover, the tests themselves are not cheap. See, Schatz, The AIDS Insurance Crisis: Underwriting or Overreaching? 100 Harv.L.Rev. 1783 (1987).

Finally, if insurers successfully screen out persons with AIDS, the medical costs of AIDS must still be paid. These costs will have to be borne by others, individuals who have AIDS and their families, the government, and providers. A recent projection estimates that by 1992 the cost of personal medical care for AIDS will be six billion dollars, of which 5.5% will be borne by patients, 29.5% by providers, and 28.5% by the government. 21.5% will be covered by insurers, 11% by employer self-insurers, and 4% by HMOs. Greeley, AIDS and the American Health Care Financing System, 51 U.Pitt.L.Rev. 73, 96–97 (1989). See also, Fox, Financing Health Care for Persons with HIV Infection: Guidelines for State Action, 26 Am.J.L. & Med. 223 (1990). Are the costs of AIDS most fairly and efficiently borne by individuals, insurers, providers, or the government?

The three most common approaches used by insurers to limit their obligations in the face of adverse selection are to refuse to insure persons infected with the AIDS virus or belonging to groups identified as at risk of being infected; to limit coverage for pre-existing conditions; or to void policies or limit coverage under them where the company can establish misrepresentation in the application. The latter approach is usually limited by "incontestability" clauses, required by state law or regulation, which provide that a policy or coverage may not be avoided for misrepresentation after the policy has been in force for a specified period of time, usually two years for individual policies and one year for group policies. Why might these protections be of less use where a person purchases insurance knowing himself to be HIV seropositive? When will the condition develop into AIDS? Will the AIDS be a "pre-existing" condition when it does? See, Clifford & Iuculano, AIDS and Insurance: The Rationale for AIDS–Related Testing, 100 Harv.L.Rev. 1806 (1987): Hoffman & Kincaid, AIDS: The Challenge to Life and Health Insurers' Freedom of Contract, 35 Drake L.Rev. 710, 726–739 (1986–87).

Underwriting based on sexual orientation is rejected by guidelines adopted by the National Association of Insurance Commissioners (NAIC):

NAIC, MEDICAL/LIFESTYLE QUESTIONS AND UNDER-WRITING GUIDELINES, PROPOSED BULLETIN
(1989).

* * *

I. GENERAL PROPOSITIONS

A. No inquiry in an application for health or life insurance coverage, or in an investigation conducted by an insurer or an insurance support organization on its behalf in connection with an application for such coverage, shall be directed toward determining the applicant's sexual orientation.

B. Sexual orientation may not be used in the underwriting process or in the determination of insurability.

C. Insurance support organizations shall be directed by insurers not to investigate, directly or indirectly, the sexual orientation of an applicant or a beneficiary.

* * *

II. MEDICAL LIFESTYLE APPLICATIONS QUESTIONS AND UNDERWRITING STANDARDS

A. No question shall be used which is designed to establish the sexual orientation of the applicant.

B. Questions relating to the applicant having or having been diagnosed as having AIDS or ARC are permissible if they are factual and designed to establish the existence of the condition.

For Example: Insurers should not ask "do you believe you may have ...?", but rather "do you know or have reasons to know ...?"

C. Questions relating to medical and other factual matters intending to reveal the possible existence of a medical condition are permissible if they are not used as a proxy to establish the sexual orientation of the applicant, and the applicant has been given an opportunity to provide an explanation for any affirmative answers given in the application.

For Example: "Have you had chronic cough, significant weight loss, chronic fatigue, diarrhea, enlarged glands, ...?" These types of questions should be related to a finite period of time preceding completion of the application and should be specific. All of the questions above should provide the applicant the opportunity to give a detailed explanation.

D. Questions relating to the applicant's having or having been diagnosed as having or having been advised to seek treatment for a sexually transmitted disease are permissible.

E. Neither the marital status, the "living arrangements," the occupation, the gender, the medical history, the beneficiary designation, nor the zip code or other territorial classification of an applicant may be used to establish, or aid in establishing, the applicant's sexual orientation.

F. For purposes of rating an applicant for health and life insurance, an insurer may impose territorial rates, but only if the rates are based on sound actuarial principles or are related to actual or reasonably anticipated experience.

G. No adverse underwriting decision shall be made because medical records or a report from an insurance support organization shows that the applicant has demonstrated AIDS-related concerns by seeking counselling from health care professionals. This subsection does not apply to an applicant seeking treatment and/or diagnosis.

* * *

H. Whenever an applicant is requested to take an AIDS-related test in connection with an application for insurance, the use of such a test must be revealed to the applicant and his or her written consent obtained. No adverse underwriting decision shall be made on the basis of such a positive AIDS-related test unless an established test protocol [conforming to medical standards for AIDS testing] has been followed.

* * *

These guidelines have been explicitly adopted by insurance departments in four states, while several others have adopted other regulations prohibiting insurers from denying insurance on the basis of sexual orientation or from asking questions about sexual orientation.

States have been much more reluctant to outlaw other means of excluding persons with AIDS from health insurance, though there are some exceptions. California law provides:

> (f) The results of a blood test to detect antibodies to the probable causative agent of acquired immune deficiency syndrome, which identifies or provides identifying characteristics of the person to whom the test results apply, shall not be used in any instance for the determination of insurability or suitability for employment.

West's Ann.Cal.Health & Safety Code, § 199.21(f).

A handful of other states have similar laws. Several states adopted laws or regulations in the mid–1980s banning or limiting the use of HIV tests for determining insurability. The regulations of New York and Massachusetts banning use of such tests for determining insurability were nullified by the courts. See Health Insurance Association of American v. Corcoran, 531 N.Y.Supp.2d 456 (1988); Life Insurance Assoc. of Mass. v. Singer, 403 Mass. 410, 530 N.E.2d 168 (1988). Other states repealed or modified their laws as the reliability of HIV testing became better established.

More common are state laws requiring informed consent for AIDS testing, imposing strict confidentiality requirements on test results, or specifying which tests are permissible or testing procedures that must be followed. Several states that permit AIDS testing prohibit by statute or regulation inquiry concerning previous AIDS tests. What explains these laws?

Do these state insurance laws and regulations apply to self-insured employer group health plans? Why or why not? If an employer discharges an HIV positive employee or one that has contracted AIDS or ARC, is the employee without remedy? Section 510 of ERISA makes it unlawful:

> for any person to discharge, fine, suspend, expel, discipline, or discriminate against a participant or beneficiary for exercising any right to which he is entitled under the provisions of an employee benefit plan, [or this title] ... or for the purpose of interfering with the attainment of any right to which such participant may become entitled under the plan, [or this title].

29 U.S.C.A. § 1140.

Might Section 503 of the Rehabilitation Act, which mandates that contracts between the federal government and employers must require the employer to engage in affirmative action to employ the handicapped, be of use to an employee discharged as HIV positive? Might the fact that section 503 is enforceable only administratively and not through private litigation limit its usefulness? Is Section 102 of the Americans with Disabilities Act of 1990 (ADA) relevant?

"No covered entity shall discriminate against a qualified individual with a disability because of the disability of such individual in regard to job application procedures, the hiring, advancement, or discharge of employees, employee compensation, job training, and other terms, conditions, and privileges of employment."

Note also Section 501(c) of the ADA, which states that the Act shall not be construed to prohibit or restrict insurance underwriting or risk-classification not otherwise prohibited by state law. Might COBRA be relevant to the discharged employees situation?

Another common response of states to the high cost of medical care for persons with AIDS is high-risk insurance pools. High-risk pools offer insurance to those who cannot buy individual health insurance commercially. Premiums are usually set by statute at a level of 150% to 200% of premiums paid by the average healthy insured in the state. High risk insureds are either assigned pro rata to insurers that sell insurance in the state or are insured by the pool, which is subsidized by a tax on insurance premiums. Why might this not be a solution to the insurance problem for many persons with AIDS? Can self-insured employers be forced to participate in high-risk pools?

High cost case management techniques have also been suggested as a means of limiting the cost of treating AIDS. See chapter 7 below for a discussion of this approach. Finally, some have argued that AIDS can be handled most appropriately through a federal catastrophic insurance program or through national health insurance. See Greeley, AIDS and the American Health Care System, 51 U.Pitt.L.Rev. 73, 135–149 (1989).

Problem: AIDS and Insurance Coverage

Your client, Gary Henderson, was discharged from his job two weeks ago. Henderson has worked at his job in an auto plant for ten years. He was told that he was discharged because his position is being eliminated. He believes that the real reason he was discharged was because of his physical condition. He has always had an exemplary work record, but in the last several months he has missed several days of work because of persistent diarrhea, fever and chills, and lack of energy. He has also noted that his lymph nodes are swollen. Henderson had plenty of sick leave and his absences from work were not causing problems of which he is aware. Henderson believes that he has been fired because his employer knows that he is gay, fears that he is exhibiting the symptoms of AIDS-Related Complex, and is afraid of the costs that the company might incur if Henderson's condition developed into AIDS. Henderson's employer is self-insured, and has become very concerned recently about its health care costs.

Since his discharge, Henderson has subsequently tried to get health insurance but has encountered a number of barriers. One company to which he applied for insurance sent him an application form which had several questions about sexual practices and orientation and about "living arrangements". Another company informed him that it required all applicants for health insurance to submit to an HIV antibody test. Another application form asked whether the applicant believed he might have AIDS or ARC. A fourth policy limited payment for any AIDS-related medical expenses to $10,000. Henderson finds these practices objectionable, and doubts that any of the companies that engage in them will insure him adequately given his present symptoms. He also is very reluctant to get an HIV antibody test at this point, since he doubts that its results will be kept confidential and any disclosure would make it even more difficult for him to find another job. Advise Mr. Henderson.

D. PRIVATE INSURANCE BENEFITS: ERISA

A determination of whether a particular medical procedure or problem is covered by a particular health insurance policy is primarily a matter of contractual interpretation. Denial of coverage can, that is, result in a breach of contract suit. If an insured asserts that an insurance company denied a claim in bad faith, suit may also be brought in tort. See Taylor v. Prudential Insurance Co., 775 F.2d 1457 (11th Cir.1985); Aetna Life Ins. Co. v. Lavoie, 470 So.2d 1060 (Ala.1984).

A common source of dispute is whether a particular procedure is (or was) "experimental" or not "medically necessary" when a policy prohibits payment for experimental or unnecessary procedures. Some courts, applying a general principle of contract interpretation that ambiguous terms will be interpreted against the insurer who drafted the contract, find such limitations ambiguous and permit the insured's physician the final say on whether a procedure was necessary, Van Vactor v. Blue Cross Association, 50 Ill.App.3d 709, 8 Ill.Dec. 400, 365 N.E.2d 638 (1977). Other courts, more attuned to the cost-implications of giving treating physicians free rein, have been willing to allow insurers to second-guess doctors on questions of necessity and appropriateness, see Sarchett v. Blue Shield of California, 43 Cal.3d 1, 233 Cal.Rptr. 76, 729 P.2d 267 (1987). Where, however, suit is brought against a group benefits plan covered by ERISA, federal, rather than state law, may become determinative.

REILLY v. BLUE CROSS AND BLUE SHIELD UNITED OF WISCONSIN.

United States Court of Appeals, Seventh Circuit, 1988.
846 F.2d 416.

* * *

WILL, SENIOR DISTRICT JUDGE.

Kathryn and Joseph Reilly, plaintiffs-appellants, Wisconsin residents, brought this action against Blue Cross and Blue Shield United of Wisconsin ("Blue Cross"), defendant-appellee, a Wisconsin non-profit corporation, alleging that Blue Cross arbitrarily and capriciously denied their insurance claim for Mrs. Reilly's in vitro fertilization ("IVF"). The plaintiffs' original complaint claims that Blue Cross breached the insurance contract, acted in bad faith, intentionally inflicted emotional distress and caused a loss of consortium. The plaintiffs seek compensatory and punitive damages.

Mr. Reilly is a Milwaukee public school teacher. He and his wife were covered under a self-insured group health plan which is part of the collective bargaining agreement between the Milwaukee Teachers Education Association ("MTEA") and the Milwaukee Public Schools ("MPS"). The plan was administered by Blue Cross for a fee "based, subject to certain limitations, on the dollar volume of covered charges approved for payment," [   ]. Blue Cross is not at risk for any health care costs.

Pursuant to Blue Cross' motion, the case was removed from the Waukesha County Circuit Court to the Eastern District of Wisconsin because it raises questions governed by the federal Employee Retirement Income Security Act of 1974 ("ERISA"), 29 U.S.C. § 1001, *et seq.* * * *

* * *

* * * On June 1, 1987, Blue Cross moved for summary judgment against the plaintiffs' (1) ERISA claim, arguing that its decision to deny coverage was not arbitrary, capricious or motivated by bad faith, and (2) state law claims, arguing that these claims are preempted by ERISA. * * *

Judge Curran granted Blue Cross' motion for summary judgment. * * * He concluded that (1) the defendant's decision was not arbitrary, capricious or motivated by bad faith; (2) ERISA preempted the plaintiffs' state law claims; and (3) even if state law claims were not preempted, he would not take pendent jurisdiction over them. The plaintiffs appeal both the decisions on the parties' motions and the preemption conclusion as to the claims for punitive damages and of bad faith.

We find that material issues of fact exist as to whether Blue Cross' decision was arbitrary, capricious or motivated by bad faith and we therefore reverse the district court's order granting Blue Cross' motion for summary judgment with respect to the plaintiffs' ERISA claim. * * * We find that the plaintiffs' demand for punitive damages and claim of bad faith are preempted under ERISA because the health plan at issue is self-insured and state laws arguably "regulating insurance" are preempted by ERISA as to self-insured plans. We therefore affirm the district court's order dismissing those claims. * * *

FACTS

By 1978 Kathryn Reilly had received treatment for infertility. In 1982, she was diagnosed as having an independently treatable condition called endometriosis, which affects a woman's ability to conceive. Blue Cross paid for her initial treatments. Thereafter she was treated with artificial insemination, among other things, which was unsuccessful. On October 15, 1984, Mrs. Reilly underwent a successful IVF procedure

at Waukesha Memorial Hospital in Wisconsin. On May 22, 1985, she
gave birth to a baby girl, Nora.

* * *

Blue Cross denied coverage for the expenses incurred by Kathryn
Reilly's IVF procedure on the grounds that: (1) IVF was an experimental procedure, which was excludable under the master contract's general provision excluding experimental procedures; and (2) the contract
specifically excluded coverage for an IVF procedure. Blue Cross
claimed that the IVF was experimental under the general exclusion
because it had a success rate of less than 50%. * * *

The contract at issue was effective from July 1, 1984 to June 30,
1985. At the time of Mrs. Reilly's IVF, October 15, 1984, MTEA had
not received the renewed contract for that period. According to the
plaintiffs, as of October 1984, the MTEA was unaware of any exclusion
under the master contract for IVF, either under the general provision
excluding experimental procedures or as a specific exclusion.

Also, according to the plaintiffs, the MTEA first received notice
that IVF procedures were excluded on September 19, 1985, long after
the baby's birth in May and nearly one year after Mrs. Reilly's IVF.
Notice was sent by Rhonda Koprowski, a Blue Cross supervisor, in a
letter stating that "the wording in this contract was updated in October
of 1984 [the effective date is July 1, 1985]. Due to the timing of the
services and the updating of the contract, the group may want to
consider paying these charges as an exception." [ ]. Blue Cross did
not make an exception.

The district court assumed, for the purpose of its decision, that at
the time of Kathryn Reilly's IVF, the parties were bound by the
previous (1983–84) agreement which did not specifically list IVF either
as being experimental or an excludable procedure. Accordingly, the
district court assumed that the general provision in the 1983–84 contract excluding expenses for experimental and investigative procedures
was the only provision under which Blue Cross could defend its decision. Our review is necessarily based on these same assumptions.

The 1983–84 contract's general provision excluding expenses for
experimental and investigative procedures reads as follows:

> Services and procedures which are experimental/investigative in
> nature. Experimental/investigative means the use of any treat-
> ment, procedure, facility, equipment, drugs, devices or supplies not
> yet recognized as accepted medical practice by Blue Cross & Blue
> Shield United and any of such items requiring federal or other
> governmental agency approval and for which approval has not
> been granted at the time services were rendered.

Blue Cross claims that at the time of Kathryn Reilly's IVF, October,
1984, IVF was deemed experimental. The plaintiffs allege that IVF
was not deemed experimental by the general expert medical community at the time of Kathryn Reilly's IVF and Blue Cross' formula

employed to determine whether IVF is experimental leads to an arbitrary and capricious conclusion.

STANDARD OF REVIEW

We must decide (1) if viewing the evidence in a light most favorable to the plaintiffs, there is a material issue of fact as to whether Blue Cross' decision was arbitrary, capricious or motivated by bad faith and violated ERISA; * * * and (3) whether the plaintiffs' state law claims for bad faith and punitive damages are preempted under ERISA.

LIABILITY UNDER ERISA

The plaintiffs' health plan is governed by ERISA. 29 U.S.C. 1002(1) and 1003(a)(3). They may bring a civil action to recover benefits allegedly due under the plan. 29 U.S.C. 1132(a)(1)(B). As the administrator of the employee benefit plan, Blue Cross is a fiduciary for ERISA purposes. 29 U.S.C. 1002(21)(B); [ ]. Accordingly, Blue Cross' duties and responsibilities for managing and administering the plaintiffs' plan are defined as follows:

(1) * * * a fiduciary shall discharge his duties with respect to a plan solely in the interest of the participants and beneficiaries and—

(A) for the exclusive purpose of:

(i) providing benefits to participants and beneficiaries; and

(ii) defraying reasonable expenses of administering the plan;

(B) with the care, skill, prudence, and diligence under the circumstances then prevailing that a prudent man acting in a like capacity and familiar with such matters would use in the conduct of an enterprise of a like character and with like aims;

. . . .

. . . . (D) in accordance with the documents and instruments governing the plan . . . .

29 U.S.C. 1104(a)(1).

To hold Blue Cross liable for denying them benefits under the plan, the plaintiffs must establish that Blue Cross' decision or conduct was arbitrary, capricious or motivated by bad faith. [ ] We may not undertake a de novo review as to whether we agree with Blue Cross' decision. [ ]

* * *

ANALYSIS

I.

Blue Cross' Decision

The plaintiffs contend that material issues of fact exist as to whether Blue Cross' administration of the plan was fair and reasonable because of the formula used to categorize IVF as experimental and in light of the evidence establishing that IVF was not in fact experimental in 1984. The plaintiffs submitted expert opinions from several doctors, including members of the American College of Obstetricians and Gynecologists and the American Fertility Society, in addition to three other fertility experts, who stated that by 1982, IVF procedures were no longer experimental. In addition, government approval was not required prior to performing an IVF procedure in October, 1984.

* * *

In contrast, Blue Cross did not submit any affidavit or deposition testimony from anyone with personal knowledge about IVF procedures indicating that IVF was experimental in 1984. Blue Cross proffered the deposition testimony of Edward Seitz, Blue Cross Assistant Vice President, Political Subdivision–Business for Blue Cross, that Blue Cross decided that IVF was an experimental procedure because its success rate was less than 50%. Seitz testified that Blue Cross' decision was based on information provided by the national Blue Cross and Blue Shield Association ("National Association") and its own Blue Cross and Blue Shield United Medical Review Committee ("Medical Review Committee").

* * *

After briefly summarizing the deposition testimony and affidavits submitted by the plaintiffs, the district court granted the defendant's motion for summary judgment. * * *

* * *

* * * The district court apparently simply accepted Blue Cross' conclusion based on Seitz' hearsay testimony. No expert testified that in 1984 IVF was experimental and no comparison with the plaintiffs' experts' testimony was made. In addition, the validity of Blue Cross' rationale, the success ratio, was not reviewed.

A decision may be arbitrary and capricious if Blue Cross "offered an explanation for its decision that runs directly counter to the evidence before [it]. * * * " Motor Vehicles [Mfrs. Ass'n v. State Farm], 463 U.S. [29] at 43, 103 S.Ct. [2856] at 2867 [1983]. The evidence proffered by the plaintiffs' experts runs counter to Blue Cross' decision and creates a material issue of fact as to whether Blue Cross' decision was arbitrary, capricious or motivated by bad faith. We do not suggest that, faced with equally conflicting evidence that IVF was or was not experimental in October, 1984, Blue Cross would necessarily face liability. However, the question of whether Blue Cross' decision was arbitrary, capricious or motivated by bad faith remains a disputed question of fact in light of the substantial contradictory evidence, as well as the reasonableness of employing a success ratio per se, particularly the 50% ratio used. These questions were not addressed by the district court.

Based on the district court's analysis, Blue Cross could immunize itself from liability for its decisions as a plan administrator simply by creating a plan which provides that it will deny claims for medical procedures if Blue Cross' internal advisory committees deem them experimental. ERISA's provisions do not permit such potential abuses; decisions and their rationales are reviewable. In this case, the reasonableness of the decision to characterize IVF as experimental is ultimately Blue Cross' responsibility.

The fact that Blue Cross allegedly relied on the advice of its own advisory groups who presumably assist Blue Cross in the administration of its health plans nationwide, those for which it is also an insurer, creates an inherent risk of abuse. Moreover, we do not have here direct evidence that Blue Cross medical review committees found IVF experimental in 1984, only Seitz' statement that Krutz, another Blue Cross employee, had told him so. Dr. Shapiro noted that Blue Cross, understandably, was concerned with the cost of IVF. When Blue Cross sought his independent advice, however, he gave them a different conclusion than they reached.

The plaintiffs contend that a procedure's success ratio alone cannot determine whether it is experimental and material issues of fact exist as to whether the decision to classify procedures apparently based on this factor alone is arbitrary and capricious. Otherwise, they contend, Blue Cross has too much discretion and could deny coverage, for example, for treatments administered to terminally ill patients. A success ratio for such treatments might well approach 0%.

Not only may the decision to grant or deny coverage based solely on a success ratio per se be arbitrary and capricious, but the particular ratio selected, in this case, for IVF, may well be arbitrary and capricious. No evidence was presented to the district court on either of these questions.

* * *

Blue Cross also suggests that because the plan at issue is self-insured, it has no risk and thus no incentive to deny claims which could lead to arbitrary and capricious decisions. That is not necessarily true. In the long run, if Blue Cross were to grant too many claims, as perceived by MPS, it might be replaced as the plan's administrator. Moreover, the ultimate issue in the case is whether Blue Cross acted arbitrarily and capriciously, not whether it had an incentive to do so.

In addition to the unresolved issues we have already noted, several other questions which remain include the following: (1) Who made the ultimate decision by Blue Cross that IVF is experimental? (2) What are their qualifications and on what basis was that decision made? (3) How many IVF procedures were analyzed to make this conclusion? (4) What other evidence was reviewed by the decisionmakers which suggested that it was not experimental? (5) How are the decisionmakers compensated by Blue Cross? (6) How did this decision affect other Blue Cross health plans?

Notwithstanding the deferential standard given to the administrator of an ERISA health benefit plan, there are clearly disputed material issues of fact as to the basis of the defendant's decision and whether it was arbitrary, capricious or motivated by bad faith. Accordingly, the district court's order granting the defendant's motion for summary judgment with respect to the plaintiffs' ERISA claim is reversed.

II.

Are the Plaintiffs' State Law Claim of Bad Faith and Demand for Punitive Damages Preempted by ERISA?

In its order the district court concluded that the plaintiffs' state law claims were preempted by ERISA or, alternatively, were without an independent basis for jurisdiction and he declined to take pendent jurisdiction.

* * *

With respect to the state law claims in their original complaint, the plaintiffs challenge the district court's preemption conclusion only as to their claim for bad faith and demand for punitive damages and they argue that pendent jurisdiction is appropriate. We therefore affirm the district court's dismissal of the plaintiffs' claims of intentional infliction of emotional distress and loss of consortium, on the theory that these claims are preempted under 29 U.S.C. § 1144(a). [ ] * * *

ERISA is a comprehensive scheme regulating health and benefit plans. ERISA's "preemption clause" provides as follows:

> Except as provided in subsection (b) of this section, the provisions of this subchapter and subchapter III of this chapter shall supercede any and all State laws insofar as they may now or hereafter relate to any employee benefit plan ....

29 U.S.C. § 1144(a). ERISA's "savings clause" provides as follows:

> Except as provided in subparagraph (B), nothing in this subchapter shall be construed to exempt or relieve any person from any law of any State which regulates insurance, banking or securities.

29 U.S.C. § 1144(b)(2)(A). The savings clause is modified by the so-called "deemer clause":

> Neither an employee benefit plan described in section 1003(a) of this title, which is not exempt under section 1003(b) of this title (other than a plan established primarily for the purpose of providing death benefits), nor any trust established under such a plan, shall be deemed to be an insurance company or other insurer, ... or to be engaged in the business of insurance ... for purposes of any law of any State purporting to regulate insurance companies, insurance contracts, banks, trust companies, or investment companies.

29 U.S.C. § 1144(b)(2)(B).

If a plan purchases insurance, as opposed to being self-insured, it is "directly affected by state laws that regulate the insurance industry." Metropolitan Life Insurance Co. v. Massachusetts, 471 U.S. 724, 732,

105 S.Ct. 2380, 2385, 85 L.Ed.2d 728 (1985). In Metropolitan Life Insurance Co. v. Massachusetts, the Court was faced with a Massachusetts statute requiring that all insurance contracts affecting Massachusetts citizens or written in Massachusetts provide minimum mental health coverage. [   ]. The statute applied to both insured (those that purchase insurance) and uninsured (self-insured) plans. [   ] The state argued that its law, as applied to insured plans, was not preempted by ERISA. The Court noted that Massachusetts was in effect acknowledging that its statute as applied to self-insured plans would not be saved from preemption because of the "deemer clause." [   ]

We need not decide whether Wisconsin law concerning punitive damages and bad faith "regulates insurance." In this case, the plan administered by Blue Cross is self-insured. It is entirely funded by the MPS and MTEA. Neither entity is an insurer and, accordingly, the deemer clause applies. The benefit plan, therefore, cannot avoid preemption. In addition, although Blue Cross is a national insurance company, in this context it is acting simply as an administrator of a self-insured plan.

We are aware that our decision results in a distinction between insured and uninsured plans, leaving the former open to indirect regulation while the latter are not. By doing so we merely give life to a distinction created by Congress in the "deemer clause," a distinction Congress is aware of and one it has chosen not to alter. [Metropolitan Life, 471 U.S. at 748, 105 S.Ct. at 2393].

* * *

Reversed in part, affirmed in part, and remanded.

POSNER, CIRCUIT JUDGE, concurring and dissenting.

I would affirm the district judge's decision in its entirety. There is no basis for supposing that Blue Cross of Wisconsin * * * acted arbitrarily or capriciously in denying Mrs. Reilly's claim. She underwent in vitro fertilization in 1984, at a cost of something under $3,000. The employee benefits plan under which she seeks to recoup this expense excludes "services and procedures which are experimental/investigative in nature," defined as any treatment "not yet recognized as accepted medical practice by" Blue Cross of Wisconsin. In deciding that in vitro fertilization was still an experimental procedure in 1984, and in denying her claim on that ground, the defendant consulted both its own medical advisory committee and a national association of Blue Cross–Blue Shield plans that evaluates and makes recommendations concerning medical procedures. Both groups advised it that in vitro fertilization, in part because of its success rate (below 50 percent, and perhaps as low as 10 percent), was still experimental.

The denial of benefits may be right or wrong but it is a reasonable interpretation of the plan, and that should be the end of the case. * * *

* * *

* * * Instead of questioning the qualifications of the members of the advisory bodies on which the defendant relied, she presented affidavits by physicians who believe that in vitro fertilization had by 1984 moved beyond the experimental stage. As it happens these physicians are specialists in the treatment of fertility and naturally want to encourage the use of an exciting and promising treatment. All that their affidavits show, however, is that there is a difference of opinion in the medical community on the experimental character of the treatment. The existence of such a disagreement does not begin to demonstrate that Blue Cross of Wisconsin acted arbitrarily or capriciously in relying on its medical advisors.

Notes and Questions

1. A recent Supreme Court decision has held that de novo review, as applied under trust law generally, rather than an arbitrary and capricious review standard, is appropriate for review of benefit determinations under ERISA unless the benefit plan explicitly gives the plan's administrators discretionary power. Firestone Tire & Rubber Co. v. Bruch, 489 U.S. 101, 109 S.Ct. 948, 103 L.Ed.2d 80 (1989). Will this simply result in redrafting of benefit plans to give such discretion to the trustees? Should the fact that insurers make more money by denying benefits and have interests conflicting with those of beneficiaries be relevant to the standard of review? See Brown v. Blue Cross & Blue Shield of Alabama, Inc., 898 F.2d 1556 (11th Cir.1990) (yes).

2. *Reilly's* absolute reading of the "deemer" clause to preclude state law challenges to self-insured plans was recently adopted by the Supreme Court in FMC Corporation v. Holliday, ___ U.S. ___, 111 S.Ct. 403, 112 L.Ed.2d 356 (1990). See, Note, Defining the Contours of ERISA Preemption of State Insurance Regulation: Making Employee Benefit Plan Regulation an Exclusively Federal Concern, 42 Vanderbilt L.Rev. 607 (1989).

3. If *Reilly* had been brought against a traditional Blue Cross employee group insurance plan, rather than a self-insured plan, would ERISA still preempt the state bad faith claim? See Pilot Life Ins. Co. v. Dedeaux, 481 U.S. 41, 107 S.Ct. 1549, 95 L.Ed.2d 39 (1987) (yes). If a hospital sues an insurer under a state unfair and deceptive trade practices act, claiming the insurer had misrepresented the insured status of a patient, does ERISA preempt the hospital's claim? See Memorial Hospital System v. Northbrook Life Insurance Co., 904 F.2d 236 (5th Cir.1990) (no).

4. Many states have attempted to broaden the health insurance coverage of insured employees through mandatory benefits laws, requiring, for example, coverage of mental health or substance abuse programs. States have also attempted to protect health care providers from discrimination through mandatory provider laws, which require insurers to cover services provided by osteopaths or chiropractors, for example. A recent study found 735 state laws mandating benefits or coverage of specified providers, one state having 38 such requirements. Gabel & Jensen, The Price of State Mandated Benefits, 26 Inquiry 419–431 (1989) What explains such laws? Are they merely due to the political strength of interest groups favored by them, such as chiropractors or purveyors of mental

health services? Or do they address genuine failures in the insurance market?

Cost-conscious employers may argue that ERISA preempts such laws, permitting their health insurance programs to offer more limited coverage. This seems to be true as to self-insured plans if such laws "relate to" employee benefit plans. See 29 U.S.C. § 1144(a). However, ERISA's saving clause, quoted in the principal case exempts from preemption state laws that regulate insurance, 29 U.S.C. § 1144(b)(2)(A). Do mandatory benefit laws or mandatory provider laws regulate insurance? See, Metropolitan Life Ins. Co. v. Massachusetts, 471 U.S. 724, 105 S.Ct. 2380, 85 L.Ed.2d 728 (1985), Note, ERISA Preemption of State Mandated–Provider Laws, 1985 Duke L.J. 1194. Might mandatory benefit or provider laws discourage employers from offering insurance or encourage them to self-insure? See, Gabel & Jensen, supra.

5. Note that ERISA not only preempts state law, but also permits defendants to remove cases that raise ERISA issues into federal court, as was done in Reilly. ERISA cases are also within the federal question jurisdiction of the federal courts.

6. ERISA also has implications for state efforts to expand access to health care for the uninsured by imposing requirements on employee benefit plans. Standard Oil Co. of Calif. v. Agsalud, 442 F.Supp. 695 (N.D.Cal.1977), affirmed, 633 F.2d 760 (9th Cir.1980), affirmed mem., 454 U.S. 801, 102 S.Ct. 79, 70 L.Ed.2d 75 (1981), for example, held that Hawaii's attempt to require most employers to provide employee health insurance was preempted by ERISA. See also, General Split Corp. v. Mitchell, 523 F.Supp. 427 (E.D.Wis.1981); St. Paul Elec. Workers Welfare Fund v. Markman, 490 F.Supp. 931 (D.Minn.1980).

Legislation like the recent Massachusetts comprehensive health coverage law, which taxes employers who do not provide health insurance rather than mandating coverage, may also prove vulnerable to ERISA challenge if it is found to "relate to" employee benefit plans. See, Perkins, ERISA Preemption Affecting Indigent Health Care Coverage, 20 Clearinghouse Rev. 1506 (1987). See also Law & Ensminger, Negotiating Physician's Fees: Individual Patients or Society? (A Case Study in Federalism), 61 N.Y.U.L. Rev. 1, 74–82 (1986) (on ERISA's effect on state attempts to decrease cost or increase accessibility of health care).

7. The extensive protection afforded by ERISA to self-insured plans goes far toward explaining why nearly 60% of all employees who are insured through their work are in self-insured plans, and nearly 85% of large employers self-insure, as compared to a negligible number at the time ERISA was enacted. A recent study determined that, though self-insured plans offered fewer benefits and required greater cost-sharing (employee deductibles and co-insurance) than did commercial or Blue Cross/Blue Shield plans, their premiums were still higher, Jensen & Gabel, The Erosion of Purchased Insurance, 25 Inquiry 328 (1988). See also, discussing the politics behind the federal policy, Fox & Schaffer, Health Policy and ERISA: Interest Groups and Semipreemption, 14 J. Health Pol., Pol'y & L 239 (1989).

II. GOVERNMENT HEALTH CARE PROGRAMS: MEDICARE AND MEDICAID

A. INTRODUCTION

Government sponsorship of health care has a long history in the United States. The first federal medical program was established in 1798 to provide care for sick seamen in the coastal trade. State hospitals for the mentally ill and local public hospitals were well established by the mid-nineteenth century. Today government at all levels finances a plethora of health care institutions and programs. In 1990 government accounted for $269 billion or 42% of the total national expenditures on personal health care. The federal government provides health care to veterans in 172 veterans' hospitals and in the community; to the active and retired military and their dependents in 168 military hospitals and through the Civilian Health and Medical Program of the Uniformed Services (CHAMPUS); to nearly a million native Americans in over 600 hospitals, health centers and clinics run by the Indian Health Service; and to a variety of special groups through block grants to the states for maternal and child health, alcohol and drug abuse treatment, mental health, preventive health, and primary care. States provide health care through mental and tuberculosis hospitals, state university hospitals, and aid to the medically indigent (AMI) and worker's compensation programs. County and local governments operate local hospitals and AMI programs. By far the largest public health care programs, however, are the federal Medicare program, which spent $96 billion in 1989, and the state and federal Medicaid program, which spent $71 billion in 1990.

Medicare is available to social security and railroad retirement recipients who are over the age of 65 or disabled. It has two parts. Part A, the Hospital Insurance (HI) program, is paid for out of payroll taxes and primarily covers institutional care. HI recipients must pay a set deductible and coinsurance [1] amount to receive services. Part B, the Supplementary Medical Insurance (SMI) program, covers primarily physicians' services and related expenses. It is subject to an annual deductible and usually pays 80% of reasonable charges. SMI is financed by premiums and from general revenue funds. The Medicare program is administered by the Health Care Financing Administration (HCFA) of the Department of Health and Human Services (HHS), but benefits are paid out by private insurers or data processors, called intermediaries in the HI program and carriers in the SMI program.

---

1. A deductible is the portion of the cost of medical services that the insured must pay before the insurance program begins to pick up the remaining medical costs. Coinsurance is the proportion of the remaining costs that are not covered by insurance, and thus must be paid by the insured. For example, if a patient is covered by a program that requires a deductible of $100 and a coinsurance payment of 20%, and the insured incurred a $1100 medical bill, the insured would pay $300 ($100 plus 20% of the remaining $1000); the insurance program would pay $800.

Medicaid is a joint federal-state program (or, rather, 56 different programs operated jointly by the federal and state or territorial governments) to provide funds to the deserving poor: those persons whose income and assets fall below certain levels and who are aged, blind, disabled, pregnant or members of families with dependent children. The federal government contributes from 50–80% of program costs (depending on the per capital income of the state) and the state covers the rest. Income and asset eligibility levels are set by the states and vary widely. States that participate in the program must cover the categorically needy, persons who are eligible to receive cash welfare benefits, and may also cover medical benefits for the "medically needy," those who have incomes high enough to disqualify them for cash assistance, but not high enough to pay their medical bills. State Medicaid programs must provide the categorically needy with certain services enumerated in the Medicaid act, including hospital and physicians' services. States may also cover a variety of optional services, including drugs, dental care, eyeglasses, hearing aids, and intermediate care. Coverage varies by state and tends to expand or contract depending on the economic health of the particular state. Medicaid programs are administered by state agencies, but are subject to federal regulatory guidelines.

Anyone designing or seeking to understand a government medical care program must begin by considering several basic questions.

First, who will be eligible for the program? Will eligibility be determined by economic need, medical condition, employment status, age, or by a combination of these and other characteristics?

Second, what benefits will be provided? For example, should the program stress institutional services such as hospitalization or nursing home care, or non-institutional alternatives such as home health care? Should the program be limited to services commonly covered by private insurance, such as physician care, or should it also cover services such as drugs, dental care, and eyeglasses, that are not normally covered by private insurance because middle class insureds can afford to pay for them, but that are inaccessible to the poor unless the program covers them? Should the program cover medically controversial services, such as care provided by chiropractors or midwives? Should a public program cover socially controversial services such as abortions? Should it cover services that render small marginal benefits at a very high cost, such as some organ transplants? Might it be politically expedient to omit services such as prenatal or preventive care whose immediate cost is not offset by immediate benefits?

Third, how should the program provide benefits? Should it deliver services directly, as do veterans' hospitals, or by reimbursing private providers? Should such "vendor payments" pay providers what they charge their private customers, or simply cover all of their costs, or pay an average, fixed, or negotiated rate? Should recipients be expected to share in the costs through coinsurance or deductibles? Should the program rely on traditional fee-for-service providers, or pay for services on a capitation basis?

Finally, who should play what role in administering the program? Should it be a federal, state, or local program? Should policy be set by the legislature or by an administrative agency? Should vendor payments be administered by the government or by private insurers? Should the courts take an active role in overseeing the program, or defer to the administrators?

This section will describe the Medicare and Medicaid programs briefly and then proceed to examine the first, second, and fourth of these issues. The question of how services are provided or paid for will be examined in the next chapter, which discusses provider payment in the context of cost containment issues.

B. ELIGIBILITY

A good way to begin to understand a public benefit program is to determine who receives its benefits. Are the targeted recipients characterized by economic need, a particular disease, advanced age, disability, residence in a particular geographic jurisdiction, employment in a certain industry, or status as an enrollee and contributor to a social insurance fund? From this question others follow: Who in fact receives most of the program's benefits? Who does the program leave out? Why are some groups included and others excluded?

1. Medicare

Medicare eligibility is generally linked to the Social Security program, the other major social insurance program of the United States. Persons eligible for retirement benefits under Social Security are automatically eligible for Medicare upon reaching age 65. If a person eligible for social security decides to continue working beyond age 65, he or she may still begin receiving Medicare at 65. Spouses or former spouses who qualify for Social Security as dependents may also begin receiving Medicare at 65, as may former federal employees eligible for Civil Service Retirement and Railroad Retirement beneficiaries, 42 U.S.C.A. § 426(a).

Disabled persons who are eligible for Social Security or Railroad Retirement benefits may also receive Medicare, but only after they have been eligible for cash benefits for at least two years, 42 U.S.C.A. § 426(b). Finally, benefits are available to two groups of persons who need not be Social Security beneficiaries. First, any person over 65 who is a United States citizen or has legally resided in the United States for at least five years may voluntarily enroll in Medicare if he or she is willing and able to pay a premium for the insurance, 42 U.S.C.A. § 1395i–2(a). In the final analysis, therefore, Medicare insurance is available to all elderly persons. Second, persons with end-stage renal (kidney) disease may receive Medicare benefits after a three-month waiting period, 42 U.S.C.A. § 426–1.

Medicare has been generally successful in assuring broad and equitable access to health care for the elderly. When the program began, the poor and nonwhite elderly received substantially less medical care than did the wealthier or white elderly, but these disparities have been substantially reduced. Some disparities still remain, notably between southern blacks and whites, and between the urban and rural elderly, Long & Settle, Medicare and the Disadvantaged Elderly: Objectives and Outcomes, 62 Milbank Mem. Fund Q. 609 (1984). Even greater disparities exist in the actual benefits received by recipients. In particular, the very old and those who are near death receive a much greater proportion of benefits than do younger recipients. See Fuchs, "Though Much is Taken": Reflections on Aging, Health and Medical Care, 62 Milbank Mem. Fund Q. 143, 151–154 (1984); Lubitz & Phihoda, The Use and Costs of Medicare Services in the Last Two Years of Life, 5 Health Care Fin.Rev. 117 (Spring 1984). Are these disparities troublesome? Why or why not?

2. *Medicaid*

Medicaid eligibility is much more complex. Medicaid is a state administered program, and each state establishes its own eligibility requirements, although the discretion of the states is limited by federal laws and regulations. Because Medicaid is a welfare program, eligibility is generally related to economic need and every Medicaid applicant must show that his or her income and resources fall below certain levels set by the states pursuant to broad federal guidelines. Medicaid represents a policy decision to provide welfare only to the deserving poor. It is targeted to assist certain favored groups of the needy, considerably complicating eligibility requirements. The CCH Medicare and Medicaid Guide identifies twenty-one discrete groups that must be covered by state Medicaid programs under federal law, and seventeen groups that may, but need not, be covered, 3 Medicare & Medicaid Guide (CCH), ¶¶ 14,231, 14,251, 14,271. Moreover, eligibility varies significantly among the 56 state and territorial Medicaid programs.

Who are the "deserving" poor? First, they are the aged, blind, and permanently and totally disabled, who are either eligible for assistance under the Federal Supplemental Security Income Program (SSI) or, if a state elects under the "209(b)" option,[2] persons who would have been

---

2. Section 209(b) was adopted in 1972 when the federal SSI program replaced preexisting state Aid to the Aged, Blind and Disabled (AABD) programs as the primary welfare program for adults. Prior to that time states had tied Medicaid eligibility for adults to AABD financial eligibility levels. In many states these eligibility levels were much lower than the new federal SSI eligibility levels. These states, there-

fore, faced the possibility of a sudden dramatic increase in the number of adults eligible for Medicaid, and thus of Medicaid expenditures, upon the implementation of SSI. To avoid this problem, Section 209(b) permits states to use any Medicaid financial eligibility level between that they used in 1972 and current SSI levels. Fourteen states have adopted the § 209(b) option.

eligible for state assistance under the eligibility requirements in effect in 1972. They are also dependent children and their families eligible for assistance under the federal/state Aid to Families with Dependent Children Program (AFDC), 42 U.S.C.A. § 1396a(a)(10)(A). These groups are called the "categorically needy" because they are eligible by virtue of their membership in categories of persons eligible for financial assistance. States that elect to have Medicaid programs must cover the categorically needy, and a variety of other groups, such as indigent pregnant women, children under the age of 5 poor enough to qualify for AFDC and persons eligible for SSI except for various social security increases. About 75% of Medicaid recipients in 1979 were categorically needy, though they consumed only just over half of Medicaid expenditures, Medicare and Medicaid Date Book, Tables 4.4 and 4.15 (1988).

The deserving poor also include the "optional categorically needy," a variety of small groups that states may choose to cover, but who then must be provided the full scope of benefits provided the categorically needy. Such groups include nursing home residents whose incomes are less than three times the SSI standards, 42 C.F.R. §§ 435.231, 435.1005, and persons who would be eligible for cash assistance, but who have not applied, 42 C.F.R. § 435.210.

States may also elect to cover a third group, the medically needy. The medically needy are categorically related (aged, disabled, blind, or families with dependent children) persons whose income exceeds the financial eligibility levels established by the state programs but who incur regular medical expenses that, when deducted from their income, bring their net disposable income below the eligibility level for financial assistance. Thirty-five Medicaid programs currently cover the medically needy, 3 Medicare & Medicaid Guide (CCH) ¶ 15,504. The medically needy are generally persons in need of expensive nursing home or hospital care. Therefore, although the medically needy constitute only about a quarter of Medicaid recipients they consume nearly half of Medicaid expenditures. The medically needy program is effectively a catastrophic health insurance program for those who fall into the categories favored by the welfare system.

Finally, recent amendments found in the Omnibus Budget Reconciliation acts of 1986, 1987, 1989, and 1990 and the Medicare Catastrophic Coverage Act of 1988 have expanded Medicaid's restrictive definition of the "worthy poor" to cover several additional groups, and, in doing so, notably separated Medicaid eligibility from cash assistance eligibility. Specifically, states are required under these acts to extend Medicaid coverage to pregnant women and to children up to age six with incomes at or below 133 percent of the federal poverty level ($13,380 for a family of three as of 1990). 42 U.S.C.A. §§ 1396a(a)(10)-(A)(ii)(VI), 1396a(l). Under OBRA 1990, coverage will gradually expand to include all children under age 18. States may also, at their option, extend Medicaid to pregnant women and infants with incomes up to

185% of the poverty level and to certain children aged 7 or 8 whose family income does not exceed the federal poverty level. For pregnant women, services must be pregnancy-related, but children may receive any services AFDC-related children could receive. State Medicaid programs are also required to pay Medicare Part B premiums and deductibles for persons earning less than 90% of the poverty level, and by 1995 persons with incomes below 120% of the poverty level. Why were pregnant women and small children chosen as targets for expanded eligibility? Why were Medicare recipients?

Who is *not* covered by Medicaid? Most poor single people and childless couples—the "undeserving" poor—are not. Medicaid covers only about 55% of these whose income falls below the 115% of the federal poverty standard. As AFDC eligibility levels have fallen farther and farther behind inflation in most states, the percentage of poor people eligible for Medicaid is dropping. The absolute number of Medicaid recipients reached its highest level in 1976 and has dropped since.

Eligibility varies widely from state to state. The maximum AFDC eligibility level (which is the Medicaid standard of eligibility for families) for a family of three in 1988 ranged from $1416 a year in Mississippi to $9140 a year in Alaska. In 1979 the ratio of Medicaid recipients to persons below the poverty level ranged from 115% in Massachusetts to 24% in Texas. Over 20% of national Medicaid expenditures are spent by New York, another 11% by California. The ten largest state programs consume 62% of the program's funds. Medicaid also tends to favor older over younger recipients. While AFDC eligibility levels have dropped in recent years as welfare increases have failed to keep pace with inflation, recipients under the federal SSI program have enjoyed regular cost-of-living increases that have increased SSI-related Medicaid eligibility levels. Although 8% of Medicaid recipients are aged and disabled, they consume 73% of Medicaid funds. Conversely, children constitute 43% of recipients but consume only 12.3% of the funds.

See, describing Medicaid eligibility and inequities within the Medicaid program, Congressional Budget Office, Medicaid: Choices for 1982 and Beyond 37–43 (1981); J. Holahan & J. Cohen, Medicaid: The Trade–Off Between Cost–Containment and Access to Care (1986); Rowland & Gaus, Reducing Eligibility and Benefits: Current Policies and Alternatives, in R. Blendon & T. Moloney, New Approaches to the Medicaid Crisis (1982) [hereafter Rowland & Gaus]; Carpenter, Medicaid Eligibility for Persons in Nursing Homes, 10 Health Care Fin.Rev. 67 (Winter 1988); Joe, Meltzer & Yu, Arbitrary Access to Care: The Case for Reforming Medicaid Eligibility, 4 Health Aff. 59 (Spring 1984); Schoen, Medicaid and the Poor, 60 Bull.N.Y.Acad.Med. 54 (Jan./Feb. 1984).

Problem: Harold and Lydia

Harold and Lydia Mueller are respectively 75 and 74 years of age. Two days ago Harold was hospitalized after he fell in the bathroom, breaking his hip. Harold's mental and physical condition have declined dramatically in the last two years, and Lydia has decided that she can no longer care for him at home. After he is well enough to be released from the hospital, he must go to a nursing home. The only satisfactory nursing home with beds available, however, costs $2000 a month, and Lydia knows that they cannot afford care for Harold at that rate for long. She has, therefore, sought out your help to determine if Harold is eligible for Medicaid.

Harold retired from his job in a factory 10 years ago, and Lydia has never held a paying job. Their only income is Harold's $500 a month social security check, Lydia's $250 a month social security check, and Harold's $600 a month pension check. They own a small condominium they bought when Harold retired. It is currently worth about $40,000. They pay about $300 a month on their mortgage, and a $30 a month maintenance fee. The state's standard utility allowance is $30 a month. They also own about $5000 worth of furniture, two certificates of deposit each worth $10,000, and a joint bank account containing about $5,000.

The state Medicaid plan currently allows institutionalized Medicaid recipients to keep a $30 monthly personal needs allowance. The current non-farm poverty level for a family of two is $8410 a year. Assuming that the state Medicaid plan otherwise tracks the requirements of the federal Catastrophic Care Act, reproduced below, advise Lydia as to: 1) how much income she can retain if Harold is institutionalized with Medicaid paying for his care; 2) what resources she and Harold can retain; 3) the steps she can take if her share of the income or resources proves insufficient to meet her needs?

42 U.S.C.A. § 1396r–5. TREATMENT OF INCOME AND RE- SOURCES FOR CERTAIN INSTITUTIONALIZED SPOUSES

(b) Rules for treatment of income

(1) Separate treatment of income.—During any month in which an institutionalized spouse is in the institution, except as provided in paragraph (2), no income of the community spouse shall be deemed available to the institutionalized spouse.

(2) Attribution of income.—In determining the income of an institutionalized spouse or community spouse, after the institutionalized spouse has been determined to be eligible for medical assistance, except as otherwise provided in this section and regardless of any State laws relating to community property or the division of marital property, the following rules apply:

(A) Non-trust property.—Subject to subparagraphs (C) and (D) in the case of income not from a trust, unless the instrument providing the income otherwise specifically provides—

(i) if payment of income is made solely in the name of the institutionalized spouse or the community spouse, the income shall be considered available only to that respective spouse;

(ii) if payment of income is made in the names of the institutionalized spouse and the community spouse, one-half of the income shall be considered available to each of them;

* * *

(D) Rebutting ownership.—The rules of subparagraphs (A) * * * are superseded to the extent that an institutionalized spouse can establish, by a preponderance of the evidence, that the ownership interests in income are other than as provided under such subparagraphs.

(c) Rules for treatment of resources.—

(1) Computation of spousal share at time of institutionalization.—

(A) Total joint resources.—There shall be computed (as of the beginning of a continuous period of institutionalization of the institutionalized spouse)—

(i) the total value of the resources to the extent either the institutionalized spouse or the community spouse has an ownership interest, and

(ii) a spousal share which is equal to ½ of such total value.

(B) Assessment.—At the request of an institutionalized spouse or community spouse, at the beginning of a continuous period of institutionalization of the institutionalized spouse and upon the receipt of relevant documentation of resources, the State shall promptly assess and document the total value described in subparagraph (A)(i) and shall provide a copy of such assessment and documentation to each spouse and shall retain a copy of the assessment for use under this section. * * *

(2) Attribution of resources at time of initial eligibility determination. —In determining the resources of an institutionalized spouse at the time of application for benefits under this subchapter, regardless of any State laws relating to community property or the division of marital property—

(A) except as provided in subparagraph (B), all the resources held by either the institutionalized spouse, community spouse, or both, shall be considered to be available to the institutionalized spouse, and

(B) resources shall be considered to be available to an institutionalized spouse, but only to the extent that the amount of such resources exceeds the amount computed under subsection (f)(2)(A) of this section (as of the time of application for benefits).

* * *

(4) Separate treatment of resources after eligibility for benefits established.—During the continuous period in which an institutionalized spouse is in an institution and after the month in which an institutionalized spouse is determined to be eligible for benefits under this subchapter, no resources of the community spouse shall be deemed available to the institutionalized spouse.

(5) Resources defined.—In this section, the term "resources" does not include—

(A) resources excluded under subsection (a) or (d) of section 1382b of this title, [including a home and burial plot] and

(B) resources that would be excluded under section 1382b(a)(2)(A) of this title [household goods] but for the limitation on total value described in such section.

(d) Protecting income for community spouse.—

(1) Allowances to be offset from income of institutionalized spouse.— After an institutionalized spouse is determined to be eligible for medical assistance, in determining the amount of the spouse's income that is to be applied monthly to payment for the costs of care in the institution, there shall be deducted from the spouse's monthly income the following amounts in the following order:

(A) A personal needs allowance * * *.

(B) A community spouse monthly income allowance (as defined in paragraph (2)), but only to the extent income of the institutionalized spouse is made available to (or for the benefit of) the community spouse.

(C) A family allowance, for each family member, equal to at least ⅓ of the amount by which the amount described in paragraph (3)(A)(i) exceeds the amount of the monthly income of that family member.

(D) Amounts for incurred expenses for medical or remedial care for the institutionalized spouse * * *.

In subparagraph (C), the term "family member" only includes minor or dependent children, dependent parents, or dependent siblings of the institutionalized or community spouse who are residing with the community spouse.

(2) Community spouse monthly income allowance defined.—In this section (except as provided in paragraph (5)), the "community spouse monthly income allowance" for a community spouse is an amount by which—

(A) except as provided in subsection (e) of this section, the minimum monthly maintenance needs allowance (established under and in accordance with paragraph (3)) for the spouse, exceeds

(B) the amount of monthly income otherwise available to the community spouse * * *

(3) Establishment of minimum monthly maintenance needs allowance.—

(A) In general—Each State shall establish a minimum monthly maintenance needs allowance for each community spouse which, subject to subparagraph (C), is equal to or exceeds—

(i) the applicable percent (described in subparagraph (B)) of ¹⁄₁₂ of the income official poverty line (* * *) for a family unit of 2 members; plus

(ii) an excess shelter allowance (as defined in paragraph (4)).

* * *

(B) Applicable percent.—For purposes of subparagraph (A)(i), the "applicable percent" described in this paragraph, effective as of—

(i) September 30, 1989, is 122 percent,

(ii) July 1, 1991, is 133 percent, and

(iii) July 1, 1992, is 150 percent.

(C) Cap on minimum monthly maintenance needs allowance.—The minimum monthly maintenance needs allowance established under subparagraph (A) may not exceed $1,500 * * *

(4) Excess shelter allowance defined.—In paragraph (3)(A)(ii), the term "excess shelter allowance" means, for a community spouse, the amount by which the sum of—

(A) the spouse's expenses for rent or mortgage payment (including principal and interest), taxes and insurance and, in the case of a condominium or cooperative, required maintenance charge, for the community spouse's principal residence, and

(B) the standard utility allowance (used by the State under * * * [the Food Stamp Act]) or, if the State does not use such an allowance, the spouse's actual utility expenses,

exceeds 30 percent of the amount described in paragraph (3)(A)(i), except that, in the case of a condominium or cooperative, for which a maintenance charge is included under subparagraph (A), any allowance under subparagraph (B) shall be reduced to the extent the maintenance charge includes utility expenses.

(5) Court ordered support.—If a court has entered an order against an institutionalized spouse for monthly income for the support of the community spouse, the community spouse monthly income allowance for the spouse shall be not less than the amount of the monthly income so ordered.

(e) Notice and fair hearing.—

* * *

(2) Fair hearing.—

* * *

(B) Revision of minimum monthly maintenance needs allowance. —If either such spouse establishes that the community spouse needs income, above the level otherwise provided by the minimum monthly maintenance needs allowance, due to exceptional circumstances resulting in significant financial duress, there shall be substituted, for the minimum monthly maintenance needs allowance in subsection (d)(2)(A) of this section, an amount adequate to provide such additional income as is necessary.

(C) Revision of community spouse resource allowance.—If either such spouse establishes that the community spouse resource allowance (in relation to the amount of income generated by such an allowance) is inadequate to raise the community spouse's income to the minimum monthly maintenance needs allowance, there shall be substituted, for the community spouse resource allowance under subsection (f)(2) of this section, an amount adequate to provide such a minimum monthly maintenance needs allowance.

(f) Permitting transfer of resources to community spouse.—

(1) In general.—An institutionalized spouse may, without regard to section 1396p of this title, transfer an amount equal to the community spouse resource allowance (as defined in paragraph (2)), but only to the extent the resources of the institutionalized spouse are transferred to (or for the sole benefit of) the community spouse. * * *

(2) Community spouse resource allowance defined.—In paragraph (1), the "community spouse resource allowance" for a community spouse is an amount (if any) by which—

(A) the greatest of—

(i) $12,000 * * *, or, if greater (but not to exceed the amount specified in clause (ii)(II)) an amount specified under the State plan,

(ii) the lesser of (I) the spousal share computed under subsection (c)(1) of this section, or (II) $60,000 (subject to adjustment under subsection (g) of this section,

(iii) the amount established under subsection (e)(2) of this section; or

(iv) the amount transferred under a court order under paragraph (3);

exceeds

(B) the amount of the resources otherwise available to the community spouse (determined without regard to such an allowance).

(3) Transfers under court orders.—If a court has entered an order against an institutionalized spouse for the support of the community spouse, section 1396p of this title shall not apply to amounts of resources transferred pursuant to such order for the support of the spouse or a family member (as defined in subsection (d)(1) of this section).

Notes and Questions

Prior to the adoption of this statute in 1988, institutionalized individuals with spouses in the community and income or assets in their own name (or held jointly with their spouse) could only become eligible for Medicaid after they had consumed all of the income and assets down to SSI (or 209(b)) eligibility levels ($2850 in liquid resources for a couple at the time the statute was adopted). An institutionalized individual could support a spouse in the community from his own money, but only at welfare eligibility levels. Conversely, if income was received in the name of the community spouse, the income would not be considered available to the institutionalized spouse for eligibility purposes after the first month of institutionalization. Assets held by a community spouse not eligible for SSI would likewise not be considered available to the institutionalized spouse after the first month of institutionalization. Transfers by the community spouse of his or her own property to another did not affect eligibility of the institutionalized spouse. How is this law changed by the provisions reproduced above? Who is favored and who harmed by these changes? What justification can be offered for the changes? See, Schreiber, Medicaid Financial Planning After the Medicare Catastrophic Coverage Act of 1988: Essential Changes Governing the Transfer of Assets, 63 Conn.Bar J. 211 (1989).

Problem: Mary's Farm

Mary Montgomery is 78 years old and recently widowed. For 50 years she and her husband Bill farmed together on the 320 acre farm they inherited from her parents. The farm was homesteaded by her grandparents in 1882 and has been in the family ever since. For the past 15 years, Mary's oldest son, Owen, has done most of the farming, and she and her husband intended to leave the farm to Owen when they passed away. Making a living on the farm was never easy, but over the years Mary and Bill managed to pay off mortgages they had put on the farm. Mary received $30,000 in life insurance at Bill's death which she has saved. Mary now lives on this sum and on her Social Security. Mary has been bothered by arthritis for several years and her condition has recently worsened. She is finding herself more and more forgetful, and although she jokes about this, she is worried that her mind may be going altogether. Owen's wife, Jane, comes by several times a week to straighten up Mary's house and to make sure that she eats well.

Mary has come to you because she is concerned about her future. Although she has no immediately life-threatening medical problems, she knows that her health is deteriorating and that sooner or later she will have to go into a nursing home. She recently went down to Park Acres Home (which is run by her church) and talked to the administrator. She was surprised to learn that skilled care in the home costs $2400 a month. She had always assumed that Medicare would cover any nursing home care she might need, and was shocked to discover that it would only cover at most 100 days, and perhaps none at all. The administrator told her that many of the patients in the home were on Medicaid, but that to become eligible for Medicaid she would have to sell the farm and liquidate the sum she would receive, plus her savings, because in her state Medicaid covers only persons with less than $1900 in savings.

Mary wants to know whether there is some way she can pass the farm and her savings on to Owen and Jane and make herself eligible for Medicaid. She knows Owen cannot afford to buy it from her, and is heart-broken at the thought of it being sold out of the family. Moreover, after all of the work Owen and Jane have done on the farm for her, they deserve it.

The state plan conforms to the federal law:

42 U.S.C.A. § 1396p(c). TAKING INTO ACCOUNT CERTAIN TRANSFERS OF ASSETS

(1) * * * the State plan must provide for a period of ineligibility for nursing facility services and for [home health services] * * * in the case of an institutionalized individual [ ] who, at any time during or after the 30–month period immediately before the date the individual becomes an institutionalized individual (if the individual is entitled to

medical assistance under the State plan on such date) or, if the individual is not so entitled, the date the individual applies for such assistance while an institutionalized individual disposed of resources for less than fair market value. The period of ineligibility shall begin with the month in which such resources were transferred and the number of months in such period shall be equal to the lesser of—

(A) 30 months, or

(B)(i) the total uncompensated value of the resources so transferred, divided by (ii) the average cost, to a private patient at the time of the application, of nursing facility services in the State or, at State option, in the community in which the individual is institutionalized.

(2) An individual shall not be ineligible for medical assistance by reason of paragraph (1) to the extent that—

(A) the resources transferred were a home and title to the home was transferred to—

(i) the spouse of such individual;

(ii) a child of such individual who (I) is under age 21, or (II) * * * is blind or permanently and totally disabled, * * *

(iii) a sibling of such individual who has an equity interest in such home and who was residing in such individual's home for a period of at least one year immediately before the date the individual becomes an institutionalized individual; or

(iv) a son or daughter of such individual (other than a child described in clause (ii)) who was residing in such individual's home for a period of at least two years immediately before the date the individual becomes an institutionalized individual, and who (as determined by the State) provided care to such individual which permitted such individual to reside at home rather than in such an institution or facility;

(B) the resources were transferred (i) to (or to another for the sole benefit of) the community spouse, * * *, or (ii) to the individual's child described in subparagraph [who is blind or disabled];

(C) a satisfactory showing is made to the State (in accordance with any regulations promulgated by the Secretary) that (i) the individual intended to dispose of the resources either at fair market value, or for other valuable consideration, or (ii) the resources were transferred exclusively for a purpose other than to qualify for medical assistance; or

(D) the State determines that denial of eligibility would work an undue hardship.

* * *

What do you advise Mary to do under this law? What are your thoughts on its fairness? See Case Study, Why Won't Medicaid Let Me Keep My Nest Egg?, 13 Hastings C.Rep., 23–25 (April 1983). The federal Medicaid statute originally permitted asset transfers prior to application, see Buckner v. Maher, 424 F.Supp. 366 (D.Conn.1976), affirmed memorandum, 434 U.S. 898, 98 S.Ct. 290, 54 L.Ed.2d 184 (1977); Caldwell v. Blum, CCH Medicare & Medicaid Guide, ¶ 30,093 (N.D.N.Y.1979), affirmed 621 F.2d 491 (2d Cir.1980), cert. denied, 452 U.S. 909, 101 S.Ct. 3039, 69 L.Ed.2d 412 (1981). Amendments in 1980, 1982, 1988, and 1989 have made such transfers very difficult, see Finberg & Schwartz, Implementation of the Medicaid Provisions of the Medicare Catastrophic Coverage Act, 23 Clearinghouse Rev. 370 (1989).

Notes and Questions

The problems illustrate one of the pervasive tensions in welfare programs—the conflict between familial and social responsibility. This conflict confronts Medicaid programs in other situations as well. Should adult children, for example, be responsible for the medical expenses of their indigent elderly parents? Is it fair for elderly persons to expect the taxpayers to finance their medical care through Medicaid rather than look to their children for help? On the other hand, is it fair to require children of indigent parents to contribute to their support, when our society does not otherwise expect adult children to support their parents? What effect would such a requirement have on parent-child relationships? Would it perpetuate a cycle of poverty? Might the cost of collecting exceed the funds collected? See N. Daniels, Just Health Care (1985); Brecher & Knickman, A Reconsideration of Long–Term–Care Policy, 10 J.Health Pol., Pol'y and L. 245, 264–6 (1985); D. Callahan, What Kind of Life: The Limits of Medical Progress (1990), Callahan, Diamond, Giele & Morris, Responsibility of Families for their Severely Disabled Adults, 1 Health Care Fin. Rev. 29 (Winter, 1980); Daniels, Family Responsibility Initiatives and Justice Between Age Groups, 13 Law, Medicine & Health Care 153 (1985); Patrick, Honor Thy Father and Mother: Paying the Medical Bills of Elderly Parents, 19 U.Rich.L.Rev. 69 (1984).

The Medicaid act expressly forbids holding adult children responsible for the care of their parents, 42 U.S.C.A. § 1396a(a)(17)(D). In 1982, however, the Health Care Financing Administration (HCFA) suggested that the states could compel filial support through their family responsibility laws, see Edelman, Family Supplementation in Nursing Homes, 18 Clearinghouse Rev. 504 (1984). Many states have such laws, which date back to the Elizabethan poor laws, on the books, but they are seldom enforced, and the states have not taken up HCFA's suggestion.

C. BENEFITS

The Medicare Hospital Insurance (HI) program, Part A, pays for hospital, nursing home, home health and hospice services. The Medicare Supplemental Medical Insurance (SMI) program, Part B, is designed to cover physicians' services, but also covers a variety of other goods and services including outpatient hospital services, physical and occupational therapy, prosthetic devices, durable medical equipment, and ambulance services. Medicare covers only 150 days of hospital services in a single benefit period ("spell of illness").[3] A one time

---

3. A spell of illness begins when a pa-   tient is hospitalized, and continues until

deductible, set at $592 in 1990, must be paid before hospital coverage begins, and a daily copayment of $198 (in 1990) must be paid after the sixtieth day of hospital care, 42 U.S.C.A. § 1395e. Though the Medicare statute provides for up to 100 days of coverage for skilled nursing care, 42 U.S.C.A. § 1395d(a)(2), the nursing home benefit has been defined so restrictively by HHS as to be largely illusory. Hospice benefits are provided on a very limited basis, 42 U.S.C.A. § 1395d(a)(4). Physicians' services are provided subject to an annual deductible ($100 for 1991) and 20% coinsurance amount. Mammography screening is provided under a new program added by OBRA 1990.

Benefits provided by state Medicaid programs vary from state to state. The Medicaid statute lists specific services that states may cover, but also permits coverage under an eighteenth category of "any other medical care, and any other type of remedial care recognized under State law, specified by the Secretary"; 42 U.S.C.A. § 1396d(a)(18). At least one state has covered acupuncture under this category. The original Medicaid law required the states to provide comprehensive services by 1975, Public Law No. 89–97, § 1903(e), but this deadline was first delayed and then abandoned. Currently states must provide the categorically needy with six services (inpatient hospital services, outpatient hospital services and rural health clinic services, other laboratory and X-ray services, skilled nursing facility services, physicians' services, and nurse-midwife and practice or other nurse practitioner services) and may provide any of the other listed services, 42 U.S.C.A. § 1396a(a)(10)(A).

States have considerably more discretion in covering the medically needy. There are some limits to this discretion, however. States that elect to offer coverage to the medically needy must provide ambulatory care for children and prenatal and delivery services for pregnant women, 42 U.S.C.A. § 1396a(a)(10)(C)(iii)(II) and states that provide institutional services for any group must also cover ambulatory services, 42 U.S.C.A. § 1396a(a)(10)(C)(iii)(I). Moreover, if a state covers institutional care for the mentally ill or retarded, it must provide either all of the services provided to the categorically needy or any seven services provided generally to Medicaid recipients, 42 U.S.C.A. § 1396a(a)(10)(C)(iv). What political considerations explain the latter provision?

There are practical as well as legal constraints on a state's discretion to determine benefits. Although the federal statute does not require coverage of intermediate care facility services, for example, every state covers such services. If they did not, many nursing home residents would go into more expensive skilled nursing homes (which must be covered) or come under state or local indigent care programs, for which federal matching funds are not available.

the patient has been out of a hospital or nursing home for at least 60 days. 42 U.S.C.A. § 1345x(a). Thus, a chronically ill person could remain indefinitely in a single spell of illness.

A striking feature of the benefit packages provided by Medicare and Medicaid is their emphasis on institutional care. In 1987, 66% of Medicare and 72% of Medicaid payments went to hospitals and nursing homes (compared to about 56% of personal health care expenditures generally for these services). While all state Medicaid programs cover hospital, skilled nursing care, and intermediate care services, many states do not cover optional services such as podiatry, dental care, eyeglasses, or dentures. Further, when economic conditions or federal cutbacks have resulted in state Medicaid cutbacks, as they did in the early 1980s, these services are the first to go.

What explains the choice of services covered under Medicare and Medicaid or dropped in lean times? Do the programs cover services that are most vital to health or that are most cost-effective? Are covered services those that poor persons or elderly persons would themselves choose to have covered if they were purchasing insurance? Why do Medicaid or Medicare cover some services for which private insurance is not generally available, such as nursing home care? What role might provider associations, their lawyers and lobbyists play in determining benefit coverage? Might services currently available under Medicaid mirror those covered by health programs previously financed by the states with their own money before federal matching funds became available?

Beyond the broad political decisions of what categories of medical care will be paid for by Medicare and Medicaid are the infinitely more numerous decisions as to whether a particular item or service will be covered at all or for a particular beneficiary. When Medicare is asked to finance a new technology, a panel of HCFA physicians and health professionals reviews the technology and determines whether to (1) allow individual Medicare carriers or intermediaries discretion to cover or not cover a service, (2) commission a special study (as was done with heart transplants), or (3) ask the Public Health Service (PHS) to assess the technology. If the technology is referred to the PHS, the PHS Office of Health Technology Assessment publishes a notice in the Federal Register soliciting comments, conducts its own extensive literature search, and makes a recommendation. See, describing this process further, Hays, From the Health Care Financing Administration: Medicare Coverage, 262 JAMA 2794 (1989).

When decisions address coverage of particular services for particular individuals, and especially when low-tech services such as home health or nursing home care are concerned, processes that are much less formal and visible come into play. Ultimately, whether any particular service is provided to any particular Medicare beneficiary will depend on the decision of a private carrier or intermediary (or perhaps of a Peer Review Organization) interpreting federal policy as mediated by Medicare regulations, manuals and manual transmittals, regional office instructions, rumor and innuendo. By restrictive interpretations applied through informal processes the Medicare program has on occasion worked dramatic changes in coverage. Strict interpretation of coverage of Medicare skilled nursing home care, for example, led to a 47% decline in coverage between 1967 and 1983 at a time when inpatient hospitalization increased 31% and home health participation 608%.

Occasionally, such restrictive interpretation results in litigation, which in turn broadens benefit coverage. Thus, a number of suits have successfully challenged the restrictive definition that HHS has devised for limiting a beneficiary's "spell of illness" and, thus, Part A benefits. See Levi v. Heckler, 736 F.2d 848 (2d Cir.1984) (per curiam); Kaufman v. Harris, 731 F.2d 370 (6th Cir.1984) (per curiam); and Mayburg v. Secretary of Health & Human Services, 740 F.2d 100 (1st Cir.1984). See also, Fox v. Bowen, 656 F.Supp. 1236 (D.Conn.1986) (overturning a Medicare contractor's denial of physical therapy services based on a rule of thumb terminating coverage when a beneficiary could walk fifty feet unaided).

Litigation concerning the scope of coverage can also broaden the discussion to include Congress. Duggan v. Bowen, 691 F.Supp. 1487 (D.D.C.1988), for example, rejected HCFA's informal position that the statutory requirement permitting coverage of home health benefits only for "part-time or intermittent care" limited coverage to home health care provided less than five days a week. Congress subsequently adopted the court's position, including in the Medicare Catastrophic Coverage Act of 1988 (MCCA) a provision specifying that "intermittent" benefits could be provided up to seven days a week for 38 days. In its pique at the rejection of the MCCA by Medicare beneficiaries, however, Congress repealed this provision in 1989, leaving the meaning of "intermittent" again uncertain. Significantly, Congress has strictly limited judicial review of national coverage decisions concerning medical technology, see Section D.1. below.

Professor Eleanor Kinney has written an excellent series of articles discussing, inter alia, Medicare coverage policy: Kinney, Setting Limits: A Realistic Assignment for the Medicare Program, 33 St. Louis U.L.J. 631 (1989); Kinney, National Coverage Policy Under the Medicare Program: Problems and Proposals for Change, 32 St. Louis U.L.J. 869 (1988); Kinney, The Medicare Appeals System for Coverage and Payment Disputes: Achieving Fairness in a Time of Constraint, 1 Admin. L.J. 1 (1987).

States must also determine coverage of particular items and services, and of particular persons, under their Medicaid programs. In so doing, they face only vague federal constraints, such as 42 C.F.R. 440.230:

§ 440.230 Sufficiency of amount, duration, and scope.

   (a) The plan must specify the amount, duration, and scope of each service that it provides for—* * *

   (b) Each service must be sufficient in amount, duration, and scope to reasonably achieve its purpose.

(c) The Medicaid agency may not arbitrarily deny or reduce the amount, duration, or scope of a required service [ ] to an otherwise eligible recipient solely because of the diagnosis, type of illness, or condition.

(d) The agency may place appropriate limits on a service based on such criteria as medical necessity or on utilization control procedures.

Consider the alternate approaches taken by the state of Missouri, the 8th Circuit Federal Court of Appeals, and the state of Oregon to the problem of who should make coverage decisions in the following materials:

WEAVER v. REAGEN

United States Court of Appeals, Eighth Circuit, 1989.
886 F.2d 194.

Ross, Senior Circuit Judge.

Appellees/plaintiffs Glenn Weaver, T.G., and Mark Momot are members of a class of Medicaid eligible individuals (plaintiffs) who are disabled by the disease Acquired Immunodeficiency Syndrome (AIDS). Plaintiffs filed suit against Michael Reagan, Director of the Missouri Department of Social Services, and Jane Kruse, Director of the Missouri Division of Medical Services (defendants) claiming that defendants had violated their statutory right to Medicaid benefits by denying coverage of the drug Retrovir (formerly known as azidothymidine or AZT) for treatment of their AIDS. Finding that AZT was medically necessary treatment, the United States District Court for the Western District of Missouri granted plaintiffs' motion for summary judgment and enjoined Missouri officials from denying coverage of AZT to the plaintiff class. We affirm.

I.

* * *

On March 20, 1987, the Food and Drug Administration (FDA) announced its approval of AZT under the brand name Retrovir, for the treatment of AIDS. The labeling approved by the FDA for AZT stated:

> Retrovir capsules are indicated for the management of certain adult patients with symptomatic HIV infection (AIDS and advanced ARC) who have a history of cytologically confirmed Pneumocystis carinii pneumonia (PCP) or an absolute CD4 (T4 helper/inducer) lymphocyte count of less than 200/mm in the peripheral blood before therapy is begun.

At the time this action was filed on July 6, 1987, the State of Missouri did not provide any Medicaid coverage for AZT. Three days after the suit was filed, the Missouri Department of Social Services promulgated an emergency rule, providing Medicaid coverage of AZT under certain diagnoses or conditions. Adopted as a permanent rule with minor modifications effective November 12, 1987, Missouri regulations now provide coverage for AZT as follows:

> The availability of the drug Zidovudine, formerly known as Azidothymidine, for Missouri Medicaid coverage shall be limited to only those eligible recipients for whom the prescribing physician has established a medical diagnosis of acquired immunodeficiency syndrome (AIDS) and who have a history of cytologically confirmed Pneumocystis carinii pneumonia (PCP) or an absolute CD4 (T4 helper/inducer) lymphocyte count of less than two hundred (200) per cubic millimeter in the peripheral blood before therapy is begun.   Mo.Code Regs. tit. 13, § 70–20.110.

This language is virtually identical to FDA's approval statement for the drug.

At the present time, the drug AZT is the only approved treatment of AIDS or ARC.   While there are treatments for particular opportunistic infections which the AIDS patient may develop, AZT is the only approved drug which acts on the HIV virus itself.

* * *

[The district court certified a class defined as:] All persons in Missouri who would have or will be determined eligible for Medicaid and who are infected with the [AIDS virus] and whose physicians have or will in the future prescribe the drug Retrovir for their treatment and who do not meet the medical criteria set forth in [Missouri's Medicaid rule] for Medicaid coverage of AZT.

The trial court held that defendants' rule limiting Medicaid coverage of AZT to only those recipients who meet certain diagnostic criteria or conditions violated federal Medicaid law, 42 C.F.R. §§ 440.230(b), 440.240(b), and 42 U.S.C. § 1983.   The district court found that AZT is medically necessary treatment for individuals in the plaintiff class who do not fit within the restrictive criteria of Missouri's Medicaid rule. The court, therefore, enjoined Missouri officials from denying coverage of AZT to "persons eligible for Medicaid and infected with the AIDS virus."

II.

In reviewing nonadjudicatory federal agency action, a court is limited to deciding whether the action is arbitrary, capricious, an abuse of discretion or otherwise not in accordance with the law. [ ] "Although the answer is far from clear," at least one court has assumed without deciding that a court "is entitled to review the actions of a state agency administering federal Medicaid funding as it would review the actions of a federal agency."   Mississippi Hosp. Ass'n, Inc. v. Heckler, 701 F.2d 511, 516 (5th Cir.1983). [ ]

Title XIX of the Social Security Act, 42 U.S.C. §§ 1396–1396s, commonly known as the Medicaid Act, is a federal-state cooperative program designed to provide medical assistance to persons whose income and resources are insufficient to meet the costs of medical care.

Although a state's participation is voluntary, once a state chooses to participate in the program it must comply with federal statutory and regulatory requirements, Alexander v. Choate, 469 U.S. 287, 289 n. 1, 105 S.Ct. 712, 714 n. 1, 83 L.Ed.2d 661 (1985); Ellis v. Patterson, 859 F.2d 52, 54 (8th Cir.1988); 42 U.S.C. § 1396a, including the requirement that participating states provide financial assistance for in-patient hospital services, out-patient hospital services, laboratory and x-ray services, skilled nursing facilities and physicians' services. See 42 U.S.C. § 1396a(a)(10) and § 1396d(a)(1)–(5).

The participating state may also elect to provide other optional medical services such as prescription drugs. See 42 U.S.C. § 1396d(a)(12). Once a state chooses to offer such optional services it is bound to act in compliance with the Act and the applicable regulations in the implementation of those services, [ ], including the requirement that "[e]ach service must be sufficient in amount, duration, and scope to reasonably achieve its purpose." 42 C.F.R. § 440.230(b).

Although a state has considerable discretion in fashioning its Medicaid program, the discretion of the state is not unbridled: "[A state] may not arbitrarily deny or reduce the amount, duration, or scope of a required service * * * to an otherwise eligible recipient solely because of the diagnosis, type of illness or condition." 42 C.F.R. § 440.230(c). "[A]ppropriate limits [may be placed] on a service based on such criteria as medical necessity or utilization control procedures." Id. at § 440.230(d). Moreover, the state's plan for determining eligibility for medical assistance must be " 'reasonable' and 'consistent with the objectives' of the Act." Beal v. Doe, 432 U.S. 438, 444, 97 S.Ct. 2366, 2371, 53 L.Ed.2d 464 (1977) (quoting 42 U.S.C. § 1396a(a)(17)). This provision has been interpreted to require that a state Medicaid plan provide treatment that is deemed "medically necessary" in order to comport with the objectives of the Act. See id. at 444–45, 97 S.Ct. at 2370–71 ("serious statutory questions might be presented if a state Medicaid plan excluded necessary medical treatment from its coverage"); Pinneke v. Preisser, 623 F.2d 546, 548 n. 2 (8th Cir.1980).

In the present case, defendants argue that their reliance on the FDA's approval statement in limiting coverage of AZT to only those patients who meet certain medical criteria is a reasonable exercise of their discretion to place limitations on covered services based on medical necessity and utilization controls. We do not find this argument persuasive.

Contrary to defendants' assertions, FDA approved indications were not intended to limit or interfere with the practice of medicine nor to preclude physicians from using their best judgment in the interest of the patient. Instead, the FDA new drug approval process is intended to ensure that drugs meet certain statutory standards for safety and effectiveness, manufacturing and controls, and labeling, 21 C.F.R. § 314.105(c) (1988), and to ensure that manufacturers market their drugs only for those indications for which the drug sponsor has demonstrated "substantial evidence" of effectiveness. Id. at § 314.126.

According to a drug bulletin issued by the FDA,

> The [Food, Drug and Cosmetic] Act does not, * * * limit the manner in which a physician may use an approved drug. Once a product has been approved for marketing, a physician may prescribe it for uses or in treatment regimens or patient populations that are not included in approved labeling. Such "unapproved" or, more precisely, "unlabeled" uses may be appropriate and rational in certain circumstances, and may, in fact, reflect approaches to drug therapy that have been extensively reported in medical literature.

> The term "unapproved uses" is, to some extent, misleading. It includes a variety of situations ranging from unstudied to thoroughly investigated drug uses * * *. [A]ccepted medical practice often includes drug use that is not reflected in approved drug labeling. With respect to its role in medical practice, the package insert is informational only.

"Use of Approved Drugs for Unlabeled Indications," 12 FDA Drug Bulletin 4 (April 1982).

Thus, the fact that FDA has not approved labeling of a drug for a particular use does not necessarily bear on those uses of the drug that are established within the medical and scientific community as medically appropriate. It would be improper for the State of Missouri to interfere with a physician's judgment of medical necessity by limiting coverage of AZT based on criteria that admittedly do not reflect current medical knowledge or practice.

It is also defendants' position on appeal that prescribing AZT outside the FDA approved indications is per se "experimental" in the sense that there is no scientific data derived from clinical trials documenting the efficacy and safety of AZT use outside the FDA guidelines. According to defendants, because such AZT use is experimental, it can never be deemed medically necessary treatment.

In our view, defendants' definition of "experimental" in this context is overly broad. In Rush v. Parham, 625 F.2d 1150 (5th Cir.1980), the Fifth Circuit, in considering the "experimental" nature of treatment for purposes of Medicaid coverage, defined "experimental" as a treatment not "generally accepted by the professional medical community as an effective and proven treatment for the condition" or "rarely used, novel or relatively unknown." Id. at 1156 n. 11.

Under the Rush definition, the prescription of AZT beyond its labeled indications is not experimental. The record here establishes that physicians commonly prescribe AZT for patients who have neither a history of PCP nor a CD4 count below 200. Plaintiffs' experts stated that based on their own practice, professional literature, conferences, and contacts with other physicians, AZT is generally accepted by the medical community as an effective and proven treatment for AIDS patients who do not meet the criteria in the FDA indications. * * *

* * *

Our decision in Pinneke v. Preisser, 623 F.2d 546 (8th Cir.1980), is controlling on the issue presently before us. In Pinneke, the Iowa Medicaid agency had a policy which stated "an irrebuttable presumption that the procedure of sex reassignment surgery can never be medically necessary when the surgery is a treatment for transsexualism," and accordingly denied Medicaid benefits for such surgery. Id. at 549. However, because sex reassignment surgery was the only available treatment for transsexualism, the Eighth Circuit held that Iowa's policy denying Medicaid coverage for sex reassignment surgery, where it was deemed medically necessary by the applicant's own physician, conflicted with the objectives of the Medicaid program. The court held, "a state plan absolutely excluding the only available treatment * * * for a particular condition must be considered an arbitrary denial of benefits based solely on the 'diagnosis, type of illness, or condition.'" Id. Relying on Beal v. Doe, supra, 432 U.S. at 445 n. 9, 97 S.Ct. at 2371 n. 9, this court emphasized the importance of professional medical judgment in the determination of medical necessity. "The decision of whether or not certain treatment or a particular type of surgery is 'medically necessary' rests with the individual recipient's physician and not with clerical personnel or government officials." Pinneke v. Preisser, supra, 623 F.2d at 550. * * *.

As in Pinneke, Missouri's Medicaid rule constitutes an irrebuttable presumption that AZT can never be medically necessary treatment for AIDS patients who have neither a history of PCP nor a CD4 count below 200. The record here establishes that such a presumption is unreasonable in light of the widespread recognition by the medical community and scientific literature that AZT is the only known antiviral treatment for individuals with AIDS.

The Medicaid statute and regulatory scheme create a presumption in favor of the medical judgment of the attending physician in determining the medical necessity of treatment. In denying coverage of AZT to the plaintiff class, the defendants have done nothing to overcome that presumption except to rely on the FDA approval process in a manner expressly rejected by the FDA. In the face of widespread recognition by the medical community and the scientific and medical literature that AZT is the only available treatment for most persons with AIDS, we find that Missouri Medicaid's approach to its coverage of the drug AZT is unreasonable and inconsistent with the objectives of the Medicaid Act. * * *

In sum, we hold that pursuant to the objectives of the Act, Missouri Medicaid may not deny coverage of AZT to AIDS patients who are eligible for Medicaid and whose physicians have certified that AZT is medically necessary treatment.

* * *

As modified, the judgment of the district court is affirmed.

OREGON LISTS ILLNESSES BY PRIORITY TO SEE WHO GETS MEDICAID CARE.

New York Times, May 3, 1990.

* * *

After months of public debate over life-and-death questions, the Oregon Health Services Commission today made public the main tool for their program: a list of 1,600 medical procedures, ranked by computer according to a formula that balances their costs against how many people would benefit.

* * *

Later this year Oregon's legislature will decide where to draw a line across the computer list. Those ailments and injuries below the line will not be covered by the Medicaid program, which is jointly financed by the state and Federal governments. Conditions above the line will be fully covered.

It is far from clear at this point where the line might be drawn.

The Oregon plan would not reduce coverage for the aged, disabled and the blind. All Medicaid coverage to those groups, no matter the procedure, would continue as before.

By eliminating a handful of expensive operations, Oregon officials say they may be able to nearly double the number of people receiving some coverage under Medicaid. About 130,000 people now receive some care in this state.

* * *

Ranking near the top of the Oregon list of ailments and injuries were such things as bacterial meningitis, bone cancer, multiple sclerosis and acute headaches.

But the list does not necessarily reflect the suffering that a particular disease can inflict on a human being. Thus, several other ailments—thumb sucking, for instance—are high on the list, not because they are the most painful or serious but because they are easily treated at a relatively low cost and affect a large number of people.

Among the diseases ranked near the middle were agoraphobia, cystic fibrosis and certain kinds of arthritis.

* * *

Near the bottom of the list, those ailments likely to be dropped from Medicaid coverage, are chronic ulcers, sleep disorders, viral herpes, varicose vein treatment, impacted teeth and sex change operations.

Detection and prevention of AIDS are high on the list, but treatment for advanced acquired immune deficiency syndrome, when a patient is close to death, is near the bottom.

The final list, which may still be changed later this year by a legislative committee, was drawn up computer. It is based on a ranking produced by a computer under a formula involving the cost of care based on the current Federal standard for the treatment in the Medicaid program, the length of time before the ailment would recur and the health of a patient after treatment, a category that Oregon called "the quality of well-being."

It was put together by a panel of doctors, consumer advocates, health care administrators and medical ethics experts. They were faced with such choices as whether a $100,000 organ transplant may be less valuable than regular tests for breast cancer.

* * *

The Oregon Legislature's health committee was ordered by the State Legislature to draw up the list after Oregon cut off Medicaid funds for organ transplants in 1987. At the time, state officials decided to concentrate their medical funds on such things as pre-natal care.

The decision spurred a debate over where the state's portion of Medicaid could best be spent.

* * *

The Oregon list reflects public sentiment from more than 50 community meetings in the last year. In the hearings, prevention of illness and early detection were ranked much higher than operations that may prolong the life of somebody who is profoundly ill, according to a state study of the meetings.

"We picked up a very strong feeling from the general public that the American system pays too little attention to illness prevention," said Dr. Michael Garland, a bio-ethicist who is president of a group that sampled opinion in the last year. "It's like the old line: You can pay me or you can pay me later. The cost of health care is increasing at a rate that is unsustainable, and people want to put the brakes on somewhere."

* * *

Notes and Questions

1. What are the reasons for and consequences of the permitting coverage decisions to be made by the various decisionmakers presented above: the personal physicians of beneficiaries, low level bureaucrats, national professional consensus groups, grass roots consensus panels? How would the Oregon plan fare under the standards applied in Weaver? Oregon intends to apply for a waiver from federal Medicaid requirements to implement the program under 42 U.S.C.A. § 1315, which permits HHS to waive the requirements of Title XIX for " * * * any experimental, pilot

or demonstration projects which is likely to assist in promoting the objectives of Title * * * XIX." Should such a waiver request be granted?

2. Does the Constitution have any relevance to the question of whether certain items or services should be covered by public benefits programs? Harris v. McRae, 448 U.S. 297, 100 S.Ct. 2671, 65 L.Ed.2d 784 (1980) addressed the constitutionality of the Hyde Amendment, which prohibited federal funding for abortion services, even if necessary to save the life of the mother. In upholding the limitation against due process and equal protection challenges, Mr. Justice Stewart wrote for the court:

* * *

 * * * [R]egardless of whether the freedom of a woman to choose to terminate her pregnancy for health reasons lies at the core or the periphery of the due process liberty recognized in *[Roe v.] Wade,* [410 U.S. 113 (1973)] it simply does not follow that a woman's freedom of choice carries with it a constitutional entitlement to the financial resources to avail herself of the full range of protected choices. The reason why was explained in *Maher* [v. Roe, 432 U.S. 464 (1977)]: although government may not place obstacles in the path of a woman's exercise of her freedom of choice, it need not remove those not of its own creation. Indigency falls in the latter category. The financial constraints that restrict an indigent woman's ability to enjoy the full range of constitutionally protected freedom of choice are the product not of governmental restrictions on access to abortions, but rather of her indigency. * * *

 Although the liberty protected by the Due Process Clause affords protection against unwarranted government interference with freedom of choice in the context of certain personal decisions, it does not confer an entitlement to such funds as may be necessary to realize all the advantages of that freedom. To hold otherwise would mark a drastic change in our understanding of the Constitution. * * *

* * *

 It remains to be determined whether the Hyde Amendment violates the equal protection component of the Fifth Amendment. This challenge is premised on the fact that, although federal reimbursement is available under Medicaid for medically necessary services generally, the Hyde Amendment does not permit federal reimbursement of all medically necessary abortions.

* * *

 The * * * question * * * is whether the Hyde Amendment is rationally related to a legitimate governmental objective. It is the Government's position that the Hyde Amendment bears a rational relationship to its legitimate interest in protecting the potential life of the fetus. We agree. * * *

 The Hyde Amendment, by encouraging childbirth except in the most urgent circumstances, is rationally related to the legitimate governmental objective of protecting potential life. By subsidizing the medical expenses of indigent women who carry their pregnancies to term while not subsidizing the comparable expenses of women who undergo abortions (except those whose lives are threatened), Congress has established incentives that make childbirth a more attractive alternative than abortion for persons eligible for Medicaid. These incentives bear a direct relationship to the legitimate congressional interest in protecting potential life.

* * *

In dissent Justice Brennan, joined by Justices Marshall and Blackmun, wrote:

* * *

Roe v. Wade held that the constitutional right to personal privacy encompasses a woman's decision whether or not to terminate her pregnancy.   * * * The proposition for which [Roe and its progeny] stand is not that the State is under an affirmative obligation to ensure access to abortions for all who may desire them; it is that the State must refrain from wielding its enormous power and influence in a manner that might burden the pregnant woman's freedom to choose whether to have an abortion. The Hyde Amendment's denial of public funds for medically necessary abortions plainly intrudes upon this constitutionally protected decision, for both by design and in effect it serves to coerce indigent pregnant women to bear children that they would otherwise elect not to have.

* * *

The fundamental flaw in the Court's due process analysis, then, is its failure to acknowledge that the discriminatory distribution of the benefits of governmental largesse can discourage the exercise of fundamental liberties just as effectively as can an outright denial of those rights through criminal and regulatory sanctions. Implicit in the Court's reasoning is the notion that as long as the Government is not obligated to provide its citizens with certain benefits or privileges, it may condition the grant of such benefits on the recipient's relinquishment of his constitutional rights.

* * *

Justice Stevens also dissented, stating:

* * *

Having decided to alleviate some of the hardships of poverty by providing necessary medical care, the government must use neutral criteria in distributing benefits. It may not deny benefits to a financially and medically needy person simply because he is a Republican, a Catholic, or an Oriental—or because he has spoken against a program the government has a legitimate interest in furthering. In sum, it may not create exceptions for the sole purpose of furthering a governmental interest that is constitutionally subordinate to the individual interest that the entire program was designed to protect. The Hyde Amendments not only exclude financially and medically needy persons from the pool of benefits for a constitutionally insufficient reason; they also require the expenditure of millions and millions of dollars in order to thwart the exercise of a constitutional right, thereby effectively inflicting serious and long-lasting harm on impoverished women who want and need abortions for valid medical reasons. In my judgment, these Amendments constitute an unjustifiable, and indeed blatant, violation of the sovereign's duty to govern impartially. * * *

3. In *McRae* the Supreme Court broke no new ground in rejecting a constitutional right to government payment for health care. But can the Court's decision be reconciled with earlier decisions, such as Sherbert v. Verner, 374 U.S. 398, 83 S.Ct. 1790, 10 L.Ed.2d 965 (1963); and Memorial Hospital v. Maricopa County, 415 U.S. 250, 94 S.Ct. 1076, 39 L.Ed.2d 306 (1974), invalidating state statutes denying welfare benefits because of the exercise of a constitutional right? Can a state encourage childbirth without discouraging the alternative of abortion? Can a state discourage abortion with passing a moral judgment against abortion? Does not *Roe v. Wade* forbid such a judgment by elevating the choice of an abortion to a constitutional right? On the other hand are not the rights of a person who finds abortion morally abhorrent violated if he or she must pay for abortions through taxes? See, Appleton, Beyond the Limits of Reproductive Choice, 81 Columbia L.Rev. 721 (1981); Goldstein, A Critique of the Abortion Funding Decisions: On Private Rights in the Public Sector, 8 Hastings Const.L.Q. 313 (1981); Perry, Why the Supreme Court was Plainly Wrong in the Hyde Amendment Case: A Brief Comment on Harris v. McRae, 32 Stan.L.Rev. 1113 (1980). For a more detailed discussion of the Supreme Court's abortion decisions, see chapter 9.

4. Is it possible to imagine a situation in which the provisions of a federal or state health benefit program would be found to violate the federal equal protection or due process clauses? Could the government refuse to pay for treatment for sickle cell anemia, a condition that afflicts primarily blacks? Could it refuse to pay for circumcisions done in accordance with Jewish law? Could it refuse to pay for AIDS treatment?

5. Since *Maher v. Roe* and *Harris v. McRae*, several state supreme courts have recognized a state constitutional right to have Medicaid pay for abortions as it does other medical procedures. See Right to Choose v. Byrne, 91 N.J. 287, 450 A.2d 925 (1982); Moe v. Secretary of Administration and Finance, 382 Mass. 629, 417 N.E.2d 387 (1981); Committee to Defend Reproductive Rights v. Myers, 29 Cal.3d 252, 172 Cal.Rptr. 866, 625 P.2d 779 (1981).

6. Various civil rights acts might also limit state discretion in determining what benefits to provide under the Medicaid program. For example, Section 504 of the Rehabilitation Act of 1973 prohibits discrimination against the handicapped in federally funded programs, 29 U.S.C.A. § 794. In Alexander v. Choate, 469 U.S. 287, 105 S.Ct. 712, 83 L.Ed.2d 661 (1985), the handicapped plaintiffs argued that Tennessee's decision to cover only 14 days of inpatient care for a recipient per fiscal year disproportionately affected, and thus discriminated against, the handicapped, who, on the average, require more inpatient care. Justice Marshall, writing for a unanimous court, rejected this argument, noting that the state requirement was neutral on its face and provided the handicapped and nonhandicapped with an equally accessible benefit. Might a regulation that prohibits state payment for AZT violate § 504 or another of the civil rights laws?

Note: The Role of Medicare and Medicaid in Shaping the Health Care Industry

Large sectors of the health care industry have emerged or developed in particular ways because of the availability of Medicare or Medicaid coverage. The American nursing home industry exists primarily because of the Medicaid program and its predecessors, and nursing homes are designed, constructed, and administered to conform to federal regulations. The home health care industry has burgeoned under the nourishment of the Medicare program. In 1967, when Medicare began, there were 1,850 Medicare-certified home health agencies and by 1981 there were 3,110. In the three years following 1981, when Medicare home health benefits were dramatically expanded, about 1,600 new home health agencies were certified. In 1981 the Medicare law, which previously had paid only for home health care provided by non-profit agencies, was also amended to permit coverage of proprietary home health. Between 1980 and 1984 the proportion of proprietary home health agencies increased almost three-fold, from 7.1% to 20.5%, Callahan, Medicare Use of Home Health Services, 7 Health Care Financing Review 89 (Winter 1985).

In 1972 the Medicare law was amended to extend renal dialysis to all persons who were fully or currently insured or entitled to monthly insurance benefits under Social Security as well as to their spouses or dependent children, even if they had not reached age 65. As of 1980 the ESRD program covered 50,000 beneficiaries and consumed 10% of total SMI benefit payments. Medicare pays for virtually all renal dialysis in the United States. In large part because of this program, far more dialysis is performed in the United States than anywhere else in the world: in 1978 the United States had a rate of 209 dialysis per million, compared to 144 in Israel (the country with the second highest prevalence) and 53 in the United Kingdom. See Rettig, The Politics of Health Cost Containment: End Stage Renal Disease, 56 Bull.N.Y.Acad.Med. 115 (Jan.–Feb. 1980); Relman & Rennie, Treatment of End–Stage Renal Disease, Free but Not Equal, 303 New Eng.J.Med. 996 (1980).

D. ADMINISTRATION AND APPEALS

1. Medicare

The major decisions about federal Medicare and Medicaid policy are ultimately made by the United States Congress. These decisions are in turn fleshed-out by the Health Care Financing Administration (HCFA) of the Department of Health and Human Services (HHS) and implemented by the carriers and intermediaries that make individual claims determinations. Though some of the provisions of the Medicare Act are overly detailed, it is often in the interest of Congress to make general pronouncements and leave the hard and politically dangerous work of hammering out the details of the program to HHS. In the early years of the program, HHS frequently deferred to the medical industry, and attempted to make program decisions by consensus. Since the late 1970s it has exercised its authority more aggressively, as is illustrated by the DRG hospital reimbursement and RBRVS physician payment programs discussed in Chapter 7. See Brown, Technocratic Corporatism and Administrative Reform in Medicare, 10 J.Health Pol., Pol'y and L. 579 (1985).

The courts have had little part in making major policy decisions about Medicare, but have been quite active at the fringes, trying to correct some of the programs worst bureaucratic excesses. Their role has been circumscribed by the strict limits placed on judicial review by the Supreme Court's interpretation of the Social Security Act. 42 U.S.C.A. § 1395ii makes applicable to the Medicare program 42 U.S.C.A. § 405(h). Section 405(h) provides, in part, that "No findings of fact or decision of the Secretary shall be reviewed by any person, tribunal, or governmental agency except as herein provided. No action against the United States, the Secretary, or any officer or employee thereof shall be brought under section 1331 or 1346 of title 28 to recover on any claim arising under this subchapter."

This section has been interpreted in several Supreme Court cases to preclude review of Social Security or Medicare decisions for which the Social Security Act did not otherwise provide review despite repeated attempts by the lower courts to find some jurisdictional toehold. Successive cases rejected arguments for review under 28 U.S.C.A. § 1331, Weinberger v. Salfi, 422 U.S. 749, 95 S.Ct. 2457, 45 L.Ed.2d 522 (1975); through the Administrative Procedures Act, Califano v. Sanders, 430 U.S. 99, 97 S.Ct. 980, 51 L.Ed.2d 192 (1977); or in the Court of Claims, United States v. Erika, 456 U.S. 201, 102 S.Ct. 1650, 72 L.Ed.2d 12 (1982).

In Heckler v. Ringer, 466 U.S. 602, 104 S.Ct. 2013, 80 L.Ed.2d 622 (1984), the court rejected a challenge to a Part A policy even though the challenge was cast as a procedural challenge (rather than a challenge to the denial of the claim itself) and though one of the claimants, who had not yet received a treatment for which coverage was denied, had no other practical means of review.

The judicial review preclusion provisions have resulted in such extensive litigation because up until recently the Medicare statute did not explicitly provide any form of judicial review for large categories of Medicare disputes. In particular, the statute made no provision for review of Part B claims. In 1986 two developments brought about a major change in the prior law. First, in Bowen v. Michigan Academy of Family Physicians, 476 U.S. 667, 106 S.Ct. 2133, 90 L.Ed.2d 623 (1986), the Supreme Court held that courts could hear challenges to the "method by which Part B awards are computed (as opposed to the computation)." 476 U.S. at 676, 106 S.Ct. at 2139. Second, section 9341 of the Omnibus Budget Reconciliation Act of 1986 amended 42 U.S.C.A. § 1395ff to permit judicial review of Part B decisions where the amount in controversy was $1000 or more. Part B procedures were further amended by section 4082 of the Omnibus Budget Reconciliation Act of 1987, permitting administrative law judges to certify legal issues to the federal district court when they determine, on motion of an appellant, that no factual issues exist in a case.

Serious questions still remain, however, as to whether judicial review is available for several classes of cases. First, the 1986 Act bars review of decisions based on payment methods established under Part B prior to 1981, 42 U.S.C.A. § 1395ff(b)(4). Second, there is still no judicial review for Part A and B claims involving less than $1000. Third, situations can still arise, as in Heckler v. Ringer, where providers will not provide services that HCFA refuses to cover, and therefore it is impossible for a recipient to file a claim and exhaust administrative remedies. Fourth, review of national coverage determinations deciding whether a particular class of items or services are covered under Medicare is subject to significant limitations. Such determinations may not be reviewed by any administrative law judge; may not be held unlawful or set aside on the ground that a requirement of the APA relating to publication in the Federal Register or opportunity for public comment was not satisfied; and, if a court determines that the rule-making record for such a determination was incomplete or otherwise lacked adequate information to support the validity of the determination, the court must remand the matter to the Secretary for additional proceedings to supplement the record and may not determine that an item or service is covered except upon review of the supplemented record. 42 U.S.C.A. § 1395ff(b)(3).

Collectively, these exceptions cover a large proportion of the Medicare issues worth litigating. Indeed, in adopting the 1986 provision, Congress may have ended up restricting rather than expanding judicial review of Medicare decisions.

Moreover, recent court decisions have interpreted *Michigan Academy* very narrowly, continuing to require exhaustion of administrative remedies under almost all circumstances, see Bodimetric Health Services, Inc. v. Aetna Life & Cas., 903 F.2d 480 (7th Cir.1990); Anderson v. Bowen, 881 F.2d 1 (2d Cir.1989); Texas Medical Ass'n v. Sullivan, 875 F.2d 1160 (5th Cir.1989); Association of Seat Lift Mfrs. v. Bowen, 858 F.2d 308 (6th Cir.1988); Kuritzky v. Blue Shield of Western New York, Inc., 850 F.2d 126 (2d Cir.1988); but see, Duggan v. Bowen, 691 F.Supp. 1487 (D.C.D.C.1988) (excusing exhaustion, finding it futile.)

Do the jurisdictional exclusions of the Medicare act still leave room for quibbling over jurisdiction in the tradition of the earlier cases? If claims in which review is explicitly precluded raise constitutional issues, is the denial of review a violation of due process? The Supreme Court avoided this question in *Michigan Academy*, but offered a telling footnote in which it suggested that such a bar of review of constitutional issues might be unconstitutional, 476 U.S. at 681, note 12, 106 S.Ct. at 2141, note 12.

Note: Medicare Administrative Appeals

1. An administrative appeal is available for Medicare HI (Part A) claims including $100 or more and SMI (Part B) claims involving $500 or

more. The only administrative review available to Medicare recipients denied SMI claims between $100 and $500 is a review on the written record or an oral hearing before a hearing officer appointed by the private insurance carrier that administers the program in the recipient's area. Even in cases involving more than $500, HCFA has insisted that the claim first be reviewed on the record and then submitted to a carrier fair hearing before the case can be submitted to an administrative law judge, a procedure upheld in Issacs v. Bowen, 865 F.2d 468 (2d Cir.1989). Until 1986 review by a carrier-appointed hearing officer was the only remedy for all SMI claims. Does this procedure satisfy due process? Will hearing officers selected by a private insurance company be biased towards upholding the decisions of that carrier? Does it make any difference that the carrier is paying claims from federal funds and the hearing officers' salaries are paid by the federal government? Is due process violated because the hearing officers are often not attorneys? See Schweiker v. McClure, 456 U.S. 188, 102 S.Ct. 1665, 72 L.Ed.2d 1 (1982). Is due process violated because an oral hearing is not available for SMI denials involving less than $100. See Gray Panthers v. Schweiker, 652 F.2d 146 (D.C.Cir.1980), appeal after remand, 716 F.2d 23 (D.C.Cir.1983).

2. The Medicare statute and regulations provide a variety of other procedures for administrative appeals and judicial review. First, eligibility for HI and SMI is determined by the Social Security Administration and is subject to administrative review through SSA's reconsideration administrative hearing, and Appeals Council procedures. The initial decision as to payment of an HI claim is made by the private intermediary processing the claim. A beneficiary can ask the intermediary to reconsider this decision, 42 C.F.R. § 405.710. This consideration is a paper review performed by an employee of the intermediary other than the initial decisionmaker. Though HI recipients seek review of very few (.05%) claims, 25% of the reviewed decisions are reversed at the reconsideration stage. A beneficiary dissatisfied with the reconsideration decision may obtain an oral, evidentiary hearing before an administrative law judge (ALJ) of the Social Security Administration, 42 C.F.R. § 405.720. Claimants enjoy a 50–60% reversal rate at this stage of review. If the ALJ decision is not satisfactory, the beneficiary may appeal to the Social Security Appeals Council, 42 C.F.R. § 405.724.

A provider denied or terminated from participation in Medicare is entitled to review by a Social Security ALJ and by the Appeals Council, and, in most cases, to judicial review, 42 C.F.R. §§ 405.1501–405.1595. An HI provider dissatisfied with the amount of reimbursement may receive a hearing before an intermediary hearing officer if the amount at issue is between $1,000 and $10,000. 42 C.F.R. §§ 405.1803–405.1813. If the amount is $10,000 or more (or if smaller claims involving a common controversy can be aggregated in an amount of $50,000 or more), the provider can receive a hearing before the Medicare Provider Reimbursement Review Board (PRRB), 42 U.S.C.A. § 1395oo(a)(2), (b). For a review of Medicare appeal procedures, see 2 CCH, Medicare & Medicaid Guide, ¶¶ 13,470–13,540; National Senior Citizens Law Center, Representing Older Persons, An Advocates Manual, 42–44 (1985); Coleman, Legal Aspects of Medicare and Medicaid Reimbursement, 135–146 (1990), Neeley–Kvarme,

Administrative and Judicial Review of Medicare Issues: A Guide Through the Maze, 57 Notre Dame Law. 1 (1981); Waxman and Chiplin, Medicare Part B Appeals—And You Thought the System was Fixed, 23 Clearinghouse Review 384 (1989); Gilcrist, Appealing Denial of Payments Under Part B of the Medicare Program, 3 Medical Staff Counselor 9 (Winter 1989); Note, Medicare Provider Reimbursement Disputes: Mapping the Contorted Borders of Administrative and Judicial Review, 21 Ind.L.Rev. 705 (1989).

2. Medicaid

Policy is formulated and implemented quite differently in the Medicaid program than in the Medicare program. While the ultimate decisions are made by Congress and elaborated by HCFA, these federal decisions merely form the skeleton for the state programs, which are also subject to the authority of state legislatures and state Medicaid agencies. Medicaid decisions that affect individual recipients and providers are ultimately subject to review in the state and federal courts.

Because Medicaid is a federal-state program, Congress has often enacted purposely flexible Medicaid provisions, leaving the states to make many fundamental policy decisions. For example, 42 U.S.C.A. § 1396a(a)(13) (the provision governing hospital reimbursement discussed in the next chapter) has permitted the states to adopt a wide variety of mechanisms—and payment levels—for hospital reimbursement. A state must submit a Medicaid state plan to HCFA demonstrating that its program conforms with the federal statutes and regulations. If a state Medicaid program ceases to be in substantial compliance with federal requirements, HCFA may, after a hearing, terminate its federal funding. Because this remedy is so drastic, HCFA has rarely convened a hearing and has never terminated a state program. See Butler, Legal Problems in Medicaid, in R. Roemer and G. McCray, Legal Aspects of Health Policy: Issues and Trends, 214, 225 (1980). Additional statutory provisions permit HHS to disallow reimbursement claimed by the state where the services covered by the state (such as elective abortions) are not eligible for reimbursement, 42 U.S.C.A. § 1316d. These provisions occasionally result in litigation between the federal government and the states. See Illinois Department of Public Aid v. Schweiker, 707 F.2d 273 (7th Cir.1983); New Jersey v. Department of Health and Human Services, 670 F.2d 1262 (3d Cir.1981); 670 F.2d 1284 (3d Cir.1982), cert. denied, 459 U.S. 824, 103 S.Ct. 56, 74 L.Ed.2d 60 (1982); Texas v. Califano, 556 F.2d 326 (5th Cir.1977), cert. denied, 439 U.S. 818, 99 S.Ct. 78, 58 L.Ed.2d 108 (1978). For an excellent review of the range of administrative law issues involved in the governance of the Medicaid Program, see Kinney, Rule and Policy Making for the Medicaid Program: A Challenge to Federalism for the Administrative Conference of the United States, 51 Ohio St.L.J. 855 (1990).

The substantial federal contribution to state-operated programs has enabled the federal government to force the states to toe the federal line on other issues of health policy, such as initiating certificate of need programs. This use of the federal spending power has generally been upheld. See North Carolina ex. rel. Morrow v. Califano, 445 F.Supp. 532 (E.D.N.C.1977), affirmed mem., 435 U.S. 962, 98 S.Ct. 1597, 56 L.Ed.2d 54 (1978), Wing and Stilton, Constitutional Authority For Extending Federal Control over the Delivery of Health Care, 57 N.C.L. Rev. 1423 (1979).

Under federal law a state must provide a recipient with a notice and fair hearing before it can deny or terminate medical assistance, 42 U.S.C.A. § 1396a(a)(3), 42 C.F.R. § 431.220, unless the action is dictated by a federal or state law requiring an automatic change, 42 C.F.R. § 431.220(b). The procedures afforded must provide due process, 42 C.F.R. § 431.205(d).

However, recipients are only guaranteed review of Medicaid decisions that directly affect their participation in the program or their benefits. Thus, even though termination of a nursing home from the program may force the transfer or discharge of a resident from a facility, the state need not afford the resident a hearing prior to the termination, since only the facility, not the resident, is terminated, O'Bannon v. Town Court Nursing Center, Inc., 447 U.S. 773, 100 S.Ct. 2467, 65 L.Ed.2d 506 (1980). The state also need not provide a hearing to a recipient who is transferred out of a Medicaid financed nursing home at the instance of the home or of a physician, even though the transfer results in lessened Medicaid benefits, Blum v. Yaretsky, 457 U.S. 991, 102 S.Ct. 2777, 73 L.Ed.2d 534 (1982).

Though review of state Medicaid decisions will generally be available in state court, most Medicaid litigation that raises federal statutory, regulatory, or constitutional issues is brought in federal court under 42 U.S.C.A. § 1983 and 28 U.S.C.A. § 1331. The Supreme Court has recently recognized the right of providers to sue state Medicaid agencies under 42 U.S.C.A. § 1983 to enforce federally created rights to reasonable reimbursement, Wilder v. Virginia Hospital Association, ___ U.S. ___, 110 S.Ct. 2510, 110 L.Ed.2d 455 (1990).

Litigation in federal court can lead to prospective declaratory or injunctive relief, but may a recipient denied benefits or a provider denied payment recover damages or restitution against the state? Is such relief barred by the 11th Amendment? Edelman v. Jordan, 415 U.S. 651, 94 S.Ct. 1347, 39 L.Ed.2d 662 (1974). Does the state consent to damage suits in federal court by agreeing to abide by the terms of the federal Medicaid act in paying providers? See Florida Department of Health and Rehabilitative Services v. Florida Nursing Home Association, 450 U.S. 147, 101 S.Ct. 1032, 67 L.Ed.2d 132 (1981), rehearing denied, 451 U.S. 933, 101 S.Ct. 2008, 68 L.Ed.2d 319 (1981); Perkins, Lawlor & Billey, That Was Then, This is Now: Reviewing the Supreme Court's Eleventh Amendment Activities, 23 Clearinghouse Rev. 966 (1989).

The multiplicity of actors involved in shaping the Medicaid program has resulted in incredible complexity. This complexity may benefit as well as burden the attorney involved in Medicaid litigation. Consider the following:

* * * HOW I LEARNED TO STOP WORRYING AND LOVE THE MEDICAID STATUTE

National Senior Citizens Law Center, Representing Older Persons: An
Advocate Manual, 23 (1985).

One of the few pleasant aspects of slogging through the federal Medicaid statute, regulations, and guidelines, and trying to understand their interrelationship with a given state's Medicaid program, is that the natural confusion which this effort engenders places one in the company of numerous distinguished jurists. The list of judges who have figuratively wept in the face of this program's complexity is a decidedly impressive one. Judge Friendly, describing a particularly arcane portion of the statute, called it "almost unintelligible to the uninitiated." Friedman v. Berger, 547 F.2d 724, 727 n. 7 (2d Cir.1976), cert. denied 430 U.S. 984 (1977). Justice Powell, discussing the Social Security Act in the context of a Medicaid case, described it as "Byzantine" and "among the most intricate ever drafted by Congress." Schweiker v. Gray Panthers, 453 U.S. 34, 43 (1981). Chief Justice Burger, in the unusual posture of the sole dissenter opposing a majority opinion authored by Justice Rehnquist, termed "the Medicaid program * * * a morass of bureaucratic complexity," and accused Court majority of "get[ting] lost in the Medicaid maze." Herweg v. Ray, 455 U.S. 265, 279, 282 (1982). District court judges have been no less kind; one called the Medicaid statute "an aggravated assault on the English language, resistant to attempts to understand it," Friedman v. Berger, 409 F.Supp. 1225, 1226 (S.D.N.Y.1976) while another, in perhaps the most abstruse and literary reference, referred to the federal Medicaid regulations as "so drawn that they have created a Serbonian bog from which the agencies are unable to extricate themselves." Feld v. Berger, 424 F.Supp. 1356, 1357 (S.D.N.Y.1976).

The point of this recital is not to needle the nation's judges for their inability to fathom this nearly incomprehensible system, but, rather, to underscore a phenomenon which, at one time or another, strikes all advocates forced to deal with the Medicaid statute. That is that understanding Medicaid is often, quite literally, impossible. The basic terminology alone is intimidating: categorically needy, medically needy, optional categorically needy, spenddowns, "209(b)" states, Pickle Amendment, comparability (vertical and horizontal), co-payments, amount-scope-and-duration, deeming, non-institutionalized spouses, personal needs allowance. The list goes on, and, to be sure, is probably no more confusing to the beginner than is any jumble of jargon in a given benefits program. But when experienced lawyers and respected judges are all befuddled by the nearly geometric possibilities created by the statute, it should encourage the "uninitiated," rather than discourage them, to wade into the morass.

There are a few things about Medicaid which can be stated with some certainty. On the other hand, there are many more to which the "right" answer is anyone's guess, so that the relatively knowledgeable Medicaid advocate is in an excellent position to present a convincing case. Instead of discouragement over the confusion which is Medicaid, newcomers should accept it as a given, and then welcome the opportunity to twist the statute, regulations, action transmittals, Medicaid Manual, state regulations, state transmittals, state Medicaid manuals, and whatever else is available to the best ends of their clients. The key concept about Medicaid is that no one really knows what it means—most especially the Health Care Financing Administration (HCFA) of the Department of Health and Human Services (DHHS), which is allegedly responsible for its implementation—so that everyone armed with a little knowledge, some equities, and confidence can go a long way.

III. THE UNINSURED AND UNCOMPENSATED CARE

About 31.5 million Americans [4], constituting 14.7% of the United States population under the age of 65, were uninsured in the fourth quarter of 1988, the most recent date for which data are available. During the 28 month period from February 1985 to August 1987, 63 million Americans, about 28% of the population, were uninsured for at least one month. These persons had no legal rights to health care financed by a third-party payer. For every person who is uninsured, another is underinsured, that is, does not have insurance to cover basic health care costs such as emergency services, physician office visits or hospital outpatient care.

The uninsured are young—one half were under the age of 25. More than half are employed, another quarter are dependents of employees, thus three quarters are attached to the work force. Most are poor, more than one third have incomes below the poverty level. Of the uninsured who are employed, most work for small businesses. Only 46% of private firms with fewer than ten employees offer health benefits, compared to 100% of those with more than 500 employees. Eighty-four percent of employed persons without health benefits work for employers with fewer than 26 employees. Workers in certain industries such as agriculture, forestry, fishery, and personal services, are most likely not to receive job related insurance. African–Americans are almost twice as likely as whites to be uninsured; Hispanics are even less likely than African–Americans to be insured. The uninsured population grew in the early 1980s as Medicaid enrollments were cut

4. Estimates range from 31 to 37 million, See Moyer, A Revised Look at the Number of Uninsured Americans, 8 Health Affairs 102 (Summer 1989) and Schwartz & Purcell, Letters: Counting Uninsured Americans, 8 Health Affairs 193 (Winter 1989). The figures used in the text are from the most recent Census Bureau publication on the subject, Bureau of the Census, Health Insurance Coverage, 1986–1988 (1990).

and first unemployment grew and then employment moved to service jobs where insurance is less likely. Since the mid–1980s the number of uninsured has fallen slowly.

The uninsured use less health services than the insured, and are more likely to receive health services in an institutional setting. In particular, they are less likely to use prenatal or preventive care. Adverse birth outcomes, such as low birth rate and fetal malnutrition, are, according to one study, 30% more common among the uninsured than among the insured. See, Braveman, et al., Adverse Outcomes and Lack of Health Insurance Among Newborns in An Eight–County Area of California, 1982–1986, 321 New Eng.J.Med. 508 (1989). Another study found that uninsured patients hospitalized for chest pain or circulatory disorders were far less likely than the insured to receive angiography, bypass grafting, or angioplasty. See, Wenneker, et al. The Association of Payer with Utilization of Cardiac Procedures in Massachusetts, 264 JAMA 1255 (1990).

When the uninsured need medical care (most typically for maternity care or accidents), they generally seek it from hospitals. While nearly 72% of charges billed by medical providers to uninsured patients are paid, another 28% are not. These unpaid charges, added to other bad debt and charity losses (such as unpaid coinsurance and deductibles from insured patients) and losses from underpayment by Medicare and Medicaid, resulted in $7.5 billion in uncompensated care provided by American hospitals in 1987, 5% of hospital expenses. The incidence of this burden is distributed very unevenly among hospitals: 5% of all hospitals provide 37% of uncompensated care. Teaching hospitals and public hospitals bear the majority of the losses.

The traditional solution to the problem of financing uncompensated care was charge-shifting: insured patients were charged more to cover the costs hospitals incurred in caring for the uninsured. In the competitive environment of the late 1980s charge-shifting has become increasingly difficult as insurers demand discounts and refuse to pay inflated charges. The only strategies left to hospitals that cannot shift charges to the insured are to reduce services (preferably those most used by the uninsured such as emergency rooms or obstetric programs); consume endowments or depreciation accounts (postponing capital improvements); or close.

Federal law has done little to address the problems on the uninsured and of uncompensated care. Medicaid has always been only a partial solution to the problem of the uninsured. Moreover, contraction of Medicaid expenditures in the late 1970s and early 1980s expanded the pool of the uninsured. Medicaid covered 65% of those below the poverty level in 1976, by 1984 it only covered 46%. Expansion of Medicaid eligibility in the late 1980s, discussed earlier in this chapter, may reverse this trend, but many persons in poverty are still not eligible. COBRA offers continuation coverage to some unemployed workers. ERISA, on the other hand, complicates state efforts to address the problems of the uninsured by limiting the ability of the states to regulate employment-related benefit plans.

The problems of the uninsured and of uncompensated care have traditionally been the responsibility of the states. State and local governments have long been involved in providing care to the medically indigent. In all but three states, state or local governments are obligated under state statutes or the state constitution to provide some health services to the medically indigent. State funding of these programs totaled 3.9 billion in 1982. Often indigent care has been provided through state or county hospitals. State and local government spent $11.6 billion on such hospitals in 1988. In other states it is provided in conjunction with state general assistance or general relief programs, which provide assistance to very poor persons who are not eligible for Medicaid. Aid to the Medically Indigent programs in other states have provided payments to hospitals that care for the medically indigent. See, regarding these laws, Dowell, State and Local Government Legal Responsibilities to Provide Medical Care for the Poor, 3 J.L. & Health 1 (1988–89).

In recent years there has been a great deal of activity at the state level to address the problem of access to health care for the uninsured. A few states have adopted catastrophic illness programs, which make the state the payer of last resort for poor persons once very high coinsurance and deductible amounts are paid. Eighteen states have adopted risk-sharing pools, in which insurers are required to provide health insurance for high-risk individuals and families who are otherwise uninsurable. ERISA threatens the viability of these pools, however, by forbidding them from requiring the participation of self-insured health plans. Hawaii has since the mid–1970s required employers to provide their employees with health insurance under a special exemption from ERISA. Massachusetts, in an attempt to circumvent ERISA, has enacted a "pay or play" requirement, under which employers that do not provide health insurance for their employees will be taxed to subsidize health insurance for the uninsured. Several states are experimenting with programs that would make insurance more affordable to small employers, effectively relying on incentives rather than mandates. Arizona is experimenting with allowing small employers to purchase HMO care through the state's Medicaid managed care plan; other states are assisting small employers to pool their risk to gain access to more affordable group policies. Finally, several states are offering subsidized insurance policies to some of their uninsured.

An alternate strategy is to focus on assisting institutions that provide uncompensated care rather than uninsured individuals. States with all-payer rate setting systems have used these systems to compensate institutions with large uncompensated care burdens, either by explicitly permitting charge-shifting or by giving these institutions access to a special pool of uncompensated care funds. Other states have established revenue pools, financed by taxes on hospitals and general funds, to subsidize hospitals with heavy uncompensated care losses.

See generally, on the uninsured: P. Butler, Too Poor to Be Sick (1988); Brown, Access to Health Insurance in the United States, 46 Medical Care Rev. 349 (1989); Wilensky, Filling the Gaps in Health Insurance: Impact on Competition, 7 Health Affairs 133 (Summer 1988). On uncompensated care, see F. Sloan, J. Blumstein, & J. Perrin, Uncompensated Hospital Care, Rights and Responsibilities (1986); Friedman, Hospital Uncompensated Care: Crisis? 262 JAMA 2975 (1989).

A. NATIONAL HEALTH INSURANCE

An obvious, though obviously controversial, solution to the problem of the uninsured is to adopt a national health insurance program. In fact, virtually every developed nation in the world except the United States assures universal access to medical care. This is accomplished through a variety of mechanisms, including direct government provision of health care, as in the United Kingdom and Sweden; government financing of privately provided health care, as in Canada; or mandatory employer provision of health insurance, as in Germany.

In the very recent past there has been a flurry of interest in creating a national health insurance program in the United States. This interest is stimulated, however, as much by increases in the cost of medical care as by problems with access to health care. For this reason, we will hold consideration of national health insurance until the next chapter.

B. THE OBLIGATION OF PROVIDERS TO FURNISH CARE

Another strategy is to compel providers to care for patients regardless of ability to pay.

1. Physicians' Duty to Treat

RICKS v. BUDGE

Supreme Court of Utah, 1937.
91 Utah 307, 64 P.2d 208.

EPHRAIM HANSON, JUSTICE.

This is an action for malpractice against the defendants who are physicians and surgeons at Logan, Utah, and are copartners doing business under the name and style of the "Budge Clinic." * * * [P]laintiff alleges that he was suffering from an infected right hand and was in immediate need of medical and surgical care and treatment, and there was danger of his dying unless he received such treatment; that defendants for the purpose of treating plaintiff sent him to the Budge Memorial Hospital at Logan, Utah; that while at the hospital and while he was in need of medical and surgical treatment, defendants refused to treat or care for plaintiff and abandoned his case. * * *

* * *

[T]he evidence shows that when plaintiff left the hospital on March 15th, Dr. Budge advised him to continue the same treatment that had been given him at the hospital, and that if the finger showed any signs of getting worse at any time, plaintiff was to return at once to Dr. Budge for further treatment; that on the morning of March 17th, plaintiff telephoned Dr. Budge, and explained the condition of his hand; that he was told by the doctor to come to his office, and in pursuance of the doctor's request, plaintiff reported at the doctor's office at 2 p.m. of that day. Dr. Budge again examined the hand and told plaintiff the hand was worse; he called in Dr. D.C. Budge, another of the defendants, who examined the hand, scraped it some, and indicated thereon where the hand should be opened. Dr. S.M. Budge said to plaintiff: "You have got to go back to the hospital." * * * Within a short time after the arrival of plaintiff, Dr. S.M. Budge arrived at the hospital. Plaintiff testified: "He [meaning Dr. S.M. Budge] came into my room and said, 'You are owing us. I am not going to touch you until that account is taken care of.'" (The account referred to was, according to plaintiff, of some years' standing and did not relate to any charge for services being then rendered.) Plaintiff testified that he did not know what to say to the doctor, but that he finally asked the doctor if he was going to take care of him, and the doctor replied: "No, I am not going to take care of you. I would not take you to the operating table and operate on you and keep you here thirty days, and then there is another $30.00 at the office, until your account is taken care of." Plaintiff replied: "If that is the idea, if you will furnish me a little help, I will try to move."

Plaintiff testified that this help was furnished, and that after being dressed, he left the Budge Memorial Hospital to seek other treatment. At that time it was raining. He walked to the Cache Valley Hospital, a few blocks away, and there met Dr. Randall, who examined the hand. Dr. Randall testified that when the plaintiff arrived at the Cache Valley Hospital, the hand was swollen with considerable fluid oozing from it; that the lower two-thirds of the forearm was red and swollen from the infection which extended up in the arm, and that there was some fluid also oozing from the back of the hand, and that plaintiff required immediate surgical attention; that immediately after the arrival of plaintiff at the hospital he made an incision through the fingers and through the palm of the hand along the tendons that led from the palm and followed those tendons as far as there was any bulging, and opened it up thoroughly all the way to the base of the hand and put drain tubes in. Plaintiff remained under the care of Dr. Randall for approximately a month. About two weeks after the plaintiff entered the Cache Valley Hospital, it became necessary to amputate the middle finger and remove about an inch of the metacarpal bone.

* * *

Defendants contend: (1) That there was no contract of employment between plaintiff and defendants and that defendants in the absence of a valid contract were not obligated to proceed with any treatment; and (2) that if there was such a contract, there was no evidence that the refusal of Dr. S.M. Budge to operate or take care of plaintiff resulted in any damage to plaintiff.

* * *

Under this evidence, it cannot be said that the relation of physician and patient did not exist on March 17th. It had not been terminated after its commencement on March 11th. When the plaintiff left the hospital on March 15th, he understood that he was to report to Dr. S.M. Budge if the occasion required and was so requested by the doctor. Plaintiff's return to the doctor's office was on the advice of the doctor. While at the doctor's office, both Dr. S.M. Budge and Dr. D.C. Budge examined plaintiff's hand and they ordered that he go at once to the hospital for further medical attention. That plaintiff was told by the doctor to come to the doctor's office and was there examined by him and directed to go to the hospital for further treatment would create the relationship of physician and patient. That the relationship existed at the time the plaintiff was sent to the hospital on March 17th cannot be seriously questioned.

We believe the law is well settled that a physician or surgeon, upon undertaking an operation or other case, is under the duty, in the absence of an agreement limiting the service, of continuing his attention, after the first operation or first treatment, so long as the case requires attention. The obligation of continuing attention can be terminated only by the cessation of the necessity which gave rise to the relationship, or by the discharge of the physician by the patient, or by the withdrawal from the case by the physician after giving the patient reasonable notice so as to enable the patient to secure other medical attention. A physician has the right to withdraw from a case, but if the case is such as to still require further medical or surgical attention, he must, before withdrawing from the case, give the patient sufficient notice so the patient can procure other medical attention if he desires.
[ ]

* * *

We cannot say as a matter of law that plaintiff suffered no damages by reason of the refusal of Dr. S.M. Budge to further treat him. The evidence shows that from the time plaintiff left the office of the defendants up until the time that he arrived at the Cache Valley Hospital his hand continued to swell; that it was very painful; that when he left the Budge Memorial Hospital he was in such condition that he did not know whether he was going to live or die. That both his mental and physical suffering must have been most acute cannot be questioned. While the law cannot measure with exactness such suffering and cannot determine with absolute certainty what damages, if any, plaintiff may be entitled to, still those are questions which a jury under proper instructions from the court must determine.

* * *

FOLLAND, JUSTICE (concurring in part, dissenting in part).

* * *

* * * The theory of plaintiff as evidenced in his complaint is that there was no continued relationship from the first employment but that a new relationship was entered into. He visited the clinic on March 17th; the Doctors Budge examined his hand and told him an immediate operation was necessary and for him to go to the hospital. I do not think a new contract was entered into at that time. There was no consideration for any implied promise that Dr. Budge or the Budge Clinic would assume the responsibility of another operation and the costs and expenses incident thereto. As soon as Dr. Budge reached the hospital he opened negotiations with the plaintiff which might have resulted in a contract, but before any contract arrangement was made the plaintiff decided to leave the hospital and seek attention elsewhere. As soon as he could dress himself he walked away. There is conflict in the evidence as to the conversation. Plaintiff testified in effect that Dr. Budge asked for something to be done about an old account. The doctor's testimony in effect was that he asked that some arrangement be made to take care of the doctor's bill and expenses for the ensuing operation and treatment at the hospital. The result, however, was negative. No arrangement was made. The plaintiff made no attempt whatsoever to suggest to the doctor any way by which either the old account might be taken care of or the expenses of the ensuing operation provided for. Of course, for the purpose of deciding the rightfulness of the trial court's action in directing a verdict, we must take plaintiff's version as true. The jury might well have found that the doctor's version was far more reasonable and the true version of what actually happened. Under either view Dr. Budge had a right to refuse to incur the obligation and responsibility incident to one or more operations and the treatment and attention which would be necessary. If it be assumed that the contract relationship of physician and patient existed prior to this conversation, either as resulting from the first employment or that there was an implied contract entered into at the clinic, yet Dr. Budge had the right with proper notice to discontinue the relationship. While plaintiff's condition was acute and needed immediate attention, he received such immediate attention at the Cache Valley Hospital. There was only a delay of an hour or two, and part of that delay is accounted for by reason of the fact that the doctor at the Cache Valley Hospital would not operate until some paper, which plaintiff says he did not read, was signed. Plaintiff said he could not sign it but that it was signed by his brother before the operation was performed. We are justified in believing that by means of this written obligation, provision was made for the expenses and fees about to be incurred. I am satisfied from my reading of the record that no injury or damage resulted from the delay occasioned by plaintiff leaving the Budge Hospital and going to the Cache Valley Hospital. He was not in such desperate condition but that he was able to walk the three or four blocks between the two hospitals. Dr. Randall testified he gave the same treatment and performed the same operation as would have been given and performed two or three hours earlier.

CHILDS v. WEIS

Court of Civil Appeals of Texas, 1969.
440 S.W.2d 104.

WILLIAMS, J.

On or about November 27, 1966 Daisy Childs, wife of J.C. Childs, a resident of Dallas County, was approximately seven months pregnant. On that date she was visiting in Lone Oak, Texas, and about two o'clock A.M. she presented herself to the Greenville Hospital emergency room. At that time she stated she was bleeding and had labor pains. She was examined by a nurse who identified herself as H. Beckham. According to Mrs. Childs, Nurse Beckham stated that she would call the doctor. She said the nurse returned and stated "that the Dr. said that I would have to go to my doctor in Dallas. I stated to Beckham that I'm not going to make it to Dallas. Beckham replied that yes, I would make it. She stated that I was just starting into labor and that I would make it. The weather was cold that night. About an hour after leaving the Greenville Hospital Authority I had the baby while in a car on the way to medical facilities in Sulphur Springs. The baby lived about 12 hours."

[Dr. Weis] said that he had never examined or treated Daisy Childs and in fact had never seen or spoken to either Daisy Childs or her husband, J.C. Childs, at any time in his life. He further stated that he had never at any time agreed or consented to the examination or treatment of either Daisy Childs or her husband. He said that on a day in November 1966 he recalled a telephone call received by him from a nurse in the emergency room at the Greenville Surgical Hospital; that the nurse told him that there was a negro girl in the emergency room having a "bloody show" and some "labor pains". He said the nurse advised him that this woman had been visiting in Lone Oak, and that her OB doctor lived in Garland, Texas, and that she also resided in Garland. The doctor said, "I told the nurse over the telephone to have the girl call her doctor in Garland and see what he wanted her to do. I knew nothing more about this incident until I was served with the citation and a copy of the petition in this lawsuit."

* * *

Since it is unquestionably the law that the relationship of physician and patient is dependent upon contract, either express or implied, a physician is not to be held liable for arbitrarily refusing to respond to a call of a person even urgently in need of medical or surgical assistance provided that the relation of physician and patient does not exist at the time the call is made or at the time the person presents himself for treatment.

* * *

Applying these principles of law to the factual situation here presented we find an entire absence of evidence of a contract, either express or implied, which would create the relationship of patient and physician as between Dr. Weis and Mrs. Childs. Dr. Weis, under these circumstances, was under no duty whatsoever to examine or treat Mrs. Childs. When advised by telephone that the lady was in the emergency room he did what seems to be a reasonable thing and inquired as to the identity of her doctor who had been treating her. Upon being told that the doctor was in Garland he stated that the patient should call the doctor and find out what should be done. This action on the part of Dr. Weis seems to be not only reasonable but within the bounds of professional ethics.

We cannot agree with appellant that Dr. Weis' statement to the nurse over the telephone amounted to an acceptance of the case and affirmative instructions which she was bound to follow. Rather than give instructions which could be construed to be in the nature of treatment, Dr. Weis told the nurse to have the woman call her physician in Garland and secure instructions from him.

The affidavit of Mrs. Childs would indicate that Nurse Beckham may not have relayed the exact words of Dr. Weis to Mrs. Childs. Instead, it would seem that Nurse Beckham told Mrs. Childs that the doctor said that she would "have to go" to her doctor in Dallas. Assuming this statement was made by Nurse Beckham, and further assuming that it contained the meaning as placed upon it by appellant, yet it is undisputed that such words were uttered by Nurse Beckham, and not by Dr. Weis. * * *

We have carefully reviewed this record in the light of the well established rules concerning judicial review of summary judgments and having done so we conclude that appellee has sustained his burden of demonstrating the nonexistence of issuable facts and that appellant could not recover against him, as a matter of law.

* * *

Affirmed.

HISER v. RANDOLPH

Court of Appeals of Arizona, 1980.
126 Ariz. 608, 617 P.2d 774.

JACOBSON, JUDGE.

* * *

[The trial court enters] summary judgment in favor of the defendant physician, Dr. W. Alan Randolph, and the decedent's spouse has appealed.

* * *

Mohave County General Hospital is the only hospital serving the community of Kingman, Arizona. It maintains an emergency room for the treatment of people in need of immediate medical service. Dr. Randolph and seven other doctors, comprising the medical profession in the Kingman area with admitting privileges at the hospital, established a program with the hospital by which each would take turns in manning the emergency room as the "on call physician" for a 12 hour period.

* * *

From the record it appears that plaintiff's wife, Bonita Hiser, went with her husband to the emergency room at the hospital at approximately 11:45 p.m. on June 12, 1973. She was in a semi-comatose condition and the nurse in charge of the emergency room evaluated her as appearing to be very ill. Mrs. Hiser had an acute diabetic condition described as juvenile onset diabetes of the "brittle" variety. She had been treated in the emergency room at the hospital on the preceding day by Dr. Arnold of Kingman, her regular physician.

The emergency room nurse, after viewing Mrs. Hiser, immediately contacted Dr. Randolph, the "on call physician" at that time. Upon being advised as to who the patient was, Dr. Randolph stated to the nurse, at 11:50 p.m., that he would not attend or treat Mrs. Hiser, and that the nurse should call Dr. Arnold. When the nurse called Dr. Arnold he responded by stating that he would not come to the hospital at that time and that the on call physician should attend Mrs. Hiser. The nurse relayed this information to Dr. Randolph who again refused to attend to or see Mrs. Hiser. The nurse then called Dr. Lingenfelter, Chief of Staff of the hospital. After a subsequent telephone conversation between Dr. Lingenfelter and Dr. Randolph in which Dr. Randolph reiterated that he would not treat Mrs. Hiser, Dr. Lingenfelter came to the hospital and attended Mrs. Hiser, arriving at approximately 12:30 a.m. Dr. Lingenfelter immediately commenced tests and treatment for Mrs. Hiser, whom he regarded as being very ill at the time. Dr. Lingenfelter stayed at the hospital throughout the night until Dr. Arnold arrived in the morning. Mrs. Hiser died at 11:00 a.m. on June 13.

As to the reason for Dr. Randolph's refusal to attend to Mrs. Hiser, a factual dispute exists. Dr. Randolph testified by deposition that the refusal was based upon his inability to adequately treat diabetes. From the evidence presented, however, a trier of fact could conclude that the refusal was based upon a personal animosity between Dr. Randolph and Mrs. Hiser or the fact that Mrs. Hiser's husband was a lawyer. Because the fact that Dr. Randolph refused to treat is undisputed and because of the posture in which this matter reaches us, we assume the refusal was medically unjustified.

* * *

In examining this issue we start with the general rule, with which we agree, that a medical practitioner is free to contract for his services as he sees fit and in the absence of prior contractual obligations, he can refuse to treat a patient, even under emergency situations.[1] [ ]

The question remains whether Dr. Randolph has contracted away this right, while being the doctor "on call" in charge of the emergency room at Mohave General Hospital and being paid the sum of $100 a day to perform those services.

* * *

In our opinion, Dr. Randolph, by assenting to these bylaws [describing the duties of the on-call physician] and rules and regulations, and accepting payment from the hospital to act as the emergency room doctor "on call," personally became bound "to insure that all patients * * * treated in the Emergency Room receive the best possible care," and agreed to insure "in the case of emergency the provisional diagnosis shall be started as soon after admission as possible." Moreover, these services were to be performed for all persons whom the "hospital shall admit * * * suffering from all types of disease."

* * *

Reversed and remanded.

Notes and Questions

1. Why did the doctor refuse to treat Mr. Ricks? Ms. Childs? Ms. Hiser? How did the courts approach the claims of the plaintiffs? On what foundation did they place the doctor's duty to treat? Did they examine the reason for the doctor's refusal to treat the patient in these cases? Should the courts distinguish among such cases on the basis of the reason for the physician's refusal?

Persons with AIDS often have limited access to health care for a variety of reasons. Although some persons with AIDS need very specialized treatment, most need the same medical services as other generally healthy individuals (such as dental care) and as other chronically or intermittently disabled patients. In 1988, the AMA Council on Ethical and Judicial Affairs announced that "a physician may not ethically refuse to treat a patient whose condition is within the physician's current realm of competence solely because the patient is (HIV) seropositive." Council Report on Ethical Issues, 259 JAMA 1360 (1988). What is the meaning of the AMA's use of the phrase "solely because [he or she] is seropositive" in describing unethical refusals to treat? Does the AMA's statement address

1. We speak here only of legal obligations. As to ethical obligations, see § 5, Code of Ethics of the American Medical Association which in part provides:

"A physician may choose whom he shall serve. In an emergency, however, he *should* render service to the best of his ability." (Emphasis added.)

the actual risk of transmission in certain medical situations? Does it intend to address unsupported fears of transmission? Homophobia? Racism? Should any health care decisions be based on the risk of transmission from a particular procedure? Again, should the reason for refusing to take a patient make a difference?

The AMA Council statement builds on a historical ethical duty to treat patients in "times of pestilence," even at jeopardy of the physician's own life, found in the first Code of Ethics adopted by the AMA in 1847. In 1912, the AMA asserted that physicians have the freedom to choose which patients they will serve. In the 1957 Code of Ethics, the duty to treat patients described in 1847 was eliminated, as was the previously stated duty to provide charity care. See, Friedlander, On The Obligation of Physicians to Treat AIDS: Is There a Historical Basis?, 12 Rev.Infect.Dis. 191 (1990). Some have argued that a compulsory physician-patient relationship violates doctors' personal and professional autonomy and would result in doctors' leaving areas that have a high number of AIDS patients. See, Zinberg, AIDS: The Duty to Treat: A Physician–Lawyer's Perspective, 56 Mt. Sinai J.Med. 259 (1988).

A few states have passed statutes that prohibit individual health care providers from refusing to treat patients because they have AIDS. See, for example, Wisc.Stat. § 146.024 which provides, *inter alia:*

No health care provider [including doctors, nurses, dentists and others], home health agency or inpatient health care facility may do any of the following with respect to an individual who has acquired immunodeficiency syndrome or has a positive test for the presence of HIV, antigen or nonantigenic products of HIV or an antibody to HIV, solely because the individual has HIV infection or an illness or medical condition that is caused by, arises from or is related to HIV infection:

(a) Refuse to treat the individual, if his or her condition is within the scope of licensure or certification of the health care provider, home health agency or inpatient health care facility.

(b) Provide care to the individual at a standard that is lower than that provided other individuals with like medical needs.

(c) Isolate the individual unless medically necessary.

(d) Subject the individual to indignity, including humiliating, degrading or abusive treatment.

Persons violating this provision would be liable to the patient for actual damages plus exemplary damages of up to $5000. For individual health care providers, the court must consider their ability to pay.

In other states, patients with AIDS have sued doctors over refusal to treat under state statutes prohibiting discrimination against the handicapped. One issue in this litigation is whether seropositivity is a handicap within the meaning of the particular statute. In addition, many such statutes do not explicitly prohibit doctors from discriminating in selecting patients but, rather, prohibit discrimination in "public accommodations." In New York, a court reversed a Human Rights Commission decision in which the Commission held that it had jurisdiction over a private dentist's office within the state's statute prohibiting discrimination in public accommodations. An appellate court, however, held that the question of whether a private practitioner was a "public accommodation" within the meaning of the statute would have to be decided in an administrative hearing before review by a court. Hurwitz v. N.Y.C.Com'n on Human Rights, 159 A.D.2d 417, 553 N.Y.S.2d 323 (1990). See also, Law's Coverage of Dentist's Offices Unclear After Rulings in AIDS Cases, 5(6) AIDS Policy and Law 1 (April 4, 1990). For a comprehensive review of AIDS discrimination legislation see, S. Renner, J. Parry & R. Horowitz, AIDS and Persons With Developmental Disabilities: The Legal Perspective (1989). The Americans with Disabilities Act of 1990 prohibits discrimination in public accommodations against persons with disabilities. The statutory definition of "public accommodations" specifically includes doctor's offices. 101 Pub.L. 336 (1990).

2. In a footnote in *Hiser,* the court referred to the ethical duty of a doctor to render emergency treatment and noted the distinction between legal obligation and ethical obligation. This approach is typical of common law cases involving claims that a physician has a duty to treat. Would you support a statute that required physicians to render a certain amount of charity care as a condition of licensure? Would you support such a rule established by a local medical society as a condition of membership? By a hospital, as a condition of staff privileges?

See, for example, Massachusetts Medical Society v. Dukakis, 815 F.2d 790 (1st Cir.1987); cert. denied, 484 U.S. 896, 108 S.Ct. 229, 98 L.Ed.2d 188 (1987), in which the U.S. Court of Appeals for the First Circuit upheld a Massachusetts licensure requirement that doctors treating Medicare patients accept the Medicare fee as payment in full and may not require the patient to pay an additional amount. Does this raise the same issues as a duty to provide charity care? See also, the Emergency Medical Treatment and Active Labor Act, 42 U.S.C.A. § 1395dd, discussed infra, which subjects both doctors and hospitals to civil fines for refusing to provide emergency care within a facility.

3. Once the court in *Hiser* decided that Dr. Randolph had a duty to treat Mrs. Hiser, it went on to discuss whether Dr. Randolph's breach of this duty, and thus the 40-minute delay in treatment, was the proximate cause of Mrs. Hiser's death. The court held that the plaintiff must prove that Mrs. Hiser "probably died as a result of the 40 minutes delay in treatment." At 778. It stated that "the mere loss of an unspecified increment of the chance for survival is, of itself, insufficient to meet the standard of probability." At 779. Would you support changing the standard from "probability" to "possibility"? See discussion of the problem of causation and damages in Chapter 2.

4. The physician may be relieved of abandonment liability for a variety of reasons suggested in the caselaw, including:

1. mutual consent;

2. explicit dismissal by the patient;

3. services required by the patient that are outside the physician's competence and training;

4. services outside the scope of the original doctor-patient agreement, where the physician has limited the contract to a type of procedure, to an office visit, or to consultation only;

5. failure of the patient to cooperate with the physician.

The "lack of cooperation" cases require actions by the patient that suggest an implied unilateral termination of the relationship by the patient. This may occur for example when the patient refuses to comply with the prescribed course of treatment or fails to return for further treatment. See, e.g., Payton v. Weaver, 131 Cal.App.3d 38, 182 Cal.Rptr. 225 (1982).

Problem: Cheryl Hanachek

Cheryl Hanachek, a resident of Boston, discovered she was pregnant during an "action" called by the city's obstetricians in protest against rising malpractice insurance rates. Ms. Hanachek first called Dr. Cunetto, who had been her obstetrician for the birth of her first child two years earlier. Dr. Cunetto's receptionist informed Ms. Hanachek that Dr. Cunetto was not able to take any new patients because her practice was "full." In fact, Dr. Cunetto had limited her practice due to her patient load.

About two weeks later, Ms. Hanachek called Dr. Simms, who had been recommended by her friends. Dr. Simms' receptionist told Ms. Hanachek that Dr. Simms was not taking any new patients so long as his malpractice insurance rates were so high and that he was even considering discontinuing his obstetrical practice. Ms. Hanachek reported to the receptionist that she was having infrequent minor cramping, and the receptionist told her that this was "nothing to worry about at this stage." Later that night Ms. Hanachek was admitted to the hospital on an emergency basis. Ms. Hanachek was in shock from blood loss due to a ruptured ectopic pregnancy. As a result of the rupture and other complications, Ms. Hanachek underwent a hysterectomy.

She has brought suit against Dr. Cunetto and Dr. Simms. If you were representing Ms. Hanachek, how would you proceed in arguing and proving your case?

2. Hospitals' Duty to Provide Treatment

a. State Law

THOMPSON v. SUN CITY COMMUNITY HOSPITAL, INC.

Supreme Court of Arizona, 1984.
141 Ariz. 597, 688 P.2d 605.

FELDMAN, J.

[Michael Jessee, plaintiff's 13–year–old son, suffered a transected or partially transected femoral artery which interrupted the flow of blood to the leg. Upon arrival at the emergency room of private Boswell Memorial Hospital fluids and blood were administered. Two surgeons agreed upon consultation that Jessee needed surgery. The emergency room physician determined that Jessee was "medically transferable" but stated that "Michael Jessee was transferred for economic reasons after we found him to be medically transferable." The orthopedic surgeon agreed that he was transferable. Jessee was transferred to County Hospital where he underwent surgery. He suffers residual impairment to the leg and claims that the injury was caused by the delay in surgery. Hospital counsel stipulated that the plaintiff was transferred for "financial reasons * * * no question about it."]

THE STANDARD OF CARE

The Hospital

In this state, the duty which a hospital owes a patient in need of emergency care is determined by the statutes and regulations interpreted by this court in *Guerrero v. Copper Queen Hospital*, 112 Ariz. 104, 537 P.2d 1329 (1975). Construing the statutory and regulatory scheme governing health care and the licensing of hospitals as of 1972, we held that it was the "public policy of this state" that a general "hospital may not deny emergency care to any patient without cause." *Id.* at 106, 537 P.2d at 1331.

In *Guerrero*, we referred primarily to former A.R.S. § 36–405(A) in construing the statutes governing the licensing of hospitals. *Id.* We then referred to specific regulations promulgated under the authority of that statute. *Id.* at 106 n. 1, n. 2, 537 P.2d at 1331 n. 1, n. 2. Subsequently, as a part of a general rewriting of title 36 in 1973, the Director of Health Services was required to adopt regulations for the licensure of health care facilities. A.R.S. § 36–405.

As guidelines for minimum requirements, the director was mandated to use the standards of the Joint Commission for Accreditation of Hospitals (JCAH). * * * The emergency services section of the JCAH [manual] states that:

> no patient should arbitrarily be transferred if the hospital where he was initially seen has means for adequate care of his problem.

JCAH, *Accreditation Manual for Hospitals* 69 (1976). The "Patient's Rights" section of the JCAH manual makes it clear that the financial resources of a patient are among the "arbitrary" considerations within the contemplation of the above language:

> no person should be denied impartial access to treatment or accommodations that are available and *medically indicated,* on the basis of such considerations as . . . the nature of the source of payment for his care.

Id. at 23 (emphasis supplied).

[The court discussed the statutory duty of the county government to pay for the emergency treatment of indigent patients, concluding that this duty resolved a serious financial problem for hospitals.]

* * * Interpreting the standard of care in accordance with the public policy defined in *Guerrero,* we hold that reasonable "cause" for transfer before completion of emergency care refers to medical consid-

erations relevant to the welfare of the patient and not economic considerations relevant to the welfare of the hospital. A transfer based on the forbidden criterion of economic considerations may be for the convenience of the hospital but it is hardly "medically indicated." Given the duty imposed in Arizona—that a general hospital may not deny emergency care to any person without valid cause—there are three possible defenses a hospital may raise in an appropriate fact situation: (1) that the hospital is not obligated (or capable) under its state license to provide the necessary emergency care, (2) there is a valid medical cause to refuse emergency care, (3) there is no true emergency requiring care and thus no emergency care which is medically indicated.

Neither of the first two defenses are at issue under the facts of this case. The third is more troublesome. Many people who enter the doors of an emergency room do not truly require "emergency care." The statutes and regulations do not apply to those who go to an "emergency room;" they apply to those in need of "emergency care." What constitutes an emergency is a matter of some disagreement. There are various definitions; the need for immediate attention seems to be the common thread. Ordinarily it is for the jury to determine the factual question of the duration of an emergency and the treatment modalities that are a necessary component of emergency care.

Given the stipulation that Boswell ordered the transfer of Jessee to County Hospital because of financial reasons, the relevant inquiries in the case at bench did not relate to "stabilization" and "transferability," but rather to the nature and duration of the emergency. The question was whether, before transfer, the hospital had rendered the emergency care medically indicated for this patient. The facts of this case indicate that emergency surgery was indicated for Jessee. Dr. Hillegas testified that "once the diagnosis is made, you should move on with definitive treatment," and that "you want to repair the arterial injury just as soon as you can." Dr. Lipsky knew Jessee needed surgery. Dr. Sabanas believed Jessee needed emergency surgery. Dr. Krigsten, an orthopedic surgeon called to testify on behalf of Dr. Sabanas, believed it would have been advantageous for two surgical teams to have worked simultaneously on Jessee at County Hospital in order to promptly revasculate the leg. Plaintiff's experts were even more insistent on the need for emergency surgery. Thus, the judge's view that the patient's condition was one requiring emergency care which included surgery to repair a transected artery was clearly supported by the evidence in addition to the defendant's concessions on this issue. Given this view of the case it was error for the trial judge to refuse plaintiff's request for a peremptory instruction on the issue of the hospital's breach of its duty of care. The undisputed evidence established that the patient was transferred for financial reasons while emergency care was medically indicated. As a matter of law this was a breach of the hospital's duty. Thus, the only question before the jury on the issue of the hospital's liability was whether its breach of duty was a cause of some compensable damage.

* * *

[The judgment in favor of the hospital was reversed and the case remanded.]

Notes and Questions

1. In a footnote, the Arizona Supreme Court distinguishes the statutory basis of *Thompson* from Wilmington Gen. Hospital v. Manlove, 54 Del. (4 Storey) 15, 174 A.2d 135 (1961), in which the Delaware Supreme Court found a common law duty on the part of a hospital to provide emergency care:

> "It may be conceded that a private hospital is under no legal obligation to the public to maintain an emergency ward * * *.
>
> * * * If a person, seriously hurt, applies for such aid at an emergency ward, relying on the established custom to render it, is it still the right of the hospital to turn him away without any reason?
>
> Such a set of circumstances is analogous to the case of the negligent termination of gratuitous services, which creates a tort liability."   At 139.

In New Biloxi Hospital, Inc. v. Frazier, 245 Miss. 185, 146 So.2d 882 (1962), the Mississippi Supreme Court held a hospital liable for the death of a patient who had been taken to the hospital's emergency room by ambulance after suffering a gunshot wound. The patient remained untreated in the emergency room for two hours, despite heavy blood loss and shock, and died twenty-five minutes after transfer to a Veterans Administration hospital. The Mississippi Supreme Court based their holding on the hospital's breach of the duty to exercise reasonable care once treatment was "undertaken." The Court found that the hospital had undertaken treatment of the patient by virtue of the patient's presence in the emergency room for two hours and his being recorded as an emergency room patient. Do the varying theories of these cases make a difference in litigating a duty to provide emergency care? The scope of that duty? For an overview and discussion of the emergency room cases, see Note, To Treat or Not to Treat: A Hospital's Duty to Provide Emergency Care, 15 U.C.D.L.Rev. 1047 (1982); Dougherty, The Right to Health Care: First Aid in the Emergency Room, 4 Pub.L.Forum 101 (1984); and Note, The Private Hospital's Role in the Dumping of the Indigent, 4 Pub.L.Forum 141 (1984).

For an excellent analysis of the history and scope of this legal doctrine see, Rothenberg, Who Cares? The Evolution of the Legal Duty to Provide Emergency Care, 26 Hous.L.Rev. 21 (1989).

2. Several other states have enacted statutes requiring hospitals to maintain emergency rooms or requiring that certain hospitals must provide emergency treatment. See, e.g., N.Y.—McKinney's Pub. Health Law § 2805–b(2).

3. A recent empirical study of emergency room patient "dumping" reported that transfers from private hospitals to the public hospital in the

District of Columbia increased from 169 in 1981 to nearly 1000 in 1984. In Chicago, the number of such transfers rose from 1295 in 1980 to 6769 in 1983. In a detailed study of transfers to Cook County Hospital's emergency room, the study found that the average delay in treatment was 5.1 hours (ranging from 1 to 18 hours, with a median of 4.6) and that the proportion of patients transferred to the medical service who died (9.4%) was more than twice that of medical-service patients who had not been transferred (3.8%). The mortality rate for surgical patients did not differ between those who had been transferred and those who had not. Comparison of fatality rates suffers from the fact that the transferred and nontransferred patient may have different characteristics. The investigators reported that 24% of transferred patients were in an unstable condition at the transfer-ring hospital although they noted that "stability" is a clinical judgment. Seventy-seven percent of the transferred patients were Black and 12%, Hispanic. Lack of insurance was the reason for 87% of the transfers. Medical care for the 467 transferred patients studied cost Cook County Hospital $3.35 million, of which $2.81 million would not be reimbursed by insurance or federal health care programs. The study projected unreim-bursed costs to Cook County Hospital for emergency room transfer patients *alone* of $24.1 million in 1983, 12% of the total operating budget. Schiff, et al., Transfers to a Public Hospital, 314 New Eng.J.Med. 552 (1986).

A 1988 study of a publicly subsidized hospital in Memphis found that, during the 92 day study, private hospitals made 190 requests to transfer patients to the public facility. Almost all patients transferred (91%) were sent for primarily economic reasons. One fourth of these patients were unstable, according to explicit clinical criteria, upon arrival at the public hospital. See, Kellerman & Hackman Emergency Department Patient "Dumping": An Analysis of Interhospital Transfers to the Regional Medi-cal Center at Memphis, Tennessee, 78 Am.J.Pub.Health 1287 (1988).

b. *Federally Imposed Obligations*

OWENS v. NACOGDOCHES COUNTY HOSPITAL DISTRICT

United States District Court, Eastern District of Texas, 1990.
741 F.Supp. 1269.

Justice, District Judge

Plaintiff has brought suit against the hospital and its board of directors in their official capacities, seeking damages, and declaratory and injunctive relief pursuant to 42 U.S.C. § 1395dd, the Emergency Medical Treatment and Active Labor Act, which forms part of the Consolidated Omnibus Budget Reconciliation Act of 1986 (COBRA).

It is clear beyond peradventure first, that no attempt was made by defendant hospital to comply with the transfer requirements of § 1395dd; second, that the sole reason for the instruction to Rebecca Owens to go to John Sealy Hospital was that she was without funds; third, that this action constituted "dumping," the very evil which § 1395dd was designed to prevent; fourth, that this incident was not an isolated one, but part of a pattern of dumpings of indigent patients that continued virtually until the time of trial in this civil action—a pattern caused by the unwillingness of defendant hospital to take the steps requisite for adequate performance of its statutory responsibilities for the care of indigent patients under both federal and state law; and finally, that what occurred to Rebecca Owens is capable of repetition, yet might evade review. Accordingly, judgment in this civil action will be entered for plaintiff, damages and attorney's fees in accordance with the stipulation of the parties will be awarded to her, and defendant hospital will be permanently enjoined from refusing her delivery in any future pregnancy in violation of 42 U.S.C. § 1395dd.

I. BACKGROUND—42 U.S.C. § 1395DD

* * * The Act was a response to a national epidemic of "dumping," the practice by hospitals of refusing emergency care to indigent patients outright or of transferring such patients, without regard to the necessity for stabilizing their condition, to other—typically public—hospitals. [ ].

* * *

[The court describes the provisions of the Act, which was amended after the violation that is the subject of this case. The transfer here, according to the court, would also violate the Act as amended.]

* * *

The definitional section of the Act clearly establishes the basis for judging the acts of the physician and hospital. That is, the physician cannot, by a mere assertion that in his judgment neither an emergency medical situation nor active labor exists, evade or negate the plain intent of the statute. To hold otherwise would render the statutory scheme merely precatory, which, as the above citation of the history of the Act makes clear, is not what Congress intended.

II. NARRATIVE OF EVENTS

Rebecca Owens, a sixteen year old indigent female resident of Nacogdoches County, was pregnant with her first child in 1987. During the course of her pregnancy she received pre-natal care and counseling from the East Texas Health Services Clinic in Lufkin, Texas, under the auspices of the Maternal and Infant Health Improvement Act (M.I.H.I.A.) program, a program established by the State of Texas to provide such services for indigent, and especially adolescent, expectant mothers.

All pertinent records concerning Rebecca's pre-natal care were turned over to the Owens family by the clinic at the end of July, 1987. Further, the East Texas Health Services clinic advised the Owenses "from day one that [Rebecca] could go to any county hospital," to deliver her child.

On the afternoon of August 3, 1987, Rebecca Owens began to experience labor pains. At approximately 3:00 p.m., she went to the emergency room at Memorial Hospital. After initial processing, she was taken to the Labor and Delivery room, where she was examined by Dr. Bruce Thompson.

In the course of his examination, Dr. Thompson relied upon the notes of the nurse who had made the preliminary examination for his conclusion that her water bag had not burst and her membranes were intact. He did not check this conclusion by performing an acidity test, a test which by his testimony would have taken "minutes" and cost "a few dollars." The whole of his instruction to Rebecca Owens was to go to Galveston, to the University of Texas Medical Branch at John Sealy Hospital, and not to speed getting there.

Dr. Thompson's diagnosis on August 3, 1987, was that Rebecca Owens was in early, latent labor. Under cross-examination, Dr. Thompson repeatedly admitted that Rebecca Owens was not in false labor.

Dr. Thompson did not call John Sealy Hospital to alert them that Rebecca Owens was on her way, and to make certain that John Sealy had a bed for her and was willing to accept her. He did not write a transfer memo, listing in writing his reasons for judging that the transfer's benefits outweighed its risks. He did not provide any medical treatment to minimize the risks to the mother and baby, unless one counts as medical treatment his advice that Rebecca Owens not speed to Galveston. He did not offer, or provide, an ambulance and crew or any other necessary and medically appropriate life support measures. Indeed, when asked how she was to transport herself to Galveston, he shrugged his shoulders. He does not appear to have provided her with the medical records to give John Sealy Hospital, which, even were one to accept his claim that he did not have the M.I.H.I.A. records, would have included those records generated in the emergency and labor and delivery rooms at Memorial on August 3, 1987.

After being told that she would not be admitted to the hospital, Rebecca Owens was in a state of some fear and confusion. She sat in the hallway at the hospital until approximately 5:30 p.m., when a nurse came up to her and told her she was supposed to be on her way to Galveston. At that point, she walked across the street to her mother's place of employment. According to Betty Owens, her daughter was "doubled over in pain." Thereafter she went to the office of East Texas Legal Services where she filled out some papers, including an application for pregnancy care. She then went to her mother's house, and subsequently to the home of Gary Dempsey, the father of her child. At some point during the afternoon, she and Geneva Dempsey, Gary Dempsey's aunt, timed her contractions. According to their calculations, the contractions were approximately 3 minutes apart.

That evening, Rebecca Owens and Gary Dempsey, who were apparently unaware that the efforts of East Texas Legal Services to obtain a temporary restraining order in this civil action were bearing fruit, went to the home of Gary Dempsey's grandfather, from whom they borrowed

$100.00 for the trip to Galveston, and departed for John Sealy Hospital in the middle of the night in a 1976 Pinto in bad condition. They arrived on the morning of August 4, 1987. At John Sealy, according to Rebecca Owen's testimony, the doctors examined her to see the extent of her dilation and had her walk around. She was told she would not be admitted because she was not dilated to three centimeters. The medical records of John Sealy Hospital reflect that she was in early labor, and that the fundal height of her baby—one of the measures by which the size of the baby in the womb is determined—was thirty-three inches.

While Rebecca Owens and Gary Dempsey were driving to Galveston, the temporary restraining order enjoining Memorial Hospital from refusing to deliver her child already referred to was issued. Dr. Thompson became aware of the temporary restraining order at midnight on August 3, but did not look at it until the following day. He was, as a result of seeing the temporary restraining order, fearful of the possibility of a malpractice suit. He did not want to deliver Rebecca Owens. He admits to anger at the prospect of having to deliver Rebecca Owens.

Rebecca Owens became aware of the temporary restraining order after her return from Galveston. Her bag of water ruptured on August 7. She returned to Memorial that afternoon. Dr. Thompson administered Oxytocin to speed her contractions, and Christopher Dempsey was born at 5:52 p.m. on August 7, 1987. When Christopher was born, the records indicate a nuchal cord—that is, the umbilical cord was wrapped around his neck. According to Dr. Thompson, it is not certain whether the cord was around the baby's neck on August 3.

According to the testimony of Rebecca Owens and Mamie Dempsey, the mother of Gary Dempsey, Dr. Thompson engaged in an abusive tirade against Rebecca Owens in the delivery room, denouncing her for involving a lawyer and a federal court. Dr. Thompson does not deny that the incident occurred, but avers that he has no memory of it. Considering the weight of the evidence and the relative credibility of the parties, the court finds it established as a matter of fact that Dr. Bruce Thompson engaged in the abusive and vilificatory language alleged.

As a result of the acts of Memorial Hospital and Dr. Bruce Thompson, Rebecca Owens asserts that she suffered great mental anguish and fear, both on the night of August 3 and 4 of 1987, during the birth of her child, and thereafter, and remains gravely concerned as to whether she can deliver future children at Memorial Hospital. The court accepts the testimony of Rebecca Owens, and finds as a matter of fact that sending Rebecca Owens, a sixteen year old girl pregnant with her first child who was experiencing labor pains, to a hospital two hundred miles away in a 1976 Ford Pinto, did occasion her great fear, mental anguish, and emotional distress.

III.   TRANSFER REQUIREMENTS UNDER 42 U.S.C. § 1395DD

[Defendants] contend that because Rebecca Owens was a M.I.H.I.A. patient, and because the University of Texas–Medical Branch at John Sealy Hospital in Galveston had, as Memorial did not, a contract to provide delivery services under M.I.H.I.A., Rebecca Owens was a patient of John Sealy Hospital; hence, they argue that the direction to go to John Sealy cannot be a transfer.

* * *

Contrary to defendants' assertions, however, Rebecca Owens was not a patient of John Sealy Hospital on August 3, 1987. She had not presented herself for admission to John Sealy Hospital. She had come to Nacogdoches Memorial Hospital. She was obviously Memorial's patient, and defendants' artful quibbling on this point avails them nothing. The definition of "transfer" unquestionably encompasses the direction to proceed to Galveston.

This is yet clearer when one considers that Rebecca Owens had never been a patient of John Sealy Hospital. She had received no treatment or care at John Sealy Hospital. All her pre-natal care had occurred at the East Texas Health Clinic in Lufkin, Texas. The blanket equation that a M.I.H.I.A. patient was a high risk patient to be sent to Galveston on which Dr. Thompson relied had no necessary warrant in her case, and was, as he admitted, not based on his examination of her.

* * *

Given that the order to go to Galveston was a transfer order, it is apparent that it violated all the standards set down for a transfer in the Act, as the narrative of events has already noted. * * *

As to the requirement of providing adequate transportation for the transfer, it is uncontroverted that no transport was provided. At best, the defendants rely on a document which asserts that according to Rebecca Owens, she had a car. Even were one willing to accept the assertions of this document, a 1976 Ford Pinto with no medical equipment, whose only other occupant besides the patient is her boyfriend, is not the equivalent of an ambulance for the purposes of the Anti–Dumping Act.

IV.   REASONS FOR THE TRANSFER

Defendants offer two arguments as reasons for the transfer of Rebecca Owens on August 3, 1987. First, they argue that Rebecca Owens announced that it was her intent to go to John Sealy Hospital when she came to Memorial. Second, they argue that it was preferable for Rebecca Owens, because she was a M.I.H.I.A. patient, to deliver at John Sealy Hospital since it is a Level–III hospital with a neonatal unit. Neither of these arguments is availing.

* * *

Many of the defendants' claims that—despite her testimony, the testimony of her mother and Gary Dempsey, and the inferences any person of ordinary common sense would make based on her actions on August 3, 1987—Rebecca Owens in fact wished to go to Galveston and asserted that she had adequate transportation to go to Galveston are based on a document labelled as an "OB Outpatient observation record" for Rebecca Owens on August 3, 1987. * * * However, as the cross examination of the nurse who alleged that she had prepared the document demonstrated, there are clear indications that the statements on which the defense relies were written in after the fact, and a very strong suggestion attaches that statements in this document were deliberately fabricated for the purposes of this litigation. * * *

Given the relative credibility of the witnesses and the inferences that may be drawn from the behavior of Rebecca Owens on August 3, 1987, the court finds that as a matter of fact, Rebecca Owens expressed no intent to go to Galveston, Texas to deliver her child, but rather requested that she be delivered at Memorial Hospital.

* * *

Dr. Thompson testified that his conclusion that there were high risks associated with Rebecca Owens's delivery was based on the fact that she had been a M.I.H.I.A. patient. He further testified that had she not been a M.I.H.I.A. patient, he would not have sent her to Galveston.

When asked to list the risks he thought possible on the basis of the fact that Rebecca Owens was a M.I.H.I.A. patient which would have justified in sending her to Galveston, Dr. Thompson, after some hesitation, was able to list four problems: that there were problems that might be associated with poor nutrition; that there was a potential for Rebecca Owens to have a growth-retarded baby; that there was a possibility that Rebecca Owens might require a Caesarean section; and that it was possible that Rebecca Owens might have a sexually transmitted disease such as Acquired Immune Deficiency Syndrome (AIDS). Under further questioning, however, Dr. Thompson admitted that poor nutrition was not corrigible during labor. He further agreed that he was fully capable of performing a caesarean section, had Rebecca Owens required one. He testified that, if a women whom he thought likely to require a Caesarean section were to go into labor, it "would not be the thing to do" to have her drive to a hospital four hours away, because there were serious risks that, should the mother give birth on the road in such a situation, either the mother or the child, or both, could die.

Dr. Thompson further admitted that he had no reason on August 3, 1987, to suspect that Rebecca Owens had AIDS, and knew of no reason related to AIDS to transfer Rebecca Owens. He finally relied on one possible risk which would justify a transfer to John Sealy Hospital—the possibility that Rebecca Owen's child was a growth-retarded, or small for gestational age (SGA) baby. On further examination, however, Dr.

Thompson testified that Memorial Hospital could have provided the nutrition necessary to counteract growth retardation, and that he could have competently delivered an SGA baby at Memorial. He further testified that it would be better for an SGA baby to be born at Memorial Hospital than in a car bound for Galveston. He stated at least twice that SGA was "not a concern of [his] back August 3rd" and was not a medical reason to transport on August 3, 1987. * * *

* * *

The explanations proffered by Dr. Thompson for the transfer are best described as inadequate, stumbling and incredible. The assertion that the risks associated with sending a frightened adolescent girl on a four hour trip by private car are markedly less severe than those of admitting her for delivery, when the only serious medical risk the physician identifies is stunted growth—a risk which, under further questioning, he then admits was not his concern at the time—is entirely unworthy of credence.

* * *

Much of the defendants' case rests on the fact that Rebecca Owens did not deliver her child for four days.

[I]mminent childbirth does not exhaust the statutory meaning of active labor pursuant to 42 U.S.C. § 1395dd. When it is established, as it is by Dr. Thompson's testimony, that the woman was in labor, the inquiry turns to the questions of whether there was sufficient time for a transfer, and most pertinently to the question of whether the transfer posed undue risk to mother and child.

There is no reason to recite yet again the dangers which all the physicians agreed would have attended a birth somewhere on the two hundred miles of highway between Nacogdoches and Galveston. They are all a matter of record. Not even Dr. Thompson, when pressed, denies that they exist. It is found that, as a matter of fact, the transfer by private car of plaintiff Rebecca Owens from Nacogdoches to Galveston while she was undergoing labor pains on the night of August 3, 1987, did pose significant and wholly unnecessary risks to both Rebecca Owens and her unborn child.

Moreover, it is transparent that the sole reason for the illegal transfer was Rebecca Owens's indigence. Dr. Thompson repeatedly admitted that, had Rebecca Owens not been a M.I.H.I.A. patient, she would not have been sent to Galveston. He was aware that Rebecca Owens's status as a M.I.H.I.A. patient indicated her indigence. * * *

Further, since under substantive Texas personal injury law, which governs pursuant to 42 U.S.C. § 1395dd, proof of physical injury is not a prerequisite for recovery for negligent infliction of mental anguish, St. Elizabeth Hospital v. Garrard, 730 S.W.2d 649 (Tex.1987), and since it has already been found that the decision to transfer her to Galveston caused Rebecca Owens severe mental anguish, it is found that the violation of the Anti–Dumping Act by Memorial Hospital through its agent Dr. Bruce Thompson caused Rebecca Owens personal injury within the meaning of the statute.

Pursuant to the joint stipulation of the parties regarding damages entered into on the morning trial commenced, the court assesses against Memorial Hospital the sum of $25,000.00 in damages and the sum of $25,000.00 in attorneys' fees.

V. DECLARATORY AND INJUNCTIVE RELIEF

By its terms, the Anti–Dumping Act provides not only for damages for personal injury, but also for "such equitable relief as is appropriate." Accordingly, plaintiff Rebecca Owens has moved for injunctive relief as well as declaratory relief pursuant to 28 U.S.C. § 2201.

* * *

Plaintiff's evidence demonstrates a long-standing pattern of patient dumping, caused by staffing policies that in the opinion of a series of medical experts would inevitably lead to standards of care at Memorial Hospital that patently did not meet state or federal statutory requirements. Bluntly stated, Memorial Hospital has callously and negligently allowed a situation to develop in which all emergency obstetric and gynecological services to indigent patients—an enormous and ever-increasing load—have been left to on-call private physicians like Dr. Thompson, and the dumping of pregnant women has been the inevitable result.

* * *

The evidence given by plaintiff's expert Dr. F. Barry Roberts, who practiced for nine and one-half years at Memorial Hospital, that Memorial has been continuously obstructionist whenever physicians attempted to bring the problem of indigent health care to the attention of the Board, is also found credible. The weight of the evidence—especially considering the fact that when this civil action came on for trial, a private practitioner was the only OB–GYN delivering poor babies at Memorial—convincingly establishes a disturbing pattern of negligent behavior on the part of the administrators of Memorial Hospital which has inevitably led to the pattern of patient dumping.

In the light of this pattern of either negligent or deliberate flouting by Memorial Hospital of its obligations under the Anti–Dumping Act, plaintiff Rebecca Owens has amply demonstrated that she has standing, and that there is a real threat of injury to her. The complained of acts are capable of repetition, and indeed have been repeated. Plaintiff is awarded permanent injunctive relief to prevent these egregious acts from evading review in the future.

Notes and Questions

1. The Emergency Medical Treatment and Active Labor Act (COBRA) provides in part:

(b)(1) In general

If any individual (whether or not eligible for [Medicare] benefits) comes to a hospital and the hospital determines that the individual has an emergency medical condition, the hospital must provide either—

(A) within the staff and facilities available at the hospital, for such further medical examination and such treatment as may be required to stabilize the medical condition, or

(B) for transfer of the individual to another medical facility in accordance with subsection (c).

(c) Restricting transfers until patient stabilized

(1) Rule

If an individual at a hospital has an emergency medical condition which has not been stabilized (within the meaning of subsection (e)(3) of this section), the hospital may not transfer the individual unless—

(A)(i) the individual (or a legally responsible person acting on the individual's behalf) after being informed of the hospital's obligation under this section and the risk of transfer, in writing requests, transfer to another medical facility;

(ii) a physician ... has signed a certification that, based upon the reasonable risks and benefits to the patient, and based upon the information available at the time of transfer, the medical benefits reasonably expected from the provision of appropriate medical treatment at another medical facility outweigh the increased risks to the individual and, in the case of labor, to the unborn child from effecting the transfer; or

(B) the transfer is an appropriate transfer (within the meaning of paragraph (2)) to that facility.

(2) Appropriate transfer

An appropriate transfer to a medical facility is a transfer—

(A) in which the transferring hospital provides the medical treatment within its capacity which minimizes the risks to the individual's health and, in the case of a woman in labor, the health of the unborn child;

(B) in which the receiving facility—

(i) has available space and qualified personnel for the treatment of the patient, and

(ii) has agreed to accept transfer of the patient and to provide appropriate medical treatment;

(C) in which the transferring hospital provides the receiving facility all medical records ... related to the emergency condition for which the individual has presented, available at the time of transfer ...,

(D) in which the transfer is effected through qualified personnel and transportation equipment, as required including the use of necessary and medically appropriate life support measures during the transfer; and

(E) other requirements as the Secretary may find necessary.

(d) Enforcement

[A hospital or "responsible physician" that knowingly or negligently violates the Act is subject to termination or suspension of its Medicare provider agreement. A hospital or "responsible physician" that knowingly violates the Act is subject to a civil penalty of not more than $50,000.]

(3) Civil enforcement

(A) Personal harm

Any individual who suffers personal harm as a direct result of a participating hospital's violation of a requirement of this section may, in a civil action against the participating hospital, obtain those damages available for personal injury under the law of the State in which the hospital is located, and such equitable relief as is appropriate.

(B) Financial loss to other medical facility

Any medical facility that suffers a financial loss as a direct result of a participating hospital's violation of a requirement of this section may, in a civil action against the participating hospital, obtain those damages available for financial loss, under the law of the State in which the hospital is located, and such equitable relief as is appropriate.

(e) Definitions

In this section:

(1) The term "emergency medical condition" means—

(A) a medical condition manifesting itself by acute symptoms of sufficient severity (including severe pain) such that the absence of immediate medical attention could reasonably be expected to result in—

(i) placing the health of the individual (or, with respect to a pregnant woman, the health of the woman or her unborn child) in serious jeopardy.

(ii) serious impairment to bodily functions, or

(iii) serious dysfunction of any bodily organ or part.

(B) with respect to a pregnant woman who is having contractions—

(i) there is inadequate time to effect safe transfer to another hospital before delivery, or

(ii) a transfer may pose a threat to the health and safety of the woman or the unborn child.

(2) The term "participating hospital" means hospital that has entered into a provider agreement under section 1395cc of this title.

(3)(A) The term "to stabilize" means, with respect to an emergency medical condition, to provide such medical treatment of the condition as may be necessary to assure, within reasonable medical probability, that no material deterioration of the condition is likely to result from or occur during the transfer of the individual from a facility or, with respect to an emergency medical condition described in (1)(B) to deliver (including the placenta).

(B) The term "stabilized" means, with respect to an emergency medical condition, that no material deterioration of the condition is likely, within reasonable medical probability, to result from the transfer of the individual from a facility or, with respect to [a pregnant woman with contractions] that the woman has delivered. . . .

(5) The term "transfer" means the movement (including the discharge) of an individual outside a hospital's facilities at the direction of any person employed by (or affiliated or associated, directly or indirectly, with) the hospital, but does not include such a movement of an individual who (A) has been declared dead or (B) leaves the facility without the permission of any such person.

2. The court in *Owens* awarded damages for emotional distress because Texas law allows such a claim in the absence of physical injury. If instead, state law required physical injury for recovery for emotional distress, could the court have awarded Owens damages? Could Owens have gotten broader equitable relief; for example, could the court enjoin the financially based transfer of any women in labor? Would this be useful? Could Owens have sued John Sealy Hospital? Could John Sealy sue Memorial? Would Owens have succeeded under any of the theories supporting a duty to provide emergency treatment discussed earlier? What does this Act add?

3. At least two cases considering this Act have granted summary judgment in favor of the hospital. In both of these cases, the courts viewed the plaintiffs' claims as ordinary malpractice claims, rather than claims founded on the Act, because neither plaintiff offered proof that care was denied due to inability to pay. Both plaintiffs had come to the emergency room with complaints that raised a suspicion of heart attack but were diagnosed otherwise. Both subsequently suffered heart attacks, one fatal. Both courts concluded that the Act was passed specifically to prohibit economically motivated transfers. Stewart v. Myrick, 731 F.Supp. 433 (D.Kan.1990); Evitt v. University Heights Hospital, 727 F.Supp. 495 (S.D. Ind.1989). But see Deberry v. Sherman Hosp. Ass'n, 741 F.Supp. 1302 (N.D.Ill.1990) concluding that an allegation of economic discrimination is not required. Why might a plaintiff who was misdiagnosed in the emergency room want to bring a claim under this Act?

4. In Thornton v. Southwest Detroit Hospital, 895 F.2d 1131 (6th Cir.1990), the U.S. Court of Appeals considered a case that tested the limits of the hospital's duty under this Act. Elease Thornton suffered a stroke and was admitted to the hospital's intensive care unit through its emergency room. Ms. Thornton spent ten days in the ICU and an additional eleven days as an in-patient. Her doctor then wanted her admitted to the Detroit Rehabilitation Institute for post-stroke therapy, but the Institute refused to admit Thornton because her insurance would not cover their services. The doctor then discharged Thornton from the hospital to her sister's home

where she received basic home nursing care. During the several months she spent at her sister's home, her condition deteriorated until she was finally admitted to the Rehabilitation Institute.

Thornton sued the hospital for violation of the Act claiming that the hospital had discharged her before her condition stabilized. She had blood in her urine, an IV, a catheter, high blood pressure and very limited function. The trial court granted summary judgment in favor of the hospital and the Court of Appeals affirmed. In affirming the summary judgment, the court stated that the Act was not limited to the emergency room and that hospitals could not "circumvent the requirements of the Act merely by admitting an emergency room patient to the hospital, then immediately discharging the patient." It based its affirmance instead on the trial court's finding that no genuine issue of fact existed as to whether her condition had stabilized. A concurring opinion states that the hospital had provided no affidavits to contradict Thornton's claim that her condition had not stabilized, but further stated that this case was "clear-cut" and that the release by Thornton's personal physician was "enough evidence" that her condition had stabilized. Was the court's reliance on the attending physician's release appropriate under the Act? The Act requires treatment in emergency situations and not under other circumstances. Is this distinction supportable? Is the line drawn in *Thornton* persuasive? What other claims might a patient bring for "premature discharge"?

5. Although the terms of COBRA clearly apply to the transferring hospital, one court has held that these provisions also apply to the receiving hospital. In Thompson v. St. Anne's Hospital, 716 F.Supp. 8 (N.D.Ill. 1989), a pregnant woman sought emergency medical treatment for premature labor. She was refused treatment at one hospital, and transferred to another. The patient alleged that the receiving hospital had accepted her, but failed to give her stabilizing treatment, as required by COBRA. The receiving hospital contended that the patient dumping laws did not apply to them because they had not transferred the patient. The court, however, found that COBRA was intended to prevent both patient transfer and outright rejection, or refusal to treat due to the patient's economic status. Thus, the district court refused to grant the receiving hospital's motion to dismiss for a failure to state a claim.

6. In February, 1989, the American Medical News reported the first case in which an individual physician was charged under the provisions of this Act. The physician had ordered the transfer of a woman who was hypertensive and allegedly in active labor to another hospital 170 miles distant. The patient had received no pre-natal care, had come to the hospital's emergency room and had been in the hospital's labor and delivery area for more than two hours before being transferred by ambulance. Her child was born in the ambulance thirty miles from the transferring hospital. Testimony indicated that the physician had signed a certificate authorizing transfer without reading the document and had commented to the nurse that until the hospital paid his malpractice insurance, he would "pick and choose" his patients as he did in his own practice.

According to the report in the News, the transferring physician testified that he believed that the transfer was required for the safety of the infant because the infant was likely to have a low birth weight and the transferring hospital did not have the capacity to provide appropriate care. The transferring physician also testified that the patient was not in active labor.

The physician expert witness testifying at the request of the Office of Inspector General stated that the patient was in active labor and needed medication for hypertension immediately. Two nurses from the hospital testified that they agreed with the expert witness and questioned the appropriateness of the transfer because they believed the baby would be born en route to the receiving hospital. (American Medical News, February 3, 1989, p. 1 col. 2)

In *Inspector General v. Burditt,* the administrative law judge found that the physician acted with "reckless disregard or deliberate ignorance by not actually engaging in any meaningful weighing of the risks and benefits of transfer." The Office of Inspector General had sought a fine of $25,000, but the ALJ reduced the fine to $20,000.

Note: Hill–Burton, Title VI and § 504

First enacted in 1946 in response to post-World War II and Depression needs, the Hill–Burton Act provided federal financing for the construction and expansion of health care facilities. The statute required that States provide adequate health facilities for all persons in the state and necessary services for those unable to pay. It also authorized the federal agency to require assurances from individual applicants for financing that they would make the federally financed facility "available to all persons residing in the territorial area of the applicant" and would provide in the financed facility "a reasonable volume of services to persons unable to pay therefor, [unless] such a requirement is not feasible from a financial viewpoint." In 1975, a new program replaced the first Hill–Burton program. The statute authorizing the 1975 program required that applicants for this program also provide the assurances.

In American Hospital Association v. Schweiker, 721 F.2d 170 (7th Cir.1983), the court reviewed regulations issued by the Secretary of Health and Human Services requiring facilities that gave the assurances to meet quantified standards of uncompensated care. These regulations specified that care provided to Medicare or Medicaid patients was not to be included in meeting the standard for uncompensated care and that any amount unmet because of financial infeasibility would be carried over to subsequent years. The AHA challenged the regulations as beyond the scope of the Secretary's statutory authority and as arbitrary and capricious. The court upheld the regulations:

> We think it is clear that the Secretary was acting within the scope of his statutory mandate. * * * Although the AHA contends that the Hill–Burton Act was merely a construction statute with a non-discrimination clause attached, such a contention is difficult to reconcile with the specific statutory language requiring assurances. * * *

> In any event, one may infer from the provisions' mere presence in the statute that the free care obligation was intended to have some

effect. Moreover, the very fact that the Act authorized an exception to the obligation to provide uncompensated care, if a facility was financially unable to furnish it, indicates that the Act contemplated that the hospital would be required to devote some of its own resources to fulfilling the assurances.

The premise, assumed in 1945, that hospitals would voluntarily provide services to all residents, including the indigent, out of their history of charitable service, proved to be unjustified; their apparent failure resulted in litigation to enforce the federally assisted hospitals' community service and uncompensated care obligations in the early 1970s. [The Secretary had in 1972 and 1974 issued regulations quantifying the assurance obligations in response to that litigation.]

The AHA also challenged the regulations on a contractual basis, claiming that hospitals accepting federal financing assistance and making assurances prior to 1979 were now being held to new requirements. The court rejected these claims: "Rather than a voluntary agreement negotiated between two parties, a grant-in-aid program like that under the Hill–Burton Act is an exercise by the federal government of its authority under the spending power to bring about certain public policy goals. * * * The 'conditions' of the arrangement are not the result of a negotiated agreement between the parties but rather are provided by the statute under which the program is administered. Determination of statutory intent, therefore, is of more relevance to the interpretation of these conditions than is an inquiry into the intent of the two parties at the moment of the initial agreement."

Rejecting the Seventh Circuit's conclusion, James Blumstein maintains that the legislative history indicates that Hill–Burton was a "public works" program to provide capital for hospital construction and modernization in response to postwar shortages and to provide jobs. Professor Blumstein argues that the original statutory access provisions simply required hospitals to continue the tradition of nonprofit hospitals in serving their communities and was not intended to create any new obligations. He further argues that the statutory provisions on access were primarily symbolic and, in fact, were designed for passive, rather than aggressive, administrative enforcement. He argues that "advocates for indigent plaintiffs spectacularly succeeded in completely reorienting a federal health program * * *". Blumstein, Court Action, Agency Reaction: The Hill–Burton Act as a Case Study, 69 Iowa L.Rev. 1227, 1227 (1984).

In contrast, Kenneth Wing defends the position ultimately adopted by the Seventh Circuit in a detailed analysis of the statute and its legislative history. Wing, The Community Service Obligation of Hill–Burton Health Facilities, 23 B.C.L.Rev. 577 (1982). Do you think the result in *AHA* would have been different if the Secretary had issued regulations allowing facilities to claim the difference in rates between government payers and private payers as uncompensated care and continuing forgiveness of the obligation in any year the facility found meeting the obligation financially infeasible?

Other federal laws impose a duty on hospitals as well. For example, Title VI of the Civil Rights Act of 1964 (42 U.S.C.A. § 2000d et seq.) prohibits discrimination on the basis of race, color or national origin under any program or activity receiving Federal financial assistance. Hospitals receiving Medicare payments are subject to Title VI. Decisions of private and public hospitals to discontinue services to communities with a high percentage of minority citizens have been challenged under Title VI. See, e.g., Bryan v. Koch, 627 F.2d 612 (2d Cir.1980) and NAACP v. Medical Center, Inc., 657 F.2d 1322 (3d Cir.1981). In each case, the court found that the defendant hospital's closing or relocation did not violate Title VI, finding that legitimate nondiscriminatory reasons supported the decisions of the facility. For comments on *Wilmington Medical Center, Inc.,* see 1981 Duke L.J. 1033 and 27 Villanova L.Rev. 797 (1982). For a critical review and analysis of the problem of racial discrimination by health care institutions and the relationship of Title VI to this problem, see Wing, Title VI and Health Facilities: Form Without Substance, 30 Hastings L.J. 137 (1978). See also, Institute of Medicine, Health Care in the Context of Civil Rights, National Academy of Sciences (1981). Title VI was used successfully in challenging a state's Medicaid plan in Linton v. Tennessee Commissioner of Health and Environment, No. 3–87–0941 (April 1990). In *Linton,* the district court ordered the state of Tennessee to submit a plan for court approval to remedy violations of Title VI. The court found that the Tennessee Medicaid plan allowed nursing homes to limit the number of "beds" certified for Medicaid reimbursement despite the federal requirement that all beds in a facility, or in a "distinct part" of a facility, be certified. The limited bed certification policy allowed facilities to transfer or discharge current nursing home residents who, having exhausted personal resources, now required Medicaid payment for care. The reason given the resident for such transfer or discharge was that the bed occupied by the resident was not Medicaid certified. The court found that the reason for these transfers or discharges was the difference in payment between Medicaid and the higher paying private pay residents. The court further found that the policy had a disparate impact on racial minorities, particularly African–Americans, because of their disproportionately high representation among the poor, and among those dependent on Medicaid. The impact was evidenced by the under-representation of African–Americans in Tennessee nursing homes. The court held that the limited bed policy violated the Medicaid statute and Title VI.

Federal law also prohibits discrimination against the handicapped under any program or activity receiving financial assistance. Section 504 of the Rehabilitation Act of 1973 (29 U.S.C.A. § 794). Health care institutions receiving Medicare funds are subject to this act. The Supreme Court has held that § 504 protects an infant born with congenital defects from discrimination if the infant is "otherwise qualified for benefits under a program or activity receiving federal financial assistance." Bowen v. American Hospital Association, 476 U.S. 610, 106 S.Ct. 2101, 2111, 90 L.Ed.2d 584, 595 (1986). The Court noted that "handicapped infants are entitled to 'meaningful access' to medical services provided by hospitals, and that a hospital rule or state policy denying or limiting such access would be subject to challenge under § 504." *Bowen,* 476 U.S. at 624, 106 S.Ct. at 2111. The Supreme Court, however, found the "Baby Doe" regulations at issue in that case to be beyond the scope of the authority of the

Secretary of Health and Human Services under the statute. See Chapter 11.

The Rehabilitation Act has been raised in suits alleging discrimination by health care facilities against persons with AIDS. In Doe v. Centinela Hospital, 1988 WL 81776 (C.D.Cal.), for example, the court considered the case of a seropositive person who was excluded from an in-patient chemical dependency program and offered only out-patient services. The court granted plaintiff's motion for summary judgment on the questions of whether the hospital, as a Medicare contractor, was covered by the Act and whether plaintiff was a handicapped individual under the Act. The court concluded that plaintiff was a handicapped individual because the program had perceived plaintiff as handicapped. The court held that triable issues remained as to the Act's requirement that plaintiff be "otherwise qualified" for the program and whether the program had made "reasonable accommodation" for the plaintiff's handicap.

A recent survey of neonatal intensive care unit clinicians indicated that a large number would make treatment decisions for infants based on the HIV status of the mother. Only half of the clinicians surveyed would recommend cardiac resuscitation for a baby whose mother tested positive for the AIDS virus. Although 89% would recommend kidney dialysis for infants, only 52% would recommend dialysis if they knew that the mother was HIV positive. The surveyors reported that one-third of the neonatal clinicians surveyed mistakenly believed that half of the babies born to seropositive women would themselves have the AIDS virus and that one in seven believed that the infection rate of such infants was 90% or better. According to the researchers, experts now believe that only one in three infants born to HIV positive women are infected with the virus. Pediatric AIDS, AIDS Policy and Law, June 27, 1990. Does § 504 of the Rehabilitation Act address the issue of individual medical treatment decisions such as these? The Americans with Disabilities Act also prohibits discrimination against persons with disabilities and is not limited to federally-funded programs. 101 Pub.L. 336 (1990).

Problem: Emmaus House I

You are a volunteer attorney for a nonprofit organization that provides services to the homeless through a community center called Emmaus House. You and several other attorneys come to Emmaus House to offer legal services a couple of hours each week. While you are there, the director of the center comes rushing into the cubicle where you are conducting interviews and tells you there is an emergency. Mr. Jack Larkin, a homeless man who comes frequently to the center, is complaining of chest pains and shortness of breath. He has had these episodes before and, in fact, went to the public hospital very early this morning because he "didn't feel right." They examined him thoroughly and concluded that he was not having a heart attack but rather was suffering from influenza. You and the director get Mr. Larkin into your car and take him to the nearest hospital which happens to be Eastbrook Memorial, a private hospital. Their emergency room physician examines Mr. Larkin and then comes to tell you that they are going to transfer Mr. Larkin to the public hospital, twenty minutes away. What do you do?

Problem: Emmaus House II

You are still volunteering at Emmaus House. The director and the board have asked the volunteer attorneys for assistance in securing adequate health care for the homeless in the city. They would like your advice on filing a lawsuit on behalf of the homeless in need of health care. What approach would you take? What would your goal be? Exactly what remedy would you want included in the court's order? What legal theories could support that remedy? Is a lawsuit the best approach? Are there other political or administrative bodies you could approach? What would be your strategy?

Assume that they have also told you of the case of a homeless family who took their infant to the emergency room of Eastbrook Memorial after the infant had had a high fever and diarrhea for 48 hours. The emergency room nurse told them to take their child to Charity Hospital, a private, nonprofit hospital, and called them a cab, paying the cabdriver in advance. When they arrived at Charity, the emergency room staff had no idea they were coming and was in the midst of treating five seriously injured victims of an accident who had arrived just moments before. The parents waited for an hour before their child was examined, a total of three hours since they had presented themselves at Eastbrook. The child was admitted to Charity, but died within a few days. The parents are convinced that the delays contributed to their child's death. If you brought suit against Eastbrook and Charity, what would you have to prove?

IV. ACCESS TO ADVANCED, EXPENSIVE TECHNOLOGY

A. ALLOCATION AND RATIONING

Until this point the focus of this chapter has been on provision of access to health care for those who cannot otherwise afford it. The remainder of the chapter will consider a somewhat different, though related, topic: rationing of available health care. The primary means through which health care is rationed in our society is through the market: those who can afford health care get it, those who cannot afford it often do not. To the extent that a society chooses to provide equal access to health care regardless of ability to pay, it must either countenance limitless expenditure of resources for health care or find some non-market means of rationing it. Moreover, some medical resources may be so limited in availability that virtually any society would seek some other way to allocate them than to give them to the highest bidder. For example, one-third of American heart transplant candidates die each year while awaiting organs. In 1988, the average wait for a kidney was almost three years. It is unlikely that anyone would advocate that those organs be allocated to the patients who will offer the most for them. This section will briefly consider general questions raised by rationing, and then turn to the problem of organ transplantation, which dramatically raises questions of rationing.

First, two distinctions must be made that play an important role in an understanding of rationing. The first is the distinction between allocation (or macroallocation) and rationing (or microallocation). Through allocation decisions a society determines how much of its resources to devote to a particular purpose (for example, how much money to allocate to Medicare, or to the End Stage Renal Dialysis program, or to transplantation of hearts). Through rationing, a society decides who gets the resources allocated in a particular way; which individual gets the dialysis or the heart. Obviously, allocation decisions affect rationing decisions: the more resources allocated to a particular purpose, the fewer difficult rationing decisions need be made as to who gets the resources. Perhaps less obviously, rationing decisions affect allocation decisions; the more poignant rationing decisions become, the more likely is a society to allocate enough resources to avoid uncomfortable rationing decisions.

A second distinction that often emerges in discussions of rationing is the distinction between statistical and identifiable lives. The statistical life is one of the 50 lives that will be lost in a year because of a government decision not to pursue a particular mine safety regulation, the identifiable life is the one miner trapped in the collapsed mine. It is a commonplace that society will expend almost limitless resources to save the identifiable life, but is willing to sacrifice statistical lives at much lower cost. The more overtly and explicitly a government decision affects an identifiable person for whom the government is responsible, the more difficulty the government will face in saying no, in refusing to provide the resources necessary to save a life or to relieve suffering. This distinction is related to the preceding one, in that allocation decisions usually affect statistical lives—rationing, identifiable lives.

How does allocation and rationing of resources occur? As already noted, in the United States, absent a decision to the contrary, both are accomplished by the market. The advantage of this, of course, is that the market moves resources to uses that are valued most, and to persons who most value them. The problem with using the market to allocate and ration important resources like health care is that it can only move valued resources to those who already have valuable resources. If the distribution of resources in society is inequitable, the market cannot make it less so. Arguably, distributing "necessary" resources like health care through the market makes an unjust situation less just.

A second option is to allocate and ration resources through political processes. In fact allocation decisions are often made this way. Government decisions to spend money or to regulate competitive processes frequently involve allocation decisions. The Medicare and Medicaid programs allocate resources to various purposes, as do state certificate of need or rate regulation programs. For an account of Oregon's plan to ration services for Medicaid patients explicitly, see above. Public rationing programs are more problematic, as they deal with identifiable lives and thus provoke much more emotional responses, subjecting the government to what some call "symbolic blackmail," which forces the government to allocate unjustifiably large sums of resources to certain purposes to avoid sacrificing an identifiable life. For example, Oregon decided to move some Medicaid finding from organ transplantation to pre-natal care. In 1987, one child—Coby Howard—was turned into a rationing martyr when his attempts to collect donations to pay for a bone marrow transplant fell short of the cost and he died. In 1990 a chastened Oregon restored Medicaid finding for organ transplants.

Some advocate addressing this problem by leaving rationing decisions to "aresponsible" agencies, like juries or draftboards, that need not explain their decision and are thus less subject to public pressure. On the other hand, others are troubled by "aresponsible" decisionmakers, arguing that they are irrational and biased.

Another option is for medical professionals and institutions to make allocation and rationing decisions. In fact, hospitals have always made allocation decisions—determining how much of what resources to have available—and physicians have long played the role of rationers— deciding what services to provide and prescribe for their patients. But in the new era of HMO's and DRG's, these decisions are becoming more painfully apparent. Some commentators embrace these developments, but others express dismay at the change these developments will bring about in the physician's traditional role as patient advocate.

Assuming a decisionmaker is identified, by what criteria should it make medical rationing decisions? Medical criteria certainly must play some role, excluding those for whom a medical procedure will do no or little good. But medical criteria can only give limited assistance; several claimants to an artificial heart may have essentially the same prognosis. Moreover medicine does not always provide an obvious answer to rationing questions: should resources be given to a patient whose medical condition is the most serious, or to another who can benefit most from the smallest application of resources?

Decisions based on social worth are also possible. During the 1960s, before the artificial kidney became widely available, the Seattle Artificial Kidney Center selected patients for hemodialysis patients in part on the basis of: " * * * age and sex of patient; marital status and number of dependents; income; net worth; emotional stability, with particular regard to the patient's capacity to accept treatment; educational background; the nature of occupation; past performance and future potential; the names of people who could serve as references." Alexander, They Decide Who Lives, Who Dies, 53 Life 102–104 (Nov. 9,

1962), quoted in Mehlman, Rationing Expensive Lifesaving Medical Treatments, 1985 Wisc.L.Rev. 239, 256.

Social worth allocations are inherently troubling, as they deny a fundamental equality of persons. They are also often indeterminate: perhaps it would be easy to choose the brilliant surgeon over the skid row bum, but how do you choose between the brilliant surgeon and the brilliant lawyer; or between the aging surgeon, who has made substantial contributions to society, and the young medical student who promises to do so in the future? Regardless of how one regards rationing based on social criteria, it is clear that non-medical factors, like residency or age, often play a role in decisions rationing medical resources.

Rationing can also be accomplished through procedures that purport to treat all equally, through a lottery or on a first come-first served basis. While these procedures are more egalitarian, they risk results that clearly seem unwise, potentially favoring the criminal condemned to death for multiple murders over the promising law student for a heart transplant. Moreover, a first come-first served approach capriciously favors those whose needs arise at certain times.

Finally a decision can be made not to decide, by allocating sufficient resources to avoid any rationing decisions. This is the approach the United States eventually took to the problem of rationing renal dialysis, but it has turned out to be a very expensive solution.

For consideration of the fascinating problems involved in rationing of resources see, G. Calabresi and P. Bobbitt, Tragic Choices (1978); Callahan, Setting Limits (1987); Shapiro, On Not Watering All the Flowers; Regulatory Theory and the Funding of Heart Transplantation, 28 Jurimetrics J. 21 (1987); Besharov and Silver, Rationing Access to Advanced Medical Techniques, 8 J.Leg.Med. 507 (1987); Evans, Health Care Technology and the Inevitability of Rationing Decisions, 249 JAMA 2047 and 2208 (1983); Mehlman, Rationing Expensive Lifesaving Medical Treatments, 1985 Wisc.L.Rev. 239. See also, debating the appropriate role of the market in rationing "normal" health care, Blumstein, Rationing Medical Resources: A Constitutional, Legal and Policy Analysis, 59 Texas L.Rev. 1345 (1981); Rosenblatt, Rationing "Normal" Health Care: The Hidden Legal Issues, 59 Texas L.Rev. 1401 (1981); Blumstein, Distinguishing Government's Responsibility in Rationing Public and Private Medical Resources, 60 Texas L.Rev. 899 (1982); Rosenblatt, Rationing "Normal" Health Care Through Market Mechanisms: A Response to Professor Blumstein, 60 Texas L.Rev. 919 (1982). Finally, for a cross-cultural approach to the problem of rationing, see Kilner, Who Shall be Saved? An African Answer, Hastings Center Report 18 (June 1984).

B. A CASE STUDY IN THE DISTRIBUTION OF NEW TECHNOLOGY: ORGAN TRANSPLANTATION

One of the most impressive achievements of modern medical technology has been the development of organ transplantation. The first kidney transplant took place only four decades ago, but today kidney transplantation has become fairly routine, as have cornea and bone marrow transplants. Transplants of hearts, livers, lungs, and pancreases are becoming increasingly common, and virtually any organ is potentially transplantable. About 95% of kidney transplant patients survive at least a year; the figure is 85% for heart transplants and 80% for liver transplants. Today, even heart-lung transplant patients have a better than even chance of one-year survival, and all of the transplant survival rates are improving quickly.

1. *Patient Access to Organ Transplantation*

Organ transplantation poses important rationing questions. First it raises questions of allocation of resources. Transplantation of major organs is very expensive. A Massachusetts study estimated that the average costs of a liver transplant patient were from $230,000 to $340,000 a year, and a heart transplant costs from $170,000 to $200,000 a year. Moreover, the benefits of organ transplantation are questionable, even if the survival rates are improving.

The number of transplants is increasing rapidly. In 1982 there were 103 heart transplants and 62 liver transplants in the United States; in 1988 there were 1646 heart transplants and 1680 liver transplants. In light of the general scarcity of medical resources, it is possible to conclude that these resources could better be allocated to other uses.

Medicare covers kidney transplantation (which has a long term cost lower than dialysis and thus saves money for the Medicare renal dialysis program). It has only recently begun to cover heart transplants on a limited basis, and still does not generally cover other organs. The explanation for this is probably historical. Is the policy justified, however, by the fact that kidney failure is normally due to genetic or organic conditions that are not the fault of the patient, while the vast majority of patients needing heart, liver, or lung transplantation are suffering the results of a lifetime of tobacco or alcohol consumption? Caplan, Organ Transplants, The Cost of Success, 13 Hastings Center Report 23, 30 (December 1983). Would the refusal of the federal government to fund liver transplants, while funding kidney transplants, violate any constitutional rights? Consider *Harris v. McCrae,* supra. Would your answer be different if the federal government decided to forbid all hospitals from carrying out organ transplants, regardless of payment source, or restricted transplantation to a limited number of regional transplant centers? Would it matter whether the government's reasons were medical cost control or reduction of risk to patients from the procedure? Would it make any difference if the prohibition were imposed on hospitals as a condition of participating in the Medicare program? See, Merrikan and Overcast, Government Regulation of Heart Transplantation and the Right of Privacy, 11 J.Contemp.L. 481 (1985).

Because the number of available organs is usually less than the demand, organ transplantation also raises questions of rationing. Consider the following problem:

Problem: Selecting an Organ Transplant Recipient

You are awakened in the middle of the night by an urgent phone call from an administrative staff member of the large urban teaching hospital that you represent. The hospital has encountered the following problem. For the last weeks two patients have been under treatment at the hospital for acute liver failure. One, James Patterson, is a sixty-year-old alcoholic. James has been in and out of the hospital for several years for problems secondary to his alcoholism. Though he has been through detoxification programs several times, he always returns to his drinking. He was found totally disabled one year ago. He has no health insurance and he is not eligible for Medicaid. His wife left him years ago and his children are grown. His liver is in advanced stages of deterioration because of cirrhosis. The second patient is Antonia Friedman, 45, a successful businesswoman, with five children, aged 7 through 15. Friedman is a member of the local city council, and has contributed generously in the past year to the hospital's building fund. Friedman has a rare congenital liver condition which has destroyed most of her liver. Within the last week both patients have taken a turn for the worse, and both will die within the next few days if they do not receive a liver transplant.

A few hours ago a patient was admitted to the hospital with massive head trauma caused by an automobile accident. The patient is now brain dead, but is being kept on life support systems to preserve his organs for transplantation. The liver is undamaged, and normal legal procedures have already been followed to assure that it is available for transplantation. Tissue matching shows that it would be an acceptable organ for either Patterson or Friedman.

The policy of the hospital heretofore has been to make organs available to patients on a first come-first served basis, though this policy has never been officially adopted or reduced to writing. Under this rule Patterson would be the recipient, as his physician, a second year resident, was first to request an organ transplant, a step he took three days ago. On the other hand, the other physicians involved in the case are troubled by this result, not only because of the social considerations, but also because they question how long the liver would last if Patterson would, as expected, return to drinking.

The caller wants to know first whether the hospital and physicians must follow any particular procedure in making the decision. They receive extensive federal funding through Medicaid and government research grants, and received Hill–Burton funds for the construction of the hospital. Are they obligated under the Constitution to provide certain procedures or to treat all candidates equally? Assuming the hospital to be a municipal hospital, what procedures would you recommend? Notice and hearing? Cross examination? Representation by Counsel? Do they have any obligations under the Hill–Burton Act or under the Medicaid Program to treat Patterson and Friedman nondiscriminately? What would that mean under the circumstances? Patterson's physician is concerned that he may be found liable for malpractice if he accedes in the decision for Friedman. He also wonders whether he has any obligation to inform Patterson of the decision against him if it is made. Finally, your caller asks for your ethical judgment as a fellow professional as to what ought to be done. What is your response?

Notes and Questions

1. Many hospitals refuse to consider a person for an organ transplant unless he or she can pay for the transplant through private means or can demonstrate third party coverage. It has been reported that "a few hospitals demand full cash payments in advance before they will even enter a candidate's name on a waiting list for a liver or pancreas." Caplan, supra at 30.

2. Section 504 of the Rehabilitation Act of 1973 forbids discrimination against the handicapped in federally funded programs. Hospitals receiving Medicare are considered to be federally funded, and alcoholism is considered a handicap. If your client chose Patterson over Friedman, would it violate Sec. 504? See, Merrikan and Overcast, Patient Selection for Heart Transplantation: When is a Discriminating Choice Discrimination? 10 Journal of Health Politics, Policy and Law 7 (1985). Does it make any difference that the handicap is related to the treatment sought? See Bowen v. American Hospital Association, 476 U.S. 610, 106 S.Ct. 2101, 90 L.Ed.2d 584 (1986) reprinted in Chapter 11.

3. States may not arbitrarily refuse medically necessary treatment to Medicaid eligible patients. At least one Federal court has determined that a two year abstinence requirement for an alcoholic who needs a liver transplant is arbitrary and thus an impermissible basis for denying the transplant. Allen v. Mansour, 681 F.Supp. 1232 (E.D.Mich.1986).

2. Increasing the Supply of Organs

a. Cadaver Organs

The need for rationing of organs is necessitated in substantial part because of the lack of donated organs. Ten thousand people are now on waiting lists for kidneys, livers, hearts, corneas and other organs. Over two million people die each year; only 50,000 are organ or tissue donors. The primary strategy used for locating organ donors is the Uniform Anatomical Gift Act (UAGA).

UNIFORM ANATOMICAL GIFT ACT (1987)

§ 1. Definitions.

As used in this [Act]:

(1) "Anatomical gift" means a donation of all or part of a human body to take effect upon or after death.

(2) "Decedent" means a deceased individual and includes a still-born infant or fetus.

(3) "Document of gift" means a card, a statement attached to or imprinted on a motor vehicle operator's or chauffeur's license, a will, or other writing used to make an anatomical gift.

(4) "Donor" means an individual who makes an anatomical gift of all or part of the individual's body.

(5) "Enucleator" means an individual who is [licensed] [certified] by the [State Board of Medical Examiners] to remove or process eyes or parts of eyes.

(6) "Hospital" means a facility licensed, accredited, or approved as a hospital under the law of any state or a facility operated as a hospital by the United States government, a state, or a subdivision of a state.

(7) "Part" means an organ, tissue, eye, bone, artery, blood, fluid, or other portion of a human body.

(8) "Person" means an individual, corporation, business trust, estate, trust, partnership, joint venture, association, government, governmental subdivision or agency, or any other legal or commercial entity.

(9) "Physician" or "surgeon" means an individual licensed or otherwise authorized to practice medicine and surgery or osteopathy and surgery under the laws of any state.

(10) "Procurement organization" means a person licensed, accredited, or approved under the laws of any state for procurement, distribution, or storage of human bodies or parts.

(11) "State" means a state, territory, or possession of the United States, the District of Columbia, or the Commonwealth of Puerto Rico.

(12) "Technician" means an individual who is [licensed] [certified] by the [State Board of Medical Examiners] to remove or process a part.

§ 2. Making, Amending, Revoking, and Refusing to Make Anatomical Gifts by Individual.

(a) An individual who is at least [18] years of age may (i) make an anatomical gift for any of the purposes stated in Section 6(a), (ii) limit an anatomical gift to one or more of those purposes, or (iii) refuse to make an anatomical gift.

(b) An anatomical gift may be made only by a document of gift signed by the donor. If the donor cannot sign, the document of gift must be signed by another individual and by two witnesses, all of whom have signed at the direction and in the presence of the donor and of each other, and state that it has been so signed.

(c) If a document of gift is attached to or imprinted on a donor's motor vehicle operator's or chauffeur's license, the document of gift must comply with subsection (b). Revocation, suspension, expiration, or cancellation of the license does not invalidate the anatomical gift.

(d) A document of gift may designate a particular physician or surgeon to carry out the appropriate procedures. In the absence of a designation or if the designee is not available, the donee or other person authorized to accept the anatomical gift may employ or authorize any physician, surgeon, technician, or enucleator to carry out the appropriate procedures.

(e) An anatomical gift by will takes effect upon death of the testator, whether or not the will is probated. If, after death, the will is declared invalid for testamentary purposes, the validity of the anatomical gift is unaffected.

(f) A donor may amend or revoke an anatomical gift, not made by will, only by:

(1) a signed statement;

(2) an oral statement made in the presence of two individuals;

(3) any form of communication during a terminal illness or injury addressed to a physician or surgeon; or

(4) the delivery of a signed statement to a specified donee to whom a document of gift had been delivered.

(g) The donor of an anatomical gift made by will may amend or revoke the gift in the manner provided for amendment or revocation of wills, or as provided in subsection (f).

(h) An anatomical gift that is not revoked by the donor before death is irrevocable and does not require the consent or concurrence of any person after the donor's death.

(i) An individual may refuse to make an anatomical gift of the individual's body or part by (i) a writing signed in the same manner as a document of gift, (ii) a statement attached to or imprinted on a donor's motor vehicle operator's or chauffeur's license, or (iii) any other writing used to identify the individual as refusing to make an anatomical gift. During a terminal illness or injury, the refusal may be an oral statement or other form of communication.

(j) In the absence of contrary indications by the donor, an anatomical gift of a part is neither a refusal to give other parts nor a limitation on an anatomical gift under Section 3 or on a removal or release of other parts under Section 4.

(k) In the absence of contrary indications by the donor, a revocation or amendment of an anatomical gift is not a refusal to make another anatomical gift. If the donor intends a revocation to be a refusal to make an anatomical gift, the donor shall make the refusal pursuant to subsection (i).

§ 3. Making, Revoking, and Objecting to Anatomical Gifts, by Others.

(a) Any member of the following classes of persons, in the order of priority listed, may make an anatomical gift of all or a part of the decedent's body for an authorized purpose, unless the decedent, at the time of death, has made an unrevoked refusal to make that anatomical gift:

(1) the spouse of the decedent;

(2) an adult son or daughter of the decedent;

(3) either parent of the decedent;

(4) an adult brother or sister of the decedent;

(5) a grandparent of the decedent; and

(6) a guardian of the person of the decedent at the time of death.

(b) An anatomical gift may not be made by a person listed in subsection (a) if:

(1) a person in a prior class is available at the time of death to make an anatomical gift;

(2) the person proposing to make an anatomical gift knows of a refusal or contrary indications by the decedent; or

(3) the person proposing to make an anatomical gift knows of an objection to making an anatomical gift by a member of the person's class or a prior class.

(c) An anatomical gift by a person authorized under subsection (a) must be made by (i) a document of gift signed by the person or (ii) the person's telegraphic, recorded telephonic, or other recorded message, or other form of communication from the person that is contemporaneously reduced to writing and signed by the recipient.

(d) An anatomical gift by a person authorized under subsection (a) may be revoked by any member of the same or a prior class if, before procedures have begun for the removal of a part from the body of the decedent, the physician, surgeon, technician, or enucleator removing the part knows of the revocation.

(e) A failure to make an anatomical gift under subsection (a) is not an objection to the making of an anatomical gift.

§ 4. Authorization by [Coroner] [Medical Examiner] or [Local Public Health Official].

(a) The [coroner] [medical examiner] may release and permit the removal of a part from a body within that official's custody, for transplantation or therapy, if:

(1) the official has received a request for the part from a hospital, physician, surgeon, or procurement organization;

(2) the official has made a reasonable effort, taking into account the useful life of the part, to locate and examine the decedent's medical records and inform persons listed in Section 3(a) of their option to make, or object to making, an anatomical gift;

(3) the official does not know of a refusal or contrary indication by the decedent or objection by a person having priority to act as listed in Section 3(a);

(4) the removal will be by a physician, surgeon, or technician; but in the case of eyes, by one of them or by an enucleator;

(5) the removal will not interfere with any autopsy or investigation;

(6) the removal will be in accordance with accepted medical standards; and

(7) cosmetic restoration will be done, if appropriate.

(b) If the body is not within the custody of the [coroner] [medical examiner], the [local public health officer] may release and permit the removal of any part from a body in the [local public health officer's] custody for transplantation or therapy if the requirements of subsection (a) are met.

(c) An official releasing and permitting the removal of a part shall maintain a permanent record of the name of the decedent, the person making the request, the date and purpose of the request, the part requested, and the person to whom it was released.

§ 5. Routine Inquiry and Required Request; Search and Notification.

(a) On or before admission to a hospital, or as soon as possible thereafter, a person designated by the hospital shall ask each patient who is at least [18] years of age: "Are you an organ or tissue donor?" If the answer is affirmative the person shall request a copy of the document of gift. If the answer is negative or there is no answer and the attending physician consents, the person designated shall discuss with the patient the option to make or refuse to make an anatomical gift. The answer to the question, an available copy of any document of gift or refusal to make an anatomical gift, and any other relevant information, must be placed in the patient's medical record.

(b) If, at or near the time of death of a patient, there is no medical record that the patient has made or refused to make an anatomical gift, the hospital [administrator] or a representative designated by the [administrator] shall discuss the option to make or refuse to make an anatomical gift and request the making of an anatomical gift pursuant to Section 3(a). The request must be made with reasonable discretion and sensitivity to the circumstances of the family. A request is not required if the gift is not suitable, based upon accepted medical standards, for a purpose specified in Section 6. An entry must be made in the medical record of the patient, stating the name and affiliation of the individual making the request, and of the name, response, and relationship to the patient of the person to whom the request was made. The [Commissioner of Health] shall [establish guidelines] [adopt regulations] to implement this subsection.

(c) The following persons shall make a reasonable search for a document of gift or other information identifying the bearer as a donor or as an individual who has refused to make an anatomical gift:

(1) a law enforcement officer, fireman, paramedic, or other emergency rescuer finding an individual who the searcher believes is dead or near death; and

(2) a hospital, upon the admission of an individual at or near the time of death, if there is not immediately available any other source of that information.

(d) If a document of gift or evidence of refusal to make an anatomical gift is located by the search required by subsection (c)(1), and the individual or body to whom it relates is taken to a hospital, the hospital must be notified of the contents and the document or other evidence must be sent to the hospital.

(e) If, at or near the time of death of a patient, a hospital knows that an anatomical gift has been made pursuant to Section 3(a) or a release and removal of a part has been permitted pursuant to Section 4, or that a patient or an individual identified as in transit to the hospital is a donor, the hospital shall notify the donee if one is named and known to the hospital; if not, it shall notify an appropriate procurement organization. The hospital shall cooperate in the implementation of the anatomical gift or release and removal of a part.

(f) A person who fails to discharge the duties imposed by this section is not subject to criminal or civil liability but is subject to appropriate administrative sanctions.

§ 6. Persons Who May Become Donees; Purposes for Which Anatomical Gifts may be Made.

(a) The following persons may become donees of anatomical gifts for the purposes stated:

(1) a hospital, physician, surgeon, or procurement organization, for transplantation, therapy, medical or dental education, research, or advancement of medical or dental science;

(2) an accredited medical or dental school, college, or university for education, research, advancement of medical or dental science; or

(3) a designated individual for transplantation or therapy needed by that individual.

(b) An anatomical gift may be made to a designated donee or without designating a donee. If a donee is not designated or if the donee is not available or rejects the anatomical gift, the anatomical gift may be accepted by any hospital.

(c) If the donee knows of the decedent's refusal or contrary indications to make an anatomical gift or that an anatomical gift by a member of a class having priority to act is opposed by a member of the same class or a prior class under Section 3(a), the donee may not accept the anatomical gift.

§ 7. Delivery of Document of Gift.

(a) Delivery of a document of gift during the donor's lifetime is not required for the validity of an anatomical gift.

(b) If an anatomical gift is made to a designated donee, the document of gift, or a copy, may be delivered to the donee to expedite the appropriate procedures after death. The document of gift, or a copy, may be deposited in any hospital, procurement organization, or registry office that accepts it for safekeeping or for facilitation of procedures after death. On request of an interested person, upon or after the donor's death, the person in possession shall allow the interested person to examine or copy the document of gift.

§ 8. Rights and Duties at Death.

(a) Rights of a donee created by an anatomical gift are superior to rights of others except with respect to autopsies under Section 11(b). A donee may accept or reject an anatomical gift. If a donee accepts an anatomical gift of an entire body, the donee, subject to the terms of the gift, may allow embalming and use of the body in funeral services. If the gift is of a part of a body, the donee, upon the death of the donor and before embalming, shall cause the part to be removed without unnecessary mutilation. After removal of the part, custody of the remainder of the body vests in the person under obligation to dispose of the body.

(b) The time of death must be determined by a physician or surgeon who attends the donor at death or, if none, the physician or surgeon who certifies the death. Neither the physician or surgeon who attends the donor at death nor the physician or surgeon who determines the time of death may participate in the procedures for removing or transplanting a part unless the document of gift designates a particular physician or surgeon pursuant to Section 2(d).

(c) If there has been an anatomical gift, a technician may remove any donated parts and an enucleator may remove any donated eyes or parts of eyes, after determination of death by a physician or surgeon.

§ 9. Coordination of Procurement and Use.

Each hospital in this State, after consultation with other hospitals and procurement organizations, shall establish agreements or affiliations for coordination of procurement and use of human bodies and parts.

§ 10. Sale or Purchase of Parts Prohibited.

(a) A person may not knowingly, for valuable consideration, purchase or sell a part for transplantation or therapy, if removal of the part is intended to occur after the death of the decedent.

(b) Valuable consideration does not include reasonable payment for the removal, processing, disposal, preservation, quality control, storage, transportation, or implantation of a part.

(c) A person who violates this section is guilty of a [felony] and upon conviction is subject to a fine not exceeding [$50,000] or imprisonment not exceeding [five] years, or both.

§ 11. Examination, Autopsy, Liability.

(a) An anatomical gift authorizes any reasonable examination necessary to assure medical acceptability of the gift for the purposes intended.

(b) The provisions of this [Act] are subject to the laws of this State governing autopsies.

(c) A hospital, physician, surgeon, [coroner], [medical examiner], [local public health officer], enucleator, technician, or other person, who acts in accordance with this [Act] or with the applicable anatomical gift law of another state [or a foreign country] or attempts in good faith to do so is not liable for that act in a civil action or criminal proceeding.

(d) An individual who makes an anatomical gift pursuant to Section 2 or 3 and the individual's estate are not liable for any injury or damage that may result from the making or the use of the anatomical gift.

* * *

Notes and Questions

1. Assume in the Problem above that the potential donor has just arrived at the hospital. Within minutes of arrival a doctor determines that the patient is brain dead, though his bodily functions are being maintained artificially. Assuming that several organs are suitable for transplantation, what steps should the doctor take under the UAGA prior to removing the organs from the body for transplantation?

2. The 1987 UAGA was adopted in eight states within two years of its promulgation; every other state has adopted some version of the 1968 UAGA.

The 1987 Act was developed upon the recognition that the earlier version simply was not producing enough donated organs. The major difference in the two Acts are summarized in the Prefatory Note to the 1987 Act:

> The proposed amendments simplify the manner of making an anatomical gift and require that the intentions of a donor be followed. For example, no witnesses are required on the document of gift and consent of next of kin after death is not required if the donor has made an anatomical gift. The identification of actual donors is facilitated by a duty to search for a document of gift and of potential donors by the provisions for routine inquiry and required request. A gift of one organ, e.g., eyes, is not a limitation on the gift of other organs after death, in the absence of contrary indication by the decedent. The right to refuse to make an anatomical gift and the manner of expressing the refusal are specified. Revocation by a donor of an anatomical gift that has been made is effective without communication of the revocation to a specified donee. Hospitals have been substituted for attending physicians as donees of anatomical gifts, and they are required to establish agreements or affiliations with other hospitals and procurement organizations in the region to coordinate the procurement and utilization of anatomical gifts. If a request for an anatomical gift has been made for transplant or therapy by a person specified in the Act and if there is no contrary indication by the decedent or known objection by the next of kin to an anatomical gift, the [coroner] [medical examiner] or [local

public health official] may authorize release and removal of a part subject to specific requirements. * * * The sale or purchase of parts is prohibited. Persons who act, or attempt to act, in good faith in accordance with the terms of the Act are not liable in any civil action or criminal proceeding. * * *

The 1987 UAGA was designed to overcome the "key problems that hinder organ donation" that were identified by the Hastings Center's working group on "Ethical, Legal and Policy Issues Pertaining to Solid Organ Procurement:"

1. Failure of persons to sign written directives.

2. Failure of police and emergency personnel to locate written directives at accident sites.

3. Uncertainty on the part of the public about circumstances and timing of organ recovery.

4. Failure on the part of medical personnel to recover organs on the basis of written directives.

5. Failure to systemically approach family members concerning donation.

6. Inefficiency on the part of some organ procurement agencies in obtaining referrals of donors.

7. High wastage rates on the part of some organ procurement agencies in failing to place donated organs.

8. Failure to communicate the pronouncement of death to next of kin.

9. Failure to obtain adequate informed consent from family members.

3. What additional steps should be taken to increase the availability of donated organs? Surveys normally show widespread support for organ donation programs, but little willingness to actually donate organs. Why are people reluctant to identify themselves as potential donors? Aversion to thinking about death? Fear that physicians will not try quite so hard to save a life if they see it as a potential organ harvest? Fear that doctors may jump the gun in finding brain death to get at available organs? Why have you not signed that card on the back of your driver's license?

The drafters of the 1987 UAGA recognized in the Prefatory Note that organ donation was far more popular in theory than in practice:

A 1985 Gallup Poll commissioned by the American Council on Transplantation reported that 98 percent of Americans surveyed knew about organ transplantation and, of these, 75 percent approved of the concept of organ donation. Although a large majority approves of organ donation, only 27 percent indicate that they would be very likely to donate their own organs, and only 17 percent have actually completed donor cards. Of those who were very likely to donate, nearly half have not told family members of their wish, even though family permission is usually requested before an organ is removed. Report of the Task Force on Organ Transplantation pursuant to the 1984 National Organ Transplant Act—P.L. 98–507—"Organ Transplantation: Issues and Recommendations" (April 1986).

One study found that families were much more willing to agree to organ donation if they knew donation to be the wish of the deceased. Since the family usually ends up making the decision, the most useful thing that can be done to encourage organ donation may be publicity that will encourage potential donors to discuss organ donation with their families and express their desire to serve as donors. Prottas, Encouraging Altruism, 61 Milbank Mem.Fund.Q. 278 (1983).

4. Because many potential donors die under violent circumstances, conflicts frequently arise between the duties of the medical examiner or coroner to establish the cause of death, and the need to harvest organs while they are still fresh. Premature organ removal could destroy important evidence. Moreover, if organs are removed prematurely, counsel defending a homicide defendant could argue that the doctors, not their client, caused the death. How does the UAGA reconcile the forensic obligations of the coroner with the need for the organs? How should they be reconciled? See Overcast, Merrikan and Evans, Malpractice Issues in Heart Transplantation, 10 Am.J.L. & Med. 363, 372–4 (1985); Rose, Medicolegal Problems Associated with Organ and Tissue Transplantations, Medical Trial Technique Q. 99, 108–9 (1984).

5. Compare the approach of Section 5 of the UAGA to 42 U.S.C.A. § 1320b–8.

(a)(1) The Secretary shall provide that a hospital meeting the requirements of title XVIII or XIX may participate in the program established under such title only if—

(A) the hospital establishes written protocols for the identification of potential organ donors that—

(i) assure that families of potential organ donors are made aware of the option of organ or tissue donation and their option to decline,

(ii) encourage discretion and sensitivity with respect to the circumstances, views, and beliefs of such families, * * *

Does the UAGA add anything to the federal law?

6. Several commentators have proposed more radical changes to develop a greater pool of cadaver organs for transplants. One proposal is that a statute be adopted recognizing "presumed consent" to donation, permitting a physician to remove organs from an appropriate cadaver without formal consent or even notification to the next of kin. As the name implies, there is an irrebuttable presumption that all appropriate and useful donors would consent. This strategy is in fact followed in a number of other countries, including France, Israel, Switzerland, and Denmark. Would this regime violate the due process or just compensation clauses? Might it violate the First Amendment free exercise clause? See, Silver, The Case for a Post–Mortem Organ Draft and a Proposed Model Organ Draft Act, 68 B.U.L.Rev. 681 (1988), Note, "She's Got Bette Davis['s] Eyes: Assessing the Nonconsensual Removal of Cadaver Organs under the Takings and Due Process Clauses, 90 Colum.L.Rev. 528 (1990). A few

religions, including Orthodox Judaism and the traditional Navajo religion, forbid removal of organs from dead bodies. See Steinbrook, Kidneys for Transplantation? 6 J.Health Pol., Pol'y and L. 504 (1981). A more common proposal is to presume consent of the proposed donor, but have that consent be rebuttable by either the donor or family, Matas, Arras, Muysken, Tellis and Veith, Routine Removal of Cadaver Organs, 10 J.Health Pol., Pol'y and L. 231 (1985), or only by the donor, Dukeminier and Sanders, Organ Transplantation: A Proposal for Routine Salvaging of Cadaver Organs, 279 New Eng.J.Med. 413 (1968). Is this proposal likely to yield more organs? Is it more or less sensitive to the feelings of the bereaved? Would it make it easier or harder for physicians to get at the organs? In fact, some countries with presumed consent laws have been able to harvest few organs; apparently, doctors feel uncomfortable harvesting the organs without the family's consent, and the law discourages the appropriate discussions with the proposed donor and the family.

7. Another proposal that could be implemented on a national level would be the allowance of a tax credit or deduction for organ donors. Donors could be allowed to take a credit when they execute the irrevocable promise to donate, or they could be allowed an estate tax deduction after actual donation. A proposal to allow the second was introduced in the House of Representatives in the early 1980s, but it died without serious consideration.

8. A final, more radical, proposal for increasing the supply of cadaver organs is sale, by the potential donor while living (for immediate use, or for use upon death) or by the next of kin at death. See Buc and Bernstein, Buying and Selling Human Organs is Worth a Harder Look, 1 Health Scan 3 (Oct.1984); Note, Retailing Human Organs Under the Uniform Commercial Code, 16 John Marshall L.Rev. 393 (1983). If the proposal were limited to cadaver organs, what problems would this regime raise? See, Annas, Life, Liberty and the Pursuit of Organ Sales, 14 Hastings Center Report 22 (Feb.1984); Capron, Buying and Selling Human Organs, The Problems, 1 Health Scan 5 (Oct.1984). One solution to some of the problems is the creation of futures market in organs. See Cohen, Increasing the Supply of Transplant Organs: The Virtues of a Futures Market, 58 George Washington L.Rev. 1 (1989). This debate has been resolved at the federal level, at least for the time being:

42 U.S.C.A. § 274(e) Prohibition of Organ Purchases

(a) Prohibition

It shall be unlawful for any person to knowingly acquire, receive, or otherwise transfer any human organ for valuable consideration for use in human transplantation if the transfer affects interstate commerce.

(b) Penalties

Any person who violates subsection (a) of this section shall be fined not more than $50,000 or imprisoned not more than five years, or both.

(c) Definitions

For purposes of subsection (a) of this section:

(1) The term "human organ" means the human (including fetal) kidney, liver, heart, lung, pancreas, bone marrow, cornea, eye, bone, and skin or any subpart thereof and any other human organ (or any subpart thereof, including that derived from a fetus) specified by the Secretary of Health and Human Services by regulation.

(2) The term "valuable consideration" does not include the reasonable payments associated with the removal, transportation, implantation, processing, preservation, quality control, and storage of a human organ or the expenses of travel, housing, and lost wages incurred by the donor of a human organ in connection with the donation of the organ.

* * *

What is the effect of the exception in this statute and the exceptions in Section 10(b) of the UAGA? Could a hospital with an active trauma center thwart the transplant programs at competing hospitals by charging high fees for removal, transportation, processing, preservation and storage of organs removed? Could a hospital with a trauma center simply refuse to provide harvested organs to competing hospitals? Could it refuse to provide those organs unless it had no qualified in-house recipients for the organ?

b. Organs From Live Donors

Hearts, lungs, and livers can, of course, be removed only from the dead. A living person who donated these organs would be a suicide; a physician who removed them would be guilty of homicide. Kidneys and bone marrow, however, may be donated by the living. Transplants of these organs from living donors with similar tissue have been more successful than cadaver transplants. Thus there has been substantial use of live related donors for these organs.

When the potential donor is a live adult family member few legal problems arise. Although organ removal is major surgery and bone marrow aspiration is extremely painful, a family member, motivated by heroism, altruism and guilt, is frequently willing to serve as a donor. In the case where the potential donor refuses, the law will not compel the gift. See McFall v. Shimp, 10 Pa.D. & C.3d 90 (1978) (request by leukemia victim to compel cousin to donate bone marrow refused), described in Frost, Review Essay, The New Body Snatchers, 1983 A.B.F.Res.J. 718, 727. See also *Hall v. Colloden,* infra. In a number of cases, however, the potential donor is a minor or incompetent. Courts have reached varying results in these cases:

STRUNK v. STRUNK
Court of Appeals of Kentucky, 1969.
445 S.W.2d 145.

OSBORNE, JUDGE.

The specific question involved upon this appeal is: Does a court of equity have the power to permit a kidney to be removed from an incompetent ward of the state upon petition of his committee, who is also his mother, for the purpose of being transplanted into the body of his brother, who is dying of a fatal kidney disease? We are of the opinion it does.

The facts of the case are as follows: Arthur L. Strunk, * * * and Ava Strunk, * * * are the parents of two sons. Tommy Strunk is 28 years of age, married, an employee of the Penn State Railroad and a part-time student at the University of Cincinnati. Tommy is now suffering from chronic glomerulus nephritis, a fatal kidney disease. He is now being kept alive by frequent treatment on an artificial kidney, a procedure which cannot be continued much longer.

Jerry Strunk is 27 years of age, incompetent, and through proper legal proceedings has been committed to the Frankfort State Hospital and School, which is a state institution maintained for the feeble-minded. He has an I.Q. of approximately 35, which corresponds with the mental age of approximately six years. * * * When it was determined that Tommy, in order to survive, would have to have a kidney the doctors considered the possibility of using a kidney from a cadaver if and when one became available or one from a live donor if this could be made available. The entire family, his mother, father and a number of collateral relatives were tested. Because of incompatibility of blood type or tissue none were medically acceptable as live donors. As a last resort, Jerry was tested and found to be highly acceptable. This immediately presented the legal problem as to what, if anything, could be done by the family, especially the mother and the father to procure a transplant from Jerry to Tommy. The mother as a committee petitioned the county court for authority to proceed with the operation. The court found that the operation was necessary, that under the peculiar circumstances of this case it would not only be beneficial to Tommy but also beneficial to Jerry because Jerry was greatly dependent upon Tommy, emotionally and psychologically, and that his well-being would be jeopardized more severely by the loss of his brother than by the removal of a kidney.

* * *

A psychiatrist, in attendance to Jerry, who testified in the case, stated in his opinion the death of Tommy under these circumstances would have "an extremely traumatic effect upon him" (Jerry).

The Department of Mental Health of this Commonwealth has entered the case as amicus curiae and on the basis of its evaluation of the seriousness of the operation as opposed to the traumatic effect upon Jerry as a result of the loss of Tommy, recommended to the court that Jerry be permitted to undergo the surgery. Its recommendations are as follows:

* * *

"In view of this knowledge, we now have particular interest in this case. Jerry Strunk, a mental defective, has emotions and reactions on a scale comparable to that of normal person. He identifies with his brother Tom; Tom is his model, his tie with his family. Tom's life is vital to the continuity of Jerry's improvement at Frankfort State Hospital and School. The testimony of the hospital representative reflected the importance to Jerry of his visits with his family and the constant inquiries Jerry made about Tom's coming to see him. Jerry is aware he plays a role in the relief of this tension. We the Department of Mental Health must take all possible steps to prevent the occurrence of any guilt feelings Jerry would have if Tom were to die.

"The necessity of Tom's life to Jerry's treatment and eventual rehabilitation is clearer in view of the fact that Tom is his only living sibling and at the death of their parents, now in their fifties, Jerry will have no concerned, intimate communication so necessary to his stability and optimal functioning.

"The evidence shows that at the present level of medical knowledge, it is quite remote that Tom would be able to survive several cadaver transplants. Tom has a much better chance of survival if the kidney transplant from Jerry takes place."

* * * We are fully cognizant of the fact that the question before us is unique. Insofar as we have been able to learn, no similar set of facts has come before the highest court of any of the states of this nation or the federal courts. The English [and American] courts have apparently taken a broad view of the inherent power of the equity courts with regard to incompetents. * * * The inherent rule in these cases is that the chancellor has the power to deal with the estate of the incompetent in the same manner as the incompetent would if he had his faculties. This rule has been extended to cover not only matters of property but also to cover the personal affairs of the incompetent. * * *

* * *

The right to act for the incompetent in all cases has become recognized in this country as the doctrine of substituted judgment and is broad enough not only to cover property but also to cover all matters touching on the well-being of the ward. * * *

* * *

The medical practice of transferring tissue from one part of the human body to another (autografting) and from one human being to another (homografting) is rapidly becoming a common clinical practice. In many cases the transplants take as well where the tissue is dead as when it is alive. * * * The chance of success in the transfer of these organs is greatly increased when the donor and the donee are genetically related. * * *

The renal transplant is becoming the most common of the organ transplants. This is because the normal body has two functioning kidneys, one of which it can reasonably do without, thereby making it possible for one person to donate a kidney to another.   * * *

* * *

We are of the opinion that a chancery court does have sufficient inherent power to authorize the operation.   The circuit court having found that the operative procedures in this instance are to the best interest of Jerry Strunk and this finding having been based upon substantial evidence, we are of the opinion the judgment should be affirmed.   * * *

GUARDIANSHIP OF PESCINSKI

Supreme Court of Wisconsin, 1975.
67 Wis.2d 4, 226 N.W.2d 180.

WILKIE, CHIEF JUSTICE.

* * *

On January 31, 1974, Janice Pescinski Lausier petitioned for permission to Dr. H.M. Kauffman to conduct tests to determine whether Richard Pescinski was a suitable donor for a kidney transplant for the benefit of his sister, Elaine Jeske.   Elaine had both kidneys surgically removed in 1970 because she was suffering from kidney failure diagnosed as chronic glomerulonephritis.   In order to sustain her life, she was put on a dialysis machine, which functions as an artificial kidney. Because of the deterioration of Elaine, the petition contended that a kidney transplant was needed.   Subsequent tests were completed establishing that Richard was a suitable donor, and a hearing was then held on the subject of whether permission should be granted to perform the transplant.   * * *

At the time of the hearing Elaine was thirty-eight and her brother Richard was thirty-nine.   Evidence was produced at the hearing that the other members of the Pescinski family had been ruled out as possible donors on the basis of either age or health.   * * *

The testimony showed that Richard was suffering from schizophrenia—catatonic type, and that while he was in contact with his environment there was marked indifference in his behavior.   Dr. Hoffman, the medical director at the Good Samaritan Home, West Bend, Wisconsin, testified that in layman's terms Richard's mental disease was a flight from reality.   He estimated Richard's mental capacity to be age twelve. No evidence in the record indicates that Richard consented to the transplant.   Absent that consent, there is no question that the trial court's conclusion that it had no power to approve the operation must be sustained.

"A guardian of the person has the care of the ward's person and must look to the latter's health, education, and support."   The guardian must act, if at all, "loyally in the best interests of his ward."   There is absolutely no evidence here that any interests of the ward will be served by the transplant.

As far as the court's own power to authorize the operation, we are satisfied that the law in Wisconsin is clearly to the contrary. There is no statutory authority given the county court to authorize a kidney transplant or any other surgical procedure on a living person. We decline to adopt the concept of "substituted judgment" which was specifically approved by the Kentucky Court of Appeals in Strunk v. Strunk. * * * In the instant case the county court had no power to authorize the procedure, and the question is whether this supreme court can by using the doctrine of substituted judgment.

As the dissenting opinion in Strunk v. Strunk points out, "substituted judgment" is nothing more than an application of the maxim that equity will speak for one who cannot speak for himself. Historically, the substituted judgment doctrine was used to allow gifts of the property of an incompetent. If applied literally, it would allow a trial court, or this court, to change the designation on a life insurance policy or make an election for an incompetent widow, without the requirement of a statute authorizing these acts and contrary to prior decisions of this court.

We conclude that the doctrine should not be adopted in this state.

We, therefore, must affirm the lower court's decision that it was without power to approve the operation, and we further decide that there is no such power in this court. An incompetent particularly should have his own interests protected. Certainly no advantage should be taken of him. In the absence of real consent on his part, and in a situation where no benefit to him has been established, we fail to find any authority for the county court, or this court, to approve this operation.

Order affirmed. No costs on this appeal.

Notes and Questions

1. The *Presinski* court explicitly rejects the "substituted judgment" rule of *Strunk,* but would Pescinski have been decided differently if the facts were the same as those in *Strunk?* Would *Strunk* have been decided differently if a "best-interests" rather than substituted judgment test were applied? See, discussing these cases, Robertson, Organ Donations by Incompetents and the Substituted Judgment Doctrine, 76 Colum.L.Rev. 48 (1976).

2. In Strunk, a sibling donor for the needy brother already existed. What if he had not? Could his parents have deliberately conceived another child to be an organ donor for him? In 1989 the parents of Anissa Ayala, who suffered from leukemia and needed a bone marrow transplant, decided to have another child. Although they hoped that the new sibling could donate bone marrow to Anissa, they realized that there was only a one in four chance she would be a match. Anissa's sister, Marissa, was born in 1990, and she will qualify as a match. She will be physically able to donate

marrow at six months. Extracting bone marrow for transplantation is risky and painful. Should she be required to do so? Should she be forbidden to do so?

Even if we do not force family members who are potential donors to make their donations, should we require those who might be potential donors to undergo blood tests to determine if there is a bone marrow match? In late 1990 the Illinois Supreme Court upheld a ruling that 3½ year old twin half siblings to a thirteen year old with leukemia could not be forced to submit to the blood tests against the wishes of their mother, who was never married to the twins' father. The father of all three children had sought the order. Following the decision the attorney for the father said, "It is clear from whatever reasons the court gives that [the twins' mother's] legal position was sound, but certainly I have no respect for her moral position." See Fegelman, Boy Seeking Marrow Loses in High Court, Chicago Tribune, Sept. 29, 1990, at 5. Do you agree that her legal position was sound? Do you agree that her moral position was unsound?

———

Donations can also be made by unrelated donors. The likelihood of a tissue match between an unrelated donor and donee, however, is relatively small, and thus a large pool of potential donors must be assembled before a match can be made. Assembly of such a pool is most easily accomplished under experimental conditions where confidentiality can be assured.

HEAD v. COLLOTON

Supreme Court of Iowa, 1983.
331 N.W.2d 870.

McCORMICK, JUSTICE.

This appeal presents a question concerning the right of access of a member of the general public to a hospital's record of the identity of a potential bone marrow donor. * * *

* * *

Plaintiff William Head is a leukemia victim who is currently undergoing chemotherapy in a Texas clinic. His illness is in relapse, and the prognosis is grim.

The University of Iowa Hospitals and Clinics include a bone marrow transplant unit. That unit maintains a bone marrow transplant registry, listing persons whose blood has been tissue-typed by the hospital. The tissue typing reveals blood antigen characteristics which must be known for determining whether a donor's bone marrow will be a suitable match-up for the bone marrow of a donee. A bone marrow transplant consists of removing bone marrow from a healthy person and infusing it into the body of a patient in the hope it will generate healthy white blood cells. The procedure is experimental between unrelated persons.

Late in 1982, plaintiff phoned the transplant unit and, through a series of conversations with a staff member, learned that the hospital's registry included the name of a woman who might, upon further testing, prove to be a suitable donor to him. Only one in approximately 6,000 persons would have blood with the necessary antigen characteristics.

The tissue typing of the woman, referred to in the record as "Mrs. X," had not been done for reasons of her own health but to determine her suitability as a blood platelet donor to a member of her family who was ill. The hospital subsequently placed her name in its platelet donor registry. Then, when it later established an experimental program involving bone marrow transplants between unrelated persons, the hospital, without Mrs. X's knowledge or consent, placed her name in the bone marrow transplant registry. When the hospital established the new program, its institutional review board approved a procedure for contacting persons listed on the registry to determine whether they would act as donors. The procedure involved sending a letter informing the person of the program, its nature and goals, and inviting the person's participation in it. If the letter was not answered, a staff member was authorized to telephone the person and ask a series of general questions designed to determine whether the person would volunteer as a donor.

After plaintiff's contact with the bone marrow unit, the unit staff on December 31, 1982, sent Mrs. X the general letter informing her about the program and encouraging her to participate in it. When no response to the letter was received, a staff member telephoned Mrs. X on January 10, 1983, and asked her the series of questions. In responding to those questions, Mrs. X said she was not interested in being a bone marrow donor. When asked if she might ever be interested in being a donor, she said, "Well, if it was for family, yes. Otherwise, no." Despite plaintiff's subsequent request that the hospital make a specific inquiry of Mrs. X in plaintiff's behalf or to disclose her identity to him so he could contact her, the hospital refused to contact her or to disclose her identity to plaintiff. He then brought the present action.

Defendants John Colloton and Lloyd J. Filer are hospital employees with access to the bone marrow transplant registry. Plaintiff asked for a mandatory injunction to require them to disclose the name and identity of the potential donor either to the court or to his attorney. He proposed that the court or counsel then be permitted to write the woman to notify her of plaintiff's need and her possible suitability as a donor, asking her if she would consider being a donor to plaintiff.

* * *

This case involves application of the provisions of chapter 68A, Iowa's public records statute. Under section 68A.1, "public records" include "all records and documents of or belonging to this state * * *." § 68A.1. Defendants concede that the records of the University of Iowa hospital, a state hospital, are public records within the meaning of this provision. Thus the bone marrow donor registry is a public record. Section 68A.2 provides for public access to all public records "unless some other provision of the Code expressly limits such right or requires such records to be kept confidential."

Defendants contend that the registry is required to be kept confidential pursuant to section 68A.7(2). In material part, section 68A.7 provides:

> The following public records shall be kept confidential, unless otherwise ordered by a court, by the lawful custodian of the records, or by another person duly authorized to release information:
>
> * * *
>
> 2. Hospital records and medical records of the condition, diagnosis, care, or treatment of a patient or former patient, including outpatient.
>
> * * *

Chapter 68A is Iowa's freedom of information statute. [ ] Its purpose is "to open the doors of government to public scrutiny—to prevent government from secreting its decision-making activities from the public, on whose behalf it is its duty to act." [ ] The act establishes a liberal policy of access from which departures are to be made only in discrete circumstances. [ ] The specific exemptions in section 68A.7 are to be construed narrowly. * * *

* * *

[Plaintiff] contends section 68A.7(2) is inapplicable on two bases. One is that a hospital record is not confidential unless it is a patient record. The other basis is that the tissue-typing record of Mrs. X is not a patient record. Defendants also offer a two-pronged argument. One prong is that a hospital record need not be a patient record to be confidential. The other is that the tissue-typing record is a hospital record of a patient within the meaning of the statute. We are thus confronted with a legal issue, requiring interpretation of section 68A.7(2).

* * *

* * * We agree with plaintiff that the only hospital records made confidential by the statute are those "of the condition, diagnosis, care, or treatment of a patient or former patient, including outpatient." * * *

We must next determine whether the record to which plaintiff seeks access is that kind of hospital record. * * *

* * *

The critical issue is whether Mrs. X was a hospital patient for purposes of section 68A.7(2) when she submitted to tissue typing as a potential platelet donor. The ordinary meaning of the word "patient" is "a person under medical or surgical treatment." [ ] The word "treatment" is broad enough to embrace all steps in applying medical arts to a person. * * *

The evidence shows the hospital believed Mrs. X became a patient when she submitted to tissue typing. Dr. Roger Gingrich, director of the hospital's bone marrow transplant program, testified she was a patient. He said: "I would regard any person who interfaces themselves with the medical profession and out of that interaction there's biologic information obtained about the * * * person, in fact to be a patient, to [have] established a doctor-patient relationship." * * * Although this testimony is not conclusive on the issue, it is consistent with the broad dictionary definition of the treatment concept.

It is also consistent with caselaw that recognizes the same duty between physician and donor as exists between physician and patient generally. [ ] In [one] case the court said the relationship is the same: "Once a [blood] donor is accepted (medical reasons rule out some donors) his person is unquestionably placed under the control of the hospital personnel operating the laboratory, and he must rely on their professional skills as in any other hospital-patient relationship." [ ]

Perhaps even more importantly the doctors' testimony is consistent with the reality of the situation. When a person submits to a hospital procedure, the hospital's duty should not depend on whether the procedure is for that person's benefit or the potential benefit of someone else. The fiduciary relationship is the same, and the standard of care is the same. In addition, just as with patients generally, a potential donor has a valuable right of privacy.

An individual's interest in avoiding disclosure of personal matters is constitutionally based. [ ] This right is also recognized at common law. [ ] A valuable part of the right of privacy is the right to avoid publicity concerning private facts. This right can be as important to a potential donor as to a person in ill health. The Hippocratic Oath makes no distinction based on how medical confidences are acquired. [ ] Nor does the American Medical Record Association make such a distinction in its model policy for maintenance of confidentiality of patient health information adopted in 1977. *See* 26 *Medical Trial Technique Quarterly* 195 (Fall 1979).

The conclusion that a potential donor is a patient and should have the privacy rights of a patient is merely reenforced by the testimony in the present record concerning the possible chilling effect of disclosure upon medical research. That evidence is not determinative of the issue.

We conclude that the hospital record of Mrs. X is the hospital record of the "condition, diagnosis, care or treatment of a patient, or former patient" within the meaning of section 68A.7(2). Therefore the record is confidential.

* * *

Notes and Questions

1. The court seems to weigh the confidentiality of the anonymous potential donor more highly than the life of Mr. Head. Is the issue really confidentiality or coercion? Obviously, revealing the name of Mrs. X to Mr. Head, and thus to the media, would have been an egregious breach of confidentiality, but he did not seek this. Rather he sought one more appeal, made by the court or his counsel. What would the effect of such an appeal have been on Mrs. X? If this coercive effect is the court's real concern, how does it differ from the coercion faced by a family member asked for an organ? Ironically, since the *Head* case received widespread media coverage at the time, Mr. Head's appeal may have reached Mrs. X even though he lost the case.

A problem similar to that faced by *Head* also emerges where a transplant candidate who has been adopted is seeking her natural family. Here the interest of the potential donee may conflict with the confidentiality policy of the adoption laws. See In re George, 630 S.W.2d 614 (Mo.App. 1982).

2. The issue of organ sales also arises with respect to live "donors", who are potential sources of kidneys, eyes, and bone marrow. Such sales raise even more poignant ethical problems than do sale of cadaver organs: should an impoverished individual be allowed to sell a kidney to raise money to support himself or his family? To pay for necessary medical care for a child? Will the federal law, which permits sale of "soft tissues" like blood but prohibits sales of organs, merely export the market to some other country? Will Americans who need organs seek to purchase them in Ethiopia or India, or somewhere else where the price will be low? Will this lead to the development of organ colonies, where impoverished families will be bred to provide organs for wealthy foreigners?

At one Indian clinic live kidney donors are paid $1800 per kidney, six times what the average Indian could expect to earn in a year. The Indian clinic doctor explains the plight of his patients directly. "Either I buy, or they die." See Bailey, Should I Be Allowed to Buy Your Kidney? Forbes, May 28, 1990, at 365. Is it appropriate for the United States government to tell governments in impoverished countries that they cannot permit this conduct?

In fact, these who regularly deal with live organ "donations" in the United States say that "donors" in this country often end up with some economic gain. Some American ethicists have suggested that outlawing this market has simply forced it underground where it cannot be appropriately regulated.

3. The possibility of organ sales has generated creative, if somewhat whimsical, comment on legal issues far afield from the traditional concerns of law and medicine. Consider, for example, the income tax consequences of organ sales. Would sale of an organ result in taxable income? If so would it be ordinary income or capital gain? If capital gain, how would one value the basis? If an organ is donated, does it result in a charitable deduction? See, Note, Tax Consequences of Transfers of Body Parts, 73 Colum.L.Rev. 842 (1973). If the purchase of an organ were financed, could

it be repossessed if the donee defaulted on payments? See Francis, Artificial and Transplanted Organs: Moveable Parts and the Unmoving Law, 11 J.Contemp.L. 29, 54–55 (1984).

4. Despite a lack of litigation, organ transplantation does raise a number of liability issues. First, what does informed consent mean in the organ transplantation setting? What risks should the potential donee be informed of? What treatment alternatives? What should be said about the probability of success? If the donee is not fully informed and an undisclosed risk results in injury or death, what problems will the patient face in seeking damages? See, Overcast, Merrikan and Evans, Malpractice Issues in Heart Transplantation, 10 Am.J.L. & Med. 363, 377–386 (1985).

5. If the organ proves defective does the patient have any recourse against the donor, the donor's estate, or the organization or institution that procured the organ, under a warranty or strict liability theory? Consider the effect of Iowa Code Ann. § 142A.8, which is exemplary of legislation in many states.

Iowa Code Ann. § 142A.8. Service but not a sale

The procurement, processing, distribution or use of whole blood, plasma, blood products, blood derivatives and other human tissues such as corneas, bones or organs for the purpose of injecting, transfusing or transplanting any of them into the human body is declared to be, for all purposes, the rendition of a service by every person participating therein and, whether or not any remuneration is paid therefor, is declared not to be a sale of such whole blood, plasma, blood products, blood derivatives or other tissues, for any purpose, subsequent to July 1, 1969. However, any person or entity that renders such service warrants only under this section that due care has been exercised and that acceptable professional standards of care in providing such service according to the current state of the medical arts have been followed. Strict liability, in tort, shall not be applicable to the rendition of such service.

Even if a donee cannot establish a claim based upon a strict liability or warranty theory, he may be able to prevail if the institution that supplied the organ was negligent. See Ravenis v. Detroit General Hospital, 63 Mich.App. 79, 234 N.W.2d 411 (1975). Litigation may also result if a donor's organs are removed before the donor is dead, if the donor is improperly pronounced dead, if the organs are removed without proper consent, or if negligence on the part of the institution or professional that removed the organs contributed to the donor's death. How much protection does the UAGA offer physicians in these circumstances? See Williams v. Hofmann, 66 Wis.2d 145, 223 N.W.2d 844 (1974).

6. Finally, might a physician whose negligence necessitated an organ transplant be liable to the *donor,* whose donation was caused by the negligence? Consider Moore v. Shah, 90 A.D.2d 389, 458 N.Y.S.2d 33 (1982), in which a kidney donor sued a physician whose alleged negligence upon the donee's father resulted in the need for the donation. The Court ultimately determined that the defendant owed no duty to potential kidney donors and rejected the claim.

The predicate for holding a defendant liable must be that a duty is owed the plaintiff, the breach of which duty is the proximate cause of plaintiff's injury [   ]. In order to establish the existence of such duty, a defendant must foresee that his negligence could cause injury, in this case not only to his patient, but to the patient's son as well. * * * Plaintiff contends, however, that the rescue doctrine serves to establish the requisite foreseeability between the doctor's negligence in treatment of his father and injury to himself as the rescuer. * * *

It is true that a wrong perpetrated upon a victim is also a wrong to his rescuer [   ] and that so long as the rescue is not a rash or wanton act, the rescue doctrine extends a defendant's liability to the rescuer. * * * However, we find that foreseeability alone is not enough to impose liability. Since plaintiff was never defendant's patient, no duty to him originally existed. Therefore, we are here involved with a question of whether foreseeability should be employed as the sole means to create a duty where none existed before [   ]. It is obvious that extension of liability of a physician to every person who conceivably might come forward as a kidney donor could create a group beyond manageable limits. * * *

458 N.Y.S. at 34. Should organ donors be treated differently from other rescuers in tort law?

Chapter 7

HEALTH CARE COST CONTROL

INTRODUCTION

A. THE PROBLEM OF HEALTH CARE COST INFLATION

Until quite recently quality was the chief concern of legal intervention in the health care system. The first five chapters of this book, therefore, primarily concern legal responses to problems in the quality of medical care. In recent years, however, health care regulation has become even more concerned—indeed obsessed—with another problem: the high and rapidly increasing cost of medical care.

Recent increases in the cost of medical care are alarming. National expenditures on health care have increased from $12.7 billion in 1950 to $41.9 billion in 1965 to $647 billion in 1990. Per capital spending on medical care has grown from $82 per year in 1950 to $211 in 1965 to $2511 in 1990. Since much of the growth in absolute expenditures reflects the general declining value of the dollar, it is more useful to compare increases in the cost of medical care to increases in consumer prices generally or to measure them as a proportion of the gross national product. Throughout the past two decades the rate of inflation in medical costs has substantially exceeded the rate of inflation generally. Between 1980 and 1988, the medical care component of the consumer price index increased 85% compared to a general increase of inflation of 43%. The proportion of the gross national product devoted to medical care has also risen from 4.4% in 1950 to 6% in 1965 to 12% in 1990. Americans spend more money on health care than they spend on groceries, owner-occupied housing, or transportation.

The growth in government expenditures for medical care has been even more dramatic. In 1967 the federal government spent $12 billion on health care, the state and local governments $7 billion; in 1990 the federal government spent $196 billion, the state and local governments $73 billion. In 1988 federal health care expenditures consumed 12% of the federal budget. Health care cost inflation has also hit private industry hard. The health insurance bill of General Motors for 1987 absorbed revenue equivalent to the sale of 270,000 cars. Finally, inflation in certain key sectors of the health care industry has exceeded even the impressive growth rates of industry costs generally. While the overall cost of personal health care increased from $35.6 to $478.3 billion from 1965 to 1988, the cost of nursing home care increased from $1.7 billion to $43.1 billion during the same period.

Why do health care costs continue to rise faster than other expenditures? To some extent the answer lies with demographic changes and with new approaches to disease and its treatment. Throughout the past two decades the American population has been aging. The elderly, particularly the very old, consume much more health care than do younger persons. Those over 65 constitute 11% of the population, yet they are responsible for 33% of health care expenditures. The focus of medical treatment has also been changing and expanding. As fewer persons die from simple infectious diseases, more and more medical care has been devoted to chronic and intractable conditions that require much greater expenditures. Conditions formerly viewed solely as criminal conduct or moral failings, such as drug abuse or alcoholism, are now treated as diseases, at great cost. Medical care is increasingly used not just to cure acute diseases but also to improve functioning and well-being. Environmental and behavioral risk factors affecting health have multiplied, while the family systems that formerly delivered much supportive health care have weakened.

By themselves, however, these changes explain only a fairly small proportion of the increase in health care expenditures. By most estimates, the rise in per capita hospital admissions over the past decade (itself a fact only partially explained by demographic changes) accounts for only about 10% of the increase in hospital costs. Population growth accounts for even less. The main reason that health care costs are rising faster than general inflation is that health care resources are being used more and more intensively. Hospitalized individuals, in particular, are consuming services at an increasing rate, and these services are increasingly expensive. But do increased expenditures on health care and growing use of medical resources produce a proportionate improvement in health? Are increased expenditures justified by the benefits they purchase?

Many believe that the increased use of health care resources has not resulted in improvement of health, or even of health care, but is rather a result of distortions in the market for health care. Some argue that these distortions necessitate more regulation of health care. Others advocate laws that would remove impediments to market competition. This section considers distortions in the market for health care. The remainder of the chapter examines proposed solutions.

B. DEMAND DISTORTIONS

The demand for health care is different in kind from the demand for cars or television sets. How different is a matter of much conjuncture and debate, but the difference is uncontrovertible. When I am really sick or seriously injured, I want medical care in a different way than I may want a new videotape recorder. I am anxious. I may fear death, impairment or disability. My personal integrity is under assault. I will often have little time to research my options and decide on the most appropriate treatment. Even if I had time, such information would be difficult and expensive to obtain. Moreover, as medical emergencies are relatively infrequent events, I will have little experience on which to base such a decision. My capacity for making an informed choice is further limited by the complex, technical nature of the judgments that need to be made and by the fact that many medical judgments are based on professional experience or intuition, which cannot be fully communicated. I must to a large extent trust a physician to direct the use of medical resources to diagnose and treat my condition. Even when the episode is completed I will often be unable to evaluate the physician's judgment. I may have done just as well with a different course of treatment, or with no treatment at all. If I am suffering from a chronic condition demanding repeated treatment, or if I am seeking a relatively common, simple form of treatment—a well-baby check or uncomplicated delivery—I may have more basis for evaluating the care I observe. In general, however, consumers cannot evaluate health care in the same way they select a box of soap or cereal.

Most health care consumers rely on physicians to make medical treatment decisions. Although physicians receive only approximately 22% of the money spent on personal health care, they direct the expenditure of about 70% of such funds. Physicians are thus the true purchasers of health care, even if they are not its ultimate consumers. This causes several problems. First, physicians are trained to view medical services as objectively necessary, rather than as goods that compete for the consumer's dollar with other goods and services. The physician is driven by the technological imperative: "If there is a technique for addressing this problem, my patient deserves it, regardless of cost." However commendable these attitudes may be, their cost implications are obvious. Moreover, physicians confront an obvious conflict of interest. They not only diagnose the patient's problem and direct the patient's consumer decisions, they also sell to the patient their own testing and treatment services. They are thus both the buyer, as agent, and the seller of medical care. Yet physicians and patients may only dimly perceive this conflict, for in most instances health insurance, rather than the patient, is paying for the care.

Major illnesses and injuries are uncertain in their occurrence and can be devastating in their effect. Most persons are risk-adverse: rather than face a small risk of incurring a large expense, they prefer to pay a smaller certain sum to pool the risk. Therefore, most Americans, about 87%, are covered either by private health insurance or by a government insurance program. Coverage is more likely for non-routine or expensive services. Thus, in 1988 only 5.3% of hospital expenditures were paid directly by patients, while 35.4% were covered by private insurance and 54.4% by public programs. On the other hand,

55.4% of dentists' services were paid for by individuals, as compared to 42.2% by private insurance, and 2.4% by public programs.

One insurance-induced distortion is the problem known as "moral hazard." Each individual who decides whether or not to consume (and each physician deciding whether or not to prescribe) a service for which the patient is fully insured is essentially deciding whether or not to consume a free good. If the service would be of any benefit at all, the logical decision is to "purchase" it. The obvious aggregate effect of many such decisions is, however, to increase health care costs. Insurance companies, of course, have an incentive to control costs, yet insurers have traditionally chosen to pass increased costs on to their insureds rather than to try aggressively to restrain costs. This choice is explained in part by the difficulty of monitoring utilization decisions of individual patients and physicians and by historic ties between insurers and providers.

Eighty-nine percent of private health insurance is provided by group policies, most of which are job related; thus, employers are the immediate purchasers of most health care insurance. Employers have traditionally been reluctant to alienate workers by being parsimonious with health care benefits (though this attitude now seems to be changing). Workers have also jealously protected these benefits. Seventy-eight per cent of strikes in 1989 involved health benefit issues. Moreover, employer contributions for health insurance have not been included in their employees' taxable income, making the dollar spent on health insurance worth more to employees than a dollar received in wages. Finally, for those covered by public insurance programs, predominantly Medicare and Medicaid, excess consumption of services does not even result in increased insurance payments. Consumption of those services is restrained only by the time it takes to obtain them, the self-restraint of patients or providers, and, in some programs, patient cost-sharing. Thus there has been—until recently—little to check the excess consumption of health insurance and of insured medical services.

The form of payment used by insurance companies has further increased health care costs. Until recently government programs, Blue Cross and Blue Shield, and many commercial insurers paid hospitals on a cost basis (i.e., they reimbursed hospitals their actual costs of providing care) and physicians on a charge basis (i.e., they reimbursed physicians what the physician charged for a service, so long as the charge was reasonable). Payments to physicians were separate from payments for physician-directed services, leaving physicians completely unaware of the cost of the services they were prescribing. It is hard to think of a more inflationary method of payment than to pay providers whatever they choose to charge for or to spend on service delivery; yet until recently this form of payment was the norm.

Finally, generous private insurance payment levels have until recently afforded health care institutions sufficient income to provide uncompensated care to the uninsured or underinsured while remaining in relatively strong financial health. Thus health care institutions have been spared the political scrutiny they have recently begun to receive as some institutions have turned away non-paying patients to maintain financial viability.

C. SUPPLY DISTORTIONS

For the past several decades, physicians have been able to maintain extraordinarily high incomes, over twice those of other professionals such as dentists and lawyers. For much of this period their earnings have increased faster than the rate of general inflation. The market for physicians has been in many respects uncompetitive. Entry into the market is subject to severe restrictions, including the limited number and high cost of medical schools and the necessity of obtaining state licenses and private certification. Professionals with more limited training have been strictly constrained from competing with physicians by the licensing and scope of practice laws, discussed in chapter 1. Physician associations have until recently prohibited dissemination of price information through ethical prohibitions on advertising and have fixed prices through fee or relative value schedules. The predominant form of pricing, fee-for-service, has encouraged physicians to overuse medical services. Fee-for-service has also facilitated price discrimination by permitting physicians to base fees on the patient's ability to pay. Innovative forms of practice that could have cut costs have until recently been strenuously and effectively opposed. Because physicians largely direct the consumption of their own services, some economists believe they can generate demand for these services, explaining the paradox that physician incomes are often higher in markets where there are more physicians per capita. Given these market conditions, doctors have been in a position to contribute to medical cost inflation.

The hospital market has also not behaved competitively. To the extent that hospitals have vied with each other, they have, some argue, competed primarily for physicians, who in turn produce patients needing services. This competition has often led to inefficiencies. It has caused hospitals to purchase expensive and unnecessary equipment to attract physicians, or to engage in cross-subsidization to finance physician teaching or research. It has been argued that doctors have been able to determine the shape and direction of hospitals to their benefit through the control they have exercised through their medical staff organizations and through the JCAHO (which they largely control). Most hospitals are nonprofit corporations. Though this structure may permit more choice of organizational objectives, those objectives will not necessarily include the economical delivery of care. Some have speculated that nonprofit hospitals are more likely to direct their energies to serving physicians, or to producing excessive services, excessive quality, or management perquisites, any of which may result in greater inefficiencies than would a profit motive.

D. THE ROLE OF GOVERNMENT

Government has played a significant role in increasing health care costs. Government currently pays directly for 41% of all personal health care and 54% of hospital care. Though increased government expenditures on health care have made health care available to many who could not otherwise afford it (see chapter 6), they have also increased demand for health care dramatically, and thus increased the overall amount society spends on health care, and probably costs experienced by other payers. The "free" nature of government care, and the cost-based form of reimbursement relied on until recently, have further contributed to the inefficient consumption of health care, by encouraging excess use of services by beneficiaries and excess expenditures by providers. The federal tax subsidy for employee health insurance has also contributed to high expenditures on insurance, which in turn has funded health cost escalation.

Many believe that the courts also contribute to the high cost of health care through medical malpractice litigation. Though malpractice premiums only account for about 1% of health care costs, defensive medicine in response to the threat of litigation may be a significant contributor to the cost of medical care. Finally, licensing laws, whatever their merits otherwise (see chapter 1), have probably maintained the cost of professional services at an artificially high level.

E. BIBLIOGRAPHY

More extensive analysis of health care cost concerns from the point of view of economists can be found in, P. Feldstein, Health Care Economics (2d Ed., 1983) [hereafter Feldstein]; P. Jacobs, The Economics of Health Care (1980); and P. Joskow, Controlling Hospital Costs (1981) [hereafter Joskow]. Short summaries of health care market failures can be found in A. Enthoven, Health Plan, 16–32 (1980); and Bovbjerg, Competition Versus Regulation in Medical Care: An Overdrawn Dichotomy, 34 Vand.L.Rev. 965, 966–73 (1981). For a contrary view, arguing that the market for medical care is perhaps not that radically different from other markets, see Pauly, Is Medical Care Different, in Federal Trade Commission, Competition in the Health Care Sector: Past, Present, and Future, 19 (1978); Pauly, Is Medical Care Different: Old Questions, New Answers, 13 J. Health Pol. Pol'y & L. 227 (1988).

F. CHAPTER COVERAGE

In the middle and late–1970s, as the problem of rising health care costs began to reach crisis proportions, comprehensive controls on health care costs were proposed. Little action was taken on these proposals, however, and such actions as were taken were on the whole unsuccessful. As we enter the 1990s, the search for a silver bullet to control health care costs nationally seems to have been abandoned for a time. The federal and state governments seem, by and large, preoccupied with controlling the costs of their own health care programs and show little interest in designing general solutions to the larger problem of health care costs. In the absence of comprehensive government action, each private insurer and employer is also striving to control its own costs, either by limiting those costs or by shifting them on to others.

This chapter begins by considering the two primary approaches that have been put forward for solving the problem of health care costs: competition and regulation. This discussion sets the stage for examining specific regulatory or competitive approaches in the materials that follow. Next, two comprehensive approaches to the problem of health care costs, holdovers from the 1970s, are considered: health planning and rate review. Then private approaches to cost containment are considered: utilization review, health maintenance organizations and preferred provider organizations. Government attempts to control the costs of government health care programs are examined next: Medicare prospective payment for hospitals and relative value payment schedules for doctors, Medicare and Medicaid fraud and abuse laws, and Peer Review Organizations. Finally, we return to the issue of national health insurance, left in abeyance at the end of the last chapter.

Although approaches to cost containment are discussed either as public or private strategies, it is important to note that most strategies are used in both the public and private sector. Utilization review, HMOs, or diagnosis-related group prospective payment, for example, play a role in both public and private strategies. In the materials that follow, however, approaches are organized for convenience as public or private strategies depending on where they currently seem to be playing the largest role.

I. COMPETITIVE AND REGULATORY APPROACHES TO COST CONTROL

A. THE COMPETITIVE DIAGNOSIS AND PRESCRIPTION

In the late 1970s a group of academics in economics, health policy and law began to assert that regulatory solutions to the problem of high and increasing health care costs were inevitably doomed to failure. They argued that efforts should be directed towards correcting fundamental defects in the market for health care, thereby unleashing the forces of market competition to bring down health care costs without counter-productive regulatory interventions. A procompetitive market approach to medical care cost-containment was consistent with the dominant conservative political culture that characterized the 1980s, and was warmly endorsed by federal policymakers in the early years of the Reagan presidency. Although competitive market reforms have nowhere been totally implemented, they have been extensively relied on for cost-containment in the private sector and play a small, but important role, in public insurance approaches to cost-containment.

The advocates of health care market competition begin by positing that health care is merely one commodity among many that contribute to the utility of consumers, and therefore ought to compete with other goods and services in the marketplace. Health care should, therefore, be subject to the either/or decisions that each of us face every day in deciding how to allocate our resources to maximize their value to us. However, market defects discussed in the introduction to this chapter, in particular, the effects of insurance and lack of information accessible to consumers, impede this form of decisionmaking. Moreover, where there has been competition, it has often been perverse. Insurance companies do not compete for insurance business by forcing providers to cut costs, but rather by offering the most comprehensive coverage. Hospitals, feeling no pressure from consumers or from insurers to cut costs, have traditionally competed to procure the latest technology and to keep beds full.

From this perspective government is part of the problem, not the solution. Advocates of competition particularly object that employees are not taxed for employer contributions to employee health insurance. This subsidy, which, it is estimated, will amount to $37.3 billion in foregone federal revenue in 1990 (compared to a projected $36 billion federal budget for Medicaid) creates incentives for the purchase of excessive insurance, which in turn encourages the purchase of medical care that is not cost-effective. Competition advocates also attack federal and state regulatory programs for creating producer protectionism and cross-subsidies and discouraging efficiency and innovation. They argue (1) that government is incapable of making hard choices concerning the rationing of health resources, because of the symbolic importance of health care, and (2) that unless health care is allocated by the market, health care costs will never be brought under control.

For pro-competitive critiques of the health care industry and of regulatory strategies for cost control, see Blumstein, Rationing Medical Resources: A Constitutional, Legal and Policy Analysis, 59 Tex.L.Rev. 1345 (1981) [hereafter Blumstein, Rationing]; Blumstein & Sloan, Redefining Government's Role in Health Care: Is a Dose of Competition What the Doctor Should Order? 34 Vand.L.Rev. 849 (1981); Havighurst, Competition in Health Services: Overview, Issues and Answers, 34 Vand.L.Rev. 1117 (1981); C. Havighurst, Deregulating the Health Care Industry (1982); Havighurst, Health Care Cost Containment Regulation: Prospects and an Alternative, 3 Am.J.L. & Med. 309 (1977).

Solutions proposed by competition advocates share a common focus: reintroducing an element of consumer choice into health care markets. They vary, however, with respect to the point at which consumer choice should be exercised. Some advocate forcing consumers to consider cost-benefit tradeoffs at the time they purchase health care services by increasing consumer cost-sharing through increased co-insurance and deductibles. Others advocate restructuring the market for health insurance to assure that consumers make a choice among several different insurance plans at the point where they, or their employer, purchase insurance. This section will discuss these two strategies. A third strategy for increasing competition—removing restraints on competition through the antitrust laws—will be discussed in the next chapter.

Before we consider differences between the two strategies, however, areas of common ground among all competition advocates should be noted. Competition advocates all agree that current tax incentives need to be changed substantially. Most concur that public health care benefits (i.e., Medicare and Medicaid) should be restructured to remove current incentives to overuse. Most favor a voucher or similar system that would give government medical aid recipients the ability to buy health care, but would otherwise require them to purchase in the same markets as other consumers.

The advocates of cost-sharing, the first strategy, argue that first-dollar insurance coverage (which totally covers medical care without requiring the insured to pay any part of the cost) renders it impossible for health care consumers to act as discriminating economic actors. Their solution to this problem is to restructure health insurance so that consumers are forced to make cost-benefit comparisons at the time medical care is delivered, and physicians are forced to acknowledge that their treatment decisions will have a direct financial impact on their patients. They would encourage consumers (through tax credits, for example) to secure insurance policies with high deductibles and coinsurance amounts. These deductible and co-insurance amounts would vary with income, and be set at the highest tolerable level for each class. (For example, one advocate proposes requiring a policy with a $1,250 deductible and 20% coinsurance to a maximum of $2500 a year for a family earning $20,000 a year). A medical loan program could be created to assist those who did not have money available for care at the time medical costs were incurred.

Cost-sharing advocates assert that patients, aware of the cost consequences of their decisions, would avoid purchasing unnecessary care and seek to purchase from the most efficient providers. Physicians, in turn, would also consider the cost of services they provided and order only cost-effective services, aware that their patients were paying for a large proportion of medical care out of pocket. Physicians would redefine their fiduciary obligation to their patients to require the delivery of cost-effective care.

Pro-competitive reform proposals that emphasize increasing consumer cost-sharing include Feldstein, The High Cost of Hospitals—and What to do About it, 48 Pub.Int. 40 (1977); M. Pauly, An Analysis of National Health Insurance Proposals (1971); Schwartz, The Inevitable Failure of Current Cost–Containment Strategies: Why They Can Provide Only Temporary Relief, 257 J.A.M.A. 228 (1987); and Seidman,

Consumer Choice Health Plan and Patient Cost–Sharing Strategy: Can They be Reconciled? [hereafter Seidman], in a New Approach to the Economics of Health Care (M. Olson, ed. 1981); Seidman, Income–Related Consumer Cost Sharing: A Strategy for the Health Sector, in National Health Insurance: What Now, What Later, What Never (M. Pauly, ed. 1980).

The cost-sharing strategy is criticized both by those skeptical of competitive strategies and by pro-competition advocates who favor reorganizational competitive solutions. For a sampling of criticism of cost-sharing, see Bovbjerg, Competition Versus Regulation in Medical Care: An Overdrawn Dichotomy, 34 Vand.L.Rev. 965, 979, 989 (1981); A. Enthoven, Health Plan: The Only Practical Solution to the Soaring Cost of Medical Care, 32–36 (1981); Gabel & Monheit, Will Competition Plans Change Insurer–Provider Relationships? 61 Milbank Mem. Fund Q. 614, 618–620 (1983) [hereafter Gabel & Monheit]; Luft, On the Potential Failure of Good Ideas: An Interview with the Originator of Murphy's Law, 7 J. Health Pol. Pol'y & L. 45, 46–7 (1982); Rosenblatt, Health Care, Markets, and Democratic Values, 34 Vand.L.Rev. 1067, 1079 (1981) [hereafter Rosenblatt]; Vladeck, The Market vs. Regulation: The Case for Regulation, 59 Milbank Me. Fund Q. 209, 211–2 (1981) [hereafter Vladeck, Regulation].

A thorough study of cost-sharing conducted by the Rand Corporation in the late 1970s found that cost-sharing could result in significant reductions in health care expenditures without significant negative effects on health status. It also found, however, that cost-sharing resulted in a dramatic reduction in the use of medical care by poor children, that effective care was as likely to be foregone as ineffective care, and that the health status of some persons, particularly poor adults with high blood pressure, was adversely affected by cost-sharing. Manning et al., Health Insurance and the Demand for Medical Care: Evidence from a Randomized Experiment, 77 Am.Econ.Rev. 251 (1987); Lohr, Use of Medical Care in the Rand Health Insurance Experiment: Diagnosis and Service Specific Analysis of a Randomized Controlled Trial, 24 Medical Care 51 (Supplement 1986).

The best known market restructuring proposals are a book and a series of articles published by Alain Enthoven of Stanford. See Enthoven, Health Plan: The Only Practical Solution to the Soaring Cost of Medical Care (1980); Enthoven & Kronick, A Consumer–Choice Health Plan for the 1990s, 320 New Eng.J.Med. 29, 101 (1989); Consumer Choice Health Plan, 298 New Eng.J.Med. 709 (1978). Most such proposals would require employers to offer employees a choice of insurance packages varying in price according to coverage. Alteration of tax incentives—including elimination or substantial diminution of the current exclusion of employer contributions to health insurance, and, possibly, the creation of tax credits or rebates—and limitations on employer contributions to health benefits would increase employee consciousness of the cost of health insurance and encourage cost-benefit judgments in the purchase of health care. This would, in turn, compel

insurers to compete with each other, primarily by creating or contracting with alternative health care delivery organizations, such as Health
Maintenance Organizations (HMOs) and Preferred Provider Organizations (PPOs). You have already been introduced to these entities
elsewhere in this text (Chapters 2 and 5). They will be discussed later
in this chapter.

In addition to Enthoven's proposals, see also, setting out market-re-
structuring proposals, Committee for Economic Development, Reform-
ing Health Care: A Market Prescription (1987); Enthoven, A Consumer
Choice Health Plan for the 1990s, 320 New Eng.J.Med. 2994 (1989);
McClure, Implementing a Competitive Medical Care System through
Public Policy, 7 J. Health Pol. Pol'y & L. 2 (1982); McClure, Structure
and Incentive Problems in Economic Regulation of Medical Care, 59
Milbank Mem. Fund Q. 107 (1981); McClure, On Broadening the
Definition of and Removing Regulatory Barriers to a Competitive
Health Care System, 3 J. Health Pol. Pol'y & Law 303 (1978). A
version of Enthoven's plan has recently been adopted in the Nether-
lands.

The market reorganization proposals of Enthoven and others have
been much criticized by those who favor regulatory approaches or are
skeptical about the potential for competition within the health care
industry. Among the most informative critical sources are Brown,
Competition and Health Cost Containment: Cautions and Conjectures,
59 Millbank Memorial Fund Q. 145 (1981); Gabel & Monheit, supra;
Homer, Some Pitfalls in Creating Competition Between HMOs and
Fee-for-Service Delivery, 7 J. Health Pol. Pol'y & L. 686 (1982); Luft,
Potential Failures; Marmour, Boyer, & Greenberg, Medical Care Com-
petition: Are Tax Incentives Enough in M. Olson, New Approach to the
Economics of Health Care, 424 (1981) [hereafter "Olson"].

Critics note in particular that after a decade of dramatic expansion,
competitive approaches to health care delivery have not yet had an
appreciable effect on diminishing the cost of health care and health
insurance. Indeed, the rate of these costs seem to be increasing, see
Fuchs, The Competition Revolution in Health Care, Health Affairs, 5
(Summer 1988); Gabel, et al., The Changing World of Group Health
Insurance, Health Affairs, 48 (Summer 1988); McLaughlin, Market
Response to HMOs: Price Competition or Rivalry? 25 Inquiry 207–18
(1988). See, generally, on the state of health care competition in the
late 1980s, Symposium, The Managed Care Revolution, Health Affairs,
Summer 1988; Special Issue on Competition in the Health Care Sector:
Ten Years Later, 13 J. Health Pol. Pol'y & L. 223 (1988), and on a
program for further reform, Greaney, Competitive Reform in Health
Care: The Vulnerable Revolution, 1988 Yale J.Reg. 179 (1988).

As you review cost-control strategies discussed in the remainder of
this chapter, consider which are properly considered competitive strategies, and evaluate the extent to which they are meeting the expectations of competitive reform advocates.

B. REGULATORY SOLUTIONS

Regulatory approaches to the problem of health care cost control have on the whole not elicited the same ideological fervor garnered by market approaches. Arguments in favor of regulatory strategies are found principally in articles challenging market solutions, see Marone, American Political Culture and the Search for Lessons from Abroad, 15 J. Health Pol. Pol'y & L. 129 (1990); Rosenblatt, Health Care, Markets, and Democratic Values, 34 Vand.L.Rev. 1067 (1981), Vladeck, The Market vs. Regulation: The Case for Regulation, 59 Milbank Mem. Fund.Q. 209 (1981). One of the most persistent and influential advocates of increased government intervention to control the cost of medical care has been a Canadian economist, Robert Evans. Excerpts from one of his recent articles, which follow, argue that, absent greater regulatory involvement, a "free" market may lead to higher health care costs and put the problem of controlling health care costs in the United States in an international perspective.

EVANS, TENSION, COMPRESSION, AND SHEAR: DIRECTIONS, STRESSES, AND OUTCOMES OF HEALTH CARE COST CONTROL

15 J.Health Pol., Pol'y, & L. 101 (1990).

* * *

Health "Costs" Paid, Passed on, or Pocketed?

The public rhetoric surrounding the costs of health care invests them with an almost elemental quality, like gravity or the tides. Vast impersonal forces drive them upward, and the task of health care policy, in every developed society, is to find ways of "controlling" those costs. *Controlling*, almost self-evidently, refers to slowing their growth and limiting their share of overall national income and wealth.

Yet the meaning of *control* is by no means restricted to the placing of limits. The controls of an automobile include the accelerator and the steering wheel, as well as the brakes. *Controlling health care costs* can refer equally well to efforts to *increase* such costs, or to reallocate them across the members of a society.

* * *

The providers of health care, in every society, have a powerful economic, but also professional and psychological, interest in "controlling" the costs of health care—driving them upward—in the process of drawing more resources into their sector, to respond to their priorities [ ]. And in every society, they possess a number of powerful forms of influence enabling them to do so.

* * *

The organizations and individuals responsible for reimbursing the costs of health care have a somewhat different view of those costs, and correspondingly a more complex form of interest in control. It is useful to distinguish between organizations which simply administer the payments process—social and private insurers—and those which ultimately bear the costs—firms, governments, workers and their unions, and individual patients or insurance subscribers. The latter have a clear interest in limiting the extent of their own outlays. But the objectives of the administering organizations are more ambiguous.

Insurers, public or private, derive the resources available for their own purposes from the spread between total premiums and other contributions, and total outlays. They may therefore have an interest in controlling their own outlays *for given levels of receipts*. But increases in total costs of health care also increase the demand/need for insurance and the volume of funds under administration. Moreover, aggressive attempts to limit the growth of costs may alienate providers and threaten other institutional objectives. Correspondingly, insurers have tended over the years to make rhetorical rather than effective responses to escalation.

The concern of reimbursers, however, whether they are the ultimate payers or simply administrators of others' payments, is for their own fiscal situation. Transferring the burden of costs to some other individual or group is equivalent to reducing it, as far as the institution is concerned, and may be a great deal less stressful managerially and politically. The consequences of such "cost pass-through" for overall, system wide performance (and for the incomes of providers) are of course very different from those of actual reduction and are quite apparent in the aggregate data. But collective consequences do not show up on the bottom line of the individual transactor, at least not directly and in an identifiable form.

CONFLICTING INTERESTS: SOURCES AND DIRECTIONS OF STRESS

These alternative objectives for the control of health care costs, up, down, and sideways, suggest an analogy with concepts from engineering. The stresses generated in a society by the application of forces to control health care costs can be analyzed as tension, compression, and shear.

The attempts by some organized groups to keep overall costs rising create tension stresses as the resources of the rest of society are stretched to provide a combination of larger incomes and wider professional opportunities for the providers (and would-be providers) of health care. These include not only individual doctors, nurses, druggists, and dentists, but also the large and powerful organizations and associations in which they are combined—hospitals, health science centers, professional associations, and private corporations. Added to them are the whole range of suppliers of pharmaceuticals, equipment, insurance and consulting services, and, more generally, all those whose incomes are generated in the health industry.

Against these forces are arrayed those who have an interest in compressing the industry, in resisting its growth dynamic. Their concerns may be simply over relative income shares—higher incomes for health care providers imply lower for everyone else, ceteris paribus —or, more generally, they may be concerned that the expansion of the health care sector represents a distortion of a society's priorities such that too few resources are left available for other more important objectives.

But for most individuals and paying organizations, the shifting of costs to someone else can be a strategy as effective as, and perhaps less costly than, the actual control of costs. Such sideways shifts build up shear stresses as the "target" groups attempt to resist the cost transfer. In this environment, attention shifts from the levels and trends in overall costs to the distributional issues of who shall carry the principal burdens of paying for them, whatever those burdens turn out to be.

* * *

The buildup of stresses within the health care system of all countries, the long-perpetuated sense of crisis, is thus a reflection of the influences of these three types of forces. The tensions created by the expansionary dynamic of the health care system itself lead either to offsetting compressive forces or to shear stresses as individual components of the system try to relieve themselves of the tension by transferring the stress to other participants, who in turn resist.

* * *

HEALTH CARE SPENDING AND HEALTH: THE LINKS ARE MISSING

Utilization patterns within health care appear to be determined neither by the objective needs of the patient nor by the characteristics of the available technology, but by a very subjective process of interpretation by individual practitioners. This leads to widely varying patterns of care (and costs) from place to place, time to time, and practitioner to practitioner, without any evidence of corresponding variations in health outcomes. * * *

But it is not at all foolish to *claim* the existence of such a tight linkage between inputs and outputs, if one is trying to convince individuals or communities to contribute more resources to the health care sector. * * *

"Shroud waving," or threatening the noncompliant patient or society with dire consequences ("You don't want your baby to die, do you?") is an ancient strategy. The modern allegation that attempts to restrain cost escalation must lead to rationing and unnecessary pain, suffering, and perhaps death is simply "your money or your life" in more roundabout language.

Indeed, even if utilization patterns were externally determined by the objective needs of patients, this would still not imply that *expenditures* were beyond the control of public policy. It would leave open the question of the levels of income—fees, wages, and profits—to be paid to those who provide them [ ]. If the provision of health care were carried out under circumstances which in any way approximated those of the "perfectly competitive market" of the economic textbooks, such income levels would be externally determined by those markets. But it isn't, and they aren't [   ]. Prices of medical services, in particular, show extreme variation between countries, and (where permitted) within countries, which bear no relation to market forces [   ]. Such price variations have a powerful influence on provider incomes.

Relative incomes in the health care sector are, at least in the short run, largely influenced by political and policy choices [   ]. Indeed, it is quite conceivable that much of the rhetoric about the externally determined nature of health expenditures is motivated precisely by the desire to deflect attention from incomes, particularly in those countries (the United States, West Germany, and Canada) where professional incomes are relatively high.

DIFFERENT COUNTRIES, DIFFERENT COSTS, DIFFERENT POLICIES

While the sources of explanatory pressure are largely internal to health care systems themselves, the compressive stresses arise from the action of external forces of various kinds operating principally through the systems of reimbursement, and from the overall public regulatory process. The strength of these forces, and their mode of application, vary considerably from country to country.

All developed nations participate in the common cultural enterprise represented by the development of clinical capabilities and their underlying bases in science and medical technology. Furthermore, the institutions and personnel—doctors, hospitals, nurses, pharmacists, dentists—seem to be similar across national boundaries. But the organization of and payment for the delivery of health services vary much more from one jurisdiction to another. In a sense, different countries have "experimented" with alternative institutional arrangements for applying a common technology to common health problems [   ].

The result of this uncontrolled experimentation has turned out to be a wide variation in levels of and trends in health expenditures, both per capita and as a share of national income. Trends in spending also vary markedly from country to country in the short term, although in the 1980s there has been a significant convergence of trends in the OECD countries—except in the United States [where expenditures have remained higher and continued to grow at a faster rate].

* * *

The data from the OECD countries, * * * display a number of other interesting and suggestive patterns. For our purposes, however, they suggest two significant conclusions. First, the comparative international experience clearly reflects the varying timing and impact of public policies to influence health care costs—first expansion and then compression. * * * Second, as one might anticipate from the more detailed studies of health care use and effectiveness, the substantial international variations in levels of health care spending do not appear to be associated with any corresponding differences in either health outcomes or public satisfaction. * * *

THE NORTH AMERICAN "EXPERIMENT" WITH ALTERNATIVE
REIMBURSEMENT POLICIES

One pair of countries, however, stands out in sharp relief because of their remarkable degree of overall similarity—cultural, linguistic, and geographic. Canada and the United States are by no means scale models of each other, but their differences are rather subtle and not always apparent to the external observer. Moreover, their systems of organization of health services delivery are, or were until quite recently, also very similar. And finally, and very importantly, the health expenditure statisticians of the two countries maintain contact with each other, to try to reconcile their data concepts and categories and to preserve, if not identity, at least effective comparability.

But starting in the 1950s, their ways of *reimbursing* health care began to diverge sharply. By 1971, Canada had universal coverage of hospital and medical care for all of its citizens, within provincially based, government-run plans financed from tax revenue, and with no parallel private system of either insurance or delivery. The United States, in contrast, chose to rely on a patchwork of public and private plans, with a level of direct patient payment which is easily the highest in the developed world.

The experience of these two countries is thus the closest we are ever likely to come to a "quasi-controlled experiment," conducted in real time with real bullets. * * *

* * * [T]he differing Canadian and U.S. experiences are traceable to their differences in the subsectors of hospital and medical spending— precisely those which are covered by the Canadian public plans—and they date from 1971, the year in which coverage became universal across Canada. By now, the cost differential has grown to about 2.5 percentage points of GNP, a massive savings on the Canadian side. Moreover, after some suggestion in the early 1980s of convergence, the gap is now widening again.

* * *

The United States is itself an outlier relative to the more general OECD pattern of health care funding [ ]. It shows both the highest (relative) costs and the lowest level of public coverage, along with a number of other peculiar characteristics in organization and ideology. But the Canadian expenditure trends are also notable relative to the overall pattern of the OECD countries, [in that its share of income spent on health care has declined relative to other countries since 1971.] * * *.

* * *

THE CONCEPT OF CONTROL

A full and detailed account of the process of control in Canada is far beyond the ambitions or capacities of this paper. [   ] It is possible, however, to identify quite briefly the results of this process, as reflected in the major cost components which differ most sharply between the two countries. These can then be related to specific institutional characteristics of the two systems. The major discrepancies are in the costs of administering the payment system itself, the rate of escalation of physicians' fees, and the intensity of servicing per patient and per patient day in the hospital system.

CONTROLLING OVERHEAD COSTS: THE "BUREAUCRACY"

The most dramatic proportional differences between a universal public insurance program and a multiple-source, predominantly private system are in the costs of the insurance process itself. * * * [T]hese "overhead costs" of managing and paying for, as opposed to providing, health care are accounting for a rapidly, though irregularly, increasing share of the United States GNP. Moreover, this explicit measure of administrative costs greatly understates their true magnitude. A substantial and apparently growing portion of the budget of American hospitals is allocated to administrative and billing functions, although in the aggregate statistics these are included as hospital costs rather than as costs of prepayment and administration. Similar costs are incurred, although on a smaller scale, in physicians' private practices and in nursing homes [ ].

* * *

* * * A large and growing share of the American total is spent, not on doctors and nurses, but on accountants, management consultants, and public relations specialists. Their contribution to the health of the American public is difficult to discern (unless one is trained in neoclassical economics and able to see with the eye of faith).

Moreover, the expansion of these expenditure categories creates, simultaneously, another large group of beneficiaries from, and advocates of, *rising* health care costs. * * * These administrative overheads, which, from the Canadian perspective, are just so much waste motion, add $50–100 billion to American costs. But the firms and individuals who earn these sums as their incomes can be expected to fight very hard to protect and expand their profits and livelihoods, however useless their activities may be from an overall social perspective.

* * * The general message, * * * is that the more diverse and complex the funding system, the more expensive it is likely to be. Sophisticated systems of "managed care," like competitive markets, are not free. In the economics textbooks, we take no account of the overhead costs of running a market system; they are assumed away, like friction. But the American example shows that the "frictional" costs of multisourced funding systems can become very large indeed.

* * *

CONTROLLING PHYSICIAN FEES

Even after allowing for the differing growth of overhead costs, however, the expenditures on actually providing care are significantly lower in Canada, for both physicians' services and hospital costs. * * * In the case of physicians' services, however, we find that there is remarkably little difference, * * * in the number or rates of growth of physician supply per capita in Canada and the United States. Nor is there much difference in the growth of productivity per physician * * *, although the Canadian rate of increase is somewhat higher. Since 1971, the growth in services per capita has been remarkably similar in both countries [   ]. The major difference is in trends in fees. In the United States, physicians' fees have risen faster than the general rate of inflation in almost every year of the last forty. Prior to 1971, a similar, though less pronounced, pattern of sector-specific inflation was seen in Canada as well. But after 1971, physicians' fees in Canada *dropped* sharply in real terms—running well behind inflation until the mid–1970s—and since then have on average risen at about the same level as prices generally.

The American environment, regulated, competitive, or whatever, has thus permitted physicians to push their fees steadily upward, in the face of rapid and sustained increases in their numbers and output. * * * In Canada, the introduction of universal public insurance coverage coincided with the introduction of periodically bargained uniform fee schedules in each province that were binding on all practitioners. Under this fee-setting process, fee levels have roughly stabilized in real terms.

Essentially, the public system is able to act as a monopoly in confronting physicians; Canada does not have socialized medicine but socialized insurance. Using this monopoly power, the reimburser can offset the still very significant political and organizational power of physicians. The fragmented, multiple-source payment system in the United States has, up till now, completely failed to develop any alternative method of containing medical fee inflation.

There is, of course, a great deal of evidence suggesting that particular American institutions, in particular settings, have been quite effective in cost control: HMOs, PPOs, IPAs and various other organizations. All of this may be true. * * * The key question is whether such partial successes can be shown to have had any effect on overall expenditure patterns, for the nation or even for those regions in which they are most prevalent. To date the answer is unambiguously negative [   ].

There has been a great deal of speculation in the United States as to how competitive pressures might be created, in a multiple-payer environment and/or when patients are paying most of their own bills, so as to exert effective downward pressure on fees—or just keep them from rising. But evidence of such effects is conspicuous by its absence. The speculation has, however, been able to survive the uncooperative behavior of the real world. It is surprisingly often presented to external observers as if it were a factual description of American experience, rather than a collection of hypotheses.

CONTROLLING HOSPITAL USE AND TECHNOLOGY

The third area of major difference in costs, hospitals, is somewhat more complex than the other two. Costs are lower, per capita, in Canada but utilization rates are higher. * * *

But the procedural intensity [in Canada] is much lower, and has been growing less rapidly, for the last two decades [ ]. * * *

* * * More, and more expensive things are done, on average, to patients in American hospitals, for any particular diagnosis or problem; this probably accounts for a large part of the difference in hospital costs between the two systems [ ].

Again, the reasons for the difference are traceable to the differences in reimbursement systems. Canadian hospitals receive their operating budgets from a single source, the provincial reimbursement agency. Capital budgets come largely from the same source but are controlled and allocated separately. Thus the amounts and locations of expensive diagnostic and therapeutic equipment can be directly controlled, subject to all the usual political pressures from within and outside the health care system, by the reimbursing agency; the provincial government.

* * *

CONCENTRATING AND MOTIVATING THE CONTROLLERS

The comparison of the Canadian and American experiences in health care funding has numerous fascinating aspects and is particularly gratifying for a Canadian. But the more important point for a wider audience is that it underscores the importance of a unified, single-source funding system as a way of concentrating the interests in cost containment—in applying compressive forces.

* * *

But the critical feature of the Canadian system is that provincial governments cannot slide away from their financial responsibilities for virtually all hospital and medical care funding. They have no option but to engage in the difficult and politically dangerous process of compression. If they do not, they must satisfy the ambitions of the health care system by cutting other forms of public spending—whose advocates also sit in Cabinet—or by raising taxes or public debt. All are unattractive. The true costs of health spending are thus brought to confront its advocates.

* * *

FACING AND MANAGING THE INEVITABLE

The North American experience therefore shows that *if* one's objective is really cost control, the only demonstrably successful approach is through monopsonistic control of the payment process. This may be through a single payer, or through multiple payers whose behavior is strictly coordinated by regulation, to create a de facto unity, as in West Germany. In this environment, and assuming that there is a political will to do so, cost escalation can be contained. The experience of Western European countries in the 1980s has confirmed the significance of this "sole-source funding," which students of North American health care have emphasized for a decade or more.

Successful cost control, however, must inevitably thwart, to a greater or lesser degree, the professional and economic ambitions of providers, both clinical and administrative/financial. Powerful offsetting forces generate severe strains. One must expect, therefore, continuing proposals from providers to modify, "make more flexible," the payment environment. "More consumer choice" is a common form of this rhetoric: Let the public, or the monopsony, payment system provide some basic minimum or safety net form of coverage, and let "consumers" make their own decisions about the form of coverage or payment they would like above this level.

It is striking, however, that such proposals seem to come only from provider groups, or from payers looking for a way to ease the financial pressure on themselves. They are rarely if ever initiated by the "consumer" patients they are supposed to benefit. The intellectual framework of consumer choice is of course almost totally irrelevant to the circumstances in which the bulk of medical care is provided. The average patient is very different from the average citizen; activity and expense is heavily concentrated on a relatively small part of the population, and the concentration is increasing. * * *

For this and other reasons, the pressures of the marketplace transmitted by individual patients have been totally ineffective, and no civilized country relies on them in any serious way. Market pressures transmitted by organizations acting on the consumer/patient's behalf have much more appeal in theory, but as yet no record of success. Pressures exerted by a government, or quasi-governmental agency backed up by regulation, actually do work, because they mobilize and strongly motivate those with the capacity to do the job.

* * *

Conversely, the policy objectives of providers are best served by an environment in which no organization has effective responsibility for or control over costs, but in which funds flow through numerous and complex channels and the opportunities for shifting are legion. This creates a form of prisoner's dilemma for payers. The optimal individual strategy is to spend one's energy on efforts to shift costs, thereby increasing them in total, because individual efforts to constrain the total have almost no chance of being effective. It is hard to imagine a more satisfactory environment for providers.

* * *

... AND MOVING ON

But ultimately, the really important questions have to do with the impact of health care on health, and the appropriate amount of mix of resources to be devoted to this task. This raises questions both about the allocation within the health sector itself and about the balance of resources between health care and other things. Since there is extensive evidence that the health of both individuals and populations depends on much more than health care alone, one cannot exclude the possibility that excessive health spending can actually threaten health, by diverting resources from other more effective activities. This is the other end of the spectrum from the argument, which seems at least plausible, that there must be some irreducible minimum below which containment of health spending results in a threat to the health of patients.

* * *

The objective which appeals to the policy analyst, and presumably to the Rawlsian representative citizen, is served by a combination of improved outcomes and reduced outlays—more for less. To the representative citizen, such outlays refer to *all* outlays, regardless of whose budget they flow through. Since all the citizens of a country must pay all its health care costs, though whichever channel they flow, costs transferred are not costs saved. (Indeed, they are usually costs increased.) Procedural activity is not a good in itself; most rational individuals would rather forego interventions. The level of activity is thus either a neutral element or a "bad," a form of cost.

* * *

A generation of experience with international health care funding, * * *, has produced a good deal of information about the process of cost containment; what works and what does not. Failure is apparently a result of institutional frameworks which present compressive forces from being mobilized and concentrated, and which divert them into shear forces while permitting the inherent tensile forces in all health care systems to proceed unchecked. Success comes from containing the shear forces.

* * *

Notes and Questions

1. See, for further discussion of international approaches to cost containment, Symposium, 11 Health Care Financing Review (1989 Annual Supplement); Pfaff, Differences in Health Care Spending Across Countries: Statistical Evidence, 15 J. Health Pol. Pol'y & L. 1 (1990); Fuchs & Hahn, How Does Canada Do It? 323 New Eng.J.Med. 884 (1990).

2. It may well be that by adopting a typical American approach of "muddling through" we have ended up with neither effective competition nor regulation, Altman & Rodwin, Halfway Competitive Markets and Ineffective Regulation: The American Health Care System, 13 J. Health

Pol., Pol'y & L. 323 (1988). Might we be better off if we opted clearly for one approach or the other? Might such decisiveness be impossible, however, given traditional American pluralism and incrementalism?

II. COMPREHENSIVE REGULATORY APPROACHES

A. HEALTH PLANNING AND CERTIFICATE OF NEED

1. Introduction

From the mid 1970s until the early 1980s the primary federal and state regulatory strategy for controlling health care costs was to constrain the supply of health care resources through health planning, primarily through certificate of need programs that required hospitals to obtain government approval for capital investments. Although the federal government has now largely abandoned this strategy, certificate of need programs and health planning are still very much alive in the majority of the states.

Constricting supply seems an odd way to control costs. Artificial constriction of supply ought to increase rather than decrease prices. Yet health planning as a cost-control strategy is founded on a plausible hypothesis: that demand for medical treatment (unlike the demand for other commodities) increases as supply increases, and without lowering costs. The argument supporting this hypothesis develops as follows. First, patients understand neither the cause of nor the solution to their medical problems, and therefore must trust physicians to decide what medical care to purchase. Realizing this, hospitals, at least under cost-based reimbursement, compete primarily to attract physicians, rather than patients, and make capital expenditures to increase their bed capacity or to acquire expensive new technology desired by their physicians. Physicians—believing that if there is a beneficial treatment, the patient should receive it—admit patients to the hospital or prescribe tests or treatment to the extent of available supply.

Because of the interplay of these factors, the demand for care will always expand to the limits of the supply. As the price need not fall for demand to increase, the cost of medical care will correspondingly rise. This theory, first proposed by Milton Roemer, and thus identified as Roemer's law, is aphorized as "A bed built is a bed filled is a bed billed." [1] See Roemer, Bed Supply and Hospital Utilization: A Natural Experiment, 35 Hosp. 37 (Nov. 1, 1961). See, further describing the theory, J. Gelman, Competition and Health Planning: An Issues Paper, 101–09 (1982) [hereafter Gelman]; Joskow, Controlling Hospital Costs

---

1. Note that the key to this hypothesis may be full insurance reimbursement for capital costs. As long as hospitals can expect insurers to reimburse them fully for any capital expenditures, they have no incentive not to spend money to enhance their size and therapeutic capacity. To the extent that insurers have switched to reimbursement policies that do not fully reimburse capital costs, however, the hypothesis may no longer be valid.

57–71 (1981); Blumstein & Sloan, Health Planning and Regulation through Certificate of Need: An Overview, 1978 Utah L.Rev. 3, 4–5 [hereafter Blumstein & Sloan]; Bovbjerg, Problems and Prospects for Health Planning: The Importance of Incentives, Standards, and Procedures in Certificate of Need, 1978 Utah L.Rev. 83, 85–97; Payton & Powsner, Regulation Through the Looking Glass: Hospitals, Blue Cross, and Certificate-of-Need, 79 Mich.L.Rev. 203, 253, 268–277 (1980).

One regulatory strategy for discouraging such excessive capital investment is to require health care institutions to demonstrate a "need" to expand or to acquire new health technology in order to obtain the state's consent for a purchase. This consent is granted through a "certificate of need." This health planning process defines "need" by first discerning the appropriate level of demand for health services and then determining what amount of health resource is needed to meet this demand. Both demand and supply are determined using a scientific or political process described below. The permitted level of health resources supply is then allocated among institutional health providers through a certificate of need program. Finally, providers ration among their patients the beds and technology permitted them so that only those who truly "need" services will receive them.

Though Roemer's law is the principal argument for health planning as a cost-control strategy, others have emerged. First, health planning could reduce the cost of health care by eliminating duplication and promoting consolidation of services to achieve economies of scale. The health planning process could permit only one hospital to install a particular kind of equipment, but also require the hospital to share it. A second hospital would then be permitted to install (and required to share) a different piece of expensive technical equipment. Health planning could also eliminate excess empty hospital beds through closings and consolidations. Finally, health planning could improve public health by promoting health education, preventive care, and primary care over high-cost medical technology. See Joskow, supra, at 80–85; 1 Inst. of Med., Health Planning in the United States; Selected Policy Issues, 48 (1982) [hereafter I.O.M.].

While cost control may be the most controversial justification for health planning, it may not be the most important. Indeed, although health planning has been around for at least a half century, cost control has emerged only recently as a significant justification for planning, which was originally designed to assure the orderly and coordinated development of health services. Health planning has also been put forward as a means of assuring equitable access to health services for diverse geographic areas and age and income groups. Planning can also assist in providing comprehensive and integrated services and in matching services with needs. In particular, it could gather and analyze data, identifying needs and facilitating the development of programs to fit those needs. Finally, some have argued that the planning process is a valuable vehicle for a community to democratically articulate its own health needs and desires. See articulating alternative rationales for health planning, 1 I.O.M., supra, at 8–9; B. Lefkowitz, Health Planning: Lessons for the Future, 138–39 (1983) [hereafter Lefkowitz]; Blumstein & Sloan, supra, at 6–7; Grosse, The Need for Health Planning, in Havighurst, Regulating Constructions, supra, at 29–30; Rohrer, Health Planning As Social Evolution, 7 Health Matrix 27 (Winter, 1989–90).

2. *History and Structure*

Though federal funding of state and local health planning first appeared in the 1940s, the most important federal health planning initiative was the National Health Resource Planning and Development Act of 1974, Public Law No. 93–641, which was in place from 1974 until its repeal in 1986. The NHRPDA, the result of a complex and lively political debate, created a series of agencies at the federal, state, and local level, and gave them a variety of planning and regulatory functions. The most important tools created by the NHRPDA were health plans, which were to be developed at both the state and local level, and certificates of need (CON), which had to be approved at both the state and local level before health care institutions could undertake major capital expenditures.

With the repeal of the NHRPDA in 1986 states have charted their own course in health planning. While there was an initial rush to repeal health planning statutes in states where the idea had never been popular, about two-thirds of the states have retained certificate of need programs at the state level. (Local programs have been largely eliminated). While some states have retained the structure of the NHRPDA largely intact at the state level, most states have taken advantage of their freedom from federal constraints to experiment. In particular, many states have raised review thresholds and streamlined procedures and several have exempted certain categories of care from review. In particular several states have deregulated hospitals and related acute care services. The major concern of states that have retained CON programs seems to be on long-term care facilities and on expensive, high-technology, services. See, Bovbjerg, New Directions for Health Planning, in Cost, Quality and Access, supra at 206; Shay, Developments in Certificate of Need, in 1989 Health Law Handbook 187, (Gosfield, ed. 1989); Simpson, Full Circle: The Return of Certificate of Need Regulation of Health Facilities to State Control, 19 Ind.L.Rev. 1025 (1986); Note, Certificate of Need for Health Care Facilities: A Time for Reexamination, 7 Pace L.Rev. 491 (1987).

Abolition of CON in some states was accompanied by a dramatic increase in health facility construction. Nine new hospitals, including five psychiatric hospitals, opened in Texas in the year following CON repeal. In the five years following CON repeal in Arizona, nursing home capacity grew from 8,313 to 14,643 beds. Ten hospitals in Arizona started open-heart surgery units following deregulation, accompanied by a 35% increase in mortality for Medicare patients undergoing by-pass surgery. In Utah, the number of nursing home beds grew by 25% in the two years following deregulation. In other states, on the other hand, little new construction occurred, and nowhere has rapid expansion of acute-care hospital construction been a problem. What factors might explain these differences?

What explains the continued interest of the states in constraining the construction of long term care facilities (accomplished in some states by construction moratoria in lieu of CON requirements)? Is the continued interest of some states in controlling the adoption of new technology justified? See, Robinson, Garnick & McPhee, Market and Regulatory Influences on the Availability of Coronary Angioplasty and Bypass Surgery in U.S. Hospitals, 317 New Eng.J.Med. 85 (1987) (arguing that new technologies are adopted more rapidly in competitive rather than regulated markets, and may be adopted in facilities that do not do procedures frequently enough to assure quality care.)

In considering the material that follows, however, consider what other strategies could be used to restrict capital investment. Could restrictions on insurance reimbursement for capital costs limit investment more effectively than CON programs? (Return to this question when studying Diagnosis–Related Group reimbursement and rate-setting, infra). What would be the effect of amending the tax code to deny hospitals tax exempt bonds? All of these approaches would restrict hospital investment generally. What effects might general strategies have on hospitals with special investment needs (e.g, inner city hospitals with deteriorating facilities)? Could these effects be avoided by a more precise surgical approach such as the CON program?

3. Health Planning: Legal Issues

DEPARTMENT OF HEALTH OF THE STATE OF NEBRASKA v. LUTHERAN HOSPITALS AND HOMES SOCIETY OF AMERICA

Supreme Court of Nebraska, 1987.
227 Neb. 116, 416 N.W.2d 222.

PER CURIAM.

The applicant, Lutheran Hospitals and Homes Society of America, doing business as Grand Island Memorial Hospital, filed an application for a certificate of need for the acquisition and installation of a linear accelerator and for development of radiation therapy services. The Nebraska Department of Health recommended denial of the application. The Certificate of Need Review Committee found that the applicant had failed to demonstrate that the proposed project met the review criteria specified in Neb.Admin.Code tit. 182, ch. 2, § 005 (1983), and denied the application. The applicant then appealed to an appeal board of the Nebraska Certificate of Need Appeal Panel, which reversed the decision of the review committee and approved the application. The appeal board's decision was affirmed by the district court. The Department of Health has appealed to this court.

* * *

At the time of the hearing there were two hospitals in health planning subarea III which were equipped to furnish radiation therapy. Good Samaritan Hospital in Kearney, Nebraska, had a Linac 6 unit and The Mary Lanning Memorial Hospital in Hastings, Nebraska, had a Cobalt–60 unit. * * *

The project proposed by the applicant was the acquisition of a 6–MeV medical linear accelerator, with the intent to expand the hospital's present abilities to treat oncology patients. Locally, the linear accelerator would be shared with St. Francis Medical Center and the Veterans Administration Medical Center, in addition to providing service for patients who travel to Grand Island from outlying communities.

In addition to purchasing the linear accelerator, a 3,700– to 4,000–square-foot building was to be constructed to accommodate the radiation equipment and to provide three examination rooms, office space, and a waiting room. The estimated cost of the entire project was $885,191; the equipment and furnishings to total $413,075, while construction of the therapy center (including architectural and engineering fees) was estimated at $472,116. Financing for the equipment was to be through Nebraska financing authority at 8.875 percent interest. Construction costs were to be financed with $300,000 of donated funds; the remaining balance of $172,116 was to be commercially financed at an estimated 13.5–percent interest.

The useful life of the linear accelerator would be about 7 to 10 years. The annual anticipated total cost of operation was estimated to be $217,000. From this data, it was calculated that the break-even point for operating costs would be 163 patients or 4,075 treatments per year. The approximate cost per treatment to the patient for the first year of operation was estimated to be $65, which was comparable to existing services.

* * *

The [Nebraska CON] statutes require the Nebraska Department of Health to promulgate criteria by which to assess applications for certificates of need. According to the rules adopted by the Department of Health, the applicant "bears the burden of demonstrating in its application that the proposal satisfies all of the review criteria" applicable to the proposal at hand. [ ] However, in an appeal from a decision granting a certificate of need, the party appealing bears the burden of proof that the application does not meet the applicable criteria. [ ]

* * *

The controversy in this case centers around the following provisions of the certificate of need regulations (Neb.Admin.Code tit. 182, ch. 2 (1983)) adopted by the state Department of Health:

006.07   THERAPEUTIC RADIOLOGY

006.07A   A megavoltage radiation therapy unit shall treat at least 300 new cancer cases annually within three years after initiation.

006.07B   There shall be no additional megavoltage units opened unless all existing megavoltage units in the health planning subarea are performing at least 6,000 treatments per year, and such new units will decrease access time to care.   Adjustments downward may be justified when travel time to available services exceeds one hour for 50 percent of the population in health planning subareas I through IV * * *

In addition to the regulations of the Department of Health, the Nebraska state health plan sets forth goals and objectives in reference to therapeutic radiology.   Those relevant in this case are:

5.3.7.3   GOALS AND OBJECTIVES

GOAL 1   Access to megavolt radiation therapy units should be increased.

GOAL 2   There should be no additional megavoltage units opened unless (1) access to care is increased, and (2) all existing megavoltage units in the health service area(s) are performing an average of at least 6,000 treatments per year.

OBJECTIVE 2(A)   By 1985, hospitals with single units failing to meet established goal levels in the Midlands should consider phasing out this service.

GOAL 3   Adjustments downward in economic utilization rates (6,000 per year) may be justified when travel time to an alternate unit exceeds: (a) one hour for 50 percent of the population in Greater Nebraska, * * *

Nebraska State Health Plan 1982–1987, supra at V–242.

The appeal board found there is a need for radiation therapy services in the service area; that the area to be served by the proposed project has been defined; that a linear accelerator to be located in Grand Island Memorial Hospital in Grand Island, Nebraska, for a cost of $885,000, is the least costly alternative for providing such service or, if not the least costly, is the most effective alternative; that the increase in costs or charges resulting from the project is justified by the need and that the project is financially feasible for the life of the linear accelerator; that the proposed project coordinates with the existing health care system and that the need established is consistent with the need projections in Neb.Admin.Code, supra, § 006, and with the state health plan; that even if the need established is inconsistent with the need projections in Neb.Admin.Code, supra, § 006, and with the state health plan, exceptions to the state health plan and Neb.Admin.Code, supra, § 006, shall be made when justification is shown by a preponderance of the evidence and the preponderance of the evidence herein justifies such exception; and that the applicant has carried its burden of proving that the project meets all the applicable criteria.

The primary contention of the Department of Health is that the evidence is insufficient to support the appeal board's determination that all applicable review criteria have been met. In support of its position, the department asserts that the proposed unit would not treat 300 new cancer cases annually within 3 years of its initiation unless it drew patients from existing units.

Charles Myers, the assistant administrator of the applicant, testified as a witness for the applicant. * * *

* * * By multiplying the population of the service area by the risk factor [for cancer projected by the state health plan], Myers concluded that there would be 1,456 new cancer cases per year in the combined service area.

According to the state health plan about 60 percent of all new cancer cases will be treated with radiation therapy, and the average number of treatments per patient is 25. Thus, Myers concluded there would be approximately 21,850 total treatments each year in the combined service area.

Similarly, Myers conducted a statistical analysis of the Grand Island service area (not the combined service area) and concluded that the number of treatments per year in the Grand Island service area would be 7,550.

Based on the above data, Myers concluded there would be 504 new cancer cases in the Grand Island service area annually, thus meeting the 300–case requirement of the Nebraska Administrative Code. Additionally, Myers concluded that the projected 7,550 treatments per year exceeded the 6,000–per–year requirements of both the Nebraska Administrative Code and the state health plan.

In its brief, the Department of Health criticizes the statistics relied on by the applicant. The department asserts that despite the applicant's showing of 504 new cancer cases annually for the Grand Island service area, and thus approximately 302 cases requiring radiation, Grand Island cannot assume that all 302 patients would choose to undergo the treatment and, even if they did, that they would choose the Grand Island hospital. There is evidence tending to show that, travel-time aside, many patients opt not to undergo radiation therapy because less than one-half obtain curative results, because of the associated physical discomforts, and finally, because of the trend toward dying at home and refusal of life-prolonging treatment.

In regard to the impact of the proposed Grand Island unit on already existing units in the subarea, Myers stated:

* * *

These three communities serve, for the most part, distinct populations. They are the three largest cities in central Nebraska. They're going to have their people in their counties and their service area that are going to continue to use these services. I think the impact is not that great.

* * *

Dr. Hrnicek, an internist in Grand Island whose practice relates extensively to cancer, stated that the impact on existing radiation units in Hastings and Kearney would be "minimal." As a basis for his opinion, Dr. Hrnicek stated that the distance from the Grand Island service area to Kearney is so great that he has only referred one patient to Kearney in 4 years.   * * *

* * *

Based on this testimony, it appears that significant numbers of patients would not be drawn from Hastings or Kearney.   * * *

Despite the fact that the applicant has shown that the proposed equipment and facility at Grand Island would realistically treat the required number of patients, the Department of Health asserts that the applicant must also show that "all existing megavoltage units in the health planning subarea are performing at least 6,000 treatments per year" before a new unit may be "opened." [   ]

[The court rejected application of the regulation because of ambiguity in the definition of "treatment." It also noted the possibility of a downward adjustment from the 6000 treatments requirement to recognize travel time.]

* * *

The regulation permits adjustments downward when traveltime to available services exceeds 1 hour for 50 percent of the population in the subarea.   * * * The exhibits show that at this time approximately 42 percent of patients living in the Grand Island service area must travel for more than 1 hour to obtain radiation therapy. Neither chart satisfies the requirement stated in the regulation, but they tend to support the board's finding that exceptions are justified in this case.

* * *

[The applicant also argued that an exception was appropriate.]

The provisions for exceptions contained in both the regulations and the statute permit the board to grant a certificate of need when there is an unmet need for health care services for a specific population, even though there is not full compliance with the requirements of Neb.Admin.Code, supra, § 006.

The issue of an unmet need for health care services for a specific population was addressed in the testimony of medical personnel from Grand Island. Dr. Rusthoven, a diagnostic radiologist, testified that there was no linear accelerator in the Grand Island service area and that if one were installed, patients from the Grand Island area would use the facility. Dr. Rusthoven stated that Grand Island hospitals can currently treat cancer patients with surgery and chemotherapy, but then "lose them because we have to let them go somewhere else for radiation therapy." Dr. Rusthoven stated that not only is the situation frustrating to physicians, but it also presents a serious problem to the patients involved. Such a situation, according to Dr. Rusthoven, results in a fragmentation of care, where the patient experiences a loss in continuity as the patient travels from doctor to doctor and hospital to hospital. Additionally, the patient may encounter increased medical expenses because of duplicative testing as well as a decrease in the effectiveness of treatment when travel is impossible due to weather conditions or the physical status of a patient.

* * *

[Other medical experts testified similarly.]

Joan Muhvic, hospice coordinator and oncology nurse at the applicant, supported the hospital's application for a linear accelerator. * * *

Muhvic stated that communications between doctor and patient break down when the patient travels to a new facility for treatment. She also stated that during the course of therapy, patients become weak and tired and may experience nausea and vomiting. She, too, has experienced patients who have looked at various locations for treatments in an attempt to minimize traveltime.

Finally, Myers, the assistant administrator of the applicant, stated that Grand Island needed its own unit rather than relying on Hastings and Kearney because: "We are attempting to become a comprehensive cancer center to be able to provide those three modalities of care. We have the two modalities. We have the support services set up. This is the last modality which we need to take care of those cancer patients."

* * *

The record shows that cancer is the second leading cause of death. It is primarily a disease of the elderly, and the Grand Island area has a higher percentage of elderly persons as residents than other areas. Not only is the number of elderly persons increasing as a proportion of the population, but the rate of cancer has increased from 3.7 new cases per 1,000 population per year (which was the basis for the calculations made in the application) to 4 new cases per 1,000 population per year.

From our review of the record, we find that the appellant has not carried its burden of proof and that the judgment of the district court should be affirmed.

Affirmed.

Caporale, Justice, dissenting.

* * *

The true basis for the applicant's effort is best revealed, perhaps unconsciously, by the local medical practitioner's lament that the Grand Island hospitals lose patients "because we have to let them go somewhere else for radiation therapy." While such a parochial concern is understandable, it has no legal significance.   * * *

The Legislature in its wisdom has enacted legislation designed to eliminate unnecessary duplication of certain medical facilities in an effort to reduce the overall cost of health care for the citizens of the state. This court is obligated to adhere to that legislatively declared policy.

* * *

Notes and Questions

1. How should the planning agency decide on whether or not a particular hospital should get a linear accelerator if it cannot rely on numerical targets based on utilization rates? Should the agency be able to weigh the additional cost of the equipment against the cost of other desirable medical equipment or facilities? Should it explicitly consider who will pay for the added equipment and how? How should the agency respond if the applicant hospital argues that it will not refer its patients to the underutilized accelerators of other hospitals because it questions the ability of the physicians using the equipment in those hospitals or the quality of their work? Should the cost of transportation and the delay incurred when the work must be performed elsewhere play a role in the planning decision? How should the planning agency view the plight of those patients who cannot receive the benefit of radiation therapy because they are too sick to travel? Is government control over the diffusion of technology politically dangerous because it forces explicit health care rationing decisions into the public arena? Note that CON programs only allocate medical resources among hospitals, leaving to hospitals and doctors the decision of who shall fill those beds. The latter decisions would certainly be far more controversial if made by the government. See Havighurst, Deregulating, supra, at 37.

2. Is it possible to reconcile health planning with the requirements of the Equal Protection Clause? Is it rational to deny Grand Island a linear accelerator, while allowing another hospital this equipment if the only reason for the decision is that only one accelerator is needed in the area?

3. Should the hospitals located in Kearney and Hastings be allowed to intervene in the Grand Island CON proceeding? Do they suffer any legally cognizable injury from its grant? Compare Community Care Centers, Inc. v. Missouri Health Facilities Review Committee, 735 S.W.2d 13, 15 (Mo. 1987) ("There is no legal right to enjoy a monopoly or to bar others from trade.") with Charter Medical–Jacksonville, Inc. v. Department of Health and Rehabilitative Services, 503 So.2d 381 (Fla.App.1987) (granting standing to a psychiatric hospital to oppose the grant of a CON to a potential competitor.)

4. The use of CON programs to control the adoption of linear accelerators and other high-tech medical equipment has been one of the most controversial aspects of health planning. One study found that regulatory controls over the adoption of technology avoid large expenditures on early, unperfected and quickly outmoded models, and allow time for efficient

techniques of using the technology to develop.   But the study also found
the controls ultimately did not stop the diffusion of technology and limited
access during the phase-in period, Higgins, Taft, & Hodgman, The Impact of
Need on CT Scanning in Massachusetts, 9 Health Care Management
Review 71 (1984).   See also Cohen & Cohodes, Certificate of Need and Low
Capital–Cost Medical Technology, 60 Milbank Mem. Fund Q. 307 (1982).

   5.   The health planning laws have generated a tremendous volume of
litigation.   Most of this litigation has involved issues of state administrative law or civil procedure: questions of standing, administrative adjudication procedure, and proper rulemaking.   Competitors of institutions granted CONs bring actions to delay, or if possible avoid, their implementation.
Providers denied CONs bring actions to challenge the basis of the decision
or the method through which it was reached.   For a digest of decisions, see
J. Simpson & T. Bogue, The Guide to Health Planning Law: A Topical
Digest of Health Planning and Certificate of Need Law (3d ed. 1985).   For a
good recent summary of developments see Shay, Developments in Certificate of Need in 1989, Health Law Handbook (A. Gosfield ed. 1989).

   The most interesting legal conundrum that emerged from the
NHRPDA was the question of how to reconcile health planning with the
antitrust laws.   On their face they seem diametrically opposed: the health
planning program is based on the notion that competition does not work in
the health care industry and therefore must be replaced by planning;
antitrust law, on the other hand, exists to remove impediments to competition, one of which would seem to be planning.   See chapter 8, infra,
discussing these problems.

Problem: Representing the Hospital in the Health Planning Process

   You are the in-house counsel for Davis Memorial Hospital, a 600 bed
nonprofit community hospital.   Your institution, located in a moderate size
northern city, is the largest of four hospitals in the area.   Despite belt-
tightening over recent years, Memorial is in fairly good financial shape:
revenues routinely equal and frequently exceed costs and the small endowment continues to grow.   Memorial is currently engaged in strategic
planning for the next decade.

   One of the concerns of the hospital is that the state legislature has
recently reaffirmed its commitment to health planning and to its certificate
of need program.   It has increased the jurisdictional amounts so that CONs
are required only for capital expenditures exceeding $1,000,000 and for
major medical equipment costing more than $500,000.   * * * The state
planning agency has taken a strong stance against hospital expansion,
turning down several recent applications for new beds or equipment.   Even
the applications it has approved have been delayed significantly.   Another
concern is increased competition from other hospitals in your area.   One of
the hospitals in town, a small proprietary hospital previously owned by a
group of physicians, has just been purchased by a national for-profit chain.
Another of the hospitals is owned by a religious group that controls 15
other hospitals in the region, and has recently adopted a strategy of
vigorous expansion.   Both hospitals have announced plans to expand,

adding respectively 50 and 100 beds, and to upgrade their medical technology.

What strategies do you suggest in the face of these facts? How can your hospital continue to expand its services while avoiding the certificate of need process? Can you think of methods of expansion that would avoid large capital expenditures? Might your knowledge of corporate organization and joint ventures, gained in chapter 5, be of use to you here?

How would you use the certificate of need process to deal with your competition? Would you advise the hospital to routinely contest the CON applications of the other hospitals in town? Could you use the CON process offensively, to block competitors from obtaining new equipment before you do? Might these strategies raise legal problems? Do they raise ethical problems? Are these problems of legal, medical, or business ethics, or a combination of all of these?

Problem: Representing a Planning Agency

You are a lawyer on the staff of a state planning agency in a state that has retained an active health planning and certificate of need program. Your agency has recently received two certificate of need applications, and you have been asked to make recommendations on both. Both applications originate from Rockville, a small city (population 60,000) whose health care institutions serve a larger suburban and rural area containing another 80,000 persons. The community currently has two hospitals, University Hospital, a 300 bed teaching hospital, affiliated with a state university located eight miles west of the heart of the city, and Mercy Hospital, a smaller (120 bed) Catholic community hospital, located on the north side of town.

The first application is from Mercy Hospital, which wants to purchase a CT scanner. University Hospital has a CT scanner, which it purchased five years ago, and on which it performs about 2000 scans a year. Mercy Hospital states that its CT scanner would cost about $700,000 initially and $250,000 a year to operate, and that it expects it would do at least 1000 scans a year. It argues that its patients and physicians have been seriously inconvenienced by having to travel twelve miles to University Hospital for scans. It has had a hard time competing with University Hospital for qualified medical staff because of its generally inferior technology. Its application is strongly supported by the local Catholic community, and generally supported by local business, political, and medical leaders. It is strongly opposed by University Hospital, which notes that its CT scanner is underused, and argues that there is no justification for another in the community.

The second application from Interhospital, Inc., an aggressive and fast growing for-profit hospital chain, is to build an 80 bed hospital in Arlington, a wealthy suburb five miles west of Rockville. Interhospital argues that this area has traditionally been underserved by the other two hospitals, and needs a primary and secondary care facility. It intends to establish a preferred provider organization and a wellness center (including a health club) and to market its services aggressively. Its application is supported by doctors and community leaders from the Arlington area, and is opposed by University and Mercy Hospitals. University and Mercy hospitals have been experiencing declining occupancy in recent years and currently average about 80% occupancy (though occupancy varies between 65% and 90% at University, and 70% and 92% at Mercy depending on the time of week or year). University Hospital has been particularly dependent on Medicare and Medicaid patients, and both hospitals have experienced significant losses due to bad debts and cutbacks in public programs in recent years. They argue there is no need in the community for a new hospital. They note that about 50% of their costs are fixed, and will need to be paid no matter how low their occupancy drops, thus increasing community bed capacity will necessarily increase costs.

Though your state has experienced some tapering off of medical cost escalation in recent years, growth is still above the national average, and medical costs are an important concern of political and business leaders. The state Medicaid program is the second largest expenditure category in the state budget, and despite recent cutbacks in eligibility and benefits, Medicaid expenditures continue to grow. How do you go about making your recommendation?

B. RATE–REGULATION

Health care rate-setting programs are commonly referred to as prospective payment programs. Under prospective payment (in contrast to traditional cost- or charge-based retrospective reimbursement), hospitals are paid for services on the basis of a predetermined fixed rate rather than on the basis of charges they set or costs they have experienced. Under prospective payment, hospitals should face incentives to spend less than the set rate (and thus make a "profit"), or at least not to spend more than the rate. Depending on how low rates are set, the rate of increase in hospital expenditures may be significantly reduced by prospective payment schemes.

Hospital rate-setting superficially resembles traditional public utility rate regulation, and draws much of its conceptual framework and technology from that quarter. The problems addressed by the two programs are, however, quite different. Traditional public utility rate regulation addresses the problem of natural monopoly. Utility rate regulation (at least in theory) restrains utility prices while expanding access to utility service by regulating rate structures and by allowing rates that only cover costs plus a fair rate of return.

Hospitals are not natural monopolies, and many areas are served by several hospitals. There is little problem in the hospital industry with unmet potential demand. The prevalence of public and private insurance has created a situation in which health care services are provided even when they are not cost-effective by any measure—and in which services are demanded, and demand is met, even though the demand is inflated because consumers do not pay the full cost of health care out of pocket. Hospital rate regulation responds to excess demand with a supply constraint strategy: by limiting the income of hospitals, it forces them to spend less. In turn, limits on spending force hospitals to become more efficient and to reduce their ability to supply medical services. As hospitals are forced to limit supply, they are also forced to ration services, eliminating, it is hoped, wasteful and unnecessary services first.

Some rate regulation programs also address a second problem, that of rate structure. Hospitals generally engage in cross-subsidization; that is, certain departments like radiology and pathology charge high rates to subsidize other departments like the outpatient clinic or obstetrics, where hospitals are otherwise less competitive and where they serve lower income patients. Hospitals also discriminate among payers: Blue Cross, Medicaid and Medicare can force hospitals to accept payments substantially less than the hospitals can require from commercial insurers or private pay patients for the same services. Some states have attempted to limit cross-subsidization and discounting under a conviction that having all payers and services pull their own weight will lead to greater equity and efficiency. Some rate-setting programs have also attempted to encourage cross-subsidization of the uninsured.

Helpful introductions to rate review can be found in P. Joskow, Controlling Hospital Costs: The Role of Government Regulation, 100–37 (1981); Bauer, Hospital Rate Setting—This Way to Salvation?, in M. Zubkoff, I. Raskin, and R. Hanft, Hospital Cost Containment: Selected Notes for Future Policy (1978) [hereafter Hospital Cost Containment]. For criticism of hospital rate setting, see Friedman, State Rate Review: The High Cost of Saving, 54 Hospitals 67 (March 16, 1980); Mitchell, Issues, Evidence and The Policymaker's Dilemma, 1 Health Aff. 84 (Summer, 1982).

About twelve states currently have rate regulation programs in which participation by providers is mandatory for at least some payers. The first of these programs was established by New York in 1970. State rate regulation programs multiplied slowly throughout the 1970s, nourished by the encouragement of the federal government and supported by hospital associations, which see state regulation as preferable to federal controls. With the antiregulatory mood of the early 1980s, some states stepped back from rate regulation. For information on the current status of state rate setting programs, see IIA, Hospital Law Manual, Financial Management, App. C (1985); Crozier, State Rate Setting: A Status Report, 1 Health Aff. 66 (Summer 1982); K. Davis, et al. Health Care Cost Containment, 93–103 (1990); Rosko, A Comparison of Hospital Performance Under the Partial Payer Medicare PPS and State All–Payer Rate–Setting Systems, 26 Inquiry 48 (1989).

The most important variable distinguishing rate-setting programs is whether participation in the program is mandatory or voluntary. All private programs and several state programs are voluntary. Predictably, voluntary programs have only a limited effect on costs, as hospitals may always withdraw from a program if its effects become too harsh. A second important variable is whether hospitals are legally bound to charge only rates set by the regulator, or whether the rates adopted by the regulator are merely advisory. A third variable is the nature of the state agency implementing the regulatory program. Several states have established independent regulatory commissions, following the public utility model. Others place the function in an existing state agency. The latter approach may avoid duplication of functions and facilitate access to data accumulated for other purposes, but causes potential conflicts of interest if the rate-regulator is located in the state Medicaid agency. Fourth, programs vary as to which payers are covered by the program. Only one program (Maryland) currently covers all payers, i.e., Medicare, Medicaid, Blue Cross, commercial insurers, and private payers, though New York, Massachusetts, and New Jersey cover virtually all payers, excluding Medicare. To the extent that a program covers some, but not all payers, it risks merely shifting costs to the uncovered payers rather than comprehensively limiting health care costs.

The most complex variable distinguishing state programs is the method through which they set rates. Traditionally programs have been classified as formula-based, budget-based or negotiated. Formula-based programs attempt to determine reasonable costs for a hospital's base year, and then use a formula to project those costs forward to establish prospective rates. Budget-based programs review a hospital's proposed budget to determine if it is reasonable. Negotiated programs negotiate rates. Once overall revenue goals are set for hospitals by whatever method, these are allocated to payers on some basis: per admission, per diem, or per service, for example.

Evaluations of the reasonableness of rates are normally based on reported costs of comparable hospitals. Judgments of comparability may be more or less complex, and may take into account factors such as case mix, size, and location. A small community hospital in upstate New York will be able to provide services for a lower cost than a major trauma center in Manhattan. That is, the reasonable cost of the same services may differ at the two hospitals. Projections for costs in future years are generally based on estimates of inflation, which may be more or less fine-tuned to reflect inflation specifically relevant to the health care sector, and may be modified upward or downward to effect policy goals.

Formula-based programs are the most common but tend to raise troublesome equity problems, such as how to handle university hospitals or inner-city hospitals or rural hospitals. Budget-based programs can interfere excessively in internal hospital management, and can be limited in their overall effectiveness by their narrower focus on the budgets of particular hospitals. As programs have matured, they have tended to pick up elements of the different approaches, and to add refinements of their own.

The best accounts of the complexity of rate regulation programs have come out of the sophisticated program in Maryland. See, e.g., Cohen & Schramm, A Design for Resolving the Conflict Resulting from Separate Regulation of Hospital Rates and Hospital Capacity, [hereafter Cohen & Schramm] in M. Olson, A New Approach to the Economics of Health Care, 258 (1981); Cohen, Experiences of a State Cost Control Commission, in M. Zubkoff, I. Raskin & R. Hanft, Hospital Cost Containment, 401 (1978) [hereafter Cohen, Experiences]; Cohen & Colmers, Reviews: A State Rate–Setting Commission, 1 Health Aff. 99 (1981); Cohen & Keane, The Regulator's View of Hospital Costs, 10 Topics in Health Care Fin. 68 (Winter 1983). Professor Schramm, formerly with the Maryland Commission, has drafted a model statute based on his experience. See Schramm, A State–Based Approach to Hospital Cost Containment, 18 Harv.J.Legis. 603 (1981). Descriptions of other state programs can be found in the Fall, 1979 issue of Topics in Health Care.

There is a broad consensus that mature rate-setting programs have been effective in reducing the rate of increase of health care costs. In the late 1970s, inflation in health care costs was from 1 to 4 percentage points a year lower in states with mandatory rate setting programs than in states without it. (Voluntary programs have had no significant effect). The most successful programs have cut the rate of health care inflation in excess of the rate of general inflation by about one half. The earliest analyses of rate-setting failed to detect this effect for a variety of reasons, but studies dating from the late 1970s, including both descriptive studies and studies applying regression analysis, have uniformly confirmed this result. The effect varies by state, and also varies by method of measurement: expense per admission and per diem generally were reduced more in most states than expense per capita (indicating that savings may have been offset by increased utilization in some states). See, analyzing the effect of rate review, Biles, Schramm, & Atkinson, Hospital Cost Inflation Under State Rate–Setting Programs, 303 New Eng.J.Med. 664 (1980); Coellen & Sullivan, The Analysis of the Effects of Prospective Reimbursement Programs and Hospital Expenditures, 1 Health Care Fin.Rev. 1 (Winter 1981); Eby & Cohodes, What do we Know About Rate–Setting?, 10 J.Health Pol. Pol'y L. 299 (1985); Hadley and Schwartz, The Impact on Hospital Costs Between 1980 and 1984 of Hospital Rate Regulation, Competition, and Changes in Health Insurance Coverage, 26 Inquiry 35 (1989); Holahan, The Impact of Alternative Hospital Payment Systems on Medicaid Costs, 25 Inquiry 517 (1988); Rosko, A Comparison of Hospital Performance Under the Partial–Payer Medicare PPS and State All–Payer Rate Setting Systems, 26 Inquiry 48 (1989); Schramm, Renn & Biles, Controlling Hospital Cost Inflation: New Perspectives on State Rate Setting, 5 Health Affairs 22 (1986); Schramm, State Hospital Cost Containment: An Analysis of Legislative Initiatives, 19 Ind.L.Rev. 919 (1986); Sloan, Rate Regulation as a Strategy for Hospital Cost Control: Evidence from the Last Decade, 61 Milbank Memorial Fund Q. 195 (1983);

Zuckerman, Rate Setting and Hospital Cost Containment: All Payer vs. Partial Payer Approaches, 22 Health Services Research 307 (1988).

Rate regulation programs have generated much litigation. Early cases challenged the constitutionality of the programs, Massachusetts General Hospital v. Weiner, 569 F.2d 1156 (1st Cir.1978). More recent cases have challenged the programs as conflicting with federal Medicaid law, Rodden v. Axelrod, 95 A.D.2d 932, 463 N.Y.S.2d 940 (1983); New England Memorial Hospital v. Rate Setting Commission, 394 Mass. 296, 475 N.E.2d 740 (1985); or as imposing requirements on employee health plans in conflict with ERISA, Rebaldo v. Cuomo, 749 F.2d 133 (2d Cir.1984), cert. denied, 472 U.S. 1008, 105 S.Ct. 2702, 86 L.Ed.2d 718 (1985); Bonser v. New Jersey, 605 F.Supp. 1227 (D.N.J. 1985). State cases have tended to turn on issues of state administrative procedure or on the reasonableness of particular decisions. See, e.g., Brockton Hospital v. Rate Setting Commission, 376 Mass. 569, 382 N.E.2d 1035 (1978); Pentucket Manor Chronic Hospital, Inc. v. Rate Setting Commission, 394 Mass. 233, 475 N.E.2d 1201 (1985); Prince George's Doctors' Hospital, Inc. v. Health Services Cost Review Commission, 302 Md. 193, 486 A.2d 744 (1983); Brooklyn Hospital v. Axelrod, 97 A.D.2d 493, 467 N.Y.S.2d 687 (1983), affirmed, 61 N.Y.2d 1012, 475 N.Y.S.2d 381, 463 N.E.2d 1233 (1984).

If a hospital enters into a collective bargaining agreement, must a rate-setting commission permit it to pass on the increased wages in increased reimbursement? See Washington State Nurses Association v. Washington State Hospital Commission, 773 F.2d 1044 (9th Cir.1985); Massachusetts Nurses Association v. Dukakis, 726 F.2d 41 (1st Cir. 1984). If it does so, will this put the Commission in the position of having to negotiate with the unions itself?

III. PRIVATE SECTOR COST CONTAINMENT

A. INTRODUCTION

Private health insurance accounts for 31% of all personal health care expenditures in the United States, including 37% of spending on hospital care and 43% of spending on physicians services. Most of this insurance is provided through employer-sponsored group health plans. In 1989 employer health insurance payments averaged 7.1% of total payroll. If employer expenditures for Medicare payroll taxes, worker's compensation taxes, disability payments, and paid sick leave are added, the burden placed by health care costs on American employers becomes even more evident. Group health insurance premiums paid by businesses have in the late 1980s been increasing at double digit levels annually, averaging 12% in 1988 and 18% in 1989. Small businesses, which account for over half of the American work force and have created two out of three new jobs in recent years, have been particularly hard hit, with premium increases in 1988 in the 20–35% range. Increased health care costs have also strained labor-management relationships, accounting for 78% of striking workers in 1989. Clearly American business, facing rising competition from foreign countries with much lower rates of expenditures on health care, are very concerned about health care costs.

Because the federal government and most states have not adopted a comprehensive strategy for addressing health care costs, and because private business itself obviously cannot exercise regulatory authority, private business has largely relied on competitive approaches to health care cost containment. These approaches—self-insurance, utilization review, cost-sharing, and contracting with alternative delivery systems—are discussed in this section.

B. SELF-INSURANCE

Perhaps the most dramatic change in American health financing in recent years has been the movement toward self-insurance by employers who offer health benefits. In 1975 only about 5% of employers self-insured, that is, carried the risk of paying the health care bills of their employees themselves. By 1987 that figure had grown, according to one study, to 52% of employers covering 60% of enrolled employees. Eighty-five percent of firms with over 1000 employees self-insured, Gabel, et al., The Changing World of Group Health Insurance, 7 Health Affairs, 48 (1988).

Self-insured plans are often administered by third-party administrators (TPAs), firms that provide many of the services provided by insurers, such as claims processing and utilization review, but do not carry insurance risk. By 1987, TPAs and self-administered plans held 37% of the health insurance market. The market share of Blue Cross/Blue Shield had diminished to 24%, down from 38% a decade earlier, while the market share held by commercial insurers had declined from 53 to 40% over the same time period.

Why are employers so eager to assume the risk of their employees health care costs? Clearly one important consideration is the Employment Retirement Income and Security Act of 1974, 29 U.S.C. § 1001 et seq. As discussed in the previous chapter, ERISA exempts qualified self-insured employee health benefit plans from state health insurance regulations, including taxes on health insurance premiums, laws mandating coverage of certain benefits or providers, or persons, capital and financial reserve requirements, and laws mandating participation in risk pools for covering the uninsurable. It also exempts ERISA plans from state tort suits for bad faith breach of contract, Pilot Life Insurance Co. v. Dedeaux, 481 U.S. 41, 107 S.Ct. 1549, 95 L.Ed.2d 39 (1987) and probably from breach of contract suits under state common law. Although ERISA plans can be sued under the fiduciary duties imposed by ERISA itself, recovery is limited to denied benefits and jury trial is not available, 29 U.S.C.A. §§ 1132(a)(1)(B), (a)(3). Self-insurance also gives employers greater control over insurance reserves and the interest they earn.

Self-insurance is not primarily a cost-containment strategy. It does, however, affect the cost-containment efforts of employers in several respects. First, self-insurance itself may lower administrative costs and thus make its own contribution towards cost containment. Second, it makes the stake of employers in health care costs more visible, since payments for health care costs are made directly out of the employers' pockets and any unanticipated increases in cost are borne directly by the employer. Third, and most importantly, ERISA permits self-administered plans flexibility to adopt a variety of strategies otherwise barred by state law, as the next section illustrates.

C. UTILIZATION REVIEW

The most common strategy adopted by employers for controlling health care costs is utilization review or management. As of 1989, 49% of employees enrolled in employment-related health benefits plans belonged to a "managed conventional" plan, which normally means a conventional insurance plan with a utilization review component. An additional 34% belonged to alternative delivery systems, most of which included a utilization review function. Only 18% belonged to a conventional plan with no utilization review.

Utilization review refers to external case by case evaluation conducted by third-party payers, purchasers, health care organizers, or utilization review contractors to evaluate the necessity and appropriateness (and sometimes the quality) of medical care. It is a strategy that attempts to control costs by limiting demand. The utilization review strategy for cost-containment is based on the knowledge that there are wide variations in the use of many medical services (discussed in chapter 1), and the belief that considered review of medical care can eliminate wasteful and unnecessary care, and might eliminate some care that is actually harmful.

Utilization review can take several forms. The oldest form is retrospective review, under which an insurer denies payment for care already rendered, normally by judging it to be medically unnecessary, experimental, or cosmetic. Retrospective review is of limited value for containing costs, since the cost of the care has already been incurred by the time the review takes place, and thus review often leads to costly disputes between the insurer resisting payment and the provider who has already incurred the cost of the care as to whether the care was in fact necessary. Compare Sarchett v. Blue Shield of California, 43 Cal.3d 1, 233 Cal.Rptr. 76, 729 P.2d 267 (1987); Van Vactor v. Blue Cross Association, 50 Ill.App.3d 709, 8 Ill.Dec. 400, 365 N.E.2d 638 (1977).

More recently, utilization review programs have stressed prior or concurrent review and high-cost case management. Prior review techniques include preadmission review (before elective hospital admissions); admission review (within 24 to 72 hours of emergency or urgent admissions); continued stay review (to assess length of stay and some-times accompanied by discharge planning); preprocedure or preservice review (to review specific proposed procedures) and voluntary or man-datory second-opinions. High-cost case management addresses a small number (1–7%) of very expensive cases that may account for 30 to 60% of benefit plan costs. Case managers create individualized treatment plans for high-cost beneficiaries. Compliance with the plan is usually voluntary, but may be rewarded by the plan paying for services not otherwise covered by the insurer (such as home health or nursing home care) but less costly than covered alternatives. The traditional con-cerns of utilization review has been to assure that care is provided in the least expensive appropriate setting and that hospitalization is not unnecessarily prolonged. More recently, utilization review has also considered the necessity or appropriateness of particular procedures.

Utilization review can be conducted by free-standing utilization review contractors, by payers (employers and insurers, with or without direct contracts with providers) or by providers. Review is usually initiated by plan beneficiaries or by physicians or hospitals, who are aware that admissions or procedures must be preapproved to secure payment. Requests for approval are usually first reviewed by nurses, who apply established criteria (often computerized) to determine appro-priateness. Nurses may approve care, but if the care does not comply with applicable criteria, the case must be referred to a physician adviser for denial. Physician advisers will often contact the attending physician and negotiate an appropriate care plan, though some plans deny payment without direct contact with the attending physician. Plans usually have a formal or informal appeals process or provide other opportunity for further discussion of proposed denials.

Utilization review seems clearly to have reduced inpatient hospital use and inpatient costs experienced by health plans that have used it. One of the best studies found that it reduced admission of groups by 12.3%, inpatient days by 8%, and hospital expenditures by 11.9%. In particular, it reduced patient days by 34% and hospital expenditures by 30% for groups that had previously had high admission rates. Feld-stein, Wickizer and Wheeler, Private Cost Containment, 318 New Eng.J.Med. 1310 (1988). It is less clear that utilization review reduces total health care costs, since it often moves care from inpatient to outpatient settings (the Feldstein study found that it reduced total medical expenditures by 8.3%). Moreover, utilization review is most effective in the short run and has less effect on long-term cost increases. Nevertheless, it is one of the most acceptable cost-containment strate-gies to employers and employees, and thus has proved more popular than other, more drastic, strategies.

See, on utilization review generally, Institute of Medicine, Control-ling Costs and Changing Patient Care?: The Role of Utilization Management (1989).

WILSON v. BLUE CROSS OF SOUTHERN CALIFORNIA

Court of Appeal, Second District, Division 5, 1990.
271 Cal.Rptr. 876, 222 Cal.App.3d 660.

TURNER, ASSOCIATE JUSTICE.

I. INTRODUCTION

On March 1, 1983, Howard Wilson, Jr. (the decedent) was admitted to College Hospital in Los Angeles while suffering from major depression, drug dependency, and anorexia. His treating physician determined that he needed three to four weeks of in-patient care at the hospital. On March 11, 1983, through its agents, the decedent's insurance company announced that it would not pay for any further hospital care. Because nobody could afford to pay for any further in-patient hospital care, the decedent was discharged from College Hospital. On March 31, 1983, the decedent committed suicide. Because a triable issue exists as to whether the conduct of the decedent's insurance company and certain related entities was a substantial factor in causing the decedent's death, we conclude that the trial court incorrectly granted the summary judgment motions.

II. RESOLUTION OF PRINCIPAL LEGAL ISSUE

This is an appeal from several judgments imposed following orders granting summary judgment motions brought by four defendants. The orders granting summary judgment were premised upon the application of the holding of *Wickline v. State of California* (1986) 192 Cal. App.3d 1630, 239 Cal.Rptr. 810, a decision of this division. * * *

Unlike a normal opinion where procedural and factual matters are initially developed, this case lends itself to the resolution of the key legal issue at the outset—the extent to which *Wickline* extends beyond the context of Medi–Cal patients to an insured under an insurance policy issued in the private sector. Because *Wickline* should be limited to its facts and the legal issues properly decided in that case, it may not serve as a basis for the orders granting the summary judgment motions filed in this case.

A. *The Wickline Decision*

In *Wickline*, the plaintiff was a Medi–Cal patient who was hospitalized. Her physician sought Medi–Cal authorization for an additional eight-day period of hospitalization but a board-certified surgeon employed as a consultant by Medi–Cal authorized payment for only four additional days of hospitalization. As a result, her principal treating physician, with the concurrence of two other treating doctors, discharged plaintiff after four additional days of hospitalization. (*Wickline v. State of California, supra,* 192 Cal.App.3d at pp. 1636–1637, 239 Cal.Rptr. 810.) The plaintiff's principal treating physician did not utilize a reconsideration procedure within the Medi–Cal funding process to seek an additional extension of benefits for further hospitalization. All of the expert opinion testimony indicated that the discharge decision "was ... within the standards of practice of the medical community...." (*Id.* at pp. 1640, 1646, 239 Cal.Rptr. 810.) After her discharge, the plaintiff in *Wickline* experienced further medical problems which led to the loss of her leg.

* * *

B. *The Three Key Elements of Wickline*

In essence, *Wickline,* is a case involving three key legal and factual components. First, as a matter of law, the discharge decision met the standard of care for physicians. * * *

Second, the funding process was not pursuant to a contract; rather, the determination as to whether the state had a duty to provide funds was made pursuant to statute and provisions of the California Administrative Code. These statutes and regulations altered the normal course of tort liability set forth in Civil Code section 1714 which provides that " '[e]very one is responsible, not only for the result of his [or her] willful acts, but also for an injury occasioned by another by his [or her] want of ordinary care or skill....' " (*Id.* at p. 1643, 239 Cal.Rptr. 810.) * * *

Third, *Wickline* was not a case where a cost limitation program such as the Medi–Cal review process was "permitted to corrupt medical judgment." (*Wickline v. State of California, supra,* 192 Cal.App.3d at p. 1647, 239 Cal.Rptr. 810.) The *Wickline* court emphasized that a patient "who requires treatment and who is harmed when care which should have been provided is not provided should recover for the injuries suffered from all those responsible for the deprivation of such care, including, when appropriate, health care payors." (*Id.* at p. 1645, 239 Cal.Rptr. 810.) As will be noted, none of these three factors were directly applicable to any of the summary judgment motions in the present case. Therefore, the holding of *Wickline* does not extend to this present case.

C. *The Wickline Dicta*

Before proceeding to evaluate the three summary judgment motions in this case, an additional comment is in order concerning *Wickline.* The moving parties in the trial court in their papers focused on language in *Wickline* which must frankly be categorized as dicta. For example, the opinion states: "However, the physician who complies without protest with the limitations imposed by a third party payor, when [her or] his medical judgment dictates otherwise, cannot avoid his [or her] ultimate responsibility for [her or] his patient's care. He [or she] cannot point to the health care payor as the liability scapegoat when the consequences of [her or] his own determinative medical decisions go sour." (*Id.* at p. 1645, 239 Cal.Rptr. 810.) This broadly stated language was unnecessary to the decision and in all contexts does not correctly state the law relative to causation issues in a tort case. * * *

III. The Issues Raised by the Pleadings

The third amended complaint contains three causes of action which arise out of the March 31, 1983, death of the decedent. Plaintiff Howard E. Wilson, Sr., as the special administrator of the decedent's estate as well as his wife, the decedent's mother, filed suit against Blue Cross and Blue Shield of Alabama (Alabama Blue Cross), Blue Cross of Southern California and Blue Cross of California (California Blue Cross), Western Medical Review Organization, Area 23 doing business as Western Medical Review (Western Medical) and Dr. John Wasserman (Dr. Wasserman), a physician and employee of Western Medical. The first cause of action alleged that an Alabama Blue Cross and California Blue Cross tortiously breached an insurance contract. Further, it was alleged that there was an insurance contract between the decedent and Alabama Blue Cross and through an entity entitled "Inter–Plan Service Benefit Bank," California Blue Cross was obligated to provide the benefits of the insurance contract between Alabama Blue Cross and the decedent. The contract provided in-patient hospital benefits under the following clause:

"INPATIENT HOSPITAL SERVICE.

While a Member is covered under this Contract and is a registered bed patient in a Hospital, and during such time * * * as the Member's attending Physician determines that hospitalization is necessary, * * *"

Benefits for mental and nervous disorders were [also] provided * * *

* * *

It was also alleged that California Blue Cross and Alabama Blue Cross hired Western Medical for purposes of "denying payment for medically necessary hospitalization" and that nothing in the insurance contract allowed for review by an outside entity of an attending physician's conclusion that hospitalization was necessary. * * * As a result of the medical review conducted by a nurse and Dr. Wasserman, Alabama Blue Cross and California Blue Cross tortiously violated the contract by informing the decedent, the hospital administrator where the decedent was being treated, and the decedent's treating physician that the decedent would not be reimbursed for further medical treatment. As a result of this tortious contract breach, it was alleged that defendant was denied medical treatment and this was a proximate cause of his death.

The second cause of action was against Western Medical for inducing a breach of contract between Alabama Blue Cross and the decedent. * * * The third amended complaint alleged that all of the defendants were agents of one another and that they were negligent in selecting one another as their agents. Also, it was alleged that the defendants knew that the decedent needed additional care, his attending physician had determined that up to four weeks of further care was necessary, the decedent had no other funds, and that defendants' course of conduct resulted in the premature termination of needed medical treatment which proximately caused the decedent's death.

IV. The Western Medical, Dr. Wasserman, and Alabama Blue Cross Summary Judgment Motions

A. Defendants' Separate Statement

Western Medical, Dr. Wasserman, and Alabama Blue Cross submitted a terse separate statement of undisputed facts which identified four "issues" and cited to four separate pieces of evidence in support of the summary judgment motion. The evidence cited in the separate statement indicated that on March 1, 1983, the decedent admitted himself to College Hospital because of mental and drug addiction problems and that his attending physician was Dr. Warren R. Taff. Dr. Taff made the decision to discharge the decedent on March 11, 1983, and did not file an appeal of an utilization review determination made by Western Medical. * * *

B. Plaintiffs' Separate Statement

In contrast to the foregoing sparse evidentiary showing made by the three moving parties, plaintiffs submitted a separate statement containing an extensive array of facts. The evidence submitted by plaintiffs indicated that the Alabama Blue Cross policy which covered the decedent had no provisions for concurrent utilization review. Western Medical and Dr. Wasserman knew that Alabama Blue Cross covered the decedent. In 1983, Alabama Blue Cross delegated authority to California Blue Cross to adjust claims through the Inter–Plan Bank and in 1983 Western Medical contracted with California Blue Cross to perform "utilization review of the 'medical necessity'" of hospitalizations of all Blue Cross insureds. Western Medical had no contract with Alabama Blue Cross. Western Medical performed concurrent utilization reviews of the "medical necessity" for Blue Cross insureds at College Hospital in March, 1983.

The decedent was admitted to College Hospital on March 1, 1983, for major depression and loss of 20 pounds in two months. Dr. Taff's treatment plan called for the decedent to remain hospitalized for three to four weeks. Dr. Taff believed that "reasonable treatment" of the decedent required in-patient treatment on March 11, 1983. In 1983, Western Medical applied federal Medi–Care utilization review standards to private insurance patients. Prior to March 11, 1983, Dr. Taff was impressed with the decedent's prognosis. However, he was informed by Western Medical that the decedent's stay was "not justified or approved." In Dr. Taff's opinion the decedent required further in-patient treatment and the appropriate medical care could not be provided on an out-patient basis. Dr. Taff testified that it was reasonably probable to assume that there was a "reasonably medical probability" that the decedent would have been alive if his hospital stay had not been prematurely terminated.

Dr. Taff informed the decedent of Western Medical's decision "that the patient did not meet the admission criteria for his particular insurance policy and that his further stay was not justified or approved." The decedent was informed that he would "not be covered financially by his insurance company and that the liability [for hospital costs] would then be his." The decedent was "not happy with the decision...." The decedent cried while talking to an aunt about the determination that he was to be released from the hospital because the insurance company would not pay for the benefits. The decedent's aunt testified at her deposition that the family did not have enough money to pay for the cost of in-patient hospitalization. Dr. Taff told the aunt of the decedent "to come and get him." Dr. Taff told the decedent's mother and father that Western Medical "terminated his [the decedent's] stay" and the decedent's father was told that this was a "problem" that had occurred on other occasions.

C.   The Motions Were Incorrectly Granted

* * *

3.   Western Medical

As to Western Medical, it contends that it is not liable under the authority of *Wickline*. In this regard, Western Medical raises three contentions. First, Western Medical argues that when a treating physician makes a decision to discharge a patient because an insurance company refuses to pay benefits that the sole liability rests with the physician. This argument is premised on the language in *Wickline* which states that the exclusive responsibility for a discharge decision rests with the physician. (*Wickline v. State of California, supra*, 192 Cal.App.3d at p. 1645, 239 Cal.Rptr. 810.) As we have previously noted, this language constitutes dicta because it was unnecessary for the decision on *Wickline*. The evidence in *Wickline* indicated that the denial of benefits as a matter of law was proper because the standard for determining whether to extend the term of the hospital stay, i.e., whether the standard of medical practice in the community required that care be provided, was satisfied.

However, apart from the fact that Western Medical's contention that it is not liable because all tort responsibility for the discharge rests exclusively with the treating physician is premised on dicta in *Wickline*, the argument is likewise invalid because it misconstrues the test for joint liability for tortious conduct. The test for joint tort liability is set forth in section 431 of the Restatement of Torts 2d which provides, "The actors' negligent conduct is a legal cause of harm to another if (a) his [or her] conduct is a substantial factor in bringing about the harm, and, (b) there is no rule of law relieving the actor from liability because of the manner in which [her or] his negligence has resulted in the harm." (Rest.2d Torts, § 431.) [ ] In the present case, there is substantial evidence that Western Medical's decision not to approve further hospitalization was a substantial factor in bringing about the decedent's demise. It was Western Medical which conducted the concurrent utilization review and directed that no further benefits be paid. * * * Once the insurance benefits were terminated, there were no other funds to pay for the decedent's hospitalization. The sole reason for the discharge, based on the evidence adduced in connection with the summary judgment motion, was that the decedent had no insurance or money to pay for any further in-patient benefits. Dr. Taff, the decedent's treating physician, believed that had the decedent completed his planned hospitalization that there was a reasonable medical probability that he would not have committed suicide. The foregoing constitutes sufficient evidence to raise a triable issue of material fact as to whether Western Medical's conduct was a substantial factor in causing the decedent's death.

Western Medical argues that it was entitled to summary judgment because there are important public policy considerations which warrant protecting insurance companies and related entities which conduct concurrent utilization review. Western Medical cites language in *Wickline* which indicates that utilization review procedures involve "issues of profound importance to the health care community and to the general public." (*Wickline v. State of California, supra,* 192 Cal.App.3d at p. 1633, 239 Cal.Rptr. 810.) Western Medical contends that the *Wickline* decision can be construed to extend an immunity to a health care payor which refuses to provide insurance benefits on the advice of an entity such as Western Medical because "public policy" considerations which support the use of the concurrent utilization process. * * *

* * *

No such clear public policy exists to provide an immunity to Western Medical. In *Wickline,* there was a clearly expressed public policy reflected in the California Administrative Code and the Welfare and Institutions Code which mandated the use of a utilization review process. [ ] Also in *Wickline,* there was a specific statute that provided for the denial of benefits to a person seeking acute hospital care when to do so was " 'in accordance with the usual standards of medical practice in the community.' " [ ] There is no similar clearly expressed public policy which applies to the decedent's contract with Alabama Blue Cross.

Third, Western Medical argues that a treating physician must pursue avenues of appeal when insurance benefits are denied in the context of the utilization review process. In *Wickline,* there was testimony that the plaintiffs treating physician had a duty to file another request to extend her hospital stay when the Medi–Cal consulting physician only authorized a four-day rather than an eight-day extension of the initial period of acute care. (*Id.* at p. 1639, 239 Cal.Rptr. 810.) Based on this uncontradicted testimony, the court in *Wickline* later noted that the doctor who "complies without protest with the limitations imposed by a third party payor, when [her or] his medical judgment dictates otherwise, cannot avoid his [or her] ultimate responsibility for [her or] his patient's care." (*Id.* at p. 1645, 239 Cal.Rptr. 810.) As noted previously, this dicta has no application to this case. The present case involves a claim by a decedent's estate and relatives directly against insurance companies and their agents, not against a physician. In any event, the failure of Dr. Taff to follow an informal policy allowing for reconsideration by Western Medical did not warrant granting summary judgment. Not only is there a substantial controversy as to whether utilization review can be pursued under the terms of the decedent's policy, but no defendant has proven that such a reconsideration request would have been granted. Also, there is a triable issue as to whether the refusal to allow the decedent to stay in the hospital was a "substantial factor" in bringing about his death and the availability of an avenue of appeal fails to prove as a matter of law that his demise was unrelated to his denial of benefits. In summary, *Wickline* is a different case from the present lawsuit. There remain triable issues of material fact as to Western Medical's liability for tortious interference with the contract of insurance between the decedent and Alabama Blue Cross and its role in causing the wrongful death of the decedent.

* * *

VAROL v. BLUE CROSS AND BLUE SHIELD

United States District Court, Eastern District of Michigan, 1989.
708 F.Supp. 826.

NEWBLATT, DISTRICT JUDGE.

FACTS

A. Background and development of the pilot program.

[The court quoted the statement of facts from the joint brief of Amicus Curiae, the International Union, The United Automobile and Agricultural Implement Workers of America and the General Motors Corporation.]

"Basic health care benefits are delivered to GM's enrollees under the General Motors Health Care Program, which is an 'employee benefit plan' subject to the provisions of the Employee Retirement Income Security Act, 29 U.S.C. § 1001 *et seq.* Under this Program, primary enrollees (GM employees, retirees or eligible surviving spouses) generally have the choice of selecting one of three health care delivery options: traditional fee for service coverage (the 'Traditional Option'), health maintenance organizations ('HMO's') or preferred provider organizations ('PPO's'). [   ]

"The psychiatric managed care pilot program which is at issue in this lawsuit applied to General Motors enrollees, non-Medicare retirees, sponsored defendants and their eligible dependents, who are employed in Genessee, Lapeer and Shiawassee counties, and who receive mental health services in those counties under the Traditional Option. The GM Health Care Program, including the Traditional Option, is administered for GM in Michigan by Blue Cross & Blue Shield of Michigan ('BCBSM') under an 'administrative services only' contract. GM reimburses BCBSM for the covered health care charges paid by BCBSM on behalf of program enrollees and GM also pays BCBSM a fee for administering the Program. Thus, all claims payment risk is retained by GM. Blue Cross provides only administrative services and not insurance coverage. [   ]

"The cost of the medical benefits by GM for its employees has sharply increased in recent years. A significant factor in the increase has been the cost of mental health benefits, which has risen [18.5% between 1984 and 1987, from $70 to $83 million] * * *

* * *

"In light of the sharply escalating cost of benefits for mental health coverage, and the need to assure delivery of quality mental health care, [G.M. and the U.A.W.] agreed in the health care supplement to the 1984 collective bargaining agreement to have the Corporation–Union Committee on Health Care Benefits ('CUCHCB') 'explore development of a predetermination process for psychiatric services.' [ ]

* * *

" * * * The CUCHCB, at a number of meetings, has discussed the concept of a psychiatric managed care pilot program and considered several proposals. CUCHCB's consideration of such a pilot program was promoted, not only by the sharply escalating cost of mental health benefits but also, by information supplied to the CUCHCB showing improper and inefficient utilization of mental health benefits. Various proposals were presented to and considered by the CUCHCB. Pursuant to the authority granted to it in the 1984 and 1987 collective bargaining agreements and health care supplements, the CUCHCB ultimately agreed to proceed with the BCBSM pilot program which is the subject of this litigation. * * *

* * *

B.   Plaintiff's challenge to the pilot program.
* * *

"Plaintiffs in this case are 10 of the 20 participating psychiatrists in the pilot program. Plaintiffs executed provider agreements containing [pre-authorization and concurrent utilization review provisions] in December of 1987, but now claim, in their complaint filed in February of 1988, that the preauthorization and managed care requirements violate a variety of state laws and deprive plaintiffs of due process. Plaintiffs also contend that 'participation in this Pilot Program is not voluntary,' [ ] and that '[a]t the time they signed new provider agreements, plaintiffs were not aware of all of the details or ramifications of the new program.' [ ]

"Several of the plaintiffs own or operate out-patient mental health clinics which were *not* invited to participate in the pilot program. Two such plaintiffs, namely Dr. Swart and Dr. Forrer who owns Psychiatric Services, P.C., a plaintiff in this lawsuit, are *suing in the state court to force Blue Cross to accept their clinics as providers for the pilot program.* [ ] Thus, those plaintiffs are suing in state court to gain entry *into* the same program which they attack in this case as illegal and oppressive."

DISCUSSION

Plaintiffs assert a number of state law claims and one claim under the United States Constitution. In Counts I and II, plaintiffs claim that the prior authorization and concurrent review procedures under the Pilot Program violate Act 350 of the Public Acts of 1980, the Michigan Non Profit Health Care Corporation Reform Act, M.C.L.A. § 550.1101, in that the requirement to obtain prior approval requires the plaintiffs to deal with unlicensed personnel of BCBSM. It is further alleged that the power lodged in BCBSM personnel to withhold approval violates Sections 502(2) and 502(3) of that statute, which require that BCBSM contacts "shall provide that the private provider-patient relationship shall be maintained" and that a "health care corporation shall not restrict the methods of diagnosis or treatment of professional health care providers who treat members." Plaintiffs claim that the pilot program "impinges on a provider's utilization of his own best judgment in treating patients * * * and transfers to BCBSM the right to have significant and perhaps, dominant influence in deciding what shall be accepted as the correct diagnosis and the proper treatment." [ ] Plaintiff's theory is that the pilot program provides powerful economic incentives for a physician to disregard his best judgment at the behest of one not licensed to render medicine [sic] and "is in direct contradiction to the policy of this state with respect to this relationship." [ ]

In support of these theories, plaintiffs argue in Count IV that the requirements of the Pilot Program compel the plaintiffs to delegate delivery of health care services improperly to BCBSM's personnel, who are unlicensed to provide health care services. Plaintiffs argue that it is their function to deliver medical services and this delegation is in violation of the Public Health Code, MCLA §§ 333.16215 and 333.16221.

* * *

Plaintiff's constitutional claim will be set aside for the moment, to deal with defendant's claims that (a) such state laws are preempted by the Employee Retirement Income Security Act (ERISA), 29 U.S.C. § 1001 *et seq.,* * * *

* * *

[The court held that the state law claims were preempted by ERISA, see chapter 6 supra, but nonetheless proceeded to address the claims on the merits.]

Turning, however, to the actual merits—the direct challenge that the Plan's preauthorization requirement violates Act 350 and the Public Health Code—plaintiffs essentially claim that requiring preauthorization interferes with the plaintiffs' "right" to determine methods of diagnosis and treatment and would result in the unauthorized practice of medicine by BCBSM personnel. As the defendant and Amici point out, BCBSM personnel can approve a plaintiff's proposed treatment, but cannot reject it. If the BCBSM personnel cannot or do not approve the proposed treatment, the matter is referred to a staff psychiatrist, who discusses the matter with the provider or treating psychiatrist before a decision may be made that the proposed service is not medically necessary. If no approval to the provider's proposed treatment is then given, the treating psychiatrist can appeal to the Physician Director and then to an independent review organization.

As the Amici point out, the purpose of the Pilot Program is to determine in advance whether the GM plan will pay for the proposed treatment. *Whether of not the proposed treatment is approved, the physician retains the right and indeed the ethical and legal obligation to provide appropriate treatment to the patient.* Thus, there is no *direct* interference with the physician-patient relationship nor in the treatment rendered.

But plaintiffs claim that when there is a threat that the physician will not be paid or fully paid because approval has been withheld, the physician will be influenced unfairly and improperly to render treatment other than what the physician in good faith believes should be rendered; and thus, although the influence is indirect, the treatment is influenced improperly because the Plan injects BCBSM into the physician patient relationship and in the selection of the treatment. Plaintiffs say that decisions as to payment influence, in fact, decisions concerning actual treatment and thus the laws are *in effect* violated.

The Amici respond, and the Court completely concurs, that the Program in no way prevents providers from obtaining full payment even for rendering services that are not concurrently review or preapproved. If the treating psychiatrist renders the service, that psychiatrist can still obtain 80 percent of his fee directly from BCBSM and collect the balance from the patient. So denial of approval does *not* have the effect plaintiffs have urged; it merely changes from whom providers collect the 20 percent.

But suppose it did; what then? There are two points to be stressed here. First, these psychiatrists have joined this Plan. Having sought to be members and contractually agreed to be members, how can they now be heard to challenge the provisions to which they agreed? How can they voluntarily enter a contract and then challenge its terms? And if challenged, why would the contract not simply be void? How can plaintiffs challenge only the provisions they do not like and ask the Court, in effect, to modify the contract to their liking? Plaintiffs do not address this.

But the most persuasive argument against the plaintiffs, it seems to me is the argument plaintiffs themselves assert. Plaintiffs say, in effect, "Irrespective of any obligation I have to my patients and to my profession, my judgment as to what is in the best interests of my patients will not be determined by the exercise of my medical judgment, but by how much I will be paid for my services." Plaintiffs are saying in effect, "Since I am weak in my resolve to afford proper treatment, BCBSM's preauthorization program would induce me to breach my ethical and legal duties, and the Court must protect me from my own weakness." In other words, protect me from my own misconduct. This is strange stuff indeed from which to fashion a legal argument.

After all, the program is designed to make certain that only medically necessary services are provided and paid for. This is a legitimate objective, whether applied to a post-service reimbursement program or a concurrent review and preauthorization program. *If the same criteria* to determine medical necessity were applied in a program based on a post-service audit and the BCBSM claim for repayment for unnecessary treatment were to be made after the services were rendered, no one would claim it violated any of the laws cited by plaintiffs. As a matter of fact, that is precisely what the plaintiffs are urging here. If the criteria for determining medical necessity are the same, why would a concurrent review or preauthorization program be illegal?

* * * Cost containment in any program must deal with policing the necessity of the services rendered and payment therefor. GM and the U.A.W. are entitled to join together to make that effort. And it appears altogether inappropriate for the plaintiffs to say that the program will induce them to breach their duties to their patients. This, of course, is also a full answer to any substantive due process claims plaintiffs may make on the basis that the program is arbitrary, capricious, or irrational. [ ]

Turning lastly to plaintiffs' constitutional claims, these are easily disposed of, for there is no state action here. BCBSM is not a state agency nor does it act for the state. * * * Even if there were to be state action, the provider contracts signed by each of the plaintiffs establish what their rights are—and those agreements provide that plaintiffs will be paid by BCBSM if the preauthorization and concurrent review procedures of the program are followed. Moreover, those agreements provide an elaborate appeal procedure for plaintiffs if they should be aggrieved by BCBSM's decision. * * * The Motion to Dismiss thus will be Granted.

Notes and Questions

1. Wilson addresses the difficult question of when a utilization review program should be held liable to a patient for the denial of medical care that ultimately turns out to have been necessary and appropriate. Such cases must be analyzed under standard tort law, examining the existence and breach of a duty and the causation of damages. First, the court must address the duty of the utilization reviewer to the patient. Though the reviewer is only denying payment and not the care itself, harm from an inappropriate denial is clearly foreseeable, and the finding of a duty is appropriate. Second, there is the question of compliance with the standard of care, a question resolved in favor of the defendant in *Wickline* but not reached in *Wilson*. Are the reviewer's procedures and the criteria it applies reasonable and in compliance with the standards of the industry? Are the standards of the industry reasonable? The third and most difficult question is that of causation. Did Blue Cross's denial of payment cause Mr. Wilson's injuries or were the injuries caused by the independent actions of his doctor? How do the doctrines of proximate cause, joint liability, or superceding intervening cause apply here? See Helverstine, Legal Implications of Utilization Review, IOM, supra, 169, 171–179.

A utilization review program may obtain some protection from tort liability by making clear in its contracts and communications with providers and patients that it is only passing judgment on its financial responsibility for care, not on the clinical advisability of the care itself. See, Key,

Avoiding Liability Risks in Utilization Review, MGM J, 30 (Sept./Oct. 1989). See also Hughes v. Blue Cross of Northern California, 263 Cal.Rptr. 850, 215 Cal.App.3d 832 (1989) (Insurer liable for damages, including punitive damages, for breach of covenant of good faith where standard of medical necessity applied in denying psychiatric hospitalization varied significantly from community standard for utilization review and claim not properly investigated).

2.   Where the utilization review entity is independent of the payer, might the beneficiary also sue the payer for the reviewer's negligence? How can negligent selection or design, agency, or ostensible agency theories be used to argue the liability of a payer for the reviewer's negligence? How should the possibility of such negligence liability be addressed in drafting a contract for a payer with a utilization review entity? See Helverstine, supra at 188–190. Might the beneficiary also sue the individual reviewer? Would the malpractice insurance of the individual reviewer cover such liability? See Helverstine, supra, 185–186.

3.   An organization that does utilization review may also be sued for breach of contract or for bad faith breach of contract if an inappropriate denial of care results in injury. If the reviewer is independent of the payer and thus not in privity with the beneficiary, the beneficiary might sue the payer for breach of its contract with the beneficiary. Alternatively, the beneficiary might sue the reviewer, claiming third party beneficiary status to the contract between the payer and reviewer, See Helverstine, supra at 179–181.

4.   As *Varol* illustrates, however, suits under any of these theories against a qualified self-insured employer plan that conducts utilization review in house or against an independent reviewer treated as a plan "fiduciary" under ERISA might be preempted by ERISA. Under such circumstances the beneficiary would be limited to the much more restricted remedies afforded by ERISA. See Blum, An Analysis of Legal Liability in Health Care Utilization Review and Case Management, 26 Houston L. Review 191, 200–212 (1989). See also, Firestone Tire and Rubber Co. v. Bruch, 489 U.S. 101, 109 S.Ct. 948, 103 L.Ed.2d 80 (1989) (discussing the appropriate standard of review under ERISA).

5.   Might a doctor whose care was determined to be "unnecessary" or "inappropriate" by a utilization reviewer sue the reviewer for defamation or interference with a contractual relationship? See Slaughter v. Friedman, 32 Cal.3d 149, 185 Cal.Rptr. 244, 649 P.2d 886 (1982); Teale v. American Manufacturers Mutual Ins. Co., 687 S.W.2d 218 (Mo.App.1984)?

6.   The scope of practice questions raised by *Varol* are discussed in Blum, supra, at 221–225. Is a nurse reviewer outside of her scope of practice if she challenges the diagnosis and treatment plan of an attending physician? Is a physician reviewer retained by a utilization review entity engaged in unauthorized practice of medicine if she reviews a case in a state in which she is not licensed? Might the acts of a utilization review entity violate a state's corporate practice of medicine statute?

7.   Can a physician who determines a surgery to be urgently necessary for a patient in her care refuse to perform that surgery once the patient's insurer decides not to pay for the care because it is unnecessary? If the

physician does refuse to perform the surgery after payment is denied and the patient subsequently sues for abandonment, are the physician's vigorous arguments to the reviewer that the care was necessary sufficient to establish liability? What information must the physician provide the patient regarding the physician's own opinion and that of the utilization reviewer to fulfill obligations imposed by the doctrine of informed consent? Who is ultimately liable for the cost of care determined by the reviewer to be unnecessary but delivered anyway—the doctor or the patient? See Helverstine, supra, 190–192, 194–195.

8. Does the following statute (one of several adopted by states to address the phenomena of utilization review) solve these problems? What interests are furthered by the statute?

LSA–Rev.Stat. 22:657 Payment of claims; health and accident policies; prospective review; penalties; self-insurers

* * *

D. (1) In any event where the contract between an insurer or self-insurer and the insured is issued or delivered in this state and contains a provision whereby in non-emergency cases the insured is required to be prospectively evaluated through a pre-hospital admission certification, pre-inpatient service eligibility program, or any similar pre-utilization review or screening procedure prior to the delivery of contemplated hospitalization, inpatient or outpatient health care, or medical services which are prescribed or ordered by a duly licensed health care provider who possesses admitting and clinical staff privileges at an acute care health care facility or ambulatory surgical care facility, the insurer, self-insurer, third party administrator, or independent contractor shall be held liable in damages to the insured only for damages incurred or resulting from unreasonable delay, reduction or denial of the proposed medically necessary services or care according to the information received from the health care provider at the time of the request for a prospective evaluation or review by the duly licensed health care provider as provided in the contract; which damages shall be limited solely to the physical injuries which are the direct and proximate cause of the unreasonable delay, reduction, or denial as further defined in this Subsection together with reasonable attorney fees and court costs.

(2) Any requirement that the insured be prospectively evaluated through a pre-hospital admission certification, pre-inpatient service eligibility program, or any similar pre-utilization review or screening procedure shall be inapplicable to an emergency certified and determined as such by the attending physician in his medical judgment to be a physical condition which places the insured in imminent danger of death or permanent disability.

* * *

The statute further defines review within two days as reasonable and delay beyond two days as potentially unreasonable, depending on the circumstances; unreasonable reduction of services as decreasing or limiting of services previously approved or of continuing services without a means of extension; and unreasonable denial as denial without review of a timely request from an insured or an insured health care provider for a service or extension of a service, or of services previously approved, or of services "deemed medically necessary according to current established medical criteria."

D. COST–SHARING

Another important development in the last decade has been greater reliance on employee cost-sharing. Employees are increasingly required to pay part of the premiums of their health insurance. In 1982, 49% of employees were required to pay part of the premiums for family coverage, 29% for individual coverage. By 1986, 65% had to contribute to family coverage, 46% to individual coverage. The amount of employee contributions for premiums increased as well to an average of $13 for individual coverage, $41 for family coverage. Co-insurance and deductible requirements have also been raised in recent years. Between 1977 and 1987 the percentage of employees with first-dollar coverage for physicians services declined from 15% to 5%, the proportion with less than 20% copayment declined from 21% to 9%.

On the other hand, benefits have expanded in recent years: the percent of workers with vision coverage grew from 25% to 40% between 1982 and 1986 as coverage for alcoholism treatment expanded from 50% to 70% and home health care from 37% to 66%. Catastrophic stop-loss coverage also expanded. Between 1977 and 1987 the percentage of employees with out-of-pocket maximums expanded from 49% to 90%, while the proportion of workers with unlimited maximum benefits grew from 10% to 17%. DiCarlo and Gabel, Conventional Health Insurance: A Decade Later, 10 Health Care Fin.Rev. 77 (Spring 1989); Gabel, et al., Employer–Sponsored Health Insurance, 1989, 9 Health Affairs 161 (Fall 1990); Short, Trends in Employee Benefits, 7 Health Affairs 186 (Summer 1988).

What impact might increased employee cost-sharing have on health care costs? What impact might it have on health care costs as experienced by employers? What problems might increased employee cost-sharing cause for employees? What are the tax effects of increased employee cost-sharing? How might increased employee contributions for health care premiums affect two wage-earner families? Are employees benefited or harmed by a shift towards higher co-insurance and deductible levels accompanied by increasing stop-loss coverage and higher maximum benefits? Should cost-sharing levels in employment-related group insurance be left to private contract, or is there a public interest in regulating them in some way?

E. ALTERNATIVE DELIVERY SYSTEMS

There has been a dramatic growth in enrollment in alternative health care delivery systems by employees enrolled in employer-sponsored health plans. In 1989, 17% of employees were enrolled in Health Maintenance Organizations (HMOs) and 16% in Preferred Provider Organizations (PPOs), compared to only 4% enrollment in HMOs and PPOs as recently as 1981. In the western region of the country, over half of employee members of health plans are currently enrolled in HMOs and PPOs. Clearly employers in the private sector are heavily invested in competitive strategies as a cure for their health care cost problems.

1. Health Maintenance Organizations

A Health Maintenance Organization (HMO) is an entity that provides comprehensive health care services to an enrolled membership for a fixed, per capita, fee. HMOs are thus both insurers and providers of medical care. HMOs are usually classified into four categories based on their relationship with medical care providers: staff model HMOs directly employ physicians to provide medical care; group model HMOs contract with an independent, multi-specialty corporation or partnership of physicians to delivery care; network HMOs contract with a number of groups of physicians who also may serve patients not belonging to the HMO; and individual practice association (IPA) HMOs contract with an IPA, which in turn contracts with individual physicians to provide care in their own offices. A recent study of HMOs found that 48% were IPAs, 14% networks, and 38% staff or group-model HMOs.

HMOs are governed by both state and federal law. Most states have HMO enabling acts, which address both the insurance and health care delivery aspects of HMOs. A federal statute adopted in 1973 to encourage the growth of HMOs establishes federal recognition of HMOs as well, 42 U.S.C.A. §§ 280c, 300c, et seq. Initially this law gave federally qualified HMOs substantial advantages over non-qualified HMOs, including access to federal grants, loans, and loan guarantees and a requirement that employers with more than 25 employees afford their employees the option to enroll in a federally qualified HMO with the employer paying the same amount to the HMO as the employer paid to other health benefit plans. 1988 Amendments eliminated the "mandated dual choice option" requirement (effective 1995) and repealed the equal contribution requirement.

The law also imposed substantial burdens on federally qualified plans, however. To qualify for federal support under the 1973 law, HMOs had to offer comprehensive benefits and meet onerous requirements, such as consumer representation on governing boards, community rating (all insureds must be charged the same rate regardless of usage), open enrollment, and mandatory inclusion of low-income and elderly patients. These requirements have been eased by subsequent amendments, most notably by 1988 amendments which eliminated consumer representation requirements and adjusted the community rating requirement to permit HMOs to recognize prior experience with member groups. Nevertheless, federal requirements have still discouraged some HMOs from becoming federally qualified. A 1988 survey, for example, found that 28% of HMOs were not federally qualified.

Efforts are currently underway to enroll Medicare beneficiaries in HMOs under capitation payments set at a risk adjusted rate tied to 95% of average community costs. Several states have also begun contracting care of Medicaid patients on a prepaid capitation fee basis. Because such programs generally require a waiver of federal regulatory requirements (like monthly eligibility determinations), they have required both federal and state approval. The federal government has generally been supportive of market-based innovations by state Medicaid agencies. See chapter 6, supra, for further discussion.

On federal policy regarding HMOs, see L. Brown, Politics and Health Care Organizations: HMOs as Federal Policy (1983). On Medicare and HMOs, see Ginsburg & Hackbarth, Alternative Delivery Systems and Medicare, 5 Health Aff. 6 (Spring, 1986); Homer, Medicare Reimbursement Issues, 1 Topics Hosp.L. 1 (June 1986); Inglehart, Medicare Turns to HMOs, 312 New Eng.J.Med. 132 (1985). For a discussion of the antitrust issues raised by alternative forms of health care, see chapter 7, infra. For consideration of the tax, contract, and state regulatory issues raised by alternative practice forms, see supra at chapter 5 and Holmquist, Physician Hospital Alternative Delivery Systems, 1 Topics Hosp.L. 47 (June 1986); Lemkin, Alternative Delivery Systems: HMOs, PPOs, and CMPs, in McNair, Health Care, Legal Responses to New Economic Forces (1985); Miller, Hospital Contracts with Alternative Delivery Systems, 1 Topics Hosp.L. 69 (June 1986); Ruffner, Tax Issues Concerning Alternative Delivery Systems, 1 Topics Hosp.L. 13 (June 1986). For a good recent review of the range of legal issues affecting HMOs, see McCann, The Uncertainty of Success: Recent Developments in HMO Law, in 1990 Health Law Handbook, 89 (A. Gosfield ed., 1990).

There is substantial evidence that HMOs deliver medical care at a total annual cost per person substantially lower than non-HMO health care plans. Studies have found that HMOs cost from 10–40% less than fee for service plans. Luft, Health Maintenance Organizations: Dimensions of Performance (1981); Manning, et. al., A Controlled Trial of the Effect of a Prepaid Group Practice on the Use of Services, 310 New Eng.J.Med. 1505 (1984). In particular, studies have found that HMOs admit patients to hospitals 40% less often than do fee for service plans and use 40% less hospital days, Manning, supra and Group Health Association of American HMO Industry Profile: Utilization Patterns (1988). Differences between utilization by HMO and non-HMO plans of discretionary surgery seem particularly large. Arguably HMOs can provide cost savings, and these cost savings are attributable to the incentives created by per capita fixed fees.

There is, however, considerable, though not undisputed, evidence that some of the comparative cost advantage of HMOs is due to favorable selection. See Luft and Miller, Patient Selection in a Competitive Health Care System, 7 Health Affairs 97 (Summer 1988); Strumwasser, et al., The Triple Option Choice: Self–Selection Bias in Traditional Coverage, HMOs and PPOs, 26 Inquiry 432 (1989). Because switching HMOs usually means changing to an HMO-affiliated doctor, HMOs are less likely to attract persons with chronic illnesses already attached to a doctor and are more likely to attract younger, healthier, individuals without a regular doctor. They are also likely to attract healthier individuals who are favorably inclined towards their preventive care philosophy. Moreover, the competitive edge enjoyed by HMOs because of their lower use of hospital care may fade as traditional plans use utilization review to diminish their hospital use. Finally, IPAs, the most common and fastest growing form of HMOs, tend to be much more similar to conventional plans in cost than are group or staff model HMOs.

One recent study of employer-sponsored health insurance found that HMO premiums for family coverage were higher on average than those for conventional plans, though it also found that if consideration is limited to only employers that offer conventional, HMO, and PPO options, HMO premiums are lower than the PPO or conventional premiums. Gabel, et al. Employer–Sponsored Health Insurance in America, 8 Health Affairs 116 (Summer 1989). Moreover, the 16.5% average increase in HMO premiums in 1989 approached the 20.4% rise in conventional premiums, raising questions as to the actual capacity of HMOs to lower health care costs dramatically. In any event, HMOs remain an important tool for employers concerned about health care costs.

HMOs, as complex health care organizations, raise a host of legal issues. Some of these—including liability of HMOs for the negligent acts of affiliated physicians, legal relationships between HMOs and other health care providers, the tax status of HMOs, and antitrust problems of HMOs—are considered elsewhere in this text. Two legal issues are of particular concern here, however, where our primary concern is the cost of health care.

First, states have become increasingly concerned with the solvency of HMOs and with their responsibility to regulate HMOs as insurers. In the late 1980s a number of HMOs, facing simultaneously strong competitive pressure to lower prices and steep increases in medical costs, became insolvent. Particularly noteworthy were the bankruptcies of Maxicare, the nation's second largest HMO with over two million members, and International Medical Centers, which allegedly defrauded the federal government out of millions of dollars of Medicare payments. In response a number of states adopted laws to protect the members of HMOs.

Several legal requirements have been adopted to address these problems. First, a number of states have either adopted statutory requirements or authorized insurance commissioners to take steps to assure the fiscal soundness of HMOs. These requirements include restricted reserves, net worth requirements, and strict accounting standards and reporting requirements. Reserve and net worth requirements are often quite low, however, particularly when compared to those required of other health insurers. A second approach is to establish state HMO guaranty funds. All HMOs are required to contribute to these funds, the assets of which are available to protect members of HMOs that fail.

What effects might such requirements have? In, particular, what incentives might guaranty funds cause for poorly managed funds and what problems might they create for well managed funds. Are there any lessons to be learned here from the Savings and Loan crisis? See, Underwood and Luecke, The HMO Industry, and What We Should Learn from the S & L Crisis, 7 Health Matrix 41 (Winter 1989–90).

A third approach to the solvency problem is illustrated by the following statute:

Ill.Rev.Code Ch. 111½ ¶ 1407.01.   Provider agreements

§ 2–8. Provider agreements. (a) All provider contracts * * * shall contain the following "hold-harmless" clause: "The provider agrees that in no event, including but not limited to nonpayment by the organization of amounts due the hospital provider under this contract, insolvency of the organization or any breach of this contract by the organization, shall the hospital provider or its assignees or subcontractors have a right to seek any type of payment from, bill, charge, collect a deposit from, or have any recourse against, the enrollee, persons acting on the enrollee's behalf (other than the organization), the employer or group contract holder for services provided pursuant to this contract except for the payment of applicable co-payments or deductibles for services covered by the organization or fees for services not covered by the organization. The requirements of this clause shall survive any termination of this contract for services rendered prior to such termination, regardless of the cause of such termination. The organization's enrollees, the persons acting on the enrollee's behalf (other than the organization) and the employer or group contract holder shall be third party beneficiaries of this clause. * * *

How do such provisions assure plan solvency? What effects might they have on the cost-effectiveness and competitiveness of HMOs?

A second concern is the effect of the incentives that HMOs create for providers on the quality of care received by plan beneficiaries.

BUSH v. DAKE

State of Michigan, Circuit Court, County of Saginaw, 1989.
File No. 86–25767 NM–2.

PRESENT: Honorable Robert L. Kaczmarek, Circuit Judge

Defendant Group Health Services of Michigan, Inc. (hereinafter referred to as GHS) has filed a Motion for Partial Summary Disposition pursuant to MCR 2.116(C)(10), in which defendants Network Family Physicians, P.C., Scott, Gugino, Mulhern, and Brasseur have joined. The motion seeks dismissal of the allegations in Plaintiffs' Complaint a) that GHS's system of financial incentives, risk sharing, and utilization review is contrary to public policy and medical ethics and b) that the use of this system constituted negligence, gross negligence, fraud, a breach of trust, and a tortious breach of the relationship between plaintiff Sharon Bush and her doctors in this particular case. Defendants contend that there is no genuine issue as to any material fact regarding these allegations and that they are therefore entitled to judgment as a matter of law.

This case arises out of the alleged failure of Dr. Dake and Dr. Foltz to timely diagnose and treat plaintiff's uterine cancer. During the period in question, Mrs. Bush was insured by GHS through her husband's employer. As the GHS system requires, she had chosen a primary care physician, Dr. Dake. For any medical problem she might have, it was necessary for Mrs. Bush to first see Dr. Dake and obtain his permission to be examined by a specialist, in order for the specialist's service to be covered by her insurance.

Dr. Dake was one of five physicians comprising Network Family Physicians, P.C. (Network). * * * Network had an agreement with GHS whereby GHS would pay Network a certain amount per month per patient, called a "capitation," for primary care services. In exchange, the physicians would see the patients an unlimited number of times, whenever the patients sought medical care.

GHS set aside a certain amount of money each year for a "referral pool" and a "hospital/ancillary pool" for the Network physicians. The money in these pools would be depleted with each referral to a specialist or hospitalization of a patient during the year. At the end of the year, any money left over in these pools would be divided between GHS and the individual physicians in Network. The result was that the fewer referrals a doctor made and the fewer hospitalizations he ordered for his patients, the more money he made.

The plaintiffs contend that it was this arrangement which led in part to the deficient medical care that Sharon Bush received in this case. Mrs. Bush first consulted Dr. Dake in late August of 1985 with regard to vaginal bleeding and mucous discharge unrelated to menstruation. Dr. Dake prescribed various medications to cure what he considered to be an infection. The condition nevertheless persisted over a period of several months. In January of 1986, the plaintiff asked Dr. Dake for a referral to Dr. Foltz, a specialist in obstetrics and gynecology. Dr. Dake agreed to make the referral, and Mrs. Bush then saw Dr. Foltz on February 18, 1986. Dr. Foltz took a vaginal smear to test for chlamydia, a sexually transmitted disease. When the results of that test came back negative, Dr. Foltz's office advised Mrs. Bush to wait until after her next menstrual period, and then if the bleeding persisted to return to Dr. Foltz for a follow-up visit. When the bleeding did persist and Mrs. Bush attempted to obtain a second referral to Dr. Foltz from Dr. Dake, he refused to make the referral. Eventually, on May 13, 1986, Mrs. Bush presented herself at the emergency room of Saginaw General Hospital, a biopsy was taken, and a diagnosis of cervical cancer was made.

It turned out, in retrospect, that a pap smear, if it had been done, would have revealed the cancer at a earlier stage. In the GHS system, pap smears are to be done by the primary care physician only. However, the primary care physician is not paid anything in addition to the existing capitation for performing pap smears.

The plaintiffs contend that the system in question is wrongful, in that it provides the physicians involved with financial disincentives to properly treat, refer, and hospitalize patients. They contend that this Court should find a) that the system violates public policy and b) that there is a jury question presented as to whether the system itself contributed to the malpractice in this case.

After examining the briefs and statutory and case authority submitted by the parties, the Court agrees with the defendants that it is not for this Court to say whether the HMO system represents sound social policy. It is the Legislature, and not this Court, that determines public policy in this state. * * * In this instance, the Legislature has approved the existence of HMO's, MCLA 333.21001, et seq.; MSA 14.15(21001), et seq., and their use of health care provider incentives, MCLA 333.21023(3); MSA 14.15(21023)(3), risk sharing, MCLA 333.-21075; MSA 14.15(21075), and utilization review, MCLA 333.21083(d); MSA 14.15(21083)(d) in an effort to contain health care costs. This Court will not second-guess the wisdom of this legislation.

The Court therefore grants defendants partial summary disposition with regard to the plaintiffs' allegations that GHS's system of financial incentives, risk sharing, and utilization review is contrary to public policy. MCR 2.116(C)(10).

With regard to the second portion of defendants' motion, the Court finds that there is a genuine issue of material fact presented as to whether GHS's system in and of itself proximately contributed to the malpractice in this case. * * * Documentary evidence has been presented which supports the plaintiffs' theory that the manner in which the system operated in this case contributed to the improper treatment and delay in diagnosis of Mrs. Bush's cancerous condition. See *Wickline v. California,* 228 Cal.Rptr. 661, 670 (Cal.App. 2 Dist., 1986). The question should be submitted to the jury for determination at trial.

The Court therefore denies defendants' motion for partial summary disposition with regard to plaintiffs' allegations that the use of the GHS system in this case constituted negligence, gross negligence, fraud, a breach of trust, and a tortious breach of the relationship between Sharon Bush and her doctors.

Notes and Questions

1. The principal case, an unpublished opinion, is one of the few cases raising the issue of the effect of HMO incentives on the medical care received by beneficiaries. While on appeal it was settled. See also, Sweede v. Cigna Healthplan of Delaware, Inc., 1989 WL 12608 (Del.Super.) (claim that doctor withheld necessary care because of financial incentives rejected on facts of case) and Teti v. U.S. Healthcare, Inc., Civ.A. Nos. 88–9808, 88–9822 (E.D.Pa.1989). (RICO claim against HMO for failing to disclose physician incentives to withhold medical care dismissed). What explains the paucity of such cases, which are greatly outnumbered by articles in the popular and trade press noting their potential?

2. A few states immunize HMOs from liability for negligence. See N.J.Stat.Ann. § 26:2J–25(c)–(d). What policies support such immunity? See Harrell v. Total Health Care, 781 S.W.2d 58 (Mo.1989). Should HMOs be permitted to contract with their members to limit their liability for the acts of their physicians, or to require claims against the HMO to be submitted to arbitration? Should courts hold HMO physicians to a different standard of care than fee-for-service physicians, recognizing the different approach to care that HMOs have adopted to control costs? Or do malpractice doctrines like the respectable minority exception or simply the definition of reasonable care accomodate the more conservative style of practice found in HMOs?

Problem: Malpractice and the HMO

You are an attorney with a substantial malpractice practice. You have been approached by the local Blue Cross/Blue Shield plan, which is in the process of establishing an HMO. The HMO will operate on a prepaid, capitation basis to serve BC/BS subscribers who choose the HMO option. It will hire a staff of primary care physicians and contract with a large group of specialists for care on a discounted fee-for-service basis. HMO patients will only be hospitalized or have access to specialists at the instance of a HMO primary care physician. The HMO will have a policy of conservative treatment and will only hire physicians who are committed to this policy. It hopes to reduce hospitalization by at least 40%, compared to general hospitalization rates in the community. It will pass the savings from this on to its members in lower rates and broader benefits.

The HMO's concerns are various, though they all relate to malpractice. First, it wants to know whether it will be liable for the negligent acts of the physicians on its staff and with whom it contracts. Second, will its physicians be held to the same legal standard of care observed in fee-for-service practice, and thus forced to practice expensive defensive medicine? How will this affect its ability to cut costs? Third, must it, or its physicians, inform patients of its treatment philosophy to secure informed consent to treatment? If so, how should this be done? Does your answer depend on whether your jurisdiction evaluates informed consent by a reasonable patient or reasonable doctor standard? Finally, what steps can the HMO's members and community relationship program take to minimize malpractice exposure, both before and after medical errors occur?

The HMO administrator who contacted you recently attended a conference at which a number of ideas for reducing HMO malpractice liability were discussed, and he would like your opinion on these. First, if the HMO includes a provision in its membership contract requiring HMO members to submit malpractice claims against the HMO to binding arbitration in consideration for their reduced insurance rates, will it be enforceable? Alternatively, what about a provision exculpating the HMO altogether from liability? What is your response to these questions?

See, Bovbjerg, The Medical Malpractice Standard of Care: HMOs and Customary Practice 1975 Duke L.J. 1375; Blumstein, Rationing Medical Resources: A Constitutional, Legal and Policy Analysis, 59 Tex.L.Rev. 1345, 1395–1399 (1981); Rationing, supra at 1395–1399; Boyd, Cost Containment and the Physician's Fiduciary Duty to the Patient, 39 DePaul L.Rev. 131 (1989); Furrow, Medical Malpractice and Cost Containment: Tightening the Screws, 36 Case West.Res.L.Rev. 985 (1986), Furrow, The Ethics of Cost–Containment: Bureaucratic Medicine and the Doctor as Patient–Advocate, 3 Notre Dame J.L. Ethics & Pub.Pol'y 187 (1988); Hall, The Malpractice Standard Under Health Care Cost Containment, 17 Law, Med.Health Care 347 (1989); Havighurst, Reforming Malpractice Law Through Consumer Choice, 3 Health Aff. 63 (Winter 1984); Morreim, Cost Containment and the Standard of Medical Care, 75 Calif.L.Rev. 1719 (1987); Rosenblatt, Rationing "Normal" Health Care: The Hidden Legal Issues, 59 Tex.L.Rev. 1401, 1411–19 (1981); Schuck, Malpractice Liability and the Rationing of Care, 59 Tex.L.Rev. 1421 (1981).

3. Other concerns affecting HMOs addressed by state statutory requirements include fraudulent advertising, handling of patient complaints, claim settlement procedures, scope of coverage and conversion privileges. See generally, on HMO regulation, Monahan and Willis, Special Legal Status for HMOs: Cost Containment Catalyst or Marketplace Impediment, 18 Stetson L.Rev. 353 (1989); Michaels and Rinn, Legal Trends and Developments in Alternative Delivery Systems, in 1989 Health Law Handbook, 153 (A. Gosfield ed.).

2. *Preferred Provider Organizations*

A preferred provider organization (PPO) is an organized system of health care providers that agrees to provide services on a negotiated basis to subscribers. PPO subscribers are not limited to plan providers (as they would be in an HMO) but face financial disincentives, such as deductibles or larger copayments, if they choose non-preferred providers. PPOs usually pay providers on a fee-for-service rather than a capitation basis, in contrast to HMOs. PPOs also usually have utilization review and sometimes quality assurance requirements. PPOs may be sponsored by hospitals, physician groups, commercial insurers, Blue–Cross/Blue Shield plans, investors, union trusts, or others.

PPOs offer employers potential cost controls through negotiated rate discounts and utilization review. Some PPOs further enhance their ability to control costs by attempting to select providers on the basis of cost-consciousness or by using primary care gate-keepers to control access to specialist care. At the same time PPOs offer employees a wider choice of providers than do HMOs, and free access to any provider if the employee is willing to assume the additional costs. PPOs also often offer employees greater coverage of preventive care than do conventional plans. Finally, they are more acceptable to many physicians than are HMOs—since they pay on a fee-for-service basis— and more attractive than conventional plans as they offer preferred access to the beneficiary pool and more efficient claims processing than that offered by conventional plans. They are also very attractive to hospitals, which see them as an opportunity to increase occupancy by securing patient and preferred physician allegiance.

PPOs have grown very rapidly in the late 1980s and now include 16% of employees in employer-sponsored health plans. Whether they will prove a significant ally in attempts to control costs, however, remains to be seen. A recent study, for example, found that PPO premium rates tend to be higher than either HMO or conventional coverage premiums, See Gabel, et. al., Employer Sponsored Health Insurance in America, 8 Health Aff., 116 (Summer 1989). During 1987–1988, increases in PPO premiums exceeded those of HMOs and conventional plans. Cost-savings such as those found in HMOs have not yet been established for PPOs.

PPOs are heavily concentrated in a few states. California, for example, has 25% of all PPOs and 62% of enrollees. Colorado, Illinois, Florida, and Ohio share another 25% of PPOs. In the eastern region of the country, by contrast, less than 1% of employees belong to PPOs. The differential growth of PPOs is undoubtedly due in part to the legal environment they face in various states.

As PPOs began to emerge they encountered in many states free-choice-of-provider statutes that prohibit insurers from restricting in any way their subscriber's right to obtain medical care from any licensed physician. See, e.g., Ga. Official Code Ann. § 33–18–17. They also encountered statutes prohibiting insurers from unfairly discriminating among covered individuals in the level of premiums, fees, or benefits. Finally, some state statutes prohibited insurers from paying different rates to different providers or forbade hospitals from charging different rates to different insurers unless the differentials were cost-justified. What purposes were such statutes designed to address? What problems might they cause PPOs? See, I and II, Rolph, et al., State Laws and Regulations Governing Preferred Provider Organizations (1986); Elden & Hinden, Legal Issues in Creating PPOs, 1 J.L. & Health, 1, 23–25 (1985–86); Greaney, Competitive Reform in Health Care: The Vulnerable Revolution, 5 Yale J.Reg. 179, 185–189 (1988).

Many states have now adopted laws explicitly authorizing PPOs. Such laws frequently include, however, "any-willing-provider-requirements" requiring PPOs to contract with any providers willing to accept the PPOs' conditions of membership. Some such statutes further require PPOs to contract with willing non-physicians. PPO enabling acts also often include "differential payment" or "differential benefit" statutes, limiting the difference between payments or benefits paid to PPO and non-PPO providers to 10–30%. Finally, some states prohibit primary care gatekeeper arrangements. What motivates these statutes? What effect might they have on PPO development and cost-control efforts?

States have also adopted a variety of consumer protection measures governing PPOs, including minimum access, benefit disclosure, emergency service coverage, grievance procedure and quality assurance requirements.

PPOs sponsored by self-insured employer sponsored group-health plans are probably exempt from state regulation under ERISA. What problems and opportunities might this create?

Since PPOs are inherently exclusionary and since many are run by providers who are collaborating to form the PPO but otherwise maintain independent practices, they raise obvious antitrust concerns. These have proven among the most thorny legal problems affecting PPOs. They are discussed in Chapter 8.

On legal problems affecting PPOs see generally, Rolph, supra, Elden & Hinden supra, Elden and Hinden, Legal Issues in Networking with Alternative Delivery Systems, 10 J.Ambulatory Care Management 51 (May 1987); Michaels & Rinn, supra., and Comment, Cost v. Quality in the Regulation of Preferred Provider Arrangements: A "Green Light to the Gold Rush"? 41 Southwestern L.J. 1155 (1988).

Problem: Private Cost Containment

You are an attorney representing Amtech Inc., which employs about 1500 employees. Since its founding in 1978 Amtech's business has grown rapidly and profits have been high. Amtech has accordingly offered generous salaries and an extensive benefits plan to attract the well-trained and educated employees it needs. In the last two years, however, growth and profits have flagged. Moreover, Amtech has recently been purchased on a highly-leveraged basis and must cut costs to service its high debt. Finally, last year the premiums of Amtech's group health plan, which it has always purchased from a conventional insurer, increased 25%. The new management has decided, therefore, that dramatic action is necessary to control corporate costs generally and health care costs in particular.

The group health plan Amtech has offered its employees for the last decade is a traditional conventional insurance plan. Individual coverage has been free. Family coverage has been offered subject to payment of a small premium, which has risen slowly to its present level of about $50.00 a month. The health plan covers basic hospitalization on a first dollar basis. It pays hospitals directly on a reasonable charge basis. Major medical is provided on an indemnity basis, subject to a $50.00 deductible and 10% copayment for which the employee is responsible. There is no maximum for plan benefits, nor is there a maximum out-of-pocket expenditure limit.

Amtech's benefits manager has devised the following plan for controlling benefit's costs. Amtech will offer its employees a triple option. Employees may opt for coverage through an HMO, PPO, or conventional indemnity plan. They must make their choice within two months of the plan's adoption, and will only be able to change plans once a year during a one month open enrollment period.

Amtech will enter into a competitive bidding process with the five HMOs currently operating in the area, and will select the one that offers it the lowest price for coverage similar to the existing conventional plan. Employees who choose the HMO option will have to pay no more for coverage than they do currently, but will be strictly limited to the HMO for medical care and receive no payment for care covered outside of the HMO.

Amtech will next offer to contract with Community Memorial, a large hospital located near Amtech's plant, to form a PPO. Initial contacts with Community Memorial, which has recently experienced a sharp drop in occupancy, indicate that it is very interested in such a contract and would be willing to offer a substantial discount from its normal charges. Community Memorial will identify primary care physicians and specialists with privileges at Community Memorial to participate in the plan on a contract basis, and negotiate discounts with them. Primary care physicians will operate as gatekeepers, and access to specialists will only be through the plan primary care physicians.

Coverage for care through Community Memorial and plan physicians will be available to employees who joined the PPO with cost-sharing terms similar to those now available through the current conventional plan. PPO enrollees can receive care out-of-plan, but will be responsible for a $500 deductible and 25% copayments.

Amtech will also contract with a utilization management firm to review employee use of PPO care, and require preadmission and length of stay review for hospitalization and preprocedure review for ambulatory surgery. Unapproved care will not be covered. The utilization management contract will establish performance goals, including denial of about 5% of claims per year, given estimates from the literature that the incidence of unnecessary care is much higher than this.

Finally, Amtech will renegotiate its current conventional contract, to raise the deductible to $200 and extend it to hospitalization coverage, and to raise the coinsurance amount to 20% for physician's services and 5% for hospitalization. Conventional care will be subject to utilization review on the same terms as care delivered by the PPO.

Amtech will only make the same employer contribution for the PPO and conventional plans that it makes for the HMO plan. Any additional premium costs will be covered by employees.

Amtech asks you to review the proposal and identify any potential legal problems. Management also asks you to comment on any potential problems you see with the plan and to make suggestions as to how it could be improved.

IV. COST CONTAINMENT IN GOVERNMENT–SPONSORED PROGRAMS

A. MEDICARE PROSPECTIVE PAYMENT UNDER DIAGNOSIS–RELATED GROUPS

1. Introduction

Because of its considerable market share, the federal Medicare program is better positioned than other payers to face the problem of the cost of medical care. Paying for over one quarter of hospital care, it is able to offer payment rates to hospitals on a take it or leave it basis. On October 1, 1983, the Medicare program put in place a program that essentially does this. This new prospective payment system (PPS) was initiated in the face of medical care cost increases that threatened to bankrupt the Medicare trust fund unless drastic steps were taken.

When Medicare was established in the mid 1960s, it borrowed from the Blue Cross programs a cost-based system of reimbursement. The inflationary possibilities discussed in the introduction of this chapter in fact materialized: between 1967 and 1983 Medicare hospital expenditures (which then constituted two-thirds of program expenditures) increased elevenfold from $3 billion to $33 billion. In 1982 Congress, impressed by the success of state rate regulation systems in controlling costs, mandated the implementation of a prospective payment system. One of the models that it looked to was that of New Jersey, where diagnosis-related groups (DRG) prospective payment, implemented through an all payer reimbursement system, had dramatically reduced hospital costs. Between 1980 and 1982, New Jersey experienced the second lowest hospital per diem cost increase in the country and dropped from 18th to 32nd in health care costs. Congress sought to emulate this success.

This section will first explain how Medicare prospective payment works. It will then review recent research examining how DRG reimbursement affects the health care system. It will conclude by considering the legal issues raised by PPS.

2. DRG PPS

A DRG is a means of categorizing patients to reflect relative intensity of services. DRGs were initially developed by a team of Yale researchers for utilization review purposes. DRG–based payment considers hospitals as entities that do not provide an unrelated set of services, but rather coordinate services to produce particular products: the diagnosis and treatment of specific conditions such as heart attacks, ulcers, and tumors. DRGs group patients primarily by principal (admitting) diagnoses, which are themselves categorized by body system into 23 systems or major diagnostic categories (MDCs). These groupings are then broken down into 467 separate categories by considering principal and secondary diagnoses, whether a surgical procedure was performed, and, in cases where relevant, by further considering age, gender and discharge status. Cases are sorted into the correct DRG by the GROUPER computer program. The purpose of this analysis is to yield groups of hospital patients, each covered by a distinct DRG, that require the same consumption of medical resources. Once DRGs were defined, HHS, using data from a 20% sample of Medicare bills, arrayed DRGs by relative intensity of resource consumption, with the average resource used defined as 1. Thus, for 1990, DRG 49, surgery, major head and neck procedures, is weighted at 2.8633 (or nearly three times the average admission cost); DRG 59, tonsillectomy and/or adnoidecotomy only on a patient over 17 years of age, at .3878, or about $^4/_{10}$ the average cost. DRG weights are recalibrated annually to recognize changes in treatment patterns, technology, or other changes that might affect relative use of resources for providing hospital care.

To determine a hospital's actual payment for caring for a Medicare patient, the relative DRG weight assigned to that patient is first multiplied times a standardized amount, which in theory represents the cost to an efficient hospital of an average case. There are currently three such standardized amounts, one for large urban areas (with populations in excess of one million), one for smaller urban areas, and one for rural areas outside metropolitan statistical areas. The standardized amount was initially based on a national survey of allowable reported costs from a base year of 1981. This standardized amount has been updated annually, taking into consideration changes in the PPS program and inflation experienced by hospitals, though annual percentage increases have usually been far below the actual rate of hospital cost inflation. Initially during a transition period, PPS rates for any particular hospital also included components that recognized the historical costs of the particular hospitals (hospital specific costs) and regional variations in hospital costs. This blend has now been completely phased out and replaced by national rates.

This national rate is only the starting point for determining PPS hospital reimbursement, however. The product of the DRG weight and standardized amount (or rather the product of the total DRG weights of all Medicare cases treated in the hospital during the payment period and the standardized amount) is adjusted in several respects to determine a hospital's actual PPS payment. About three quarters of PPS payments are attributable to labor costs, which vary greatly throughout the country. Accordingly, this labor-related portion of the PPS payment is adjusted by an area wage index factor. This adjustment results in hospitals in high cost labor markets receiving significantly higher Medicare payments than those in low labor cost markets.

PPS payments are further adjusted to recognize the cost of extraordinarily expensive cases. Cases in which the length of stay or the cost of care greatly exceed the norm for the DRG assigned to the case can qualify as "outliers" for which Medicare will pay part (currently 75%) of the additional costs hospitals incur. PPS payments are also enhanced to compensate teaching hospitals for the indirect costs of operating educational programs. Finally, PPS payments are increased or otherwise adjusted to benefit special categories of hospitals: Disproportionate Share Hospitals (which serve large numbers of low income patients, which presumably cost more to treat); Sole Community Hospitals (which serve communities distant from other hospitals, protected by federal policy); and Rural Referral Centers (hospitals located in rural areas that resemble larger urban hospitals in the complexity of cases that they handle.) These adjustments can be very important for hospitals in particular situations. Whereas straight unadjusted PPS reimbursement accounts for 75% of the Medicare payments for acute care hospitals generally, it accounts for only 53% of the reimbursement for major teaching hospitals, with outliers accounting for 7%, the indirect medical education adjustment for 16%, and the direct medical education adjustment for 9% of the total Medicare revenues for these institutions.

Finally, some categories of hospital costs continue to be reimbursed on a cost basis. Capital costs, for example, are reimbursed on a cost basis, reflecting the extraordinary variation of such costs among hospitals depending on factors such as the age and location of the facility. The current goal of Congress is to reimburse capital costs on a DRG basis by late 1991, but the method that will be used has not been decided as of this writing. The direct costs of medical education programs are also reimbursed on a pass-through cost basis, as are hospital bad debts related to uncollectible Medicare deductible and co-insurance amounts and a few other miscellaneous expenses. Finally, a variety of special hospitals, including psychiatric, rehabilitation, and long-term hospitals continue to be reimbursed on a cost basis outside of the PPS program.

Good descriptions of PPS reimbursement are found in T. Coleman, Legal Aspects of Medicare and Medicaid Reimbursement, 21–56 (1990) and Philips and Wineberg, Medicare Prospective Payment: A Quiet Revolution, 87 W.Va.L.Rev. 13, 30–9 (1984).

3. The Effects of Medicare PPS

The effects of Medicare DRG payment on the American health care system in the second half of the 1980s have been profound. These effects are compounded by the use of DRG or other case-mix reimbursement systems by over a third of the federal-state Medicaid programs and by some private insurance companies. PPS was greeted with dire predictions that it would result in hospital closures, poorer quality and less accessible care for beneficiaries, and massive cost-shifting to other payers. In fact, PPS must be adjudged at least a modest success, particularly compared to other cost-saving strategies. Its effects on the utilization of health care services by Medicare beneficiaries, on Medicare costs, on hospitals, and on beneficiaries will now be explored.

a. Effects on Use of Medicare Financed Services

The effects of PPS on the health care system were immediate and dramatic. In the first year of PPS, 1984, the average length of stay for Medicare beneficiaries dropped to 8.95 days from 9.68 days the previous year. Though the average length of stay for the elderly had been declining at a rate of 1% to 2% per year for more than a decade, this 7.5% drop in one year was unprecedented and clearly attributable to PPS. One hospital reported a decline in average length of stay for hip fracture patients from 16.6 to 10.3 days, another from 29.9 to 12.6 days with the initiation of PPS. Several studies also found decreases in the use of intensive care units and in the number of routine tests and procedures used for Medicare patients. Most surprisingly, the initiation of PPS was accompanied by a decline in hospital admissions of the elderly. Hospital admissions had been growing in the years preceding the introduction of PPS, and it was widely believed that per-case payment would create significant incentives to increase admissions. Nevertheless, admissions declined annually from 1983 until 1987, only then beginning to rise slowly. The combination of declining length of stay and admissions led to a decrease in occupancy rates from 74% in 1983 to 64% in 1987.

These decreases in the use of hospital services were accompanied, however, by sharp increases in the use of services in other medical care settings. A rapid growth in the use of home health care accompanied the initiation of PPS. Discharges from hospitals to nursing homes did not grow dramatically with the introduction of PPS, as had been anticipated, but patients discharged to nursing homes seemed to be more acutely ill. PPS was also accompanied by a dramatic move of surgery from inpatient to outpatient settings. In 1983 80% of Medicare surgical charges were for inpatient surgery, 7% for outpatient surgery, and 13% for surgery in physician's offices. By 1986 57% of charges were for inpatient, 26% for outpatient, and 16% for office surgery. By 1986 40% of surgical procedures performed in hospitals were performed on an outpatient basis. A particularly dramatic drop was experienced in cataract surgery. Ophthalmologists, who account for 29% of all surgical charges paid by Medicare, billed 87% of their charges for inpatient surgery in 1980. By 1985 only 25% of their billings were for inpatient surgery.

b. Cost Savings for the Medicare Program

The implementation of PPS has clearly and dramatically moderated the growth of hospital costs as experienced by the Medicare program. Medicare Part A inpatient hospital costs, which were growing at a rate of 19.8% in 1981, and 11.2% as late as 1983 and 1984, fell to a historic low growth rate of 3.1% in 1987 before climbing again to a growth rate of 7.8% in 1989. In constant dollars, Medicare spending for inpatient hospital care has stayed almost constant since the initiation of PPS. Indeed, costs for 1990 are now expected to be 18 billion dollars less than those predicted for 1990 by the trustees of the Medicare Hospital Insurance Trust fund in their reports for the five years preceding PPS.

The majority of this increase in hospital costs is attributable to the increasing complexity of hospital case-mix rather than to inflation pass-throughs. That is to say, the hospital bills submitted to Medicare claim that patients being treated are sicker and thus have higher DRGs than was true when PPS began. How much of this change in case-mix is real, and how much is attributable to "DRG–creep" (the tendency of hospitals to upcode for higher DRGs to maximize reimbursement) is unclear. Undoubtedly, however, the decline in admissions mentioned above and the relocation of minor surgery to outpatient settings would support the belief that hospitals are now treating sicker patients, for whom they are claiming higher payments.

Decreases in Part A inpatient hospital payments have been accompanied by dramatic increases elsewhere in the Medicare program, however. Between 1984 and 1989 payments for Part B services increased 92%, leading in turn to Congressional action to control Part B costs. Outpatient hospital costs more than doubled during that period. Whereas Part A inpatient costs accounted for 64% of total Medicare payments in 1984, they accounted for only 53.8% in 1989. Nevertheless, total Medicare expenditures grew at only single digit inflation levels throughout most of the second half of the 1980s, compared to double digit inflation levels in the Medicare program during the preceding half decade and in the private sector during the late 1980s. Perhaps most tellingly, the Medicare Hospital Insurance Trust fund, which as recently as 1984 seemed destined for bankruptcy by 1991, now seems secure into the next century.

c. Effects on Hospitals and Other Payers

Has PPS merely shifted the cost of treating Medicare patients to hospitals or to other payers? Substantial cost-shifting to other payers has not taken place. Indeed, it appears that other payers have also benefited from the decline in admissions and more conservative practice patterns that have caused a decline in Medicare payments.

The effect of PPS on hospitals, however, is more complex. Hospitals fared very well under PPS initially. Hospital operating margins (profits) hit an historic high of 6% in 1984. During 1984 and 1985 the PPS–operating margin (the difference between what hospitals received from prospective payments and expenditures for Medicare patients) exceeded 14%. Teaching hospitals fared particularly well due to Medicare's liberal reimbursement for educational costs. In the following years, however, hospital costs increased much more quickly than PPS reimbursement. By 1990 it was estimated that PPS margins would approximate on average minus 2.5%. Since the cost containment efforts of other payers leave little room for cost-shifting, hospitals with below average PPS margins found themselves in the late 1980s in serious trouble. Rural hospitals were disproportionately represented among this group, leading to congressional efforts in 1989 to shift Medicare resources towards rural hospitals. See, discussing the effect of DRG PPS on hospitals, Oday and Dobson, Paying Hospitals Under Medicare's Prospective Payment System: Another Perspective, 7 Yale J. Reg. 529 (1990).

Hospitals have reacted to PPS by tightening their belts. Hospital employment, which had grown at about 4% a year from 1980 to 1983, dropped in 1984 and 1985 and grew very slowly thereafter. Hospital investment in capital also seems to be declining. Finally, the number of hospital closures in recent years have been growing, particularly among rural hospitals.

d. Quality and Technology Diffusion

It was widely predicted at the time that PPS was implemented that it would lead to "quicker and sicker" discharge of Medicare beneficiaries. While anecdotal evidence of quality problems under PPS surfaced earlier, they have by and large not been confirmed by subsequent research. The most recent and comprehensive study of the effects of PPS on quality of care concludes that by most measures the quality of hospital care has remained unchanged or improved since the introduction of PPS, though the incidence of patients discharged in an unstable condition has increased. See, Rogers, et al., Quality of Care Before and After Implementation of the DRG–Based Prospective Payment System, 264 J.A.M.A. 1989 (1990).

PPS does not seem to have adversely affected the diffusion of new medical technologies. A study of adoption of CT scanners, MRIs, lithotripters, cardiac catherization labs, cancer programs, neonatal intensive care units, and open-heart surgery determined that rates of adoption after PPS were equivalent to those before. Where particular technologies are undervalued by the DRG assigned to them, however, as may have been the case with cochlear implants, diffusion may be slowed. Kane and Manoukian, The Effect of the Medicare Prospective Payment System on the Adoption of New Technology, 321 New Eng.J. Med. 1378 (1989).

In sum, PPS seems to have at least had a modest effect on controlling the cost of health care experienced by the federal government, while not demonstrably diminishing the quality of care received by Medicare beneficiaries. On the other hand, PPS seems to be at the point of seriously affecting the financial viability of many hospitals, and its long term effects here must be monitored closely.

For good summaries of the literature on the effects of PPS see, Prospective Payment Assessment Commission, Medicare Prospective Payment and The American Health Care System: Report to Congress, June 1990; L. Russell, Medicare's New Hospital Payment System: Is it Working? (1989); Lave, The Impact of the Medicare Prospective Payment System and Recommendations for Change, 7 Yale J. Reg. 499 (1990); Schramm & Gabel, Prospective Payment, Some Retrospective Observations, 318 New Eng.J.Med. 1681 (1988); and McCarthy, DRGs— Five Years Later, 318 New Eng.J.Med. 1683 (1988).

4. PPS and the Business of Lawyers

PPS does not seem to be making much business for lawyers. This is in marked contrast to Medicare cost reimbursement which preceded PPS. If cost-based reimbursement was a gold mine for hospitals, it was also a gold mine for lawyers. Cost-based reimbursement continually raised questions of the sort that lawyers (and accountants) love to argue about. Should the fact that Medicare patients benefit from a relatively small proportion of malpractice recoveries be taken into account in determining the share of a hospital's malpractice costs that should be borne by the Medicare program? See Tallahassee Memorial Regional Medical Center v. Bowen, 815 F.2d 1435 (11th Cir.1987); St. Marys Hospital Medical Center v. Heckler, 753 F.2d 1362 (7th Cir.1985). Should a woman in a labor or delivery room bed at a hospital's census hour be counted as an inpatient (increasing the hospital's occupancy and decreasing Medicare's proportionate share of its costs, since few women on Medicare have babies)? See Central Dupage Hospital v. Heckler, 761 F.2d 354 (7th Cir.1985) Saint Mary of Nazareth Hosp. Center v. Schweiker, 718 F.2d 459 (D.C.Cir.1983). Litigation about such cost-finding and apportionment questions, and about the timing and procedures for review of cost-reimbursement issues, the appropriateness of HHS rulemaking on cost-reimbursement issues, and interest rates on eventual judgments against HHS, continue to occupy the courts still six years into PPS. See, Mazer & Hedlund, Developments in Medicare Reimbursement for Hospital Services, in 1990 Health Law Handbook, 311 (A. Gosfield, ed. 1990).

By contrast, PPS raises remarkably few justiciable issues. Issues raised by PPS are either political questions, such as what the standardized amount update level should be for any particular year, or technical questions, such as how a particular DRG should be weighted or which DRG should be assigned by a hospital to a particular admission. Congress has made it clear that it does not want the court's getting involved in these determinations:

> There shall be no administrative or judicial review under Section 1395oo of this title or otherwise of—
>
> (A) the determination of the requirement, or the proportional amount of any adjustment effected pursuant to subsection (e)(1) of this section [providing for updates in the standardized amount], and
>
> (B) the establishment of diagnosis-related-groups, of the methodology for the classification of discharges under within groups, and of the appropriate weighting of factors thereof * * *

42 U.S.C.A. § 1395ww(d)(7)

Congress has established a tri-partite dialogue among itself, HHS, and an independent body called the Prospective Payment Assessment Commission, to determine these questions and has left no place for the courts. See Kinney, Making Hard Choices Under the Medicare Prospective Payment System: One Administrative Model for Allocating Resources under a Government Health Insurance Program, 19 Ind.L. Rev. 1151 (1986).

Remarkably few cases have been brought so far involving PPS. Most reported cases raising PPS issues involve the hospital specific portion of the blended rate that applied during the first several years of transition from cost reimbursement to PPS. They are thus, in fact, cost reimbursement cases. Most involve the question of what notice HHS must give a hospital before it can appeal the hospital specific portion of its rate, See Sunshine Health Systems, Inc. v. Bowen, 809 F.2d 1390 (9th Cir.1987); Georgetown University Hosp. v. Bowen, 862 F.2d 323 (D.C.Cir.1988); Doctors Hosp. v. Bowen, 811 F.2d 1448 (11th Cir.1987). A few raise the question of whether a particular hospital qualifies for special treatment under PPS, e.g. as a disproportionate share hospital. See Samaritan Health Center v. Heckler, 636 F.Supp. 503 (D.D.C.1985) or a rural referral center, Providence Hosp. v. Bowen, CCH Medicare and Medicaid, ¶ 35,430.

To the extent that some costs, most notably capital costs, are still passed through under PPS, the opportunity exists for raising traditional accounting type questions. Treatment of funded depreciation accounts and interest on them, for example, has recently been much debated by lawyers who closely follow these issues. Finally, there is also still the possibility of a constitutional challenge to the whole edifice, though such a challenge will almost certainly be turned back by the rational basis test. See Good Samaritan Hosp. v. Heckler, 605 F.Supp. 19 (S.D.Ohio 1984) (challenge to urban-rural distinction).

Insofar as PPS makes work for lawyers, it is primarily in the area of advising clients how to live with PPS. Consider the following problem:

Problem: DRGs

You are in-house counsel for a 400 bed teaching hospital in a major metropolitan area. The CEO of the hospital has requested your advice on a matter that has come to her attention. Your hospital is heavily dependent on Medicare reimbursement, which provides about 40% of its revenues. You are located in the Northeast, a high cost region, and in a downtown location, and have been hit heavily by DRG reimbursement, which has not begun to cover your high costs. The hospital lost $400,000 last year, and is consuming its endowment at an alarming rate. Your fiscal planning department has been working hard trying to analyze the average and marginal costs your institution experiences for various procedures and to identify DRGs that are revenue winners and losers, so that your institution can alter its marketing strategy to improve its revenue position. In doing so they have noticed that one of your biggest revenue losers is DRG 107, coronary artery bypass with catheterization, a surgical approach to improve heart functioning, and one of your biggest winners is DRG 124, angina with catheterization, a primarily medical intervention for the same problem. Your hospital's costs for the former procedure over the past year have ranged from $18,800 to $85,855 per case, while the DRG reimbursement is $14,000. Costs for the latter treatment have ranged from $214 to $7460 per case, while DRG reimbursement is $7396. The two treatment forms are not wholly fungible: the surgical approach is more intrusive and is slightly more risky (about 2% death rate resulting from the procedure), largely because of the need for the procedure to be performed under general anesthesia. On the other hand, the surgical intervention is more successful in prolonging life and improving the quality of life of the recipient. Moreover, in about 30% of cases in which the medical intervention is attempted, surgery is eventually performed anyway.

The CEO has suggested asking the medical staff director to present this information to the next medical staff meeting, together with a request that medical staff consider the financial problems of the hospital in determining the appropriate course of treatment for their patients. She has asked your advice as to any potential legal problems this approach may entail. In particular, she is concerned as to what, if anything, patients should be told if a physician follows this advice. She also wonders whether it might be appropriate eventually to terminate the staff privileges of physicians who insist on using the form of treatment more costly to the facility. What is your response?

B. MEDICARE PAYMENT OF PHYSICIANS

Reform of Medicare payment for physicians has lagged behind hospital payment reform, but with OBRA 1989 seems finally to be underway. Since the inception of the Medicare program Part B physician services have been reimbursed on a "reasonable charge" basis.

This "reasonable charge" for a service is the lowest of (1) the physician's actual charge; (2) the physician's "customary charge" to Medicare beneficiaries for similar services and (3) the "prevailing charge" for similar services in the locality. 42 U.S.C.A. § 1395u(b)(3). Prior to 1984 the customary and prevailing charges were updated annually based on the prior years data, though since 1973 the increase in prevailing charges has been limited by a national economic index that has caused reasonable charges lag behind actual charges.

Unlike hospitals, physicians are not required to bill Medicare directly or to accept Medicare payment rates as payment in full for Medicare services. A physician may agree to accept assignment of a beneficiary's claim, bill the Medicare carrier directly, and accept the reasonable charge (plus copayments and deductibles for which the beneficiary is responsible) as payment in full. Alternatively, the physician may bill the beneficiary directly, who then must turn to the carrier for indemnification. Until 1984 the physician could decide on a case by case basis whether or not to accept assignment, and in non-assignment cases bill the beneficiary any charge the physician chose, with the beneficiary being responsible for the difference between the actual charge and the reasonable charge as determined by Medicare. As Medicare reasonable charges diverged further and further from actual charges in the early 1980s, assignment became less and less common, and beneficiaries became responsible for ever increasing physician charges.

The Deficit Reduction Act of 1984 (DEFRA) and the Omnibus Budget Reconciliation Act of 1986 (OBRA) made significant changes in physician reimbursement aimed at remedying the rapid escalation of physician charges and of beneficiary liability for them. First, DEFRA established a "participating physician" program, which offered incentives to physicians who would accept assignment from all of their Medicare patients. Second, DEFRA froze reasonable charges at 1983–1984 levels, and also temporarily prohibited even physicians who did not accept assignment from billing Medicare beneficiaries charges in excess of their actual charges during the second quarter of 1984.

OBRA 1986 went a step further towards controlling fees and encouraging assignment. First, it raised the amount Medicare paid participating physicians while holding the amount paid non-participating physicians constant. Second, it established for non-participating physicians a "maximum allowable actual charge" or MAAC, which capped the amount such physicians could bill Medicare beneficiaries. A monitoring system, enforced through civil fines, was established to assure compliance with the MAAC. A constitutional challenge to these reforms was rejected in Issacs v. United States, 865 F.2d 264 (9th Cir.1988).

For further information on physician payment prior to OBRA of 1989, see Wieland, Medicare Reimbursement of Physicians, 1989 Health Law Handbook, 109 (A. Gosfield ed. 1989); Dechene, Reform of

Medicare Reimbursement for Physician Services, 23 J. Health Hosp.L. 33, 333–36 (February 1990)

The restrictions imposed by DEFRA and OBRA ultimately failed to stem the tide of increases in physician payments under Part B, which grew nearly three times faster than expenditures for Part A between 1985 and 1989, nearly doubling between 1983 and 1988. Even during years in which physician fees were frozen, expenditures for physician services continued to grow rapidly because of increases in the volume and intensity of the services physicians provided. Concern about beneficiary access to affordable services also continued to grow during the late 1980s. The participating physician incentive program had some effect—by 1989 41% of physicians billing Medicare were participating physicians and over 80% of claims were billed on an assigned basis. Several states also enacted laws either requiring physicians to take assignment for all or for low-income Medicare beneficiaries. See Massachusetts Medical Society v. Dukakis, 815 F.2d 790 (1st Cir.1987) cert. denied, 484 U.S. 896, 108 S.Ct. 229, 98 L.Ed.2d 188 (1987) (upholding such legislation in Massachusetts). Yet participation rates remained low in some specialties, and balance billing (billing beneficiaries for charges above the Medicare payment amount) has continued to stretch the resources of some Medicare beneficiaries.

Awareness also increased in the late 1980s of the inequities inherent in charge-based reimbursement. Charge-based reimbursement merely accepts the charge structure existing in the market for physician services without questioning the rationality of that structure. If the market were competitive and free from distortions, this might be acceptable. Given the severe distortions found in the market for physician services, discussed at the outset of this chapter, this structure has become increasingly unacceptable. In particular, the disparity between the generous reimbursement offered by Medicare for technical procedures and the parsimonious payments for cognitive services have become impossible to rationalize.

Finally, policy-makers also became increasingly concerned that Medicare physician reimbursement did not do enough to encourage the quality and appropriateness of care provided beneficiaries. In 1989 a political consensus came together around a package of reforms designed to address these problems described in the following excerpt, and codified at 42 U.S.C.A. §§ 1395w–4(a)—1395w–4(j).

PHYSICIAN PAYMENT REVIEW COMMISSION, ANNUAL REPORT TO CONGRESS

19–21, 24–32 (1990).

Medicare Fee Schedule

A cornerstone of the payment reform legislation is the creation of the Medicare Fee Schedule. In January 1992 the Medicare program will begin to replace the current payment system that bases fees on what physicians charge with a fee schedule that reflects the resources used in providing services to patients. This policy is intended to realign payments that, under a charge-based system, have come to overvalue most surgical and technical procedure relative to visits and consultations. Over a five-year transition period, the fee schedule will play an increasing role in determining what physicians are paid.

Setting payment under the fee schedule begins with a relative value scale (RVS) that indicates the value of each service relative to other services. The RVS is translated into a schedule of fees when it is multiplied by a dollar conversion factor and a geographic adjustment factor that indicates how fees should vary from one locality to another. The fee schedule does not include specialty differentials. The Congress believes that there should be no difference in the fee paid to different specialists for providing the same service.

* * *

RELATIVE VALUE SCALE

The resource basis of the Medicare Fee Schedule is embodied in the relative value scale specified in the legislation. The RVS will have three cost components: a physician work component that reflects the time and intensity of the physician's effort in providing a service; a practice expense component that includes costs such as office rent, salaries, equipment, and supplies; and a separate malpractice component that reflects professional liability premium expenses. While the proportion of a relative value represented by each component varies by service, on average physician work accounts for slightly more than half the relative value.

RELATIVE PHYSICIAN WORK VALUES

The legislation specifies that the physician work component is to reflect the time and intensity involved in providing a service. * * *

* * *

PRACTICE EXPENSE

Practice expense constitutes almost half the resources that need to be allocated to different services in the RVS. Much of practice expense consists of overhead, in that a given resource is used to produce all or most physician services. Office rent is an example. But some practice expense—X-ray equipment, for instance—supports only a limited range of services.

* * *

MALPRACTICE EXPENSE

The legislation specifies a separate RVS component for the costs of malpractice coverage. The Commission suggested the distinction to highlight the magnitude of malpractice insurance costs and to permit a method of allocating these costs that differs from that for other practice costs. Malpractice premiums in an area are determined primarily on the basis of a physician's specialty. A separate component for malpractice permits calculating this expense according to a physician's specialty in a relative value scale that does not otherwise incorporate specialty differentials.

* * *

Transition to the Medicare Fee Schedule

The legislation calls for a five-year transition from the current payment system to the Medicare Fee Schedule. The first step of that transition is particularly significant. Fees for services in a locality whose 1991 payments, as defined by the legislation, are within 15 percent of the fee schedule will shift to the fee schedule amounts in that first step in 1992.

* * *

For services for which payments do not move to the fee schedule in the first year of the transition, payments will be a blend of the payment amount from the previous year and the fee schedule amount. In each of the next four years, the percentage of the Medicare payment attributable to the fee schedule amount will increase, beginning with 25 percent in 1993, 33 percent in 1994, and 50 percent in 1995. In 1996 all payments will be based on the fee schedule.

* * *

Geographic Adjustment Factor

Under the new payment system, fees will be adjusted to reflect geographic variation in costs of practice. The adjustment will reflect the full variation in an index of cost items such as office rent, salaries of nonphysician employees, and malpractice premiums and a partial adjustment for geographic differences in the cost of living. Cost of living is represented by an index of earnings of professional workers other than physicians.

* * *

Beneficiary Financial Protection

The Medicare program has always allowed physicians to charge patients more than the approved Medicare payment amount. This practice is often referred to as balance billing. The payment reform legislation continues that policy, while placing clearer and, in many cases, tighter limits on what physicians can charge. The policy standardizes the percentage by which charges can exceed the fee schedule amount, replacing a complicated system of physician-specific charge limits known as maximum allowable actual charges. In 1991 physicians will no longer be able to charge patients more than 125 percent of the Medicare fee. That percentage will decline to 120 percent in 1992 and to 115 percent in 1993 and thereafter.

Because of the way the policy defines the payment amount to which the limit is applied, however, its impact will be even more than is apparent. The charge limits are based on Medicare payments to nonparticipating physicians (those who have not signed an agreement to accept what Medicare pays as payment in full on all claims), which are to be 95 percent of the fee schedule amounts. Because the 115 percent limit is applied to this lower fee, nonparticipating physicians can actually charge no more than 9.25 percent of the full fee schedule amount received by participating physicians.

The payment reform legislation also contains several provisions that are particularly important in assuring beneficiary financial protection and access to physicians' services. The Secretary of HHS must monitor charges by nonparticipating physicians and changes in the proportion of expenditures attributable to services provided by participating physicians or on an assigned basis. The Secretary must develop a plan to address any significant decreases in these assignment and participation trends.

The legislation also requires the Secretary to monitor changes in beneficiary utilization and access to services, possible sources of inappropriate utilization, and factors influencing these developments. Each year the Secretary must report the Department's findings to the Congress along with recommendations to address any problems identified through the monitoring process.

* * *

Medicare Volume Performance Standards

The VPS policy is the major component of the payment reform to address the problem of increasing program costs. Under the policy, the fee schedule conversion factor will be updated on the basis of how expenditure increases compare to a previously determined goal. * * *.

CONTROLLING COSTS THROUGH APPROPRIATE USE OF SERVICES

The VPS policy expresses the Congress' determination to slow the growth of expenditures to an affordable rate. Its underlying concept is that by basing fee updates on how expenditure growth compares to a performance standard, the medical profession is given a collective incentive to foster approaches to cost containment. While these incentives are not intended to influence the decisions of individual practitioners directly, they do provide a reason for physicians to become more involved in efforts to contain medical costs. Approaches that medical organizations can pursue include developing and disseminating practice guidelines, expanding continuing education, and providing both technical and political support to carriers and Peer Review Organizations (PROs) in their utilization review activities.

* * *

The federal government will support the efforts of the medical profession to increase appropriate use of medical resources in a number of ways. It will provide financial support for the profession's efforts to develop guidelines and review criteria. It will also generate information on utilization patterns to help focus these efforts and increase the effectiveness of peer review.

The VPS will be the federal government's main tool to control aggregate spending for physician services under Medicare. Once a specific standard for the rate of increase in expenditures is adopted, fee increases two years later will be adjusted up or down to guide expenditures toward this goal. The ability of Medicare to control costs in the long run through the VPS policy will depend both on whether the annual standards are met through slowed growth in service volume or through reduced fee updates and on how private insurers respond to disparities between Medicare and private payment levels. If private insurers maintain current payment levels and Medicare performance standards are met through reductions in fee updates, physicians may be less willing to see Medicare patients. This in turn could limit the federal government's ability to control growth in spending without compromising access to care. On the other hand, if private insurers adjust their fees in response to reductions in Medicare fee updates, potential access problems for Medicare patients would be diminished.

SETTING THE PERFORMANCE STANDARD AND UPDATING THE CONVERSION FACTOR

The specifics of the VPS policy are complex because the Congress left little discretion in the implementation of the policy to HHS. The legislation calls for the Congress to make annual decisions on the performance standard (the target rate of increase in expenditures) and on the conversion factor update. But leaving these decisions to the Congress required provisions concerning what will happen if the Congress does not act. Thus, the legislation contains a series of formulas that HHS will use to determine the standard and the update if the Congress does not specify it each year.

While those who drafted the legislation envision the Congress acting each year, the default formulas are nevertheless very important. First, they signal the Congress' current thinking about the proper level of the performance standard and how the subsequent conversion factor update will depend on it. Second, the presence of a default option will inevitably influence deliberations, as various parties compare potential options with what the default formulas would yield.

To show how the VPS mechanism works, the following outlines how the expenditure change from 1990 to 1991 will influence the conversion factor update for 1993. In April 1990, HHS will recommend a performance standard rate of increase for fiscal year 1991. One month later, the Commission will comment and make its recommendation to the Congress. Then the Congress will either set a performance standard or allow the default formula to go into effect. The 1991 default performance standard is the sum of (1) the 1990–1991 increase in Medicare fees, (2) the average annual rate of growth in volume and intensity over the 1986–1990 period and (3) the effects of changes in law other than those affecting fees, less (4) a VPS factor of 1 percentage point. This VPS factor is 0.5 percentage points for 1990, 1 percentage point in 1991, 1.5 percentage points in 1992, and 2 percentage points for

1993 and later years. This suggests an intention to slow the expenditure growth rate gradually. * * *

* * *

If the Congress does not act, the default formula will determine the update. The formula starts with the Medicare Economic Index (MEI), a measure of general inflation relevant to medical practices, and adjusts it by the difference between the performance standard and the actual change in expenditures. Thus, if the performance standard is 11 percent and expenditures increase by 12 percent, the update will be the MEI minus 1 percentage point. The default formula places a floor on how much less than the MEI the update can be. The limit is 2 percentage points for 1992 or 1993, 2.5 percentage points for 1994 or 1995, and 3 percentage points for 1996 and thereafter. There is no upper limit for the update. If the Congress makes the update decision, the limitation in the default formula does not apply.

* * *

A Program of Research and Dissemination to Improve Clinical Practice

The fourth component of the payment reform legislation expands federal support of health care research and dissemination of what is learned. It establishes the Agency for Health Care Policy and Research. The new agency has been given a broad charge to conduct and support research on the quality, appropriateness, effectiveness, and cost of health care services and to use the results of this research to promote improvements in clinical practice and in the organization, financing, and delivery of health care services.

* * *

DISSEMINATION OF INFORMATION AND PRACTICE GUIDELINES

AHCPR will support efforts to disseminate and use the knowledge gained by research through a Forum for Quality and Effectiveness in Health Care. The Forum will sponsor the development of practice guidelines, clinical standards, and review criteria that will summarize much that is learned about effective and appropriate practice. Guidelines and clinical standards will help physicians and patients decide what care each patient should receive.

* * *

Notes

See also, explaining the reforms, Dechene, Reform of Medicare Physician Reimbursement for Physician Services, 23 J. Health & Hosp. L. 33 (Feb.1990); Furrow, Physician Payment Reform: Plugging the Drain, 34 St. Louis U.L.J. 821 (1990); Ginsburg, Physician Payment Policy in the 101st Congress, 8 Health Aff. 5 (Spring 1989); Ginsburg, Medicare Physician Payment Reform, 34 St. Louis U.L.J. 759 (1990); Holahan, Physician Payment Reform, 34 St. Louis U.L.J. 867 (1990); Iglehart, The New Law on Medicare's Payments to Physicians, 322 New Eng.J.Med. 1247 (1990);

Scott, Physician Payment Reform—Implementing Resource–Based Relative Value Schedules, 4 Med.Staff.Couns. 1 (Summer 1990).

Problem: Cutting Lawyers Fees

Sometime in the mid–1990s it becomes apparent to Congress that the high cost of legal services is having a substantial negative effect on the American economy and on our international competitive position. Congress also becomes concerned that there are gross and irrational disparities among the payments lawyers receive for legal services. Congress, therefore, adopts a resource-based relative value schedule, limiting lawyers to the charges allowed by such a schedule (plus 15% where the client agrees). Adherence to the charges is enforced by criminal laws plus civil penalties ($2000 per infraction).

Legal services for representing corporations in corporate takeovers and tax and securities work and for representing individuals in estate planning, domestic relations, real estate transactions or criminal defense matters, are all evaluated considering the (1) time, (2) mental effort and judgment, and (3) psychological stress [2] involved in delivering each service. Geographic variations in practice overhead are also recognized in fee-setting, though historic geographical variations in payments for the time of lawyers are recognized only to a very limited extent (i.e. a lawyer will be paid for his or her own time—as opposed to overhead—the same payment for similar work whether it is performed in Manhattan or in Peoria). No explicit recognition is given in the fee schedule for experience, skill, or law school class standing of individual practitioners.

How might such a fee schedule affect access to legal services? The volume of legal services provided? The geographic and specialty distribution of lawyers? The quality of legal services? Innovation in developing new legal theories? Your plans after law school? How hard you study for the final in this class?

Where does the analogy between this problem and RBRVS break down? How, that is, does the market for physician services differ from the market for legal services?

Notes and Questions

1. As with PPS, there will probably be little work for lawyers created directly by Medicare physician payment reform. 42 U.S.C.A. 1395w–4(i) provides

There shall be no administrative or judicial review * * * of—

   (A) the determination of the historical payment basis * * *

   (B) the determination of relative values and relative value units
* * *

2. These factors plus technical skill and physical effort are all being considered in setting the physician RBRVS, see Hsiao, et. al., Estimating Physicians' Work for A Resource–Based Relative–Value Scale, 319 New Eng.J.Med. 835 (1988). Unless the additional physical exertion on the golf course consumed in serving corporate clients is considered, this latter factor does not seem relevant to legal services.

(C) the determination of conversion factors * * *

(D) the establishment of geographic adjustment factors * * *, and

(E) the establishment of the system for the coding of physicians' service under this section.

2. Predictions as to how the RBRVS physician payment reforms will affect the problems it is designed to correct vary. Reducing fees chargeable by specialists, for example (fees for a coronary artery bypass are predicted to decrease by 65% and a cataract removal with lens insertion by 56%), may result in such specialists attempting to increase the volume of their services or in their refusing to treat Medicare patients. Primary care doctors, on the other hand, whose fees will increase under RBRVS, will charge higher copayments, perhaps discouraging beneficiary access to primary care. Assignment rates, which have been climbing steadily, may decrease as specialists attempt to recoup lost income and stricter limits on balance billing may discourage physicians from treating beneficiaries. A rigid RVS might discourage innovation or encourage more labor intensive services that may be less efficient and effective than less labor intensive services. The fact that individual physicians are generally better able to get along without Medicare patients than are hospitals, might make reform of physician payment harder than was hospital payment reform.

3. It is hoped that volume and intensity increases will be moderated by clinical practice guidelines that will discourage unnecessary and inappropriate procedures. What legal issues are raised by the creation and enforcement of such standards? Would a professional or specialty group violate the antitrust laws if it drafted practice guidelines itself? If it attempted to enforce them by denying membership or other benefits to those who refused to comply with them? Should such guidelines be narrow and focused or broad and flexible? Should a variety of groups be encouraged to develop a variety of approaches to practice guidelines, to enhance consumer choice and competitiveness in the health care environment? Will the existence of such guidelines encourage or facilitate the resolution of malpractice disputes? See Physician Payment Review Commission, Annual Report to Congress, 235–245 (1990) Brook, Practice Guidelines and Practicing Medicine, Are They Compatible? 262 J.A.M.A. 3027 (1989); Havighurst, Practice Guidelines for Medical Care: The Policy Rationale, 34 St. Louis L.J. 777 (1990).

4. The inclusion of a separate component of the physician payment package for malpractice premium costs is likely to spotlight the costs of malpractice to the Medicare program and keep malpractice reform on the federal agenda. Relative to the malpractice reform debate, it is of interest that one of the studies of recent increases in the volume of physician services determined that increasing malpractice premiums had a negative, rather than a positive, effect on the volume of services provided by physicians, raising questions about the role of defensive medicine in medical care cost increases. See Holahan, Dor & Zuckerman, Understanding the Recent Growth in Medicare Physician Expenditures, 263 J.A.M.A. 1658 (1990).

5. Adopting the RBRVS administered price approach to Medicare physician payment necessarily means rejecting, at least for a time, alternative approaches. Alternatives that have been proposed include payments to hospital medical staffs rather than individual physicians to encourage greater oversight of practice patterns (Welch, Prospective Payment to Medical Staffs: A Proposal, 8 Health Aff. 34 (1989)); competitive bidding to reintroduce market controls (McCombs, A Competitive Bidding Approach to Physician Payment, 8 Health Aff. 50 (1989)); or payments related to outcomes to encourage quality and efficiency, (Furrow, supra).

6. States have also responded to budget constraints by cutting Medicaid payments to physicians. During the 1981 to 1984 period Medicaid payments to physicians declined 5.4% per year in constant dollars. To accomplish these cuts, states abandoned charge-based reimbursement in favor of other payment methods. A majority of states (31 in 1986) now reimburse physicians based on fee schedules. Moreover, some of the states that retain charge-based reimbursement use such low level charge screens that they effectively are using a fee schedule. By 1984 Medicaid physician payment levels in the median state were less than $2/3$ Medicare payment levels—in some states Medicaid rates were less than $1/4$ Medicare payment levels. Declining physician payment levels has led to a decline in participation by physicians in the Medicaid program. From 1976 to 1983, for example, the percentage of obstetricians and gynecologists who accept Medicaid patients dropped from 60 to 46 per cent. Physicians who accept Medicaid patients also seem to be treating fewer of them. This has in turn led, it seems, to increased use by Medicaid recipients of outpatient hospital and emergency room care, which has in turn increased Medicaid costs. See J. Holahan and J. Cohen, Medicaid: The Trade-off between Cost Containment and Access to Care, Urban Institute (1986), 61–69; Physician Payment Review Commission, 1990 Ann.Rep. to Congress, 246–275.

The 1989 OBRA contains two provisions that might affect Medicaid Physician payment. First is 42 U.S.C. 1396a(a)(30), which requires payment levels, "sufficient to enlist enough providers so that services . . . are available to . . . recipients at least to the extent that those services are available to the general population." Second, states must annually specify their payment rates and provide to HHS data demonstrating their compliance with the equal access requirement. It remains to be seen, however, whether this requirement will be enforceable. As to litigation involving an identical earlier regulatory requirement, compare Degregorio v. O'Bannon, 500 F.Supp. 541 (E.D.Pa.1980); Dental Society of the State of New York v. Carey, 61 N.Y.2d 330, 474 N.Y.S.2d 262, 462 N.E.2d 362 (1984) with District of Columbia Podiatry Society v. District of Columbia, 407 F.Supp. 1259 (D.D.C.1975).

C. MEDICAID AND MEDICARE HMOs

Government sponsored payment programs, like private insurance programs, have also shown great interest in competitive alternatives. In 1989 1.4 million Medicare beneficiaries were enrolled in 166 MHOs. Under the Tax Equity and Fiscal Responsibility Act of 1982 (TEFRA), HMOs may provide services to Medicare beneficiaries on a risk or capitated basis. Risk-based payments may either be made to federally qualified HMOs or to competitive medical plans (CMPs).[3] Beneficiaries who enroll in a risk-contract HMO are "locked-in" and can only receive Medicare covered services through that HMO. Risk contract HMOs are paid 95% of the average adjusted per capita cost (AAPCC) paid for fee-for-service Medicare beneficiaries, a capitation payment adjusted both geographically and also to consider the age, sex, and institutional, disability, and Medicaid status of enrolled beneficiaries. Risk contract HMOs must return the difference between Medicare payments and the HMOs normal adjusted community rate to beneficiaries through increased services or lower premiums. HMOs may also provide services to Medicare beneficiaries on a cost-reimbursement basis.

In theory everybody wins with Medicare HMOs: Medicare only pays 95% of what it would otherwise pay for care; the HMOs have access to members they would not otherwise serve and thus to greater profits; and the beneficiary receives more services than would otherwise be covered by Medicare or pays lower premiums. Experience has been less positive. Because HMOs seem to benefit from favorable selection not wholly compensated for by the AAPCC, Medicare may be paying more for services than it would have absent HMO enrollment. See Langwell and Hadley, Evaluation of Medicare Competition Demonstrations, 11 Health Care Fin.Rev. 65 (Winter 1989) (estimating that HCFA paid 15% to 33% more for beneficiaries enrolled in risk HMOs studied than it would have paid had they remained in the fee-for-service sector). HMOs, on the other hand, have had difficulty dealing with mid-year "clarifications" of benefit packages expanding their obligations without additional compensation and Gramm–Rudman sequestrations diminishing their contracted rates. Beneficiaries have experienced questionable recruiting practices and difficulties in gaining redress through appeal or grievance procedures when services are denied.

Potential quality problems in HMOs are to some extent addressed by review of HMO care by Medicare Peer Review Organizations. (Landwell and Hadley, supra, found that the quality of care provided by Medicare demonstration HMOs was as good or better than that provided in the fee-for-service sector). Further, certain harmful practices can result in civil fines ranging from $25,000 to $100,000 per offense, 42 U.S.C.A. § 1395mm(i)(6)(A), 2(B). These include failure to provide medically necessary items and services, imposing unpermitted charges, improper disenrollment of beneficiaries, failure to provide prompt payment for proper out-of-plan services (such as emergency care), providing false information to plan members, or improperly discouraging high-cost beneficiaries from enrollment.

For further information on Medicare HMOs, see Michaels and Rinn, Legal Trends and Developments in Alternative Delivery Systems, in 1989 Health Law Handbook, 153, 161–164 (A. Gosfield, ed.1989);

3. CMPs are HMOs that do not meet the strict requirements for federal qualifications, but do meet more flexible Medicare requirements.

Krasner, New Directions in Medicare and Medicaid Managed Care, 2 The Medical Staff Counselor 23, 23–27 (Fall 1988); Parks and Waxman, The Medicare/HMO "Partnership" " Some Problems for Beneficiaries, 21 Clearinghouse Rev. 236 (1987).

The 1981 Omnibus Budget Reconciliation Act also authorized Medicaid HMOS. Prior to 1981 the Medicaid statute had guaranteed recipients the right to choose their own providers, 42 U.S.C.A. § 1396a(a)(23). The 1981 amendments authorized HHS to permit states to limit recipients to certain providers. For example, a state may require a Medicaid beneficiary to choose one primary case manager (internist, family practitioner, or pediatrician) from a selected list. That provider is then responsible for the delivery of all non-emergency care. Under this system, called primary case management, the recipient cannot see a specialist, obtain drugs, or be hospitalized without a referral from the case manager, 42 U.S.C.A. § 1396n(b)(1). Alternatively, states may require recipients to obtain services from certain hospitals or suppliers of medical services (like eyeglasses or lab services) with which the state has negotiated a "prudent buyer" contract. 42 U.S. C.A. § 1396n(b)(4).

What values are served by Medicaid's traditional policy of permitting recipients the freedom to choose any provider who participates in Medicaid (or Medicare)? What abuses might a free choice system permit or encourage? How does limiting choice help cut costs? What problems might recipients encounter in a system of limited choice? Is it possible that under some conditions enrolling Medicaid beneficiaries in an HMO might increase rather than limit free choice of providers? See Welch and Miller, Mandatory HMO Enrollment in Medicaid: The Issue of Freedom of Choice, 66 Milbank Q. 618 (1988).

By 1987 2.3 million Medicaid beneficiaries (about 10 per cent of all beneficiaries) were enrolled in Medicaid managed care plans in 29 states. Arizona, the last state to adopt a Medicaid program, is the only state that requires beneficiary participation in capitated programs on a statewide basis.

While commentators frequently advocate expanded reliance by Medicaid on managed care options to control costs while expanding services, research on Medicaid managed care does not establish it as a panacea. A careful study of Medicaid competition demonstration projects, for example, found that though they reduced utilization, the costs of the projects to the states were the same or higher than fee for service comparison sites. Freund, et. al., Evaluation of the Medicaid Competition Demonstrations, 11 Health Care Financing Review 81 (Winter 1989). Another study of primary care case management programs in six states found that the states had experienced savings on the order of .5 to 3.4%. Johns and Adler, Evaluation of Recent Changes in Medicaid, 8 Health Affairs 171, 178 (1989). On the other hand, studies have not confirmed widespread problems with access, quality, and patient satisfaction alleged by critics of managed care alternatives. See

McCall, et al. Access and Satisfaction in the Arizona Health Care Cost Containment System, 11 Health Care Financing Review 65 (Fall 1989); Freund, supra at 92–94. See, critical of Medicaid Managed care, Dallek, Parks, and Waxman, Medicaid Primary Care Case Management Systems: What We've Learned, 18 Clearinghouse Rev. 270 (1984); Dallek & Wulsin, Limits on Medicaid Patients Rights to Choose Their Own Doctors and Hospitals, 17 Clearinghouse Rev. 280 (1983); Perkins, Medicaid Primary Care Case Management Update, 22 Clearinghouse Rev. 348 (1988).

V. POLICING COST–CONTAINMENT

A. INTRODUCTION

Any method through which a payer such as the federal or state governments determines the prices it will pay health care providers for services inevitably creates undesired, and sometimes undesirable, incentives. Cost- and charge-based payment create substantial incentives for providing excessive services. By contrast, PPS per-case payment might encourage the provision of too few services to patients admitted to the hospital, since the hospital is paid the same per-case amount whether it provides few or many services. PPS could also result in excessive hospital admissions, since the hospital is paid more with each admission. When (as is often the case) provision of health care depends on a collective enterprise—requiring, for example, the combined services of doctors, hospitals, allied health professionals, clinical laboratories, or providers of drugs or durable medical equipment—service providers who can reap greater profits from greater volume have reason to share those profits (through kickbacks and bribes) with those in a position to increase their business through referrals.

The federal government has been concerned about excessive utilization of health care and the costs of excessive utilization. The federal government has also been concerned that patients might be harmed by poor quality care resulting from underprovision of care caused by PPS, or overprovision or inappropriate care resulting from unnecessary referrals. Finally, federal law has attempted to encourage a professional fiduciary relationship between providers and patients that puts the best interest of patients above profits.

These concerns have resulted in two programs. First, the Medicare and Medicaid fraud and abuse laws attempt to police provider conduct to control costs, protect quality, and encourage professional fidelity to patient interests. Second, the Medicare Utilization and Quality Peer Review (PRO) program (like the Professional Standards Review Organization (PSRO) program which preceded it) attempts to police the utilization and quality of Medicare financed care.

If there is little work for lawyers in PPS or RBRVS reimbursement, the fraud and abuse laws (and to a lesser extent the PRO program) more than make up for it. Indeed, a health care trade journal referred to recent changes in the fraud and abuse laws as a "Lawyers Relief Act," and as a "pot of gold" for lawyers. The pay-off for lawyers for mastering the intricacies of Medicare and Medicaid reimbursement, comes, therefore, in enforcing, defending against, or interpreting the fraud and abuse and PRO laws through which federal cost-containment efforts are policed.

B. FRAUD AND ABUSE

1. *The Statute: 42 U.S.C.A. § 1320a–7b*

(a) Whoever—

(1) knowingly and willfully makes or causes to be made any false statement or representation of a material fact in any application for any benefit or payment under a program under subchapter XVIII or a State health care program (as defined in section 1320a–7(h) of this title),

(2) at any time knowingly and willfully makes or causes to be made any false statement or representation of a material fact for use in determining rights to such benefit or payment,

* * *

shall (i) in the case of such a statement, representation, concealment, failure, or conversion by any person in connection with the furnishing (by that person) of items or services for which payment is or may be made under the program, be guilty of a felony and upon conviction thereof fined not more than $25,000 or imprisoned for not more than five years or both, or (ii) in the case of such a statement, representation, concealment, failure, or conversion by any other person, be guilty of a misdemeanor and upon conviction thereof fined not more than $10,000 or imprisoned for not more than one year, or both.   * * *

(b)(1) Whoever knowingly and willfully solicits or receives any remuneration (including any kickbacks, bribe, or rebate) directly or indirectly, overtly or covertly, in cash or in kind—

(A) in return for referring an individual to a person for the furnishing or arranging for the furnishing of any item or service for which payment may be made in whole or in part under subchapter XVIII of this chapter or a State health care program, or

(B) in return for purchasing, leasing, ordering, or arranging for or recommending purchasing, leasing, or ordering any good, facility, service, or item for which payment may be made in whole or in part under subchapter XVIII of this chapter or a State health care program,

shall be guilty of a felony and upon conviction thereof, shall be fined not more than $25,000 or imprisoned for not more than five years, or both.

(2) Whoever knowingly and willfully offers or pays any remuneration (including any kickback, bribe or rebate) directly or indirectly, overtly or covertly, in cash or in kind to any person to induce such person—

    (A) to refer an individual to a person for the furnishing or arranging for the furnishing of any item or service for which payment may be made in whole or in part under subchapter XVIII of this chapter or a State health care program, or

    (B) to purchase, lease, order, or arrange for or recommend purchasing, leasing, or ordering any good, facility, service, or item for which payment may be made in whole or in part under subchapter XVIII of this chapter or a State health care program,

shall be guilty of a felony and upon conviction thereof shall be fined not more than $25,000 or imprisoned for not more than five years, or both.

* * *

[Section (c) prohibits knowing and willful false statements or representations of material facts with respect to the conditions or operation of any entity in order to qualify such an entity for Medicare or Medicaid certification. Section (d) prohibits knowingly and willfully charging patients for Medicaid services where such charges are not otherwise permitted.]

2. *Problems: Advising Under the Fraud and Abuse Laws*

Do any of the following transactions violate the fraud and abuse laws? Is there anything else wrong with them from either a legal, ethical, or public policy perspective?

1. Doctor Molloy, an allergist, leaves all of his billing to his trusted billing clerk of ten years, Tammi. Upon examining or treating a patient Dr. Molloy checks the services rendered on a "superbill" form he purchases from a medical supply firm, and then gives the form to Tammi. Tammi bills Medicare, Medicaid, a private insurer, or the patient based on information she takes from the superbill. She routinely codes visits as extended rather than brief, regardless of the length, and codes injections as including multiple rather than single allergins, regardless of their actual content. Dr. Molloy never reviews the billings, but admonishes Tammi from time to time to maximize reimbursement, while at the same time coding services properly so as not to get him in trouble. His practice has prospered in recent years, and each year Tammi has received a generous Christmas bonus and raise, as have other office staff.

2. Bio–Laboratories Ltd. is a partnership of which Flacco Schwartz is the general partner. Bio–Lab sells limited partnership interests to physicians, who must invest at least $2000 to become

limited partners. Bio–Lab has little laboratory equipment of its own, but has a contract with a well-known and well-regarded national laboratory to do most of its testing for it. Bio–Lab's partner physicians routinely refer lab work to it. Bio–Lab sends all but the most routine lab work on to the national laboratory, bills Medicare, Medicaid, or private insurers for the lab work, and pays the national laboratory 70% of the payments it receives. Partner physicians are not required to refer their work to Bio-lab, but all partners are given a monthly list of all partners and the number of referrals for which each is responsible. Partners are paid dividends based on Bio-lab's revenues, and are currently earning about a 50% return on their initial investment annually.

3. Starkville Community Hospital is located in a rural area in a distant corner of a large mid-western state. Recently Dr. McPherson, the hospital's only obstetrician, announced his retirement. Few new physicians have settled in Starkville in recent years, and the community and hospital are very concerned about the loss of obstetric services. The hospital has decided, therefore, to implement a plan to attract a new obstetrician. It is offering to provide any board-certified obstetrician who will settle in Starkville and obtain privileges at Starkville Memorial the following for the first two years the physician is at the hospital: 1) a guaranteed annual income of $90,000, 2) free malpractice insurance through the hospital's self-insurance plan, and 3) free rent in the hospital's medical practice building. The new obstetrician would not be required to refer patients to Starkville Community, though the closest alternative hospital is 60 miles away. The obstetrician would also be expected to assume some administrative duties in exchange for the compensation package Starkville is offering. Starkville Community is currently engaged in negotiations with a young doctor who has just finished her residency and appears likely to accept this offer. There is a potential problem, however. Dr. Waxman, who came to Starkville two years ago and is the hospital's only cardiologist, has threatened that he will leave unless he gets the same terms.

4. Dr. Ness, a successful ophthalmologist, advertises in the weekly suburban shopping newspaper, offering free cataract examinations for senior citizens. He in fact does not charge those who respond to the offer for the Medicare deductible or co-insurance amounts, but bills Medicare for the maximum charge allowable for the service.

5. A market study recently concluded by Samaritan Hospital has revealed that it is receiving few admissions from Arlington, a rapidly growing affluent suburb eight miles to the northwest. To remedy this problem, it has entered into negotiations to purchase the Arlington Family Practice Center, a successful group practice containing five board-certified family practitioners. Samaritan has offered a generous price for the practice. The practice would be renamed Samaritan–Arlington Family Practice Center and its doctors would become salaried employees of Samaritan hospital. They would thereafter be required to admit patients only at Samaritan and to refer only to specialists who

have privileges at Samaritan. The five doctors, who are weary of the administrative hassles of private practice, are eager to sell.

6. Community Memorial has clearly become a PPS loser. Despite its efforts to educate its medical staff as to the financial realities of PPS, they continue to order tests and prolong patient stays like they did in the good old cost-reimbursement days. To counter this trend, a consultant has suggested a plan. Each month Community Memorial will provide each of its doctors with a print-out, identifying the average length of stay and costs of medical tests ordered for that physician's patients for each DRG under which the physician admitted patients, comparing these numbers with averages for the hospital and for the region. For each month in which a physician is able to hold average length of stay and lab costs below regional norms, the physician will receive a $50.00 gift certificate redeemable at any restaurant in town.

7. Community Memorial's consultant has also suggested a strategy to increase its flagging census, which has dropped to 60% in the last year. Many of Community Memorial's doctors rent space in Community Memorial's Medical office building. Many of these doctors, however, have admitting privileges at one of the other two hospitals in town. Often they admit to one of those hospitals rather than to Community Memorial. The consultant has recommended that Community Memorial reduce the monthly rental payments of any doctor in its building .5% for each patient that doctor admits to Community Memorial during that month.

8. Twenty-three small rural hospitals in a mid-western state have entered into a contract with a group-purchasing agent to purchase medical equipment and supplies for them. The agent will take advantage of volume discounts and of careful market research to significantly lower the cost of supplies and equipment purchased for the hospitals. The agent obtains, on average, a 5% rebate from suppliers for all goods it purchases.

3. Penalties for Fraud and Abuse

Violations of the false billing, illegal remuneration (bribes and kickbacks), misrepresentation of compliance with conditions of participation, illegal supplementation of Medicaid payments, or assignment provisions of 42 U.S.C.A. § 1320a–7b are federal crimes, in most instances felonies. Providers who attempt to defraud the government may also be prosecuted under federal laws prohibiting false statements or mail fraud, or under RICO (under which a Florida chiropractor who had defrauded Medicare recently forfeited his chiropractic clinics, home, automobiles and yacht.) Many states also have criminal laws addressing Medicaid fraud, fee-splitting, or improper patient referrals, which may be broader or more specific than federal law.

Equally of concern to providers, however, are the civil penalty and exclusion powers of the Department of Health and Human Services.

Federal criminal prosecutions can only be brought by the Justice Department, which has not always placed fraud and abuse as its highest priority. Civil penalties and program exclusion under the federal statute, however, are the prerogative of the Office of Inspector General (OIG) of HHS, which has aggressively pursued enforcement in recent years. Moreover, for many providers, dependent on Medicare and Medicaid for a large share of their business, exclusion from these programs can be effectively a death warrant, at least as serious as a felony conviction. Finally, civil sanction proceedings are administrative in nature, criminal intent need not be shown, and the standard of proof is preponderance of the evidence rather than beyond a reasonable doubt.

The list of behaviors for which HHS can assess civil money penalties is long and grows with every annual budget reconciliation act. For example, civil penalties of up to $2,000 per item or service plus twice the amount claimed can be assessed for an item or service that a person "knows or should know" was "not provided as claimed" 42 U.S.C.A. § 1320a–7a(a)(1)(A). If a physician bills, therefore, 100 claims of $20 each for services not provided, a penalty of up to $204,000 could be assessed by HHS. Penalties of up to $2000 can be imposed against participating doctors who bill in violation of Medicare assignment or participation agreements or non-participating physicians who bill in excess of charge limitations. 42 U.S.C.A. §§ 1320a–7a(a)(2)(A); 1395u(j)(1)(B). Civil money penalties of up to $15,000 can be assessed against any person who provides false and misleading information that could reasonably be expected to influence the decision of when to discharge a Medicare beneficiary from a hospital, 42 U.S.C.A. § 1320a–7a(3). Medicare or Medicaid HMOs that fail substantially to provide medically necessary services with a substantial likelihood of adversely affecting beneficiaries, or that impose premiums in excess of permitted amounts can be penalized up to $25,000. 42 U.S.C.A. § 1395mm(i)(6)(A)(i). Penalties of up to $2000 may be imposed against hospitals that make direct or indirect payments to physicians as incentives for reducing or limiting services provided to beneficiaries or against physicians who accept such payments. 42 U.S.C.A. § 1320a–7a(b). Penalties of up to $2000 per violation may be imposed on doctors who fail to provide diagnosis codes on non-assigned Medicare claims, 42 U.S.C.A. § 1395u(p)(3); of $5000 per violation on persons who knowingly sell duplicate Medigap policies, 42 U.S.C.A. § 1395ss(d); and of $5000 ($25,000 in the case of a broadcast or telecast) on persons who advertise using the terms Social Security, Medicare or HCFA so as to give a false impression that their product is approved by the federal government. 42 U.S.C.A. § 1320b–10. The list goes on and on.

The OIG must exclude from the Medicare program individuals or entities convicted of criminal Medicare or Medicaid fraud or of criminal patient neglect or abuse. 42 U.S.C.A. § 1320a–7(a)(1) & (2). The OIG also has discretion to exclude providers for seventeen other categories of offenses, including conviction of a controlled substances offense, loss of professional license, submission of bills substantially in excess of usual charges or costs, substantial failure of an HMO to provide medically necessary services, substantial failure of a hospital to comply with a corrective plan for unnecessary admissions or other inappropriate practices to circumvent PPS, or default by health professionals on student loans. 42 U.S.C.A. § 1320a–7(b). Exclusions are normally for a fixed period of years, after which the provider may apply for reinstatement. Exclusion or criminal conviction frequently results in disciplinary action by state professional licensure boards, and can thus end the professional career of even a professional who sees few Medicaid and Medicare patients.

On Medicare and Medicaid fraud generally, see E. Hogue, S. Teplitzky, & H. Sollins, Preventing Fraud and Abuse: A Guide for Medicare and Medicaid Providers (1988); Teplitzky, Holden, Sollins, Medicare and Medicaid Fraud and Abuse, in 1989 Health Law Handbook, 507 (A. Gosfield ed., 1989); Hyman and Williamson, Fraud and Abuse: Regulatory Alternatives in a "Competitive" Health Care Era, 19 Loyola U.L.J. 1133 (1988); Teplitzky & Holden, 1989 Developments in Medicare and Medicaid Fraud and Abuse, 1990 Health Law Handbook, 433 (A. Gosfield, ed. 1990).

4. Ramifications of the Kickback Provisions of the Fraud and Abuse Laws for Collective Activity in the Provision of Health Care

Sharing the profits of collective economic activity is common throughout the economy generally. Landlords rent commercial properties under percentage leases, agents sell goods and services produced by others on commission, merchants grant discounts to those who use their services or encourage others to do so. Such activity has, however, long been frowned on in health care. It is widely believed that patients lack the knowledge and information (or even the legal right, in the case of prescription drugs) to make health care decisions themselves (choosing appropriate drugs or specialists, for example). Therefore providers have a fiduciary obligation to recommend goods and services for patients considering only the patient's medical needs, not the provider's own economic interest. With the advent of government financing of health care this concern has been supplemented by another: that financial rewards to providers for patient referrals might drive up program costs by encouraging the provision of unnecessary or inordinately expensive medical care.

For these reasons, the fraud and abuse statutes reproduced above prohibit paying or receiving any remuneration (directly or indirectly, overtly or covertly) for referring, ordering, purchasing, or ordering goods, facilities, items or services paid for by Medicare or Medicaid. As interpreted most broadly, however, these provisions seem to proscribe a wide variety of transactions common in the economy generally and arguably of value in the health care setting. In particular, a number of practices that might encourage competition or efficient production of health care might, under a literal reading of the fraud and abuse statute, be felonies under the federal law. Considerable effort, therefore, has gone into identifying approaches to interpreting the statute that might more properly separate beneficial and detrimental conduct. These approaches to interpreting the statute are discussed below.

a. Licit or Illicit Motivation

UNITED STATES v. GREBER

United States Court of Appeals, Third Circuit, 1985.
760 F.2d 68, cert. denied, 474 U.S. 988, 106 S.Ct. 396, 88 L.Ed.2d 348 (1985).

WEIS, CIRCUIT JUDGE.

In this appeal, defendant argues that payments made to a physician for professional services in connection with tests performed by a laboratory cannot be the basis of Medicare fraud. We do not agree and hold that if one purpose of the payment was to induce future referrals, the Medicare statute has been violated. * * *

After a jury trial, defendant was convicted on 20 of 23 counts in an indictment charging violations of the mail fraud, Medicare fraud, and false statement statutes. Post-trial motions were denied, and defendant has appealed.

Defendant is an osteopathic physician who is board certified in cardiology. In addition to hospital staff and teaching positions, he was the president of Cardio–Med, Inc., an organization which he formed. The company provides physicians with diagnostic services, one of which uses a Holter-monitor. This device, worn for approximately 24 hours, records the patient's cardiac activity on a tape. A computer operated by a cardiac technician scans the tape, and the data is later correlated with an activity diary the patient maintains while wearing the monitor.

Cardio–Med billed Medicare for the monitor service and, when payment was received, forwarded a portion to the referring physician. The government charged that the referral fee was 40 percent of the Medicare payment, not to exceed $65 per patient.

Based on Cardio–Med's billing practices, counts 18–23 of the indictment charged defendant with having tendered remuneration or kickbacks to the referring physicians in violation of 42 U.S.C. § 1395nn(b)(2)(B) (1982).

* * *

The proof as to the Medicare fraud counts (18–23) was that defendant had paid a Dr. Avallone and other physicians "interpretation fees" for the doctors' initial consultation services, as well as for explaining the test results to the patients. There was evidence that physicians received "interpretation fees" even though defendant had actually evaluated the monitoring data. Moreover, the fixed percentage paid to the referring physician was more than Medicare allowed for such services.

The government also introduced testimony defendant had given in an earlier civil proceeding. In that case, he had testified that " * * * if the doctor didn't get his consulting fee, he wouldn't be using our service. So the doctor got a consulting fee." In addition, defendant told physicians at a hospital that the Board of Censors of the Philadelphia County Medical Society had said the referral fee was legitimate if the physician shared the responsibility for the report. Actually, the Society had stated that there should be separate bills because "for the monitor company to offer payment for the physicians * * * is not considered to be the method of choice."

The evidence as to mail fraud was that defendant repeatedly ordered monitors for his own patients even though use of the device was not medically indicated. As a prerequisite for payment, Medicare requires that the service be medically indicated.

The Department of Health and Human Services had promulgated a rule providing that it would pay for Holter-monitoring only if it was in operation for eight hours or more. Defendant routinely certified that the temporal condition had been met, although in fact it had not.
* * *

* * *

I. MEDICARE FRAUD

The Medicare fraud statute was amended by P.L. 95–142, 91 Stat. 1183 (1977). Congress, concerned with the growing problem of fraud and abuse in the system, wished to strength the penalties to enhance the deterrent effect of the statute. To achieve this purpose, the crime was upgraded from a misdemeanor to a felony.

Another aim of the amendments was to address the complaints of the United States Attorneys who were responsible for prosecuting fraud cases. They informed Congress that the language of the predecessor statute was "unclear and needed clarification." H.Rep. No. 393, PART II, 95 Cong., 1st Sess. 53, reprinted in 1977 U.S.CODE CONG. & AD.NEWS 3039, 3055.

A particular concern was the practice of giving "kickbacks" to encourage the referral of work. Testimony before the Congressional committee was that "physicians often determine which laboratories would do the test work for their medicaid patients by the amount of the kickbacks and rebates offered by the laboratory. * * * Kickbacks take a number of forms including cash, long-term credit arrangements, gifts, supplies and equipment, and the furnishing of business machines." *Id.* at 3048–3049.

To remedy the deficiencies in the statute and achieve more certainty, the present version of 42 U.S.C. § 1395nn(b)(2) was enacted. It provides:

"whoever knowingly and willfully offers or pays any remuneration (including any kickback, bribe or rebate) directly or indirectly, overtly or covertly in cash or in kind to induce such person—

* * *

(B) to purchase, lease, order, or arrange for or recommend purchasing * * * or ordering any * * * service or item for which payment may be made * * * under this title, shall be guilty of a felony."

The district judge instructed the jury that the government was required to prove that Cardio–Med paid to Dr. Avallone some part of the amount received from Medicare; that defendant caused Cardio–Med to make the payment; and did so knowingly and willfully as well as with the intent to induce Dr. Avallone to use Cardio–Med's services for patients covered by Medicare. The judge further charged that even if the physician interpreting the test did so as a consultant to Cardio–Med, that fact was immaterial if a purpose of the fee was to induce the ordering of services from Cardio–Med.

Defendant contends that the charge was erroneous. He insists that absent a showing that the only purpose behind the fee was to improperly induce future services, compensating a physician for services actually rendered could not be a violation of the statute.

The government argues that Congress intended to combat financial incentives to physicians for ordering particular services patients did not require.

The language and purpose of the statute support the government's view. Even if the physician performs some service for the money received, the potential for unnecessary drain on the Medicare system remains. The statute is aimed at the inducement factor.

The text refers to "any remuneration." That includes not only sums for which no actual service was performed but also those amounts for which some professional time was expended. "Remuneration" is defined as "to pay an equivalent for service." Webster Third New International Dictionary (1966). By including such items as kickbacks and bribes, the statute expands "remuneration" to cover situations where no service is performed. That a particular payment was a remuneration (which implies that a service was rendered) rather than a kickback, does not foreclose the possibility that a violation nevertheless could exist.

In *United States v. Hancock,* 604 F.2d 999 (7th Cir.1979), the court applied the term "kickback" found in the predecessor statute to payments made to chiropractors by laboratories which performed blood tests. The chiropractors contended that the amounts they received were legitimate handling fees for their services in obtaining, packaging, and delivering the specimens to the laboratories and then interpreting the results. The court rejected that contention and noted, "The potential for increased costs to the Medicare–Medicaid system and misapplication of federal funds is plain, where payments for the exercise of such

judgments are added to the legitimate cost of the transaction ....
[T]hese are among the evils Congress sought to prevent by enacting the
kickback statutes. ..." *Id.* at 1001.

Hancock strongly supports the government's position here, because
the statute in that case did not contain the word "remuneration." The
court nevertheless held that "kickback" sufficiently described the defendants' criminal activity. By adding "remuneration" to the statute
in the 1977 amendment, Congress sought to make it clear that even if
the transaction was not considered to be a "kickback" for which no
service had been rendered, payment nevertheless violated the Act.

We are aware that in *United States v. Porter,* 591 F.2d 1048 (5th
Cir.1979), the Court of Appeals for the Fifth Circuit took a more narrow
view of "kickback" than did the court in *Hancock.* *Porter*'s interpretation of the predecessor statute which did not include "remuneration" is
neither binding nor persuasive. We agree with the Court of Appeals
for the Sixth Circuit, which adopted the interpretation of "kickback"
used in *Hancock* and rejected that of the *Porter* case. *United States v.
Tapert,* 625 F.2d 111 (6th Cir.1980). *See also United States v. Duz–Mor
Diagnostic Laboratory, Inc.,* 650 F.2d 223, 227 (9th Cir.1981).

We conclude that the more expansive reading is consistent with the
impetus for the 1977 amendments and therefore hold that the district
court correctly instructed the jury. If the payments were intended to
induce the physician to use Cardio–Med's services, the statute was
violated, even if the payments were also intended to compensate for
professional services.

A review of the record also convinces us that there was sufficient
evidence to sustain the jury's verdict.

* * *

Having carefully reviewed all of the defendant's allegations, we
find no reversible error. Accordingly, the judgment of the district
court will be affirmed.

Notes and Questions

1. Conviction of a crime usually requires a finding of criminal intent.
Where, as in the *Greber* case, remuneration appears to be both for legitimate (test interpretation) and illegitimate (referral fee) purposes, a variety
of approaches to application of the statute are possible. These can be
arrayed along a continuum. At one end, it could be argued that as long as
there is some legitimate purpose for the remuneration, the conduct is not
criminal. Alternatively, the primary purpose of the remuneration could be
considered. If the primary purpose is legitimate, the conduct is not
criminal, but if the primary purpose of the payment is to solicit referrals,
the payment violates the law. At the opposite end of the spectrum, any
illegitimate purpose renders the conduct illegal. Early cases interpreting
the fraud and abuse statutes, such as the *Porter* case cited in *Greber* and
United States v. Zacher, 586 F.2d 912 (2d Cir.1978) strictly limited its
application. *Greber*'s reading of the statute (which was amended in the

interim to expand its reach) falls at the opposite extreme. Transactions violate the statute if they are in any way tainted by an illegitimate purpose.

Though *Greber*'s strict interpretation of the statute was for a time considered to be an aberration, it has recently been followed in two other cases, United States v. Kats, 871 F.2d 105 (9th Cir.1989) and United States v. Bay State Ambulance, 874 F.2d 20 (1st Cir.1989). Its position has also explicitly been adopted by proposed regulations published by the OIG for the enforcement of its civil money penalty and exclusion authority. These regulations state that the OIG "May exclude any individual or entity that it determines has knowingly and willfully solicited, received, offered or paid any remuneration in the manner and for the purposes described therein, irrespective of whether the individual or entity may be able to prove that the remuneration was also intended for some other purpose * * * " proposed 42 C.F.R. § 1001.951(a)(2)(i), 55 FR 12205, 12219 (April 2, 1990).

Cases like *Greber* cannot but leave providers who want to engage in transactions that may serve legitimate goals, but could also be interpreted as involving illegal remuneration, with a profound sense of discomfort. This discomfort has undoubtedly been exacerbated by the aggressive enforcement posture of the OIG, as demonstrated in the recent fraud alert on joint ventures:

OFFICE OF INSPECTOR GENERAL, SPECIAL FRAUD ALERT: JOINT VENTURE ARRANGEMENTS

(1989).

* * *

The Office of Inspector General has become aware of a proliferation of arrangements between those in a position to refer business, such as physicians, and those providing items or services for which Medicare or Medicaid pays. Some examples of the items or services provided in these arrangements include clinical diagnostic laboratory services, durable medical equipment (DME), and other diagnostic services. Sometimes these deals are called "joint ventures." * * * Of course, there may be legitimate reasons to form a joint venture, such as raising necessary investment capital. However, the Office of Inspector General believes that some of these joint ventures may violate the Medicare and Medicaid anti-kickback statute.

Under these suspect joint ventures, physicians may become investors in a newly formed joint venture entity. The investors refer their patients to this new entity, and are paid by the entity in the form of "profit distributions." These suspect joint ventures may be intended not so much to raise investment capital legitimately to start a business, but to lock up a stream of referrals from the physician investors and to compensate them indirectly for the referrals. Because physician investors can benefit financially from their referrals, unnecessary procedures and tests may be ordered or performed, resulting in unnecessary program expenditures.

* * *

To help you identify these suspect joint ventures, the following are examples of questionable features, which separately or taken together may result in a business arrangement that violates the anti-kickback statute. Please note that this is not intended as an exhaustive list, but rather gives examples of indicators of potentially unlawful activity.

INVESTORS

— Investors are chosen because they are in a position to make referrals.

— Physicians who are expected to make a large number of referrals may be offered a greater investment opportunity in the joint venture than those anticipated to make fewer referrals.

— Physician investors may be actively encouraged to make referrals to the joint venture, and may be encouraged to divest their ownership interest if they fail to sustain an "acceptable" level of referrals.

— The joint venture tracks its sources of referrals, and distributes this information to the investors.

— Investors may be required to divest their ownership interest if they cease to practice in the service area, for example, if they move, become disabled or retire.

— Investment interests may not be transferable.

BUSINESS STRUCTURE

— The structure of some joint ventures may be suspect. For example, one of the parties may be an ongoing entity, already engaged in a particular line of business. That party may act as the reference laboratory or DME supplier for the joint venture. In some of these cases, the joint venture can be best characterized as a "shell".

In the case of a shell laboratory, for example:

— It conducts very little testing on the premises, even though it is Medicare certified.

— The reference laboratory may do the vast bulk of the testing at its central processing laboratory, even though it also serves as the "manager" of the shell laboratory.

— Despite the localities of the actual testing, the local "shell" laboratory bills Medicare directly for these tests.

* * *

FINANCING AND PROFIT DISTRIBUTIONS

— The amount of capital invested by the physician may be disproportionately small and the returns on investment may be disproportionately large when compared to a typical investment in a new business enterprise.

— Physician investors may invest only a nominal amount, such as $500 to $1500.

— Physician investors may be permitted to "borrow" the amount of the "investment" from the entity, and pay it back through deductions from profit distributions, thus eliminating even the need to contribute cash to the partnership.

— Investors may be paid extraordinary returns on the investment in comparison with the risk involved, often well over 50 to 100 percent per year. * * *

* * *

2. How would you advise the entities and individuals involved in the problems above if the only authority you had to rely on was *Greber*?

b. A Transactional Approach

An alternative approach to interpretation of the fraud and abuse laws is to list and describe exhaustively transactions that are alternatively legitimate or illegal under the fraud and abuse laws either by statute or regulation. The recently adopted Stark Amendment, addressing the problem of physician referrals to laboratories owned by physicians, establishes a bright line test in this particular area.

The Stark bill prohibits physicians from making referrals for Medicare-financed services to clinical laboratories in which the physician (or an immediate family member) has an ownership interest, or with which the physician (or an immediate family member) has a compensation arrangement. It is also illegal for a clinical laboratory to bill for services provided subject to such illegal referrals.

The Act is subject to a number of exceptions. First, physicians may refer to laboratories supervised by other members of a group practice or HMO of which they are a part. Second, physicians may refer to laboratories in which they own publicly-traded stock if the assets of the corporation exceed $100,000,000. Third rural clinical laboratories are exempt. Finally, physicians may refer to the laboratories of hospitals in which they have an ownership interest, by which they are employed, or from which they rent office space or have received physician recruitment incentives, if specific statutory requirements are met to assure that arrangements are in good faith and at arms length. 42 U.S.C.A. § 1395nn.

The Stark bill is in part the response of Congress to a study by the OIG of HHS of 2690 practicing physicians, which determined that 12% of them had ownership interests in and 8% had compensation arrangements with businesses to which they referred their patients. It further determined that nationally 25% of independent clinical laboratories, 27% of independent physiological laboratories, and 8% of durable medical equipment supplies were owned at least in part by referring physicians. Beneficiaries treated by physicians who owned or invested in independent clinical laboratories received 45% and 34% more laboratory services from the independent clinical laboratories than Medicare beneficiaries in general. Iglehart, The Debate Over Physician Ownership of Health Care Facilities, 321 New Eng.J.Med. 198, 202 (1989).

Do the bright lines drawn by the Stark bill make sense? Why are referrals within group practices excepted? Why are referrals to hospitals in which the physician has an ownership interest, or with which he has a financial relationship through physician recruitment plans, employment and service arrangements, or rental agreements? Why are patients in rural areas left unprotected? Are the distinctions justifiable in principle or mere political compromises.

The Medicare Patient and Provider Protection Act of 1987 also drew some bright lines to delineate conduct that did not violate the fraud and abuse laws:

42 U.S.C.A. § 1320a–7b(b)(3)

(3) Paragraphs (1) and (2) [outlawing bribes & kickbacks] shall not apply to—

(A) a discount or other reduction in price obtained by a provider of services or other entity under subchapter XVIII of this chapter or a State health care program if the reduction in price is properly disclosed and appropriately reflected in the costs claimed or charges made by the provider or entity under subchapter XVIII of this chapter or a State health care program;

(B) any amount paid by an employer to an employee (who has a bona fide employment relationship with such employer) for employment in the provision of covered items or services;

(C) any amount paid by a vendor of goods or services to a person authorized to act as a purchasing agent for a group of individuals or entities who are furnishing services reimbursed under subchapter XVIII of this chapter or a State health care program if—

(i) the person has a written contract with each such individual or entity, which specifies the amount to be paid the person, which amount may be a fixed amount or a fixed percentage of the value of the purchases made by each such individual or entity under the contract, and

(ii) in the case of an entity that is a provider of services (as defined in section 1395x(u) of this title), the person discloses (in such form and manner as the Secretary requires) to the entity and upon request to the Secretary the amount received from each such vendor with respect to purchases made by or on behalf of the entity.

* * *

Subsection (D) of this act authorized the Secretary of HHS to promulgate so called "Safe Harbor" regulations to describe conduct that is not criminal under the fraud and abuse laws. It is a most unusual provision, because it permits an administrative agency to designate conduct otherwise illegal under federal law as not subject to prosecution by the Justice Department. It allows HHS to do formally what it had been doing informally in the early 1980s, before it was informed by the Department of Justice in 1985 that it was improper, absent statutory authorization, to bind the prosecutorial discretion of Justice.

The promulgation of Safe Harbor Regulations has been a complex process. Proposed regulations involving 10 specific types of conduct were promulgated on January 23, 1989 (54 Fed.Reg. 3088). Draft proposed regulations addressing other transactions were also leaked to the industry in 1989. Drafts of final regulations were subsequently leaked, and an entire industry suddenly appeared offering conferences and writing articles in the trade press scrutinizing and responding to draft final and draft proposed Safe Harbor Regulations.

PROPOSED RULES: PART 1001—PROGRAM INTEGRITY: MEDICARE

54 Fed.Reg. 3088 (January 23, 1989).

42 CFR § 1001.952   Exceptions.

The following payment practices shall not be treated as a criminal offense under section [1320a–7b] of the Act and shall not serve as the basis for an exclusion.

(a) Investment interests. As used in section [1320a–7b] of the Act "remuneration" does not include any payment that is a return, such as a dividend, capital gains distribution, or interest income from an investment obtained for fair market value in the investment securities (including shares in a corporation, bonds, debentures, notes, or other debt instruments) of a corporation that at the end of the corporation's fiscal year preceding the purchase of the securities had—

(1) Total assets exceeding $5,000,000 and

(2) A class of equity security held of record by at least 500 persons.

(b) Space rental: As used in section [1320a–7b] of the Act "remuneration" does not include payments made by a lessee to a lessor for the use of premises, as long as—

(1) The lease agreement is set out in writing and signed by the parties;

(2) The lease specifies the premises covered by the lease;

(3) If the lease is intended to provide the lessee with access to the premises for periodic intervals of time, rather than on a full-time basis for the term of the lease, the lease specifies exactly the schedule of such intervals, their precise length, their periodicity, and the exact rent for such intervals;

(4) The term of the lease is not less than one year, and

(5) The rental charge is consistent with fair market value in arms-length transactions and is not determined in a manner that takes

into account the volume or value of any referrals of business between the parties reimbursed under Medicare or Medicaid.

For purposes of this section, the term "fair market value" means the value of the rental property for general commercial purposes (not taking account of its intended use), but shall not be adjusted to reflect the additional value the prospective lessee or lessor would attribute to the property as a result of its proximity or convenience to the lessor where the lessor is a potential source of patient referrals to the lessee.

* * *

(e) Sale of practice: As used in section [1320a–7b] of the Act "remuneration" does not include payments made to a practitioner by another practitioner where one practitioner is selling his or her practice to another practitioner as long as—

(1) The period from the date of any agreement pertaining to the sale to the completion of the sale is not more than one year; and

(2) The practitioner who is selling his or her practice will not be in a professional position to make referrals to the purchasing practitioner after one year from the date of the agreement.

* * *

Notes and Questions

What justifies the conduct protected by each of the Safe Harbor Regulations? Do these regulations help you resolve the problems presented at the beginning of this section? Do they strike you as covering a wide or limited range of beneficial economic activities? (Are they broad bays or narrow slips?) What effect will they have on development of novel approaches to health care organization that might contribute to efficiency or to superior health care but that involve sharing of the profits of collective economic activity? What is the consequence of a transaction that falls in a general area addressed by the Safe Harbor Regulations not fitting within the terms of the appropriate regulation? What other limitations are inherent in a transactional approach to defining fraud and abuse? See Hall, Making Sense of Referral Fee Statutes, 13 J.H.P.P.L. 623, 625–26 (1988).

c. Disclosure

An alternative approach to the problem of referrals would be to permit doctors to refer patients to any source of care regardless of the doctor's financial relationship with the source of care, as long as that relationship was disclosed. The patient could then choose whether to accept the referral or, instead, to seek care from a different physician who had no financial relationships with other providers of care. Disclosure of financial conflicts of interest in referrals is required by the laws of some states, West's Ann.Cal.Bus. & Prof.Code §§ 654.1, 654.2; West's Fla.Stat.Ann. §§ 458.327(2)(c)(1)(2) & (3); M.G.L.A. c. 112, Sec. 1; and advocated as a solution to the referral problem by the AMA Council on Ethical and Judicial Affairs, Conflicts of Interest: Report A (I–86) (1986).

What limitations are there in this approach? Are patients capable of evaluating the risks they face in accepting referrals from a doctor with a financial interest in the referred product or service? Can patients realistically be expected to refuse self-interested referrals or to change physicians to avoid such referrals? What effect would such disclosures have on the physician-patient relationship? What predictions would you make about the operation of a disclosure requirement based on your knowledge of informed consent? Does a disclosure requirement address the effect of kickbacks on the cost of medical care? See Morreim, Conflicts of Interest: Profits and Problems in Physician Referrals, 262 J.A.M.A. 390 (1989); Morreim, Physician Investment and Self–Referral: Philosophical Analysis of a Contentious Debate, 15 J.Med. and Philosophy 425 (1990); Rodwin, Physicians Conflicts of Interest, The Limitations of Disclosure, 321 New Eng.J.Med. 1405 (1989).

d. Other Approaches

Another potential solution to the problem is to distinguish between "earned" and "unearned" referral fees. If the doctors who cooperated with Dr. Greber were only compensated for the market value of their services in interpreting the tests, they did no wrong, and should not be punished. To the extent, however, that the payment was only for the referral itself and not otherwise earned, a sanction would be appropriate. See Hall, supra, 628–632.

Will it always be possible to distinguish between the earned and unearned portion of referral fees? Moreover, if the test for measuring the fairness of earned compensation for services is market value, how is market value determined in the health care market where prices are often administrative constructs created by financing programs? Moreover, is it possible to determine the market value of legitimate conduct in markets that do not discriminate between that portion of the value of a transaction attributable to legitimate conduct and that attributable to illegitimate conduct? Might not the market value of conduct itself depend on whether the conduct is legitimate or illegitimate, thus creating a problem of circularity? See Frankford, Creating and Dividing the Fruits of Collective Economic Activity: Referrals Among Health Care Providers, 89 Col.L.Rev. 1862, 1889–1900 (1989). Finally, does the test adequately address the ethical as well as the economic problems raised by the referral problem? See Hyman and Williamson, supra at 1189–90.

Perhaps the entire attempt to solve the problem through statutory or regulatory approaches is misguided. Perhaps any attempt to adequately distinguish between efficient, ethical, and procompetitive conduct on the one hand, and wasteful, fraudulent, and unethical conduct on the other, is doomed to generate more heat than light and consume considerable resources in the process. Perhaps the problem is already adequately addressed by the common law. Patients already have a right to information affecting their care (including cost information) and doctors have an obligation to disclose such information as they possess relevant to such care (including information about the cost and quality of goods and services which they advise the patient to purchase for health care purposes.) Doctors already have a fiduciary obligation to put their patients' welfare above their own financial gain when the two come in conflict. Patients who are harmed by incompetent medical services provided pursuant to a referral from their physician, based on their physician's financial interest, might well be able to recover against the physician for medical negligence. What more is needed? See, Morreim, Physician Investment and Self–Referral: Philosophical Analysis of a Contentious Debate, 15 J.Med.Phil. 425 (1990) and Chapter 3, supra.

Are common law solutions really adequate however? To the extent that they rely on disclosure of conflicts of interest, they are subject to all of the objections raised to disclosure above. How likely is it, moreover, that any one patient would bring a lawsuit to enforce common law obligations when the only injury suffered by the patient would be an excessive medical fee of a few hundred dollars? What difficulties in proof would be encountered by a patient who attempted to prove that a doctor made a referral to an inferior source of medical care for financial gain, particularly if the patient suffered no serious injury as a result? Do the common law remedies of patients address the cost problems caused by financially motivated referrals?

Finally, is it possible that the problem of illegitimate referrals is greatly overrated, and that any cure may be worse than the problem itself? Arguably all solutions leave untouched one of the most serious conflicts of interest present in our current health care system: the incentives created by fee-for-service reimbursement for doctors to perform excessive services for patients and to treat patients themselves rather than referring them to others, to maximize their own reimbursement. In fact, it can be argued that when fee-for-service reimbursement is pervasive, fee-splitting is useful to counter-balance the incentives against referrals created by fee-for-service reimbursement where referrals are appropriate. See Pauly, The Ethics and Economics of Kickbacks and Fee Splitting, 10 Bell J.Econ. 344 (1979).

Will preoccupation with sharing of profits among health care providers force vertical integration of providers? Referrals within entities by their members or employees are generally permitted by interpretations of the fraud and abuse laws. Physicians may refer patients, for example, to laboratories operated within the group practice to which the physician belongs. Physician recruitment plans that result in the physician becoming an employee of the hospital are less suspect than those in which the physician is compensated by the hospital yet remains independent. Perhaps the ultimate result of the law will be increasingly to force the integration of the provision of medical services. Whether this will result in greater efficiency and higher quality care is an open question, but it can certainly be argued that it will not. See Frankford, supra., Wiehl, "Physician Integration": The Legal Pressures for Consolidation of Health Care Services, 34 St. Louis U.L.J. (1990).

Problem: Sorting It Out

When you have completed your analysis of the problems at the beginning of this section, reconstruct the arrangements there presented to accomplish as substantially as possible the legitimate goals of the parties to the transaction without offending the fraud and abuse laws. Having done so, determine whether any of the solutions you have attempted would create problems if one of the parties to the transaction was a tax-exempt organization under the Internal Revenue Code, referring to chapter 5.

C. THE MEDICARE UTILIZATION AND QUALITY CONTROL PEER REVIEW ORGANIZATION (PRO) PROGRAM

Undesirable provider responses to Medicare cost containment initiatives are also policed through the PRO program, which is described in the following excerpt:

JOST, ADMINISTRATIVE LAW ISSUES INVOLVING THE MEDICARE UTILIZATION AND QUALITY CONTROL PEER REVIEW ORGANIZATION (PRO) PROGRAM: ANALYSIS AND RECOMMENDATIONS
50 Ohio St.L.J. 1 (1989).

* * *

The initial Medicare law adopted in 1965 gave little attention to regulating the medical necessity, appropriateness, and quality of services provided Medicare beneficiaries. * * * By the early 1970s * * * it was becoming apparent that further controls were needed to limit excessive utilization of Medicare services. Out of this concern grew the PSRO program, which used regional nonprofit physicians groups to review independently the use of medical services by beneficiaries of federal medical assistance programs, including Medicare. * * * PSROs never succeeded in meeting the expectations of their supporters or overcoming the criticisms of their increasingly vocal detractors. In 1982 the Tax Equity and Fiscal Responsibility Act (TEFRA) abolished the PSRO program and created in its stead the PRO program.

The PRO program was intended to be a leaner and more effective program than its predecessor. The 195 PSRO regions were trimmed to 54 statewide areas. The old system of grant-funding was replaced by biennial (now triennial) contracts, to be awarded by competitive bidding. Ineffective PROs were to be terminated. PROs could no longer delegate utilization review functions to hospitals, as had the PSROs.

Though PROs were initially to be physician-sponsored organizations (as were the old PSROs), the statute allows HHS to turn to other organizations, including insurance companies or Medicare fiscal intermediaries, for PRO services if initial physician-sponsored contractors prove ineffective. Unlike PSROs, PROs could be for-profit entities. Finally, the PROs were given enhanced sanction and payment denial authority to enforce their power.

* * *

The primary tasks of the PROs are to process data concerning health care services provided to Medicare beneficiaries and to intervene when these data indicate that services have been provided unnecessarily, inappropriately, or with inadequate quality. Because hospitals consume over two-thirds of Medicare expenditures, PROs have focused their review traditionally on care provided to beneficiaries by doctors in hospitals. Recently many of the PROs have begun to review care provided by health maintenance organizations and competitive medical plans (HMOs/CMPs) with Medicare risk-sharing contracts. The Omnibus Budget Reconciliation Act of 1986 (OBRA '86) also requires PROs to stretch their review capacity to cover services provided in other settings, including post-acute care provided by skilled nursing facilities and home health agencies; ambulatory and hospital outpatient care; and beginning in 1989 care provided by physicians in their offices.
* * *

The principal source of data for PRO review is the hospital record. PROs regularly receive from fiscal intermediaries (the insurance companies and other entities that handle Medicare reimbursement to providers) data on bills paid for services rendered to Medicare beneficiaries. The PRO selects a sample of these cases for review and requests medical records on these cases from the hospitals, which are reviewed at the hospital or at the PRO office. The sampling criteria that PROs use for selecting cases for review, and the focus of their review in examining the records, have varied over the three contract cycles during which PROs have been in operation. During each contract cycle, the screening criteria and focus of PRO activity have been established by a scope of work [a document that defines the terms of the HHS–PRO contract during a particular contract period].

The sampling criteria mandated by the *Third Scope of Work,* currently being implemented, require a PRO to review, for each PPS hospital (hospitals reimbursed under the DRG prospective payment system) under its jurisdiction, a 3% random sample of all discharges; 50% of cases involving transfers from one PPS hospital to another; * * * 25% of cases in which a patient discharged from a PPS hospital is readmitted within thirty-one days; 20% of cases in the 25% discharge and readmission sample just mentioned, in which the patient received care from a nursing home, home health agency, or hospital outpatient area during the period intervening between hospitalizations; 25%, 50%, or 100% of cases coded with certain problem DRGs; 25% of day and cost outliers (cases in which hospitals received extra payment beyond the DRG reimbursement because the case required an extraordinarily long or expensive hospital stay); all cases with targeted principal diagnoses, such as obesity or pacemaker fitting or adjustment; all cases in which a hospital has requested that a case be adjusted from a lower to a higher DRG; all cases in which a hospital has determined that an admission was not covered but the patient required Medicare-covered care at some time during the stay; and all cases referred to the PRO by the fiscal intermediary or by HCFA. When reviews indicate that a hospital is committing errors in more than 5% of its cases (or six cases if this amount is greater), the PRO is to intensify review to 50% or 100%, depending upon the problem, of the hospital's Medicare cases.

To this point, all the reviews listed are retrospective. The PROs must also perform preadmission or preprocedure review of ten specific procedures and the use of assistants for cataract surgery. Finally, a separate HMO/CMP *Scope of Work* provides a sampling procedure for identifying HMO/CMP cases to be reviewed. The intensity of sampling of HMO/CMP cases is related to the confidence that the PRO has in the HMO/CMP's own internal quality control capacity. In total, sample cases under the second contract cycle totaled about 26% of all Medicare hospital admissions.

* * * [M]edical records fitting these sample criteria * * * are reviewed by professional reviewers (usually nurses), who apply criteria screens to identify utilization of quality problems.   * * *

Once a PRO identifies a problem through this review of medical records, the case is routed to a physician reviewer. If the physician confirms the problem, the case can go in one of two directions. First, if a quality problem is identified, the case is routed to the PRO quality assurance system, which can interpose various interventions (including sanctions ultimately) to correct the problem. If, on the other hand, the problem is identified as a utilization problem, the case is considered for a payment denial. PROs also continually assemble profile data in an effort to identify aberrant providers and physicians. Profiles are kept on patients, physicians, hospitals, DRGs, diagnoses, and procedures to monitor PRO impact and identify problems for further study.

PROs have a number of other functions unrelated to their data gathering and analysis functions. They are responsible for reviewing cases when hospitals inform patients that their care is not, or is no longer, covered by Medicare. PROs are also responsible for monitoring to assure that hospitals provide beneficiaries with a statement of their rights to PRO discharge review at the time of admission. They are required to investigate complaints by Medicare beneficiaries about the quality of Medicare-covered services received from Medicare-certified hospitals, nursing homes, home health agencies, or ambulatory surgical centers. Finally, PROs are responsible for educating beneficiaries and providers as to their existence and functions.

* * *

Notes and Questions

1. What explains the items reviewed under the Third Scope of Work described in the excerpt? How does PRO review respond to potential problems caused by PPS?

2. The PRO program relies predominantly on retrospective review. Where the PRO determines that care was rendered unnecessarily, it must instruct the Medicare intermediary or carrier to deny payment, 42 U.S.C.A. § 1320c–3(a)(3)(A). To mitigate the effect of this provision on Medicare recipients, who could be left with huge medical bills for medical care subsequently determined unnecessary, 42 U.S.C.A. § 1395pp provides that payment will be made if both the recipient and provider of services "did not know, and could not reasonably have been expected to know" that the services would not be covered. If the provider knew or should have known that the services would not be covered, but the recipient was innocent, Medicare will reimburse the recipient for any payments he or she has made to the provider and recover the payment from the provider. If comparable situations arise after a recipient or provider has already previously received the benefit of the waiver of liability provisions, the recipient or provider will be deemed to have knowledge of non-coverage. Determinations on whether a beneficiary or provider had reason to know unnecessary care would not be covered will be made on a case by case basis. 42 C.F.R. §§ 405.334–405.336.

3. If the PRO denies a recipient or provider Medicare payment for care, the practitioner or provider is entitled to discuss a potential denial with the PRO before an initial denial, 42 U.S.C.A. § 1320c–3(a)(3)(B). A patient denied reimbursement may seek a reconsideration from the PRO, 42 C.F.R. § 473.20. If a reconsideration decision is unfavorable, the patient may appeal a PRO determination involving more than $200.00 to the Social Security Administration, 42 C.F.R. § 473.40; and obtain judicial review of a decision involving more than $2000, 42 U.S.C.A. § 1320c–4. A provider is not entitled to review beyond the reconsideration stage of a payment denial, though it may appeal an adverse waiver of liability determination, 42 U.S.C.A. § 1395pp. See, Manning & Miller, Strategies for Appeals of PRO Payment Denials, 4 Med.Staff.Couns. 21 (1990).

4. What procedures should be followed at a hearing involving denial of payment for utilization of unnecessary medical care? Who should bear the burden of proof on the question of whether institutionalization is necessary or not? Does the patient have to prove that she needs care, or must the utilization review program establish that the utilization was unnecessary? What evidence should be considered? Will it make any difference that an individual hearing examiner will be hearing the case of a particular patient instead of determining in the abstract what cases are appropriate for hospital care? See 42 C.F.R. Part 473 (providing for reconsideration and appeals for PRO decisions).

If a private physician or medical institution, rather than a government-sponsored utilization review program, decides that further institutional care is unnecessary, and that decision results directly in termination of care financed by Medicare or Medicaid, the Constitution does not require that the patient be given due process to review the decision of the doctor or hospital, because there is no state action. See Blum v. Yaretsky, 457 U.S. 991, 102 S.Ct. 2777, 73 L.Ed.2d 534 (1982).

5. Utilization and quality review requires access to data on particular patients and providers by persons and institutions external to the medical care delivery process. Moreover, an effective utilization and quality review program could turn up information on providers that would be of great interest to others: to professional licensure and discipline boards concerned about the practices of specific providers, to patients concerned about the advisability of particular forms of treatment, to consumers comparing the quality of particular physicians or institutions. On the other hand, as the price for cooperating with peer review, professionals demand confidential treatment of potentially embarrassing information, and patients are legitimately concerned that private medical information not be made public.

PROs are not federal agencies, and are thus not subject to the FOIA. Under the PRO statute, PROs may disclose only information they assemble where disclosure is necessary to carry out their functions and then only in the manner consistent with HHS regulations, 42 U.S.C.A. § 1320c–9(a). In particular, a PRO may disclose information to federal and state agencies responsible for investigating fraud and abuse, and state licensing and disciplinary agencies and national accrediting bodies where information is requested, 42 U.S.C.A. § 1320c–9(b). They may also disclose information regarding physicians to hospitals in which those physicians practice. Unauthorized disclosure of information by a PRO is a federal crime, 42 U.S.C.A. § 1320c–9(c). See also, on information collection and dissemination by PROs, 42 C.F.R. §§ 476.101–476.143.

6. Because the PRO program is administered by private entities under contracts with the federal government, because the responsibilities of the program change virtually with every budget reconciliation act, and because of the notorious sluggishness of HHS in promulgating formal rules, the program has largely been governed through scopes of work, contracts, manuals, manual transmittals, program instructions, rumor and innuendo. What practical and legal problems does this mode of governance raise? Several such manual and contract provisions were challenged by a national provider organization as violating the rulemaking provisions of the Administrative Procedures Act in American Hospital Association v. Bowen, 834 F.2d 1037 (D.C.Cir.1987). The court upheld the provisions, relying on the procedural rules and general statement of policy exceptions to APA rulemaking requirements. Congress in OBRA 1987 subsequently arrived at a compromise, requiring HHS to publish in the Federal Register policies, procedures, criteria and standards affecting PROs, and to accept comments on criteria and standards, but stopping short of uniformly requiring full compliance with APA rulemaking requirements, 42 U.S.C.A. § 1320c–2(h). See Jost, supra at 9–19.

The most controversial aspect of the PRO program has undoubtedly been the PROs' sanction authority. PROs may recommend that the Office of Inspector General of HHS exclude from participation in the Medicare program or assess a civil money penalty against practitioners or providers who have "failed in a substantial number of cases substantially to comply" or "grossly and flagrantly violated * * * in one or more instances" obligations to provide services to Medicare beneficiaries economically, only when medically necessary, and of a quality that meets professional standards of care. 42 U.S.C.A. § 1320c–5(b). Though only about one hundred of the hundreds of thousands of doctors who treat Medicare patients have been sanctioned under the PRO program, the sanction authority of the PROs has been met with vehement criticism by the medical community. In part this is no doubt due to the minimal procedural protections afforded practitioners and providers, particularly in the early years of the program. These procedural protections, however, have been uniformly upheld by the courts.

LAVAPIES v. BOWEN

United States Court of Appeals, Sixth Circuit, 1989.
883 F.2d 465.

MERRITT, CIRCUIT JUDGE.

In this Medicare exclusion case arising under § 1156 of the Social Security Act, 42 U.S.C. § 1320c–5, the plaintiff-physician seeks an injunction setting aside her one-year suspension from participation in Medicare, Title XVIII. She challenges the District Court's dismissal of her case on grounds that she failed to exhaust her administrative remedies, and its finding that none of her challenges presented "colorable constitutional claims." Her primary claim is that the administrative process by which she has been excluded denies her due process. [   ] Specifically, she asserts two constitutional claims:

1) She has a right to a full pre-exclusion hearing, or at minimum a face-to-face encounter with the ultimate decision maker, especially on the question of whether she was unable or unwilling to meet her § 1156 obligations.

2) She was excluded under a standard that was unconstitutionally vague.

She also asserts two statutory claims:

3) She was excluded under a standard set forth in a procedural manual not adopted under the Administrative Procedure Act.

4) The statutory and regulatory scheme for peer review creates and permits biased decision-making.

Upon review of the entire record, the District Court denied the physician's request for an injunction and dismissed the case, finding that the plaintiff had not exhausted her administrative remedies and had presented no cognizable constitutional claim which would create an exception to the exhaustion requirement.

I.

Nermin Lavapies is a family practice physician in Belmont County, Ohio, a county designated as a rural health manpower shortage area ("HMSA") in the areas of podiatry and psychiatry only. Over 40% of her patients are eligible for Medicare. In 1984, Peer Review Systems,

Inc., whose function it is to determine whether a health care petitioner has violated her statutory obligations established under the Medicare scheme, identified several quality of care problems in Dr. Lavapies' cases and considered sanctioning her. After a meeting in November 1985, Dr. Lavapies, represented by counsel, and six physicians agreed to a corrective action plan in February 1986 which included among other requirements the demand that she see her patients in a timely fashion. PRS continued to monitor Dr. Lavapies' care. On March 19, 1987, PRS notified Dr. Lavapies that in five cases she had violated her obligation under § 1156 of the Social Security Act to provide medical services which meet professionally recognized standards. Dr. Lavapies' counsel did respond to the PRS letter; and both Dr. Lavapies and her counsel met with PRS physicians on June 4, 1987.

On September 11, 1987, PRS notified Dr. Lavapies that she had failed to comply with her § 1156 obligations; one violation was gross and flagrant and the other two were substantial. They recommended to the Office of Inspector General that she be suspended for two years from participation in the Medicare Program. PRS provided Dr. Lavapies with a copy of the material upon which they based their decision, copies of which were also forwarded to the OIG. This material included the PRS rationale for its recommended exclusion that Dr. Lavapies had failed to personally evaluate a patient until seventeen hours after admission, a criticism she was supposed to remedy under her 1986 corrective action plan. Additionally, PRS specifically mentioned that Dr. Lavapies had been under a corrective action plan since February 1986, concerning previous sanction activity involving quality of care violations identified during the 1984 to 1986 PRS contract period. They went on to state that she exhibited a pattern of inappropriate care that did not meet professionally recognized standards. PRS also indicated that Dr. Lavapies' exclusion would not adversely affect Medicare beneficiaries because of the availability of an ample number of family practitioners in the surrounding metropolitan area. PRS informed her that under the Medicare statute she could submit additional written information to the OIG which might affect their exclusion recommendation.

Dr. Lavapies availed herself of this administrative process. She submitted through counsel and by affidavit a detailed rebuttal of the PRS criticisms. On January 11, 1988, the OIG informed Dr. Lavapies that she was excluded from the Medicare Program for one year. In his notification, the OIG specifically mentioned the receipt of Dr. Lavapies' rebuttal material. He relied on the fact that Dr. Lavapies had "grossly and flagrantly violated [her] obligation to provide care that meets professionally recognized standards of quality," and had "demonstrated an inability and unwillingness substantially to comply with the obligations imposed on [her] by section 1156(a). * * *" The OIG went on to find support for the latter statement in Dr. Lavapies' history of quality care problems and in her failure to follow her corrective action plan. Specifically, the OIG noted that Dr. Lavapies did not see a patient for seventeen hours after admission and issued orders for the patient's care without a personal evaluation. Dr. Lavapies concedes that, when she filed suit in federal District Court, she had not exhausted the administrative review procedures set out in 42 U.S.C. § 1320c–5(b)(4). These procedures provide a post-exclusion hearing before an administrative law judge and appeal to the Secretary's Appeal Council. Judicial review of that decision is then available.

II.

The Supreme Court recognized in Mathews v. Eldridge, 424 U.S. 319, 96 S.Ct. 893, 47 L.Ed.2d 18 (1976), an exception to the statutory requirement of exhaustion of administrative remedies. In order to fall within this exception a plaintiff must: (1) raise a colorable constitutional claim collateral to her substantive claim of entitlement; (2) show that she would be irreparably harmed by enforcement of the exhaustion requirement; and (3) show that the purposes of exhaustion would not be served by requiring further administrative procedures. Id. at 329–31, 96 S.Ct. at 900–01; see also Bowen v. City of New York, 476 U.S. 467, 484, 106 S.Ct. 2022, 2032, 90 L.Ed.2d 462 (1986). Here the plaintiff has failed to demonstrate valid claims of constitutional deprivation under the Due Process Clause.

Pre–Exclusion Hearing. Although this is a case of first impression in this circuit, six of our sister circuits have considered the question of whether due process requires that a physician receiving Medicare payments be given a pre-exclusion evidentiary hearing before the OIG. They have been unanimous in their conclusion that it does not. We concur. [ ]

Lavapies also argues that she did not get minimal due process because she was never on notice that she had violated her corrective action plan nor was she able to fully respond to the OIG on the issue of her unwillingness or inability to follow this plan. The evidence belies Dr. Lavapies' position. A reading of the transcript of Lavapies' 1985 hearing makes it clear that she was aware of the need to evaluate promptly newly admitted patients in person. Her inability to correct this behavior was a part of the PRS's recommendation, and her own extensive point-by-point response to the PRS materials submitted to the OIG further undermines her position that she had deficient notice and lacked the opportunity to respond adequately to PRS criticism.

Vagueness. Lavapies also claims that the term "gross and flagrant" used in the Medicare statute is unconstitutionally vague. 42 U.S.C. § 1320c–5(b)(1)(B). The regulations define a "gross and flagrant" violation as

> "a violation of an obligation [which] has occurred in one or more instances which presents an imminent danger to the health, safety or well-being of a Medicare beneficiary or places the beneficiary unnecessarily in high-risk situations."

42 C.F.R. § 1004.1(b) (1986), formerly codified at 42 C.F.R. § 474.0(b) (1985). The First and Eighth Circuits have found that the statutory term at issue is not unconstitutionally vague. We concur. [   ] ("[t]he definition of adequate medical care cannot be boiled down to a precise mathematical formula").

Exhaustion of Administrative Remedies. The Supreme Court in Weinberger v. Salfi, 422 U.S. 749, 95 S.Ct. 2457, 45 L.Ed.2d 522 (1975), pointed to the need for exhaustion of administrative remedies:

> Exhaustion is generally required as a matter of preventing premature interference with agency processes, so that the agency may function efficiently and so that it may have an opportunity to correct its own errors, to afford the parties and the courts the benefit of its experience and expertise, and to compile a record which is adequate for judicial review.

Id. at 765, 95 S.Ct. at 2467. The following nonconstitutional claims must fail because plaintiff has failed to exhaust administrative remedies:

(1) Dr. Lavapies claims that § 4095 of P.L. 100–203 entitles her to a pre-exclusion hearing because she allegedly is located in a rural health manpower shortage area. Alternatively, she argues that while she is "located" in Belmont County, she provides services "located" in Harrison and Monroe Counties which have been designated as health manpower shortage areas in the specialty of primary care.

(2) Dr. Lavapies challenges the section of the PRS manual in which a phrase is added to the term "gross and flagrant violation" in 42 C.F.R. § 1004.1. She claims the statement was not adopted pursuant to the rulemaking procedures of the Administrative Procedure Act.

(3) Finally, Lavapies contends that the reviewing physicians have a potentially direct financial stake in their decisions to exclude. She contends that PRS was under a contractual pressure to meet a "quota" of sanctions.

Because we find that none of Dr. Lavapies' claims present constitutional violations, and because the remainder of her claims must be exhausted administratively, her contention that she is entitled to a preliminary injunction fails.

Accordingly, the decision of the District Court declining to issue an injunction is affirmed.

Notes and Questions

1. One of the claims of Dr. Lavapies is based on a provision of OBRA 1987 that established special procedural protections for rural physicians and hospitals. Before rural providers and practitioners may be excluded from the Medicare program they must be afforded a preliminary hearing before an Administrative Law Judge. Unless the ALJ determines that the hospital or doctor will pose a serious risk to Medicare recipient if allowed to continue delivering services, the exclusion will not go into effect until an

ALJ hearing is held. 42 U.S.C.A. § 1320c–5(b)(5). What justifies special treatment for rural physicians and providers? (Consider that from 1985 to 1987, 65% of the physicians sanctioned by the HHS on recommendation of the PROs were from rural areas, despite the fact that only 11% of physicians in the U.S. practice in rural areas.)

2. How should the PRO define "professionally recognized standards of quality." Should the PRO apply the same standards applied in malpractice cases? 42 U.S.C.A. § 1320c–6 provides that a physician or provider cannot be held liable for malpractice if he, she, or it complies with or relies on professionally developed norms or care and treatment applied by PROs and exercises due care in so doing. Does this imply that standards applied by PROs should be the same or different than malpractice standards?

Should PROs apply national or local standards? PRO regulations permit the use of variant norms to accommodate local variations in practice, 42 C.F.R. § 466.100(d); Greene v. Bowen, 639 F.Supp. 554 (E.D. Cal.1986) held that the question of whether rural standards must be applied to rural physicians raised a question substantial enough to warrant the grant of a preliminary injunction against the application of national standards; and OBRA 87 required PRO consideration of "special problems associated with delivering care in remote rural areas," 42 U.S.C.A. § 1320c–3(a)(6). What explains the use of a similar locality rule by the PROs, when many states have moved to a national standard for malpractice cases?

3. Before the OIG can exclude a practitioner or provider from Medicare on the basis of a PRO recommendation, it must find that the practitioner or provider has "demonstrated an unwillingness or a lack of ability substantially to comply" with program obligations, 42 U.S.C.A. § 1320c–5(b). What explains the existence of this requirement? How would you prove that a practitioner has not only grossly and flagrantly (or substantially and often) violated standards in the past, but is unwilling or unable to do better in the future, particularly in the face of the practitioner's protestations of reform?

4. The conflict of interest argument raised by Dr. Lavapies also appears in other cases. Since the PROs are contractually obligated to sanction providers, the argument goes, the PROs' financial interest makes them inherently biased against providers who are accused of violations of professional standards. This argument has uniformly been rejected by the courts. Doyle v. Bowen, 660 F.Supp. 1484 (D.Me.1987), reversed on other grounds, 848 F.2d 296 (1st Cir.1988).

5. Under 42 U.S.C.A. § 1320c–3(a)(1)(B), an amendment of COBRA 85, PROs are obligated to deny payment for Medicare services when the quality of those services does not meet professionally recognized standards of care. When the PRO denies payment for care as substandard, the beneficiary must be notified and is not liable to pay for the care. This provision has proved intensely controversial, and, as of this writing, has still not been implemented. Can you see why the provision bothers practitioners and providers? OBRA 1989 amended the provision to require prior notification and an opportunity for reconsideration for the practitioners or providers before the beneficiary is notified. It also requires that the notice beneficiaries will receive must state: "In the judgment of the peer

review organization, the medical care received was not acceptable under the Medicare program. The reasons for the denial have been discussed with your physician and hospital." sec. 6224. Proposed regulations for the substandard care denial initiative are found at 54 Fed.Reg. 1956, January 18, 1989.

6. See, further describing the PRO program, Gosfield, PROs: A Case Study in Utilization Management and Quality Assurance, in 1989 Health Law Handbook, (A. Gosfield ed., 1989); Jost, supra; Melette, The Changing Focus of Peer Review under Medicare, 20 U.Rich.L.Rev. 325 (1986).

VI. NATIONAL HEALTH INSURANCE

Finally, we return to national health insurance. In the recent past a host of proposals have emerged for national health insurance programs, aimed both at expanding access to medical care and controlling its cost. One such proposal follows:

PEPPER COMMISSION RECOMMENDATIONS ON ACCESS TO HEALTH CARE

STRUCTURE OF JOB–BASED/FEDERAL PUBLIC HEALTH INSURANCE PLAN

1. Employer Responsibilities (in businesses with more than 100 employees; in smaller businesses only if a specified coverage target is not met):

— All businesses are required to provide private health insurance for at least the specified benefit package to all employees (and non-working dependents) or contribute to the public plan on their behalf.

— If employers choose to provide private insurance, they must pay at least 80% of the premium for full-time workers and their non-working dependents and a share of the premium for part-time workers and their non-working dependents.

— Alternatively, employers may contribute to the public plan for coverage for their employees and non-working dependents. The contribution will be equal to a percentage of payroll, set at a level to encourage employers who now purchase private insurance to retain that coverage and to establish a fair balance of additional coverage responsibilities between the private and public sectors.

* * *

2. Individual responsibilities

— All workers receive the specified benefit package through their own employer, although they may receive extra benefits from their spouse's employer.   Rules, consistent with tax policy, determine the plan to which children are assigned.

— Individuals pay up to 20% of the private insurance premium.

— To participate in the public plan, working individuals pay a percentage of wages as their share of the premium. Self-employed and non-working individuals pay the cost of the plan, subject to their ability to pay. People with incomes below 100% of poverty (and pregnant women and children to age six below 185% of poverty) pay nothing and people with incomes below 200% of poverty would pay no more than three percent of income for the premium for adults or one percent of income for the premium for children and pregnant women.

— Premiums and cost-sharing for low income people, whether covered by the public plan or private insurance, are subsidized by the federal government. Individuals or families whose income is under 100% of the federal poverty level pay no premiums, deductibles or coinsurance. Individuals or families with income up to 200% of poverty, at a minimum pay premiums, deductibles and coinsurance on a sliding scale.

— At full implementation, individuals must obtain health insurance through their employer or the public plan.

3. Public Plan

— At full implementation, the public plan is financed and administered primarily by the federal government. As under Medicare, insurers may administer claims and may, under contract, offer managed care options. States also may administer claims.

— The public plan pays providers for the specified services with rates set according to the rules of the Medicare program.

— The public plan subsumes Medicaid for the specified benefits. Medicaid remains intact for all services not covered by the package.

— Participation in the public plan is financed through:

    — employer contributions

    — individual contributions

    — federal revenues

    — state contributions equal to Medicaid expenditures for covered services, adjusted for general inflation.

4. State Role

— State governments no longer have responsibility for providing the specified benefit package for their low income residents.

The new public plan replaces Medicaid for those services. Medicaid is retained for services not included in the package.

— States contribute to the public program as specified above.

— A state, at its option and subject to federal rules, can administer the public plan. All aspects of the administration must be conducted through a new agency which is unconnected to the welfare or Medicaid departments.

— States retain the responsibility for regulating financial stability of insurers.

5. Specified Benefit Package

— Basic services, including hospital and surgical services, physician services, diagnostic tests and limited mental health services (45 inpatient days and 25 outpatient visits).

— Preventive services, including prenatal care, well-child care, mammograms, pap smears, colorectal and prostate cancer screening procedures and other preventive services that evidence shows are effective relative to cost.

— Early, periodic screening, diagnosis and treatment services (EPSDT) are included for children in the public program. Privately insured families can buy this coverage for their children from the public plan at cost (or at a subsidized rate for families under at least 200% of poverty).

— Deductibles are $250 for an individual and $500 for a family. Coinsurance is 20% for all services except prenatal care, well-child care, and other preventive services, which have no coinsurance, and the limited outpatient mental health benefit which has a 50% coinsurance. The maximum, annual out-of-pocket expense per person or family is $3,000.

— One year after the effective date of this plan, the Office of Technology Assessment shall report to the Secretary on an assessment of the cost-effectiveness of prescription drugs for the purpose of inclusion in the benefit package as a preventive service.

ASSISTANCE FOR SMALL BUSINESS

1. Insurance reforms and a minimum benefit package will make obtaining private insurance for small groups more predictable and affordable. (See below.)

2. To stimulate voluntary coverage, employers with fewer than 25 workers and average payroll below $18,000 will be eligible for tax credits/subsidies for 40% of the cost of health insurance for workers and their dependents. After the tax credit/subsidy for employers of fewer than 25 employees ends, businesses of ten employees or less,

previously eligible for the credit, who are at extreme financial risk, would be allowed to purchase coverage from the public plan at a percentage of payroll, set consistently at a relatively low rate to ensure affordability.

* * *

INSURANCE MARKET REFORM

1. For all employment-based health insurance:

— No pre-existing condition exclusions.

— No denial of coverage for any individual in the group.

2. For those who wish to sell a health insurance product to employers in the small group market new rules would apply:

— Guaranteed acceptance of all groups wishing to purchase insurance.

— Insurers set rates on the same terms to all groups in specified areas.

— Rates may not be increased selectively for any group enrolled in a plan.

— Enrollment for a specified minimum period.

— States are restricted from regulating the content of health insurance benefits, but benefits are standardized, to the extent possible, across carriers. At least one basic benefit package must be offered by each insurer in the small group market.

— If managed care plans are available to larger employers in the area, then such plans must also be offered to small groups.

— A self-financed voluntary reinsurance mechanism through which insurers could reinsure high-risk persons or groups would be established.

QUALITY ASSURANCE

1. The federal government should develop and implement a comprehensive national system of quality assurance which includes:

— The development of national practice guidelines and standards of care, already begun by the newly created Agency for Health Care Policy and Research. Physicians and physician organizations should be widely utilized in developing and reviewing practice guidelines and parameters.

— The development and implementation of a uniform data system that covers all health care encounters, regardless of payment source or setting. These data would provide a common foundation for all payers' quality assessment activities and for examining the effectiveness of medical care and identifying health policy and research concerns.

— The development and testing of new, more effective methods of quality assurance and assessment.

— The development and oversight of local review organizations that have skills in data integration and analysis, quality assessment and quality assurance.

2. The Prospective Payment Assessment Commission and the Physician Payment Review Commission will be directed to convene experts, providers, lawyers and consumers to study and conduct demonstration projects related to medical malpractice reform in order to make recommendations to Congress on actions to be taken on the federal level. The appropriate committees of jurisdiction in Congress should also hold hearings on the malpractice issue, and the access legislation should incorporate professional liability reform.

Cost Containment Initiatives

1. Insuring all Americans through a job-based/public program and reforming the private insurance market will distribute the costs of insurance more fairly by:

— Reducing the cost-shift that now occurs from the uninsured to the insured population.

— Reducing the cost-shift that now occurs from employers who do not provide insurance to employers who cover their workers and dependents.

— Assuring small businesses access to a minimum benefit package at a predictable rate, regardless of employees' health status.

2. Adoption of a quality assurance strategy (described above) and reform of the medical malpractice system will assure greater value for the dollar in the delivery of medical services.

3. Measures to promote efficiency in provider payment would include:

— Cost-sharing in the minimum benefit package that makes consumers sensitive to price.

— Insurance reform that leads insurers to compete around efficient service delivery, rather than for "good" risks.

— Extending "managed care" to small employers and including it as a means to provide the minimum benefit package in private insurance and the public plan.

— Extending Medicare payment rules to the public program, which, in turn, serves as a model for private insurance.

* * *

2. The federal government should:

— Promote an adequate supply and appropriate mix of personnel and facilities for underserved areas and populations through mechanisms including:

— Provider payment methods in public programs that promote the availability of primary care practitioners and facilities and assure access to other needed services;

— Special initiatives (such as the National Health Service Corps and other financial incentives) to attract a range of providers (physicians and other practitioners) to underserved areas, and to assist such providers through mechanisms such as professional backup systems and support networks for rural providers (e.g., telecommunications with other professionals and facilities, mobile medical services).

— Support local efforts to develop outreach and facilitating services, such as health education, transportation, home visiting, and translation services—preferably linked to health care delivery programs—to facilitate access to services and to encourage patients to seek and continue participation in health care.

— Support local efforts to reduce organizational and bureaucratic barriers to access through efforts such as the coordination and/or co-location of medical, welfare and social services (e.g., medical referrals, nutrition counseling, and eligibility determinations for welfare and housing programs).

— Undertake and support research and evaluation efforts to determine the effectiveness of primary care models and services aimed at addressing the needs of underserved communities.

— Support programs of health promotion, disease prevention, risk reduction and health education toward the reduction of excess morbidity and mortality and toward the increase of healthy lifestyles. Federal support for such programs should total at least $1 billion annually beyond current federal efforts.

— Support an effective continuum of care, including short-term hospital-based and/or longer-term community based alcoholism and other drug treatment services.

* * *

REVENUES FOR HEALTH CARE

A. Although some of the revenues necessary to support the above recommendations could come from savings achieved elsewhere in the federal budget, the Commission is committed to raising whatever additional revenues are necessary.

B. In considering what revenue options to adopt, the Commission recommends that the choice be guided by the following three criteria:

1.   The final tax package ought to be progressive, requiring a higher contribution from those most able to bear increased tax burdens. That is, families with higher incomes would be asked to contribute a greater share of their incomes than required of lower income families.

2.   Since persons of all ages would benefit, persons of all ages should contribute to financing the recommendations.

3.   Revenues chosen should grow fast enough to keep up with benefit growth so that new sources of revenue will not need to be enacted over time. Rates of growth would need to be in excess of eight to nine percent per year.

The Commission report will include illustrations of the extent to which various revenue sources meet these criteria.

C. Various combinations of revenue sources may be used that together meet these criteria, even if individual tax sources may fall short in one category.

* * *

The Pepper Commission was a bipartisan commission whose mandate was to come up with a consensus proposal for health insurance. It failed to reach a consensus—the preceding proposal was voted out of the commission 8 to 7. A major barrier to the plan was its $86.2 billion price tag. See, on the Commission Report, Rockefeller, The Pepper Commission Report on Comprehensive Health Care, 323 New Eng.J. Med. 1005 (1990). Other recent proposals include the American Medical Association's Health Access America plan; the AFL–CIO's National Health Care Program; the Heritage Foundation's National Health System for America (S. Butler & E. Haislmaier, eds. 1989); the National Leadership Commission on Health Care's proposal (NLCHC, For the Health of a Nation (1989)); and Physicians for a National Health Program's, National Health Program for the United States (320 New Eng.J.Med. 102 (1989)).

Problem: National Health Insurance

Divide the class into attorney/lobbyists representing the following interests: the American Medical Association, the American Hospital Association, the Health Insurance Association of America, the AFL–CIO, an association representing small businesses, an association representing large manufacturers, the Committee to Save Social Security, the National Welfare Rights Organization, a national HMO group, and a national taxpayers organization. Which provisions of the Pepper proposal does each group like most? Which provisions are least acceptable to each group? Which group finds the proposal most acceptable? Which least? Why? What changes would each group make in the proposal? Why? How likely is it that the class will arrive at a consensus proposal for a national health insurance program?

Chapter 8

ANTITRUST

INTRODUCTION

The purpose of the antitrust laws is to prohibit private conduct that restrains trade, i.e. that impedes competition in markets for goods and services. It should be clear from the preceding chapter that many impediments exist in health care markets and that some of these obstacles are attributable to intentional conduct on the part of health care professionals and institutions. Recent years have seen vigorous enforcement activity to remove these barriers, thus a competent health care attorney must have some familiarity with the antitrust laws.

The principal federal statutes creating causes of action for restraint of trade are the Sherman Act, the Federal Trade Commission Act and the Clayton Act. (In addition, most states also have antitrust statutes and there are common law doctrines that prohibit unfair competition. Neither of these is covered in this chapter.) These are not recent statutes: Congress enacted the Sherman Act in 1890 and the Federal Trade Commission and Clayton Acts in 1914. For most of this century, however, medical professionals and organizations engaged in health care escaped serious scrutiny. Beginning only in 1975, when the Supreme Court rejected the conventional wisdom that health care providers were exempt from antitrust enforcement as "learned professions," (in Goldfarb v. Virginia State Bar, 421 U.S. 773, 95 S.Ct. 2004, 44 L.Ed.2d 572 (1975)), has antitrust law begun to play an important role in regulating the health care industry.

The application of the federal antitrust statutes to health care, however, continues to present problems related to the peculiarity of health care enterprises as compared to other businesses: What place is there for defenses related to concerns over the quality of health care in a statutory regime designed to enhance competition and to leave such issues to the market? Do not-for-profit health care providers conform to traditional economic assumptions about competitors? If they do not, should they somehow be treated differently under the statutes? What impact do regulatory controls such as certificate of need and professional licensure have on the application of federal antitrust law? Do market failures in health care, particularly imperfect information, suggest special approaches to applying antitrust law?

Section 1 of the Sherman Act provides: "Every contract, combination * * * or conspiracy, in restraint of trade or commerce among the several States * * * is hereby declared to be illegal." 15 U.S.C. § 1. This short statement raises three major issues requiring explanation. First, the activities prohibited by Section 1—contracts, combinations and conspiracies—require joint or collusive action. They require that two or more persons have acted together. A claim based on Section 1, then, must include proof of a concerted activity. One of the questions this presents in health care is whether a hospital and its medical staff are capable of conspiring or whether they should be treated, in effect, as one person. Second, the federal antitrust laws only proscribe restraints of "interstate commerce." Though the Supreme Court has shown a willingness to interpret this provision quite liberally, whether it reaches to the denial of staff privileges by a single hospital of a single doctor, for example, remains to be finally decided. Third, what kind of agreements restraining trade are prohibited by the Act? *All* contracts restrain trade, as they represent a commitment to provide particular services or goods to one party and set the price to the contracting buyer such that price thereafter is no longer allowed to change in response to competitive bids from other potential buyers or sellers. It was necessary, therefore, early in the history of Section 1, for the courts to interpret the statute to prohibit only "unreasonable" restraints of trade.

The courts have developed two approaches to testing the "reasonableness" of restraints under Section 1. Some activities, such as group boycotts, tying and price-fixing (each described below), are considered so likely to restrict trade unreasonably that they are held to be *per se* illegal. If a plaintiff can prove that the defendant's anti-competitive conduct fits within one of the *per se* categories (those listed above and a few others), the inquiry ends; the conduct would be held to have violated the statute. In effect, the *per se* characterization establishes a conclusive presumption of illegality.

Other activities, those not fitting within the categories listed above, are subject to a broader examination of competitive factors under the "rule of reason." Under the rule of reason, defendants escape liability if they prove that the pro-competitive benefits of the challenged activity outweigh its anti-competitive effects, with the result that competition, the singular policy concern of the statute, is strengthened, rather than restrained, overall. The classic articulation of the rule-of-reason methodology is Justice Brandeis' formulation in Chicago Board of Trade v. United States, 246 U.S. 231, 238, 38 S.Ct. 242, 242, 62 L.Ed. 683 (1918):

> The true test of legality is whether the restraint imposed is such as merely regulates and perhaps promotes competition or whether it is such as may suppress or even destroy competition. To determine that question the court must ordinarily consider the facts peculiar to the business * * *; its conditions before and after the restraint was imposed; the nature of the restraint and its effect, actual or probable. The history of the restraint, the evil believed to exist, the reason for

adopting the particular remedy, the purpose or end sought to be attained are all relevant facts.

In recent years the Supreme Court and others have moved away from a rigid dichotomy between *per se* and rule of reason analysis, and now view the two forms as complementary modes of analysis. Thus, as some of the cases in this chapter demonstrate, the courts will now consider, however briefly, procompetitive justifications for suspect practices before attaching the *per se* label. Similarly, courts will truncate the inquiry under the rule of reason when they find convincing proof (such as a reduction in output or an absence of plausible justifications) that the conduct unreasonably restrains trade. During the past few years, the Supreme Court and others have at times indicated dissatisfaction with the *per se* rule. As the courts have begun to consider the application of the *per se* rule to activities in the health care setting, some have shied away from the presumptive illegality required by a *per se* violation, perhaps as a remnant of the deference that historically had been granted the "learned professions." As the courts have modified the *per se* rule at least in health care cases, some have used a "shorthand" form of the rule of reason in which the court examines the apparent effects of the activity but does not engage in the rather intensive examination required for full treatment under the rule of reason. This approach is still evolving but has been used in a number of health care cases.

Courts generally view horizontal restraints, as compared to vertical restraints, as more likely to violate the statute. Horizontal restraints are those among competitors at the same level of production or distribution. Examples include an agreement among area hospitals to charge the same *per diem* room prices (possibly, price-fixing); an agreement among physicians to refuse to admit patients to hospitals that employ non-physician health care professionals (possibly, a group boycott); or agreements between two hospitals in adjacent towns to market their services only in their own town or between two hospitals not to develop ancillary services already offered by the other (possibly, division of markets). Vertical restraints involve concerted action between competitors at different levels of production or distribution; for example, between buyers and sellers or manufacturers and retailers. Economic analysis of vertical restraints suggests that these restraints are likely to have significant pro-competitive effects and so may be inappropriate for the *per se* rule. A possible exception, still appropriate for *per se* treatment, is the tying arrangement, where a seller refuses to sell a product as to which it has power to control the market unless the buyer also purchases another "tied" product. Where do staff privileges decisions fit in this analysis? Are they horizontal restraints among competing physicians? Or are they vertical restraints between the "buyer" of physician services (the hospital) and the "seller" (the physicians)?

The concept of market power is critical to most Section 1 and all Section 2 claims. Under the rule of reason, Section 1 claims require that the plaintiff prove that the defendant has "market power." Section 2 of the Sherman Act prohibits monopolization and attempts to monopolize. A claim of illegal monopolization requires proof that the defendant enjoys sufficient market power to allow it to exclude competitors or control price. A second requirement to establish monopolization is the willful acquisition or maintenance of power as distinguished from growth or development resulting from a superior product, business skill or accident. To satisfy this requirement, courts tend to require plaintiff to show that the power was achieved or is maintained through illegitimate business practices.

Definition of a market for discerning market power requires two determinations. What is the relevant product market? And, what is the relevant geographic market? For example, for a hospital, is the relevant product in-patient services only, or does the hospital's product also include out-patient services? What range of products compete with the hospital's products? May consumers, for example, substitute non-hospital-based out-patient surgery for in-patient surgery? Is the relevant geographic market for a hospital the political subdivision (i.e., the city or the county) in which it is located; or its standard metropolitan statistical area; or all zip code areas from which the hospital draws any, or a significant number, of patients? Once the market is defined, the defendant's share of that market must be determined as a proxy for the defendant's market power. Other factors in addition to market share, such as ease of entry, may bear importantly on whether the market share data actually reflects market power.

Market definition is also critical to a major prohibition of the Clayton Act relevant to the health care industry. Section 7 of the Clayton Act prohibits mergers and acquisitions where the effect may be to "substantially lessen competition" or to "tend to create a monopoly." 15 U.S.C.A. § 18. (The Clayton Act also prohibits tying or exclusive dealing contracts and price discrimination.) In order to test the legality of a proposed merger or acquisition, a court must define the market share of the entities prior to the transaction and of the resulting organization after the transaction. As hospitals consolidate in response to cost containment and more intense competition, merger cases will become much more frequent.

Finally, Section 5 of the Federal Trade Commission Act prohibits unfair methods of competition (which include all Sherman Act and Clayton Act violations) and unfair deceptive acts or practices (including deceptive advertising). Section 5 has been interpreted to grant the FTC the authority to enforce in civil suits the provisions of the Sherman Act and the Clayton Act. The FTC has no jurisdiction over not-for-profit organizations under the FTC Act, limiting its relevance to health care institutions. It may, however, have jurisdiction over not-for-profits for purposes of enforcing the merger provisions of the Clayton Act. The Department of Justice has authority to enforce the Sherman Act through both civil and criminal proceedings and the Clayton Act through civil actions. Finally, any person "injured" by a violation of the antitrust laws may bring a civil suit to enjoin the illegal act or practice or to recover treble damages. A prevailing plaintiff is also entitled to attorney's fees and costs. Not surprisingly, private parties have brought the vast majority of antitrust suits in health care. Individual physicians have sued hospitals over the denial of staff privileges. Nurse practitioners have sued doctors and hospitals over lack of access to facilities. Everyone has sued the private professional associations, such as the American Medical Association, that dominate health care.

There are several statutory and judicially-crafted defenses to antitrust liability, some of which are of importance to health care antitrust litigation. The antitrust state action doctrine exempts from antitrust liability actions taken pursuant to a clearly expressed state policy to restrict free competition, where the challenged conduct is under the active control and supervision of the state. The high degree of state regulation of health care has spawned state action defenses, in, for example, staff privileges cases, ultimately with little success. The McCarran–Ferguson Act generally exempts the "business of insurance" from antitrust enforcement to the extent that the particular insurance activities are regulated by state law. (This should not be taken to mean, however, that "insurance companies" are exempt from antitrust scrutiny). The Noerr–Pennington doctrine, developed in two Supreme Court cases in the 1960s, protects the exercise of the First Amendment right to petition the government, so long as the "petitioning" is not merely a "sham" to cover anti-competitive behavior. This defense is relevant in lobbying efforts on health care issues and to participation in administrative proceedings, such as certificate of need, each of which may lead to an outcome that lessens competition. The most recent statutory defense relevant to health care is the Health Care Quality Improvement Act, enacted by Congress in 1986, which grants limited immunity for peer review activities. Each of these defenses is discussed in this chapter where applicable.

Good basic introductions to antitrust law are available in the standard antitrust hornbooks. A very brief and very useful introduction is presented in Gellhorn, Antitrust Law and Economics in a Nutshell (West 1986). Sullivan and Harrison, Understanding Antitrust and Its Economic Implications (1988), is also good and is accessible to non-specialists. Health care antitrust sources include, Hall and Ellman, Health Care Law and Ethics in a Nutshell (West 1989); The Antitrust Health Care Handbook (ABA 1988); and the symposium on Antitrust and Health Care, in Law and Contemporary Problems, Spring 1988 (edited by Blumstein and Sloan).

I. STAFF PRIVILEGES

For most doctors, hospital admitting and clinical privileges are indispensable to the practice of their profession. It is not surprising, then, that the denial or revocation of privileges generates litigation. While most states, whether through the courts or the legislature, have developed at least limited immunity from liability for peer review actions, the expansion of federal antitrust law to the health care setting provided a new route for challenging privileges decisions.

Staff privileges decisionmaking in the traditional hospital governance model, in which doctors exercised nearly unrestrained control over privileges for their competitors, has been particularly vulnerable to anticompetitive behavior. But the hospital credentialing system has also been one of the most important tools in enhancing the quality of institution-based health care services. Further, the traditional "doctor's workshop" model of hospital governance no longer fully describes the relative power of institution and medical staff. What level of antitrust scrutiny is appropriate in the application of antitrust law to credentialing decisions?

A. ANTITRUST CLAIMS

WEISS v. YORK HOSPITAL

United States Court of Appeals, Third Circuit, 1984.
745 F.2d 786.

I. INTRODUCTION AND GENERAL BACKGROUND

This antitrust case arises from the refusal to grant hospital staff privileges to a physician. The plaintiff, Malcolm Weiss, is an osteopath [1] who was denied staff privileges at York (Pennsylvania) Hospital. Dr. Weiss brought this suit, both individually and as representative of the class of all osteopathic physicians in the York Medical Service Area (York MSA), against York Hospital ("York"), the York Medical and Dental Staff, and ten individual physicians who served on the York Medical Staff Executive Committee and the York Judicial Review Committee. York is controlled by, and, at the time Dr. Weiss applied for staff privileges, was exclusively staffed by doctors who graduated from allopathic medical schools.[3]

The gravamen of Weiss' lawsuit is that, although allopaths (hereinafter referred to as medical doctors or M.D.s) and osteopaths (D.O.s) are equally trained and qualified to practice medicine, his application for staff privileges at York Hospital was turned down solely because of his status as an osteopath. * * *

---

1. Dorland's Illustrated Medical Dictionary defines Osteopathy as:

a system of therapy founded by Andrew Taylor Still (1828–1917) and based on the theory that the body is capable of making its own remedies against disease and other toxic conditions when it is in normal structural relationship and has favorable environmental conditions and adequate nutrition. It utilizes generally accepted physical, medicinal, and surgical methods of diagnosis and therapy, while placing chief emphasis on the im-

portance of normal body mechanics and manipulative methods of detecting and correcting faulty structure.

3. Allopathy is defined as a system of remedial treatment in which it is sought to cure a disease by producing, through medicines, a condition incompatible with the disease. *See* Funk & Wagnalls New Standard Dictionary of the English Language (1942). Allopathy constitutes the common or "regular" system of medical practice. Allopathic doctors, signify their degree as M.D.

In addition, Weiss alleged that the treatment that he received at the hands of the M.D.s who control York sent a message to other D.O.s in the York MSA not to apply for staff privileges at York. In Weiss' submission, this scheme to exclude D.O.s from York Hospital was motivated by a desire to restrict the ability of D.O.s to compete with M.D.s, thereby increasing the profits of the M.D.s. Weiss contends that this conduct violates sections 1 and 2 of the Sherman Act, 15 U.S.C. §§ 1 & 2. * * *

II. THE FACTS

A. Hospital Services in the York MSA

There are two providers of in-patient hospital services in the York MSA: York, which is run by M.D.s, and Memorial Hospital ("Memorial"), which is run by D.O.s. York is by far the larger of the two, with approximately 450 beds and 2,500 employees. Memorial has 160 beds. The testimony at trial established that York had a market share of 80% of the patient-days of hospitalization in the York MSA.

In addition to York's overall market dominance, testimony at trial established that certain complex, highly technical "tertiary care" services and facilities are, for a number of reasons, only available at York.[8]

* * *

B. Discrimination Against D.O.s at York

Prior to 1974, both York Hospital's corporate charter and the bylaws of the York medical staff barred D.O.s from obtaining staff privileges at York. * * * Consequently, whenever a patient of a D.O. wanted to go to York for treatment, either because the patient preferred the reputation and size of York over Memorial, or because the patient required tertiary care services that were available only at York, the treating D.O. had no choice but to refer the patient to an M.D. with staff privileges at York. [ ]

The evidence adduced at trial indicated several ways in which D.O.s were economically disadvantaged as a result of this discrimination. First, D.O.s lost fees directly when one of their patients was admitted for treatment at York. * * *

D.O.s were also indirectly disadvantaged as the result of York's discriminatory policy. When patients of D.O.s were referred to M.D.s in order that they could be treated at York, they sometimes did not return to the referring D.O. after the treatment at York was completed, but instead remained in the care of the referred M.D.

---

8. Since most tertiary care equipment is highly sophisticated and thus very expensive, and since York already possesses the equipment and can handle the total patient demand for the York MSA, Memorial cannot obtain the required "certificates of need" to purchase tertiary care equipment for itself. * * * Tertiary care is only provided by highly specialized physicians. Because most D.O.s do not highly specialize, * * * there are few who are qualified to provide tertiary care services. By contrast, M.D.s tend to highly specialize, even outside large metropolitan areas, hence an M.D. hospital like York is a natural place for providing tertiary care services.

* * * Additionally, the evidence established that the absence of staff privileges is a competitive disadvantage, in that it indicates to patients that the doctor is a second-class practitioner. * * *

In 1974 York amended its corporate charter to allow osteopathic physicians to practice at York. Osteopaths were still barred from admission to York, however, because of the prohibition in the medical staff bylaws. Nevertheless, in early 1976, Weiss and another osteopath named Dr. Michael Zittle, both of whom were engaged in family practice in the York MSA, applied for staff privileges at York. Dr. Weiss informed representatives of the York medical staff that if York excluded him because of his osteopathic training he would institute legal action.

The York medical staff considered the applications and Weiss' threat of legal action, and in November of 1976 amended its bylaws to permit admission of osteopaths at York. Dr. Weiss contends that the amendment of the bylaws was purely cosmetic, and that since 1976 the York medical staff has engaged in a deliberate covert policy of discrimination against osteopaths. In support of this contention Weiss offered evidence that York had a historical presumption in favor of admitting any M.D. who applied for staff privileges, regardless of the applicant's medical ability or social graces,[12] but that in the case of D.O. applicants York engaged in "strict scrutiny" of the applicant's medical qualifications, and, in addition, considered the applicant's social acceptability. If the D.O. was found lacking, even minimally, in either area, his application was denied. * * * Because "[t]he denial of hospital staff privileges to a physician or the revocation of such privileges is a serious adverse professional event which is likely to besmirch the professional reputation of such a physician," [ ] the district court found that application of the strict scrutiny standard to Weiss' application for staff privileges, and the consequent denial of Weiss' application, "could reasonably be anticipated to cause [other] osteopathic physicians to refrain from applying for staff privileges at York Hospital." [ ]

In addition to discriminating against D.O.s in the admissions process, Weiss also offered evidence that York automatically gave any D.O. who survived the strict scrutiny of that process the lowest category of

---

12. In the ten years preceding the date of the trial, York and its staff received approximately 200 applications by M.D.s. During this period the only M.D. to ever be denied privileges was suffering from psychiatric problems. The presumption enjoyed by M.D.s was even strong enough to permit the admission to staff privileges at York of a certain Dr. "A" [actual name held confidential by the district court] even after the following report was made to the medical staff by one of its senior members based on extensive personal evaluation:

[Dr. A] has demonstrated poor judgment in decisions about therapy without obtaining all the facts at hand or necessary

to make these judgments or decisions. Moreover he has proceeded in an over-confident manner such as administration of hydrochloric acid * * * to correct metabolic alkalosis where other modes of therapy were indicated. I have discussed these actions with him but they tend to recur. He answers questions about events and dates on patients without knowing the facts. He is not able to provide total patient care. He has serious deficiencies in medical knowledge. And moreover compounds these deficiencies by neglecting to obtain the facts before treatment of patients.

staff privileges offered by York, that of "Assistant Staff," regardless of the D.O.'s actual skill level. Under the Assistant Staff category of privileges the physician is required to consult with other members of the department in the care and treatment of his patients. By contrast, M.D.s who applied for and received staff privileges at York were given different levels of staff privileges depending on their level of skill as certified by the various M.D. specialty Boards.

* * *

D. Doctor Weiss' Application for Staff Privileges

In 1976 Doctors Weiss and Zittle applied for staff privileges in York's Family Practice Department. In accordance with the [hospital's] procedures, * * * the Family Practice Department Credentials Committee and the chairman of the Family Practice Department considered the applications. On January 17, 1977, the department recommended that they be accepted. The Medical Staff Credentials Committee then reviewed the applications and also recommended acceptance. The Medical Staff Executive Committee, however, did not approve either application. Instead, it took the unusual step of deciding to conduct a further investigation. The Committee made extensive oral and written inquiries concerning the professional competence and moral character of both Weiss and Zittle. No such survey had ever before been conducted by the hospital before [sic]. Ultimately the investigation turned up some questions about Dr. Weiss' personality. The investigation also raised some glimmer of a question about Dr. Weiss' medical competence, but the sole "evidence" that was adduced was hearsay, often second or third level hearsay. Nevertheless, the Medical Staff Executive Committee, apparently based on this "new evidence" decided not to recommend Weiss for staff privileges.

On June 30, 1977, the hospital Board of Directors considered the recommendations of the various committees which had considered Weiss' and Zittle's applications. The Board voted to approve Zittle's application and deny Weiss' application. Notice of the Board's action was sent to Weiss the same day.

On August 19, 1977, following meetings with York officials, Weiss requested that his application be reactivated and hence reconsidered. * * * On February 28, 1978, the Medical Staff Credentials Committee voted to recommend again that Weiss' renewed application be accepted. However, on March 6, 1978, the Medical Staff Executive Committee again voted to recommend that the application be denied.

Weiss' application was next referred to the Medical Affairs Committee of the hospital's Board of Directors. This committee directed that the members of the Family Practice Department Credentials Committee, the Medical Staff Credentials Committee, and the Medical Staff Executive Committee meet informally to attempt to reach a consensus on Weiss' application. The members of these committees then met on March 20, 1978, and voted to recommend that Weiss' application be denied. The Medical Staff Executive Committee then met on April 19, 1978, to re-reconsider Weiss' application and, for the third time, voted to recommend that the hospital Board of Directors deny the application.

On April 21, 1978, York sent Weiss written notice of the April 19, 1978, unfavorable recommendation of the Medical Staff Executive Committee. Upon being advised of the decision of that Committee, Weiss requested and received a statement of reasons. Weiss' status as a D.O. rather than an M.D. was not one of the reasons cited by the Committee in its official statement of reasons. Weiss also requested an appeal to a "judicial review" committee as provided for in the hospital bylaws.

A "Judicial Review" Committee was impanelled and a hearing was held. Weiss was present and represented by counsel at this proceeding. After reviewing all the evidence, the committee, on December 28, 1978, determined unanimously that the decision of the Medical Staff Executive Committee not to recommend Weiss for staff privileges was not unreasonable, arbitrary, or capricious. The committee also determined, with one member dissenting, that the Medical Staff Executive Committee was not in error in its recommendation.

The Hospital Board of Directors then held a special meeting at which presentations were made by counsel for Weiss and special counsel for the Hospital. On March 13, 1979, the Board voted to deny Weiss staff privileges.

* * *

IV. THE SHERMAN ACT CLAIMS

* * *

A. *Section 1 of the Sherman Act*

In order to establish a violation of section 1 of the Sherman Act, 15 U.S.C. § 1 (1982), a plaintiff must establish three elements: (1) a contract, combination, or conspiracy; (2) restraint of trade; and (3) an effect on interstate commerce. * * *

1. *Proof of an Agreement: Is There a Sufficient Number of Conspirators?*

In order to establish a violation of section 1, a plaintiff must prove that two or more distinct entities agreed to take action against the plaintiff. Before the district court, Weiss contended that the hospital and its medical staff were legally distinct entities and therefore capable of conspiring in violation of section 1. He also asserted that the doctors who joined together to form the medical staff were separate economic entities who competed against each other so that, as a matter of law, the medical staff was a "combination" of doctors within the meaning of section 1. Finally, Weiss argued that even if the individual doctors who made up York's medical staff were deemed by the court to be the equivalent of "officers or employees" of the hospital and therefore ordinarily not capable of conspiring with the hospital, nevertheless the doctors were acting for their own benefit in discriminating against osteopaths, and therefore fell within an exception to the ordinary rule that "officers or employees of the same firm do not provide the plurality of actors imperative for a § 1 conspiracy." [43] [ ]

The defendants countered that York and its medical staff were legally one entity and therefore incapable of conspiring. In addition the defendants asserted that the individual doctors who made up the medical staff were the equivalent of "employees or officers" of the hospital and hence legally incapable of conspiring with the hospital.
* * *

We agree with the plaintiffs that, as a matter of law, the medical staff is a combination of individual doctors and therefore that any action taken by the medical staff satisfies the "contract, combination, or conspiracy" requirement of section 1. * * * In addition, because the medical staff itself is a combination as a matter of law, we conclude that the absence of evidence of any other co-conspirator(s) is irrelevant. We do, however, agree with the district court that the hospital cannot legally conspire with its medical staff.

* * *

The York medical staff is a group of doctors, all of whom practice medicine in their individual capacities, and each of whom is an independent economic entity in competition with other doctors in the York medical community. Each staff member, therefore, has an economic interest separate from and in many cases in competition with the interests of other medical staff members. Under these circumstances, the medical staff cannot be considered a single economic entity for purposes of antitrust analysis.

* * *

Two recent Supreme Court cases reaffirm that a single entity made up of independent, competing economic entities satisfies the joint action requirement of Sherman Act section 1. In *Arizona v. Maricopa County Medical Society,* 457 U.S. 332, 102 S.Ct. 2466, 73 L.Ed.2d 48 (1982), the defendants, the Maricopa Foundation for Medical Care and the Pima Foundation for Medical Care, were non-profit Arizona corporations composed of licensed doctors of medicine, osteopathy, and podiatry engaged in private practice. The Foundations were "organized for the purpose of promoting fee-for-service medicine and to provide the community with a competitive alternative to existing health insurance plans." *Id.* at 339, 102 S.Ct. at 2470. The Court simply assumed without discussion that the actions of each foundation satisfied the "contract combination * * * or conspiracy" element of section 1. Similarly, in *National Society of Professional Engineers v. United States,* 435 U.S. 679, 98 S.Ct. 1355, 55 L.Ed.2d 637 (1978), the defendant, an

43. If corporate officers or employees act for their own interests, and outside the interests of the corporation, they are legally capable of conspiring with their employer for purposes of section 1. [ ] Because the jury did not find any of the named individual defendants to be conspirators, we do not have occasion to discuss this exception further.

association of professional engineers organized to deal with "the non-technical aspects of engineering practice," *id.* at 682, 98 S.Ct. at 1360, had adopted an ethics canon prohibiting competitive bidding. Once again the Court simply assumed, without discussion, that the defendant was a combination of its members. [ ]

On the basis of these cases, we believe that the actions of the York medical staff are the actions of a combination of the individual doctors who make it up. * * * Where such associations exist, their actions are subject to scrutiny under section 1 of the Sherman Act in order to insure that their members do not abuse otherwise legitimate organizations to secure an unfair advantage over their competitors. * * * The district court found that the medical staff was an unincorporated division of the hospital, and as such the court determined that the two could not conspire. Although we do not necessarily agree with the district court's characterization of the medical staff as an unincorporated division of the hospital, we agree with its basic conclusion that, with respect to the issues in this case, the hospital could not, as a matter of law, conspire with the medical staff. The medical staff was empowered to make staff privilege decisions on behalf of the hospital. As such, with regard to these decisions, the medical staff operated as an officer of a corporation would in relation to the corporation. Although the members of the medical staff had independent economic interests in competition with each other, the staff as an entity had no interest in competition with the hospital. Accordingly, we conclude that the district court correctly charged the jury that there could not be a conspiracy between the hospital and the medical staff. [ ]

2. *Proof of Restraint of Trade*

a. *Introduction*

Read literally, Section 1 prohibits every agreement "in restraint of trade." In *United States v. Joint Traffic Ass'n,* 171 U.S. 505, 19 S.Ct. 25, 43 L.Ed. 259 (1898), the Supreme Court recognized that Congress could not have intended a literal interpretation of the word "every," and since *Standard Oil Co. of New Jersey v. United States,* 221 U.S. 1, 31 S.Ct. 502, 55 L.Ed. 619 (1911), courts have analyzed most restraints under the so-called "rule of reason." As its name suggests, the rule of reason requires the factfinder to decide whether, under all the circumstances of the case, the restrictive practice imposes an unreasonable restraint on competition.

The courts have also, however, applied a rule of *per se* illegality to certain types of business practices. * * * In this case, the plaintiffs argued that the actions of the defendants were the equivalent of a boycott, or as it is sometimes called, a concerted refusal to deal, and thus illegal *per se.* We now turn to that inquiry.

b. *Is Defendants' Exclusionary Conduct the Equivalent of a Concerted Refusal to Deal ("Boycott")?*

The jury found that the defendants had engaged in a policy of discrimination against Dr. Weiss and the other D.O.s in the York MSA by applying unfair, unequal, and unreasonable procedures in reviewing their applications. [ ] In addition, the district court concluded that this unfair, unreasonable, and unequal treatment "could reasonably be anticipated [by the defendants] to cause osteopathic physicians to refrain from applying for staff privileges at the York Hospital." [ ] The question before us is whether these actions should properly be characterized as a "group boycott" or "concerted refusal to deal," in which case they are illegal *per se* under section 1. [ ] If the defendants' actions cannot be so characterized, the rule of reason analysis would apply and the outcome of the case could be different. [ ] We conclude that the defendants' actions, as found in the district court, are the equivalent of a concerted refusal to deal.

The classic example of a concerted refusal to deal is the situation in which businesses at one level of production or distribution, e.g., retailers, use the threat of a boycott to induce businesses at another level, e.g., manufacturers, not to deal with competitors of the retailers. As Professor Sullivan has observed, "The boycotting group members, in effect, say to their suppliers or to their customers, 'If you don't stop dealing with non-group members, we will stop dealing with you.' If continued trade with group members is more important to a supplier or customer than is trading with non-group members, this threat will be effective." L. Sullivan, *Handbook of the Law of Antitrust* § 83 at 230 (1977).

In this case York is a provider of hospital services; for the purpose of our analysis, the equivalent of the manufacturer in the example of a classical boycott. Similarly, the M.D.s are the equivalent of the retailers in the example, in the sense that physicians require access to a hospital in order to effectively treat patients. The difficulty with this analogy, at first blush, is that there is no evidence that the M.D.s have used coercion for the purpose of inducing York to exclude their competitors, the D.O.s. Upon closer analysis, however, the absence of coercion is irrelevant. A boycott is not illegal under the antitrust laws because of opposition to the use of coercion, but because it involves the use by businesses of an existing relationship with a supplier to exclude competition. In the paradigm case, coercion is necessary to induce the supplier not to deal with the competitors. In this case, because of the M.D.s' control over York's admission decisions, no coercion is necessary. The underlying antitrust violation is the same: a group of firms at one level of distribution, i.e., the doctors' level, have used their existing relationship with a supplier to exclude their competitors from dealing with the supplier.[58]

58. We note that in this case York possesses monopoly power in the York MSA with respect to inpatient hospital health care services. * * * We therefore need not reach the question whether, in order to constitute a *per se* illegal boycott, a conspiracy to exclude a group of potential competitors from hospital staff privileges requires that the hospital—i.e., the entity at the other level of "production"—possess

We recognize that the facts of this case do not precisely fit into the mold of the classical refusal to deal. The refusal to deal is less than total insofar as York admitted Dr. Zittle and a number of other osteopaths. [ ] Arguably then, what is at issue is not a boycott but mere discrimination, which sounds less like a *per se* antitrust violation. However, given the evidence of the different standards applied to osteopaths and M.D.s and the second class citizenship afforded D.O.s upon admission to staff privileges at York, and in view of the adverse impact of these factors upon D.O. applications for York staff privileges, we are satisfied that the restrictive policy is, in purpose and effect, sufficiently close to the traditional boycott, that the characterization is appropriate.

The Medical Staff is, however, entitled to exclude individual doctors, including osteopaths, on the basis of their lack of professional competence or unprofessional conduct. * * * If York's policy toward D.O.s could be viewed as a form of industry self-regulation of this type, the rule of reason, rather than a *per se* rule, would be applicable. [ ]

* * *

c. The "Learned Profession" Exception

In *Goldfarb v. Virginia State Bar,* 421 U.S. 773, 788 n. 17, 95 S.Ct. 2004, 2013 n. 17, 44 L.Ed.2d 572 (1975), in which the Supreme Court made clear that the medical profession is not exempt from the antitrust laws, the Court stated that the "public service aspect, and other features of the professions, may require that a particular practice, which could properly be viewed as a violation of the Sherman Act in another context, be treated differently." *See also National Society of Professional Engineers v. United States,* 435 U.S. 679, 696, 98 S.Ct. 1355, 1367, 55 L.Ed.2d 637 (1978). In *Arizona v. Maricopa County Medical Society,* 457 U.S. 332, 348–49, 102 S.Ct. 2466, 2475–2476, 73 L.Ed.2d 48 (1982), the Court partially explained this exception by stating that conduct which is normally subject to *per se* condemnation under section 1 will instead be subject to rule of reason analysis where the challenged conduct is "premised on public service or ethical norms." * * *

In this case the defendants have offered no "public service or ethical norm" rationale for their discriminatory treatment of D.O.s. Indeed, their defense at trial was that they did not discriminate against D.O.s. Since the jury believed otherwise, we conclude that the *per se* rule governs this case, except to the extent that the defendants may defend as to the damage claims of Weiss or any class member on grounds of lack of professional capacity or unprofessional conduct.[61]

substantial market power in the relevant market. This distinguishing factor might render the analysis in this case different from the analysis in a large metropolitan area. *Cf. Jefferson Parish Hosp. Dist. No. 2 v. Hyde,* 466 U.S. 2, 104 S.Ct. 1551, 1559, 80 L.Ed.2d 2 (1984) ("Accordingly, we have condemned tying arrangements [only] when the seller has some special ability— usually called 'market power'—to force a purchaser to do something that he would not do in a competitive market.")

61. Even if we were to conclude that a rule of reasons analysis governs in this case simply because a learned profession is

* * *

B. Section 2 of the Sherman Act

Section 2 reads in pertinent part:

Every person who shall monopolize, or attempt to monopolize, or combine or conspire with any other person or persons, to monopolize any part of the trade or commerce among the several States, or with foreign nations, shall be deemed guilty of a misdemeanor. * * *

15 U.S.C. § 2. The test for determining whether a defendant has monopolized in violation of section 2 has been articulated by the Supreme Court as: "(1) the possession of monopoly power in the relevant market and (2) the willful acquisition or maintenance of that power as distinguished from growth or development as a consequence of a superior product, business acumen, or historic accident." *United States v. Grinnell Corp.*, 384 U.S. 563, 570–571, 86 S.Ct. 1698, 1703–1704, 16 L.Ed.2d 778 (1966). [ ] The district court found the defendant York liable to both Weiss and the plaintiff class for unlawful monopolization in violation of section 2. York has appealed that finding.

York contends that the jury incorrectly concluded that the appropriate market was inpatient health care services provided by hospitals and their staffs; that it incorrectly concluded that York had monopoly power in that market; and that it incorrectly concluded that York acquired or maintained that power by means of "willful" conduct. We conclude that, although there was sufficient evidence to support the jury's conclusion as to relevant market and monopoly power, there was no evidence of willful conduct designed to acquire or maintain monopoly power, and therefore the judgment against York under section 2 must be reversed.

(1) Relevant Market

In order to define the relevant market for purposes of a section 2 claim, it is necessary to examine two aspects of that market: the product market and geographic market. York does not challenge the jury's finding that the relevant geographic market is the York MSA. York does, however, challenge the jury's finding on the product market. In answer to special verdict question number 14, the jury found that the relevant product market was "inpatient hospital health care services supplied by hospitals and their medical staffs." [ ] Market definition is a question of fact, [ ] and we therefore must affirm the jury's conclusion unless the record is devoid of evidence upon which the jury might reasonably base its conclusion.

involved, we would conclude that the defendants' conduct here was an unreasonable restraint because: (1) Weiss met his burden of production and persuasion that the purpose and effect of the defendants' discriminatory conduct was to "foreclose so much of the market from penetration by [the M.D.s'] competitors [i.e., the D.O.s] as to unreasonably restrain competition in the affected market, the market for [inpatient medical care]," *see Jefferson Parish Hosp. Dist. No. 2 v. Hyde*, 466 U.S. 2, 104 S.Ct. 1551, 1568 n. 51, 80 L.Ed.2d 2 (1984), and (2) the defendants—who relied solely on the defense they had not discriminated against D.O.s—made no attempt to counter this evidence.

* * *

Defendants argue that "inpatient health care services" is not a single market, but an amalgam of numerous markets for individual types of services. Where, however, several goods or services are generally offered by the same providers, it is not unreasonable for a jury to conclude that the market for antitrust purposes includes all of those goods or services. * * * The jury could reasonably have concluded * * * that a consumer of hospital services makes one "purchase decision"—where to be hospitalized—and that further decisions concerning his treatment are relatively insulated from any competitive effect. This conclusion was clearly supported by the evidence, and therefore we affirm the jury's finding that the relevant product market was inpatient hospital health care. [ ]

(2) Monopoly Power

Monopoly power is defined as the ability to control price in or to exclude or restrict competition from a relevant geographic market.

* * *

A primary criterion used to assess the existence of monopoly power is the defendant's market share. [ ] In this case, the plaintiffs' expert testified that York possessed a market share in excess of eighty percent, and that in his expert opinion the defendants possessed "the power to exclude competition" and "the power to raise and control prices." [ ] Since monopoly power is a question of fact, [ ] and since we believe that the expert's testimony and York's market share is sufficient evidence upon which the jury could reasonably have concluded that monopoly power existed in this case, we affirm the jury's and district court's finding on this point. [ ]

(3) Willful Acquisition or Maintenance of Monopoly Power

In addition to proving monopoly power in the relevant market, an antitrust plaintiff must also show that the defendant willfully acquired or maintained that power.[73] [ ]

The plaintiffs concede that York lawfully acquired its monopoly power; therefore, the relevant issue is whether the plaintiffs adduced sufficient evidence to demonstrate that York "willfully" *maintained* this power. The only evidence that plaintiffs offered on this point was the testimony of their expert that M.D.s have a strong economic interest in excluding D.O.s from access to York Hospital because, if D.O.s are given access to York on the same terms and conditions as M.D.s, M.D.s will be forced to compete directly and on equal terms with D.O.s. This testimony is a sufficient basis on which to imply an anticompetitive purpose on the part of the M.D.s in excluding the D.O.s,

---

73. This requirement represents a policy judgment that a firm that has acquired and maintained its position as a monopolist because of "growth or development as a result of superior product, business acumen, or historic accident," [ ] and not through anticompetitive conduct, should not be liable under the antitrust laws for its success.

but it does not explain an economic motive on the part of the hospital to discriminate against D.O.s.

On this point, the uncontradicted evidence of both the plaintiffs' and the defendants' experts was that York, like any hospital, would maximize its revenues by giving staff privileges to every qualified doctor who applied. Hospitals are in the business of providing facilities (rooms and equipment) and support staff (nurses, administrators, etc.). These resources are fixed in the short run, and the hospital maximizes its revenues by encouraging competition for its hospital beds and operating rooms. Since only physicians with staff privileges can admit and treat patients, York can maximize competition for its facilities by granting staff privileges to every qualified doctor who applies. Excluding D.O.s on the other hand, is likely to weaken York's monopoly position in the long run, since a potential rival, such as Memorial Hospital, would have an incentive to provide competing services for the D.O.s excluded from York.

Recognizing this problem with their section 2 claim, plaintiffs assert that, although the hospital itself has no economic reason to discriminate against D.O.s, the hospital's medical staff, which as a matter of law is a single entity with the hospital, [ ] is a combination of M.D.s, each of whom have a strong economic motive to exclude D.O.s. Thus, the plaintiffs argue, we should ascribe the anticompetitive motives of the individual M.D.s to the hospital.

There are two problems with this argument. First, the fact that the individual M.D.s who make up the medical staff have parallel anticompetitive motives was the reason we concluded that, as a matter of law, the medical staff is a combination of doctors within the meaning of section 1. We believe, however, that it would be improper to attribute the economic motive of the M.D.s to York because the M.D.s' motive is to restrict competition in a market in which York is not involved, and because in fact York's economic interest is directly contradictory to that of the individual doctors. Second, even if the anticompetitive motive of the individual doctors could be attributed to the hospital, the actions taken in furtherance of that motive have nothing to do with the maintenance of York's monopoly position; restricting the access of D.O.s to York will not aid York in maintaining that monopoly power.

In sum, we conclude that there is no evidence that York "willfully" maintained its monopoly position as the dominant provider of inpatient health care services in the York MSA. For this reason we reverse the district court's finding that York violated section 2 of the Sherman Act.

* * *

Notes and Questions

1. The court in *Weiss* concludes that hospital-medical staff action in credentialing does not meet the statutory conspiracy requirement in § 1 of the Sherman Act. The Third Circuit adhered to its analysis of conspiracy

in *Weiss* in Nanavati v. Burdette Tomlin Memorial Hospital, 857 F.2d 96 (3d Cir.1988). Several circuits, however, have differed with *Weiss* and have concluded that a conspiracy between a hospital and its medical staff is not impossible as a matter of law. See, for example, Oksanen v. Page Memorial Hospital, 912 F.2d 73 (4th Cir.1990); Bolt v. Halifax Hosp. Medical Center, 891 F.2d 810 (11th Cir.1990); Oltz v. St. Peter's Community Hospital, 861 F.2d 1440 (9th Cir.1988). See also, Pinhas v. Summit Health, Ltd., 880 F.2d 1108, 894 F.2d 1024 (9th Cir.1989), in which the Ninth Circuit did not explicitly resolve the question of a hospital-medical staff conspiracy, but did find that Pinhas "sufficiently alleges that [the hospital attorneys] exerted their influence over [defendants] so as to direct them to engage in the complained of acts for an anticompetitive purpose."

What is at stake in this issue? Are the purposes of antitrust law better served by a rule that a hospital and medical staff either can or cannot conspire or by a case-by-case, fact-specific approach? Is the *Pinhas* decision that a hospital's attorneys can conspire with the hospital consistent with the underlying analysis of *Weiss?*

2. The Sherman Act makes illegal restraints and monopolization of "trade or commerce among the several states." It thus requires that plaintiff prove a substantial effect on interstate commerce. A dispute among the circuits concerning the interstate effect required by the Act for antitrust litigation against hospitals has existed for some time.

The Supreme Court has granted *cert* in Pinhas v. Summit Health, Ltd., 894 F.2d 1024 (9th Cir.1989), *cert.* granted ___ U.S. ___, 110 S.Ct. 3212, 110 L.Ed.2d 660 (1990) on the question of the interstate commerce requirement for staff privileges.

3. The court characterized the credentialing decision in *Weiss* as a group boycott, one of the horizontal restraints that historically has been viewed as a *per se* violation of the Sherman Act. The court's willingness to shift to rule-of-reason analysis evidences an erosion of *per se* analysis, at least in medical contexts.

Subsequent to *Weiss,* the Supreme Court considered the antitrust analysis of concerted refusals to deal. The Court stated that the *per se* rule was to be applied only where the action appears to present a great likelihood of anticompetitive conduct. The Court identified a threshold inquiry for the application of the *per se* rule: "In these cases [in which a group boycott was subject to the *per se* rule], the boycott often cut off access to a supply, facility, or market necessary to enable the boycotted firm to compete [ ] and frequently the boycotting firms possessed a dominant position in the relevant market. [ ] In addition, the practices were generally not justified by plausible arguments that they were intended to enhance overall efficiency and make markets more competitive. Under such circumstances the likelihood of anticompetitive effects is clear and the possibility of countervailing procompetitive effects is remote. * * * A plaintiff seeking application of the *per se* rule must present a threshold case that the challenged activity falls into a category likely to have predominantly anticompetitive effects. The mere allegation of a concerted refusal to deal does not suffice because not all concerted refusals to deal are predominantly anticompetitive." Northwest Wholesale Stationers, Inc. v. Pacific Stationery and Printing Co., 472 U.S. 284, 105 S.Ct. 2613, 86 L.Ed.2d 202 (1985).

In Goss v. Memorial Hospital System, 789 F.2d 353 (1986), the Fifth Circuit, relying on *Northwest Wholesale,* rejected a physician's claim that the denial of his staff privileges was the result of a group boycott that warranted application of the *per se* rule: "[A]ppellant's challenged expulsion from the staffs of Memorial and Sharpstown * * * does not imply anticompetitive state of mind. Review procedures are necessary to insure that hospital staff members are competent medical practitioners. Also, the summary judgment evidence fails to show that the hospitals possess 'market power or unique access to a business element necessary for effective competion.' " The defendant hospitals controlled less than 7% of the beds in the county in which they were located. The court held that the physician's claim of anticompetitive animus should be considered in a rule-of-reason analysis of this claim.

Would Dr. Weiss' claim be entitled to *per se* consideration under these criteria? James Blumstein and Frank Sloan have suggested that *per se* rules have passed out of fashion and are generally inappropriate for credentialing decisions. They argue that certain credentialing actions that pose the "most significant potential for anticompetitive effects" ought to trigger a "rebuttable presumption of invalidity" within a rule-of-reason analysis. If the plaintiff is able to show that the credentialing policies or decisions excluded a particular class of practitioners (e.g., osteopaths); excluded practitioners who engaged in particular practices (e.g., working with HMOs or advertising); or excluded practitioners who were not members of particular physician groups or partnerships, the burden would shift to the credentialing body to rebut the presumption of illegality. Although the hospital or medical staff bears a heavy burden in this scheme, it does at least allow for some defense. Blumstein and Sloan, Antitrust and Hospital Peer Review, 51 L. & Contemp. Probs. 7 (1988).

4. As in *Weiss,* hospitals granting exclusive contracts for the provision of certain medical services such as radiology, pathology, and anesthesiology exclude entire classes of physicians; i.e., those who are not members of the group or partnership that holds the exclusive contract. Plaintiffs challenging exclusive contracts on antitrust grounds have attempted to characterize the contracts as "tying" arrangements which are *per se* illegal. This claim requires the plaintiff to prove that a seller with market power in one product (the tying product) has forced a buyer to purchase another product (the tied product) that the buyer ordinarily would prefer to purchase separately.

In Jefferson Parish Hospital Dist. No. 2 v. Hyde, 466 U.S. 2, 104 S.Ct. 1551, 80 L.Ed.2d 2 (1984), the Supreme Court considered an antitrust challenge to an exclusive contract for anesthesia services. The plaintiff claimed that the exclusive contract tied hospital services and anesthesiology. The plurality opinion held that, although there were two products involved, the plaintiff failed to prove that the hospital had market power in the tying product. A concurring opinion signed by four justices argued that tying should not be subject to *per se* liability, but rather should be judged in the context of its economic effects in each case. The concurring justices identified significant economic benefit to the hospital in the exclusive arrangement.

Plaintiff doctors generally have been unsuccessful in challenging exclusive contracts as illegal tying arrangements. See, for example, Collins v. Associated Pathologists, Ltd., 844 F.2d 473 (7th Cir.1988) and White v. Rockingham Radiologists, Ltd., 820 F.2d 98 (4th Cir.1987), in which the courts held that plaintiffs alleging illegal tying in the case of exclusive contracts for pathology, in the first case, and CT reading, in the latter case, failed to prove the existence of two products. It is difficult to fit such contracts into the tying characterization unless the hospital shares directly or indirectly in the doctor's profits.

Exclusive contracts may be vulnerable to attack as "exclusive-dealing arrangements" under § 1 of the Sherman Act. Exclusive-dealing arrangements are examined under the rule of reason. The concurring opinion in *Hyde* rejected plaintiff's claim: "Exclusive dealing is an unreasonable restraint of trade only when a significant fraction of buyers or sellers are frozen out of a market by the exclusive deal. * * * There is no suggestion that East Jefferson Hospital is likely to create a 'bottle-neck' in the availability of anesthesiological services, or that the [contracting anesthesiology group] have unreasonably narrowed the range of choices available to other anesthesiologists in search of a hospital or services that will buy their services. A firm of four anesthesiologists represents only a very small fraction of the total number of anesthesiologists whose services are available for hire by other hospitals, and East Jefferson is one among numerous hospitals buying such services. Even without engaging in a detailed analysis of the size of the relevant markets we may readily conclude that there is no likelihood that the exclusive-dealing arrangement challenged here will either unreasonably enhance the hospital's market position relative to other hospitals, or unreasonably permit [the contracting anesthesiologist group] to acquire power relative to other anesthesiologists."

In *Collins,* supra, the court rejected the plaintiff pathologist's exclusive-dealing claim. The court identified the appropriate market as the job market for pathologists and concluded that the market for pathologists was a national market, which the contracting hospital did not dominate.

The plaintiff nurse anesthetist was successful in Oltz v. St. Peter's Community Hospital, 861 F.2d 1440 (9th Cir.1988). Tafford Oltz provided nurse anesthetist services for St. Peter's hospital, one of two hospitals in Helena, Montana. Mr. Oltz was popular among surgeons at the hospital, and he charged approximately two-thirds what the anesthesiologists charged. After three of the four M.D. anesthesiologists with privileges at the hospital repeatedly threatened to leave, the hospital's Board of Trustees decided to enter into an exclusive contract for anesthesiology services. St. Peter's advertised nationally and then contracted with three of the anesthesiologists who already had privileges at the hospital. After Oltz left St. Peter's, each of Helena's anesthesiologists experienced a 40 to 50% increase in earnings. Oltz sued the hospital and the anesthesiologists, claiming that the exclusive contract violated § 1 of the Sherman Act. The doctors settled for over $400,000. The jury found for Oltz and awarded him nearly $500,000, although the trial court found this to be excessive and ordered a new trial on damages. On appeal, St. Peter's challenged the trial court's use of Helena as the relevant product market, arguing that the market for anesthetists was national. The appellate court concluded that, although the market for anesthetists was national, the market for patient anesthesia services was also relevant. The court held that the patient services market was properly confined to the city of Helena. The court distinguished *Oltz* from *Collins* because the evidence in *Oltz* revealed a demand for individual anesthesia service providers. St. Peter's argued that under the court's analysis "no rural hospital could lawfully grant an exclusive contract." The court responded that "the conspiracy St. Peter's joined involved more than the establishment of an exclusive contract. The absence of a goal to remove Oltz and reduce the competition for the patients whom he served would have dramatically altered the outcome of this case."

5. Hospitals, such as St. Peter's, that have market power probably do have to be somewhat more careful in their credentialing processes. Blumstein and Sloan, supra, suggest that such hospitals should consider intermediate disciplinary remedies; use external peer review; and be especially aggressive in asserting the institution's control over privileges decisions.

In Doctors and Hospitals: An Antitrust Perspective on Traditional Relationships, 1984 Duke L.J. 1071, Clark Havighurst recommends application of an "essential-facilities doctrine" to staff privileges cases. Havighurst's doctrine would require that the court find, first "that the [particular] hospital is truly an essential resource, access to which is necessary for a competitor to compete effectively in the market place at all." At 1114. Second, the court would have to find that the privileges decision was controlled by the applicant's competitors; i.e. the medical staff, rather than the hospital's governing board.

If the "essential-facilities doctrine" is not applicable because of the absence of either of these two factors, the court is to refrain from further scrutiny of the hospital's action. If the "essential-facilities doctrine" applies, Havighurst argues that the court should subject the decisionmaking process to "strict requirements and close oversight" as to its procedures and substantive requirements. At 1123–1125. In cases in which there is evidence of concerted action between the hospital and the medical staff, the court should examine only "whether the collaboration * * * was structured to avoid undue risks to competition." At 1129. How would Havighurst's approach alter the analysis or result in *Weiss,* if at all? How does his approach differ from the Supreme Court's approach in *Northwest Wholesale?*

6. *Weiss* states that "the Medical Staff is * * * entitled to exclude individual doctors, including osteopaths, on the basis of their lack of professional competence or unprofessional conduct." Concerns over "professional competence or unprofessional conduct" are articulated in the record for most adverse credentialing decisions. How does a court distinguish those cases that violate the requirements of the antitrust laws from

those that are proper peer review actions? Can the distinction be made short of a full trial or must every case be tried?

Consider Miller v. Indiana Hospital, 843 F.2d 139 (3d Cir.1988):

Plaintiff Ralph J. Miller is a licensed physician and surgeon specializing in urology. He was a teaching fellow at the University of Pittsburgh for several years and has published numerous articles in the area of his medical specialty. He established a practice in Indiana, Pennsylvania in 1959 after obtaining staff privileges in the Department of Surgery at Indiana Hospital. Indiana Hospital is the only general hospital in the County of Indiana, a county with a population of approximately 93,000 persons and an area of 825 square miles.

According to the affidavits of Miller and others, the administrators of Indiana Hospital perceived Miller and his expansion plans as a threat to the hospital. [Miller had built a medical office building and a medical services building in which he offered laboratory and radiology services, allegedly in competition with the hospital, and in which he planned to establish a "comprehensive family-oriented medical center."] For example, William Peters, Administrator of the hospital in the 1960's, averred that in the mid–1960's Henry Hild, Chairman of the Board of the hospital, told Peters that he disliked Miller and was concerned about Miller's plans to expand his health care holdings. Robert Knight, Comptroller of the hospital in the early 1970's, averred that people within the hospital administration were fearful that Miller and his expansion plans posed a threat to the hospital and that they wanted to "gather sufficient medical staff support to keep Dr. Miller from hiring good doctors to staff his medical center." [ ] Don Gaydos, Director of Fiscal Services at the hospital in the early to mid 1970's averred that Donald Smith, President of the hospital, told Gaydos, "to befriend Dr. Miller so that I [Gaydos] could gather information on what and how Dr. Miller was planning as to expansion of his medical office building and his health care center so that I could report these things back to Mr. Smith." [ ]

In 1977, a patient under Miller's care at the hospital died. [A letter from a member of the medical staff's executive committee triggered an investigation.]

[After a three-day hearing], the hearing committee found that Miller had exhibited "disruptive, insulting, intimidating, disrespectful, disparaging, abusive and other improper behavior" toward various members of the staff; [ ] that he had acted improperly in the case of the deceased patient by failing to request a medical consultation, by failing to order certain tests, and by making improper entries in the patient's record; that he had failed to comply with an order of the Bureau of Medical Assistance barring him from writing Medical Assistance prescriptions; that he had acted unprofessionally by discussing confidential medical information with a layperson; and that he had failed to carry out certain administrative duties. [Miller's staff privileges were revoked.]

* * *

Miller filed an action against the hospital, alleging, *inter alia,* breach of contract, defects in the hearing proceedings, and Fourteenth Amendment due process violations. * * * The Superior Court of Pennsylvania affirmed the trial court's denial of injunctive relief, finding that "the charges against [Miller] were supported by sufficient evidence" and that Miller "was dismissed in a fair and impartial manner in accordance with the hospital bylaws." * * *

In 1977 and 1978, Miller applied for and was denied staff privileges. In 1979 the hospital refused even to consider his application for staff privileges for 1980, and for the next three years it refused even to furnish him with an application. [In 1981 Miller filed this antitrust suit.]

The district court * * * ruled that in order for a plaintiff physician to withstand summary judgment in an antitrust action arising out of a hospital's decision to terminate the physician's staff privileges, "the plaintiff must demonstrate on the basis of the record before the hospital at the time of its decision, that the hospital lacked substantial evidence in support of its ultimate decision." [ ] The court further stated that "whether there is substantial evidence to support the decision of the hospital committee to discharge a physician or to deny staff privileges to that physician is a question of law for a reviewing court and the resolution of that question need not await trial." [ ]

[T]he court found the requisite "substantial evidence." It therefore granted the hospital's motion for summary judgment, denied Miller's motion for summary judgment, and dismissed the pendent state law claims. [ ] Miller appeals.

* * * The hospital argues that because this court stated in *Weiss v. York Hospital,* that a medical staff "is * * * entitled to exclude individual doctors * * * on the basis of their lack of professional competence or unprofessional conduct," the threshold inquiry in an antitrust staff privilege case is the professional competency of the individual physician. The hospital misreads *Weiss.* Nothing in that case suggests that the usual antitrust inquiry may be avoided merely because the conspiracy alleged involves a hospital.

* * *

In this case, Miller contends that his hospital staff privileges were revoked and his applications for reinstatement denied because defendants wished to stifle his competition. He contends that the outcome of the hearing pursuant to which his privileges were revoked was predetermined and that he was treated more severely than other physicians whose competence was in question but who presented no economic threat to the defendants. Defendants' argument that they revoked Miller's staff privileges because of his professional incompetence and unprofessional conduct is a defense they may present before the jury which, if convinced, will absolve them of any antitrust liability. It is inappropriate and unprecedented, however, to pretermit the jury's consideration of the parties' various contentions under the rubric of the substantial evidence test. Such a test defers to the manner in which defendants themselves, who are parties in interest, weighed the evidence and drew inferences. Moreover, the substantial evidence test effectively eliminates any application of the antitrust laws to defendants' actions. It is apparent therefore that the district court erred as a matter of law in applying a substantial evidence test to determine if there were genuine issues of material fact to withstand summary judgment.

Miller concedes for the purpose of this appeal that a rule of reason analysis is applicable to the hospital's conduct. The hospital argues that its conduct was patently reasonable because Miller, after a full hearing approved by the state court, was found to have demonstrated professional incompetence and unprofessional conduct. However, Miller has produced evidence which, if believed by the jury, would show that, in fact, the hospital's revocation of his privileges, although ostensibly for professional incompetence and unprofessional conduct, was motivated by the anticompetitive purpose of destroying Miller's competition or prospective competition.

The affidavits of former hospital administrators, referred to above, provide evidence that even before the death of Miller's patient, the hospital expressed concern about Miller's competition. Miller's affidavit sets forth evidence of at least one example of the hospital's interference with his recruitment of medical staff for his proposed medical center by encouraging a pediatrician to break his contract with Miller; of its failure to terminate the staff privileges of other physicians whose professional infractions were allegedly more substantial than Miller's; and of irregularities and possible conflicts of interests in the hearing process itself, such as the fact that the presiding officer of the hearing was counsel for the hospital and that the chairman was a physician against whom Miller had previously filed charges of unethical conduct with the state board of licensure.

The evidence produced by Miller is sufficient to raise a genuine issue of material fact as to whether the hospital's conduct in revoking Miller's staff privileges was, as the hospital claims, because of his incompetence and hence a reasonable restraint or whether it was a result of anticompetitive motivation and thereby constituted a prohibited restraint of trade * * *.

For the foregoing reasons, we will reverse the district court's order granting the hospital's motion for summary judgment, and remand for further proceedings consistent with this opinion.

7. Dr. Miller was able to reach the jury because he had evidence that strongly indicated that the credentialing decision was intended to eliminate competition. Absent that evidence, should the case have reached the jury?

8. How should a jury be instructed in the *Miller* trial? Is the question strictly one of motive? Or was motive simply enough to reach the jury? What should the result be if the jury believes that the action was motivated both by anticompetitive animus and by the low quality of Miller's work? The rule of reason requires that anticompetitive effects be balanced against procompetitive effects, not against "good intentions." How can a rule-of-reason examination of a medical staff privileges decision accommodate legitimate quality issues? Clearly, a defendant hospital or

medical staff could claim that its concern for quality in a particular case has procompetitive effects. How could defendant prove this? Is there a difference between allowing a hospital or medical staff to claim its role in quality control as a defense and allowing a hospital to prove that its behavior in pursuing quality achieves procompetitive effects? See, Greaney, Quality of Care and Market Failure Defenses in Antitrust Health Care Litigation, 21 Conn.L.Rev. 605 (1989).

9. Hospitals seeking protection from antitrust scrutiny may restructure the credentialing process: "Because the primary focus on antitrust concern in this area lies with competitor collaboration that restrains trade, antitrust law should not impede a wide array of quality assurance mechanisms. [The author describes quality assurance programs controlled by and operated for the benefit of "third parties," including hospitals, in which the third party actually controls the decision while competitor-physicians provide information and expertise to the decisionmaker]. * * * Despite the availability of alternative means of structuring quality assurance mechanisms, competitor collaboration of the kind raising the most serious antitrust issue remains an important part of the health care industry." Greaney, Quality of Care and Market Failure Defenses in Antitrust Health Care Litigation, 21 Conn.L.Rev. 605, 605–606 (1989). Blumstein and Sloan suggest that hospitals re-orient the peer review process toward giving the facility's governing body real independence in credentialing decisions by treating medical staff decisions as recommendations; by using outside consultants; and by establishing a quality assurance plan that periodically audits performance rather than initiating investigations only upon receiving complaints. Blumstein and Sloan, Antitrust and Hospital Peer Review, 51 L. & Contemp.Probs. 7 (1988) What obstacles confront a hospital in restructuring its peer review process?

B. ANTITRUST IMMUNITY: HEALTH CARE QUALITY IMPROVEMENT ACT

AUSTIN v. McNAMARA

United States District Court, Central District of California, 1990.
731 F.Supp. 934.

GADBOIS, DISTRICT JUDGE.

Plaintiff George M. Austin, M.D. ("Dr. Austin"), is a neurosurgeon and brings this action alleging violations of the Sherman Antitrust Act, 15 U.S.C.A. §§ 1, 2 (1982), * * * against five individual physicians and the Santa Barbara Cottage Hospital ("Cottage Hospital"). Plaintiff's claims arise out of the alleged conspiracy and concerted actions of the individual Defendant physicians to shut down Dr. Austin's neurosurgery practice in Santa Barbara by having his staff privileges suspended at Cottage Hospital.

* * * Defendant Cottage Hospital brings the "main" Summary Judgment Motion, asserting that it is immune from federal antitrust liability by virtue of the provisions of the Health Care Quality Improve-

ment Act of 1986 ("HCQIA"), 42 U.S.C.A. §§ 11101 et seq. (West Supp.1989).

[T]he Court grants the Summary Judgment Motions of the Defendants Cottage Hospital, Dr. Jones, and Dr. St. John for the reasons enumerated below.

FACTUAL BACKGROUND

* * *

When Plaintiff arrived in Santa Barbara in 1981, there were only three other practicing neurosurgeons in the area, Defendants Dr. Brown, Dr. St. John, and Dr. Schweinfurth. The patient-to-neurosurgeon ratio in Santa Barbara was already close to saturation when Plaintiff arrived to set up shop. Defendant Dr. Jones came to Santa Barbara a few months after the Plaintiff and established his own neurosurgery practice.

* * *

Dr. Austin alleges in his Complaint that although the Defendant neurosurgeons often "covered" patients for each other, shortly after his arrival, all of them refused to "cover" for the Plaintiff. In his deposition, however, Dr. Austin admits that Defendants Dr. Brown, Dr. Jones, and Dr. Schweinfurth did in fact "cover" for him, but only a few times over a seven-year period. Defendant Dr. St. John is the only one who has refused to "cover" for the Plaintiff from the outset and has never done so. In October of 1986, Dr. Brown sent the Plaintiff a letter confirming that he would never "cover" for Dr. Austin again.

The Plaintiff admits that "covering" patients for other physicians is merely professional courtesy and that there is no legal or ethical obligation to do so. With the exception of Dr. St. John, the other Defendant neurosurgeons testified in their depositions that they "covered" for the Plaintiff when their schedules allowed them to, and attributed any refusals to scheduling conflicts or last-minute notice. Plaintiff Dr. Austin admits that he has refused to "cover" or assist the various Defendant neurosurgeons on occasion due to scheduling conflicts.

As additional evidence of the conspiracy against him, Plaintiff alleges that Defendants Dr. Jones and Dr. St. John "openly demeaned [his] work to nurses on staff at Cottage Hospital in order to develop animosity over [sic] him." Dr. Austin also contends that the Defendant neurosurgeons would "aggressively attack" his judgment at various monthly Cottage Hospital neurosurgical group meetings. The Defendant neurosurgeons counter that there were legitimate concerns with the Plaintiff's treatment of patients at Cottage Hospital.

* * *

On January 29, 1986, Defendant Dr. McNamara, as Chief of Staff, informed Plaintiff that an internal evaluation of his cases would take place. This was done in response to concerns expressed by the nursing and technical staffs, as well as Dr. Austin's colleagues, about the quality of care some of the Plaintiff's patients were receiving. Defendant Dr. McNamara instructed his Chief of Surgery, Defendant Dr. Brown, to review all of the Plaintiff's cases in 1985.

On April 24, 1986, Defendant Dr. Brown presented his findings to Cottage Hospital's Surgical Audit Committee ("SAC"). Defendant Dr. Schweinfurth sat as a member of the SAC. In his presentation, Dr. Brown outlined what he perceived to be deficiencies in 26 out of the 30 cases handled by the Plaintiff in 1985. Dr. Brown also presented three additional "problematic" cases from 1986 to the SAC. The SAC voted to have an outside reviewer further evaluate Dr. Austin's charts and to continue monitoring his work.

On June 10, 1986, Chief of Staff Dr. McNamara requested Cottage Hospital's Medical Executive Committee ("MEC") to establish an *Ad Hoc* Committee ("AHC") of five doctors to investigate concerns voiced by the staff that Plaintiff Dr. Austin was providing substandard care to his patients at the Hospital. Defendant Dr. Jones served on the AHC which met four times between June 25, 1986 and August 15, 1986 to discuss the possible revocation of Plaintiff's staff privileges at Cottage Hospital.

In addition to the internal investigation by the AHC, Defendant Dr. McNamara also had an external, independent review conducted by Dr. Sidney Tolchin and Dr. David G. Sheetz, two neurosurgeons appointed by the California Medical Association. Dr. Tolchin and Dr. Sheetz spent a day at Cottage Hospital talking to various staff members and reviewing Dr. Austin's charts. The outside reviewers also spent an hour and a half interviewing Dr. Austin himself. Both Dr. Tolchin and Dr. Sheetz gave the Plaintiff a generally favorable evaluation, but both expressed serious concerns in some areas and recommended further monitoring.

[A]fter considering the findings of the independent reviewers, the *Ad Hoc* Committee voted to establish a six-month period of monitoring of the Plaintiff's cases by the Surgical Audit Committee. As a member of the AHC, Defendant Dr. Jones recommended and voted for the continued monitoring. From August 15, 1986 to November 16, 1986, five of the Plaintiff's cases were reviewed by the SAC. Defendant Dr. St. John reviewed three cases and Defendants Dr. Brown and Dr. Jones reviewed one each.

On November 17, 1986, Defendant Dr. McNamara, as Chief of Staff, informed Plaintiff that his staff privileges at Cottage Hospital were summarily suspended. This action was taken after Dr. McNamara had presented certain cases handled by Dr. Austin to the Medical Executive Committee. These cases had been monitored by members of the SAC since early October of 1986. On November 19, 1986, Plaintiff appeared before the MEC to defend his actions in the three cases that Defendant Dr. St. John had reviewed and found substandard, as well as the case of patient C.P. that Defendant Dr. Jones declared substandard. Following the discussion, the MEC passed a motion recommending to the Board of Directors corrective action to revoke the clinical privileges of Dr. Austin. * * *

In a letter dated December 3, 1986 ("December 3rd Letter"), Dr. Robert A. Reid, Vice President of the Medical Staff, advised Plaintiff that the reason for the recommendation was that his professional conduct was lower than the applicable standard of practice. The December 3rd Letter set out 14 specific categories of allegedly substandard practice with patient chart numbers designated as to each specification. The December 3rd Letter alleges 103 instances of substandard professional conduct on the part of Dr. Austin.

* * *

Plaintiff Dr. Austin's suspension from Cottage Hospital lasted approximately seven months, from November 19, 1986 to June 3, 1987. During this time, Plaintiff continued to enjoy staff privileges at several other local hospitals including St. Francis, Goleta Valley, Santa Ynez, Lompoc, and Ojai. Plaintiff continued to see patients during this time period and performed neurosurgery at St. Francis Hospital while suspended from Cottage Hospital.

Plaintiff requested and received a hearing before the Judicial Review Committee ("JRC") to appeal the revocation of his staff privileges. The JRC was comprised of six impartial doctors and the Honorable William Reppy, retired Justice of the California Appeals Court presided over the hearings. Plaintiff admits that he was given adequate time to prepare and present all the witnesses and evidence he desired.

Both sides were represented by counsel at the JRC hearings * * *

* * * The JRC found that the MEC's decision to revoke the Plaintiff's staff privileges "was unreasonable" and reinstated Dr. Austin to the Cottage Hospital medical staff. The JRC's findings, however, were far short of complete vindication for the Plaintiff. The JRC found Dr. Austin's treatment of patient C.P. to be "below the applicable standard" and expressed concern in several other areas.

In reinstating the Plaintiff, the JRC concluded "that the totality of problems reasonably warrants some appropriate conditions on the continued exercise of clinical privileges by Dr. Austin." Specifically, the JRC recommended to the Board of Directors of Cottage Hospital:

[t]hat the continued exercise of clinical privileges by Dr. Austin be conditioned in two respects:

1) for assurance of proper patient management, that Dr. Austin obtain Internal Medicine, Pathology and Radiological procedural consultations;

2) that there be periodical outside independent neurosurgical case review. The Committee feels that it has been demonstrated that

objective monitoring by the neurosurgeons of Cottage Hospital could not be done.

While the Plaintiff attempts to gloss over these conditions on his staff privileges in his papers, there is no question that these are significant restrictions that are out of the ordinary for a surgeon of Plaintiff's experience.

* * *

CONCLUSIONS OF LAW

The Court finds no genuine issue of material fact precluding the application of the Health Care Quality Improvement Act of 1986 ("HCQIA"), 42 U.S.C.A. §§ 11101 et seq., to this action. As a matter of law, the Court holds that all five of the individual doctor Defendants, as well as Defendant Cottage Hospital, qualify for immunity from federal antitrust liability pursuant to the provisions of the HCQIA. * * *

II. Requirements to Qualify for Immunity Under the HCQIA

The Defendants can qualify for immunity under the HCQIA if they can demonstrate that:

A) the professional review actions complied with the standards set forth in 42 U.S.C.A. § 11112;

B) the results of the professional review actions were properly reported to the State authorities in compliance with 42 U.S.C.A. §§ 11131(c)(1), 11151(2);

C) the professional review actions occurred on, or after November 14, 1986, the effective date of the HCQIA.

As detailed below, the Defendants have successfully shown that both professional review actions have complied with each of these three requirements.

A. Standards for Professional Review Actions

1. Section 11112(a)(1) Analysis

In order to satisfy the due process requirements as outlined in 42 U.S.C.A. § 11112(a)(1)–(4),[5] the Defendants must first show that the professional review actions were taken "in the reasonable belief that the action was in the furtherance of quality health care." § 11112(a)(1).

5. Section 11112(a) provides in pertinent part:

"(a) In General

For purposes of the protection set forth in section 11111(a) of this title, a professional review action must be taken—

(1) in the reasonable belief that the action was in the furtherance of quality health care,

(2) after a reasonable effort to obtain the facts of the matter,

(3) after adequate notice and hearing procedures are afforded to the physician involved or after such other procedures as are fair to the physician under the circumstances,

(4) in the reasonable belief that the action was warranted by the facts known after such reasonable effort to obtain facts and after meeting the requirement of paragraph (3)."

With regards to the November 19th MEC Meeting, the Court is satisfied that the MEC voted to revoke the Plaintiff's staff privileges in the interest of furthering quality health care at Cottage Hospital. The Defendant doctors came to believe that the Plaintiff's treatment in various cases was below the acceptable standard of care at Cottage Hospital through their own observations and from concerns voiced by the nursing and technical staffs. This concern for patient safety prompted nearly ten months' worth of both internal and external evaluations and monitoring of the Plaintiff's cases conducted by the Defendant neurosurgeons and other members of Cottage Hospital's Surgical Audit Committee and *Ad Hoc* Committee, as well as the two neurosurgeons appointed by the California Medical Association who had no connection to Cottage Hospital. All of the findings from these numerous evaluations and periods of monitoring were considered before the MEC voted to revoke the Plaintiff's staff privileges.

The Court also finds that the JRC Hearings were conducted "in the reasonable belief that the action was in furtherance of quality health care." § 11112(a)(1). After hearing over 70 hours of testimony at the JRC Hearings that extended from March 16, 1987 to May 14, 1987, the independent panel of five voting (six physicians sat on the panel during the hearings) physicians concluded that "the totality of problems reasonably warrants some appropriate conditions on the continued exercise of clinical privileges by Dr. Austin." JRC Final Report, at 3. The nature of the conditions placed on Plaintiff's reinstatement, that he obtain consultations in internal medicine, pathology, and radiology, and that his cases be periodically monitored by outside independent neurosurgeons, demonstrates that it was the JRC's intent to "restrict incompetent behavior" and "protect patients" through their recommendations.

2. *Section 11112(a)(2) Analysis*

The Defendants must next demonstrate that there was a "reasonable effort to obtain the facts of the matter" before the professional review actions were undertaken. § 11112(a)(2). As more fully detailed in the Factual Background section, the November 19th MEC Meeting was the culmination of nearly ten months' worth of evaluations and monitoring of the Plaintiff's work. These reviews were conducted internally by the Defendant neurosurgeons as well as the other physicians on Cottage Hospital's Surgical Audit Committee and *Ad Hoc* Committee.

A comprehensive, external review of the Plaintiff's work was conducted by Dr. Tolchin and Dr. Sheetz, two independent neurosurgeons appointed by the California Medical Association. These outside reviewers spent an entire day at Cottage Hospital reviewing the Plaintiff's charts as well as interviewing officials of the hospital staff and Dr. Austin himself. With regards to the JRC Hearings, Dr. Austin admits that he was allowed adequate time to prepare and was able to present all of the witnesses and evidence he desired to the panel. The Court concludes that both the November 19th MEC Meeting and the JRC Hearings were preceded by very diligent efforts to gather the relevant facts in compliance with Section 11112(a)(2).

3. *Section 11112(a)(3) Analysis*

Section 11112(a)(3) requires that the professional review actions comply with the due process requirements of "adequate notice and hearing" in order to merit immunity.[6] The notice procedures outlined in § 11112(b)(1)–(2) contemplate the professional review action being initiated by the health care entity, thereby necessitating adequate notice to the targeted physician. The facts of this case however, are somewhat unique in that Plaintiff requested a second professional review action, the JRC Hearings, to appeal the outcome of an earlier professional review action, the November 19th MEC Meeting.

While the legislative history indicates that "[t]he due process requirement can always be met by the procedures specified in [§ 11112(b)]," 1986 U.S.Code Cong. & Admin.News, at 6393, both the text of § 11112(b) and the legislative history agree that these procedures need not be followed to the letter in order to satisfy the due process requirement. Taking into consideration the factual twist in this case, the Court concludes that under these circumstances, the closing paragraph of the December 3rd Letter gave Plaintiff sufficient notice of the JRC Hearings.

The Court further finds that the JRC Hearings were conducted in compliance with the procedures outlined in § 11112(b)(3)(A)–(D), thereby satisfying the "adequate hearing" requirement of subsection (a)(3). First off, Plaintiff admits that he was afforded a "fair and impartial hearing." The JRC Hearings were held before a panel of six impartial, independent physicians appointed by the Cottage Hospital, none of whom were in direct economic competition with the Plaintiff. § 11112(b)(3)(A)(iii).

Dr. Austin was represented throughout the hearings by counsel and all of the proceedings were recorded by court reporters and 12 volumes of transcripts were produced. § 11112(b)(3)(C)(i), (ii). Plaintiff admits that he was given the opportunity to call witnesses and to present all of the evidence he desired. § 11112(b)(3)(C)(iii), (iv). Plaintiff submitted a written statement at the close of the hearings on June 15, 1987, and the JRC issued its final report and recommendations along with the underlying reasoning on June 30, 1987. §§ 11112(b)(3)(C)(v), 11112(b)(3)(D)(i).

The Court finds that the initial professional review action, the November 19th MEC Meeting, satisfies the subsection (a)(3) due process requirement by virtue of § 11112(c)(2), which allows "an immediate suspension or restriction of clinical privileges, subject to subsequent

---

6. Section 11112(a)(3) provides that in order for a professional review action to merit immunity, it must be taken: "(3) after adequate notice and hearing proce-   dures are afforded to the physician involved or after such other procedures as are fair to the physician under the circumstances * * *."

notice and hearing * * * where the failure to take such an action may result in imminent danger to the health of an individual." The legislative history reveals that "[t]he Committee felt strongly that it was necessary to establish these exceptions * * * to allow quick action where it would be reasonable to conclude that someone's health might otherwise suffer." 1986 U.S.Code Cong. & Admin.News, at 6394.

While the Court acknowledges that the JRC eventually found the revocation of Plaintiff's staff privileges to be "unreasonable," it must be noted that the JRC reached this conclusion only after considering over 70 hours of testimony in a series of hearings that lasted two months. The Court is convinced that based on the information available at the time of the special meeting on November 19, 1986, it was reasonable for the MEC to conclude that the health of Dr. Austin's patients "might otherwise suffer" unless immediate action was taken. This conclusion finds support in the fact that the JRC found Dr. Austin's treatment of patient C.P. to be substandard, expressed concerns regarding the treatment of other patients, and placed significant restrictions on Plaintiff's continued exercise of clinical privileges at Cottage Hospital. The Court further finds that the December 3rd Letter and the JRC Hearings satisfy the "subsequent notice and hearing" component of § 11112(c)(2).
* * *

Plaintiff's Inability to Rebut the Presumption of Immunity Created by Section 11112(a)

As outlined above, the Defendants have successfully demonstrated that both professional review actions at issue in this case warrant immunity under the HCQIA because both have satisfied the standards set forth in Section 11112(a)(1)–(4). The burden is now on the Plaintiff to rebut this showing, as Section 11112(a) declares that "A professional review action shall be presumed to have met the preceding standards necessary for the protection set out in section 11111(a) of this title unless the presumption is rebutted by a preponderance of the evidence."

The Plaintiff has failed to even address, much less rebut, the Defendants' evidentiary showing. Despite the fact that all three Defendants seeking summary judgment argue for immunity under the HCQIA in their moving papers, the Plaintiff's consolidated opposition papers make no mention of the statute. The Plaintiff does not attempt to refute or contest any of the Defendants' efforts to apply the immunity provisions of the HCQIA to the facts of this case. The Court finds the Plaintiff's naked allegations of a conspiracy against him, based largely on the Defendant neurosurgeons' refusals to cover for him and unsubstantiated hearsay, insufficient to rebut the presumption of immunity conferred on the professional review actions.

B.   Compliance With the HCQIA's Reporting Requirements

[The court finds that the hospital made the required reports.]
* * *

Notes and Questions

1. The Health Care Quality Improvement Act provides immunity for "damages under any law of the United States or of any State (or political subdivision thereof)." Plaintiffs may bring actions for injunctive relief. The Act excludes from the scope of the immunity actions "relating to the civil rights of any person or persons." The Act also does not provide immunity for actions relating to "nurses, other licensed health care practitioners, or other health professionals who are not physicians."

2. Would the defendants in *Weiss* and *Miller* be entitled to immunity under the Act? Why or why not? Did the court in *Austin* do what the trial court in *Miller* had attempted? If not, what was different?

3. On the application of the Health Care Quality Improvement Act immunity provisions see, Blumstein and Sloan, Antitrust and Hospital Peer Review, 51 L. & Contemp.Probs. 7 (1988); Bierig and Portman, The Health Care Quality Improvement Act of 1986, 32 St. Louis U.Law J. 977 (1988). For a comprehensive legislative history of the statute, see Reams, The Health Care Quality Improvement Act of 1986: A Legislative History of Pub.L. 99–660 (1990).

Part of the impetus for this statute, insofar as it applies to antitrust immunity, was litigation arising from a denial of staff privileges in which the jury awarded Dr. Timothy Patrick $650,000 (which was trebled by the District Court) for antitrust violations by several physicians, as individuals and as partners in a primary care clinic, during the peer review process; $20,000 in compensatory and $90,000 in punitive damages against the physicians on a state law claim; and $228,600 in attorney's fees. Patrick came to Astoria, Oregon, a town of 10,000, and became an employee of the Astoria Clinic. The majority of the medical staff of the local hospital were employees or partners of the Astoria Clinic. When Patrick refused an offer of partnership in the Clinic, Clinic physicians stopped referring patients to Patrick, a surgeon; refused to provide back-up or consultation services; and criticized Patrick for failing to secure consultations and back-up.

On appeal, however, the Ninth Circuit Court of Appeals reversed the judgment, holding that the physicians' activities in the staff privileges decision at the hospital (as well as the participation of one of the defendant physicians as a member of the state's Board of Medical Examiners) were exempt from antitrust liability under the state action doctrine. Patrick v. Burget, 800 F.2d 1498 (9th Cir.1986). The state action doctrine requires that the conduct [in this case, staff privileges decisions] "must be taken pursuant to a clearly articulated and affirmatively expressed state policy and must be subject to active supervision by the state." Id. at 1505. The Court found that the staff privileges process met this standard. Because the state action doctrine applied, according to the Court, the fact that there was strong evidence that the physicians had acted in bad faith was irrelevant. The Court of Appeals reversed the decision as to the state law claim as well for the District Court's failure to instruct the jury as to immunities available under state law for the activities complained of and remanded the case to the District Court.

The Supreme Court reversed the Ninth Circuit in Patrick v. Burget, 108 S.Ct. 1658 (1988). The Supreme Court, in a unanimous decision, held that the staff privileges process in *Patrick* was not immune under state action because the anticompetitive conduct was not "actively supervised by the State itself." At 1663.

The Court defined active supervision as requiring that the state review and disapprove of acts not in accord with state policy. The defendants in *Patrick,* according to the Court, failed to prove that the state's Health Division, the Board of Medical Examiners or the state judicial system "reviews—or even could review—private decisions regarding hospital privileges to determine whether such decisions comport with state regulatory policy and to correct abuses." At 1663. In regard to judicial review as active supervision, the Court stated that it would not decide "the broad question whether judicial review of private conduct even can constitute active supervision, because judicial review of privilege-termination decisions in Oregon, if such review exists at all, falls far short of satisfying the active supervision requirement." At 1665.

The Court noted that no state statute in Oregon required judicial review and that the Oregon courts had not clearly stated that judicial review was available. The Oregon courts in fact, had stated that a court should not review the merits of a dismissal and that a court should only require that some reasonable procedure occur and that there be evidence which support a finding that there was a threat to patient care. At 1665.

Several circuits have since refused to extend state action immunity to staff privileges decisions. See, for example, Bolt v. Halifax Hosp. Medical Center, 891 F.2d 810 (11th Cir.1990) (The Eleventh Circuit Court of Appeals had held Florida peer review exempt under the state action doctrine. At 851 F.2d 1273. The Court vacated its decision, at 861 F.2d 1233 (1988), and on en banc reargument, defendants dropped their claim of state action immunity.); Tambone v. Memorial Hospital, 825 F.2d 1132 (7th Cir.1987) (Illinois); Pinhas v. Summit Health, Ltd., 880 F.2d 1108, 894 F.2d 1094 (9th Cir.1989), cert. granted, ___ U.S. ___, 110 S.Ct. 3212, 110 L.Ed.2d 660 (1990) [on an unrelated issue].

II. PRIVATE ACCREDITATION AND PROFESSIONAL ORGANIZATIONS

One of the most challenging problems in antitrust litigation over the policies and rules of private accreditation and professional organizations is the relevance of "quality-of-care" justifications. Although antitrust analysis explicitly considers only the competitive effects of the association's challenged canons, evidence of quality goals frequently enters the process, sometimes appropriately and sometimes not.

KOEFOOT v. AMERICAN COLLEGE OF SURGEONS

United States District Court, Northern District of Illinois, 1985.
610 F.Supp. 1298.

ROVNER, DISTRICT JUDGE.

The controversy in this case centers around the "itinerant surgery" rule of the defendant American College of Surgeons ("ACS"). That rule defines itinerant surgery as follows:

The performance of surgical operations (except on patients whose chances of recovery would be prejudiced by removal to another hospital) under circumstances in which the responsibility for diagnosis or care of the patient is delegated to another who is not fully qualified to undertake it.

In practice, the rule essentially requires that a surgeon who does not undertake the post-operative care of a patient himself may only delegate that care to another surgeon.

Plaintiffs are Robert Koefoot ("Dr. Koefoot"), a surgeon residing in the metropolitan area of Grand Island, Nebraska; three local hospitals in the vicinity of Grand Island at which Dr. Koefoot performs surgery; and three general practitioners to whom Dr. Koefoot delegates post-operative care for his patients at the plaintiff hospitals. Defendants are the ACS and two of its executives, Dr. C. Rollins Hanlon and Dr. Frank Padberg.

In Count I of the complaint, plaintiffs allege that the defendants combined, conspired, or contracted to restrain trade and commerce in violation of Section 1 of the Sherman Act, 15 U.S.C. § 1, by adopting and enforcing the itinerant surgery rule. Dr. Koefoot was suspended in June, 1979 and expelled one year later by the ACS for his violation of that rule.

* * *

Plaintiffs provide medical care in the State of Nebraska, largely a rural state consisting of 92 counties, comprising approximately 70,000 square miles. In 1980, there were approximately 2,300 doctors in Nebraska, of whom 181 were general surgeons such as Dr. Koefoot. Over 70% of the state's population resides in 21 of the 92 counties, located in and around the major cities of Omaha and Lincoln. Those 21 counties had 89% of the physician population, leaving only 247 physicians to serve the remaining 71 counties with their 457,000 residents. The state has 116 hospitals. The area outside that known as the "Fish Hook" has only 247 physicians to serve over 63,000 square miles and 450,000 people, a ratio of 1,850 people per doctor. * * *

According to the plaintiffs, the ACS is the largest, oldest, most prestigious, and most influential surgical organization and accrediting body in the world. At the end of 1982, its membership included more than 46,000 surgeons; in 1980, more than 60% of Board Certified surgeons in the United States were members of the ACS. Membership as a Fellow of the ACS commands considerable prestige within the medical profession and provides assurance to the patient that the Fellow is fully qualified in the field of surgery. In 1983, the ACS had total assets of $26 million, budgeted receipts of over $13 million, and an endowment fund of more than $11 million, thereby indicating that it has substantial financial power. The ACS also influences medical education through programs in medical schools and through its service as the accrediting organization for residency review programs in several surgical areas. It plays a considerable role in Board Certification. It is involved in the accreditation process of thousands of hospitals and other health treatment facilities. Most importantly, the ACS has substantial influence on hospital staff privileges for surgeons. A statement issued by the ACS places special emphasis on either Board Certification or Fellowship in the ACS as a minimum requirement for surgical staff privileges. That statement was adopted by the Joint Commission On Accreditation Of Hospitals.

Dr. Koefoot is a general surgeon who practices surgery at each of three hospitals in Grand Island, Nebraska, a city of 45,000 people. He also practices surgery currently at two of the plaintiff hospitals, Howard County Community Hospital in St. Paul, Nebraska, and Litzenberg Memorial County Hospital in Central City, Nebraska. * * * Grand Island falls within the area of Nebraska known as the "Fish Hook," but the three plaintiff hospitals are located in counties that fall outside the "Fish Hook."

* * *

After surgery in one of the hospitals located in Grand Island, Dr. Koefoot manages the post-operative care of his surgical patients by seeing them at least once daily. * * *

For operations performed at the plaintiff hospitals, typically less complex and more routine than those he performs at the Grand Island hospitals, Dr. Koefoot schedules elective surgery generally from 3:00 a.m. to 5:30 a.m. so that he can return to Grand Island for surgery scheduled there at 7:30 a.m. His travel time to either of the plaintiff hospitals at which he currently operates is approximately 20 minutes. He generally arrives at these hospitals approximately 30 minutes before the scheduled surgery and is assisted at the surgery by the general practitioner plaintiff who referred the case. Dr. Koefoot sees the patient following the surgery in the recovery room and writes post-operative orders but then delegates the post-operative management of his surgical patient to the referring general practitioner plaintiff. Dr. Koefoot does not see the patient post-operatively unless he is in the community for another purpose or unless the referring physician believes it is necessary.

* * *

Dr. Koefoot's expulsion from the ACS resulted from his own admissions to the College regarding the nature of his surgical practice in 1978. His associate, Dr. William Fowles, had applied to the College for Fellowship. The College deferred Dr. Fowles' application for one year pending further investigation because it appeared from his application that he was engaging in the practice of itinerant surgery. Dr. Koefoot's protests against the deferral of Dr. Fowles' application led to a series of communications with the ACS in which Dr. Koefoot admitted that he himself delegated the post-operative care of his surgical patients at the plaintiff hospitals to the referring general practitioners and did not see those patients post-operatively. * * * Dr. Koefoot's position essentially is that it is not necessary for him personally to manage the post-operative care of patients for whom he performs surgery at the plaintiff hospitals because the general practitioner plaintiffs who refer those patients to him are sufficiently competent to do so. According to Dr. Koefoot, his position is supported by his extremely low rate of post-operative complications in the 25 years he has been performing surgery, and he thus believes the facts justify his contention that the general practitioner plaintiffs are as qualified as surgeons to monitor the post-operative care of his patients. Not surprisingly, the position of the ACS is that Dr. Koefoot's practice violates its rule against itinerant surgery, a rule which it maintains is designed to assure the highest quality post-operative care to surgical patients of Fellows who are members of the ACS. It has been the consistent position of the ACS that a physician is not fully qualified to assume responsibility for the post-operative management of a surgical patient unless he is as well qualified as the operating surgeon. The ACS maintains that Dr. Koefoot's point that he does not routinely see his patients post-operatively at the plaintiff hospitals because it is unnecessary for him to do so and because he does not have time is in fact motivated by economic considerations. The position of the ACS is succinctly set forth as follows:

> The College believes that the surgeon has a moral, ethical and legal obligation to give patients upon whom he has operated his personal attention, and to attend his patients post-operatively. If Dr. Koefoot chooses not to drive 20 miles to [plaintiff hospitals] to see his patients, if Dr. Koefoot disagrees with the College policy, or if Dr. Koefoot chooses to spend his time on pursuits other than surgery, that is his perfect right. But he may not call himself a Fellow of the American College of Surgeons. [ ]

Thus, while plaintiffs characterize the itinerant surgery rule as the method by which the ACS has inhibited the ability of rural community hospitals to compete with hospitals in major metropolitan areas, of surgeons in Dr. Koefoot's position to compete with local surgeons, and of general practitioners to compete with surgeons in the provision of post-operative care, the ACS has defended the rule by asserting ethical motivations for its promulgation out of a concern for the public welfare. It is readily apparent that a dispute of fact exists over the motive of the ACS in promulgating the itinerant surgery rule. * * *

[S]ufficient evidence exists that the itinerant surgery rule may be *per se* illegal as a horizontal market allocation. Plaintiffs have attached documents as exhibits to their brief opposing the motion for summary judgment which suggest that at least one of the purposes of the itinerant surgery rule was to protect young surgeons residing in a community from outside competition. * * * On its face, the rule certainly seems to allow local surgeons to block competition with visiting surgeons by refusing to accept responsibility for post-operative care of patients. Defendants point out that there are no local surgeons residing in the communities in which Dr. Koefoot practices itinerant surgery. But that fact is irrelevant to whether the itinerant surgery rule sets up a horizontal allocation of markets because the rule may well be working in reverse as well: it may prevent surgeons from establishing residence in rural communities by prohibiting them from caring for patients in other rural communities and in metropolitan areas. The rule also prohibits general practitioners from competing with surgeons for post-operative treatment. Finally, it purportedly inhibits competition between local hospitals and metropolitan hospitals for surgical patients. Indeed, plaintiffs characterize the rule as a threat to the ability of local hospitals to survive and to the practice of medicine in rural communities in general because of the vital necessity of having adequate surgical services.

* * *

Plaintiffs argue here that there is sufficient evidence from which a jury can conclude that conduct constituting a *per se* violation has occurred. Nonetheless, plaintiffs concede that the issue is one for the jury to decide:

> Since conduct which would constitute per se violations could be found by the jury, the procedure at trial [as defined in *Wilk,*] is for the jury to determine what the College's motive was for the rule and Dr. Koefoot's expulsion; the "money motive", the "public interest" motive or the "patient care" motive. If the jury determines that the "money motive" was predominant, it can go on to determine if conduct constituting a per se offense existed. Contrarily, if the "patient care" motive predominated, the jury could consider only the rule of reason issues.

Although evidence exists that the itinerant surgery rule is indeed motivated by a concern for patient care, this Court finds that an insufficient record exists at this time by which a decision may be reached as to whether a *per se* analysis or a rule of reason analysis is applicable to this case. The Court need not reach this question, however, because, on the defendants' motion for summary judgment, it is clear that an issue of material fact exists over the ACS' motive in promulgating the itinerant surgery rule. * * *

Antitrust Injury

Only those who have suffered an injury of a kind that the antitrust laws are designed to prevent may seek relief under Section 4 of the Clayton Act.

* * *

The defendants contend that the record demonstrates that Dr. Koefoot has not been hampered by the rule against itinerant surgery in his ability to perform surgery at the rural plaintiff hospitals because his practice in those hospitals has continued unaffected by his expulsion as a Fellow of the ACS. The general practitioner plaintiffs continue to refer their surgical patients to him regardless of whether the surgery is performed at a plaintiff hospital or in Grand Island. Moreover, Dr. Koefoot has not been prevented from practicing surgery in the plaintiff hospitals; nor has he been denied staff privileges at any hospital despite his expulsion from the ACS. Fellowship in the ACS is not a prerequisite to the practice of surgery in any state, and his exclusion as a Fellow did not affect his surgical privileges at any hospital in Grand Island or at the plaintiff hospitals. Indeed, defendants contend that to the extent that Fellows of the ACS who compete with Dr. Koefoot and who are still subject to the itinerant surgery rule spend more time providing care for their patients after surgery personally, Dr. Koefoot's competitive position may actually be strengthened. In addition, the defendants contend that the record demonstrates that Dr. Koefoot's expulsion has not prevented him from association with Fellows of the College, from taking advantage of the educational and scientific programs of the College, and from maintaining his reputation as a surgeon of the "highest order."

Plaintiffs respond by referring to the great degree of prestige associated with being a Fellow of the ACS and the associated referrals engendered therefrom. The ACS receives numerous calls requesting referrals to surgeons, who, quite naturally, are referred to ACS members. Moreover, plaintiffs emphasize the importance of ACS membership in obtaining staff privileges at hospitals.

In addition, plaintiffs emphasize that expulsion from membership injured Dr. Koefoot's reputation. First, Dr. Koefoot lost the services of his associate, Dr. Fowles, who refused to continue performing surgery at the plaintiff hospitals when he was faced with deferral and possible denial of his ACS application. According to Dr. Koefoot, he subsequently encountered significant problems in finding a replacement for Dr. Fowles. Second, at the time of the disciplinary action, one of his fellow Regents on the Board of Regents of the University of Nebraska, Dr. Robert Prokop, called for Dr. Koefoot's impeachment or resignation as a Regent. Third, Dr. Koefoot has allegedly been injured in his ability to act as an expert witness in surgical matters in litigation. Before 1978, Dr. Koefoot testified ten to fifteen times per year; after the disciplinary charges were brought, his expert witness testimony has decreased to three to four times per year. Opposing counsel has raised his suspension and expulsion from the ACS as impeachment of his credentials when Dr. Koefoot has testified. Fourth, surgeons who formerly sought Dr. Koefoot's advice and counsel, including the President of the Nebraska Medical Association, will not speak to him today.

More importantly for purposes of this motion, plaintiffs allege that the level of Dr. Koefoot's referrals from other physicians has declined since his suspension and expulsion from the ACS. * * * Dr. Koefoot, of course, will be required strictly to establish at trial that the level of his referrals and income has decreased as a direct result of his expulsion from the ACS. * * *

* * * Because this Court finds that a material dispute of fact exists as to the existence of antitrust injury, and because it declines to find on the state of the present record that any such injury is purely speculative or conjectural, defendants' motion for summary judgment as to plaintiffs' claims for injunctive relief under general equitable principles and under Section 16 of the Clayton Act, 15 U.S.C. § 26, is * * * denied.

Notes and Questions

1. The policy against itinerant surgery at issue in *Koefoot* began with the publication in 1877 of Joseph Lister's results with the antiseptic postsurgical treatment of amputations. Lister's results indicated that post-operative dressings should be subject to the same level of antiseptic controls as the surgery itself. This work proved that "rigorous post-operative care by surgeons was essential to the well-being of their patients. No longer could they turn them over to the dressers or general practitioners once the operation was finished." This fact also made the surgeon "the leading power in the hospital itself." Thompson, "The Uneasy Alliance," in Physicians and Hospitals 13–14 (Duke Univ. Press 1985).

The court in *Koefoot* stated that the "motive" of ACS in promulgating the itinerant surgery rule would determine the question of whether a rule of reason or *per se* analysis should be used to judge the acceptability of the rule. The court held that a material issue of fact existed as to ACS' motive. How would you prove whether ACS has a substantial patient care motive or a "money motive" in this case?

2. The District Court again had an opportunity to rule on motions in *Koefoot* in December, 1986, this time resolving the issues of 1) the application of the *per se* rule v. the rule of reason; 2) the use of the patient care defense; and 3) the relevance of the motive behind the rule. 1987–1 CCH Trade Cases ¶ 67,508.

As to the *per se*/rule of reason issue, the court commented that "plaintiffs have attempted to force the defendants' conduct into three separate *per se* categories—horizontal allocation of markets, tying arrangements, and group boycotts. * * * In their relentless pursuit of categorization, the plaintiffs have failed to detect a consistent theme present in cases applying the antitrust laws to the professions." The court reviewed the leading Supreme Court cases involving the professions and concluded that "rule of reason analysis is appropriate when facially legitimate ethical canons are challenged under the Sherman Act. [This] Court defines facially legitimate ethical canons as being rules of professional practice which, on their face, establish professional standards of care without reference to the economic interests of the professionals. * * * The Court further holds that the ACS itinerant surgery rule, both by its terms and by the ACS interpretation, is a facially legitimate ethical canon. Therefore, the rule of reason governs this case." The District Court specifically noted that their decision to apply rule of reason analysis did not rely on the fact that the case involved the medical profession "as opposed to any other learned profession."

The *Koefoot* case went to trial in early 1987. Defendant ACS prevailed, and plaintiffs motion for a new trial was denied. 1987–1 CCH Trade Cases ¶ 67,511. Is this result surprising?

WILK v. AMERICAN MEDICAL ASS'N

United States Court of Appeals, Seventh Circuit, 1990.
895 F.2d 352, cert. denied, ___ U.S. ___, 111 S.Ct. 513, 112 L.Ed.2d 524 (1990).

MANION, CIRCUIT JUDGE.

The district court held that the American Medical Association ("AMA") violated § 1 of the Sherman Act, 15 U.S.C. § 1, by conducting an illegal boycott in restraint of trade directed at chiropractors generally, and the four plaintiffs in particular. The court granted an injunction [ ] requiring, among other things, wide publication of its order. * * * *Wilk v. American Medical Association*, 671 F.Supp. 1465 (N.D.Ill. 1987). The AMA appeals the finding of liability, and contends that, in any event, injunctive relief is unnecessary. * * * We affirm.

I.

* * * Plaintiffs Chester A. Wilk, James W. Bryden, Patricia B. Arthur, and Michael D. Pedigo, are licensed chiropractors. Their complaint, originally filed in 1976, charged several defendants with violating §§ 1 and 2 of the Sherman Act, 15 U.S.C. §§ 1 and 2. It sought both damages and an injunction. * * * At the first trial, plaintiffs' primary claim was that the defendants engaged in a conspiracy to eliminate the chiropractic profession by refusing to deal with plaintiffs and other chiropractors. * * *

A jury returned a verdict for the defendants. An earlier panel of this court, however, reversed that judgment. *Wilk v. American Medical Association*, 719 F.2d 207 (7th Cir.1983) (*Wilk I*). In reversing and ordering a new trial, we held that, in applying the rule of reason, the jury had been allowed to consider factors beyond the effect of the AMA's conduct on competition. The district court had improperly failed to confine the jury's consideration to the "patient care motive as contrasted with [the] generalized public interest motive." *Id.* at 229.

[The court recounts the history of the AMA's opposition to and actions against chiropractic.]

At trial, the AMA raised the so-called "patient care defense" which this court had formulated in its earlier opinion in this case. * * * That defense required the AMA generally to show that it acted because of a genuine, and reasonable, concern for scientific method in patient care and that it could not adequately satisfy this concern in a way that was less restrictive of competition. The district court rejected the defense. The court found the AMA failed to establish that throughout the relevant period (1966–1980) their concern for scientific methods in patient care had been objectively reasonable. The court also found the AMA similarly failed to show it could not adequately have satisfied its concern for scientific method in patient care in a manner less restrictive of competition than a nationwide conspiracy to eliminate a licensed profession.

* * *

The AMA's present position regarding chiropractic is that it is ethical for a medical physician to professionally associate with chiropractors, if the physician believes that the association is in his patient's best interests. The district court found that the AMA had not previously communicated this position to its membership.

Based on these findings, the court held that the AMA and its members violated § 1 of the Sherman Act by unlawfully conspiring to restrain trade. According to the court, the AMA's boycott's purpose had been to eliminate chiropractic; the boycott had substantial anticompetitive effects; the boycott had no counterbalancing pro-competitive effects; and the AMA's unlawful conduct injured the plaintiffs.

Despite the fact that the district court found the conspiracy ended in 1980, it concluded that the illegal boycott's "lingering effects" still threatened plaintiffs with current injury and ordered injunctive relief. The court concluded that the boycott caused injury to chiropractors' reputations which had not been repaired, and current economic injury to chiropractors. Further, the AMA never affirmatively acknowledged that there are no impediments to professional association and cooperation between chiropractors and medical physicians, except as provided by law. Thus, chiropractors continued to suffer because the boycott's negative effects (namely, inhibiting AMA members' individual decision-making in their relationships with chiropractors) still remained. The district court believed it was important that the AMA make its members aware of the present AMA position (i.e., it is ethical for medical physicians to professionally associate with chiropractors, if the physician believes it is in the patient's best interest) to eliminate the illegal boycott's lingering effects, and ordered an injunction designed to accomplish that result. [The district court required the AMA to mail the court's order to all AMA members; to publish the order in JAMA; and to revise other publications.]

* * *

Unreasonable Restraint of Trade

The central question in this case is whether the AMA's boycott constituted an unreasonable restraint of trade under § 1 of the Sherman Act.

* * *

The threshold issue in any rule of reason case is market power. [ ] Market power is the ability to raise prices above the competitive level by restricting output. [ ] Whether market power exists in an appropriately defined market is a fact-bound question, and appellate courts normally defer to district court findings on that issue. * * * Several facts demonstrated the AMA's market power within the health care services market. AMA members constituted a substantial force in the provision of health care services in the United States and they constituted a majority of medical physicians. AMA members received a much greater portion of fees paid to medical physicians in the United States than non-AMA members. The evidence showed that AMA members received approximately 50% of all fees paid to health care providers. Finally, according to plaintiffs' expert, the AMA enjoyed substantial market power. The district court also found there was substantial evidence that the boycott adversely affected competition, and that a showing of such adverse effects negated the need to prove in any elaborate fashion market definition and market power * * *.

The AMA first contests the district court's finding of market power. It challenges the court's reliance on market share evidence as a basis to find market power and the district court's lumping together all AMA members as a group in assessing market share as a basis for its market power finding. We are not convinced the trial court erred. The district court properly relied on the AMA membership's substantial market share in finding market power. While we cautioned against relying solely on market share as a basis for inferring market power [   ], we did not rule out that approach. [   ] This is especially so where there are barriers to entry and no substitutes from the consumer's perspective. * * *

The district court also relied on substantial evidence of adverse effects on competition caused by the boycott to establish the AMA's market power. In *Indiana Federation of Dentists*, the Supreme Court explained that since "the purpose of the inquiries into market definition and market power is to determine whether an arrangement has the potential for genuine adverse effects on competition, 'proof of actual detrimental effects, such as reduction of out-put' can obviate the need for an inquiry into market power, which is but a 'surrogate for detrimental effects.' " 476 U.S. at 460–61, 106 S.Ct. at 2018–19, quoting 7 P. Areeda, *Antritrust Law* ¶ 1511, p. 429 (1986). [   ] Thus, the district court recited the boycott's anticompetitive effects:

> It is anticompetitive and it raises costs to interfere with the consumer's free choice to take the product of his liking; it is anticompetitive to prevent medical physicians from referring patients to a chiropractor; it is anticompetitive to impose higher costs on chiropractors by forcing them to pay for their own x-ray equipment rather than obtaining x-rays from hospital radiology departments or radiologists in private practice; and it is anticompetitive to prevent chiropractors from improving their education in a professional setting by preventing medical physicians from teaching or lecturing to chiropractors.

These findings eliminated the need for an inquiry into market power.

* * * Moving on, the AMA argues that even if market power existed, it escapes liability under the rule of reason because [the AMA rule against associating with chiropractors] had overriding pro-

competitive effects. The AMA's argument is not unpersuasive in the abstract; but unfortunately it relies on evidence which the district court rejected as "speculative." Essentially, the AMA argues that the market for medical services is one where there is "information asymmetry." In other words, health care consumers almost invariably lack sufficient information needed to evaluate the quality of medical services. This increases the risk of fraud and deception on consumers by unscrupulous health care providers possibly causing what the AMA terms "market failure": consumers avoiding necessary treatment (for fear of fraud), and accepting treatment with no expectation of assured quality. The AMA's conduct, the theory goes, ensured that physicians acquired reputations for quality (in part, by not associating with unscientific cultists), and thus allowed consumers to be assured that physicians would use only scientifically valid treatments. This in effect simultaneously provided consumers with essential information and protected competition.

Getting needed information to the market is a fine goal, but the district court found that the AMA was not motivated solely by such altruistic concerns. Indeed, the court found that the AMA intended to "destroy a competitor," namely, chiropractors. It is not enough to carry the day to argue that competition should be eliminated in the name of public safety.

* * *

In sum, we agree with the district court that the AMA's boycott constituted an unreasonable restraint of trade under § 1 of the Sherman Act under the rule of reason. Therefore, the district court's findings that the AMA's boycott was anticompetitive, and was not counter-balanced by any procompetitive effects were not erroneous.

Patient Care Defense

In the AMA's first appeal, we modified the rule of reason to allow the AMA to justify its boycott of chiropractors if it could show that it was motivated by a concern for "patient care." We were persuaded that measuring former Principle 3's reasonableness required a more flexible approach than the traditional rule of reason inquiry provided. Thus, we explained that if plaintiffs met their burden of persuasion on remand by showing that [the rule against chiropractic] and the implementing conduct had restricted competition rather than promoting it, the burden of persuasion would shift to the defendants to show:

(1) that they genuinely entertained a concern for what they perceive as scientific method in the care of each person with whom they have entered into a doctor-patient relationship; (2) that this concern is objectively reasonable; (3) that this concern has been the dominant motivating factor in defendants' promulgation of [the rule] and in the conduct intended to implement it; and (4) that this concern for scientific method in patient care could not have been adequately satisfied in a manner less restrictive of competition.

* * *

The district court held that the AMA failed to meet the defense's second and fourth elements: that its concern for scientific method in patient care was objectively reasonable, and that the concern for scientific method in patient care could not have been satisfied adequately in a manner less restrictive of competition, respectively. While only those two rulings are at issue, it is useful to summarize the district court's treatment of the entire defense.

Although doubting the AMA's genuineness regarding its concern for scientific method in patient care, the district court concluded that the AMA established that element. While it was attacking chiropractic as unscientific, the AMA simultaneously was attacking other unscientific methods of disease treatment (e.g., the Krebiozen treatment of cancer), and, as the district court noted, the existence of medical standards or guidelines against unscientific practice was relatively common. The court, however, found that the AMA failed to carry its burden of persuasion as to whether its concern for scientific method in patient care was objectively reasonable.

The court acknowledged that during the period that the Committee on Quackery was operating, there was plenty of material supporting the belief that all chiropractic was unscientific. But, according to the court (and this is unchallenged), at the same time, there was evidence before the Committee that chiropractic was effective, indeed more effective than the medical profession, in treating certain kinds of problems, such as back injuries. The Committee was also aware, the court found, that some medical physicians believed chiropractic could be effective and that chiropractors were better trained to deal with musculoskeletal problems than most medical physicians. Moreover, the AMA's own evidence suggested that at some point during its lengthy boycott, there was no longer an objectively reasonable concern that would support a boycott of the entire chiropractic profession. Also important was the fact that "it was very clear" that the Committee's members did not have open minds to pro-chiropractic arguments or evidence.

Next, the court found that the AMA met its burden in establishing that its concern about scientific method was the dominant motivating factor for promulgating [the rule], and in the conduct undertaken and intended to implement it. But even so, the court acknowledged there was evidence showing that the AMA was motivated by economic concerns, as well.

Finally, the court concluded that the AMA failed to meet its burden in demonstrating that its concern for scientific method in patient care could not have been satisfied adequately in a manner less restrictive of competition. The court stated that the AMA had presented no evidence of other methods of achieving their objectives such as public education or any other less restrictive approach.

* * *

Notes and Questions

1. The District Court, in ruling on motions in the *Koefoot* case in 1986, refused to allow defendant ACS to use the *Wilk* patient care defense: "[T]he dispute in this case between licensed medical doctors, all of whom share common training and belief concerning human pathology, is fundamentally different from the dispute * * * between rival professions whose fundamental concepts of the treatment of disease are radically at odds." 652 F.Supp. 882, 891 (N.D.Ill.1986). The court rejected defendants' attempt to use a "patient care motive" defense as inconsistent with recent Supreme Court decisions. The court did hold that evidence of motive would be admissible, not as a defense, but for its relevance to the proof of anticompetitive or procompetitive effect. The court strongly cautioned defendants on the use of evidence of the patient care rationale for the itinerant surgery rule because of its highly prejudicial nature. Why would such a defense be "prejudicial"? Why would the courts in *Wilk* be willing to admit motive at all? This defense requires the court to judge that the defendant's "concern" was "objectively reasonable." How is the court to test this? Should this defense be called the "allopathic-chiropractic defense," or are there other situations in which it may apply?

The District Court in *Koefoot* expanded on these issues. The defendants represented to the court that they intended to argue to the jury that "[i]t is patently procompetitive for a professional association to adopt a rule that improves the quality of care provided to consumers." The court rejected this argument: "Having lost their patient care motivation *defense* in the Court's prior opinion, the defendants seek to replace it with a patient care motivation *procompetitive advantage*. The defense and the procompetitive advantage are two sides of the same coin and both are improper * * *". At 900.

ACS also claimed that designation as a Fellow of the American College of Surgery (FACS) was a "seal of approval." Its informational value to consumers, according to ACS, could be judged procompetitive only if itinerant surgery is actually harmful and, therefore, that evidence of harm must be admissible. The court rejected defendants' argument stating that "the possible procompetitive informational effect of the FACS label in the instant case does not depend on a finding that itinerant surgery is either good or bad for patients." At 902. The court further stated:

> The ACS cannot claim to be an independent standard-making organization similar to [Underwriters Laboratory] for the simple reason that the ACS is not truly an independent third party setting standards of general applicability. The defendants admit that ACS members are in competition with itinerant surgeons. [ ] Additionally, the ACS appears to perform no true testing function. The ACS has never claimed that it routinely "tests" whether its members comply with the ACS rules of professional conduct.

* * *

The defendants fervently desire to argue to the jury that the FACS label is procompetitive because it enables consumers to choose better surgeons. Once the smoke surrounding this argument has been cleared away, the true desire of the defendants is found. The defendants, again, are attempting to convince the jury that the itinerant surgery rule is procompetitive because it results in better patient care. As the Court has taken great pains to explain, that is not a proper antitrust argument.

There is a possible procompetitive effect provided by the FACS label that is independent of a value judgment on the merits of itinerant surgery. If a label enables consumers to more quickly find a product or service that they desire, then the label increases efficiency by reducing needless delay. A way for the ACS to prove that the FACS label has procompetitive value is not for it to prove that itinerant surgery is harmful, but rather for it to prove that the FACS label provides consumers with a shorthand method of locating something they already desire, which in this case would be post-operative care rendered by a surgeon. The ACS can argue that by finding an ACS surgeon, the consumer has found a surgeon who does not delegate post-operative care to non-surgeons. Whether the ACS is correct in an abstract sense that the itinerant surgery rule enhances patient care, is irrelevant to the advantage to consumers that follows from having a reliable labeling mechanism.

The Court has never hindered the defendants from making the argument outlined above. All the Court has done is to limit the parties to relevant evidence. If the defendants can prove that consumers desire post-operative care to be rendered by surgeons, then the defendants are free to argue that the FACS label has a procompetitive use.

It is a safe assumption that all consumers desire the best possible surgical care. What Congress and the Supreme Court have made clear is that the "best" product or service will be selected by consumers when their choice is made in an open market free of restraints. Eventually, the marketplace will determine the best medical care, not judges, juries, or even doctors. If in a free market consumers prefer post-operative care to be rendered by a surgeon then they will choose it. And, if in a free market rural consumers prefer local hospitalization with post-operative care rendered by a non-surgeon then they will choose that. In all situations the choice must be left to the consumers. At 903, 904.

2. Although each of these cases allows some limited role for quality-of-care justifications, they all express hostility toward such evidence and strive to limit its influence. What is the basis for this position?

Professor Thomas Greaney argues that "recognition of noneconomic defenses would be inconsistent with the [antitrust] law's fundamental design." This does not mean that private accreditation associations, or other entities involved in quality assurance, cannot pursue quality-of-service strategies: "By allowing providers to unite to offer services that are of high quality and to freely dispense comparative information about quality, antitrust law promotes rivalry and innovation. At the same time, curbing coercion assures that consumers will have the opportunity to make choices on the merits. A legal standard more tolerant of professional coercion would explicitly sanction overriding consumer choice." One very limited form of patient-care defense Greaney would allow is a "market failure defense." If this defense is adopted, the balance of anti-competitive and pro-competitive effects of a restraint would include an analysis of the functioning of the market in which the restraint operates. The health care market is generally observed to suffer from market imperfections, such as problems with information, and from market failures, such as a comparatively higher incidence of natural monopolies. In a "market failure defense," the private association or other defendant would be allowed to prove that the challenged restraint improved competition by offsetting a market failure. To limit the use of such a defense, Greaney suggests that the defense be most narrowly drawn in cases involving a "naked restraint" such as explicit restrictions on price or output; that the defendant bear the burden of coming forward with evidence that the market failure addressed by the restraint actually does interfere with competition; that if the particular market failure were eliminated competitive results would improve; and that the restraint be no broader than necessary to achieve the goal identified by defendant. Greaney, Quality of Care and Market Failure Defenses in Antitrust Health Care Litigation, 21 Conn.L.Rev. 605 (1989).

The AMA attempted to rely on market failure before the Seventh Circuit, but the Court rejected the defense. Would the AMA have succeeded under Greaney's structure?

3. In applying the patient-care defense, the District Court in *Wilk*, affirmed by the Court of Appeals, held that the AMA failed to prove that its quality-of-care concern could not be achieved in a "manner less restrictive of competition." What other possible strategies existed for the AMA?

4. The AMA claimed protection under the Noerr–Pennington doctrine in *Wilk*. The Court of Appeals affirmed the District Court's handling of the issue: "[T]o the extent that the Committee's work regarding influencing legislation on the state and federal levels or in informational activities to inform the public on the nature of chiropractic was involved, [the district court] did not consider such conduct in reaching its decision." The Court of Appeals specifically pointed to the AMA's circulation of its Judicial Council opinion on chiropractic to its members and to 56 medical specialty boards and its success in persuading JCAHO to adopt the AMA's bar as part of its own standards as conduct outside the Noerr–Pennington protection.

5. Several scholars have proposed approaches to the application of antitrust laws and other government regulation to the activities of private credentialing organizations in a manner that will preserve the organizations' beneficial activities but that will discourage undesirable anticompetitive activities. See, e.g., Havighurst and King, Private Credentialing of Health Care Personnel—Part One, 9 Am.J.Law & Med. 131 (1983) and Part Two, 9 Am.J.Law & Med. 263 (1983); Jost, The Joint Commission on Accreditation of Hospitals: Private Regulation of Health Care and the Public Interest, 24 B.C.L.Rev. 835 (1983); and Kissam, Government Policy Toward Medical Accreditation and Certification: The Antitrust Laws and Other Procompetitive Strategies, 1983 Wisc.L.Rev. 1.

Problem: Home Births

Assume that you are counsel for the Accreditation Association of Nurse–Midwives. Nearly 70% of nurse-midwives are members of the association. Membership in the association is highly regarded, by nurse-midwives as well as by doctors and hospitals, as an indication of professionalism. The Association's governing board has been reviewing two situations.

First, Association members are concerned about the participation of some nurse-midwives in home births. Although there is some support for home births among its members, the Association's governing body is not supportive of the practice in general, believing that it presents unnecessary risks to mother and child and that recent reforms have alleviated many of the objections against hospital-based birthing practices. It also is concerned that if its members are free to offer home births, doctors' support for nurse-midwives, which has never been particularly strong, will erode. The governing board has before it a proposed rule that would establish very restrictive standards for nurse-midwife-assisted home births and that would provide for the expulsion of Association members who violate the standards.

Second, the Association's membership is nearly unanimous in opposing assistance at births by lay-midwives. The Association believes that professional training as a nurse is a prerequisite to high-quality midwifery. It is concerned that consumers may be uninformed of the difference between nurse-midwives and lay-midwives. The governing body is considering a number of actions. First, it has prepared a brochure and television commercial about nurse-midwifery that clearly condemns lay-midwifery. Second, it has drafted model state legislation that would make lay-midwifery illegal and model medical staff by-laws that would allow for limited clinical privileges for nurse-midwives but would exclude lay-midwives. Third, it has developed an ethical canon that prohibits nurse-midwives from using lay-midwives as assistants or from participating in enterprises in which lay-midwives assist at births. This canon would be enforced by expulsion from the Association.

What are the risks in each of these proposals? Are there other strategies that might be less risky?

III. MERGERS, ACQUISITIONS AND OTHER INTER–INSTITUTIONAL ARRANGEMENTS

HOSPITAL CORPORATION OF AMERICA

3 Trade Reg.Rep. (CCH) ¶ 22,301 (FTC Oct. 25, 1985).

CALVANI, COMM'R

I. INTRODUCTION TO THE CASE

A. *The Acquisitions*

In August 1981, Respondent Hospital Corporation of America ("HCA"), the largest proprietary hospital chain in the United States, acquired Hospital Affiliates International ("HAI") in a stock transaction valued at approximately $650 million. * * * At the time of the acquisition, HAI owned or leased 57 hospitals and managed 78 hospitals nationwide. [ ] Prior to its acquisition by HCA, HAI owned or managed five acute care hospitals in the general area of Chattanooga, Tennessee, and HCA acquired ownership or management of these hospitals through the transaction. Some four months later HCA acquired yet another hospital corporation, Health Care Corporation ("HCC"), in a stock transaction valued at approximately $30 million. [ ] At the time of the acquisition, HCC owned a single acute care hospital in Chattanooga. These two transactions provide the genesis for the instant case.

As a result of the HCA–HAI acquisition, Respondent increased its hospital operations in Chattanooga and its suburbs from ownership of one acute care hospital to ownership or management of four of the area's eleven acute care hospitals. Within the six-county Chattanooga Metropolitan Statistical Area ("Chattanooga MSA"), HCA changed its position from owner of one hospital to owner or manager of six of fourteen acute care hospitals. With the acquisition of HCC, HCA obtained yet another acute care hospital in Chattanooga. Thus, HCA became owner or manager of five of the eleven acute care hospitals within the Chattanooga urban area and seven of the fourteen in the Chattanooga MSA.

On July 30, 1982, the Commission issued a complaint charging that the effect of HCA's acquisitions of HAI and HCC, both together and separately, may be substantially to lessen competition or to tend to create a monopoly in the acute care hospital services market in the Chattanooga, Tennessee area in violation of Section 7 of the Clayton Act, 15 U.S.C. Sec. 18 (1982), and Section 5 of the Federal Trade Commission Act, 15 U.S.C. Sec. 45 (1982). Judge Parker issued his Initial Decision on October 30, 1984. He found that the acquisitions violated Section 7 of the Clayton Act and Section 5 of the Federal Trade Commission Act, and ordered HCA to divest two of the hospitals of which it had acquired ownership. Judge Parker also ordered that HCA provide prior notification to the Commission of certain of its future hospital acquisitions. HCA appeals the Initial Decision on several grounds; Complaint Counsel appeal certain of Judge Parker's findings as well.

* * * We affirm Judge Parker's finding of liability and modify his opinion only as stated below.

B. The Structure of Health Care Markets

Both parties agree that the health care industry is unique in some respects. Before considering the merits of this case, it is important to have a fundamental understanding of the role of physicians and third-party payors in the health care transaction.

* * *

With respect to our analysis, there is one extremely important effect on the hospital services market of third-party payment: The extent to which a patient is insured determines the extent to which he is sensitive to the price of hospital care. If he is fully insured, once he becomes ill his interest lies in receiving the best quality care possible, including the highest quality comforts and surroundings if he is in the hospital, no matter what the costs. Who, then, is concerned about price? * * * When hospital prices rise, the increased payments made by an insurance company are spread over all its subscribers, both patients and non-patients (*i.e.*, prospective patients); premiums rise less than proportionally to the increase in hospital prices. Thus, not every significant increase in hospital prices will bring a significant market reaction from insurance consumers. However, if insurance premiums rise sufficiently, even after the cost of health care is spread over so many people, then consumer reaction should reverberate into the health care market. To avoid losing business and to minimize their costs, insurance companies will, through the insurance mechanism, take whatever actions they can to hold down the prices they pay for hospital and physician care.

We are thus confronted in this case with a very peculiar market indeed. Because of the uncertainty of illness and injury and the grossly imperfect information available to consumers of hospital services, patients generally rely on physicians to determine the nature and extent of the medical care they receive and on third-party payors to provide the financial assurances that such care will be paid for. Any analysis of hospital markets under Section 7 must bear in mind both the role that physicians play on behalf of patients and the role of the insurance market in financing hospital care. With this in mind, we now turn to the merits of the case before us.

* * *

III. THE PRODUCT MARKET

An acquisition violates Section 7 of the Clayton Act "where in any line of commerce in any section of the country, the effect of such acquisition may be substantially to lessen competition, or to tend to create a monopoly." 15 U.S.C. Sec. 18 (1982). Accordingly, we now turn to the definition of the relevant "line of commerce" or "product market" in which to measure the likely competitive effects of these acquisitions. In measuring likely competitive effects, we seek to define a product or group of products sufficiently distinct that buyers could not defeat an attempted exercise of market power on the part of sellers of those products by shifting purchases to still different products. Sellers might exercise market power by raising prices, limiting output or lowering quality. [   ]

Complaint Counsel argued below that the product market was properly defined as the provision of acute inpatient hospital services and emergency hospital services provided to the critically ill. This definition would exclude non-hospital providers of outpatient services,

e.g., free standing emergency centers, as well as non-hospital providers
of inpatient services, e.g., nursing homes, from the product market. It
would also exclude the outpatient business of hospitals, except for that
provided to the critically ill in the emergency room. The rationale for
excluding outpatient care is that inpatient services are the reason for
being of acute care hospitals; inpatient services are needed by and
consumed by patients in combination and therefore can be offered only
by acute care hospitals. Inpatients in almost all cases will purchase a
range of services and not just one test or procedure; they will typically
consume a "cluster" of services involving 24–hour nursing, the services
of specialized laboratory and X-ray equipment, the services of equipment needed to monitor vital functions or intervene in crises, and so
forth. An acutely ill patient must be in a setting in which all of these
various services can be provided together. [ ] According to this
reasoning, outpatient services are not an integral part of this "cluster
of services" offered by acute care hospitals, and therefore must be
excluded.

Respondent, on the other hand, urged that the market be defined to
include outpatient care as well as inpatient care. Respondent's expert
witness, Dr. Jeffrey E. Harris, testified that outpatient care is growing
rapidly for hospitals, as well as for free-standing facilities such as
emergency care and one-day surgery centers, which compete with
hospitals for outpatients. [ ] Moreover, because of substantial
changes in medical technology, there are a growing number of procedures that can be provided on an outpatient basis that previously could
have been done on only an inpatient basis. [ ]

Judge Parker agreed that the market should include outpatient
services provided by hospitals but excluded outpatient services provided
by non-hospital providers, holding that only hospitals can provide the
"unique combination" of services which the acute care patient needs.
[ ] He defined the relevant product market to be the cluster of
services offered by acute care hospitals, including outpatient as well as
inpatient care, "since acute care hospitals compete with each other in
offering both kinds of care and since * * * acute care outpatient
facilities feed patients to the inpatient facilities."

Neither HCA nor Complaint Counsel appeal Judge Parker's product market definition. See Commission Rule of Practice 3.52(b). Accordingly, for purposes of this proceeding only we accept Judge Parker's
finding on this issue.

However, we do note that Judge Parker's definition does not
necessarily provide a very happy medium between the two competing
positions; the evidence in this case tended to show *both* that free-standing outpatient facilities compete with hospitals for many outpatients
and that hospitals offer and inpatients consume a cluster of services
that bears little relation to outpatient care. [ ] If so, it may be that
defining the cluster of hospital inpatient services as a separate market
better reflects competitive reality in this case. * * * Certainly, it is

clear that anticompetitive behavior by hospital firms could significantly lessen competition for hospital inpatients that could not be defeated by competition from non-hospital outpatient providers. Our analysis will hence proceed with primary reference to the cluster of services provided to inpatients.

IV. THE GEOGRAPHIC MARKET

* * * Because we are concerned only with an area in which competition could be harmed, the relevant geographic market must be broad enough that buyers would be unable to switch to alternative sellers in sufficient numbers to defeat an exercise of market power by firms in the area. Again, sellers may exercise market power by raising prices, reducing output or reducing quality. [ ] If an exercise of market power could be defeated by the entry of products produced in another area, both areas should be considered part of the same geographic market for Section 7 purposes, since competition could not be harmed in the smaller area. That is, the geographic market should determine not only the firms that constrain competitors' actions by currently selling to the same customers, but also those that would be a constraint because of their ability to sell to those customers should price or quality in the area change. [ ]

* * *

HCA would have us adopt Hamilton County, Tennessee, together with Walker, Dade and Catoosa counties in Georgia, the "Chattanooga urban area," as the relevant geographic market. HCA predicates its conclusion largely on an analysis of evidence concerning physician admitting patterns.

* * * With few exceptions, every physician who admitted to Chattanooga urban area hospitals admitted exclusively to other hospitals in the Chattanooga urban area. [ ] Conversely, physicians admitting and treating patients at hospitals outside the Chattanooga urban area rarely admitted and treated patients at hospitals in the Chattanooga urban area. [ ]

* * *

Additionally, the weight of the evidence concerning patient origin suggests that patients admitted to Chattanooga urban area hospitals who live outside of the Chattanooga urban area are, with few exceptions, in need of specialized care and treatment unavailable in their own communities. * * * Hospitals in outlying communities do not always provide quite the same product that the urban area hospitals provide such patients, and therefore patient inflows are not necessarily indicative of the willingness of patients to leave their home areas for services that are available in those areas. * * * Judge Parker agreed with HCA that the Chattanooga urban area is the relevant geographic market in this case.

On appeal, Complaint Counsel agree that the Chattanooga urban area is an appropriate geographic area in which to assess the competitive effects of these acquisitions. However, they claim that a much more appropriate geographic market is the federally designated Metropolitan Statistical Area that includes Chattanooga. In effect, Complaint Counsel would have us add the Tennessee counties of Marion and Sequatchie to the market proffered by HCA and adopted by Judge Parker. By adding this area, three additional hospitals—South Pittsburg Municipal Hospital, Sequatchie General Hospital, and Whitwell Community Hospital—would be included in the relevant market. Both South Pittsburg and Sequatchie were acquired by HCA from HAI, and Complaint Counsel seek divestiture by HCA of its long-term lease arrangement with South Pittsburg.

* * *

* * * Geopolitical designations such as "MSA" may reflect a host of considerations that do not concern the issue of competition between hospitals. * * * Nor do we find any evidence that MSA designations were ever intended to reflect an economic market for purposes of Section 7. We do not here conclude that an MSA will never accurately reflect the relevant geographic market in a hospital merger case. But where, as here, the MSA designation excludes important sources of potential competition, it must be rejected. * * *

* * *

V. THE EFFECT ON COMPETITION

A. The Effect of HCA–Managed Hospitals

One of the major dimensions of HCA's purchase of HAI was the acquisition of some 75 to 80 hospital management contracts. Two of these were management contracts HAI had with two hospitals in the Chattanooga urban area—Downtown General Hospital and Red Bank Community Hospital. * * *

HCA argues, and Judge Parker agreed, that Downtown General and Red Bank hospitals should be treated as entities completely separate from HCA, incapable of being significantly influenced by HCA in its role as administrator. * * *

We conclude that treating the two managed hospitals as entities completely independent of HCA is contrary to the overwhelming weight of the evidence in this case. As manager, HCA controls the competitive variables needed for successful coordination with the activities of HCA-owned hospitals in Chattanooga. Moreover, as manager it knows the competitive posture of managed hospitals so well that the likelihood of any anticompetitive behavior HCA wished to engage in is greatly increased.

* * *

Indeed, the very reason that a management firm is hired, as reflected in the management contracts, is to direct the competitive operations of the managed hospital. The evidence shows clearly that management recommendations, including proposed rate increases, are almost invariably followed by the boards of directors of Downtown General and Red Bank. * * *

* * *

* * * In Chattanooga, HCA held meetings for both owned and managed hospital administrators "to initiate them into the HCA philosophy." * * *

In the case of Downtown General HCA owns assets important to the continuing existence of the institution. HCA owns not only the land on which the hospital is located, but also the physician office building situated adjacent to the facility. [ ] Physicians with offices in the adjacent building account for approximately 95% of the hospital's admissions. [ ] Moreover, the hospital board acknowledges that the hospital would not survive without the medical office building. * * *

* * *

* * * The evidence compels us to consider the market shares of Downtown General and Red Bank as part of HCA's market share in considering the effect on competition in this case. Even were the evidence not as compelling, we would consider HCA's management of the two hospitals to greatly enhance the likelihood of collusion in this market.

* * *

B. The Nature of Competition Among Chattanooga Hospitals

Traditionally, hospitals have competed for patients in three general ways: first, by competing for physicians to admit their patients; second, by competing directly for patients on the basis of amenities and comfort of surroundings; and third, by competing to a limited degree on the basis of price. [ ] The first two constitute "non-price" or "quality" competition, and by far have been in the past the most important of the three. [ ]

Non-price competition for physicians includes the provision of up-to-date equipment, a qualified and reliable nursing staff and other technically trained personnel, convenient office space to make it easier for the physician to concentrate both his ambulatory and inpatient work within the same location, a nice doctors' lounge with a good selection of journals—everything that will convince physicians that their patients are receiving the best care possible and make physicians' lives more comfortable. [ ] Competition directed at patients themselves has traditionally been through the provision of amenities, such as pleasant surroundings, attractive rooms, televisions and telephones, high nurse-to-patient ratios, convenient parking—everything that will make patients more comfortable. [ ]

* * *

Over the last decade, two major trends increasing competition among hospitals beyond its traditional limits have developed. [ ] First, both non-price and price competition are now being directed much more toward patients themselves than in the past. Second, beginning in the late 1970s the hospital industry has been [sic] the clear emergence of direct price competition. At the same time, traditional non-price competition for patients on the basis of amenities has intensified somewhat, through the provision of such amenities as private rooms. Non-price competition for physicians remains pervasive, since physicians still largely determine the disposition and treatment of their patients.

* * *

* * * [T]his increasing concern of employers and employees with the costs of insurance means that differences in prices between hospitals matter to them and their third-party payors, since insurance will cost less when hospital care costs less. [ ] The result is that hospitals are now far more likely to present themselves to insurers, employers and employee groups as less costly than their competitors as one method of attracting more business. Price competition, fostered by these new insurance mechanisms, is therefore growing in the hospital industry. [ ]

* * *

Thus, it is obvious that price has been a competitively sensitive matter among Chattanooga hospitals. [ ] We do not here conclude that price has been the prime arena in which hospitals in Chattanooga compete. However, we do think it clear that even though rates are not constantly adjusted due to a changing price structure, they have been periodically set with some reference to what the market will bear in face of the prices of other hospitals. [ ]

It is clear that Section 7 protects whatever price competition exists in a market, however limited. * * *

* * *

C. Respondent's Market Share and Concentration in the Chattanooga Urban Area

Three ways to measure a hospital's share of the acute care hospital services market are by using: (1) bed capacity; (2) inpatient days; and (3) net revenues. Bed capacity and inpatient days measure a hospital's position with regard to the cluster of inpatient services, the heart of hospital care. Net revenues, on the other hand, account for both inpatient and outpatient services.

Naturally, because of their proposed market definitions, Complaint Counsel advocate use of inpatient measures, while HCA urges net revenues as the preferable measure since it accounts for outpatient services. We conclude, however, that the three measures are so similar in this case that they yield the same result whatever measure is used.

* * *

The Herfindahl–Hirschman Index ("HHI") of market concentration is calculated by summing the squares of the individual market shares of

all the firms in the market.   The HHI reflects the distribution of
market shares between firms and gives proportionately greater weight
to the market shares of the larger firms, which likely accords with their
relative importance in any anti-competitive interaction.   [   ] * * *
[U]sing any measure of market power the Herfindahl index was above
1900 before the acquisitions.   Thus, the acquisitions occurred in a
market already highly concentrated.   [   ] Following HCA's acquisition
of HAI, the HHI increased some 295 points using net patient revenues
and over 300 using beds or patient days.   With the acquisition of HCC,
the HHI additionally increased well over 100 points using any measure.
Again using any measure, the HHI at the very least rests at 2416 after
the acquisitions.   We consider such an increase in concentration in an
already concentrated market to be of serious competitive concern, all
other things being equal.   [   ]

More traditional measures of market share also support this conclusion.   For example, using patient days HCA's market share increased from 13.8% to 25.8% in the Chattanooga urban area, while
four-firm concentration increased to almost 92% and two-firm concentration to 61%.   The figures for approved beds and net patient revenues are almost identical.   These figures support an inference of harm
to competition, all other things equal.   [   ]

Moreover, all other things being equal, an increase in market
concentration through a reduction in the absolute number of competitive actors makes interdependent behavior more likely.   [   ] These
acquisitions decreased the number of independent firms in the market
from 9 to 7.   The costs of coordination or of policing any collusive
agreement are less with fewer participants, and the elimination of
competitive forces in this market facilitates joint anticompetitive behavior.   [   ]

In sum, evidence of the increased concentration caused by these
acquisitions points toward a finding of likely harm to competition, all
other things being equal.   HCA's acquisitions have made an already
highly concentrated market more conducive to collusion by eliminating
two of the healthiest sources of competition in the market and increasing concentration substantially.   But all other things are not equal in
this market, and statistical evidence is not the end of our inquiry.   In
the absence of barriers to entry, an exercise of market power can be
defeated or deterred by the entry or potential entry of new firms
regardless of the structure of the existing market.   [   ] We now turn to
the issue of entry barriers and conclude that they confirm and even
magnify the inference to be drawn from the concentration evidence in
this case.

D. Barriers to Entry

* * *

* * * [T]here is hardly free entry into the acute care hospital
industry in either Tennessee or Georgia.   Indeed, the CON [certificate
of need] laws at issue here create a classic "barrier to entry" under

every definition of that term. In *Echlin Manufacturing Co.,* we defined a "barrier to entry" to include "additional long-run costs that must be incurred by an entrant relative to the long-run costs faced by incumbent firms." [   ] We explained that "[t]he rationale underlying this definition is that low-cost incumbent firms can keep prices above the competitive level as long as those prices remain below the level that would provide an incentive to higher-cost potential entrants." [   ]

If a potential entrant desires to build a new hospital in Chattanooga, he must incur all the costs in time and money associated with obtaining a CON. The cost of starting a new hospital includes not only the start-up costs that any firm would incur to enter the market but also the costs of surviving the administrative process. Incumbents in this market, however, did not incur such costs during initial construction. They have only had to incur those costs for additions made to bed capacity since the enactment of the CON laws a decade ago. Incumbents thus have a long run cost advantage over potential entrants. The result is that market power could be exercised by incumbents without attracting attempts at entry as long as supracompetitive profits are not high enough for a potential entrant to justify incurring all the ordinary costs of starting a hospital *plus* the significant costs of obtaining a CON.

The evidence is clear that those costs are significant in this market. We agree with Judge Parker that because incumbent hospitals can oppose new entry, even an unsuccessful opposition to a CON application may delay its disposition by several years. * * *

Thus the CON process provides existing hospitals in the Chattanooga urban area ample opportunity to significantly forestall the entry of a new hospital or the expansion of an existing hospital within the area. Indeed, the evidence shows that existing hospitals frequently oppose CON applications when they feel competitively threatened. * * *

* * *

In sum, it is not merely the costs of obtaining a CON that a potential entrant faces, but the significant risk of being denied entry once those costs have been incurred. This risk, which incumbents did not have to face when building their hospitals, in effect raises the costs of entry a significantly greater amount. As a result, many potential entrants may decide not to even attempt entry. [   ] Indeed, the evidence shows that CON regulation has had a deterrent effect in the Chattanooga market. [   ] * * *

* * *

Interestingly, HCA's executive leadership recognizes the barrier to entry quality of CON regulation. In an interview published in a 1981 issue of the *Harvard Business Review,* Dr. Thomas J. Frist, Jr., HCA's president and chief executive officer, observed:

> Federal and state health planning laws have erected formidable barriers to entry into the hospital industry by creating literal monopolies for physicians and hospitals. If the health planning

laws state that a community can have only one cardiac surgery program, they might as well give the physician who performs that surgery an exclusive franchise. It's the same for hospitals.

* * * Dr. Frist also observed that such barriers to entry benefit HCA because they "protect our hospitals from competitors who might build new facilities and take away our market. We know what the market for a particular institution is going to be like 5 or 10 years down the road." [ ] He noted further that "regulation severely restricts new hospitals from entering our markets." [ ]

* * *

E. *The Nature and Likelihood of Anticompetitive Behavior in the Chattanooga Hospital Market*

1. *The Nature of Anticompetitive Behavior*

* * *

Some of the most likely forms of collusion between hospitals would involve collective resistance to emerging cost containment pressures from third-party payors and alternative providers. For example, joint refusals to deal with HMOs or PPOs may occur, or perhaps joint refusals to deal on the most favorable terms. Conspiracies to boycott certain insurance companies that are generating price competition may occur. Utilization review programs may also be resisted. Hospitals could concertedly refuse to provide the information desired by third-party payors—information that would otherwise be provided as hospitals vie to attract the business of those payors and their subscribers. The result of any such boycott would be to raise prices, reduce quality of services or both.

* * *

Quality competition itself might also be restricted. For example, the group of hospitals in a relevant market might agree to staff their wards with fewer nurses yet continue to maintain current rates for inpatient services. Patients would be harmed by the resulting drop in quality of services without any compensating reduction in price of services. Colluding hospitals in the market, however, would profit from their agreement by cutting costs without cutting revenues. Again, hospitals could accomplish anticompetitive ends not only by fixing staff-patient ratios but by agreeing on wages or benefits to be paid certain personnel—for example, laboratory technicians. Indeed, wage and salary surveys are common in this market. [ ] The result would be the same—to hold the cost of inputs down with probable harm to the quality of output of health care services. Hospitals could also agree not to compete for each other's personnel or medical staff. Indeed, some Chattanooga urban area hospital firms have already engaged in such behavior. [ ]

Moreover, under certificate of need legislation, the addition of new services and purchases of certain kinds of new equipment require a demonstration of need for the expenditure, and the existence of need is determined in part by the facilities already provided in the community. [ ] It would thus be to the advantage of competing hospitals to enter into agreements among themselves as to which competitor will apply for which service or for which piece of equipment. * * * Such market division by private agreement would save hospitals the expense of applying for numerous CONs but may harm the quality of care that would be available to patients were CON approval sought independently by each hospital with reference to its own merits and expertise.

Concerted opposition to the CON application of a potential new entrant is yet another manner in which Chattanooga hospitals could successfully collude. * * *

Anticompetitive pricing behavior could also take several forms. For example, hospitals could work out agreements with respect to pricing formulas. * * *

Hospitals could also successfully collude with respect to price by agreeing not to give discounts to businesses, insurers and other group purchasers such as HMOs and PPOs. * * *

In sum, we conclude that hospitals compete in a myriad of ways that could be restricted anticompetitively through collusion. Thus, it appears that a merger analysis in this case need be no different than in any other case; market share and concentration figures, evidence of entry barriers and other market evidence taken together appear to yield as accurate a picture of competitive conditions as they do in other settings. Nevertheless, although HCA concedes that many of the above described forms of collusion *could* occur, the heart of HCA's case is that collusion in this market is inherently unlikely, and to that contention we now turn.

2. The Likelihood of Anticompetitive Behavior

Section 7 of the Clayton Act prohibits acquisitions that may have the effect of substantially lessening competition or tending to create a monopoly. Because Section 7 applies to "incipient" violations, actual anticompetitive effects need not be shown; an acquisition is unlawful if such an effect is reasonably probable. [ ]

The small absolute number of competitors in this market, the high concentration and the extremely high entry barriers indicate a market in which anticompetitive behavior is reasonably probable after the acquisitions. The fact that industry members recognize the enormity of entry barriers makes collusion even more probable. In addition, hospital markets have certain features that evidence a likelihood of collusion or other anticompetitive behavior when they become highly concentrated. [ ]

First, price elasticity of demand for hospital services is very low [ ], which makes anticompetitive behavior extremely profitable and hence attractive. [ ] Second, because consumers of hospital services cannot arbitrage or resell them as is often possible with goods, discrimination among different groups of consumers is possible. That is, collusion may be directed at a certain group or certain groups of consumers, such as a particular insurance company, without the necessity of anticompetitive behavior toward other groups. [ ] Third, the traditions of limited price competition and disapproval of advertising [ ] provide an incentive for future anticompetitive restrictions of those activities. Fourth, and in the same vein, the advent of incentives to resist new cost containment pressures may create a substantial danger of hospital collusion to meet pressures. [ ] Fifth, the hospital industry has a tradition of cooperative problem solving which makes collusive conduct in the future more likely. Hospitals have historically participated in voluntary health planning in a coordinated manner, and along with other professional organizations, such as medical societies, have participated in developing joint solutions to industry problems. [ ]

     * * * The most convincing evidence of the facility with which such collusion could occur is a blatant market allocation agreement executed in 1981 between Red Bank Community Hospital and HCC. [ ] The parties actually *signed a contract* under which Red Bank agreed that for a period of three years it would not "file any application for a Certificate of Need for psychiatric facilities or nursing home facilities." [ ] Moreover, the parties agreed that they would not compete for each other's personnel and medical staff during that time period, and that they would not oppose each other's CON applications in certain areas. [ ] Such an overt agreement to refrain from competition at the very least demonstrates the predisposition of some firms in the market to collude when it is in their interest; at worst it shows a callous disregard for the antitrust laws.

* * *

     Furthermore, a basis for collusion is provided by the exchanges of rate, salary and other competitively sensitive information that occur in this market. * * *

* * *

     * * * It is true that the undisputed evidence shows that more vigorous competition, including more direct price competition, is emerging in the health care industry, but it is a fallacy to conclude that growing competition in health care markets means that these acquisitions pose no threat to that competition. In fact, it is just that emerging competition that must be protected from mergers that facilitate the suppression of such competition. * * *

a. Non-profit Hospitals and the Likelihood of Collusion

     HCA contends that the most fundamental difference between hospitals in Chattanooga is that several of the hospitals are "non-profit" institutions. Economic theory presumes that businesses in an industry are profit-maximizers and that output will be restricted in pursuit of profits. Non-profit hospitals, the argument goes, have no incentive to maximize profits, rather, they seek to maximize "output" or the number of patients treated. [ ] HCA contends that non-profit hospitals may have other goals as well, such as providing the most sophisticated and highest quality care possible, or pursuing religious or governmental goals. [ ] In short, HCA argues that collusion would not occur because the "for-profit" and "non-profit" competitors have no common goal. [ ]

We disagree that non-profit hospitals have no incentive to collude with each other or with proprietary hospitals to achieve anticompetitive ends. First, we note that non-profit status of market participants is no guarantee of competitive behavior. * * *

* * *

In addition, administrators of non-profit hospitals may seek to maximize their personal benefits and comfort through what would otherwise be known as profit-seeking activity. * * *

* * *

Moreover, specific characteristics of non-profit hospitals in this market make anticompetitive behavior a reasonable probability. First, two of the six non-profit hospitals in the Chattanooga urban area, Downtown General and Red Bank, are managed by HCA. [ ] Indeed, the non-profit hospitals in the Chattanooga area managed by HCA are considered to be proprietary hospitals by their competitors and others in the industry. [ ]

Second, two major non-profit hospitals, Erlanger and Tri–County, have a tremendous incentive to participate in price collusion. Erlanger has sole responsibility for unreimbursed indigent care in Hamilton County. * * * Because it must subsidize unreimbursed care out of the rates charged to paying customers, Erlanger cannot compete effectively through price cutting. [ ] Erlanger's rates are 50 dollars per day *or 10%* higher than they would be if such cross-subsidization between paying and non-paying patients were not necessary. [ ] Because it cannot price below a level that covers the direct costs it incurs for indigent care, Erlanger would in fact benefit from a decrease in price competition through interdependent behavior. [ ] The same analysis applies to Tri–County, which must provide care for indigent residents of Walker, Dade and Catoosa counties in Georgia, and shift costs from non-paying to paying patients. * * *

* * *

b. *Purported Obstacles to Successful Coordination*

Relying entirely upon the testimony of its expert, Dr. Harris, HCA argues that even if hospitals in Chattanooga were inclined to collude, the administrators of those hospitals would find it difficult to reach anticompetitive agreements or understandings, or to sustain them if they ever were reached. This is so because the ideal market circumstances for collusion are not present, i.e. where manufacturers are selling "some simple, relatively homogeneous good, well characterized by a single price." [ ] HCA contends that hospital services are heterogeneous and influenced by a variety of complicating factors.

Hospitals provide a large number of varied medical tests and treatments and each patient receives unpredictable personalized service the extent of which is determined by physicians. [ ] Moreover, HCA claims costs and demand vary between hospitals. And because the dominant avenues of competition relate to the quality of medical care and patient amenities, hospitals would have to agree on a whole host of things to eliminate competition in a manner sufficient to earn monopoly returns, it is alleged.

* * *

HCA's analysis of the likelihood of collusion distorts competitive reality. HCA would have us believe that the world of possible collusion is limited to complicated formulae concerning every aspect of hospital competition—that market power can only be exercised with respect to the entire cluster of services that constitutes the acute care hospital market through a conspiracy fixing the overall quantity or quality of treatment running to each patient in the market. Rather than focus on the likely avenues of collusion among hospitals, HCA assumes into existence a world in which collusion is infeasible.

* * *

HCA offers an additional reason why the acquisitions allegedly create no risk that Chattanooga hospitals will collude to eliminate price competition, arguing that price collusion is unlikely because of the role of Blue Cross in this market. * * *

We cannot accept HCA's claims that Blue Cross has both the omniscience and market power to halt successful collusion by Chattanooga hospitals. First, under the current Blue Cross charge approval system, collusion could be difficult to detect. [ ] If all the hospital firms in Chattanooga attempt to raise prices a similar amount in the review process, coordinated pricing could be overlooked; there is no *a priori* reason why Blue Cross would consider this to be the result of collusion rather than a rise in costs. * * *

Furthermore, even if detected, we do not think such collusion could be easily deterred by Blue Cross. HCA ignores the fact that Blue Cross has a contract not only with participating hospitals but also with its subscribers. Blue Cross must serve its subscribers in the Chattanooga area, and HCA does not explain how Blue Cross could reject a concerted effort by the hospitals there even if it wanted to; certainly, Blue Cross could not ask its subscribers to all go to Knoxville for hospital care if Chattanooga urban area hospitals colluded. * * *

* * *

VII. CONCLUSION

We hold that HCA's acquisitions of HAI and HCC may substantially lessen competition in the Chattanooga urban area acute care hospital market in violation of Section 7 of the Clayton Act and Section 5 of the Federal Trade Commission Act. The only remaining issue is the appropriate remedy to be accorded the public in this case.

VIII. REMEDY

The appropriate remedy in this case is yet another hotly contested issue. Because we find that HCA violated Section 7 of the Clayton Act first in purchasing HAI and second in purchasing HCC, we order the divestiture of hospitals purchased—Diagnostic Center Hospital and North Park Hospital—and their adjacent facilities. We also order the divestiture of the Downtown General management contract acquired by HCA from HAI, since it is integral to the HAI acquisition and its likely pernicious effect on competition. [   ]

* * *

We agree with Complaint Counsel that a prior approval requirement for future HCA hospital purchases and assumption of hospital management contracts in the Chattanooga urban area is appropriate here. The record evidence shows that any horizontal acquisition or assumption of a management arrangement by HCA in the Chattanooga urban area, like those in this proceeding, poses such a potential for harm to competition that prior Commission approval is warranted. A Commission approval requirement does not amount to a ban on acquisitions; but in view of the substantial danger of competitive harm in the Chattanooga urban area we think it is the most efficient way to screen out those mergers and management contracts that are potentially anticompetitive. Moreover, we do not believe that imposing a prior approval requirement in one local market, the Chattanooga urban area, will substantially harm HCA's competitive position in the market for hospital acquisitions as a whole.

* * *

[The Commission rejected Complaint Counsel's recommendation for a prior approval requirement outside the Chattanooga urban area.]

Notes and Questions

1. The Seventh Circuit reviewed and upheld the decision of the Federal Trade Commission in Hospital Corporation of America v. FTC, 807 F.2d 1381 (7th Cir.1986). In his opinion for the Court, Judge Posner comments that the Clayton Act permits HCA to seek judicial review in any circuit in which it does business and that "for unexplained reasons it has chosen this circuit." Judge Posner faulted HCA for failing to address the scope of review over the FTC's decision:

> Hospital Corporation has argued the case to us as if we were the FTC, which assuredly we are not. Our only function is to determine whether the Commission's analysis of the probable effects of these acquisitions on hospital competition in Chattanooga is so implausible, so feebly supported by the record, that it flunks even the deferential test of substantial evidence.

Calling the FTC's decision a "model of lucidity," Judge Posner reviewed the Commission's analysis of the merger:

When an economic approach is taken in a section 7 case, the ultimate issue is whether the challenged acquisition is likely to facilitate collusion. In this perspective the acquisition of a competitor has no economic significance in itself; the worry is that it may enable the acquiring firm to cooperate (or cooperate better) with other leading competitors on reducing or limiting output, thereby pushing up the market price. Hospital Corporation calls the issue whether an acquisition is likely to have such an effect "economic," which of course it is. But for purposes of judicial review, as we have said, it is a factual issue subject to the substantial evidence rule.   * * *

* * *

Considering the concentration of the market, the absence of competitive alternatives, the regulatory barrier to entry (the certificate of need law), the low elasticity of demand, the exceptionally severe cost pressures under which American hospitals labor today, the history of collusion in the industry, and the sharp reduction in the number of substantial competitors in this market brought about by the acquisition of four hospitals in a city with only eleven (one already owned by Hospital Corporation), we cannot say that the Commission's prediction [of a danger to competition] is not supported by substantial evidence.

Judge Posner discussed Hospital Corporation's arguments that collusion is unlikely because of the heterogeneity of hospital markets, the rapid technological and economic change experienced by the hospital industry, and the size of third party payers. Judge Posner concluded: "Most of these facts do detract from a conclusion that collusion in this market is a serious danger, but it was for the Commission—it is not for us—to determine their weight."

2. Complaint Counsel in *Hospital Corporation of America* recommended that the Commission require HCA to submit to the Commission for prior approval the following: (1) purchases of hospitals and (2) assumption of hospital management contracts in areas where there is a certificate of need requirement for new hospitals; where the acquisition would increase an HHI of at least 1800 by 100 or more points; and where HCA is already operating a hospital or would operate two or more hospitals as the result of the acquisition. Complaint Counsel argued that the relevant market for calculation of market share should be the Metropolitan Statistical Area and the share be calculated based upon state-licensed acute care bed capacity. Although these are only rough approximations of the analysis required for proof of violation of the Clayton Act, as illustrated in *HCA*, a dissenting Commissioner advocated the Counsel's proposal for prior approval of HCA purchases and management contracts outside the Chattanooga urban area against the Commission's rejection. Should the Commission have adopted prior approval requirements for areas meeting the Complaint Counsel's standards?

3. Miles and Philp offer the following equation to illustrate the calculation of the Herfindahl–Hirschmann Index: "[The HHI] is calculated by squaring the market share of each firm in the market and then adding the squares. For example, suppose Firm A with 10% of the market and Firm B with 12%. Suppose also that Firms C, D, E, F, and G are in the

market with shares of 25%, 15%, 10%, 8%, and 20%. Then the postmerger $HHI = (10 + 12)^2 + (25)^2 + (15)^2 + (10)^2 + (8)^2 + (20)^2 = 1898$. [I]t also is important to ascertain by how much the merger increases the HHI. This can be calculated simply by multiplying the shares of the merging firms and then multiplying that product by 2. In the example above, the change in $HHI = (10)(12)(2) = 240$." Miles and Philp, Hospitals Caught in the Antitrust Net, 24 Duquesne L.Rev. 489, 668 (1986). The use of this index as a measure of the potential market impact of a merger or acquisition is analyzed by Schramm and Renn, Hospital Mergers, Market Concentration and the Herfindahl–Hirschmann Index, 33 Emory L.J. 869 (1984).

Using data from the California Health Facilities Commission, Schramm and Renn conclude that "in eighty percent of the markets [of the 131 in the study], any consolidation within the market would likely be challenged" and comment that "any market having six or fewer hospitals with roughly equal market shares (specifically, no one hospital having a share of less than 10 percent) is in what one might think of as a 'static' violation. Any merger must necessarily result in an Index in excess of 1,800 points and an accompanying increase of at least 100 points." Id. at 874. Does this argue in favor of or against the use of the Herfindahl–Hirschmann Index by the Commission in such markets? What implications does this result have for financially threatened institutions in highly concentrated markets?

4. In applying § 7 of the Clayton Act, the courts, the Commission and the Department of Justice take into account efficiencies that might be produced by the acquisition and balance these efficiencies against the acquisition's anti-competitive effects. In *Hospital Corporation of America,* the Commissioner noted that "HCA has provided no more than speculation as its 'evidence' of efficiencies." How could HCA have proven that the acquisition of HAI and HCC facilities in Chattanooga created efficiencies? If the Commission were persuaded that these efficiencies occurred, how should they be balanced against the acquisition's anti-competitive effects?

Note: Antitrust Analysis of Mergers of Nonprofit Providers

Two hospital merger cases filed by the Department of Justice subsequent to *HCA* have raised significant questions concerning the application of antitrust merger law to not-for-profit institutions. The first of these is whether § 7 of the Clayton Act reaches mergers of such institutions.

In United States v. Carilion Health System, Community Hospital of Roanoke Valley, 707 F.Supp. 840 (W.D.Va.1989), affirmed without opinion, 892 F.2d 1042 (4th Cir.1989), the district court granted defendant's motion to dismiss the government's § 7 claim. Section 7 governs acquisitions of "stock or other share capital." The court in *Roanoke* held that the acquired hospital, as a not-for-profit organization, had not issued stock or share capital. Section 7 also controls the acquisition of "assets" by a "person subject to the jurisdiction" of the FTC. The *Roanoke* court considered the jurisdiction of the FTC under § 4 of the FTC Act, which grants the FTC jurisdiction over "any company, trust * * * or association, incorporated or unincorporated, which is organized to carry on a business for its own profit or that of its members." Because a not-for-profit corporation does not carry on a business for profit, the court concluded that the FTC did not have jurisdiction over the nonprofit hospital and, therefore, § 7 of the Clayton Act did not govern the proposed merger.

In United States v. Rockford Memorial Corp., SwedishAmerican Corp., 898 F.2d 1278 (7th Cir.1990), Judge Posner, writing for a unanimous panel, considered the merger of two nonprofit hospitals. Judge Posner rejected the government's theory that § 7 of the Clayton Act applied to such a merger because the merger of the two nonprofit entities would "in effect" be the same as any other merger. But Judge Posner also rejected the conclusion in *Roanoke* that § 7 does not apply to the acquisition or merger of nonprofits. Instead, Posner argues that § 7 of the Clayton Act applies via the Act's § 11. Section 11 of the Clayton Act provides that certain agencies have enforcement power over particular entities (e.g., the FCC as to common carriers) and that the FTC has enforcement authority over any persons subject to the Act in "all other character of commerce." Posner concludes that the assets acquisition language of § 7 is intended to exclude only regulated industries, which does not include hospitals. Posner dismissed the government's § 7 claim, however, because the government failed to make the argument he himself made and found persuasive.

The second question raised in *Roanoke* and *Rockford* concerns whether not-for-profit health care institutions conform to traditional economic analysis of competitor behavior. Both *Roanoke* and *Rockford* ultimately were tried under § 1 of the Sherman Act.

Applying the rule of reason, the court in *Roanoke* found that the merger did not violate § 1. This case involved the merger of two of three hospitals in Roanoke. The court, disagreeing with the government's definition of the relevant geographic market, rejected the government's claim that the merger would result in a 70% market share for the merging hospitals. In addition, the court found that the defendants intended the merger to enhance competition and that Roanoke Memorial wanted to expand with its acquisition of Community Hospital, which itself was underoccupied. The court also speculated that the hospitals' nonprofit structure, with a board that included business leaders "who can be expected to demand that the institutions use the savings achieved through the merger to reduce hospital charges," would adequately restrain the merged hospitals. Overall, the court found that the proposed merger would strengthen competition, relying in part on its finding that hospital rates are lower where there are fewer hospitals. The court was not persuaded that entry barriers existed that would prohibit competitors from entering the market.

The Seventh Circuit affirmed the geographic market definition adopted by the district court in *Rockford*. It affirmed the court's finding that the merger of the two largest hospitals in Rockford would result in a 64% to 72% market share for these hospitals and a 90% share for the three largest hospitals remaining in Rockford after the merger.

In responding to defendants' argument that not-for-profit organizations would behave differently in uncompetitive circumstances, Posner stated:

> * * * We are aware of no evidence—and the defendants present none, only argument—that nonprofit suppliers of goods or services are more likely to compete vigorously than profit-making suppliers. Most

people do not like to compete, and will seek ways of avoiding competition by agreement tacit or explicit, depending of course on the costs of agreeing. The ideology of nonprofit enterprise is cooperative rather than competitive. If the managers of nonprofit enterprises are less likely to strain after that last penny of profit, they may be less prone to engage in profit-maximizing competition. [ ]

* * * We would like to see more effort put into studying the actual effect of concentration on price in the hospital industry as in other industries. If the government is right in these cases, then, other things being equal, hospital prices should be higher in markets with fewer hospitals. This is a studiable hypothesis, by modern methods of multivariate statistical analysis, and some studies have been conducted correlating prices and concentration in the hospital industry. [ ]

Unfortunately, this literature is at an early and inconclusive stage, and the government is not required to await the maturation of the relevant scholarship in order to establish a prima facie case. * * * The government showed large market shares in a plausibly defined market in an industry more prone than many to collusion. The defendants responded with conjectures about the motives of nonprofits, and other will o' the wisps, that the district judge was free to reject, and did.

* * *

Both the question concerning the scope of § 7 of the Clayton Act and the issue of competitive behavior by nonprofit entities reflect the relatively recent expansion of antitrust enforcement against not-for-profit organizations. In fact, the Roanoke and Rockford mergers are the first mergers of not-for-profit hospitals challenged by the U.S. Department of Justice in an action for injunctive relief.

Review the material in Chapter 5 on not-for-profit hospitals. Can you state any hypotheses that should be tested in the research desired by Judge Posner?

Note: Health Planning and Antitrust Law

The planning and antitrust strategies for controlling health care cost inflation seem diametrically opposed. Health planning seeks to control costs by cooperative activity to limit supply; antitrust law by removing cooperative restraints on competition. Thus, while the federal health planning laws were in effect the courts faced a difficult task in reconciling the two legislative programs. See Hospital Building Company v. Trustees of Rex Hospital, 691 F.2d 678 (4th Cir.1982) cert. denied 464 U.S. 890, 104 S.Ct. 231, 78 L.Ed.2d 224 (1983). Further, a continuing question exists as to the extent to which state health planning activities are exempt from antitrust scrutiny.

If a state health planning agency grants a certificate of need that creates a monopoly or restrains trade, can the agency itself be held liable under the antitrust laws? Clearly not, as the Parker v. Brown (or state action) exemption protects activities carrying out clearly articulated and supervised state policies from antitrust sanctions. See Miller, Antitrust and Certificate of Need: Health Systems Agencies, the Planning Act and Regulatory Capture, 68 Georgetown L.J. 873, 843–900 (1981). If one private institution acquires another with the approval of the state certificate of need agency and the acquisition creates a monopoly in a local market, is the private action immunized under Parker v. Brown? See North Carolina ex rel. Edmisten v. P.I.A. Asheville, Inc., 740 F.2d 274 (4th Cir.1984), cert. denied, 471 U.S. 1003, 105 S.Ct. 1865, 85 L.Ed.2d 159 (1985) (Parker v. Brown does not apply as the state merely authorizes private conduct, but does not supervise it).

Efforts by providers to exclude competitors from their market by urging disapproval of the proposals of those competitors by state planning agencies may be protected by the Noerr–Pennington antitrust immunity. Noerr–Pennington protects from antitrust sanctions attempts to influence the passage or enforcement of laws, even if these attempts stem from anticompetitive motives. The Noerr–Pennington immunity (so named because of the two cases in which it was enunciated) insures that the antitrust laws do not unduly impose on free expression and political advocacy. It is subject, however, to a "sham" exception: if frivolous and baseless actions are taken with the intent to interfere with competition, Noerr–Pennington immunity may not apply. For a discussion of the application of Noerr–Pennington and the sham exception to health planning activities, see Hospital Bldg. Co. v. Trustees of Rex Hosp., 691 F.2d 678 (4th Cir.1982), cert. denied, 464 U.S. 890, 104 S.Ct. 231, 78 L.Ed.2d 224 (1983); Huron Valley Hosp., Inc. v. City of Pontiac, 650 F.Supp. 1325 (E.D.Mich.1986), affirmed, 849 F.2d 262 (6th Cir.1988).

IV. HEALTH CARE FINANCING

The preceding chapter examined at length the inefficiencies that have plagued the markets for health care and for health care financing for the last half-century. Many of the strategies proposed in Chapter 7 for lowering health care costs and improving efficiency in the health care industry involve reorganization of these markets. Some of these efforts rely directly on traditional antitrust law to remove restraints on competition imposed by providers. An example of this approach is the 1979 FTC ruling that ethical restrictions imposed by the American Medical Association restricting price competition between physicians violated the antitrust laws, American Medical Association v. Federal Trade Commission, 94 F.T.C. 701 (1979), modified and enforced, 638 F.2d 443 (2d Cir.1980), affirmed memorandum by an equally divided court, 455 U.S. 676, 102 S.Ct. 1744, 71 L.Ed.2d 546 (1982), rehearing denied 456 U.S. 966, 102 S.Ct. 2048, 72 L.Ed.2d 491 (1982).

Other strategies, on the other hand, may violate the antitrust laws. Some approaches rely on organization of independent providers into new entities or joint ventures that arguably can compete more effectively, or on empowering purchasers to bargain more effectively with providers through collective action. HMOs, IPAs, PPOs, and purchasing coalitions are in this category. These approaches often involve concerted action and usually result in reducing the number of competitors in a market and are therefore subject to review under the antitrust laws. Other cost control efforts rely on constraining the purchase of services through utilization review, or controlling prices through maximum fee schedules or relative value schedules. Artificial constraints on output or on prices run contrary to normal notions of competition, and thus are suspect under the antitrust laws. Efforts to organize providers or to bargain with them collectively or to constrain utilization or prices often exclude or diminish the income of some providers. Excluded providers have in several instances sued under the antitrust laws, erroneously believing that the purpose of the antitrust laws is to protect competitors from competition. The area of health care financing offers a fruitful field for antitrust litigation.

ARIZONA v. MARICOPA COUNTY MEDICAL SOCIETY

Supreme Court of the United States, 1982.
457 U.S. 332, 102 S.Ct. 2466, 73 L.Ed.2d 48.

JUSTICE STEVENS delivered the opinion of the Court.

The question presented is whether § 1 of the Sherman Act, 26 Stat. 209, as amended, 15 U.S.C. § 1, has been violated by agreements among competing physicians setting, by majority vote, the maximum fees that they may claim in full payment for health services provided to policyholders of specified insurance plans. The United States Court of Appeals for the Ninth Circuit held that the question could not be answered without evaluating the actual purpose and effect of the agreements at a full trial. 643 F.2d 553 (1980). Because the undisputed facts disclose a violation of the statute, we granted certiorari, 450 U.S. 979, 101 S.Ct. 1512, 67 L.Ed.2d 813 (1981), and now reverse.

I

In October 1978 the State of Arizona filed a civil complaint against two county medical societies and two "foundations for medical care" that the medical societies had organized. The complaint alleged that the defendants were engaged in illegal price-fixing conspiracies. * * * The District Court * * * entered an order pursuant to 28 U.S.C. § 1292(b), certifying for interlocutory appeal the question "whether the FMC membership agreements, which contain the promise to abide by maximum fee schedules, are illegal *per se* under section 1 of the Sherman Act."

The Court of Appeals, by a divided vote, affirmed the District Court's order refusing to enter partial summary judgment,[4] * * *.

---

4. Judge Sneed explained his reluctance to apply the *per se* rule substantially as follows: The record did not indicate the actual purpose of the maximum-fee arrangements or their effect on competition in the health care industry. It was not clear whether the assumptions made about typical price restraints could be carried over to that industry. Only recently had this Court applied the antitrust laws to the professions. Moreover, there already were such significant obstacles to pure competi-

Because the ultimate question presented by the certiorari petition is whether a partial summary judgment should have been entered by the District Court, we must assume that the respondents' version of any disputed issue of fact is correct. We therefore first review the relevant undisputed facts and then identify the factual basis for the respondents' contention that their agreements on fee schedules are not unlawful.

II

The Maricopa Foundation for Medical Care is a nonprofit Arizona corporation composed of licensed doctors of medicine, osteopathy, and podiatry engaged in private practice. Approximately 1,750 doctors, representing about 70% of the practitioners in Maricopa County, are members.

The Maricopa Foundation was organized in 1969 for the purpose of promoting fee-for-service medicine and to provide the community with a competitive alternative to existing health insurance plans. The foundation performs three primary activities. It establishes the schedule of maximum fees that participating doctors agree to accept as payment in full for services performed for patients insured under plans approved by the foundation. It reviews the medical necessity and appropriateness of treatment provided by its members to such insured persons. It is authorized to draw checks on insurance company accounts to pay doctors for services performed for covered patients. In performing these functions, the foundation is considered an "insurance administrator" by the Director of the Arizona Department of Insurance. Its participating doctors, however, have no financial interest in the operation of the foundation.

The Pima Foundation for Medical Care, which includes about 400 member doctors, performs similar functions. For the purposes of this litigation, the parties seem to regard the activities of the two foundations as essentially the same. No challenge is made to their peer review or claim administration functions. Nor do the foundations allege that these two activities make it necessary for them to engage in the practice of establishing maximum-fee schedules.

At the time this lawsuit was filed, each foundation made use of "relative values" and "conversion factors" in compiling its fee schedule. The conversion factor is the dollar amount used to determine fees for a particular medical specialty. Thus, for example, the conversion factors for "medicine" and "laboratory" were $8 and $5.50, respectively, in 1972, and $10 and $6.50 in 1974. The relative value schedule provides a numerical weight for each different medical service—thus, an office

tion in the industry that a court must compare the prices that obtain under the maximum-fee arrangements with those that would otherwise prevail rather than with those that would prevail under ideal competitive conditions. Furthermore, the Ninth Circuit had not applied *Keifer–Stewart Co. v. Joseph E. Seagram & Sons, Inc.*, 340 U.S. 211, 71 S.Ct. 259, 95 L.Ed. 219 (1951), and *Albrecht v. Herald Co.*, 390 U.S. 145, 88 S.Ct. 869, 19 L.Ed.2d 998 (1968), to horizontal agreements that establish maximum prices; some of the economic assumptions underlying the rule against maximum price fixing were not sound.

consultation has a lesser value than a home visit. The relative value was multiplied by the conversion factor to determine the maximum fee. The fee schedule has been revised periodically. The foundation board of trustees would solicit advice from various medical societies about the need for change in either relative values or conversion factors in their respective specialties. The board would then formulate the new fee schedule and submit it to the vote of the entire membership.[10]

The fee schedules limit the amount that the member doctors may recover for services performed for patients insured under plans approved by the foundations. To obtain this approval the insurers—including self-insured employers as well as insurance companies[11]—agree to pay the doctors' charges up to the scheduled amounts, and in exchange the doctors agree to accept those amounts as payment in full for their services. The doctors are free to charge higher fees to uninsured patients, and they also may charge any patient less than the scheduled maxima. A patient who is insured by a foundation-endorsed plan is guaranteed complete coverage for the full amount of his medical bills only if he is treated by a foundation member. He is free to go to a nonmember physician and is still covered for charges that do not exceed the maximum-fee schedule, but he must pay any excess that the nonmember physician may charge.

The impact of the foundation fee schedules on medical fees and on insurance premiums is a matter of dispute. The State of Arizona contends that the periodic upward revisions of the maximum-fee schedules have the effect of stabilizing and enhancing the level of actual charges by physicians, and that the increasing level of their fees in turn increases insurance premiums. The foundations, on the other hand, argue that the schedules impose a meaningful limit on physicians' charges, and that the advance agreement by the doctors to accept the maxima enables the insurance carriers to limit and to calculate more efficiently the risks they underwrite and therefore serves as an effective cost-containment mechanism that has saved patients and insurers millions of dollars. * * * We must assume that the respondents' view of the genuine issues of fact is correct.

This assumption presents, but does not answer, the question whether the Sherman Act prohibits the competing doctors from adopting, revising, and agreeing to use a maximum-fee schedule in implementation of the insurance plans.

10. The parties disagree over whether the increases in the fee schedules are the cause or the result of the increases in the prevailing rate for medical services in the relevant markets. There appears to be agreement, however, that 85–95% of physicians in Maricopa County bill at or above the maximum reimbursement levels set by the Maricopa Foundation.

11. Seven different insurance companies underwrite health insurance plans that have been approved by the Maricopa Foundation, and three companies underwrite the plans approved by the Pima Foundation. The record contains no firm data on the portion of the health care market that is covered by these plans. The State relies upon a 1974 analysis indicating that insurance plans endorsed by the Maricopa Foundation had about 63% of the prepaid health care market, but the respondents contest the accuracy of this analysis.

III

The respondents recognize that our decisions establish that price-fixing agreements are unlawful on their face. But they argue that the *per se* rule does not govern this case because the agreements at issue are horizontal and fix maximum prices, are among members of a profession, are in an industry with which the judiciary has little antitrust experience, and are alleged to have procompetitive justifications. Before we examine each of these arguments, we pause to consider the history and the meaning of the *per se* rule against price-fixing agreements.

A

Section 1 of the Sherman Act of 1890 literally prohibits *every* agreement "in restraint of trade." In *United States v. Joint Traffic Assn.,* 171 U.S. 505, 19 S.Ct. 25, 43 L.Ed. 259 (1898), we recognized that Congress could not have intended a literal interpretation of the word "every"; since *Standard Oil Co. of New Jersey v. United States,* 221 U.S. 1, 31 S.Ct. 502, 55 L.Ed. 619 (1911), we have analyzed most restraints under the so-called "rule of reason." As its name suggests, the rule of reason requires the factfinder to decide whether under all the circumstances of the case the restrictive practice imposes an unreasonable restraint on competition.

The elaborate inquiry into the reasonableness of a challenged business practice entails significant costs. Litigation of the effect or purpose of a practice often is extensive and complex. [   ] Judges often lack the expert understanding of industrial market structures and behavior to determine with any confidence a practice's effect on competition. [   ] And the result of the process in any given case may provide little certainty or guidance about the legality of a practice in another context. [   ]

The costs of judging business practices under the rule of reason, however, have been reduced by the recognition of *per se* rules. Once experience with a particular kind of restraint enables the Court to predict with confidence that the rule of reason will condemn it, it has applied a conclusive presumption that the restraint is unreasonable. As in every rule of general application, the match between the presumed and the actual is imperfect. For the sake of business certainty and litigation efficiency, we have tolerated the invalidation of some agreements that a fullblown inquiry might have proved to be reasonable.

* * *

The application of the *per se* rule to maximum-price-fixing agreements in *Kiefer–Stewart Co. v. Joseph E. Seagram & Sons, Inc.,* 340 U.S. 211, 71 S.Ct. 259, 95 L.Ed. 219 (1951), followed ineluctably from [proscription of maximum price fixing in] *Socony–Vacuum* :

"For such agreements, no less than those to fix minimum prices, cripple the freedom of traders and thereby restrain their ability to sell in accordance with their own judgment. We reaffirm what we said in *United States v. Socony–Vacuum Oil Co.*, 310 U.S. 150, 223 [60 S.Ct. 811, 844, 84 L.Ed. 1129]: 'Under the Sherman Act a combination formed for the purpose and with the effect of raising, depressing, fixing, pegging, or stabilizing the price of a commodity in interstate or foreign commerce is illegal *per se.*'" 340 U.S., at 213, 60 S.Ct., at 839.

Over the objection that maximum-price-fixing agreements were not the "economic equivalent" of minimum-price-fixing agreements, *Kiefer–Stewart* was reaffirmed in *Albrecht v. Herald Co.*, 390 U.S. 145, 88 S.Ct. 869, 19 L.Ed.2d 998 (1968):

"Maximum and minimum price fixing may have different consequences in many situations. But schemes to fix maximum prices, by substituting the perhaps erroneous judgment of a seller for the forces of the competitive market, may severely intrude upon the ability of buyers to compete and survive in that market. Competition, even in a single product, is not cast in a single mold. Maximum prices may be fixed too low for the dealer to furnish services essential to the value which goods have for the consumer or to furnish services and conveniences which consumers desire and for which they are willing to pay. Maximum price fixing may channel distribution through a few large or specifically advantaged dealers who otherwise would be subject to significant nonprice competition. Moreover, if the actual price charged under a maximum price scheme is nearly always the fixed maximum price, which is increasingly likely as the maximum price approaches the actual cost of the dealer, the scheme tends to acquire all the attributes of an arrangement fixing minimum prices." *Id.*, at 152–153, 88 S.Ct., at 872–873. * * *

* * *

B

Our decisions foreclose the argument that the agreements at issue escape *per se* condemnation because they are horizontal and fix maximum prices. *Kiefer–Stewart* and *Albrecht* place horizontal agreements to fix maximum prices on the same legal—even if not economic—footing as agreements to fix minimum or uniform prices. The *per se* rule "is grounded on faith in price competition as a market force [and not] on a policy of low selling prices at the price of eliminating competition." [ ] In this case the rule is violated by a price restraint that tends to provide the same economic rewards to all practitioners regardless of their skill, their experience, their training, or their willingness to employ innovative and difficult procedures in individual cases. Such a restraint also may discourage entry into the market and may deter experimentation and new developments by individual entrepreneurs. It may be a masquerade for an agreement to fix uniform prices, or it may in the future take on that character.

Nor does the fact that doctors—rather than nonprofessionals—are the parties to the price-fixing agreements support the respondents' position. In *Goldfarb v. Virginia State Bar,* 421 U.S. 773, 788, n. 17, 95 S.Ct. 2004, 2013, n. 17, 44 L.Ed.2d 572 (1975), we stated that the "public service aspect, and other features of the professions, may require that a particular practice, which could properly be viewed as a violation of the Sherman Act in another context, be treated differently." [ ] The price-fixing agreements in this case, however, are not premised on public service or ethical norms. The respondents do not argue, as did the defendants in *Goldfarb* [ ], that the quality of the professional service that their members provide is enhanced by the price restraint. The respondents' claim for relief from the *per se* rule is simply that the doctors' agreement not to charge certain insureds more than a fixed price facilitates the successful marketing of an attractive insurance plan. But the claim that the price restraint will make it easier for customers to pay does not distinguish the medical profession from any other provider of goods or services.

We are equally unpersuaded by the argument that we should not apply the *per se* rule in this case because the judiciary has little antitrust experience in the health care industry. The argument quite obviously is inconsistent with *Socony–Vacuum.* * * * [Y]et the Court of Appeals refused to apply the *per se* rule in this case in part because the health care industry was so far removed from the competitive model.[20] Consistent with our prediction in *Socony–Vacuum,* 310 U.S., at 221, 60 S.Ct., at 843, the result of this reasoning was the adoption by the Court of Appeals of a legal standard based on the reasonableness of the fixed prices, an inquiry we have so often condemned. Finally, the argument that the *per se* rule must be rejustified for every industry that has not been subject to significant antitrust litigation ignores the rationale for *per se* rules, which in part is to avoid "the necessity for an incredibly complicated and prolonged economic investigation into the entire history of the industry involved, as well as related industries, in an effort to determine at large whether a particular restraint has been unreasonable—an inquiry so often wholly fruitless when undertaken." [ ]

The respondents' principal argument is that the *per se* rule is inapplicable because their agreements are alleged to have procompetitive justifications. The argument indicates a misunderstanding of the *per se* concept. The anticompetitive potential inherent in all price-fixing agreements justifies their facial invalidation even if procompetitive

---

20. "The health care industry, moreover, presents a particularly difficult area. The first step to understanding is to recognize that not only is access to the medical profession very time consuming and expensive both for the applicant and society generally, but also that numerous government subventions of the costs of medical care have created both a demand and supply function for medical services that is artifically high. The present supply and demand functions of medical services in no way approximate those which would exist in a purely private competitive order. An accurate description of those functions moreover is not available. Thus, we lack baselines by which could be measured the distance between the present supply and demand functions and those which would exist under ideal competitive conditions." 643 F.2d, at 556.

justifications are offered for some. Those claims of enhanced competition are so unlikely to prove significant in any particular case that we adhere to the rule of law that is justified in its general application. Even when the respondents are given every benefit of the doubt, the limited record in this case is not inconsistent with the presumption that the respondents' agreements will not significantly enhance competition.

The respondents contend that their fee schedules are procompetitive because they make it possible to provide consumers of health care with a uniquely desirable form of insurance coverage that could not otherwise exist. The features of the foundation-endorsed insurance plans that they stress are a choice of doctors, complete insurance coverage, and lower premiums. The first two characteristics, however, are hardly unique to these plans. Since only about 70% of the doctors in the relevant market are members of either foundation, the guarantee of complete coverage only applies when an insured chooses a physician in that 70%. If he elects to go to a nonfoundation doctor, he may be required to pay a portion of the doctor's fee. It is fair to presume, however, that at least 70% of the doctors in other markets charge no more than the "usual, customary, and reasonable" fee that typical insurers are willing to reimburse in full. Thus, in Maricopa and Pima Counties as well as in most parts of the country, if an insured asks his doctor if the insurance coverage is complete, presumably in about 70% of the cases the doctor will say "Yes" and in about 30% of the cases he will say "No."

It is true that a binding assurance of complete insurance coverage—as well as most of the respondents' potential for lower insurance premiums[25]—can be obtained only if the insurer and the doctor agree in advance on the maximum fee that the doctor will accept as full payment for a particular service. Even if a fee schedule is therefore desirable, it is not necessary that the doctors do the price fixing.[26] The

---

25. We do not perceive the respondents' claim of procompetitive justification for their fee schedules to rest on the premise that the fee schedules actually reduce medical fees and accordingly reduce insurance premiums, thereby enhancing competition in the health insurance industry. Such an argument would merely restate the long-rejected position that fixed prices are reasonable if they are lower than free competition would yield. It is arguable, however, that the existence of a fee schedule, whether fixed by the doctors or by the insurers, makes it easier—and to that extent less expensive—for insurers to calculate the risks that they underwrite and to arrive at the appropriate reimbursement on insured claims.

26. According to a Federal Trade Commission staff report: "Until the mid-1960's, most Blue Shield plans determined in advance how much to pay for particular procedures and prepared fee schedules reflecting their determinations. Fee schedules are still used in approximately 25 percent of Blue Shield contracts." Bureau of Competition, Federal Trade Commission, Medical Participation in Control of Blue Shield and Certain Other Open–Panel Medical Prepayment Plans 128 (1979). We do not suggest that Blue Shield plans are not actually controlled by doctors. Indeed, as the same report discusses at length, the belief that they are has given rise to considerable antitrust litigation. See also D. Kass & P. Pautler, Bureau of Economics, Federal Trade Commission, Staff Report on Physician Control of Blue Shield Plans (1979). Nor does this case present the question whether an insurer may, consistent with the Sherman Act, fix the fee schedule and enter into bilateral contracts with individual doctors. That question was not reached in *Group Life & Health Insurance Co. v. Royal Drug Co.,* 440 U.S.

record indicates that the Arizona Comprehensive Medical/Dental Program for Foster Children is administered by the Maricopa Foundation pursuant to a contract under which the maximum-fee schedule is prescribed by a state agency rather than by the doctors. This program and the Blue Shield plan challenged in *Group Life & Health Insurance Co. v. Royal Drug Co.*, 440 U.S. 205, 99 S.Ct. 1067, 59 L.Ed.2d 261 (1979), indicate that insurers are capable not only of fixing maximum reimbursable prices but also of obtaining binding agreements with providers guaranteeing the insured full reimbursement of a participating provider's fee. In light of these examples, it is not surprising that nothing in the record even arguably supports the conclusion that this type of insurance program could not function if the fee schedules were set in a different way.

The most that can be said for having doctors fix the maximum prices is that doctors may be able to do it more efficiently than insurers. The validity of that assumption is far from obvious, but in any event there is no reason to believe that any savings that might accrue from this arrangement would be sufficiently great to affect the competitiveness of these kinds of insurance plans. It is entirely possible that the potential or actual power of the foundations to dictate the terms of such insurance plans may more than offset the theoretical efficiencies upon which the respondents' defense ultimately rests.

* * *

IV

Having declined the respondents' invitation to cut back on the *per se* rule against price fixing, we are left with the respondents' argument that their fee schedules involve price fixing in only a literal sense. For this argument, the respondents rely upon *Broadcast Music, Inc. v. Columbia Broadcasting System, Inc.*, 441 U.S. 1, 99 S.Ct. 1551, 60 L.Ed.2d 1 (1979).

In *Broadcast Music* we were confronted with an antitrust challenge to the marketing of the right to use copyrighted compositions derived from the entire membership of the American Society of Composers, Authors and Publishers (ASCAP). The so-called "blanket license" was entirely different from the product that any one composer was able to sell by himself. Although there was little competition among individual composers for their separate compositions, the blanket-license arrangement did not place any restraint on the right of any individual copyright owner to sell his own compositions separately to any buyer at any price. But a "necessary consequence" of the creation of the blanket license was that its price had to be established. *Id.*, at 21, 99 S.Ct., at 1563. We held that the delegation by the composers to ASCAP

205, 99 S.Ct. 1067, 59 L.Ed.2d 261 (1979). See *id.*, at 210, n. 5, 99 S.Ct., at 1072, n. 5. In an *amicus curiae* brief, the United States expressed its opinion that such an arrangement would be legal unless the plaintiffs could establish that a conspiracy among providers was at work. Brief for United States as *Amicus Curiae*, O.T.1978, No. 77–952, pp. 10–11. Our point is simply that the record provides no factual basis for the respondents' claim that the doctors must fix the fee schedule.

of the power to fix the price for the blanket license was not a species of the price-fixing agreements categorically forbidden by the Sherman Act. The record disclosed price fixing only in a "literal sense." *Id.*, at 8, 99 S.Ct., at 1556.

This case is fundamentally different. Each of the foundations is composed of individual practitioners who compete with one another for patients. Neither the foundations nor the doctors sell insurance, and they derive no profits from the sale of health insurance policies. The members of the foundations sell medical services. Their combination in the form of the foundation does not permit them to sell any different product. Their combination has merely permitted them to sell their services to certain customers at fixed prices and arguably to affect the prevailing market price of medical care.

The foundations are not analogous to partnerships or other joint arrangements in which persons who would otherwise be competitors pool their capital and share the risks of loss as well as the opportunities for profit. In such joint ventures, the partnership is regarded as a single firm competing with other sellers in the market. The agreement under attack is an agreement among hundreds of competing doctors concerning the price at which each will offer his own services to a substantial number of consumers. It is true that some are surgeons, some anesthesiologists, and some psychiatrists, but the doctors do not sell a package of three kinds of services. If a clinic offered complete medical coverage for a flat fee, the cooperating doctors would have the type of partnership arrangement in which a price-fixing agreement among the doctors would be perfectly proper. But the fee agreements disclosed by the record in this case are among independent competing entrepreneurs. They fit squarely into the horizontal price-fixing mold.

The judgment of the Court of Appeals is reversed.

It is so ordered.

Justice Blackmun and Justice O'Connor took no part in the consideration or decision of this case.

Justice Powell, with whom The Chief Justice and Justice Rehnquist join, dissenting.

The medical care plan condemned by the Court today is a comparatively new method of providing insured medical services at predetermined maximum costs. It involves no coercion. Medical insurance companies, physicians, and patients alike are free to participate or not as they choose. On its face, the plan seems to be in the public interest.

* * * I do not think today's decision on an incomplete record is consistent with proper judicial resolution of an issue of this complexity, novelty, and importance to the public. I therefore dissent.

* * *

II

This case comes to us on a plaintiff's motion for summary judgment after only limited discovery. Therefore, as noted above, the inferences to be drawn from the record must be viewed in the light most favorable to the respondents. [   ] This requires, as the Court acknowledges, that we consider the foundation arrangement as one that "impose[s] a meaningful limit on physicians' charges," that "enables the insurance carriers to limit and to calculate more efficiently the risks they underwrite," and that "therefore serves as an effective cost-containment mechanism that has saved patients and insurers millions of dollars." [   ] The question is whether we should condemn this arrangement forthwith under the Sherman Act, a law designed to *benefit* consumers.

Several other aspects of the record are of key significance but are not stressed by the Court. First, the foundation arrangement forecloses *no* competition. Unlike the classic cartel agreement, the foundation plan does not instruct potential competitors: "Deal with consumers on the following terms and no others." Rather, physicians who participate in the foundation plan are free both to associate with other medical insurance plans—at any fee level, high or low—and directly to serve uninsured patients—at any fee level, high or low. Similarly, insurers that participate in the foundation plan also remain at liberty to do business outside the plan with any physician—foundation member or not—at any fee level. Nor are physicians locked into a plan for more than one year's membership. [   ] Thus freedom to compete, as well as freedom to withdraw, is preserved. The Court cites no case in which a remotely comparable plan or agreement is condemned on a *per se* basis.

Second, on this record we must find that insurers represent consumer interests. Normally consumers search for high quality at low prices. But once a consumer is insured—*i.e.,* has chosen a medical insurance plan—he is largely indifferent to the amount that his physician charges if the coverage is full, as under the foundation-sponsored plan.

The insurer, however, is *not* indifferent. To keep insurance premiums at a competitive level and to remain profitable, insurers—including those who have contracts with the foundations—step into the consumer's shoes with his incentive to contain medical costs. Indeed, insurers may be the only parties who have the effective power to restrain medical costs, given the difficulty that patients experience in comparing price and quality for a professional service such as medical care.

On the record before us, there is no evidence of opposition to the foundation plan by insurance companies—or, for that matter, by members of the public. Rather seven insurers willingly have chosen to contract out to the foundations the task of developing maximum-fee schedules. Again, on the record before us, we must infer that the foundation plan—open as it is to insurers, physicians, and the public—has in fact benefited consumers by "enabl[ing] the insurance carriers to limit and to calculate more efficiently the risks they underwrite." [ ] Nevertheless, even though the case is here on an incomplete summary judgment record, the Court conclusively draws contrary inferences to support its *per se* judgment.

III

It is settled law that once an arrangement has been labeled as "price fixing" it is to be condemned *per se*. But it is equally well settled that this characterization is not to be applied as a talisman to every arrangement that involves a literal fixing of prices. Many lawful contracts, mergers, and partnerships fix prices. But our cases require a more discerning approach. * * *

* * *

* * * [T]he fact that a foundation-sponsored health insurance plan *literally* involves the setting of ceiling prices among competing physicians does not, of itself, justify condemning the plan as *per se* illegal. Only if it is clear from the record that the agreement among physicians is "so plainly anticompetitive that no elaborate study of [its effects] is needed to establish [its] illegality" may a court properly make a *per se* judgment. [ ] And, as our cases demonstrate, the *per se* label should not be assigned without carefully considering substantial benefits and procompetitive justifications. This is especially true when the agreement under attack is novel, as in this case. * * *

IV

The Court acknowledges that the *per se* ban against price fixing is not to be invoked every time potential competitors *literally* fix prices. [ ] One also would have expected it to acknowledge that *per se* characterization is inappropriate if the challenged agreement or plan achieves for the public procompetitive benefits that otherwise are not attainable. The Court does not do this. And neither does it provide alternative criteria by which the *per se* characterization is to be determined. It is content simply to brand this type of plan as "price fixing" and describe the agreement in *Broadcast Music*—which also literally involved the fixing of prices—as "fundamentally different." [ ]

In fact, however, the two agreements are similar in important respects. Each involved competitors and resulted in cooperative pricing. Each arrangement also was prompted by the need for better service to the consumers. And each arrangement apparently makes possible a new product by reaping otherwise unattainable efficiencies. The Court's effort to distinguish *Broadcast Music* thus is unconvincing.[12]

12. The Court states that in *Broadcast Music* "there was little competition among individual composers for their separate compositions." [ ] This is an irrational ground for distinction. Competition *could* have existed, 441 U.S., at 6, 99 S.Ct., at 1555; see also 562 F.2d, at 134–135, 138, but did not because of the cooperative agreement. That competition yet persists among *physicians* is not a sensible reason to invalidate their agreement while refusing, similarly to condemn the *Broadcast Music* agreements that were *completely* effective in eliminating competition.

* * *

Notes and Questions

1. The position of the defendant in *Maricopa County* that *per se* rules should not be applied in the peculiar circumstances of the health care industry reflects a belief held by some prior to *Maricopa County* that rule of reason analysis would be the norm in litigation involving medical professionals. Does *Maricopa County* close the door to special antitrust treatment of the health care industry? Is it important that the restraints to which *Maricopa County* applies a *per se* rule were intended to set prices rather than to maintain professional quality? Does the court apply an absolute *per se* rule, or does it first take a peek at the effects of the practices under review before applying *per se* treatment? See Harrison, Price Fixing, The Professions and Ancillary Restraints, Coping with Maricopa County, 1982 U.Ill.L.Rev. 925. Consider also the discussion of the "learned profession exception" in *Weiss,* supra.

2. How are consumers hurt by an agreement among doctors to charge no more than a maximum price? Might not an arrangement like the Maricopa County Medical Society's (1) assist insurers and patients in the otherwise difficult task of identifying low cost providers, (2) decrease the transaction costs involved in negotiation of fees between insurers and providers, and (3) diminish the adverse selection problem that would be faced if a few physicians agreed to work for a fixed fee but most did not? Does not maximum price fixing allow insurers to project their exposure for medical costs better, lowering transaction costs and thus rates? How likely is it that maximum fees will be set so low as to discourage entry, innovation or quality? If the real problem is that maximum price fixing will become minimum price fixing, why not address the problem of minimum price fixing directly if it develops? See Easterbrook, Maximum Price Fixing, 48 U.Chi.L.Rev. 886 (1981); Gerhart, The Supreme Court and Antitrust Analysis: The Near Triumph of the Chicago School, 1982 Sup.Ct. Rev. 319, 346–7. On the other hand, should any form of provider collusion, including maximum fee setting, be especially suspect in the health care industry, where a long history of concerted provider activity to limit price

The Court also offers as a distinction that the foundations do not permit the creation of "any different product." [ ] But the foundations provide a "different product" to precisely the same extent as did *Broadcast Music's* clearinghouses. The clearinghouses provided only what copyright holders offered as individual sellers— the rights to use individual compositions. The clearinghouses were able to obtain these same rights more efficiently, however, because they eliminated the need to engage in individual bargaining with each individual copyright owner. See 441 U.S., at 21–22, 99 S.Ct., at 1563.

In the same manner, the foundations set up an innovative means to deliver a basic service—insured medical care from a wide range of physicians of one's choice—in a more economical manner. The foundations' maximum-fee schedules replace the weak cost containment incentives in typical "usual, customary, and reasonable" insurance agreements with a stronger cost control mechanism: an absolute ceiling on maximum fees that can be charged. The conduct of the insurers in this case indicates that they believe that the foundation plan as it presently exists is the most efficient means of developing and administering such schedules. At this stage in the litigation, therefore, we must agree that the foundation plan permits the more economical delivery of the basic insurance service—"to some extent, a different product." *Broadcast Music,* 441 U.S., at 22, 99 S.Ct., at 1563.

competition and of insurer disinterest in lowering prices make cartelization likely? Weller, "Free Choice" as a Restraint of Trade in American Health Care Delivery and Insurance, 69 Iowa L.Rev. 1351, 1378–82 (1984) [hereafter Weller, Free Choice].

Note: Antitrust Law and PPOs

The foundations for medical care at issue in *Maricopa County* resemble preferred provider organizations (PPOs), which are discussed in chapter 7. Though PPOs vary considerably in structure, they must exercise some control over prices charged by preferred providers to the PPO, either through agreed maximums or discounts. How should a PPO be organized to avoid violating the antitrust laws after *Maricopa County?*

First, does *Maricopa County* outlaw all "price-fixing" or only price-fixing by providers? If a PPO is established by an insurer, broker, or employer, does *Maricopa County* forbid it from negotiating fixed fees with providers individually? Can providers work collectively in any way in setting fees, for example, by providing suggestions for ranking the value of services for relative value schedules? How should a provider-sponsored PPO go about setting its fees? Might it avoid liability under *Maricopa County* by hiring an independent manager to set fees, and keeping information concerning fees charged by or paid to individual providers confidential from other providers? See Classen, Provider–Based Preferred Provider Organizations: A Viable Alternative Under Present Federal Antitrust Policies? 66 North Carolina L.Rev. 253 (1988); Costillo & Kazon, Preferred Provider Plans: Avoiding Problems of Horizontal Price–Fixing, 29 Antitrust Bull. 403 (1984); Miles & Philp, Hospitals Caught in the Antitrust Net: An Overview, 24 Duq.L.Rev. 439, 585–594 (1984); Steele, Minimizing Risks of Blue Cross and Blue Shield Plans, 4 J. Contemp. Health L. & Pol'y 227, 251–254 (1988); Walsh & Feller, Provider–Sponsored Alternative Health Care Delivery Systems: Reducing Antitrust Liability after Maricopa, 19 U.Rich.L.Rev. 207, 215–220 (1984) [hereafter Walsh & Feller]; Youle & Daw, Preferred Provider Organizations: An Antitrust Perspective, 29 Antitrust Bull. 301, 305–341 (1984) [hereafter Youle & Daw]; Commentary, Preferred Provider Organizations: Can Doctors Do the Price Fixing? 37 Okla.L.Rev. 733 (1984).

A jury in a recent case against an HMO awarded $101 million to participating physicians who claimed to have been injured by the physician-controlled board setting fees at an illegally low level. The case was settled for $37.5 million before an opinion was published in the case. See, criticizing its apparent reasoning, Kopit, Moses & Kenyon, Through the Looking Glass and Back: Sherman Act Claims by Health Care Providers Demanding Higher Fees From Health Insuring Organizations, 34 St. Louis U.L.J. 241 (1990).

Maricopa County also suggests, discussing *Broadcast Music,* that price-fixing by providers might be more tolerable if it were ancillary to a joint venture in which providers had pooled capital and risk. What degree of pooling of risk should be necessary before a court would find that a PPO was in effect a joint venture? Is it enough that a provider-sponsored PPO retains some of the fees payable to a physician to cover the costs of excess utilization, as many do? Would it help if the PPO also centralized marketing, billing and debt collection of participating providers? Or is a greater degree of risk-pooling necessary? See Walsh & Feller, supra, at 220–226; Youle & Daw, supra, at 331–341. If a court were to find a PPO to be a joint venture, the court would analyze restraints the PPO imposed on trade under a rule of reason rather than a *per se* rule. In particular, a court would be concerned with whether the joint venture was bona fide and not created to restrain competition, whether restraints were necessary and ancillary to a cooperative purpose that promoted competition, and whether the joint venture did not significantly reduce competition. It would also consider whether the joint venture was a merger that violated Section 7 of the Clayton Act. See Walsh & Feller, supra, at 222; Weller, Antitrust Aspects of PPOs, in D. Cowan, Preferred Provider Organizations: Planning, Structure and Operation 189, 193–197 (1984) [hereafter Weller, PPOs]. See generally, Brodley Joint Ventures and Antitrust Policy, 85 Harv.L.Rev. 1521 (1982). A spokesman for the Justice Department indicated that PPOs should be analyzed using this framework, McGrath, Remarks Concerning Preferred Provider Organizations and the Antitrust Laws (Mar. 22, 1985), reprinted in ALI–ABA, Health Care Industry, New Trends and New Problems, 44, 51 (1985) [hereafter McGrath].

An excellent recent analysis of the competitive risks and benefits of physician-sponsored PPOs structured as joint ventures is found in Greaney and Sindelar, Physician–Sponsored Joint Ventures: An Antitrust Analysis of Preferred Provider Organizations, 18 Rutgers L.J. 513 (1987). See, applying such analysis to an IPA and an HMO, Hassan v. Independent Practice Associates, P.C., 698 F.Supp. 679 (E.D.Mich.1988); Northwest Medical Laboratories, Inc. v. Blue Cross and Blue Shield of Oregon, 97 Or.App. 74, 775 P.2d 863 (1989).

The Maricopa County FMC is also distinguishable from many PPOs by its market share. The Maricopa County FMC contained 70% of the physicians in Maricopa County, and the insurers who subscribed to the FMC allegedly served about 63% of the prepaid health care market, Arizona v. Maricopa Medical Society, 457 U.S. at 341, 102 S.Ct. at 2471, 73 L.Ed.2d at 56, note 11. Substantial market share may indicate the presence of monopolization, proscribed by Section 2 of the Sherman Act, and may enable a PPO to cooperate with its providers to engage in practices restraining trade forbidden by Section 1. What are the relevant numbers for evaluating market share—the proportion of providers or of purchasers enrolled in the plan? Does it make a difference whether the PPO permits employers or insurers to allow their subscribers or employees to choose between several PPOs or permits providers to belong to several PPOs simultaneously? What proportion of the market is excessive? See Weller, PPOs, supra, at 202–204; Walsh & Feller, supra, at 223–224. The Justice Department has threatened to sue a PPO containing 50% of the physicians in one market and 90% in another, which was allegedly formed to eliminate HMO competition, McGrath, supra, at 49. On the other hand, the FTC has approved an IPA containing 65% of the physicians in an area, but serving only 12% of the population, Walsh & Feller, supra, at 224. And Judge Easterbrook held in Ball Memorial Hospital, Inc. v. Mutual Hospital Insurance, Inc., 784 F.2d 1325 (7th Cir.1986) that Blue Cross and Blue

Shield of Indiana, which intended to establish a PPO, lacked market power though the Blues had enlisted over half of the hospitals in the state for the PPO, and 27% of the patients in Indiana were insured by the Blues. The court noted in reaching this conclusion the highly competitive nature of the health insurance industry, Ball Memorial, 748 F.2d at 1332. See, Discussing Market Share Issues, Greaney & Sindelar, 576–578.

To limit its market power a PPO must necessarily exclude some providers. It should also have the power to exclude providers to control quality, utilization, and cost. Excluded providers can argue that they are the victims of a group boycott—a concerted refusal to deal—which is illegal under the Sherman Act. Klor's, Inc. v. Broadway–Hale Stores, Inc., 359 U.S. 207, 79 S.Ct. 705, 3 L.Ed.2d 741 (1959). If the PPO is provider-sponsored, rather than purchaser-sponsored, this claim is more likely to succeed, as the antitrust laws are not generally concerned with purchasers' choices of suppliers, but will intervene to protect some sellers excluded by other sellers from a market. Rule of reason treatment seems more appropriate for the exclusionary practices of PPOs in any event, since procompetitive justifications for exclusion of some physicians may often outweigh the anticompetitive effects of exclusion. See Hoffman v. Delta Dental Plan, 517 F.Supp. 564 (D.Minn.1981); Manasen v. California Dental Service, 1981–1 Trade Reg.Cas. (CCH) ¶ 63,959 (N.D.Cal.1980); Youle & Daw, supra, at 341–56; Walsh & Feller, supra, at 226–32; Weller, supra, at 204–08. However, if denial of participation in a provider-sponsored PPO excludes a provider from a facility essential to his practice (e.g., if the PPO were the only insurer in the market), a court might find an illegal group boycott. Closer scrutiny may also be appropriate where physician-dominated plans boycott non-physician providers, see Hahn v. Oregon Physicians' Service, 868 F.2d 1022 (9th Cir.1988). Note that considerations, and the law, here are very similar to those applicable in the staff privilege area discussed above. For a recent comprehensive view of antitrust issues affecting PPOs, see, Health Care Committee, Section of Antitrust Law, American Bar Ass'n, Managed Care and Antitrust: The PPO Experience (1990).

Note: Antitrust Protection for Innovative Approaches to Health Care Delivery and Financing

Antitrust law is a potential weapon HMOs, PPOs and other health care financing innovations may use to combat concerted opposition from traditional fee-for-service medicine. As early as 1943 the American Medical Association was convicted of criminal violation of the antitrust laws for its efforts to surpress HMOs, American Medical Association v. United States, 317 U.S. 519, 63 S.Ct. 326, 87 L.Ed. 434 (1943). More recently the Federal Trade Commission has proscribed AMA professional ethical restrictions on physician participation in financing arrangements that restricted choice of provider or encouraged physicians to discount fees, American Medical Association v. FTC, 94 F.T.C. 701 (1979), modified and enforced, 638 F.2d 443 (2d Cir.1980), affirmed memorandum by an equally divided court, 455 U.S. 676, 102 S.Ct. 1744, 71 L.Ed.2d 546 (1982). See Weller, Free Choice, supra. Cases have also been brought challenging boycotts directed at HMO's, United States v. Halifax Hosp. Medical Center, 1981–1 Trade Cases

(CCH) ¶ 64,151 (N.D.Fla.1981); Blue Cross v. Kitsap Physicians Service, 1982–1 Trade Cases (CCH) ¶ 64,558 (W.D.Wash.1981).

The foundations at issue in *Maricopa County* have been viewed as attempts by traditional fee for service medicine to stifle innovation in health care marketing. See generally, discussing use of the antitrust laws to support HMO development or other innovations in health care financing, Havighurst, Professional Restraints on Innovation in Health Care Financing, 1978 Duke L.J. 303; Kissam, Health Maintenance Organizations and the Role of Antitrust Law, 1978 Duke L.J. 487; Kopit & Klothen, Antitrust Implications of the Activities of Health Maintenance Organizations, 25 St. Louis U.L.J. 247 (1981); Thompson, Antitrust and Unfair Competition Issues Concerning Alternative Delivery Systems, 5 Health Aff. 35 (June 1986); Weller, Antitrust, Joint Ventures and the End of the AMA's Contract Practice Ethics: New Ways of Thinking About the Health Care Industry, 14 N.C.Cent.L.Rev. 3 (1984).

KARTELL v. BLUE SHIELD OF MASSACHUSETTS, INC.

United States Court of Appeals, First Circuit, 1984.
749 F.2d 922, cert. denied, 471 U.S. 1029, 105 S.Ct. 2040, 85 L.Ed.2d 322 (1985).

BREYER, CIRCUIT JUDGE.

Blue Shield pays doctors for treating patients who are Blue Shield health insurance subscribers, but only if each doctor promises not to make any additional charge to the subscriber. The basic issue in this case is whether this Blue Shield practice—called a "ban on balance billing"—violates either Sherman Act § 1 forbidding agreements "in restraint of trade," 15 U.S.C. § 1, or Sherman Act § 2 forbidding "monopolization" and "attempts to monopolize," *id.* § 2. The district court, 582 F.Supp. 734 (D.Mass.1984) held that the practice constituted an unreasonable restraint of trade in violation of section 1. We conclude that the practice does not violate either section of the Sherman Act; and we reverse the district court.

As the district court noted, the relevant facts are "not . . . generally . . . disputed." Blue Shield provides health insurance for physician services while its sister, Blue Cross, insures against hospital costs. The consumers of Blue Shield insurance, at least those who buy "full service" prepaid medical benefits, can see any "participating doctor," *i.e.*, a doctor who has entered into a standard Participating Physician's Agreement with Blue Shield. (If a doctor has not signed the Agreement, Blue Shield will reimburse him only if he provides emergency or out-of-state services.) Under the standard agreement, a participating doctor promises to accept as payment in full an amount determined by Blue Shield's "usual and customary charge" method of compensation. The district court found that the method has evolved, through the use of various "capping" devices, towards payment of a "fixed fee," determined by Blue Shield, for each particular type of service. Blue Shield pays this amount directly to the doctor; the patient pays nothing out of his own pocket and therefore receives no reimbursement.

The district court also found that Blue Shield provides some form of health insurance to about 56 percent of the Massachusetts population. (About 45 percent has coverage carrying a "balance billing" ban.) If one subtracts from the total population universe those Massachusetts residents who rely on government sponsored health care (*e.g.,* Medicare or Medicaid), then Blue Shield (and Blue Cross) provide insurance coverage for about 74 percent of the rest, namely those Massachusetts residents who *privately* insure against health costs. (About 23 percent of that group have coverage with commercial insurers; and about 4 percent subscribe to Health Maintenance Organizations.) Virtually all practicing doctors agree to take Blue Shield subscribers as patients and to participate in its fee plan. Blue Shield payments made under that plan account for about 13 to 14 percent of all "physician practice revenue."

The district court found that, because of the large number of subscribers, doctors are under "heavy economic pressure" to take them as patients and to agree to Blue Shield's system for charging the cost of their care. The court believed that the effect of this payment system, when combined with Blue Shield's size and buying power, was to produce an unreasonably rigid and unjustifiably low set of prices. In the court's view, the fact that doctors cannot charge Blue Shield subscribers more than the Blue Shield payment-schedule amounts interferes with the doctors' freedom to set higher prices for more expensive services and discourages them from developing and offering patients more expensive (and perhaps qualitatively better) services. For these and related reasons, the district court held that Blue Shield's ban on "balance billing" unreasonably restrains trade, and thereby violates Sherman Act § 1. Blue Shield appeals from this holding. The plaintiff doctors cross-appeal from other rulings of the district court in Blue Shield's favor.

* * *

I

We disagree with the district court because we do not believe that the facts that it found show an unreasonable restraint of trade. We can best explain our reasons by first discussing the basic antitrust issue in general terms, then turning to the specific, detailed arguments advanced by the parties, and finally noting several special reasons here that militate against a finding of liability.

A

We disagree with the district court's finding of "restraint." To find an unlawful restraint, one would have to look at Blue Shield as if it were a "third force," intervening in the marketplace in a manner that prevents willing buyers and sellers from independently coming together to strike price/quality bargains. Antitrust law typically frowns upon behavior that impedes the striking of such independent bargains. The persuasive power of the district court's analysis disappears, however, once one looks at Blue Shield, not as an inhibitory "third force," but as itself the purchaser of the doctors' services. * * * Antitrust Law rarely stops the buyer of a service from trying to determine the price or characteristics of the product that will be sold. Thus, the more closely Blue Shield's activities resemble, in essence, those of a purchaser, the less likely that they are unlawful.

Several circuits have held in antitrust cases that insurer activity closely analogous to that present here amounts to purchasing, albeit for the account of others. And, they have held that an insurer may lawfully engage in such buying of goods and services needed to make the insured whole. The Second Circuit has held lawful a Blue Shield plan requiring pharmacies to accept Blue Shield reimbursement as full payment for drugs they supply to Blue Shield subscribers. *Medical Arts Pharmacy of Stamford, Inc. v. Blue Cross & Blue Shield of Connecticut, Inc.,* 675 F.2d 502 (2d Cir.1982). The Third Circuit has allowed a hospital cost insurer (Blue Cross) to reimburse hospitals directly (and apparently completely) for services to subscribers. *Travelers Insurance Co. v. Blue Cross of Western Pennsylvania,* 481 F.2d 80 (3d Cir.), *cert. denied,* 414 U.S. 1093, 94 S.Ct. 724, 38 L.Ed.2d 550 (1973). * * *

At the same time, the facts before us are unlike those in cases where courts have forbidden an "organization" to buy a good or service—cases in which the buyer was typically a "sham" organization seeking only to combine otherwise independent buyers in order to suppress their otherwise competitive instinct to bid up price. *Mandeville Island Farms, Inc. v. American Crystal Sugar Co.,* 334 U.S. 219, 235, 68 S.Ct. 996, 1005, 92 L.Ed. 1328 (1948) (horizontal price-fixing by purchasers held *per se* illegal); * * *. No one here claims that Blue Shield is such a "sham" organization or anything other than a legitimate, independent medical cost insurer. *But cf. Virginia Academy of Clinical Psychologists v. Blue Shield of Virginia,* 624 F.2d 476 (4th Cir.1980) (Blue Shield found to be a combination, not of policyholders, but of *physicians*), *cert. denied,* 450 U.S. 916, 101 S.Ct. 1360, 67 L.Ed.2d 342 (1981).

Once one accepts the fact that, from a commercial perspective, Blue Shield in essence "buys" medical services for the account of others, the reasoning underlying the Second, Third, and Seventh Circuit views indicates that the ban on balance billing is permissible. To understand that reasoning, consider some highly simplified examples. Suppose a father buys toys for his son—toys the son picks out. Or suppose a landlord hires a painter to paint his tenant's apartment, to the tenant's specifications. Is it not obviously lawful for the father (the landlord) to make clear to the seller that the father (the landlord) is in charge and will pay the bill? Why can he not then forbid the seller to charge the child (the tenant) anything over and above what the father (the landlord) pays—at least if the seller wants the buyer's business? To bring the example closer to home, suppose that a large manufacturing company hires doctors to treat its employees. Can it not insist that its doctors not charge those employees an additional sum over and above what the company agrees to pay them to do the job? In each of these instances, to refuse to allow the condition would disable the buyer from holding the seller to the price of the contract. Yet, if it is lawful for the buyer to buy for the third party in the first place, how can it be unlawful to bargain for a price term that will stick? Given this argument, it is not surprising the courts have unanimously upheld contracts analogous in various degrees to the one at issue here—contracts in which those who directly provide goods or services to insureds have agreed to cap or forego completely additional charges to those insureds in return for direct payment by the insurer. * * *

Two arguments might be made in an effort to distinguish these cases. First, the doctors may claim that Blue Shield is not, in essence, a buyer. Traditionally, doctors have opposed financial arrangements that involved the "selling" of their services to anyone but the patient. *See* Comment, 63 Yale L.J. 938, 978–80 (1954). And medical associations in the past sometimes have argued that selling services to third parties or related "corporate practice" might interfere with the absolute ethical obligation that a doctor owes to the patient. *Id.,* (citing, *e.g.,* AMA, Principles of Medical Ethics, ch. 3, art. 5, § 4). Medical associations have not, however, opposed reimbursement by third party insurers, such as Blue Shield, a fact that arguably suggests an important distinction between "insurance reimbursement" and "purchasing."

In our view, however, any such distinction is irrelevant for antitrust purposes. The relevant antitrust facts are that Blue Shield pays the bill and seeks to set the amount of the charge. Those facts led other courts in similar circumstances to treat insurers as if they were "buyers." The same facts convince us that Blue Shield's activities here are *like* those of a buyer. Whether for ethical, medical, or related professional purposes Blue Shield is, or is not, considered a buyer is beside the point. We here consider only one specific argued application of the antitrust laws and we do not suggest how Blue Shield ought to be characterized in any other context.

Second, the doctors seek to distinguish these precedents by pointing to an important district court finding either not present or not discussed in depth in these other cases. The district court here found that Blue Shield is a buyer with significant "market power"—*i.e.,* the power to force prices below the level that a freely competitive market would otherwise set. They argue that Blue Shield's "market power" makes a significant difference. We do not agree.

At the outset, we note that Blue Shield disputes the existence of significant "market power." It points out that the district court relied heavily upon participation by 99 percent of all Massachusetts doctors in Blue Shield's program, as "prov[ing] * * * Blue Shield's economic power." But, Blue Shield says, this by itself proves little. Participating in Blue Shield's program does not stop doctors from taking other patients or from charging those other patients what they like. As long as Blue Shield's rates are even marginally remunerative, 99 percent of all doctors might sign up with Blue Shield if it had only ten policyholders or ten thousand instead of several million.

Blue Shield adds that the record does not prove the existence of the single harm most likely to accompany the existence of market power on the buying side of the market, namely lower seller output. [ ] Indeed, here the district court found that the supply of doctors in Massachusetts has "increased steadily during the past decade." Blue Shield also claims that whatever power it possesses arises from its ability as an "expert" to prevent doctors from charging unknowledgeable patients *more* than a free (and informed) market price. *See generally* Comment, 75 Nw.U.L.Rev. [506 (1980)].

On the other hand, several doctors testified that low prices discouraged them from introducing new highly desirable medical techniques. And, they argue that fully informed patients would have wanted to pay more for those techniques had they been allowed to do so.

To resolve this argument about the existence of market power—an issue hotly debated by the expert economists who testified at trial—would force us to evaluate a record that the district court described as "two competing mountains of mostly meaningless papers." Rather than do so, we shall assume that Blue Shield possesses significant market power. We shall also assume, but purely for the sake of argument, that Blue Shield uses that power to obtain "lower than competitive" prices.

We next ask whether Blue Shield's assumed market power makes a significant legal difference. As a matter of pure logic, to distinguish the examples previously mentioned one must accept at least one of the following three propositions: One must believe either (1) that the law forbids a buyer with market power to bargain for "uncompetitive" or "unreasonable" prices, or (2) that such a buyer cannot buy for the account of others, or (3) that there is some relevant difference between obtaining such price for oneself and obtaining that price for others for whom one can lawfully buy. In our view, each of these propositions is false, as a matter either of law or of logic.

First, the antitrust laws interfere with a firm's freedom to set even uncompetitive prices only in special circumstances, where, for example, a price is below incremental cost. Such a "predatory" price harms competitors, cannot be maintained, and is unlikely to provide consumer benefits. [ ] Ordinarily, however, even a monopolist is free to exploit whatever market power it may possess when that exploitation takes the form of charging uncompetitive prices. As Professor Areeda puts it, "Mere monopoly pricing is not a violation of the Sherman Act." [ ] * * *.

The reasons underlying this principle include a judicial reluctance to deprive the lawful monopolist (say a patent monopolist) of its lawful

rewards, and a judicial recognition of the practical difficulties of determining what is a "reasonable," or "competitive," price. * * * Thus,
where a monopoly is unlawful, antitrust courts typically seek to change
the market's structure, "to break up or render impotent the monopoly
power which violates the Act." [   ] Courts only rarely try to supervise
the price bargain directly. [   ] And, where monopoly power is regulated, the regulator, not the court, bears the burden of determining
whether prices are reasonable. [   ]

The district court did not suggest here that the prices subject to the
"balance billing" ban were "predatory." Nor (with one possible exception, see [infra]) do the parties point to evidence of any price below
anyone's "incremental cost." [   ] Rather, the district court suggested
that Blue Shield's prices were "uncompetitively low," "unreasonably
low," lower than the doctors might have charged to individual patients
lacking market power. That is to say, Blue Shield obtained prices that
reflected its market power. For the reasons just mentioned then, if
Blue Shield had simply purchased those services for itself, the prices
paid, in and of themselves, would not have amounted to a violation of
the antitrust laws. [   ]

Second, as we previously mentioned, there is no law forbidding a
legitimate insurance company from itself buying the goods or services
needed to make its customer whole. The cases that we have cited are
unanimous in allowing such arrangements. The rising costs of medical
care, the possibility that patients cannot readily evaluate (as competitive buyers) competing offers of medical service, the desirability of
lowering insurance costs and premiums, the availability of state regulation to prevent abuse—all convince us that we ought not create new
potentially far-reaching law on the subject. And, the parties have not
seriously argued to the contrary.

Third, to reject the first two propositions is, as a matter of logic, to
reject the third. If it is lawful for a monopoly buyer to buy for the
account of another, how can it be unlawful for him to insist that no
additional charge be made to that other? To hold to the contrary is, in
practice, to deny the buyer the right to buy for others, for the seller
would then be free to obtain a different price from those others by
threatening to withhold the service. This reasoning seems sound
whether or not the buyer has "market power."

In essence, then, the lawfulness of the term in question stems from
the fact that it is an essential part of the price bargain between buyer
and seller. Whether or not that price bargain is, in fact, reasonable is,
legally speaking, beside the point, even in the case of a monopolist. As
Blue Shield stresses in its brief, health maintenance organizations,
independent practice associations, and preferred provider organizations
all routinely agree with doctors that the doctors will accept payment
from the plan as payment in full for services rendered to subscribers.
We can find no relevant analytical distinction between this type of

purchasing decision and the practice before us—even on the assumption that Blue Shield possesses market power.

B

We now consider more closely the specific arguments raised by the district court and the parties to show that Blue Shield's "balance billing ban" is anticompetitive in practice. The Rodkey plaintiffs' brief sets forth in summary form the following allegedly harmful effects of the ban:

(1) Price competition among physicians for services covered by Blue Shield's service benefit policies is "virtually eliminated."

(2) Doctor's prices have tended to cluster around Blue Shield's "maximum price levels."

(3) Doctors wanting to compete by offering innovative or "premium" services are inhibited from doing so because Blue Shield's pricing structure assumes that physicians' services are fungible and mandates the same price ceilings for virtually all physicians.

(4) Doctors just entering practice are discouraged from doing so by particularly low levels of Blue Shield reimbursement.

(5) Blue Shield's low prices lead doctors to charge higher prices to others.

(6) Blue Shield discourages doctors from charging others low prices by insisting that its subscribers be given the benefit of any such low prices.

(7) Blue Shield's pricing system discourages doctors from trying out more expensive services that could bring about lower total medical costs, *e.g.,* a "colonoscopy with polypectomy," an expensive service that is nonetheless cheaper than the surgery that would otherwise be needed to cure the patient.

(8) Blue Shield, by reason of its pricing practices, has been able to attract more subscribers, extending its "competitive edge" over other health insurers, and increasing its dominance in the health insurance business.

The first seven of these arguments attack the price term in the agreement between Blue Shield and the doctors. To argue that Blue Shield's pricing system is insufficiently sensitive to service differences, or that it encourages high costs, or does not give the patients what they really need, or to claim that the buyer is making a bad decision is like arguing that the buyer of a fleet of taxicabs ought to buy several different models, or allow the seller to vary color or horsepower or gearshift because doing so either will better satisfy those passengers who use the fleet's services, or will in the long run encourage quality and innovation in automobile manufacture. The short—and conclusive—answer to these arguments is that normally the choice of what to seek to buy and what to offer to pay is the buyer's. And, even if the buyer has monopoly power, an antitrust court (which might, in appropriate circumstances, restructure the market) will not interfere with a buyer's (nonpredatory) determination of price.

* * * A legitimate buyer is entitled to use its market power to keep prices down. The claim that Blue Shield's price scheme is "too rigid" because it ignores qualitative differences among physicians is properly addressed to Blue Shield or to a regulator, not to a court. There is no suggestion that Blue Shield's fee schedule reflects, for example, an effort by, say, one group of doctors to stop other doctors from competing with them. [ ] Here, Blue Shield and the doctors "sit on opposite sides of the bargaining table" [ ]. And Blue Shield seems simply to be acting "as every rational enterprise does, *i.e.,* [to] get the best deal possible" [ ]. The first seven adverse consequences to which appellees point are the result of this unilateral behavior.

Plaintiffs' eighth argument focuses on the health insurance business: Blue Shield's "ban on balance billing," by attracting more subscribers, augments its share of the health insurance business, thereby enabling it to secure still lower doctor charges. This argument, however, comes down to saying that Blue Shield can attract more subscribers because it can charge them less. If Blue Shield is free to insist upon a lower doctor charge, it should be free to pass those savings along to its subscribers in the form of lower prices. * * *

Finally, the district court rested its decision in large part upon the Supreme Court's recent case, *Arizona v. Maricopa County Medical Society,* 457 U.S. 332, 102 S.Ct. 2466, 73 L.Ed.2d 48 (1982). *Maricopa,* however, involved a *horizontal* agreement among competing doctors about what to charge. A horizontal agreement among competitors is typically unlawful because the competitors prevent themselves from making *independent* decisions about the terms as to which they will bargain. * * * The unlawfulness of the agreement does not necessarily depend upon the undesirability of the contractual term as to which competitors agree not to compete.

The district court saw a similarity between the horizontal agreement cases and this one in the fact that Blue Shield can extract an "uncompetitive price" from doctors while the *Maricopa* court feared that "price-fixing" by competitors might bring about uncompetitive prices. But, the antitrust problems at issue when a single firm sets a price—whether, when, and how courts can identify and control an individual exercise of alleged market power—are very different from those associated with agreements by competitors to limit independent decision-making. A decision about the latter is not strong precedent for a case involving only the former. *Maricopa* is simply not on point. * * *

C

Three additional circumstances militate strongly here against any effort by an antitrust court to supervise the Blue Shield/physician price bargain. * * *

First, the prices at issue here are low prices, not high prices. [ ] Of course, a buyer, as well as a seller, can possess significant market power; and courts have held that *agreements* to fix prices—whether maximum or minimum—are unlawful. [ ] Nonetheless, the Congress that enacted the Sherman Act saw it as a way of protecting consumers against prices that were too *high,* not too low. * * *

Second, the subject matter of the present agreement—medical costs—is an area of great complexity where more than solely economic values are at stake. * * * This fact, too, warrants judicial hesitancy to interfere.

Third, the price system here at issue is one supervised by state regulators. [ ] While that fact does not automatically carry with it antitrust immunity, see *Cantor v. Detroit Edison Co.,* 428 U.S. 579, 96 S.Ct. 3110, 49 L.Ed.2d 1141 (1976), it suggests that strict antitrust scrutiny is less likely to be necessary to prevent the unwarranted exercise of monopoly power. * * *

These general considerations do not dictate our result in this case. They do, however, counsel us against departing from present law or extending it to authorize increased judicial supervision of the buyer/seller price bargain. * * *

III

We turn now to four issues that the plaintiff doctors raise in their cross-appeal from other rulings of the district court—rulings that dismissed various parts of their case against Blue Shield (and against Blue Cross, Blue Shield's sister organization). The fact that we have found Blue Shield's ban on balance billing to be lawful simplifies the issues on the cross-appeal and virtually determines an outcome in defendants' favor.

First, the doctors argue that the district court wrongly dismissed their claim that Blue Shield's refusal to reimburse nonparticipating doctors (except for emergency or out-of-state services) violated the antitrust law. The district court found that Blue Shield's actions were immunized from antitrust attack by a prong of the "state action" doctrine which removes actions required (or forbidden) by state laws from the scope of the federal antitrust laws. [ ] The Massachusetts Supreme Judicial Court has held that state law, namely Mass.Gen.Laws ch. 176B, § 7 prohibits Blue Shield from generally reimbursing nonparticipating doctors * * *.

* * * We need not trace the labyrinthine path of this preemption argument, however, for we uphold the district court's ruling for a simpler reason. [The plaintiffs failed to establish an antitrust violation.] * * *

The doctors charge that Blue Shield simply refuses to deal with doctors who do not agree to participate in its program. The doctors strongly argued that this "refusal to deal" helped Blue Shield implement its ban on balance billing. Were that ban unlawful, the "refusal to deal" conceivably could have been found unlawful, too, as an unjustified means towards that unlawful end. If the ban is lawful, however, the "refusal to deal" charge must rise, or fall, on its own. And, on its own, it runs squarely into basic antitrust law that a firm "generally has a right to deal, or refuse to deal, with whomever it likes, as long as it does so independently." [ ] There is nothing special here to take this case outside the general rule. There is neither evidence of a horizontal conspiracy nor any charge that Blue Shield agreed with one of its competitors not to deal with nonparticipating doctors. * * * In a nutshell, Blue Shield's independent determination of the terms on which it will deal, of the customers to whom it will sell, and of the suppliers from whom it will purchase is a manifestation of the competitive process, not an effort to suppress or to destroy that process. * * *

* * *

Notes and Questions

1. Do you agree that Blue Shield is correctly described as a purchaser of medical services, or does it resemble more closely a manufacturer that tries to set prices charged by retailers of its products, a practice that is illegal under the antitrust laws? See Note, Preferred Provider Organizations and Provider Contracting: New Analyses Under the Sherman Act, 37 Hast.L.J. 377, 393–99 (1985). Does the court in *Kartell* give adequate consideration to the market power of Blue Shield? Id. at 399–406. Miller, Vertical Restraints and Powerful Health Insurers: Exclusionary Conduct Masquerading as Managed Care?, 51 L. & Contemp.Prob. 195 (1988). Is its treatment of the monopoly issue consistent with the *Hospital Corporation of America* case? With *Weiss*?

2. The Blue Cross and Blue Shield plans occupy a dominant position in many health insurance markets and have therefore been defendants in a number of antitrust suits brought by disgruntled providers or consumers. *Kartell* is only one of several suits brought by physicians, dentists, hospitals and pharmacists claiming that the Blues have used their market power to keep rates artificially low. *Kartell* is typical of these cases in rejecting these claims. See, in addition to the cases cited in *Kartell*, Brillhart v. Mutual Medical Insurance, Inc., 768 F.2d 196 (7th Cir.1985); Westchester Radiological Associated P.C. v. Empire Blue Cross and Blue Shield, 707 F.Supp. 708 (S.D.N.Y.1989). See also, on antitrust challenges to insurer cost containment efforts, Batavia, Blue Cross–Blue Shield Payment Policies: Antitrust Aspects and Implications for the Health Care and Insurance Industries, 33 Fed'n Ins.Cons.Q. 173 (1983); Heiter, Antitrust and Third Party Insurers, 8 Am.J.L. & Med. 251 (1983); Heiter & Ader, Blue Cross and Blue Shield Contracts with Providers, 2 J.L.Med. 265 (1981); Kallstrom, Health Care Cost Control by Third Party Payors: Fee Schedules and the Sherman Act, 1978 Duke L.J. 645; Note, Prepaid Prescription Drug Plans Under Antitrust Scrutiny: A Stern Challenge to Health Care Cost Containment, 75 Nw.U.L.Rev. 506 (1980). If employers join together in coalitions to force lower rates on providers, rather than relying on insurance intermediaries to do so, what potential antitrust issues are raised? See Colton, Hospital Involvement in Health Care Coalitions, 14 N.C.Cent.L.

Rev. 33 (1983); Steele, Minimizing Antitrust Risks of Blue Cross and Blue Shield Plans, 4 J.Contemp.L. & Pol'y 227 (1988).

3. As competition has increasingly threatened the long dominant position of the Blues in many states, they have responded by creating their own PROs and HMOs and by using their dominant position in the health insurance market to stave off competitors. Blues that have formed their own HMOs or PPOs have attempted to improve their competitive position by the use of vertical restraints on providers such as exclusive dealing arrangements (refusing to deal with facilities that contract with HMOs other than the Blue HMO) and "most favored nation" clauses (refusing to pay providers more than the discounted prices those providers offer other PPOs or HMOs).

Must the analysis applied in *Kartell* change if Blue Shield is a player in both the health insurance and health care market? Does Blue Shield's market power become more significant if it is competing in both markets? Could vertical restraints that have the immediate effect of lowering prices providers charge Blue Shield ever be violations of the Sherman Act? Is Blue Shield's conduct in raising its prices for employers who also offer another HMO option (ostensibly to compensate for adverse selection) anti-competitive?

Ocean State Physicians Health Plan, Inc. v. Blue Cross & Blue Shield of Rhode Island, 883 F.2d 1101 (1st Cir.1989) involved a challenge to a "most favored nations" clause contract. Blue Cross/Blue Shield allegedly controlled 80% of the Rhode Island private health insurance market. When Ocean State, a new HMO, began to make significant inroads into its market, the Blues responded by imposing a requirement that participating physicians grant the Blues the same discount they granted Ocean State. Thereafter about 350 of Ocean State's 1200 participating physicians left the plan. A jury found the Blues guilty of Section 2 violations and of tortious interference with Ocean State's contractual relationships and awarded Ocean State $3.2 million. The First Circuit affirmed a judgment notwithstanding the verdict, finding that the "most favored nations" clause was a legitimate competitive strategy to assure that the Blues could get the lowest price for services rather than an attempt to monopolize the health insurance market.

In Reazin v. Blue Cross and Blue Shield of Kansas, Inc., 899 F.2d 951 (10th Cir.1990), however, a verdict for $5.4 million (plus $2.2 million in attorney's fees) against the Blues was upheld for similar conduct. In *Reazin* the Blues proposed the termination of the provider status of Wesley Hospital, which had been acquired by the Hospital Corporation of America which owned the most successful HMO in the Wichita market. The Blues simultaneously notified all other hospitals in Kansas that they would face similar sanctions if they attempted to compete with the Blues in the insurance market. The Blues allegedly acted in concert with two other Wichita hospitals that granted discounts to attract Blue Cross insured patients away from Wesley. The Tenth Circuit Court of Appeals held, in affirming the verdict, that the Blues had attempted to monopolize trade and unreasonably restrained trade by threatening the growth of new alternative delivery systems. Can *Ocean State* and *Reazin* be distinguished?

See, discussing *Ocean State* and *Reazin,* Baker, Vertical Restraints Among Hospitals, Physicians and Health Insurers that Raise Rivals' Costs, 14 Am.J.L. & Med. 147 (1988); Miller, supra. See also, Celnicker, A Competitive Analysis of Most Favored Nations Clauses in Contracts Between Health Care Providers and Insurers, 69 N.C.L.Rev. (1991), arguing that most favored nations clauses eliminate a dynamic mechanism whereby prices are racheted down, reduce the total output (by prohibiting price discrimination) and prevent the market from rewarding efficient producers.

4. Providers have at times banded together to oppose insurer attempts to control health care costs. FTC v. Indiana Federation of Dentists, 476 U.S. 447, 106 S.Ct. 2009, 90 L.Ed.2d 445 (1986), involved a group of dentists who formed a fictitious "union" which promulgated a "work rule" forbidding dentists to provide insurance companies with x-rays for use in evaluating patients' benefit claims. The dentists argued that their policy promoted quality care by encouraging fuller examinations. If insurers had access to the x-rays, the dentists argued, the insurers would rely on them as the sole basis for granting or denying payment for claims, even though a full examination and not just x-rays were needed for adequate evaluation of a patient's needs. The FTC issued a cease and desist order against the Federations' policy, arguing that it restrained trade by keeping from consumers a service they desired, forwarding of x-rays to insurers. The Supreme Court upheld the FTC's position. In rejecting the dentist's quality of care argument, it noted: "The argument is, in essence, that an unrestrained market in which consumers are given access to the information they believe to be relevant to their choices will lead them to make unwise or even dangerous choices. Such an argument amounts to "nothing less than a frontal assault on the basic policy of the Sherman Act." 476 U.S. at 463, 106 S.Ct. at 2020. It also rejected the argument on the basis of the factual findings of the FTC.

5. The Blues were formed by provider associations and until recently were largely dominated by providers. See Law, Blue Cross, What Went Wrong (2d ed. 1976). There is some evidence that provider control has increased the costs of these plans, Kass & Pautler, F.T.C. Staff Report on Physician Control of Blue Shield Plans (1979); though others have argued that provider controlled plans cost less, Lynk, Regulatory Control of the Membership of Corporate Boards of Directors: The Blue Shield Case, 24 J.L. & Econ. 159 (1981). Challenges to physician control have usually involved claims of group boycotts directed against non-physician or non-participating providers rather than price-fixing. See Blue Shield of Virginia v. McCready, 457 U.S. 465, 102 S.Ct. 2540, 73 L.Ed.2d 149 (1982); Virginia Academy of Clinical Psychologists v. Blue Shield, 624 F.2d 476 (4th Cir.1980), cert. denied, 450 U.S. 916, 101 S.Ct. 1360, 67 L.Ed.2d 342 (1981); Ballard v. Blue Shield, 543 F.2d 1075 (4th Cir.1976), cert. denied, 430 U.S. 922, 97 S.Ct. 1341, 51 L.Ed.2d 601 (1977); Hoffman v. Delta Dental Plan, 517 F.Supp. 564 (D.Minn.1981); Johnson v. Blue Cross/Blue Shield of New Mexico, 677 F.Supp. 1112 (D.N.M.1987). In *Virginia Academy* the court found that the Blue Shield plan was itself a conspiracy of the participating physicians, and not a single entity, as it claimed. Though the

FTC has expressed concern about provider control of Blue plans, it has decided to consider problems with provider control on a case-by-case basis rather than to proscribe it altogether. See Physician Agreements to Control Medical Prepayment Plans, Notice of Initiation of Case-by-Case Law Enforcement Program, 46 Fed.Reg. 27,768 (1981), 48,982 (1981).

6. The McCarran–Ferguson Act, which exempts state regulated insurance industry activities, was thought until recently to protect the cost-containment efforts of insurance companies from antitrust scrutiny. Two cases, Group Life and Health Insurance v. Royal Drug Co., 440 U.S. 205, 99 S.Ct. 1067, 59 L.Ed.2d 261 (1979) rehearing denied, 441 U.S. 917, 99 S.Ct. 2017, 60 L.Ed.2d 389 (1979) and Union Labor Life Insurance Co. v. Pireno, 458 U.S. 119, 102 S.Ct. 3002, 73 L.Ed.2d 647 (1982), have interpreted the McCarran–Ferguson Act very restrictively, limiting its protection to activities involving risk-spreading and transferring in the insurance-insured relationship. This leaves the cost-containment activities of insurers generally subject to antitrust oversight, see Crump & Maxwell, Health Care, Cost Containment, and the Antitrust Laws: A Legal and Economic Analysis of the Pireno Case; 56 S.Cal.L.Rev. 913 (1983); Kennedy, The McCarran Act: A Limited "Business of Insurance" Antitrust Exemption Made Ever Narrower—Three Recent Decisions, 18 Forum 528 (1983). See, however, Ocean State Physician Health Plan v. Blue Cross, 883 F.2d 1101 (1st Cir.1989) (finding that the McCarran–Ferguson Act immunized an insurer's marketing and pricing policies in offering HMO coverage and imposition of higher rates on employers that also offered a competing HMO option). Insurance companies have enjoyed somewhat more success in arguing that the activities mandated by state law such as exclusion of certain providers are exempt from antitrust scrutiny under the state action exemption. See Llewellyn v. Crothers, 765 F.2d 769 (9th Cir.1985); Alonzo v. Blue Cross of Greater Philadelphia, 611 F.Supp. 310 (E.D.Pa.1984). The mere fact that a practice is consistent with state policy, if it is neither compelled nor supervised by the state, is not sufficient to immunize it from antitrust scrutiny. See FTC v. Indiana Federation of Dentists, 476 U.S. 447, 106 S.Ct. 2009, 90 L.Ed.2d 445 (1986).

Problem: Healthcare First

You represent Healthcare First, an HMO which is in the process of being formed in Carterville, a town in a Rocky Mountain state. Healthcare First is wholly owned by Carterville Community Hospital, one of the two hospitals in town (the other is a smaller for-profit hospital, MedAmerica, that opened about five years ago). Healthcare First has hired about a dozen primary care physicians with staff privileges at the hospital. It has also contracted with two dozen specialists to deliver services to its subscribers at discounted rates negotiated with each of the specialists by Healthcare First. Subscribers will be limited to Carterville Community Hospital except in emergencies, and will only have access to the specialists or to the hospital upon referral or admission by a plan physician. The plan only covers subscribers for primary care delivered by plan physicians, and for laboratory work and pharmaceuticals from the hospital's lab and pharmacy (except in emergencies). Primary care physicians employed by the plan may not carry on an outside practice, but specialists under contract will continue their fee-for-service practice, and are permitted to contract with other HMOs or PPOs.

Healthcare First has negotiated agreements to cover the employees of several of the largest employers in town, including the only two substantial industries. These employees (all non-union) will be offered only Healthcare First coverage through their employer. Healthcare First is also negotiating with the state Medicaid agency to cover Medicaid patients in the area under a program the state has initiated under a federal waiver to limit freedom of choice for Medicaid recipients. Under these arrangements, Healthcare First will cover about 40% of the patients in the Carterville area. Healthcare First offers rates substantially under those offered by other insurers and providers, as it expects to realize substantial economies through utilization control and more efficient use of hospital capacity.

The plan has troubled many in Carterville. First, MedAmerica, the other hospital in town, is upset at losing its patients who are employees of the businesses that have signed on with Healthcare First, and who were previously covered by Blue Cross. Second, primary care providers who were not hired by the plan anticipate a substantial loss of business. Several also believe that the plan is unethical, because it restricts patients to a small group of providers whose practice will be subject to review by the HMO. Third, several specialists who chose to contract with the plan are upset by the sharply discounted rates the plan has insisted on. Finally, several employees of the companies that have signed on with Healthcare First are concerned that they will no longer be covered by health insurance unless they leave nonparticipating physicians who have cared for their families for years. Healthcare First fears an antitrust suit, and has sought your advice as to possible theories and the likelihood of their success. Please advise.

Chapter 9

HUMAN REPRODUCTION
AND BIRTH

The rights, obligations, privileges, and relationships previously described in this book are generally rights, obligations, privileges, and relationships of people. But who ought to be recognized as a person, subject to the principles that apply to persons, and not to human limbs, individual cells, hair pieces, animals, disembodied souls, hospitals, state legislatures or other entities? While a fertilized ovum is "life" in some form, so is a single still-functioning liver cell taken from the body of a person who died yesterday. Is there a difference in these two entities? When does a person, entitled to formal legal respect as such, come into existence? When does one who is so defined go out of existence? The obvious answers—at the point of life and at the point of death—are fraught with ambiguities that can be resolved only through an analysis of medicine, ethics, law, social history, anthropology, theology and other disciplines which seek to answer the basic questions of human existence. Physicians and lawyers have been deeply involved in determining when life begins and when it ends, and it is therefore appropriate to consider these issues in this text. The first portion of this chapter deals with the definition of human life; the definition of death is taken up in the next chapter.

Physicians and lawyers have also been deeply involved in developing and defining new forms of procreation, and in determining the role that the society ought to play in limiting and facilitating reproduction. Issues surrounding contraception, genetic screening (and control and protection of those involved in this process), sterilization, abortion, the social allocation of the cost of failed reproductive control and potential fetal-maternal conflicts have all been addressed by law-makers, in either a judicial or legislative forum. In addition, newly developed forms of facilitating reproduction, including artificial insemination, *in vitro* fertilization, ovum transfer and surrogacy have also been addressed in legal fora. The second portion of this chapter examines the interdisciplinary debate that has given rise to legal intervention that may result in limiting or facilitating reproduction. As you read chapters 9, 10, and 11 consider this problem:

Problem: Death During Pregnancy

Ms. Masterson was carrying a fetus in the thirty-fifth week of gestation when the automobile she was driving was struck by a truck racing away from a convenience store and pursued by a city police car. The driver of the truck, who was unlicensed and highly intoxicated, was attempting to escape after committing an armed robbery at the convenience store when the collision occurred. The truck struck the driver's door of Ms. Masterson's car and flung her through the passenger window onto the ground about thirty feet from the car. The chasing police officer arrested the intoxicated driver, who was subsequently charged with armed robbery, driving while intoxicated, and driving without a license. The police officer did not call for medical help for Ms. Masterson, and no ambulance came for her until a passing motorist called the fire department. The ambulance arrived to find her unconscious.

When Ms. Masterson arrived at the hospital, physicians immediately provided her cardiopulmonary support. An examination revealed that the fetus she was carrying had suffered serious cranial injuries which could result in severe brain dysfunction if the child were born alive. Tests done about 24 hours after Ms. Masterson's admission to the hospital indicated no spontaneous activity in any part of her brain. Physicians have determined that maintaining Ms. Masterson on the cardiopulmonary support systems would provide the only chance for the fetus to be born alive.

Ms. Masterson was widowed in the seventh month of her pregnancy, two months ago. Her only living relatives are her two sisters, whom she despises. In fact, to avoid the possibility that they might inherit some of her wealth, last month she executed a will leaving all of her property to the National Abortion Rights League and the American Eugenics Society.

What actions should the hospital staff take in this case? Should Ms. Masterson be maintained on cardiopulmonary support, or should she be removed?

Consider the medical, social, political and legal (both civil and criminal) consequences of your actions as you read this chapter.

I. WHEN DOES HUMAN LIFE BECOME A "PERSON"?

This society has had difficulty defining who is a "person." In part, this arises out of the different and inconsistent purposes for which we seek a definition. The "person" from whom we wish to harvest a kidney for transplantation is likely to be different from the "person" who is protected by the Fourteenth Amendment, federal civil rights laws, and various other federal and state laws. Even when the purpose of the definition is settled—as when we seek to know who is a person able to bring an action under state tort law—there is no consensus on when the status of "personhood" first attaches. The most obvious definition of personhood is a recursive one: a human being (and thus, a "person") is the reproductive product of other human beings. Even if we accept this "human stock" definition of person, however, the inquiry remains open. Does that human stock become a person, for tort law or other purposes, upon conception? Upon quickening? Upon viability? Upon birth? A year after birth? Upon physical maturity?

The definition of "person" is not limited to various stages in the development of human stock. "Personhood" could commence upon ensoulment, upon the development of self concept, upon the development of a sense of personal history, or upon the ability to communicate through language. The resolution of the question appears to require a resort to first principles.

In the vast majority of cases, it is not difficult to identify an object as being a person or something else. You are easily distinguishable from your arms, your dog, your insurance company and your Mazda Miata, as close as you may feel to each of them. The most difficult questions tend to arise at the very beginning and at the very end of human life. Just as you may be able to identify the fact that you were in love, but not be able to identify exactly when it began, or the moment when it ended, it is clear that human stock constitutes a "person," at least from a few years after birth into the competent elderly years. The beginnings and the endings of "personhood" are the fuzzy portions.

There are limits to what may reasonably be considered a "person," even when we limit our consideration to human stock. No one suggests that anything independent of the unified sperm and ovum, or its consequences, ought to be considered a person. A great many religious groups consider "personhood" to attach at conception. Aristotle viewed the development of the person as a three stage process, going from vegetable (at conception), to animal (in utero), to rational (sometime after birth). For many centuries, Christian theology fixed the point of "immediate animation" when the fetus was "ensouled" as forty days after conception for males and eighty days after conception for females. St. Thomas Aquinas determined that the ensoulment took place at the time of quickening, usually fourteen to eighteen weeks after conception, and his determination had a very substantial effect on the development of the common law in England and in this country. Recently some philosophers have suggested that "personhood," at least to the extent that it includes a right to life, depends on attributes that are not likely to be developed until sometime after birth. For example, Michael Tooley, a philosopher, defends infanticide on the grounds that it is indistinguishable from abortion and that neither constitutes the improper killing of a human being because there can be no human being until the being possesses a concept of self as a continuing subject of experiences and other mental states, and recognizes that it is such a continuing entity. Professor Tooley suggests that this occurs sometime after birth, perhaps many weeks after birth. M. Tooley, *Abortion and Infanticide* (1983).

The most comprehensive set of attributes of personhood has been developed by Joseph Fletcher, a bioethicist. Consider his fifteen criteria, described below, and determine whether some or all of them can be used to properly define who is your colleague in personhood and who is not. Consider whether the fact that many of these criteria disqualify fetuses, newborns, and the seriously developmentally disabled affects their acceptability as standards. Further, does the fact that some animal or some man-made machine might eventually fulfill all of these criteria cause you to doubt their validity? What are the consequences of our failure to define a cloned person, a highly intelligent and communicative ape, or a robot as a "person" in terms of our conceptions of "democracy" and "slavery," for example?

A. THE ATTRIBUTES OF PERSONHOOD

FLETCHER, "HUMANNESS," IN HUMANHOOD: ESSAYS IN BIOMEDICAL ETHICS
12–16 (1979).

Synthetic concepts such as human and man and person require operational terms, spelling out the which and what and when. Only in that way can we get down to cases—to normative decisions. There are always some people who prefer to be visceral and affective in their moral choices, with no desire to have any rationale for what they do. But ethics is precisely the business of rational, critical reflection (encephalic and not merely visceral) about the problems of the moral agent—in biology and medicine as much as in law, government, education, or anything else.

To that end, then, for the purposes of biomedical ethics, I now turn to a *profile of man* in concrete and discrete terms. As only one man's reflection on man, it will no doubt invite adding and subtracting by others, but this is the road to be followed if we mean business. As a dog is said to worry a bone, let me worry out loud and on paper, hoping for some agreement and, at the least, consideration. There is time only to itemize the inventory, not to enlarge upon it, but I have fifteen positive propositions. Let me set them out, in no rank order at all, and as hardly more than a list of criteria or indicators, by simple title.

1. MINIMUM INTELLIGENCE

Any individual of the species *Homo sapiens* who falls below an I.Q. grade of 40 in a standard Stanford–Binet test, amplified if you like by other tests, is questionably a person; below the mark of 20, not a person. * * * Mere biological life, before minimal intelligence is achieved or after it is lost irretrievably, is without personal status.

2. SELF-AWARENESS

Self-consciousness, as we know, is the quality we watch developing in a baby; we watch it with fascination and glee. Its essential role in personality development is a basic datum of psychology. Its existence or function in animals at or below the primate level is debatable. It is clearly absent in the lower vertebrates, as well as in the nonvertebrates. In psychotherapy non-self-awareness is pathological; in medicine, unconsciousness when it is incorrigible at once poses quality-of-life judgments—for example, in neurosurgical cases of irreversible damage to the brain cortex.

3. SELF-CONTROL

If an individual is not only not controllable by others (unless by force) but not controllable by the individual himself or herself, a low level of life is reached about on a par with that of a paramecium. * * *

4. A SENSE OF TIME

* * *

5. A SENSE OF FUTURITY

How "truly human" is any man who cannot realize there is a time yet to come as well as the present? Subhuman animals do not look forward in time; they live only on what we might call visceral strivings, appetites. Philosophical anthropologies (one recalls that of William Temple, the Archbishop of Canterbury, for instance) commonly emphasize purposiveness as a key to humanness. Chesterton once remarked that we would never ask a puppy what manner of dog it wanted to be when it grows up. * * *

6. A SENSE OF THE PAST

* * *

7. THE CAPABILITY TO RELATE TO OTHERS

Interpersonal relationships, of the sexual-romantic and friendship kind, are of the greatest importance for the fullness of what we idealize as being truly personal. * * * Man's society is based on culture—that is, on a conscious knowledge of the system and on the exercise in some real measure of either consent or opposition.

8. CONCERN FOR OTHERS

Some people may be skeptical about our capacity to care about others (what in Christian ethics is often distinguished from romance and friendship as "neighbor love" or "neighbor concern"). The extent to which this capacity is actually in play is debatable. But whether concern for others is disinterested or inspired by enlightened self-interest, it seems plain that a conscious extra-ego orientation is a trait of the species * * *.

9. COMMUNICATION

Utter alienation or disconnection from others, if it is irreparable, is de-humanization. * * *

10. CONTROL OF EXISTENCE

It is of the nature of man that he is not helplessly subject to the blind workings of physical or physiological nature. He has only finite knowledge, freedom, and initiative, but what he has of it is real and effective. * * *

* * *

11. CURIOSITY

To be without affect, sunk in *anomie,* is to be not a person. Indifference is inhuman. Man is a learner and a knower as well as a tool maker and user. * * *

12. CHANGE AND CHANGEABILITY

To the extent that an individual is unchangeable or opposed to change, he denies the creativity of personal beings. It means not only the fact of biological and physiological change, which goes on as a condition of life, but the capacity and disposition for changing one's mind and conduct as well. Biologically, human beings are developmental: birth, life, health, and death are processes, not events, and are to be understood progressively, not episodically. All human existence is on a continuum, a matter of becoming. * * *

13. BALANCE OF RATIONALITY AND FEELING

* * * As human beings we are not coldly rational or cerebral, nor are we merely creatures of feeling and intuition. It is a matter of being both, in different combinations from one individual to another. To be one rather than the other is to distort the *humanum.*

14. IDIOSYNCRASY

The human being is idiomorphous, a distinctive individual. * * * To be a person is to have an identity, to be recognizable and callable by name.

15. NEOCORTICAL FUNCTION

In a way, this is the cardinal indicator, the one all the others are hinged upon. Before cerebration is in play, or with its end, in the absence of the synthesizing function of the cerebral cortex, the person is nonexistent. Such individuals are objects but not subjects. This is so no matter how many other spontaneous or artificially supported functions persist in the heart, lungs, neurologic and vascular systems. Such noncerebral processes are not personal. Like the Harvard Medical School's *ad hoc* committee report on "brain death," some state statutes require the absence of brain function. * * * But what is definitive in determining death is the loss of cerebration, not just of any or all brain function. Personal reality depends on cerebration and to be dead "humanly" speaking is to be excerebral, no matter how long the body remains alive.

Notes and Questions

1. Which attributes does Fletcher consider to be necessary for personhood? Are any sufficient? Would you add any others to his list? Is there any underlying principle that describes the fifteen attributes selected by Fletcher? Are they all really a subset of the first?

2. Which attributes of personhood, if any, does Ms. Masterson or her fetus possess?

3. Dr. Fletcher commenced a serious debate over whether the persons protected by law ought to be defined in terms of attributes we wish to protect or in terms of the human stock from which the person is created. Both forms of definition may be valuable for different purposes. We provide some rights to people because they possess many or all of the attributes that distinguish human beings. The right to make medical decisions, based on the autonomy of individuals, is not accorded to those who would score below twenty on an I.Q. test (and who would fail many of Dr. Fletcher's tests for humanness). On the other hand, we provide minimally adequate housing, food, medical care, and other necessities for those of human stock, even when they do not meet some of Dr. Fletcher's criteria, and even when we do not provide those same benefits to others, (e.g., animals) who fail the same criteria. In the end, the Fletcher propositions may be useful in determining some of the rights of persons and the "human stock" definition may be helpful in determining others. Just as property is often described as a bundle of rights, it may turn out that "personhood" is a bundle of rights that need to be separated out and individually analyzed.

4. As we saw earlier, even the adoption of a "human stock" definition does not answer the question of when that human stock becomes a person. What is the attribute of the human stock that makes it a person—genetic uniqueness? Responsiveness? The potential to be born? The appearance of a human being? Consider the following list of the alternative medical points of personhood from C.R. Austin, Human Embryos: The Debate on Assisted Reproduction 22–31 (1989):

When does a person's life really begin?

* * * Probably most people who were asked this question would answer 'at fertilization' (or 'conception'). Certainly, several interesting and unusual things happen then—it is really the most *obvious* event to pick—but for biologists the preceding and succeeding cellular processes are *equally* important. Nevertheless, 'fertilization' continues to be the cry of many religious bodies and indeed also of the august World Medical Association, who, in 1949, adopted the Geneva Convention Code of Medical Ethics, which contains the clause: 'I will maintain the utmost respect for human life from the time of conception'. So we do need to look more closely at this choice, for a generally acceptable 'beginning' for human life would be a great help in reaching ethical and legal concensus.

In the first place human *life,* as such, obviously begins before fertilization, since the egg or oocyte is alive before sperm entry, as were innumerable antecedent cells, back through the origin of species into the mists of time. A more practical starting point would be that of the life of the human *individual,* so it is individuality that we should be looking for, at least as one of the essential criteria. Now the earliest antecedents of the eggs, as of sperm, are the primordial germ cells, which can be seen as a group of distinctive little entities migrating through the tissues of the early embryo. When they first become recognizable, they number only about a dozen or two, but they multiply fast and soon achieve large numbers, reaching a peak of 7–10 million about 6 months after conception. Then, despite continued active cell division, there is a dramatic decline in the cell population, which has tempted people to suggest that some sort of 'selection of the fittest' occurs, but there is no good evidence in support of this idea; nor is there any good reason to look for individuality in that mercurial population. In due course, the primordial germ cells, while still undergoing cell divisions, settle down in the tissues of the future ovary, change subtly in their characteristics, and thus become oogonia; and then, soon after birth, *cell division ceases,* the cells develop large nuclei and are now recognizable as primary oocytes. From now on, there are steady cell losses but no further cell divisions * * * ; it is the same entity that was a primary oocyte, becomes a fertilized egg, and then develops as an embryo. The primary oocytes are very unusual cells, for they have the capacity to live for much longer than most other body cells; the *same* oocytes can be seen in the ovaries of women approaching the menopause—cells that have lived for about 40 years or longer. And it is with the emergence of the primary oocytes that we can hail the start of *individuality.* Then, in those oocytes that are about to be ovulated, the first meiotic division takes place—another important step, for the 'shuffling' of genes that occurs at that point bestows *genetic uniqueness* on the oocyte. So both individuality and genetic uniqueness are established before sperm penetration and fertilization; these processes have distinctly different actions—providing the stimulus that initiates cleavage and contributing to biparental inheritance. Thus, the preferred choice for the start of the human individual should surely be the formation of the primary oocyte, but there is certainly no unanimity on this score.

Passing over now the popularity of fertilization, for many people it is instead the emergence of the embryonic disc and primitive streak that most appeals as the stage in which to identify the start of 'personhood' (one or more persons, in view of the imminent possibility of twinning), and there is much to support this opinion. Here, for the first time, are structures that are designed to have a different destiny than *all the rest of the embryo* —they represent the primordium of the fetus, and the developmental patterns of embryo and fetus progressively diverge from this stage onwards. An additional point is that this new emergence is not inevitable, for in around one in two-thousand pregnancies the embryo grows, often to quite a large size, but there is no fetus; the clinical conditions are known as blighted ovum, dropsical ovum, hydatidiform mole, etc. Evidence suggests that hydatidiform mole is attributable to fertilization of a faulty egg, the embryo developing only under the influence of the sperm chromosomes.

At the time of appearance of the embryonic disc, and shortly beforehand, the process of implantation is occurring, and this is considered by many to have special significance in relation to embryonic potential—so far as we know, implantation cannot occur once the development of the embryo has passed the stage when interaction with * * * the uterus normally takes place.

But despite all that has been said, there are still many folk who remain unconvinced—is the being at this stage sufficiently 'human' to qualify as the start of a person? After all, the disc is just a collection of similar cells, virtually undifferentiated, poorly delineated from its surroundings, about a fifth of a millimetre long, non-sentient, and without the power of movement. It is in no way a 'body' and it does not bear the faintest resemblance to a human being—*and* the soul cannot enter yet, for the disc may yet divide in the process of twinning, and the soul being unique is indivisible. Also, it is argued that we should be looking for some spark of personality, and a moral philosopher has proposed that some sort of 'responsiveness' is an essential feature.

One of the earliest succeeding changes in the direction of humanness could be the development of the heart primordium, and soon after that the beginnings of a circulatory system; the first contractions of the heart muscle occur possibly as early as day 21, with a simple tubular heart at that stage, and in the fourth week a functional circulation begins. With the heart beats we have the first movements initiated within the embryo (?fetus) and thus in a way the first real 'sign of life'. The conceptus is now about 6 mm long. During the fifth and sixth weeks, nerve fibres grow out from the spinal cord and make contact with muscles, so that at this time or soon afterwards, a mechanical or electrical stimulus might elicit a muscle twitch; this is important for it would be the first indication of sentient existence—of 'responsiveness'. At this stage, too, the embryo could possibly feel pain. But, still, some would find cause to demur: only an expert could tell that this embryo/fetus, now 12–13 mm in length, with branchial arches (corresponding to the 'gill-slits' in non-mammalian embryos), stubby limbs, and a prominent tail, is human. A marginally more acceptable applicant is the fetus at 7½ weeks, when the hands and feet can be seen to have fingers and toes, and thereafter physical resemblance steadily improves; also at this time, a special gene on the Y-chromosome (the 'testis-determining factor' or TDF) is switched on, and the fetuses that have this chromosome, the males, proceed thenceforward to develop *as* males, distinguishable from females.

At about 12 weeks, electrical activity can be detected in the brain of the fetus, which could signal the dawn of consciousness. Here, we would seem to have a very logical stage marking the *start* of a person, for the cessation of electrical activity in the brain ('brain death') is accepted in both medical and legal circles as marking the *termination* of a person—as an indication that life no longer exists in victims of accidents or in patients with terminal illnesses. Around the fourth or fifth month of pregnancy, the mother first experiences movements of the fetus ('quickening'), which were regarded by St. Thomas Aquinas as the first indication of life, for he believed that life was distinguished by two features, knowledge and movement; moreover, it would seem logical that the fetus would move when the *animus* (life or soul) took up residence.[†] * * *

† The modern equivalent would be at about day 21, when the heart begins to beat.

At about 24 weeks, the fetus reaches a state in which it can commonly survive outside the maternal body, with assistance. * * * Just which stage marks the start of a person's life is a matter of personal opinion. Much of the foregoing argumentation may seem to some people difficult to comprehend, especially if they have not had formal training in biology, and to others may even seem irrelevant, in view of the firm line taken by many church authorities. But it really is important that we should try to reach a concensus on just when a person's life should be held to begin, for the decision does have important practical consequences—it directly affects the rights of other embryos, of fetuses, and of people.

STAGES AT WHICH THE LIFE OF 'A PERSON' COULD BEGIN

Developmental stage	Activity	Significance for 'start of life'	Approximate numbers [per woman]
Primordial germ cells; oogonia	Successive divisions	Earliest generative cells	5–10 million
Primary oocytes	Cell growth— no division	Origin of individuality	Up to hundreds of thousands
Emission of first polar body	First meiosis; ovulation	Genetic uniqueness established	About 500 [c]
Secondary oocyte	Fertilization; second meiosis	Activation; has paternal genes	About 100 [d]
Cleavage embryo	Cell division	Potential plurality	80 [e]
Blastocyst	Implantation	First maternal response	60
Embryonic disc —neural folds	Primordium of fetus	Logical period for soul entry	30
Day 21 embryo	First heart beat	First 'sign of life'	30
5–6 Week embryo	Nerve reflex possible	Responsiveness	25
Fetus at 12 weeks	Electrical activity—brain	Clinical match for end of life	15
Fetus at 4–5 months	'Quickening'	First 'awareness' by mother	10
Infant	Born and surviving	Full legal status	5 [f]

c Based on the calculation that with a fertile life of 40 years an 'average' woman would have about 480 menstrual cycles in which an average of 1.1 eggs would be ovulated: total 528 or say 500.

d A fertilization rate of 20 per cent overall seems reasonable, since intercourse would often occur too early or too late for successful fertilization; and some allowance is made for the use of contraceptives.

e This and the next six figures are broad estimates, with some basis on published data for early loss rates.

f This figure is based on the assumption that the world average starting family would be about five, after allowing for perinatal deaths.

B. LEGAL RECOGNITION OF THE BEGINNING OF HUMAN LIFE

The law is increasingly forced to confront the question of when rights and privileges of persons attach to fetuses and young children. While children have always been treated differently from adults in the law, those fundamental common law and constitutional rights that uniformly extend to both competent and incompetent adults also have been extended to children from the time of birth. Courts have had greater difficulty determining which rights, if any, attach to a fetus.

The trend over the past fifteen years has been for states to expand the common law rights of the fetus and to recognize that the fetus can be an independent victim for purposes of the criminal law. For example, most states now permit a tort action to be filed by an estate of a stillborn child. Just a decade ago, the vast majority of states required that the child be born alive before any right to sue would attach. Similarly, many states now extend the protection of their homicide law to fetuses; several years ago that extension was very unusual. The extent of any constitutional protection of fetuses is far less certain.

1. Constitutional Recognition

While the Supreme Court has never formally determined when a fetus becomes a "person" for constitutional purposes, it has not been able to completely avoid that question despite its several attempts to finesse it. Indeed, some commentators thought that the matter was finally resolved in the watershed case of Roe v. Wade, 410 U.S. 113, 93 S.Ct. 705, 35 L.Ed.2d 147 (1973), in which the Supreme Court was called upon to determine whether a fetus was a person for purposes of the protections of the Fourteenth Amendment. While *Roe v. Wade* will be considered in some greater detail below, it is significant to know that the Court held that the term "person," at least as that term appears in the Fourteenth Amendment, was not intended to encompass the fetus. After reviewing over 2,000 years of the history of abortion the Court addressed the question directly:

> The appellee and certain amici argue that the fetus is a "person" within the language and meaning of the Fourteenth Amendment. In support of this, they outline at length and in

detail the well-known facts of fetal development. If this suggestion of personhood is established, the appellant's case, of course, collapses, for the fetus' right to life is then guaranteed specifically by the Amendment. The appellant conceded as much on reargument. On the other hand, the appellee conceded on reargument that no case could be cited that holds that a fetus is a person within the meaning of the Fourteenth Amendment.

The Constitution does not define "person" in so many words. Section 1 of the Fourteenth Amendment contains three references to "person." The first, in defining "citizens," speaks of "persons born or naturalized in the United States." The word also appears both in the Due Process Clause and in the Equal Protection Clause. "Person" is used in other places in the Constitution: in the listing of qualifications for Representatives and Senators, Art I, § 2, cl 2, and § 3, cl 3; in the Apportionment Clause, Art I, § 2, cl 3;[53] in the Migration and Importation provision, Art I, § 9, cl 1; in the Emolument Clause, Art I, § 9, cl 8; in the Electors provisions, Art II, § 1, cl 2, and the superseded cl 3; in the provision outlining qualifications for the office of President, Art II, § 1, cl 5; in the Extradition provisions, Art IV, § 2, cl 2, and the superseded Fugitive Slave Clause 3; and in the Fifth, Twelfth, and Twenty-second Amendments, as well as in §§ 2 and 3 of the Fourteenth Amendment. But in nearly all these instances, the use of the word is such that it has application only postnatally. None indicates, with any assurance, that it has any possible prenatal application.[54]

* * *

All this, together with our observation * * * that throughout the major portion of the 19th century prevailing legal abortion practices were far freer than they are today, persuades us that the word "person," as used in the Fourteenth Amendment, does not include the unborn.[55] * * * 410 U.S. at 156–157, 93 S.Ct. at 728–729.

53. We are not aware that in the taking of any census under this clause, a fetus has ever been counted.

54. When Texas urges that a fetus is entitled to Fourteenth Amendment protection as a person, it faces a dilemma. Neither in Texas nor in any other State are all abortions prohibited. Despite broad proscription, an exception always exists. The exception contained in Art 1196, for an abortion procured or attempted by medical advice for the purpose of saving the life of the mother, is typical. But if the fetus is a person who is not to be deprived of life without due process of law, and if the mother's condition is the sole determinant, does not the Texas exception appear to be out of line with the Amendment's command?

There are other inconsistencies between Fourteenth Amendment status and the typical abortion statute. It has already been pointed out [ ] that in Texas the woman is not a principal or an accomplice with respect to an abortion upon her. If the fetus is a person, why is the woman not a principal or an accomplice? Further, the penalty for criminal abortion specified by Art 1195 is significantly less than the maximum penalty for murder prescribed by Art 1257 of the Texas Penal Code. If the fetus is a person, may the penalties be different?

55. Cf. the Wisconsin abortion statute, defining "unborn child" to mean "a human being from the time of conception until it is born alive," and the new Connecticut statute, declaring it to be the public policy

The Supreme Court recognized that there were protectable interests beyond those specified in the Constitution and determined:

> [W]e do not agree that, by adopting one theory of life, Texas may override the rights of the pregnant woman that are at stake. We repeat, however, that the state does have an important and legitimate interest in preserving and protecting the health of the pregnant woman * * *, and that it has still *another* important and legitimate interest in protecting the potentiality of human life. 410 U.S. at 162, 93 S.Ct. at 731.

Thus, a state may be able to define and protect rights in the fetus, but these are not the Fourteenth Amendment rights of "persons." Despite the uncertainty of the Constitutional basis of the right of the fetus, the Court went so far as to point out that the right could be sufficiently compelling to overcome the mother's Fourteenth Amendment right to control her body and choose to have an abortion.

> With respect to the state's important and legitimate interest in potential life, the "compelling" point is at viability. This is so because the fetus then presumably has the capability of meaningful life outside the mother's womb. State regulations protective of fetal life after viability thus have both logical and biological justifications. If the state is interested in protecting fetal life after viability, it may go so far as to proscribe abortion during that period, except when it is necessary to preserve the life or health of the mother. 410 U.S. at 163–164, 93 S.Ct. at 731–32.

Thus, the Supreme Court determined that the state may define the point at which a fetus becomes a "person," but that point may not be defined as arising earlier than viability or subsequent to birth. Because virtually every state had substantially limited the mother's right to an abortion even before viability, the effect of *Roe v. Wade* was to legitimize abortions that had been prohibited by state law. On the other hand, while those who say that *Roe v. Wade* removed "personhood" from the fetus are right, those who say it removed all rights from all fetuses are clearly wrong. In reaching its conclusion, the Supreme Court reviewed those state cases that found rights of one sort or another in fetuses:

> In a recent development, generally opposed by the commentators, some states permit the parents of a stillborn child to maintain an action for wrongful death because of prenatal injuries. Such an action would appear to be one to vindicate the parents' interest and is thus consistent with the view that the fetus, at most, represents only the potentiality of life. Similarly, unborn children have been recognized as acquiring rights or interests by way of inheritance or other devolution of property, and have been represented by guardians *ad litem*. Perfections of the interests involved, again, has

of the State and the legislative intent "to protect and preserve human life from the   moment of conception."

generally been contingent upon live birth. In short, the unborn have never been recognized in the law as persons in the whole sense. 410 U.S. at 162, 93 S.Ct. at 731.

The continued viability of *Roe v. Wade* itself was called into question in Webster v. Reproductive Health Services, 492 U.S. 490, 109 S.Ct. 3040, 106 L.Ed.2d 410 (1989), in which the Supreme Court reviewed a Missouri statute that restricted the availability of abortions in several ways. In addition, that statute included a preamble that defined personhood:

    1. The general assembly of this state finds that:

        (1) the life of each human being begins at conception;

        (2) unborn children have protectable interests in life, health, and well being; * * *

    2. * * * the laws of this state shall be interpreted and construed to acknowledge on behalf of the unborn child at every stage of development, all the rights, privileges, and immunities available to other persons, citizens, and residents of this state, subject only to the Constitution of the United States, and decisional interpretations thereof. * * *

    3. As used in this section, the term "unborn children" or "unborn child" shall include all unborn child or children or the offspring of human beings from the moment of conception until birth at every stage of biological development. * * *

Vernon's Ann.Mo.Stat. § 1.205 (1986). This preamble was attacked on the grounds that it was beyond the constitutional authority of the state legislature to define personhood, at least to the extent that the definition extended personhood to pre-viable fetuses. The Supreme Court sidestepped that question by concluding that the preamble was nothing more than a state value judgment favoring childbirth over abortion, and that such a value judgment was clearly within the authority of the legislature. The Court explained that "the extent to which the preamble's language might be used to interpret other state statutes or regulations is something that only the courts of Missouri can definitively decide. State law has offered protections to unborn children in tort and probate law [ ], and [this section] can be interpreted to do no more than that." 109 S.Ct. at 3050. More significantly, probably, the Supreme Court went on to cast doubt about the continuing constitutional viability of *Roe v. Wade* itself. Four justices (Chief Justice Rehnquist and Justices White, Scalia and Kennedy) indicated that *Roe* should be overturned either explicitly or implicitly; four justices (Justices Brennan, Marshall, Blackmun and Stevens) insisted that it remain intact. Justice O'Connor resisted entreaties from both sides arguing that "[w]hen the constitutional invalidity of a state's abortion statute actually turns on the constitutional validity of *Roe v. Wade,* there will be time enough to reexamine *Roe.* And to do so carefully." 109 S.Ct. at 3061. That time will not come, of course, until a state promulgates a statute that is on its face clearly and unambiguously inconsistent with *Roe v. Wade*. In the year following the *Webster* decision, the two state statutes that would have raised the issue most clearly—one passed by the legislature of Louisiana and one passed by the legislature of Idaho—were vetoed and never became law. A subsequent Utah statute may supply the Supreme Court with an appropriate case.

The four dissenting justices in *Webster* made several arguments. Unlike the majority, they did address the question of personhood:

> I think it obvious that the state's interest in the protection of an embryo—even if that interest is defined as "protecting those who will be citizens" * * *—increases progressively and dramatically as the organism's capacity to feel pain, to experience pleasure, to survive, and to react to its surroundings increases day by day. * * * [I]f distinctions may be drawn between a fetus and a human being in terms of the state interest in their protection—even though the fetus represents one of "those who will be citizens"—it seems to me quite odd to argue that distinctions may not also be drawn between the state interest in protecting the freshly fertilized egg and the state interest in protecting the nine-month-gestated, fully sentient fetus on the eve of birth. Recognition of this distinction is supported not only by logic, but also by history and by our shared experiences. 109 S.Ct. 3040 (Blackmun, J., dissenting, quoting Stevens, J., in Thornburgh v. American College of Obstetricians and Gynecologists, 476 U.S. 778–779.)

There are two separate constitutional issues that surround the definition of person. First, is there a definition of "person" for purposes of the Constitution? Second, do the substantive provisions of the Constitution put any limit on the way that *states* may define "person" for any other purpose? Could each state define "person" differently for constitutional purposes? States did so before the Thirteenth Amendment, of course. Could the definition of "person" for constitutional purposes be different from that definition for other purposes? The current status of abortion law suggests that there is no definitive answer to any of these questions.

Is there any reason that an estate of a viable or nonviable fetus ought to have the right to bring a tort action and yet the fetus should not be entitled to the rights of a person under the Fourteenth Amendment or for purposes of protection of the criminal law? What social values are served by the right to bring a tort action? What social values are served by the Fourteenth Amendment?

2. Statutory Recognition

As Justice Blackmun pointed out in *Roe v. Wade*, courts have generally considered killing a fetus to be substantially different from killing a person who was born alive. This is reflected in the different penalties that usually attach to feticide and other forms of homicide and the fact that feticide itself has been distinguished from murder or manslaughter in most jurisdictions. Over the past several years, however, several states have made the penalties for feticide commensurate with the penalties for homicide, and several have promulgated new homicide statutes that explicitly include fetuses as those whose death may give rise to homicide prosecutions. In 1986 the Minnesota legislature passed its "unborn child homicide" statute which provides, in part:

Minn.Stat.Ann. § 609.2661 (1988):

Whoever does any of the following is guilty of murder of an unborn child in the first degree and must be sentenced to imprisonment for life:

(1) causes the death of an unborn child with premeditation and with intent to effect the death of the unborn child or of another * * *.

Minn.Stat.Ann. § 609.2662 (1988):

Whoever does either of the following is guilty of murder of an unborn child in the second degree and may be sentenced to imprisonment for not more than forty years:

(1) causes the death of an unborn child with the intent to effect the death of that unborn child or another, but without premeditation * * *.

The statute found its way to the Minnesota Supreme Court in 1990.

STATE v. MERRILL

Supreme Court of Minnesota, 1990.
450 N.W.2d 318.

SIMONETT, JUSTICE.

Defendant has been indicted for first- and second-degree murder of Gail Anderson and also for first- and second-degree murder of her "unborn child." The trial court denied defendant's motion to dismiss the charges relating to the unborn child but certified for appellate review two questions:

1. Do Minn.Stat. §§ 609.2661(1) and .2662(1) (1988) [the unborn child homicide statutes] violate the fourteenth amendment of the United States Constitution as interpreted by the United States Supreme Court in *Roe v. Wade,* by failing to distinguish between viable fetuses and nonviable fetuses and embryos, and by treating fetuses and embryos as persons?

2. Are [said statutes] void for vagueness?

On November 13, 1988, Gail Anderson died from gunshot wounds allegedly inflicted by the defendant. An autopsy revealed Ms. Anderson was pregnant with a 27- or 28–day–old embryo. The coroner's office concluded that there was no abnormality which would have caused a miscarriage, and that death of the embryo resulted from the death of Ms. Anderson. At this stage of development, a 28–day–old embryo is 4– to 5–millimeters long and, through the umbilical cord, completely dependent on its mother. The Anderson embryo was not viable. Up to the eighth week of development, it appears that an "unborn child" is referred to as an embryo; thereafter it is called a fetus. The evidence indicates that medical science generally considers a fetus viable at 28 weeks following conception although some fetuses as young as 20 or 21 weeks have survived. The record is unclear in this case whether either Ms. Anderson or defendant Merrill knew she was pregnant at the time she was assaulted.

Defendant was indicted for the death of Anderson's "unborn child" under two statutes entitled, respectively, "Murder of an Unborn Child in the First Degree" and "Murder of an Unborn Child in the Second Degree." These two statutes, enacted by the legislature in 1986, follow precisely the language of our murder statutes, except that "unborn child" is substituted for "human being" and "person." The term "unborn child" is defined as "the unborn offspring of a human being conceived, but not yet born." Minn.Stat. § 609.266(a) (1988).

This legislative approach to a fetal homicide statute is most unusual and raises the constitutional questions certified to us. Of the 17 states that have codified a crime of murder of an unborn, 13 create criminal liability only if the fetus is "viable" or "quick." Additionally, two noncode states have expanded their definition of common law homicide to include viable fetuses. [ ] [Two states] impose criminal liability for causing the death of a fetus at any stage, as does Minnesota, but the statutory penalty provided upon conviction is far less severe. Arizona [ ] (5–year sentence); Indiana [ ] (2–year sentence).

* * *

I.

Defendant first contends that the unborn child homicide statutes violate the Equal Protection Clause. Defendant premises his argument on *Roe v. Wade,* which, he says, holds that a nonviable fetus is not a person. He then argues that the unborn child criminal statutes have impermissibly "adopted a classification equating viable fetuses and nonviable embryos with a person."

Assuming the relevance of defendant's stated premise, defendant has failed to show that the statutory classification impinges upon any of his constitutional rights. * * *

If we understand defendant correctly, he is claiming the statutory classification, by not distinguishing between viable and nonviable fetuses, exposes him to conviction as a murderer of an unborn child during the first trimester of pregnancy, while others who intentionally destroy a nonviable fetus, such as a woman who obtains a legal abortion and the doctor who performs it, are not murderers. In other words, defendant claims the unborn child homicide statutes expose him to serious penal consequences, while others who intentionally terminate a nonviable fetus or embryo are not subject to criminal sanctions. In short, defendant claims similarly situated persons are treated dissimilarly.

We disagree. The situations are not similar. The defendant who assaults a pregnant woman causing the death of the fetus she is carrying destroys the fetus without the consent of the woman. This is not the same as the woman who elects to have her pregnancy terminated by one legally authorized to perform the act. In the case of abortion, the woman's choice and the doctor's actions are based on the woman's constitutionally protected right to privacy. This right encompasses the woman's decision whether to terminate or continue the pregnancy without interference from the state, at least until such time as the state's important interest in protecting the potentiality of human life predominates over the right to privacy, which is usually at viability. *Roe v. Wade* [ ]. *Roe v. Wade* protects the woman's right of choice; it does not protect, much less confer on an assailant, a third-party unilateral right to destroy the fetus.

As defendant points out, the United States Supreme Court has said that an unborn child lacks "personhood" and is not a person for purposes of the Fourteenth Amendment. *Roe v. Wade* [ ]. The focus of that case, however, was on protecting the woman from governmental interference or compulsion when she was deciding whether to terminate or continue her pregnancy. Significantly, the *Roe v. Wade* court also noted that the state "has still *another* important and legitimate interest in protecting the potentiality of human life." * * * In our case, the fetal homicide statutes seek to protect the "potentiality of human life," and they do so without impinging directly or indirectly on a pregnant woman's privacy rights.

The state's interest in protecting the "potentiality of human life" includes protection of the unborn child, whether an embryo or a nonviable or viable fetus, and it protects, too, the woman's interest in her unborn child and her right to decide whether it shall be carried *in utero*. * * *

* * *

II.

A more difficult issue, as the trial court noted, is whether the unborn child criminal statutes are so vague as to violate the Due Process Clause of the Fourteenth Amendment.

* * *

A.

Defendant first contends that the statutes fail to give fair warning to a potential violator. Defendant argues it is unfair to impose on the murderer of a woman an additional penalty for murder of her unborn child when neither the assailant nor the pregnant woman may have been aware of the pregnancy.

The fair warning rule has never been understood to excuse criminal liability simply because the defendant's victim proves not to be the victim the defendant had in mind. Homicide statutes generally provide that a person is guilty of first- or second-degree murder upon proof that the offender caused the death of a person with intent to cause the death of that person *or another*. [   ] Because the offender did not intend to kill the particular victim, indeed, may not even have been aware of that victim's presence, does not mean that the offender did not have fair warning that he would be held criminally accountable the same as if the victim had been the victim intended. [   ]

* * *

B.

Defendant next contends that the unborn child criminal statutes are fatally vague because they do not define the phrase "causes the death of an unborn child." As a result, defendant argues, the statutes invite or permit arbitrary and discriminatory enforcement. [   ]

Defendant argues that the statute leaves uncertain when "death" occurs, or, for that matter, when "life" begins. People will differ on whether life begins at conception or at viability. People may differ on whether death is the cessation of brain activity (an activity not present in an embryo) or the cessation of a functioning circulatory system. The problem, says defendant, is that absent statutory criteria, judges and juries will provide their own definitions which will differ, leaving the statutes vulnerable to arbitrary and discriminatory enforcement. This argument, we think, attempts to prove too much.

* * * Traditionally, the crime of feticide imposed criminal liability for the death of a "viable" fetus, that is, a fetus at that stage of development which permits it to live outside the mother's womb, or a fetus that has "quickened," that is, which moves within the mother's womb.

[Our legislature] has enacted very unusual statutes which go beyond traditional feticide, both in expanding the definition of a fetus and in the severity of the penalty imposed. The statutes in question impose the criminal penalty for murder on whoever causes the death of "the unborn offspring of a human being conceived, but not yet born."

Whatever one might think of the wisdom of this legislation, and notwithstanding the difficulty of proof involved, we do not think it can be said the offense is vaguely defined. An embryo or nonviable fetus when it is within the mother's womb is "the unborn offspring of a human being." Defendant argues, however, that to cause the death of an embryo, the embryo must first be living; if death is the termination of life, something which is not alive cannot experience death. In short, defendant argues that causing the death of a 27–day–old embryo raises the perplexing question of when "life" begins, as well as the question of when "death" occurs.

The difficulty with this argument, however, is that the statutes do not raise the issue of when life as a *human person* begins or ends. The state must prove only that the implanted embryo or the fetus in the mother's womb was living, that it had life, and that it has life no longer. To have life, as that term is commonly understood, means to have the property of all living things to grow, to become. It is not necessary to prove, nor does the statute require, that the living organism in the womb in its embryonic or fetal state be considered a person or a human being. People are free to differ or abstain on the profound philosophical and moral questions of whether an embryo is a human being, or on whether or at what stage the embryo or fetus is ensouled or acquires "personhood". These questions are entirely irrelevant to criminal liability under the statute. Criminal liability here requires only that the genetically human embryo be a living organism that is growing into a human being. Death occurs when the embryo is no longer living, when it ceases to have the properties of life.

* * *

KELLEY, JUSTICE (concurring in part, dissenting in part):

* * *

Each of the statutes under attack in this appeal employs the phrase "causes the death of an unborn child." As appellant points out, neither statute defines the phrase, nor does either set out particularized standards to afford guidance to a court or a jury for use in construing the phrase. In short, both statutes leave when "death" occurs, or, for that matter, when "life" commences undefined. Absent such definition, it seems to me the phrase "causes the death of an unborn child" is burdened with ambiguity which, by its very nature, invites arbitrary and discriminatory enforcement. The result, as I see it, is that by necessity trial courts are left to wrestle with metaphysical, medical and legal concepts relative to the commencement and cessation of life in order to apply these statutes in a criminal prosecution.

* * *

It cannot be gainsaid that few topics today compel as fierce public debate and evoke the passionate convictions of as many of our citizens as does the issue of when "life" in a fetus begins. In view of the stridency of that debate, it appears conceivable, perhaps even predictable, that two juries having the same evidence could arrive at the same factual conclusions, but due to divergent and strongly held beliefs arrived at a dissimilar legal result. By way of example, in the case before us, one jury sharing a common viewpoint of when life commences could find the defendant guilty of fetal murder, whereas another whose members share the view that life was nonexistent in a 26 to 28–day–old embryo, could exonerate the appellant.

The likelihood of discriminatory enforcement is further enhanced when the discretionary charging function possessed by a grand jury is considered. The decision to charge must be concurred in by only a majority of the panel. Minn.R.Crim.P. 18.07. Thus, the decision to charge or not may well pivot on the personal philosophical and moral tenets of a majority of the potential panel—a majority whose beliefs may vary from grand jury panel to grand jury panel.

* * *

WAHL, JUSTICE (dissenting).

* * *

* * * The constitutional requirement of due process not only concerns matters of criminal procedure, but also limits "the manner and extent to which conduct may be defined as criminal in the substantive criminal law." [   ]

By failing to distinguish between viable fetuses and nonviable fetuses and embryos, [the statute] run[s] afoul of the defendant's right to substantive due process.

Defendant is charged with murder of an unborn child * * *. [T]he actor, to be guilty of murder and to be sentenced for murder, must cause the death, not of a human being, but of an unborn child. An unborn child is the unborn offspring of a human being conceived, but not yet born [   ] Thus an unborn child can be a fertilized egg, an embryo, a nonviable fetus or a viable fetus.

The law with regard to murder is clear. Murder is the "unlawful killing of a human being by another * * *." [   ] The term murder implies a felonious homicide, which is the wrongful killing of a human being. [   ] A nonviable fetus is not a human being, nor is an embryo a human being, nor is a fertilized egg a human being. None has attained the capability of independent human life. [   ] * * *

* * *

* * * "When a fundamental right is involved, due process requires a state to justify any action affecting that right by demonstrating a compelling state interest." * * *

The fundamental right involved in the case before us as far as defendant is concerned is his liberty. He is charged with two counts of murder of a woman who was 26 to 28 days pregnant at the time of her death. * * * The state does not have a compelling interest in this potential human life until the fetus becomes viable. [   ] [The statute is] not narrowly drawn to distinguish between viable fetuses, nonviable fetuses and embryos, so as to express "only the legitimate state interests at stake." Unless the words "unborn child" are construed to read "viable unborn child," the reach of these statutes is unconstitutionally broad. * * *

Notes and Questions

1. The majority distinguishes human life from "personhood" and determines that the statute was designed to protect human life, not persons. Would the majority permit the legislature to protect other forms of human life—human blood cells, for example—in the same way that it has decided to protect the "nonperson" human life in this case, or is the potential personhood of the embryo fundamental to the majority's decision that this statute's protection of human life is constitutional?

2. In this case the court could have depended upon the interests of several different parties and nonparties. The pregnant woman has an interest, as do the criminal defendant, the state, and, perhaps, the embryo or fetus. The majority depends upon the pregnant woman's interest in being able to maintain her pregnancy, while the dissent looks to the interest of the criminal defendant. None of the justices depends independently upon the interest of the embryo or the fetus. Could you craft an opinion that would depend upon that interest rather than the interest of the pregnant woman, the criminal defendant or the state?

3. In her dissent, Justice Wahl argues that *Roe v. Wade* forbids a state from treating a nonviable fetus like a person, at least for purposes of criminal law. Is she right? For purposes of the homicide laws, is there any reason to draw a line between a viable and nonviable fetus when the mother of each intends to carry the fetus in utero full term? Courts have had little trouble upholding harsh feticide statutes that protect only *viable* fetuses; perhaps this is because by the point of viability the fact of the pregnancy is likely to be obvious to the assailant. Are any goals of the criminal law served by the application of this Minnesota statute to a case where neither the pregnant woman nor the assailant knew of the pregnancy? In People v. Smith, 188 Cal.App.3d 1495, 234 Cal.Rptr. 142 (1987), a man who killed a woman he knew to be pregnant was held to be on notice that he could be convicted for two murders under California law. See also, United States v. Spencer, 839 F.2d 1341 (9th Cir.1988); Smith v. Newsome, 815 F.2d 1386 (11th Cir.1987).

4. Minnesota is not alone in extending its homicide statute to protect fetuses before viability. The former feticide statute in Illinois, which applied only to fetuses whose viability was proven beyond a reasonable doubt, carried a penalty that was "the same as for murder, except that the death penalty may not be imposed." Shortly after the statute was upheld in People v. Shum, 117 Ill.2d 317, 111 Ill.Dec. 546, 512 N.E.2d 1183 (1987), the Illinois legislature replaced the feticide statute with a statute prescribing "intentional homicide of an unborn child." In that statute "unborn child" is defined as "any individual of the human species from fertilization until birth." Ill.—S.H.A. ch. 38, § 9–1.2 (1988 Supp.) Although the Illinois statute applies to previable fetuses and embryos, it is narrower than its Minnesota counterpart in that it can be applied only when the assailant knows that his victim is pregnant. Is this mens rea requirement reasonable? Is it reasonable to have a statute, like Minnesota's, without this knowledge requirement?

3. *Common Law Recognition*

AMADIO v. LEVIN

Supreme Court of Pennsylvania, 1985.
509 Pa. 199, 501 A.2d 1085.

PAPADAKOS, JUSTICE.

Once again this Court is called upon to decide whether a right of recovery exists under our Wrongful Death Act and Survival Statute on behalf of a stillborn child who died as a result of injuries received en ventre sa mere.

The facts are not complicated and can be quickly summarized. Jennifer Amadio was the full-term unborn child of Joseph and Regina Amadio (Appellants), due to be delivered on September 28, 1979. On October 15, 1979, Jennifer was born stillborn at Methodist Hospital, Philadelphia, Pennsylvania. At delivery, Jennifer was a fully matured and perfectly proportioned seven pound eight ounce female.

On September 22, 1981, Joseph and Regina Amadio, in their own right, and as Administrators of the estate of Jennifer, filed a Complaint in Trespass * * * claiming that, as a result of negligence, there were incurred medical expenses, burial expenses, a loss of earnings, loss of enjoyment of life, and physical pain and mental anguish.

* * *

Prior decisions of this Court [ ] uniformly held that in order for a survival action to lie, there must be an independent life in being, surviving birth, which could have brought the action prior to death. Five reasons were usually cited for limiting survival and wrongful death actions to children born alive.

First, the Court surmised that the real objective of such a lawsuit was to compensate the parents of the deceased child for their emotional distress, and that since parents already had the ability in their own right to institute such an action, it would only be duplication to permit parents to file a second action on behalf of the estate of the child.

Second, because wrongful death actions are derivative, and since the Court refused to acknowledge that a stillborn child was an individual under the wrongful death or survival statutes, it was concluded that the Acts were not intended to provide for recovery by the estate of a stillborn child.

Third, extending causes of actions to the estates of stillborn children was felt to increase problems of causation and damages.

Fourth, the prior cases arose out of an era when most jurisdictions did not permit the filing of such actions. * * *

Fifth, it was reasoned that since only children born alive may take property by descent under our Intestate Laws, the Court assumed that the Legislature had already limited the creation of causes of actions to those instances where the existence or estate of a child was recognized by the laws of intestacy.

Appellants urge us to abandon these prior decisions requiring survival at birth in order to maintain an action for fatal injuries caused en ventre sa mere, and to adopt the majority view that requires only that the death dealing injuries occur when the child is viable en ventre sa mere.   * * *

* * *

* * * [W]e acknowledge a child en ventre sa mere to be an "individual," "having existence as a separate creature from the moment of conception." [ ] Henceforth, injuries received by a child while en ventre sa mere can form the basis for survival or wrongful death actions as maintained on behalf of a child born alive. Live birth can no longer be a limiting prerequisite to the maintenance of such an action. This is consistent with [a dissent in an earlier case, which] argues against drawing a line at the birth of a child, its viability, or some other arbitrary period of gestation, and instead concludes that the action should proceed to trial and let the orderly production of evidence by the adversaries prove or disprove causation, injury and damages in each case.

* * *

This Court's former view that the real objective of these lawsuits was to compensate the parents of their deceased children twice for the parents' emotional distress is not only incorrect, but if accepted, merely perpetuates the notion that a child is inseparable from its mother while en ventre sa mere. That view lumped medical and funeral costs incurred due to the injury to the child as elements of damages recoverable by the mother. Once the child is recognized as a separate individual, however, medical and funeral costs incurred as well as any economic losses are recoverable by the child's estate, not the mother.

* * *

Since we recognize that the child's wrongful death is a separate injury from that of the mother's, the child's wrongful death is compensable in damages and the child's estate is the proper party to seek recovery for the decedent child's funeral and medical expenses and pecuniary losses under the Wrongful Death Statute and for the loss of earning power less the costs of maintenance and for the decedent's pain and suffering under the Survival Statute.

* * *

Today's holding merely makes it clear that the recovery afforded the estate of a stillborn is no different than the recovery afforded the estate of a child that dies within seconds of its release from its mother's womb. In view of the current attitude throughout our sister states to let the representatives of the stillborn's estate prove their losses, it would be illogical to continue to deny that such claims could be established, when we permit them for the child that survives birth for an instant.

* * *

* * * We do not decide the criminal liability, if any, attendant upon causing the death of a child en ventre sa mere, for such is not the case before us today.

* * *

ZAPPALA, JUSTICE, concurring.

* * *

* * * Mindful of the virtue of avoiding redundance, I repeat what has been said elsewhere and long ago, in hope that the repeating will make clear the full impact of these concepts which have been accepted but nevertheless largely ignored. As previously noted this Court as early as 1960 recognized that a child in the womb is not merely a part of its mother's body but is in fact a distinct individual [ ]. * * *

> While it is a fact that there is a close dependence by the unborn child on the organism of the mother, it is not disputed today that the mother and the child are two separate and distinct entities; that the unborn child has its own system of circulation of the blood separate and apart from the mother; that there is no communication between the two circulation systems; that the heart beat of the child is not in tune with that of the mother but is more rapid; that there is no dependence by the child on the mother except for sustenance. It might be remarked here that even after birth the child depends for sustenance upon the mother or upon a third party. It is not the fact that an unborn child is part of the mother, but that rather in the unborn state it lived with the mother, we might say, and from conception on developed its own distinct, separate personality.

401 Pa. at 273, 164 A.2d at 96.

The essence of this view of mother and child as independent beings was distilled in the rhetorical questioning of the Michigan Supreme Court:

> If the mother can die and the fetus live or the fetus die and the mother live, how can it be said there is only one life? If tortious conduct can injure one and not the other, how can it be said there is not a duty owing to each?

[ ] And lest it be thought that this approach partakes of intellectual machinations detached from realities, it should be noted that the leading medical text on obstetrical practice speaks in identical terms.

> Happily, we have entered an era in which the fetus can be rightfully considered and treated as our second patient. * * *

* * *

* * * [T]his Court has already acknowledged the existence of a distinct life in the child developing itself in the mother's womb. There

is, therefore, no "legal certainty" to be gained by imposing a requirement of birth upon the recognition of that life.

"The alternative to drawing an arbitrary line anywhere is to recognize the cause of action generally while, of course, maintaining the not-insubstantial burden of proving causation in each case." * * * An illusory "certainty" whose only benefit is a reduced caseload for the judicial system cannot be permitted to deny injured parties the opportunity to prove and recover their damages. The live birth requirement "might aid the judiciary but hardly justice." [ ]

* * *

* * * "Personhood" as a legal concept arises not from the humanity of the subject but from the ascription of rights and duties to the subject. Black's Law Dictionary 1299, 1300 (4th ed. 1968), *citing* Pollock, First Book of Jurisprudence 110, *and* Gray, Nature and Sources of Law, ch. II.[5]

* * *

For the foregoing reasons I agree that our prior cases precluding wrongful death and survival actions on behalf of stillborn children should be overruled and the present case be reversed and remanded to the Court of Common Pleas of Philadelphia County for further proceedings.[7]

Nix, Chief Justice, dissenting.

* * *

Regrettably, the concept of a "deep pocket" has become pervasive in this area and has frequently influenced decisions as to when a cause of action should arise and as to the appropriate recovery to allow for the claimed loss. The "deep pocket" theory springs from the "desire to insure that victims of tortious injury can reach a defendant with sufficient wealth to provide adequate compensation." [ ] This motive has had a tendency to obscure the basis of the finding of liability and the extent to which reimbursement can be justified.

* * *

Turning to the instant case, I would agree with the majority that it would be unfair to preclude a just recovery for an injury negligently caused because the expiration of the life of the child occurs prior to, rather than after, birth. However, I do not believe such a disparity

---

5. *But see* Black's Law Dictionary 1029 (5th ed. 1979) *citing Roe v. Wade*, 410 U.S. 113, 93 S.Ct. 705, 35 L.Ed.2d 147 (1973) for the proposition that an unborn child is not a "person". Because the Court in that case sought to define "person" only for purposes of the Fourteenth Amendment to the United States Constitution, that definition is not binding here. Furthermore, the reasoning of the Court in *Roe* has been subject to widespread criticism and, at least as to the protectibility of "viable" unborn children, suffers from internal inconsistency.

7. Because the Complaint in this case asserts that Jennifer was "viable" at the time the allegedly negligent conduct of the defendants caused her death, the questions involved in circumstances implicating "viability" in other ways must be left for another day.

does in fact exist. The legitimate elements of compensatory damages following from the injury are recoverable in either event. The only difference is that where the child expires before birth these elements are subsumed in the claim of the mother.

* * *

My second concern is that the extension here urged falls within the province of the legislature and not the courts. It would appear that what we are presently being requested to do is a matter appropriately addressed to the legislative branch of government.

* * *

Notes and Questions

1. What is the holding of the *Amadio* court? Is it that a fetus is a "person" for purposes of commencing a tort action when that fetus is viable, or even when the fetus is not viable? Does the holding define the fetus as a "person" only for purposes of commencing a tort action, or does it extend that definition for all state law purposes?

2. The *Amadio* court points out that there is no reason to distinguish between a still birth and a baby who dies a few minutes after birth for purposes of permitting the commencement of a tort action. Many courts distinguish between a viable and a pre-viable fetus for these purposes. Is such a distinction justifiable? If a fetus becomes a "person" for purposes of commencing a tort action only upon viability, the court must address several questions when it hears a tort action commenced on behalf of a fetus. First, what is the legally relevant moment when the fetus must be viable for that fetus to possess a cause of action—is it the time of the injury or the time of the tortious action? Second, when is a fetus viable as a general matter? Is this a matter of law or fact? Third, was the plaintiff-fetus viable at the legally relevant time in the instant case?

All of these questions were before the court upon a motion for summary judgment in In re Air Crash Disaster at Detroit Metropolitan Airport on August 16, 1987, Rademacher v. McDonnell Douglas Corporation, 737 F.Supp. 427 (E.D.Mich.1989), an action brought on behalf of the fetus of a flight attendant killed in the crash. The District Court determined that Michigan law would permit recovery on behalf of the fetus only if the fetus were "viable at the time of the injury." Further, the court rejected evidence from a right-to-life advocate that fetuses could be viable as early as twenty weeks, and adopted the "generally accepted *Roe [v. Wade]* proposition that viability occurs at twenty-four weeks." Finally, the court concluded:

> [The plaintiff] submits a sonogram report from July 13, 1987, which concludes that the "[e]stimated gestational age is 15.8 +/− 2 weeks." The fatal accident involving Northwest Flight 255 occurred five weeks later. Therefore, on the date of the accident the * * * fetus was 20.8 weeks old +/− 2 weeks. Therefore, the fetus was, at most, 22.8 weeks old. * * *

Thus, the subject fetus in this case was nonviable as a matter of law [and has no cause of action under Michigan law].

3.   While *Amadio* deals with survival and wrongful death statutes, the principles they discuss are general tort principles and are derived from the common law of tort rather than the formal language of the statutes.   Could a legislature, as part of a survival or wrongful death statute, define who constitutes a "person" for purposes of bringing an action under the statute?

4.   The *Rademacher* case described in note 2 discusses the irony in allowing the estate of a fetus to recover damages even if the tortious act was committed at a time when the mother could have chosen to abort the fetus.   The court suggests that while a mother's interest in terminating a pregnancy may outweigh a state's interest in maintaining the life of a pre-viable fetus, a third party's interest does not overcome both the state's and the mother's interest in continuing the pregnancy.   Is this distinction sound?

5.   Consider the Masterson problem on pages 883–884.   Would the estate of Ms. Masterson or the estate of her fetus have a tort action against a police department that negligently failed to seek medical assistance for her?   Suppose Ms. Masterson is declared dead and then gives birth to a child who lives for two days.   Should Ms. Masterson's estate be distributed to the beneficiaries listed in her will, or might her sisters be able to argue successfully that her child inherited at least a portion of her estate, and that they were among the heirs of that child?   Would your answer be different if Ms. Masterson were declared dead and the fetus were subsequently stillborn?   What if Ms. Masterson died before the fetus were even viable?   Should any of these distinctions make a legal difference?

6.   A host of cases have considered the issue of whether a wrongful death action may be brought on behalf of a fetus who dies in utero.   Among those that have allowed such actions for viable fetuses are DiDonato v. Wortman, 320 N.C. 423, 358 S.E.2d 489 (1987), Luff v. Hawkins, 551 A.2d 437 (Del.1988); Farley v. Mount Marty Hosp. Ass'n, 387 N.W.2d 42 (S.D. 1986); Summerfield v. Superior Court, 144 Ariz. 467, 698 P.2d 712 (1985); Hopkins v. McBane, 359 N.W.2d 862 (N.D.1984); O'Grady v. Brown, 654 S.W.2d 904 (Mo.1983); Volk v. Baldazo, 103 Idaho 570, 651 P.2d 11 (1982); Craig v. IMT Insurance Company, 407 N.W.2d 584 (Iowa 1987) (parents of fetus killed in automobile accident may recover for loss of consortium from their insurance company because of ambiguities of the language of the policy).   See also Johnson v. Ruark Obstetrics, 327 N.C. 283, 395 S.E.2d 85 (1990) (permitting recovery for physician's failure to treat maternal diabetes which resulted in the death of a viable fetus) and Terrell v. Rankin, 511 So.2d 126 (Miss.1987) (also permitting a wrongful death action on behalf of a viable fetus for whose mother the physician prescribed medicine for symptoms typical of pregnancy up to the eighth month without ever diagnosing the pregnancy itself).

In addition, consider Johnson v. Verrilli, 134 Misc.2d 582, 511 N.Y.S.2d 1008 (1987), modified, 139 A.D.2d 497, 526 N.Y.S.2d 600 (1988) (since a fetus is not a person under New York law, it must be a part of the mother. Thus, its death in utero constitutes a physical injury to the mother).   For cases which have not permitted wrongful death recovery for the death of a fetus in utero, see Smith v. Columbus Community Hospital, Inc., 222 Neb. 776, 387 N.W.2d 490 (1986) (excellent dissent suggests that the live birth requirement is inconsistent with the developing theories of causation), Witty v. American General Capital Distributors, Inc., 727 S.W.2d 503 (Tex.1987) (while not a person, a fetus is not a chattel either; thus, mother cannot recover for negligent destruction of a chattel), Chamness v. Fairtrace, 158 Ill.App.3d 325, 110 Ill.Dec. 662, 511 N.E.2d 839 (1987) (parental tort immunity applies to suits by one spouse against the other for death of their viable fetus; the prenatal absence of a parent-child relationship is irrelevant since the benefits of any recovery would go to the tortfeasor), Abdelaziz v. A.M.I.S.U.B. of Florida, Inc., 515 So.2d 269 (Fla.App. 3 Dist. 1987) (viable fetus died while its mother awaited transfer from a private to a public hospital), Milton v. Cary Medical Center, 538 A.2d 252 (Me.1988) (majority depends upon legislative history to show that wrongful death statute intended to include only children born alive; dissent would find power in the courts to interpret the statute in matters unanticipated by the legislature when it first promulgated it).

II. MEDICAL INTERVENTION IN REPRODUCTION

The law has been invoked regularly to order the relationships of private individuals and to constrain government to its appropriate role with regard to the control of reproduction through medical and other interventions designed to limit reproduction, such as contraception, sterilization and abortion. The law has also been engaged to regulate medical interventions designed to facilitate reproduction, such as artificial insemination, ovum and embryo transfer, in vitro fertilization, and surrogacy. While the propriety of legal intervention in these matters will undoubtedly remain a matter of dispute, the sexual nature of the issues, as well as their novelty and moral complexity, is likely to cause society to maintain a high interest in regulating them. This section of this chapter is not intended to be a comprehensive analysis of all of these questions; many related issues are discussed elsewhere in this text or in other courses. For example, the tort actions of "wrongful life", "wrongful birth", and "wrongful conception" are forms of medical malpractice, which is discussed in Chapter 2. Similarly, a full discussion of the constitutional issues surrounding contraception and abortion must be left for a constitutional law course. It is the intent of this section of this chapter to provide structure to those issues surrounding procreation and reproduction that are likely to be of special concern to attorneys representing health care professionals, institutions and their patients.

A. LIMITING REPRODUCTION

1. *Government Prohibitions on Reproduction*

Is there a role for the government in prohibiting reproduction, at least in some circumstances? To control population growth, as China has attempted to do? To serve political, economic, or environmental goals? For eugenic purposes? Dr. Joseph Fletcher has argued that there is a moral obligation to prevent the birth of genetically diseased or defective children, and a failure to carry out that obligation to those children "who would suffer grievously if conceived or born * * * would be tantamount to rejecting the whole notion of preventive medicine, sanitation, environmental protection law, and all the other ways in which we express our obligation to the unborn." Although the history of the eugenics movement demonstrates that governmental intervention can be misdirected, there is a strong analytical argument in favor of permitting the government to safeguard the human gene pool. Consider the following argument and determine whether it is strong enough to overcome (1) the potential abuses inherent in allowing governments to choose appropriate genetic traits for the next generation, and (2) the possible scientific error that might lead a regulating government to allow the disappearance of a currently unvalued gene that will become valuable generations from now.

> My fundamental commitment is that survival of the human species is a good and that it is a good of such importance and value that it can be accredited as a right. From this I deduce that individuals and social units have the concomitant obligation to pursue courses of actions that will foster and protect the right of the species' survival. Among these acknowledged and traditional courses of action is general health care. One segment of that health care involves the protection of the population from the transmission of identifiable, seriously deleterious genes and from debilitating and costly (in terms of natural, economic and human resources) genetic disease which can neither be cured nor treated with any preservation of the quality of life and relative independence of the afflicted. Because individual human rights are negotiable according to their historical context, and because there is legal precedent for restricting the exercise of reproductive rights, those who are at high risk for passing on clearly identifiable and severely deleterious genes and debilitating genetic disease should not be allowed to exercise their reproductive prerogative.

Ulrich, Reproductive Rights and Genetic Disease, in J. Humber and R. Almender, Biomedical Ethics and the Law, 351, 360 (1976).

Of course, manipulation of the gene pool, which will be discussed below in Section IV, is not the only reason governments seek to regulate procreation. Because of the theological, ethical, and social values related to sexual conduct and its consequences, governments have often regulated techniques designed to limit reproduction. In the United States, legislatures and courts have often considered the propriety of contraception, sterilization, and abortion. Because these issues are considered in detail in constitutional law courses, they are only briefly addressed here.

2. *Contraception*

Historical and religious reasons explain why some states made the use of contraceptives a crime. The question of the propriety of those statutes reached the Supreme Court in Griswold v. Connecticut, 381 U.S. 479, 85 S.Ct. 1678, 14 L.Ed.2d 510 (1965). An official of the Planned Parenthood League of Connecticut and a Yale physician were charged with aiding and abetting "the use of a drug, medicinal article, or instrument for the purpose of preventing conception," a crime under Connecticut law, by providing contraceptives to a married couple. The Supreme Court reversed their conviction, although it remains difficult to understand the legal basis of the Court's determination. Justice Douglas, writing for the Court, concluded:

> [s]pecific guarantees in the Bill of Rights have penumbras, formed by emanations from those guarantees that helped give them life and substance. Various guarantees create zones of privacy. The rights of association contained in the penumbra of the first amendment is one * * * the third amendment in its prohibition against the quartering of soldiers "in any house" in time of peace without the consent of the owner is another facet of that privacy. The fourth amendment explicitly affirms the right of the people to be secure in their persons, houses, papers, and effects against unreasonable searches and seizures. The fifth amendment in its self-incrimination clause enables the citizen to create a zone of privacy which government may not force him to surrender to his detriment. The ninth amendment provides "the enumeration in the constitution of certain rights will not be construed to deny or disparage others retained by the people."

> The present case * * * concerns a relationship lying within the zone of privacy created by several fundamental constitutional guarantees * * *.

> We deal with a right of privacy older than the Bill of Rights—older than our political parties, older than our school system. Marriage is a coming together for better or worse, hopefully enduring, and intimate to the degree of being sacred. It is an association that promotes a way of life, not causes; a harmony in living, not political faith; a bilateral loyalty, not commercial or social projects. Yet it is an association for as noble a purpose as any involved in our prior decisions.

381 U.S. at 484, 85 S.Ct. at 1681. Although a majority concurred in Justice Douglas's opinion, Chief Justice Warren and Justices Brennan and Goldberg based their determination on the Ninth Amendment. Justice Harlan based his concurrence entirely on the due process clause of the Fourteenth Amendment. Separately, Justice White concurred in the judgment and based his determination on the fourteenth amendment. Justices Black and Stewart dissented. Justice Black wrote:

There is no single one of the graphic and eloquent strictures and criticisms fired at the policy of this Connecticut law either by the court's opinion or by those of my concurring brethren to which I cannot subscribe—except their conclusion that the evil qualities they see in the law make it unconstitutional * * *

I like my privacy as well as the next one, but I am nevertheless compelled to admit the government has a right to invade it unless prohibited by some specific constitutional provision. For these reasons, I cannot agree with the court's judgment and the reasons it gives for holding this Connecticut law unconstitutional.

381 U.S. at 510, 85 S.Ct. at 1696. The *Griswold* case left open the question of whether this new right of privacy extended only to married couples or to single people as well. It also left open the question of whether it extended only to decisions related to procreation or whether it extended to all health care decisions. The first of these questions was answered in 1972 when the Court determined that a law that allowed married people, but not unmarried people, to have access to contraceptives violated the equal protection clause of the Fourteenth Amendment because there could be no rational basis for distinguishing between married and unmarried people in permitting access to contraceptives. The Court suggested that "if the right of privacy means anything, it is the right of the individual, married or single, to be free from unwarranted government intrusion into matters so fundamentally affecting a person as a decision whether to bear a child." Eisenstadt v. Baird, 405 U.S. 438, 453, 92 S.Ct. 1029, 1038, 31 L.Ed.2d 349 (1972). In Carey v. Population Services International, 431 U.S. 678, 97 S.Ct. 2010, 52 L.Ed.2d 675 (1977), the Supreme Court confirmed that since *Griswold* declared it unconstitutional for a state to deny contraceptives to married couples, and *Eisenstadt* declared it unconstitutional for a state to distinguish between married couples and unmarried people in controlling access to contraceptives, a state was without authority to ban the distribution of contraceptives to any adult.

The political battle over the nomination of Robert Bork to the Supreme Court in the late 1980s left little doubt about the political popularity of the *Griswold* decision; indeed, approval of this case appears to be a litmus test virtually all United States senators are willing to apply to Supreme Court nominees. Further, in *Webster v. Reproductive Health Services* the majority takes pains to point out that the Missouri statute, which is ultimately upheld, will not impinge upon the right to contraception guaranteed by *Griswold*. See 109 S.Ct. at 3059.

3. *Abortion*

The right to privacy discussed (and perhaps invented) in *Griswold* found its most significant articulation in Roe v. Wade, 410 U.S. 113, 93 S.Ct. 705, 35 L.Ed.2d 147 (1973), the abortion case. Imagine Justice Blackmun writing this opinion, going through medicine and history texts hoping to find out just when a person protected by the Fourteenth Amendment really did come into existence. Justice Blackmun, who had been counsel to the Mayo Clinic earlier in his legal career, was keenly aware of the medical consequences of his determination. A comparison of Justice Blackmun's approach to this problem, and Justice Douglas's approach, which appears in his concurring opinion, suggests that Justice Blackmun viewed abortion as a medical problem, while Justice Douglas viewed it as a personal issue. In any case, *Roe v. Wade* firmly established a constitutionally based right of privacy which extended to personal procreative decisions. Further, this right was based on the due process clause of the Fourteenth Amendment, not the penumbras and emanations that formed the unstable foundation for *Griswold.* While *Roe* remains good law (at least in 1991), its breadth was severely limited in the late 1980s, and the call for its formal death was made explicit in *Webster v. Reproductive Health Services* in 1989.

ROE v. WADE

Supreme Court of United States, 1973.
410 U.S. 113, 93 S.Ct. 705, 35 L.Ed.2d 147.

MR. JUSTICE BLACKMUN delivered the opinion of the Court.

This Texas federal appeal and its Georgia companion, Doe v. Bolton, [ ] present constitutional challenges to state criminal abortion legislation. * * *

We forthwith acknowledge our awareness of the sensitive and emotional nature of the abortion controversy, of the vigorous opposing views, even among physicians, and of the deep and seemingly absolute convictions that the subject inspires. One's philosophy, one's experiences, one's exposure to the raw edges of human existence, one's religious training, one's attitudes toward life and family and their values, and the moral standards one establishes and seeks to observe, are all likely to influence and to color one's thinking and conclusions about abortion.

In addition, population growth, pollution, poverty, and racial overtones tend to complicate and not to simplify the problem.

Our task, of course, is to resolve the issue by constitutional measurement, free of emotion and of predilection. We seek earnestly to do this, and, because we do, we have inquired into, and in this opinion place some emphasis upon, medical and medical-legal history and what that history reveals about man's attitudes toward the abortion procedure over the centuries. We bear in mind, too, Mr. Justice Holmes' admonition in his now-vindicated dissent in Lochner v. New York, 198 U.S. 45, 76, 49 L.Ed. 937, 25 S.Ct. 539 (1905):

"[The Constitution] is made for people of fundamentally differing views, and the accident of our finding certain opinions natural and familiar or novel and even shocking ought not to conclude our judgment upon the question whether statutes embodying them conflict with the Constitution of the United States."

* * *

The principal thrust of appellant's attack on the Texas statutes is that they improperly invade a right, said to be possessed by the pregnant woman, to choose to terminate her pregnancy. Appellant would discover this right in the concept of personal "liberty" embodied in the Fourteenth Amendment's Due Process Clause; or in personal, marital, familial, and sexual privacy said to be protected by the Bill of Rights or its penumbras, [   ]; or among those rights reserved to the people by the Ninth Amendment [   ]. Before addressing this claim, we feel it desirable briefly to survey, in several aspects, the history of abortion, for such insight as that history may afford us, and then to examine the state purposes and interests behind the criminal abortion laws.

VI

It perhaps is not generally appreciated that the restrictive criminal abortion laws in effect in a majority of States today are of relatively recent vintage. Those laws, generally proscribing abortion or its attempt at any time during pregnancy except when necessary to preserve the pregnant woman's life, are not of ancient or even of common-law origin. Instead, they derive from statutory changes effected, for the most part, in the latter half of the 19th century.

[The Court then reviewed, in great detail, ancient attitudes, the Hippocratic Oath, the common law, English statutory law, American Law, the position of the American Medical Association, the position of the American Public Health Association, and the position of the American Bar Association.]

VII

Three reasons have been advanced to explain historically the enactment of criminal abortion laws in the 19th century and to justify their continued existence.

[The first, Victorian sexual morality, is dismissed as an anachronism.]

A second reason is concerned with abortion as a medical procedure. When most criminal abortion laws were first enacted, the procedure was a hazardous one for the woman. This was particularly true prior to the development of antisepsis. Antiseptic techniques, of course, were based on discoveries by Lister, Pasteur, and others first announced in 1867, but were not generally accepted and employed until about the turn of the century. Abortion mortality was high. Even after 1900, and perhaps until as late as the development of antibiotics in the 1940's, standard modern techniques such as dilation and curettage were not nearly so safe as they are today. Thus, it has been argued that a State's real concern in enacting a criminal abortion law was to protect the pregnant woman, that is, to restrain her from submitting to a procedure that placed her life in serious jeopardy.

Modern medical techniques have altered this situation. Appellants and various amici refer to medical data indicating that abortion in early pregnancy, this is, prior to the end of the first trimester, although not without its risk, is now relatively safe. Mortality rates for women undergoing early abortions, where the procedure is legal, appear to be as low as or lower than the rates for normal childbirth. Consequently, any interest of the State in protecting the woman from an inherently hazardous procedure, except when it would be equally dangerous for her to forgo it, has largely disappeared. Of course, important state interests in the area of health and medical standards do remain. The State has a legitimate interest in seeing to it that abortion, like any other medical procedure, is performed under circumstances that assure maximum safety for the patient. This interest obviously extends at least to the performing physician and his staff, to the facilities involved, to the availability of aftercare, and to adequate provision for any complication or emergency that might arise. The prevalence of high mortality rates at illegal "abortion mills" strengthens, rather than weakens, the State's interest in regulating the conditions under which abortions are performed. Moreover, the risk to the woman increases as her pregnancy continues. Thus, the State retains a definite interest in protecting the woman's own health and safety when an abortion is proposed at a late stage of pregnancy.

The third reason is the State's interest—some phrase it in terms of duty—in protecting prenatal life. Some of the argument for this justification rests on the theory that a new human life is present from the moment of conception. The State's interest and general obligation to protect life then extends, it is argued, to prenatal life. Only when the life of the pregnant mother herself is at stake, balanced against the life she carries within her, should the interest of the embryo or fetus not prevail. Logically, of course, a legitimate state interest in this area need not stand or fall on acceptance of the belief that life begins at conception or at some other point prior to live birth. In assessing the State's interest, recognition may be given to the less rigid claim that as long as at least *potential* life is involved, the State may assert interests beyond the protection of the pregnant woman alone.

Parties challenging state abortion laws have sharply disputed in some courts the contention that a purpose of these laws, when enacted, was to protect prenatal life. Pointing to the absence of legislative history to support the contention, they claim that most state laws were designed solely to protect the woman. Because medical advances have lessened this concern, at least with respect to abortion in early pregnancy, they argue that with respect to such abortions the laws can no longer be justified by any state interest. There is some scholarly support for this view of original purpose. The few state courts called upon to interpret their laws in the late 19th and early 20th centuries did focus on the State's interest in protecting the woman's health rather than in preserving the embryo and fetus. Proponents of this view point out that in many States, including Texas, by statute or judicial interpretation, the pregnant woman herself could not be prosecuted for self-abortion or for cooperating in an abortion performed upon her by another. They claim that adoption of the "quickening" distinction through received common law and state statutes tacitly recognizes the greater health hazards inherent in late abortion and impliedly repudiates the theory that life begins at conception.

It is with these interests, and the weight to be attached to them, that this case is concerned.

VIII

The Constitution does not explicitly mention any right of privacy. In a line of decisions, however, going back perhaps as far as [   ] 1891 the Court has recognized that a right of personal privacy, or a guarantee of certain areas or zones of privacy, does exist under the Constitution. In varying contexts, the Court or individual Justices have, indeed, found at least the roots of that right in the First Amendment, [   ] in the Fourth and Fifth Amendments, Terry v. Ohio, [   ] in the penumbras of the Bill of Rights, Griswold v. Connecticut, [   ] the Ninth Amendment, [   ] or in the concept of liberty guaranteed by the first section of the Fourteenth Amendment. [   ] These decisions make it clear that only personal rights that can be deemed "fundamental" or "implicit in the concept of ordered liberty," [   ] are included in this guarantee of personal privacy. They also make it clear that the right has some extension to activities relating to marriage, [   ] family relationships, [   ] and child rearing and education [   ].

This right of privacy, whether it be founded in the Fourteenth Amendment's concept of personal liberty and restrictions upon state action, as we feel it is, or, as the District Court determined, in the Ninth Amendment's reservation of rights to the people, is broad enough to encompass a woman's decision whether or not to terminate her pregnancy. The detriment that the State would impose upon the pregnant woman by denying this choice altogether is apparent. Specific and direct harm medically diagnosable even in early pregnancy may be involved. Maternity, or additional offspring, may force upon the woman a distressful life and future. Psychological harm may be imminent. Mental and physical health may be taxed by child care. There is also the distress, for all concerned, associated with the unwanted child, and there is the problem of bringing a child into a family already unable, psychologically and otherwise, to care for it. In other cases, as in this one, the additional difficulties and continuing stigma of unwed motherhood may be involved. All these are factors the woman and her responsible physician necessarily will consider in consultation.

On the basis of elements such as these, appellant and some amici argue that the woman's right is absolute and that she is entitled to terminate her pregnancy at whatever time, in whatever way, and for whatever reason she alone chooses. With this we do not agree. Appellant's arguments that Texas either has no valid interest at all in regulating the abortion decision, or no interest strong enough to support any limitation upon the woman's sole determination, is unpersuasive. The Court's decisions recognizing a right of privacy also acknowledge that some state regulation in areas protected by that right is appropriate. As noted above, a State may properly assert important interests in safeguarding health, in maintaining medical standards, and in protecting potential life. At some point in pregnancy, these respective interests become sufficiently compelling to sustain regulation of the factors that govern the abortion decision * * *.

We, therefore, conclude that the right of personal privacy includes the abortion decision, but that this right is not unqualified and must be considered against important state interests in regulation.

* * *

This means, on the other hand, that, for the period of pregnancy prior to this "compelling" point, the attending physician, in consultation with his patient, is free to determine, without regulation by the State, that, in his medical judgment, the patient's pregnancy should be terminated. If that decision is reached, the judgment may be effectuated by an abortion free of interference by the State.

With respect to the State's important and legitimate interest in potential life, the "compelling" point is at viability. This is so because the fetus then presumably has the capability of meaningful life outside the mother's womb. State regulation protective of fetal life after viability thus has both logical and biological justifications. If the State is interested in protecting fetal life after viability, it may go so far as to proscribe abortion during that period, except when it is necessary to preserve the life or health of the mother.

* * *

XI

To summarize and to repeat:

1. A state criminal abortion statute of the current Texas type, that excepts from criminality only a *lifesaving* procedure on behalf of the mother, without regard to pregnancy stage and without recognition of the other interests involved, is violative of the Due Process Clause of the Fourteenth Amendment.

(a) For the stage prior to approximately the end of the first trimester, the abortion decision and its effectuation must be left to the medical judgment of the pregnant woman's attending physician.

(b) For the stage subsequent to approximately the end of the first trimester, the State, in promoting its interest in the health of the mother, may, if it chooses, regulate the abortion procedure in ways that are reasonably related to maternal health.

(c) For the stage subsequent to viability, the State in promoting its interest in the potentiality of human life may, if it chooses, regulate, and even proscribe, abortion except where it is necessary, in appropriate medical judgment, for the preservation of the life or health of the mother.

* * *

This holding, we feel, is consistent with the relative weights of the respective interests involved, with the lessons and examples of medical and legal history, with the lenity of the common law, and with the demands of the profound problems of the present day. The decision leaves the State free to place increasing restrictions on abortion as the period of pregnancy lengthens, so long as those restrictions are tailored to the recognized state interests. The decision vindicates the right of the physician to administer medical treatment according to his professional judgment up to the points where important state interests provide compelling justifications for intervention. Up to those points, the abortion decision in all its aspects is inherently, and primarily, a medical decision, and basic responsibility for it must rest with the physician. If an individual practitioner abuses the privilege of exercising proper medical judgment, the usual remedies, judicial and intraprofessional, are available.

* * *

MR. JUSTICE DOUGLAS, concurring.

While I join the opinion of the Court, I add a few words.

The questions presented in the present cases * * * involve the right of privacy, one aspect of which we considered in Griswold v. Connecticut, [ ] when we held that various guarantees in the Bill of Rights create zones of privacy.

* * *

The Ninth Amendment obviously does not create federally enforceable rights. It merely says, "The enumeration in the Constitution, of certain rights, shall not be construed to deny or disparage others retained by the people." But a catalogue of these rights includes customary, traditional, and time-honored rights, amenities, privileges, and immunities that come within the sweep of "the Blessings of Liberty" mentioned in the preamble to the Constitution. Many of them, in my view, come within the meaning of the term "liberty" as used in the Fourteenth Amendment.

First is the autonomous control over the development and expression of one's intellect, interests, tastes, and personality.

* * *

Second is freedom of choice in the basic decisions of one's life respecting marriage, divorce, procreation, contraception, and the education and upbringing of children.

* * *

Third is the freedom to care for one's health and person, freedom from bodily restraint or compulsion, freedom to walk, stroll, or loaf.

* * *

Notes and Questions

1. The Court's opinion stirred into action political forces opposed to abortion. They have encouraged state legislatures to seek creative ways to discourage abortions without running afoul of the requirements of *Roe v. Wade.* The Supreme Court at first resisted attempts to intrude upon the underlying rights recognized in 1973, although the number of justices supporting that decision has declined over time. *Roe* was reaffirmed more than a dozen times in its first decade, but in 1986 the 7–2 majority was down to 5–4. Thornburgh v. American College of Obstetricians and Gynecologists, 476 U.S. 747, 106 S.Ct. 2169, 90 L.Ed.2d 779 (1986). As we shall see, by 1989 the Court appeared to be divided 4–4, with Justice O'Connor not willing to address the issue.

2. *Roe v. Wade* has been vigorously criticized, both as a matter of policy and a matter of law. Despite the sincere commitment of those who oppose abortion and the presence of a sympathetic administration in Washington, the Congress has not taken sufficient action to promulgate a constitutional amendment allowing states to prohibit abortions. On the other hand, government funding for abortions has been limited and the restrictions on the use of government funds for abortions have generally been upheld by the courts. In 1977, the Supreme Court upheld state statutes and Medicaid plans that refused to fund nontherapeutic abortions as well as a city's determination that its hospitals would not provide nontherapeutic abortions. Beal v. Doe, 432 U.S. 438, 97 S.Ct. 2366, 53 L.Ed.2d 464 (1977); Maher v. Roe, 432 U.S. 464, 97 S.Ct. 2376, 53 L.Ed.2d 484 (1977); Poelker v. Doe, 432 U.S. 519, 97 S.Ct. 2391, 53 L.Ed.2d 528 (1977). Three years later in Harris v. McRae, 448 U.S. 297, 100 S.Ct. 2671, 65 L.Ed.2d 784 (1980), the Supreme Court upheld the Hyde amendment, which provided that federal funds could not be used for virtually any abortion.

3. There have been two legal lines of attack on the Supreme Court's decision in *Roe v. Wade.* The first argues that the Supreme Court has returned to the unhappy Lochnerian days of substantive due process, during which the Court acted as if it were free to make social policy without regard to legal or constitutional restrictions. It is this argument which seems to have captured the attention of the four justices now willing to overturn *Roe.* See *Webster,* below.

There is little doubt that the authors of the Fourteenth Amendment were not thinking of the right to an abortion when the amendment was drafted and promulgated, and while the Fourteenth Amendment has been broadly interpreted, *Roe v. Wade* and the subsequent abortion cases are among the very few examples of the application of a "right to privacy" that arise out of that amendment. It is a difficult jurisprudential feat to support the creation and application of that right. The Supreme Court has refused to extend this right of privacy to other areas, even within the health care system. For example, that right does not extend to the use of laetrile, even assuming laetrile to be a harmless substance when it is used under the supervision of a physician. United States v. Rutherford, 442

U.S. 544, 99 S.Ct. 2470, 61 L.Ed.2d 68 (1979). The Supreme Court also explicitly rejected the application of the right of privacy to protect those engaging in homosexual conduct. Bowers v. Hardwick, 478 U.S. 186, 106 S.Ct. 2841, 92 L.Ed.2d 140 (1986). In the first right to die case considered by the Court, none of the Justices even used the word "privacy" to describe the underlying constitutional right; instead they depended upon the apparently more limited "liberty interest" explicitly mentioned in the Fourteenth Amendment. Cruzan v. Director, Missouri Dept. of Health, 110 S.Ct. 2841, 111 L.Ed.2d 224 (1990) [See Chapter 11]. In a strictly legal, conceptual sense, *Roe v. Wade* remains a barely afloat derelict on the waters of the law.

The second line of attack focuses on the opinion's scientific foundation. *Roe v. Wade* made two kinds of distinctions. First, it identified that point at which it became more dangerous to abort than to bear the child; second, it identified that point at which the fetus was viable. The court identified those points as occurring at the end of the first and second trimesters. As the science of obstetrics improves and safer techniques of abortion are developed, the first point is being moved back, closer to the time of delivery, and the second point is being moved forward, closer to the time of conception. It is now quite safe to have an abortion long after the end of the first trimester, and a fetus may be viable before the end of the second trimester. Should the Supreme Court stick to its scientifically justifiable points (the point of increased danger and the point of viability), which would create an ambiguity because it changes with the latest medical developments, or should it stick with the arbitrary first and second trimester timelines, which are easy to apply, even though they are no longer supported by science? The Court answered this question in City of Akron v. Akron Center for Reproductive Health, Inc., 462 U.S. 416, 103 S.Ct. 2481, 76 L.Ed.2d 687 (1983):

> *Roe* identified the end of the first trimester as the compelling point because until that time—according to the medical literature available in 1973—"mortality in abortion may be less than mortality in normal childbirth" * * * . There is substantial evidence that the developments in the past decade, particularly the development of a much safer method of performing second trimester abortions * * * have extended the period in which abortions are safer than childbirth * * * .

> We think it prudent, however, to retain *Roe's* identification of the beginning of the second trimester as the approximate time at which the state's interest in maternal health becomes sufficiently compelling to justify significant regulation of abortion * * * .

> The *Roe* trimester standard * * * continues to provide a reasonable legal framework for limiting a state's authority to regulate abortions.

462 U.S. at 429 n. 11, 103 S.Ct. at 2492 n. 11.

In any case, at least one of the scientific flash points significant to the holding in *Roe*—the point of viability—does not appear likely to change without a dramatic and unexpected change in medical technology (and, most likely, the development of an artificial womb). In the absence of such a development, no fetus will be viable before 23½ or 24 weeks of gestation.

See Webster v. Reproductive Health Services, 109 S.Ct. 3040, 3075 n. 9, 106 L.Ed.2d 410 (1989) (Blackmun, dissenting).

The best discussion of the effect scientific development should have on the trimester division of *Roe v. Wade* is found in Rhoden, Trimesters and Technology: Revamping Roe v. Wade, 95 Yale L.Rev. 639 (1986). Rhoden argues that the real basis for the Court's distinction between the second and third trimester in *Roe v. Wade* is not viability but rather "the ethical precept that late in gestation a fetus is so like a baby that elective abortion can be forbidden." She suggests that rational support for the *Roe v. Wade* dividing line could be found in analysis of "medical factors, social realities, and the need for all women to have sufficient time to exercise their constitutional right," even if the opinion can no longer stand on its original biological justification.

4. Should the Supreme Court abandon the holding of *Roe v. Wade*? There are two ways in which the Court could do this; it could overturn *Roe's* finding that there was a right of privacy that included the right to an abortion in the Fourteenth Amendment, or it could simply abandon the trimester distinctions of *Roe* and assert that the state's interest in preserving the fetus could be compelling at any stage of the pregnancy. Some justices of the Supreme Court appeared to be interested in each of these approaches when the landmark case of *Webster v. Reproductive Health Services* came before the Court.

WEBSTER v. REPRODUCTIVE HEALTH SERVICES

Supreme Court of the United States, 1989.
492 U.S. 490, 109 S.Ct. 3040, 106 L.Ed.2d 410.

CHIEF JUSTICE REHNQUIST announced the judgment of the Court and delivered the opinion of the Court with respect to Parts I, II–A, II–B, and II–C, and an opinion with respect to Parts II–D and III, in which JUSTICE WHITE and JUSTICE KENNEDY join.

This appeal concerns the constitutionality of a Missouri statute regulating the performance of abortions.   * * *

I

In June 1986, the Governor of Missouri signed into law Missouri Senate Committee Substitute for House Bill No. 1596 (hereinafter Act or statute), which amended existing state law concerning unborn children and abortions. The Act consisted of 20 provisions, 5 of which are now before the Court. The first provision, or preamble, contains "findings" by the state legislature that "[t]he life of each human being begins at conception," and that "unborn children have protectable interests in life, health, and well-being." Mo.Rev.Stat. §§ 1.205.1(1), (2) (1986). The Act further requires that all Missouri laws be interpreted to provide unborn children with the same rights enjoyed by other persons, subject to the Federal Constitution and this Court's precedents. § 1.205.2. Among its other provisions, the Act requires that, prior to performing an abortion on any woman whom a physician has reason to believe is 20 or more weeks pregnant, the physician ascertain whether the fetus is viable by performing "such medical examinations and tests as are necessary to make a finding of the gestational age, weight, and lung maturity of the unborn child." § 188.029. The Act also prohibits the use of public employees and facilities to perform or assist abortions not necessary to save the mother's life, and it prohibits the use of public funds, employees, or facilities for the purpose of "encouraging or counseling" a woman to have an abortion not necessary to save her life. §§ 188.205, 188.210, 188.215.

* * *

II

Decision of this case requires us to address four sections of the Missouri Act: (a) the preamble; (b) the prohibition on the use of public facilities or employees to perform abortions; (c) the prohibition on public funding of abortion counseling; and (d) the requirement that physicians conduct viability tests prior to performing abortions. We address these *seriatim*.

A

[The preamble is discussed in Section I(B)(1) of this chapter, above.]

B

Section 188.210 provides that "[i]t shall be unlawful for any public employee within the scope of his employment to perform or assist an abortion, not necessary to save the life of the mother," while § 188.215 makes it "unlawful for any public facility to be used for the purpose of performing or assisting an abortion not necessary to save the life of the mother."   * * *

* * *

* * * As in [the public funding cases], the State's decision here to use public facilities and staff to encourage childbirth over abortion "places no governmental obstacle in the path of a woman who chooses to terminate her pregnancy." [   ] Just as Congress' refusal to fund abortions in *McRae* left "an indigent woman with at least the same range of choice in deciding whether to obtain a medically necessary abortion as she would have had if Congress had chosen to subsidize no health care costs at all," [   ], Missouri's refusal to allow public employees to perform abortions in public hospitals leaves a pregnant woman with the same choices as if the State had chosen not to operate any public hospitals at all. The challenged provisions only restrict a woman's ability to obtain an abortion to the extent that she chooses to use a physician affiliated with a public hospital. This circumstance is more easily remedied, and thus considerably less burdensome, than indigency, which "may make it difficult—and in some cases, perhaps, impossible—for some women to have abortions" without public funding.
* * *

* * *

* * * Nothing in the Constitution requires States to enter or remain in the business of performing abortions. Nor, as appellees suggest, do private physicians and their patients have some kind of constitutional right of access to public facilities for the performance of abortions. * * *

* * *

C

[Here the Court reiterated its position that the state could limit the expenditure of public funds to support abortions.]

D

Section 188.029 of the Missouri Act provides:

"Before a physician performs an abortion on a woman he has reason to believe is carrying an unborn child of twenty or more weeks gestational age, the physician shall first determine if the unborn child is viable by using and exercising that degree of care, skill, and proficiency commonly exercised by the ordinarily skillful, careful, and prudent physician engaged in similar practice under the same or similar conditions. In making this determination of viability, the physician shall perform or cause to be performed such medical examinations and tests as are necessary to make a finding of the gestational age, weight, and lung maturity of the unborn child and shall enter such findings and determination of viability in the medical record of the mother."

As with the preamble, the parties disagree over the meaning of this statutory provision. * * *

* * *

We think the viability-testing provision makes sense only if the second sentence is read to require only those tests that are useful to making subsidiary findings as to viability. If we construe this provision to require a physician to perform those tests needed to make the three specified findings *in all circumstances,* including when the physician's reasonable professional judgment indicates that the tests would be irrelevant to determining viability or even dangerous to the mother and the fetus, the second sentence of § 188.029 would conflict with the first sentence's *requirement* that a physician apply his reasonable professional skill and judgment. * * *

* * *

We think that the doubt cast upon the Missouri statute by these cases is not so much a flaw in the statute as it is a reflection of the fact that the rigid trimester analysis of the course of a pregnancy enunciated in *Roe* has resulted in subsequent cases making constitutional law in this area a virtual Procrustean bed. * * *

Stare decisis is a cornerstone of our legal system, but it has less power in constitutional cases, where, save for constitutional amendments, this Court is the only body able to make needed changes. [   ]

We have not refrained from reconsideration of a prior construction of the Constitution that has proved "unsound in principle and unworkable in practice." [ ] We think the *Roe* trimester framework falls into that category.

In the first place, the rigid *Roe* framework is hardly consistent with the notion of a Constitution cast in general terms, as ours is, and usually speaking in general principles, as ours does. The key elements of the *Roe* framework—trimesters and viability—are not found in the text of the Constitution or in any place else one would expect to find a constitutional principle. Since the bounds of the inquiry are essentially indeterminate, the result has been a web of legal rules that have become increasingly intricate, resembling a code of regulations rather than a body of constitutional doctrine. As Justice White has put it, the trimester framework has left this Court to serve as the country's "*ex officio* medical board with powers to approve or disapprove medical and operative practices and standards throughout the United States." [ ]

In the second place, we do not see why the State's interest in protecting potential human life should come into existence only at the point of viability, and that there should therefore be a rigid line allowing state regulation after viability but prohibiting it before viability. * * *

The tests that § 188.029 requires the physician to perform are designed to determine viability. The State here has chosen viability as the point at which its interest in potential human life must be safe-guarded. See Mo.Rev.Stat. § 188.030 (1986) ("No abortion of a viable unborn child shall be performed unless necessary to preserve the life or health of the woman"). It is true that the tests in question increase the expense of abortion, and regulate the discretion of the physician in determining the viability of the fetus. Since the tests will undoubtedly show in many cases that the fetus is not viable, the tests will have been performed for what were in fact second-trimester abortions. But we are satisfied that the requirement of these tests permissibly furthers the State's interest in protecting potential human life, and we therefore believe § 188.029 to be constitutional.

The dissent takes us to task for our failure to join in a "great issues" debate as to whether the Constitution includes an "unenumerat-ed" general right to privacy as recognized in cases such as *Griswold v. Connecticut,* and *Roe.* But *Griswold v. Connecticut,* unlike *Roe,* did not purport to adopt a whole framework, complete with detailed rules and distinctions, to govern the cases in which the asserted liberty interest would apply. As such, it was far different from the opinion, if not the holding, of *Roe v. Wade,* which sought to establish a constitutional framework for judging state regulation of abortion during the entire term of pregnancy. That framework sought to deal with areas of medical practice traditionally subject to state regulation, and it sought to balance once and for all by reference only to the calendar the claims of the State to protect the fetus as a form of human life against the claims of a woman to decide for herself whether or not to abort a fetus she was carrying. * * *

The dissent also accuses us, *inter alia,* of cowardice and illegitimacy in dealing with "the most politically divisive domestic legal issue of our time." * * * But the goal of constitutional adjudication is surely not to remove inexorably "politically divisive" issues from the ambit of the legislative process, whereby the people through their elected representatives deal with matters of concern to them. The goal of constitutional adjudication is to hold true the balance between that which the Constitution puts beyond the reach of the democratic process and that which it does not. We think we have done that today. * * *

III

Both appellants and the United States as *Amicus Curiae* have urged that we overrule our decision in *Roe v. Wade.* [ ] The facts of the present case, however, differ from those at issue in *Roe.* Here, Missouri has determined that viability is the point at which its interest in potential human life must be safeguarded. In *Roe,* on the other hand, the Texas statute criminalized the performance of *all* abortions, except when the mother's life was at stake. This case therefore affords us no occasion to revisit the holding of *Roe.* * * * To the extent indicated in our opinion, we would modify and narrow *Roe* and succeeding cases.

JUSTICE O'CONNOR, concurring in part and concurring in the judgment.

* * *

* * * I agree with the plurality that it was plain error for the Court of Appeals to interpret the second sentence [of the Statute] as meaning that "doctors *must* perform tests to find gestational age, fetal weight and lung maturity." * * *

Unlike the plurality, I do not understand these viability testing requirements to conflict with any of the Court's past decisions concerning state regulation of abortion. Therefore, there is no necessity to accept the State's invitation to reexamine the constitutional validity of *Roe v. Wade.* [ ] * * * When the constitutional invalidity of a State's abortion statute actually turns on the constitutional validity of *Roe v. Wade,* there will be time enough to reexamine *Roe.* And to do so carefully.

* * *

JUSTICE SCALIA, concurring in part and concurring in the judgment.

I join Parts I, II-A, II-B, and II-C of the opinion of The Chief Justice. As to Part II-D, I share Justice Blackmun's view, that it effectively would overrule *Roe v. Wade.* I think that should be done, but would do it more explicitly. Since today we contrive to avoid doing it, and indeed to avoid almost any decision of national import, I need not set forth my reasons, some of which have been well recited in dissents of my colleagues in other cases. [   ]

* * *

* * * Ordinarily, speaking no more broadly than is absolutely required avoids throwing settled law into confusion; doing so today preserves a chaos that is evident to anyone who can read and count. Alone sufficient to justify a broad holding is the fact that our retaining control, through *Roe*, of what I believe to be, and many of our citizens recognize to be, a political issue, continuously distorts the public perception of the role of this Court. We can now look forward to at least another Term with carts full of mail from the public, and streets full of demonstrators, urging us—their unelected and life-tenured judges who have been awarded those extraordinary, undemocratic characteristics precisely in order that we might follow the law despite the popular will—to follow the popular will. * * *

* * * Given the Court's newly contracted abstemiousness, what will it take, one must wonder, to permit us to reach that fundamental question? The result of our vote today is that we will not reconsider that prior opinion, even if most of the Justices think it is wrong, unless we have before us a statute that in fact contradicts it—and even then (under our newly discovered "no-broader-then-necessary" requirement) only minor problematical aspects of *Roe* will be reconsidered, unless one expects State legislatures to adopt provisions whose compliance with *Roe* cannot even be argued with a straight face. It thus appears that the mansion of constitutionalized abortion law, constructed overnight in *Roe v. Wade*, must be disassembled door-jamb by door-jamb, and never entirely brought down, no matter how wrong it may be.

Of the four courses we might have chosen today—to reaffirm *Roe*, to overrule it explicitly, to overrule it *sub silentio*, or to avoid the question—the last is the least responsible. * * * I concur in the judgment of the Court and strongly dissent from the manner in which it has been reached.

JUSTICE BLACKMUN, with whom JUSTICE BRENNAN and JUSTICE MARSHALL join, concurring in part and dissenting in part.

Today, *Roe v. Wade*, and the fundamental constitutional right of women to decide whether to terminate a pregnancy, survive but are not secure. Although the Court extricates itself from this case without making a single, even incremental, change in the law of abortion, the plurality and Justice Scalia would overrule *Roe* (the first silently, the other explicitly) and would return to the States virtually unfettered authority to control the quintessentially intimate, personal, and life-directing decision whether to carry a fetus to term. Although today, no less than yesterday, the Constitution and the decisions of this Court prohibit a State from enacting laws that inhibit women from the meaningful exercise of that right, a plurality of this Court implicitly invites every state legislature to enact more and more restrictive abortion regulations in order to provoke more and more test cases, in the hope that sometime down the line the Court will return the law of procreative freedom to the severe limitations that generally prevailed in this country before January 22, 1973. Never in my memory has a plurality announced a judgment of this Court that so foments disregard for the law and for our standing decisions.

Nor in my memory has a plurality gone about its business in such a deceptive fashion. At every level of its review, from its effort to read the real meaning out of the Missouri statute, to its intended evisceration of precedents and its deafening silence about the constitutional protections that it would jettison, the plurality obscures the portent of its analysis. With feigned restraint, the plurality announces that its analysis leaves *Roe* "undisturbed," albeit "modif[ied] and narrow[ed]." But this disclaimer is totally meaningless. The plurality opinion is filled with winks, and nods, and knowing glances to those who would do away with *Roe* explicitly, but turns a stone face to anyone in search of what the plurality conceives as the scope of a woman's right under the Due Process Clause to terminate a pregnancy free from the coercive and brooding influence of the State. The simple truth is that *Roe* would not survive the plurality's analysis, and that the plurality provides no substitute for *Roe's* protective umbrella.

I fear for the future. I fear for the liberty and equality of the millions of women who have lived and come of age in the 16 years since *Roe* was decided. I fear for the integrity of, and public esteem for, this Court.

* * *

The plurality opinion is far more remarkable for the arguments that it does not advance than for those that it does. The plurality does not even mention, much less join, the true jurisprudential debate underlying this case: whether the Constitution includes an "unenumerated" general right to privacy as recognized in many of our decisions, most notably *Griswold v. Connecticut,* and *Roe,* and, more specifically, whether and to what extent such a right to privacy extends to matters of childbearing and family life, including abortion. [ ] These are questions of unsurpassed significance in this Court's interpretation of the Constitution, and mark the battleground upon which this case was fought, by the parties, by the Solicitor General as *amicus* on behalf of petitioners, and by an unprecedented number of *amici.* On these grounds, abandoned by the plurality, the Court should decide this case.

* * *

Finally, the plurality asserts that the trimester framework cannot stand because the State's interest in potential life is compelling throughout pregnancy, not merely after viability. The opinion contains not one word of rationale for its view of the State's interest. This "it-is-so-because-we-say-so" jurisprudence constitutes nothing other than an attempted exercise of brute force; reason, much less persuasion, has no place.

* * *

For my own part, I remain convinced, as six other Members of this Court 16 years ago were convinced, that the *Roe* framework, and the viability standard in particular, fairly, sensibly, and effectively functions to safeguard the constitutional liberties of pregnant women while recognizing and accommodating the State's interest in potential human life. The viability line reflects the biological facts and truths of fetal development; it marks that threshold moment prior to which a fetus cannot survive separate from the woman and cannot reasonably and objectively be regarded as a subject of rights or interests distinct from, or paramount to, those of the pregnant woman. At the same time, the viability standard takes account of the undeniable fact that as the fetus evolves into its postnatal form, and as it loses its dependence on the uterine environment, the State's interest in the fetus' potential human life, and in fostering a regard for human life in general, becomes compelling. As a practical matter, because viability follows "quickening"—the point at which a woman feels movement in her womb—and because viability occurs no earlier than 23 weeks gestational age, it establishes an easily applicable standard for regulating abortion while providing a pregnant woman ample time to exercise her fundamental right with her responsible physician to terminate her pregnancy. Although I have stated previously for a majority of this Court that "[c]onstitutional rights do not always have easily ascertainable boundaries," to seek and establish those boundaries remains the special responsibility of this Court. In *Roe*, we discharged that responsibility as logic and science compelled. The plurality today advances not one reasonable argument as to why our judgment in that case was wrong and should be abandoned.

* * *

Having contrived an opportunity to reconsider the *Roe* framework, and then having discarded that framework, the plurality finds the testing provision unobjectionable because it "permissibly furthers the State's interest in protecting potential human life." This newly minted standard is circular and totally meaningless. Whether a challenged abortion regulation "permissibly furthers" a legitimate state interest is the *question* that courts must answer in abortion cases, not the standard for courts to apply. In keeping with the rest of its opinion, the plurality makes no attempt to explain or to justify its new standard, either in the abstract or as applied in this case. Nor could it. The "permissibly furthers" standard has no independent meaning, and consists of nothing other than what a majority of this Court may believe at any given moment in any given case. The plurality's novel test appears to be nothing more than a dressed-up version of rational-basis review, this Court's most lenient level of scrutiny. One thing is clear, however: were the plurality's "permissibly furthers" standard adopted by the Court, for all practical purposes, *Roe* would be overruled.

The "permissibly furthers" standard completely disregards the irreducible minimum of *Roe:* the Court's recognition that a woman has a limited fundamental constitutional right to decide whether to terminate a pregnancy. That right receives no meaningful recognition in the plurality's written opinion. Since, in the plurality's view, the State's interest in potential life is compelling as of the moment of conception, and is therefore served only if abortion is abolished, every hindrance to a woman's ability to obtain an abortion must be "permissible." Indeed, the more severe the hindrance, the more effectively (and permissibly) the State's interest would be furthered. A tax on abortions or a criminal prohibition would both satisfy the plurality's standard. So, for that matter, would a requirement that a pregnant woman memorize and recite today's plurality opinion before seeking an abortion.

* * *

For today, at least, the law of abortion stands undisturbed. For today, the women of this Nation still retain the liberty to control their destinies. But the signs are evident and very ominous, and a chill wind blows.

JUSTICE STEVENS, concurring in part and dissenting in part.

* * *

In my opinion the preamble to the Missouri statute is unconstitutional for two reasons. To the extent that it has substantive impact on the freedom to use contraceptive procedures, it is inconsistent with the central holding in *Griswold.* To the extent that it merely makes "legislative findings without operative effect," as the State argues, it violates the Establishment Clause of the First Amendment [by adopting one religious view as the formal policy of the state]. Contrary to the theological "finding" of the Missouri Legislature, a woman's constitutionally protected liberty encompasses the right to act on her own belief that—to paraphrase St. Thomas Aquinas—until a seed has acquired the powers of sensation and movement, the life of a human being has not yet begun.

Notes and Questions

1. The granting of certiorari in the *Webster* case generated a nearly unprecedented wave of nervous anticipation. Indeed, the case attracted 78 amicus briefs, more than any other case in history. Virtually the entire country expected *Webster* to be the watershed abortion case of this era, an expectation which arose out of the recognition that the Court was fundamentally reshaped by President Reagan's appointees. The public debate over the merits of *Webster* quickly polarized into two factions—one advocating the overruling of *Roe,* and the other advocating the reaffirmation of *Roe's* principles. Both perspectives were passionately advanced while the country awaited the Court's decision. The eventual opinions not only failed to satisfy either faction, but they revealed a degree of vehemence and

personal involvement rarely disclosed by sitting justices of the Supreme Court.

2. Is *Roe v. Wade* still good law? Does the trimester division still have meaning, or may a state act to protect a fetus or an embryo at any stage of development, at least if its interest in that fetus or embryo is strong enough? Chief Justice Rehnquist describes the progeny of *Roe* as making a "Procrustean bed". Procrustes is a mythical figure who required his guests to fit his bed. If they were too large, he simply lopped off portions of their body. If they were too small, he stretched them to the corners of the bed. Is the Chief Justice suggesting that the holding in *Roe* had been stretched to meet whatever purpose the Court desired? If Rehnquist himself did lop off large parts of the holding in that case, as the dissents apparently believe, what, exactly, is left?

3. The ink on *Roe v. Wade* was barely dry when state legislatures turned their attention to means of regulating abortion rights. Although *Webster* represents one of the most significant Supreme Court decisions on the scope of states' right to limit abortion access, it remains only one of a series of cases delineating that scope. To date, state attempts to regulate abortion fall into four categories: a) consent requirements, b) notification requirements, c) funding restrictions, and d) regulations of medical procedures for abortions. Although only consent requirements appear to constitute a potentially complete bar to abortion, each of the other regulatory means is likely to have a chilling effect. Restrictions on funding, for example, erect a de facto bar for many women. Similarly, both notification and procedural requirements will dissuade women who feel unable to face either the repercussions of notification, or the ordeal of some procedural requirement (such as forced viewing of fetal development photographs).

Consent and Notification Requirements

The issue of third party consent as a prerequisite to a pregnant woman's abortion arises primarily when the woman is a minor or incapacitated in some way. A competent, adult pregnant woman need not obtain anyone's consent prior to obtaining an abortion. The consent issue has been typically addressed in reference to a pregnant minor's parents; occasionally the issue also arises in reference to her spouse or the father of the child. The Supreme Court has upheld parental consent requirements only where the state statute provides for a "judicial bypass" alternative, which allows the minor to substitute judicial consent where obtaining parental consent would be impossible or detrimental. See Akron v. Akron Center for Reproductive Health, Inc., 462 U.S. 416, 103 S.Ct. 2481, 76 L.Ed.2d 687 (1983); Bellotti v. Baird, 443 U.S. 622, 99 S.Ct. 3035, 61 L.Ed.2d 797 (1979); Planned Parenthood of Central Missouri v. Danforth, 428 U.S. 52, 96 S.Ct. 2831, 49 L.Ed.2d 788 (1976).

The Supreme Court has also upheld parental notification requirements if the statute provides for some alternative when the requirement would "unduly burden" the pregnant woman's decision, or not be in her best interest. See Hodgson v. Minnesota, 110 S.Ct. 2926, 111 L.Ed.2d 344 (1990); Ohio v. Akron Ctr. for Reproductive Health, 110 S.Ct. 2972, 111 L.Ed.2d 405 (1990). Although a pregnant minor need merely notify her parent or parents under these statutes, and can proceed without their consent, for many pregnant teenagers such a requirement is an insurmountable obstacle.

The debate for and against consent and notification requirements reveals an even deeper debate about the current role of the family in contemporary life. While most agree that a teenager's abortion should be a decision made in consultation with her parents, that belief rests upon several assumptions. First, it assumes that the family dynamics are such that the daughter's disclosure will not trigger domestic violence or other forms of family abuse. Second, it assumes that the daughter lives within a traditional nuclear family, or can readily reach her biological parents. Finally, and most critically, it assumes that parents will act in the daughter's best interest. Some of these assumptions may, sadly, be based upon an idealized view of contemporary family life.

Those who support these consent and notification statutes offer many stories of girls who had abortions secretly and now regret not discussing it with their parents. Those who oppose these statutes offer stories about girls who committed suicide rather than go through the notification procedures. Is this anecdotal evidence offered by both sides of much value? Could valuable data on these sociological issues be developed? Why do you think it has not been developed in any reliable way? Does it seem ironic that under a consent or notification statute a court could declare a pregnant minor to be too immature to proceed without parental consultation, and thus order her to become a mother?

Funding Restrictions

Perhaps the most common means of both federal and state regulation of abortion access is by restrictions on governmental funding. The Supreme Court has consistently upheld a state's right to withhold funding for abortions, and in *Webster* the Court went one step further and allowed the state to prohibit use of state facilities for performing abortions.

Regulation of Medical Procedures

The Supreme Court has been considerably less willing to give it's approval to various state statutes which attempt to regulate medical procedures for performing abortions and obtaining informed consent for abortions. The Court has refused to allow a state to impose a 24-hour waiting period between the decision to seek an abortion and the surgical procedure. *Akron v. Akron Ctr. for Reproductive Health, Inc.*, supra. States have also been precluded from requiring that second trimester abortions be performed in hospitals, where they are far more expensive than in equally well equipped clinics. Id. Considering more psychological aspects, the Court has also refused to allow a state to impose some kinds of "informed consent" procedures. Specifically, states have been precluded from requiring that doctors show patients pictures of fetuses, or explain fetal development in a graphic way with the goal of dissuading the woman from having an abortion. Such requirements were found to improperly burden the pregnant woman's right to an abortion. Compare the analysis of "reasonable" consent requirements in *Planned Parenthood of Missouri*, supra, with the "unreasonably burdensome" ones in *Akron,* supra. See also, Thornburgh v. American College of Obstetricians and Gynecologists, 476 U.S. 747, 106 S.Ct. 2169, 90 L.Ed.2d 779 (1986). The Supreme Court has yet to deal with the First Amendment implications of statutes that limit dissemination of information about abortion; those cases are now on their way to the Court, however.

4. If the range of abortion related cases addressed by the Supreme Court is large, the range of cases addressed by other courts is truly remarkable. Dozens of other courts have considered dozens of other implications and attempted limitations on whatever is left of *Roe v. Wade.* For example, in Monmouth County Correctional Institution Inmates v. Lanzaro, 834 F.2d 326 (3d Cir.1987), cert. denied, 486 U.S. 1006, 108 S.Ct. 1731, 100 L.Ed.2d 195 (1988), the Court determined that a prisoner has a right to an abortion that cannot be limited by the requirement that there be a court-ordered "release." In addition, the Third Circuit determined that prison inmates may not be required to obtain their own financing to have an abortion if requiring them to do so would limit their right. In an entirely different context, the Oklahoma Supreme Court determined in Spencer v. Seikel, 742 P.2d 1126 (Okl.1987), that a doctor has no duty to inform his patient that she could get an abortion in another state after he discovered her 23 or 24-week fetus—which was arguably viable and not subject to abortion in Oklahoma—was suffering from hydrocephalus. In another case, the Supreme Court of Rhode Island, applying the theory of substituted judgment, allowed for an abortion to be performed on a profoundly retarded woman suffering from a seizure disorder and cerebral palsy, whose pregnancy was the result of a sexual assault, over the objection of her mother, who was also her temporary custodian. See In re Jane Doe, 533 A.2d 523 (R.I.1987).

5. Even if *Roe v. Wade* were to survive, could states limit the right to seek abortions for particular purposes? For example, Pennsylvania has considered making abortion for the purpose of sex selection illegal. Could such a ban be applied at any point during the pregnancy? Are there other reasons that a state could justifiably limit abortions? For example, could a state limit abortions where abortion is used as a primary method of birth control? Is there any way to draft or implement a statute which would have this effect?

6. Although abortion is a divisive issue that has driven a wedge between groups in our society, the Supreme Court's apparent decision to return the issue—or, at least, a great deal of it—to state legislatures may allow for the development of a consensus among those who find flaws in both the pro-choice arguments and the pro-life arguments. For example, both sides may support expanded state funding for prenatal care and post-natal care, each of which may make abortion a less attractive alternative to pregnant women. In addition, better welfare support for families, and more thorough and complete sex education may make resort to abortion necessary in fewer cases. Similarly, the increase in education about the availability of effective contraception is likely to decrease the number of abortions that are performed.

There may even be some basic value issues upon which the pro-choice and pro-life partisans agree. While pro-choice supporters argue that an abortion should be among the choices of a pregnant woman, no one views an abortion as a happy event. Both sides would be pleased if society reached a point where there were no need for abortions. Similarly, while some pro-life supporters believe that every fetus is entitled to be born alive, many recognize that there are some times when the mother's interest does trump that of the fetus—when the mother's life is at stake, for example, and, perhaps, when the pregnancy is a result of rape or incest—and many recognize that the quality of life of the fetus is a relevant consideration. Very few people oppose abortions of anencephalic fetuses, for example, or early abortions of other fetuses who are virtually certain to be stillborn or to die within the first few minutes of birth. Is there a common ground that could give rise to some kind of generally acceptable state policy on abortion, at least in some states? If pro-choice partisans and pro-life partisans were to sit with you and enumerate their common concerns, would there be some basic issues and basic principles upon which they would agree?

7. The amount, nature and diversity of the academic writing on abortion is truly remarkable. The writings range from the polemic to the theological, and sometimes both are contained in the same books and articles (on both sides of the issue). A good general introduction to the issue, with an interesting international perspective, is L. Tribe, Abortion: The Clash of Absolutes (1990), which describes simply the medical, ethical, political, and legal issues. The November 1989 University of Pennsylvania Law Review has a good discussion of the *Webster* case. See Dellinger and Sperling, Abortion and the Supreme Court: The Retreat from Roe v. Wade, 138 U.Pa.L.Rev. 83 (1989); Bopp, What Does Webster Mean?, 138 U.Pa.L. Rev. 157 (1989); and Johnsen, From Driving to Drugs: Governmental Regulation of Pregnant Women's Lives After Webster, 138 U.Pa.L.Rev. 179 (1989). Some of the amicus briefs filed in Webster are reprinted in the summer-fall 1989 issue of the American Journal of Law and Medicine. For an interesting account of the interest of potential fathers, see Sharrin, Potential Fathers and Abortion: A Woman's Womb Is Not a Man's Castle, 55 Brooklyn L.Rev. 1359 (1990). For a good debate on the still unresolved First Amendment issues, see Hirt, Why the Government Is Not Required to Subsidize Abortion Counseling and Referral, 101 Harv.L.Rev. 1895 (1988), and Benshoof, The Chastity Act: Governmental Manipulation of Abortion Information and the First Amendment, 101 Harv.L.Rev. 1916 (1988). For a remarkable and cross-cultural view on abortion, see Note, The Law of Abortion in the U.S.S.R. and China: Women's Rights in Two Socialist Countries, 40 Stan.L.Rev. 1027 (1988).

Note: The Blurry Distinction Between Contraception and Abortion

If contraception refers to any process designed to prevent a pregnancy, and abortion refers to any process designed to end an established pregnancy, then the point at which the process of contraception becomes the process of abortion is at the commencement of the pregnancy. There is some ambiguity, however, about when the pregnancy begins, just as there is some ambiguity about when "conception" takes place.

The Missouri statute defines "conception" as "the fertilization of the ovum of a female by a sperm of a male," [ ] even though standard medical texts equate "conception" with implantation in the uterus occurring about six days after fertilization.

Webster v. Reproductive Health Services, 109 S.Ct. at 3080 (Stevens, J., concurring in part and dissenting in part). When does the pregnancy begin? Does the fact that a large number of fertilized eggs—perhaps 50%—never implant, suggest that pregnancy does not begin until implantation? Is the fact that cells of the fertilized ovum are identical for about three days, and then begin to separate into differentiated cells that will become the placenta, on one hand, and cells that will become the embryo and fetus, on the other, relevant? For a somewhat more detailed discussion of this biological process, see pages 956–959, below.

If there is to be a legal difference between contraception and abortion, the courts will have to determine when "conception" takes place and when a pregnancy begins. As Justice Stevens points out, many forms of what we now consider contraception are really devices designed to stop the fertilized egg from implanting in the uterus, not devices designed for avoiding fertilization of the egg in the first place.

An intrauterine device, commonly called an IUD "works primarily by preventing a fertilized egg from implanting" [ ]; other contraceptive methods that may prevent implantation include "morning-after pills" high-dose estrogen pills taken after intercourse, particularly in cases of rape, [ ] and the French RU 486, a pill that works "during the indeterminant period between contraception and abortion", [ ] low level estrogen "combined" pills—a version of the ordinary, daily ingested birth control pill—also may prevent the fertilized egg from reaching the uterine wall and implanting[ ].

109 S.Ct. at 3081 (Stevens, J., concurring in part and dissenting in part). If the law recognizes a distinction between contraception and abortion, should the law also be required to define that point at which contraception becomes abortion? Justice Stevens suggests that we must depend upon a medical definition of pregnancy, because any alternative would constitute the legal adoption of a theological position and thus be a violation of the establishment clause of the First Amendment. Do you agree? Can you develop a coherent legal argument that the state may regulate abortion in any way it sees fit, but *may not* prohibit a woman's choice to stop a fertilized ovum from reaching her uterus and implanting?

Problem: Drafting Abortion Legislation

As the legislative counsel responsible for drafting proposed legislation in your state, consider the requests of two groups of state legislators. The first asks you to draft the most restrictive abortion statute that would be constitutional under current law. The second group asks you to draft a consensus statute that would regulate abortion, but do so in such a way that it is likely to be supported by both pro-choice and pro-life constituents. Draft the two statutes and be prepared to defend each one—the first on the basis of its constitutionality, and the second on the basis of its political acceptability and good policy.

4. Sterilization

The sterilization of the mentally retarded has given rise to considerable discussion beginning with the development of the eugenics movement in the late 19th century. While there is no significant evidence that most forms of mental retardation are genetic and inheritable, there remains a residue of social support for the notion that this society can purify its gene pool by sterilizing those who would pollute it, such as the mentally retarded and criminals. The aim of the eugenics movement was confirmed by Justice Holmes in Buck v. Bell, 274 U.S. 200, 47 S.Ct. 584, 71 L.Ed. 1000 (1927), which dealt with an attempt by the State of Virginia to sterilize Carrie Buck, who had been committed to the State Colony for Epileptics and the Feeble Minded. The State was opposed on the grounds that the statute authorizing sterilization violated the Fourteenth Amendment by denying Ms. Buck due process of law and the equal protection of the law. Justice Holmes responded:

> Carrie Buck is a feeble minded white woman who was committed to the State Colony above mentioned in due form. She is the daughter of a feeble minded mother in the same institution and the mother of an illegitimate feeble minded child * * *.

> [The lower court found] "that Carrie Buck is the probable potential parent of socially inadequate offspring, likewise afflicted, that she may be sterilized without detriment to her general health and that her welfare and that of society will be promoted by her sterilization." * * * We have seen more than once that the public welfare may call upon the best citizens for their lives. It would be strange if it could not call upon those who already sapped the strength of the state for these lesser sacrifices, often not felt to be such by those concerned, in order to prevent our being swamped with incompetence. It is better for all the world if instead of waiting to execute degenerate offspring for crime, or to let them starve for their imbecility, society can prevent those who are manifestly unfit from continuing their kind. The principle that sustains compulsory vaccination is broad enough to cover cutting the fallopian tubes. [   ] Three generations of imbeciles are enough.

* * *

The Supreme Court has never overturned the decision in *Buck v. Bell,* although it is of questionable precedential value today. Society's perception of the mentally incompetent has changed and, especially after the Nazi experience, arguments based upon eugenics are held in low regard. In fact, when Carrie Buck was discovered in the Appalachian Hills in 1980, she was found to be mentally competent and extremely disappointed that throughout her life she was unable to bear another child.

The Supreme Court addressed eugenic sterilizations once more, in Skinner v. Oklahoma, 316 U.S. 535, 62 S.Ct. 1110, 86 L.Ed. 1655 (1942).

The Court determined that the equal protection clause prohibited Oklahoma from enforcing its statute which required sterilizing persons convicted of repeated criminal acts, but only if the crimes were within special categories. White collar crimes were exempted from these categories, and the Supreme Court's determination was based on the state's irrational distinction between blue collar (sterilizable) and white collar (unsterilizable) crimes. The Court was asked to, but did not, overrule *Buck v. Bell.*

Recent programs to sterilize individual mentally retarded people have been based on the convenience of sterilization for the patient and his (or, virtually always, her) family. Some who have sought sterilization for the mentally retarded have been worried about the consequences of sexual exposure to people who can barely cope with the minimal requirements of daily life; some have suggested that it would be much easier to care for patients, especially menstruating women, if they were sterilized; and others have suggested that sterilization might make it practical for mentally retarded people, who would otherwise be institutionalized, to live at home. Generally, courts have acted to protect the mentally retarded from sterilization if there is any less restrictive alternative that would serve the same interests.

Not all of the protection has come out of the judiciary, however. In California, for example, the Probate Code was amended to prohibit the sterilization of mentally retarded persons. This statute was challenged by the conservator of an incompetent mentally retarded woman who argued that the legislature had denied her a procreative choice that was extended to all other women in the community. She argued that to deny her the opportunity for a sterilization when there would be no other safe and effective method of contraception available to her would be to deny her important constitutionally protected rights. While a mentally retarded person may have a right not to be unfairly sterilized, she argued, she has a correlative right not to be unfairly and arbitrarily denied a sterilization.

In Conservatorship of Valerie N., 40 Cal.3d 143, 219 Cal.Rptr. 387, 707 P.2d 760 (1985), the California Supreme Court, through Justice Grodin, upheld the challenge and threw out the statute:

> True protection of procreative choice can be accomplished only if the state permits the court supervised substituted judgment of the conservator to be exercised on behalf of the conservatee who is unable to personally exercise this right. Limiting the exercise of that judgment by denying the right to effective contraception through sterilization to this class of conservatees denies them a right held not only by conservatees who are competent to consent but by all other women. Respondent has demonstrated neither a compelling state interest in restricting this right nor a basis upon which to conclude that the prohibition contained [in the statute] is necessary to achieve the identified purpose of furthering the incompetent's right not to be sterilized.

Chief Justice Bird, who did not frequently disagree with Justice Grodin, wrote a particularly strong dissent:

> Today's holding will permit the state, through the legal fiction of substituted consent, to deprive many women permanently of the right to conceive and bear children. The majority run roughshod over this fundamental constitutional right in a misguided attempt to guarantee a procreative choice for one they assume has never been capable of choice and never will be.   * * *
>
> The majority opinion opens the door to abusive sterilization practices which will serve the convenience of conservators, parents, and service providers rather than incompetent conservatees. The ugly history of sterilization abuse against developmentally disabled persons in the name of seemingly enlightened social policies counsels a different choice.

Rather than place an absolute prohibition upon the sterilization of the developmentally disabled as the California legislature attempted to do, most courts attempt to safeguard those who may be subject to sterilization by applying very strict procedural requirements to any proposed sterilization. For example, the standard that has been most often emulated is that provided in In re Guardianship of Hayes, 93 Wash.2d 228, 608 P.2d 635 (1980), where the court set out the procedural requirements simply and explicitly:

> The decision can only be made in a superior court proceeding in which (1) the incompetent individual is represented by a disinterested guardian ad litem, (2) the court has received independent advice based upon a comprehensive medical, psychological, and social evaluation of the individual, and (3) to the greatest extent possible, the court has elicited and taken into account the view of the incompetent individual.
>
> Within this framework, the judge must first find by clear, cogent and convincing evidence that the individual is (1) incapable of making his or her own decision about sterilization, and (2) unlikely to develop sufficiently to make an informed judgment about sterilization in the foreseeable future.
>
> Next it must be proved by clear, cogent and convincing evidence that there is a need for contraception. The judge must find that the individual is (1) physically capable of procreation, and (2) likely to engage in sexual activity at the present or in the near future under circumstances likely to result in pregnancy, and must find in addition that (3) the nature and extent of the individual's disability, as determined by empirical evidence and not solely on the basis of standardized tests, renders him or her permanently incapable of caring for a child, even with reasonable assistance.
>
> Finally, there must be no alternatives to sterilization. The judge must find that by clear, cogent and convincing evidence (1) all less drastic contraceptive methods, including supervision, edu-

cation and training, have been proved unworkable or inapplicable, and (2) the proposed method of sterilization entails the least invasion of the body of the individual. In addition, it must be shown by clear, cogent and convincing evidence that (3) the current state of scientific and medical knowledge does not suggest either (a) that a reversible sterilization procedure or other less drastic contraceptive method will shortly be available or (b) that science is on the threshold of an advance in the treatment of the individual's disability.

The court recognized that there was "a heavy presumption against sterilization of an individual incapable of informed consent" and that the burden "will be even harder to overcome in the case of a minor incompetent * * *." Some have read the procedural requirements of *Hayes* as effectively removing the possibility of the sterilization of the developmentally disabled. Can you imagine a case that would meet the stiff "procedural" requirements of *Hayes?*

For a history of sterilization of the mentally retarded in this country, see Ross, Sterilization of the Developmentally Disabled: Shielding Some Myth–Conceptions, 9 Fla.St.U.L.Rev. 599 (1981) and Sherlock and Sherlock, Sterilizing the Retarded: Constitutional, Statutory and Policy Alternatives, 60 N.C.L.Rev. 943 (1982). The best overview of the medical, social, and legal issues at stake in sterilization of the mentally retarded is American Association on Mental Deficiency, Consent Handbook (1977). For a representative sample of litigation involving sterilization of the mentally retarded, see Ruby v. Massey, 452 F.Supp. 361 (D.Conn.1978), Wentzel v. Montgomery Gen. Hosp., Inc., 293 Md. 685, 447 A.2d 1244 (1982); Matter of Grady, 85 N.J. 235, 426 A.2d 467 (1981), In re Moe, 385 Mass. 555, 432 N.E.2d 712 (1982). Compare, In re Moore's Sterilization, 289 N.C. 95, 221 S.E.2d 307 (1976) with North Carolina Assoc. for Retarded Children v. North Carolina, 420 F.Supp. 451 (M.D.N.C.1976). See also Guardianship of Matejski, 419 N.W.2d 576 (Iowa 1988) (court has jurisdiction to order sterilization even though legislature abolished "Eugenics Board"; dissent would not find jurisdiction without express grant of authority from the legislature.)

5. Tort Remedies for Failed Reproductive Control: Wrongful Birth, Wrongful Life and Wrongful Conception

SMITH v. COTE

Supreme Court of New Hampshire, 1986.
128 N.H. 231, 513 A.2d 341.

BATCHELDER, JUSTICE.

* * *

* * * Plaintiff Linda J. Smith became pregnant early in 1979. During the course of her pregnancy Linda was under the care of the

defendants, physicians who specialize in obstetrics and gynecology. Linda consulted the defendants on April 8, 1979, complaining of nausea, abdominal pain and a late menstrual period.   * * *

On August 3, 1979, nearly four months after the April visits, Linda underwent a rubella titre test at the direction of the defendants. The test indicated that Linda had been exposed to rubella. At the time the test was performed, Linda was in the second trimester of pregnancy.

Linda brought her pregnancy to full term. On January 1, 1980, she gave birth to a daughter, Heather B. Smith, who is also a plaintiff in this action. Heather was born a victim of congenital rubella syndrome. Today, at age six, Heather suffers from bilateral cataracts, multiple congenital heart defects, motor retardation, and a significant hearing impairment. She is legally blind, and has undergone surgery for her cataracts and heart condition.

In March 1984 the plaintiffs began this negligence action. They allege that Linda contracted rubella early in her pregnancy and that, while she was under the defendants' care, the defendants negligently failed to test for and discover in a timely manner her exposure to the disease. The plaintiffs further contend that the defendants negligently failed to advise Linda of the potential for birth defects in a fetus exposed to rubella, thereby depriving her of the knowledge necessary to an informed decision as to whether to give birth to a potentially impaired child.   * * *

The plaintiffs do not allege that the defendants caused Linda to conceive her child or to contract rubella, or that the defendants could have prevented the effects of the disease on the fetus. Rather, the plaintiffs contend that if Linda had known of the risks involved she would have obtained a eugenic abortion.

The action comprises three counts, only two of which are relevant here. In Count I, Linda seeks damages for her emotional distress, for the extraordinary maternal care that she must provide Heather because of Heather's birth defects, and for the extraordinary medical and educational costs she has sustained and will sustain in rearing her daughter.

* * *

In Count III, Heather seeks damages for her birth with defects, for the extraordinary medical and educational costs she will sustain, and for the impairment of her childhood attributable to her mother's diminished capacity to nurture her and cope with her problems.

* * * [T]he Superior Court transferred to us the following questions of law:

"A. Will New Hampshire Law recognize a wrongful birth cause of action by the mother of a wilfully conceived baby suffering from birth defects[?]

B. If the answer to question A is in the affirmative, will New Hampshire law allow recovery in such a cause of action for damages for emotional distress, extraordinary maternal child care, and the extraordinary medical, institutional and other special rearing expenses necessary to treat the child's impairments?

C. Will New Hampshire law recognize a cause of action for wrongful life brought by a minor child suffering from birth defects[?]

D. If the answer to question C is in the affirmative, what general and specific damages may the child recover in such an action?"

* * *

We recognize that the termination of pregnancy involves controversial and divisive social issues. Nonetheless, the Supreme Court of the United States has held that a woman has a constitutionally secured right to terminate a pregnancy. *Roe v. Wade* [   ]. It follows from *Roe* that the plaintiff Linda Smith may seek, and the defendants may provide, information and advice that may affect the exercise of that right. The basic social and constitutional issue underlying this case thus has been resolved; we need not cover ground already traveled by a court whose interpretation of the National Constitution binds us. Today we decide only whether, given the existence of the right of choice recognized in *Roe,* our common law should allow the development of a duty to exercise care in providing information that bears on that choice.

For the sake of terminological clarity, we make some preliminary distinctions. A wrongful birth claim is a claim brought by the parents of a child born with severe defects against a physician who negligently fails to inform them, in a timely fashion, of an increased possibility that the mother will give birth to such a child, thereby precluding an informed decision as to whether to have the child. * * *

A wrongful life claim, on the other hand, is brought not by the parents of a child born with birth defects, but by or on behalf of the child. The child contends that the defendant physician negligently failed to inform the child's parents of the risk of bearing a defective infant, and hence prevented the parents from choosing to avoid the child's birth.

I. WRONGFUL BIRTH: CAUSE OF ACTION

We first must decide whether New Hampshire law recognizes a cause of action for wrongful birth. Although we have never expressly recognized this cause of action, we have considered a similar claim, one for "wrongful conception." In *Kingsbury v. Smith,* 122 N.H. 237, 442 A.2d 1003 (1982), the plaintiffs, a married couple, had had three children and wanted no more. In an attempt to prevent the conception of additional offspring, Mrs. Kingsbury underwent a tubal ligation. The operation failed, however, and Mrs. Kingsbury later gave birth to a fourth child, a normal, healthy infant. The plaintiffs sued the physicians who had performed the operation, alleging that in giving birth to an unwanted child they had sustained an injury caused by the defendants' negligence.

We held that the common law of New Hampshire permitted a claim for wrongful conception, an action "for damages arising from the birth of a child to which a negligently performed sterilization procedure or a negligently filled birth control prescription which fails to prevent conception was a contributing factor." We reasoned that failure to recognize a cause of action for wrongful conception would leave "a void in the area of recovery for medical malpractice" that would dilute the standard of professional conduct in the area of family planning. [ ]

In this case, the mother contends that her wrongful birth claim fits comfortably within the framework established in *Kingsbury* and is consistent with well established tort principles. The defendants argue that tort principles cannot be extended so as to accommodate wrongful birth, asserting that they did not cause the injury alleged here, and that in any case damages cannot be fairly and accurately ascertained.

* * *

* * * In general, at common law, one who suffers an injury to his person or property because of the negligent act of another has a right of action in tort. [ ] In order to sustain an action for negligence, the plaintiff must establish the existence of a duty, the breach of which proximately causes injury to the plaintiff. [ ]

The first two elements of a negligence action, duty and breach, present no conceptual difficulties here. If the plaintiff establishes that a physician-patient relationship with respect to the pregnancy existed between the defendants and her, it follows that the defendants assumed a duty to use reasonable care in attending and treating her. [ ] Given the decision in *Roe v. Wade,* we recognize that the "due care" standard, may have required the defendants to ensure that Linda had an opportunity to make an informed decision regarding the procreative options available to her. [ ] It is a question of fact whether this standard required the defendants, at an appropriate stage of Linda's pregnancy, to test for, diagnose, and disclose her exposure to rubella. The standard is defined by reference to the standards and recommended practices and procedures of the medical profession, the training, experience and professed degree of skill of the average medical practitioner, and all other relevant circumstances.

We note that this standard does not require a physician to identify and disclose every chance, no matter how remote, of the occurrence of every possible birth "defect," no matter how insignificant. [ ] If (1) the applicable standard of care required the defendants to test for and diagnose Linda's rubella infection in a timely manner, and to inform her of the possible effects of the virus on her child's health; and (2) the defendants failed to fulfill this obligation; then the defendants breached their duty of due care.

The third element, causation, is only slightly more troublesome. The defendants point out that proof that they caused the alleged injury depends on a finding that Linda would have chosen to terminate her pregnancy if she had been fully apprised of the risks of birth defects. The defendants argue that this hypothetical chain of events is too remote to provide the basis for a finding of causation.

We do not agree. No logical obstacle precludes proof of causation in the instant case. Such proof is furnished if the plaintiff can show that, but for the defendants' negligent failure to inform her of the risks of bearing a child with birth defects, she would have obtained an abortion. * * *

We turn to the final element of a negligence action, injury. Linda contends that, in bearing a defective child after being deprived of the opportunity to make an informed procreative decision, she sustained an injury. The defendants argue that, because both benefits (the joys of parenthood) and harms (the alleged emotional and pecuniary damages) have resulted from Heather's birth, damages cannot accurately be measured, and no injury to Linda can be proved. The defendants in effect assert that the birth of a child can never constitute an injury to its parents; hence, when an actor's negligence causes a child to be born, that actor cannot be held liable in tort.

We do not agree. We recognize * * * that in some circumstances parents may be injured by the imposition on them of extraordinary liabilities following the birth of a child. Under *Roe,* prospective parents may have constitutionally cognizable reasons for avoiding the emotional and pecuniary burdens that may attend the birth of a child suffering from birth defects. Scientific advances in prenatal health care provide the basis upon which parents may make the informed decisions that *Roe* protects. We see no reason to hold that as a matter of law those who act negligently in providing such care cannot cause harm * * *.

The defendants' emphasis on the inherent difficulty of measuring damages is misplaced. An allegation of "injury," an instance of actionable harm, is distinct from a claim for "damages," a sum of money awarded to one who has suffered an injury. We have long held that difficulty in calculating damages is not a sufficient reason to deny recovery to an injured party. [ ] Other courts have recognized that the complexity of the damages calculation in a wrongful birth case is not directly relevant to the validity of the asserted cause of action. [ ]

We hold that New Hampshire recognizes a cause of action for wrongful birth. Notwithstanding the disparate views within society on the controversial practice of abortion, we are bound by the law that protects a woman's right to choose to terminate her pregnancy. Our holding today neither encourages nor discourages this practice, [ ] nor does it rest upon a judgment that, in some absolute sense, Heather Smith should never have been born. We cannot (and need not, for purposes of this action) make such a judgment. We must, however, do our best to effectuate the first principles of our law of negligence: to deter negligent conduct, and to compensate the victims of those who act unreasonably.

II. Wrongful Birth: Damages

We next must decide what elements of damages may be recovered in a wrongful birth action. The wrongful birth cause of action is unique. Although it involves an allegation of medical malpractice, it is not (as are most medical malpractice cases) a claim arising from physical injury. It is instead based on a negligent invasion of the parental right to decide whether to avoid the birth of a child with congenital defects. When parents are denied the opportunity to make this decision, important personal interests may be impaired, including an interest in avoiding the special expenses necessitated by the condition of a child born with defects, an interest in preventing the sorrow and anguish that may befall the parents of such a child, and an interest in preserving personal autonomy, which may include the making of informed reproductive choices. [ ] The task of assessing and quantifying the tangible and intangible harms that result when these interests are impaired presents a formidable challenge.

Linda seeks compensation for the extraordinary medical and educational costs that she will sustain in raising Heather, as well as for the extraordinary maternal care that she must provide her child. In addition, she asks for damages for her "emotional distress, anxiety and trauma," which she claims is a natural and foreseeable consequence of the injury she has sustained, and hence should be included as an essential element in the calculation of general damages. We consider these claims for tangible and intangible losses in turn.

A. Tangible Losses

The usual rule of compensatory damages in tort cases requires that the person wronged receive a sum of money that will restore him as nearly as possible to the position he would have been in if the wrong had not been committed. [ ] In the present case, if the defendants' failure to advise Linda of the risks of birth defects amounted to negligence, then the reasonably foreseeable result of that negligence was that Linda would incur the expenses involved in raising her daughter. According to the usual rule of damages, then, Linda should recover the entire cost of raising Heather, including both ordinary child-rearing costs and the extraordinary costs attributable to Heather's condition.

However, "few if any jurisdictions appear ready to apply this traditional rule of damages with full vigor in wrongful birth cases." [ ] Although at least one court has ruled that all child-rearing costs should be recoverable, most courts are reluctant to impose liability to this extent. A special rule of damages has emerged; in most jurisdictions the parents may recover only the extraordinary medical and educational costs attributable to the birth defects. In the present case, in accordance with the rule prevailing elsewhere, Linda seeks to recover, as tangible losses, only her extraordinary costs.

The logic of the "extraordinary costs" rule has been criticized. * * * The rule in effect divides a plaintiff's pecuniary losses into two categories, ordinary costs and extraordinary costs, and treats the latter category as compensable while ignoring the former category. At first glance, this bifurcation seems difficult to justify.

The disparity is explained, however, by reference to the rule requiring mitigation of tort damages. The "avoidable consequences" rule specifies that a plaintiff may not recover damages for "any harm that he could have avoided by the use of reasonable effort or expenditure" after the occurrence of the tort. Rigidly applied, this rule would appear to require wrongful birth plaintiffs to place their children for adoption. [ ] Because of our profound respect for the sanctity of the family, [ ] we are loathe to sanction the application of the rule in these circumstances. If the rule is not applied, however, wrongful birth plaintiffs may receive windfalls. Hence, a special rule limiting recovery of damages is warranted.

Although the extraordinary costs rule departs from traditional principles of tort damages, it is neither illogical nor unprecedented. The rule represents an application in a tort context of the expectancy rule of damages employed in breach of contracts cases. Wrongful birth plaintiffs typically desire a child (and plan to support it) from the outset. [ ] It is the defendants' duty to help them achieve this goal. When the plaintiffs' expectations are frustrated by the defendants' negligence, the extraordinary costs rule "merely attempts to put plaintiffs in the position they expected to be in with defendant's help." [ ]

Under this view of the problem, ordinary child-rearing costs are analogous to a price the plaintiffs were willing to pay in order to achieve an expected result. According to contract principles, plaintiffs "may not have a return in damages of the price and also receive what was to be obtained for the price." [ ] We note that expectancy damages are recoverable in other kinds of tort cases, [ ] and that contract principles are hardly unknown in medical malpractice litigation, which has roots in contract as well as in tort. [ ] In light of the difficulty posed by tort damages principles in these circumstances, we see no obstacle—logical or otherwise—to use of the extraordinary costs rule. [ ]

The extraordinary costs rule ensures that the parents of a deformed child will recover the medical and educational costs attributable to the child's impairment. At the same time it establishes a necessary and clearly defined boundary to liability in this area. [ ] Accordingly, we hold that a plaintiff in a wrongful birth case may recover the extraordinary medical and educational costs attributable to the child's deformities, but may not recover ordinary child-raising costs.

Three points stand in need of clarification. First, parents may recover extraordinary costs incurred both before and after their child attains majority. Some courts do not permit recovery of post-majority expenses, on the theory that the parents' obligation of support terminates when the child reaches twenty-one. [   ] In New Hampshire, however, parents are required to support their disabled adult offspring. [   ]

Second, recovery should include compensation for the extraordinary maternal care that has been and will be provided to the child. Linda alleges that her parental obligations and duties, which include feeding, bathing, and exercising Heather, substantially exceed those of parents of a normal child. One court has ruled that parents "cannot recover for services that they have rendered or will render personally to their own child without incurring financial expense." [   ] We see no reason, however, to treat as noncompensable the burdens imposed on a parent who must devote extraordinary time and effort to caring for a child with birth defects. * * * Avoiding these burdens is often among the primary motivations of one who chooses not to bear a child likely to suffer from birth defects. We hold that a parent may recover for his or her ministrations to his or her child to the extent that such ministrations:

(1) are made necessary by the child's condition;

(2) clearly exceed those ordinarily rendered by parents of a normal child; and

(3) are reasonably susceptible of valuation.

* * *

Third, to the extent that the parent's alleged emotional distress results in tangible pecuniary losses, such as medical expenses or counseling fees, such losses are recoverable. [   ]

B. Intangible Losses

Existing damages principles do not resolve the issue whether recovery for emotional distress should be permitted in wrongful birth cases. Emotional distress damages are not uniformly recoverable once a protected interest is shown to have been invaded. [The court discussed New Hampshire precedent which denied parents damages for emotional distress resulting from the death of their children.]

This case arises from a child's birth, not a child's injury or death. Nonetheless, we are struck by the parallels between the claims for emotional distress in [cases involving the death of children] and the claim before us. Moreover, we are mindful of the anomaly that would result were we to treat parental emotional distress as compensable. The negligent conduct at issue in [those cases] was the direct cause of injuries to or the death of otherwise healthy children. By contrast, in wrongful birth cases the defendant's conduct results, not in injuries or death, but in the birth of an unavoidably impaired child. It would be curious, to say the least, to impose liability for parental distress in the latter but not the former cases.

We also harbor concerns of proportionality. "[T]he unfairness of denying recovery to a plaintiff on grounds that are arbitrary in terms of principle may be outweighed by the perceived unfairness of imposing a burden on defendant that seems much greater than his fault would justify."

We hold that damages for emotional distress are not recoverable in wrongful birth actions. [ ]

III. WRONGFUL LIFE

The theory of Heather's wrongful life action is as follows: during Linda's pregnancy the defendants owed a duty of care to both Linda and Heather. The defendants breached this duty when they failed to discover Linda's exposure to rubella and failed to advise her of the possible effects of that exposure on her child's health. Had Linda been properly informed, she would have undergone an abortion, and Heather would not have been born. Because Linda was not so informed, Heather must bear the burden of her afflictions for the rest of her life. The defendant's conduct is thus the proximate cause of injury to Heather.

This theory presents a crucial problem, however: the question of injury. * * *

In order to recognize Heather's wrongful life action, then, we must determine that the fetal Heather had an interest in avoiding her own birth, that it would have been best *for Heather* if she had not been born.

This premise of the wrongful life action—that the plaintiff's own birth and suffering constitute legal injury—has caused many courts to decline to recognize the claim. * * * As one court has written,

"[w]hether it is better never to have been born at all than to have been born with even gross deficiencies is a mystery more properly to be left to the philosophers and the theologians. Surely the law can assert no competence to resolve the issue, particularly in view of the very nearly uniform high value which the law and mankind has placed on human life, rather than its absence."

Becker v. Schwartz, 46 N.Y.2d 401, 411, 386 N.E.2d 807, 812, 413 N.Y.S.2d 895, 900 (1978).

Moreover, compelling policy reasons militate against recognition of wrongful life claims. The first such reason is our conviction that the courts of this State should not become involved in deciding whether a given person's life is or is not worthwhile. * * *

* * *

The second policy reason militating against recognition of Heather's claim is related to the first.

"[L]egal recognition that a disabled life is an injury would harm the interests of those most directly concerned, the handicapped. * * * Furthermore, society often views disabled persons as burdensome misfits. Recent legislation concerning employment, education, and building access reflects a slow change in these attitudes. This change evidences a growing public awareness that the handicapped can be valuable and productive members of society. To characterize the life of a disabled person as an injury would denigrate both this new awareness and the handicapped themselves." [ ]

The third reason stems from an acknowledgment of the limitations of tort law and the adjudicative process. Wrongful life actions are premised on the ability of judges and juries accurately to apply the traditional tort concept of injury to situations involving complex medical and bioethical issues. Yet this concept applies only roughly. In the ordinary tort case the *existence* of injury is readily and objectively ascertainable. In wrongful life cases, however, the finding of injury necessarily hinges upon subjective and intensely personal notions as to the intangible value of life. * * * The danger of markedly disparate and, hence, unpredictable outcomes is manifest.

In deciding whether to recognize a new tort cause of action, we must consider the "defendant's interest in avoiding an incorrect judgment of liability because of the court's incompetence to determine certain questions raised by application of the announced standard." [ ] Wrongful life claims present problems that cannot be resolved in a "reasonably sensible, even-handed, and fair" manner from case to case. [ ] As Chief Justice Weintraub of the Supreme Court of New Jersey recognized nearly twenty years ago, "[t]o recognize a right not to be born is to enter an area in which no one could find his way." *Gleitman v. Cosgrove,* 49 N.J. 22, 63, 227 A.2d 689, 711 (1967) (Weintraub, C.J., dissenting in part).

* * *

We recognize that our rejection of the [wrongful life action] is not without cost. In the future recovery of an impaired child's necessary medical expenses may well depend on whether the child's parents are available to assert a claim for wrongful birth. * * * But this cost is the price of our paramount regard for the value of human life, and of our adherence to fundamental principles of justice. We will not recognize a right not to be born, and we will not permit a person to recover damages from one who has done him no harm.

* * *

IV. CONCLUSION

We answer the transferred questions as follows:

A. New Hampshire recognizes a cause of action for wrongful birth.

B. The damages that may be recovered are the extraordinary medical and educational costs of raising the impaired child. Such damages should reflect costs that will be incurred both before and after the child attains majority, and should include compensation for extraordinary parental care. In addition, the mother may recover her tangible losses attributable to her emotional distress.

C. New Hampshire does not recognize a cause of action for wrongful life.

* * *

SOUTER, JUSTICE, concurring:

I concur in the majority opinion and add this further word, not because that opinion fails to respond to the questions transferred to us, but because those questions fail to raise a significant issue in the area of malpractice litigation that we address today. The trial court did not ask whether, or how, a physician with conscientious scruples against abortion, and the testing and counselling that may inform an abortion decision, can discharge his professional obligation without engaging in procedures that his religious or moral principles condemn. To say nothing about this issue could lead to misunderstanding.

In response to the questions transferred, the court holds that a sphere of medical practice necessarily permitted under *Roe* is not exempt from standards of reasonable medical competence. Consequently we hold that the plaintiff alleges a violation of the physician's duty when she claims, in the circumstances of the case, that prevailing standards of medical practice called for testing and advice, which the defendants failed to provide.

It does not follow, however, and I do not understand the court to hold, that a physician can discharge the obligation of due care in such circumstances only by personally ordering such tests and rendering such advice. The court does not hold that some or all physicians must make a choice between rendering services that they morally condemn and leaving their profession in order to escape malpractice exposure. The defensive significance, for example, of timely disclosure of professional limits based on religious or moral scruples, combined with timely referral to other physicians who are not so constrained, is a question open for consideration in any case in which it may be raised.

Notes and Questions

1. Judge Souter's concurring opinion in *Smith v. Cote* received a great deal of attention four years later when he was nominated to the United States Supreme Court. During his confirmation process, many commentators looked to this opinion as the only evidence of his view of the propriety of *Roe v. Wade*, and most agreed that it was ambiguous on that issue.

2. Although courts have used the terms in different ways over the past two decades, "wrongful birth", "wrongful life", and "wrongful conception" have come to describe identifiably different kinds of actions. An action for wrongful birth is one commenced by parents against a defendant whose negligence led to the birth of a child with birth defects. An action for wrongful life is one commenced by a child born with birth defects against a defendant whose negligence resulted in the birth of the child. An action for wrongful conception (or wrongful pregnancy) is an action brought by a healthy child or that child's parents against a defendant whose negligence (in performing a tubal ligation, for example) resulted in the

birth of the child. Is there any justification for distinguishing between "wrongful life", "wrongful birth", and "wrongful conception"? Are these distinctions based upon any real legal difference? An economic difference? A philosophical analysis? Social policy consequences?

3. While wrongful birth cases were not initially well received by the judiciary, see Gleitman v. Cosgrove, 49 N.J. 22, 227 A.2d 689 (1967) (first "modern" wrongful birth action; recovery denied), no court has refused to entertain such an action since *Roe v. Wade* was decided in 1973. As the *Smith* court pointed out,

> Two developments help explain the trend toward judicial acceptance of wrongful birth actions. The first is the increased ability of health care professionals to predict and detect the presence of fetal defects.

> *Roe v. Wade* [ ] and its progeny constitute the second development explaining the acceptance of wrongful birth actions.

513 A.2d at 345–346. Obviously, medicine's ability to do prenatal diagnosis will only improve. On the other hand, the future of the second factor necessary to the acceptance of wrongful birth actions—*Roe v. Wade*—is less certain. The *Smith* court made it clear that "[W]e believe that Roe is controlling; we do not hold that our decision would be the same in its absence." 513 A.2d at 346. Given the policies for wrongful birth actions discussed in the *Smith* case, if *Roe* is overruled, will that lead state courts to overrule decisions recognizing wrongful birth actions? Among those decisions that have recognized wrongful birth actions are Siemieniec v. Lutheran Gen. Hosp., 117 Ill.2d 230, 111 Ill.Dec. 302, 512 N.E.2d 691 (1987), Berman v. Allan, 80 N.J. 421, 404 A.2d 8 (1979) (overruling *Gleitman*), James G. v. Caserta, 332 S.E.2d 872 (W.Va.1985), and Becker v. Schwartz, 46 N.Y.2d 401, 413 N.Y.S.2d 895, 386 N.E.2d 807 (1978). See also Robak v. United States, 658 F.2d 471 (7th Cir.1981).

4. Wrongful life actions have been far less successful than wrongful birth actions. Only the California, New Jersey and Washington courts have recognized wrongful life actions. See Turpin v. Sortini, 31 Cal.3d 220, 182 Cal.Rptr. 337, 643 P.2d 954 (1982), Procanik v. Cillo, 97 N.J. 339, 478 A.2d 755 (1984) and Harbeson v. Parke–Davis, Inc., 98 Wash.2d 460, 656 P.2d 483 (1983). To the extent that a wrongful life action seeks the same damages that could be recovered in a wrongful birth action, it hardly makes sense to allow one and not the other. In fact, in such cases permitting the wrongful life action simply has the effect of extending the statute of limitations, which is usually longer for an injured newborn than for an injured adult in medical malpractice cases. See Procanik v. Cillo, 97 N.J. 339, 478 A.2d 755 (1984) (justice requires allowing the wrongful life action because the wrongful birth action is barred by the statute of limitations). Despite this, the vast majority of the cases that have considered the issue have reached the same result that was reached in New Hampshire; they permit wrongful birth actions but not wrongful life actions. See, e.g., Lininger v. Eisenbaum, 764 P.2d 1202 (Colo.1988), and Gildiner v. Thomas Jefferson Univ. Hosp., 451 F.Supp. 692 (E.D.Pa.1978).

There are several reasons that courts are reluctant to accept wrongful life actions. The first argument against such actions is that a defendant cannot have a duty to a putative plaintiff who did not exist at the time that the tortious action took place. Of course, the law does recognize such a duty under other circumstances. As John Robertson has pointed out, one would be liable to an injured party for a bomb planted in a newborn nursery and set to go off a year later; the fact that the injured party was not even conceived at the time the bomb was planted would not be dispositive. See also Renslow v. Mennonite Hosp., 67 Ill.2d 348, 10 Ill.Dec. 484, 367 N.E.2d 1250 (1977) (doctor liable to child born to a woman several years after the doctor negligently transfused the woman).

The second argument against permitting a child to sue the party whose negligence caused his birth is the presumption that being born is always better than not being born; one cannot have suffered damages because one was born alive. Do you agree? Is the general acceptance of "right to die" cases, discussed below in Chapter 11, a refutation of this "life is always better than death" argument? The *Smith* court distinguished the "right to die" cases from the wrongful life cases quite directly:

> Simply put, the judiciary has an important role to play in protecting the privacy rights of the dying. It has no business declaring that among the living are people who never should have been born.

513 A.2d at 353.

Another argument raised against permitting wrongful life actions is that legal recognition of these lawsuits would constitute a social judgment that handicapped lives are worth less than other lives. Is the legal decision not to recognize wrongful life actions an appropriate way to indicate society's desire to respect the handicapped?

5. Those wrongful conception cases brought by parents to recover the costs of a pregnancy have fared well in the courts. See, e.g., O'Toole v. Greenberg, 64 N.Y.2d 427, 488 N.Y.S.2d 143, 477 N.E.2d 445 (1985) (failed tubal ligation), Hartke v. McKelway, 707 F.2d 1544 (D.C.Cir.1983) (tubal cauterization). On the other hand, wrongful conception cases seeking damages that include the cost of raising the healthy child have run into the same barriers that have faced wrongful life actions.

6. The measure of damages is a significant legal issue in most wrongful birth, wrongful life, and wrongful conception cases. As a matter of general course, the courts have allowed special damages for the pregnancy itself in wrongful birth and wrongful conception cases, and they have permitted recovery of some child rearing costs where those costs exceed the costs of raising a normal healthy child in wrongful birth actions. Some courts deny any recovery of the cost of raising a healthy child on the rationale that a healthy child can never be an injury, as a matter of public policy. O'Toole v. Greenberg, 64 N.Y.2d 427, 488 N.Y.S.2d 143, 477 N.E.2d 445 (1985); Hartke v. McKelway, 707 F.2d 1544 (D.C.Cir.1983). Other courts have fashioned a curious hybrid, allowing child-rearing costs but deducting a quantified estimate of the "benefit" of parenthood. A minority of courts allow child-rearing costs without any offset. In Marciniak v. Lundborg, 153 Wis.2d 59, 450 N.W.2d 243 (1990), an action to recover damages for a negligent sterilization that resulted in a normal healthy child, the public policy arguments for limiting recovery in such cases were enumerated and rejected:

Defendants first argue that child rearing costs are too speculative and that it is impossible to establish with reasonable certainty the damages to the parents. We do not agree that the damages are too speculative. * * * [S]imilar calculations are routinely performed in countless other malpractice situations. Juries are frequently called on to make far more complex damage assessments in other tort cases. There may thus actually be a less speculative calculation involved than in many other malpractice actions which are routinely allowed, such as those involving pain, suffering, and mental anguish. Population studies are readily available to provide figures for the costs of raising a child.

Defendants next argue that because the costs of raising a child are so significant, allowing these costs would be wholly out of proportion to the culpability of the negligent physician. We find no merit in that contention. Admittedly, the cost of raising a child is substantial. However, the public policy of this state does not categorically immunize defendants from liability for foreseeable damages merely because the damages may be substantial.

Defendants next argue that "awarding damages to the parents may cause psychological harm to the child when, at a later date, it learns of its parents' action for its wrongful birth thereby creating an 'emotional bastard.'" Again, we do not agree. The parents' suit for recovery of child rearing costs is in no reasonable sense a signal to the child that the parents consider the child an unwanted burden. The suit is for costs of raising the child, not to rid themselves of an unwanted child. They obviously want to keep the child. The love, affection, and emotional support any child needs they are prepared to give. But the love, affection, and emotional support they are prepared to give do not bring with them the economic means that are also necessary to feed, clothe, educate and otherwise raise the child. That is what this suit is about and we trust the child in the future will be well able to distinguish the two.

Defendants also argue that allowing these costs would in some way debase the sanctity of human life, stating that "(T)he courts have been loath to adopt a rule, the primary effect of which is to encourage or reward the parents' disparagement of the value of their child's life." We do not perceive that the Marciniaks in bringing this suit are in any way disparaging the value of their child's life. They are, to the contrary, attempting to enhance it.

Defendants further argue that allowing these costs would shift the entire cost of raising the child to the physician, thereby creating a new category of surrogate parent. This suit is not an attempt to shift the responsibility of parenting from the Marciniaks to the physician. The Marciniaks are assuming that responsibility. To equate the responsibility of parenting with the responsibility of paying for the costs of child raising is illogical.

Defendants further argue that allowing these costs would enter a field that has no sensible or just stopping point. To the extent that the defendants base this proposition on the concern that the damages would be too speculative, we have answered that argument above. Juries are frequently called on to answer damage questions that are far less predictable than those presented here.

We do not agree that the refusal of the Marciniaks to abort the unplanned child or give it up for adoption should be considered as a failure of the parents to mitigate their damages. The rules requiring mitigation of damages require only that reasonable measures be taken. We do not consider it reasonable to expect parents to essentially choose between the child and the cause of action.

450 N.W.2d at 245–247. The court then concluded:

One of the basic principles of traditional damages is the concept that the wrongdoer compensate those who are injured by his or her negligence. Where the purpose of the physician's actions is to prevent conception through sterilization, and the physician's actions are performed negligently, traditional principles of tort law require that the physician be held legally responsible for the consequences which have in fact occurred. We therefore conclude that the parents of a healthy child may recover the costs of raising the child from a physician who negligently performs a sterilization.

450 N.W.2d at 248. Finally, the court decided not to apply the "benefit rule" that would allow an offset for the joy of having the child to the damages awarded:

We conclude that it is not equitable to apply the benefit rule in the context of the tort of negligent sterilization. The parents made a decision not to have a child. It was precisely to avoid that "benefit" that the parents went to the physician in the first place. Any "benefits" that were conferred upon them as a result of having a new child in their lives were not asked for and were sought to be avoided. With respect to emotional benefits, potential parents in this situation are presumably well aware of the emotional benefits that might accrue to them as the result of a new child in their lives. When parents make the decision to forego this opportunity for emotional enrichment, it hardly seems equitable to not only force this benefit upon them but to tell them they must pay for it as well by offsetting it against their proven emotional damages.

450 N.W.2d at 450. The cost of raising a healthy child is, in fact, less than the special damages sought in many other kinds of medical malpractice cases, and it is far less than those damages related to the medical care of a seriously ill newborn. See Comment, Wrongful Pregnancy: Child Rearing Damages Deserve Full Judicial Consideration, 8 Pace L.Rev. 313, 333–34 (1988).

7. Because wrongful birth, wrongful life and wrongful conception actions may expand the areas in which physicians are liable for malpractice, and because they implicate abortion, about half of the state legislatures have considered legislative resolutions of these issues. While one state has promulgated a statute allowing for wrongful birth and wrongful life actions, 24 Me.Rev.Stat.Ann. § 2931 (Supp.1988), several others have promulgated legislation forbidding both wrongful birth and wrongful life

actions. Most have language similar to that adopted in Minnesota, which provides that "no person shall maintain a cause of action or receive an award of damages on the claim that but for the negligent conduct of another, a child would have been aborted." Minn.Stat.Ann. § 145.424(2) (1989). The Minnesota Supreme Court upheld that statute in an action brought by a thirty-four year old mother of a child born with Down's syndrome. The mother alleged that the physician defendant negligently discouraged her from undergoing a test which would have revealed the Down's syndrome and resulted in the abortion of the fetus. The court rejected the argument that the statute violated interests protected by *Roe v. Wade,* and that it violated the equal protection of the Fourteenth Amendment. First, the court decided that there was no state action alleged, and thus no constitutionally protected right at stake. Even if there were state action, the court concluded, the statute did not constitute a legally impermissible burden on the mother's right to seek an abortion. Three justices dissented, finding the statute to be an improper state interference with the mother's right to an abortion, Hickman v. Group Health Plan, Inc., 396 N.W.2d 10 (Minn.1986).

8. There are a number of articles on the propriety of wrongful birth, wrongful life and wrongful conception actions. See, e.g., Capron, Tort Liability in Genetic Counselling, 79 Colum.L.Rev. 618 (1979); Rogers, Wrongful Life and Wrongful Birth: Medical Malpractice in Genetic Counselling and Prenatal Testing, 33 S.C.L.Rev. 713 (1982); Collins, An Overview and Analysis: Prenatal Torts, Preconception Torts, Wrongful Life, Wrongful Death, and Wrongful Birth: Time for a New Framework, 22 J.Fam.L. 677 (1984). The propriety of wrongful birth and wrongful life actions in the context of genetic counselling is well discussed in Note, Wrongful Birth and Wrongful Life Actions Arising from Negligent Genetic Counselling: The Need for Legislation Supporting Reproductive Choice, 17 Fordham Urban L.J. 27 (1989). The question of whether life can ever be "wrongful" is nicely discussed in Roberts, Distinguishing Wrongful from "Rightful" Life, 6 J. Contemporary Health L. & Policy 59 (1990). Finally, a good response to recent legislation is found in Note, Wrongful Birth Actions: The Case Against Legislative Curtailment, 100 Harv.L.Rev. 2017 (1987) (arguing that statutory limitations infringe on parents' right to make informed procreative decisions).

B. FACILITATING REPRODUCTION

Problem: Reproductive Arrangements Go Awry

Avery and Alma Kleb wanted a child for years, but Avery proved infertile. Artificial insemination of Alma also proved unsuccessful because her uterus is unable to maintain a fertilized ovum. A year ago they consulted Dr. Lopez, a specialist in the treatment of infertility. He suggested *in vitro* insemination of Alma's ovum, which could then be implanted in the womb of a surrogate. The Klebs agreed, and Dr. Lopez arranged to have fertile sperm delivered from Nobel Labs Incorporated for impregnation of one of Alma's ova, which he surgically removed from her. He then implanted the fertilized ovum in the uterus of Alice Thompkins, a healthy

25–year old single woman who was referred to Dr. Lopez by Motherhood Incorporated, a surrogate mother brokering company. The Klebs agreed to the selection of Ms. Thompkins, whom they had never met, and they agreed to pay Dr. Lopez his fee of $15,000, and Motherhood Incorporated their administrative fee of $40,000, which included "all legal and medical expenses of carrying the child to term." The Klebs agreed to adopt the child at birth, and Motherhood Incorporated agreed to hold the $40,000 in escrow until the adoption was complete.

One month ago the child, Alfred, was born with some serious problems. He is likely to be mildly developmentally disabled as a consequence of an automobile accident Ms. Thompkins suffered during the eighth month of the pregnancy, in which Alfred's skull was partially crushed *in utero.* The automobile accident was the result of Ms. Thompkins' negligence in going through a red light. In addition, the child is likely to develop mottled, discolored teeth as a consequence of the administration to Ms. Thompkins of tetracycline in the emergency room after the automobile accident. Discolored teeth is a well known consequence of the use of that antibiotic in pregnant women. Finally, the infant suffers from Von Willebrand disease, which is a form of hemophilia that is apparently the result of a genetic defect in the biological father. The defect could have been discovered before impregnation, but only through a genetic analysis of the father. That analysis was not undertaken because the sperm, according to Nobel Incorporated, "came from a very healthy, very smart man."

The Klebs have refused to adopt the infant, and they have demanded a refund of the $40,000 from Motherhood's escrow agent. Motherhood Incorporated demands the $40,000. Ms. Thompkins is willing to keep the baby, as long as the Klebs pay support, which they refuse. She is threatening a maternity action against Alma and a contract action against Avery. Who has what rights against whom? What kind of a contract would you have drawn as counsel to the Klebs? Nobel Incorporated? Motherhood Incorporated? Ms. Thompkins? Dr. Lopez? Which of those contracts, if any, would be enforceable?

1. *Introduction*

a. *The Process of Human Reproduction*

Those seeking medical help in facilitating reproduction do so because they want a child. The birth of a child requires the growth of a fetus in a woman's uterus. This, in turn, requires the implantation of a fertilized ovum (also called an egg or an oocyte) in the uterine wall. The ovum can implant in the uterine wall only if it has been fertilized by a sperm in the fallopian tube.

Despite the development of a variety of techniques to accomplish this, most people still use coitus as the preferred process for initiating pregnancy. Typically, an ovum leaves a woman's ovary when the wall of follicular cells in which it has been residing breaks and it is carried upon a wave of escaping follicular fluid into the upper end of the fallopian tube; this process is called ovulation and it occurs once each menstrual cycle, usually between the ninth and fourteenth day. During this stage, if a man ejaculates semen which contains motile spermatozoa (sperm) into the woman's vagina, the sperm move (at a rate of a little less than five inches per hour) through her uterus and into her fallopian tubes. Although one ejaculation may contain a billion sperm pursuing the ovum, only a much smaller number reach the upper portion of the one fallopian tube that contains the freshly released ovum. An even smaller number of sperm actually reach the ovum. Of these, the first sperm head to embed in the outer wall of the ovum releases a substance that changes the ovum's outer wall, making it impermeable to other sperm. Sperm remain alive and capable of fertilization in the uterine environment for only 48 hours after ejaculation. Because the ovum is estimated to have a fertilizable life of less than 24 hours after it is released from the ovary, the timing of fertilization is important.

Within a day, the fertilized ovum has divided twice, into a two- and then a four-celled "embryo," and it is here that we must pause to consider the impact that our language has on our conceptualization and therefore our law. The terminology of early pregnancy is rife with alternative phraseology. For example, a fertilized ovum/egg/oocyte is also called a "zygote," or a cluster of dividing "blastomeres" which eventually divide into a "blastocyst" or hollow cellular ball (see illustration page 958). Some will argue that because there is no differentiated living matter generated in forming the blastocyst (i.e., there are no fetal or placental cells yet), this division of cell material is not a constructive development of living substance. It is a process which does nothing to distribute particular developmental qualities to particular parts of a resulting fetus. On the other hand, it is the preliminary stage which makes it possible for the blastocyst cell ball to implant and use materials from the uterine wall to grow and develop into a fetus. Obviously, the fertilization of the ovum by the sperm begins the embryonic process, although some use the term "embryo" only to apply to later stages of development. See *Davis v. Davis,* below, page 970.

At any rate, whether it is called an embryo or not, the fertilized ovum continues its migration through the fallopian tube toward the uterus. The fertilized and subdividing ovum arrives at the lower end of the fallopian tube, hesitating for about two days before being expelled into the uterus. This delay allows the uterine lining to build up for successful implantation. The implantation of this cell cluster is a complicated biological process that takes several days. Where the fertilized ovum cell cluster adheres to the uterine lining is variable, although there is less risk of some subsequent complications if implantation occurs in the upper half of the uterus.

Even when all other conditions are met, not all fertilized ova actually do implant and not all implanted ova survive until birth. About 50% of fertilized ova are expelled from the body before the woman has reason to know that she is pregnant. Some of these spontaneous expulsions occur before implantation, and some occur during the first few days after the commencement of the implantation process.

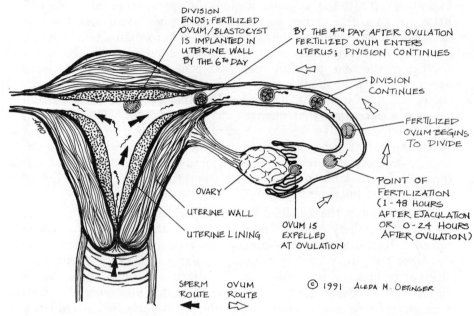

There are several reasons that those who wish to raise children may not conceive them through this natural process. First, some are unable to participate in coital sexual relations, or choose not to participate in such relations. Others are infertile—that is, normal coitus does not result in a fertilized ovum that implants in the uterine wall and grows into a fetus and then a child. About 10% of American couples are infertile. Of these, one third are infertile because the man does not produce sperm that is capable of fertilizing the ovum and about two-thirds are infertile because of some problem in the woman's reproductive system. Some women are unable to produce ova, for example, and others have fallopian tubes that cannot adequately accept ova to be fertilized, or do not permit the travel of fertilized ova to the uterus. In other cases, the uterus is incapable of allowing for implantation of the fertilized ovum or maintaining the implanted embryo through the pregnancy. In all of these cases, some form of intervention may allow those who could not become parents through unassisted coitus to achieve parenthood nonetheless.

The variety of problems that results in the need to assist reproduction give rise to a wide variety of alternative interventions. These interventions, in turn, require the involvement of a host of other people. A sperm source (who is not necessarily a sperm donor—he is usually a sperm vendor) is necessary where the problem is the lack of a man or a man's inability to produce physiologically adequate sperm; an ovum source is necessary where the problem is a woman's inability to provide a potentially fertile ovum; a uterus source (or "surrogate mother") is necessary where a woman is unable or unwilling to carry the fertilized ovum through the pregnancy in her own uterus. Sometimes a combination of these needs requires that there be a series of interventions to produce a pregnancy and a child. A woman may be unable to produce ova and unable to carry a fertilized ovum in her uterus, for example. There may be several options available to allow her to obtain both an ovum that can be fertilized (from an ovum source) and a uterus for the gestation of that fertilized ovum (from a surrogate).

b. The Role of the Law

The law's involvement in human reproduction has not been limited to evaluating the propriety of techniques used to avoid bearing children: the law is also involved in regulating processes designed to facilitate reproduction. These processes include AIH (artificial insemination-homologous: artificial insemination of a woman with the sperm of the person who is intended to be the biological and nurturing father, usually the husband), AID (artificial insemination-donor: artificial insemination of the woman with the sperm of someone who is presumed to have no continuing relationship with the child), IVF (*in vitro* fertilization: fertilizing an ovum outside of the uterus and then implanting it), embryo transfer, egg transfer, and surrogacy (carrying a fetus expected to be raised by an dentifiable person other than the pregnant woman). There are other techniques that may be applied to aid fertilization problems—such as full IVP (*in vitro* pregnancy) and cloning—but these are unlikely to be of much practical concern over the next several decades. There are hundreds of thousands of children now alive in the United States who were conceived by AID; there are thousands who are the result of *in vitro* fertilization, and hundreds carried by surrogate mothers. Questions surrounding their legal status are real, substantial, and immediate.

It is not hard to imagine the variety of unusual legal relationships which can develop as a consequence of medical and non-medical reproductive techniques. It is possible to have a child who is the product of sperm from one source (whose sperm may be mixed with sperm from several sources), an ovum extracted from one woman, implanted in another, and carried for the benefit of yet another set of parents who intend to nurture the child from the time of its birth. Such a child would have two genetic parents, another mother providing a uterus, and two nurturing parents. Who ought to be treated as the legal parents? Should the others involved in the process have any rights whatsoever? For example, if the nurturing parents have the rights normally associated with parenthood, should any rights—visitation, for example—be extended to the carrying mother, or the genetic parents? Should we consider parenthood to be a bundle of rights, much as we have come to view property, and should these rights be separated out and split among several people, each of whom would share in the privileges and responsibilities of parental status?

For one taxonomy of relationships resulting from reproductive technology, consider the following table of reproductive possibilities that has been provided by Professor Alexander Capron:

Reproductive possibilities

No	Name of Method	Genetic Source	Fertilization	Gestation	Social Parents
1	Traditional Reproduction	X_M & Y_M	Natural	M	M & M
2	Artificial Insemination, Husband	X_M & Y_M	AI	M	M & M
3	Test Tube Baby	X_M & Y_M	IVF	M	M & M
4	Artificial Insemination, Donor	X_M & Y_D	AI	M	M & M
5A	Donated Egg	X_D & Y_M	IVF	M	M & M
5B	Transferred Egg	X_D & Y_M	AI with embryo flushing	M	M & M
6	Surrogate Motherhood	X_D & Y_M	AI	D	M & M
7A	Test Tube Baby in Rented Womb	X_M & Y_M	IVF	D	M & M
7B	Transfer to Rented Womb	X_M & Y_M	Natural or AI w/embryo flushing	D	M & M
8	Postnatal Adoption	X_D & Y_D	Natural, AI, or IVF	D	M & M
9	Substitute Father	X_M & Y_D	IVF	M	M & M
10	Brave New World	X_1 & Y_2	IVF or Natural/AI/w/embryo flushing	3	4 & 5

Abbreviations: X = female, Y = male, AI = artificial insemination, IVF = *in vitro* fertilization, D = donor, M = member of married couple [Ed. note: "embryo flushing" occurs when an ovum is fertilized in one woman and the resulting embryo is washed out of that woman and captured for implantation in another woman.]

Capron, Alternative Birth Technologies: Legal Challenges, 20 U.Cal. Davis L.Rev. 679, 682 (1987). For another and more complex table of reproductive options, see Dickens, Reproduction Law and Medical Consent, 35 Toronto L.J. 255, 280 (1985). An excellent account of the various alternatives is found in I. Kennedy and A. Grubb, Medical Law 607–738 (1989). A good comparatively early classification of forms of alternative reproduction is found in Wadlington, Artificial Conception: The Challenge for Family Law, 69 Va.L.Rev. 465, 488–496 (1983). The most comprehensive general account of the technology and law (as of 1985) is L. Andrews, New Conceptions: A Consumer's Guide to the Newest in Fertility Treatments including In Vitro Fertilization, Artificial Insemination and Surrogate Mothering (Rev. ed. 1985). See also L. Andrews, Between Strangers (1989).

c. Facilitating Reproduction and the Definition of the Family

We are so concerned about the use of new technology to facilitate reproduction in part because of its potential effect on family structure, and because any consequent changes in family structure may also have an impact on social structure. Courts and legislatures have been tentative at best in actually defining what constitutes a "family" of the kind which we wish to preserve and protect. Perhaps this should not come as a surprise; others who have attempted to define "family" have not been any more successful. As R.D. Laing explained,

> [w]e speak of families as though we all knew what families are.
> We identify, as families, networks of people who live together over
> periods of time, who have ties of marriage and kinship to one
> another. The more one studies family dynamics, the more *unclear*
> one becomes as to the ways *family* dynamics compare and contrast
> with the dynamics of other groups not called families, let alone the
> ways families differ themselves. As with dynamics, so with struc-
> ture (patterns, more stable and enduring than others): Again,
> comparisons and generalizations must be very tentative.

Laing, The Politics of the Family and Other Essays, 3 (1971). Since
1971 American social living arrangements, and the consequent notions
of the family, have become even more uncertain. Early this century a
society of extended families (which were extended both horizontally, to
include near relatives, and vertically, to include near generations) was
transformed through increased mobility, increased urbanization, and
increased industrialization into a society of nuclear families, each
family possessing an identifiable head of a household (generally the
father) a mother, and children; a dog is optional.

This model of the family has been tested by many forces, including
those that come from women's reassessment of their roles. Even
greater changes have driven us from a society of nuclear families to a
society of "constructed" families—designer families, really—where relationships between adults, and between adults and children, are arranged on an *ad hoc* basis or by agreement. Of course, these *ad hoc*
arrangements may provide for a different relationship between adults
and their parents, and between these new social units and the state,
than those which traditionally have been recognized in law. Further,
while many of these new "constructed" families look very much like
the families of a few decades ago, many do not. Many are one parent
families, some include more than two parents and some include two
parents of the same gender.

The law has struggled to deal with the social and medical developments that made these families possible with only limited success.
While courts have been able to develop processes to accommodate the
breakup of nuclear families—custody and support arrangements, primarily—neither the courts nor legislatures have done very well in
developing institutions that are capable of dealing with these previously legally unrecognized families. Ultimately this society will call upon
the law to define families, declare family relationships, and allocate
power within families. The solutions to the problems thus raised will
depend upon the answer to the question the law has not yet asked: why
does this society recognize families? Why do we strive to protect
families? Why are the institutions of government so interested in
preserving and restoring the authority of families? These questions
have been unanswered—indeed, unasked—by the law until now because the law has not been called to address them. However, social
and medical changes over the last several years have forced these
questions into the legal spotlight. This society must determine first,

descriptively, the role families do play in society, and, second, prescriptively, the role they ought to play in this society.

As you read the rest of this section of this chapter, ask yourself whether the law reflects forethought and purpose behind its definitional conclusions (be they explicit or implicit). Is the law consistent in this area? Is it just? For the classic academic structure of these issues, see Skolnick and Skolnick, Family in Transition: Rethinking Marriage, Sexuality, Childbearing, and Family Organization (1971). For an entirely different approach, see Hutter, The Changing Family: Comparative Perspectives (2d 1988). An excellent history of the legal treatment of the family is found in Teitelbaum, Family History and Family Law, 1985 Wis.L.Rev. 1135.

2. *Artificial Insemination*

The Process of Artificial Insemination

Artificial insemination is the placement of the semen in the vagina (or in the cervical canal) by means other than the penis. The sperm source produces semen through masturbation and ejaculation. The ejaculate is then put into a syringe and injected directly into the woman who intends to become pregnant. This process, using "fresh" semen, need not be a medical procedure; it can be done successfully at home by anyone who understands the underlying biological principles. Ideally, the insemination is done at about the time of ovulation, a time that can be determined with increasing accuracy through home ovulation prediction tests.

Medically performed artificial insemination now generally employs frozen semen rather than fresh semen. Although freezing semen permits subsequent tests upon the donor to determine the presence of any latent contaminant (HIV, for example), the freezing process is medically difficult and expensive. The semen is mixed with a preservative before it is frozen, and it must be carefully thawed before it is used. Once the semen is frozen, however, it is unlikely to undergo substantial deterioration; one estimate is that the risk of genetic mutation will double if the semen is kept frozen for 5,000 years. In 1990 one Seattle man successfully inseminated his wife with sperm he deposited in a New York sperm bank fourteen years earlier. The man, who became sterile after his deposit, had paid $50 each year to keep his deposit on ice.

There are about 200,000 women artificially inseminated medically each year in the United States. The service is provided by over 10,000 doctors throughout the country. While frozen sperm costs only about $50 per vial (average use—2 per cycle); the total cost per cycle is between $200 and $500.

a. *Artificial Insemination—Homologous (AIH)*

Virtually no legal questions have arisen surrounding the use of the sperm of a husband to inseminate his wife, even if the sperm is artificially injected into the vagina or cervical canal. Such a process may be used within a marriage to allow for processing of the semen to overcome low sperm count. In these cases, there is no question about the identity of the mother and the father of the child. While there are some religious objections to masturbation (which, obviously, is required) and to any process that alters the "natural" arrangement, AIH has now become well accepted as a social and medical matter, and it is not a matter of substantial legal concern.

b. *Artificial Insemination—Donor (AID)*

When the sperm is not that of the husband of the woman whose pregnancy results, the question of who ought to be considered the father of the resulting child may arise. For the most part this matter has been resolved by the adoption of the Uniform Parentage Act or another statute that serves the same purposes.

UNIFORM PARENTAGE ACT (1973)

§ 1. [Parent and Child Relationship Defined.]

As used in this Act, "parent and child relationship" means the legal relationship existing between a child and his natural or adoptive parents incident to which the law confers or imposes rights, privileges, duties, and obligations. It includes the mother and child relationship and the father and child relationship.

§ 2. [Relationship Not Dependent on Marriage.]

The parent and child relationship extends equally to every child and to every parent, regardless of the marital status of the parents.

* * *

§ 5. [Artificial Insemination.]

(a) If, under the supervision of a licensed physician and with the consent of her husband, a wife is inseminated artificially with semen donated by a man not her husband, the husband is treated in law as if he were the natural father of a child thereby conceived. The husband's consent must be in writing and signed by him and his wife. The physician shall certify their signatures and the date of the insemination, and file the husband's consent with the [State Department of Health], where it shall be kept confidential and in a sealed file. However, the physician's failure to do so does not affect the father and child relationship. All papers and records pertaining to the insemination, whether part of the permanent record of a court or of a file held by the supervising physician or elsewhere, are subject to inspection only upon an order of the court for good cause shown.

(b) The donor of semen provided to a licensed physician for use in artificial insemination of a married woman other than the donor's wife is treated in law as if he were not the natural father of a child thereby conceived.

* * *

§ 23. [Birth Records.]

(a) Upon order of a court of this State or upon request of a court of another state, the [registrar of births] shall prepare [an amended birth registration] [a new certificate of birth] consistent with the findings of the court [and shall substitute the new certificate for the original certificate of birth].

(b) The fact that the father and child relationship was declared after the child's birth shall not be ascertainable from the [amended birth registration] [new certificate] but the actual place and date of birth shall be shown.

(c) The evidence upon which the [amended birth registration] [new certificate] was made and the original birth certificate shall be kept in a sealed and confidential file and be subject to inspection only upon consent of the court and all interested persons, or in exceptional cases only upon an order of the court for good cause shown.

Notes and Questions

1. The Uniform Parentage Act applies only if the woman who is inseminated is a wife (i.e., is married), if she proceeds with the consent of her husband and the procedure is carried out under the supervision of a licensed physician. If any of these conditions is not met, the statute is inapplicable and the common law will define the rights and interests of all of the parties. Some common law cases have treated the source of the sperm to be the father, with all of the rights (including visitation) and obligations (including child support) that come with such a designation; others have not. Compare Gursky v. Gursky, 39 Misc.2d 1083, 242 N.Y. S.2d 406 (Sup.Ct.1963) (child born of AID is illegitimate) with In re Adoption of Anonymous, 74 Misc.2d 99, 345 N.Y.S.2d 430 (Sup.Ct.1973). See also In re Baby Doe, 291 S.C. 389, 353 S.E.2d 877 (1987) (one who assists his wife's efforts to conceive by artificial insemination must be treated as the legal father of the resulting child); Strnad v. Strnad, 190 Misc. 786, 78 N.Y.S.2d 390 (Sup.Ct.1948) (husband of woman who receives AID with his consent has rights and obligations of father); People v. Sorensen, 68 Cal.2d 280, 66 Cal.Rptr. 7, 437 P.2d 495 (1968) (husband of wife impregnated by AID with his consent is liable for support of child) and C.M. v. C.C., 152 N.J.Super. 160, 377 A.2d 821 (1977) (natural father by AID liable for support). For an analysis of the sperm donor's constitutional rights to maintain a relationship with the child when the woman promised she

would permit such a relationship, see McIntyre v. Crouch, 98 Or.App. 462, 780 P.2d 239 (1989) aff'd 308 Or. 593, 784 P.2d 1100 (1989).

2. In addition to the moral arguments that are made against AIH, there are four additional arguments against the moral propriety of AID. First, some believe that it constitutes adultery. Second, the uncertainty of the screening of the sperm source in AID can provide for uncertainty in the health of the child, and the anonymity of the sperm source can impose upon the woman or her child unforeseen emotional consequences. Of course, these problems can be overcome by adequate screening of the sperm source and procedures that permit a child born of artificial insemination to obtain some information about the sperm source at some point in his or her life—perhaps when the child becomes an adult. Third, there is a worry that the availability of AID will reshape and dilute family structure, replacing the nuclear family with unusual and inappropriate combinations of adults and children. Finally, there is an argument that AID is inappropriate because if there is no limit on the number of times one man may donate sperm there may be a genetically unacceptably large number of "test tube" children who unknowingly have the same genetic father. This may lead to the dilution of the genetic pool of some communities. Is this a scientifically reasonable worry? Is this a good reason to prohibit the practice, or to regulate it?

3. Should the source of the sperm in an artificial insemination procedure remain anonymous? Should a woman being inseminated be able to choose the man who will be the source of the sperm? At the least, should she be able to designate some of the attributes that she wishes the source of the sperm to possess? Alternatively, should the source of the sperm remain unknown to the child, the inseminated woman, and, perhaps, even the inseminating physician? Some sperm banks do provide profiles of their various donors, and some issue catalogs of these profiles allowing their consumers to choose the profile that seems most appropriate. Is a profile that reads "tall, thin stockbroker of eastern European Jewish descent, interested in Republican Party politics and skiing" very helpful? In addition to relevant health information, what kind of information, if any, about the sperm source ought to be provided to the woman who is going to be inseminated? In considering the appropriate policy for Britain, a government commission considered the American practice:

> It is the practice of some clinics in the U.S.A. to provide detailed descriptions of donors, and to permit couples to exercise choice as to the donor they would prefer. In the evidence there was some support for the use of such descriptions. It is argued that they would provide information and reassurance for the parents and, at a later date, for the child. They might also be of benefit to the donor, as an indication that he is valued for his own sake. A detailed description also offers some choice to the woman who is to have the child, and lack of such choice can be said to diminish the importance of the woman's right to choose the father of her child.

> The contrary view, also expressed in the evidence, is that detailed donor profiles would introduce the donor as a person in his own right. It is also argued that the use of profiles devalues the child who may

HUMAN REPRODUCTION AND BIRTH

seem to be wanted only if certain specifications are met, and this may become a source of disappointment to the parents if their expectations are unfulfilled.

Report to the Committee of Inquiry into "Human Fertilization and Embryology" (Cmnd 9314) (the "Warnock Commission") Paragraphs 4.19–20 (1984). The committee went on to recommend "that on reaching the age of 18 the child should have access to the basic information about the donor's ethnic origin and genetic health and that legislation be enacted to provide the right of access to this." *Id.* ¶ 4.21.

Physicians in the United States are responsive to requests of women for sperm from sources with particular characteristics. A 1987 Office of Technology Assessment survey found that over 90% of the surveyed physicians who engaged in artificial insemination were willing to match for race (97%), eye color (94%), complexion (90%) and height (90%), if requested to do so. A majority were also willing to match ethnic/national origin, weight, body type, hair texture, educational attainment, age, I.Q., and religion. A majority were not willing to match for special abilities and hobbies or interests, and almost three-fourths were unwilling to match for income.

4. What kind of screening ought to be done on sperm sources? In 1987 the Office of Technology Assessment found that half of the physicians who had four or more artificial insemination patients in the previous year tested the sperm source for HIV. About one-fourth tested for gonorrhea, hepatitis, and chlamydia, about one-fifth tested for blood type and rh factor. Half of the physicians accepting semen donations did not check to see if the donors possessed any genetic disease, and 25% did not screen the donors for fertility. Office of Technology Assessment, Artificial Insemination Practice in the United States (1988). Some commercial sperm banks do far more thorough screening of their sources and their products.

5. Physicians also screen those who seek to be inseminated. The 1987 study found that over half of the physicians doing artificial insemination had rejected, or would be likely to reject, a request for artificial insemination from a potential recipient with any one of the following attributes: unmarried (and with no partner), psychologically immature, homosexual, welfare dependent, evidence of child abuse, evidence of drug abuse, evidence of alcohol abuse, history of serious genetic disorder, HIV positive, under 18 years old or criminal record. Id. Does the determination by these physicians not to inseminate the poor or those with criminal records harken back to the era of *Buck v. Bell* and *Skinner v. Oklahoma,* when there was a presumption that wealth and criminal proclivity were inheritable, or do such screening processes merely suggest that the physicians, who can choose whom they will make parents, are determining which of the proposed patients are likely to be the best parents? Should a determination of who will be inseminated be left to physicians who perform this procedure? Should a physician ever be required to perform artificial insemination in a case where she believes that the woman being inseminated is not capable of the physical, mental or emotional obligations of motherhood?

6. The ability to freeze and preserve sperm gives rise to the possibility that the father of a child conceived through artificial insemination could have died years before that child's birth. In a French case, the court had to confront an action by a woman to recover a sperm bank deposit made by her paramour shortly before he underwent treatment for cancer of the testicles which resulted in his sterility, and, ultimately, his death. The court, recognizing that the woman seeking the sperm and the sperm donor had actually married two days before his death, concluded,

> [n]either the preservation or the redelivery of the sperm of the deceased husband nor the insemination of his widow are prohibited or even provided for by any legislation or regulation.
>
> Moreover, they are not an infringement of natural law, since one of the aims of marriage is procreation. * * *
>
> On these various grounds the court has decided that the request should be granted.

Parpalaix v. CECOS, quoted in I. Kennedy and A. Grubb, Medical Law 622 (1989). Is sperm simply property that can be passed on like any other property upon death? Ought there be any limitation on the people to whom sperm can be willed or sold? Is a child born of sperm from a "father" who died years before an heir of that man? Is the only limitation upon that heir's opportunity to partake in the estate the statute of limitations? Does this problem implicate the rule against perpetuities?

7. What is the tort liability that arises out of the provision of inadequate sperm for purposes of artificial insemination? Might the physician or the sperm bank be liable in negligence for inadequately screening the count, health and motility of the sperm? What is the standard of care for screening sperm? How would you find out? In any case, might the doctor or the sperm bank be strictly liable without negligence (on a products liability theory) for the provision of defective sperm?

Of course, the physician and the physician's staff could also be liable in negligence for failing to carry out properly the procedure or failing to adequately inform and counsel the woman to be inseminated about the risks, benefits and alternatives of the procedure.

Might there be a contract action against the physician or the sperm bank who deals commercially in the sale of sperm? If the sperm is sold to the woman who is to be inseminated, is it sold with any implied warranty—perhaps a warranty of fitness for a particular purpose—under the Uniform Commercial Code?

Could the sperm source himself be liable for providing defective sperm? What if the sperm source knew that his semen carried some venereal disease or that he had some unmanifested or secretly manifested genetic defect?

3.   *In Vitro Fertilization, Egg Transfer and Embryo Transfer*

The Process of *In Vitro* Fertilization and Related Techniques

In vitro (literally, "in glass") fertilization is a highly technical medical intervention. Unlike artificial insemination, it cannot be performed with instruments that one finds in a kitchen. In the normal *in vitro* case, an ovum that is ready to be released from the ovary is identified through laparoscopy or ultrasound and removed from the ovary by surgery or aspiration through a hollow needle. The ovum (or ova—there usually is an attempt to get more than one) is placed in a container with the appropriate amount of semen containing fertile sperm. The fertilized ovum is then placed in the woman's uterus, where it is permitted to implant and develop.

In the United States clinics conducting *in vitro* fertilization programs try to remove several eggs so that three or four will be fertilized *in vitro* and can be replaced in the uterus. In many cases there is no fertilization or inadequate fertilization *in vitro,* and, thus, no return to the uterus. If the fertilized ovum is placed in the uterus, there is a relatively high chance of miscarriage; the rate of miscarriage for *in vitro* fertilization pregnancies is about twice the rate of spontaneous miscarriages in other pregnancies. In 1987 success of *in vitro* fertilization ranged from 5% to almost 15% per attempt.

Because the chances of success are substantially increased if several fertilized ova are returned to the uterus, and because of the high cost of repeating the procedure, women undergoing *in vitro* fertilization are generally given drugs to increase the number of ova that become ripe and ready for release and fertilization in one cycle. While this "superovulation" increases the chances of successful fertilization and implantation, inducing ovulation itself may have adverse side effects. In addition, the simultaneous placement of multiple fertilized ova results in a high rate of multiple births—one study found that almost one fourth of successful *in vitro* fertilization pregnancies resulted in multiple births.

The perinatal (i.e., birth) and neonatal (i.e., newborn) mortality rates for *in vitro* fertilization babies are higher than for others and the rate of caesarian section births is much higher for *in vitro* fertilization babies than for babies conceived in other ways.

The medical cost of this process is about $5,000 per ovulation cycle. Given the current success rate, this means an average cost of $40,000 to $50,000 per live birth. While many infertile couples are thus priced out of *in vitro* fertilization, it is the only process available to women whose fallopian tubes cannot accommodate the fertilization process, and tens of thousands of happy and healthy children (and parents) have resulted from this process.

The development and common use of *in vitro* fertilization has given rise to several other related procedures and some variations on the original process. In gamete intra-fallopian transfer (GIFT) the ova are collected just as they would be for *in vitro* fertilization, but both the ova and the semen containing fertile sperm are then injected into the fallopian tubes, where fertilization takes place. Peritoneal oocyte and sperm transfer (POST) involve the same thing, except that the fertilization takes place after the sperm and ova are inserted into the peritoneum.

In addition, it is now possible to freeze ova either before or after fertilization. This permits evaluation of the genetic structure of the ova or embryo before it is thawed and implanted. While the insertion of the fertilized ovum may be the most difficult portion of the procedure from a medical point of view, the removal of the ovum is the most difficult process from the point of view of the woman. Thus, removing extra ova and freezing them, either before or after they are fertilized, may save an additional retrieval process if the first insertion is unsuccessful. While cryopreservation of ova is a new technology, it is quite commonly employed with fertilized ova. About half of frozen embryos are capable of use upon thawing, although the long term medical consequences of freezing embryos remains unknown.

The legal issues that arise out of *in vitro* fertilization multiply when the fertilized ova are placed in a woman other than the one who produced them. In such a case, the pregnant woman is not the genetic mother of the child that she is carrying. Of course, the man expecting to raise the child may not be the genetic father either. Such a case may be a variant on surrogacy, which is discussed below.

Notes and Questions: The Status of the Parents

1. *In vitro* fertilization using the ova of a woman into whom they are replaced and the sperm of that woman's husband should raise no more moral or legal questions, at least as to the status of the parents, than AIH. Is the essential religious argument—that procreation should be a natural process and that the consequences of intervening are too serious and unknown for us to permit it—stronger in the case of the more highly medicalized *in vitro* fertilization than in the case of artificial insemination?

2. Analogously, *in vitro* fertilization using the ova supplied by the woman into whom it is replaced and the sperm of a man not her husband ought to be treated very much like AID, at least as regards the status of the parents. Is there any reason to give the sperm source greater (or lesser) rights as against the mother just because the fertilization process has been *in vitro* rather than *in vivo?*

3. The most difficult questions arise when the ova of one woman are placed in the uterus of another, whatever the source of the sperm. Under such circumstances, who is the mother? Perhaps the simplest case is where the ova of one woman is placed in the uterus of a second after it has been fertilized by the sperm of that second woman's husband, with the expectation of all parties that the pregnant woman and her husband will raise the child. In some respects, this is simply a gender reversed version of AID. Does the Uniform Parentage Act apply in such cases? If it does not, should it be amended so that the legal result of such "ovum transfer-donor" is the same as the result of AID?

Of course, providing an egg is not the same as providing sperm; retrieving the egg is far more invasive than retrieving the sperm. On the other hand, there is no male activity that is analogous, in time commitment, physical commitment, and emotional consequences, to carrying the pregnancy. Should that commitment and the fact that the fetus is nurtured by the pregnant woman's body make the pregnant woman the legal mother, whatever the source of the ovum? While there is a presumption that the woman from whose womb the baby emerges is that baby's mother, that presumption arose before there was any possibility that the source of the ovum and the source of the womb could be different women. In considering this issue, Britain's Warnock Commission concluded:

> Egg donation produces for the first time circumstances in which the genetic mother (the woman who donates the egg), is a different woman from the woman who gives birth to the child, the carrying mother. The law has never, til now, had to face this problem. There are inevitably going to be instances where the stark issue arises of who is the mother. In order to achieve some certainty in this situation it is our view that where a woman donates an egg for transfer to another the donation should be treated as absolute and that, like a male donor, she should have no rights or duties with regard to any resulting child. **We recommend that legislation should provide that when a child is born to a woman following donation of another's egg the woman giving birth should, for all purposes, be regarded in law as the mother of that child and that the egg donor should have no rights or obligations in respect of the child.**

Report to the Committee of Inquiry into "Human Fertilisation and Embryology", (Cmnd 9314) (1984), ¶ 6.8 (emphasis in original). One state in Australia, which has been at the forefront of the medical development of treatment for infertility, does treat the pregnant woman (at least when she is married and acts in accord with the consent of her husband) as the mother, whatever the source of the ovum. Victoria (Australia) Status of Children (Amendment) Act 1984, paragraph 10E. Does this resolution make sense? Are there any circumstances in which you would want to treat the ovum source, rather than the pregnant woman, as the mother? Should a woman with fertile ova but no uterus who wishes to bear a child with her husband (or someone else) be able to enter a binding contract with another woman to have that second woman carry and give birth to her child for her? See the discussion of surrogacy, below.

4. The legal issues raised by embryo transfer are roughly the same as those raised by ovum transfer. The hardest questions do not relate to the status of the parents but, rather, to the status of the embryos themselves. The question of the status of frozen embryos first came to the appellate courts in 1990 in the context of a divorce of a couple undergoing *in vitro* fertilization.

DAVIS v. DAVIS
Court of Appeals of Tennessee, 1990.
59 U.S.L.W. 2205 app. granted, Supreme Court of Tennessee, 1990.

FRANKS, J.

In this divorce action, the sole issue on appeal is essentially who is entitled to control seven of Mary Sue's ova fertilized by Junior's sperm through the *in vitro* fertilization process. The fertilized ova are cryopreserved at the Fertility Center of East Tennessee in Knoxville. The trial judge awarded "custody" of the fertilized ova to Mary Sue and directed that she "be permitted the opportunity to bring these children to term through implantation."

At the outset, it should be emphasized no pregnancy is involved. Both Mary Sue and Junior are now married to other spouses; moreover, neither wants a child with the other as parent.[1]

There are significant scientific distinctions between fertilized ova that have not been implanted and an embryo[2] in the mother's womb. * * * It is important to remember when these ova were fertilized through mechanical manipulation, their development was limited to the 8 cell stage. At this juncture there is no development of the nervous system, the circulatory system, or the pulmonary system and it is thus possible for embryonic development to be indefinitely arrested at this stage by cryopreservation or "freezing".[3]

* * *

The parties, after concluding a normal pregnancy was unlikely, jointly decided to attempt to have a child by in vitro fertilization and, after several attempts, nine of Mary Sue's ova were successfully fertilized in December of 1988. For the first time, their doctors advised that freezing was an option and would enable them to avoid all but the implantation phase of in vitro fertilization if later attempts were undertaken. The couple agreed to attempt implantation of two of the fertilized ova and to preserve the others.[5] There was no discussion between them or their doctors about the consequences of preservation should the Davises divorce while the fertilized ova were stored. Mary Sue testified she had no idea that a divorce might be imminent and she would not have undergone the in vitro fertilization procedure had she contemplated divorce. Junior testified he believed the marriage was foundering but believed that having a child would improve the marriage and did not anticipate a divorce at the time of the in vitro fertilization procedure.[6]

On appeal, Junior asserts the trial court's judgment is not in accord with state and federal law and essentially argues the trial court's grant to Mary Sue of unilateral control over the implantation of the fertilized ova is tantamount to the court's deciding that Junior may be required to become a parent against his will, thus denying to him the right to control reproduction.

1. Mary Sue's appellate brief states:

Since the conclusion of this trial, appellee has moved to Florida where she has remarried, and she now goes by the name of Mary Stowe. She has directed the undersigned to inform this Court that her intention should the Court uphold the lower court's judgment is not to implant the embryos, and she wants authority to donate the embryos so that another childless couple may use them.

2. Webster's Medical Desk Dictionary defines the human embryo as: "The developing human individual from the time of implantation to the end of the eighth week after conception."

3. At the time of trial, there was no data available as to the effects on the fertilized ovum when cryopreserved for more than two years.

5. The implantation proved unsuccessful.

6. The fertility center did not require the Davises to sign any agreement as to the terms of storage or disposition at the time the fertilized ova were cryopreserved.

The United States Supreme Court [has] recognized the right to procreate is one of a citizen's "basic civil rights." Conversely, the court has clearly held that an individual has a right to prevent procreation. "The decision whether to bear or beget a child is a constitutionally protected choice." [ ]

Awarding the fertilized ova to Mary Sue for implantation against Junior's will, in our view, constitutes impermissible state action [7] in violation of Junior's constitutionally protected right not to beget a child where no pregnancy has taken place. We have carefully analyzed Tennessee's legislative Acts and case decisions and conclude there is no compelling state interest to justify our ordering implantation against the will of either party.

The policy of the state on the subject matter before us may be gleaned from the state's treatment of fetuses in the womb. [The court reviewed the Tennessee statutory and case law of wrongful death and abortion.] This statutory scheme indicates that as embryos develop, they are accorded more respect than mere human cells because of their burgeoning potential for life. But, even after viability, they are not given legal status equivalent to that of a person already born. * * *

The trial court in his fact finding and legal conclusions ignored the public policy implicit in the Tennessee statutes, the case holdings of the Tennessee Supreme Court and the teachings of the United States Supreme Court. We are required to resolve the issue consistent with the existing Tennessee law and the parties' constitutional rights. On the facts of this case, it would be repugnant and offensive to constitutional principles to order Mary Sue to implant these fertilized ova against her will. It would be equally repugnant to order Junior to bear the psychological, if not the legal, consequences of paternity against his will.

Jointly, the parties share an interest in the seven fertilized ova. [ ]

Accordingly, the cause is remanded to the trial court to enter a judgment vesting Mary Sue and Junior with joint control of the fertilized ova and with equal voice over their disposition. Cost of the appeal is assessed one-half to each party.

Notes and Questions: The Status of the Embryo

1. The trial court in *Davis* treated the frozen embryos as children and awarded custody to their mother because she was committed to nurturing

7. A haunting reminder of the evils of uncontrolled state action is found in Schuman's contemporary account of the state's control of reproduction in Nazi Germany:

Under the Sterilization Law a series of "Hereditary Health Courts" were established throughout the Reich with appellate courts and a Supreme Hereditary Health Court with power to deliver final judgments. Before these bodies all persons suspected of hereditary disease are obliged to appear and show cause why they should not be rendered sterile through a surgical operation.

Schuman, The Nazi Dictatorship 382, (2nd ed. 1939).

them by assuring their return to someone's uterus. Many argue that this "best interest" standard is appropriate when parents fight over the custody of an embryo, as it is the standard that is applied when parents fight over the custody of a child. Others suggest that the embryos are more like property and should be divided according to the principles that are used in dividing property upon a divorce. This could mean that the embryos would be divided between the two parties, or it could mean that the ovum source would get title to the property because the woman's contribution to the embryo (through surgery or the aspiration of the ova following a course of medication) is so much greater than the man's contribution.

In any case, does it make sense to treat frozen embryos as children *or* property? While they have the potential to be children, they are not. While they may have some of the attributes of property, they seem to be very different from cuisinarts, sofas, and other property often contested in divorce proceedings. Some view the determination of the *Davis* court —that frozen embryos are one stage along the joint project of a man and a woman to create a child—to be the most reasonable solution. Effectively, this conclusion gives both parties veto power over the use of the embryos.

2.   If you conclude that the approach of the *Davis* case is appropriate, is the constitutional path used by the court to reach it correct? Is there a greater constitutional right in the sperm source to avoid being the genetic father of a child than there is in the ovum source to become the genetic mother? Would the constitutional considerations have been different if the ovum source still wanted to carry these embryos herself? Would the result be different if the ovum source were no longer able to produce ova, and, thus, could never have genetically related children unless she had access to the frozen embryos?

3.   What is the warden of the freezer to do with frozen embryos whose contributors cannot agree upon their disposition? If the embryos are people, must there be an attempt to find wombs for all of them? If they are merely property, can they be destroyed (or sold to the highest bidder) when the storage fee remains unpaid? If one of the parties who contributed to the embryos dies, does that party's interest pass to the other? What if both die? That second circumstance arose several years ago in Australia:

> In 1984 in Melbourne, Australia the question arose as to what should be done with two embryos which had been frozen at the request of Mr. and Mrs. Rios following IVF procedures using donor sperm. If the first implantation with Mrs. Rios failed it had been planned to use one of the stored embryos. The Rios were, however, killed in an airplane crash in Chile before this could be done.
>
> The Waller Committee [set up to address the ethical and legal issues of new reproductive technologies] was asked to advise on the disposition of the embryos. Having initially advised that they should be destroyed, the committee subsequently changed its mind and proposed that the embryos be removed from storage and set aside, likening this to "the removal of life support systems from a terminally-ill person. Life is allowed to end."

The Victorian government took a different view, however.   * * *
[T]he Infertility (Medical Procedures) Act 1984 provides that, in a case
such as the Rios['s] where there is no recommendation by the parents
at the time of the storage:

> * * * the Minister shall direct the designated officer of the
> approved hospital where the embryo is stored to insure that the
> embryo is made available for use in a relevant procedure.

What does this tell us about the status of the embryo in law?

I. Kennedy and A. Grubb, Medical Law 660 (1989). If another woman were
to have access to one of the embryos and were to gestate it to birth, would
that embryo be an heir to Mr. and Mrs. Rios, who were exceptionally
wealthy?

4. The new reproductive technologies of *in vitro* fertilization and
ovum and embryo cryopreservation can give rise to a host of different kinds
of liability. Of course, the physician and medical institution could be liable
in an ordinary medical malpractice case for negligently performing the
procedure. Would the duty of due care extend to the fetus as well as the
parents? Would it extend to a fetus not born alive? To an aborted fetus?
Negligently freezing an ovum or embryo, or negligently thawing it and thus
destroying or damaging it, would also subject the appropriate professionals
to malpractice liability.

Presumably, an ovum source would also be liable in contract to the
same extent as would a sperm source. Any warranty that would come with
an ovum would be analogous to that which would come with sperm, and the
nature of any such warranty under the U.C.C. could depend upon whether
the ovum is a good or a service.

4. Surrogacy

The Process of Surrogacy

Surrogacy may be the least technological of reproductive technologies. It is also the oldest; Genesis tells of Abraham's servant Hagar
bearing a child to be raised by the genetic father, Abraham, and his
wife Sarah. Genesis 16:1–16. Surrogacy is that arrangement in which
a woman carries a child to term intending at the initiation of the
pregnancy for another woman to raise the child as the social mother.
As was the case with Hagar, fertilization may take place through
normal coitus. It also may be a consequence of artificial insemination,
in vitro fertilization or embryo transfer. While the genetic father is
often the husband of the woman who expects to raise the child as its
mother, that need not be the case. While the genetic mother is usually
the pregnant woman, that is not required either. It is possible to take
the sperm from one source, the ovum from another and place the
subsequently developed embryo in the uterus of a third person.

Although there is some debate about whether surrogacy is a
"medical treatment" for infertility, it provides the only way for a
woman without a uterus to be the genetic mother of a child (through

embryo transfer), or to be the mother of a child whose genetic father is her husband (through artificial insemination of the surrogate with the husband's sperm). In addition, some women may choose to avoid pregnancy because it poses grave physical or emotional risk to them, or because it would be inconvenient.

It is hard to estimate the cost of the "average" surrogacy arrangement. In some cases the carrying mother is a friend or relative of the woman who expects to raise the child and seeks no compensation for her efforts. Other unrelated women may also be willing to act as surrogates for entirely altruistic reasons. Yet others engage in surrogacy for entirely economic reasons. A couple wishing to contract for a surrogate through a commercial service may pay over $50,000 for the medical and legal fees and the expenses of the surrogate herself.

Commercial surrogacy arrangements have given rise to a great deal of controversy. In some states the process itself has been challenged before any particular case has arisen on the grounds that commercial surrogacy constitutes baby selling *per se*. See *Surrogate Parenting Associates, Inc. v. Commonwealth*, below. When there is no pre-pregnancy challenge to surrogacy itself, a dispute between the parties will require the courts to determine the rights and responsibilities of all of those involved, and the propriety and enforceability of any contractual arrangements of the parties. See *In re Baby M*, below at 979.

SURROGATE PARENTING ASSOCIATES, INC. v. COMMONWEALTH EX REL. ARMSTRONG

Supreme Court of Kentucky, 1986.
704 S.W.2d 209.

Leibson, Justice.

In March 1981, the Attorney General instituted proceedings against Surrogate Parenting Associates, Inc. (SPA), a Kentucky corporation, seeking to revoke SPA's corporate charter on grounds of abuse and misuse of its corporate powers detrimental to the interest and welfare of the state and its citizens. The suit alleges that SPA's surrogate parenting procedure is in violation of the following Kentucky statutes:

KRS 199.590(2), which prohibits sale, purchase or procurement for sale or purchase of "any child for the purpose of adoption."

* * *

SPA operates a medical clinic which assists infertile couples in obtaining a child biologically-related to the husband (the biological father) through artificial insemination of a "surrogate mother." The contract for conception and delivery is between the biological father and the surrogate mother. The arrangement contemplates that after delivery of the child the parental rights of the surrogate mother will be terminated, leaving the biological father with custody. The husband of the surrogate mother, if there is one, also agrees to give up any claim to the child. The paternity of the biological father is confirmed by new methods of genetic testing with almost complete scientific certainty.

The wife of the biological father, if there is one, is not party to these contractual arrangements. Of course, after entry of a judgment terminating the parental rights of the surrogate mother, the wife of the biological father can avail herself of the legal procedure available for adoption by a stepparent. [ ]

Before being artificially inseminated, the prospective surrogate mother agrees with the prospective father that she will voluntarily terminate all parental rights subsequent to the birth, thereby extinguishing any rights she might have to participate in any subsequent adoptive proceeding by the biological father's wife.

The surrogate mother receives a fee from the biological father, part of which is paid before delivery of the child and the remainder of which is paid after entry of a judgment terminating the parental rights of the surrogate mother. In addition, the father assumes responsibility for medical, hospital, travel, laboratory and other necessary expenses of the pregnancy.

Each party must be represented by independent counsel, and the father's counsel is to prepare all agreements and documents in connection with the surrogate parenting process. The biological father pays the attorney's fees.

SPA and its president are paid a fee by the biological father for selection and artificial insemination of the surrogate mother, for obstetrical care and testing during pregnancy, and for actual delivery.

* * *

The question for us to decide is one of statutory interpretation: Has the legislature spoken? The fundamental question is whether SPA's involvement in the surrogate parenting procedure should be construed as participation in the buying and selling of babies as prohibited by KRS 199.590(2). We conclude that it does not, that there are fundamental differences between the surrogate parenting procedure in which SPA participates and the buying and selling of children as prohibited by KRS 199.590(2) which place this surrogate parenting procedure beyond the purview of present legislation.

There is no doubt but that KRS 199.590 is intended to keep baby brokers from overwhelming an expectant mother or the parents of a child with financial inducements to part with the child. But the central fact in the surrogate parenting procedure is that the agreement to bear the child is entered into *before* conception. The essential considerations for the surrogate mother when she agrees to the surrogate parenting procedure are *not* avoiding the consequences of an unwanted pregnancy or fear of the financial burden of child rearing. On the contrary, the essential consideration is to assist a person or couple who desperately want a child but are unable to conceive one in the customary manner to achieve a biologically related offspring. The problem is caused by the wife's infertility. The problem is solved by artificial insemination. The process is not biologically different from the reverse situation where the husband is infertile and the wife conceives by artificial insemination.

No one suggests that where the husband is infertile and conception is induced by artificial insemination of the wife that the participants involved, the biological father, the physicians who care for the mother and deliver the child, or the attorneys who arranged the procedure, have violated the statutes now in place. Although this is tampering with nature in the same manner as the surrogate parenting procedure here involved, we recognize "[t]he decision whether or not to beget or bear a child is at the very heart * * * of constitutionally protected choices." [   ]

* * *

SPA has freely acknowledged that the initial contractual arrangements regarding the mother's surrender of custody and termination of parental rights are voidable. * * * The policy of the voluntary termination statute and the consent to adoption statute is to preserve to the mother her right of choice regardless of decisions made before the birth of the child. This policy is not violated by the existence of the contractual arrangements previously made. The policy of these statutes is carried out because the law gives the mother the opportunity to reconsider her decision to fulfill the role as surrogate mother and refuse to perform the voluntary termination procedure. Should she elect to do so, the situation would be no different than had she never entered into the procedure. She would be in the same position vis-a-vis the child and the biological father as any other mother with a child born out of wedlock. The parental rights and obligations between the biological father and mother, and the obligations they owe to the child, would then be the rights and obligations imposed by pertinent statutes rather than the obligations imposed by the contract now vitiated.

* * *

The courts should not shrink from the benefits to be derived from science in solving these problems simply because they may lead to legal complications. The legal complications are not insolvable. Indeed, we have no reason to believe that the surrogate parenting procedure in which SPA participates will not, in most instances, proceed routinely to the conclusion desired by all of the parties at the outset—a woman who can bear children assisting a childless couple to fulfill their desire for a biologically-related child.

* * *

VANCE, JUSTICE, dissenting.

When the activities of Surrogate Parenting Associates are placed in their best light by the majority, the fact remains that its primary purpose is to locate women who will readily, for a price, allow themselves to be used as human incubators and who are willing to sell, for a price, all of their parental rights in a child thus born.

The parties stipulate that a surrogate mother is paid a fee, part of which is paid to the mother before delivery of the child, and the rest to be paid after she carries the child to term and upon entry of a judgment terminating her parental rights. In other words, a portion of the fee is paid in advance for the use of her body as an incubator, but a portion of the payment is withheld and is not paid until her living child is delivered unto the purchaser, along with the equivalent of a bill of sale, or quit-claim deed, to wit—the judgment terminating her parental rights. How can it be denied that this last portion of the payment is in fact a payment for the baby, because if the baby is not delivered and parental rights not surrendered, the last part of the fee need not be paid.

* * *

It is stipulated that Surrogate Parenting Associates is an intermediary which offers to assist infertile couples in obtaining a child biologically related to the father through the process of artificial insemination of a surrogate mother. I view the subsequent delivery of the child together with an agreed judgment terminating the parental rights of the natural mother in exchange for a monetary consideration to be no less than the sale of a child. It cannot be gainsaid that Surrogate Parenting Associates is an intermediary in this process, and thus it violates the statute. * * *

* * *

WINTERSHEIMER, JUSTICE, dissenting.

* * *

In my view, the people of the Commonwealth of Kentucky have not abdicated their sovereignty to a self-appointed group of scientists-kings. The tolerance of the many can easily lead to the tyranny of a few. The attractiveness of assistance to childless couples should not be a cosmetic facade for unnecessary tampering with human procreation.

Animals are reproduced; human beings are procreated.

The procedure endorsed by the majority is nothing more than a commercial transaction in which a surrogate mother receives money in exchange for terminating her natural and biological rights in the child. This permits the infant to be adopted by the infertile wife and apparent biological father.

The apparent biological father is obviously not adopting his own child but actually purchasing the right to have the child adopted by his own infertile wife. Regardless of the good intentions that may give rise to such a practice, the commercialization of this type of personal problem is exactly what KRS 199.590(2) is intended to prevent.

* * *

IN THE MATTER OF BABY M

Supreme Court of New Jersey, 1988.
109 N.J. 396, 537 A.2d 1227.

WILENTZ, C.J.:

In this matter the Court is asked to determine the validity of a contract that purports to provide a new way of bringing children into a family. For a fee of $10,000, a woman agrees to be artificially inseminated with the semen of another woman's husband; she is to conceive a child, carry it to term, and after its birth surrender it to the natural father and his wife. The intent of the contract is that the child's natural mother will thereafter be forever separated from her child. The wife is to adopt the child, and she and the natural father are to be regarded as its parents for all purposes. The contract providing for this is called a "surrogacy contract," the natural mother inappropriately called the "surrogate mother."

We invalidate the surrogacy contract because it conflicts with the law and public policy of this State. While we recognize the depth of the yearning of infertile couples to have their own children, we find the payment of money to a "surrogate" mother illegal, perhaps criminal, and potentially degrading to women. Although in this case we grant custody to the natural father, the evidence having clearly proved such custody to be in the best interests of the infant, we void both the termination of the surrogate mother's parental rights and the adoption of the child by the wife/stepparent. We thus restore the "surrogate" as the mother of the child. We remand the issue of the natural mother's visitation rights to the trial court, since that issue was not reached below and the record before us is not sufficient to permit us to decide it *de novo*.

We find no offense to our present laws where a woman voluntarily and without payment agrees to act as a "surrogate" mother, provided that she is not subject to a binding agreement to surrender her child. Moreover, our holding today does not preclude the Legislature from altering the current law, however, the surrogacy agreement before us is illegal and invalid.

I.

Facts

In February 1985, William Stern and Mary Beth Whitehead entered into a surrogacy contract. It recited that Stern's wife, Elizabeth, was infertile, that they wanted a child, and that Mrs. Whitehead was willing to provide that child as the mother with Mr. Stern as the father.

[The Court reviewed the facts of the case with excruciating detail, and then reviewed the lower court's holding that the contract was valid, but that placement of the child—called Melissa by the Sterns and Sara by Mary Beth Whitehead—should depend upon the best interest of the child.]

* * *

II.

Invalidity and Unenforceability of Surrogacy Contract

We have concluded that this surrogacy contract is invalid. Our conclusion has two bases: direct conflict with existing statutes and conflict with the public policies of this State, as expressed in its statutory and decisional law.

One of the surrogacy contract's basic purposes, to achieve the adoption of a child through private placement, though permitted in New Jersey "is very much disfavored." [ ] Its use of money for this purpose—and we have no doubt whatsoever that the money is being paid to obtain an adoption and not, as the Sterns argue, for the personal services of Mary Beth Whitehead—is illegal and perhaps criminal. * * * In addition to the inducement of money, there is the coercion of contract: the [natural mother's] irrevocable agreement, prior to birth, even prior to conception, to surrender the child to the adoptive couple. Such an agreement is totally unenforceable in private placement adoption. [ ] Even where the adoption is through an approved agency, the formal agreement to surrender occurs only *after* birth * * *, and then, by regulation, only after the birth mother has been counseled. * * * Integral to these invalid provisions of the surrogacy contract is the related agreement, equally invalid, on the part of the natural mother to cooperate with, and not to contest, proceedings to terminate her parental rights, as well as her contractual concession, in aid of the adoption, that the child's best interests would be served by awarding custody to the natural father and his wife—all of this before she has even conceived, and, in some cases, before she has the slightest idea of what the natural father and adoptive mother are like.

The foregoing provisions not only directly conflict with New Jersey statutes, but also offend long-established State policies. These critical terms, which are at the heart of the contract, are invalid and unenforceable; the conclusion therefore follows, without more, that the entire contract is unenforceable.

A. Conflict with Statutory Provisions

The surrogacy contract conflicts with: (1) laws prohibiting the use of money in connection with adoptions; (2) laws requiring proof of parental unfitness or abandonment before termination of parental rights is ordered or an adoption is granted; and (3) laws that make surrender of custody and consent to adoption revocable in private placement adoptions.

[The court discusses the terms of the New Jersey statutes in each of these areas.]

B. Public Policy Considerations

The surrogacy contract's invalidity, resulting from its direct conflict with the above statutory provisions, is further underlined when its goals and means are measured against New Jersey's public policy. The contract's basic premise, that the natural parents can decide in advance of birth which one is to have custody of the child, bears no relationship to the settled law that the child's best interests shall determine custody.
* * *

The surrogacy contract guarantees permanent separation of the child from one of its natural parents. Our policy, however, has long been that to the extent possible, children should remain with and be brought up by both of their natural parents. * * * This is not simply some theoretical ideal that in practice has no meaning. The impact of failure to follow that policy is nowhere better shown than in the results of this surrogacy contract. A child, instead of starting off its life with as much peace and security as possible, finds itself immediately in a tug-of-war between contending mother and father.[9]

The surrogacy contract violates the policy of this State that the rights of natural parents are equal concerning their child, the father's right no greater than the mother's. * * * The whole purpose and effect of the surrogacy contract was to give the father the exclusive right to the child by destroying the rights of the mother.

* * *

Under the contract, the natural mother is irrevocably committed before she knows the strength of her bond with her child. She never makes a totally voluntary, informed decision, for quite clearly any decision prior to the baby's birth is, in the most important sense, uninformed, and any decision after that, compelled by a pre-existing contractual commitment, the threat of a lawsuit, and the inducement of a $10,000 payment is less than totally voluntary. Her interests are of little concern to those who controlled this transaction.

Although the interest of the natural father and adoptive mother is certainly the predominant interest, realistically the *only* interest served, even they are left with less than what public policy requires. They know little about the natural mother, her genetic makeup, and her psychological and medical history. Moreover, not even a superficial attempt is made to determine their awareness of their responsibilities as parents.

Worst of all, however, is the contract's total disregard of the best interests of the child. There is not the slightest suggestion that any

---

9. And the impact on the natural parents, Mr. Stern and Mrs. Whitehead, is severe and dramatic. The depth of their conflict about Baby M, about custody, visitation, about the goodness or badness of each of them, comes through in their telephone conversations, in which each tried to persuade the other to give up the child. The potential adverse consequences of surrogacy are poignantly captured here—Mrs. Whitehead threatening to kill herself and the baby, Mr. Stern begging her not to, each blaming the other. The dashed hopes of the Sterns, the agony of Mrs. Whitehead, their suffering, their hatred—all were caused by the unraveling of this arrangement.

inquiry will be made at any time to determine the fitness of the Sterns as custodial parents, or Mrs. Stern as an adoptive parent, their superiority to Mrs. Whitehead, or the effect on the child of not living with her natural mother.

This is the sale of a child, or, at the very least, the sale of a mother's right to her child, the only mitigating factor being that one of the purchasers is the father. Almost every evil that prompted the prohibition of the payment of money in connection with adoptions exists here.

The differences between an adoption and a surrogacy contract should be noted, since it is asserted that the use of money in connection with surrogacy does not pose the risks found where money buys an adoption. * * *

First, and perhaps most important, all parties concede that it is unlikely that surrogacy will survive without money. * * *

Second, the use of money in adoptions does not *produce* the problem—conception occurs, and usually the birth itself, before illicit funds are offered. With surrogacy, the "problem," if one views it as such, consisting of the purchase of a woman's procreative capacity, at the risk of her life, is caused by and originates with the offer of money.

Third, with the law prohibiting the use of money in connection with adoptions, the built-in financial pressure of the unwanted pregnancy and the consequent support obligation do not lead the mother to the highest paying, ill-suited, adoptive parents. * * * In surrogacy, the highest bidders will presumably become the adoptive parents regardless of suitability, so long as payment of money is permitted.

Fourth, the mother's consent to surrender her child in adoptions is revocable, even after surrender of the child * * *. In surrogacy, consent occurs so early that no amount of advice would satisfy the potential mother's need, yet the consent is irrevocable.

The main difference, that the plight of the unwanted pregnancy is unintended while the situation of the surrogate mother is voluntary and intended, is really not significant. Initially, it produces stronger reactions of sympathy for the mother whose pregnancy was unwanted than for the surrogate mother, who "went into this with her eyes wide open." On reflection, however, it appears that the essential evil is the same, taking advantage of a woman's circumstances (the unwanted pregnancy or the need for money) in order to take away her child, the difference being one of degree.

In the scheme contemplated by the surrogacy contract in this case, a middleman, propelled by profit, promotes the sale. Whatever idealism may have motivated any of the participants, the profit motive predominates, permeates, and ultimately governs the transaction. The demand for children is great and the supply small. The availability of contraception, abortion, and the greater willingness of single mothers to bring up their children has led to a shortage of babies offered for adoption. [ ] The situation is ripe for the entry of the middleman who will bring some equilibrium into the market by increasing the supply through the use of money.

Intimated, but disputed, is the assertion that surrogacy will be used for the benefit of the rich at the expense of the poor. [ ] In response it is noted that the Sterns are not rich and the Whiteheads not poor. Nevertheless, it is clear to us that it is unlikely that surrogate mothers will be as proportionately numerous among those women in the top twenty percent income bracket as among these in the bottom twenty percent. [ ] Put differently, we doubt that infertile couples in the low-income bracket will find upper income surrogates.

* * *

The point is made that Mrs. Whitehead *agreed* to the surrogacy arrangement, supposedly fully understanding the consequences. Putting aside the issue of how compelling her need for money may have been, and how significant her understanding of the consequences, we suggest that her consent is irrelevant. There are, in a civilized society, some things that money cannot buy. In America, we decided long ago that merely because conduct purchased by money was "voluntary" did not mean that it was good or beyond regulation and prohibition. * * * There are, in short, values that society deems more important than granting to wealth whatever it can buy, be it labor, love, or life. Whether this principle recommends prohibition of surrogacy, which presumably sometimes results in great satisfaction to all of the parties, is not for us to say. We note here only that, under existing law, the fact that Mrs. Whitehead "agreed" to the arrangement is not dispositive.

The long-term effects of surrogacy contracts are not known, but feared—the impact on the child who learns her life was bought, that she is the offspring of someone who gave birth to her only to obtain money; the impact on the natural mother as the full weight of her isolation is felt along with the full reality of the sale of her body and her child; the impact on the natural father and the adoptive mother once they realize the consequences of their conduct. Literature in related areas suggests these are substantial considerations, although, given the newness of surrogacy, there is little information. [ ]

* * *

In sum, the harmful consequences of this surrogacy arrangement appear to us all too palpable. In New Jersey the surrogate mother's agreement to sell her child is void. Its irrevocability infects the entire contract, as does the money that purports to buy it.

III.

Termination

We have already noted that under our laws termination of parental rights cannot be based on contract, but may be granted only on proof of the statutory requirements. * * *

* * *

There is simply no [statutory] basis * * * to warrant termination of Mrs. Whitehead's parental rights. We therefore conclude that the natural mother is entitled to retain her rights as a mother.

IV.

Constitutional Issues

Both parties argue that the Constitutions—state and federal—mandate approval of their basic claims. The source of their constitutional arguments is essentially the same: the right of privacy, the right to procreate, the right to the companionship of one's child, those rights flowing either directly from the fourteenth amendment or by its incorporation of the Bill of Rights, or from the ninth amendment, or through the penumbra surrounding all of the Bill of Rights. They are the rights of personal intimacy, of marriage, of sex, or family, or procreation. Whatever their source, it is clear that they are fundamental rights protected by both the federal and state Constitutions. * * * The right asserted by the Sterns is the right of procreation; that asserted by Mary Beth Whitehead is the right to the companionship of her child. We find that the right of procreation does not extend as far as claimed by the Sterns. As for the right asserted by Mrs. Whitehead,[12] since we uphold it on other grounds (*i.e.*, we have restored her as mother and recognized her right, limited by the child's best interests, to her companionship), we need not decide that constitutional issue, and for reasons set forth below we should not.

* * * The right to procreate very simply is the right to have natural children, whether through sexual intercourse or artificial insemination. It is no more than that. Mr. Stern has not been deprived of that right. Through artificial insemination of Mrs. Whitehead, Baby M is his child. The custody, care, companionship, and nurturing that follow birth are not parts of the right to procreation; they are rights that may also be constitutionally protected, but that involve many considerations other than the right of procreation. To assert that Mr. Stern's right of procreation gives him the right to custody of Baby M would be to assert that Mrs. Whitehead's right of procreation does *not* give her the right to the custody of Baby M; it would be to assert that the constitutional right of procreation includes within it a constitutionally protected contractual right to destroy someone else's right of procreation.

We conclude that the right of procreation is best understood and protected if confined to its essentials, and that when dealing with rights concerning the resulting child, different interests come into play. There is nothing in our culture or society that even begins to suggest a fundamental right on the part of the father to the custody of the child

---

12. Opponents of surrogacy have also put forth arguments based on the thirteenth amendment, as well as the Peonage Act, 42 U.S.C. Section 1993 (1982). We need not address these arguments because we have already held the contract unenforceable on the basis of state law.

as part of his right to procreate when opposed by the claim of the mother to the same child.   * * *

Mr. Stern also contends that he has been denied equal protection of the laws by the State's statute [analogous to the Uniform Parentage Act] granting full parental rights to a husband in relation to the child produced, with his consent, by the union of his wife with a sperm donor * * *. The claim really is that of Mrs. Stern. It is that she is in precisely the same position as the husband in the statute: she is presumably infertile, as is the husband in the statute; her spouse by agreement with a third party procreates with the understanding that the child will be the couple's child. The alleged unequal protection is that the understanding is honored in the statute when the husband is the infertile party, but no similar understanding is honored when it is the wife who is infertile.

It is quite obvious that the situations are not parallel. A sperm donor simply cannot be equated with a surrogate mother. The State has more than a sufficient basis to distinguish the two situations—even if the only difference is between the time it takes to provide sperm for artificial insemination and the time invested in a nine-month pregnancy—so as to justify automatically divesting the sperm donor of his parental rights without automatically divesting a surrogate mother. Some basis for an equal protection argument might exist if Mary Beth Whitehead had contributed her egg to be implanted, fertilized or otherwise, in Mrs. Stern, resulting in the latter's pregnancy. That is not the case here, however.

Mrs. Whitehead, on the other hand, asserts a claim that falls within the scope of a recognized fundamental interest protected by the Constitution. As a mother, she claims the right to the companionship of her child. This is a fundamental interest, constitutionally protected. Furthermore, it was taken away from her by the action of the court below. Whether that action under these circumstances would constitute deprivation, however, we need not and do not decide. By virtue of our decision Mrs. Whitehead's constitutional complaint—that her parental rights have been unconstitutionally terminated—is moot. We have decided that both the statutes and public policy of this state require that termination be voided and that her parental rights be restored. It therefore becomes unnecessary to decide whether that same result would be required by virtue of the federal or state Constitutions.   * * *

V.

Custody

* * * With the surrogacy contract disposed of, the legal framework becomes a dispute between two couples over the custody of a child produced by the artificial insemination of one couple's wife by the other couple's husband. Under the Parentage Act the claims of the natural father and the natural mother are entitled to equal weight, *i.e.*, one is not preferred over the other solely because it is the father or the

mother.   * * * The applicable rule given these circumstances is clear: the child's best interests determine custody.

* * *

The circumstances of this custody dispute are unusual and they have provoked some unusual contentions. The Whiteheads claim that even if the child's best interests would be served by our awarding custody to the Sterns, we should not do so, since that will encourage surrogacy contracts—contracts claimed by the Whiteheads, and we agree, to be violative of important legislatively-stated public policies. Their position is that in order that surrogacy contract be deterred, custody should remain in the surrogate mother unless she is unfit, regardless of the best interests of the child. We disagree. Our declaration that this surrogacy contract is unenforceable and illegal is sufficient to deter similar agreements. We need not sacrifice the child's interests in order to make that point sharper.   * * *

* * *

There were eleven experts who testified concerning the child's best interests, either directly or in connection with pattern related to that issue. Our reading of the record persuades us that the trial court's decision awarding custody to the Sterns (technically to Mr. Stern) should be affirmed since "its findings * * * could reasonably have been reached on sufficient credible evidence present in the record."   * * *

Our custody conclusion is based on strongly persuasive testimony contrasting both the family life of the Whiteheads and the Sterns and the personalities and characters of the individuals.   * * * [The Court addressed the instability of the Whitehead household, Mrs. Whitehead's controlling nature, and the Sterns' "loving, giving, nurturing" nature.]

* * *

Based on all of this we have concluded, independent of the trial court's identical conclusion, that Melissa's best interests call for custody in the Sterns. Our * * * disagreements with the trial court do not, as we have noted, in any way diminish our concurrence with its conclusions. We feel, however, that those disagreements are important enough to be stated. They are disagreements about the evaluation of conduct. They also may provide some insight about the potential consequences of surrogacy.

It seems to us that given her predicament, Mrs. Whitehead was rather harshly judged—both by the trial court and by some of the experts. She was guilty of a breach of contract, and indeed, she did break a very important promise, but we think it is expecting something well beyond normal human capabilities to suggest that this mother should have parted with her newly born infant without a struggle. Other than survival, what stronger force is there? We do not know of, and cannot conceive of, any other case where a perfectly fit mother was expected to surrender her newly born infant, perhaps forever, and was then told she was a bad mother because she did not. We know of no authority suggesting that the moral quality of her act in those circumstances should be judged by referring to a contract, made before she became pregnant. We do not countenance, and would never countenance, violating a court order as Mrs. Whitehead did, even a court order that is wrong; but her resistance to an order that she surrender her infant, possibly forever, merits a measure of understanding. We do not find it so clear that her efforts to keep her infant, when measured against the Sterns' efforts to take her away, make one, rather than the other, the wrongdoer. The Sterns suffered, but so did she. And if we go beyond suffering to an evaluation of the human stakes involved in the struggle, how much weight should be given to her nine months of pregnancy, the labor of childbirth, the risk to her life, compared to the payment of money, the anticipation of a child and the donation of sperm?

* * *

VI.

Visitation

The trial court's decision to terminate Mrs. Whitehead's parental rights precluded it from making any determination in visitation. [ ] Our reversal of the trial court's order, however, requires delineation of Mrs. Whitehead's rights to visitation. It is apparent to us that this factually sensitive issue, which was never addressed below, should not be determined *de novo* by this Court. * * *

* * *

We also note the following for the trial court's consideration: First, this is not a divorce case where visitation is almost invariably granted to the non-custodial spouse. To some extent the facts here resemble cases where the non-custodial spouse has had practically no relationship with the child * * *; but it only "resembles" those cases. In the instant case, Mrs. Whitehead spent the first four months of this child's life as her mother and has regularly visited the child since then. Second, she is not only the natural mother, but also the legal mother, and is not to be penalized one iota because of the surrogacy contract. Mrs. Whitehead, as the mother (indeed, as a mother who nurtured her child for its first four months—unquestionably a relevant consideration), is entitled to have her own interest in visitation considered. Visitation cannot be determined without considering the parents' interests along with those of the child.

In all of this, the trial court should recall the touchstones of visitation: that it is desirable for the child to have contact with both parents; that besides the child's interests, the parents' interests also must be considered; but that when all is said and done, the best interest of the child is paramount.

We have decided that Mrs. Whitehead is entitled to visitation at some point, and that question is not open to the trial court on this remand. The trial court will determine what kind of visitation shall be granted to her, with or without conditions, and when and under what circumstances it should commence.   * * *

* * *

Conclusion

This case affords some insight into a new reproductive arrangement: the artificial insemination of a surrogate mother. The unfortunate events that have unfolded illustrate that its unregulated use can bring suffering to all involved. Potential victims include the surrogate mother and her family, the natural father and his wife, and most importantly, the child. Although surrogacy has apparently provided positive results for some infertile couples, it can also, as this case demonstrates, cause suffering to participants, here essentially innocent and well-intended.

We have found that our present laws do not permit the surrogacy contract used in this case. Nowhere, however, do we find any legal prohibition against surrogacy when the surrogate mother volunteers, without any payment, to act as a surrogate and is given the right to change her mind and to assert her parental rights. Moreover, the Legislature remains free to deal with this most sensitive issue as it sees fit, subject only to constitutional constraints.

* * *

Notes and Questions

1. Upon remand, the superior court determined that Mary Beth Whitehead Gould should have "unsupervised uninterrupted liberal visitation" with Baby M. Under the court's schedule, the visitations would be increased until they included a two-day (and one overnight) visit every other week, and an annual two-week visit. See 14 Fam.L.Rep. 1276 (1988).

2. Most of the arguments against surrogacy are outlined in the dissents in *Surrogate Parenting Associates* and the opinion of the court in *Baby M.* Generally, these objections fall into three categories—those related to the contracting parties; those related to the child; and those related to the effect of the process on society as a whole.

The first argument generally advanced against surrogacy is that it exploits women who are willing to give or rent their bodies as vessels to carry other people's children. Could the inducement of payment for pregnancy cause a woman to consent to something that otherwise would be an unthinkable intrusion upon her body? Will the development of commercial surrogacy lead to a class of poor women who will become child bearers for wealthy women who do not want to spend the time or energy on pregnancy? Is it likely that the fact that there is a relationship between ethnicity and the distribution of wealth in this society mean that we will develop separate childbearing races and child-raising races?

Feminists are divided on this issue. Some are deeply offended by the overt use of the woman's body that is the whole goal of a surrogacy arrangement; others believe it is merely misguided paternalism that leads courts (and others) to conclude that women are incapable of deciding for themselves whether they should enter surrogacy contracts. Some economists argue that making surrogacy contracts unenforceable will merely lower the amount that is paid to surrogates. Thus, they suggest, making surrogacy contracts unenforceable is just another in a long history of allegedly protectionist regulations that restrict what a woman may choose to do with her body.

Some argue that surrogacy contracts ought to be prohibited or discouraged because they advance only the best interests of the contracting parties, not the best interest of the child. Normally in a custody dispute between those with claims as parents, the court will look to the best interest of the child in determining the appropriate placement. Enforcing a surrogacy contract is necessarily inconsistent with this principle. In addition, some believe that children who find out that they were carried by a surrogate will be injured by that discovery, and others argue that surrogacy contracts render children instruments for the use of parents, not ends in themselves, and that this is necessarily harmful for children.

Finally, some believe that the fabric of society as a whole is weakened by surrogacy arrangements, at least commercial ones. As Justice Wilentz points out in *Baby M*, there are some things that money cannot buy. How, exactly, does he define this class of things? Why does he conclude that surrogacy is one of them?

Perhaps a surrogacy contract, which is a contract to put one's body to work for the benefit of another, is nothing more than a form of slavery. Since the Thirteenth Amendment we have prohibited contracts for slavery, even if the contracting parties are all competent adults who are acting voluntarily. One argument for the Thirteenth Amendment is that in addition to whatever it offers those who might be or become slaves, society as a whole is better off if the status of "slave" is impossible for everyone. Are all people in this society—including those who would never participate in a surrogacy contract in any way—better off if the society simply eliminates surrogacy?

3. Both *Surrogate Parenting Associates* and *Baby M* investigate the commercial nature of the surrogacy arrangement. Would the result in *Baby M* be the same, and its consequences the same, if the arrangement were not one that involved the exchange of money? Which ethical and legal arguments depend upon the commercial nature of the arrangement, and which remain just as strong whether or not any money changes hands?

4. In addressing one constitutional issue, Judge Wilentz announces that the "right to procreate very simply is the right to have natural children, whether through sexual intercourse or artificial insemination. It is no more than that." Why does he limit the right in this way? Why does he include artificial insemination, but not *in vitro* fertilization (even between husband and wife) among those actions protected by the constitutional "right to procreate"? How far do you think the "right to procreate" should go? Should it include *in vitro* fertilization? Egg transfer? Embryo transfer? Surrogacy? In which of these circumstances might one person's "right to procreate" conflict with another's?

5. Surrogacy contracts are often condemned on the ground that they constitute baby selling, which is illegal in every state. There is confusion over the purpose of statutes that prohibit baby selling, though: they may be intended to protect parents from financial inducements to give up their children, or they may be intended to protect children from being reduced to the status of an ordinary commodity. Are baby selling statutes merely anachronisms left over from the 19th century practice of selling children into effective slavery? Should baby selling be prohibited? Why? Should surrogacy arrangements be governed by baby selling statutes?

6. There is no doubt that the remedy of specific performance is not available to those who offer some consideration in return for the surrogate's labor. For this reason, surrogacy contracts drafted by careful lawyers do not provide for any substantial payment to the surrogate until the baby is delivered to the commissioning party and the surrogate mother (and her husband, if necessary) relinquish their parental rights. There remains the risk that the surrogate mother will not relinquish her parental rights, and that it will be impossible to have a court order termination of those rights. Indeed, this was the case in *Baby M.* In such a case a sperm source who has commissioned the surrogate may find himself liable for child support (and eligible for visitation rights) for a child who bears no legal or physical relationship to his own wife. After *Baby M,* is there any way to draft a contract to avoid these consequences? *Should* there be a way to do so? The *Baby M* court appended to their opinion a copy of the surrogacy contract and the contract between Mr. Stern and the surrogacy agency. To see exactly what the court determined to be unenforceable, see 537 A.2d 1265–1273. Another interesting surrogate mother contract, including comments on each paragraph, is found in Brophy, A Surrogate Mother Contract to Bear a Child, 20 J.Fam.L. 263, 266–288 (1982).

7. One argument against the use of surrogacy arrangements is the legal uncertainty they cause. Is this a good argument when those uncertainties could be resolved by judicial or legislative action? While many have called for legislative action to prohibit surrogacy arrangements, others have called for legislative action to regulate such arrangements so that the legal uncertainties can be avoided. There is a plethora of model acts designed to define, refine, limit or prohibit surrogacy. See, for example, Model Human Reproductive Technologies and Surrogacy Act, 72 Iowa L.Rev. 943 (1987); Family Law Section Adoption Committee and Ad Hoc Surrogacy Committee, Draft ABA Model Surrogacy Act, 22 Fam.L.Q. 123 (1988).

In its mid-year meeting in 1989, the American Bar Association House of Delegates approved a model act that provides some guidelines for surrogacy contracts. This ABA model act provides two alternative avenues for interested state legislators. One version of the act declares that surrogacy contracts are void on public policy grounds; the other accepts such contracts and defines the legal positions of all the legal parties. The ABA "alternative" act was originally drafted by the National Conference of Commissioners on Uniform State Laws as the Uniform Status of Children of Assisted Conception Act and was adopted in preference to the one sponsored by the ABA Family Law Section. For the text of the act, see 15 Fam.L.Rep. 2009 (1989).

Several state legislatures have taken up the invitation to legislate in this area. While Nevada has explicitly removed surrogacy from the acts prohibited by its baby selling statute, 1987 Nev.Rev.Stat. 773, other states have outlawed surrogacy contracts. See, e.g., 1987 LSA–R.S. § 9:2713 (West Supp.1989); West's Ann.Ind.Code §§ 31–8–1–1 to 31–8–1–5 (West 1988); Ky.Rev.Stat. 199.590(3) (Baldwin 1988); Neb.Rev.Stat. § 25–21,200 (Supp.1988). See also Mich.Comp.Laws Ann. § 722.859 (West 1988) (making entering a surrogacy contract a felony).

8. The complexities that may surround surrogacy arrangements is illustrated by the facts of Johnson v. Calvert, Orange County 633190 (Cal.Super.Ct.1990). Mark and Crispina Calvert, who are married to each other, are the source of both the sperm and the ovum that together made the embryo that was placed in Anna Johnson's uterus. Mrs. Calvert could not carry the fetus herself because she had undergone a hysterectomy and had no uterus. As the time for the birth of the child drew near, Ms. Johnson claimed that she was the mother of the child and she wanted to be treated as such by the law. She thus became the first surrogate to seek custody of a child not genetically related to her. The ovum source, Mrs. Calvert, also claimed to be the mother. In the course of this dispute, Johnson argued that the Calverts failed to treat her properly and pay her adequately. The Calverts argued that Johnson, who admitted to welfare fraud during the course of the pregnancy, was merely trying to extort additional money from them. To add complexity to the case, Johnson, who is African–American, also raised a claim that she had some Indian blood (which was, of course, coursing through the fetus) and, thus, the disposition of the child should be subject to the Indian Child Welfare Act. The Orange County court appointed both an "independent guardian" and a guardian ad litem for the fetus. Shortly after the birth of the child the court awarded custody to the Calverts and declared that Ms. Johnson had no rights cognizable in family law to maintain a relationship with a genetically unrelated child.

Note: Facilitating Reproduction and the Singles Scene

The technology for facilitating reproduction is not only of interest to married couples. Single men and women, and single sex couples, have a special need for this technology. Outside of adoption, the use of a surrogate mother is the only way that a single man could expect to have a child to whom he would be genetically related. Similarly, the use of artificial insemination may be an especially attractive way for a single woman, or a lesbian couple, to have a child. While the law has put no formal restriction on the availability of reproductive techniques, some physicians and hospitals are reluctant to provide the full range of infertility services to single people or non-traditional families. Local and state statutes restricting discrimination on the basis of sexual preference may provide avenues of relief for those homosexual potential parents who are denied reproductive services. *Eisenstadt v. Baird,* which threw out a statute forbidding single people access to contraceptives under some circumstances in which they were available to married people, might suggest that the equal protection clause of the Fourteenth Amendment would also protect single people who are denied access to infertility treatment provided to married people by state hospitals and other state facilities. On the other hand, the Supreme Court's opinion in Bowers v. Hardwick, 478 U.S. 186, 106 S.Ct. 2841, 92 L.Ed.2d 140 (1986), which upheld the Georgia sodomy law, undermined the equal protection argument, at least for homosexuals. Justice White, for the Court, specifically reserved ruling on whether such sodomy statutes might be enforceable against married couples. There is a strong suggestion, if not a holding, that the law may treat the sexual (and presumably, procreative) relationship of homosexuals differently than it treats such relationships between married couples. Whether unmarried heterosexual couples may be treated differently remains uncertain:

> We first register our disagreement with the Court of Appeals and with respondent that the Court's prior cases have construed the Constitution to confer a right of privacy that extends to homosexual sodomy and for all intents and purposes have decided this case. The reach of this line of cases was sketched in Carey v. Population Services International, [ ] and deals with child rearing and education; with family relationships; with procreation; with marriage; with contraception; and with abortion. The latter three [issues were discussed in] cases [which] were interpreted as construing the Due Process Clause of the Fourteenth Amendment to confer a fundamental individual right to decide whether or not to beget or bear a child. [ ]

> Accepting the decisions in these cases and the above description of them, we think it evident that none of the rights announced in these cases bears any resemblance to the claimed constitutional right of homosexuals to engage in acts of sodomy that is asserted in this case. No connection between family, marriage, or procreation on the one hand and homosexual activity on the other has been demonstrated either by the Court of Appeals or by respondent. Moreover, any claim that these cases nevertheless stand for the proposition that any kind of private sexual conduct between consenting adults is constitutionally insulated from state proscription is unsupportable. * * * [T]he Due Process Clause did not reach so far.

Bowers v. Hardwick, 478 U.S. at 189–92, 106 S.Ct. at 2843–44.

Bibliographical Note: Facilitating Reproduction

For an excellent account of the medical technology that has been developed to facilitate reproduction and its legal and ethical consequences, see L. Andrews, Between Strangers (1989). Some well considered solutions to the problems raised by nontraditional reproduction are found in Robertson, Embryos, Families and Procreative Liberty: The Legal Structure of the New Reproduction, 59 S.Cal.L.Rev. 939 (1986) and Hollinger, From Coitus to Commerce: Legal and Social Consequences of Noncoital Reproduction, 18 U.Mich.J.L.Ref. 865 (1985). An excellent bibliography on artificial insemination is found in Patt, A Pathfinder on Artificial Insemination, 8 L.Ref.Servs.Q. 117 (1988). For a thoughtful and thorough account of the status of the embryo between fertilization and implantation, see Robertson, In the Beginning: The Legal Status of Early Embryos, 76 Va.L.Rev. 437 (1990) and Martin and Lagod, The Human Embryo, The

Progenitors and the State: Toward a Dynamic Theory of Status, Rights, and Research Policy, 5 High Tech.L.J. 257 (1990).

For an interesting debate on the propriety of the development of a commercial market for babies, see Landes and Posner, The Economics of The Baby Shortage, 7 J.Leg.Stud. 323 (1978) and Prichard, A Market for Babies?, 34 Toronto L.J. 341 (1984). See also Eisenman, Fathers, Biological and Anonymous, and Other Legal Strangers, 45 Ohio St.L.J. 383 (1984), and Rushevsky, Legal Recognition of Surrogate Gestation, 7 Women's Rts.L. Rep. 107 (1982). For a good feminist account of many of these issues, see G. Corea, The Mother Machine (1986). The summer 1988 issue of the Family Law Quarterly is a special issue on surrogacy. It includes Sedillo Lopez, Privacy and the Regulation of the New Reproductive Technologies: A Decision Making Approach, 22 Fam.L.Q. 173 (1988) and Garrison, Surrogate Parenting: What Should Legislatures Do?, 22 Fam.L.Q. 149 (1988). Both are very thoughtful new approaches to the problem. That issue also includes a fine comprehensive bibliography of the subject, Peritore, A Select Bibliography on Surrogacy, 22 Fam.L.Q. 213 (1988).

For a good medical account of the processes available to facilitate reproduction, as well as a medical perspective on their social and legal consequences, see C.R. Austin, Human Embryos: The Debate on Assisted Reproduction (1989). See also Office of Technology Assessment, Infertility: Medical and Social Choices (1988). Cascades of writing on reproductive technology continue to come, and much more, no doubt, is still gestating.

III. FETAL MATERNAL CONFLICT

Problem: Children Bearing Children

Elsie McIntosh is a fifteen year-old high school dropout in the fourth month of her first pregnancy. She lives at home with her mother, whose primary source of income is Aid to Families with Dependent Children (i.e., state welfare) and food stamps. Elsie and her mother, who has been a desperate alcoholic for the past eight years, have spoken barely ten words in the past year. They live more like roommates than a mother-daughter family, and Elsie lives on her share of her mother's state aid, supplemented by a modest income from her own prostitution. Her prostitution has led to her arrest twice, and each of the arrests resulted in a night in juvenile detention, a morning in court, and a deferred finding of delinquency that was subsequently dismissed.

Elsie has been a heavy drinker and a heavy user of cocaine for the past three or four years, and her drinking and cocaine use have continued during her pregnancy. Knowing all of this, what should her state-assigned welfare worker do? If she were being seen by an obstetrician who knew all of this about Elsie, what should the obstetrician do? If this information about a patient came to the attention of a medical clinic legal counsel, what should that legal counsel do? If this information were to come to the attention of the district attorney, what should the district attorney do?

A. MEDICAL AND LIFESTYLE CHOICES

In re A.C.

District of Columbia Court of Appeals, 1990.
573 A.2d 1235.

TERRY, ASSOCIATE JUDGE:

* * *

We are confronted here with two profoundly difficult and complex issues. First, we must determine who has the right to decide the course of medical treatment for a patient who, although near death, is pregnant with a viable fetus. Second, we must establish how that decision should be made if the patient cannot make it for herself—more specifically, how a court should proceed when faced with a pregnant patient, *in extremis,* who is apparently incapable of making an informed decision regarding medical care for herself and her fetus. We hold that in virtually all cases the question of what is to be done is to be decided by the patient—the pregnant woman—on behalf of herself and the fetus. If the patient is incompetent or otherwise unable to give an informed consent to a proposed course of medical treatment, then her decision must be ascertained through the procedure known as substituted judgment. * * *

I

This case came before the trial court when George Washington University Hospital petitioned the emergency judge in chambers for declaratory relief as to how it should treat its patient, A.C., who was close to death from cancer and was twenty-six and one-half weeks pregnant with a viable fetus. After a hearing lasting approximately three hours, which was held at the hospital (though not in A.C.'s room), the court ordered that a caesarean section be performed on A.C. to deliver the fetus. * * * The caesarean was performed, and a baby girl, L.M.C., was delivered. Tragically, the child died within two and one-half hours, and the mother died two days later.

* * *

II

A.C. was first diagnosed as suffering from cancer at the age of thirteen. In the ensuing years she underwent major surgery several times, together with multiple radiation treatments and chemotherapy. A.C. married when she was twenty-seven, during a period of remission, and soon thereafter she became pregnant. She was excited about her pregnancy and very much wanted the child. Because of her medical history, she was referred in her fifteenth week of pregnancy to the high-risk pregnancy clinic at George Washington University Hospital.

On Tuesday, June 9, 1987, when A.C. was approximately twenty-five weeks pregnant, she went to the hospital for a scheduled check-up.

Because she was experiencing pain in her back and shortness of breath, an x-ray was taken, revealing an apparently inoperable tumor which nearly filled her right lung. On Thursday, June 11, A.C. was admitted to the hospital as a patient. By Friday her condition had temporarily improved, and when asked if she really wanted to have her baby, she replied that she did.

Over the weekend, A.C.'s condition worsened considerably. Accordingly, on Monday, June 15, members of the medical staff treating A.C. assembled, along with her family, in A.C.'s room. The doctors then informed her that her illness was terminal, and A.C. agreed to palliative treatment designed to extend her life until at least her twenty-eighth week of pregnancy. The "potential outcome [for] the fetus," according to the doctors, would be much better at twenty-eight weeks than at twenty-six weeks if it were necessary to "intervene." A.C. knew that the palliative treatment she had chosen presented some increased risk to the fetus, but she opted for this course both to prolong her life for at least another two weeks and to maintain her own comfort. When asked if she still wanted to have the baby, A.C. was somewhat equivocal, saying "something to the effect of 'I don't know, I think so.' " As the day moved toward evening, A.C.'s condition grew still worse, and at about 7:00 or 8:00 p.m. she consented to intubation to facilitate her breathing.

The next morning, June 16, the trial court convened a hearing at the hospital in response to the hospital's request for a declaratory judgment. The court appointed counsel for both A.C. and the fetus, and the District of Columbia was permitted to intervene for the fetus as *parens patriae*. * * *

* * *

There was no evidence before the court showing that A.C. consented to, or even contemplated, a caesarean section before her twenty-eighth week of pregnancy. There was, in fact, considerable dispute as to whether she would have consented to an immediate caesarean delivery at the time the hearing was held. A.C.'s mother opposed surgical intervention, testifying that A.C. wanted "to live long enough to hold that baby" and that she expected to do so, "even though she knew she was terminal." Dr. Hamner [a treating obstetrician] testified that, given A.C.'s medical problems, he did not think she would have chosen to deliver a child with a substantial degree of impairment. * * *

After hearing this testimony and the arguments of counsel, the trial court made oral findings of fact. It found, first, that A.C. would probably die, according to uncontroverted medical testimony, "within the next twenty-four to forty-eight hours"; second, that A.C. was "pregnant with a twenty-six and a half week viable fetus who, based upon uncontroverted medical testimony, has approximately a fifty to sixty percent chance to survive if a caesarean section is performed as soon as possible"; third, that because the fetus was viable, "the state has [an] important and legitimate interest in protecting the potentiality of human life"; and fourth, that there had been some testimony that the operation "may very well hasten the death of [A.C.]," but that there had also been testimony that delay would greatly increase the risk to the fetus and that "the prognosis is not great for the fetus to be delivered post-mortem * * *." Most significantly, the court found:

> The court is of the view that it does not clearly know what [A.C.'s] present views are with respect to the issue of whether or not the child should live or die. She's presently unconscious. As late as Friday of last week, she wanted the baby to live. As late as yesterday, she did not know for sure.

Having made these findings of fact and conclusions of law, * * * the court ordered that a caesarean section be performed to deliver A.C.'s child.

The court's decision was then relayed to A.C., who had regained consciousness.

[When the court reconvened later in the day, Dr. Hamner testified that A.C. then consented to the procedure.] When the court suggested moving the hearing to A.C.'s bedside, Dr. Hamner discouraged the court from doing so, but he and Dr. Weingold, together with A.C.'s mother and husband, went to A.C.'s room to confirm her consent to the procedure. What happened then was recounted to the court a few minutes later:

* * *

> DR. WEINGOLD: She does not make sound because of the tube in her windpipe. She nods and she mouths words. One can see what she's saying rather readily. She asked whether she would survive the operation. She asked [Dr.] Hamner if he would perform the operation. He told her he would only perform it if she authorized it but it would be done in any case. She understood that. She then seemed to pause for a few moments and then very clearly mouthed words several times, *I don't want it done, I don't want it done.* Quite clear to me.
>
> I would obviously state the obvious and that is this is an environment in which, from my perspective as a physician, this would not be an informed consent one way or the other. She's under tremendous stress with the family on both sides, but I'm satisfied that I heard clearly what she said. * * *

Dr. Weingold later qualified his opinion as to A.C.'s ability to give an informed consent, stating that he thought the environment for an informed consent was non-existent because A.C. was in intensive care, flanked by a weeping husband and mother. He added:

> I think she's in contact with reality, clearly understood who Dr. Hamner was. Because of her attachment to him [she] wanted him to perform the surgery. Understood he would not unless she consented and did not consent.

That is, in my mind, very clear evidence that she is responding, understanding, and is capable of making such decisions.   * * *

After hearing this new evidence, the court found that it was "still not clear what her intent is" and again ordered that a caesarean section be performed.   * * * The operation took place, but the baby lived for only a few hours, and A.C. succumbed to cancer two days later.

* * *

IV
* * *

A.   *Informed Consent and Bodily Integrity*
* * *

* * * [O]ur analysis of this case begins with the tenet common to all medical treatment cases: that any person has the right to make an informed choice, if competent to do so, to accept or forgo medical treatment.   * * *

In the same vein, courts do not compel one person to permit a significant intrusion upon his or her bodily integrity for the benefit of another person's health.   See, e.g., *McFall v. Shimp,* 10 Pa.D. & C.3d 90 (Allegheny County Ct.1978).   In *McFall* the court refused to order Shimp to donate bone marrow which was necessary to save the life of his cousin, McFall:

> The common law has consistently held to a rule which provides that one human being is under no legal compulsion to give aid or to take action to save another human being or to rescue.   * * *

Even though Shimp's refusal would mean death for McFall, the court would not order Shimp to allow his body to be invaded.   It has been suggested that fetal cases are different because a woman who "has chosen to lend her body to bring [a] child into the world" has an enhanced duty to assure the welfare of the fetus, sufficient even to require her to undergo caesarean surgery.   [ ] Surely, however, a fetus cannot have rights in this respect superior to those of a person who has already been born.[8]

* * *

What we distill from the cases discussed in this section is that every person has the right, under the common law and the Constitution, to accept or refuse medical treatment.   This right of bodily integrity belongs equally to persons who are competent and persons who are not.   Further, it matters not what the quality of a patient's life may be; the right of bodily integrity is not extinguished simply because

---

8. There are also practical consequences to consider.   What if A.C. had refused to comply with a court order that she submit to a caesarean?   Enforcement could be accomplished only through physical force or its equivalent.   A.C. would have to be fastened with restraints to the operating table, or perhaps involuntarily rendered unconscious by forcibly injecting her with an anesthetic, and then subjected to unwanted major surgery.   Such actions would surely give one pause in a civilized society, especially when A.C. had done no wrong.

someone is ill, or even at death's door. To protect that right against intrusion by others—family members, doctors, hospitals, or anyone else, however well-intentioned—we hold that a court must determine the patient's wishes by any means available, and must abide by those wishes unless there are truly extraordinary or compelling reasons to override them. When the patient is incompetent, or when the court is unable to determine competency, the substituted judgment procedure must be followed.

From the record before us, we simply cannot tell whether A.C. was ever competent, after being sedated, to make an informed decision one way or the other regarding the proposed caesarean section. The trial court never made any finding about A.C.'s competency to decide. * * *

* * * We have no reason to believe that, if competent, A.C. would or would not have refused consent to a caesarean. We hold, however, that without a competent refusal from A.C. to go forward with the surgery, and without a finding through substituted judgment that A.C. would not have consented to the surgery, it was error for the trial court to proceed to a balancing analysis, weighing the rights of A.C. against the interests of the state.

There are two additional arguments against overriding A.C.'s objections to caesarean surgery. First, as the American Public Health Association cogently states in its *amicus curiae* brief:

> Rather than protecting the health of women and children, court-ordered caesareans erode the element of trust that permits a pregnant woman to communicate to her physician—without fear of reprisal—all information relevant to her proper diagnosis and treatment. An even more serious consequence of court-ordered intervention is that it drives women at high risk of complications during pregnancy and childbirth out of the health care system to avoid coerced treatment.

Second, and even more compellingly, any judicial proceeding in a case such as this will ordinarily take place—like the one before us here—under time constraints so pressing that it is difficult or impossible for the mother to communicate adequately with counsel, or for counsel to organize an effective factual and legal presentation in defense of her liberty and privacy interests and bodily integrity. * * *

* * *

B. *Substituted Judgment*

* * * Sometimes, however, as our analysis presupposes here, a once competent patient will be unable to render an informed decision. In such a case, we hold that the court must make a substituted judgment on behalf of the patient, based on all the evidence. This means that the duty of the court, "as surrogate for the incompetent, is to determine as best it can what choice that individual, if competent, would make with respect to medical procedures." [ ]

* * *

We have found no reported opinion applying the substituted judgment procedure to the case of an incompetent pregnant patient whose own life may be shortened by a caesarean section, and whose unborn child's chances of survival may hang on the court's decision. Despite this precedential void, we conclude that substituted judgment is the best procedure to follow in such a case because it most clearly respects the right of the patient to bodily integrity. * * *

* * *

Because it is the patient's decisional rights which the substituted judgment inquiry seeks to protect, courts are in accord that the greatest weight should be given to the previously expressed wishes of the patient. This includes prior statements, either written or oral, even though the treatment alternatives at hand may not have been addressed. * * *

Courts in substituted judgment cases have also acknowledged the importance of probing the patient's value system as an aid in discerning what the patient would choose. We agree with this approach. [The court then discussed the ways in which it could determine the substituted judgment of the patient. For a fuller discussion of this issue, see chapter 11.]

C. The Trial Court's Ruling

* * * The [trial] court did not * * * as it should have * * *, * * * make a finding as to what A.C. would have chosen to do if she were competent. Instead, the court undertook to balance the state's and [the fetus's] interests in surgical intervention against A.C.'s perceived interest in not having the caesarean performed.

* * *

* * * What a trial court must do in a case such as this is to determine, if possible, whether the patient is capable of making an informed decision about the course of her medical treatment. If she is, and if she makes such a decision, her wishes will control in virtually all cases. If the court finds that the patient is incapable of making an informed consent (and thus incompetent), then the court must make a substituted judgment. * * *

Having said that, we go no further. We need not decide whether, or in what circumstances, the state's interests can ever prevail over the interests of a pregnant patient. * * * Indeed, some may doubt that there could ever be a situation extraordinary or compelling enough to justify a massive intrusion into a person's body, such as a caesarean section, against that person's will. Whether such a situation may someday present itself is a question that we need not strive to answer here. * * *

* * *

BELSON, ASSOCIATE JUDGE, concurring in part and dissenting in part:

* * *

I think it appropriate * * * to state my disagreement with the very limited view the majority opinion takes of the circumstances in which the interests of a viable unborn child can afford such compelling reasons. The state's interest in preserving human life and the viable unborn child's interest in survival are entitled, I think, to more weight than I find them assigned by the majority when it states that "in virtually all cases the decision of the patient * * * will control." I would hold that in those instances, fortunately rare, in which the viable unborn child's interest in living and the state's parallel interest in protecting human life come into conflict with the mother's decision to forgo a procedure such as a caesarean section, a balancing should be struck in which the unborn child's and the state's interest are entitled to substantial weight.

* * *

Turning to the rights of the child, tort law has long recognized the right of a living child to recover for injuries suffered when she was a viable unborn child. * * *

* * *

The holdings [that a fetus is a person under the wrongful death and survival statutes] establish that for purposes that are, at least, relevant to this case, a viable unborn child is a *person* at common law who has legal rights that are entitled to the protection of the courts. In a case like the one before us, the unborn child is a patient of both the hospital and any treating physician, and the hospital or physician may be liable to the child for the child's prenatal injury or death if caused by their negligence. [   ]

* * *

The balancing test should be applied in instances in which women become pregnant and carry an unborn child to the point of viability. This is not an unreasonable classification because, I submit, a woman who carries a child to viability is in fact a member of a unique category of persons. Her circumstances differ fundamentally from those of other potential patients for medical procedures that will aid another person, for example, a potential donor of bone marrow for transplant. This is so because she has undertaken to bear another human being, and has carried an unborn child to viability. Another unique feature of the situation we address arises from the singular nature of the dependency of the unborn child upon the mother. A woman carrying a viable unborn child is not in the same category as a relative, friend, or stranger called upon to donate bone marrow or an organ for transplant. Rather, the expectant mother has placed herself in a special class of persons who are bringing another person into existence, and upon whom that other person's life is totally dependent. Also, uniquely, the viable unborn child is literally captive within the mother's body. No other potential beneficiary of a surgical procedure on another is in that position.

* * *

Thus, I cannot agree with the conclusion of the majority opinion that while we "do not quite foreclose the possibility that a conflicting state interest may be so compelling that the patient's wishes must yield * * * we anticipate that such cases will be extremely rare and truly exceptional." While it is, fortunately, true that such cases will be rare in the sense that such conflicts between mother and viable unborn child are rare,[7] I cannot agree that in cases where a viable unborn child is in the picture, it would be extremely rare, within that universe, to require that the mother accede to the vital needs of the viable unborn child.[8]

* * *

I next address the sensitive question of how to balance the competing rights and interests of the viable unborn child and the state against those of the rare expectant mother who elects not to have a caesarean section necessary to save the life of her child. The indisputable view that a woman carrying a viable child has an extremely strong interest in her own life, health, bodily integrity, privacy, and religious beliefs necessarily requires that her election be given correspondingly great weight in the balancing process. In a case, however, where the court in an exercise of a substituted judgment has concluded that the patient would probably opt against a caesarean section, the court should vary the weight to be given this factor in proportion to the confidence the court has in the accuracy of its conclusion. Thus, in a case where the indicia of the incompetent patient's judgment are equivocal, the court should accord this factor correspondingly less weight. The appropriate weight to be given other factors will have to be worked out by the development of law in this area, and cannot be prescribed in a single court opinion. Some considerations obviously merit special attention in the balancing process. One such consideration is any danger to the mother's life or health, physical or mental, including the relatively small but still significant danger that necessarily inheres in any caesarean delivery, and including especially any danger that exceeds that level. The mother's religious beliefs as they relate to the operation would appear to deserve inclusion in the balancing process.

On the other side of the analysis, it is appropriate to look to the relative likelihood of the unborn child's survival. * * * The child's

---

7. The majority opinion quotes Opinion No. 55 of the Ethics Committee of the American College of Obstetricians and Gynecologists as follows: "[t]he welfare of the fetus is of the utmost importance to the majority of women; thus only rarely will a conflict arise." Another observer described the attitude of most expectant mothers more graphically: "The vast majority of women will accept significant risk, pain, and inconvenience to give their babies the best chance possible. One obstetrician who performs innovative fetal surgery stated that most of the women he sees 'would cut off their heads to save their babies.'" [ ]

8. To the contrary, it appears that a majority of courts faced with this issue have found that the state's compelling interest in protection of the unborn child should prevail. [ ] I add that in mapping this uncharted area of the law, we can draw lines, and a line I would draw would be to preclude the use of physical force to perform an operation. The force of the court order itself as well as the use of the contempt power would, I think, be adequate in most cases.

interest in being born with as little impairment as possible should also be considered. This may weigh in favor of a delivery sooner rather than later. The most important factor on this side of the scale, however, is life itself, because the viable unborn child that dies because of the mother's refusal to have a caesarean delivery is deprived, entirely and irrevocably, of the life on which the child was about to embark.

* * *

Notes and Questions

1. As the opinions in *A.C.* suggest, potential fetal-maternal conflicts force courts to answer two questions. First, should the court balance the interests of the fetus (or the interests of the state in protecting the fetus) with the interests of the mother? If the answer to that question is "no," as it was for the majority in *A.C.,* the issue becomes the comparatively simple one of determining the wishes of the mother. If there is a decision to balance the interests, however, as the dissenting opinion in *A.C.* suggests, the court must also face the question of what standards to apply. Are the interests of the fetus or the state as strong as the interests of the mother? Can the relative strengths of these different interests vary from case to case, depending upon the stage of development of the fetus, the consequences of the decision to be made, or other factors?

2. *In Re A.C.* was not the first case in which a court was asked to order a pregnant woman to undergo medical treatment for the benefit of her fetus. In Raleigh–Fitkin–Paul Morgan Memorial Hospital v. Anderson 42 N.J. 421, 201 A.2d 537 (1964), the New Jersey Supreme Court ordered blood transfusions to save an "unborn child" over the objections of the Jehovah's Witness mother. See also In re Application of Jamaica Hospital, 128 Misc.2d 1006, 491 N.Y.S.2d 898 (Sup.Ct.1985) (blood transfusion to save fetus who was not yet viable). In Jefferson v. Griffin Spalding County Hospital Authority, 247 Ga. 86, 274 S.E.2d 457 (1981), the Georgia Supreme Court ordered a caesarean section against the religiously motivated wishes of the mother when physicians argued that failure to do so would result in the death of both the mother and the fetus. The court acted because of the "duty of the state to protect a living, unborn human being from meeting * * * death before being given the opportunity to live." 274 S.E.2d at 460.

3. Cases that address the conflict between what is presumed to be the interest of the fetus (usually the interest in being born healthy, or, at least, the interest in being born) and the articulated wishes of the mother can arise from very different facts. As note 2 indicates, sometimes conflicts arise when a pregnant woman chooses to forgo blood transfusions and there is a claim that the refusal will lead to the death of her fetus. Others have arisen from the insistence by a pregnant woman on giving birth vaginally when physicians insist that the health of the fetus (and sometimes the mother) require delivery by caesarean section. In addition, fetal surgery is now a reality, and over the next several years a wide range of fetal therapies may become available. It is not unreasonable to expect litigation to result from a mother's failure to make "correct" medical choices for her fetus. Finally, some cases have arisen from a pregnant woman's unhealthy

lifestyle choices. Does the fetus have a legally cognizable right to make sure that his or her (or its) mother does not drink too much, or misuse drugs, or over- (or under-) exercise, or otherwise engage in activities that might adversely affect the fetus?

4. One reason that many physicians have been so intolerant of judicial intervention to require pregnant women to undergo medical care for the benefit of their fetuses is the fact that medical diagnosis in this area is often wrong. Doctors seem willing to testify that intervention is necessary to save the fetus even when the prognosis following nonintervention is quite uncertain. There is a series of cases that suggests that when doctors testify that a caesarean is necessary for the health of the fetus, but the mother "escapes" and attempts a normal vaginal birth, there is a good chance the child will be born without complication. Fletcher, Drawing Moral Lines in Fetal Therapy, 29 Clin. Obstetrics & Gynecology 595 (1986). Fletcher summarizes his review of six cases:

> First, inaccuracies and possible misdiagnosis appear to be involved in half of the cases * * * since babies were born healthy after vaginal delivery. If precedents flow from examples flawed by faulty assumptions or mistaken evaluations, errors may be replicated. These outcomes also should remind all concerned of the possibility of misdiagnosis before fetal therapy. Forced fetal therapy on the basis of misdiagnosis would constitute an ethical megadisaster.

29 Clin. Obstetrics and Gynecology at 599.

5. Not all moral obligations are enforceable through the use of the legal process. First, we must ask if a pregnant woman has a *moral* obligation to act to preserve the health of her fetus. Only if we find such a moral obligation must we address the second question: Should this obligation be enforceable in law? Some (including the majority in *A.C.*) argue that the wishes of the mother (who is unquestionably a person) always trump the presumed interests of the fetus (whose "personhood" status is uncertain). Some argue that the interests of the fetus (who has yet to experience life) always trump the wishes of the mother.

If you adopt neither absolute, you must address the balancing issue raised above in note 1. How do you weigh the wishes of the pregnant woman against the interests of the fetus (or the interest of the state in protecting fetal life)? What are the relevant factors? Is the viability status of the fetus relevant? Is the likely outcome of the proposed medical procedure relevant? Is the burden this procedure places on the mother relevant? Is the determination by the mother that she will bear the child—that she definitely will not have an abortion, even if that is legally permitted—relevant? Some have argued that this last factor is especially important because where the mother has decided to carry her fetus to term and give birth to a child, the mother's interest must be weighed against the greater interest of this yet-to-be-born person, not the lesser interest of a fetus who may yet be aborted. See Robertson and Schulman, Pregnancy and Prenatal Harm to Offspring: The Case of Mothers with PKU, 17 Hastings Center Rep. (4) 23 (Aug./Sept.1987).

6. If society were to enforce the moral obligation of a mother to care for the health of her fetus by law, it could do so in many ways.

a. Civil Remedies

Civil remedies could include mandatory injunctions (or their equivalents) like those sought in *A.C.* and granted in *Jefferson.* Could a court permit a state child protective services agency to take custody of a fetus under civil abuse and neglect law? Can taking custody of a fetus be distinguished from taking custody of the pregnant woman whose body contains the fetus? Is the fact that a pregnant woman exposed her baby to illegal drugs prenatally sufficient to show neglect? See In re Stefanel C., 16 Fam.L.Rep. 1377 (N.Y.App.Div.1990). See also "Coke Baby" Actions Increasing, American Medical News 2 (June 8, 1990).

In a large number of high risk pregnancies the pregnant woman is herself a child, and there seems to be some relationship between drug and alcohol use and teenage pregnancy. If the pregnant woman is herself a minor, is *her* parents' inability to control her conduct to assure the safety of the fetus itself evidence that the pregnant woman is a neglected child who can be taken into custody to protect her (and, indirectly, her fetus)?

Should civil damages be available to a child born alive who is injured by the pre-birth conduct of her mother? See Grodin v. Grodin, 102 Mich.App. 396, 301 N.W.2d 869 (1980) (suit by child against mother who took tetracycline during pregnancy, resulting in discoloration of child's teeth; potential liability in insurance company that issued mother a homeowner's policy). If we allow children born alive to seek tort damages against others who injure them prenatally, is there a reason to treat their tort-feasing parents differently and more favorably?

b. Criminal Remedies

The law could also apply criminal penalties to those who put their fetuses at risk. States could apply the criminal law of child abuse and neglect to a mother's care for her fetus. Since these criminal statutes generally make failing to provide adequate medical care to a child a form of neglect, they could be interpreted to mean that failing to provide adequate medical care to a fetus would constitute neglect. Such an interpretation of the criminal law might turn any pregnant woman who fails to follow her doctor's advice into a criminal, and this might discourage women at risk from seeking adequate prenatal care.

Other criminal laws also could be used to protect fetuses. Some lifestyle choices that put a fetus at risk (like use of cocaine or heroin) are illegal and can result independently in criminal sanctions against the pregnant woman. There have been several prosecutions for prenatal delivery of illegal drugs by a pregnant woman to her fetus. Should the fact that a subsequently born child is neither addicted nor disabled in any other way be relevant to such a prosecution against that child's mother? Should the fact that the mother is an addict be relevant? To the extent that some criminal sanctions (such as imprisonment) might protect the fetus, are they particularly appropriate for pregnant women who would continue their risky behavior unless they were confined? If a mother is imprisoned for the term of her pregnancy *in order to protect her fetus,* is she being punished for the crime she committed, or for her pregnancy? Is there any deterrence value in imprisoning a pregnant woman who violates the criminal law in a way that adversely affects her fetus?

c. Civil Commitment

Finally, the remedy of civil commitment may be available to protect fetuses from abuse by mentally ill, drug abusing, or alcoholic mothers under some state laws that permit commitment to treat these conditions. Is the use of the civil commitment remedy any less troublesome than the use of the criminal sanction?

7. What should be done if the generally appropriate commitment and treatment is inconsistent with the best interest of the fetus? For example, heroin addicts are often "treated" by replacing their heroin addiction with a methadone addiction. Methadone is a safer addiction because its use doesn't result in the ups and downs brought on by heroin, and its supply and purity can be regulated by medical authorities. On the other hand, it is harder to withdraw from methadone than from heroin, and a fetus may be put at great risk if the pregnant woman switches addictions during the pregnancy. A fetus may also be put at great risk if the pregnant woman withdraws from heroin "cold turkey" during pregnancy.

Should a pregnant heroin addict who wishes to start methadone (or stop taking drugs altogether) be allowed to do so? Should she be encouraged to do so? How should a doctor legally and ethically treat a pregnant heroin addict? May she tell her patient that she should continue using heroin throughout her pregnancy? Must she tell her that?

Some have suggested that a substantial number of places in drug rehabilitation programs be put aside for pregnant women. With the very long waiting lines for admission to these programs, would this be a good idea? Might it encourage women who are desperate for treatment to get pregnant so they will qualify for expedited assistance?

8. Of course, not all behavior that is unhealthy for the fetus is also illegal for the mother. Consumption of any amount of alcohol during pregnancy may result in fetal alcohol syndrome, which is now the most common known cause of mental retardation at birth in the United States. Is there any reason to distinguish a woman who puts her child at risk of fetal alcohol syndrome from a woman who puts her fetus at risk through the use of another proscribed drug? For an informative and moving account of fetal alcohol syndrome and its consequences on families and communities, see M. Dorris, The Broken Cord (1989). Author Michael Dorris raised an adopted fetal alcohol syndrome child, and it made him sensitive to the need to protect children who face a lifetime of deprivation due to the addiction of their alcoholic mothers.

9. In A.C. the court appointed a guardian ad litem to represent the fetus. This is a rather unusual process; guardians ad litem generally are appointed to represent persons, not potential persons. Should courts appoint guardians ad litem in cases that implicate the interests of a fetus? Is there any disadvantage in appointing a guardian ad litem under such circumstances? Does the appointment of such a guardian ad litem (or the failure to appoint one) effectively prejudge the issue of the fetus's standing to participate in the litigation, and, thus, the fetus's interest?

10. For a good short summary of the issue of fetal-maternal conflict, see Robertson, Legal Issues in Prenatal Therapy, 29 Clin. Obstetrics & Gynecology 603 (1986). See also Noble–Allgire, Court–Ordered Caesarian Sections, 10 J. Legal Med. 211 (1989); Johnsen, The Creation of Fetal Rights: Conflicts with Women's Constitutional Rights to Liberty, Privacy, and Equal Protection, 95 Yale L.J. 599 (1986); Goldberg, Medical Choices During Pregnancy: Whose Decision Is It Anyway? 41 Rutgers L.Rev. 591 (1989); Nelson and Milliken, Compelled Medical Treatment of Pregnant Women, 259 J.A.M.A. 1060 (1988); Note, Maternal Substance Abuse: The Need to Provide Legal Protection for the Fetus, 60 S.Cal.L.Rev. 1209 (1987); Note, Maternal Rights and Fetal Wrongs: The Case Against the Criminalization of "Fetal Abuse", 101 Harv.L.Rev. 994 (1988) (a response to the previous note); Rhoden, The Judge in the Delivery Room: The Emergence of Court–Ordered Caesareans, 74 Calif.L.Rev. 1951 (1986); Sedillo Lopez, Privacy and the Regulation of the New Reproductive Technologies: A Decision–Making Approach, 22 Fam.L.Q. 173 (1988); Note, Of Women's First Disobedience: Forsaking a Duty of Care to her Fetus—Is This Mother's Crime? 53 Brooklyn L.Rev. 807 (1987) (a good account from the fetal rights side despite the title).

B. EMPLOYMENT CHOICES AND EMPLOYER "FETAL PROTECTION" POLICIES

There is another area that may give rise to potential fetal-maternal conflict, and that is the workplace. Some employment environments that are safe for workers may not be safe for workers' fetuses. Employers may seek to exclude pregnant women (or even women who may become pregnant) from jobs that could put the fetuses at risk—either because the employers wish to protect the fetuses, or because the employers wish to protect themselves from adverse publicity, increased health insurance costs and potential litigation. The employee and her fetus may have interests in conflict: the financial advantage and emotional fulfillment of the employee may come at an increased risk of serious damage to her yet-to-be-born (or even yet-to-be-conceived) child. Should an employer be able to force women in the workplace to choose between ineligibility to work in certain jobs and ineligibility (through sterilization, for example) to conceive children? The United States Supreme Court resolved this issue—at least for employers covered by Title VII of the Civil Rights Act—in 1991.

AUTOMOBILE WORKERS v. JOHNSON CONTROLS

Supreme Court of the United States, 1991.
111 S.Ct. 1196.

JUSTICE BLACKMUN delivered the opinion of the Court.

In this case we are concerned with an employer's gender-based fetal-protection policy. May an employer exclude a fertile female employee from certain jobs because of its concern for the health of the fetus the woman might conceive?

I.

Respondent Johnson Controls, Inc., manufactures batteries. In the manufacturing process, the element lead is a primary ingredient. Occupational exposure to lead entails health risks, including the risk of harm to any fetus carried by a female employee. [Until 1977 Johnson Controls employed no women in its battery manufacturing business. From 1977 until 1982 the company did employ women in the at-risk jobs, but it warned them of the potential dangers. In 1982 Johnson Controls changed back to its policy of exclusion after eight employees with potentially excessive levels of lead in their blood became pregnant despite the warnings.]

* * *

II.

In April 1984, petitioners filed * * * a class action challenging Johnson Controls' fetal-protection policy as sex discrimination that violated Title VII of the Civil Rights Act of 1964. [ ] Among the individual plaintiffs were petitioners Mary Craig, who had chosen to be sterilized in order to avoid losing her job, Elsie Nason, a 50-year-old divorcee, who had suffered a loss in compensation when she was transferred out of a job where she was exposed to lead, and Donald Penney, who had been denied request for a leave of absence for the purpose of lowering his lead level because he intended to become a father. Upon stipulation of the parties, the District Court certified a class consisting of "all past, present and future production and maintenance employees" in United Auto Workers bargaining units at nine of Johnson Controls' plants "who have been and continue to be affected by [the employer's] Fetal Protection Policy implemented in 1982." [ ]

The District Court granted summary judgment for defendant-respondent Johnson Controls. 680 F.Supp. 309 (1988). * * *

The Court of Appeals for the Seventh Circuit, sitting en banc, affirmed the summary judgment by a 7-to-4 vote. 886 F.2d 871 (1989). * * *

[The first question for the Supreme Court was the standard to be applied in determining the propriety of the Johnson Controls policy. Does a classification by gender amount to disparate treatment by sex—i.e., does it discriminate against women on its face, or is it merely a classification with a disparate effect on women? If it were the first, the employer would be required to show that the inability to become pregnant was a bona fide occupational qualification (BFOQ)—that it was "reasonably necessary to the operation of [the] business." 42 U.S.C.A. Sec. 2000e–2(e)(I) (1982). If it were the second, the employer need only show "business necessity"—that excluding potentially pregnant workers "serves, in a significant way, the legitimate employment goals of the employer." Wards Cove Packing Co., Inc. v. Atonio, 490 U.S. 642, 109 S.Ct. 2115, 2125–26, 104 L.Ed.2d 733 (1989).]

III.

The bias in Johnson Controls' policy is obvious. Fertile men, but not fertile women, are given a choice as to whether they wish to risk their reproductive health for a particular job. Section 703(a) of the Civil Rights Act of 1964 prohibits sex-based classifications in terms and conditions of employment, in hiring and discharging decisions, and in other employment decisions that adversely affect an employee's status.[2] Respondent's fetal-protection policy explicitly discriminates against women on the basis of their sex. The policy excludes women with childbearing capacity from lead-exposed jobs and so creates a facial classification based on gender.

* * *

First, Johnson Controls' policy classifies on the basis of gender and childbearing capacity, rather than fertility alone. Respondent does not seek to protect the unconceived children of all its employees. Despite evidence in the record about the debilitating effect of lead exposure on the male reproductive system, Johnson Controls is concerned only with the harms that may befall the unborn offspring of its female employees.
* * *

Our conclusion is bolstered by the Pregnancy Discrimination Act of 1978 (PDA), 42 U.S.C. § 2000e(k), in which Congress explicitly provided that, for purposes of Title VII, discrimination "on the basis of sex" includes discrimination "because of or on the basis of pregnancy, childbirth, or related medical conditions." * * *

We concluded above that Johnson Controls' policy is not neutral because it does not apply to the reproductive capacity of the company's male employees in the same way as it applies to that of the females. Moreover, the absence of a malevolent motive does not convert a facially discriminatory policy into a neutral policy with a discriminatory effect. Whether an employment practice involves disparate treatment through explicit facial discrimination does not depend on why the employer discriminates but rather on the explicit terms of the discrimination. * * *

* * *

IV.

Under § 703(e)(1) of Title VII, an employer may discriminate on the basis of "religion, sex, or national origin in those certain instances

---

2. The statute reads:

"It shall be an unlawful employment practice for an employer—

"(1) to fail or refuse to hire or discharge any individual, or otherwise to discriminate against any individual with respect to his compensation, terms, conditions, or privileges of employment, because of such individual's race, color, religion, sex, or national origin; or

"(2) to limit, segregate, or classify his employees or applicants for employment in any way which would deprive or tend to deprive any individual of employment opportunities or otherwise adversely affect his status as an employee, because of such individual's race, color, religion, sex, or national origin."

where religion, sex, or national origin is a bona fide occupational qualification reasonably necessary to the normal operation of that particular business or enterprise." 42 U.S.C. § 2000e–2(e)(1). We therefore turn to the question whether Johnson Controls' fetal-protection policy is one of those "certain instances" that come within the BFOQ exception.

* * *

The wording of the BFOQ defense contains several terms of restriction that indicate that the exception reaches only special situations. The statute thus limits the situations in which discrimination is permissible to "certain instances" where sex discrimination is "reasonably necessary" to the "normal operation" of the "particular" business. Each one of these terms—certain, normal, particular—prevents the use of general subjective standards and favors an objective, verifiable requirement. But the most telling term is "occupational"; this indicates that these objective, verifiable requirements must concern job-related skills and aptitudes.

* * *

Our case law * * * makes clear that the safety exception [portion of the BFOQ defense] is limited to instances in which sex or pregnancy actually interferes with the employee's ability to perform the job. This approach is consistent with the language of the BFOQ provision itself, for it suggests that permissible distinctions based on sex must relate to ability to perform the duties of the job. Johnson Controls suggests, however, that we expand the exception to allow fetal-protection policies that mandate particular standards for pregnant or fertile women. We decline to do so. Such an expansion contradicts not only the language of the BFOQ and the narrowness of its exception but the plain language and history of the Pregnancy Discrimination Act.

* * *

V.

We have no difficulty concluding that Johnson Controls cannot establish a BFOQ. Fertile women, as far as appears in the record, participate in the manufacture of batteries as efficiently as anyone else. Johnson Controls' professed moral and ethical concerns about the welfare of the next generation do not suffice to establish a BFOQ of female sterility. Decisions about the welfare of future children must be left to the parents who conceive, bear, support, and raise them rather than to the employers who hire those parents. Congress has mandated this choice through Title VII, as amended by the Pregnancy Discrimination Act. Johnson Controls has attempted to exclude women because of their reproductive capacity. Title VII and the PDA simply do not allow a woman's dismissal because of her failure to submit to sterilization.

* * *

VI.

A word about tort liability and the increased cost of fertile women in the workplace is perhaps necessary. One of the dissenting judges in this case expressed concern about an employer's tort liability and concluded that liability for a potential injury to a fetus is a social cost that Title VII does not require a company to ignore. [ ] It is correct to say that Title VII does not prevent the employer from having a conscience. The statute, however, does prevent sex-specific fetal-protection policies. These two aspects of Title VII do not conflict.

More than 40 States currently recognize a right to recover for a prenatal injury based either on negligence or on wrongful death. [ ] According to Johnson Controls, however, the company complies with the lead standard developed by OSHA and warns its female employees about the damaging effects of lead. It is worth noting that OSHA gave the problem of lead lengthy consideration and concluded that "there is no basis whatsoever for the claim that women of childbearing age should be excluded from the workplace in order to protect the fetus or the course of pregnancy." [ ] Instead, OSHA established a series of mandatory protections which, taken together, "should effectively minimize any risk to the fetus and newborn child." [ ] Without negligence, it would be difficult for a court to find liability on the part of the employer. If, under general tort principles, Title VII bans sex-specific fetal-protection policies, the employer fully informs the woman of the risk, and the employer has not acted negligently, the basis for holding an employer liable seems remote at best.

[In any case, the Court points out, if state tort law "furthers discrimination in the workplace and prevents employers from hiring women who are capable of manufacturing the product as men, then it will impede the accomplishment of Congress' goals in enacting Title VII" and thus probably be pre-empted by the federal law.] * * * Because Johnson Controls has not argued that it faces any costs from tort liability, not to mention crippling ones, the pre-emption question is not before us. * * *

The tort-liability argument reduces to two equally unpersuasive propositions. First, Johnson Controls attempts to solve the problem of reproductive health hazards by resorting to an exclusionary policy. Title VII plainly forbids illegal sex discrimination as a method of diverting attention from an employer's obligation to police the workplace. Second, the spectre of an award of damages reflects a fear that hiring fertile women will cost more. The extra cost of employing members of one sex, however, does not provide an affirmative Title VII defense for a discriminatory refusal to hire members of that gender. * * *

We, of course, are not presented with, nor do we decide, a case in which costs would be so prohibitive as to threaten the survival of the employer's business. We merely reiterate our prior holdings that the incremental cost of hiring women cannot justify discriminating against them.

VII.

* * *

It is no more appropriate for the courts than it is for individual employers to decide whether a woman's reproductive role is more important to herself and her family than her economic role. Congress has left this choice to the woman as hers to make.

The judgment of the Court of Appeals is reversed and the case is remanded for further proceedings consistent with this opinion.

JUSTICE WHITE, with whom THE CHIEF JUSTICE and JUSTICE KENNEDY join, concurring in part and concurring in the judgment.

The Court properly holds that Johnson Controls' fetal protection policy overtly discriminates against women, and thus is prohibited by Title VII unless it falls within the bona fide occupational qualification (BFOQ) exception. The Court erroneously holds, however, that the BFOQ defense is so narrow that it could never justify a sex-specific fetal protection policy. I nevertheless concur in the judgment of reversal because on the record before us summary judgment in favor of Johnson Controls was improperly entered by the District Court and affirmed by the Court of Appeals.

* * *

* * * [A] fetal protection policy would be justified under the terms of the statute if, for example, an employer could show that exclusion of women from certain jobs was reasonably necessary to avoid substantial tort liability. Common sense tells us that it is part of the normal operation of business concerns to avoid causing injury to third parties, as well as to employees, if for no other reason than to avoid tort liability and its substantial costs. * * *

* * *

In enacting the BFOQ standard, "Congress did not ignore the public interest in safety." [ ] The Court's narrow interpretation of the BFOQ defense in this case, however, means that an employer cannot exclude even pregnant women from an environment highly toxic to their fetuses. It is foolish to think that Congress intended such a result, and neither the language of the BFOQ exception nor our cases requires it.

* * *

[The opinion of Justice Scalia, concurring in the judgment only, is omitted.]

Notes and Questions

1. Is there any kind of fetal protection policy that would be legal after *Johnson Controls*? Could an employer still exclude a pregnant woman

(rather than a merely potentially pregnant woman) from a work environment that is known to put the fetus at great risk, or, as Justice White's concurring opinion suggests, is even that prohibited by the majority opinion? Can you imagine any case in which a pregnant woman would choose to continue working in an environment that puts her fetus at risk?

2. At what point, if any, would the cost of accommodating a pregnant employee justify not hiring one? In his concurring opinion Justice Scalia suggests that "for example, a shipping company may refuse to hire pregnant women as crew members on long voyages because the on-board facilities for foreseeable emergencies, though quite feasible, would be inordinately expensive." Would it make a difference if the foreseeable emergencies involved the health of the worker or the health of someone else—like her child or fetus?

3. The primary cost to Johnson Controls of hiring potentially pregnant women is the risk of tort liability. The majority suggests that the problem is an insignificant one if the company is not otherwise negligent, and that Title VII may pre-empt state tort law anyway. Justice White argues that "[s]uch speculation will be small comfort to employers" because (1) Title VII may not pre-empt state tort law, (2) warnings to employees, and their waiver of tort actions against their employers, will not preclude actions by children born to those employees, and (3) "it will be difficult for employers to determine in advance what will constitute negligence." Would you be willing to represent a child born to a woman employed at Johnson Controls after this case was decided? How would you cast an action against Johnson Controls for injury that resulted from the very hazards about which the company warned your client's mother?

4. Would it violate ERISA to refuse to hire women (or pregnant women) for certain jobs because of the consequences for employer-paid health insurance premiums? Would it violate ERISA for an employer to drop employee health insurance coverage altogether if the employer were required to hire women (or pregnant women) under circumstances that it feared would put its premiums at risk? Could an employer worried about the effect of a job environment on women drop dependent coverage from an employer-paid health insurance plan? Could that employer buy coverage that excludes treatment for diseases "contracted through exposure to toxic substances or conditions *in utero*"? For a discussion of the application of ERISA generally, see Chapter 6.

5. In *Johnson Controls* the Seventh Circuit had applied a heightened version of the "business necessity" standard rather than the BFOQ standard. The Court of Appeals would have permitted discrimination based upon potential pregnancy only upon "(1) a demonstration of the existence of a substantial health risk to the unborn child, and (2) establishment that transmission of the hazard to the unborn child occurs only through women." The Court also said it would "allow the employee to present evidence of less discriminatory alternatives equally capable of preventing the health hazard to the unborn." 886 F.2d 871, 885. Ultimately the Seventh Circuit also held that the practice of Johnson Controls would pass the BFOQ test, too, if that were to be applied.

6. The *en banc* Seventh Circuit consideration of this case resulted in several opinions revealing different perspectives on fetal protection policies and the role of the courts in applying them. In a brief dissent, Judge Cudahy raised the potential gender difference in approaches to this question:

> It is a matter of some interest that, of the twelve federal judges to have considered this case to date, none has been female. This may be quite significant because this case, like other controversies of great potential consequence, demands, in addition to command of the disembodied rules, some insight into social reality. What is the situation of the pregnant woman, unemployed or working for the minimum wage and unprotected by health insurance, in relation to her pregnant sister, exposed to an indeterminate lead risk but well-fed, housed and doctored? Whose fetus is at greater risk? Whose decision is this to make? We, who are unfortunately all male, must address these and other equally complex questions through the clumsy vehicle of litigation. At least let it be complete litigation focusing on the right standard.

Also dissenting were Judges Posner and Easterbrook, two leading scholars of the law and economics movement, which has not been closely identified with feminist values or labor unions. Each would have applied the BFOQ defense rather than the "business necessity" defense because, they each concluded, the Johnson Controls policy is one of disparate treatment rather than merely disparate impact. As Judge Easterbrook concludes:

> Title VII requires employers to evaluate applicants and employees as individuals rather than as members of a group defined by sex. The statute has its costs; prenatal injuries are among these. Appeals to the "flexibility" with which the Supreme Court has allocated burdens of proof and persuasion get us nowhere. No amount of "flexibility" justifies sex discrimination without a BFOQ, unless by "flexibility" we mean a prerogative to disregard the statute when it requires decisions antithetical to our beliefs. Although my colleagues refer to many constitutional cases, [ ] for the proposition that sex discrimination sometimes is permissible, cases showing that Congress *may* authorize sex-based decisions hardly shows that in this instance it *did*. Title VII forbids rather than requires resort to sex as a basis of decision.
>
> Risk to the next generation is incident to all activity, starting with getting out of bed. (Staying in bed all day has its own hazards.) To insist on *zero* risk, which the court says Johnson may do, is to exclude women from the industrial jobs that have been a male preserve. By all means let society bend its energies to improving the prospects of those who come after us. Demanding zero risk produces not progress but paralysis. Defining tolerable risk, and seeking to reduce that limit, is more useful—but it is a job for Congress or OSHA in conjunction with medical and other sciences. Laudable though its objective be, Johnson may not reach its goal at the expense of women.

7. If there is a real workplace risk to a fetus, who should decide if the benefit of the job to the mother is worth the risk to the potential child? Should the decision be made by the employee, the employer, the government (either administratively, judicially, or through legislative action), or by someone else? What factors are relevant to such a decision? The chance of birth defects? The chance of pregnancy? Alternative employment prospects for the employees? The social status of the job?

8. For more analysis of this issue, see three other federal cases dealing with fetal protection policies: Hayes v. Shelby Memorial Hospital, 726 F.2d 1543 (11th Cir. 1984); Zuniga v. Kleberg County Hosp., 692 F.2d 986 (5th Cir. 1982), and Wright v. Olin Corp., 697 F.2d 1172 (4th Cir. 1982). A California court found Johnson Controls' policy illegal under state law. Johnson Controls, Inc. v. Fair Employment and Housing Commission, 218 Cal.App.3d 517, 267 Cal.Rptr. 158 (1990). See also Buss, Getting Beyond Discrimination: A Regulatory Solution to the Problem of Fetal Hazards in the Workplace, 95 Yale L.J. 577 (1986) and the clear note on the Seventh Circuit decision in Johnson Controls, Note, 103 Harv.L.Rev. 977 (1990). The Supreme Court oral argument in this case is summarized in interesting detail at 59 U.S.L.W. 3304 (S.Ct., November 23, 1990).

IV. GENETIC SCREENING AND ENGINEERING

A. INTRODUCTION

Americans have always been fascinated with dreams of transformation. Raised on a steady diet of Hollywood movies featuring men transformed into werewolves and research labs accidentally unleashing bizarre semi-human forms of life, deep in our imaginations always lay a future full of genetic engineers. While science fiction writers spun out stories of societies breeding only "preferred" genetic stock, in the real world, the notion became a horrifying obsession in Nazi Germany. Now, the future has arrived, and indeed, the future is full of genetic engineers. We stand, collectively, facing the proverbial pandora's box. Chief Justice Burger considered the possible consequences of opening the box in a case involving whether a live "human-made" organism is patentable:

[T]he petitioner * * * points to the grave risks that may be generated by research endeavors such as respondent's. The briefs present a gruesome parade of horribles. Scientists, among them Nobel laureates, are quoted suggesting that genetic research may pose a serious threat to the human race, or at the very least, that the dangers are far too substantial to permit research to proceed apace at this time. We are told that genetic research and related technological developments may spread pollution and disease, that it may result in a loss of genetic diversity, and that its practice may tend to depreciate the value of human life. These arguments are forcefully, even passionately, presented; they remind us that, at times, human ingenuity seems unable to control fully the forces it creates—that, with Hamlet, it is sometimes better 'to bear those ills we have than to fly to others that we know not of.' "

Diamond v. Chakrabarty, 447 U.S. 303, 316, 100 S.Ct. 2204, 2211, 65 L.Ed.2d 144 (1980). In finding that the grant or denial of the patent would not appreciably resolve these issues, the Court concluded that policies regarding genetic research should be made through the legislative process, not by the courts. Id. at 317, 100 S.Ct. at 2212.

The debate over the ethical, medical, and legal consequences of genetic screening and engineering remains far from resolved. The bright promise of prevention and treatment of genetic diseases is partially obscured by increasingly apparent ethical and legal concerns. Rarely have human beings been entrusted with such potentially powerful knowledge about each other. Just as testing for HIV raises issues of confidentiality and discrimination, the growing debate over genetic testing raises similar concerns. Will genetic knowledge be used with integrity, and rescue millions from an otherwise deadly genetic fate? Or will genetic knowledge be used to create new classes of discrimination? For a broad sampling of issues raised by genetic testing, see The Randolph W. Thrower Symposium: Genetics and the Law, 39 Emory L.J. 620 (1990).

1. *The Human Genome*

Each somatic cell in the body (all cells except for the ova and sperm) contain the full human genome, a complete account of all inherited attributes. The genome consists of 46 chromosomes in 23 pairs. Each chromosome is a long strand of DNA which is composed of basic chemical constituents called "base pairs". Each chromosome contains an average of 4,000 genes, each made up of an average of about 35,000 base pairs. Genes are consistent by species, so a gene found in a particular location on a particular chromosome in one person will control the same trait as will a gene that is found in the same location on the same chromosome in another person. The trait itself is determined by the structure of the base pairs within the gene. Although about 90% of the DNA, the "junk" DNA, is not directly related to the genetic message of the genome, variations in the other 10% result in variations in form or "phenotype" among the human species.

The germ-line cells (ovum and sperm) contain 23 individual chromosomes, and when a sperm and an ovum combine they possess the full complement of 46 paired chromosomes. In 22 of the 23 pairs of chromosomes the two chromosomes that make up the pair contain genes for the same trait. The final two chromosomes determine sex, and any sex linked genetic trait must be related, in some way, to this last pair of chromosomes.

Sometimes a trait will manifest itself if the DNA sequence which codes for that trait is located in the gene of either of the paired chromosomes; this is a dominant trait. Sometimes a trait will manifest itself only if the appropriate DNA sequence is located on both genes; in this case the gene is called "recessive" and a person with one gene for this trait is a "carrier". The relationship between the gene and its physical manifestation is sometimes a simple one and sometimes a very complex one. Some genes manifest themselves only if certain other genes are also present, and some manifest themselves only if other "suppressor" genes are absent. Some attributes are the result of many pairs of genes, and some are the result of many pairs of genes and environmental factors working together. While much of what constitutes each one of us is found in our genetic material, much is not. Alcoholism and obesity, for example, may be genetic, they may be environmental, and they may involve the complex interaction of many genes (which are yet to be identified) with non-genetic factors.

There are now over 4,000 inherited disorders that have been identified. These include some that we have known about for decades (like sickle cell anemia) and some that have been discovered very recently (the gene for cystic fibrosis was discovered in 1990, for example). Some of the disorders that can be traced to particular genes or combinations of genes do not have adverse consequences until the one who possesses them becomes an adult, although some manifest themselves at birth or before. Some of these genetic disorders can be treated through nongenetic means (phenylketonuria—PKU—has its adverse effects minimized if those who possess it are given diets without phenylalanine), and others (like sickle cell anemia and cystic fibrosis) currently lack any effective treatment other than the hope held out by future genetic therapy. For an excellent overview, see M. Shapiro and R. Spece, Bioethics and the Law, 342–348 (1981).

2. *The Human Genome Project*

The United States government, through the National Institutes of Health and the Department of Energy, have undertaken the largest biology project in the history of science—mapping and understanding the entire human genome. This effort is expected to take 15 years and cost $3 billion, and even that budget presumes scientific breakthroughs in the techniques necessary to map each of the three billion base pairs that make up the human genome. There is opposition to the human genome project. Some scientists believe that the information it will develop will be largely useless. After all, 90% of the base pairs appear to have no genetic purpose, and the location and attributes of some genes have been discovered outside of the human genome project. Some believe that the project will also siphon off already decreasing research funds for basic biology even though, theoretically, the human genome initiative will be funded separately from other scientific research.

There is also concern that the knowledge gained through the project will be used for sinister purposes. The history of eugenic movements, both in this country and in Europe, might well make us worry about the way that this information could be employed. Finally, the knowledge that will be gained through the human genome project may cause us to reevaluate some very basic principles. How will the argument for determinism fare when we know the complete genetic structure of the human being, and we know with greater certainty (or, ultimately, perhaps perfect certainty) what is genetically guided? In addition, how will our genetic discoveries reshape what we consider to be a normal, or exemplary, or minimally acceptable human being? As one scholar points out,

> [w]e know that most "diseases" and "abnormalities" are social constructs, not facts of nature. Myopia, for example, is considered acceptable, whereas obesity is not. We won't discover a "normal" or "standard" human genome, but we may invent one. If we do, how much variation from the norm will society permit before an individual's genome is labeled "substandard" or "abnormal"? And what impact will such a concept of genetic normalcy have on society and on "substandard" individuals?

Annas, Impact of Gene Maps on Law and Society, Trial 42, 48 (July 1990). Ultimately, most scientists view the project as inevitable and appropriate as a matter of science; others view the project as merely inevitable. The role it will play in our society, and some of the questions it will raise, are identified by Professor Sinsheimer, a biologist and a thoughtful commentator on the social use of genetic information.

SINSHEIMER, WHITHER THE GENOME PROJECT?

20 Hastings Center Report (4) (July/August 1990) 5.

The Human Genome Project represents the convergence of three billion years of biological evolution and ten thousand or more years of cultural evolution—and their interaction is bound to change both, profoundly. From now on, their futures will be indissolubly linked.

Actually, these streams, coursing through time, have already unwittingly made contact. With the invention of sanitation and the introduction of modern medicine, the role of natural selection in the perpetuation of the species was markedly reduced, with inevitable influence on the human gene pool.

Now we foresee a more conscious interaction. Those who fear, even dread, its uncertain consequences, argue that we should prevent or abort this meeting. To do so would, of course, consign humanity forever to the cruelties and opportunities of the genetic lottery—statistical cruelties that mean blighted lives for those afflicted; statistical opportunities that provide the rare genius who, appearing at the right time, forever changes our civilization. Must we accept the former to have the latter?

And though rarely noted, to do so implies that our present genetic endowment—with all of its admixed ancient baggage and recent innovation—is beyond human grasp and appreciation, much less improvement, an acme, or the expression of a divine will.

To some, even increased *knowledge* of the genetic basis of human characteristics is an assault upon human dignity. But is human dignity best affirmed by willful ignorance, or by increasing human self-knowledge?

Some, seeking an intermediate course, argue that biology and culture should meet at arms length. They fear the consequence of unrestrained interaction. They seek a decorous relationship in which the culture may pick and choose from the biological knowledge acquired to alleviate a few grievous genetic ailments, but avoid large-scale biological, and inevitably cultural, change.

Others would set no a priori limits to this interaction, but would advocate great caution. We know so little about the complexity and tolerances of either our biological or cultural organization, they argue, that either or both could easily be destabilized with catastrophic consequence. In their view any experiments should be of small scale and slow pace. Still others, no doubt, full of confidence, would simply permit free enterprise to reign.

The human genome project per se is intended solely to acquire knowledge. Yet in the ethos of modern society, it is feckless to suppose that knowledge, once available, will not be used. While ethicists may properly debate the morality of experimentation with sentient beings—in either the biological or cultural mode—heuristically, in a secular age dominated by the twin pillars of power—commerce and politics—what in fact is *likely* to happen?

Specific concerns most often relate to invasion of privacy—who shall have access to genetic information—or eugenics—who shall determine genetic choices. Rights of privacy are, of necessity, increasingly circumscribed in an increasingly interactive society. The balance between autonomy and restriction will depend in turn upon the expectations the individual may place upon the society.

The feasibility of eugenics—the planned "improvement" of the human genetic endowment is often met, either with a shudder and reference to the Nazi atrocities and the Holocaust or with glib assurance that such distortions would never happen again. Quite aside from the more abstract possible degradation of human individuality and dignity if eugenics should become a reality (subject to the forces of commerce and politics?), the Nazi experience raises starkly the question as to whether human beings can ever be entrusted with the control of their own inheritance. And yet, conversely, is it conceivable that at some time, it might be thought outrageous to leave a future genome to the whims of chance?

Presently, concerns about the morality of the experimentation necessary to establish "desired" genetic combinations pose grievous questions that at minimum will slow the acquisition of knowledge of links between genetics and behavior, and that may, unless great ingenuity can be exercised, bring any such program to a halt. Indeed, this difficulty may link the twin concerns of privacy and eugenics, for one research approach may be to seek to correlate individual genetic patterns with distinctive behavioral patterns.

Progeny genetic structure may join the classic list of decisions to be shared in some proportion between the individual and the society. In what proportions, along what dimensions, within what societal vision? It would seem unlikely that the varied cultures of the planet will come to a common understanding of such issues. The moral traditions of Christianity, Judaism, Islam, Buddhism, seem unlikely to provide a common view. Evolution may well have found a new arena for Darwinian selection.

As sentient organisms, each of us might like to be able to choose his or her genome, but given the arrow of time, this will (mostly) never be possible. We cannot cut free from our genetic moorings. We (collectively) can only ever choose between genomes determined by chance—as have served us thus far—and, someday, genomes determined by the best intentions of our predecessors.

Thus the human condition evolves.

———

For good accounts of this remarkable undertaking, see Wingerson, Mapping Our Genes: The Genome Project and the Future of Medicine (1990) and Bishop and Waldholz, Genome: The Story of the Most Astonishing Adventure of Our Time—The Attempt to Map All the Genes in the Human Body (1990).

3. Potential Uses of Genetic Information

Obviously, there are a wide range of potential uses of genetic information. "Gene therapy", medical procedures designed to change the genetic composition of somatic cells, could help those with genetic diseases overcome the consequences of their genetic structure. Similarly, changes in the gene structure of ova or sperm could allow those with genetic diseases, or those who are merely carriers, to avoid passing genetic disorders to their children. Genetic information may also be helpful to people engaged in their own reproductive decisionmaking and to those who are doing medical or non-medical planning and want to know something of their future. Genetic information may also be useful to employers, insurers, schools, the courts, and to state agencies dealing with immigration and adoption, for a start. Finally, the dissemination of information about the genetic structure of a person—

to that person, and, separately, to others—may itself have substantial consequences.

B. GENE THERAPY

Gene therapy is the process by which a normal gene is inserted in cells to replace a malfunctioning gene that is causing some genetic disease. The process is simply explained in the following government pamphlet.

DEPARTMENT OF HEALTH AND HUMAN SERVICES, GENE THERAPY FOR HUMAN PATIENTS: INFORMATION FOR THE GENERAL PUBLIC
4–5 (1990).

* * *

Human gene therapy is a possible alternative approach to the treatment of some genetic diseases. The basic idea behind gene therapy is to insert normal genes with correct information into the DNA of the cells that contain malfunctioning genes. Adding genes in this way is called "gene insertion." The added genetic information would allow these cells to function properly and might reduce or eliminate the signs or symptoms of the disease. For example, instead of repeatedly treating a hemophiliac with clotting factor, one could insert the correct genetic information into his cells to allow those cells to make their own clotting factor.

It seems likely that human gene therapy will also be used to combat certain diseases that may not be genetic. For example, malignancies are usually treated with surgery, radiation and/or chemotherapy. For cancer patients who are not helped by these therapies, researchers are now planning to treat the patients' disease with genetically altered white blood cells.

Scientists have developed methods for inserting genes into human somatic cells. The techniques for isolating human genes and making multiple copies of them in the laboratory are well established. Now scientists are studying how to insert those genes into cells and how to make those genes work properly once inside the cells. One method for inserting genes into cells is to link the genes with a virus that has been crippled and rendered harmless. As part of the modification, such a virus, sometimes called a vector or vehicle, has been deliberately altered so that it can carry genes into cells but cannot then escape to infect other cells. After the cells to be treated have been temporarily removed from a patient's body, the virus or vector is used to carry the desired gene into them. The final step will be to return the treated cells, which now contain the correct genetic information, to the patient's body. For example, bone marrow, liver cells, or white blood cells could be removed from the body of a patient, treated in the laboratory, and returned to the patient.

Whether bone marrow cells or some other type of human cells were used, the added genes would be inserted only into somatic (nonreproductive) cells and not into germ line (reproductive) cells. Therefore, newly inserted genes could not be passed to patients' children. The therapy would be called somatic cell gene therapy and would not attempt to affect the germ line cells, which carry genetic information to the next generation.

The best outcome of human gene therapy would be a single treatment that would correct enough cells to provide a permanent cure for the patient's disease. This kind of complete success is unlikely in the beginning stages of human gene therapy but will remain the long-term goal of research scientists working in this field.

———

Even with the obvious promise of gene therapy, the specter of genetic research and treatment has attracted considerable concern. Responding to fears that research involving recombinant or "active" DNA might pose a risk to society, the government established the Recombinant DNA Advisory Committee to review federally funded research in 1974. After weathering two decades of fear about potential "escape" of DNA which could infect the public, the advisory committee is now concerned with a variety of ethical issues surrounding genetic research. All research proposals involving human gene therapy now must be approved by their Human Gene Therapy Subcommittee. In 1990 the committee approved the first gene therapy protocol designed to be of therapeutic value. The protocol is designed to provide treatment for children with severe combined immunodeficiency (SCID). This fatal disease is also known as "Bubble–Boy disease" because some children with this genetic trait must live in a plastic bubble free of potential contaminants. The plan for this gene therapy makes it a prototype for other proposals that are likely to arise in the next few years:

> [B]lood will be drawn from SCID patients at the clinical center of NIH. Their white cells will be cultured and then exposed to an engineered retrovirus containing a working virus of the gene the patients lack. The virus will infect and transfer the gene to them, but it is designed to be self limiting. If tests confirm that cells have started to produce the missing enzyme [the absence of which causes the disease] and that no infectious virus is present, the cells will be infused back into the patient.
>
> If it works, the gene therapy could be a life saver for children who can not receive the principal alternative treatment, bone-marrow transplantation. * * *

Beardsley, Profile: Gene Doctor, Scientific American 33, 33B (August 1990). Gene therapy may be available at many stages of development. For example, genetic disfunctions that can be diagnosed before birth and that manifest themselves at birth may be correctable *in utero*. See Anderson, Prospects for Human Gene Therapy in the Born and Unborn Patient, 29 Clinical Obstetrics and Gynecology 586 (1986). If prenatal gene therapy is appropriate, would it also be appropriate to go back one step further and do genetic engineering of germ-line cells? Is there any ethical difference, and ought there be any legal difference, between treatment of a born patient, treatment of a fetus, and treatment of a "patient" who is not yet conceived? See, generally, Institute of Medicine, Human Gene Therapy (1988); President's Commission for the Study of Ethical Problems in Medicine and Biomedical and Behavioral Research, Splicing Life: A Report on the Social and Ethical Issues of Genetic Engineering with Human Beings (1982), and Office of Technology Assessment, Human Gene Therapy: Background Paper (1984).

C. GENETIC SCREENING

A genetic screen is a medical determination of the genetic structure of a person. A genetic screen can be designed to discover the existence of one or more identified genes or traits. Screening can be done through a genetic probe, which looks directly at the DNA in the identified gene, or through a test for genetic markers, which provide indirect knowledge about the presence of a gene. Genetic probes are available for only a few traits; most are investigated by a search for genetic markers. Testing by genetic probe is extremely accurate; testing through genetic markers has variable accuracy. Commercial interest in genetic screening and the huge infusion of research funds through the Human Genome Project will undoubtedly result in an increase in the number of genetic probes that are available and the number and quality of the tests for genetic markers.

Problem: Genetic Testing

Ibrahim Abdul Salaam decided to seek genetic testing to determine whether he was a carrier of the sickle cell trait when he and his wife, who are both African American, decided to have children. Mr. Salaam had a cousin who died of sickle cell disease, and several of his wife's relatives have been afflicted with the disease. Mr. Salaam was assured by the testing physician that the testing was simple and painless, and that the results would be confidential. The genetic screen for sickle cell trait came back positive—i.e., Mr. Salaam is a carrier of the recessive trait for sickle cell anemia.

While Mr. Salaam was discussing the results of the test with his physician he mentioned that his sister was recently married, and that her husband knows that he is a carrier for sickle cell trait. The physician suggested that she be told of her brother's test result because of the increased chance that she, too, could be a carrier. Mr. Salaam decided against telling his sister because he was embarrassed by his carrier status and he did not want others in his family to know about it. As he pointed out to his physician, he did not intend to tell even his wife because his family is Islamic and neither his wife nor his sister would ever consider amniocentesis or abortion; he was merely seeking some personal reassurance (which he did not get, of course) through his own test.

Shortly after Mr. Salaam was given his test result his employer, Ringding Aircraft, switched to a new provider for its employer-paid group health policy. The new health insurance company, First Intergalactic Big Insurance (FIB), asked each employee to fill out a medical history which inquired about the employee's "knowledge of any genetic disease or defect." While FIB agreed to cover all employees without regard to their medical history, it did condition coverage on filling out the form. Further, it conditioned the issuance of supplemental hospitalization insurance and term life insurance (which could be purchased by the employees, without employer contribution) on the "current policies of the company." Although this was unknown to Mr. Salaam at the time, the company policy does not permit the issuance of any insurance other than group health to anyone with any "genetic defect," and company policy defines "genetic defect" to include carrying the sickle cell trait. FIB also has a policy of releasing the medical forms of anyone covered by employer-paid group health insurance to the employer. Ringding has an unhappy history of racial discrimination, and Mr. Salaam fears that if the information about his sickle cell carrier status is provided to the company it will find some excuse to fire him.

Is Mr. Salaam or his physician obliged to provide information about his sickle cell carrier status to his wife? To his sister? Is the physician permitted to provide this information to Mr. Salaam's wife or sister without his permission? Must Mr. Salaam fill out the medical history in such a way that he reveals his sickle cell carrier status? Can he stop the insurance company from providing the information to his employer? Can the insurance company deny him any individual coverage because of his genetic status? Can it deny Ringding group health insurance coverage if "too many" of its employees are sickle cell carriers?

1.   Uses of Genetic Screening

a.   Medical Planning

The most obvious beneficial use of genetic information is the medical planning that can be done by those who know their own genetic structure. In some cases, people will learn that they have a genetic disorder that can be treated, either through gene therapy or by some other method. On the other hand, it is far less clear that genetic screening ought to be encouraged for conditions for which there is no treatment. Would it be helpful to know that you will suffer from Huntington's Disease, an untreatable, cruel and disabling disorder, sometime later in life? If it were possible to make such a genetic deduction, would you want to know that you will develop Alzheimer's Disease? Cancer? If genetic information can be discovered, must it be? Could the medical profession, or the state or federal government, decide to restrict patients' access to their own genetic structure if they conclude that the information will be misunderstood or misused?

b. Reproductive Decisionmaking

For a couple considering pregnancy, fears of passing on genetic diseases may either cloud the pregnancy with anxiety, or dissuade the couple from taking the risk altogether. Although amniocentesis testing is widely available for genetic testing of the fetus in the second trimester, it forces decision-making to wait until the second trimester when there are fewer medical and legal options. Preconception testing offers a woman an opportunity to know whether she or her partner carry problematic genes, and allows her to make informed reproductive decisions.

The relationship between genetic traits and ethnicity can make this a difficult issue, however. Sickle cell trait is far more common among African–Americans than other Americans, and Tay–Sachs disease is found almost exclusively in Jews of Eastern European extraction. Thus, politics has entered the national debate over what kind of genetic testing ought to be encouraged or required. Statutes have attempted to finesse the relationship between sickle cell trait and race, which has been the most politically charged. One state legislature required a sickle cell test for anyone who is not "Caucasian, Indian, or Oriental" to get a marriage license. Other states still provide for mandatory or voluntary testing of infants, school children, and others. If there is to be widespread screening for the sickle cell trait, do infants and school children seem like appropriate target populations? Is it ever appropriate for a state to target a population for genetic screening by ethnicity, or is the risk of improper use of the information too great under that circumstance? The 1990 discovery of the gene that causes cystic fibrosis led to discussion of the propriety of screening the whole population to find those who were carriers of this disease. The National Institutes of Health convened a workshop to review that issue. The workshop promulgated a thoughtful and careful consensus statement.

SPECIAL REPORT: STATEMENT FROM THE NATIONAL INSTITUTES OF HEALTH WORKSHOP ON POPULATION SCREENING FOR THE CYSTIC FIBROSIS GENE

323 N. England J. Med. 70 (1990).

Cystic Fibrosis is an autosomal [i.e., not sex linked] recessive genetic disorder clinically characterized by chronic lung disease and pancreatic insufficiency. Median survival is 25 years, with an increasing number of patients surviving into their 30s. This disease affects about 1 in 2500 persons of European ancestry. It is less frequent among black and Hispanic Americans and is rare in Asians. One in 25 persons of European ancestry is a carrier, having one normal and one abnormal cystic fibrosis gene.

The cloning of the cystic fibrosis gene and identification of the most common mutation in the gene were major advances in medical genetics.

These break-throughs provide a basis for understanding the patho-physiology of the disease and offer the hope that improved therapy can be developed. In addition, there are immediate implications for the identification of carriers of a mutant cystic fibrosis gene.

Currently, DNA analysis can identify a single mutation in the cystic fibrosis gene that is present in 70 to 75 percent of carriers of European ancestry. Many additional mutations producing cystic fibrosis, currently about 20, have been identified. The identification of multiple individually rare mutations rather than a small number of common mutations will make carrier testing more difficult. The inability to detect all carriers creates complexities for the use of carrier testing at this time.

A major question is whether population-based screening for cystic fibrosis carriers could or should be implemented at present. Population-based screening implies offering a program of carrier testing, with appropriate informed consent and genetic counseling, to potentially millions of healthy people. The purpose of such screening would be to allow people to make more informed reproductive decisions with regard to the risk of cystic fibrosis in their offspring.

Unlike testing in the general population, testing for carriers in families in which the disease has occurred is nearly 100 percent informative. This is because carrier testing can be performed with linkage analysis in addition to mutation analysis when there is a DNA sample available from an affected person in a family. Therefore, testing should be offered to all individuals and couples with a family history of cystic fibrosis. This makes it more important than ever for providers of medical care to obtain family histories, particularly for patients of reproductive age.

In contrast, for a number of reasons there is a consensus that under the current circumstances population-based screening [i.e., screening the whole population, not just likely candidates] should not be recommended for individuals and couples with a negative family history. First among these reasons is the fact that currently the test will detect only 70 to 75 percent of carriers. Therefore, only about half the couples at risk can be identified. Second, the frequency of the disease and the different mutations vary according to racial and ethnic background, so that important laboratory and counseling modifications would be required in different populations. Third, there are substantial limitations on the ability to educate people regarding the use of an imperfect test. Fourth, without more definitive tests, about 1 in 15 couples—those in which one partner has a positive test and the other has a negative test—would be left at increased risk (approximately 1 in 500) of bearing a child with cystic fibrosis.

These difficulties would be substantially reduced if testing could detect at least 90 to 95 percent of carriers. There is a consensus that population-based screening for carriers could be offered to all persons of reproductive age if a 95 percent level of carrier detection were achieved. The offering of population-based screening would still require that substantial educational and counseling guidelines be satisfied. Benefits and risks of population-based screening and its feasibility are uncertain if this level of carrier detection cannot be achieved. When people without a family history of cystic fibrosis request testing, the physician should explain the risks and benefits of the test, either directly or through a center for genetic counseling.

Regardless of when or whether population-based screening becomes widespread, there is consensus on a number of screening guidelines. First, screening should be voluntary, and confidentiality must be assured. Second, screening requires informed consent. Pretest educational material should explain the hazards (for example, psychosocial effects and the loss of insurability) and benefits of choosing to be tested or choosing not to be tested. Third, providers of screening services have the obligation to ensure that adequate education and counseling are included in the program. Fourth, quality control of all aspects of the laboratory testing, including systematic proficiency testing, is required and should be implemented as soon as possible. And finally, there should be equal access to testing.

In view of the importance of the voluntary nature of screening and anticipated rapid changes in current information, legislative action to require cystic fibrosis screening is undesirable at present. There is consensus, however, that cystic fibrosis carriers should not be discriminated against with regard to insurability or employment. If evidence of discrimination emerges, corrective legislative action should be considered.

When population-based screening becomes available, who should be offered testing and in what setting? The most appropriate group for population-based screening comprises those of reproductive age. Although it is recognized that testing will often be provided to couples during pregnancy, it is preferable to offer screening before conception. Preconception testing offers a couple that has a one-in-four risk of having an affected child a broader range of reproductive options.

The optimal setting for carrier testing is through primary health care providers. Community-based screening programs provide an alternative setting. At present, newborn screening primarily to detect carriers is inappropriate, as are screening programs directed at children below reproductive age.

Education of the lay community and health care providers concerning the disease, its genetic transmission, and carrier testing is an important goal. Both traditional and innovative methods should be used for community education. Education regarding carrier testing for cystic fibrosis could have a major effect on the level of genetic knowledge in the population.

In addition to obtaining informed consent, providers of carrier screening must ensure the availability of appropriate genetic counseling. Those with a negative carrier test should require minimal counseling but should be reminded of the limitations of the test. Those identified as carriers should be informed of the personal and family implications of their status. Group and individual counseling services should be available. After specialized training, physicians, nurses, social workers, and other health care personnel could provide much of this counseling service. A range of teaching devices to be shared with family members should be developed and evaluated as an adjunct to counseling.

Couples found to have a one-in-four risk require comprehensive individual genetic counseling by a qualified professional. This counseling should be non-directive and should help the couple to make reproductive decisions consonant with their own beliefs. Educational materials that present a range of views and options should be developed.

Pilot programs investigating research questions in the delivery of population-based screening for cystic fibrosis carriers are urgently needed. These programs should address clearly defined questions, including the effectiveness of educational materials, the level of utilization of screening, laboratory aspects, counseling issues, costs, and the beneficial and deleterious effects of screening. One important issue is to determine the effect on couples who are at increased risk because only one partner has an identified cystic fibrosis mutation. Pilot programs should examine alternative models of delivery that could be generalized. Federal funds are critically needed to carry out these programs.

The development of carrier-screening programs for cystic fibrosis should not detract from the current scientific efforts to improve the treatment of this disease. Currently, about 30,000 Americans have cystic fibrosis, and additional children with the disease are born every day. The ability to identify couples at risk will continue to be important even if more successful treatments are developed.

Note: Post–Conception Genetic Screening and Genetic Counseling

Reproductive decisionmaking is not limited to the choice of a mate; as long as the opportunity to choose an abortion is available that decisionmaking will continue after the pregnancy begins. Some screening devices that are now available, such as amniocentesis, provide some information about the chromosomal structure and genetic makeup of a fetus. Presumably, the human genome project will result in the availability of much more genetic information, and, possibly, in the development of a technique that will allow for the discovery of the complete genetic profile of the fetus.

Most women considering genetic testing are initially referred to genetic counselors who undertake the difficult process of helping them understand the advantages and risks of testing during pregnancy. The process of genetic counseling is a complex one. For a woman to give informed consent to the procedure, she must understand the risks and benefits. Ideally, the counselor will explain the process of amniocentesis, the risk to the fetus, the information which can be obtained, and the possible implications of the information. The counselor will also try to elicit a detailed medical history, and be responsive to the woman's questions and concerns. To this counseling session, each woman will bring her own unique understanding of her pregnancy, reflecting her cultural, economic, religious and familial experiences. Her pre-existing views on abortion, disabilities, and child-bearing will all shape her receptiveness to genetic testing. As one commentator describes,

> When viewed culturally, * * * the process of obtaining "informed consent" is not simply the exchange of information-for-signature negotiated at the intake interview. It is based on all the assumptions, fears, and norms concerning healthy and sickly children with which any given woman undertakes a pregnancy. It includes the meaning of illness in family history: the shame and pride attached to the bearing (or non-bearing) of children; beliefs about fertility, abortion, femininity and masculinity; and the social consequences and prejudices surrounding disability * * *.

Rapp, Chromosomes and Communication: The Discourse of Genetic Counseling, 2 Med. Anthropology Q. 143 (1988).

Complicating this genetic counseling is the fact that much genetic data is inherently ambiguous. For example, a chromosome may often indicate the presence of a disease without indicating whether it is only a slight manifestation or a severe one. This imprecision in the test results may make it extremely difficult for a pregnant woman to decide whether to terminate the pregnancy. The genetic counselor faces a series of decisions in this regard. Is there any genetic information which should be kept from the mother because its use would be inappropriate in decision-making? Who should define what is appropriate?

There is little disagreement that information that the fetus carries a genetic disease that will lead to an early and painful death should be provided to the mother. However, there is greater debate about whether the Downs Syndrome status of the child, a primary reason for amniocentesis, is a justifiable basis for abortion. Whose decision should that be? Should parents have a legal right to abort a fetus with a relatively minor genetic defect? Or because the fetus is not the gender they hoped for? Pennsylvania, for example, has considered prohibiting abortions based on the gender of the child. How far should parental discretion be allowed in selecting the traits of their child? Would screening be justifiable solely to determine the fetus's eye color, height, or athletic promise?

c. Employment

Some employers are already using genetic tests to determine the susceptibility of their workers to occupational illnesses because there are several identifiable genetic traits that can give rise to illness under circumstances likely to arise in particular occupational settings. For example, exposure to aromatic nitro and amino compounds exacerbates the consequences of NADH dehydrogenase deficiency, a genetic defect disproportionally affecting Native Alaskans, Navajos and Puerto Ricans, and oxidizing chemicals appear to exacerbate glucose-phosphate dehydrogenase deficiency, a sex linked trait that only affects males. See Rowinski, Genetic Testing in the Work Place, 4 J. Contem. Health L. & Pol. 375 n. 3 (1988). As Ms. Rowinski points out, there are several reasons that employers may wish to screen their employees for genetic traits:

> First, employers may have a sincere concern for the health of their employees, believing that protection through exclusion is the most effective paternalistic policy available. Second, with increasing insurance costs, employers have a strong economic incentive to minimize their liabilities created by occupational health hazards, and to avoid lawsuits arising from resulting injuries. Third, genetic predictions could increase productivity by decreasing absenteeism due to illness. Finally, many employers contend that it is not economically feasible to maintain a work place safe for all employees, as required under the Occupational Safety and Health Act. Genetic tests could make this a more realistic objective, however, by screening out those employees with the lowest tolerance levels, and thereby minimizing the need for expensive safety equipment and procedures.

Id. at 387 (Footnotes omitted).

On the other hand, there is a risk that employers could use this information inappropriately to subvert other legal requirements. For example, there is little doubt that refusing employment to those with the sickle cell trait—as the United States Air Force did for some time—is little more than a cover for racism. Similarly, screening for other genetic diseases could be a cover to avoid the obligation of maintaining a safe workplace or to avoid the consequences of Title VII of the Civil Rights Act, the Rehabilitation Act or the Americans With Disabilities Act. See Note, Employment Discrimination Implications of Genetic Screening in the Workplace Under Title VII and the Rehabilitation Act, 10 Am.J.L. and Med. 323 (1984). Because of the uncertainty of the reach of federal law, some states have acted to eliminate potential employment discrimination based on genetic structure. See, e.g., N.J. Stat. Ann. § 10:5–12 (West 1986) (outlawing discrimination on the basis of any genetic trait), and West's Fla.Stat.Ann. § 488.075 (West 1986) and N.C.Gen.Stat. § 95–28.1 (1985) (both outlawing discrimination on the basis of sickle cell trait).

Should employers be able to eliminate hypersusceptible workers from jobs where their unusual genetic structure creates a risk of illness that will not be faced by other potential employees? Does any employee have the right to cause the employer or the employer's insurer to bear the potential economic burden of an increased risk of occupational disease? For an excellent review of these questions, see M. Rothstein,

Occupational Safety and Health Law (1990) and M. Rothstein, Medical Screening and the Employee Health Cost Crisis (1989). See also Office of Technology Assessment, Role of Genetic Testing in the Prevention of Occupational Disease, (1983).

d. *Insurance*

While insurance companies are doing very little genetic testing now, they are interested in the development of the technology. After all, insurance decisions are based upon classifications which are themselves based upon the likelihood, timing and amount of any potential claim. To the extent that genetic information is useful in predicting illness or death, it will be useful in classifying those who apply for health insurance or life insurance. Should an insurance company treat a genetic likelihood of early death any differently from a recently diagnosed cancer? While forbidding insurance companies from denying coverage to those with identifiable genetic traits will transfer the cost of their illness or death to the rest of the population, that cost sharing may be the very purpose of insurance.

One problem that could arise from failure to do a genetic screen on those who apply for insurance is the problem of moral hazard. If a potential insured knows that he has a genetic trait that will lead to his early death, for example, and the insurance company does not know that, the potential insured has an incentive to buy more insurance than he would if the premium were set at a level that reflected his knowledge. Insurance is a gamble. If you know more than the insurance company you may be tempted to buy more insurance because you can beat the odds—although only your beneficiaries will benefit. The problem of moral hazard is reduced if an insurance company is permitted to ask the potential insured whether he knows that he has any relevant genetic trait. Even then, some would suggest that a minimum amount of life insurance and health insurance should be permitted to those whose defect is beyond their control; the value of fairness to those with genetic defects may outweigh the problem of moral hazard.

While the federal government puts no real limitation on genetic testing by insurance companies, two states have promulgated statutes and both permit insurance companies to use genetic screening and its results as long as there is an actuarial basis for doing so. See, West's Ann.Cal.Ins.Code § 10143 (West Supp.1988), Md.Ann.Code 1986, Art. 48 A, § 223 (1986). For an interesting account of this entire question, see Miller, Genetic Testing and Insurance Classification: National Action Can Prevent Discrimination Based on the "Luck of the Genetic Draw", 93 Dickinson L.Rev. 729 (1989).

e. *Other Purposes*

There are a range of other potential uses for information gleaned from genetic screening. As a matter of policy, should immigration decisions be made to strengthen the gene pool of the country? Should those whose genetic screening demonstrates they are most likely to succeed in school be afforded a better education? Should those who are most likely to succeed in certain substantive areas be directed to those areas? Should the concept of mens rea be altered in the criminal law to reflect genetic propensity to commit acts of violence? Is there a particular genetic configuration that is likely to make someone a better parent, and should such genetic information be relevant to a court making a custody determination? Should that information be available to a court in an adoption action? To what extent might consideration of the genetic structure of a person be relevant to decisionmaking by others? To what extent should the state intervene to forbid the use of that genetic knowledge in decisionmaking?

2. Confidentiality and Genetic Information

Obviously, a person upon whom a genetic screen has been performed has a very strong interest in maintaining the confidentiality of the results. How is this to be weighed against the claimed interest of employers, insurers, genetic researchers, and others who might have a direct interest in the test? These "others" include relatives of the patient who unknowingly might be carrying the same genetic defect. Does the person conducting the test have an obligation to inform a patient's sister, for example, when that sister may put her children at risk of a genetic disorder for which she can be tested? Consider the following set of guidelines for disclosure of the results of genetic screening to third parties.

KOBRIN, COMMENT: CONFIDENTIALITY OF GENETIC INFORMATION
30 U.C.L.A. L.Rev. 1283, 1313–1314 (1983).

GUIDELINES FOR THE DUTY TO DISCLOSE

Effective guidelines for the physician/counselor must reflect two goals: first, the preservation of the privacy rights of the counselee, and second, the prevention of harm to third parties.[213] The first goal can be met by careful definition of situations where the harm is serious enough to require disclosure. When such a situation is identified, there must be controls to insure that only information necessary to prevent the harm is revealed and that it is disclosed only to those who may be affected.

Achieving the second goal, effective prevention of harm to third parties, may turn upon the timeliness of disclosure. Suppose a female

213. The President's Commission has framed this issue as follows: "It is worth emphasizing that the harm-prevention argument for compelled disclosure merely shows that the commitment to confidentiality is not absolute in cases of the sort described. It does not establish that a general practice of breaching the confidentiality of genetic information would have acceptable consequences." [ ]

counselee, a carrier of an X-linked disorder, refuses to disclose that information to her pregnant sister. If the counselor is permitted or obligated to inform the sister immediately of her potential difficulties, she may, if she wishes, obtain screening and counseling. She will then be able to make an informed and timely decision regarding her pregnancy. An untimely disclosure would defeat the purpose of excepting this information from traditional confidentiality restraints.[214]

This Comment proposes legislative guidelines for disclosure as part of statutory regulation of genetic counseling. This legislation, designed to meet both disclosure goals, should do the following:

1. Specify the party or parties with an unconditional right of access to the information obtained, and the duties of the counselor to disclose that information. This disclosure should be limited to the counselees.

2. Guarantee non-disclosure to all other parties unless:

(a) explicit signed consent is obtained from the counselee for each specific disclosure; or

(b) the situation falls within one of the exceptions set forth below.

3. Define the exceptions to confidentiality and create specific guidelines to determine each exception. These exceptions should be:

(a) disclosure to relatives who the genetic information indicated are at risk; and [215]

(b) disclosure for research purposes.

4. Provide for civil and/or criminal penalties for unauthorized disclosure.

* * *

The author of this comment proposes a legislative solution to the problem of balancing the interests in confidentiality with the interest of third parties in gaining access to genetic information. Is this kind of policy best developed through the legislative process, or might it better be developed by health care providers, institutions, and professional organizations? Might the knowledge that a doctor will tell relatives of

214. The President's Commission has suggested that "[s]ince the decision to breach professional confidentiality is such a weighty one, it may * * * be advisable to seek review by an appropriate third party." *Id.* at 44–45. This Comment takes the position that any procedural requirements for review may delay disclosure to the extent that the prospective harm can no longer be prevented.

215. The probability of risk of specific disorders for various relatives would be determined with the help of specialists in genetics. Policy-makers would then decide how serious the disorder must be and how high the probability of occurrence must be to require disclosure. Guidelines based on these decisions would specify who must be notified in a given situation. This will protect the counselee from wholesale distribution of sensitive information to family members and underscore the policy objectives of harm-prevention.

a patient's genetic defect discourage patients from being tested for the defect—at least in some cases?   Should patients be allowed to consent to genetic testing on the condition that no one—not even those at risk—be told of the results?   Is current legal protection of the confidentiality of all medical information enough to protect the confidentiality of genetic information, or is there the need for additional legal protection of such a sensitive kind of medical information?   For a general account of the legal protection of confidential medical information, see chapter 3, above.

Chapter 10

DEFINING DEATH

Problem: When Does Death Occur?

Alberto Arcturus was face down by the side of the road, apparently after being run down by a hit-and-run driver, when a passing motorist saw him and called the local emergency medical services. An ambulance with two paramedics arrived on the scene about fifteen minutes after the call, and they found that Mr. Arcturus was not breathing and that he had no pulse. They also discovered that a substantial portion of his head (including his forehead and forebrain) was crushed. One paramedic looked at the other and said, "He's dead; let's call the morgue." The second, less experienced paramedic insisted on trying to resuscitate Mr. Arcturus, as was required by the emergency medical services manual for paramedics. They placed him in the ambulance and administered cardiopulmonary resuscitation throughout the fifteen minute ride to the nearest hospital emergency room.

At the emergency room physicians confirmed that Mr. Arcturus did not breathe spontaneously and had no spontaneous cardiac activity. One doctor told the charge nurse that he was dead, and that "dead on arrival" should be marked on his chart. A young intern balked at this, however, because the hospital emergency room protocol required more before a brain injured patient could be declared dead. The physicians then administered drugs and used paddles that sent an electric current through Mr. Arcturus's chest in an effort to start his heart. After some time they managed to get a weak pulse, and they placed Mr. Arcturus on a ventilator and moved him to the intensive care unit. A neurology consult revealed that Mr. Arcturus's neocortex was completely and irreversibly destroyed—most of it was literally gone, left on the highway—although his brain stem remained intact. Another consult revealed that Mr. Arcturus had a healthy kidney and liver, each of which could be transplanted to save the life of another patient in the hospital. With the help of a ventilator (necessary because of the head and chest injuries to the patient), Mr. Arcturus's body could continue functioning indefinitely.

After considerable investigation, police have captured a person who, they believe, was the hit-and-run driver who ran into Mr. Arcturus. They wish to know whether to charge him with vehicular homicide (a felony), or something else (all other potential offenses would be misdemeanors). The doctors and Mr. Arcturus's family want to know

1034

whether he is dead or alive. Further, if he is dead, they want to know when he died—at the roadside, in the hospital emergency room, in the intensive care unit, or somewhere else. Mr. Arcturus's health insurer is denying coverage because "we only pay for necessary medical services, and no services are necessary when the patient is dead." Finally, the transplant team at the hospital wants to know if Mr. Arcturus's organs are available for transplantation.

I. "SOCIAL–MORAL" AND "MEDICAL–SCIENTIFIC" PERSPECTIVES OF DEATH

As we saw in Chapter 9, defining "personhood" has vexed commentators for centuries. Determining when a "person" died, however, was simple until the last few decades. Death occurred when several simultaneous physical changes occurred. These changes included the cessation of all cardiopulmonary (heart and lung) function, the cessation of all cognitive activity, the cessation of all responsive activity, and with only slight delay, the onset of rigormortis, livormortis, and, eventually, putrification. There could be no question about whether death would occur if all cognitive and responsive activity ceased but cardiopulmonary function continued because those functions were so closely related that the existence of one without the other would be impossible for more than a few hours. Because the cessation of cardiopulmonary functions was so much easier to observe than the cessation of cognitive ability, responsive activity, and other delayed attributes of death, the cessation of cardiopulmonary functions became, informally and practically, the definition of death. This test was never really anything more significant than the most convenient *evidence* of death; there is no suggestion that there was any basis for making cardiopulmonary functions definitional.

The development of mechanical substitutes for hearts and lungs has forced reconsideration of the definition of death. It is now possible for a person to be without cognitive or responsive activity (i.e., without any brain activity), and yet maintain cardiopulmonary functions with the assistance of technological devices. Logically, this temporal division of these formerly contemporaneous attributes requires a determination of what death is. Is it the cessation of cardiopulmonary functions or is it the cessation of some, or all, brain functions?

The definition of death, like any other definition in law, ought to be functional. It is impossible to determine what ought to constitute death before the purpose of the definition is articulated. It should not be surprising that the legal function of defining death might be very different from the psychological function, which might be very different from the historical, sociological, anthropological, and medical functions. For example, the law must establish a time to distribute property from the estate, to require the payment of death contracts (i.e., life insurance), and to purge voting lists. Psychologists, however, may determine that death is a period of settling relationships, mourning, and healing. Physicians may view it as a time when their obligation to act in the interest of the patient ceases. There are many definitions of death, and, ultimately, attempts to develop an interdisciplinary consensus on the definition of death may be futile. This section will review two perspectives on death and the dying process, the "social-moral" perspective and the "medical-scientific" perspective. As you read these accounts, try to determine which, if either, provides the more useful philosophical basis for creating a legal definition of death. After a consideration of these philosophical bases, this section will review the distinction between the cardiopulmonary death and brain death models, and seek to evaluate whether they are inconsistent in any way. Finally, it will review the development of a legal definition of death over the last several years and consider the legal consequences of the general acceptance of a brain death or combined brain death-cardiopulmonary death definition.

MORISON, DEATH: PROCESS OR EVENT?
173 Science 694 (Aug.1971)

Most discussions of death and dying shift uneasily, and often more or less unconsciously, from one point of view to another. On the one hand, the common noun "death" is thought of as standing for a clearly defined event, a stop function that puts a sharp end to life. On the other, dying is seen as a long-drawn-out process that begins when life itself begins and is not completed in any given organism until the last cell ceases to convert energy.

* * *

It should be quite clear that, just as we do not observe a fluid heat, but only differences in temperature, we do not observe "life" as such. Life is not a thing or a fluid anymore than heat is. What we observe are some unusual sets of objects separated from the rest of the world by certain peculiar properties such as growth, reproduction, and special ways of handling energy. These objects we elect to call "living things." From here, it is but a short step to the invention of a hypothetical entity that is possessed by all living things and that is supposed to account for the difference between living and nonliving things. We might call this entity "livingness," following the usual rule for making abstract nouns out of participles and adjectives. This sounds rather awkward, so we use the word "life" instead. This apparently tiny change in the shape of the noun helps us on our way to philosophical error. The very cumbersomeness of the word "livingness" reminds us that we have abstracted the quality for which it stands from an array of living things. The word "life," however, seems much more substantial in its own right. Indeed, it is all too easy to believe that the word, like so many other nouns, stands for something that must have an existence of its own and must be definable in general terms, quite apart from the particular objects it characterizes. Men thus find themselves thinking more and more about life as a thing in itself, capable of entering inanimate aggregations of material and turning them into living things. It is then but a short step to believing that, once life is there, it can leave or be destroyed, thereby turning living things into dead things.

* * *

Death is no more a single, clearly delimited, momentary phenomenon than is infancy, adolescence, or middle age. The gradualness of the process of dying is even clearer than it was in Shakespeare's time, for we now know that various parts of the body can go on living for months after its central organization has disintegrated. Some cell lines, in fact, can be continued indefinitely.

* * * The integrated physiological system does not inevitably fail all at once. Substitutes can be devised for each of the major components, and the necessary integration can be provided by a computer. All the traditional vital signs are still there—provided in large part by the machines. Death does not come by inevitable appointment. He must sit patiently in the waiting room until summoned by the doctor or nurse.

* * *

We must now ask ourselves how much sense it makes to try to deal with this complex set of physiological, social, and ethical variables simply by "redefining" death or by developing new criteria for pronouncing an organism dead. Aside from the esoteric philosophical concerns discussed so far, it must be recognized that practical matters of great moment are at stake. Fewer and fewer people die quietly in their beds while relatives and friends live on, unable to stay the inevitable course. More and more patients are subject to long, continued intervention; antibiotics, intravenous feeding, artificial respiration, and even artificially induced heartbeats sustain an increasingly fictional existence. All this costs money—so much money, in fact, that the retirement income of a surviving spouse may disappear in a few months. There are other costs, less tangible but perhaps more important—for example, the diversion of scarce medical resources from younger people temporarily threatened by acute but potentially curable illnesses. Worst of all is the strain on a family that may have to live for years in close association with a mute, but apparently living corpse.

* * *

As our skill in simulating the physiological processes underlying life continues to increase in disproportion to our capacity to maintain its psychological, emotional, or spiritual quality, the difficulty of regarding death as a single, more or less coherent event, resulting in the instantaneous dissolution of the organism as a whole, is likely to become more and more apparent.

* * * [I]t is clear that it is the complex interactions that make the characteristic human being. The appropriate integration of these interactions is only loosely coupled to the physiological functions of circulation and respiration. The latter continue for a long time after the integrated "personality" has disappeared. Conversely, the natural

rhythms of heart and respiration can fail, while the personality remains intact. The complex human organism does not often fail as a unit. The nervous system is, of course, more closely coupled to personality than are the heart and lungs (a fact that is utilized in developing the new definitions of death), but there is clearly something arbitrary in tying the sanctity of life to our ability to detect the electrical potential charges that managed to traverse the impedance of the skull.

* * *

[T]he life of the dying patient becomes steadily less complicated and rich, and, as a result, less worth living or preserving. The pain and suffering involved in maintaining what is left are inexorably mounting, while the benefits enjoyed by the patient himself, or that he can in any way confer on those around him, are just as inexorably declining. As the costs mount higher and higher and the benefits become smaller and smaller, one may well begin to wonder what the point of it all is. These are the unhappy facts of the matter, and we will have to face them sooner or later. Indeed, attempts to face the facts are already being made, but usually in a gingerly and incomplete fashion. As we have seen, one way to protect ourselves is to introduce imaginary discontinuities into what are, in fact, continuous processes.

* * *

Once it is recognized that the process of dying under modern conditions is at least partially controlled by the decisions made by individual human beings, it becomes necessary to think rather more fully and carefully about what human beings should be involved and what kinds of considerations should be taken into account in making the decisions.

* * *

It is not only probable, but highly desirable that society should proceed with the greatest caution and deliberation in proposing procedures that in any serious way threaten the traditional sanctity of the individual life. As a consequence, society will certainly move very slowly in developing formal arrangements for taking into account the interests of others in life-and-death decisions. It may not be improper, however, to suggest one step that could be taken right now. Such a step might ease the way for many dying patients without impairing the sanctity or dignity of the individual life: instead it should be enhanced. I refer here to the possibility of changing social attitudes and laws that now restrain an individual from taking an intelligent interest in his own death.

* * *

KASS, DEATH AS AN EVENT, A COMMENTARY ON ROBERT MORISON
173 Science 698 (Aug.1971)

As I understand R.S. Morison's argument, it consists of these parts, although presented in different order. First: He notes that we face serious practical problems as a result of our unswerving adherence to the principle, "always prolong life." Second: Although *some* of these problems could be solved by updating the "definition of death," such revisions are scientifically and philosophically unsound. Third: The reason for this is that life and death are part of a continuum; it will prove impossible, in practice, to identify any border between them because theory tells us that no such border exists. Thus: We need to abandon both the idea of death as a concrete event and the search for its definition; instead, we must face the fact that our practical problems can only be solved by difficult judgments, based upon a complex cost-benefit analysis, concerning the value of the lives that might or might not be prolonged.

I am in agreement with Morison only on the first point. I think he leads us into philosophical, scientific, moral, and political error. * * *

The difficulties begin in Morison's beginning, in his failure to distinguish clearly among aging, dying, and dead.

* * *

* * * We must keep separate two distinct and crucial questions facing the physician: (i) When, if ever, is a person's life no longer worth prolonging? and (ii) When is a person in fact dead? The first question translates, in practice, to: When is it permissible or desirable for a physician to withhold or withdraw treatment so that a patient (still alive) may be allowed to die? The second question translates, in practice, to: When does the physician pronounce the (ex)patient fit for burial? Morison is concerned only with the first question. He commendably condemns attempts to evade this moral issue by definitional wizardry. But regardless of how one settles the question of whether and what kind of life should be prolonged, one will still need criteria for recognizing the end. * * *

In considering the definition and determination of death, we note that there is a difference between the meaning of an abstract concept such as death (or mass or gravity or time) and the operations used to determine or measure it. * * * [T]he various proposals for updating the definition of death, their own language to the contrary, are not offering a new definition of death but merely refining the procedure stating that a man has died. Although there is much that could be said about these proposals, my focus here is on Morison's challenge to the concept of death as an event, and to the possibility of determining it.

* * *

What dies is the organism as a whole. It is this death, the death of the individual human being, that is important for physicians and for the community, not the "death" of organs or cells, which are mere parts.

Lacking a concept of the organism as a whole, and confusing the concept of death with the criteria for determining it, Morison errs by trying to identify the whole with one of its parts and by seeking a single "infallible physiological index" to human personhood. One might as well try to identify a watch with either its mainspring or its hands; the watch is neither of these, yet it is "dead" without either. Why is the concept of the organism as a whole so difficult to grasp? Is it because we have lost or discarded, in our reductionist biology, all notions of organism, of whole?

In my opinion, the question, "Is he dead?" can still be treated as a question of fact, albeit one with great moral and social consequences. I hold it to be a medical-scientific question in itself, not only in that physicians answer it for us. Morison treats it largely as a social-moral question. This is because, as I indicated above, he does not distinguish the question of when a man is dead from the question of when his life is not worth prolonging. Thus, there is a conjoined issue: Is the determination of death a matter of the true, or a matter of the useful or good?

We are all in Morison's debt for inviting us to consider the suffering that often results from slavish and limitless attempts to prolong life. But there is no need to abandon traditional ethics to deal with this problem. The Judeo–Christian tradition, which teaches us the duty of preserving life, does not itself hold life to be the absolute value. The medical tradition, until very recently, shared this view. Indeed, medicine's purpose was originally *health,* not simply the unlimited prolongation of life or the conquest of disease and death. Both traditions looked upon death as a natural part of life, not as an unmitigated evil or as a sign of the physician's failure. We sorely need to recover this more accepting attitude toward death and, with it, a greater concern for the human needs of the dying patient. We need to keep company with the dying and to help them cope with terminal illness. We must learn to desist from those useless technological interventions and institutional practices that deny to the dying what we most owe them—a good end. These purposes could be accomplished in large measure by restoring to medical practice the ethic of allowing a person to die.

But the ethic of allowing a person to die is based solely on a consideration of the welfare of the dying patient himself, rather than on a consideration of benefits that accrue to others. This is a crucial point. It is one thing to take one's bearings from the patient and his interests and attitudes, to protect his dignity and his right to a good death against the onslaught of machinery and institutionalized loneliness; it is quite a different thing to take one's bearings from the interests of, or costs and benefits to, relatives or society. The first is in keeping with the physician's duty to act as the loyal agent of his patient; the second is a perversion of that duty, because it renders the physician, in this decisive test of his loyalty, merely an agent of society, and ultimately, her executioner. The first upholds and preserves the respect for human life and personal dignity; the second sacrifices these on the evershifting altar of public opinion.

* * *

SUMMARY

1) We have no need to abandon either the concept of death as an event or the efforts to set forth reasonable criteria for determining that a man has indeed died.

2) We need to recover both an attitude that is more accepting of death and a greater concern for the human needs of the dying patient. But we should not contaminate these concerns with the interests of relatives, potential transplant recipients, or "society." To do so would be both wrong and dangerous.

3) We should pause to note some of the heavy costs of technological progress in medicine: the dehumanization of the end of life, both for those who die and for those who live on; and the defogging of the minds of intelligent and moral men with respect to the most important human matters.

II. RELIGIOUS PERSPECTIVE ON DEATH

In attempting to develop a legal definition of death, there is no particular reason to be bound by the social-moral perspective or the medical-scientific perspective. There are a variety of other social conceptions of death; many of the most pervasive of those considerations are theological. For many people, death is significant not just because it ends life, but because it begins something else.

> For Christians, death is not seen as the destruction or annihilation of the person. Although dissolution of the spirit-body bond that exists during our life is painful, death, viewed as transformation of the person to a new state of existence, is not. Furthermore, the Christian belief is that he will be resurrected, that the body in some way will share in the new life promised by Jesus Christ. Thus, the Christian is able to view the determination of death from a wider perspective than purely medical. This understanding provides the proper perspective for approaching the legal aspects of the determination of death.

Showalter, Determining Death: The Legal and Theological Aspects of Brain–Related Criteria, 27 Catholic Lawyer 112, 116 (1982). Whatever the consequences of death, the determination of the moment of death has generally been perceived to be a medical function, essentially independent of its legal, theological, social, psychological, and other consequences. For example, Pope Pius XII indicated that "it remains for the doctor * * * to give a clear and precise definition of 'death' and the 'moment of death' of a patient who passes away in a state of unconsciousness." Pope Pius XII, The Prolongation of Life (Nov. 24, 1957).

III. THE DEVELOPMENT OF THE "BRAIN DEATH" DEFINITION

Given that even the religious perspective of death treats the issue as one for medical expertise, it is not surprising that the first well-accepted definition of death to include brain death came from the Harvard Medical School and was published in the Journal of the American Medical Association. The Ad Hoc Committee of the Harvard Medical School used the term "irreversible coma" to define what is now generally called brain death and suggested that "no statutory change in the law should be necessary since the law treats this question essentially as one of fact to be determined by physicians."

The Ad Hoc Committee was explicit in describing its purpose in promulgating its new definition of death:

> Our primary purpose is to define irreversible coma as a new criterion for death. There are two reasons why there is need for a definition: (1) Improvements in resuscitative and supportive measures have led to increased efforts to save those who are desperately injured. Sometimes these efforts have only partial success so that the result is an individual whose heart continues to beat but whose brain is irreversibly damaged. The burden is great on patients who suffer permanent loss of intellect, on their families, on the hospitals, and on those in need of hospital beds already occupied by these comatose patients. (2) Obsolete criteria for the definition of death can lead to controversy in obtaining organs for transplantation.

Report of the Ad Hoc Committee of the Harvard Medical School to Examine the Definition of Brain Death, 205 J.A.M.A. 85 (Aug.1968). In addition to listing the characteristics of irreversible coma—unreceptivity and unresponsivity, no movements or breathing, no reflexes, and flat electro-encephalogram—the Ad Hoc Committee recommended that death be declared before the respirator is turned off ("in our judgment it will provide a greater degree of legal protection to those involved"), that the physician in charge consult with others before the declaration of death is made, that the physician (rather than the family) make the decision, and that the decision to declare death be made by physicians who are not involved "in any later effort to transplant organs or tissue from the deceased individual." Id.

The Ad Hoc Committee's determination that brain death ought to constitute death met surprisingly little medical opposition. There has been debate over the precise nature of the characteristics of "irreversible coma" that can give rise to brain death and over whether the issue should be left to physicians or be brought into the domain of public debate and converted into a formal legal standard. The Ad Hoc Committee contributed substantially to this debate by the publication of its report. They also contributed to the confusion that subsequently has surrounded the issue by using such terms as "irreversible coma," which is now generally used to refer to something less than brain death, and "hopelessly damaged," as synonyms for brain death. The consensus that brain death is in fact death of the human being confirms that the cessation of heart-lung activity may never have been more than evidence of death. The real defining characteristic was that there be, in the words of the Ad Hoc Committee, "no discernable central nervous system activity."

The Ad Hoc Committee concluded:

> From ancient times down to the recent past it was clear that, when the respiration and heart stopped, the brain would die in a few minutes; so the obvious criterion of no heart beat as synonymous with death was sufficiently accurate. In those times the heart was considered to be the central organ of the body; it is not surprising that its failure marked the onset of death. This is no longer valid when modern resuscitative and supportive measures are used. These improved activities can now restore "life" as judged by the ancient standards of persistent respiration and continuing heart beat. This can be the case even when there is not the remotest possibility of an individual recovering consciousness following massive brain damage. In other situations "life" can be maintained only by means of artificial respiration and electrical stimulation of the heart beat, or in temporarily by-passing the heart, or, in conjunction with these things, reducing with cold the body's oxygen requirement.

Id. As the leading legal and medical experts point out, the Ad Hoc Committee marked the beginning of the public debate over brain death; closure was not to come until some time later.

> Not surprisingly, disquiet over the change in medical attitude and practice arose in lay as well as medical circles. The prospect of physicians agreeing amongst themselves to change the rules by which life is measured in order to salvage a larger number of transplantable organs met with something short of universal approval. Especially with increasing disenchantment over heart transplantation (the procedure in which the traditional criteria for determining death posed the most difficulties), some doubt arose whether it was wise to adopt measures which encouraged a medical "advance" that seemed to have gotten ahead of its own basic technology. Furthermore, many people—doctors included—found themselves with nagging if often unarticulated doubts about how to proceed in the situation, far more common than transplantation, in which a long-comatose patient shows every prospect of "living" indefinitely with artificial means of support. As a result of this growing public and professional concern, elected officials, with the encouragement of the medical community, have urged public discussion and action to dispel the apprehension created by the new

medical knowledge and to clarify and reformulate the law. Some commentators, however, have argued that public bodies and laymen in general have no role to play in this process of change. Issue is therefore joined on at least two points: (1) ought the public to be involved in "defining" death? and (2) if so, how ought it to be involved—specifically, ought governmental action, in the form of legislation, be taken?

Capron and Kass, A Statutory Definition of the Standards for Determining Human Death: An Appraisal and a Proposal, 121 U.Pa.L.Rev. 87, 91–92 (1972).

The first state to promulgate a statute adopting brain death was Kansas. The 1970 Kansas statute provided alternatively for both brain death and traditional cardiopulmonary death:

> A person will be considered medically and legally dead if, in the opinion of a physician, based on ordinary standards of medical practice, there is the absence of spontaneous respiratory and cardiac function and, because of the disease or condition which caused, directly or indirectly, these functions to cease, or because of the passage of time since these functions ceased, attempts at resuscitation are considered hopeless; and, in this event, death will have occurred at the time these functions ceased; or

> A person will be considered medically and legally dead if, in the opinion of a physician, based on ordinary standards of medical practice, there is the absence of spontaneous brain function; and if based on ordinary standards of medical practice, during reasonable attempts to either maintain or restore spontaneous circulatory or respiratory function in the absence of aforesaid brain function, it appears that further attempts at resuscitation or supportive maintenance will not succeed, death will have occurred at the time when these conditions first coincide. Death is to be pronounced before artificial means of supporting respiratory and circulatory function are terminated and before any vital organ is removed for purposes of transplantation.

> These alternative definitions of death are to be utilized for all purposes in this state, including the trials of civil and criminal cases, any laws to the contrary notwithstanding.

Kan.Stat.Ann. § 77–202.

The statute was quickly copied and just as quickly criticized. The primary criticism was directed to the alternative definitions of death, which some believed might lead to the conclusion that a person could be either dead or alive depending on which paragraph of the definition the determining physician invoked. It is hard to believe, however, that these alternative definitions would result in any confusion in fact, and there has been no case that has engendered such confusion in Kansas or any other state with a similar statute. Professor Capron and Dr. Kass proposed an alternative to the Kansas statute. Their proposal grew out of the Research Group on Death and Dying at the Hastings Center. It would provide:

A person will be considered dead if in the announced opinion of a physician, based on ordinary standards of medical practice, he has experienced an irreversible cessation of spontaneous respiratory and circulatory functions. In the event that artificial means of support precluded a determination that these functions have ceased, a person will be considered dead if in the announced opinion of a physician, based on ordinary standards of medical practice, he has experienced an irreversible cessation of spontaneous brain functions. Death will have occurred at the time when the relevant functions ceased.

Capron and Kass defended their alternative statute, and compared it to the Kansas statute:

The legislation suggested here departs from the Kansas statute in its basic approach to the problem of "defining" death: the proposed statute does not set about to establish a special category of "brain death" to be used by transplanters. Further, there are a number of particular points of difference between them. For example, the proposed statute does not speak of persons being "medically and legally dead," thus avoiding redundancy and, more importantly, the mistaken implication that the "medical" and "legal" definitions could differ. Also, the proposed legislation does not include the provision that "death is to be pronounced before" the machine is turned off or any organs removed. Such a *modus operandi,* which was incorporated by Kansas from the Harvard Committee's report, may be advisable for physicians on public relations grounds, but it has no place in a statute "defining" death. The proposed statute already provides that "Death will have occurred at the time when the relevant functions ceased." If supportive aids, or organs, are withdrawn after this time, such acts cannot be implicated as having caused death. The manner in which, or exact time at which, the physician should articulate his finding is a matter best left to the exigencies of the situation, to local medical customs or hospital rules, or to statutes on the procedures for certifying death or on transplantation if the latter is the procedure which raises the greatest concern of medical impropriety. The real safeguard against doctors killing patients is not to be found in a statute "defining" death. Rather, it inheres in physicians' ethical and religious beliefs, which are also embodied in the fundamental professional ethic of *primum non nocere* and are reinforced by homicide and "wrongful death" laws and the rules governing medical negligence applicable in license revocation proceedings or in private actions for damages.

The proposed statute shares with the Kansas legislation two features of which [some commentators are] critical. First, it does not require that two physicians participate in determining death, as recommended by most groups which set forth suggestions about transplantation. The reasons for the absence of such a provision

should be obvious. Since the statute deals with death in general
and not with death in relation to transplantation, there is no
reason for it to establish a general rule which is required only in
that unusual situation. If particular dangers lurk in the transplantation setting, they should be dealt with in legislation on that
subject, such as the Uniform Anatomical Gift Act. If all current
means of determining "irreversible cessation of spontaneous brain
functions" are inherently so questionable that they should be
double-checked by a second (or third, fourth, etc.) physician to be
trustworthy, or if a certain means of measuring brain function
requires as a technical matter the cooperation of two, or twenty,
physicians, then the participation of the requisite number of experts would be part of the "ordinary standards of medical practice"
that circumscribe the proper, non-negligent use of such procedures.
It would be unfortunate, however, to introduce such a requirement
into legislation which sets forth the general standards for determining who is dead, especially when it is done in such a way as to
differentiate between one standard and another.

[The] second objection, that a death statute ought to provide
"for the separation and insulation of the physician (or physicians)
attending the patient donor and certifying death, from the recipient of any organ that may be salvaged from the cadaver," is
likewise unnecessary. As was noted previously, language that
relates only to transplantation has no place in a statute on the
determination of death.

Capron and Kass, supra at 115–117.

The Capron and Kass analysis and recommendation had a very
substantial effect on the development of the law. Combined with the
ABA's Definition of Death Act proposed in 1975 and the ABA's pressure on the National Conference of Commissioners on Uniform State
Laws, it led to the Uniform Brain Death Act, which was adopted by the
Commissioners in 1978. This uniform act was adopted by only a couple
of states before it was superseded by the Uniform Determination of
Death Act (UDDA) in 1980. That act was promulgated as a political
compromise that could be supported by those who had been supporting
the Uniform Brain Death Act, the Definition of Death Act, and AMA
model act, and other versions of statutes that recognized brain death as
conclusive evidence of death. The 1980 uniform act, which gives
explicit credit to Capron and Kass in its prefatory note, returns to the
alternative definitions of death. This is not because the Commissioners
determined that there were two independent definitions of death.
Rather, it treated death as a phenomenon that could be *tested* by two
alternative criteria.

UNIFORM DETERMINATION OF DEATH ACT (1980)

§ 1. [Determination of Death]

An individual who has sustained either (1) irreversible cessation of
circulatory and respiratory functions, or (2) irreversible cessation of all

functions of the entire brain, including the brain stem, is dead. A determination of death must be made in accordance with accepted medical standards.

————

Since 1980 there have been some suggested modifications to the Uniform Determination of Death Act. In 1982 three Dartmouth Medical School professors argued:

> The UDDA statute is not desirable, we believe, because it too is ambiguous and it elevates the irreversible cessation of cardiopulmonary functioning to the level of a standard of death, when it is really only a test, although a test that may be used in most circumstances. Permanent cessation of spontaneous cardiopulmonary functioning works as a test of death only in the absence of artificial cardiopulmonary support because only there does it produce the true standard of death—the irreversible cessation of all brain functions. A conceptually satisfactory statute would not need to mention cessation of cardiopulmonary function at all. It would be sufficient to include only irreversible cessation of whole brain functioning and allow physicians to select validated and agreed-upon tests (prolonged absence of spontaneous cardiopulmonary function would be one) to measure irreversible cessation of whole brain function.

Bernat, Culver and Gert, Defining Death in Theory and Practice, 12 Hastings Center Report 5 (Feb. 1982). They proposed their own statute, which begins, "An individual who has sustained irreversible cessation of all functions of the entire brain, including the brain stem, is dead." Id. The proposed statute then lists two ways to determine whether there has been irreversible cessation of all functions of the entire brain—the prolonged absence of spontaneous circulatory and respiratory functions, or, as an alternative in the presence of artificial means of cardiopulmonary support, direct tests of brain function. Id. In part because the difference between the Uniform Determination of Death Act and the Dartmouth professors' alternative amounts to little more than a legal quibble with insubstantial practical, legal or medical consequences, there has been little interest in formally changing the language of the Uniform Act, even among those who find the unitary brain death definition (with alternative *criteria* for determining whether the entire brain is dead) intellectually preferable to the alternative-definitions form employed by the Uniform Act.

The Uniform Determination of Death Act has now been adopted, more or less as proposed by the Commission, in 26 states and the District of Columbia. Bernat and his colleagues were not completely unsuccessful; there is now a consensus among philosophers that it is really the irreversible cessation of all brain function that constitutes death, whether it be measured through tests of the brain function itself or tests for cardiopulmonary activity.

Note: Higher Brain Death

Why is there such a consensus that it is brain death, not cardiopulmonary death, that is the true defining characteristic of the death of a person? The President's Commission reached that conclusion from its premise that death was "the permanent cessation of functioning of the organism as a whole." How should we deal with a person with no cerebral function, but with continued brain stem function? Such a person would be incapable of any cognitive activity—incapable of any communication, self concept, pleasure or pain—yet still be capable of breathing, maintaining heart activity, and responding reflexively. Can that person be said to be functioning as a whole organism? Is the absence of higher brain function, rather than merely *any* brain function, the real attribute of the disintegration of the functioning of the organism as a whole, and thus the real attribute of death? The Dartmouth professors support the conclusion of the President's Commission that whole brain death, not merely death of those portions of the brain that are responsible for higher brain function, must occur before brain death can be declared. There are two primary objections to the "higher brain death" proposal. As they point out:

An important weakness of the higher brain formulation of death is the "slippery slope" problem. Just how much neocortical damage is necessary for death? By this definition, would not severely demented patients also be considered dead? Then what about those somewhat less severely brain damaged? Because personhood is an inherently vague concept, strict criteria for its loss are difficult to identify.

Bernat, Culver and Gert, Defining Death in Theory and Practice, 12 Hastings Center Report (Feb.1982) at 6. Robert Veatch, a leading proponent of the "higher brain death" definition, disagrees:

It does not follow that advocates of higher-brain formulations are more vulnerable to the slippery-slope problem than defenders of whole-brain grounds for pronouncing a person dead. Advocates of whole brain pronouncement of death must, as Harry Beecher quickly discovered, rule out spinal cord reflexes. They must rule out isolated cellular activity that continues to produce micro-volt electron potentials on an electroencephalogram. Their own question could be forced back on them: "Just how much brain tissue damage is necessary for death?" Would they consider someone alive who had a few brain stem cells functioning? What about one or two intact brain stem reflexes? The advocates of higher-brain concepts of death are in no better, but no worse a position. They think it is as easy to draw a hard and fast line between higher-brain (cortical) functions and other brain functions as between the brain stem and the high spinal cord. They can say *any cortical* function signals protectable life, just as the whole-brainers can say *any brain* function does. One is not on any slipperier slope than the other. If there is a slippery slope, anyone who leaves the comfortable confines of the pericardium and begins ascending the spinal cord toward the cerebral cortex is already on it.

Those of us who favor some version of the higher-brain formulations do so precisely because we believe that a person does not function as a whole unless some higher brain function is present. The argument goes back to old Judeo–Christian notions of what it means to be whole. While the Greeks gave priority to the soul, the Judeo–Christian tradition consistently affirms that the human is a necessarily integrated unity of body and mind. Yet [some] hold that a person can function as a whole even when all mental function is totally and irreversibly gone. What a vitalistic, animalistic, biological view of the nature of the human! It confuses the person with the body as badly as the old heart/lung formulations did.

It is all right if some people want to hold that view. If we cannot accurately measure the irreversible loss of all mental capacity today anyway, it may be better to have a conceptually inadequate formulation of what it means to be dead in order to prevent some muddled clinician from pronouncing someone dead prematurely. The problem of false positive diagnoses of life is worth thinking about, however. It protects us from confusing the person as a whole from his or her flesh and blood. If we were not worried about false positive diagnoses of life, we might as well retreat to the safe and sure heart/lung based formulations and be done with it.

Veatch, Correspondence, 12 Hastings Center Report (5) at 45 (Oct. 1982).

The primary objection to the "higher brain death" proposal is a practical one. Remember, any legal definition of death ought to serve the function of such a definition. While the "higher brain function" definition may allow for the distribution of a decedent's property and his purge from voting lists, many people would feel uncomfortable burying a person who is still breathing. Is this discomfort simply irrational and anachronistic or is it supported by some principle that ought to be recognized in law?

Note: Brain Death and Anencephalic Infants as Organ Donors

The debate over the adoption of a new definition of death—one that would increase the "pool" of those defined as dead—has been revived by the potential availability of anencephalic infants as organ donors. An anencephalic infant is one born without a forebrain—that is, without cerebral hemispheres. Such a newborn has a brain stem, but no other brain tissue. The transplantable organs within the body of an anencephalic infant are often healthy and given the very short life span of anencephalic newborns (few live longer than 3 or 4 days, and virtually none survive for more than two weeks), some have viewed them as a particularly rich source of transplantable organs. Although the extent of the need is unclear, there is some need for hearts, kidneys and livers for other newborns with healthy brain function but organ dysfunction. In fact, if organs are to be transplanted into newborns, the organs will almost certainly have to come from newborn donors. In addition, organs from newborns may be transplanted into older children and teenagers with great success.

Under current law, can anencephalic infants' organs be transplanted? Anencephalics are not dead under the Uniform Determination of Death Act because they have some brain stem activity. In any case, a Task Force of the American Academy of Pediatrics recently published guidelines recommending that no brain death definition should be applied to children under seven days of age—making the definition useless in dealing with most anencephalic infants. Obviously, taking a heart or a liver from a living anencephalic infant would result in the infant's death. It would be plainly inconsistent with the principle that we can not kill one person for the benefit of another. In fact, the removal of an organ from a living person would ordinarily constitute murder when that removal results in death. Prima facie, then, it seems that anencephalic infants are not legally permissible organ donors.

Many people—including transplant surgeons, parents of children who need organ transplants to remain alive, parents of anencephalic infants, and others—view the arid and inflexible application of the Uniform Determination of Death Act (and the law of homicide) in these cases as being misdirected and counterproductive. They argue that it makes no sense whatsoever to require the death of an otherwise healthy infant with heart or liver disease by forbidding transplantation from a cerebrum-less infant with a life span that is unlikely to be longer than a few days. Because anencephalic infants' organs are likely to deteriorate during the few-day dying process of the infant, they are unlikely to be transplantable after the infant dies unless they have been artificially well maintained during the infant's short life. Thus, even permitting the transplantation of an anencephalic's organs after the infant's death will often require putting the anencephalic on life support systems to maintain the quality of the organs—not to extend or maintain the quality of the infant's life. There is no other area of medicine where living people are maintained on life support systems solely for the benefit of others.

Those who want access to anencephalic infants' organs suggest two ways of overcoming the apparent disutility of the current law. The first is to redefine brain death to include anencephalic infants. If the definition of death is a social construct, not a medical "fact," this is an attractive, if worrisome, suggestion. Second, some have suggested that the law should recognize a new category of persons—not brain dead, but "brain absent" persons. While good social policy would have us treat these "brain absent" children as living for some purposes, good social policy might also make them available as organ donors.

Those who are troubled by the development of this new source of organs raise two major arguments. The first is that any decision to use some group of living human beings for the benefit of others is a violation of the essential principle of respect for human beings, and this violation is exacerbated when those who are "used" are among the most vulnerable members of society. The second, and related, argument against the use of anencephalic infant donors is that it puts society on the slippery slope of deciding who may be required to give up a life for the benefit of another. Are anencephalic infants so different from other infants with some, but very little, brain function? If we allow for anencephalic infant organ donors, even with their parents' consent or encouragement, who will be the next class of involuntary organ donors? This sinister prospect is made all the more real by the calls to Loma Linda University Medical Center, where these transplants have taken place over the last few years, from physicians and parents of newborns who are "not quite anencephalic" but who have very limited brain function.

In the relatively few places where anencephalic infants' organs are used for transplant, there have been a variety of approaches to the problem. In England, forebrain-absent infants are generally considered available sources for organ transplantation. In Canada, there has been a determination that researchers should investigate 1) the length of time that anencephalic infants can live with the intensive intervention of life support systems, 2) whether anencephalic infants can experience pain, 3) the duration and conditions under which the transplantable organs in anencephalic infants maintain their health for transplant purposes, and 4) whether anencephally is a truly unique condition that is clearly distinguishable from other conditions of infants.

In the United States, the Loma Linda University Medical Center issued a policy on this issue, and amended it several times. Although most of the original transplant operations conducted at the Medical Center were conducted with organs from infants who could not be considered brain dead, the December 18, 1987 Loma Linda protocol required the donor to be brain dead, but it allowed the donor to be maintained on life support systems until brain death to maintain the quality of the organs. In April, 1988, Loma Linda modified its protocol so that potential donor infants would not be placed on life support systems until death was imminent because "it is obvious that provision of full intensive care from birth alters the natural course of dying, resulting in prolongation of the dying process." Modification of Protocol (April 15, 1988). Loma Linda subsequently discontinued the use of anencephalic infants' organs for transplantation.

The Ethics and Social Impact Committee of the Transplant Policy Center in Ann Arbor, Michigan, has adopted the position that "a special category for the infant born without a brain" ought to be created. The Committee concluded that "only in this way can we cut through the tangle to attend, quickly and with mercy, to the desperate needs of anguished parents and dying babies." This position, the Committee claims, "looks toward a rethinking of the moral issues raised by the possibilities of organ transplantation, and provides a formulation of them in such a way that the life-saving transplantation of organs from anencephalics—intuitively thought right by virtually all of us—may be effectively defended in morals and in law." The Committee's transparent attempt to justify, rationally, its intuitive conclusion reveals a great deal about the moral complexity of this argument.

Note: Brain Death and Homicide Statutes

Brain death has not been adopted into the law wholly through statutes. In some states courts have been willing to adopt the brain death definition. This issue necessarily comes before the court in criminal cases where the defendant argues that he cannot be charged with homicide because the victim, although without any brain activity because of the criminal conduct, could have been kept "alive" with mechanically assisted heart and lungs indefinitely (or at least for a year and a day, which is all that is usually required for the defendant to avoid the homicide charge). Some homicide defendants have argued that the victims were not dead until brain death was declared by the physicians, and that the physicians really made the declaration so that organs could be removed for transplantation. They argue that the harvesting of the organs, not their underlying criminal acts, was the proximate cause of death. Several states which have faced various manifestations of this very clever and obviously desperate argument have denied this defense; in no case has it been successful.

A representative set of facts comes from People v. Eulo, 63 N.Y.2d 341, 482 N.Y.S.2d 436, 472 N.E.2d 286 (1984), where the New York Court of Appeals dealt explicitly with the New York Legislature's failure to define death. The facts of that case provide a useful background:

On the evening of July 19, 1981, defendant and his girlfriend attended a volunteer firemen's fair in Kings Park, Suffolk County. Not long after they arrived, the two began to argue, reportedly because defendant was jealous over one of her former suitors, whom they had seen at the fair. The argument continued through the evening; it became particularly heated as the two sat in defendant's pick-up truck, parked in front of the home of the girlfriend's parents. Around midnight, defendant shot her in the head with his unregistered handgun.

The victim was rushed by ambulance to the emergency room of St. John's Hospital. A gunshot wound to the left temple causing extreme hemorrhaging was apparent. A tube was placed in her windpipe to enable artificial respiration and intravenous medication was applied to stabilize her blood pressure.

Shortly before 2:00 a.m., the victim was examined by a neurosurgeon, who undertook various tests to evaluate damage done to the brain. Painful stimuli were applied and yielded no reaction. Various reflexes were tested and, again, there was no response. A further test determined that the victim was incapable of spontaneously maintaining respiration. An electroencephalogram (EEG) resulted in "flat," or "isoelectric", readings indicating no activity in the part of the brain tested.

Over the next two days, the victim's breathing was maintained solely by a mechanical respirator. Her heartbeat was sustained and regulated through medication. Faced with what was believed to be an imminent cessation of these two bodily functions notwithstanding the artificial maintenance, the victim's parents consented to the use of certain of her organs for transplantation.

On the afternoon of July 23, a second neurosurgeon was called in to evaluate whether the victim's brain continued to function in any manner. A repetition of all of the previously conducted tests led to the same diagnosis: the victim's entire brain had irreversibly ceased to function. This diagnosis was reviewed and confirmed by the Deputy Medical Examiner for Suffolk County and another physician.

The victim was pronounced dead at 2:20 p.m. on July 23, although at that time she was still attached to a respirator and her heart was still beating. Her body was taken to a surgical room where her kidneys, spleen, and lymph nodes were removed. The mechanical respirator was then disconnected, and her breathing immediately stopped, followed shortly by a cessation of the heartbeat.

Defendant was indicted for second degree murder. After a jury trial, he was convicted of manslaughter. * * *

472 N.E.2d at 289.

The court held that "a recognition of brain-based criteria for determining death is not unfaithful to prior judicial definitions of 'death', as presumptively adopted in the many statutes using that term. Close examination of the common-law conception of death and the traditional criteria used to determine when death has occurred leads inexorably to this conclusion." Id. at 294. The court determined that "[d]eath remains the single phenomenon identified at common law," and that the courts could appropriately adapt criteria "to account for the 'changed conditions' that a dead body may be attached to a machine so as to exhibit demonstrably false indicia of life." Id. The *Eulo* court went on:

> This court searches in vain for evidence that, apart from the concept of death, the legislature intended to render immutable the criteria used to determine death. By extension, to hold to the contrary would be to say that the law could not recognize diagnostic equipment such as the stethoscope or more sensitive equipment even when it became clear that these instruments more accurately measured the presence of signs of life.

Id. Thus, the court concluded,

> when a determination has been made according to accepted medical standards that a person has suffered an irreversible cessation of heartbeat and respiration, or, when these functions are maintained solely by extraordinary mechanical means, an irreversible cessation of all functions of the entire brain, including the brain stem, no life traditionally recognized by the law is present in that body.

Id. The Court of Appeals described with some precision just when medical intervention could constitute a superseding cause that would relieve a defendant from criminal homicide liability:

> If the victims were properly diagnosed as dead, of course, no subsequent medical procedure such as organ removal would be deemed a cause of death. If victims' deaths were prematurely announced due to a doctor's negligence, the subsequent procedures may have been a cause of death, but that negligence would not constitute a superseding cause of death relieving defendants of liability [ ]. If, however, the pronouncements of death were premature due to the gross negligence or the intentional wrongdoing of doctors, as determined by a grave deviation from accepted medical practices or disregard for legally cognizable criteria for determining death, the intervening medical procedure would interrupt the chain of causation and become the legal cause of death [ ].

Id. at 297. Surprisingly, the *Eulo* defense has come up in more subtle ways since 1984. In People v. Hall, 134 Misc.2d 515, 511 N.Y.S.2d 532 (1987), the court held that a defendant could be convicted of the murder of a viable fetus which had to be delivered prematurely after the shooting of its mother. The court concluded that the fact that the infant was maintained on a ventilator after the C-section birth did not alter its status as one who was "born alive," and thus a "person" under the murder statute. In People v. Lai, 131 A.D.2d 592, 516 N.Y.S.2d 300 (1987), the court announced that *Eulo* would allow the jury to determine whether the brain death standard or the heart-lung standard ought to be applied in a homicide case to determine the time of death. Does this seem like an issue of fact properly within the province of the jury?

See also State v. Matthews, 291 S.C. 339, 353 S.E.2d 444 (1986) (depending on *Eulo*); State v. Velarde, 734 P.2d 449 (Utah 1986); Poppe, People v. Eulo: New York Adopts the Brain Death Standard for Homicide cases, 29 Cath.Lawyer 375 (1984). Two courts have expressly limited their judicial acceptance of brain death to homicide cases. Commonwealth v. Golston, 373 Mass. 249, 366 N.E.2d 744 (1977); State v. Meints, 212 Neb. 410, 322 N.W.2d 809 (1982).

Should the judicially created definition of death in *Eulo* extend to criminal actions only, or should it also apply in civil actions (in tort actions, for example)? See Strachan v. John F. Kennedy Memorial Hosp., 109 N.J. 523, 538 A.2d 346 (1988).

Bibliographical Note on Brain Death

There is a superb bibliography on the legal definition of death written by someone who understands both the legal and medical subtleties of the issue. Leahy, Legal Death: A Pathfinder to the Current State of the Law and Its Implications, 74 Leg. Reference Serv's. Q. 73 (1989). Among the sources Leahy discovers is this excellent conclusion to this section:

> If we treat the dead as if they were wholly dead it shows want of affection;
>
> If we treat them as wholly alive it shows want of sense.
>
> Neither should be done.

Confucius, The Book of Rites II, quoted at 74 Leg.Reference Services Q. at 73.

For a complete account of the argument supporting cardiopulmonary definition of death, whole brain death, and neocortical death, see President's Commission for the Study of Ethical Problems in Medicine and Biomedical and Behavioral Research, Defining Death: A Report on the Medical, Legal, and Ethical Issues In the Determination of Death (1981). An international perspective is provided in Pallis, Brain Stem Death—The Evolution of a Concept, 55 Medico–Legal J. 84 (1987). See also Bernat, Culver, Gert, On Definition and Criteria of Death, 94 Annals of Internal Med. 389 (1981). Various definitions of whole brain death are compared in Walker, Current Concept of Brain Death, 15 J. Neurosurgical Nursing 261 (1983). For an excellent judicial history of the adoption of the brain death standard, see People v. Mitchell, 132 Cal.App.3d 389, 183 Cal.Rptr. 166 (1982).

The best account of arguments in support of (and in opposition to) neocortical death are found in Smith, Legal Recognition of Neocortical

Death, 71 Cornell L.Rev. 850 (1986) which includes a proposed neocortical death statute. See also Veatch, The Definition of Death: Ethical, Philosophical and Policy Confusion, 315 Annals N.Y.Acad. of Sci. 307 (1978); Dworkin, Death in Context, 48 Ind.L.J. 623 (1973).

A great deal has been written about anencephalic infants and the use of their organs for transplantation. A good summary is found in Botkin, Anencephalic Infants as Organ Donors, 82 Pediatrics 250 (August 1988). A fine account of Loma Linda's most famous use of an anencephalic infant's organ—the "Baby Gabrielle" case—is found in Annas, From Canada With Love: Anencephalic Newborns as Organ Donors? 17 Hastings Center Report 36 (December 1987). The October/November 1988 Hastings Center Report contains a forum on the use of anencephalic infants as organ donors. See Frost, Organs from Anencephalic Infants: An Idea Whose Time Has Not Yet Come, 18 Hastings Center Report 5 (October–November 1988), Shewmon, Anencephally: Selected Medical Aspects, 18 Hastings Center Report 11 (October–November 1988) (an excellent account of the relevant medical factors), Walters and Ashwall, Organ Prolongation in Anencephalic Infants: Ethical and Medical Issues, 18 Hastings Center Report 19 (October–November 1988), Ethics and Social Impact Committee, Anencephalic Infants as Sources of Transplantable Organs, 18 Hastings Center Report 28 (October–November 1988) (a report of the Committee that determined anencephalics should be treated as "a special category"), and Willke and Andrusko, Personhood Redux, 18 Hastings Center Report 30 (October–November 1988) (a right-to-life perspective on the use of anencephalic infants as organ donors). See also Landwirth, Should Anencephalic Infants be Used as Organ Donors? 82 Pediatrics 257 (August 1988); Arras & Shinnar, Anencephalic Newborns as Organ Donors: A Critique, 259 J.A.M.A. 2284 (1988).

Chapter 11

LIFE AND DEATH DECISIONS

I. PRINCIPLES OF AUTONOMY AND BENEFICENCE

Over the last several years the law has been invoked regularly by physicians and other health care providers concerned about the ethical, legal, and medical propriety of discontinuing what is now generally referred to as "life sustaining treatment." A number of questions taken to the courts and legislatures arguably are outside the competence of the law. For example, consider what might constitute a "terminal illness," a concept that some have considered relevant in bioethical decision making. While there surely is a medical element to a determination that a patient is "terminally ill," reflection upon the suggestion that there could be a lab test for this condition indicates that it is more than that. Classifying a patient as "terminally ill" depends on a combination of the patient's medical condition and the social, ethical, and legal consequences of the classification. If such a classification triggers a living will provision, for example, it might be treated differently than if it triggers the patient's relocation from one room to another within a hospital.

If a determination of terminal illness is not solely a medical decision, but rather a hybrid medical, ethical, and legal determination, where is the locus of appropriate decision making? Should the decision be made by medical personnel alone? By a patient and his family? By a hospital committee? By some external committee? By a court appointed guardian? By the court itself? By the state legislature? By Congress? Should the decision be based upon principles and rules that emerge from medicine, ethics, litigation, or legislative social policy making? Finally, what substantive principles ought to govern the decision-maker?

The difficulties in allocating decision-making authority and developing appropriate substantive principles are not limited to the "terminal illness" classification. They extend to such defining terms as "irreversible coma," "life-sustaining treatment," "death prolonging," "maintenance medical care," "extraordinary means," "heroic efforts," and even breathing and feeding. For almost every question that arises within the bioethics sphere, we must make two determinations: (1) where should the problem be resolved, and (2) what substantive principles should apply. Thus, the questions become ones of process (who will decide and how) and substance (what principles must form the basis of a recognized decision). As one might expect, the substantive questions are often hidden in apparently procedural inquiries.

Substantive Principles. Three substantive principles form the basis of virtually all bioethics debates: autonomy, beneficence, and social justice. Autonomy and beneficence are the principles most directly implicated in the questions considered in this chapter, although questions of cost allocation and rationing generally implicate social justice.

The principle of autonomy declares that each person is in control of his own person, including his body and mind. This principle, in its purest form, presumes that no other person or social institution ought to intervene to overcome a person's desires, whether or not those desires are "right" from any external perspective. If Mr. Smith wants to die, then Mr. Smith is entitled to die as he sees fit, at least as long as he chooses a method that does not substantially affect anyone else.

The principle of beneficence declares that what is best for each person should be accomplished. The principle incorporates both the negative obligation of nonmaleficence ("primum non nocere"—"first of all, do no harm"—the foundation of the Hippocratic oath) and the positive obligation to do that which is good. Thus, a physician is obliged, under the principle of beneficence, to provide the highest quality medical care for each of his patients. Similarly, a physician ought to treat a seriously ill newborn in a way that is most medically beneficial for that infant, whatever he may think the infant "wants" and whatever the baby's parents may desire.

When a person does not desire what others determine to be in his interest, the principles of autonomy and beneficence conflict. For example, if we treat the continued life of a healthy person to be in that person's interest, the values of autonomy and beneficence become inconsistent when a healthy competent adult decides to take his own life. As a general matter, the principle of autonomy is now recognized as the first principle of medical ethics and that has been confirmed repeatedly by the courts. The principle of beneficence has become a secondary principle generally applied by courts and bioethics scholars only when autonomy is meaningless, as where the patient is a newborn infant who cannot be expected to have any articulated wishes or desires. As we will soon see, though, the primacy of the principles can be changed by legislative enactments, and they may also change in accord with prevailing judicial philosophies.

Because issues of bioethics have only recently started to come before the courts, the courts have looked elsewhere to find principles upon which to base their judgments. Courts have regularly looked both to the traditions of the common law and the traditions of ethics and medicine. See Capron, Borrowed Lessons: The Role of Ethical Distinctions in Framing Law on Life–Sustaining Treatment, 1984 Ariz.L.Rev. 647. Analogously, judicial decisions have often formed the basis for new ethical and medical approaches. In fact, the debate over appropriate ethical policy in determining when life support systems should be initiated or discontinued now involves lawyers as much as bioethics scholars, and the debate has centered on the judicial resolution of these cases as much as on any other source of formal principles. The law is not merely looking to ethics for potential methods of analysis, it is usurping ethics in debate on these issues.

The law is not developed only through rationally justified and formally articulated judicial opinions. The law also comes out of political compromises, legislative action, and public perceptions of well-publicized bioethical issues. Congress's decision to fund kidney dialysis through an expansion of the Medicare program for all those who need it, for example, has had a substantial effect on determining who shall live and who shall die. Infants have names, and cry, and can be cuddled; fetuses do none of these things. Not surprisingly, we are willing to spend a great deal more to treat seriously ill newborns than we are to provide adequate prenatal care. See Trachtman, Why Tolerate the Statistical Victim?, 15 Hastings Center Report (2) 14 (Feb. 1985). Finally, the increasingly overtly political nature of some questions—such as the question of whether nasogastric tubes or other forms of artificial feeding may be withheld from the terminally ill—has brought formerly nonpolitical, personal questions into the political sphere. In 1985, Governor Lamm of Colorado was considered the unusual, unrestrained politician when he suggested that the elderly may have an obligation to die, yet the social consequences of health care decisions become a matter of real concern to those who realize that all of their family assets easily could be consumed by a final illness. Additionally, there is real controversy over whether there is any truth to the public perception that medical resources are being used (much less, wasted) to prolong the dying process. See Scitovski, The High Cost of Dying: What Do the Data Show? 62 Milbank Mem. Fund Q. 591 (1984); Bayer et al., The Care of the Terminally Ill: Morality and Economics, 309 New England J. of Med. 1490 (1983). Compare D. Callahan, Setting Limits (1988) and D. Callahan, What Kind of Life (1989) with Eglit, Health Care Allocation for the Elderly: Age Discrimination by Another Name, 26 Hous.L.Rev. 813 (1989).

In reading this chapter, consider what role individuals, families, hospitals, the medical community, courts, legislatures, and others ought to play in dealing with the ethical, medical, legal, social and political questions that often arise out of our new found technical ability to maintain life. As you review the way courts and others have considered individual cases, attempt to distill reasoned principles from their judgments and apply them to the following problem. What issues arise at each point in the course of the problem? Do the issues change? Is your analysis a procedural or substantive one? Who ought to be involved in the decision making at each point? Are the principles of autonomy and beneficence equally relevant at each point?

Problem: Right to Die

Mr. Karl, an otherwise healthy 62 year–old man, arrived at the Pleasant City General Hospital emergency room by ambulance. He had serious stab wounds to his chest and back, and he was losing blood quickly. The emergency technician on the ambulance explained to the emergency room physicians that he was called to the Howdy Podner Bar by its owner, who telephoned to report a fight and request an ambulance. He said that Mr. Karl complained that he had been knifed by his son and that Mr. Karl was generally uncooperative, but was too weak to successfully oppose the ambulance attendants on the four block drive to the hospital. Mr. Karl's wife, who was called by another patron at the bar, arrived at the emergency room at the same time as Mr. Karl.

When an emergency room physician explained to Mr. Karl that he required several units of blood, Mr. Karl absolutely refused to accept that form of treatment. He said that he understood the consequences of not receiving blood under the circumstances—that death would be likely, if not inevitable. However, he explained that his Jehovah's Witness faith did not allow him to consent to a blood transfusion. In any case, he explained, religion or not, he "had his own reasons" for not wanting to survive this stabbing, and he did not want any blood. His wife, who is also a Jehovah's Witness, begged the doctor to provide the blood and save her husband's life. She explained that her husband was misinterpreting Jehovah's Witness doctrine, which permitted a blood transfusion in certain circumstances. In fact, she argued, their faith does not require that he not be given blood, it merely requires that he not actively give his consent to receiving blood. She pointed out that they had been married for 35 years and that she knew he wanted the transfusion, but that he felt obliged by his religion to appear to oppose it. Physicians treated his wounds but did not provide any blood. They did begin intravenous fluid support, which ameliorated the effect of lost blood.

Mr. Karl was maintained in the emergency room. He continued to object to any form of blood transfusion, but after several hours of blood loss became less coherent. He began to cry about the guilt he suffered from stabbing his son, and he began talking about the Lord's revenge upon evil men. When he was approached by physicians, he demanded that they kill him—or allow him to kill himself—or, at least, allow him to die. At one point he screamed "why don't you morphine me to death like the other patients? Please, help me die; I want to die but I cannot face the pain."

About 10 hours after he arrived at the emergency room, he was afflicted with an apparent stroke and slipped into unconsciousness. He then was moved to the intensive care unit. He lost breathing capacity and the intensive care physician placed him on a ventilator. Shortly after his move, his three daughters arrived, confirmed what their mother had said earlier, and begged that their father be given all available treatment, including blood. His only son, with whom he had been fighting earlier in the evening, was arrested and remained in jail.

Within the next several hours all bleeding ceased, and he remained in stable condition. Given the consequences of the stroke, his physicians concluded that there was virtually no hope that Mr. Karl would regain any cognitive abilities. Intravenous nutritional supplementation was commenced, then replaced by a nasogastric tube (i.e., a tube inserted through the nose into the stomach) through which nutrition was passed directly to his stomach.

After her father had spent two weeks in intensive care, one of the daughters requested that her father's ventilator be removed. The doctors explained that they had several options. The ventilator could be removed at once, which would surely lead to her father's death. He could be "weaned" from the ventilator, with ventilator support slowly removed (and reinstated when necessary): a process which would not result in his immediate death, but would be likely to shorten his life substantially. He could be "terminally weaned," which would be the same as the weaning process except that the support would not be reinstated, even if it were necessary. Finally, he could be maintained on the ventilator. Mr. Karl's wife and daughters determined that he should be removed from the ventilator in whatever manner the physician thought proper, and he was successfully "weaned" from it. A week later Mr. Karl's wife asked that his feeding tube be removed. She said, "He always said that the worst thing that could ever happen to him was to be a vegetable like Quinlan." In addition, his family physician reported that he had once talked to Mr. Karl about living wills and that Mr. Karl had asked for a living will form, although he had not filled it out. He did always carry with him a Uniform Anatomical Gift Act donor card and a copy of Dylan Thomas's "Do Not Go Gentle Into That Good Night," which is reprinted below at page 1180. Two of the three daughters agreed with their mother that the feeding tube should be removed, but one strongly objected, saying that she believed it would be wrong, from a moral and religious point of view, to do so.

Mr. Karl's wife and children are his only heirs. He has always been particularly close to the daughter who does not want his feeding tube removed. His family physician reports that during a previous hospitalization for an ulcer, Mr. Karl depended heavily upon his wife, to whom he had been happily married for 35 years, and left every treatment decision to her. The current medical and hospital charges of about $4000 per day are paid by Mr. Karl's insurance (80%), and by his family (through their 20% coinsurance obligation). The family resources will be exhausted in another few weeks when the maximum annual payout on the insurance policy will also have been met. After that, his health care will be paid by Medicaid, through which the State will pay medical and hospital expenses of about $2300 per day to fully cover his treatment.

What treatment would have been appropriate at each point in Mr. Karl's hospitalization? How should that have been decided? What judicial consequences could (and should) each medical decision have? Would your answer be different if you were Mr. Karl? A member of Mr. Karl's family? One of his creditors? His lawyer? The hospital administrator? The doctor? A nurse? The hospital ethics committee? The hospital lawyer? The doctor's (or hospital's) insurance company? A judge?

II. THE UNITED STATES CONSTITUTION AND THE "RIGHT TO DIE"

CRUZAN v. DIRECTOR, MISSOURI DEPARTMENT OF HEALTH

Supreme Court of the United States, 1990.
492 U.S. ___, 110 S.Ct. 2841, 111 L.Ed.2d 224.

CHIEF JUSTICE REHNQUIST delivered the opinion of the Court.

Petitioner Nancy Beth Cruzan was rendered incompetent as a result of severe injuries sustained during an automobile accident. Co-petitioners Lester and Joyce Cruzan, Nancy's parents and co-guardians, sought a court order directing the withdrawal of their daughter's artificial feeding and hydration equipment after it became apparent that she had virtually no chance of recovering her cognitive faculties. The Supreme Court of Missouri held that because there was no clear and convincing evidence of Nancy's desire to have life-sustaining treatment withdrawn under such circumstances, her parents lacked authority to effectuate such a request. We granted certiorari and now affirm.

On the night of January 11, 1983, Nancy Cruzan lost control of her car as she traveled down Elm Road in Jasper County, Missouri. The vehicle overturned, and Cruzan was discovered lying face down in a ditch without detectable respiratory or cardiac function. Paramedics were able to restore her breathing and heartbeat at the accident site, and she was transported to a hospital in an unconscious state. An attending neurosurgeon diagnosed her as having sustained probable cerebral contusions compounded by significant anoxia (lack of oxygen). The Missouri trial court in this case found that permanent brain damage generally results after 6 minutes in an anoxic state; it was estimated that Cruzan was deprived of oxygen from 12 to 14 minutes. She remained in a coma for approximately three weeks and then progressed to an unconscious state in which she was able to orally ingest some nutrition. In order to ease feeding and further the recovery, surgeons implanted a gastrostomy feeding and hydration tube in Cruzan with the consent of her then husband. Subsequent rehabilitative efforts proved unavailing. She now lies in a Missouri state hospital in what is commonly referred to as a persistent vegetative state: generally, a condition in which a person exhibits motor reflexes but evinces no indications of significant cognitive function. The State of Missouri is bearing the cost of her care.

After it had become apparent that Nancy Cruzan had virtually no chance of regaining her mental faculties her parents asked hospital employees to terminate the artificial nutrition and hydration procedures. All agree that such a removal would cause her death. The employees refused to honor the request without court approval. The parents then sought and received authorization from the state trial court for termination. The court found that a person in Nancy's condition had a fundamental right under the State and Federal Constitutions to refuse or direct the withdrawal of "death prolonging procedures." The court also found that Nancy's "expressed thoughts at age twenty-five in somewhat serious conversation with a housemate friend that if sick or injured she would not wish to continue her life unless she could live at least halfway normally suggests that given her present condition she would not wish to continue on with her nutrition and hydration."

The Supreme Court of Missouri reversed by a divided vote. * * *

We granted certiorari to consider the question of whether Cruzan has a right under the United States Constitution which would require the hospital to withdraw life-sustaining treatment from her under these circumstances.

* * *

State courts have available to them for decision a number of sources—state constitutions, statutes, and common law—which are not available to us. In this Court, the question is simply and starkly whether the United States Constitution prohibits Missouri from choosing the rule of decision which it did. This is the first case in which we have been squarely presented with the issue of whether the United States Constitution grants what is in common parlance referred to as a "right to die."

* * *

The Fourteenth Amendment provides that no State shall "deprive any person of life, liberty, or property, without due process of law." The principle that a competent person has a constitutionally protected liberty interest in refusing unwanted medical treatment may be inferred from our prior decisions. * * *

But determining that a person has a "liberty interest" under the Due Process Clause does not end the inquiry;[7] "whether respondent's constitutional rights have been violated must be determined by balancing his liberty interests against the relevant state interests." [ ]

Petitioners insist that under the general holdings of our cases, the forced administration of life-sustaining medical treatment, and even of artifically-delivered food and water essential to life, would implicate a competent person's liberty interest. Although we think the logic of the cases discussed above would embrace such a liberty interest, the dramatic consequences involved in refusal of such treatment would inform the inquiry as to whether the deprivation of that interest is constitutionally permissible. But for purposes of this case, we assume that the United States Constitution would grant a competent person a constitutionally protected right to refuse lifesaving hydration and nutrition.

7. Although many state courts have held that a right to refuse treatment is encompassed by a generalized constitutional right of privacy, we have never so held. We believe this issue is more properly analyzed in terms of a Fourteenth Amendment liberty interest. See *Bowers v. Hardwick,* 478 U.S. 186, 194–195 (1986).

Petitioners go on to assert that an incompetent person should possess the same right in this respect as is possessed by a competent person. * * *

The difficulty with petitioners' claim is that in a sense it begs the question: an incompetent person is not able to make an informed and voluntary choice to exercise a hypothetical right to refuse treatment or any other right. Such a "right" must be exercised for her, if at all, by some sort of surrogate. Here, Missouri has in effect recognized that under certain circumstances a surrogate may act for the patient in electing to have hydration and nutrition withdrawn in such a way as to cause death, but it has established a procedural safeguard to assure that the action of the surrogate conforms as best it may to the wishes expressed by the patient while competent. Missouri requires that evidence of the incompetent's wishes as to the withdrawal of treatment be proved by clear and convincing evidence. The question, then, is whether the United States Constitution forbids the establishment of this procedural requirement by the State. We hold that it does not.

Whether or not Missouri's clear and convincing evidence requirement comports with the United States Constitution depends in part on what interests the State may properly seek to protect in this situation. Missouri relies on its interest in the protection and preservation of human life, and there can be no gainsaying this interest. As a general matter, the States—indeed, all civilized nations—demonstrate their commitment to life by treating homicide as serious crime. Moreover, the majority of States in this country have laws imposing criminal penalties on one who assists another to commit suicide. We do not think a State is required to remain neutral in the face of an informed and voluntary decision by a physically-able adult to starve to death.

But in the context presented here, a State has more particular interests at stake. The choice between life and death is a deeply personal decision of obvious and overwhelming finality. We believe Missouri may legitimately seek to safeguard the personal element of this choice through the imposition of heightened evidentiary requirements. It cannot be disputed that the Due Process Clause protects an interest in life as well as an interest in refusing life-sustaining medical treatment. Not all incompetent patients will have loved ones available to serve as surrogate decisionmakers. * * * A State is entitled to guard against potential abuses in such situations. Similarly, a State is entitled to consider that a judicial proceeding to make a determination regarding an incompetent's wishes may very well not be an adversarial one, with the added guarantee of accurate factfinding that the adversary process brings with it. [ ] Finally, we think a State may properly decline to make judgments about the "quality" of life that a particular individual may enjoy, and simply assert an unqualified interest in the preservation of human life to be weighed against the constitutionally protected interests of the individual.

In our view, Missouri has permissibly sought to advance these interests through the adoption of a "clear and convincing" standard of proof to govern such proceedings. * * * "This Court has mandated an intermediate standard of proof—'clear and convincing evidence'—when the individual interests at stake in a state proceeding are both 'particularly important' and 'more substantial than mere loss of money.' " [   ] Thus, such a standard has been required in deportation proceedings, [   ] in denaturalization proceedings, [   ] in civil commitment proceedings, and in proceedings for the termination of parental rights. Further, this level of proof, "or an even higher one, has traditionally been imposed in cases involving allegations of civil fraud, and in a variety of other kinds of civil cases involving such issues as * * * lost wills, oral contracts to make bequests, and the like." [   ]

We think it self-evident that the interests at stake in the instant proceedings are more substantial, both on an individual and societal level, than those involved in a run-of-the-mine civil dispute. But not only does the standard of proof reflect the importance of a particular adjudication, it also serves as "a societal judgment about how the risk of error should be distributed between the litigants." [   ] The more stringent the burden of proof a party must bear, the more that party bears the risk of an erroneous decision. We believe that Missouri may permissibly place an increased risk of an erroneous decision on those seeking to terminate an incompetent individual's life-sustaining treatment. An erroneous decision not to terminate results in a maintenance of the status quo; the possibility of subsequent developments such as advancements in medical science, the discovery of new evidence regarding the patient's intent, changes in the law, or simply the unexpected death of the patient despite the administration of life-sustaining treatment, at least create the potential that a wrong decision will eventually be corrected or its impact mitigated. An erroneous decision to withdraw life-sustaining treatment, however, is not susceptible of correction.

* * *

In sum, we conclude that a State may apply a clear and convincing evidence standard in proceedings where a guardian seeks to discontinue nutrition and hydration of a person diagnosed to be in a persistent vegetative state. * * *

The Supreme Court of Missouri held that in this case the testimony adduced at trial did not amount to clear and convincing proof of the patient's desire to have hydration and nutrition withdrawn. * * * The testimony adduced at trial consisted primarily of Nancy Cruzan's statements made to a housemate about a year before her accident that she would not want to live should she face life as a "vegetable," and other observations to the same effect. The observations did not deal in terms with withdrawal of medical treatment or of hydration and nutrition. We cannot say that the Supreme Court of Missouri committed constitutional error in reaching the conclusion that it did.

Petitioners alternatively contend that Missouri must accept the "substituted judgment" of close family members even in the absence of substantial proof that their views reflect the views of the patient. * * * [W]e do not think the Due Process Clause requires the State to repose judgment on these matters with anyone but the patient herself. Close family members may have a strong feeling—a feeling not at all ignoble or unworthy, but not entirely disinterested, either—that they do not wish to witness the continuation of the life of a loved one which they regard as hopeless, meaningless, and even degrading. But there is no automatic assurance that the view of close family members will necessarily be the same as the patient's would have been had she been confronted with the prospect of her situation while competent. All of the reasons previously discussed for allowing Missouri to require clear and convincing evidence of the patient's wishes lead us to conclude that the State may choose to defer only to those wishes, rather than confide the decision to close family members.[12]

* * *

JUSTICE O'CONNOR, concurring.

I agree that a protected liberty interest in refusing unwanted medical treatment may be inferred from our prior decisions, and that the refusal of artificially delivered food and water is encompassed within that liberty interest. I write separately to clarify why I believe this to be so.

As the Court notes, the liberty interest in refusing medical treatment flows from decisions involving the State's invasions into the body. Because our notions of liberty are inextricably entwined with our idea of physical freedom and self-determination, the Court has often deemed state incursions into the body repugnant to the interests protected by the Due Process Clause. [ ] The State's imposition of medical treatment on an unwilling competent adult necessarily involves some form of restraint and intrusion. A seriously ill or dying patient whose wishes are not honored may feel a captive of the machinery required for life-sustaining measures or other medical interventions. Such forced treatment may burden that individual's liberty interests as much as any state coercion. [ ]

The State's artificial provision of nutrition and hydration implicates identical concerns. Artificial feeding cannot readily be distinguished from other forms of medical treatment. * * * Whether or not the techniques used to pass food and water into the patient's alimentary tract are termed "medical treatment," it is clear they all involve some degree of intrusion and restraint. Feeding a patient by means of a nasogastric tube requires a physician to pass a long flexible tube through the patient's nose, throat and esophagus and into the stomach.

---

12. We are not faced in this case with the question of whether a State might be required to defer to the decision of a surrogate if competent and probative evidence established that the patient herself had expressed a desire that the decision to terminate life-sustaining treatment be made for her by that individual.

Because of the discomfort such a tube causes, "[m]any patients need to be restrained forcibly and their hands put into large mittens to prevent them from removing the tube." * * * A gastrostomy tube (as was used to provide food and water to Nancy Cruzan), or jejunostomy tube must be surgically implanted into the stomach or small intestine. * * * Requiring a competent adult to endure such procedures against her will burdens the patient's liberty, dignity, and freedom to determine the course of her own treatment. Accordingly, the liberty guaranteed by the Due Process Clause must protect, if it protects anything, an individual's deeply personal decision to reject medical treatment, including the artificial delivery of food and water.

I also write separately to emphasize that the Court does not today decide the issue whether a State must also give effect to the decisions of a surrogate decisionmaker. In my view, such a duty may well be constitutionally required to protect the patient's liberty interest in refusing medical treatment. Few individuals provide explicit oral or written instructions regarding their intent to refuse medical treatment should they become incompetent. States which decline to consider any evidence other than such instructions may frequently fail to honor a patient's intent. Such failures might be avoided if the State considered an equally probative source of evidence: the patient's appointment of a proxy to make health care decisions on her behalf. Delegating the authority to make medical decisions to a family member or friend is becoming a common method of planning for the future. [ ]

Several States have recognized the practical wisdom of such a procedure by enacting durable power of attorney statutes that specifically authorize an individual to appoint a surrogate to make medical treatment decisions. Some state courts have suggested that an agent appointed pursuant to a general durable power of attorney statute would also be empowered to make health care decisions on behalf of the patient. * * * Other States allow an individual to designate a proxy to carry out the intent of a living will. These procedures for surrogate decisionmaking, which appear to be rapidly gaining in acceptance, may be a valuable additional safeguard of the patient's interest in directing his medical care. Moreover, as patients are likely to select a family member as a surrogate, [ ] giving effect to a proxy's decisions may also protect the "freedom of personal choice in matters of * * * family life." [ ]

Today's decision, holding only that the Constitution permits a State to require clear and convincing evidence of Nancy Cruzan's desire to have artificial hydration and nutrition withdrawn, does not preclude a future determination that the Constitution requires the States to implement the decisions of a patient's duly appointed surrogate. Nor does it prevent States from developing other approaches for protecting an incompetent individual's liberty interest in refusing medical treatment. * * * Today we decide only that one State's practice does not violate the Constitution; the more challenging task of crafting appropriate procedures for safeguarding incompetents' liberty interests is entrusted to the "laboratory" of the States, in the first instance.

JUSTICE SCALIA, concurring.

* * *

While I agree with the Court's analysis today, and therefore join in its opinion, I would have preferred that we announce, clearly and promptly, that the federal courts have no business in this field; that American law has always accorded the State the power to prevent, by force if necessary, suicide—including suicide by refusing to take appropriate measures necessary to preserve one's life; that the point at which life becomes "worthless," and the point at which the means necessary to preserve it become "extraordinary" or "inappropriate," are neither set forth in the Constitution nor known to the nine Justices of this Court any better than they are known to nine people picked at random from the Kansas City telephone directory; and hence, that even when it *is* demonstrated by clear and convincing evidence that a patient no longer wishes certain measures to be taken to preserve her life, it is up to the citizens of Missouri to decide, through their elected representatives, whether that wish will be honored. It is quite impossible (because the Constitution says nothing about the matter) that those citizens will decide upon a line less lawful than the one we would choose; and it is unlikely (because we know no more about "life-and-death" than they do) that they will decide upon a line less reasonable.

The text of the Due Process Clause does not protect individuals against deprivations of liberty *simpliciter*. It protects them against deprivations of liberty "without due process of law." To determine that such a deprivation would not occur if Nancy Cruzan were forced to take nourishment against her will, it is unnecessary to reopen the historically recurrent debate over whether "due process" includes substantive restrictions. [ ] It is at least true that no "substantive due process" claim can be maintained unless the claimant demonstrates that the State has deprived him of a right historically and traditionally protected against State interference. [ ] That cannot possibly be established here.

* * * "[T]here is no significant support for the claim that a right to suicide is so rooted in our tradition that it may be deemed 'fundamental' or 'implicit in the concept of ordered liberty.' " [ ]

Petitioners rely on three distinctions to separate Nancy Cruzan's case from ordinary suicide: (1) that she is permanently incapacitated and in pain; (2) that she would bring on her death not by any affirmative act but by merely declining treatment that provides nourishment; and (3) that preventing her from effectuating her presumed wish to die requires violation of her bodily integrity. None of these suffices.

[Scalia points out (1) that pain and incapacity have never constituted legal defenses to a charge of suicide, (2) that the distinction between "action" and "inaction" is logically and legally meaningless, and (3) that preventing suicide often (or always) requires the violation of bodily integrity, and it begs the question of whether the refusal of treatment is itself suicide.]

The dissents of JUSTICES BRENNAN and STEVENS make a plausible case for our intervention here only by embracing—the latter explicitly and the former by implication—a political principle that the States are free to adopt, but that is demonstrably not imposed by the Constitution. "The State," says Justice Brennan, "has no legitimate general interest in someone's life, completely abstracted from the interest of the person living that life, that could outweigh the person's choice *to avoid medical treatment*." (emphasis added). The italicized phrase sounds moderate enough, and is all that is needed to cover the present case—but the proposition cannot *logically* be so limited. One who accepts it must also accept, I think, that the State has no such legitimate interest that could outweigh "the person's choice *to put an end to her life*." Similarly, if one agrees with Justice Brennan that "the State's general interest in life must accede to Nancy Cruzan's particularized and intense interest in self-determination *in her choice of medical treatment*," (emphasis added), he must also believe that the State must accede to her "particularized and intense interest in self-determination *in her choice whether to continue living or to die*." For insofar as balancing the relative interests of the State and the individual is concerned, there is nothing distinctive about accepting death through the refusal of "medical treatment," as opposed to accepting it through the refusal of food, or through the failure to shut off the engine and get out of the car after parking in one's garage after work. Suppose that Nancy Cruzan were in precisely the condition she is in today, except that she could be fed and digest food and water *without* artificial assistance. How is the State's "interest" in keeping her alive thereby increased, or her interest in deciding whether she wants to continue living reduced? It seems to me, in other words, that Justice Brennan's position ultimately rests upon the proposition that it is none of the State's business if a person wants to commit suicide. Justice Stevens is explicit on the point: "Choices about death touch the core of liberty. * * * [N]ot much may be said with confidence about death unless it is said from faith, and that alone is reason enough to protect the freedom to conform choices about death to individual conscience." This is a view that some societies have held, and that our States are free to adopt if they wish. But it is not a view imposed by our constitutional traditions, in which the power of the State to prohibit suicide is unquestionable.

* * * To raise up a constitutional right here we would have to create out of nothing (for it exists neither in text nor tradition) some constitutional principle whereby, although the State may insist that an individual come in out of the cold and eat food, it may not insist that he take medicine; and although it may pump his stomach empty of poison he has ingested, it may not fill his stomach with food he has failed to ingest. Are there, then, no reasonable and humane limits that ought not to be exceeded in requiring an individual to preserve his own life?

There obviously are, but they are not set forth in the Due Process Clause. What assures us that those limits will not be exceeded is the same constitutional guarantee that is the source of most of our protection—what protects us, for example, from being assessed a tax of 100% of our income above the subsistence level, from being forbidden to drive cars, or from being required to send our children to school for 10 hours a day, none of which horribles is categorically prohibited by the Constitution. Our salvation is the Equal Protection Clause, which requires the democratic majority to accept for themselves and their loved ones what they impose on you and me. This Court need not, and has no authority to, inject itself into every field of human activity where irrationality and oppression may theoretically occur, and if it tries to do so it will destroy itself.

Justice Brennan, with whom Justice Marshall and Justice Blackmun join, dissenting.

* * *

Today the Court, while tentatively accepting that there is some degree of constitutionally protected liberty interest in avoiding unwanted medical treatment, including life-sustaining medical treatment such as artificial nutrition and hydration, affirms the decision of the Missouri Supreme Court. The majority opinion, as I read it, would affirm that decision on the ground that a State may require "clear and convincing" evidence of Nancy Cruzan's prior decision to forgo life-sustaining treatment under circumstances such as hers in order to ensure that her actual wishes are honored. Because I believe that Nancy Cruzan has a fundamental right to be free of unwanted artificial nutrition and hydration, which right is not outweighed by any interests of the State, and because I find that the improperly biased procedural obstacles imposed by the Missouri Supreme Court impermissibly burden that right, I respectfully dissent. Nancy Cruzan is entitled to choose to die with dignity.

I

A

* * *

The question before this Court is a relatively narrow one: whether the Due Process Clause allows Missouri to require a now-incompetent patient in an irreversible persistent vegetative state to remain on life-support absent rigorously clear and convincing evidence that avoiding the treatment represents the patient's prior, express choice. If a fundamental right is at issue, Missouri's rule of decision must be scrutinized under the standards this Court has always applied in such circumstances. [ ] If a requirement imposed by a State "significantly interferes with the exercise of a fundamental right, it cannot be upheld unless it is supported by sufficiently important state interests and is closely tailored to effectuate only those interests." The Constitution imposes on this Court the obligation to "examine carefully ... the extent to which [the legitimate government interests advanced] are served by the challenged regulation." * * *   An evidentiary rule, just as a substantive prohibition, must meet these standards if it significantly burdens a fundamental liberty interest.   Fundamental rights "are protected not only against heavy-handed frontal attack, but also from being stifled by more subtle governmental interference."   [   ]

B

* * * Today, the Court concedes that our prior decisions "support the recognition of a general liberty interest in refusing medical treatment."   The Court, however, avoids discussing either the measure of that liberty interest or its application by assuming, for purposes of this case only, that a competent person has a constitutionally protected liberty interest in being free of unwanted artificial nutrition and hydration.   Justice O'Connor's opinion is less parsimonious.   She openly affirms that "the Court has often deemed state incursions into the body repugnant to the interests protected by the Due Process Clause," that there is a liberty interest in avoiding unwanted medical treatment and that it encompasses the right to be free of "artificially delivered food and water."

But if a competent person has a liberty interest to be free of unwanted medical treatment, as both the majority and Justice O'Connor concede, it must be fundamental.   * * *

The right to be free from medical attention without consent, to determine what shall be done with one's own body, *is* deeply rooted in this Nation's traditions, as the majority acknowledges.

* * *

No material distinction can be drawn between the treatment to which Nancy Cruzan continues to be subject—artificial nutrition and hydration—and any other medical treatment.   * * *   [Justice Brennan's description of the medical procedure involved in providing nutrition and hydration is provided below, p. 1141–1142].

Nor does the fact that Nancy Cruzan is now incompetent deprive her of her fundamental rights.   * * * As the majority recognizes, the question is not whether an incompetent has constitutional rights, but how such rights may be exercised.   As we explained in *Thompson v. Oklahoma*, 487 U.S. 815 (1988), "[t]he law must often adjust the manner in which it affords rights to those whose status renders them unable to exercise choice freely and rationally.   Children, the insane, and *those who are irreversibly ill with loss of brain function, for instance, all retain 'rights,'* to be sure, but often such rights are only meaningful as they are exercised by agents acting with the best interests of their principals in mind."   [   ] "To deny [its] exercise because the patient is unconscious or incompetent would be to deny the right."   [   ]

II

A

The right to be free from unwanted medical attention is a right to evaluate the potential benefit of treatment and its possible consequences according to one's own values and to make a personal decision whether to subject oneself to the intrusion. For a patient like Nancy Cruzan, the sole benefit of medical treatment is being kept metabolically alive. Neither artificial nutrition nor any other form of medical treatment available today can cure or in any way ameliorate her condition. Irreversibly vegetative patients are devoid of thought, emotion and sensation; they are permanently and completely unconscious. As the President's Commission concluded in approving the withdrawal of life support equipment from irreversibly vegetative patients:

> "[T]reatment ordinarily aims to benefit a patient through preserving life, relieving pain and suffering, protecting against disability, and returning maximally effective functioning. If a prognosis of permanent unconsciousness is correct, however, continued treatment cannot confer such benefits. Pain and suffering are absent, as are joy, satisfaction, and pleasure. Disability is total and no return to an even minimal level of social or human functioning is possible." [   ]

There are also affirmative reasons why someone like Nancy might choose to forgo artificial nutrition and hydration under these circumstances. Dying is personal. And it is profound. For many, the thought of an ignoble end, steeped in decay, is abhorrent. A quiet, proud death, bodily integrity intact, is a matter of extreme consequence. "In certain, thankfully rare, circumstances the burden of maintaining the corporeal existence degrades the very humanity it was meant to serve." * * *

Such conditions are, for many, humiliating to contemplate, as is visiting a prolonged and anguished vigil on one's parents, spouse, and children. A long, drawn-out death can have a debilitating effect on family members. [   ] For some, the idea of being remembered in their persistent vegetative states rather than as they were before their illness or accident may be very disturbing.

B

* * *

The only state interest asserted here is a general interest in the preservation of life. But the State has no legitimate general interest in someone's life, completely abstracted from the interest of the person living that life, that could outweigh the person's choice to avoid medical treatment. * * * [T]he State's general interest in life must accede to Nancy Cruzan's particularized and intense interest in self-determination in her choice of medical treatment. There is simply nothing legitimately within the State's purview to be gained by superseding her decision.

* * *

III

This is not to say that the State has no legitimate interests to assert here. As the majority recognizes Missouri has a *parens patriae* interest in providing Nancy Cruzan, now incompetent, with as accurate as possible a determination of how she would exercise her rights under these circumstances. Second, if and when it is determined that Nancy Cruzan would want to continue treatment, the State may legitimately assert an interest in providing that treatment. But *until* Nancy's wishes have been determined, the only state interest that may be asserted is an interest in safeguarding the accuracy of that determination.

Accuracy, therefore, must be our touchstone. Missouri may constitutionally impose only those procedural requirements that serve to enhance the accuracy of a determination of Nancy Cruzan's wishes or are at least consistent with an accurate determination. The Missouri "safeguard" that the Court upholds today does not meet that standard. The determination needed in this context is whether the incompetent person would choose to live in a persistent vegetative state on life-support or to avoid this medical treatment. Missouri's rule of decision imposes a markedly asymmetrical evidentiary burden. Only evidence of specific statements of treatment choice made by the patient when competent is admissible to support a finding that the patient, now in a persistent vegetative state, would wish to avoid further medical treatment. Moreover, this evidence must be clear and convincing. No proof is required to support a finding that the incompetent person would wish to continue treatment.

A

The majority offers several justifications for Missouri's heightened evidentiary standard. * * *

* * *

The majority claims that the allocation of the risk of error is justified because it is more important not to terminate life-support for someone who would wish it continued than to honor the wishes of someone who would not. * * * But, from the point of view of the patient, an erroneous decision in either direction is irrevocable. An erroneous decision to terminate artificial nutrition and hydration, to be sure, will lead to failure of that last remnant of physiological life, the brain stem, and result in complete brain death. An erroneous decision not to terminate life-support, however, robs a patient of the very qualities protected by the right to avoid unwanted medical treatment. His own degraded existence is perpetuated; his family's suffering is protracted; the memory he leaves behind becomes more and more distorted.

Even a later decision to grant him his wish cannot undo the intervening harm. But a later decision is unlikely in any event. "[T]he discovery of new evidence," to which the majority refers, is more hypothetical than plausible. The majority also misconceives the relevance of the possibility of "advancements in medical science," by treating it as a reason to force someone to continue medical treatment against his will. The possibility of a medical miracle is indeed part of

the calculus, but it is a part of the *patient's* calculus. If current
research suggests that some hope for cure or even moderate improvement is possible within the life-span projected, this is a factor that
should be and would be accorded significant weight in assessing what
the patient himself would choose.

B

Even more than its heightened evidentiary standard, the Missouri
court's categorical exclusion of relevant evidence dispenses with any
semblance of accurate factfinding. The court adverted to no evidence
supporting its decision, but held that no clear and convincing, inherently reliable evidence had been presented to show that Nancy would want
to avoid further treatment. * * * The court did not specifically define
what kind of evidence it would consider clear and convincing, but its
general discussion suggests that only a living will or equivalently
formal directive from the patient when competent would meet this
standard. [ ]

Too few people execute living wills or equivalently formal directives for such an evidentiary rule to ensure adequately that the
wishes of incompetent persons will be honored. While it might be a
wise social policy to encourage people to furnish such instructions, no
general conclusion about a patient's choice can be drawn from the
absence of formalities.

* * *

The testimony of close friends and family members, on the other
hand, may often be the best evidence available of what the patient's
choice would be. It is they with whom the patient most likely will have
discussed such questions and they who know the patient best. "Family
members have a unique knowledge of the patient which is vital to any
decision on his or her behalf." [ ] The Missouri court's decision to
ignore this whole category of testimony is also at odds with the
practices of other States. [ ]

The Missouri court's disdain for Nancy's statements in serious
conversations not long before her accident, for the opinions of Nancy's
family and friends as to her values, beliefs and certain choice, and even
for the opinion of an outside objective factfinder appointed by the State
evinces a disdain for Nancy Cruzan's own right to choose. The rules by
which an incompetent person's wishes are determined must represent
every effort to determine those wishes. The rule that the Missouri
court adopted and that this Court upholds, however, skews the result
away from a determination that as accurately as possible reflects the
individual's own preferences and beliefs. It is a rule that transforms
human beings into passive subjects of medical technology. * * *

C

* * * Of the many States which have instituted such protections,
Missouri is virtually the only one to have fashioned a rule that lessens
the likelihood of accurate determinations. In contrast, nothing in the

Constitution prevents States from reviewing the advisability of a family decision, by requiring a court proceeding or by appointing an impartial guardian ad litem.

There are various approaches to determining an incompetent patient's treatment choice in use by the several States today and there may be advantages and disadvantages to each and other approaches not yet envisioned. The choice, in largest part, is and should be left to the States, so long as each State is seeking, in a reliable manner, to discover what the patient would want. * * *

D

Finally, I cannot agree with the majority that where it is not possible to determine what choice an incompetent patient would make, a State's role as *parens patriae* permits the State automatically to make that choice itself. [ ] Under fair rules of evidence, it is improbable that a court could not determine what the patient's choice would be. Under the rule of decision adopted by Missouri and upheld today by this Court, such occasions might be numerous. But in neither case does it follow that it is constitutionally acceptable for the State invariably to assume the role of deciding for the patient. A State's legitimate interest in safeguarding a patient's choice cannot be furthered by simply appropriating it.

* * *

* * * The new medical technology can reclaim those who would have been irretrievably lost a few decades ago and restore them to active lives. For Nancy Cruzan, it failed, and for others with wasting incurable disease it may be doomed to failure. In these unfortunate situations, the bodies and preferences and memories of the victims do not escheat to the State; nor does our Constitution permit the State or any other government to commandeer them. No singularity of feeling exists upon which such a government might confidently rely as *parens patriae*. The President's Commission, after years of research, concluded:

> In few areas of health care are people's evaluations of their experiences so varied and uniquely personal as in their assessments of the nature and value of the processes associated with dying. For some, every moment of life is of inestimable value; for others, life without some desired level of mental or physical ability is worthless or burdensome. A moderate degree of suffering may be an important means of personal growth and religious experience to one person, but only frightening or despicable to another. [ ]

Yet Missouri and this Court have displaced Nancy's own assessment of the processes associated with dying. They have discarded evidence of her will, ignored her values, and deprived her of the right to a decision as closely approximating her own choice as humanly possible. They have done so disingenuously in her name, and openly in Missouri's own. That Missouri and this Court may truly be motivated only by concern

for incompetent patients makes no matter. As one of our most prominent jurists warned us decades ago: "Experience should teach us to be
most on our guard to protect liberty when the government's purposes
are beneficent. * * * The greatest dangers to liberty lurk in insidious
encroachment by men of zeal, well meaning but without understanding." *Olmstead v. United States,* 277 U.S. 438, 479 (1928) (Brandeis, J., dissenting).

I respectfully dissent.

JUSTICE STEVENS, dissenting.

Our Constitution is born of the proposition that all legitimate
governments must secure the equal right of every person to "Life,
Liberty, and the pursuit of Happiness." In the ordinary case we quite
naturally assume that these three ends are compatible, mutually enhancing, and perhaps even coincident.

The Court would make an exception here. It permits the State's
abstract, undifferentiated interest in the preservation of life to overwhelm the best interests of Nancy Beth Cruzan, interests which would,
according to an undisputed finding, be served by allowing her guardians
to exercise her constitutional right to discontinue medical treatment.

* * *

It is perhaps predictable that courts might undervalue the liberty
at stake here. Because death is so profoundly personal, public reflection upon it is unusual. As this sad case shows, however, such reflection must become more common if we are to deal responsibly with the
modern circumstances of death. Medical advances have altered the
physiological conditions of death in ways that may be alarming: highly
invasive treatment may perpetuate human existence through a merger
of body and machine that some might reasonably regard as an insult to
life rather than as its continuation.

* * *

It is against this background of decisional law, and the constitutional tradition which it illuminates, that the right to be free from unwanted life-sustaining medical treatment must be understood. That right
presupposes no abandonment of the desire for life. Nor is it reducible
to a protection against batteries undertaken in the name of treatment,
or to a guarantee against the infliction of bodily discomfort. Choices
about death touch the core of liberty. Our duty, and the concomitant
freedom, to come to terms with the conditions of our own mortality are
undoubtedly "so rooted in the traditions and conscience of our people as
to be ranked as fundamental," [   ] and indeed are essential incidents of
the unalienable rights to life and liberty endowed us by our Creator.
[   ]

The more precise constitutional significance of death is difficult to
describe; not much may be said with confidence about death unless it is
said from faith, and that alone is reason enough to protect the freedom
to conform choices about death to individual conscience. We may also,

however, justly assume that death is not life's simple opposite, or its necessary terminus, but rather its completion. Our ethical tradition has long regarded an appreciation of mortality as essential to understanding life's significance. It may, in fact, be impossible to live for anything without being prepared to die for something. Certainly there was no disdain for life in Nathan Hale's most famous declaration or in Patrick Henry's; their words instead bespeak a passion for life that forever preserves their own lives in the memories of their countrymen. From such "honored dead we take increased devotion to that cause for which they gave the last full measure of devotion."

These considerations cast into stark relief the injustice, and unconstitutionality, of Missouri's treatment of Nancy Beth Cruzan. Nancy Cruzan's death, when it comes, cannot be an historic act of heroism; it will inevitably be the consequence of her tragic accident. But Nancy Cruzan's interest in life, no less than that of any other person, includes an interest in how she will be thought of after her death by those whose opinions mattered to her. There can be no doubt that her life made her dear to her family, and to others. How she dies will affect how that life is remembered. The trial court's order authorizing Nancy's parents to cease their daughter's treatment would have permitted the family that cares for Nancy to bring to a close her tragedy and her death. Missouri's objection to that order subordinates Nancy's body, her family, and the lasting significance of her life to the State's own interests. The decision we review thereby interferes with constitutional interests of the highest order.

To be constitutionally permissible, Missouri's intrusion upon these fundamental liberties must, at a minimum, bear a reasonable relationship to a legitimate state end. [ ] Missouri asserts that its policy is related to a state interest in the protection of life. In my view, however, it is an effort to define life, rather than to protect it, that is the heart of Missouri's policy. Missouri insists, without regard to Nancy Cruzan's own interests, upon equating her life with the biological persistence of her bodily functions. Nancy Cruzan, it must be remembered, is not now simply incompetent. She is in a persistent vegetative state, and has been so for seven years. The trial court found, and no party contested, that Nancy has no possibility of recovery and no consciousness.

It seems to me that the Court errs insofar as it characterizes this case as involving "judgments about the 'quality' of life that a particular individual may enjoy." Nancy Cruzan is obviously "*alive*" in a physiological sense. But for patients like Nancy Cruzan, who have no consciousness and no chance of recovery, there is a serious question as to whether the mere persistence of their bodies is "*life*" as that word is commonly understood, or as it is used in both the Constitution and the Declaration of Independence. The State's unflagging determination to perpetuate Nancy Cruzan's physical existence is comprehensible only as an effort to define life's meaning, not as an attempt to preserve its sanctity.

This much should be clear from the oddity of Missouri's definition alone. Life, particularly human life, is not commonly thought of as a merely physiological condition or function. Its sanctity is often thought to derive from the impossibility of any such reduction. When people speak of life, they often mean to describe the experiences that comprise a person's history, as when it is said that somebody "led a good life." [20] They may also mean to refer to the practical manifestation of the human spirit, a meaning captured by the familiar observation that somebody "added life" to an assembly. If there is a shared thread among the various opinions on this subject, it may be that life is an activity which is at once the matrix for and an integration of a person's interests. In any event, absent some theological abstraction, the idea of life is not conceived separately from the idea of a living person. Yet, it is by precisely such a separation that Missouri asserts an interest in Nancy Cruzan's life in opposition to Nancy Cruzan's own interests. The resulting definition is uncommon indeed.

* * *

In short, there is no reasonable ground for believing that Nancy Beth Cruzan has any *personal* interest in the perpetuation of what the State has decided is her life. As I have already suggested, it would be possible to hypothesize such an interest on the basis of theological or philosophical conjecture. But even to posit such a basis for the State's action is to condemn it. It is not within the province of secular government to circumscribe the liberties of the people by regulations designed wholly for the purpose of establishing a sectarian definition of life. [   ]

* * *

Only because Missouri has arrogated to itself the power to define life, and only because the Court permits this usurpation, are Nancy Cruzan's life and liberty put into disquieting conflict. If Nancy Cruzan's life were defined by reference to her own interests, so that her life expired when her biological existence ceased serving *any* of her own interests, then her constitutionally protected interest in freedom from unwanted treatment would not come into conflict with her constitutionally protected interest in life. Conversely, if there were *any* evidence that Nancy Cruzan herself defined life to encompass every form of biological persistence by a human being, so that the continuation of treatment would serve Nancy's own liberty, then once again there would be no conflict between life and liberty. The opposition of life and liberty in this case are thus not the result of Nancy Cruzan's tragic accident, but are instead the artificial consequence of Missouri's effort, and this Court's willingness, to abstract Nancy Cruzan's life from Nancy Cruzan's person.

20. It is this sense of the word that explains its use to describe a biography: for example, Boswell's Life of Johnson or Beveridge's The Life of John Marshall. The reader of a book so titled would be surprised to find that it contained a compilation of biological data.

* * *

Both this Court's majority and the state court's majority express great deference to the policy choice made by the state legislature. That deference is, in my view, based upon a severe error in the Court's constitutional logic. The Court believes that the liberty interest claimed here on behalf of Nancy Cruzan is peculiarly problematic because "an incompetent person is not able to make an informed and voluntary choice to exercise a hypothetical right to refuse treatment or any other right." The impossibility of such an exercise affords the State, according to the Court, some discretion to interpose "a procedural requirement" that effectively compels the continuation of Nancy Cruzan's treatment.

* * *

* * * [T]he Court's deference seems ultimately to derive from the premise that chronically incompetent persons have no constitutionally cognizable interests at all, and so are not persons within the meaning of the Constitution. Deference of this sort is patently unconstitutional. It is also dangerous in ways that may not be immediately apparent. Today the State of Missouri has announced its intent to spend several hundred thousand dollars in preserving the life of Nancy Beth Cruzan in order to vindicate its general policy favoring the preservation of human life. Tomorrow, another State equally eager to champion an interest in the "quality of life" might favor a policy designed to ensure quick and comfortable deaths by denying treatment to categories of marginally hopeless cases. If the State in fact has an interest in defining life, and if the State's policy with respect to the termination of life-sustaining treatment commands deference from the judiciary, it is unclear how any resulting conflict between the best interests of the individual and the general policy of the State would be resolved. I believe the Constitution requires that the individual's vital interest in liberty should prevail over the general policy in that case, just as in this.

That a contrary result is readily imaginable under the majority's theory makes manifest that this Court cannot defer to any State policy that drives a theoretical wedge between a person's life, on the one hand, and that person's liberty or happiness, on the other. The consequence of such a theory is to deny the personhood of those whose lives are defined by the State's interests rather than their own. This consequence may be acceptable in theology or in speculative philosophy [ ] but it is radically inconsistent with the foundation of all legitimate government. Our Constitution presupposes a respect for the personhood of every individual, and nowhere is strict adherence to that principle more essential than in the Judicial Branch. [ ]

* * *

In this case, as is no doubt true in many others, the predicament confronted by the healthy members of the Cruzan family merely adds emphasis to the best interests finding made by the trial judge. Each of us has an interest in the kind of memories that will survive after death. To that end, individual decisions are often motivated by their impact on others. A member of the kind of family identified in the trial court's findings in this case would likely have not only a normal interest in minimizing the burden that her own illness imposes on others, but also an interest in having their memories of her filled predominantly with thoughts about her past vitality rather than her current condition. The meaning and completion of her life should be controlled by persons who have her best interests at heart—not by a state legislature concerned only with the "preservation of human life."

The Cruzan family's continuing concern provides a concrete reminder that Nancy Cruzan's interests did not disappear with her vitality or her consciousness. However commendable may be the State's interest in human life, it cannot pursue that interest by appropriating Nancy Cruzan's life as a symbol for its own purposes. Lives do not exist in abstraction from persons, and to pretend otherwise is not to honor but to desecrate the State's responsibility for protecting life. A State that seeks to demonstrate its commitment to life may do so by aiding those who are actively struggling for life and health. In this endeavor, unfortunately, no State can lack for opportunities: there can be no need to make an example of tragic cases like that of Nancy Cruzan.

I respectfully dissent.

Notes and Questions

1. Subsequent to this judgment the Missouri trial court heard newly discovered evidence, provided by Nancy Cruzan's friends and colleagues, that she had made explicit and unambiguous statements that demonstrated, clearly and convincingly, that she would not want continued the treatment that she was receiving. Without opposition from the Attorney General of Missouri, the trial court authorized Ms. Cruzan's guardians to terminate her nutrition and hydration. Nancy Beth Cruzan died on December 26, 1990.

2. Does the Opinion of the Court recognize a constitutional right to die? Many authoritative sources presume that the opinion does recognize a constitutionally protected liberty interest in a competent person to refuse unwanted medical treatment. Indeed, the syllabus prepared for the Court says just that, and the case was hailed by the New York Times as the first to recognize a right to die. On the other hand, the Chief Justice's language does not support such a conclusion. While the majority agrees that "[t]he principle that a competent person has a constitutionally protected liberty interest in refusing unwanted medical treatment *may* be inferred from our prior decisions," (emphasis added) the Court never makes the inference itself. In fact, the opinion says explicitly that "*for purposes of this case,* we assume that the United States Constitution would grant a competent person a constitutionally protected right to refuse life saving nutrition and hydration." (emphasis added)

Why is this assumption limited to the "purposes of this case"? Does the Court question (1) whether there is a constitutionally protected liberty interest in refusing unwanted medical treatment, (2) whether the right extends to life saving treatment, or (3) whether it covers hydration and nutrition?

It must have been difficult for the Chief Justice to craft an opinion that would be joined by a majority of the court. Justice Scalia most clearly does not believe that there is any constitutional right implicated. If the Chief Justice were to formally recognize a constitutional right, he might have lost Justice Scalia's signature—and thus lost an opportunity for there to be any majority opinion.

The dissents filed in this case are long and obviously heartfelt. Do the dissenters, all of whom would recognize a constitutionally protected right to die, and Justice O'Connor, who would also do so, create a majority in support of this constitutional position?

3. The majority opinion permits a state to limit its consideration to those wishes previously expressed by the patient and to ignore the decisions of another person acting on behalf of the patient. In fact, the Court explicitly does not address the question of whether a state must defer to an appropriately nominated surrogate acting on behalf of the patient. See 110 S.Ct. at 2856 n. 12. On the other hand, the dissenting justices would recognize the decisions of a surrogate under appropriate circumstances, and Justice O'Connor suggests that the duty to give effect to those decisions "may well be constitutionally required." 110 S.Ct. at 2857. What is the constitutional status of surrogate decision-making after *Cruzan*?

4. Note that none of the opinions refers to the "right of privacy," a term which has caused the Court such tremendous grief in the abortion context. The Chief Justice analyzes this issue in the more general terms of a fourteenth amendment liberty interest, and none of the counsel argued the case in terms of the right to privacy. Apparently the Court just did not wish to entangle itself any further with the "P" word.

5. Except for a glancing reference by Justice Stevens in his dissent, the opinions do not consider the cost of providing care to Nancy Cruzan. Should the cost be relevant? Should the constitutional right (to liberty or to life) be any different depending on who bears the cost? See Harris v. McRae, 448 U.S. 297, 100 S.Ct. 2671, 65 L.Ed.2d 784 (1980). Would your analysis of this case be any different if the costs were being paid by an insurance company, by Ms. Cruzan's parents, or by community fund raising in Nancy Cruzan's neighborhood, rather than by the state of Missouri? Should the one who pays the surgeon get to call the cuts?

At the oral argument of this case one Justice asked the counsel for Missouri several questions about the cost. If the cost were borne by the Cruzan family, and if the state could require the continued treatment of Nancy Cruzan, could the state also impose a duty on the family to pay for that treatment? Counsel for Missouri never argued that the state could require the family to pay for treatment that members of the family believed the patient would not want. Instead, he simply argued that the cost question was not before the Court because the entire cost was being borne by the state of Missouri. But what if the family were paying?

Would it seem especially cruel to require a family to spend all its resources on treatment it believes is terribly burdensome to the patient and that it is certain the patient would not want? Should this be a matter of constitutional law?

Justice Blackmar's dissent to the Missouri Supreme Court's opinion in *Cruzan* addresses the disutility of requiring some patients to be kept alive, at great expense, while the state is unable (or unwilling) to provide adequate care to others. He points out:

> The absolutist position is also infirm because the state does not stand prepared to finance the preservation of life, without regard to the cost, in very many cases. In this particular case the state has Nancy in its possession, and is litigating its right to keep her. Yet, several years ago, a respected judge needed extraordinary treatment which the hospital in which he was a patient was not willing to furnish without a huge advance deposit and the state apparently had no desire to help out. Many people die because of the unavailability of heroic medical treatment. It simply cannot be said that the state's interest in preserving and prolonging life is absolute.

760 S.W.2d at 429. Judge Blackmar also points out, in a footnote, that "an absolutist would undoubtedly be offended by an inquiry as to whether the state, by prolonging Nancy's life at its own expense, is disabling itself from [providing] needed treatment to others who do not have such dire prognosis." 760 S.W.2d at 429 n. 4.

6. The result of the *Cruzan* case is that most "right to die" law will be established on a state by state basis; there will be very little, if any, United States constitutional limits on what states may do. The *Cruzan* case thus may politicize the "right to die" in the way that the *Webster* decision politicized the abortion question. Indeed, there were several attempts to moot out the *Cruzan* case while it was pending before the United States Supreme Court. A legislative measure that would have allowed for the termination of nutrition and hydration after a patient remained in persistent vegetative state for some extended period (one bill put the period at three years) never made it through the Missouri legislature.

The decision of the United States Supreme Court to opt out of providing much constitutional guidance to the states may create a crazy quilt of state laws such that a patient who would have a "right to die" that could be exercised by his family in California or New Jersey would not have that right (or would not have a right that could be exercised by his family) in Missouri or New York. Indeed, the conditions and extent of, and the restrictions and exceptions to, any "right to die" might be different in each state. State policies will thus require different results in factually identical cases. Is there anything wrong with this?

What would happen if Nancy Cruzan's family had decided to move her to the Yale Medical Center "because of the more favorable medical facilities" there? Could they have moved her from Missouri to Connecticut, where removal of the gastrostomy clearly would be legally permitted, just for the purpose of removing the gastrostomy? If they could not, then Nancy Cruzan could have become a prisoner of a state that rejects her family's values—values that have been incorporated into official state policies in other jurisdictions. If they could move her, however, Missouri would have allowed the family to avoid the important policy of the state law and imperil the very life the law was designed to protect. Would it violate any criminal statute to move someone across state lines for the purpose of avoiding the termination of life support laws of the first state? Could a state make such an action a crime?

In early 1991 the father and guardian of Christine Busalacchi sought to have his daughter moved from Missouri to Minnesota for medical consultation with a nationally known neurologist. Ms. Busalacchi, who had been living in the same nursing home that had housed Nancy Cruzan, was arguably in a persistent vegetative state. The state of Missouri sought (and obtained) an order forbidding the move because of the fear that her father wanted only to find some place where his daughter could die. A divided Missouri Court of Appeals determined that the trial court was required to commence a new hearing on whether the move could be justified by other medical objectives. In deciding the case, the majority made it clear that "* * * we will not permit [the] guardian to forum shop in an effort to control whether Christine lives or dies." The dissent argued that "* * * Minnesota is not a medical or ethical wasteland * * *. There is a parochial arrogance in suggesting, as the state does, that only in Missouri can Christine's medical, physical, and legal well being be protected and only here will her best interests be considered." For an interesting commentary on the increasing need to cross state lines to make personally acceptable ethical decisions, see Goodman, Shopping for a Place to Die, Boston Globe, March 10, 1991, A31.

Might the *Cruzan* and *Busalacchi* cases give rise to medic alert bracelets that say, "If I might be in a persistent vegetative state, keep me out of Missouri?"

7. The September/October 1990 Hastings Center Report includes an excellent symposium on *Cruzan*. The symposium includes Colby, Missouri Stands Alone, 20 Hastings Center Rep. (5) 5 (1990) (written by counsel for the Cruzans); Busalacchi, How Can They? 20 Hastings Center Rep. (5) 6 (1990) (written by Christine Busalacchi's father); Baron, On Taking Substituted Judgment Seriously, 20 Hastings Center Rep. (5) 7 (1990); Robertson, Cruzan: No Rights Violated, 20 Hastings Center Rep. (5) 8 (1990); Cranford, A Hostage to Technology, 20 Hastings Center Rep. (5) 9 (1990) (written by a neurologist); Lynn and Glover, *Cruzan* and Caring for Others, 20 Hastings Center Rep. (5) 10 (1990) (written by physicians, exploring the effect of the case on the doctor-patient-family relationships).

III. THE "RIGHT TO DIE"—COMPETENT PATIENTS

For years, commentators have concluded that competent adult patients have the right to refuse any form of medical treatment, even if the refusal is certain to cause death—a view consistent with the decision of the vast majority of the states to decriminalize suicide. It was not until 1984, however, that an appellate court directly confronted a situation in which a clearly competent patient refused treatment without which he would surely die. In *Bartling v. Superior Court*, the California Court of Appeal's decision was made easier by the fact that the patient had died before the case was finally resolved. Any tentativeness in the *Bartling* opinion was overcome by the case of Elizabeth Bouvia, in which the California Court of Appeal went so far as to require the hospital to provide adequate support to Ms. Bouvia during her dying process. The court confirmed that hospitals are obliged to serve the autonomous interests of patients, as defined by those patients. This view—that the function of the hospital is to be defined by patients, not physicians or other health care providers—is considered by some to be the single most outrageous judicial intrusion upon the medical profession. The California hospital was not only required to refrain from providing life-sustaining treatment for Ms. Bouvia, the hospital was required to provide the medical assistance that would allow her to die without avoidable pain, i.e., that would allow her to die the way she wanted to.

The legal history of the right of competent patients to forgo life-sustaining treatment is provided in a clear and accurate way through these two California opinions. The very strong unanimous court in *Bouvia* demonstrates that the consensus absent in 1984 had begun to solidify by 1986. As you saw, this right was recognized explicitly as part of American common law (even if its Constitutional source is uncertain) in *Cruzan*.

BARTLING v. SUPERIOR COURT

California Court of Appeal, Second District, 1984.
163 Cal.App.3d 186, 209 Cal.Rptr. 220.

HASTINGS, ASSOCIATE JUSTICE.

In this case we are called upon to decide whether a competent adult patient, with serious illnesses which are probably incurable but have not been diagnosed as terminal, has the right, over the objection of his physicians and the hospital, to have life-support equipment disconnected despite the fact that withdrawal of such devices will surely hasten his death.

* * *

Mr. Bartling entered Glendale Adventist on April 8, 1984, for treatment of his depression. A routine physical examination, including a chest x-ray, was performed, and a tumor was discovered on Mr. Bartling's lung. A biopsy of the tumor was performed by inserting a needle in the lung, which caused the lung to collapse. Tubes were inserted in Mr. Bartling's chest and through his nasal passage and throat in order to reinflate his lung. Because of his emphysema, the hole made by the biopsy needle did not heal properly and the lung did not reinflate. While Mr. Bartling was being treated with antibiotics to promote healing of the lung, a tracheotomy was performed and he was placed on a ventilator. Mr. Bartling remained on the ventilator until the time of his death, and efforts to "wean" him from the machine were unsuccessful.

On several occasions in April, Mr. Bartling tried to remove the ventilator tubes. To prevent accidental or deliberate disconnection of the ventilator tubes (or any of the other tubes to which he was attached), Mr. Bartling's wrists were placed in "soft restraints." Despite requests from both Mr. and Mrs. Bartling, Glendale Adventist and Mr. Bartling's treating physicians refused to remove the ventilator or the restraints.

In June of this year, petitioners filed a complaint * * * in the Superior Court seeking damages for battery (unconsented medical treatment), violation of state and federal constitutional rights, breach of fiduciary duty on the part of Glendale Adventist and Mr. Bartling's treating physicians, intentional infliction of emotional distress, and conspiracy. Petitioners sought an injunction restraining real parties from administering any unconsented medical care to Mr. Bartling. This included "forcing Plaintiff to undergo mechanical breathing through the ventilator" and other medical procedures. Attached to the complaint were:

(1) A "living will," signed by Mr. Bartling with an "X" and properly witnessed, which stated in part: "If at such time the situation should arise in which there is no reasonable expectation of my recovery from extreme physical or mental disability, I direct that I be allowed to die and not be kept alive by medications, artificial means or heroic measures."

(2) A declaration from Mr. Bartling in which he stated in part: "While I have no wish to die, I find intolerable the living conditions forced upon me by my deteriorating lungs, heart and blood vessel systems, and find intolerable my being continuously connected to this ventilator, which sustains my every breath and my life for the past six and one-half (6½) weeks. Therefore, I wish this Court to order that the sustaining of my respiration by this mechanical device violates my constitutional right, is contrary to my every wish, and constitutes a battery upon my person. I fully understand that my request to have the ventilator removed and discontinued, which I have frequently made to my wife and to my doctors, will very likely cause respiratory failure and ultimately lead to my death. I am willing to accept that risk rather than to continue the burden of this artificial existence which I find unbearable, degrading and dehumanizing. I also suffer a great deal of pain and discomfort because of being confined to bed, being on this ventilator, and from the other problems which are occurring."

(3) A "Durable Power of Attorney for Health Care," executed by Mr. Bartling, appointing Mrs. Bartling as his attorney-in-fact. In this document, Mr. Bartling stated in part: "My desires concerning future medical and supportive care, which I direct my attorney-in-fact to follow, are as follows: * * * I am totally unable to care for myself, and believe that I am dependent on a mechanical ventilator to support and

sustain my respiration and life. I continuously suffer agonizing discomfort, pain and the humiliating indignity of having to have my every bodily need and function tended to by others. I do not wish to continue to live under these conditions. It is therefore my intent to refuse to continue on ventilator support and thereby to permit the natural process of dying to occur—peacefully, privately and with dignity. I direct my attorney-in-fact to honor my desires in this regard, and to refuse ventilator support, at such time as I am unable to do so for myself. I am aware that impairment, incapacity and unconsciousness may occur as a result of my refusal of ventilation, but I desire that none of these be deemed to be a medical emergency."

Mr. and Mrs. Bartling and Mr. Bartling's daughter Heather all executed documents in which they released Glendale Adventist and its doctors from any claim of civil liability should the hospital and doctors agree to honor Mr. Bartling's wishes.

Despite these strong and unequivocal statements from Mr. Bartling and his family, his treating physicians refused to remove the ventilator and refused to remove the restraints which would allow Mr. Bartling to disconnect the ventilator himself should he choose to do so.

In support of their application for injunction and this petition, petitioners supplied declarations to support their contentions that (1) Mr. Bartling had a relatively short time to live, even with the ventilator; (2) he was competent to direct what medical treatment he would or would not receive; and (3) it would not be unethical for Mr. Bartling's treating physicians to honor his wishes, even if it meant disconnection of a life-sustaining machine.

Mr. Bartling's videotape deposition was taken on the day before the Superior Court hearing, June 21. Mr. Bartling could not speak but could nod or shake his head to indicate yes or no answers. Mr. Bartling said that he wanted to live, but did not want to live on the ventilator. He did understand that if the ventilator were removed he might die.

It was the opinion of Mr. Bartling's treating physicians, presented to the trial court by way of declarations, that Mr. Bartling's illness was not terminal and that he could live for at least a year if he was "weaned" from the ventilator. However, the doctors opined in their declarations that "weaning was unlikely because of his medical and psychological problems that were not under control."

* * *

From an ethical standpoint, declarations were submitted to the effect that Glendale Adventist is a Christian hospital devoted to the preservation of life, and it would be unethical for Glendale Adventist's physicians to disconnect life-support systems from patients whom they viewed as having the potential for cognitive, sapient life.

The hospital and doctors also expressed concern about their potential civil and criminal liability should they accede to Mr. Bartling's wishes and disconnect the ventilator.

* * * [W]e turn to the major issue in this case: whether the right of Mr. Bartling, as a competent adult, to refuse unwanted medical treatment, is outweighed by the various state and personal interests urged by real parties: the preservation of life, the need to protect innocent third parties, the prevention of suicide, and maintaining of the ethics of the medical profession.

* * *

The right of a competent adult patient to refuse medical treatment has its origins in the constitutional right of privacy. This right is specifically guaranteed by the California Constitution [ ] and has been found to exist in the "penumbra" of rights guaranteed by the Fifth and Ninth Amendments to the United States Constitution. (*Griswold v. Connecticut* [ ]) "In short, the law recognizes the individual interest in preserving 'the inviolability of the person.'" (*Superintendent of Belchertown School v. Saikewicz,* [ ]). The constitutional right of privacy guarantees to the individual the freedom to choose to reject, or refuse to consent to, intrusions of his bodily integrity. [ ]

Balanced against these rights are the interests of the state in the preservation of life, the prevention of suicide, and maintaining the ethical integrity of the medical profession. The most significant of these interests is the preservation of life. This is of prime concern to Glendale Adventist, which submitted a declaration to the effect that it is a Christian, pro-life oriented hospital, the majority of whose doctors would view disconnecting a life-support system in a case such as this one as inconsistent with the healing orientation of physicians. We do not doubt the sincerity of real parties' moral and ethical beliefs, or their sincere belief in the position they have taken in this case. However, if the right of the patient to self-determination as to his own medical treatment is to have any meaning at all, it must be paramount to the interests of the patient's hospital and doctors. The right of a competent adult patient to refuse medical treatment is a constitutionally guaranteed right which must not be abridged.

* * *

Our holding that the court below erred in this case is of little consolation to Mr. Bartling. His death renders moot that portion of the petition which seeks an order compelling the Superior Court to grant the injunction sought. However, petitioners have also requested an award of costs and attorneys' fees under the "private attorney general" theory [ ]. The case is remanded to the Superior Court for a determination as to whether attorneys' fees * * * are appropriate.

BOUVIA v. SUPERIOR COURT

California Court of Appeal, Second District, 1986.
179 Cal.App.3d 1127, 225 Cal.Rptr. 297.

BEACH, ASSOCIATE JUSTICE.

Petitioner, Elizabeth Bouvia, a patient in a public hospital seeks the removal from her body of a nasogastric tube inserted and maintained against her will and without her consent by physicians who so placed it for the purpose of keeping her alive through involuntary forced feeding.

* * *

Petitioner is a 28–year–old woman. Since birth she has been afflicted with and suffered from severe cerebral palsy. She is quadriplegic. She is now a patient at a public hospital maintained by one of the real parties in interest, the County of Los Angeles. Other parties are physicians, nurses and the medical and support staff employed by the County of Los Angeles. Petitioner's physical handicaps of palsy and quadriplegia have progressed to the point where she is completely bedridden. Except for a few fingers of one hand and some slight head and facial movements, she is immobile. She is physically helpless and wholly unable to care for herself. * * * She suffers also from degenerative and severely crippling arthritis. She is in continual pain. * * *

She is intelligent, very mentally competent. She earned a college degree. She was married but her husband has left her. She suffered a miscarriage. She lived with her parents until her father told her that they could no longer care for her. She has stayed intermittently with friends and at public facilities. A search for a permanent place to live where she might receive the constant care which she needs has been unsuccessful. She is without financial means to support herself and, therefore, must accept public assistance for medical and other care.

She has on several occasions expressed the desire to die. In 1983 she sought the right to be cared for in a public hospital in Riverside County while she intentionally "starved herself to death." A court in that county denied her judicial assistance to accomplish that goal. * * * Thereafter, friends took her to several different facilities, both public and private, arriving finally at her present location. Efforts by * * * social workers to find her an apartment of her own with publicly paid live-in help or regular visiting nurses to care for her, or some other suitable facility have proved fruitless.

Petitioner must be spoon fed in order to eat. Her present medical and dietary staff have determined that she is not consuming a sufficient amount of nutrients. Petitioner stops eating when she feels she cannot orally swallow more, without nausea and vomiting. As she cannot now retain solids, she is fed soft liquid-like food. Because of her previously announced resolve to starve herself, the medical staff feared her weight loss might reach a life-threatening level. Her weight since admission to real parties' facility seems to hover between 65 and 70 pounds. Accordingly, they inserted the subject tube against her will and contrary to her express written instructions.[2]

2. Her instructions were dictated to her lawyers, written by them and signed by her by means of her making a feeble "x"

Petitioner's counsel argue that her weight loss was not such as to be life threatening and therefore the tube is unnecessary. However, the trial court found to the contrary as a matter of fact, a finding which we must accept. Nonetheless, the point is immaterial, for, as we will explain, a patient has the right to refuse any medical treatment or medical service, even when such treatment is labeled "furnishing nourishment and hydration." This right exists even if its exercise creates a "life threatening condition."

THE RIGHT TO REFUSE MEDICAL TREATMENT

"[A] person of adult years and in sound mind has the right, in the exercise of control over his own body, to determine whether or not to submit to lawful medical treatment." [ ] It follows that such a patient has the right to refuse *any* medical treatment, even that which may save or prolong her life. [ ] *Bartling v. Superior Court* (1984) [ ] In our view the foregoing authorities are dispositive of the case at bench. Nonetheless, the County and its medical staff contend that for reasons unique to this case, Elizabeth Bouvia may not exercise the right available to others. * * *

The right to refuse medical treatment is basic and fundamental. It is recognized as a part of the right of privacy protected by both the state and federal constitutions. * * *

Bartling v. Superior Court, supra, [ ] was factually much like the case at bench. Although not totally identical in all respects, the issue there centered on the same question here present: i.e., "May the patient refuse even life continuing treatment?" * * *

* * *

The description of Mr. Bartling's condition fits that of Elizabeth Bouvia. The holding of that case applies here and compels real parties to respect her decision even though she is not "terminally" ill.

But if additional persuasion be needed, there is ample. As indicated by the discussion in *Bartling* [ ], substantial and respectable authority throughout the country recognize the right which petitioner seeks to exercise. * * *

Moreover, as the *Bartling* decision holds, there is no practical or logical reason to limit the exercise of this right to "terminal" patients. The right to refuse treatment does not need the sanction or approval by any legislative act, directing how and when it shall be exercised.

* * *

A recent Presidential Commission for the Study of Ethical Problems in Medicine and Biomedical and Behavioral Research concluded in part: "The voluntary choice of a competent and informed patient should determine whether or not life-sustaining therapy will be undertaken, just as such choices provide the basis for other decisions about medical treatment. Health care institutions and professionals should

on the paper with a pen which she held in   her mouth.

try to enhance patients' abilities to make decisions on their own behalf and to promote understanding of the available treatment options * * *. Health care professionals serve patients best by maintaining a presumption in favor of sustaining life, while recognizing that competent patients are entitled to choose to forgo any treatments, including those that sustain life."

* * *

The American Hospital Association Policy and Statement of Patients' Choices of Treatment Options, approved by the American Hospital Association in February of 1985 discusses the value of a collaborative relationship between the patient and the physician and states in pertinent part: "Whenever possible, however, the authority to determine the course of treatment, if any, should rest with the patient" and "the right to choose treatment includes the right to refuse a specific treatment *or all treatment * * *.*"

* * *

Significant also is the statement adopted on March 15, 1986, by the Council on Ethical and Judicial Affairs of the American Medical Association. It is entitled "Withholding or Withdrawing Life Prolonging Medical Treatment." In pertinent part, it declares: "The social commitment of the physician is to sustain life and relieve suffering. Where the performance of one duty conflicts with the other, the choice of the patient, or his family or legal representative if the patient is incompetent to act in his own behalf, should prevail."

* * *

It is indisputable that petitioner is mentally competent. She is not comatose. She is quite intelligent, alert and understands the risks involved.

THE CLAIMED EXCEPTIONS TO THE PATIENT'S RIGHT TO CHOOSE ARE INAPPLICABLE

As in *Bartling* the real parties in interest, a county hospital, its physicians and administrators, urge that the interests of the State should prevail over the rights of Elizabeth Bouvia to refuse treatment. Advanced by real parties under this argument are the State's interests in (1) preserving life, (2) preventing suicide, (3) protecting innocent third parties, and (4) maintaining the ethical standards of the medical profession, including the right of physicians to effectively render necessary and appropriate medical service and to refuse treatment to an uncooperative and disruptive patient. Included, whether as part of the above or as separate and additional arguments, are what real parties assert as distinctive facts not present in other cases, i.e., (1) petitioner is a patient in a public facility, thereby making the State a party to the result of her conduct, (2) she is not comatose, nor incurably, nor terminally ill, nor in a vegetative state, all conditions which have justified the termination of life-support system in other instances, (3) she has asked for medical treatment, therefore, she cannot accept a part of it while cutting off the part that would be effective, and (4) she is, in truth, trying to starve herself to death and the State will not be a party to a suicide.

* * *

At bench the trial court concluded that with sufficient feeding petitioner could live an additional 15 to 20 years; therefore, the preservation of petitioner's life for that period outweighed her right to decide. In so holding the trial court mistakenly attached undue importance to the *amount of time* possibly available to petitioner, and failed to give equal weight and consideration for the *quality* of that life; an equal, if not more significant, consideration.

All decisions permitting cessation of medical treatment or life-support procedures to some degree hastened the arrival of death. In part, at least, this was permitted because the quality of life during the time remaining in those cases had been terribly diminished. In Elizabeth Bouvia's view, the quality of her life has been diminished to the point of hopelessness, uselessness, unenjoyability and frustration. She, as the patient, lying helplessly in bed, unable to care for herself, may consider her existence meaningless. She cannot be faulted for so concluding. If her right to choose may not be exercised because there remains to her, in the opinion of a court, a physician or some committee, a certain arbitrary number of years, months, or days, her right will have lost its value and meaning.

Who shall say what the minimum amount of available life must be? Does it matter if it be 15 to 20 years, 15 to 20 months, or 15 to 20 days, if such life has been physically destroyed and its quality, dignity and purpose gone? As in all matters lines must be drawn at some point, somewhere, but that decision must ultimately belong to the one whose life is in issue.

Here Elizabeth Bouvia's decision to forgo medical treatment or life-support through a mechanical means belongs to her. It is not a medical decision for her physicians to make. Neither is it a legal question whose soundness is to be resolved by lawyers or judges. It is not a conditional right subject to approval by ethics committees or courts of law. It is a moral and philosophical decision that, being a competent adult, is hers alone.

* * *

Here, if force fed, petitioner faces 15 to 20 years of a painful existence, endurable only by the constant administrations of morphine. Her condition is irreversible. There is no cure for her palsy or arthritis. Petitioner would have to be fed, cleaned, turned, bedded, toileted by others for 15 to 20 years! Although alert, bright, sensitive, perhaps even brave and feisty, she must lie immobile, unable to exist except through physical acts of others. Her mind and spirit may be free to take great flights but she herself is imprisoned and must lie physically helpless subject to the ignominy, embarrassment, humiliation and dehumanizing aspects created by her helplessness. We do not believe it is the policy of this State that all and every life must be preserved against the will of the sufferer. It is incongruous, if not monstrous, for medical practitioners to assert their right to preserve a life that someone else must live, or, more accurately, endure, for "15 to 20 years." We cannot conceive it to be the policy of this State to inflict such an ordeal upon anyone.

* * * Being competent she has the right to live out the remainder of her natural life in dignity and peace. It is precisely the aim and purpose of the many decisions upholding the withdrawal of life-support systems to accord and provide as large a measure of dignity, respect and comfort as possible to every patient for the remainder of his days, whatever be their number. This goal is not to hasten death, though its earlier arrival may be an expected and understood likelihood.

* * *

Moreover, the trial court seriously erred by basing its decision on the "motives" behind Elizabeth Bouvia's decision to exercise her rights. If a right exists, it matters not what "motivates" its exercise. We find nothing in the law to suggest the right to refuse medical treatment may be exercised only if the patient's *motives* meet someone else's approval. It certainly is not illegal or immoral to prefer a natural, albeit sooner, death than a drugged life attached to a mechanical device.

* * *

We do not purport to establish what will constitute proper medical practice in all other cases or even other aspects of the care to be provided petitioner. We hold only that her right to refuse medical treatment even of the life-sustaining variety, entitles her to the immediate removal of the nasogastric tube that has been involuntarily inserted into her body. The hospital and medical staff are still free to perform a substantial, if not the greater part of their duty, i.e., that of trying to alleviate Bouvia's pain and suffering.

Petitioner is without means to go to a private hospital and, apparently, real parties' hospital as a public facility was required to accept her. Having done so it may not deny her relief from pain and suffering merely because she has chosen to exercise her fundamental right to protect what little privacy remains to her.

Personal dignity is a part of one's right of privacy. * * *

COMPTON, ASSOCIATE JUSTICE, concurring opinion.

* * *

Elizabeth apparently has made a conscious and informed choice that she prefers death to continued existence in her helpless and, to her, intolerable condition. I believe she has an absolute right to effectuate that decision. This state and the medical profession instead of frustrating her desire, should be attempting to relieve her suffering by permitting and in fact assisting her to die with ease and dignity.

The fact that she is forced to suffer the ordeal of self-starvation to achieve her objective is in itself inhumane.

The right to die is an integral part of our right to control our own destinies so long as the rights of others are not affected. That right should, in my opinion, include the ability to enlist assistance from others, including the medical profession, in making death as painless and quick as possible.

Notes and Questions

1. Various attempts to get a rehearing at the Court of Appeal or certiorari from the California Supreme Court in the *Bouvia* case failed. The wide-spread support for the decision of the Court of Appeal may demonstrate a social consensus that no physician, no government agency and no social committee can overrule a competent individual's determination that death is preferable to life—at least when the death will be the consequence of forgoing medical treatment.

2. Do you agree that the hospital had an obligation to accept Ms. Bouvia and provide her with medical relief from her pain and suffering, even though the physicians and hospital found her conduct immoral and her request an abuse of the medical profession? Cf. Brophy v. New England Sinai Hospital, Inc., 398 Mass. 417, 497 N.E.2d 626 (1986), where the Massachusetts Supreme Judicial Court found that a patient in a persistent vegetative state could, through his family, deny consent to feeding through a gastric tube, but that the hospital need not remove or clamp the tube if it found it to be contrary to the ethical dictates of the medical profession. The *Brophy* decision required that the family move the patient to another medical institution more receptive to his apparent desires for his feeding tube to be removed. The New Jersey Supreme Court took a middle ground in In re Jobes, 108 N.J. 394, 529 A.2d 434, 450 (1987):

> The trial court held that the nursing home could refuse to participate in the withdrawal of the j-tube by keeping Mrs. Jobes connected to it until she is transferred out of that facility. Under the circumstances of this case, we disagree, and we reverse that portion of the trial court's order.

> Mrs. Jobes' family had no reason to believe that they were surrendering the right to choose among medical alternatives when they placed her in the nursing home. [ ] The nursing home apparently did not inform Mrs. Jobes' family about its policy toward artificial feeding until May of 1985 when they requested that the j-tube be withdrawn. In fact there is no indication that this policy has ever been formalized. Under these circumstances Mrs. Jobes and her family were entitled to rely on the nursing home's willingness to defer to their choice among courses of medical treatment. * * *

> We do not decide the case in which a nursing home gave notice of its policy not to participate in the withdrawal or withholding of artificial feeding at the time of a patient's admission. Thus, we do not hold that such a policy is never enforceable. But we are confident in this case that it would be wrong to allow the nursing home to discharge

Mrs. Jobes. The evidence indicates that at this point it would be extremely difficult, perhaps impossible, to find another facility that would accept Mrs. Jobes as a patient. Therefore, to allow the nursing home to discharge Mrs. Jobes if her family does not consent to continued artificial feeding would essentially frustrate Mrs. Jobes' right of self-determination. *See generally* Annas, "Transferring the Ethical Hot Potato," 17 Hastings Center Report 20–21 (Feb.1987) (explaining how patients' rights are threatened by legal decisions that allow medical institutions to discharge "patients who do not accept everything they offer").

Is the fact that Bouvia could not afford any other hospital care relevant? Do only private, not public, hospitals have the luxury of living up to what they view to be ethical mandates?

3. If refusing treatment may be an appropriate patient choice, just as choosing treatment may be an appropriate choice, then the alternatives about which patients must be informed by physicians may change and increase substantially. In fact, if we take seriously the *Bouvia* suggestion that hospitals have an obligation to provide comfort to patients who choose to forgo treatment and thus die, do physicians have an obligation to inform patients of the various ways of dying that are available to them, and the consequences of choosing any one of them?

Consider Battin, The Least Worst Death, 13 Hastings Center Rep. 13–16 (April 1983):

> In the face of irreversible, terminal illness, a patient may wish to die sooner but "naturally," without artificial prolongation of any kind. By doing so, the patient may believe he is choosing a death that is, as a contributor to the *New England Journal of Medicine* has put it, "comfortable, decent, and peaceful". "[N]atural death," the patient may assume, means a death that is easier than a medically prolonged one.

> [H]e may assume that it will allow time for reviewing life and saying farewell to family and loved ones, for last rites or final words, for passing on hopes, wisdom, confessions, and blessings to the next generation. These ideas are of course heavily stereotyped * * * : Even the very term "natural" may have stereotyped connotations for the patient: something close to nature, uncontrived, and appropriate. As a result of these notions, the patient often takes "natural death" to be a painless, conscious, dignified, culminative slipping-away.

> Now consider what sorts of death actually occur under the rubric of "natural death." A patient suffers a cardiac arrest and is not resuscitated. Result: sudden unconsciousness, without pain, and death within a number of seconds. Or a patient has an infection that is not treated. Result: * * * fever, delirium, rigor or shaking, and lightheadedness; death usually takes one or two days, depending on the organism involved.

> * * *

> But active killing aside, the physician can do much to grant the dying patient the humane death he has chosen by using the sole legally

protected mechanism that safeguards the right to die: refusal of treatment. This mechanism need not always backfire. For in almost any terminal condition, death can occur in various ways, and there are many possible outcomes of the patient's present condition. * * * What the patient who rejects active euthanasia or assisted suicide may realistically hope for is this: the least worst death among those that could naturally occur. Not all unavoidable surrenders need involve rout: in the face of inevitable death, the physician becomes strategist, the deviser of plans for how to meet death most favorably.

* * *

To recognize the patient's right to autonomous choice in matters concerning the treatment of his own body, the physician must provide information about all the legal options open to him, not just information sufficient to choose between accepting or rejecting a single proposed procedure.

* * *

In the current enthusiasm for "natural death" it is not patient autonomy that dismays physicians. What does dismay them is the way in which respect for patient autonomy can lead to cruel results. The cure for that dismay lies in the realization that the physician can contribute to the *genuine* honoring of the patient's autonomy and rights, assuring him of "natural death" in the way in which the patient understands it, and still remain within the confines of good medical practice and the law.

4. The right to choose to die is usually based upon the premise that a person rationally may decide that death is preferable to the pain, expense, and inconvenience of life. Given that the process of weighing the value of life and death is necessarily based in personal history, religious and moral values, and individual sensitivity, and given that it finds its philosophical basis in the principle of autonomy, is there any justification for independent second-party evaluation of whether the balancing was properly, or even rationally, performed by the patient? In fact, the most difficult cases have arisen over decisions that are not based upon a personal weighing of the value of life and death by the patient, but, rather, upon the dictates of religious principles. Should a court treat a Jehovah's Witness who chooses for religious reasons to forgo a necessary blood transfusion any differently than it treats Elizabeth Bouvia? Is it relevant that others consider the religious ban on the ingestion of blood irrational?

Because courts have been less able to empathize with patients who have unusual religious beliefs than with others, courts have been less willing to entertain the right to forgo life-sustaining treatment on religious grounds than on other grounds. Are the arguments used to justify judicial intervention to require blood transfusions for Jehovah's Witnesses when such transfusions are necessary to preserve life persuasive examples of the social value of law and medicine, or are they unconvincing examples of the paternalistic heritage of both professions? Consider the leading case ordering a transfusion for a Jehovah's Witness adult.

APPLICATION OF THE PRESIDENT AND DIRECTORS OF GEORGETOWN COLLEGE, INC., 331 F.2d 1000, 9 A.L.R.3d 1367 (D.C.Cir.1964).

J. SKELLY WRIGHT, Circuit Judge.

Mrs. Jones was brought to the hospital by her husband for emergency care, having lost two thirds of her body's blood supply from a ruptured ulcer. She had no personal physician, and relied solely on the hospital staff. She was a total hospital responsibility. It appeared that the patient, age 25, mother of a seven-month-old child, and her husband were both Jehovah's Witnesses, the teachings of which sect, according to their interpretation, prohibited the injection of blood into the body. When death without blood became imminent, the hospital sought the advice of counsel, who applied to the District Court in the name of the hospital for permission to administer blood. Judge Tamm of the District Court denied the application, and counsel immediately applied to me, as a member of the Court of Appeals, for an appropriate writ.

* * *

Mr. Jones, the husband of the patient * * * [s]aid, that if the court ordered the transfusion, the responsibility was not his.

* * *

I tried to communicate with her, advising her again as to what the doctors had said. The only audible reply I could hear was "Against my will." It was obvious that the woman was not in a mental condition to make a decision. I was reluctant [t]o press her because of the seriousness of her condition and because I felt that to suggest repeatedly the imminence of death without blood might place a strain on her religious convictions. I asked her whether she would oppose the blood transfusion if the court allowed it. She indicated, as best I could make out, that it would not then be her responsibility.

* * *

I thereupon signed the order allowing the hospital to administer such transfusions as the doctors should determine were necessary to save her life.

It has been firmly established that the courts can order compulsory medical treatment of children for any serious illness or injury, and that adults, sick or well, can be required to submit to compulsory treatment or prophylaxis, at least for contagious diseases, e.g., Jacobson v. Massachusetts. [ ] And there are no religious exemptions from these orders * * *.

The right to practice religion freely does not include liberty to expose the community or the child to communicable disease or the latter to ill health or death. [ ]

Of course, there is here no sick child or contagious disease. However, the sick child cases may provide persuasive analogies because she was as little able competently to decide for herself as any child would be. Under the circumstances, it may well be the duty of a court of general jurisdiction, such as the United States District Court for the

District of Columbia, to assume the responsibility of guardianship for her, as for a child, at least to the extent of authorizing treatment to save her life. And if, as shown above, a parent has no power to forbid the saving of his child's life, *a fortiori* the husband of the patient here had no right to order the doctors to treat his wife in a way so that she would die. * * *

[Another] set of considerations involved the position of the doctors and the hospital. Mrs. Jones was their responsibility to treat. The hospital doctors had the choice of administering the proper treatment or letting Mrs. Jones die in the hospital bed, thus exposing themselves, and the hospital, to the risk of civil and criminal liability in either case. * * *

[N]either the principle that life and liberty are inalienable rights, nor the principle of liberty of religion, provides an easy answer to the question whether the state can prevent martyrdom. Moreover, Mrs. Jones had no wish to be a martyr. And her religion merely prevented her consent to a transfusion. If the law undertook the responsibility of authorizing the transfusion without her consent, no problem would be raised with respect to her religious practice. Thus, the effect of the order was to preserve for Mrs. Jones the life she wanted without sacrifice of her religious beliefs.

The final, and compelling, reason for granting the emergency writ was that a life hung in the balance. There was no time for research and reflection. Death could have mooted the cause in a matter of minutes, if action were not taken to preserve the *status quo*. To refuse to act, only to find later that the law required action, was a risk I was unwilling to accept. I determined to act on the side of life.

In *Georgetown College* Judge Wright also concluded that Jehovah's Witnesses are not required to forgo blood transfusions by their religious code; they are merely required to refuse consent to those transfusions. Thus, a weak denial may be taken as a plea for medical intervention against the patient's stated, but misleading, request to be left without adequate care. Other bases for the decision in the *Georgetown College* case demonstrate why this opinion by one of the great Federal judges of this century has come to be seen as one of the most obvious examples of judicial rationalization. The hospital could hardly claim that the risk of civil or criminal liability required the transfusion after the hospital went to court to determine its legal responsibility. Finally, the presumption that anyone so ill as to need a blood transfusion to save her life is likely to be less than fully competent is simply unsupported by fact.

5. Most of the courts that have considered this issue over the past several years have concluded that Jehovah's Witnesses may choose to forgo medical treatment, whatever the results of those decisions may be, because the patient bears the consequences of choosing to forgo life-sustaining treatment. See, for example, In re Brooks' Estate, 32 Ill.2d 361, 205 N.E.2d 435 (1965), In re Osborne, 294 A.2d 372 (D.C.App.1972), Mercy Hospital, Inc.

v. Jackson, 62 Md.App. 409, 489 A.2d 1130 (App.1985), vacated on other grounds, 306 Md. 556, 510 A.2d 562 (1986) (affirming denial of petition to appoint a guardian to consent to Jehovah's witness blood transfusion during C–Section). But see Raleigh Fitkin–Paul Morgan Memorial Hospital v. Anderson, 42 N.J. 421, 201 A.2d 537 (1964), cert. denied, 377 U.S. 985, 84 S.Ct. 1894, 12 L.Ed.2d 1032 (1964) (pregnant Jehovah's Witness not permitted to refuse a necessary transfusion).

Even when others (such as children) are indirectly affected, the courts tend to recognize the competent adult's right to forgo treatment. Consider Public Health Trust of Dade County v. Wons, 541 So.2d 96 (Fla.1989):

* * *

The Court of Appeal has certified the following question as one of great public importance:

WHETHER A COMPETENT ADULT HAS A LAWFUL RIGHT TO REFUSE A BLOOD TRANSFUSION WITHOUT WHICH SHE MAY WELL DIE.

* * *

The issues presented by this difficult case challenge us to balance the right of an individual to practice her religion and protect her right of privacy against the state's interest in maintaining life and protecting innocent third parties.

Norma Wons entered * * * a medical facility operated by the Public Health Trust of Dade County, with a condition known as dysfunctional uterine bleeding. Doctors informed Mrs. Wons that she would require treatment in the form of a blood transfusion or she would, in all probability, die. Mrs. Wons, a practicing Jehovah's Witness and mother of two minor children, declined the treatment on ground that it violated her religious principles to receive blood from outside her own body. At the time she refused consent Mrs. Wons was conscious and able to reach an informed decision concerning her treatment.

The Health Trust petitioned the Circuit Court to force Mrs. Wons to undergo a blood transfusion. * * * [T]he court granted the petition, ordering the hospital doctors to administer the blood transfusion, which was done while Mrs. Wons was unconscious. The trial judge reasoned that minor children have a right to be reared by two loving parents, a right which overrides the mother's rights of free religious exercise and privacy. Upon regaining consciousness, Mrs. Wons appealed to the Third District which reversed the order. After holding that the case was not moot due to the recurring nature of Mrs. Wons condition * * *, the district court held that Mrs. Wons' constitutional rights of religion and privacy could not be overridden by the state's purported interests.

* * *

The Health Trust asserts that the children's right to be reared by two loving parents is sufficient to trigger the compelling state interest [in protection of innocent third parties]. While we agree that the nurturing and support by two parents is important in the development of any child, it is not sufficient to override fundamental constitutional rights. * * * As the district court noted in its highly articulate opinion below:

> Surely nothing, in the last analysis, is more private or more sacred than one's religion or view of life, and here the courts, quite properly, have given great deference to the individual's right to make decisions vitally affecting his private life according to his own conscience. It is difficult to overstate this right because it is, without exaggeration, the very bedrock upon which this country was founded.

A concurring opinion in *Wons* depends in part upon the fact that the children would be cared for by relatives even if Mrs. Wons were to die. In that opinion the Chief Justice points out:

> The medical profession may consider a blood transfusion a rather ordinary or routine procedure, but, given Mrs. Wons' religious beliefs, that procedure for her is extraordinary. * * * [W]e must not assume from her choice that Mrs. Wons was not considering the best interests of her children. She knows they will be well cared for by her family. As a parent, however, she also must consider the example she sets for her children, how to teach them to follow what she believes is God's law if she herself does not. The choice for her can not be an easy one, but it is hers to make. It is not for this court to judge the reasonableness or validity of her beliefs. Absent a truly compelling state interest to the contrary, the law must protect her right to make that choice.

The dissent in *Wons* depended in part upon another portion of *Application of the President and Directors of Georgetown College, Inc.,* supra note 4, where Judge Wright concluded that "[t]he state, as parens patriae, will not allow a parent to abandon a child, and so it should not allow this most ultimate of voluntary abandonments. The patient had a responsibility to the community to care for her infant. Thus the people had an interest in preserving the life of this mother." Would this rationale support state intervention and an injunction to stop a mother who had decided to take up hang-gliding, bronco-riding, working as a firefighter, or some other dangerous occupation?

6. A patient who refuses a blood transfusion during an operation may thereby exacerbate damage caused by medical negligence. Should the refusal of a blood transfusion be considered contributory or comparative negligence for purposes of a malpractice action against a negligent physician whose negligence would have had inconsequential results if blood could have been provided to the patient? We rarely consider acting on religious principle to be negligence of any sort, even when the religious principle is unusual and dangerous. On the other hand, it seems unfair that a physician, even a negligent physician, should be liable for greatly increased damages because he decided to respect his patient's religious views and thus avoid a blood transfusion that under other circumstances would have been considered a medical necessity. See Shorter v. Drury, 103 Wn.2d 645, 695 P.2d 116 (1985) (Jehovah's Witness died as a result of medical negligence and because she demanded there be no blood transfusion; court found comparative negligence). In that case, the court pointed

out that the First Amendment was not implicated because the case was a dispute between private parties. Since there was no state action, there could be no First Amendment limitation. 695 P.2d at 124. Would there be a First Amendment issue if the action were filed against a state hospital?

7. The right to choose to forgo life-sustaining treatment is not absolute, even for competent adults. In Superintendent of Belchertown State School v. Saikewicz, 373 Mass. 728, 370 N.E.2d 417 (1977), the Massachusetts Supreme Judicial Court first identified the four "countervailing State interests" that could overcome a patient's choice:

(1) preservation of life;

(2) protection of the interests of innocent third parties;

(3) prevention of suicide; and

(4) maintenance of the ethical integrity of the medical profession.

Saikewicz involved an incompetent, mentally retarded patient. Those four interests have also been reiterated in subsequent cases involving competent patients—including Bartling, Bouvia and Wons—but they have not been found to be sufficient to overcome the choice of a competent patient.

In Saikewicz the Massachusetts Supreme Judicial Court explored the significance of these four state interests and their limitations:

It is clear that the most significant of the asserted State interests is that of the preservation of human life. Recognition of such an interest, however, does not necessarily resolve the problem where the affliction or disease clearly indicates that life will end soon, and inevitably be extinguished. The interest of the State in prolonging a life must be reconciled with the interest of an individual to reject the traumatic cost of that prolongation. There is a substantial distinction in the State's insistence that human life be saved where the affliction is curable, as opposed to the State interest where, as here, the issue is not whether but when, for how long, and at what cost to the individual that life may be briefly extended. Even if we assume that the State has an additional interest in seeing to it that individual decisions on the prolongation of life do not in any way tend to "cheapen" the value which is placed on the concept of living, we believe it is not inconsistent to recognize a right to decline medical treatment in a situation of incurable illness. The constitutional right to privacy, as we conceive it, is an expression of the sanctity of individual free choice and self-determination as fundamental constituents of life. The value of life as so perceived is lessened not by a decision to refuse treatment, but by the failure to allow a competent human being the right of a choice.

A second interest of considerable magnitude, which the State may have some interest in asserting, is that of protecting third parties, particularly minor children, from the emotional and financial damage which may occur as a result of the decision of a competent adult to refuse life-saving or life-prolonging treatment. Thus, even when the State's interest in preserving an individual's life was not sufficient, by itself, to outweigh the individual's interest in the exercise of free choice, the possible impact on minor children would be a factor which might have a critical effect on the outcome of the balancing process. Similarly, in the *Georgetown* case the court held that one of the interests requiring protection was that of the minor child in order to avoid the effect of "abandonment" on that child as a result of the parent's decision to refuse the necessary medical measures. We need not reach this aspect of claimed State interest as it is not an issue on the facts of this case.

The last State interest requiring discussion [11] is that of the maintenance of the ethical integrity of the medical profession as well as allowing hospitals the full opportunity to care for people under their control. The force and impact of this interest is lessened by the prevailing medical ethical standards. Prevailing medical ethical practice does not, without exception, demand that all efforts toward life prolongation be made in all circumstances. Rather, the prevailing ethical practice seems to be to recognize that the dying are more often in need of comfort than treatment. Recognition of the right to refuse necessary treatment in appropriate circumstances is consistent with existing medical mores; such a doctrine does not threaten either the integrity of the medical profession, the proper role of hospitals in caring for such patients or the State's interest in protecting the same. It is not necessary to deny a right of self-determination to a patient in order to recognize the interest of doctors, hospitals, and medical personnel in attendance on the patient. Also, if the doctrines of informed consent and right of privacy have as their foundations in the right to bodily integrity, and control of one's own fate, then those rights are superior to the institutional considerations. 370 N.E.2d at 425–427.

In fact, generally these four interests may be even weaker than the Massachusetts court indicated:

(1) If the value of the preservation of life is the very question faced by the court in right-to-die cases, does it make sense to define it, *a priori*, as a value that is countervailing to the patient's desire to discontinue treatment? Subsequent to *Saikewicz*, the Massachusetts Supreme Judicial Court recognized this:

When we balance the State's interest in prolonging a patient's life against the rights of the patient to reject such prolongation, we must recognize that the State's interest in life encompasses a broader interest than mere corporeal existence. In certain, thankfully rare, circumstances the burden of maintaining the corporeal existence degrades the very humanity it was meant to serve. The law recognizes the individual's right to preserve his humanity,

---

11. The interest in protecting against suicide seems to require little if any discussion. In the case of the competent adult's refusing medical treatment such an act does not necessarily constitute suicide since (1) in refusing treatment the patient may not have the specific intent to die, and (2) even if he did, to the extent that the cause of death was from natural causes, the patient did not set the death producing agent in motion with the intent of causing his own death. Furthermore, the underlying State interest in this area lies in the prevention of irrational self-destruction. What we consider here is a competent, rational decision to refuse treatment when death is inevitable, and the treatment offers no hope of cure or preservation of life. There is no connection between the conduct here in issue and any State concern to prevent suicide.

even if to preserve his humanity means to allow the natural processes of a disease or affliction to bring about a death with dignity.

Brophy v. New England Sinai Hospital, Inc., 398 Mass. 417, 497 N.E.2d 626 (1986).

The nature of the state's interest in the preservation of life was also discussed in the *Cruzan* case, in which it was the only interest advanced by the state of Missouri. The Chief Justice said that "a state may properly decline to make judgments about the 'quality' of life that a particular individual may enjoy, and simply assert an unqualified interest in the preservation of human life to be weighed against the constitutionally protected interests of the individual." Not surprisingly, the dissenters viewed the state's interest in the preservation of life very differently. Justice Stevens objected to Missouri's policy of "equating [Cruzan's] life with the biological persistence of her bodily functions." He pointed out that, "[l]ife, particularly human life, is not commonly thought of as a merely physiological condition or function. Its sanctity is often thought to derive from the impossibility of any such reduction. When people speak of life, they often mean to describe the experiences that comprise a person's history. * * *" Justice Brennan was especially offended by the notion that the generalized state interest in life could overcome the liberty interest to forgo life-sustaining treatment. One's rights, he argued, may not be sacrificed just to make society feel good:

> If Missouri were correct that its interests outweigh Nancy's interests in avoiding medical procedures as long as she is free of pain and physical discomfort, [ ] it is not apparent why a state could not choose to remove one of her kidneys without consent on the ground that society would be better off if the recipient of that kidney were saved from renal poisoning * * *, patches of her skin could also be removed to provide grafts for burn victims, and scrapings of bone marrow to provide grafts for someone with leukemia. * * * Indeed, why could the state not perform medical experiments on her body, experiments that might save countless lives, and would cause her no greater burden than she already bears by being fed through her gastrostomy tube? This would be too brave a new world for me and, I submit, for our constitution.

110 S.Ct. 2841, 2869–70 n. 13.

(2) Does the protection of the interests of innocent third parties have any meaning if courts are not willing to force people to stop pursuing their own interests and to serve some undefined communal goal? Is it merely a make-weight argument in a society as individualistic as ours?

(3) Is the interest in the prevention of suicide anachronistic? Attempting suicide is no longer a crime in any state. But see Brophy, 398 Mass. 417, 497 N.E.2d 626, 640 (1986) (Nolan, J., dissenting): "suicide is direct self-destruction and is intrinsically evil. No set of circumstances can make it moral * * *." See also Section VI(B)(2), below, discussing suicide.

(4) Finally, there is no reason to believe that the ethics of the profession do not permit discontinuation of medical treatment to a

competent patient who refuses it. See AMA Ethical Opinion 2.20, Withholding or Withdrawing a Life–Prolonging Medical Treatment, Current Opinions 13 (1989). Even if there were, though, should the protection of the "ethical integrity of the medical profession" overcome an otherwise proper decision to forgo some form of treatment? Is there any reason for the judiciary to uphold the ethical integrity of the medical profession where it is inconsistent with good law and good social policy? If all other analyses point to allowing a patient to deny consent to some form of treatment, why should the medical profession be able to require the treatment in the interest of its own self-defined integrity?

8. Are there special circumstances in which the interest of the patient ought not to be recognized or the interest of the state is especially important? Does the national interest allow the military to require its soldiers to undergo life saving (or other) medical care so that they can be returned to the front? Can a prisoner refuse kidney dialysis that is necessary to save his life unless the state moves him from a medium to minimum security prison? See Commissioner of Corrections v. Myers, 379 Mass. 255, 399 N.E.2d 452 (1979) (interest in "orderly prison administration" outweighs any privacy right of the prisoner).

9. The strength of any of these countervailing interests depends upon the strength of the patient's right to choose to forgo treatment. That, in turn, may depend upon the source of that right. Although some courts have found that right in the United States Constitution, *Cruzan*'s crabbed interpretation of the Fourteenth Amendment is unlikely to provide any basis for future state court determinations that patients (competent or incompetent) possess a "right to die". Of course, state courts have other sources of law from which they may derive the right; it may be found in state common law, state statutes, or state constitutions.

The vast majority of state courts that have found a "right to die" have found that right in state common law, usually in the law of informed consent. As the Chief Justice recognized in *Cruzan*, "the informed consent doctrine has become firmly entrenched in American tort law * * * the logical corollary of the doctrine of informed consent is that the patient generally possesses the right not to consent, that is, to refuse treatment. * * *" Once a court finds a common law right, it is not necessary to determine whether the right is also conferred by statute or by the constitution. See, e.g., In re Storar, 52 N.Y.2d 363, 438 N.Y.S.2d 266, 420 N.E.2d 64 (1981). While the New Jersey court initially recognized a constitutional "right to die" in In re Quinlan, 70 N.J. 10, 355 A.2d 647, 664 (1976), it later recognized that the constitutional determination was unnecessary and retrenched: "While the right of privacy might apply in a case such as this, we need not decide that since the right to decline medical treatment is, in any event, embraced within the common law right to self determination." In re Conroy, 98 N.J. 321, 486 A.2d 1209, 1223 (1985).

Some states have gone beyond their common law and found the right in state statutes. Generally, courts that find a statutory "right to die" also find a consistent common law right. See, e.g., McConnell v. Beverly

Enterprises–Connecticut, Inc., 209 Conn. 692, 553 A.2d 596, 601–602 (1989). The Illinois Supreme Court explicitly rejected state and federal constitutional justifications for a "right to die" because of the existence of both state common law and state statutory remedies:

> Lacking guidance from the Supreme Court, we decline to address whether federal privacy guarantees the right to refuse life-sustaining medical treatment. Lacking clear expression of intent from the drafters of our 1970 state constitution, we similarly abstain from expanding the privacy provision of our state constitution to embrace this right. * * * Instead, we follow the wisdom of the Supreme Court in avoiding constitutional questions when the issue at hand may be decided upon other grounds. * * * In the present case, we find the right to refuse life-sustaining medical treatment in our state's common law and in provisions of the Illinois Probate Act.

In re Estate of Longeway, 133 Ill.2d 33, 139 Ill.Dec. 780, 549 N.E.2d 292, 297 (1989).

In addition, several state courts have found the "right to die" in their state constitutions. A decision based on the state constitution may be the strongest kind of support such a right can ever find, because it is not subject to review by the United States Supreme Court (absent an improbable argument that a state created right would itself violate the United States Constitution) and it is not subject to review by the state legislature (except through the generally cumbersome state constitutional amendment process).

Relevant state constitutional provisions take different forms. For example, the Florida Constitution provides that "[e]very natural person has the right to be let alone and free from governmental intrusion into his private life except as otherwise provided herein. * * * " Fla. Const., art. 1, section 23. The Arizona Constitution provides that "[n]o person shall be disturbed in his private affairs or his home invaded, without authority of law." Arizona Const., art. 2, section 8. Both of these constitutional provisions have given rise to state court recognized rights to forgo life-sustaining treatment. See In re Guardianship of Barry, 445 So.2d 365 (Fla. App.1984) and Rasmussen v. Fleming, 154 Ariz. 207, 741 P.2d 674 (1987). A California court of appeal also found that such a right for competent patients could be found in the California Constitution. See Bouvia, supra.

10. Recent cases have produced scores of articles evaluating the propriety of allowing competent adults to forgo life-sustaining treatment. In addition to cases cited above, see In re Farrell, 108 N.J. 335, 529 A.2d 404 (1987); Natanson v. Kline, 186 Kan. 393, 350 P.2d 1093 (1960) (patient has to be informed by doctor of risks and alternatives of forgoing life-sustaining treatment); In re Dinnerstein, 6 Mass.App.Ct. 466, 380 N.E.2d 134 (1978); and Satz v. Perlmutter, 362 So.2d 160 (Fla.App.1978), affirmed, 379 So.2d 359 (Fla.1980).

IV. THE "RIGHT TO DIE"—INCOMPETENT PATIENTS

A. DETERMINING COMPETENCY

A competent adult may choose to forgo medical care, even if that choice results in death. This necessarily follows from the principle of autonomy which underlies the physician-patient relationship. Of course, that principle is not served by allowing a patient to make a decision he is not competent to make. In order to determine whether a patient can choose to undergo (or forgo) medical care, someone must determine whether the patient is competent. Because competency is thus employed to serve the social principle of autonomy, competency determinations should not be entirely medical; social, philosophical, and political factors should also be considered. Courts have been reluctant to articulate a standard for competence. There are few reported opinions in which courts state and apply any formal principle of competency. Courts have been much more likely to finesse the issue out of the law and back into medicine by inviting physicians, especially psychiatrists, to testify about the mental state and thus, competency of a patient.

For many years, physicians were likely to find a patient competent to make a serious medical decision whenever that patient agreed with the physician. When the patient disagreed with the physician—especially if that disagreement would lead to the death of the patient—the physician, and subsequently the court, would be likely to find the patient incompetent and then seek out some surrogate decision-maker more likely to agree with the physician. In reaction to this, and as a consequence of the frustration of attempting to develop any consistent and practical definition of competence, consumerist attorneys and physicians in the 1970s suggested that any patient who could indicate an affirmative or negative ought to be considered competent. Of course, this reactionary view is no more satisfactory than the previously prevailing view. Neither serves the purpose of protecting the individual personality of the patient and the authority of the patient to control his own life in a way that is consistent with his own values.

Despite the extremes described above, some scholars have attempted to categorize the possible tests for competency that could be applied to patients of questionable competence. Five different kinds of tests for competency are outlined in the following article prepared by a psychiatrist, a lawyer, and a sociologist with extensive expertise in psychiatry.

ROTH, MEISEL, AND LIDZ, TESTS OF COMPETENCY TO CONSENT TO TREATMENT

134 Am.J. Psychiatry 279 (1977).

* * *

TESTS FOR COMPETENCY

Several tests for competency have been proposed in the literature; others are readily inferable from judicial commentary. Although there is some overlap, they basically fall into five categories: 1) evidencing a choice, 2) "reasonable" outcome of choice, 3) choice based on "rational" reasons, 4) ability to understand, and 5) actual understanding.

Evidencing a Choice

This test for competency is set at a very low level and is the most respectful of the autonomy of patient decision making. Under this test the competent patient is one who evidences a preference for or against treatment. This test focuses not on the quality of the patient's decision but on the presence or absence of a decision. * * * This test of competency encompasses at a minimum the unconscious patient: in psychiatry it encompasses the mute patient who cannot or will not express an opinion.

* * *

"Reasonable" Outcome of Choice

This test of competency entails evaluating the patient's capacity to reach the "reasonable," the "right," or the "responsible" decision. The emphasis in this test is on outcome rather than on the mere fact of decision or how it has been reached. The patient who fails to make a decision that is roughly congruent with the decision that a "reasonable" person in like circumstances would make is viewed as incompetent.

This test is probably used more often than might be admitted by both physicians and courts. Judicial decisions to override the desire of patients with certain religious beliefs not to receive blood transfusions may rest in part on the court's view that the patient's decision is not reasonable. When life is at stake and a court believes that the patient's decision is unreasonable, the court may focus on even the smallest ambiguity in the patient's thinking to cast doubt on the patient's competency so that it may issue an order that will preserve life or health. * * *

Mental health laws that allow for involuntary treatment on the basis of "need for care and treatment" without requiring a formal adjudication of incompetency in effect use an unstated reasonable outcome test in abridging the patient's common-law right not to be treated without giving his or her consent. These laws are premised on the following syllogism: the patient needs treatment; the patient has not obtained treatment on his or her own initiative; therefore, the patient's decision is incorrect, which means that he or she is incompetent, thus justifying the involuntary imposition of treatment.

* * * Ultimately, because the test rests on the congruence between the patient's decision and that of a reasonable person or that of the physician, it is biased in favor of decisions to accept treatment, even when such decisions are made by people who are incapable of weighing the risks and benefits of treatment. In other words, if patients do not

decide the "wrong" way, the issue of competency will probably not arise.

Choice Based on "Rational" Reasons

Another test is whether the reasons for the patient's decision are "rational," that is, whether the patient's decision is due to or is a product of mental illness. As in the reasonable outcome test, if the patient decides in favor of treatment the issue of the patient's competency (in this case, whether the decision is the product of mental illness) seldom if ever arises because of the medical profession's bias toward consent to treatment and against refusal of treatment.

In this test the quality of the patient's thinking is what counts.

* * *

The test of rational reasons, although it has clinical appeal and is probably much in clinical use, poses considerable conceptual problems; as a legal test it is probably defective. The problems include the difficulty of distinguishing rational from irrational reasons and drawing inferences of causation between any irrationality believed present and the valence (yes or no) of the patient's decision. Even if the patient's reasons seem irrational, it is not possible to prove that the patient's actual decision making has been the product of such irrationality. * * * The emphasis on rational reasons can too easily become a global indictment of the competency of mentally disordered individuals, justifying widespread substitute decision making for this group.

The Ability to Understand

This test—the ability of the patient to understand the risks, benefits, and alternatives to treatment (including no treatment)—is probably the most consistent with the law of informed consent. Decision making need not be rational in either process or outcome; unwise choices are permitted. Nevertheless, at a minimum the patient must manifest sufficient ability to understand information about treatment, even if in fact he or she weighs this information differently from the attending physician. What matters in this test is that the patient is able to comprehend the elements that are presumed by law to be a part of treatment decision making. How the patient weighs these elements, values them, or puts them together to reach a decision is not important.

The patient's capacity for understanding may be tested by asking the patient a series of questions concerning risks, benefits, and alternatives to treatment. By providing further information or explanation to the patient, the physician may find deficiencies in understanding to be remediable or not.

* * *

Furthermore, how potentially sophisticated must understanding be in order that the patient be viewed as competent? There are considerable barriers, conscious and unconscious and intellectual and emotional, to understanding proposed treatments. Presumably the potential understanding required is only that which would be manifested by a reasonable person provided a similar amount of information. A few attempts to rank degrees of understanding have been made. However, this matter is highly complex and beyond the scope of the present inquiry. Certainly, at least with respect to nonexperimental treatment, the patient's potential understanding does not have to be perfect or near perfect for him or her to be considered competent, although one court seemed to imply this with respect to experimental psychosurgery. A final problem with this test is that its application depends on unobservable and inferential mental processes rather than on concrete and observable elements of behavior.

Actual Understanding

Rather than focusing on competency as a construct or intervening variable in the decision-making process, the test of actual understanding reduces competency to an epiphenomenon of this process. The competent patient is by definition one who has provided a knowledgeable consent to treatment. Under this test the physician has an obligation to educate the patient and directly ascertain whether he or she has in fact understood. If not, according to this test the patient may not have provided informed consent. Depending on how sophisticated a level of understanding is to be required, this test delineates a potentially high level of competency, one that may be difficult to achieve.

* * *

The practical and conceptual limitations of this test are similar to those of the ability-to-understand test. What constitutes adequate understanding is vague, and deficient understanding may be attributable in whole or in part to physician behavior as well as to the patient's behavior or character. An advantage that this test has over the ability-to-understand test, assuming the necessary level of understanding can be specified *a priori,* is its greater reliability. Unlike the ability-to-understand test, in which the patient's comprehension of material of a certain complexity is used as the basis for an assumption of comprehension of other material of equivalent complexity (even if this other material is not actually tested), the actual understanding test makes no such assumption. It tests the very issues central to patient decision making about treatment.

Note

Roth, Meisel, and Lidz suggest that each of these tests is biased by the evaluator's analysis of whether the treatment would succeed—that is, whether the evaluator would consent or not. The authors conclude that where the benefit of treatment is likely to far outweigh the risk (i.e., the evaluator would choose to undergo it), there is likely to be a low standard for competency when the patient consents and a high standard for competency when the patient refuses. Analogously, where the risk greatly outweighs the benefit (again, of course, in the evaluator's mind), a low standard for competency will be applied if the patient refuses treatment, but a high standard will be applied when the patient consents. The authors point out:

> Of course, some grossly impaired patients cannot be determined to be competent under any conceivable test, nor can most normally functioning people be found incompetent merely by selective application of the test of competency. However, within limits and when the patient's competency is not absolutely clear cut, a test of competency that will achieve the desired medical or social end despite the actual condition of the patient may be selected. We do not imply that this is done maliciously either by physicians or by the court; rather we believe that it occurs as a consequence of the strong societal bias in favor of treating treatable patients so long as it does not expose them to serious risks. 134 Am.J.Psych. at 283.

The authors do not hold out much hope for the development of a clear test for competence that can be easily applied because no such test could be consistent with the different reasons that we seek to determine competence:

> The search for a single test of competency is a search for a Holy Grail. Unless it is recognized that there is no magical definition of competency to make decisions about treatment, the search for an acceptable test will never end. "Getting the words just right" is only part of the problem. In practice, judgments of competency go beyond semantics or straightforward applications of legal rules; such judgments reflect social considerations and societal biases as much as they reflect matters of law and medicine. Id.

The difficulty in establishing a uniform and consistent test of competency to consent to treatment is demonstrated by the practical inadequacy of the suggestion made by the President's Commission for the Study of Ethical Problems in Medicine and Biomedical and Behavioral Research. The Commission provides an analytical perspective that undoubtedly serves the underlying function of the preservation of the patient's autonomy. Unfortunately, it does not provide a test that is easily applied in practice.

PRESIDENT'S COMMISSION, 1 MAKING HEALTH CARE DECISIONS

57–60 (1980).

Elements of Capacity. In the view of the Commission, any determination of the capacity to decide on a course of treatment must relate to the individual abilities of a patient, the requirements of the task at hand, and the consequences likely to flow from the decision. Decision-making capacity requires, to greater or lesser degree: (1) possession of a set of values and goals; (2) the ability to communicate and to understand information; and (3) the ability to reason and to deliberate about one's choices.

The first, a framework for comparing options, is needed if the person is to evaluate possible outcomes as good or bad. * * * The patient must be able to make reasonably consistent choices. Reliance on a patient's decision would be difficult or impossible if the patient's values were so unstable that the patient could not reach or adhere to a choice at least long enough for a course of therapy to be initiated with some prospect of being completed.

The second element includes the ability to give and receive information, as well as the possession of various linguistic and conceptual skills needed for at least a basic understanding of the relevant information. These abilities can be evaluated only as they relate to the task at hand and are not solely cognitive, as they ordinarily include emotive elements. To use them, a person also needs sufficient life experience to appreciate the meaning of potential alternatives: what it would probably be like to undergo various medical procedures, for example, or to live in a new way required by a medical condition or intervention.

Some critics of the doctrine of informed consent have argued that patients simply lack the ability to understand medical information relevant to decisions about their care. Indeed, some empirical studies purport to have demonstrated this by showing that the lay public often does not know the meaning of common medical terms, or by showing that, following an encounter with a physician, patients are unable to report what the physician said about their illness and treatment. Neither type of study establishes the fact that patients cannot understand. The first merely finds that they do not currently know the right definitions of some terms; the second, which usually fails to discover what the physician actually did say, rests its conclusions on an assumption that information was provided that was subsequently not understood.

* * *

The third element of decisionmaking capacity—reasoning and deliberation—includes the ability to compare the impact of alternative outcomes on personal goals and life plans. Some ability to employ probabilistic reasoning about uncertain outcomes is usually necessary, as well as the ability to give appropriate weight in a present decision to various future outcomes.

Notes and Questions

1. What are the advantages and disadvantages of the five Roth, Meisel, and Lidz criteria, as compared to the President's Commission's criteria? Which defines competency better?

2. There is a necessary internal inconsistency in applying any test of competency. The purpose of determining competency is to preserve the autonomy of the patient and save the patient from an externally imposed judgment. Yet how can a second party apply a competency test that is consistent with that autonomy? Any practical test that can be applied by someone other than the patient is not likely to be consistent with the underlying principle of autonomy. Isn't any decisionmaking in the absence of competency a *per se* violation of autonomy?

3. The issue of whether a patient of questionable competence is competent to forgo life-sustaining treatment has arisen on many occasions. One case that squarely faced the question involved Robert Quakenbush, a seventy-two-year-old recluse whose gangrenous leg would have to be amputated to avoid a certain, quick death. He was rambunctious, belligerent, and "a conscientious objector to medical therapy" who had shunned medical care for 40 years. In deciding that the patient was competent, the court depended on the testimony of two psychiatrists, both of whom treated the issue of competency as entirely medical, and the judge's own visit with Mr. Quackenbush.

The testimony concerning Quackenbush's mental condition was elicited from two psychiatrists. The first, appearing for the hospital, was Dr. Michael Giuliano. Dr. Giuliano, licensed to practice in 1971, saw Quackenbush once on January 6. The doctor's conclusions are that Quackenbush is suffering from an organic brain syndrome with psychotic elements. He asserts that the organic brain syndrome is acute—i.e., subject to change—and could be induced by the septicemia * * *. [Dr. Giuliano] concluded that Quackenbush's mental condition was not sufficient to make an informed decision concerning the operation.

Dr. Abraham S. Lenzner, a Board-certified psychiatrist for 25 years and specialist in geriatric psychiatry, testified as an independent witness at the request of the court. Dr. Lenzner is Chief of Psychiatry at the Memorial Hospital and a professor at the New Jersey College of Medicine and Dentistry.

Dr. Lenzner is of the opinion, based upon reasonable medical certainty, that Quackenbush has the mental capacity to make decisions, to understand the nature and extent of his physical condition, to understand the nature and extent of the operations, to understand the risks involved if he consents to the operation, and to understand the risks involved if he refuses the operation * * *.

I visited with Quackenbush for about ten minutes on January 12. During that period he did not hallucinate, his answers to my questions were responsive and he seemed reasonably alert. His conversation did wander occasionally but to no greater extent than would be expected of a 72–year–old man in his circumstances. He spoke somewhat philosophically about his circumstances and desires. He hopes for a miracle but realizes there is no great likelihood of its occurrence. He indicates a desire—plebeian, as he described it—to return to his trailer and live out his life. He is not experiencing any pain and indicates that if he does, he could change his mind about having the operation.

* * *

The matter may be tried before a judge without a jury. My findings pursuant to this authority are that Robert Quackenbush is competent and capable of exercising informed consent on whether or not to have the operation. I do not question the events and conditions described by Dr. Giuliano but find they were of a temporary, curative, fluctuating nature, and whatever their cause the patient's lucidity is sufficient for him to make an informed choice.

* * *

In re Quackenbush, 156 N.J.Super. 282, 383 A.2d 785 at 788 (1978).

Ultimately, it is difficult to determine whether the court merely chose the more credible of the two psychiatrists, or whether the court depended upon some intuitive conclusions that followed the judge's ten minute visit with the patient. Which would be the more satisfying basis for the court's determination of competency?

Whatever one may think of the process the court employed for determining competency in *Quackenbush,* the case stands for two principles that have been repeated constantly since. The first is that a patient who fluctuates between competence and incompetence cannot be denied an opportunity to make decisions concerning medical care, even life-sustaining medical care, just because of the temporary absence of competence. The desires of that patient, articulated during a period of competence, must be respected by the physician, the hospital, and the courts. See Lane v. Candura, 6 Mass.App.Ct. 377, 376 N.E.2d 1232 (1978). The second principle assumed in *Quackenbush* is that a patient may be competent for some purposes and incompetent for others; a patient may be "variably competent." Whatever test of competence one adopts, a patient may be competent to decide to undergo (or forgo) medical treatment, and yet be incompetent to dispose of his estate. Similarly, a patient may be competent to enter a business agreement or to vote, and yet not meet the same test of competency for making health-care decisions. Indeed, a patient may be competent to make some kinds of health-care decisions, like the decision to undergo routine blood tests, and not competent to make others, like the decision to undergo a sterilization. See, e.g., Matter of Hier, 18 Mass. App.Ct. 200, 464 N.E.2d 959 (1984) (guardian authorized to consent to administration of drug treatment but not surgical treatment, which incompetent patient clearly did not want). Some state statutes explicitly recognize and protect the variably competent person. Statutes passed in the early 1990s generally use the term "decisional capacity" rather than "competency" to stress the fact that such capacity will vary from decision to decision (as well as from time to time) for each person.

4. To what extent do value judgments and prejudices enter into decisions regarding competency? Would the Quackenbush case have been a simpler one if Mr. Quackenbush were a retired lawyer leading a middle class life rather than a belligerent hermit? One fascinating review of "right to die" cases suggests that gender may be an important factor, and that the legal system takes the expressed wishes of men more seriously than those of women. Miles and August, Courts, Gender, and "The Right to Die," 18 Law, Med. & Health Care 85 (1990). For a more comprehensive recent account of judicial attempts to determine competency, see Wolff, Determining Competency in Treatment Refusal Cases, 24 Ga.L.Rev. 733 (1990).

B. DETERMINING THE PATIENT'S CHOICE

It is very difficult to serve the underlying goal of autonomy, if that goal is defined as personal choice, in patients who are not competent.

One way to serve this principle is through the application of the doctrine of substituted judgment. Under this doctrine, a person, committee, or institution attempts to determine what the patient would do if the patient were competent. Of course, there is no way to know with certainty what the patient would do under those circumstances. Some have argued that the doctrine of substituted judgment is too speculative to be applied reliably and that there is simply no way to protect the autonomy of an incompetent patient. Where there is no possible method for establishing what the autonomous patient would do, ethics analysis (and increasingly, courts) move to the second principle of bioethical decision-making, beneficence. In these circumstances, the alternative to serving autonomy is serving beneficence, and the alternative to the doctrine of substituted judgment is the doctrine of the "best interest" of the patient. As we shall see, the more difficult it becomes to decide what the patient would do if that patient were competent, the more likely it is that the court will apply the principle of beneficence rather than the principle of autonomy. See generally, President's Commission, Deciding to Forego Life Sustaining Treatment, Chapter 4 (1983).

1. Patients With Former Competence

To the extent that the purpose of autonomy is to serve the values of the patient, it is possible to review the values of a formerly competent patient to determine whether that patient would choose to undergo or forgo proposed medical care. This can be done through a thoughtful analysis of the patient's values during life or, more precisely, through review of formal statements made by the patient when the patient was competent. The most relevant considerations may be statements made by the patient about the proposed treatment itself. Indeed, such statements may provide the only *constitutionally* relevant information about an incompetent patient's wishes after *Cruzan*. These statements may include statements in living wills, durable powers of attorney, or other such documents.

a. Living Wills

Frightened by the indignity of the life of Karen Quinlan, many people began to search for a way to avoid a similar fate. Within two years of the first press reports of the *Quinlan* case several states had adopted statutes that formally recognized certain forms of written statements requesting that some kinds of medical care be discontinued. These statutes, generally referred to as "living will" legislation, "right to die" legislation, or "natural death" acts, provide a political outlet for the frustration that accompanied the empathy for Ms. Quinlan.

The statutes, now adopted in over 40 states, differ in several respects. In some states living wills may be executed by any person, at any time (and in some states they may be executed on behalf of minors), while in other states they require a waiting period, and may not be executed during a terminal illness. In most states they are of indefinite duration, although in some states they expire after a determined number of years. Some statutes address only the terminally ill, others include those in irreversible coma, and still others provide for different conditions to trigger the substantive provisions of the document. Some states require the formalities of a will for the living will to be recognized by statute, while other states require different formalities. The statutes generally relieve physicians and other health care providers of any civil or criminal liability if they properly follow the requirements of the statute and implement the desires expressed in a legally executed living will. Some of the statutes also require that any physician who cannot, in good conscience, carry out those provisions, transfer the patient to a physician who can. Some of the statutes also provide that carrying out the provisions of a properly executed living will does not constitute suicide for insurance purposes. It is hard to know whether the absence of litigation over the terms of living wills means that the institution of these documents is working well or not at all.

The structure of the statutes is more a consequence of the political vagaries of the state legislatures that enacted them than any substantive legal developments. For example, the highly political nature of the issue in California resulted in a narrow, highly restricted statute. The terms used in most of the statutes—terms like "maintenance medical care," "terminal condition," "irreversible coma," and "life sustaining treatments,"—are often ambiguous and sometimes employ circular definitions. While the statutes and executed documents are probably not technically responsible for many clinical decisions, the political climate that has been created by the legislative debate over the statutes has undoubtedly changed the way physicians in hospitals view the discontinuation of life-support systems, and the existence and widespread distribution of living will forms has caused a great many people to make explicit statements that can and have been used in subsequent periods of incompetency to apply the doctrine of substituted judgment, even if the wills have not been formally legally enforced.

While the 1989 Uniform Rights of the Terminally Ill Act has not yet been adopted by any state in its pristine form, it provides a good summary of current prevailing thought about the appropriate scope of such statutes.

UNIFORM RIGHTS OF THE TERMINALLY ILL ACT
(1989).

PREFATORY NOTE

* * *

The scope of the Act is narrow. Its impact is limited to treatment that is merely life-prolonging, and to patients whose terminal condition is incurable and irreversible, whose death will soon occur, and who are unable to participate in treatment decisions. Beyond its narrow scope, the Act is not intended to affect any existing rights and responsibilities of persons to make medical treatment decisions. The Act merely provides alternative ways in which a terminally-ill patient's desires regarding the use of life-sustaining procedures can be legally implemented.

The purposes of the Act are (1) to establish a procedure which is simple, effective, and acceptable to persons who desire to execute a declaration, (2) to provide a statutory framework that is acceptable to physicians and health-care facilities whose conduct will be affected, (3) to provide for the effectiveness of a declaration in states other than the state in which it is executed through uniformity of scope and procedure, and (4) to avoid the inconsistency in approach that has characterized early state statutes in the area.

§ 1. Definitions.

As used in this [Act], unless the context otherwise requires:

(1) "Attending physician" means the physician who has primary responsibility for the treatment and care of the patient.

(2) "Declaration" means a writing executed in accordance with the requirements of Section 2(a).

(3) "Health-care provider" means a person who is licensed, certified, or otherwise authorized by the law of this State to administer health care in the ordinary course of business or practice of a profession.

(4) "Life-sustaining treatment" means any medical procedure or intervention that, when administered to a qualified patient, will serve only to prolong the process of dying.

(5) "Person" means an individual, corporation, business trust, estate, trust, partnership, association, joint venture, government, governmental subdivision or agency, or any other legal or commercial entity.

(6) "Physician" means an individual [licensed to practice medicine in this State].

(7) "Qualified patient" means a patient [18] or more years of age who has executed a declaration and who has been determined by the attending physician to be in a terminal condition.

* * *

(9) "Terminal condition" means an incurable and irreversible condition that, without the administration of life-sustaining treatment, will, in the opinion of the attending physician, result in death within a relatively short time.

§ 2. Declaration Relating to Use of Life–Sustaining Treatment.

(a) An individual of sound mind and [18] or more years of age may execute at any time a declaration governing the withholding or withdrawal of life-sustaining treatment. The declarant may designate another individual of sound mind and [18] or more years of age to make decisions governing the withholding or withdrawal of life-sustaining treatment. The declaration must be signed by the declarant, or another at the declarant's direction, and witnessed by two individuals.

(b) A declaration directing a physician to withhold or withdraw life-sustaining treatment may, but need not, be in the following form:

DECLARATION

If I should have an incurable and irreversible condition that, without the administration of life-sustaining treatment, will, in the opinion of my attending physician, cause my death within a relatively short time, and I am no longer able to make decisions regarding my medical treatment, I direct my attending physician, pursuant to the Uniform Rights of the Terminally Ill Act of this State, to withhold or withdraw treatment that only prolongs the process of dying and is not necessary for my comfort or to alleviate pain.

Signed this _____ day of _____, _.

Signature _____

Address _____

The declarant voluntarily signed this writing in my presence.

Witness _____

Address _____

Witness _____

Address _____

(c) A declaration that designates another individual to make decisions governing the withholding or withdrawal of life-sustaining treatment may, but need not, be in the following form:

DECLARATION

If I should have an incurable and irreversible condition that, without the administration of life-sustaining treatment, will, in the opinion of my attending physician, cause my death within a relatively short time, and I am no longer able to make decisions regarding my medical treatment, I appoint _____ or, if he or she is not reasonably available or is unwilling to serve, _____, to make decisions on my behalf regarding withholding or withdrawal of treatment that only prolongs the process of dying and is not necessary for my comfort or to alleviate pain, pursuant to the Uniform Rights of the Terminally Ill Act of this State.

[If the individual(s) I have so appointed is not reasonably available or is unwilling to serve, I direct my attending physician, pursuant to the Uniform Rights of the Terminally Ill Act of this State, to withhold or withdraw treatment that only prolongs the process of dying and is not necessary for my comfort or to alleviate pain.]

Strike out bracketed language if you do not desire it.

Signed this _____ day of _____, _.

Signature _____

Address _____

The declarant voluntarily signed this writing in my presence.

Witness _____

Address _____

Witness _____

Address _____

Name and address of designees.

Name _____

Address _____

(d) The designation of an attorney-in-fact [pursuant to the Uniform Durable Power of Attorney Act or the Model Health–Care Consent Act], or the judicial appointment of an individual [guardian], who is authorized to make decisions regarding the withholding or withdrawal of life-sustaining treatment, constitutes for purposes of this [Act] a declaration designating another individual to act for the declarant pursuant to subsection (a).

(e) A physician or other health-care provider who is furnished a copy of the declaration shall make it a part of the declarant's medical record and, if unwilling to comply with the declaration, promptly so advise the declarant and any individual designated to act for the declarant.

§ 3. When Declaration Operative.

A declaration becomes operative when (i) it is communicated to the attending physician and (ii) the declarant is determined by the attending physician to be in a terminal condition and no longer able to make decisions regarding administration of life-sustaining treatment. When the declaration becomes operative, the attending physician and other health-care providers shall act in accordance with its provisions and with the instructions of a designee under Section 2(a) or comply with the transfer requirements of Section 8.

§ 4. Revocation of Declaration.

(a) A declarant may revoke a declaration at any time and in any manner, without regard to the declarant's mental or physical condition. A revocation is effective upon its communication to the attending physician or other health-care provider by the declarant or a witness to the revocation.

(b) The attending physician or other health-care provider shall make the revocation a part of the declarant's medical record.

§ 5. Recording Determination of Terminal Condition and Declaration.

Upon determining that a declarant is in a terminal condition, the attending physician who knows of a declaration shall record the determination and the terms of the declaration in the declarant's medical record.

§ 6. Treatment of Qualified Patients.

(a) A qualified patient may make decisions regarding life-sustaining treatment so long as the patient is able to do so.

(b) This [Act] does not affect the responsibility of the attending physician or other health-care provider to provide treatment, including nutrition and hydration, for a patient's comfort care or alleviation of pain.

(c) Life-sustaining treatment must not be withheld or withdrawn pursuant to a declaration from an individual known to the attending physician to be pregnant so long as it is probable that the fetus will develop to the point of live birth with continued application of life-sustaining treatment.

§ 7. Consent By Others to Withdrawal or Withholding of Treatment.

(a) If written consent to the withholding or withdrawal of the treatment, witnessed by two individuals, is given to the attending physician, the attending physician may withhold or withdraw life-sustaining treatment from an individual who:

(1) has been determined by the attending physician to be in a terminal condition and no longer able to make decisions regarding administration of life-sustaining treatment; and

(2) has no effective declaration.

(b) The authority to consent or to withhold consent under subsection (a) may be exercised by the following individuals, in order of priority:

(1) the spouse of the individual;

(2) an adult child of the individual or, if there is more than one adult child, a majority of the adult children who are reasonably available for consultation;

(3) the parents of the individuals;

(4) an adult sibling of the individual or, if there is more than one adult sibling, a majority of the adult siblings who are reasonably available for consultation; or

(5) the nearest other adult relative of the individual by blood or adoption who is reasonably available for consultation.

(c) If a class entitled to decide whether to consent is not reasonably available for consultation and competent to decide, or declines to decide, the next class is authorized to decide, but an equal division in a class does not authorize the next class to decide.

(d) A decision to grant or withhold consent must be made in good faith. A consent is not valid if it conflicts with the expressed intention of the individual.

(e) A decision of the attending physician acting in good faith that a consent is valid or invalid is conclusive.

(f) Life-sustaining treatment must not be withheld or withdrawn pursuant to this section from an individual known to the attending physician to be pregnant so long as it is probable that the fetus will develop to the point of live birth with continued application of life-sustaining treatment.

§ 8. Transfer of Patients.

An attending physician or other health-care provider who is unwilling to comply with this [Act] shall take all reasonable steps as promptly as practicable to transfer care of the declarant to another physician or health-care provider who is willing to do so.

§ 9. Immunities.

(a) A physician or other health-care provider is not subject to civil or criminal liability, or discipline for unprofessional conduct, for giving effect to a declaration or the direction of an individual designated pursuant to Section 2(a) in the absence of knowledge of the revocation of a declaration, or for giving effect to a written consent under Section 7.

(b) A physician or other health-care provider, whose action under this [Act] is in accord with reasonable medical standards, is not subject to criminal or civil liability, or discipline for unprofessional conduct, with respect to that action.

(c) A physician or other health-care provider, whose decision about the validity of consent under Section 7 is made in good faith, is not subject to criminal or civil liability, or discipline for unprofessional conduct, with respect to that decision.

(d) An individual designated pursuant to Section 2(a) or an individual authorized to consent pursuant to Section 7, whose decision is made or consent is given in good faith pursuant to this [Act], is not subject to criminal or civil liability, or discipline for unprofessional conduct, with respect to that decision.

§ 10. Penalties.

(a) A physician or other health-care provider who willfully fails to transfer the care of a patient in accordance with Section 8 is guilty of [a class _____ misdemeanor].

(b) A physician who willfully fails to record a determination of terminal condition or the terms of a declaration in accordance with Section 5 is guilty of [a class _____ misdemeanor].

(c) An individual who willfully conceals, cancels, defaces, or obliterates the declaration of another individual without the declarant's consent or who falsifies or forges a revocation of the declaration of another individual is guilty of [a class _____ misdemeanor].

(d) An individual who falsifies or forges the declaration of another individual, or willfully conceals or withholds personal knowledge of a revocation under Section 4, is guilty of [a class _____ misdemeanor].

(e) A person who requires or prohibits the execution of a declaration as a condition for being insured for, or receiving, health-care services is guilty of [a class _____ misdemeanor].

(f) A person who coerces or fraudulently induces an individual to execute a declaration is guilty of [a class _____ misdemeanor].

(g) The penalties provided in this section do not displace any sanction applicable under other law.

§ 11. Miscellaneous Provisions.

(a) Death resulting from the withholding or withdrawal of life-sustaining treatment in accordance with this [Act] does not constitute, for any purpose, a suicide or homicide.

(b) The making of a declaration pursuant to Section 2 does not affect the sale, procurement, or issuance of a policy of life insurance or annuity, nor does it affect, impair, or modify the terms of an existing policy of life insurance or annuity. A policy of life insurance or annuity is not legally impaired or invalidated by the withholding or withdrawal of life-sustaining treatment from an insured, notwithstanding any term to the contrary.

(c) A person may not prohibit or require the execution of a declaration as a condition for being insured for, or receiving, health-care services.

(d) This [Act] creates no presumption concerning the intention of an individual who has revoked or has not executed a declaration with respect to the use, withholding, or withdrawal of life-sustaining treatment in the event of a terminal condition.

(e) This [Act] does not affect the right of a patient to make decisions regarding use of life-sustaining treatment, so long as the patient is able to do so, or impair or supersede a right or responsibility that a person has to effect the withholding or withdrawal of medical care.

(f) This [Act] does not require a physician or other health-care provider to take action contrary to reasonable medical standards.

(g) This [Act] does not condone, authorize, or approve mercy-killing or euthanasia.

§ 12.   When Health–Care Provider May Presume Validity of Declaration.

In the absence of knowledge to the contrary, a physician or other health-care provider may assume that a declaration complies with this [Act] and is valid.

§ 13.   Recognition of Declaration Executed in Another State.

A declaration executed in another state in compliance with the law of that state or of this State is valid for purposes of this [Act].

§ 14.   Effect of Previous Declaration.

An instrument executed anywhere before the effective date of this [Act] which substantially complies with Section 2(a) is effective under this [Act].

§ 15.   Uniformity of Application and Construction.

This [Act] shall be applied and construed to effectuate its general purpose to make uniform the law with respect to the subject of this [Act] among states enacting it.

* * *

§ 17.   Severability Clause.

If any provision of this [Act] or its application to any person or circumstance is held invalid, the invalidity does not affect other provisions or applications of this [Act] which can be given effect without the invalid provision or application, and to this end the provisions of this [Act] are severable.

* * *

Notes and Questions

1.   While the vast majority of states have living will legislation, no two statutes are identical.   Why do you think that is the case?   What relevant

political groups are likely to be stronger in some states and weaker in others?

2.   In some states the political nature of the right to die has driven the legislature to enact virtually meaningless statutes to avoid political fallout from all sides. Of course, the existence of these impotent statutes might do more harm than good.   Justice Welliver, dissenting from the Missouri Supreme Court decision in *Cruzan,* points this out with regard to that state's living will statute:

> The principle opinion says that "[n]one of the parties argue that Missouri's living will statute applies in this case." * * * In this respect the parties are imminently correct. The opinion unnecessarily seeks to place a mantle of constitutionality on the Missouri Living Will Statute, which statute in my opinion has been a fraud on the people of Missouri from the beginning and which statute, if directly attacked, must, in my opinion, be held unconstitutional.

> * * *

> We Missourians can sign an instrument directing the withholding or withdrawing of death-prolonging procedures, but, after the Missouri amendments, "death-prolonging procedure" does not include: (1) "the administration of medication," * * * (3) "the performance of any procedure to provide nutrition," (4) "the performance of any procedure to provide * * * hydration." If we cannot authorize withdrawing or withholding "medication," "nutrition" or "hydration," then what can we authorize to be withheld in Missouri? The Missouri Living Will Act is a fraud on Missourians who believe we have been given a right to execute a living will, and to die naturally, respectably, and in peace.

Cruzan, 760 S.W.2d at 441–442.

Recognizing the proliferation of meaningless living will statutes, the Commissioners included in their comment to section 1 of the 1989 Uniform Act: "Though the act intends to err on the side of prolonging life, it should not be made wholly ineffective as to the actual situation it purports to address."   It is remarkable indeed that such an explanation had to be formally articulated.

3.   The comments to the Uniform Act also point out that the Commissioners consciously chose to define the statute's applicability in terms of "terminal condition" rather than "terminal illness," a term more common in many state statutes.   In addition, a "terminal condition" is one that is "incurable and irreversible."   Does this make sense?   Are those words any less ambiguous than "no possibility of recovery," a term which the Commissioners rejected?   As the Commissioners point out in the comment, "a condition which is reversible but incurable is *not* a terminal condition." (Emphasis in original)   A "terminal condition" also must be one that will "result in death within a relatively short time."   Is that standard clear to you?   Is it a better term than "imminent", a term used in some other statutes?

4.   The Uniform Act does not apply to those in persistent vegetative state, irreversible coma, or any other medical condition that is not a "terminal condition."   Thus, this statute would have been of no assistance

to Nancy Cruzan if it had been adopted in Missouri and if she had executed a declaration under it prior to her accident. Is there a reason to limit living will legislation to terminal conditions, or should such statutes be extended to other conditions, like persistent vegetative state, where there is broad consensus that patients should have the right to forgo life-sustaining treatment?

5. Although the Uniform Act treats nutrition and hydration as any other form of comfort care, many recent statutes specifically exclude "the performance of any procedure to provide nutrition or hydration" from the definition of death-prolonging procedures, and thus do not extend any statutory protection to those who remove nutrition or hydration from a patient. For the most famous example, see Vernon's Ann.Mo.Stat. § 459.010(3). After the United States Supreme Court decision in *Cruzan*, are such exceptions legally meaningful? Are they constitutional? The Chief Justice reviews those state cases that have treated nutrition and hydration just like any other form of medical care, apparently with approval. In her concurring opinion, Justice O'Connor cites AMA Ethical Opinion 2.20, Withholding or Withdrawing a Life–Prolonging Medical Treatment, Current Opinions 13 (1989) to support her proposition that "artificial feeding cannot readily be distinguished from other forms of medical treatment." In his dissent, Justice Brennan states without reservation: "No material distinction can be drawn between the treatment to which Nancy Cruzan continues to be subject—artificial nutrition and hydration—and any other medical treatment." For a fuller discussion on the legal position of the withdrawal of nutrition and hydration, see pages 1138–1142, below. For an example of judicial avoidance of the apparent consequences of a nutrition and hydration exception to a living will statute, see McConnell v. Beverly Enterprises–Connecticut, Inc., 209 Conn. 692, 553 A.2d 596 (1989). See also In re Guardianship of Browning, 568 So.2d 4 (Fla.1990).

6. Section 2 of the Uniform Act includes two forms of declarations. The second form would appoint a surrogate to make decisions that could have been made through the execution of the first declaration. Effectively, this permits a very narrow and constrained durable power of attorney. The Commissioners specifically anticipated that some patients would want to appoint their physicians to make these decisions for them, and in their comment they point out that "the physician may act in the appointed capacity." Is this a good idea? Is it otherwise legally acceptable? Is it ethically acceptable? As a physician, would you be willing to serve in this capacity? As counsel to a physician, would you advise her to serve (or to refuse to serve) in such a capacity?

7. Although generally a neutral document on issues of major controversy, the Uniform Act takes an explicitly pro-life position on the protection of the fetus. Life-sustaining treatment must be continued upon a pregnant woman where it is "probable" that the fetus, even if it is not viable at the moment of treatment, will eventually be born alive if the treatment is provided. Is this provision, which removes from all pregnant women a right the statute guarantees to all others, constitutional? The vigor of the Commissioner's position is demonstrated by the fact that the 1985 Uniform Act, which this draft superseded, allowed a pregnant woman to opt out of the presumption that treatment would be continued if the

fetus could be saved. The woman's right to opt out of forced continued treatment during pregnancy was removed from the 1989 Act.

8. The fetal protection portions of the Uniform Act are not the only sections to address controversial issues. The Act also provides that it does not "condone, authorize, or approve mercy-killing or euthanasia." What does that section add to the statute? Does it have any effect whatsoever? If it does not, why do you think it was included in the text?

9. Declarations valid in the state in which they were signed, or valid in a state adopting the Uniform Act, are valid in all states adopting the Uniform Act. This is one of the real advances of this Uniform Act. Most state statutes do not include such a comity provision, however. Without such a provision, what is the effect of a declaration legally executed in one state upon a patient who undergoes one of the triggering conditions in a second state? Must the second state give full faith and credit to the statute that authorized the execution of the document in the first state? Is this a particularly good reason for adopting a Uniform Act?

10. The statutory language need not limit a clever attorney in drafting a living will for a client. While an attorney ought to draft a document that is consistent with the formalities of state law, most state laws (and the Uniform Act) allow an attorney to be expansive and directive in providing for the needs of the person who will execute the document—the formal legal applicability of the uncertain language can be determined later. For example, some attorneys use living will forms that explicitly define nutrition and hydration as the kinds of treatment that may be withheld or withdrawn even though state statutes are silent on that point. Would such a clarification of the explicit wishes of the patients affect the validity of an otherwise legal document? After *Cruzan*, might such inclusions take on constitutional significance?

11. Living wills have been relied upon more as mere evidence of the desires of the patient rather than as statutorily recognized legal documents directing specific treatment. Thus, there is probably great value in the national distribution of living will forms, even if they comply with virtually none of the statutory requirements of any particular state. The first and most cited case to give value to a legally insufficient living will is John F. Kennedy Memorial Hosp., Inc. v. Bludworth, 452 So.2d 921 (Fla.1984):

> We have recognized that terminally ill incompetent persons being sustained only through use of extraordinary artificial means have the same right to refuse to be held on the threshold of death as terminally ill competent patients. Since incompetent patients may not exercise this right while they are incompetent, there must be a means by which this right may be exercised on their behalf, otherwise it will be lost. The means developed by the courts to afford this right to incompetent persons is the doctrine of "substituted judgment." Under this doctrine close family members or legal guardians substitute their judgment for what they believe the terminally ill incompetent persons, if competent, would have done under these circumstances. If such a person, while competent, had executed a so-called "living" or "mercy" will, that will would be persuasive evidence of that incompetent person's intention

and it should be given great weight by the person or persons who substitute their judgment on behalf of the terminally ill incompetent. 452 So.2d at 926.

12. Review the problem on pages 1059–1060. Would Mr. Karl's situation have been different if he had executed either form of declaration under the Uniform Act? When, if ever, would it have been relevant to his treatment? How would it have come up?

13. For a broad view of the history of the effect of living will statutes, see Gelfand, Living Wills Statutes: The First Decade, 1987 Wis.L.Rev. 737 (1987). Useful perspectives on the value of living wills may also be found in Francis, The Evanescence of Living Wills, 14 J.Contemp.L. 27 (1988) and in an excellent symposium at 13 Law, Medicine and Health Care 260–282 (1985). For a good criticism of living wills, see Johnson, Sequential Domination, Autonomy, and Living Wills, 9 Western N.Eng.L.Rev. 113 (1987). The unusual status of one common clause in living wills statutes is discussed in Note, Pregnancy Clauses in Living Wills Statutes, 87 Colum.L. Rev. 1280 (1987). Fine accounts of particular state statutes include Note, The "Terminal Condition" Condition in Virginia's Natural Death Act, 73 Va.L.Rev. 749 (1987) and Note, A Necessary Compromise: The Right to Forgo Artificial Nutrition and Hydration Under Maryland's Life–Sustaining Procedures Act, 47 Md.L.Rev. 1188 (1988).

b. *Durable Powers of Attorney*

Another means of identifying who should speak for the patient when the patient is incompetent is to allow the patient to designate a spokesperson during the patient's period of competence. This may be accomplished through the patient's execution of a durable power of attorney.

Powers of attorney have been available over the past several centuries to allow for financial transactions to be consummated by agents of a principal. A power of attorney may be executed, under oath, by any competent person. It provides that the agent designated shall have the right to act on behalf of the principal for purposes that are described and limited in the document itself. Thus, a principal may give an agent a power of attorney to enter into a particular contract, a particular kind of contract, or all contracts. The power may be limited by time, by geographic area, or in any other way. It may be granted to any person, who, upon appointment, becomes the agent and "attorney-in-fact" for the principal. At common law a power of attorney expired upon the "incapacity" of the principal. This was necessary to assure that the principal could maintain adequate authority over his agent. As long as a power of attorney expired upon the incapacity (and, thus, presumably the incompetency) of the principal, the power of attorney had no value in making medical decisions. After all, a competent patient could decide for himself; there is no reason for him to delegate authority to an agent attorney-in-fact.

In the mid 1970s it became clear that the value of the power of attorney could be increased if it could extend beyond the incapacity of the principal. For example, as an increasing number of very elderly people depended upon their children and others to handle their financial affairs, it became important that there be some device by which they could delegate their authority to these agents. For such principals it was most important that the authority remain with their agents when they did become incapacitated. The Uniform Probate Code was amended to provide for a durable power of attorney; that is, a power of attorney that would remain in effect (or even become effective) upon the incapacity of the principal. Various statutes providing for durable powers of attorney, now adopted in every state, require only that powers of attorney include a statement that they will become (or remain) effective upon the incapacity of the principal. As was the case at common law, the principal may put any limitation otherwise permitted by law in the durable power of attorney.

The question of whether general durable powers of attorney may be used for nonfinancial determinations, such as health care decisionmaking, has yet to be conclusively answered by the courts. Although a slight majority of states have now promulgated their own statutes to authorize specifically the execution of durable powers of attorney for health care purposes, many still depend upon their version of the Uniform Probate Code (this section of which is also separately codified as the Uniform Durable Power of Attorney Act).

UNIFORM PROBATE CODE
DURABLE POWER OF ATTORNEY

Section 5–501. [Definition].

A durable power of attorney is power of attorney by which a principal designates another his attorney in fact in writing and the writing contains the words "this power of attorney shall not be affected by subsequent disability or incapacity of the principal, or lapse of time," or "this power of attorney shall become effective upon the disability or incapacity of the principal," or similar words showing the intent of the principal that the authority conferred shall be exercisable notwithstanding the principal's subsequent disability or incapacity, and, unless it states a time of determination, notwithstanding the lapse of time since the execution of the instrument.

Section 5–502. [Durable power of attorney not affected by lapse of time, disability or incapacity].

All acts done by an attorney in fact pursuant to a durable power of attorney during any period of disability or incapacity of the principal have the same effect and inure to the benefit of and bind the principal and his successors in interest as if the principal were competent and not disabled. Unless the instrument states a time of termination, the power is exercisable notwithstanding the lapse of time since the execution of the instrument.

Notes and Questions

1. In her concurring opinion in the *Cruzan* case, Justice O'Connor suggests that there may be constitutional significance to a properly executed durable power of attorney:

> I also write separately to emphasize that the Court does not today decide the issue whether a state must also give effect to the decisions of a surrogate decision-maker. In my view, such a duty may well be Constitutionally required to protect the patient's liberty interest in refusing medical treatment.

110 S.Ct. at 2587. She commends those several states that have recognized "the practical wisdom of such a procedure by enacting durable power of attorney statutes" and she suggests that a written appointment of a proxy "may be a valuable additional safeguard of the patient's interest in directing his medical care." In the final paragraph of her opinion she points out that "[t]oday's decision * * * does not preclude a future determination that the Constitution requires the states to implement the decisions of a patient's duly appointed surrogate."

2. Most states have adopted statutes that formally authorize the execution of durable powers of attorney for health care decisions. There is an extremely wide variety among these statutes. One of the first, in California, turned into a nightmare of political compromise. It is long, complex, and highly technical. For example, it prescribes that a "warning to person executing this document" be included in the form durable power in 10–point boldface type. The California warning itself is longer than the entire durable power prescribed by statutes of other states. West's Ann. Cal.Civ.Code § 2433. The Illinois statute, which is generally far more permissive than the California alternative, contains a non-mandatory "Illinois statutory short form power of attorney for health care" which is several typed pages long. See Ill.—S.H.A. ch. 110½ para. 804–10 (Smith–Hurd Supp.1990). While the Illinois statute at least provides that "the form of health care agency in this article is not intended to be exclusive * * * ", the Rhode Island statute explicitly provides:

> "[t]he statutory form of durable power of attorney as set forth in [this act] shall be used and shall be the only form by which a person may execute a durable power of attorney for health care. * * * It shall not be altered in any manner and shall preclude the use of any other form to exercise the durable power of attorney for health care."

R.I.Gen.Laws §§ 23–410–1.

The New Mexico legislature dealt with the issue very simply by listing health care decisions among other kinds of decisions that principals may wish to delegate to attorneys-in-fact in more general durable powers of attorney. Among the boxes that can be initialled on the New Mexico statutory durable power form are real estate transactions, bond, share and commodity transactions, chattel and goods transactions, a host of other business transactions—and "decisions regarding life-saving and life-prolonging medical treatment," "decisions relating to medical treatment, surgical treatment, nursing care, medication, hospitalization, institutionalization in a nursing home or other facility and home health care," and, most remarkably, "transfer of property or income as a gift to the principal spouse for the purpose of qualifying the principal for governmental medical assistance." N.M.Stat.Ann., § 45–5–502 (Supp.1990). Which of these state approaches is likely to be most successful? What kinds of caveats and restrictions are necessary to avoid the potential abuse of the durable power of attorney for health care decision-making?

3. There is no reported opinion formally holding that the authority of a durable power of attorney executed under the Uniform Probate Code extends to health care decision-making. For two suggesting that there would be such authority, see In re Peter, 108 N.J. 365, 378–379, 529 A.2d 419, 426 (1987) ("Although the statute does not specifically authorize conveyance of durable authority to make medical decisions, it should be interpreted that way.") and In re Westchester Medical Center (O'Connor), 72 N.Y.2d 517, 534 N.Y.S.2d 886, 531 N.E.2d 607, 612 fn. 2 (1988).

The President's Commission assumed, without any discussion, that it could be used for this purpose. See President's Commission, Deciding to Forego Life–Sustaining Treatment, 145–149 (1983). On the other hand, two statutory sources of these acts—the Uniform Probate Code and the Model Special Power of Attorney for Small Interests Act—were conceived originally as ways of controlling property, not health care decisions. Is there any intellectual problem in extending this simple statute to health care decision-making?

4. In drafting durable powers of attorney under the Uniform Probate Code, it makes sense to be expansive and properly directive. The principal can designate any person he wishes as his attorney-in-fact, and may authorize that person to make any designated group of health care decisions or to make all health care decisions on his behalf. He may require that the agent consult with named others before making certain kinds of decisions, or he may require the agent to consider certain deeply held personal values before proceeding. In determining how you would draft a durable power of attorney, consider the effect it would have on the principal's family, the physician and health-care workers, and the person who is designated as agent. What would happen if that person refused to honor the durable power of attorney, or refused to abide by some of its provisions?

5. Some state laws now permit durable powers of attorney to arrange not only for decisionmaking after the principal's incapacity, but also for decisionmaking after the principal's death. These statutes allow the principal to provide for the disposition of his body through a durable power. See, e.g., Ill.—S.H.A. ch. 110½, para. 802–10 (Smith–Hurd Cum.Supp.1990) and Kan.Stat.Ann. § 58–625 (Cum.Supp.1989).

6. For useful discussions of durable powers of attorney, see Peters, Advance Medical Directives: the Case for the Durable Power of Attorney for Health Care, 8 J.Legal Med. 437 (1987); Martyn and Jacobs, Legislating Advance Directives for the Terminally Ill: The Living Will and Durable Power of Attorney, 63 Neb.L.Rev. 779 (1984); Note, Appointing an Agent to Make Medical Treatment Choices, 84 Columbia L.Rev. 985 (1984).

Note: The Patient Self-Determination Act

The Patient Self-Determination Act became law as a part of the Omnibus Budget Reconciliation Act of 1990, and it increases the role that advance directives—both living wills and durable powers of attorney—play in medical decision making. The statute, effective December 1, 1991, applies to hospitals, skilled nursing facilities, home health agencies, hospice programs, and HMOs which receive Medicaid or Medicare funding. It requires each of those covered by the Act to provide each patient with written information concerning:

> (i) an individual's rights under State law (whether statutory or as recognized by the courts of the State) to make decisions concerning * * * medical care, including the right to accept or refuse medical or surgical treatment and the right to formulate advance directives * * * and

> (ii) the written policies of the provider or organization respecting the implementation of such rights.

42 U.S.C.A. § 1395cc(a)(1)(f)(1)(A). In addition, those covered must document in each patient's record whether that patient has signed an advance directive, assure that the state law is followed in the institution, and provide for education of both the staff and the public concerning living wills and durable powers of attorney. A covered institution or organization that does not assure the Secretary of Health and Human Services that it is complying with all relevant portions of the Act must lose all of its Medicaid and Medicare funding; this sanction is mandatory and the Secretary has no discretion to grant exceptions or extensions.

The statute also requires states to develop written descriptions of their own state law, and it requires the Department of Health and Human Services to conduct nationwide public education on advance directives. In addition, all Social Security recipients will receive information about living wills and durable powers, and a new section on these issues will be added to the Medicare handbook. Not surprisingly, the American Medical Association, the American Hospital Association and the Health Care Financing Administration opposed the Act; the American Bar Association opposed it also. Will the non-establishment origins of this sweeping Act making it more or less effective in accomplishing its purpose?

c. Patients Without Formal Prior Directives—Substantive Principles

Most incompetent patients in need of life-sustaining treatment have executed neither a living will nor a durable power of attorney. This does not mean that the principle of autonomy need be ignored: there are other ways to determine what a patient's wishes would be. There are two parts to such an inquiry. First, there must be a determination of the substantive principles to be applied to determine what the patient would have done, if he were competent. Second, there must be a decision about the process to be employed in making this substituted judgment. While there has been substantial debate over the process that should be employed, there is virtually a consensus that courts ought to apply the substantive principle embodied in doctrine of substituted judgment and seek to discover the patient's values and desires to determine what the patient would have done under the circumstances if that patient were competent. This always involves evaluating the patient's previous statements and usually involves evaluating the patient's life style and the views of close relatives and friends about the patient.

It has become standard medical practice to seek consent to any medical procedure from close family members of an incompetent patient. There is no common law authority for this practice; it is an example of medical practice (and good common sense) being subtly absorbed by the law. The President's Commission suggests five reasons for this deference to family members:

(1) The family is generally most concerned about the good of the patient.

(2) The family will also usually be most knowledgeable about the patient's goals, preferences, and values.

(3) The family deserves recognition as an important social unit that ought to be treated, within limits, as a responsible decision-maker in matters that intimately affect its members.

(4) Especially in a society in which many other traditional forms of community have eroded, participation in a family is often an important dimension of personal fulfillment.

(5) Since a protected sphere of privacy and autonomy is required for the flourishing of this interpersonal union, institutions and the state should be reluctant to intrude, particularly regarding matters that are personal and on which there is a wide range of opinion in society.

President's Commission, Deciding to Forego Life–Sustaining Treatment, 127 (1983). Of course, consulting with family members also neutralizes potential malpractice plaintiffs: this factor probably accounts for its current popularity.

Over the past few years several states have enacted "family consent laws" that authorize statutorily designated family members to make health care decisions for their relatives in circumscribed situations. While these statutes often apply to a wide range of health care decisions (including decisions to forgo life sustaining treatment), they apply only when there has been a physician's certification of the patient's inability to make the health care decision. In addition, "family consent laws" often provide immunity from liability for family members and physicians acting in good faith, and judicial authority to resolve disputes about the authority of the family members under the statutes. The definition of "family member" varies from state to state. The statutes are generally consistent on one point—the family member must apply substituted judgment to determine what the patient would choose if that patient were competent. See, e.g., S.C.Code 1990, §§ 44–66–10 to 80 (Supp.1990).

Family members may not share all of the values of the patient, and those actually closest to the patient may be unrelated friends. As the Chief Justice pointed out in *Cruzan,* "there is no automatic assurance that the view of close family members will necessarily be the same as the patient's would have been had she been confronted with the prospect of her situation while competent." The family's role in decision making may even be in direct conflict with the interests of the patient, and family members are often the patient's heirs. Ultimately, while courts may be deferential to a family's determination under a statute or the common law, the question is what the *patient* would want. On this issue the family's conclusions, like those of friends, physicians, and others, generally are not dispositive, but merely evidentiary.

IN RE EICHNER

New York Court of Appeals, 1981.
52 N.Y.2d 363, 438 N.Y.S.2d 266, 420 N.E.2d 64.

WACHTLER, JUDGE.

For over 66 years Brother Joseph Fox was a member of the Society of Mary, a Catholic religious order which, among other things, operates Chaminade High School in Mineola. * * *

While [an] operation was being performed * * * he suffered cardiac arrest, with resulting loss of oxygen to the brain and substantial brain damage. He lost the ability to breathe spontaneously and was placed on a respirator which maintained him in a vegetative state. The attending physicians informed Father Philip Eichner, who was the president of Chaminade and the director of the society at the school, that there was no reasonable chance of recovery and that Brother Fox would die in that state.

After retaining two neurosurgeons who confirmed the diagnosis, Father Eichner requested the hospital to remove the respirator. The hospital, however, refused to do so without court authorization. Father Eichner then applied, * * * to be appointed committee of the person and property of Brother Fox, with authority to direct removal of the respirator. The application was supported by the patient's 10 nieces and nephews, his only surviving relatives. The court appointed a guardian ad litem and directed that notice be served on various parties, including the District Attorney.

At the hearing the District Attorney opposed the application and called medical experts to show that there might be some improvement in the patient's condition. All the experts agreed, however, that there was no reasonable likelihood that Brother Fox would ever emerge from the vegetative coma or recover his cognitive powers.

There was also evidence, submitted by the petitioner, that before the operation rendered him incompetent the patient had made it known that under these circumstances he would want a respirator removed. Brother Fox had first expressed this view in 1976 when the Chaminade community discussed the moral implications of the celebrated *Karen Ann Quinlan* case, in which the parents of a 19–year–old New Jersey girl who was in a vegetative coma requested the hospital to remove the respirator [   ]. These were formal discussions prompted by Chaminade's mission to teach and promulgate Catholic moral principles. At that time it was noted that the Pope had stated that Catholic principles permitted the termination of extraordinary life support systems when there is no reasonable hope for the patient's recovery and that church officials in New Jersey had concluded that use of the respirator in the *Quinlan* case constituted an extraordinary measure under the circumstances. Brother Fox expressed agreement with those views and stated that he would not want any of this "extraordinary business" done for him under those circumstances. Several years later, and only a couple of months before his final hospitalization, Brother Fox again stated that he would not want his life prolonged by such measures if his condition were hopeless.

* * *

In this case the proof was compelling. There was no suggestion that the witnesses who testified for the petitioner had any motive other than to see that Brother Fox' stated wishes were respected. The finding that he carefully reflected on the subject, expressed his views and concluded not to have his life prolonged by medical means if there were no hope of recovery is supported by his religious beliefs and is not inconsistent with his life of unselfish religious devotion. These were obviously solemn pronouncements and not casual remarks made at some social gathering, nor can it be said that he was too young to realize or feel the consequences of his statements [   ]. That this was a persistent commitment is evidenced by the fact that he reiterated the decision but two months before his final hospitalization. There was, of course, no need to speculate as to whether he would want this particular medical procedure to be discontinued under these circumstances. What occurred to him was identical to what happened in the *Karen Ann Quinlan* case, which had originally prompted his decision. In sum, the evidence clearly and convincingly shows that Brother Fox did not want to be maintained in a vegetative coma by use of a respirator.

* * *

———

Two states, Missouri and New York, reject substituted judgment except where it is based on the formally articulated desires of the patient. See *Cruzan,* supra at 1061, In re Westchester Medical Center (O'Connor), below at 1142. In these states it is almost impossible to remove life sustaining treatment from incompetent patients because it is rare indeed to have a patient foresee and describe his condition and the treatment he would wish with the specificity with which Brother Fox spoke. More often, patients have not addressed the questions and others must decide on their behalf exercising substituted judgment for the patient.

The Illinois court expressed this principle clearly and simply:

Under substituted judgment, a surrogate decisionmaker attempts to establish, with as much accuracy as possible, what decision the patient would make if he were competent to do so. Employing this theory, the surrogate first tries to determine if the patient had expressed explicit intent regarding this type of medical treatment prior to becoming incompetent. [ ] Where no clear intent exists, the patient's personal value system must guide the surrogate.
* * *

In re Estate of Longeway, 133 Ill.2d 33, 549 N.E.2d 292, 299 (1989).

In such cases, courts (except in Missouri and New York, as noted) look wherever they can to determine the patient's wishes. In Brophy v. New England Sinai Hospital, Inc., 398 Mass. 417, 497 N.E.2d 626 (1986), the Massachusetts Supreme Court based its conclusion that food and hydration could be withheld from a comatose adult on the substituted judgment analysis done by the lower court.

[After full hearing] the judge found on the basis of ample evidence which no one disputes, that Brophy's judgment would be to decline the provision of food and water and to terminate his life. In reaching that conclusion, the judge considered various factors including the following: (1) Brophy's expressed preferences; (2) his religious convictions and their relation to refusal of treatment; (3) the impact on his family; (4) the probability of adverse side effects; and (5) the prognosis, both with and without treatment. The judge also considered present and future incompetency as an element which Brophy would consider in his decision-making process. The judge relied on several statements made by Brophy prior to the onset of his illness. Although he never had discussed specifically whether a G-tube or feeding tube should be withdrawn in the event that he was diagnosed as being in a persistent vegetative state following his surgery, the judge inferred that, if presently competent, Brophy would choose to forgo artificial nutrition and hydration by means of a G-tube. The judge found that Brophy would not likely view his own religion as a barrier to that choice.

The *Conroy* court also addressed the question of whether life-support systems could be removed from patients who have never clearly expressed their desires about such treatment. The court developed three tests, depending upon the existence (vel non) of any trustworthy evidence that the patient would forego the life-sustaining treatment.

IN RE CONROY

Supreme Court of New Jersey, 1985.
98 N.J. 321, 486 A.2d 1209.

SCHREIBER, JUSTICE.

* * * [W]e hold that life-sustaining treatment may be withheld or withdrawn from an incompetent patient when it is clear that the particular patient would have refused the treatment under the circumstances involved. The standard we are enunciating is a subjective one, consistent with the notion that the right that we are seeking to effectuate is a very personal right to control one's own life. The question is not what a reasonable or average person would have chosen to do under the circumstances but what the particular patient would have done if able to choose for himself.

* * *

We * * * hold that life-sustaining treatment may also be withheld or withdrawn from a patient in Claire Conroy's situation [i.e., a patient who was competent but is now incompetent] if either of two "best interests" tests—a limited-objective or a pure-objective test—is satisfied.

Under the limited-objective test, life-sustaining treatment may be withheld or withdrawn from a patient in Claire Conroy's situation when there is some trustworthy evidence that the patient would have refused the treatment, and the decision-maker is satisfied that it is clear that the burdens of the patient's continued life with the treatment outweigh the benefits of that life for him. By this we mean that the patient is suffering, and will continue to suffer throughout the expected duration of his life, unavoidable pain, and that the net burdens of his prolonged life (the pain and suffering of his life with the treatment less the amount and duration of pain that the patient would likely experience if the treatment were withdrawn) markedly outweigh any physical pleasure, emotional enjoyment, or intellectual satisfaction that the patient may still be able to derive from life. This limited-objective standard permits the termination of treatment for a patient who had not unequivocally expressed his desires before becoming incompetent, when it is clear that the treatment in question would merely prolong the patient's suffering.

* * *

This limited-objective test also requires some trustworthy evidence that the patient would have wanted the treatment terminated. This evidence could take any one or more of the various forms appropriate to prove the patient's intent under the subjective test. Evidence that, taken as a whole, would be too vague, casual, or remote to constitute the clear proof of the patient's subjective intent that is necessary to satisfy the subjective test—for example, informally expressed reactions to other people's medical conditions and treatment—might be sufficient to satisfy this prong of the limited-objective test.

In the absence of trustworthy evidence, or indeed any evidence at all, that the patient would have declined the treatment, life-sustaining treatment may still be withheld or withdrawn from a formerly competent person like Claire Conroy if a third, pure-objective test is satisfied. Under that test, as under the limited-objective test, the net burdens of the patient's life with the treatment should clearly and markedly outweigh the benefits that the patient derives from life. Further, the recurring, unavoidable and severe pain of the patient's life with the treatment should be such that the effect of administering life-sustaining treatment would be inhumane. Subjective evidence that the patient would not have wanted the treatment is not necessary under this pure-objective standard. Nevertheless, even in the context of severe pain, life-sustaining treatment should not be withdrawn from an incompetent patient who had previously expressed a wish to be kept alive in spite of any pain that he might experience.

* * * [W]e expressly decline to authorize decision-making based on assessments of the personal worth or social utility of another's life, or the value of that life to others.

* * *

We are aware that it will frequently be difficult to conclude that the evidence is sufficient to justify termination of treatment under either of the "best interests" tests that we have described. Often, it is unclear whether and to what extent a patient such as Claire Conroy is capable of, or is in fact, experiencing pain. Similarly, medical experts are often unable to determine with any degree of certainty the extent of a nonverbal person's intellectual functioning or the depth of his emotional life. When the evidence is insufficient to satisfy either the limited-objective or pure-objective standard, however, we cannot justify the termination of life-sustaining treatment as clearly furthering the best interests of a patient like Ms. Conroy.

* * * When evidence of a person's wishes or physical or mental condition is equivocal, it is best to err, if at all, in favor of preserving life. * * *

Note: Conroy and Persistent Vegetative State

The Conroy case has been extremely influential; it is cited by most courts that have dealt with decisionmaking for incompetent patients since 1985 and its three-tiered set of tests—the subjective, limited-objective, and pure-objective tests—are generally well regarded. In 1987 the New Jersey Supreme Court decided a trilogy of cases that called into question whether every case of the discontinuation of life-sustaining treatment in an incompetent patient could be resolved by reference to one of these three *Conroy* tests. In re Farrell, 108 N.J. 335, 529 A.2d 404 (1987); In re Jobes, 108 N.J. 394, 529 A.2d 434 (1987); In re Peter, 108 N.J. 365, 529 A.2d 419 (1987).

In *Farrell* the court affirmed the right of a competent patient to discontinue life-sustaining treatment and, in dicta, approved the "subjective" test that had been adopted in Conroy. In *Jobes* and *Peter,* however, the court side-stepped the Conroy test because of the condition of the patients. Each of those cases involved a patient in persistent vegetative state. In an explanation subsequently adopted by the United States Supreme Court in *Cruzan*, 110 S.Ct. 2841 n. 1, 111 L.Ed.2d 224 (1990), the *Jobes* court explained "persistent vegetative state" by quoting the trial testimony of Dr. Fred Plum, who created the term:

> [Persistent] vegetative state describes a body which is functioning entirely in terms of its internal controls. It maintains temperature. It maintains heartbeat and pulmonary ventilation. It maintains digestive activity. It maintains reflex activity of muscles and nerves for low level conditioned responses. But there is no behavioral evidence of either self-awareness or awareness of the surroundings in a learned manner.

529 A.2d at 438.

The New Jersey Supreme Court held that "the balancing tests set forth in *Conroy* are [not] appropriate in the case of a persistently vegetative patient." As the court pointed out,

> Even in the case of a patient like Claire Conroy—the type of patient for whom the balancing tests were created—it can be difficult or impossible to measure the burdens of embarrassment, frustration, helplessness, rage and other emotional pain, or the benefits of enjoyable feelings like contentment, joy, satisfaction, gratitude, and well being that the patient experiences as a result of life-sustaining treatment. "[M]edical experts are often unable to determine with any degree of medical certainty the extent of a nonverbal person's intellectual functioning or the depth of his emotional life." [citing *Conroy*]

> While a benefits-burdens analysis is difficult with marginally cognitive patients like Claire Conroy, it is essentially impossible with patients in a persistent vegetative state. By definition such patients, like Ms. Peter, do not experience any of the benefits or burdens that the *Conroy* balancing tests are intended or able to appraise. Therefore, we hold that these tests should not be applied to patients in the persistent vegetative state.

In re Peter, 529 A.2d at 424–425.

In *Peter* the court was able to depend upon the subjective prong of the *Conroy* test, and thus it did not have to address the alternative test to be applied when an incompetent patient did not leave clear and convincing evidence of that patient's desires. In *Jobes*, however, the court was required to look for an alternative test. The court determined that the appropriate test in the case of a patient in persistent vegetative state who had not left clear and convincing evidence of the patient's desires was the test that had been applied in *Quinlan* almost a decade before. Although there was some ambiguity in the early *Quinlan* decision, the *Jobes* court made it clear that "the right of a patient in an irreversibly vegetative state to determine whether to refuse life-sustaining medical treatment may be exercised by the patient's family or close friend. If there are close and caring family members who are willing to make this decision there is no need to have a guardian appointed." 529 A.2d at 447. In effect, in

Peter and *Jobes* the New Jersey Supreme Court said that the limited-objective and pure-objective tests of Conroy make it too difficult to terminate the treatment of patients in persistent vegetative states, even if those standards could reasonably be applied to other incompetent patients.

Does it make any sense to treat a patient in a persistent vegetative state any differently from another incompetent patient? Is there any reason to permit the termination of life-sustaining treatment in a patient in persistent vegetative state when it would not be permitted in an otherwise identically situated patient with a scintilla of higher brain function? Is the New Jersey retreat from *Conroy* in the case of patients in persistent vegetative state a narrowing or a broadening of the *Conroy* rule?

For a good account of the medical issues relating to persistent vegetative state, see Cranford, The Persistent Vegetative State: The Medical Reality, 18 Hastings Center Report (1) 27 (Feb./March 1988). For a description of every case in which state and federal courts have permitted the discontinuation of life support treatments in patients in persistent vegetative state, see Justice Stevens's dissent in *Cruzan,* 110 S.Ct. 2841, 2888 n. 21. Justice Stevens points out that the *Cruzan* case itself is unique in not permitting the termination of treatment in a patient in persistent vegetative state.

Note: Irrelevant Distinctions—Active and Passive Conduct; Ordinary and Extraordinary Treatment

Courts have been called upon to determine the legal significance of the difference between active and passive conduct, and ordinary and extraordinary forms of medical intervention. These anachronistic distinctions have not found a safe harbor in the law, just as they have been increasingly recognized as meaningless in ethics. The *Conroy* opinion specifically and carefully considered each of these distinctions, and summarized the ethical and legal literature and the reasons for rejecting the distinctions.

1. As to the distinction between active and passive conduct, the *Conroy* court announced:

> We emphasize that in making decisions whether to administer life-sustaining treatment to patients such as Claire Conroy, the primary focus should be the patient's desires and experience of pain and enjoyment—not the type of treatment involved. Thus, we reject the distinction that some have made between actively hastening death by terminating treatment and passively allowing a person to die of a disease as one of limited use in a legal analysis of such a decision-making situation.

> Characterizing conduct as active or passive is often an elusive notion, even outside the context of medical decision-making * * *. The distinction is particularly nebulous, however, in the context of decisions whether to withhold or withdraw life-sustaining treatment. In a case like that of Claire Conroy, for example, would a physician who discontinued nasogastric feeding be actively causing her death by removing her primary source of nutrients; or would he merely be

omitting to continue the artificial form of treatment, thus passively allowing her medical condition, which includes her inability to swallow, to take its natural course?   [   ] The ambiguity inherent in this distinction is further heightened when one performs an act within an over-all plan of non-intervention, such as when a doctor writes an order not to resuscitate a patient.   * * *

For a similar reason, we also reject any distinction between withholding and withdrawing life-sustaining treatment. Some commentators have suggested that discontinuing life-sustaining treatment once it has been commenced is morally more problematic than merely failing to begin the treatment.   [   ] Discontinuing life-sustaining treatment, to some, is an "active" taking of life, as opposed to the more "passive" act of omitting the treatment in the first instance.

This distinction is more psychologically compelling than logically sound. As mentioned above, the line between active and passive conduct in the context of medical decisions is far too nebulous to constitute a principled basis for decisionmaking. Whether necessary treatment is withheld at the outset or withdrawn later on, the consequence—the patient's death—is the same. Moreover, from a policy standpoint, it might well be unwise to forbid persons from discontinuing a treatment under circumstances in which the treatment could permissibly be withheld. Such a rule could discourage families and doctors from even attempting certain types of care and could thereby force them into hasty and premature decisions to allow a patient to die. [   ]

486 A.2d at 1233–1234.

This policy interest was recognized by Justice Brennan in his *Cruzan* dissent:

Moreover, there may be considerable danger that Missouri's rule of decision would impair rather than serve any interest the state does have in sustaining life. Current medical practice recommends use of heroic measures if there is a scintilla of a chance that the patient will recover, on the assumption that the measures will be discontinued should the patient improve. When the President's Commission in 1982 approved the withdrawal of life support equipment from irreversibly vegetative patients, it explained that "[a]n even more troubling wrong occurs when a treatment that might save life or improve health is not started because the health care personnel are afraid that they will find it very difficult to stop the treatment if, as is fairly likely, it proves to be of little benefit and greatly burdens the patient."   [   ]

110 S.Ct. at 2870.

2. As to the distinction between ordinary and extraordinary treatment, *Conroy* pointed out:

We also find unpersuasive the distinction relied upon by some courts, commentators, and theologians between "ordinary" treatment, which they would always require, and "extraordinary" treatment, which they deem optional. * * * The terms "ordinary" and "extraordinary" have assumed too many conflicting meanings to remain useful.

To draw a line on this basis for determining whether treatment should be given leads to a semantical milieu that does not advance the analysis. [ ]

The distinction between ordinary and extraordinary treatment is frequently phrased as one between common and unusual, or simple and complex, treatment[ ]; "extraordinary" treatment also has been equated with elaborate, artificial, heroic, aggressive, expensive, or highly involved or invasive forms of medical intervention [ ]. Depending on the definitions applied, a particular treatment for a given patient may be considered both ordinary and extraordinary. [ ] Further, since the common/unusual and simple/complex distinctions among medical treatments "exist on continuums with no precise dividing line," [ ] and the continuum is constantly shifting due to progress in medical care, disagreement will often exist about whether a particular treatment is ordinary or extraordinary. In addition, the competent patient generally could refuse even ordinary treatment; therefore, an incompetent patient theoretically should also be able to make such a choice when the surrogate decision-making is effectuating the patient's subjective intent. In such cases, the ordinary/extraordinary distinction is irrelevant except insofar as the particular patient would have made the distinction.

The ordinary/extraordinary distinction has also been discussed in terms of the benefits and burdens of treatment for the patient. If the benefits of the treatment outweigh the burdens it imposes on the patient, it is characterized as ordinary and therefore ethically required; if not, it is characterized as extraordinary and therefore optional. [ ] This formulation is extremely fact-sensitive and would lead to different classifications of the same treatment in different situations.

* * * Moreover, while the analysis may be useful in weighing the implications of the specific treatment for the patient, essentially it merely restates the question: whether the burdens of a treatment so clearly outweigh its benefits to the patient that continued treatment would be inhumane.

468 A.2d at 1234–1235. See also Brophy v. New England Sinai Hospital, Inc., 398 Mass. 417, 497 N.E.2d 626 (1986) ("while we believe that the distinction between extraordinary and ordinary care is a factor to be considered, the use of such a distinction as the sole, or major, factor of decision tends * * * to create a distinction without meaning.")

Note: The Special Status of Nutrition and Hydration

The issue of withdrawing nutrition and hydration has become an especially contentious one since it found its place on some political agendas. Generally, courts have concluded that the termination of nutrition and hydration is no different from the termination of other forms of mechanical support. For example, *Conroy* suggested:

Some commentators, * * * have made yet [another] distinction, between the termination of artificial feedings and the termination of other forms of life-sustaining medical treatment. * * * According to the Appellate Division:

> If, as here, the patient is not comatose and does not face imminent and inevitable death, nourishment accomplishes the substantial benefit of sustaining life until the illness takes its natural course. Under such circumstances nourishment always will be an essential element of ordinary care which physicians are ethically obligated to provide. [ ]

Certainly, feeding has an emotional significance. As infants we could breathe without assistance, but we were dependent on others for our lifeline of nourishment. Even more, feeding is an expression of nurturing and caring, certainly for infants and children, and in many cases for adults as well.

Once one enters the realm of complex, high-technology medical care, it is hard to shed the "emotional symbolism" of food. * * * Analytically, artificial feeding by means of a nasogastric tube or intravenous infusion can be seen as equivalent to artificial breathing by means of a respirator. Both prolong life through mechanical means when the body is no longer able to perform a vital bodily function on its own.

Furthermore, while nasogastric feeding and other medical procedures to ensure nutrition and hydration are usually well tolerated, they are not free from risks or burdens; they have complications that are sometimes serious and distressing to the patient.

* * *

Finally, dehydration may well not be distressing or painful to a dying patient. For patients who are unable to sense hunger and thirst, withholding of feeding devices such as nasogastric tubes may not result in more pain than the termination of any other medical treatment. * * * Thus, it cannot be assumed that it will always be beneficial for an incompetent patient to receive artificial feeding or harmful for him not to receive it. * * *

Under the analysis articulated above, withdrawal or withholding of artificial feeding, like any other medical treatment, would be permissible if there is sufficient proof to satisfy the subjective, limited-objective, or pure-objective test. A competent patient has the right to decline any medical treatment, including artificial feeding, and should retain that right when and if he becomes incompetent. In addition, in the case of an incompetent patient who has given little or no trustworthy indication of an intent to decline treatment and for whom it becomes necessary to engage in balancing under the limited-objective or pure-objective test, the pain and invasiveness of an artificial feeding device, and the pain of withdrawing that device, should be treated just like the results of administering or withholding any other medical treatment.

486 A.2d 1209, 1235–1237.

See also, In re Jobes, 108 N.J. 394, 529 A.2d 434 (1987); In re Peter, 108 N.J. 365, 529 A.2d 419 (1987); Gray v. Romeo, 697 F.Supp. 580 (D.R.I.1988) ("Although an emotional symbolism attaches itself to artificial feeding, there is no legal difference between a mechanical device that allows a person to breathe artificially and a mechanical device that allows a person nourishment. If a person has right to decline a respirator, then a person has the equal right to decline a gastrostomy tube."); Brophy v. New England Sinai Hospital, Inc., 398 Mass. 417, 497 N.E.2d 626 (1986); Corbett v. D'Alessandro, 487 So.2d 368 (Fla.App.1986) ("we see no reason to differentiate between the multitude of artificial devices that may be available to prolong the moment of death."); Bouvia v. Superior Court, 179 Cal.App.3d 1127, 225 Cal.Rptr. 297 (1986).

In McConnell v. Beverly Enterprises–Connecticut, Inc., 209 Conn. 692, 553 A.2d 596 (1989), the court authorized the withdrawal of feeding by a gastrostomy tube despite a statute that appeared to say that under such circumstances "nutrition and hydration must be provided." The court reasoned that the nutrition and hydration that was implicated in the statute was that provided by "a spoon or a straw," and that feeding by gastrostomy tube was no different than any other mechanical or electronic medical intervention.

Medical sources have also recognized the irrelevancy of distinguishing between nutrition and hydration and other forms of medical treatment. The Council on Ethical and Judicial Affairs of the American Medical Association has determined that "[l]ife-prolonging medical treatment includes medication and artificially or technologically supplied respiration, nutrition or hydration." Current Opinions 13, Opinion 2.20 (1989).

For the best medical account of this issue see Lynn and Glover, Ethical Decision–Making in Enteral Nutrition in Rombeau and Coldwell (eds.), Enteral and Tube Feeding (2d ed. 1990) (including a chart of all tube-feeding cases). See also Steinbrook and Lo, Artificial Feeding—Solid Ground, Not a Slippery Slope, 318 N.Eng.J.Med. 286 (1988) (describing "the emerging consensus" that "artificial feeding can be viewed on a level with other medical interventions—cardiopulmonary resuscitation, mechanical ventilation, dialysis, antibiotic therapy.") For a Catholic analysis of this emerging consensus, see O'Rourke, The A.M.A. Statement on Tube Feeding: An Ethical Analysis, America 321 (Nov. 22, 1986). See also Ruark, Raffin, and The Stanford University Medical Center Committee on Ethics, Initiating and Withdrawing Life–Support, Principles and Practice in Adult Medicine, 318 N.Eng.J.Med. 25 (1988).

The Missouri Supreme Court in *Cruzan* is the only state supreme court to unambiguously adopt the vitalist position that nutrition and hydration cannot be removed under virtually any circumstance. The position of the Washington Supreme Court is ambiguous on this issue, however. In a 5–4 decision, that court refused to treat nutrition and hydration as different from any other form of medical treatment in dicta in In re Guardianship of Grant, 109 Wash.2d 545, 747 P.2d 445 (1987), which involved a patient who was not yet in need of such treatment:

> * * * The prolongation of the existence of this vegetative state for possibly years to come by artificially placing liquids and nutrients into this body to the emotional and economic destruction of the survivors is

a monstrous assault to the family concerned that we will not countenance.

We hold that the right of a terminally ill patient to have life sustaining procedures withheld includes the right to withhold nasogastric tubes, intravenous feeding, and other artificial means of nutrition and hydration. * * *

747 P.2d at 455.

A vigorous dissent by Justice Andersen, depending on Siegler and Weisbard, Against the Emerging Stream: Should Fluids and Nutritional Support Be Discontinued?, 145 Archives of Internal Med. 129 (1985), would have left it to the legislature to determine whether the court could ever authorize the withdrawal of nutrition and hydration. Seven months after the opinion was rendered, the court published a "Revision of the Listing of Concurring Justices" and ordered that the name of one of the concurring Justices be removed from the majority opinion and be "appended at the end of the opinion authored by Andersen, J." 757 P.2d 534 (1988). No other explanation was provided by the court, although this "listing" revision appears to change the balance of the court on the issue of withholding nutrition and hydration.

In 1990, at least, a majority of the Supreme Court (the four dissenters and concurring Justice O'Connor in *Cruzan*) viewed nutrition and hydration as another form of medical care. As Justice O'Connor pointed out, "artificial feeding cannot readily be distinguished from other forms of medical treatment. Whether or not the techniques used to pass food and water into the patient's alimentary tract are termed 'medical treatment,' it is clear they all involve some degree of intrusion and restraint. * * * " She concluded that "the liberty guaranteed by the due process clause must protect, if it protects anything, an individual's deeply personal decision to reject medical treatment, including the artificial delivery of food and water."

In his dissent, Justice Brennan reached the same conclusion, vividly describing the medical processes involved:

The artificial delivery of nutrition and hydration is undoubtedly medical treatment. The technique to which Nancy Cruzan is subject—artificial feeding through a gastrostomy tube—involves a tube implanted surgically into her stomach through incisions in her abdominal wall. It may obstruct the intestinal tract, erode and pierce the stomach wall, or cause leakage of the stomach's contents into the abdominal cavity. [ ] The tube can cause pneumonia from reflux of the stomach's contents into the lung. [ ] Typically, and in this case, commercially prepared formulas are used, rather than fresh food. [ ] The type of formula and method of administration must be experimented with to avoid gastrointestinal problems. [ ] The patient must be monitored daily by medical personnel as to weight, fluid intake and fluid output; blood tests must be done weekly.

Artificial delivery of food and water is regarded as medical treatment by the medical profession and the federal government. * * * The federal government permits the cost of the medical devices and formulas used in enteral feeding to be reimbursed under Medicare. [ ] The formulas are regulated by the Federal Drug Administration as "medical foods," [ ] and the feeding tubes are regulated as medical devices [ ].

110 S.Ct. at 2866–67.

d.   Patients Without Formal Prior Directives—Judicial Process and the Burden of Proof

There is a near consensus that where a patient has not left a formal prior directive, the goal of medicine should be to do what that patient, if competent, would want done.   When, if ever, is it necessary for a court to be involved in making that decision—and when should the decision be left to the family, health care providers, or others?   If the court is involved, what procedures should it employ?   The procedural issues which have caused the greatest difficulty for state courts are the nature of evidence that would be relevant in determining a patient's wishes and the burden of proof to be applied to decisions to authorize the removal of life-sustaining treatment.   As you read the next case, which formally addresses these issues, ask what kind of evidence would be (1) relevant and (2) sufficient for each of the judges of the New York Court of Appeals.

IN RE WESTCHESTER COUNTY MEDICAL CENTER (O'CONNOR)

Court of Appeals of New York, 1988.
72 N.Y.2d 517, 534 N.Y.S.2d 886, 531 N.E.2d 607.

WACHTLER, CHIEF JUDGE.

Mary O'Connor is an elderly hospital patient who, as a result of several strokes, is mentally incompetent and unable to obtain food or drink without medical assistance.   In this dispute between her daughters and the hospital the question is whether the hospital should be permitted to insert a nasogastric tube to provide her with sustenance or whether, instead, such medical intervention should be precluded and she should be allowed to die because, prior to becoming incompetent, she made several statements to the effect that she did not want to be a burden to anyone and would not want to live or be kept alive by artificial means if she were unable to care for herself.

The hospital has applied for court authorization to insert the nasogastric tube.   The patient's daughters object claiming that it is contrary to her "expressed wishes", although they conceded at the hearing that they do not know whether their mother would want to decline this procedure under these circumstances, particularly if it would produce a painful death.   The trial court denied the hospital's application, concluding that it was contrary to the patient's wishes. The Appellate Division affirmed.   * * *

We have concluded that the order of the Appellate Division should be reversed and the hospital's petition granted. On this record there is not clear and convincing proof that the patient had made a firm and settled commitment, while competent, to decline this type of medical assistance under circumstances such as these.

I.

* * *

The treating physician, Dr. Sivak, testified that Mrs. O'Connor was suffering from multiinfarct dementia as a result of [several] strokes. This condition substantially impaired her cognitive ability but she was not in a coma or vegetative state. She was conscious, and capable of responding to simple questions or requests sometimes by squeezing the questioner's hand and sometimes verbally. She was also able to respond to noxious stimuli, such as a needle prick, and in fact was sensitive to "even minimal discomfort," although she was not experiencing pain in her present condition. When asked how she felt she usually responded "fine," "all right" or "ok." The treating physician also testified that her mental awareness had improved at the hospital and that she might become more alert in the future. * * *

The doctor stated that Mrs. O'Connor was presently receiving nourishment exclusively through intravenous feeding. * * * He testified that intravenous feeding is used as a temporary measure which generally must be discontinued within several weeks. He noted that these difficulties could be overcome with a gastric tube connected to the patient's digestive tract through her nose or abdomen. * * * If the procedure were not employed and the intravenous methods could no longer be used or were otherwise discontinued, she would die of thirst and starvation within 7 to 10 days. The doctor stated that death from starvation and especially thirst, was a painful way to die and that Mrs. O'Connor would, therefore, experience extreme, intense discomfort since she is conscious, alert, capable of feeling pain, and sensitive to even mild discomfort.

The respondents' expert * * * agreed essentially with Dr. Sivak's evaluation and prognosis. In his opinion, however, Mrs. O'Connor would not experience pain if permitted to die of thirst and starvation. * * *

* * *

Neither of the doctors had known Mrs. O'Connor before she became incompetent and thus knew nothing of her attitudes toward the use of life-sustaining measures. The respondents' first witness on this point was * * * a former co-worker and longtime friend of Mrs. O'Connor. * * * He testified that his first discussion with Mrs. O'Connor concerning artificial means of prolonging life occurred about 1969. At that time his father, who was dying of cancer, informed him that he would not want to continue life by any artificial method if he had lost his dignity because he could no longer control his normal bodily functions.

The witness said that when he told Mrs. O'Connor of this she agreed wholeheartedly and said: "I would never want to be a burden on anyone and I would never want to lose my dignity before I passed away." He noted that she was a "very religious woman" who "felt that nature should take its course and not use further artificial means." They had similar conversations on two or three occasions between 1969 and 1973. During these discussions Mrs. O'Connor variously stated that it is "monstrous" to keep someone alive by using "machinery, things like that" when they are "not going to get better"; that she would never want to be in the same situation as her husband * * * and that people who are "suffering very badly" should be allowed to die.

Mrs. O'Connor's daughter Helen testified that her mother informed her on several occasions that if she became ill and was unable to care for herself she would not want her life to be sustained artificially. * * * Mrs. O'Connor's other daughter, Joan, essentially adopted her sister's testimony. She described her mother's statements on this subject as less solemn pronouncements: "it was brought up when we were together, at times when in conversations you start something, you know, maybe the news was on and maybe that was the topic that was brought up and that's how it came about."

However, all three of these witnesses also agreed that Mrs. O'Connor had never discussed providing food or water with medical assistance, nor had she ever said that she would adhere to her view and decline medical treatment "by artificial means" if that would produce a painful death. When Helen was asked what choice her mother would make under those circumstances she admitted that she did not know. Her sister Joan agreed, noting that this had never been discussed, "unfortunately, no."

* * *

II.

It has long been the common-law rule in this State that a person has the right to decline medical treatment, even life-saving treatment, absent an overriding State interest [　]. In 1981, we held, in two companion cases, that a hospital or medical facility must respect this right even when a patient becomes incompetent, if while competent, the patient stated that he or she did not want certain procedures to be employed under specified circumstances. [*Eichner*]

* * * *Eichner* had been competent and capable of expressing his will before he was silenced by illness. In those circumstances, we concluded that it would be appropriate for the court to intervene and direct the termination of artificial life supports, in accordance with the patient's wishes, because it was established by "clear and convincing evidence" that the patient would have so directed if he were competent and able to communicate. We selected the "clear and convincing evidence" standard in *Eichner* because it " 'impress[es] the factfinder with the importance of the decision' * * * and it 'forbids relief whenever the evidence is loose, equivocal or contradictory' " [　] Nothing less

than unequivocal proof will suffice when the decision to terminate life supports is at issue.

* * *

* * * The number and variety of situations in which the problem of terminating artificial life supports arises preclude any attempt to anticipate all of the possible permutations. However, this case, as well as our prior decisions, suggest some basic principles which may be used in determining whether the proof "clearly and convincingly" evinces an intention by the patient to reject life prolonged artificially by medical means.

III.

* * *

Every person has a right to life, and no one should be denied essential medical care unless the evidence clearly and convincingly shows that the patient intended to decline the treatment under some particular circumstances. This is a demanding standard, the most rigorous burden of proof in civil cases. It is appropriate here because if an error occurs it should be made on the side of life.

Viewed in that light, the "clear and convincing" evidence standard requires proof sufficient to persuade the trier of fact that the patient held a firm and settled commitment to the termination of life supports under the circumstances like those presented. As a threshold matter, the trier of fact must be convinced, as far as is humanly possible, that the strength of the individual's beliefs and the durability of the individual's commitment to those beliefs [ ] makes a recent change of heart unlikely. The persistence of the individual's statements, the seriousness with which those statements were made and the inferences, if any, that may be drawn from the surrounding circumstances are among the factors which should be considered.

The ideal situation is one in which the patient's wishes were expressed in some form of a writing, perhaps a "living will," while he or she was still competent. The existence of a writing suggests the author's seriousness of purpose and ensures that the court is not being asked to make a life-or-death decision based upon casual remarks. Further, a person who has troubled to set forth his or her wishes in a writing is more likely than one who has not to make sure that any subsequent changes of heart are adequately expressed, either in a new writing or through clear statements to relatives and friends. In contrast, a person whose expressions of intention were limited to oral statements may not as fully appreciate the need to "rescind" those statements after a change of heart.

Of course, a requirement of a written expression in every case would be unrealistic. Further, it would unfairly penalize those who lack the skills to place their feelings in writing. For that reason, we must always remain open to applications such as this, which are based upon the repeated oral expressions of the patient. In this case, however, the application must ultimately fail, because it does not meet the foregoing criteria.

Although Mrs. O'Connor's statements about her desire to decline life-saving treatments were repeated over a number of years, there is nothing, other than speculation, to persuade the fact finder that her expressions were more than immediate reactions to the unsettling experience of seeing or hearing of another's unnecessarily prolonged death. * * * If such statements were routinely held to be clear and convincing proof of a general intent to decline all medical treatment once incompetency sets in, few nursing home patients would ever receive life-sustaining medical treatment in the future. * * *

* * *

In sum, on this record it cannot be said that Mrs. O'Connor elected to die under circumstances such as these. Even her daughters, who undoubtedly know her wishes better than anyone, are earnestly trying to carry them out, and whose motives we believe to be of the highest and most loving kind, candidly admit that they do not know what she would do, or what she would want done under these circumstances.

* * *

HANCOCK, JUDGE (concurring).

* * *

[T]here are, I believe, several reasons why the present New York rule—requiring a factual finding of the patient's actual intent and precluding the exercise of judgment, in her best interests and on her behalf, by her physician and family, a court or guardian—is unrealistic, often unfair or inhumane and, if applied literally, totally unworkable.

The rule posits, as the only basis for judicial relief, the court's finding by clear and convincing proof of a fact which is inherently unknowable: what the incompetent patient would actually have intended at the time of the impending life-support decision. What is required here is not a finding of intent as the term is used in its fictional sense as, for example, to express the legal conclusion of what the Legislature intended when it enacted a statute or what parties intended when they signed a contract. What the rule literally demands is an impossibility: a factual determination of the incompetent patient's actual desire at the time of the decision [   ].

* * *

SIMONS, JUDGE (dissenting).

Respondents have established that Mary O'Connor did not wish any "artificial or mechanical support systems" used to sustain her life; if she were unable to function on her own, she wanted "nature to take its course." That being so, and inasmuch as no countervailing State interest has been asserted, she is entitled to have the court respect and implement her choice. The majority refuses to do so because it holds her statements were too indefinite. Its holding substantially rewrites the law of self-determination, at least for cases such as this, and has for all practical purposes foreclosed any realistic possibility that a patient, once rendered incompetent, will have his or her wishes to forego life-sustaining treatment enforced.   * * *

I

Courts have resolved the question of when medical treatment of the gravely ill may be terminated by using two legal theories. The first is based on the common-law right of self-determination, which gives an individual essentially unrestricted authority to limit others' contact with his or her body. [ ] This fundamental right, similar to other privacy rights recognized at common law and by the Constitution, guarantees individuals the freedom to behave as they deem fit so long as their wishes do not conflict with the precepts of society. It encompasses a patient's freedom to refuse medical treatment even when such refusal is life threatening [   ], and it particularly includes the right of a dying patient to refuse medical care or treatment that cannot restore health. [ ] Before a patient's right of self-determination can be enforced, however, his or her wishes must be ascertained. If the patient is incompetent and cannot presently express those wishes, they will be enforced if established by clear and convincing evidence. The right to reject treatment is not absolute but, absent some overriding State interest, the courts are bound to recognize and enforce it. The test for granting relief is entirely subjective: what does the patient desire done. The court's role is limited to ensuring that effectuating the patient's wishes does not violate the State's interest; it may not intrude into this area of personal autonomy and impose its paternalistic view of the patient's best interests (see, Matter of Storar, supra).

The second theory is the substituted judgment approach. Although courts apply this theory differently, generally the obligation of the court when implementing substituted judgment is to ensure that a surrogate of the patient, usually a family member or a guardian, effectuates as nearly as possible the decision the incompetent would make if he or she were able to state it [   ]. The subjective views of the patient remain important, but the absence of a clearly expressed intent is not determinative; objective factors are also considered in deciding what is best for the patient in the circumstances presented. Thus, the surrogate's decision should take into account the patient's personal values and religious beliefs, prior statements on the subject, attitudes about the impact his or her condition will have on others, and any other factors bearing on the issue. Inasmuch as the patient's wishes cannot be known with certainty, objective factors indicating that the burdens of continued life outweigh the benefits of that life for the patient are significant.

Both these theories were presented to us in Matter of Storar and its companion case, Matter of Eichner. [   ] Matter of Eichner involved Brother Fox, a member of a religious order, who, having expressed his views on the situation of Karen Quinlan, [   ] subsequently suffered from precisely the same condition.   * * *

* * *

* * * Mary O'Connor clearly expressed her wishes in the only realistic way she could and, inasmuch as none of the litigants claims the State has any interest in prolonging her life, her wishes should be recognized and the order of the Appellate Division should be affirmed. The order will not be affirmed, however, because the majority, by its decision today, narrowly restricts the only available avenue of relief. Mary O'Connor's wishes will not be recognized because her daughters cannot prove she anticipated her present condition and specifically stated that under such circumstances she chose to die rather than be nourished by artificial means.   The court has confined the *Eichner* holding to the singular facts of that case and inasmuch as few persons will be able to satisfy the new test, the right of self-determination is reduced to a hollow promise.

* * *

IV

The majority refuses to recognize Mrs. O'Connor's expressed wishes because they were not solemn pronouncements made after reflection and because they were too indefinite.

Respondents have established the reliability of the statements under any standard.   * * * These were not "casual remarks," but rather expressions evidencing the long-held beliefs of a mature woman who had been exposed to sickness and death in her employment and her personal life.   Mrs. O'Connor had spent 20 years working in the emergency room and pathology laboratory of Jacobi Hospital, confronting the problems of life and death daily.   She suffered through long illnesses of her husband, stepmother, father and two brothers who had died before her.   She herself has been hospitalized for congestive heart failure and she understood the consequences of serious illnesses.

Because of these experiences, Mrs. O'Connor expressed her wishes in conversations with her daughters, both trained nurses, and a coemployee from the hospital who shared her hospital experience.   There can be no doubt she was aware of the gravity of the problem she was addressing and the significance of her statements, or that those hearing her understood her intentions.   She clearly stated the values important to her, a life that does not burden others and its termination with dignity, and what she believed her best interests required in the case of severe, debilitating illness.   * * *

Notwithstanding this, the majority finds the statements entitled to little weight because Mrs. O'Connor's exposure was mostly to terminally ill cancer patients, or because her desire to remain independent and avoid burdening her children constituted little more than statements of self-pity by an elderly woman.   There is no evidence to support those inferences and no justification for trivializing Mrs. O'Connor's state-

ments. She is entitled to have them accepted without reservation.
* * *

* * *

V

* * *

The [majority's] rule is unworkable because it requires humans to exercise foresight they do not possess. It requires that before life-sustaining treatment may be withdrawn, there must be proof that the patient anticipated his or her present condition, the means available to sustain life under the circumstances, and then decided that the alternative of death without mechanical assistance, by starvation in this case, is preferable to continued life [   ]. The majority states that Mrs. O'Connor's instructions are rejected because the "infirmities she was concerned with and the procedures she eschewed are qualitatively different than those now presented." The implication is that courts may exercise some flexibility in applying these rigorous standards if the condition and treatment referred to in the patient's instructions and those that presently exist are qualitatively similar. If that is so, the majority's statement fails to include any test for determining when conditions and procedures are "qualitatively" the same or different. Is physical and mental incapacity caused by accident qualitatively similar to the same condition caused by illness? Is incapacity caused by cancer qualitatively similar to the same condition caused by cerebral accident? Judging from the distinction the majority has drawn between Mary O'Connor's prior experience with cancer patients and her present condition, one would guess its answer would be "no." As to support systems, is feeding by nasogastric tube qualitatively different from the surgical implantation of a feeding tube in the patient's stomach or intestine? The two options involve different procedures and present different risks. Inasmuch as it is now no longer sufficient to provide that "all" life-support systems be withdrawn, the patient must anticipate these distinctions and resolve them. If he or she fails to do so, the instructions will not be recognized.

* * *

Even if a patient possessed the remarkable foresight to anticipate some future illness or condition, however, it is unrealistic to expect or require a lay person to be familiar with the support systems available for treatment—to say nothing of requiring a determination of which is preferable or the consequences that may result from using or foregoing them. Indeed, the conditions and consequences may change from day to day. * * *

In short, Mary O'Connor expressed her wishes in the only terms familiar to her, and she expressed them as clearly as a lay person should be asked to express them. To require more is unrealistic, and for all practical purposes, it precludes the right of patients to forego life-sustaining treatment.

The rule adopted is not only unworkable, it is unwise. Given the disparity of knowledge between lay persons and doctors, medical personnel will undoubtedly be reluctant to honor a patient's instructions if they are unclear or less than complete. Inevitably, the courts will be required to intervene, not because the State has any interest in prolonging the life of the particular patient, but because the family and the doctors are uncertain that the patient's wishes meet the majority's strict standard and are justifiably concerned about the consequences of an erroneous decision. The majority holds that the instructions must be specific, solemn pronouncements, but they need not be precise. Surely, no doctor is prepared to implement that ambiguous legal direction without judicial assistance. The patient's statements will have to be construed like statutes or contract terms—and the courts necessarily must be the ones to construe them, to make the findings and draw the inferences interpreting the patient's statements, using the imprecise considerations set forth in the majority opinion—to determine if the strict, "demanding" standard of the majority has been met. Decisions under such circumstances will necessarily reflect the value choices of the Judge, rather than those of the patient, and are nothing short of arbitrary intrusions into the personal life of the patient.

* * *

Notes and Questions

1. Of course, the propriety of the "clear and convincing evidence" standard applied by the Missouri Supreme Court in the *Cruzan* case was the primary issue before the United States Supreme Court in that case. The Court concluded that "a state may apply a clear and convincing evidence standard in proceedings where a guardian seeks to discontinue nutrition and hydration of a person diagnosed to be in a persistent vegetative state." This holding, which, the Chief Justice assures us, describes only the outer limit of what the Constitution permits, is supported by a lengthy description of civil cases in which the "clear and convincing evidence" standard is applied. See *Cruzan*, supra at 1061. In his dissent, which cites Judge Simons's dissenting opinion in *O'Connor*, Justice Brennan discusses the New York law developed in the *O'Connor* case:

> New York is the only state besides Missouri to deny a request to terminate life support on the ground that clear and convincing evidence of prior, expressed intent was absent, although New York did so in the context of very different situations. Mrs. O'Connor, the subject of *In re O'Connor*, had several times expressed her desire not to be placed on life support if she were not going to be able to care for herself. However, both of her daughters testified that they did not know whether their mother would want to decline artificial nutrition and hydration under her present circumstances. Moreover, despite damage from several strokes, Mrs. O'Connor was conscious and capable of responding to simple questions and requests and the medical testimony suggested she might improve to some extent. [ ]

110 S.Ct. 2841, 2875, n. 22. In fact, most states have adopted a "clear and convincing evidence" standard in "right to die" cases, although what that evidentiary standard means varies from state to state—and, as the *O'Connor* case suggests, from judge to judge within a state. See, e.g., McConnell v. Beverly Enterprises–Connecticut, Inc., 209 Conn. 692, 553 A.2d 596 (1989); In re Conroy, 98 N.J. 321, 486 A.2d 1209 (1985); In re Jobes, 108 N.J. 394, 529 A.2d 434 (1987) (In New Jersey "evidence is 'clear and convincing' when it produce[s] in the mind of the trier of fact a firm belief or conviction as to the truth of the allegations sought to be established, evidence so clear, direct and weighty and convincing as to enable [the fact finder] to come to a clear conviction, without hesitancy, of the truth of the precise facts at issue.") While disputed evidence may still be "clear and convincing," it is also true that uncontroverted evidence may not rise to that level. In re Jobes, 529 A.2d at 441, citing In re Colyer, 99 Wash.2d 114, 143–45, 660 P.2d 738, 754–55 (1983) (Dore, J. dissenting).

The choice of the appropriate burden of proof is not always between "clear and convincing evidence" and the normal civil "preponderance" standard. In *Eichner,* in which this issue was first raised before the New York Court of Appeals, the district attorney seeking the continuation of treatment for Brother Fox argued that "proof beyond a reasonable doubt" was the appropriate burden. The Court of Appeals explained why it chose "clear and convincing evidence":

> The Supreme Court and the Appellate Division found that the evidence on [Brother Fox's decision] as well as proof of the patient's subsequent incompetency and chances of recovery was "clear and convincing." We agree that this is the appropriate burden of proof and that the evidence in the record satisfies this standard.

> Although this is a civil case in which a preponderance of the evidence is generally deemed sufficient, the District Attorney urges that the highest burden of proof beyond a reasonable doubt should be required when granting the relief may result in the patient's death. But that burden, traditionally reserved for criminal cases where involuntary loss of liberty and possible stigmatization are at issue [ ] is inappropriate in cases where the purpose of granting the relief is to give effect to an individual's right by carrying out his stated intentions. However, we agree with the courts below that the highest standard applicable to civil cases should be required. There is more involved here than a typical dispute between private litigants over a sum of money. Where particularly important personal interests are at stake, clear and convincing evidence should be required [ ]. It is constitutionally required in cases of involuntary civil commitments and we have recognized the need for the higher standard in exceptional civil matters [ ]. Clear and convincing proof should also be required in cases where it is claimed that a person, now incompetent, left instructions to terminate life sustaining procedures when there is no hope of recovery. This standard serves to "impress the factfinder with the importance of the decision" [ ] and it " 'forbids relief whenever the evidence is loose, equivocal or contradictory' "

In re Eichner, 420 N.E.2d at 72.

2.   The question of what burden of proof is appropriate is different from the issue of what kinds of evidence ought to be admissible to meet the burden.   While most courts agree on the appropriate burden of proof in these cases, there is little agreement about the admissibility or weight to be given to different kinds of potential evidence.   How should the court consider previous statements of a currently incompetent patient?   Should it make any difference that the statements were in writing?   To relatives?   In response to news events (like the *Quinlan* case—or, one expects, the *Cruzan* case)?   In response to a family emergency or a death in the family?   Would your prior statements about this issue be considered serious or off-hand by a court if tomorrow you were in a persistent vegetative state?   Obviously, the characterization a court puts upon the nature of the evidence will determine the weight it is to be accorded.   That, in turn, is likely to determine whether a petitioner can meet the generally accepted "clear and convincing evidence" standard.

3.   Because it is almost impossible to predict exactly what kinds of medical care one might need and what kind of medical condition one will suffer, some courts and scholars have suggested that the most helpful kind of advance directive would be one that deals generally with the medical interests and values of the patient.   One form of such an advance directive would have patients anticipate the nature and extent of intervention they would want in a host of clearly described alternative medical scenarios.   See Emmanuel and Emmanuel, The Medical Directive: A New Comprehensive Advance Care Document, 261 J.A.M.A. 3288 (1989).   Another possibility would be to encourage every competent person to articulate values that are likely to be significant in subsequent decisionmaking.

Perhaps the best device for encouraging such discussion (and for recording the results) is the "Values History Form," which asks prospective patients about their general values, their medical values, their relationships with family members, friends, and health care providers, their wishes in particular cases and a host of other issues likely to become relevant if they become incompetent and health care decisions must be made on their behalf.   While such a values history has no formal legal significance, and while some may be put off by such questions as "What makes you laugh?" and "What makes you cry?", there is no doubt that the existence of such a document would be of great value to a substitute decisionmaker, and to any court called upon to confirm that substitute's decision.   See Gibson, Reflecting on Values, 51 Ohio St.L.J. 451 (1990).

4.   Whether the courts have any role at all in these matters has been the subject of some debate.   On the one hand, there is a fear that the absence of judicial oversight will lead to arbitrary decisions and, thus, arbitrary deaths.   On the other hand, any attempt to bring all of these cases to the courts would yield an intolerable caseload and delay the deaths of many patients who desperately seek that relief.   The Massachusetts Supreme Judicial Court changed its view of the necessity of judicial confirmation of a guardian's decision that a patient should forgo life-sustaining treatment.   See In re Spring, 380 Mass. 629, 405 N.E.2d 115 (1980) (no review required in most circumstances; reversing prior position).   Should judicial review of all decisions to terminate life-sustaining treatment be required?   Should such judicial review be required in some cases?

In cases in which there is no written advance directive? In which there is no agreement among family members? In which there is an ambiguity in the previous statements of the patient? Is there any way to adequately categorize those cases in which judicial review ought to be required?

5. When resort to a court is required, what procedure ought to be employed by the court? Should the court's involvement be limited to the appointment of a decisionmaker, should the court make the decision itself, or should the court review every decision (or some decisions) made by an appointed decisionmaker? Should the action be a special statutory action, an injunction action, a guardianship, or does the form of the action really make much difference? Should the court always appoint a guardian *ad litem* for the patient? If so, is the role of the guardian *ad litem* to represent what that person believes the patient would want, or what that person believes is in the best interest of the patient? Alternatively, should the guardian *ad litem* always oppose the petitioner (who is usually seeking the termination of the treatment)? Every state has a nursing home ombudsman. Should the ombudsman be notified whenever discontinuation of treatment of a nursing home patient is requested? Should the ombudsman participate in every such case? See In re Conroy, 486 A.2d at 1237–1242.

In In re Guardianship of Hamlin, 102 Wash.2d 810, 689 P.2d 1372 (1984), the Washington Supreme Court announced two entirely separate processes—one to be followed where there is "total agreement among the patient's family, treating physicians and prognosis committee as to the course of medical treatment," and one to be followed where there is "an incompetent with no known family, who has never made his wishes known." No judicial process and no formal guardianship is required in the first case where "the incompetent patient is in (1) a persistent vegetative state with no reasonable chance of recovery and (2) the patient's life is being maintained by life support systems." In the second situation a guardian must be appointed by the court, but that guardian need not have judicial confirmation for any particular decision "if the treating physicians and prognosis committee are unanimous that life-sustaining efforts should be withheld or withdrawn and the guardian concurs." Of course, most cases fall between the two extremes discussed in *Hamlin*. The current state of the Washington law on this and all "right to die" issues has been muddled by In re Guardianship of Grant, 109 Wash.2d 545, 747 P.2d 445 (1987), corrected 757 P.2d 534 (1988).

6. If there is to be a judicial process, should it be an adversary process? While the Chief Justice appears to think that the adversary process is helpful in these cases, *Cruzan*, 110 S.Ct. 2841, 2853 n. 9, that part of the opinion gave Justice Stevens pause:

> The Court recognizes that "the state has been involved as an adversary from the beginning" in this case only because Nancy Cruzan "was a patient at a state hospital when this litigation commenced." * * * It seems to me, however, that the Court draws precisely the wrong conclusion from this insight. The Court apparently believes that the absence of the state from the litigation would have created a problem, because agreement among the family and the independent guardian *ad*

litem as to Nancy Cruzan's best interests might have prevented her treatment from becoming the focus of a "truly adversarial" proceeding. [ ] It may reasonably be debated whether some judicial process should be required before life-sustaining treatment is discontinued; this issue has divided the state courts. Compare *In re Estate of Longeway,* [ ] (requiring judicial approval of guardian's decision) with *In re Hamlin* [ ] (discussing circumstances in which judicial approval is unnecessary). * * * I tend, however, to agree * * * that the intervention of the state in these proceedings as an *adversary* is not so much a cure as it is part of the disease.

Cruzan 110 S.Ct. 2841, 2884, n. 13 (Stevens, J., dissenting). A decade before the Florida Supreme Court expressed the same reservations: "because the issue with its ramifications is fraught with complexity and encompasses the interests of the law, both civil and criminal, medical ethics and social morality, it is not one which is well suited for a solution in an adversary judicial proceeding." Satz v. Perlmutter, 379 So.2d 359, 360 (Fla.1980). Are the "advantages" of an adversary proceeding truly advantageous in these agonizing cases?

7. Several courts (including the Florida Supreme Court in *Satz*) have suggested that the issue is more for the legislature than for the judiciary. Is the legislature any better equipped than the courts to address questions surrounding the termination of life support systems?

8. "Right to die" cases brought to vindicate the federal privacy rights of patients against state entities (like state hospitals) may be based on 42 U.S.C.A. § 1983. When one successfully raises a federal civil rights claim under that statute, the prevailing party is entitled to attorney's fees under 42 U.S.C.A. § 1988. In Gray v. Romeo, 697 F.Supp. 580 (D.R.I.1988), the successful attorney was awarded $38,495.95. Gray v. Romeo, Order of March 8, 1989. Will the *Cruzan* case drive "right to die" cases into the federal courts or keep them in the state courts?

Bibliographical Note: Terminating Treatment for Incompetent or Arguably Incompetent Patients

In addition to those discussed and cited here, several other cases have considered when it would be appropriate to discontinue treatment for patients who are arguably incompetent. For example, see Matter of Hier, 18 Mass.App.Ct. 200, 464 N.E.2d 959 (1984) (patient refuses to have gastric feeding tube replaced); Severns v. Wilmington Medical Center, Inc., 421 A.2d 1334 (Del.1980); Matter of Conservatorship of Torres, 357 N.W.2d 332 (Minn.1984); Foody v. Manchester Memorial Hospital, 40 Conn.Sup. 127, 482 A.2d 713 (1984); In re P.V.W., 424 So.2d 1015 (La.1982).

There has been a flood of academic writing dealing with these issues, and much of it is excellent. Among the best articles are Rhoden, Litigating Life and Death, 102 Harv.L.Rev. 375 (1988); Dresser, Relitigating Life and Death, 51 Ohio St.L.J. 425 (1990) (a brief response to Rhoden); Weinberg, Whose Right Is It Anyway? Individualism, Community and the Right to Die: A Commentary on the New Jersey Experience, 40 Hastings L.J. 119 (1988); Mayo, Constitutionalizing the "Right to Die", 49 Md.L.Rev. 103 (1990); Moore, Two Steps Forward, One Step Back: An Analysis of New

Jersey's Latest Right–To–Die Decisions, 19 Rutgers L.J. 955 (1988); New-man, Treatment Refusals for the Critically and Terminally Ill: Proposed Rules for the Family, the Physician and the State, 3 N.Y.L. School J. Human Rights 35 (1985); Merritt, Equality for the Elderly Incompetent: A Proposal for Dignified Death, 39 Stan.L.Rev. 689 (1987); Comment, The Role of the Family in Medical Decisionmaking for Incompetent Adult Patients: A Historical Perspective in Case Analysis, 48 U.Pitt.L.Rev. 539 (1987).

2. *Patients Without Former Competence*

Where the patient has never been competent—where the patient had been severely retarded from birth, for example—the courts have still made an attempt to determine what the patient's choice would be. Of course, it is exceptionally difficult to imagine what an incompetent person, who had never been competent, would want to do if that person were suddenly competent. Compare the next two cases, one of which confirms the principle of substituted judgment and one of which aban-dons that approach to apply the principle of beneficence and seeks to do what is in the best interest of such a patient. *Superintendent of Belchertown State School v. Saikewicz,* involved a 67–year–old pro-foundly retarded adult suffering from leukemia. The court addressed the question of whether the chemotherapy that would be likely to be provided to others in his condition should be withheld. *Matter of Storar,* the companion case to *Matter of Eichner,* concerned a profound-ly retarded 52–year–old cancer patient and the propriety of blood transfusions.

SUPERINTENDENT OF BELCHERTOWN STATE SCHOOL v. SAIKEWICZ

Supreme Judicial Court of Massachusetts, 1977.
373 Mass. 728, 370 N.E.2d 417.

LIACOS, JUSTICE.

* * *

The question what legal standards govern the decision whether to administer potentially life-prolonging treatment to an incompetent person encompasses two distinct and important subissues. First, does a choice exist? That is, is it the unvarying responsibility of the State to order medical treatment in all circumstances involving the care of an incompetent person? Second, if a choice does exist under certain conditions, what considerations enter into the decision-making process?

We think that principles of equality and respect for all individuals require the conclusion that a choice exists * * *. We recognize a general right in all persons to refuse medical treatment in appropriate circumstances. The recognition of that right must extend to the case of an incompetent, as well as a competent, patient because the value of human dignity extends to both.

This is not to deny that the State has a traditional power and responsibility, under the doctrine of *parens patriae,* to care for and protect the *"best interests"* of the incompetent person.

The "best interests" of an incompetent person are not necessarily served by imposing on such persons results not mandated as to competent persons similarly situated. It does not advance the interest of the State or the ward to treat the ward as a person of lesser status or dignity than others. To protect the incompetent person within its power, the State must recognize the dignity and worth of such a person and afford to that person the same panoply of rights and choices it recognizes in competent persons. If a competent person faced with death may choose to decline treatment which not only will not cure the person but which substantially may increase suffering in exchange for a possible yet brief prolongation of life, then it cannot be said that it is always in the "best interests" of the ward to require submission to such treatment. Nor do statistical factors indicating that a majority of competent persons similarly situated choose treatment resolve the issue. The significant decisions of life are more complex than statistical determinations. Individual choice is determined not by the vote of the majority but by the complexities of the singular situation viewed from the unique perspective of the person called on to make the decision. To presume that the incompetent person must always be subjected to what many rational and intelligent persons may decline is to downgrade the status of the incompetent person by placing a lesser value on his intrinsic human worth and vitality.

* * * This leads us to the question of how the right of an incompetent person to decline treatment might best be exercised so as to give the fullest possible expression to the character and circumstances of that individual.

* * *

To put the above discussion in proper perspective, we realize that an inquiry into what a majority of people would do in circumstances that truly were similar assumes an objective viewpoint not far removed from a "reasonable person" inquiry. While we recognize the value of this kind of indirect evidence, we should make it plain that the primary test is subjective in nature—that is, the goal is to determine with as much accuracy as possible the wants and needs of the individual involved. This may or may not conform to what is thought wise or prudent by most people. The problems of arriving at an accurate substituted judgment in matters of life and death vary greatly in degree, if not in kind, in different circumstances. * * * Joseph Saikewicz was profoundly retarded and noncommunicative his entire life, which was spent largely in the highly restrictive atmosphere of an institution. While it may thus be necessary to rely to a greater degree on objective criteria, such as the supposed inability of profoundly retarded persons to conceptualize or fear death, the effort to bring the substituted judgment into step with the values and desires of the affected individual must not, and need not, be abandoned.

The "substituted judgment" standard which we have described commends itself simply because of its straightforward respect for the integrity and autonomy of the individual. * * *

* * * [W]e now reiterate the substituted judgment doctrine as we apply it in the instant case. We believe that both the guardian *ad litem* in his recommendation and the judge in his decision should have attempted (as they did) to ascertain the incompetent person's actual interests and preferences. In short, the decision in cases such as this should be that which would be made by the incompetent person, if that person were competent, but taking into account the present and future incompetency of the individual as one of the factors which would necessarily enter into the decision-making process of the competent person. Having recognized the right of a competent person to make for himself the same decision as the court made in this case, the question is, do the facts on the record support the proposition that Saikewicz himself would have [declined treatment]. We believe they do.

* * *

IN RE STORAR

New York Court of Appeals, 1981.
52 N.Y.2d 363, 438 N.Y.S.2d 266, 420 N.E.2d 64.

WACHTLER, JUDGE.

* * *

John Storar was profoundly retarded with a mental age of about 18 months. At the time of this proceeding he was 52 years old and a resident of the Newark Development Center, a State facility, which had been his home since the age of 5. His closest relative was his mother * * *.

In 1979 physicians at the center noticed blood in his urine and asked his mother for permission to conduct diagnostic tests. She * * * gave her consent. The tests, completed in July, 1979, revealed that he had cancer of the bladder. It was recommended that he receive radiation therapy at a hospital in Rochester. When the hospital refused to administer the treatment without the consent of a legal guardian, Mrs. Storar applied to the court and was appointed guardian of her son's person and property in August, 1979. With her consent he received radiation therapy for six weeks after which the disease was found to be in remission.

However in March, 1980, blood was again observed in his urine. The lesions in his bladder were cauterized in an unsuccessful effort to stop the bleeding. At that point his physician diagnosed the cancer as terminal, concluding that after using all medical and surgical means then available, the patient would nevertheless die from the disease.

In May the physicians at the center asked his mother for permission to administer blood transfusions. She initially refused but the following day withdrew her objection. For several weeks John Storar received blood transfusions when needed. However, on June 19 his mother requested that the transfusions be discontinued.

The director of the center then brought this proceeding, pursuant to [ ] the Mental Hygiene Law, seeking authorization to continue the transfusions, claiming that without them "death would occur within weeks." Mrs. Storar cross-petitioned for an order prohibiting the transfusions, and named the District Attorney as a party. The court appointed a guardian ad litem and signed an order temporarily permitting the transfusions to continue, pending the determination of the proceeding.

At the hearing in September the court heard testimony from various witnesses including Mrs. Storar, several employees at the center, and seven medical experts. All the experts concurred that John Storar had irreversible cancer of the bladder, * * * with a very limited life span, generally estimated to be between 3 and 6 months. They also agreed that he had an infant's mentality and was unable to comprehend his predicament or to make a reasoned choice of treatment. In addition, there was no dispute over the fact that he was continuously losing blood.

* * *

It was conceded that John Storar found the transfusions disagreeable. He was also distressed by the blood and blood clots in his urine which apparently increased immediately after a transfusion. He could not comprehend the purpose of the transfusions and on one or two occasions had displayed some initial resistance. To eliminate his apprehension he was given a sedative approximately one hour before a transfusion. He also received regular doses of narcotics to alleviate the pain associated with the disease.

On the other hand several experts testified that there was support in the medical community for the view that, at this stage, transfusions may only prolong suffering and that treatment could properly be limited to administering pain killers. Mrs. Storar testified that she wanted the transfusions discontinued because she only wanted her son to be comfortable. She admitted that no one had ever explained to her what might happen to him if the transfusions were stopped. She also stated that she was not "sure" whether he might die sooner if the blood was not replaced and was unable to determine whether he wanted to live. However, in view of the fact that he obviously disliked the transfusions and tried to avoid them, she believed that he would want them discontinued.

* * *

* * * John Storar was never competent at any time in his life.
* * * Thus it is unrealistic to attempt to determine whether he would

want to continue potentially life prolonging treatment if he were competent. * * * Mentally, John Storar was an infant and that is the only realistic way to assess his rights in this litigation. [ ] Thus this case bears only superficial similarities to *Eichner* and the determination must proceed from different principles.

A parent or guardian has a right to consent to medical treatment on behalf of an infant. [ ] The parent, however, may not deprive a child of life saving treatment, however well intentioned. * * *

In the *Storar* case there is the additional complication of two threats to his life. There was cancer of the bladder which was incurable and would in all probability claim his life. There was also the related loss of blood which posed the risk of an earlier death, but which, at least at the time of the hearing, could be replaced by transfusions. Thus, as one of the experts noted, the transfusions were analogous to food—they would not cure the cancer, but they could eliminate the risk of death from another treatable cause. Of course, John Storar did not like them, as might be expected of one with an infant's mentality. But the evidence convincingly shows that the transfusions did not involve excessive pain and that without them his mental and physical abilities would not be maintained at the usual level. With the transfusions on the other hand, he was essentially the same as he was before except of course he had a fatal illness which would ultimately claim his life. Thus, on the record, we have concluded that the application for permission to continue the transfusions should have been granted. Although we understand and respect his mother's despair, as we respect the beliefs of those who oppose transfusions on religious grounds, a court should not in the circumstances of this case allow an incompetent patient to bleed to death because someone, even someone as close as a parent or sibling, feels that this is best for one with an incurable disease.

* * *

Questions

How would the Supreme Judicial Court of Massachusetts have decided *Storar*? How would the New York Court of Appeals have decided *Saikewicz*? Might there be cases for which the principles of *Storar* and the principles of *Saikewicz* would lead to different results? Which principle is preferable? Why?

V. DO NOT RESUSCITATE ORDERS

There may be some reason to treat cardiopulmonary resuscitation (CPR) differently from the way we treat other forms of life-sustaining therapy. CPR is the only form of life-sustaining treatment that is provided routinely without consent of the patient, and it may be the only medical treatment of any sort that is generally initiated without an order of a physician. Bartholome, "Do Not Resuscitate" orders,

Accepting Responsibility, 148 Arch.Intern.Med. 2345 (1988). CPR generally is provided unless a formal "Do Not Resuscitate" (DNR) order is entered in the patient's chart. Remarkably, even patients in hospitals are infrequently asked to make their own decisions on cardiopulmonary resuscitation. See Younger et al., Do Not Resuscitate Orders, Incidents and Implications in a Medical Intensive Care Unit, 253 J.A.M.A. 5 (1985). For an account of the underlying medical-legal issues in general, see Miller, Do Not Resuscitate Orders: Public Policy and Patient Autonomy, 17 Law, Medicine and Health Care 252 (1989); and Mooney, Deciding Not to Resuscitate Hospital Patients: Medical and Legal Perspectives, 1986 Ill.L.Rev. 1025.

Why don't doctors talk to patients about DNR orders? The medical tradition of not discussing CPR was exacerbated by the mid–1980s fear among physicians that they would be liable for damages if they did not resuscitate whenever it was possible to do so—even when attempts at resuscitation were futile or inconsistent with the desires of the patient. These factors gave rise to "slow codes" or "pencil DNRs" in which the hospital staff was instructed to provide certain patients with resuscitation under circumstances that would guarantee that the resuscitation would fail (by delaying the commencement of the treatment, for example). Sometimes the hospital staff was instructed in a more straightforward way to avoid resuscitation—but the instruction was provided in some form that would leave no record—it was written in the chart in pencil or, in New York, indicated by the placement of a removable purple dot on the patient's file.

The reaction to this transparently dishonest process was the development of formal hospital policies that provided for honest and open decisionmaking on DNR. See, e.g., Committee on Policy for DNR Decisions, Yale–New Haven Hospital, Report on Do Not Resuscitate Decisions, 47 Conn.Med. 478 (1983); Levine and Nolan, Editorial, Do Not Resuscitate Decisions, A Policy, 47 Conn.Med. 511 (1983). These developments were accompanied by a more formal legal analysis of the problems of hospital decisionmaking in this area, and in 1986 the highly respected New York State Task Force on Life and the Law proposed legislation on Do Not Resuscitate orders. A statute similar to that recommended by the task force was adopted in New York in 1987.

The statute is remarkable for its precision, and, some might say, for the bureaucracy it has brought to making one kind of treatment decision. First, the statute sets the default position on DNR orders: "every person admitted to a hospital shall be presumed to consent to the administration of cardiopulmonary resuscitation in the event of cardiac or respiratory arrest, unless there is consent to the issuance of an order not to resuscitate as provided in this article." N.Y.Pub.Health Law § 2962 (Supp.1990). This default position is coupled with the requirement that patients or their surrogates be given appropriate information before they are allowed to choose to forgo resuscitation, and that any appropriately entered order "shall be included in writing in the patient's chart." Id. While the statute permits adults with decisionmaking capacity to consent to the entry of a DNR order either orally or in writing, an oral determination must be made during hospitalization in the presence of two adult witnesses, one of whom must be a doctor affiliated with the hospital. Even the written decision must be made in the presence of two adult witnesses who themselves must sign off on the determination. Id. § 2964. While the statute permits a limited therapeutic privilege, the requirements it establishes discourage decisionmaking without participation of the patient. Id.

If a patient does not have the capacity to consent to a DNR order, a surrogate may do so under some circumstances. The process for determining capacity is included in the statute. Id. § 2963. It is notable that the statute requires that notice of the determination of incapacity be given to the patient "where there is any indication of the patient's ability to comprehend such notice." Id. When a surrogate is properly identified, that person

> may consent to an order not to resuscitate on behalf of an adult patient only if there has been a determination by an attending physician with a concurrence of another physician selected by a person authorized by the hospital to make such a selection, given after personal examination of the patient that, to a reasonable degree of medical certainty:
>
> > [i] the patient has a terminal condition; or [ii] the patient is terminally unconscious; or [iii] resuscitation would be medically futile or [iv] resuscitation would impose an extraordinary burden on the patient in light of the patient's medical condition and the expected outcome of resuscitation for the patient.

Id. § 2965. If no surrogate is available, the entry of a DNR order effectively is limited to those cases in which "to a reasonable degree of medical certainty, resuscitation would be medically futile." Id. § 2966.

The statute requires that DNR policies be reviewed by the attending physician every three days (for patients in a hospital) or every 60 days or whenever the patient is required to be seen by a physician (for patients in residential health facilities). Id. § 2970.

The statute requires the establishment of dispute mediation systems at hospitals to mediate decisions to consent (or refuse to consent) to DNR orders. The medical determinations are subject to judicial review, although "the person or entity challenging the decision must show, by clear and convincing evidence, that the decision is contrary to the patient's wishes including consideration of the patient's religious and moral beliefs, or, in the absence of evidence of the patient's wishes, that the decision is contrary to the patient's best interests." Id. § 2973. Those involved (physician, health care professional, nurse's aide, hospital or person employed by or under contract with the hospital) are immune from civil and criminal liability, and may not be deemed to have engaged in unprofessional conduct, for making a determination in accord with the statute. Finally, if no surrogate "is reasonably available, willing * * * and competent" to act under the statute, a court may render a judgment:

directing the physician to issue an order not to resuscitate where the patient has a terminal condition, is permanently unconscious, or resuscitation would impose an extraordinary burden on the patient in light of the patient's medical condition and the expected outcome of the resuscitation for the patient, and issuance of an order is not inconsistent with the patient's wishes including a consideration of the patient's religious and moral beliefs or, in the absence of evidence of the patient's wishes, the patient's best interests.

Id. § 2976.

The statute became effective on April 1, 1988, and it has become the subject of great debate. Ironically the statute, which was promulgated because of the worry of overuse of CPR, has been criticized primarily because it may continue to require CPR in cases where it is inappropriate. First, the statute would seem to permit (or even require) cardiopulmonary resuscitation even when that treatment is futile unless a DNR order has been entered. Should physicians ever be required to apply futile treatment? See Rosner, Must We Always Offer the Option of CPR: The Law in New York, 260 J.A.M.A. 3129 (1988); Murphy, Do Not Resuscitate Orders: Time for Reappraisal in Long Term Care Institutions, 260 J.A.M.A. 2098 (1988); Blackhall, Must We Always Use CPR?, 317 N.Eng.J.Med., 1281 (1987).

The statute has also been criticized for its very narrow application of the therapeutic privilege—a result the drafters of the statute intended so that there would be more doctor-patient discussion about DNR orders. Those who object to the limited applicability of the therapeutic privilege may also be disappointed by the statutory requirement that the physician tell the patient when the patient has been found incapacitated to consent to a DNR order. Once again, the drafters of the statute believed that requiring this communication would encourage doctor-patient communication generally and would thus improve medical decisionmaking.

Other objections to the statute focus on its rather cumbersome process, although it has been defended as "parallel[ing] existing clinical practice." Miller, supra at 248. Of course, to the extent that the statute does parallel the current practice it institutionalizes and strengthens the current default position that CPR should be applied in every case unless a prior formal and bureaucratically correct determination has been made to enter a DNR order.

Should the processes for entering DNR orders be determined by statute? Should New York promulgate another statute to deal with ventilators, and a third to deal with nasogastric tubes? Is there something truly unique about DNR orders that requires a statute? The New York statute was promulgated at a time when most hospitals were developing policies on DNR orders anyway. These policies, although often similar to the substantive provisions of the New York statute, varied with the local structure and local culture of the hospital in which they were adopted. Should these policies be established on a patient-by-patient basis, an attending physician-by-attending physician basis, a hospital-by-hospital basis, or by the state legislature through statute? Could religious hospitals be bound by DNR statutes offensive to their mission? Why do you think that no other state has followed the New York lead?

For additional discussion of DNR orders, see Younger, Do Not Resuscitate Orders: No Longer Secret But Still a Problem, 17 Hastings Center Rep. (1) 24 (Feb.1987); Tomlinson and Brody, Ethics—Communication in Do Not Resuscitate Orders, 318 N.Eng.J.Med. 43 (1988); Brennan, Silent Decisions: Limits of Consent in the Terminally Ill Patient, 16 Law, Medicine and Health Care 204 (1988).

VI. CRIMINAL LAW AND THE "RIGHT TO DIE"

A. HOMICIDE

THE BARBER CASE

If the financial and emotional threat of a malpractice action imposes fear in health-care providers dealing with patients who are near death, the threat of criminal prosecution for homicide imposes real terror. The risk of a criminal prosecution is not entirely hypothetical; from time to time ambitious district attorneys decide to file criminal charges against physicians who permit the termination of life-support systems in patients. The contemplation of a conviction for murder, life imprisonment, and all of the other attendant consequences, can be a powerful deterrent to a physician who may otherwise believe that it is appropriate to let a patient die.

In 1983 the district attorney in Los Angeles County brought murder charges against two physicians who had discontinued ventilation and then removed the feeding tube from a patient in one of the Kaiser hospitals in Los Angeles. Clarence Herbert, the patient, had been first admitted to the hospital with a bowel obstruction in May of 1981. He was treated by Dr. Barber, Former Chief of Internal Medicine at Kaiser, and Dr. Nejdl, Chief of Surgery at the hospital. The first operation failed and sometime later he underwent an ileostomy, which diverts the gastrointestinal system directly from the small intestine out of the body through a hole in the abdomen.

Mr. Herbert returned to the hospital in July with kidney failure and was properly treated. He returned again on August 26 to have the ileostomy closed. The operation appeared to be successful, but Mr. Herbert went into cardiac arrest in the recovery room and was resuscitated only after so much time had passed that he had slipped into deep, and probably irreversible, coma. Mr. Herbert was kept on a ventilator, as there was a presumption that he would cease breathing and die when he was removed from the ventilator. On August 29, three days after the accident, the physicians, with the agreement of the family, removed the ventilator. Surprisingly, this did not lead to Mr. Herbert's death. The next day, August 30, the physicians, after consultation with the family, agreed to remove the intravenous feeding device that was continuing to keep Mr. Herbert alive. Mr. Herbert died on September 6.

The case apparently was brought to the attention of the district attorney by one of the nurses who disagreed with Dr. Nejdl's handling of the case. An information charging murder was filed against both Drs. Barber and Nejdl. The Municipal Court granted the doctors' motion to dismiss the prosecution, but a Superior Court judge reinstated the criminal information. The matter was not finally resolved until the Court of Appeal rendered its decision on whether the criminal action ought to proceed to trial. As you review this case, consider the likely reactions of Dr. Barber, Dr. Nejdl, the Kaiser Hospital, other health-care providers and hospitals in California, and the legal counsel, as the case progressed through each level of judicial review—accompanied, at each step, with substantial publicity and public debate. Ask yourself what the most important consequence of this case could be. Is it the legal precedent established by the opinion of the Court of Appeal, or is it that physicians in California may have to defend against a murder charge if they discontinue any form of life-support treatment in very ill patients?

BARBER v. SUPERIOR COURT

California Court of Appeal, Second District, 1983.
147 Cal.App.3d 1006, 195 Cal.Rptr. 484.

COMPTON, ASSOCIATE JUSTICE.

* * *

The precise issue for determination by this court is whether the evidence presented before the magistrate was sufficient to support his determination that petitioners should not be held to answer to the charges of murder [ ] and conspiracy to commit murder [ ].

As we will later discuss, this issue must be determined against a background of legal and moral considerations which are of fairly recent vintage and which as a result have not, in our opinion, been adequately addressed by the Legislature.

* * * [I]t appears to us that a murder prosecution is a poor way to design an ethical and moral code for doctors who are faced with decisions concerning the use of costly and extraordinary "life support" equipment.

Murder is the "*unlawful* killing of a human being, * * * with malice aforethought." [ ] Malice may be express or implied. It is express when there is an intent *unlawfully* to take any life. It is implied when the circumstances show an abandoned and malignant heart. [ ]

The magistrate who heard the evidence made written findings of fact and concluded that (1) petitioners did not "kill" the deceased since their conduct was not the proximate cause of death—the proximate cause * * * being diffuse encephalomalacia, secondary to anoxia, (2) the petitioners' conduct under the circumstances, being the result of good faith, ethical and sound medical judgment, was not unlawful, and (3) the petitioners' state of mind did not amount to "malice."

The superior court judge, as he was required to do under the statute before ordering reinstatement of the complaint, concluded *as a matter of law* that petitioners' conduct, however well motivated, and however ethical or sound in the eyes of the medical profession, was, under California law, "unlawful." This conclusion was reached despite his determination that the magistrate's findings were supported by substantial evidence.

The judge opined that, since everyone, sooner or later will die, homicide is simply the shortening of life by some measurable period of time and inasmuch as the petitioners' intentional conduct, which shortened Mr. Herbert's life, was not authorized by law, it constituted murder.

* * *

This gap between the statutory law and recent medical developments has resulted in the instant prosecution and its attendant legal dispute. That dispute in order to be resolved within the framework of existing criminal law must be narrowed to a determination of whether petitioners' conduct was unlawful. * * *

* * *

We thus turn to an analysis of the superior court's determination that petitioners' conduct was "unlawful" as a matter of law.

* * *

As a predicate to our analysis of whether the petitioners' conduct amounted to an "unlawful killing," we conclude that the cessation of "heroic" life support measures is not an affirmative act but rather a withdrawal or omission of further treatment.

Even though these life support devices are, to a degree, "self-propelled," each pulsation of the respirator or each drop of fluid introduced into the patient's body by intravenous feeding devices is comparable to a manually administered injection or item of medication. Hence "disconnecting" of the mechanical devices is comparable to withholding the manually administered injection or medication.

* * *

In the final analysis, since we view petitioners' conduct as that of omission rather than affirmative action, the resolution of this case turns on whether petitioners had a duty to continue to provide life sustaining treatment.

There is no criminal liability for failure to act unless there is a legal duty to act. [ ] Thus the critical issue becomes one of determining the duties owed by a physician to a patient who has been reliably diagnosed as in a comatose state from which any meaningful recovery of cognitive brain function is exceedingly unlikely.

* * *

In examining this issue we must keep in mind that the life-sustaining technology involved in this case is not traditional treatment in that it is not being used to directly cure or even address the pathological condition. It merely sustains biological functions in order to gain time to permit other processes to address the pathology.

The question presented by this modern technology is, once undertaken, at what point does it cease to perform its intended function and who should have the authority to decide that any further prolongation of the dying process is of no benefit to either the patient or his family?

* * *

The evidence presented at the preliminary hearing supports the conclusion that petitioners reasonably concluded that Mr. Herbert had virtually no chance of recovering his cognitive or motor functions. The most optimistic prognosis provided by any of the testifying experts was that the patient had an excellent chance of "recovery." However, recovery was defined in terms of a spectrum running from a persistent vegetative state to full recovery. A persistent vegetative state was described as that state in which the patient would have no contact with the environment but parts of the brain would continue to live. The doctor who was of course approaching the case after the fact and from a hindsight view, was unable to predict where on this continuum Mr. Herbert was likely to end up. Several studies on which the expert relied, however, indicated that the chances for unimpaired or full recovery were miniscule. The results of these studies coincided with the diagnoses of the physicians who had actually examined and dealt with the patient before his demise.

Given the general standards for determining when there is a duty to provide medical treatment of debatable value, the question still remains as to who should make these vital decisions. Clearly, the medical diagnoses and prognoses must be determined by the treating and consulting physicians under the generally accepted standards of medical practice in the community and, whenever possible, the patient himself should then be the ultimate decision-maker.

When the patient, however, is incapable of deciding for himself, because of his medical condition or for other reasons, there is no clear authority on the issue of who and under what procedure is to make the final decision.

* * *

The authorities are in agreement that any surrogate, court appointed or otherwise, ought to be guided in his or her decisions first by his knowledge of the patient's own desires and feelings, to the extent that they were expressed before the patient became incompetent. [   ]

* * *

Under the circumstances of this case, the wife was the proper person to act as a surrogate for the patient with the authority to decide issues regarding further treatment, and would have so qualified had judicial approval been sought. There is no evidence that there was any disagreement among the wife and children. Nor was there any evidence that they were motivated in their decision by anything other than love and concern for the dignity of their husband and father.

* * *

In summary we conclude that the petitioners' omission to continue treatment under the circumstances, though intentional and with knowledge that the patient would die, was not an unlawful failure to perform a legal duty. In view of our decision on that issue, it becomes unnecessary to deal with the further issue of whether petitioners' conduct was in fact the proximate cause of Mr. Herbert's ultimate death.

The evidence amply supports the magistrate's conclusion. The superior court erred in determining that as a matter of law the evidence required the magistrate to hold petitioners to answer.

* * *

Notes and Questions

1. Kaiser Hospital, where Drs. Nejdl and Barber treated Mr. Herbert, is part of an HMO. Is that relevant to your evaluation of this case? What if Mr. Herbert had become a very expensive patient for whom the hospital was receiving no additional payment? If that fact is relevant, should standards applied by HMOs in deciding if life support systems should be removed be different from standards applied by institutions supported by other payment schemes? What kind of standard ought to be applied by a PPO? A community hospital providing service to a Medicaid patient? A Veterans Administration hospital?

2. The case of Drs. Barber and Nejdl quickly became a cause celebre, and it generated a great deal of publicity for the prosecution and the defense lawyers. What started as a case primarily of interest to bioethics scholars became a high profile criminal case designed for those used to reading Perry Mason, not the Pacific Reporter. A sense of the deep personal adversarial nature of these proceedings can be gleaned from reviewing excerpts of the closing argument of Mr. Braun, for Dr. Nejdl, in the Municipal Court in support of his motion to dismiss the criminal information:

People v. Barber, Excerpts from the Closing Argument of Mr. Braun, Counsel for Dr. Nejdl at the Preliminary Hearing

Mr. Braun: We do have here a conspiracy—a conspiracy not by Drs. Nejdl and Barber, but a conspiracy of a small group of radical, moral cavemen who have taken over the prosecuting machinery in this county and wish to impose their radical views, through a novel theory of the criminal law, on all of us.

* * *

So all of this talk about a hopeless condition is a fraudulent subterfuge for a vitalist's position that would turn half of the population over time into Karen Quinlans.

Now, if [the prosecutors] want to impose that standard on their family, that's fine. If they want to impose that emotional burden on their family, fine. But don't impose it on my family, and don't impose it on anyone in the court who does not subscribe to such a preposterous position.

The District Attorney owes some responsibility to the rest of the community to not sit here with these preposterous positions and ask physicians like Nejdl and Barber to go out and practice medicine. He owes a duty to his constituents, seven million people in the county, not to use the law of homicide to traumatize and slander physicians. That's precisely what he's doing in this case.

The danger about this case is there are people who are afraid to go into hospitals in Los Angeles County for fear not of the physicians but for fear of the District Attorney, for fear that physicians will not be able to practice good medicine, compassionate medicine, because the vitalists, the moral radicals, who have infiltrated and taken over the District Attorney's office, are going to charge them with murder.

The moral problem is not so much with these men who may sincerely believe that this caveman position makes some sense, but the people above them who find it politically expedient to ignore what's going on here. Let them allow Drs. Nejdl and Barber to twist in the wind, let all the patients across this county suffer. But they don't wait to come out.

* * *

[The District Attorney is a] great man when there's no problems, but give us a hillside strangler case and he tries to dismiss it. Give us the first time in American history that someone has filed a case on a physician under these circumstances, and he calls them murderers and then hides in the closet.

* * *

The real problem with this case, Your Honor, is what physician is ever going to be able to practice medicine without looking over his shoulder and seeing [the prosecutors] peering over his every decision? The fact is that unless this position is clearly repudiated by the court system—the court system is our only protection. If the court does not dismiss this case, under these circumstances it seems to me that we would have to go elsewhere for medical treatment for fear that we would have to be hooked up to a machine.

* * *

Are we the masters of these machines or are we the victims of these machines? Have we lost control of our lives to the District

Attorney's office, to their crazy theories? Are they going to start practicing medicine rather than letting physicians practice medicine?

* * *

It seems to me, Your Honor, that what these physicians did was good medicine. The fact that there's never ever been a prosecution under these circumstances indicates that it defies common sense, it defies the common law, it defies the statutes in this state, and it defies all the ethical reasoning that has gone on in these areas.

* * *

The motive has some sex appeal, particularly if you are more interested in tarnishing Kaiser Hospital than you are in prosecuting murder cases. That's the motive behind this case, to get an institution which some people feel threatens their income, so that's the motive behind the motive in this case.

* * *

We need a clear signal to the medical community that this prosecution makes no sense, that physicians aren't going to have to stand for murder every time [the prosecutor] disagrees with their diagnoses. We can't have a situation like this.

Note: Homicide and Discontinuing Medical Care

Homicide statutes in the United States take many forms, but most provide for two degrees of murder, some lower degree of intentional homicide and a form of grossly negligent homicide. Murder is generally a killing that is accompanied with "malice aforethought," for which the intent to kill is sufficient. Malice aforethought does not require "malice" in the normal English sense of that word. The lower degree of intentional homicide, traditionally called voluntary manslaughter, was historically described as an intentional killing in the heat of passion and upon adequate provocation. The lowest degree of homicide, traditionally called involuntary manslaughter, is unintentional homicide and includes killings that are a result of grossly or criminally negligent conduct.

When a physician removes a respirator or feeding tube from a patient whose death is intentionally hastened by that act, his act is unlikely to be described as one committed in the heat of passion upon adequate provocation, or as one that is grossly negligent. It constitutes murder if the health-care professional who discontinues the support acts with "malice aforethought" which, as we have seen, encompasses the intent to kill. Performing an act that is known to result in the death of another is treated as an act done with the intent to cause the death of another. When a physician discontinues a ventilator or removes a feeding tube knowing that his act will cause the death of the patient he acts with "malice aforethought" for purposes of the homicide statute. Thus, if the removal of life-support systems is to constitute homicide at all, it is likely to constitute murder, and not some lesser degree of homicide.

Further, one of the characteristics that distinguishes first degree murder from second degree in many jurisdictions is the presence of "premeditation." A murder is premeditated if the perpetrator has contemplated his act, even for a moment, before performing that act. Those health care professionals who discontinue life-support systems properly have given the matter a great deal of thought and consideration. They must admit to having reflected upon the nature and consequences of their act to avoid allegations of malpractice. Thus, if their act constitutes homicide it must constitute murder, and if their act constitutes murder, it is likely to constitute first degree murder.

There are two defenses regularly raised in "mercy killing" cases, each doomed to be unsuccessful when it is raised in the context of the termination of life-support systems. First, it is tempting to argue that a physician terminating life-support systems is merely shortening the life of the patient, not ending it. After all, the patient whose life-support systems are removed is generally near death. This is an inadequate defense to a homicide charge because the most a murderer ever can do is shorten the life of his victim; no one lives forever. Second, it is argued that the health-care professional who discontinues life-support systems, or who fails to initiate them, has committed no "act," and the commission of an act is required before there can be any criminal prosecution. There are times, however, when an omission (rather than an act) can constitute a crime. Where there is a duty to act, a breach of that duty through inaction fulfills the requirement of an act under the criminal statute. The physician has a duty to act derived from the doctor/patient relationship. The physician has a duty to provide adequate care to his patient; if he fails to do so his omission is treated as an act for purposes of the criminal law. Thus, the California Court of Appeal's conclusion that the termination of life support systems constituted an omission was not sufficient to resolve the case. The Court was required to proceed to determine if there was a duty to act that had been neglected by the physician.

If all the elements for a homicide crime are present, a defendant may be found not guilty only if the homicide can be shown not to be unlawful. Normally, a killing is unlawful unless it is justifiable or excusable. The definitions of justifiable and excusable homicide are rather narrow and, once again, historically well defined. Excusable homicide includes accidental homicide and homicide committed by a person who is insane or, under some circumstances, by a person who acts under duress. Justifiable homicide includes killing in self-defense. No common law excuse or justification would cover the acts of a physician who terminates life-support systems. Thus, the decision of the California Court of Appeal to base its exculpation of the physicians on the "lawfulness" of their acts (or omissions) constitutes a uniquely broad reading of "unlawful" in the murder statute.

The American law of homicide, heir to 500 years of English common law development, is simply not adequate to deal with the proper termination of life-support systems. Applying the criminal law in this area seems wholly misdirected and utterly foolish. Nonetheless, the criminal law is generally strictly construed, and unless it is modified by the legislature its strict terms, however apparently irrelevant or anachronistic, may continue to be applied by the courts.

Note: Declaratory Judgments and Potential Homicide Liability

The *Barber* case is the most widely publicized criminal case arising out of a physician's termination of life-support systems. The issue has arisen more regularly where a physician, a hospital, or the family of a patient seeks a court order allowing the discontinuation of life-support systems and in declaratory judgments that such discontinuation will not constitute criminal conduct. Virtually every court that has been faced with this issue and that has determined that it would be appropriate that life-support systems be discontinued has also found that no criminal liability would result. This result is as obvious to the courts as it is to outside observers; it would be inconsistent for a court to declare conduct to be proper and then determine that the same conduct is criminal.

See Matter of Colyer, 99 Wash.2d 114, 660 P.2d 738, 751 (1983):

An issue that must be addressed is the potential criminal liability of those involved in the decision to terminate life sustaining support. Under Washington's criminal code, homicide is "the killing of a human being by the act, procurement or omission of another" [ ], and it is murder in the first degree when, "[w]ith a premeditated intent to cause the death of another person, [one] causes the death of such person." [ ] Thus, the potential for criminal liability for withdrawing life sustaining mechanisms appears to exist. We conclude, however, that such action, if in good faith compliance with the procedure set forth above, would not be criminal.

The *Quinlan* court reached this same conclusion based on two alternative theories: (1) that the ensuing death would not be caused by the removal of the treatment, but rather by expiration from existing natural causes, hence it would not be homicide; or (2) even if it were homicide, it would not be unlawful because the action would be based on the exercise of a constitutional right and, as such, would be protected from criminal prosecution. [ ] We concur in this reasoning.

In addition, Washington's Natural Death Act excludes from criminal liability those who act in good faith and in accordance with a directive complying with the statutory requirements. [ ] It further states that acts in accordance with a directive are not deemed suicide, they should have no effect on life or health insurance policies, and the cause of death shall be that which placed the patient in a terminal condition. [ ] We believe that the same principles should apply when the patient's right to refuse life sustaining treatment is exercised in accordance with this opinion.

B. EUTHANASIA AND SUICIDE

1. Euthanasia

Euthanasia (Greek for "good death") generally refers to an act in which one person kills another at the request of, and for the benefit of, the one who dies. Some have distinguished "active euthanasia," where there is an affirmative actus reus that causes the death of another, from "passive euthanasia," where it is an omission which results in the death. Today "euthanasia" generally is used to describe only "active" euthanasia, not the process of allowing another to die.

Suicide, of course, is the taking of one's own life. Assisting suicide may constitute euthanasia if there is a close enough causal relationship between the assistance and the death. In reviewing the following materials on euthanasia, assisted suicide, and suicide, you should keep in mind that these terms have not taken on hardened meanings in the law, and they may be used in very different ways by different commentators.

Because consent is not a defense to homicide crimes, and because the law makes no distinction between a "good death" and any other kind of death, euthanasia is criminal homicide in every state and in almost every country. Recently there have been some suggestions that this should change, and that euthanasia should be permitted, at least in some carefully limited circumstances. Can you find any flaws in the following argument?

KUHSE, THE CASE FOR ACTIVE VOLUNTARY EUTHANASIA

14 Law Medicine and Health Care 145 (1986).

The following case of active voluntary euthanasia happened in Holland in 1981:

In 1976, 89–year–old Maria Barendregt moved into a center for the aged and became the patient of Dr. Schoonheim. She was a vital and strong-willed person and set great store by her independence. During the next few years, her health deteriorated and on several occasions, Maria Barendregt asked her doctor to help her die. Dr. Schoonheim did not initially respond to her request.

By September 1981, Maria Barendregt was no longer able to leave her bed. Soon she could no longer sit up, and then even speaking became difficult. By then she was 94 years old. Totally dependent on the nursing staff for washing, evacuation of the bowels, and for general care, Maria Barendregt remained mentally alert and was fully conscious of her progressive decline. Her requests to Dr. Schoonheim to shorten her life were increasing in urgency. A series of talks took place between the patient, her son, Dr. Schoonheim and his assistant, culminating in Dr. Schoonheim's decision to accede to Maria Barendregt's request.

A few days later—in the presence of his assistant—Dr. Schoonheim gave her an injection which put her to sleep. A little later, he administered a second injection and Maria Barendregt died. Dr. Schoonheim advised the Medical Examiner that he had performed an act of active voluntary euthanasia—he had killed his patient for the patient's sake.

These facts underlie the path-breaking judgment of November 1984, in which the Supreme Court of Holland upheld the District Court's decision that a doctor may, in a situation such as this, practice active voluntary euthanasia. This, very briefly, was the reasoning: in such situations doctors have two conflicting duties. On the one hand, they have the duty to uphold the laws of the land (which do not allow a doctor to kill a patient); on the other hand, doctors have a duty to put the patient's interests first. Since doctors cannot do both—obey the law and act in the patient's best interests—they cannot be held criminally responsible for choosing to do what a doctor's professional duty demands—namely, to act in the patient's best interests.

But I do not cite this case in order to offer an explication of the legal situation in the Netherlands. Rather, the question I want to raise is this: If it is permissible to *let* some patients die, why, then, do many of those who take this view think that it is not permissible to *help* a patient die? Dr. Schoonheim could, for example, have waited until his patient contracted a disease, such as bronchitis, that if left untreated would have led to her foreseen death—just as in the case of the patient suffering from Parkinson's disease. But why should that mode of bringing death about be the preferable course of action?

Again, the patient's death would have been the outcome of a deliberate human decision, although *when* and *how* death would have occurred would have been left to chance, or nature. Moreover, would it have been voluntary euthanasia—a good and easy death as chosen by the patient? Cessation of life-sustaining treatment does not always result in a swift and painfree death. For example, as Dr. Battin points out, if a patient's kidneys fail and dialysis or transplant is not undertaken, the patient generally remains conscious and experiences nausea, vomiting, gastro-intestinal hemorrhage (evident in vomiting blood), inability to concentrate, neuromuscular irritability or twitching, and, eventually, convulsions. It may take the patient days or weeks to die, unless high potassium levels intervene.

An untreated respiratory death involves conscious air hunger. This means gasping, an increased breathing rate, a panicked feeling of inability to get air in or out. Respiratory deaths may take only minutes; on the other hand, they may take hours. Dr. Battin lists various other examples as well, where cessation of life-sustaining treatment does not result in a quick and merciful death. In a recent Melbourne case, an elderly man suffering from cancer of the stomach starved himself to death when he was refused aid in dying. Would it not have been better to help him die?

Notes and Questions

1. Several arguments are made against the case for euthanasia. These arguments fall into six categories.

(1) *Misdiagnosis.* If euthanasia were permitted, a mistake in the diagnosis of a patient could result in the quick and comparatively

unconsidered death of the patient. This risk, which is avoided when we are required to allow death to take its natural course, outweighs any benefit that euthanasia may bring with it.

(2) *Involuntariness.* It is very difficult to determine whether the application of euthanasia in any particular case is truly voluntary. What if the patient who requests euthanasia does so only because her conniving and overbearing son has convinced her that she should? When is the person who volunteers for death doing so freely and when is that person doing so because he believes (rightly or wrongly) that he is a financial or social burden upon his family, or upon the community? There is simply no way to guarantee that any euthanasia will be truly voluntary.

(3) *The Slippery Slope.* While at first euthanasia may be institutionalized only for those in terrible pain, or those who are terminally ill, or those for whom it is otherwise appropriate, the pressure of the allocation of health care resources will inevitably enlarge the class for whom euthanasia is deemed appropriate. Every society has a group who are deemed to be socially unworthy and members of that group— the uneducated, the unemployed and the disabled, for example—will become good candidates for euthanasia. The only way to avoid slipping down this slope is to refuse to permit euthanasia in any case.

(4) *Disrespect for the Disabled.* Presumably those severely disabled people who choose death would be physically unable to accomplish it by their own means. Thus, the disabled—like Bouvia—would be the most likely to take advantage of any socially permitted euthanasia. Allowing euthanasia which disproportionately affects this portion of the population is tantamount to promulgating a social policy that says that we should rid ourselves of the disabled; that the disabled are less worthy of life than the able-bodied. Because it would be unfair to limit euthanasia to the able-bodied and prohibit the disabled from doing that which others would be permitted, the only way to avoid making such a social statement is to prohibit euthanasia for everyone.

(5) *Change in the Role of Medicine.* Permitting euthanasia would turn doctors who practice it into killers, and this would change the relationship between the medical profession and the community. Doctors, who are subject to tremendous trust in the community, would no longer be viewed as those who are present to save the patient. The medical profession would be viewed as one that takes life as well as one that saves life. This additional role as community executioner would adversely affect the ability of the profession to serve in its helping role.

(6) *Promoting the Right to Die.* It has been a difficult political road to achieve the right to die, a right recognized in one form or another in most states and in most countries. The fear that the right to die would lead to euthanasia has always been a major argument against the right to die itself. To argue in favor of euthanasia now would be to give credence to those arguments and would slow the very important development of the right to die.

Many of these arguments can be found in various forms in the excellent special supplement on Mercy, Murder and Morality: Perspectives on Euthanasia, 19 Hastings Center Rep. (Jan./Feb. 1989). See especially Fenigsen, A Case Against Dutch Euthanasia, 19 Hastings Center Rep., Special Supplement, 22 (Jan./Feb. 1989); Koop, The Challenge of Death, 29 Hastings Center Rep., Special Supplement, 2 (Jan./Feb. 1989) and Callahan, Can We Return Death to Disease?, 19 Hastings Center Rep., Special Supplement, 4 (Jan./Feb. 1989). For the argument that the quest to preserve and expand the right to die will be hindered by arguments that support euthanasia, see Wolf, Holding the Line on Euthanasia, 19 Hastings Center Rep., Special Supplement, 13 (Jan./Feb. 1989). Which arguments do you find most convincing? Should euthanasia and assisted suicide remain illegal under all circumstances?

2. Why has euthanasia become such a subject of interest over the last decade? Daniel Callahan has a suggestion:

> The power of medicine to extend life under poor circumstances is now widely and increasingly feared. The combined powers of a quasi-religious tradition of respect for individual life and a secular tradition of relentless medical progress creates a bias toward aggressive, often unremitting treatment that appears unstoppable.

> How is control to be gained? For many the answer seems obvious and unavoidable: active euthanasia and assisted suicide.

19 Hastings Center Rep., Special Supplement, 4 (Jan./Feb. 1989). Dr. Callahan goes on to suggest that those who strongly oppose active euthanasia, as he does, ought to focus on "dampening * * * the push for medical progress, a return to older traditions of caring as an alternative to curing, and a willingness to accept decline and death as part of the human condition (not a notable feature of American medicine)." Id. Is he right? It used to be that people would fear that if they went to the hospital they would die there. Now people fear that if they go to the hospital they will be kept alive there. Is it this fear that gives rise to our current interest in euthanasia?

3. As we have all learned in the abortion debate, the question of whether a particular action is morally appropriate is different from the question of whether the action ought to be tolerated by law. Some argue that the law is a blunt and improper weapon with which to battle the moral ambiguity of euthanasia, and that we should learn to tolerate euthanasia.

> One will need to live with individuals' deciding with consenting others when to end their lives, not because such is good, but because one does not have the authority coercively to stop individuals from acting together in such ways. In a secular, pluralist society one will need to accept euthanasia by default. One need not look to the Netherlands or elsewhere for models of what this might be like. In Texas up until 1973, neither suicide nor aiding and abetting suicide were criminalized. In articulating what was the old law in Texas, the Texas Supreme Court drew the line between what might be morally wrong and what the state would forbid:

>> It may be a violation of morals and ethics and reprehensible that a party may furnish another poison or pistols or guns or any other

means or agency for the purpose of the suicide to take his own life, yet
our law has not seen proper to punish such persons or such acts.
[citing Sanders v. State, 54 Tex.Crim. 101, 105, 112 S.W. 68, 70 (1908)]

Like it or not, given the moral limitations of the authority of the state,
we are all probably headed for Texas.

Engelhardt, Fashioning an Ethic for Life and Death in a Post–Modern
Society, 19 Hastings Center Rep., Special Supplement 7, 9 (Jan./Feb. 1989).

4. As Dr. Engelhardt pointed out, euthanasia is permitted, under
limited circumstances, in the Netherlands. While there has been some
debate over how well it has worked there and whether it has been abused,
there is little doubt that there is still broad public support for permitting
euthanasia after several years of experience with it. An excellent and
authoritative description of the way it is actually applied is found in RIGTER,
EUTHANASIA IN THE NETHERLANDS: DISTINGUISHING FACTS FROM FICTION, 19 HAS-
TINGS CENTER REP., SPECIAL SUPPLEMENT, 31–32 (Jan./Feb. 1989):

* * *

Euthanasia is a criminal offense under article 293 of the Penal
Code of The Netherlands: Any person who terminates the life of
another person at the latter's express and earnest request is liable to a
term of imprisonment not exceeding twelve years. This article con-
strues terminating life on request as manslaughter or murder, subject
to the mitigating circumstance of the request. In the absence of a
patient request the perpetrator renders himself or herself guilty of
manslaughter or murder. Moreover, the present government has *not*
adopted a longstanding proposal to legalize euthanasia. Instead, it has
decided that physicians who terminate life on request of the patient
will not be punished only if they invoke a defense of *force majeure* and
have satisfied the criteria discussed below, and then only on condition
that the court accepts this defense. Such possible immunity from
prosecution applies only to doctors.

Thus, doctors practicing euthanasia do so in violation of the law.
In practice, however, they will not be prosecuted if they appear to have
followed strict guidelines. Three tiers of the Dutch judicial system—
district courts, appeal courts, and the Supreme Court—have handed
down judgments in which these guidelines are precisely defined. They
have been affirmed and elaborated upon by the Royal Dutch Medical
Association (KNMG), the State Commission on Euthanasia, and the
Dutch government.

In brief, these conditions require, among other things, that there
be an explicit and repeated request by the patient that leaves no
reason for doubt concerning his desire to die; that the mental or
physical suffering of the patient must be very severe with no prospect
of relief; that the patient's decision be well-informed, free, and enduring; that all options for other care have been exhausted or refused by
the patient; and that the doctor consult another physician (in addition,
he may decide to consult nurses, pastors, and others). The doctor is
advised to note down the course of events.

Unfamiliarity and unease with the legal process is probably a major reason why cases of euthanasia are underreported by physicians. The district public prosecutor of Rotterdam recently instructed a large audience of physicians on these procedures. According to the prosecutor, there is no guarantee that a doctor performing euthanasia is ever exempt from prosecution, but, for those adhering to the guidelines, judicial red tape will be minimal. At the same meeting, the Rotterdam chapter of the KNMG announced that it will appoint consultants to advise doctors prepared to honor a request for euthanasia, helping them to follow the guidelines and through the ensuing legal process. In addition, many nursing homes and hospitals have developed (or are planning) euthanasia protocols incorporating the above guidelines.

The extent of euthanasia in The Netherlands is not known. According to a recent report, there were some 200–300 cases of euthanasia in Amsterdam in 1987, 10 percent of which were reported to the public prosecutor. The frequently cited figure is 5000–8000 cases per year but the Amsterdam data suggests this figure is too high. According to one estimate, the average general physician has recourse to euthanasia once every three years.

Euthanasia is more common in family practice than in nursing homes or hospitals. The annual number of euthanasia cases in the two major cancer hospitals does not exceed twenty. The relatively low incidence of euthanasia in these hospitals is not due to their technological superiority. Rather, terminal patients themselves request to be released from the hospital, or refuse to return, preferring to die at home to make sure that dying is a family affair.

It is sometimes suggested that the need for euthanasia is reinforced by inferior terminal care. However, while there may be waiting lists for some (nonacute) health care facilities, extensive, sophisticated, sensitive terminal care is universally available in The Netherlands. Furthermore, foreign commentators occasionally wonder whether economic motives play a role in the practice of euthanasia. The answer is no. In the relatively well-funded health care system of The Netherlands there is no economic stimulus for doctors or institutions to end the lives of patients. Dutch general physicians even lose money by performing euthanasia because of the per capita reimbursement system.

Is The Netherlands unique with regard to euthanasia? Not really, or at least not any more. The existence of euthanasia in other countries is finally coming out into the open.

* * *

If the situation in our country is unique at all, it is perhaps in the wish of physicians to subject their actions to public scrutiny.

5. Doctors and medical groups generally oppose any medical participation in euthanasia. Is this because it is morally reprehensible, or because it is too morally complicated? Drs. Cassel and Meier suggest that it could be, at least in part, the second:

A strict proscription against aiding in death may betray a limited conceptual framework that seeks the safety of ironclad rules and principles to protect the physician from the true complexity of individual cases. Patients seeking comfort in their dying should not be held hostage to our inability or unwillingness to be responsible for knowing right from wrong in each specific situation.

Cassel and Meier, Morals and Moralism in the Debate Over Euthanasia and Assisted Suicide, 323 N.Eng.J.Med. 750, 751 (1990).

6. Would our highly diverse society make it more difficult for euthanasia to be effectively employed in the United States? Polls show that the legalization of euthanasia would be popular in this country also. Despite this, an attempt to put the "Humane and Dignified Death Act" on the California ballot as an initiative failed in 1988 when its supporters were unable to get the 400,000 signatures necessary for citizen initiatives. The process of placing such an initiative on the California ballot is difficult, and, most significantly, extremely expensive. It is hard to tell whether the failure was a result of lack of money, lack of interest, or opposition to the substance of the initiative. In any case, some groups intend to put similar initiatives, which would permit euthanasia under certain circumstances roughly analogous to those in which it is permitted in the Netherlands, on ballots in those states that permit the initiative process. A Washington state initiative to permit physicians to give "aid-in-dying" to their patients under some circumstances is expected on the ballot soon; attempts to get similar legislation on the ballot in Oregon and Florida also may succeed. How would you draft a statute that would permit euthanasia? Should it be an independent statute, or merely a defense available in homicide cases? Can you construct language that would be sufficiently narrow and also sufficiently unambiguous?

2. Suicide and Assisted Suicide

Although suicide was punishable under the common law in England for the past two centuries, it was not a crime until 1854. The common law of the American states is hardly monolithic on the issue of suicide. While all states have abrogated laws making suicide a crime (and they were hardly enforceable in any case), most states do prohibit assisting suicide. Some treat assisting suicide rather harshly—in Illinois, Michigan, and Ohio it constitutes murder—but Hawaii and Indiana only prohibit causing suicide, not assisting it. Nine states have no laws prohibiting causing or assisting suicide and there are very few prosecutions under those statutes that do limit participation in another's suicide in any event. For an excellent history of the statutes and the cases enforcing them, see Smith, All's Well That Ends Well: Toward a Policy of Assisted Rational Suicide or Merely Enlightened Self–Determination?, 22 U.C.Davis L.Rev. 275, 290–291 (1989) and Smith, Final Choices: Autonomy in Health Care Decisions (1989). See also Marzen, O'Dowd, Crone and Balch, Suicide: A Constitutional Right?, 24 Duq.L.Rev. 1 (1985).

While it is now apparent that state statutes criminalizing assisting suicide are constitutional, *Cruzan,* supra at 1061, there seems to be no interest in enforcing criminal limitations on assisting suicide against physicians, at least when they assist suicide in appropriate cases. As Justice Stevens pointed out in his *Cruzan* dissent, "[e]ven laws against suicide presuppose that those inclined to take their own lives have *some* interest in living, and, indeed, that the depressed people whose lives are preserved may later be thankful for the state's intervention." Consider the California Penal Code section dealing with assisting suicide, and determine the circumstances under which it could be applied to a physician who helps a patient commit suicide:

CALIFORNIA PENAL CODE SECTION 401.   SUICIDE; AIDING,
ADVISING OR ENCOURAGING

Every person who deliberately aids, or advises, or encourages another to commit suicide, is guilty of a felony.

Would this statute apply to a physician who clamps a feeding tube? To a physician who withholds antibiotics? To a physician who prescribes morphine to a patient in persistent pain, and provides enough tablets to make a lethal dose? To a physician who prescribes that same morphine and tells the patient what would constitute a lethal dose? To those who publish instructions on how to commit suicide for the use of those who are terminally ill or in excruciating pain? To those who make generally available information about how to commit suicide at home? To those who play rock music with lyrics that suggest that suicide is acceptable? Surprisingly, only this last group has been the subject of any attempt to apply the statute. See McCollum v. CBS, Inc., 202 Cal.App.3d 989, 249 Cal.Rptr. 187 (1988).

Where the decision to remove life support systems is otherwise legally justifiable, it would be senseless to define such conduct as criminal. In addition, most living will legislation provides that if removal of life-sustaining treatment is consistent with the legislation, it will not constitute suicide. The Ethics and Health Policy Council of the American Medical Association has determined that "[d]eeply rooted medical traditions and the guiding principles of medical practice" say that physicians should not be able to assist the suicide of even a hopelessly ill patient. Orentlicher, Physician Participation in Assisted Suicide, 262 J.A.M.A. 1844 (1989). As the AMA Council notes, this view is not unanimous; some physicians view assisting the death of a patient in an appropriate case as being within the appropriate role of a physician dedicated to caring for, as well as curing, the patient. See Wanzer, et al., The Physician's Responsibility Toward Hopelessly Ill Patients: A Second Look, 320 N.Eng.J.Med. 844 (1989). One response to the AMA Council's position explained the need for physician involvement in suicide of hopelessly ill patients:

Finally, Dr. Orentlicher says, "what the sick need and are entitled to seek from the efforts of physicians is health." Physicians are not always empowered to supply patients with health. Substitute the word *help* for *health* and the phrase becomes universally apt. Be aware that if physicians did not have a virtual monopoly on medications in this country, patients would not need to ask them for this kind of help. Because this is so, dedication to an exceptionless principle does not necessarily make for better patient care than an involved and conscientious physician carefully and painfully weighing each case on its merits.

Abrams, Letters to the Editor, 263 J.A.M.A. 1197 (1990). For a compelling personal account of one physician's decision to accommodate a patient's wish to end her life, see Quill, Death and Dignity: A Case of Individualized Decision Making, 324 N.Eng.J.Med. 691 (1991).

Might a patient's decision to terminate life support systems be considered suicide for civil purposes—for example, for insurance purposes—even if it is not considered so for criminal purposes? Many living will statutes explicitly provide that it is not suicide for any purpose. Even in the absence of such a statute though, there has been no litigation over this issue, apparently because insurance companies have not attempted to avoid their insurance contract obligations by claiming that such people have committed suicide. The fact that insurance companies are so certain of the way a jury would react to an "unreasonable failure to pay" action if they did deny these payments suggests that there is a fairly clear community consensus that termination of life support systems, when otherwise appropriate, does not constitute suicide for civil or criminal purposes.

Even when death is inevitable and the body is racked with pain, is there some value in resisting death? Consider Dylan Thomas's famous poem, written upon the death of his father:

DO NOT GO GENTLE INTO THAT GOOD NIGHT

Do not go gentle into that good night,
Old age should burn and rave at close of day;
Rage, rage against the dying of the light.

Though wise men at their end know dark is right,
Because their words had forked no lightning they
Do not go gentle into that good night.

Good men, the last wave by, crying how bright
Their frail deeds might have danced in a green bay,
Rage, rage against the dying of the light.

Wild men who caught and sang the sun in flight,
And learn, too late, they grieved it on its way,
Do not go gentle into that good night.

Grave men, near death, who see with blinding sight
Blind eyes could blaze like meteors and be gay,
Rage, rage against the dying of the light.

> And you, my father, there on the sad height,
> Curse, bless, me now with your fierce tears, I pray.
> Do not go gentle into that good night.
> Rage, rage against the dying of the light.

Must the rage be a personal thing, or can it be required by law?

VII. THE "RIGHT TO DIE"—SERIOUSLY ILL NEWBORNS

Problem: Newborn With Spina Bifida

Baby Roe's parents decided their child would be born at Pleasant City Birthing Center despite medical advice that the advanced age of the mother made a hospital delivery advisable. At birth, the baby appeared to have spina bifida and hydrocephalus, serious congenital heart problems, and several other less serious medical problems.

Spina bifida is a midline defect of the osseous spine. In this case there is an external sacular protrusion high on the spine, and the protruding sac, which is filled with spinal fluid, includes a portion of the spinal cord. This medical condition is known as myelomeningocele. Hydrocephalus, which is often associated with spina bifida, consists of a cranial capacity engorged by fluids. The pressure of this fluid on the brain can have substantial adverse consequences. None of those problems are related to advanced maternal age.

The physician on call for the birthing center was telephoned immediately, and he ordered the baby to be moved to the Pleasant City General Hospital Neonatal Intensive Care Unit, which he called to inform of the baby's imminent arrival. Physicians at the Neonatal Intensive Care Unit concluded that the child would die of infection within a few months if the opening in the spine were not closed. To give Baby Roe any chance of long term survival, dozens of operations and virtually full time hospitalization would be required over a two year period. With maximum intervention, he might live 60 or 70 years. During this existence, he might be able to feel pain and experience pleasure; the physicians simply could not be sure. If he had any cognitive ability whatsoever, he would be likely to be severely retarded.

The parents, who are extremely distraught, are very angry that their child was moved to the Neonatal Intensive Care Unit. They believe that he should not have been removed without their consent, which they would have denied. The parents have also denied consent for the placement of a shunt necessary to minimize the effect of the hydrocephalus by relieving pressure on the brain. In addition, they refuse consent to the heart wall repair which is necessary to keep their son alive. The family physician and all other physicians working in the Neonatal Intensive Care Unit agree that it would be medically appropriate either to provide all treatment or not to provide any treatment in this case.

One of the nurses, however, disagrees. She explains that she recognizes the awful dilemma faced by the parents, but she believes that their needs can be attained in ways that do not result in the death of their child.

As she points out, the state child protective services agency has a list of members of the local Citizens for Life organization who are willing to adopt immediately any child born with any serious birth defect. People on the list are willing to provide the full cost of any treatment required by such children. The nurse believes the case should be referred to the state child protective service agency, which can then arrange for the termination of current parental rights and the adoption of the child by someone who will provide adequate medical care.

What actions ought the parents, physicians, nurses, and others take? What judicial consequences could (and should) each medical decision have?

If it is difficult to apply the principle of autonomy to an incompetent adult who had been competent, and nearly impossible to apply that principle to serve an incompetent adult who had never been competent (but who had expressed likes and dislikes), it is simply impossible to apply that principle to a seriously ill newborn. It makes no sense to talk about serving the deeply held values and desires of a two-minute (or two-day, or two-month) old baby. Since it is utterly impossible to serve any of the interests of autonomy in such cases, the principle of beneficience must become primary. The obligation of health care professionals and institutions is to do what is in the best interest of the child. As a matter of general course, parents are presumed to be acting in the best interest of their children, and parents of seriously ill newborns traditionally have been permitted to determine whether their infants would receive treatment, and what kind of treatment that should be. Thus, if a parent of a newborn with some severe anomaly determined that it would be best for that child not to receive life-sustaining treatment, that determination traditionally was honored even though it would result in the certain death of a child whose life otherwise could be saved.

The question of what treatment must be provided to a seriously ill newborn, however, has proved to be not quite so simple. Philosophically, the difficulties arise out of the fact that parents of newborn infants with serious defects may not always act in the best interest of their children. While parents undoubtedly feel some special responsibility for all of their children, a seriously ill newborn is likely to be a financial and emotional drain on the parents and the rest of the family. If the parents can avoid the problem before they become too attached to the child, they may spare themselves years or decades of unhappiness. With such a substantial risk that the parents' interest will be in conflict with the child's best interest, should we still allow the parents to decide what is in the best interest of the child? In addition, questions surrounding seriously ill newborns often require a determination of whether life-sustaining treatment should be forgone. Is it philosophically sensible to declare that death is in the "best interest" of a child who may be capable of so little brain activity that he will be without pain? What can "best interest" mean under such circumstances? Is it any easier to apply the principle of beneficence than the principle of autonomy under these conditions?

These are precisely the kinds of questions that are generally answered at the local institutional level within our health-care system. Indeed, that is exactly what had been happening throughout the country; the ultimate determination generally was left to the parents, who were heavily influenced by the hospital medical staff. Without much public attention, and with discussion limited primarily to medical and ethical professional organizations, somewhat different standards were applied in somewhat different institutions. Then the story of Baby Doe was picked up by the press.

Baby Doe was born on April 9, 1982, in Bloomington, Indiana. He was born with Down's Syndrome and a tracheoesophageal fistula which would require repair to allow the baby to consume nutrition orally. The parents decided not to authorize the necessary surgery, and the baby was given phenobarbital and morphine until he died, six days after birth. During Baby Doe's short life he was the subject of a suit commenced by the hospital in the local children's court, which refused to order that the surgery be done. The Indiana Supreme Court denied an extraordinary writ that would have had the same effect, and the attorneys for the hospital were on their way to Washington to seek a stay from the United States Supreme Court when the issue was rendered moot by Baby Doe's death. Baby Doe presents a very clean case for philosophical and jurisprudential analysis. The physicians refused to do the operation because the parents refused to consent. The parents refused to consent because their child had Down's Syndrome. If the child had not been born with Down's Syndrome, he would have been provided the surgery.

Several political groups, including right to life groups and advocacy groups for the developmentally disabled, were outraged by the circumstances of Baby Doe's death. Looking for some way to redress this issue, the Health and Human Services Department hit upon Section 504 of the Rehabilitation Act of 1974, 29 U.S.C.A. § 794, which forbids any agency receiving federal funds from discriminating on the basis of handicap. In March of 1983 the Secretary of Health and Human Services issued emergency regulations to assure that no hospital would avoid providing necessary treatment for seriously ill newborns. These regulations, purportedly authorized by Section 504 of the Rehabilitation Act, provided for federal "Baby Doe squads" to swoop down upon any hospital that put at risk the life or health of a handicapped infant by denying that infant life-sustaining treatment. The regulations also required large signs describing federal policy in all maternity and pediatric wards and newborn nurseries, and they established a toll free number to report violations of the regulation.

The regulation was challenged by the American Academy of Pediatrics, which successfully argued that it was defective because it had not been issued after the notice and comment period required by the Administrative Procedures Act. American Academy of Pediatrics v. Heckler, 561 F.Supp. 395 (D.D.C.1983). The Department of Health and Human Services then proposed a slightly revised regulation ("Baby Doe II") and invited comments. In early 1984 the new final regulations ("Baby Doe III") were issued. These regulations were based on the articulated substantive principle that "nourishment and medically beneficial treatment (as determined with respect to reasonable medical judgments) should not be withheld from handicapped infants solely on the basis of their present or anticipated mental or physical impairments." Under the final regulations the federal government maintained its investigatory and enforcement roles, state child protective services agencies were required to develop processes to investigate cases of non-treatment of seriously ill newborns, and individual institutions were encouraged to establish "Infant Care Review Committees" to review appropriate cases.

The American Medical Association and the American Hospital Association challenged "Baby Doe III" in an action that was destined for the United States Supreme Court. Although the challenge was based in part upon substantive principles, the real crux of the litigation was the authority of the Department of Health and Human Services to issue these regulations under Section 504 of the Rehabilitation Act. A powerful argument submitted in support of the regulation came in an amicus brief submitted by the Association for Retarded Citizens and other advocacy groups for the handicapped:

> In the normal course of medical practice, it is usually the physician and not the patient (or parents of the patient) who frames and requests treatment decisions. The experience of Amici, as parents of handicapped children, has been that some physicians act differently towards parents who have infants with identical medical problems based on whether or not the infant is expected to be a handicapped child and adult. Often the very framing of a parental treatment/no-treatment decision by a physician reveals an underlying difference in assumptions regarding the value of the life of the handicapped infant. If a parent takes a sick, non-handicapped child to a hospital for an examination which reveals that the child has a life-threatening infection easily and safely cured by an injection of antibiotics, would any physician seriously ask the parent the question of whether the vitally needed medical treatment should be withheld? Physicians, however, frequently call upon parents of sick, handicapped infants to make such decisions. Parents of infants with spina bifida have been asked to consent to the withholding of antibiotics from their handicapped children with life-threatening infections. In this situation, the physician suggests to parents a decision which assumes that the withdrawal of a routine medical procedure needed to preserve the life of a handicapped child is acceptable, despite the fact that such a decision would never even be suggested if an infant with the same infection

were not handicapped. The *a priori* assumption of such a question is not that the child cannot or will not live, but rather that because of his or her handicap the infant's life has such diminished value that the child *should* not live.

This difference in the treatment of handicapped and non-handicapped children directly reflects the physician's judgment that the life of the handicapped infant is of significantly less value than is the life of the non-handicapped infant. Perhaps the bias and devaluation inherent in seriously presenting the no-treatment option would be clearer if the decision were based on race or sex (other permanent physical characteristics). If physicians in a neonatal intensive care unit, in cases where clearly beneficial treatment was safely available, routinely and seriously presented the no-treatment alternative to parents of black infants but not to parents of white infants, would there be any question of inherent and unlawful bias? Would it suffice to argue that, because of a higher incidence of poverty among black families, such a differentiation in the presentation of treatment alternatives was justified either because of the potential economic burden of another child on the family or because the quality of the child's future life, as measured from the physician's sociological viewpoint, might well be significantly lower because of the child's race? * * *

Not all medical decisions to withhold treatment from a handicapped infant are based on different assumptions regarding the value of the infant's life. The pivotal question to be answered is, "If the child were not thought to be permanently disabled, would there be any hesitation in providing a particular type of treatment?" If the answer is "yes" * * * then the treatment decision would be properly predicated on medical factors related to the infant's current physical condition rather than the infant's status as a handicapped child. However, if the answer is "no" * * * then the decision would appear clearly predicated upon the diminished value assigned to the life of that child. Thus a physician may legitimately decide not to recommend heart surgery for a black child with Down's syndrome because it is medically contraindicated. However, if the physician decides not to recommend clearly beneficial surgery *because* the child is and will be mentally retarded, or *because* the child is and will be black, the basis of the physician's decision has shifted from a medical to a sociological one. There is no more central civil rights issue than a life and death difference in treatment based on a different and lesser valuation of a human life attributable to membership in a particular group.

Brief of The Association for Retarded Citizens, at 6–9. An amicus brief submitted by the American Academy of Pediatrics and several other pediatrics organizations explained the physicians' dissatisfaction with the regulation:

In Petitioner's paradigm case, the pediatrician need only make one treatment decision: whether to perform surgery to correct an intestinal problem. [ ] Yet just as seriously ill infants do not suffer from static, isolated medical conditions, medical care of seriously ill infants rarely involves an isolated decision to treat one malady. Rather, pediatric care involves numerous treatment decisions which are typically based on an uncertain prognosis. Arras, *Toward an Ethic of Ambiguity*, 14 Hastings Center Report 25, 27 (Apr. 1984). The pediatrician must assess, often without reliable medical data, the likelihood of successful treatment, the risk of damage to the infant from the therapy, the effect on the child of protracted artificial life-support care, and the pain and suffering of continued treatment. Treatment may be life-saving, but the result of the therapy could cause other damage.

Petitioner's argument that withholding medical treatment from a disabled infant "subject[s] * * * [the infant] * * * to discrimination" within the meaning of Section 504 thus grossly over-simplifies the medical decision-making process. The spectrum of medical conditions involved, and the numerous medical decisions necessary to respond to them, change continually. The result, as explained by the Second Circuit, is that:

> [w]here the handicapping condition is related to the condition(s) to be treated, it will rarely, if ever, be possible to say with certainty that a particular decision was "discriminatory."

[ ] The treatment decision posited by the Secretary is a simple one; the reality is a far more complex one where differing medical conditions justify different treatment for individual infants. [ ] Thus, a decision which may in Petitioner's view constitute "discrimination" at one moment may become a bona fide medical judgment—concededly outside the scope of Section 504—the next. With the threat of federal intervention, adverse publicity, litigation, and possible loss of funding, the effect of the regulations would be to require treatment even where contraindicated, a gross intrusion into difficult and complex medical decisions.

Brief of the American Academy of Pediatrics, at 7–9.

Ultimately, the case was decided by a 5–3 vote, but Chief Justice Burger concurred in the result only and did not write an opinion. Thus, there is no majority opinion.

BOWEN v. AMERICAN HOSPITAL ASSOCIATION

Supreme Court of the United States, 1986.
476 U.S. 610, 106 S.Ct. 2101, 90 L.Ed.2d 584.

JUSTICE STEVENS announced the judgment of the Court and delivered an opinion in which JUSTICE MARSHALL, JUSTICE BLACKMUN, and JUSTICE POWELL joined.

This case presents the question whether certain regulations governing the provision of health care to handicapped infants are authorized by § 504 of the Rehabilitation Act of 1973. * * *

I

The American Medical Association, the American Hospital Association, and several other respondents challenge the validity of Final Rules promulgated on January 12, 1984, by the Secretary of the Department of Health and Human Services.

* * *

II

The Final Rules represent the Secretary's ultimate response to an April 9, 1982, incident in which the parents of a Bloomington, Indiana infant with Down's syndrome and other handicaps refused consent to surgery to remove an esophageal obstruction that prevented oral feeding. On April 10, the hospital initiated judicial proceedings to override the parents' decision, but an Indiana trial court, after holding a hearing the same evening, denied the requested relief. On April 12 the court asked the local Child Protection Committee to review its decision. After conducting its own hearing, the Committee found no reason to disagree with the court's ruling. The infant died six days after its birth.

* * *

IV

The Solicitor General is correct that "handicapped individual" as used in § 504 includes an infant who is born with a congenital defect. If such an infant is "otherwise qualified" for benefits under a program or activity receiving federal financial assistance, § 504 protects him from discrimination "solely by reason of his handicap." * * *

However, no such rule or policy is challenged, or indeed has been identified, in this case. Nor does this case * * * involve a claim that any specific individual treatment decision violates § 504. This suit is not an enforcement action, and as a consequence it is not necessary to determine whether § 504 ever applies to individual medical treatment decisions involving handicapped infants. Respondents brought this litigation to challenge the * * * Final Rules on their face. * * * The specific question presented by this case, then, is whether the * * * provisions of the Final Rules are authorized by § 504.

V

It is an axiom of administrative law that an agency's explanation of the basis for its decision must include "a 'rational connection between the facts found and the choice made.'" * * *

Before examining the Secretary's reasons for issuing the Final Rules, it is essential to understand the pre-existing state-law framework governing the provision of medical care to handicapped infants. In broad outline, state law vests decisional responsibility in the parents, in the first instance, subject to review in exceptional cases by the State acting as *parens patriae.* Prior to the regulatory activity culminating in the Final Rules, the federal Government was not a participant in the process of making treatment decisions for newborn infants. We presume that this general framework was familiar to Congress when it enacted § 504. * * *

The Secretary has identified two possible categories of violation of § 504 as justifications for federal oversight of handicapped infant care. First, he contends that a hospital's refusal to furnish a handicapped infant with medically beneficial treatment "solely by reason of his handicap" constitutes unlawful discrimination. Second, he maintains that a hospital's failure to report cases of suspected medical neglect to a state child protective services agency may also violate the statute. We separately consider these two possible bases for the Final Rules.

VI

In the immediate aftermath of the Bloomington Baby Doe incident, the Secretary apparently proceeded on the assumption that a hospital's statutory duty to provide treatment to handicapped infants was unaffected by the absence of parental consent. [ ] He has since abandoned that view. Thus, the preamble to the Final Rules correctly states that when "a non-treatment decision, no matter how discriminatory, is made by parents, rather than by the hospital, section 504 does not mandate that the hospital unilaterally overrule the parental decision and provide treatment notwithstanding the lack of consent." [ ] A hospital's withholding of treatment when no parental consent has been given cannot violate § 504, for without the consent of the parents or a surrogate decisionmaker the infant is neither "otherwise qualified" for treatment nor has he been denied care "solely by reason of his handicap." Indeed, it would almost certainly be a tort as a matter of state law to operate on an infant without parental consent. This analysis makes clear that the Government's heavy reliance on the analogy to race-based refusals which violate § 601 of the Civil Rights Act is misplaced. If, pursuant to its normal practice, a hospital refused to operate on a black child whose parents had withheld their consent to treatment, the hospital's refusal would not be based on the race of the child even if it were assumed that the parents based *their decision* entirely on a mistaken assumption that the race of the child made the operation inappropriate.

Now that the Secretary has acknowledged that a hospital has no statutory treatment obligation in the absence of parental consent, it has become clear that the Final Rules are not needed to prevent hospitals from denying treatment to handicapped infants.

The Secretary's belated recognition of the effect of parental nonconsent is important, because the supposed need for federal monitoring of hospitals' treatment decisions rests *entirely* on instances in which parents have refused their consent. Thus, in the Bloomington, Indiana, case that precipitated the Secretary's enforcement efforts in this area,

* * * the hospital's failure to perform the treatment at issue rested on the lack of parental consent. The Secretary's own summaries of these cases establish beyond doubt that the respective hospitals did not withhold medical care on the basis of handicap and therefore did not violate § 504. * * *

* * *

VII

As a backstop to his manifestly incorrect perception that withholding of treatment in accordance with parental instructions necessitates federal regulation, the Secretary contends that a hospital's failure to report parents' refusals to consent to treatment violates § 504, and that past breaches of this kind justify federal oversight.

By itself, § 504 imposes no duty to report instances of medical neglect—that undertaking derives from state-law reporting obligations or a hospital's own voluntary practice. * * *

The particular reporting mechanism chosen by the Secretary—indeed the entire regulatory framework imposed on state child protective services agencies—departs from the nondiscrimination mandate of § 504 in a more fundamental way. The mandatory provisions of the Final Rules omit any direct requirement that hospitals make reports when parents refuse consent to recommended procedures. Instead, the Final Rules command *state agencies* to require such reports, regardless of the state agencies' own reporting requirements * * *. Far from merely preventing state agencies from remaining calculatedly indifferent to handicapped infants while they tend to the needs of the similarly situated nonhandicapped, the Final Rules command state agencies to utilize their "full authority" to "prevent instances of unlawful medical neglect of handicapped infants." [ ] The Rules effectively make medical neglect of handicapped newborns a state investigative priority, possibly forcing state agencies to shift scarce resources away from other enforcement activities—perhaps even from programs designed to protect handicapped children outside hospitals. * * *

* * *

VIII

* * *

* * * We could not quarrel with a decision by the Department to concentrate its finite compliance resources on instances of life-threatening discrimination rather than instances in which merely elective care has been withheld. [ ] But nothing in the statute authorizes the Secretary to dispense with the law's focus on discrimination and instead to employ federal resources to save the lives of handicapped newborns, without regard to whether they are victims of discrimination by recipients of federal funds or not. Section 504 does not authorize the Secretary to give unsolicited advice either to parents, to hospitals, or to state officials who are faced with difficult treatment decisions concerning handicapped children. We may assume that the "qualified

professionals" employed by the Secretary may make valuable contributions in particular cases, but neither that assumption nor the sincere conviction that an immediate "on site investigation" is "necessary to protect the life or health of a handicapped individual" can enlarge the statutory powers of the Secretary.

The administrative record demonstrates that the Secretary has asserted the authority to conduct on-site investigations, to inspect hospital records, and to participate in the decisional process in emergency cases in which there was no colorable basis for believing that a violation of § 504 had occurred or was about to occur. The District Court and the Court of Appeals correctly held that these investigative actions were not authorized by the statute and that the regulations which purport to authorize a continuation of them are invalid.

The judgment of the Court of Appeals is affirmed.

* * *

CHIEF JUSTICE BURGER concurs in the judgment.

JUSTICE REHNQUIST took no part in the consideration or decision of this case.

[The dissenting opinion of JUSTICE WHITE is omitted.]

Notes

1. While the challenge to Baby Doe III was winding its way through the courts, principals on both sides of the issue agreed to a compromise that was turned into a statute in the form of the Child Abuse Amendments of 1984, 42 U.S.C. Sec. 5102 (1986). The final regulations under the 1984 amendments to the Child Abuse Prevention and Treatment Act were promulgated in 1987. See 52 Fed.Reg. 3990 (Feb. 6, 1987), codified at 45 C.F.R. Part 1340. In addition, the Seventh Circuit has determined that government records on the original (Bloomington) *Baby Doe* case are exempt from disclosure under the Freedom of Information Act. See Marzen v. Department of Health and Human Services, 825 F.2d 1148 (7th Cir.1987).

2. Although the issue now rarely arises in the judicial setting, courts are loathe to allow infants who can be "saved" to die. For an interesting opinion, see Iafelice v. Zarafu, 221 N.J.Super. 278, 534 A.2d 417 (App.Div. 1987) (parents may not withhold consent to a shunt to be placed in a spina bifida infant, even when substantial mental retardation is extremely likely). In the United Kingdom, on the other hand, there is far more toleration of a family decision to discontinue treatment of an infant with a "brain incapable of even limited intellectual function. * * *" The British courts are willing to explicitly consider the quality of life of a seriously ill newborn, as was demonstrated in a recent case in which treatment was not required for a newborn when "[c]oupled with her total physical handicap, the quality of her life will be demonstrably awful and intolerable." In Re C (Minor) [1989] 2 All E.R. 782 (C.A.) discussed in Brahams, Medicine and the Law: Court of Appeal Endorses Medical Decision to Allow Baby to Die, Lancet 969 (April 29, 1989).

A British commentator addressed the difference between American and British law on this subject:

[I]t seems that doctors will and should continue to bear their traditional responsibility for deciding, with the patient and family, when treatment should be withdrawn and for implementing such decisions. It would be undesirable for the courts to usurp the doctor's role and to become routinely involved in a medical decision which is the prerogative of the patient (if capable), family, and doctors in privacy. The UK courts respect the medical profession as the arbiter of clinical competence in negligence claims and will be wise to continue to leave doctors in charge of terminal treatment decisions. By contrast, the courts in the United States have taken a much more interventionist stance. Legal involvement in medical decision making for the dying and comatose is usually unwelcome and has produced some distressing and depressing decisions following prolonged US court actions.

Id. at 970. See also In re J (Minor), [1990] 3 All E.R. 930 (C.A.) (court applies principle of substituted judgment to determine that a severely mentally and physically handicapped baby would not choose to live, and thus certain treatments could be withheld from him).

Whatever the American judicial position, American medicine is now more willing to accept nontreatment of hopelessly ill newborns, even when the parents demand that treatment and threaten legal action. As a lawyer, doctor, and theologian argue:

[P]atients must be offered more than pain, suffering and costs; the use of the procedure must be justified by a realistic expectation of prolonged benefit.

Paris, Crone and Reardon, Occassional Notes: Physicians' Refusal of Requested Treatment, 322 N.Eng.J.Med. 1012, 1013 (1990), citing Moore, The Desperate Case: CARE (Cost, Applicability, Research, Ethics), 261 J.A.M.A. 1483 (1989).

Bibliographical Note: Discontinuing Treatment In Children and Infants

A great deal has been written about the Baby Doe cases; much of it polemical. Among the most interesting accounts of the matter are Rosenblum and Grant, The Legal Response to Babies Doe: An Analytical Prognosis, 1 Issues in Law and Med. 391 (1986); and Note, Withholding Lifesaving Treatment from Defective Newborns: An Equal Protection Analysis, 29 St. Louis U.L.J. 853 (1985). Children are not treated in the same way as newborns; they are generally treated as incompetent adults. See In re L.H.R., 253 Ga. 439, 321 S.E.2d 716 (1984) (15–day–old child); Guardianship of Barry, 445 So.2d 365 (Fla.App.1984) (10–month–old child); In re P.V.W., 424 So.2d 1015 (La.1982) (birth injury).

For a superb outline of these issues see Rhoden, Treatment Dilemmas for Imperiled Newborns: Why Quality of Life Counts, 585 So.Cal.L.Rev. 1283 (1985). The very helpful report of The Hastings Center's project on imperiled newborns is found in 17 Hastings Center Rep. (6) 5–32 (Dec. 1987). The structure of the legal analysis regularly applied to these issues was first described in Robertson, Involuntary Euthanasia of Defective Newborns: A Legal Analysis, 27 Stan.L.Rev. 213 (1975). See also R. Weir, Selective Nontreatment of Handicapped Newborns (1984). For an argument for not treating some impaired newborns, see Weir and Bale, Selective Treatment of Neurologically Impaired Neonates, 7 Neurologic Clinics 807 (1989). For a good account of one important legal issue, see Vitiello, Baby Jane Doe: Stating a Cause of Action Against Officious Intermeddlers, 37 Hast.L.J. 863 (1986). See also T. Murray and A. Caplan, eds., Which Babies Shall Live? Humanistic Dimensions of the Care of Imperiled Newborns (1985); Paris, Terminating Treatment for Newborns: A Theological Perspective, 10 Law, Medicine & Health Care 120 (1982); Arras, Toward an Ethic of Ambiguity, 14 Hastings Center Rep. (3) 25 (April 1984).

Chapter 12
INTERDISCIPLINARY DECISIONMAKING IN HEALTH CARE: IRBs, ETHICS COMMITTEES, AND ADVISORY COMMITTEES

INTRODUCTION

If the previous eleven chapters have made anything clear, it is that there are a great number of health care decisions that can not neatly be classified as "medical," "legal," "ethical," "social" or "economic." These issues, which range from broad social matters, such as who should have access to kidney dialysis, to particular questions dealing with individual cases, such as whether Baby Jane Doe should receive surgery, have made obvious the value of interdisciplinary decisionmaking at the societal, institutional, and individual level. Within the last ten years several forms of medical decisionmaking by interdisciplinary committees have arisen. These committees include institutional review boards (IRBs) established by federal regulation and appointed by local institutions to review research involving human subjects; institutional ethics committees (IECs) established without any legal obligation by many hospitals and some nursing homes to help review ethical policies and practices; infant care review committees (ICRCs) established pursuant to the "Baby Doe" regulations to review the quality of care given to seriously ill newborns under some circumstances; diagnosis committees established to determine whether a diagnosis that triggers an ethical and legal consequence (like "terminal illness") has been properly confirmed; medical-legal malpractice review panels established by state law in some states and by medical and legal societies in others to provide screening of potential malpractice actions; the Recombinant DNA Advisory Committee (RAC) established by federal law to review research involving DNA; presidential commissions appointed by the President under acts of Congress to investigate and help establish national policy on matters of interdisciplinary concern and parallel state commissions to establish state policy.

While the medical profession has sometimes viewed the development of these committees, panels, and commissions as an inappropriate intrusion upon its decisionmaking authority, these institutions have brought new ideas and perspectives to the debates concerning what are ultimately social issues. The function of this chapter is to provide an introduction to the needs that gave rise to such interdisciplinary agencies, the methods of their organization and operation, and the value of their existence.

Problem: Making Health Care Policy

As the commissioner and chief administrative officer of a state health department that sets state policy and also operates a large general hospital, you are confronted with the need to resolve several issues:

1.   What definition of brain death, if any, ought to be applied within the state?

2.   What level of care, if any, should the state insist that local hospitals provide to seriously ill newborns?   Should the state child abuse and neglect processes be available to unrelated third parties who wish to challenge hospital actions in providing care to seriously ill newborns?

3.   What ought to be done about the quality deficiencies within private nursing homes within the state?

4.   Should the state's determination to provide Medicaid to some, but not all, of the optional categories of Medicaid eligible persons be altered in such a way that health care will be more equitably distributed to those who need it most?

5.   What kind of policy regarding life sustaining treatment should the state's hospital adopt?

6.   Should the hospital allow medically unqualified traditional healers to perform their healing techniques?

7.   Should every person admitted to a particular hospital be asked whether he or she is willing to be an organ donor?

8.   Should patients be permitted to participate as research subjects in an experiment to test the safety and efficacy of a new sleeping pill, even though there is substantial evidence that sleeping medications are responsible for as much social harm as good?

9.   Should the hospital limit the practice of physicians or other health care providers who are HIV positive?   Should it tell patients which providers are HIV positive?   Should it test all providers for HIV?

10.   Should the hospital tell health care providers which patients are HIV positive?

Some of these questions must be answered in a way that develops a policy for the entire state; some of these questions are directed to particular cases at a single hospital.   Would it be helpful to appoint committees to recommend answers to these questions?

1.   If so, what is it about the decisionmaking that would make committees helpful under each of these circumstances?

2.   What kind of people ought to be appointed to each of these committees?

3.   What procedures ought to be applied to the committees, and how ought they go about their work?

4. Should any substantive limitations be put on the work of any of these committees?

5. Is the purpose of each committee to resolve a particular case, to develop an institution-wide or state-wide policy, or to educate other principals who will be working on the underlying question?

6. To whom should these committees report? To the physician and family? To a hospital administrator? To the commissioner of health? To the legislature? To someone else?

This first section of this chapter discusses IRBs, the earliest interdisciplinary committees to be widespread and accepted, and briefly reviews the recent history of human subjects research. The next two sections consider other kinds of individual case-oriented interdisciplinary decisionmakers. The following section reviews the work of government policy commissions established to consider bioethics questions. The final section of the chapter analyzes the problems that underlie doctor-lawyer relationships and the need for interdisciplinary training of health care professionals.

I. REGULATION OF RESEARCH UPON HUMAN SUBJECTS—IRBs

A. NAZI EXPERIMENTATION AND THE DEVELOPMENT OF THE NUREMBERG CODE

The shocking horrors that could be perpetrated by medical experimentation performed by superbly qualified scientists became apparent to the world through the Nazi war crimes trials which resulted in the prosecution of several leading German physicians. These trials unveiled conduct ignominious under any circumstances. For example, they brought to light medical research in which "volunteers," usually concentration camp inmates, were exposed to extremely low atmospheric pressure until they died in order to help the German Air Force prepare for high altitude military operations. They revealed subjects who were forced to drink seawater or breathe mustard gas, were exposed to such epidemics as malaria, jaundice, and typhus, or were placed in ice water until they froze. Several of the experiments were "open" to a wide range of concentration camp inmates, while others were limited to Jews, Gypsies, Polish priests, or other "special" groups.

This experimentation was not perceived as an abuse of medicine by its perpetrators. Rather, it was seen as appropriate conduct, done in the name of healing, and carried out consistently with the Hippocratic Oath. For an account of the professional role of physicians in the Nazi policy of extermination, see R.J. Lifton, The Nazi Doctors (1986). Most of the twenty physicians accused of participating in or directing this experimentation were convicted, and some were hanged. A few were acquitted and one escaped. In one of the tribunal's most significant and ultimately most important judgments, the court of three American judges sitting in Nuremberg promulgated a set of principles to be applied to determine when medical experimentation is appropriate.

These principles provide the basis for all subsequent discussions of the substantive limitations that ought to be put upon research involving human subjects.

NUREMBERG CODE: PERMISSIBLE MEDICAL EXPERIMENTS

The great weight of the evidence before us is to the effect that certain types of medical experiments on human beings, when kept within reasonably well-defined bounds, conform to the ethics of the medical profession generally. The protagonists of the practice of human experimentation justify their views on the basis that such experiments yield results for the good of society that are unprocurable by other methods or means of study. All agree, however, that certain basic principles must be observed in order to satisfy moral, ethical and legal concepts:

1. The voluntary consent of the human subject is absolutely essential.

This means that the person involved should have legal capacity to give consent; should be so situated as to be able to exercise free power of choice, without the intervention of any element of force, fraud, deceit, duress, over-reaching, or other ulterior form of constraint or coercion; and should have sufficient knowledge and comprehension of the elements of the subject matter involved as to enable him to make an understanding and enlightened decision. This latter element requires that before the acceptance of an affirmative decision by the experimental subject there should be made known to him the nature, duration, and purpose of the experiment; the method and means by which it is to be conducted; all inconveniences and hazards reasonably to be expected; and the effects upon his health or person which may possibly come from his participation in the experiment.

The duty and responsibility for ascertaining the quality of the consent rests upon each individual who initiates, directs or engages in the experiment. It is a personal duty and responsibility which may not be delegated to another with impunity.

2. The experiment should be such as to yield fruitful results for the good of society, unprocurable by other methods or means of study, and not random and unnecessary in nature.

3. The experiment should be so designed and based on the results of animal experimentation and a knowledge of the natural history of the disease or other problem under study that the anticipated results will justify the performance of the experiment.

4. The experiment should be so conducted as to avoid all unnecessary physical and mental suffering and injury.

5. No experiment should be conducted where there is an *a priori* reason to believe that death or disabling injury will occur; except,

perhaps, in those experiments where the experimental physicians also serve as subjects.

6. The degree of risk to be taken should never exceed that determined by the humanitarian importance of the problem to be solved by the experiment.

7. Proper preparations should be made and adequate facilities provided to protect the experimental subject against even remote possibilities of injury, disability, or death.

8. The experiment should be conducted only by scientifically qualified persons. The highest degree of skill and care should be required through all stages of the experiment of those who conduct or engage in the experiment.

9. During the course of the experiment the human subject should be at liberty to bring the experiment to an end if he has reached the physical or mental state where continuation of the experiment seems to him to be impossible.

10. During the course of the experiment the scientist in charge must be prepared to terminate the experiment at any stage, if he has probable cause to believe, in the exercise of the good faith, superior skill and careful judgment required of him that a continuation of the experiment is likely to result in injury, disability, or death to the experimental subject.

The Nuremberg Code has been restated and expanded several times since it was rendered. The World Medical Association adopted the Declaration of Helsinki, which elaborated upon the Nuremberg Code, in 1964. This comparatively sophisticated document distinguished between professional care (i.e., purely therapeutic interaction), non-therapeutic research, and medical research combined with professional care, which it called "clinical research." The Declaration included the requirement of fully informed written consent and recognized that minors, mentally ill persons, and those who are institutionalized need special protections if they are to participate as human research subjects. These principles have been fine tuned and repromulgated by several national and international medical organizations.

B. HISTORY OF RESEARCH UPON HUMAN SUBJECTS IN THE UNITED STATES

In the United States research has also been tainted by racially and politically motivated choices of subjects for medical investigation. Indeed, one of the defenses raised at the Nazi war trials was that there was no relevant distinction between what the Nazi physicians did and the contemporaneous American practice of using conscientious objectors and prisoners (including "political" prisoners, such as those convicted of treason) as subjects in research designed to improve America's military strength. The argument that the United States applied a double standard that condemned only Nazi research is bolstered by the fact that there was no effort to seek retribution against Japanese experimenters who were doing work with serious implications for biological warfare, but who cooperated with the United States after their capture.

The most famous twentieth century American breach of research ethics was the Tuskegee Syphilis Study. In this study, hundreds of poor African American men in the South were studied so that the research agency, the United States Public Health Service, could develop an understanding of the natural history of syphilis. Poor rural African Americans were chosen as subjects because of the difficulty they might have in seeking treatment for syphilis and because it was thought that African Americans, who were considered naturally more sexually active and physically and mentally weaker than whites, would be more likely to benefit from the outcome of the study. The natural history of the disease could be discovered only if any treatment provided to the subjects were ineffective. The United States Public Health Service continued this research for some forty years. Even when penicillin, the first truly effective treatment for syphilis, became available, the Public Health Service physicians failed to offer that treatment to most of their subjects, and many were regularly discouraged from getting other forms of treatment. The study came to public light in 1972 and was the topic of federal administrative and Congressional hearings in 1973. While participants in the study successfully sued the Public Health Service for compensation, no criminal actions arose out of the case. For a complete account of this tawdry episode in American medical history, see J. Jones, Bad Blood (1981).

The Tuskegee Syphilis Study is not unique as an example of American medical research failing to respect individual subjects. Other publicized cases include the Jewish Chronic Disease Hospital case, in which live cancer cells were injected into patients without their knowledge, and the Willowbrook State Hospital hepatitis study, in which children admitted to a state hospital rife with hepatitis were given the disease as a condition of admission. In each of these cases, as in the Nazi experiments, the only authorities determining whether the subjects were properly selected were the medical investigators themselves.

The first formal federal policy requiring outside review of research involving human subjects was imposed in 1966 by the Public Health Service upon those seeking grants from it. The 1966 policy required prior consideration of "the risks and potential medical benefits of the investigation" before a protocol could be submitted to the Public Health Service.

In 1974, one year after the public disclosure of the Tuskegee Syphilis Study, Congress enacted the National Research Act establishing the National Commission for Protection of Human Subjects of

Biomedical and Behavioral Research, which was to "conduct a comprehensive investigation and study to identify basic ethical principles" that should underlie the conduct of human subjects research. That Commission was also to develop procedures to assure that the research would be consistent with those ethical principles and to recommend guidelines that could apply to human subjects research supported by the Department of Health, Education and Welfare. In recognition of the interdisciplinary nature of the issue, the Act also required the establishment of institutional review boards (IRBs) at institutions under contract with the Department of Health, Education and Welfare.

By 1975, when the Department of Health, Education and Welfare issued its "Policy for the Protection of Human Research Subjects", virtually every university, medical school, and research hospital had established IRBs which operated within the requirements of both federal and state regulations. The federal regulations were revised by what had become the Department of Health and Human Services (DHHS) in 1981 to remove the necessity of IRB reviews from some low-risk research and to provide for informal consent procedures in some cases. This year in the United States, hundreds of IRBs will review thousands of research protocols. No federally funded research will be carried out at an institution without that institution's IRB approval.

C. CURRENT REGULATION OF RESEARCH UPON HUMAN SUBJECTS IN THE UNITED STATES

Consider the currently applicable regulations. Determine how they reflect the Nuremburg Code and the principle that health care policies ought not be determined at the national level, but rather should be delegated to local agencies that reflect local community values.

Problem: Rape Victims as Research Subjects

As counsel to a small community hospital that has not engaged in any research, you have been asked how the hospital trustees should react to the request of one of the staff physicians to evaluate the effectiveness of the emergency room staff in dealing with victims of rapes. She wishes to ask all such patients, some of whom are likely to be minors, to answer a series of questions on their religious, cultural, and educational background and on their knowledge of social resources for rape victims. She also intends to review those patients' medical and psychological histories. Finally, she wishes to contact them by mail several weeks after their hospital admission with a follow up questionnaire. All information will be coded so that only the investigator will be able to determine the identity of any patient. The physician believes that the research will help the hospital determine what kinds of immediate care are most helpful to rape victims (e.g., what kind of psychological counseling is most important?), what kinds of physicians are best qualified to help those patients (e.g., are women physicians more likely to provide satisfactory treatment?), and what kinds of hospital policies are most likely to encourage victims to seek medical attention (e.g., should the hospital call the police if the alleged victim has not?). She expects to publish the results of her research, which will cost about $10,000 to perform. About $1500 of the costs will be underwritten by a grant from DHHS.

Is the hospital obliged to establish an institutional review board to review this research? If so, how is one established? Who should be on it? To whom should it report? What, precisely, should it review? What standards should it apply to the review? Is there any way that this research can be done without the establishment of such a board?

45 C.F.R. §§ 46.101–46.117 (1990)
BASIC DHHS POLICY FOR PROTECTION OF HUMAN RESEARCH SUBJECTS

§ 46.101 To what do these regulations apply?

(a) Except as provided in paragraph (b) of this section, this subpart applies to all research involving human subjects conducted by the Department of Health and Human Services or funded in whole or in part by a Department grant, contract, cooperative agreement or fellowship.

(b) Research activities in which the only involvement of human subjects will be in one or more of the following categories are exempt from these regulations unless the research is covered by other subparts of this part:

(1) Research conducted in established or commonly accepted educational settings, involving normal educational practices, such as (i) research on regular and special education instructional strategies, or (ii) research on the effectiveness of or the comparison among instructional techniques, curricula, or classroom management methods.

(2) Research involving the use of educational tests.

(3) Research involving survey or interview procedures.

(4) Research involving the observation (including observation by participants) of public behavior.

(5) Research involving the collection or study of existing data, documents, records, pathological specimens, or diagnostic specimens.

(c) The Secretary has final authority to determine whether a particular activity is covered by these regulations.

(d) The Secretary may require that specific research activities or classes of research activities conducted or funded by the Department, but not otherwise covered by these regulations, comply with some or all of these regulations.

(e) The Secretary may also waive applicability of these regulations to specific research activities or classes of research activities, otherwise covered by these regulations. * * *

(f) No individual may receive Department funding for research covered by these regulations unless the individual is affiliated with or sponsored by an institution which assumes responsibility for the research under an assurance satisfying the requirements of this part, or the individual makes other arrangements with the Department.

(g) Compliance with these regulations will in no way render inapplicable pertinent federal, state, or local laws or regulations.

§ 46.102   Definitions.

* * *

(d) "Legally authorized representative" means an individual or judicial or other body authorized under applicable law to consent on behalf of a prospective subject to the subject's participation in the procedure(s) involved in the research.

(e) "Research" means a systematic investigation designed to develop or contribute to generalizable knowledge. Activities which meet this definition constitute "research" for purposes of these regulations, whether or not they are supported or funded under a program which is considered research for other purposes.

(f) "Human subject" means a living individual about whom an investigator (whether professional or student) conducting research obtains (1) data through intervention or interaction with the individual, or (2) identifiable private information. "Intervention" includes both physical procedures by which data are gathered (for example, venipuncture) and manipulations of the subject or the subject's environment that are performed for research purposes. "Interaction" includes communication or interpersonal contact between investigator and subject. "Private information" includes information about behavior that occurs in a context in which an individual can reasonably expect that no observation or recording is taking place, and information which has been provided for specific purposes by an individual and which the individual can reasonably expect will not be made public (for example, a medical record). Private information must be individually identifiable (i.e., the identity of the subject is or may readily be ascertained by the investigator or associated with the information) in order for obtaining the information to constitute research involving human subjects.

(g) "Minimal risk" means that the risks of harm anticipated in the proposed research are not greater, considering probability and magnitude, than those ordinarily encountered in daily life or during the performance of routine physical or psychological examinations or tests.

§ 46.107   IRB membership.

(a) Each IRB shall have at least five members with varying backgrounds to promote complete and adequate review of research activities commonly conducted by the institution. The IRB shall be sufficiently qualified through the experience and expertise of its members, and the diversity of the members' backgrounds including consideration of the racial and cultural backgrounds of members and sensitivity to such issues as community attitudes, to promote respect for its advice and counsel in safeguarding the rights and welfare of human subjects. In addition to possessing the professional competence necessary to review specific research activities, the IRB shall be able to ascertain the acceptability of proposed research in terms of institutional commitments and regulations, applicable law, and standards of professional conduct and practice. The IRB shall therefore include persons knowledgeable in these areas. If an IRB regularly reviews research that involves a vulnerable category of subjects, including but not limited to subjects covered by other subparts of this part, the IRB shall include one or more individuals who are primarily concerned with the welfare of these subjects.

(b) No IRB may consist entirely of men or entirely of women, or entirely of members of one profession.

(c) Each IRB shall include at least one member whose primary concerns are in nonscientific areas; for example: lawyers, ethicists, members of the clergy.

(d) Each IRB shall include at least one member who is not otherwise affiliated with the institution and who is not part of the immediate family of a person who is affiliated with the institution.

(e) No IRB may have a member participating in the IRB's initial or continuing review of any project in which the member has a conflicting interest, except to provide information requested by the IRB.

(f) An IRB may, in its discretion, invite individuals with competence in special areas to assist in the review of complex issues which require expertise beyond or in addition to that available on the IRB. These individuals may not vote with the IRB.

§ 46.109 IRB review of research.

(a) An IRB shall review and have authority to approve, require modifications in (to secure approval), or disapprove all research activities covered by these regulations.

* * *

(d) An IRB shall notify investigators and the institution in writing of its decision to approve or disapprove the proposed research activity, or of modifications required to secure IRB approval of the research activity. If the IRB decides to disapprove a research activity, it shall include in its written notification a statement of the reasons for its decision and give the investigator an opportunity to respond in person or in writing.

(e) An IRB shall conduct continuing review of research covered by these regulations at intervals appropriate to the degree of risk, but not less than once per year, and shall have authority to observe or have a third party observe the consent process and the research.

§ 46.111   Criteria for IRB approval of research.

(a) In order to approve research covered by these regulations the IRB shall determine that all of the following requirements are satisfied:

(1) Risks to subjects are minimized: (i) by using procedures which are consistent with sound research design and which do not unnecessarily expose subjects to risk, and (ii) whenever appropriate, by using procedures already being performed on the subjects for diagnostic or treatment purposes.

(2) Risks to subjects are reasonable in relation to anticipated benefits, if any, to subjects, and the importance of the knowledge that may reasonably be expected to result. In evaluating risks and benefits, the IRB should consider only those risks and benefits that may result from the research (as distinguished from risks and benefits of therapies subjects would receive even if not participating in the research). The IRB should not consider possible long-range effects of applying knowledge gained in the research (for example, the possible effects of the research on public policy) as among those research risks that fall within the purview of its responsibility.

(3) Selection of subjects is equitable. In making this assessment the IRB should take into account the purposes of the research and the setting in which the research will be conducted.

(4) Informed consent will be sought from each prospective subject or the subject's legally authorized representative, in accordance with, and to the extent required by § 46.116.

(5) Informed consent will be appropriately documented, in accordance with, and to the extent required by § 46.117.

(6) Where appropriate, the research plan makes adequate provision for monitoring the data collected to insure the safety of subjects.

(7) Where appropriate, there are adequate provisions to protect the privacy of subjects and to maintain the confidentiality of data.

(b) Where some or all of the subjects are likely to be vulnerable to coercion or undue influence, such as persons with acute or severe physical or mental illness, or persons who are economically or educationally disadvantaged, appropriate additional safeguards have been included in the study to protect the rights and welfare of these subjects.

§ 46.113   Suspension or termination of IRB approval of research.

An IRB shall have authority to suspend or terminate approval of research that is not being conducted in accordance with the IRB's requirements or that has been associated with unexpected serious harm to subjects. Any suspension or termination of approval shall include a statement of the reasons for the IRB's action and shall be reported promptly to the investigator, appropriate institutional officials, and the Secretary.

§ 46.116   General requirements for informed consent.

Except as provided elsewhere in this or other subparts, no investigator may involve a human being as a subject in research covered by these regulations unless the investigator has obtained the legally effective informed consent of the subject or the subject's legally authorized representative. An investigator shall seek such consent only under circumstances that provide the prospective subject or the representative sufficient opportunity to consider whether or not to participate and that minimize the possibility of coercion or undue influence. The information that is given to the subject or the representative shall be in language understandable to the subject or the representative. No informed consent, whether oral or written, may include any exculpatory language through which the subject or the representative is made to waive or appear to waive any of the subject's legal rights, or releases or appears to release the investigator, the sponsor, the institution or its agents from liability for negligence.

(a) Basic elements of informed consent. Except as provided in paragraph (c) or (d) of this section, in seeking informed consent the following information shall be provided to each subject:

(1) A statement that the study involves research, an explanation of the purposes of the research and the expected duration of the subject's participation, a description of the procedures to be followed, and identification of any procedures which are experimental;

(2) A description of any reasonably foreseeable risks or discomforts to the subject;

(3) A description of any benefits to the subject or to others which may reasonably be expected from the research;

(4) A disclosure of appropriate alternative procedures or courses of treatment, if any, that might be advantageous to the subject;

(5) A statement describing the extent, if any, to which confidentiality of records identifying the subject will be maintained;

(6) For research involving more than minimal risk, an explanation as to whether any compensation and an explanation as to whether any medical treatments are available if injury occurs and, if so, what they consist of, or where further information may be obtained;

(7) An explanation of whom to contact for answers to pertinent questions about the research and research subjects' rights, and whom to contact in the event of a research-related injury to the subject; and

(8) A statement that participation is voluntary, refusal to participate will involve no penalty or loss of benefits to which the subject is otherwise entitled, and the subject may discontinue participation at any time without penalty or loss of benefits to which the subject is otherwise entitled.

(b) Additional elements of informed consent. When appropriate, one or more of the following elements of information shall also be provided to each subject:

(1) A statement that the particular treatment or procedure may involve risks to the subject (or to the embryo or fetus, if the subject is or may become pregnant) which are currently unforeseeable;

(2) Anticipated circumstances under which the subject's participation may be terminated by the investigator without regard to the subject's consent;

(3) Any additional costs to the subject that may result from participation in the research;

(4) The consequences of a subject's decision to withdraw from the research and procedures for orderly termination of participation by the subject;

(5) A statement that significant new findings developed during the course of the research which may relate to the subject's willingness to continue participation will be provided to the subject; and

(6) The approximate number of subjects involved in the study.

* * *

(d) An IRB may approve a consent procedure which does not include, or which alters, some or all of the elements of informed consent set forth above, or waive the requirements to obtain informed consent provided the IRB finds and documents that:

(1) The research involves no more than minimal risk to the subjects;

(2) The waiver or alteration will not adversely affect the rights and welfare of the subjects;

(3) The research could not practicably be carried out without the waiver or alteration; and

(4) Whenever appropriate, the subjects will be provided with additional pertinent information after participation.

(e) The informed consent requirements in these regulations are not intended to preempt any applicable federal, state, or local laws which require additional information to be disclosed in order for informed consent to be legally effective.

(f) Nothing in these regulations is intended to limit the authority of a physician to provide emergency medical care, to the extent the physician is permitted to do so under applicable federal, state, or local law.

§ 46.117   Documentation of informed consent.

(a) Except as provided in paragraph (c) of this section, informed consent shall be documented by the use of a written consent form approved by the IRB and signed by the subject or the subject's legally authorized representative. A copy shall be given to the person signing the form.

(b) Except as provided in paragraph (c) of this section, the consent form may be either of the following:

(1) A written consent document that embodies the elements of informed consent required by § 46.116. This form may be read to the subject or the subject's legally authorized representative, but in any event, the investigator shall give either the subject or the representative adequate opportunity to read it before it is signed; or

(2) A "short form" written consent document stating that the elements of informed consent required by § 46.116 have been presented orally to the subject or the subject's legally authorized representative. When this method is used, there shall be a witness to the oral presentation. Also, the IRB shall approve a written summary of what is to be said to the subject or the representative. Only the short form itself is to be signed by the subject or the representative. However, the witness shall sign both the short form and a copy of the summary, and the person actually obtaining consent shall sign a copy of the summary. A copy of the summary shall be given to the subject or the representative, in addition to a copy of the "short form."

(c) An IRB may waive the requirement for the investigator to obtain a signed consent form for some or all subjects if it finds either:

(1) That the only record linking the subject and the research would be the consent document and the principal risk would be potential harm resulting from a breach of confidentiality. Each subject will be asked whether the subject wants documentation linking the subject with the research, and the subject's wishes will govern; or

(2) That the research presents no more than minimal risk of harm to subjects and involves no procedures for which written consent is normally required outside of the research context.

Notes and Questions

1. Most medical researchers, who resent the necessity of obtaining IRB approval before applying for federal grants, applauded the 1981 amendments to the basic DHHS policy. These amendments excluded from the necessity of full review many kinds of research, including some questionnaire research and most retrospective data reviews which had been included under the 1975 regulations. The new regulations also provided for an expedited approval for research with no more than "minimal risk," that is, where the risk was no greater than that encountered in daily life—for example, the risk of leaving the house, going to work, and ultimately returning home via Safeway. 45 C.F.A. § 46.110 (1990).

2. The 1981 revisions also clarified an issue that had been a matter of some dispute under the 1975 regulations: the IRB procedures set out in the regulations are required only for research performed or funded by the Department of Health and Human Services. As the 1981 amendments

make clear, the regulations do not apply to other research, even if they are conducted at the same institutions. This distinction has little practical effect, however, because Food and Drug Administration regulations apply the same principles to privately funded research that is designed to result in a new drug or medical device license. In addition, the regulations require that any institution receiving research funds from the DHHS assure the Department that research not funded by DHHS also will be reviewed for ethical propriety. Because it is difficult to maintain two IRBs—one conforming with federal regulations for DHHS funded and FDA projects, and another, not necessarily conforming, to review other research—most institutions have opted to apply the federal regulations to all research being conducted within the institution and to have all such research reviewed by the same IRB.

3. IRBs are intended to reflect local conditions and local values. They may have as few as five members or as many as the institution wishes to place on the board; some have dozens of members. IRBs are expected to have racial and cultural diversity and to be sensitive to community attitudes. Section 46.107(b), which provides that "no IRB may consist entirely of men or entirely of women, or entirely of members of one profession," assures that an IRB will not consist of only male physicians. There must be one non-scientist on each IRB (the regulations suggest a lawyer, ethicist, or member of the clergy), and there must be one member who is not affiliated with the institution. Do the regulations effectively guarantee that the IRB will represent the values that ought to be considered in making research determinations? Most IRBs include several researchers from the institution, a nurse (who usually allows the IRB to meet the "not entirely men" requirement), a local clergyman, and a lawyer. What purpose does the presence of the lawyer serve? Is there anything in the background of the lawyer that makes his or her presence on the board significant? If you were to rewrite § 46.107, which deals with IRB membership, what kind of interdisciplinary mix would you require on the IRB? Why?

4. While § 46.111 establishes seven substantive criteria for approval of a research protocol, most IRB time is spent discussing (1) whether the "risks to subjects are reasonable in relationship to anticipated benefits," and (2) whether the informed consent form is adequate. Should these be the primary substantive bases for community review of medical research? Consent forms can always be rewritten: thus, in the rare instance that a research protocol is turned down by an IRB the reason is usually that the IRB has determined that the risk to benefit ratio is not acceptable. The power to reach this determination gives a substantial amount of authority to the committee.

5. The IRB must determine that risks to the subjects are reasonable in relationship to (1) benefits to the subjects and (2) the importance of the knowledge that may reasonably be expected to result. The IRB must consider the long-range effects of the knowledge in evaluating *benefits,* but it may *not* consider the long range effects on evaluating *risks.* § 46.111(a)(2). Thus, an IRB could not refuse approval of a military study just because the results could be used only to promote offensive weaponry. Similarly, IRBs have been required to approve studies of sleeping pills that

have a minimal benefit (and no risk) to patients under clinical conditions, even though the IRB members agreed that ultimate FDA approval of the sleeping pills and their consequent public availability would have a serious adverse effect on public health.

6. When an IRB is established at a private institution under the direction of federal regulations, is the IRB a federal agency or merely a private committee? Is it the subject of federal statutory and regulatory constraints? Must an IRB respond to a Freedom of Information Act request? If a state institution—for instance, a state hospital—establishes an IRB under federal law, is the IRB a federal agency, a state agency, some hybrid of the two, or something else entirely? If there is a conflict between the Freedom of Information Act and a state public records act, which is the appropriate vehicle for obtaining information from a state hospital IRB? Can an IRB be a federal agency and a state agency at the same time?

7. Recently there has been some interest in obtaining records of IRBs for use elsewhere—for example, in malpractice cases. Are the IRB documents or records of their deliberations public information, entirely confidential, or something between the two? Are the IRBs medical review committees whose processes and documents are confidential and not discoverable? Would it affect the deliberations of the IRB if those deliberations could later be made public and the participants cross-examined? Some IRBs meet privately and admit no outsiders, some admit outsiders with advance approval of the chair or the IRB, and some IRBs meet in public arenas and allow some public participation. See Adams, Medical Research and Personal Privacy, 30 Villanova L.Rev. 1077 (1985). See also Chapter 4, supra, concerning the availability of medical records.

8. In 1983 the Department of Health and Human Services promulgated regulations which provide supplementary protection to children who are research subjects. These regulations divide research upon children into three categories: "research not involving greater than the minimal risk," "research involving greater than minimal risk but presenting the prospect of direct benefit to the individual subjects," and "research involving greater than minimal risk and no prospect of direct benefit to individual subjects, but likely to yield generalizable knowledge about the subject's disorder or condition." 45 C.F.R. §§ 46.404–46.406 (1990). In all cases IRB approval must assure that "adequate provisions are made for soliciting the assent of the children and permission of their parents or guardians."

Where there is a more than minimal risk but the research will also benefit the child, the risk must be justified "by the anticipated benefit to the subjects" (unleavened by any benefit that society may derive), and "[t]he relation of the anticipated benefit to the risk [must be] at least as favorable to the subjects as that presented by available alternative approaches." 45 C.F.R. § 46.405 (1990). Non-therapeutic research involving more than minimal risk may be approved only if there is a "minor" increase over minimal risk, the "experiences" that accompany the research are those that the child-subjects are likely to undergo anyway, and the research is aimed at a disorder or condition actually suffered by the subject. 45 C.F.R. § 46.406 (1990). The regulations require the consent (called "permission" in the regulations) of one parent before a child may participate in research, although the permission of both parents (if they are reasonably available) is required before a child becomes a subject in non-therapeutic research involving greater than minimal risk.

The regulations also require that "the IRB shall determine that adequate provisions are made for soliciting the assent of the children, when in the judgment of the IRB the children are capable of providing assent." 45 C.F.R. § 46.408 (1990). The IRB is required to consider the age, maturity, and psychological state of the subjects when determining whether the children are capable of assenting, and the IRB is entitled to make a determination of the propriety of requiring subject assent on either a protocol-by-protocol or child-by-child basis. Id.

Finally, the regulations put additional limitations on research involving "[c]hildren who are wards of the state or any other agency, institution, or entity. * * * " 45 C.F.R. § 46.409 (1990). The regulations attempt to discourage researchers from using these easy marks as subjects, and their use as subjects is prohibited unless the research is "related to their status as wards" or is conducted in such a way that most of the children who are subjects are not wards. Id.

9. The most controversial federal regulations governing research are those that severely limit fetal research. These regulations divide fetal research into two categories: research done upon fetuses *in utero,* and research done upon fetuses *ex utero.* Therapeutic research is permitted on a fetus *in utero* only if the risk is minimized. Non-therapeutic research is permitted on a fetus *in utero* only if the risk is minimized *and* the research is intended to result in "the development of important biomedical knowledge which cannot be obtained by other means." 45 C.F.R. § 46.208 (1990).

Viable fetuses *ex utero* are treated as children, of course, and non-viable fetuses *ex utero* may be subjects in research only if "(1) vital functions of the fetus will not be artificially maintained except where the purpose of the activity is to develop new methods for enabling fetuses to survive to the point of viability, (2) experimental activities which of themselves would terminate the heartbeat or respiration of a fetus will not be employed, and (3) the purpose of the activity is the development of important biomedical knowledge which cannot be obtained by other means." 45 C.F.R. § 46.209 (1990). In any case, the mother and father (unless he is unavailable or the pregnancy is the result of rape) must consent to the research before a fetus can be a subject of that research. Id.

Some believe that this effective prohibition on research upon human fetuses is slowing the development of medical treatment which could help many non-viable fetuses reach the point of viability, and which could help viable fetuses live longer and happier lives. Others argue that the special vulnerability of the fetus requires special protection by government regulation. Of course, the debate over the appropriate limitations on research involving fetal tissue is not unrelated to the debate over the propriety of abortion. Some fear that giving physicians the authority to do research upon fetal tissue will inevitably result in their acquisition of that tissue through encouraged or solicited abortions.

This fear has also resulted in a ban (called a "moratorium") on all Federal funding of all research in which human fetal tissue from induced abortions is transplanted into humans. The ban, which was instituted in 1988, has been continued despite substantial opposition from ethicists and medical researchers.

10. Other classes of subjects have been proposed as worthy of special protection by regulation. Since 1978 DHHS and FDA have proposed various regulations that would have narrowly limited research upon prisoners because "prisoners may be under constraints because of their incarceration which could affect their ability to make a truly voluntary and uncoerced decision whether or not to participate as subjects in research." 43 Fed.Reg. 53652, 53655 (1978). These regulations would have required that the IRB approving research involving prisoner subjects have at least one prisoner or prisoner representative and that a majority of the IRB be unassociated with the prison. Generally, research would have been limited to that directed to prison conditions and there would have had to be assurances that the prisoner subjects would not get substantially better treatment or earlier parole because of their participation in the research, and that the selection of the prisoner subjects would be "fair" and "immune from arbitrary intervention by prison authorities or prisoners." Id. Do you think that prisoners need special protection from medical researchers? For judicial considerations of these issues, see Bailey v. Lally, 481 F.Supp. 203 (D.Md.1979) (claim that prison conditions were so bad and inducements to participate in research so great that consent could not be voluntary and thus violated prisoners' constitutional rights) and People v. Gauntlett, 134 Mich.App. 737, 352 N.W.2d 310 (1984) (sex offender could not be forced to quench his libido as a condition of probation through experimental medical treatment).

Among others for whom additional research protections are proposed but not adopted are those institutionalized as mentally disabled. See 43 Fed.Reg. 53950 (1978). While the unadopted regulations have no legal effect, the discussion that followed the proposal of regulations aimed at prisoners and institutionalized mentally disabled subjects has had a real effect on the research community; there is now an attempt to avoid these classes of subjects if others are available.

11. One hotly debated issue is who ought to profit when medical researchers take unique human tissue from a subject and develop a commercial product from it. In Moore v. Regents of the University of California, 51 Cal.3d 120, 271 Cal.Rptr. 146, 793 P.2d 479 (1990) [reprinted in chapter 3, above] the plaintiff was a cancer patient at the U.C.L.A. Medical Center. Upon the physicians' recommendation that his spleen be removed to save his life, Moore consented to the surgery. For the next seven years he regularly returned to the U.C.L.A. Medical Center from his home in Seattle when asked to do so by his physicians. He was told that his treatment required his return to U.C.L.A. and that the procedures, which routinely included taking samples of blood, blood serum, skin, bone marrow aspirate and sperm, could only be performed there. Moore alleged that the defendants concealed from him the fact that they were engaged in several activities by which they would "benefit financially and competitively * * * by virtue of [their] ongoing physician-patient relationship * * *," 793 P.2d at 481. In fact, physicians at U.C.L.A. developed (and patented) a commercially valuable cell line from Moore's tissue. The California Su-

preme Court, appalled by the defendants' alleged conduct, found that Moore stated a cause of action for breach of fiduciary duty and lack of informed consent, but that the physicians' use of his body substances did not provide the patient with a cause of action for conversion. This decision is destined to be the subject of a great deal of academic writing. For some of the more interesting writings published before the thorough and thoughtful opinions that were issued by the California Supreme Court, see Note, Toward the Right of Commerciality: Recognizing Property Rights and the Commercial Value of Human Tissue, 34 U.C.L.A. L.Rev. 207 (1986); Howard, Biotechnology, Patients' Rights, and the *Moore* case, 44 Food Drug Cosm.L.J. 331 (1989); Danforth, Cells, Sales, and Royalties: the Patient's Right to a Portion of the Profits, 6 Yale L. & Pol'y Rev. 179 (1988); Note, Source Compensation for Tissues and Cells Used in Biotechnology Research: Why a Source Shouldn't Share in the Profits, 64 Notre Dame L.Rev. 628 (1989). For the best, very brief account of the ethics of this issue, see Murray, Who Owns the Body? On the Ethics of Using Human Tissue for Commercial Purposes, IRB: A Review of Human Subjects Research 5 (Jan./Feb.1986).

12. The federal regulations do not directly address the question that arises when an investigator believes that one arm of a therapeutic investigation is really superior to the other. Can that investigator allow his patients to be randomized to one arm or another? One thoughtful commentator suggests that such randomization is ethical when there is "present or imminent controversy in the clinical community over the preferred treatment," whatever the individual investigator may believe. Freedman, Equipoise and the Ethics of Clinical Research, 317 N.Eng.J.Med. 141 (1987).

13. The invaluable standard text on research involving human subjects is Levine, Ethics and Regulation of Clinical Research (2d ed. 1986). IRB: A Journal of Human Subjects Research is a periodical that contains timely articles on all aspects of research involving human subjects.

II. INSTITUTIONAL ETHICS COMMITTEES

While interdisciplinary medical decisionmaking is particularly well established in the area of research involving human subjects, other substantive issues could also benefit from interdisciplinary committee discussion. Only a few years ago there were a mere handful of institutional ethics committees (IECs) in this country; now virtually all major medical institutions have them. By 1990 the greatest growth area for IECs was in nursing homes, where they have been slower to catch on but where residents and staff frequently face difficult ethical decisions. Unlike IRBs, which have a structure and role defined by federal regulation and operate similarly throughout the country, the function and process of an IEC at one institution may bear virtually no relationship to the function and process of an IEC at another.

There are three general functions that an IEC can serve. First, the committee may educate itself, the hospital administration, and the hospital staff about medical-ethical issues. For example, the staff's fear of legal intervention when life support systems are removed from a terminally ill (or even brain-dead) patient can be alleviated by institutional education conducted by a thoughtful IEC. Second, an IEC may participate in policy development within a hospital. For example, an IEC may draft a "Do Not Resuscitate" policy or a hospital-wide living will policy. Third, an IEC may be involved in the resolution of particular cases. A physician and family who are uncertain about whether it would be appropriate to discontinue therapy on a patient might consult an IEC, which could consider the issue, provide information to the physician and family, confirm the physician's and the family's previous decision, or simply decide the case itself.

In fact, ethics committees have found that they are best able to serve the educational functions and that these educational functions generally lead to policy development within the institution. It is only a committee with a good reputation for education and policy development within the institution that is likely to be consulted on individual cases. IECs generally have found that they are more likely to be accepted within the institution if they are an advisory group, not a formal and binding court of appeal on pending substantive bioethics questions. The compositions of IECs vary, as do their roles. Institutional staff is always well represented, and committees will often have a clergyman, ethicist, lawyer, "community representative," or several of each of these.

JUDICIAL COUNCIL OF THE A.M.A., GUIDELINES FOR ETHICS COMMITTEES IN HEALTH CARE INSTITUTIONS
253 J.A.M.A. 2698 (1985).

These guidelines have been developed to aid in the establishment and functioning of ethics committees in hospitals and other health care institutions that may choose to form such committees, recognizing that the functions may vary depending on the type of institution.

Ethics committees in health care institutions should be voluntary, educational, and advisory in purpose so as not to interfere with the primary responsibility and relationship between physicians and their patients. Generally, the function of the ethics committee is to consider and assist in resolving unusual, complicated ethical problems involving issues that affect the care and treatment of patients within the health care institution and concern those persons who are responsible for their care and treatment. Typical are issues involving quality of life, terminal illness, and utilization of scarce, limited health resources.

The size of the ethics committee should be consistent with the needs of the institution but not so large in number as to be unwieldy. Members of the committee should be selected on the basis of their concern for the welfare of the sick and infirm, their interest in ethical matters, and their reputation in the community and among their peers for integrity and mature judgment. Preferably, a majority of the committee should consist of physicians, nurses, and other health care providers.

Persons considered for the ethics committee should be temperamentally suited to making recommendations affecting the welfare of patients and professional considerations relating to their care and treatment. Experience as a member of hospital or medical society committees concerned with ethical conduct or quality assurance should be given weight in selecting members of the committee. It is important that persons selected as committee members should not have other responsibilities that are likely to prove incompatible with their duties as members of the ethics committee.

The functions of the ethics committee should be confined exclusively to ethical matters. In hospitals, the medical staff bylaws should delineate the functions of the ethics committee, general qualifications for membership, manner of selection, and parameters of the committee's activities. The *Principles of Medical Ethics* and *Current Opinions of the Judicial Council of the American Medical Association* are recommended for the guidance of ethics committees in the making of their own recommendations.

Although the recommendations that the ethics committee may make may involve the application of moral standards that exceed those imposed by law, such recommendations should not contravene or violate applicable laws of the jurisdiction or call upon others to do so. In denominational health care institutions or those operated by religious orders, the recommendations of the ethics committee may be anticipated to be consistent with published religious tenets and principles. Where particular religious beliefs are to be taken into consideration in the committee's recommendations, this fact should be publicized to those persons concerned with the committee's recommendations.

The matters to be considered by the ethics committee should consist of ethical subjects that a majority of its members may choose to discuss on its own initiative, matters referred to it by the executive committee of the organized medical staff or by the governing board of the institution, or appropriate requests from patients, families of patients, or physicians. The ethics committee may also choose to consider requests from other health professionals who are employed by the institution and who pursued the matter through designated appropriate administrative channels.

Generally, recommendations of the ethics committee should be in writing and channeled through the executive committee of the organized medical staff in consideration of those persons who may have a direct interest in the committee's recommendations. In the absence of an organized medical staff the committee's recommendations should be channeled through the administrator of the institution or the latter's designee. The procedures followed by the ethics committee should comply with institutional policies for preserving the confidentiality of information regarding patients.

The recommendations of the ethics committee should be offered precisely as recommendations imposing no obligation for acceptance on the part of the institution, its governing board, medical staff, attending physician, or other persons. On the other hand, it is expected that the ethics committee will give patient consideration and sympathetic understanding to matters that it is called upon to study, and that the institution will provide the committee with necessary staff assistance. Typically, it should be expected that the efforts of a dedicated committee will receive serious consideration by those whose responsibility it is to function as decision makers.

Those who are selected as members of the ethics committee should be prepared to meet on short notice and to render their recommendations in a timely and prompt fashion in accordance with the demands of the situation and the issues involved.

GIBSON AND KUSHNER, ETHICS COMMITTEES: HOW ARE THEY DOING?

16 Hastings Center Report (3) 9 (June 1986).

The definition of [ethics] committees proposed * * * in 1983, "a multidisciplinary group of health care professionals within a health care institution that has been specifically established to address the ethical dilemmas that occur within the institution," is still applicable, although a kind of democratization has occurred in those committees that have extended membership to community representatives. What lay members may lack in background they more than make up for in enthusiasm and a willingness to learn.

Ethics committees today are more solidly established than in the past, and many have achieved the status of permanent standing committees of the medical staff. But although they report increased institutional acceptance, utilization, and overall support, those problems common to any all-volunteer effort continue to plague them. If committees are to meet the increased educational, policy development, and consultative demands being made on them, they will require financial support beyond xeroxing privileges, permanent staffing beyond part-time secretarial help, and administrative recognition that time devoted to committee activities is part of the members' professional duties and not merely volunteer work.

Since the early 1980s, the "big three" of ethics committee activity have been education, policy development, and case consultation—ideally taken in that order. Common advice to committees just forming was to start with self-education, move on to institutional education and later to community-wide education. Policy development could then follow with the confidence that the content would be sound and the political climate friendlier. Finally, for those committees fortunate enough to have sufficient lead time, case consultations could be undertaken by a committee whose members were well prepared and whose colleagues would be generally receptive. Of course, in the "real world" events crowd in on logic and order, and few, if any, committees have proceeded exactly according to plan. Nevertheless, education, policy development, and consultation remain the three categories committees use to explain and assess their performance.

Committees' attitudes toward education have evolved in an unusual way. Almost without exception self-education and intra-institutional education are now recognized not merely as the starting point for committee activity, but as the continuing and end points as well. Finding that they must cover the same ground repeatedly, yet surprised that seemingly similar cases do not necessarily lend themselves to generalization, committees appreciate that the ongoing collaborative nature of discussion appropriate for ethics consultation applies to their educational activities as well. Requests to repeat programs already offered, and suggestions for development of policies that have been in place for some time remind committee members that success measured only in terms of consults requested ignores the importance of ongoing education.

Emerging areas for policy development include: care of the uninsured or medically indigent, institutional procedures for organ procurement, and advocacy for the rights of incompetent or variably competent elderly patients who are transferred from nursing homes to acute care facilities. One committee chair reported that the hospital administrator, in anticipation of problems concerning premature discharges under DRGs, has formally requested the hospital ethics committee to take on the issue of quality patient care in a cost-containment environment.

Committees emphasize their role as discussants and facilitators of consensus, not as consultants whose decisions are necessarily separate, formal, or final. Yet the question remains: Are the recommendations of such committees *de facto* binding? Committee chairs and members with whom we spoke reported agreement among ethics committee consultants and primary decision makers (physicians, nurses, patient, family). If the committees' recommendations carry weight, members hypothesize, it is because those requesting the consult choose to follow their advice. In the opinion of the committee members, physicians generally make good decisions and simply need a broader forum for discussion and for support. Consultations are viewed as focusing on the process of decision making, where disposition of the *how* and the *who* of an issue takes precedence over the *what*.

Ethics committees now refer less frequently to their function as consultative bodies and more to their emerging role as the institution's "conscience." This role, they suspect, may bring them into greater conflict with the institution's administration over such issues as institutional liability, accountability, and social justice.

* * *

Overall, there is a modest sense of satisfaction with present mechanisms for dealing with ethical dimensions of patient care decisions, and a cautious optimism about the future. This is tempered by a growing, though as yet unfocused concern that emerging issues of cost, access, and quality of care will press ethics committees, now the "consciences" of institutions, into service on behalf of the community at large.

Notes and Questions

1. There is no consensus that ethics committees adequately serve the functions described by Gibson and Kushner. Dr. Mark Siegler argues that the development of ethics committees "symbolizes the dreary, depressed, and disorganized state to which American medicine has fallen." Siegler, Ethics Committees: Decisions by Bureaucracy, 16 Hastings Center Rep. (3) 22 (June 1986). While Dr. Siegler finds a host of problems arising from the movement of health care institutions to create ethics committees, his primary argument is that ethics committees inevitably limit the decision-making authority of physicians, and this, in turn, limits physicians' ability to provide adequate care. In essence, he argues that committees cannot "care" the way doctors do. Is he right when he asserts that the interposition of a committee inevitably weakens the doctor-patient relationship?

2. Dr. Siegler recommends the development of "small advisory groups possessing great clinical expertise in their own particular specialty" in place of ethics committees. Id. The current debate over the appropriate forum for ethical consultation is between those who believe that committees make the best consultants on issues of medical ethics, and those who believe that individual clinical consultants—individual expert medical ethicists—are likely to yield the most helpful information. See La Puma and Toulmin, Ethics Consultants and Ethics Committees, 249 Arch.Internal Med. 1109 (1989). Those who support individual consultants argue that ethics, like nephrology or oncology, requires analysis by those who are truly expert in the area, not some pick-up group of uncertain academic lineage, however diverse they may be. Judith Ross, author of the American Hospital Association's *Handbook for Hospital Ethics Committees* (1986) disagrees. She argues that appointing an expert to deal with ethical issues sends a message that others, including the patient and the physician, ought to defer to the ethicist who knows best. As she points out,

> "I would suggest that, no matter how non-directive, how non-judgmental an ethics consultant attempts to be (assuming he/she does make such an attempt), no matter how committed to being a resource, to opening up questions, to stimulating thought rather than to providing answers, such a role in this culture says that the individual who occupies this role has expertise and authority * * * and that others don't."

Ross, Case Consultation: The Committee or the Clinical Consultant? 2 Hosp.Ethics Comm.Forum 289, 293 (1990). She contrasts this with an ethics committee consultation:

> When it is the ethics committee that takes on individual casework as well as education and policy recommendation, the hospital communi-

cates, in a very direct and visible manner, its commitment to the creation of an *ethical community* in which all actions, all decisions, and all lives are a part of its moral vision because all actors, all decision makers, and all participants are the creators of its moral community.

Id. at 297–8. Do you agree with Ms. Ross that the very existence and process of the ethics committee contains a message that cannot be communicated through individual expert consultants?

3. Are there any legal risks or advantages that derive from consultation with an institutional ethics committee? Should a court consider relevant the fact that a physician consulted an ethics committee, and that his actions are consistent with its recommendations, in determining whether life support treatment can be removed? In determining whether the physician committed malpractice? In determining whether the physician committed a crime? If a physician decides to ignore the recommendation of the ethics committee, should that be relevant in any of the same ways? Finally, if the physician decides not to consult an available ethics committee, might that fact be used against him?

Increasingly, courts are finding themselves to be inadequate to resolve certain kinds of questions. Courts have recognized that consulting with an ethics committee, which is likely to be a better place to resolve some of these issues, may relieve patients, physicians and health care institutions from the obligation of seeking judicial approval for their actions. See, e.g., In re Guardianship of Browning, 543 So.2d 258, 269 n. 16 (Fla.App. 2 Dist.1989); In re Torres, 357 N.W.2d 332 (Minn.1984).

4. As is true with IRBs, the question of access to IEC deliberations, documents, and related information has arisen over the past few years, primarily in the context of malpractice cases, but also in medical licensing, defamation, civil rights, and other cases. Should patients, other physicians, plaintiffs' lawyers, courts, state medical licensing boards and others have access to IEC proceedings and records? Should those proceedings and records be confidential? If so, what is the legal basis of that confidentiality? See Merritt, The Tort Liability of Hospital Ethics Committees, 60 S.Cal.L.Rev. 1239 (1987). See also Cranford, Hester, and Ashley, Institutional Ethics Committees: Issues of Confidentiality and Immunity, 13 Law, Medicine & Health Care 52 (April 1985).

5. Do IECs have an ethical or legal obligation to report wrongdoing or potential danger that they discover in the course of their activities? What should an IEC (or a member of an IEC) do upon discovering that a particularly inept physician is practicing at the hospital? Is there a duty to warn the hospital or the patients? Is there a duty to report discovery of inadequate care to the state licensing board? What should an IEC (or a member of an IEC) do upon discovering some evidence of child abuse or neglect?

6. Might members of IECs be personally liable for their conduct on such committees? If a committee unanimously reaches a conclusion supporting the propriety of an act which a court later finds to be wrong, might IEC members be personally liable in negligence, under civil rights laws, or on some other theory? In other words, do IECs or IEC members owe a duty enforceable in tort law to the patients whose cases come before them?

Even if they do, might the IEC or its members partake of the statutory immunity provided to some other medical review committees?

Professor Merritt suggests that committees could be liable for aiding and abetting tortious conduct. See Merritt, supra, Note 4 at 1274–1281. He argues that "ethics committees may best avoid any liability to patients if they establish a role as the physician's 'risk management' counselor and disclaim any interest in benefitting the patient," although he recognizes that such a role would be "a sad retreat from the idealism" that gave rise to the ethics committee movement. Id. at 1297. At least one ethics committee has been named as a defendant in an action for damages. After Elizabeth Bouvia had her right to refuse a naso-gastric tube confirmed by a judicial order, she commenced an action against all of the members of the ethics committee that had gone along with the decision to place the tube against her wishes. The California Court of Appeal decision authorizing the removal of the naso-gastric tube is reprinted in Chapter 11, below. The civil action is described in Merritt, supra at 1250–1251.

Is there any way that the institution can act to limit liability of IEC members or provide them with indemnity?

7. As issues of cost and access become more important, should IECs play some role in determining what a hospital's policy on distribution of resources ought to be? Should an IEC always be supportive of the policies ultimately adopted by its institution, or should it be a critic (internally or externally) willing to be an advocate on ethical issues that have not been formally presented to it by the hospital administration or individual hospital employees?

8. Should health care institutions be required by law to have ethics committees? Only one state—Maryland—has imposed such a duty, and it has been met with a mixed reaction.

9. For a general account of the development of institutional ethics committees, see B. Hosford, Bioethics Committees: The Health Care Provider's Guide (1986). J. Ross, Handbook for Hospital Ethics Committees (1986) is an extremely useful and comprehensive guide to the operation of these committees, and a new edition of this work is expected soon. See also R. Cranford and E. Doudera, Institutional Ethics Committees and Health Care Decision Making (1984) and R. Craig and C. O'Connell, Ethics Committees: A Practical Approach (1986) (dealing with ethics committees at Catholic hospitals). For a good account of the legal position of ethics committees, see Capron, Legal Perspectives on Institutional Ethics Committees, 11 J. College and University L. 417 (1985). The clearest, brief discussion of the various voluntary and mandatory processes that could define the IEC role is Robertson, Ethics Committees in Hospitals: Alternative Structures and Responsibilities, 6 Quality Rev.Bull. (1) 10 (1984). For good accounts of the role of ethics committees in nursing homes, see Glasser, Zweibel, and Cassel, The Ethics Committee in the Nursing Home: Results of a National Survey, 36 J.Am.Geriatric Soc. 150 (1988) and Brown, Miles, and Aroskar, The Prevalence and Design of Ethics Committees in Nursing Homes, 35 J.Am.Geriatric Soc. 1028 (1987).

Note: Other Interdisciplinary Case Review Agencies

IRBs and IECs are not the only kinds of interdisciplinary committees that review individual cases. While there may be a few national interdisciplinary case review agencies—like the Recombinant DNA Advisory Committee discussed in Chapter 9, most such committees are local. For example, the PRO, discussed above in Chapter 6, provides for more than a mere medical review of the cost and quality of care provided to Medicare recipients. The development and proliferation of medical-legal panels to review malpractice cases before they are filed in the courts, a development discussed in Chapter 4, above, has provided yet another forum for interdisciplinary (even if not multidisciplinary) decisionmaking.

Interdisciplinary case review committees may provide a way for courts and agencies to finesse a question from the highly visible stage of government into a less controversial forum. For example, the New Jersey Supreme Court required that an "ethics committee" review Karen Quinlan's medical diagnosis before a determination of the propriety of the removal of life sustaining treatment could be made. Matter of Quinlan, 70 N.J. 10, 355 A.2d 647 (1976). The committee was to determine whether there was any "reasonable possibility of Karen's ever emerging from her present comatose condition to a cognitive sapient state." Thus, the committee was to review the medical prognosis only; it was not to apply any ethics principles. Is there any reason that this prognosis committee, concerned only with the medical prognosis of one patient, should be interdisciplinary? The New Jersey Supreme Court depended on an article which recommended the development of committees "of physicians, social workers, attorneys, and theologians * * * to review the individual circumstances of ethical dilemmas. * * *" 355 A.2d at 668, quoting Teel, The Physician's Dilemma: A Doctor's View: What the Law Should Be, 27 Baylor L.Rev. 6, 8 (1975).

Similarly, when the Department of Health and Human Services wished the Baby Doe spotlight to be diffused, it managed to get most major American medical associations to recommend institutional creation of committees to review the care appropriate for seriously ill newborns. These committees, Infant Care Review Committees (ICRCs), were general policy committees that were also designed to review individual cases. Under some circumstances—as when the parent and the physicians disagreed about whether treatment was appropriate or when the committee determined that treatment was appropriate and the physician and family disagreed—the committee could have some formal decisionmaking authority. These committees, like IRBs and many IECs, were expected to be broadly representative of the community, and, more significantly, they were expected to contain advocates that would support treatment for the patient. Despite the federal regulatory status of ICRCs and their approval by a wide range of health care organizations, the fact that ICRCs were foisted upon hospitals by government fiat and then given real power to review (and, under some circumstances, reverse) highly sensitive decisions made by families and their physicians led to substantial opposition within the medical, legal, and ethics communities. The sad circumstances under which ICRCs arose—the battle over the Baby Doe regulations, which is described in Chapter 11—have probably done more to slow the development of interdisciplinary ethics committees than any other single event. Despite this, however, ICRCs demonstrate how governments can avoid difficult questions by delegating authority to local "ethics committees", just as happened in the *Quinlan* case. This kind of delegation is likely to increase in the absence of social consensus on the underlying substantive principles.

III. NATIONAL AND STATE COMMISSIONS

The need for interdisciplinary decisionmaking applies to broad issues of social policy as well as to individual cases. To the extent that society wishes to develop a national policy on the definition of death, genetic engineering, access to health care, and similar issues, a full national debate on those issues is necessary. Of course, one authority ultimately responsible for the development of social policy—the legislative branch—is a sort of multidisciplinary committee. It may be wise, however, to have those issues fully argued and debated in some other forum before the power of the Congress and the state legislatures institutionalizes any apparent consensus.

The federal government has advanced debates concerning a wide range of bioethics questions by establishing national commissions, interdisciplinary in nature, to marshal the facts and arguments that relate to each of the issues and, often, to make recommendations. The first truly significant national commission was the National Commission for the Protection of Human Subjects of Biomedical and Behavioral Research, which was statutorily created in 1974, completed its work in 1978, and is responsible for the greatest part of the current federal regulations governing research involving human subjects. At least as important is the President's Commission for the Study of Ethical Problems in Medicine and Biomedical and Behavioral Research, which was created by statute in 1978, completed its work in 1983, and has already had a very substantial effect on legislative and judicial decisions in this country. Both the National Commission and the President's Commission were so important because, like most IECs, neither had any actual power to implement their recommendations. Both viewed their roles as primarily educational, and each became a vehicle for developing a national consensus on policies that would inevitably be incorporated into law. The National Commission and the President's Commission remain the most constantly cited sources on every issue they studied.

The President's Commission has not been free of criticism, however, even from those who influenced it (and were influenced by it). The conclusions of the President's Commission were based primarily on the principle of autonomy. That principle is an essentially procedural one; it tells us who has the authority to make a decision rather than what decision ought to be made. Daniel Callahan, a thoughtful philosopher and careful critic of commonly accepted presumptions, suggests that it is time to turn to the substance of these issues. As he points out:

> The debate over the right of the terminally ill to withdraw from treatment provides as good an example as any of our present predicament. On the surface, the most important part of the debate turns on whether the dying have a legal and moral right to have their treatment discontinued. The general answer to both questions is yes; that is, both morality and the law grant them such a right. * * *
>
> But all the while, the most important moral questions are neglected: under what circumstances, and by what principles, may I decide that I no longer must continue struggling against death? How should I make use of my freedom to declare that I no longer want to be treated? What do I owe to myself? What do I owe to my family or those who love me? Who am I that I may declare my life no longer worth living?
>
> * * *
>
> We have gone through an important era that has established many new rights and privileges in the face of the power and potency of biomedicine. We have been told that we are autonomous and can make free choices—that autonomy is a key ingredient in the thread of consensus that runs through the reports of the President's Commission. In the next stage, we must begin work on the content of that freedom. For it is here that consensus will most desperately be needed; otherwise, the newly gained freedoms will turn out to be either empty or dangerous.

Callahan, Morality and Contemporary Culture: The President's Commission and Beyond, 6 Cardozo L.Rev. 347 (1984).

In fact, one attempt to move a government sponsored national commission into the realm of substantive bioethics proved an utter failure. The Health Research Extension Act of 1985 created the Biomedical Ethics Board (composed of six senators and six members of the House of Representatives) and the Biomedical Ethics Advisory Committee, to be appointed by the Biomedical Ethics Board. The Advisory Committee would have been a continuing agency to carry out substantive analyses of issues within the scope of the Board, which was instructed to "study and report to the Congress on a continuing basis on the ethical issues arising from the delivery of health care and biomedical and behavioral research, including the protection of human subjects of such research and developments in genetic engineering (including activities in recombinant DNA technology) which have implications for human genetic engineering." Ultimately both the Board and the Committee were paralyzed by the issue of abortion. Partisans on both sides of that issue viewed the Committee as a potentially subversive political agency. Although Senator Gore was named vice chairman of the Board, a chair was never appointed. In fact, the membership of the Advisory Committee was not fully established until the middle of 1988, and funding was cut off by the fall of 1989. As the acting staff director of the Advisory Committee said, "Politicians have been extremely reluctant to take on not only the abortion issue, but anything that may be seen as related. And there is no area of ethical analysis that isn't somehow seen as part of this issue by activists." Hilts, Abortion Debate Clouds Research on Fetal Tissue, The New York Times 19 (October 16, 1989). Will it be possible for any national commission to deal with any bioethics questions before we reach consensus (or at least detente) on abortion? Is it best to simply avoid an allegedly neutral national governmental inquiry into these issues with the current political climate?

Perhaps more significant work towards consensus on bioethical issues could be done at the state and local level. Indeed, states also have established interdisciplinary commissions to assist in the development of bioethics policy. New York's "Task Force on Law and Life" was established in late 1984, about a year after the termination of the President's Commission's work. This task force has released several exceptionally thoughtful and comprehensive reports. More recently, New Jersey, whose judiciary has been at the forefront of many of these issues, established a bioethics commission that is expected to have a real effect on the development of policy in New Jersey and elsewhere. Most other states have established some variety of commissions, committees, panels and task forces to prepare reports and recommendations on subjects that range from malpractice reform to surrogacy to access to health care.

In addition, many local communities have set up task forces to consider bioethics issues, including the availability of health care within those communities. Is there any reason to believe that these interdisciplinary committees, whether called presidential commissions, state task forces, or community blue ribbon committees, operate best at any particular level of government? Would you expect a South Dakota task force on surrogacy to come to a different conclusion than a New York City committee?

Several states have instituted a "Health Decisions" program that is modeled on one that began in Oregon in the early 1980s. This program aims to educate the community about questions relating to health care by scheduling small discussion groups and then convening townhall meetings in an attempt to develop consensus recommendations that will influence lawmakers. The educational value of this program is immense; the political value has also proven itself in Oregon, where it has seen its recommendations taken seriously by the legislature.

A Symposium on "Commissioning Morality: A Critique of the President's Commission for the Study of Ethical Problems in Medicine and Biomedical and Behavioral Research" is the subject of 6 Cardozo L.Rev. 223–355 (1984). In addition to the Callahan article, the symposium includes: Weisbard and Arras, Commissioning Morality: An Introduction to the Symposium, 6 Cardozo L.Rev. 223 (1984); Katz, Limping is No Sin: Reflections on Making Health Care Decisions, 6 Cardozo L.Rev. 243 (1984); Burt, The Ideal of Community in the Work of the President's Commission, 6 Cardozo L.Rev. 267 (1984); Cassel, Deciding to Forgo Life Sustaining Treatment: Implications for Policy in 1985, 6 Cardozo L.Rev. 287 (1984); Bayer, Ethics, Politics, and Access to Health Care: A Critical Analysis of the President's Commission for the Study of Ethical Problems in Medicine and Biomedical and Behavioral Research, 6 Cardozo L.Rev. 303 (1984); and Arras, Retreat from the Right to Health Care: The President's Commission and Access to Health Care, 6 Cardozo L.Rev. 321 (1984). Other relevant analyses of the role of presidential commissions include Capron, Looking Back at the President's Commission, 13 Hastings Center Report 7 (Oct.1983); and Annas, Report on the National Commission: Good as Gold, Medicolegal News 4 (Dec.1980).

The current status of the "Health Decisions" movement is addressed in several articles in the Sep.–Oct. 1990 Hastings Center Report. See Garland and Hasnain, Health Care in Common: Setting Priorities in Oregon, 20 Hastings Center Rep.(5) 16 (Sep.–Oct.1990); Wallace–Brodeur, Community Values in Vermont Health Planning, 20 Hastings Center Rep.(5) 18 (Sep.–Oct.1990); Hill, Giving Voice to the Pragmatic Majority in New Jersey, 20 Hastings Center Rep.(5) 20 (Sep.–Oct.1990); Colbert, Public Input Into Health Care Policy: Controversy and Contribution in California, 20 Hastings Center Rep.(5) 21 (Sep.–Oct.1990); Crawshaw, A Vision of the Health Decisions Movement, 20 Hastings Center Rep.(5) 21 (Sep.–Oct.1990); and Jennings, Democracy and Justice in Health Policy, 20 Hastings Center Rep.(5) 22 (Sep.–Oct.1990).

IV. DOCTOR–LAWYER RELATIONS AND THE NEED FOR INTERDISCIPLINARY TRAINING

If there is a need for interdisciplinary discussion, then there is a need for people of different disciplines to be able to speak to and understand one another. If there is any place where this need remains unmet, it is in the relationship between doctors and lawyers. As physicians and lawyers become increasingly involved in working together to resolve social questions with bioethical considerations, they are going to have to learn to trust each other. As the discussion of malpractice law in Chapter 2 indicates, this will be no easy task. The failure of doctors and lawyers to understand and respect each other has led to serious problems in the development of public policy in the area of medical malpractice, research involving human subjects, the treatment of seriously ill newborns, and the discontinuation of life-support systems for the seriously ill, among other areas. An understanding of the basis for the conflict may help dispel the conflict and lead to a more open discussion of the underlying questions.

GIBSON AND SCHWARTZ, PHYSICIANS AND LAWYERS: SCIENCE, ART, AND CONFLICT
6 Am.J.L. & Med. 173 (1981).

Over the past several decades, relations between physicians and lawyers have undergone considerable change. Once based on mutual respect and even trust, the two professions' attitudes towards one another have deteriorated into mutual hostility and mistrust. With the advent in the early 1970s of what was widely perceived to be a medical malpractice insurance crisis, the divisions between them deepened, and have, if anything, grown more formidable since then.

Simultaneous with the observed loss of respect of physicians and lawyers for each other, both professions—though surely the most respected in the English-speaking world for the past two centuries—have been losing the esteem they once had in the community. The time when both physicians and lawyers were considered "men of mystery and magic, members of a sacerdotal class in close communion with God," has passed. Just as the public's perception of physicians as having unique powers to work mysterious cures has lapsed, so the powerful respect for the rule of law as formal authority has increasingly been questioned.

Undoubtedly, the decline in respect accorded both professions by the community has contributed to the defensiveness of each professional group, and to the tendency of each to denigrate the apparent self-righteousness of the other. In addition, some believe that this defensiveness is reinforced by the potentially competing economic interests of the two professions. Clearly, physicians feel attacked economically as well as professionally by the increased prosecution of medical malpractice actions.

A suggested explanation for the difficulty physicians and lawyers now have in communicating is the extent to which they intentionally attach different meanings to the same words. The words need not be part of medical or legal jargon for this problem to arise. One obvious example is the different medical and legal definitions and interpretations given the word "causation".

Similar problems arise with a number of other words—such as "illness," "injury," and "harm"—some of which have become separate terms of art in each profession. Although these sematic differences may be frustrating, they do not exemplify an essential philosophical difference, or even a substantive difference in the notion of what ought to give rise to liability. Thus, the differences in terminology, either alone or in tandem with the theories explored above, do not explain the profound levels of suspicion and hostility that divide the two professions.

* * * The most significant explanation for this deep-seated antagonism between the two professions is that physicians and lawyers do not reason and solve problems in the same way. At first glance it would

seem unlikely that these two professions would reason in radically different ways. Prospective physicians and lawyers tend to come from the same social classes and to have the same kinds of backgrounds: they grow up in the same suburbs, go to the same secondary schools, and attend the same colleges. Indeed, it would be difficult to find two groups who ought to think as much alike as physicians and lawyers. If they reason in different ways, then, the explanation must lie in the nature of the professions themselves, or in the nature of the education that socializes law and medical students into their respective professions.

Indeed, the ways in which physicians and lawyers analyze problems—for example, the ways in which they invoke the scientific method—are very different; in fact, the two professions look for truth in unrelated ways. While medicine seeks objective, absolute truths, the law, employing the adversary system, seeks relative truths. The adversary system requires that every idea and argument be tested, and that only those that remain after being assailed be accepted as the relatively better truth. In theory, therefore, a court makes a finding by having an able advocate present the best arguments on one side of an issue and then having another equally able advocate present the arguments supporting a contrasting conclusion. Out of this battle of ideas, the legal system supposes, the strongest—or stronger—argument will emerge victorious. This system of discovering truth necessarily admits that there is no single and clearly superior truth in any particular case. The question is not which argument is right and which is wrong, but which argument is the better one.

The notion of the adversary system is largely inconsistent with the way in which physicians make decisions. Despite some powerful dissent from this view, most physicians consider medicine to be more of a science than an art. Diagnoses are developed not through debate or through the challenge of ideas, but through dispassionate research and careful as well as neutral evaluation of a set of natural facts.

Are the differences in the ways in which physicians and lawyers think, reason, and argue simply the perpetuation of different teaching methods and professional traditions imposed during, and continued after, law and medical school? While these differences are reflected in the respective educational systems, they appear to go beyond methodology. Rather, they seem to be linked to the content and structure of medical "science" and law, and to the implicit theories of reality that accompany each.

Science, as an activity involving both discovery and explanation of natural phenomena, is generally understood to comprise procedures of observation, identification, description, experimental investigation, and theoretical explanation. Law, on the other hand—at least since the advent of legal realism—has been defined as constituting the development (and not just the discovery) of a system of relations for those living in a society, and as "behavioral directives about interpersonal actions."

Physicians-as-scientists view their functions (observations, identification, description, investigation, and explanation of natural phenomena) within the theoretical confines of their discipline. They usually accept the notion of scientific law as a formulation of observed recurrences, order, relationships, or interactions of natural phenomena. Even the theories to which they turn, while not, by definition, based directly on observable phenomena, must ultimately be validated by reference to confirmed experimental law—to observably simple and definitively true statements about the nature or behavior of natural phenomena. And while the term "law" is neither a precisely nor a comprehensively defined term for scientists, "[t]here is * * * agreement that a minimum necessary condition of any scientific statement proposed as lawlike is that it be a universal generalization." To have any meaning, scientific laws must accurately predict an event, a relationship, or a consequence, and to the extent that physicians see themselves as scientists, their reality is described and controlled by laws that must be empirically verifiable and universally generalizable.

The lawyer deals with laws of a very different sort. Legal rules can be prescriptive, as well as descriptive, and thus are not empirically verifiable in the same manner as "scientific" laws. While verification of a law is the hallmark of the scientific method, it is simply irrelevant to most legal inquiry. A scientific law is "truth" because it accurately describes an attribute of the universe, and thus applies to all societies and all times. A law announced by a common law court is "truth" because the community, authoritatively represented in this instance by a majority of the court's members, believes it works well in individual cases that have arisen. It is not, however, universally generalizable; it may, in fact, be inconsistent with laws adopted by different societies.

The implications of this reality are significant. Consider the earlier discussion of the different meanings physicians and lawyers assign to terms such as "causation," and it will appear now that these semantic differences themselves entail something more basic: physicians and lawyers work within, or create, qualitatively different sorts of "factual" contexts and intellectual environments out of which causal relations may be inferred. For example, experimental scientists, and physicians to the extent that they are trained as scientists, inquire into those *general* conditions that *typically* accompany, cause, or entail an instance of a certain *kind*. While this is but one of many possible notions of causal explanation, it stands in marked contrast to the legal notion of proximate cause—that cause so closely related to the undesirable end that it ought to give rise to legal liability. Whereas a physician might describe the cause of a death as cardiac arrest, a lawyer might describe the cause of the same death as a gunshot fired by a named assailant—a gunshot that triggered the particular sequence of physiological events that resulted in the victim's cardiac arrest and death. The problem is not that one description of the cause contradicts the other; they are, of course, perfectly consistent. * * * This difference in the professions' approaches to language is much more than a semantic difference in the way certain terms are used. It is a consequence of the fact that physicians and lawyers have chosen very different means to define truth, and, ultimately, that both are searching for different truths, unrelated to one another.

So long as science, without art, provides the model for the medical practitioner, the different methods physicians and lawyers use to solve problems will perpetuate mistrust between the professions. A physician who is a defendant in a malpractice case may very reasonably explain to his or her lawyer that he or she is an expert in the field, knows more about the challenged procedure than anyone else, and did not err. The physician is sure to be surprised and frustrated when the lawyer informs him or her that implicit in the legal system is the belief that justice is more likely to be done if the plaintiff presents another physician, equally knowledgeable in the field and equally articulate, who believes that the defendant did err. Until physicians recognize that the adversary system and all of its attributes—including cross examination of the physician and of other experts—do not constitute a personal attack on the competency of the physician, they will mistrust the system. Similarly, until lawyers realize that a physician's training leaves no room for an adversary inquiry, they are likely to misunderstand physicians' responses to their questions.

Notes and Questions

1. The authors suggest that the formal structure of professional education makes it difficult for doctors and lawyers to consider the same problem in the same way. How has your professional education been a broadening (or narrowing) one? Will the movement in medical schools toward the study of humanities and the development of seminars not directly related to clinical medicine improve the physician's understanding of the law? Will the law school development of legal clinics, which roughly parallel the traditional form of third and fourth year medical education, overcome the lawyers' condescending attitude toward the analytical ability of physicians? Will the development of more law and medicine, bioethics, and health care courses that are themselves interdisciplinary help overcome the mistrust that professional education appears to instill in doctors and lawyers?

2. Might a change in the composition of entering law school and medical school classes alter the relationship between the professions? The dramatic drop in medical school applications in the last half of the 1980s has changed the nature of many medical schools. Some suggest that entering medical students are much more likely to have chosen the profession for reasons of personal satisfaction rather than for reasons of lucre. Would such a change be welcome in law as well? As women make up a much larger percentage of law students and medical students, and as minorities make up a slightly larger percentage of law students and

medical students, will the values of those professions change? Will any such change affect the way the professions view each other?

3. Professional misunderstandings are not limited to doctors and lawyers. Economists, ethicists, theologians, scientists, police officers, and hospital administrators are all trained in very different ways, and their training causes them to analyze the same questions from different perspectives. Many of the "Right to Die" cases that go to court arise out of disagreements among doctors, nurses, hospital administrators, and all of their lawyers. If our attempt is to build an integrated health care system, is there anything that can be done to expose potential workers to the world view of others within the system? Is it possible for the system to work efficiently if doctors, lawyers, insurance administrators, and physical therapists all view its goals and processes in entirely different ways?

4. Not all lawyers think alike, just as not all doctors share the same world view. A legal academic will view matters entirely differently from a hospital lawyer, who may be working primarily as a risk manager. Both will perceive the same issue differently from a malpractice plaintiff's lawyer or a hospital association lobbyist. Similarly, a university pediatrician whose primary interest is Dostoyevski may view the health care system and his position in it very differently from an orthopedic surgeon whose primary interest is skiing. Any attempt to train doctors and lawyers so that they can talk with one another will also require training lawyers and doctors to be broad-minded enough to be able to talk about these issues with their colleagues.

Index

References are to Pages

1229

†